FINANCIAL ACCOUNTING

Third Edition

JERRY J. WEYGANDT Ph.D., C.P.A.
Arthur Andersen Alumni Professor of Accounting
University of Wisconsin
Madison, Wisconsin

DONALD E. KIESO Ph.D., C.P.A.
KPMG Emeritus Professor of Accounting
Northern Illinois University
DeKalb, Illinois

PAUL D. KIMMEL Ph.D., C.P.A.
Associate Professor of Accounting
University of Wisconsin–Milwaukee
Milwaukee, Wisconsin

JOHN WILEY & SONS, INC.
New York • Chichester • Weinheim • Brisbane • Singapore • Toronto

Dedicated To
(our siblings)
Richard, Dennis, and Robert
Joan and Bob
Lois, Sara, Amy, and Joel

Executive Editor   Susan Elbe
Senior Development Editor   Nancy Perry
Outside Development Editor/Proofreader   Ann Torbert
Supplements Editor   Julie Kerr
Full Service Manager   Jeanine Furino
Senior Designer   Kevin Murphy
Photo Editor   Nicole Horlacher
Illustration Editor   Anna Melhorn
Production Management   Ingrao Associates
Photo Researcher   Jennifer Atkins
Cover Photo   Horst Baender/Tony Stone Images/New York, Inc.

This book was set in Palatino by York Graphic Services, Inc. and printed and bound by Von Hoffman Press. The cover was printed by Phoenix Color Corp.

This book is printed on acid-free paper.

The specimen financial statements, Appendix A and Appendix B, are printed with permission of Kellogg Company and General Mills, Inc.

The information and trademarks offered herein are the property of Kellogg Company. TONY THE TIGER™ is a registered trademark of Kellogg Company. All rights reserved. Used with permission.

General Mills, Inc. disclaims responsibility for any reproduction or transmission errors contained in this reprinted version of portions of its 1998 Annual Report.

ISBN   0-471-34773-6

Printed in the United States of America

10   9   8   7   6   5   4   3   2

ABOUT THE AUTHORS

Jerry J. Weygandt, Ph.D., CPA, is Arthur Andersen Alumni Professor of Accounting at the University of Wisconsin-Madison. He holds a Ph.D. in accounting from the University of Illinois. Articles by Professor Weygandt have appeared in the *Accounting Review, Journal of Accounting Research,* the *Journal of Accountancy,* and other professional journals. These articles have examined such financial reporting issues as accounting for price-level adjustments, pensions, convertible securities, stock option contracts, and interim reports. He is a member of the American Accounting Association, the American Institute of Certified Public Accountants, and the Wisconsin Society of Certified Public Accountants. He has served on numerous committees of the American Accounting Association and as a member of the editorial board of the *Accounting Review.* In addition, he is actively involved with the American Institute of Certified Public Accountants and has been a member of the Accounting Standards Executive Committee (AcSEC) of that organization. He has served on the FASB task force that examined the reporting issues related to "accounting for income taxes" and is presently a trustee of the Financial Accounting Foundation. Professor Weygandt has received the Chancellor's Award for Excellence in Teaching; he also has served as President and Secretary-Treasurer of the American Accounting Association. Recently he received the Wisconsin Institute of CPA's Outstanding Educator's Award and the Lifetime Achievement Award.

Donald E. Kieso, Ph.D., CPA, received his bachelor's degree from Aurora University and his doctorate in accounting from the University of Illinois. He has served as chairman of the Department of Accountancy and is currently the KPMG Emeritus Professor of Accounting at Northern Illinois University. He has public accounting experience with Price Waterhouse & Co. (San Francisco and Chicago) and Arthur Andersen & Co. (Chicago) and research experience with the Research Division of the American Institute of Certified Public Accountants (New York). He is a recipient of NIU's Teaching Excellence Award and four Golden Apple Teaching Awards. He has served as a member of the Board of Directors of the Illinois CPA Society, the Board of Governors of the American Accounting Association's Administrators of Accounting Programs Group, the AACSB's Accounting Accreditation Committee, the State of Illinois Comptroller's Commission, as Secretary-Treasurer of the Federation of Schools of Accountancy, and as Secretary-Treasurer of the American Accounting Association. Professor Kieso is serving as Chairman of the Board of Trustees and Executive Committee of Aurora University, the Boards of Directors of Castle BancGroup Inc. and Valley West Community Hospital, and as Secretary-Treasurer of The Sandwich Hospital Resolution Board. From 1989 to 1993 he served as a charter member of the national Accounting Education Change Commission. In 1988 he received the Outstanding Accounting Educator Award from the Illinois CPA Society; in 1992 he received the FSA's Joseph A. Silvoso Award of Merit and the NIU Foundation's Humanitarian Award for Service to Higher Education; and in 1995 he received a Distinguished Service Award from the Illinois CPA Society.

Paul D. Kimmel, Ph.D., CPA, received his bachelor's degree from The University of Minnesota and his doctorate in accounting from University of Wisconsin. He is an Associate Professor at the University of Wisconsin-Milwaukee. He has public accounting experience with Deloitte & Touche (Minneapolis). He is the recipient of the UWM School of Business Advisory Council Teaching Award, the Reggie Taite Excellence in Teaching Award, a three-time winner of the Outstanding Teaching Assistant Award at the University of Wisconsin, and a recipient of the Elijah Watts Sells Award for Honorary Distinction for his results on the CPA exam. He is a member of the American Accounting Association and has published articles in the *Accounting Review, Accounting Horizons, Issues in Accounting Education,* and the *Journal of Accounting Education* as well as other journals. His research interests include accounting for financial instruments and innovation in accounting education. He has published papers and given numerous talks on incorporating critical thinking into accounting education, and helped prepare a catalog of critical thinking resources for the Federated Schools of Accountancy.

To The Instructor

In previous editions of *Financial Accounting*, we sought to create a book about business that made the subject clear and fascinating to beginning students. And that is still our passion: to provide a link between accounting principles, student learning, and the real world.

EMPOWERMENT AND THE FEELING OF ACCOMPLISHMENT

In our effort to create an even more effective text, we surveyed the market, talked personally to instructors, and held focus groups with professors and students. We heard again and again that the biggest challenges students face are becoming motivated, learning how to study, and managing their tasks. We have responded to this information by creating a complete framework for success that will empower students to meet these challenges. The pedagogy of the Third Edition of *Financial Accounting* will keep students motivated by giving them a daily sense of accomplishment. We give students the tools and the motivation they need to succeed in subsequent accounting courses and in their future business careers.

GOALS AND FEATURES OF THE THIRD EDITION

The Third Edition of *Financial Accounting* provides an opportunity to improve a textbook that has set high standards for quality. Users and reviewers continue to comment positively on the writing style, the use of real-world examples, pedagogical features, and the fact that the textbook is not only about accounting but about business as well.

The primary purpose of this revision was to maintain these successful features and improve on them. We gathered four consistent messages from all our developmental research:

- Some complex topics that were beyond the scope of the introductory accounting course needed to be eliminated. We've carefully evaluated all topics regarding their suitability for beginning accounting students. Those topics more suitable for an advanced course in accounting were deleted from this edition.
- A student's textbook should be as pedagogically effective as possible. Although we believe that our Second Edition was a market leader in pedagogical effectiveness, we've added many pedagogical elements that are truly helpful. The *accounting equation* has been inserted

in the margin next to key journal entries throughout the text. This new feature reinforces the students' understanding of the impact of an accounting transaction on the financial statements. To increase the effectiveness of our learning system, we developed a guide to the learning process, which we call *The Navigator*. The learning system, as well as The Navigator, are described below.
- The book should continue to involve the student in the learning process and ensure that the student understands the *why* as well as the *how*. The message is consistent with the Accounting Education Change Commission recommendations which encourage an emphasis on communication skills, critical thinking and decision-making skills, ethics, international accounting, and real-world emphasis.
- We have added considerable new "user" material. Our reasons were twofold: (1) to accomplish the objectives of the Accounting Education Change Commission, and (2) to demonstrate the relevance of accounting to all students, no matter what their area of study. Most of the new user material was added to the Broadening Your Perspectives section of the end-of-chapter material. These learning activities are designed to develop many skills that will be of use to students in other courses and in life after college, including financial statement analysis skills, research skills, and the ability to use the Internet. In addition, to give students the opportunity to follow an extended example, we have integrated references to the Kellogg Company financial statements throughout the book, including Review It questions, ratio presentations, and end-of-chapter assignment materials.

Simplified Presentation

As in the Second Edition, we continue to simplify and condense the textual material. To achieve this goal, the text was reviewed and carefully edited to ensure its clarity and exposition. The changes that were made can be characterized into four types:

Organizational Changes. Acting in response to adopters of the second edition, we moved the inventory chapter from 9 to 6 so that the inventory topics are now covered sequentially back to back—"Accounting for Merchandising Operation" (Chapter 5) followed immediately by "Inventories" (now Chapter 6). The simpler perpetual inventory system is covered first in Chapter 5, and the slightly more complex periodic inventory system is covered in Chapter 6, while the perpetual inventory system is still fresh in the student's mind.

Updates. This edition was subject to comprehensive updating to ensure that it is relevant and fresh. Updating involved replacing Accounting in Action boxes, problem material, real-world examples cited in the text, infographic illustrations, and chapter-opening feature stories.

To freshen the end-of-chapter assignment material, we have replaced some exercises and problems throughout the book and revised many others. At least two problems per chapter have been replaced, and both financial statement analysis assignments in the Broadening Your Perspective section are revised from Pepsi and Coca-Cola to Kellogg and General Mills. Most research assignments at the end of each chapter are new or updated. A new Surfing the Net Internet assignment now accompanies each chapter.

Condensations and Deletions. We either condensed or deleted material that was better suited for more advanced level courses, along with concepts and procedures that are little used. We made these decisions after gathering a great deal of information from instructors on how they teach the course and what they think today's beginning accounting students need to know.

Additions. In a very few cases, we added new material to the textbook. These topics had to pass a strict test to warrant their inclusion: they were added only if they represented a major concept, issue, or procedure that a beginning student should understand.

A chapter by chapter summary of these changes is provided below.

Key Changes in Each Chapter

Chapter 1: Accounting in Action

- New Feature Story on Kellogg Company and related "A Look Back" exercise with solution
- New infographics on questions asked by internal and external users of financial statements and one on the transaction identification process
- New Accounting in Action box on choosing an accounting year-end
- New Before You Go On exercise requiring transaction analysis
- Revised coverage of corporate ethics statements, including example from Kellogg Company
- New appendix on the accounting profession and career paths in public and private accounting
- New end-of-chapter (EOC) material: two new problems, financial statement analysis, comparative analysis, research assignment, and Internet-based assignment

Chapter 2: The Recording Process

- New Feature Story and related "A Look Back" exercise with solution
- New infographic on T accounts and new Technology in Action box
- Enhanced illustration related to normal account balances
- Updated terminology

- New EOC material: three new problems, financial reporting problem, comparative analysis problem, group decision case, and Internet-based assignment

Chapter 3: Adjusting the Accounts

- New Feature Story and related "A Look Back" exercise with solution
- New infographics on the revenue recognition and matching principles, and the time period assumption
- Revised illustration on summary of adjusting entries
- Condensed and simplified "Preparing the Adjusted Trial Balance" section
- New EOC material: new exercise, three new problems, financial reporting problem, comparative analysis problem, group decision case, and Internet-based assignment

Chapter 4: Completion of the Accounting Cycle

- New illustration from real companies' financials
- New infographic on liquidity
- New EOC material: numerical data revised in all problems; financial analysis problem; comparative analysis problem; and Internet-based assignment

Chapter 5: Accounting for Merchandising Operations

- New Feature Story and related "A Look Back" exercise with solution
- New infographics on purchase discount and sales discount
- New Accounting in Action box on perpetual inventory system
- New EOC material: two new brief exercises, new exercise, two new problems, financial reporting problem, comparative analysis problem, research assignment, and Internet-based assignment

Chapter 6 Inventories

- Repositioned inventories from Chapter 9 to Chapter 6 so that the coverage of the periodic inventory system immediately follows coverage of the perpetual inventory system
- New Feature Story and related "A Look Back" exercise with solution
- New infographics to illustrate each of the inventory cost flow assumptions
- New EOC material: brief exercises, exercises, two new problems, financial reporting problem, comparative analysis problem, research assignment, group discussion case, and Internet-based assignment

Chapter 7: Accounting Principles

- Deleted percentage-of-completion coverage
- New infographic on constraints in accounting (materiality and conservatism)
- New EOC material: financial reporting problem, comparative analysis problem, research assignment, and Internet-based assignment

Chapter 8: Internal Control and Cash

- New Feature Story and related "A Look Back" exercise with solution
- Numerous new infographics on principles of internal control; revised infographics on internal control for cash
- New Accounting in Action box: International Perspective on fraud at Sumitomo bank
- Additional explanation on reporting cash over and short
- New EOC material: new exercise, three new problems, financial reporting problem, comparative analysis problem, interpreting financial statements, and Internet-based assignment

Chapter 9: Accounting for Receivables

- New Feature Story and related "A Look Back" exercise with solution
- New Accounting in Action box on Sears, Roebuck's provision for credit card losses
- New Accounting in Action box on the phenomenon of unsolicited, preapproved credit card applications
- New International Note on accounts receivable write-off practices in China
- Clarification of percentage-of-sales approach, with added T accounts
- New EOC material: exercise, four new problems, financial reporting problem, comparative analysis problem, interpretation of financial statements, and Internet-based assignment

Chapter 10: Plant Assets, Natural Resources, and Intangible Assets

- New infographic on depreciation as an allocation concept
- New margin infographics to illustrate each of the depreciation methods
- New Accounting in Action box on the effect of a change in an asset's life on net income
- New Accounting in Action box on intangible assets
- New Accounting in Action box on copyrights
- New EOC material: new questions, brief exercises, and exercises; four new problems; financial reporting problem; comparative analysis problem; research assignment; and Internet-based assignment

Chapter 11: Liabilities

- New Feature Story and related "A Look Back" exercise with solution
- New real-world company illustrations
- New infographics on types of bonds
- New EOC material: four new problems, financial reporting problem, comparative analysis problem, interpreting financial statements, and Internet-based assignment

Chapter 12: Corporations: Organization, Stock Transactions, Dividends, and Retained Earnings

- New Feature Story and related "A Look Back" exercise with solution

- Revised accounting rules on treatment of organization costs
- New infographic on indirect issuance of stock
- New infographic on effect of stock dividend
- New Accounting in Action box on stock price per share
- New EOC material: two new problems, financial reporting problem, comparative analysis problem, and Internet-based assignment

Chapter 13: Investments

- New Feature Story and related "A Look Back" exercise with solution
- Expanded discussion on why companies purchase investment securities, and new infographic on why companies invest
- Enhanced discussion of temporary investments
- New Accounting in Action box on financial implications of merger of Time Warner and Turner Broadcasting
- Reduced coverage of consolidated financial statements
- New EOC material: three new problems, financial reporting problem, comparative analysis problem, research assignment, and two Internet-based assignments

Chapter 14: The Statement of Cash Flows

- New infographics on cash flows
- Integrated Kellogg Company financial data throughout all illustrations and analyses
- New EOC material: brief exercise, exercise, two problems, financial reporting problem, comparative analysis problem, and Internet-based assignment

Chapter 15: Financial Statement Analysis

- New Feature Story and related "A Look Back" exercise with solution
- Integrated Sears, Roebuck and Company financial data throughout analysis illustrations
- New Technology in Action box
- New EOC material: two new problems, financial reporting problem, comparative analysis problem, and Internet-based assignment

Appendix A: Specimen Financial Statements

- Kellogg Company financial statements

Appendix B: Specimen Financial Statements

- General Mills, Inc. financial statements

Appendix C: Time Value of Money

Appendix D: Payroll Accounting

Appendix E: Subsidiary Ledgers and Special Journals

Appendix F: Other Significant Liabilities

Proven Pedagogical Framework

Financial Accounting has always provided tools to help students learn accounting concepts and procedures and apply them to the real world. The Third Edition places increased emphasis on the processes students undergo as they learn.

Learning How to Use the Text

- A **Student Owner's Manual** begins the text to help students understand the value of the text's learning aids and how to use them.
- After becoming familiar with the text, students can take a *Learning Styles Quiz* to help them identify how they learn best (visually, aurally, through reading and writing, kinesthetically, or through a combination of those styles). They then get tips on in-class and at-home learning strategies, as well as help in identifying the text features that would be most useful to them when they study.
- Chapter 1 contains **notes** that explain each learning aid the first time it appears.
- Finally, **The Navigator** pulls all the learning aids together into a learning system designed to guide students through each chapter and help them succeed in learning the material. It consists of (1) a checklist at the beginning of the chapter, which outlines text features and study skills they will need, and (2) a series of check boxes that prompt students to use the learning aids in the chapter and set priorities as they study. At the end of the chapter, students are reminded to return to The Navigator to check off their completed work. An example of The Navigator is shown below.

THE NAVIGATOR ✔

- ■ Understand *Concepts for Review* ☐
- ■ Read *Feature Story* ☐
- ■ Scan *Study Objectives* ☐
- ■ Read *Preview* ☐
- ■ Read text and answer *Before You Go On*
  p. 370 ☐ *p. 376* ☐ *p. 385* ☐ *p. 390* ☐
- ■ Work *Demonstration Problem* ☐
- ■ Review *Summary of Study Objectives* ☐
- ■ Answer *Self-Study Questions* ☐
- ■ Complete assignments ☐

Understanding the Context

- **Concepts for Review,** listed at the beginning of each chapter from Chapter 2 on, identify concepts from previous chapters that will apply in the chapter to come. In this way, students see the relevance to the current chapter of concepts covered earlier.

- The **Feature Story** helps students picture how the chapter topic relates to the real world of accounting and business. It also serves as a running example in the chapter and is the topic of a series of review questions called **A Look Back at Our Feature Story,** toward the end of the chapter.
- **Study Objectives** form a learning framework throughout the text, with each objective repeated in the margin at the appropriate place in the main body of the chapter and again in the **Summary.** Further, end-of-chapter assignment materials are linked to the Study Objectives.
- A chapter **Preview** links the chapter-opening Feature Story to the major topics of the chapter. First, an introductory paragraph explains how the Feature Story relates to the topic to be discussed, and then a graphic outline of the chapter provides a "visual road map," useful for seeing the big picture as well as the connections between subtopics.

Learning the Material

- **Financial statements** appear regularly throughout the book. Those from real companies are usually identified by a logo or related photo. Often, numbers or categories are highlighted in colored type to draw students' attention to key information.
- **Key ratios,** using data from **Kellogg Company's 1998 Annual Report,** are examined in appropriate spots throughout the text. Integration of ratios enables students to see in a single presentation two important pieces of information about financial data: how they are presented in financial statements as well as how they are analyzed by users of financial information. In addition, a complete presentation of ratio analysis is included in Chapter 15 on financial statement analysis.
- **Accounting Equation** analyses have been inserted in the margin next to key journal entries throughout the text. This new feature reinforces the students' understanding of the impact of an accounting transaction on the financial statements.
- **Key terms** and concepts are printed in blue where they are first explained in the text and are defined again in the end-of-chapter glossary.
- **Helpful Hints** in the margins help clarify concepts being discussed.
- **Accounting in Action** boxes give students insight into how real companies use accounting in practice. The boxes, highlighted with striking photographs, cover business, ethics, and international issues.
- **Technology in Action** sections, identified by a CD icon, show how computers are used by accountants and users of accounting information.
- **Color illustrations** visually reinforce important concepts of the text.
- **Infographics,** a special type of illustration, help students visualize and apply accounting concepts to the real world. They provide entertaining and memorable visual reminders of key concepts.
- **Alternative Terminology** presents synonymous terms, since terminology may differ from discipline to discipline.

- **Before You Go On** sections occur at the end of each key topic and often consist of two parts:

    * *Review It* questions serve as a learning check by asking students to stop and answer questions about the material just covered. *Review It* questions marked with the *Tony The Tiger*™ icon (see margin) send students to find information in Kellogg Company's 1998 Annual Report (packaged with the text and excerpted in Appendix A at the end of the text). These excercises help cement students' understanding of how topics covered in the chapter are reported in real-world financial statements. Answers appear at the end of the chapter.

    * A mini-demonstration problem, in a section called *Do It*, gives immediate practice of the material just covered and is keyed to homework exercises. Solutions are provided to help students understand the reasoning involved in reaching an answer.

    The last **Before You Go On** exercise takes students back for a critical look at the chapter-opening Feature Story.

- Marginal **International Notes** introduce international issues and problems in accounting.

- Marginal **Ethics Notes** help sensitize students to the real-world ethical dilemmas of accounting.

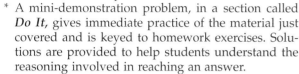

Putting It Together

- **Demonstration Problems** give students the opportunity to refer to a detailed solution to a representative problem as they do homework assignments. *Problem-solving strategies* assist students in understanding the solution and establishing a logic for approaching similar types of problems.

- The **Summary of Study Objectives** relates the study objectives to the key points of the chapter. It gives students another opportunity to review, as well as to see how all the key topics within the chapter are related.

- The **Glossary** defines all the key terms and concepts introduced in the chapter.

Developing Skills Through Practice

- **Self-Study Questions** are a practice test that enables students to check their understanding of important concepts. With questions keyed to the Study Objectives, students can go back and review sections of the chapter in which they find they need further work. Answers appear on the last page of the chapter.

- **Questions** provide a full review of chapter content and help students prepare for class discussions and testing situations.

- **Brief Exercises** build students' confidence and test their basic skills. Each Brief Exercise focuses on one of the **Study Objectives.**

- Each of the **Exercises** focuses on one or more **Study Objectives.** These tend to take a little longer to complete, and they present more of a challenge to students than Brief Exercises. The **Exercises** help instructors and students make a manageable transition to more challenging problems. Certain exercises, marked with a ▥▤▤▷ , help students practice business writing skills.

- **Problems** stress the application of the concepts presented in the chapter. Two sets—**A** and **B**—have corresponding problems keyed to the same **Study Objectives,** thus giving instructors greater flexibility in assigning homework. Certain problems, marked with a ▥▤▤▷ , help build business writing skills.

- Each **Brief Exercise, Exercise,** and **Problem** has a description of the concept covered and is keyed to **Study Objectives.**

- **General Ledger Problems,** identified by ⊡ , are selected problems that can be solved using the General Ledger Software package.

- **Spreadsheet Problems,** identified by ⬰ , are selected exercises and problems that can be solved using *Solving Financial Accounting Problems Using Excel for Windows.*

Expanding and Applying Knowledge

Broadening Your Perspective is a unique section at the end of each chapter that offers a wealth of resources to help instructors and students pull together the learning for the chapter. This section offers problems and projects for those instructors who want to broaden the learning experience by bringing in more real-world decision-making and critical thinking activities. The elements of the Broadening Your Perspective section are described below.

- A **Financial Reporting Problem** directs students to study various aspects of the financial statements in Kellogg Company's 1998 Annual Report, which is packaged with the text and excerpted in Appendix A at the end of the text.

- A **Comparative Analysis Problem** offers the opportunity to compare and contrast Kellogg's financial reporting with that of a competitor, General Mills, Inc. (whose 1998 financial statements are in Appendix B at the end of the book.)

- **Research Assignments** lead students to reports and articles published in various popular business periodicals for further study and analysis of key topics.

- **Interpreting Financial Statements** ask students to read parts of financial statements of actual companies and to interpret that information in light of concepts presented in the chapter.

- The **Real-World Focus** asks students to apply concepts presented in the chapter to specific situations faced by actual companies.

- The **Group Decision Case** helps build decision-making skills by analyzing accounting information in a less structured situation. These cases require evaluation of a manager's decision or lead to a decision among alternative courses of action. As group activities, they promote teamwork.

- **Communication Activities** ask students to engage in real-world business situations using writing, speaking, or presentation skills.

- **Ethics Cases** describe typical ethical dilemmas and ask students to analyze the situation, identify the stakeholders and the ethical issues involved, and decide on an appropriate course of action.

- **Surfing the Net** exercises guide students to Internet sites where they can find and analyze information related to the chapter topic.

Accounting Education Change Commission Recommendations Applied

As indicated earlier, we must involve the student in the learning process and ensure that he or she understands the *why* as well as the *how*. We therefore have provided material that should help students in the following areas, as recommended by the Accounting Education Change Commission.

Communication Skills. Each chapter requires answers to certain exercises and problems, identified by a pencil icon, to be in the form of written business communications such as memos or reports. In addition, the entire Broadening Your Perspective section provides students with an opportunity to use both oral and written communication skills.

Critical Thinking and Decision-Making Skills. Every chapter has a section of Critical Thinking activities. In addition, before the end of the chapter proper, students are asked to recall the opening Feature Story of each chapter in a critical thinking exercise. There is also at least one Group Decision Case per chapter. These cases require an evaluation of a manager's decision or lead to a decision concerning alternative courses of action. In addition, many exercises and problems require analysis and interpretation of financial statements.

Ethics. A discussion of ethics appears in Chapter 1 of the text. Each chapter has an Ethics Case that is relevant to the chapter. In addition, selected real-world "Accounting in Action: Ethics Insights" are provided in the text and ethics notes are provided in the margins.

International Accounting. This topic is covered in a section in Chapter 7 and in examples throughout the book. In Chapter 7, the importance of international trade is explained, and the magnitude of foreign sales for major U.S. companies is illustrated. The section concludes with an explanation of financial statements and the setting of uniform international accounting standards. In addition, "Accounting in Action: International Insights" are provided in the text, and International Notes are provided in the margins to illustrate interesting international accounting issues.

Real-World Emphasis. *Financial Accounting* has been the leader in the use of real-world vignettes. The vignettes, called Accounting in Action, are classified as (1) Business Insight, (2) International Insight, and (3) Ethics Insight. In the Third Edition, we continue to use real-world vignettes extensively in every chapter. We have also included a Real-World Focus case in each chapter, which addresses an accounting issue faced by a real corporation. In addition, the majority of the chapter-opening Feature Stories focus on accounting issues in the business world.

As in earlier editions, Appendix A at the end of the text includes the annual report of a major U.S. corporation. In this edition, we chose Kellogg Company. In addition, to allow for comparison, we have added, in a new Appendix B, the financial statements of one of Kellogg's competitors, General Mills, Inc.

In the Broadening Your Perspective activities at the end of each chapter we have a comprehensive selection of real-world activities called Financial Reporting and Analysis. The activities in the section include: Financial Reporting Problem (an analysis of Kellogg's financial statements); Comparative Analysis Problem (comparison of the financial results of Kellogg vs. General Mills); Research Assignment (designed to sharpen research skills and analytical abilities); Interpreting Financial Statements (activities that focus on interesting financial analysis challenges for real companies); Real-World Focus (an activity that looks at the financial reporting practices of a real company); and Surfing the Net (activities designed to illustrate the variety of accounting issues and information available on the Internet). In addition, financial ratios for Sears as well as department store industry data from Dun & Bradstreet are provided in Chapter 15, Financial Statement Analysis.

Technology Vignettes. *Financial Accounting* was the pioneer text in using technology vignettes. These real-world vignettes, called Technology in Action, give students an opportunity throughout the text to see how computers are used in the accounting business world.

SUPPLEMENTARY MATERIALS AND TEACHING AIDS

Financial Accounting, Third Edition, features a full line of teaching and learning resources developed and revised to help you create a more dynamic and innovative learning environment.

The success of students is a major theme of the entire supplements package. Vital current topics such as communication skills, critical thinking and decision making, ethics, and real-world emphasis are integrated throughout. These resources—including print, software, and Internet-based materials—also take an *active learning approach* to help build students' skills and analytical abilities.

Web Site at www.wiley.com/college/weygandt. Recognizing that the World Wide Web is a valuable resource for students and instructors, we have developed a Web Site at www.wiley.com/college/weygandt to provide a variety of additional resources. Internet cases, company Web sites and useful accounting links will be included. Students will also be provided with an e-mail feedback form that, when sent, goes to the authors.

Instructor's Resources. For the instructor, we have designed an extensive support package to help you maximize your teaching effectiveness. We offer useful supplements for instructors with various levels of experience and different instructional circumstances.

Instructor's Resource System on CD-ROM. Responding to the changing needs of instructors, the Supplement CD-ROM provides the instructor support material in an easy-to-use and navigate electronic format. This CD-ROM contains all the print supplements, as well as the electronic ones, for use in the classroom, for printing out material, or for downloading and modifying.

Solutions Manual. The Solutions Manual contains detailed solutions to all exercises and problems in the textbook and suggested answers to the questions and cases. Print is large and bold for easy readability in lecture settings. Each chapter includes an *assignment classification table* (identified end-of-chapter items by study objectives), an *assignment characteristics table* (describes each problem and alternate problem), a *Bloom's taxonomy table* (classifies end-of-chapter items by Bloom's taxonomy of learning skills and objectives), and identifies difficulty level and estimated completion time.

Examination Book and Test Bank. The Third Edition now features a comprehensive testing package designed to allow instructors to tailor examinations according to study objectives, learning skills and objectives, and selected content. This package consists of a Test Bank of over 2,000 examination questions and exercises accompanied by answers and solutions. Each chapter includes a *Summary of Questions by Objectives* and a *Summary of Objectives by Questions* (linking test items to Study Objectives), and an indication of placement among Bloom's taxonomy. Exercises are also identified by estimated completion time. In addition to the examination material provided for each chapter, comprehensive examinations covering three to five chapters are also included.

The Examination Book also includes a series of preprinted Achievement Tests for easy testing of major concepts. Each test covers two chapters from the textbook. The tests, easy to photocopy and distribute directly to students, consist of multiple-choice, matching, true/false, and problems and exercises (computation and journal entries). Solutions are included at the end of each Achievement Test.

Test Preparation Service. Simply call Wiley's special number (1-800-541-5602) with the questions you want on an examination. Wiley will provide a customized master exam within 24 hours. If you prefer, random selection from a number of chapters is possible.

Solutions Transparencies. Packaged in an organizer box with chapter file folders, these transparencies feature detailed solutions to all exercises and problems in the textbook, and suggested answers to the cases. They feature large, bold type for better projection and easy readability in large classroom settings. Accuracy is assured—all solutions were extensively checked by the authors and reviewers.

Teaching Transparencies. One hundred and thirty-four illustrations are available in four-color format. The authors have selected these illustrations from the text and

from original exhibits outside the text as well. Designed to support and clarify concepts in the text, the Teaching Transparencies will enhance lectures. Suggestions on how to integrate the Teaching Transparencies are included in the Instructor's Manual.

Instructor's Manual. The Instructor's Manual is a comprehensive resource guide designed to assist professors in preparing lectures and assignments. The manual is set in a print size large enough for easy reading or use as transparency masters. It includes a sample syllabus use of the textbook. A correlation chart for all end-of-chapter exercises and problems and a correlation chart of chapter contents helps instructors adapt their lecture materials for a smooth transition to the Third Edition.

Included for each chapter are an *assignment classification table,* an *assignment characteristics table,* a *list of study objectives* in extra large, bold-face print for transparencies; a *chapter review* of the significant topics and points contained in the chapter; *enhanced lecture outlines* with teaching tips and references to text material; *suggestions for integrating supplements* into the classroom; a *20-minute quiz* in the form of 10 true/false and 5 multiple-choice questions (with solutions); and illustrations, including diagrams, graphs, questions and exercises, for use as classroom hand-outs, overhead transparencies, in-class quizzes, or demonstrations (solutions are provided).

Checklist of Key Figures. A listing of key amounts for textbook problems, allowing students to verify the accuracy of their answers as they work through the assignments, is available at the *Financial Accounting* Web site at http://www.wiley.com/college/weygandt.

Additional Solutions Manuals. Solutions Manuals are also available for the following:

- University Bookstore, Inc.: A Corporate Practice Set
- Solving Financial Accounting Problems Using Excel and Lotus 1-2-3

Technology Supplements for Instructors

Computerized Test Bank. The collection of objective questions and exercises with answers for each chapter in the textbook is available for use with IBM and IBM-true compatibles. The Computerized Test Bank offers a number of valuable options. You can:

- Quickly generate a large number of test questions randomly or manually.
- Modify and customize test questions by either changing existing problems or by adding your own problems.
- Create multiple versions of the same test by scrambling questions by type, chapter, or number.
- Customize exams with headers, page and margin size, and question numbering.
- Preview tests prior to printing (the answer key prints with the test).
- Store tests on a separate disk or hard drive and retrieve them later for playback.
- Save tests as ASCII files for export into other word-processing applications.

PowerPoint Presentation Material. This powerful PowerPoint lecture aid contains a combination of key concepts, images, and problems from the textbook for use in the classroom. Designed according to the organization of the material in the textbook, this series of electronic transparencies can be used to reinforce financial accounting principles visually and graphically. PowerPoint viewer is included, so users are not required to have PowerPoint already installed. However, users with PowerPoint will be able to add their own material to the presentation, or modify existing material to meet their needs.

General Ledger Software Evaluator Disk. This program is a simple way to evaluate students' answers prepared using the General Ledger Software. It evaluates both the transactions that were posted and the ending balances for each of the accounts. The program also includes many reporting options, allowing instructors to print detailed or summary reports for a student or a class using a variety of sort sequences.

Wiley Nightly Business Report **Video.** This video contains segments from the highly respected *Nightly Business Report*, which have been selected for their applicability to accounting financial and for their reinforcement of key concepts in the text. Each of the segments is approximately 3 to 5 minutes long and can be used to introduce topics to the students, enhance lecture material, and provide real-world context for related concepts. Suggestions for integrating the material into the classroom are included in the Video Instructor's Manual.

Technical Support. If you need assistance for any Wiley technology product, please contact Wiley at one of these addresses:

Tech support e-mail: techhelp@jwiley.com
Tech support hotline: 1-212-850-6753
Tech support Web page: http://www.wiley.com/techsupport

Student Active Learning Aids

In addition to the innovative pedagogy included in the text, we offer a number of valuable learning aids for the student. These are intended to enhance true understanding so that students will be able to apply financial accounting concepts.

Working Papers. Working Papers are partially completed accounting forms for all end-of-chapter exercises, problems, and cases. A convenient resource for organizing and completing homework assignments, they demonstrate how to correctly set up solution formats and are directly tied to textbook assignments. Each page of the Working Papers has the problem number and company name, and space for students to write their name and course information, providing instructors with consistent forms to grade.

Student Study Guide. The Student Study Guide is a comprehensive review of financial accounting and a powerful tool for students to use in the classroom. It guides students through chapters by tying content to study objectives and provides resources for use during lectures. This is an excellent resource when preparing for exams. Each chapter of the Student Study Guide includes:

- Study Objectives and a chapter review consisting of 20 to 30 key points to reinforce the material in the textbook.
- A demonstration problem linked to study objectives in the textbook.
- Additional opportunities for students to practice their knowledge and skills through true/false, multiple-choice, and matching questions related to key terms, and exercises linked to study objectives.
- Solutions to the exercises explaining the hows and whys so students get immediate feedback.
- A chapter outline with space provided for students to take lecture notes.
- Blank working papers for students to record any problems and examples presented in class.

Self-Study Problems/Solutions Book. This Self-Study tutorial is designed to improve students' success rates in solving financial accounting homework assignments and exam questions. The Self-Study also provides additional insight and tips on how to study financial accounting. Each chapter includes:

- An overview of key chapter topics and a review of chapter Study Objectives.
- Purpose statements for each question, case, or exercise, and a direct link to Study Objectives.
- Tips to alert students to common pitfalls and misconceptions, as well as reminders of concepts and principles to help solve problems.
- A selection of multiple-choice questions, exercises, and cases representative of common exam questions or homework assignments to enhance student proficiency.
- Detailed solutions and explanations to assist students in the approach, setup, and completion of problems.

Take Note! This handy note-taking guide includes all the PowerPoint presentations printed out three to a page, with spaces next to them for you to take notes. Take Note! allows you to focus on the discussions at hand, instead of focusing on copying down slides projected in class.

Practice Set. **University Bookstore, Inc.** is a corporate practice set that exposes students to a real-world simulation of maintaining a complete set of accounting records for a business, integrating business events, accounting concepts, and records. Performed either independently or in a group, the set includes few transactions and thus reinforces students' analytical and creative problem-solving skills.

Technology Supplements for Students

General Ledger Software. The General Ledger Software (GLS) is one of the most exciting technology supplements that accompanies the Third Edition. Available in a Windows or Network version, the General

Ledger Software program allows students to solve selected end-of-chapter text problems, which are identified by a diskette icon in the margin in the text.

- GLS is ideal for instructors who want their students to gain a hands-on feel for a computerized accounting system. The program demonstrates the immediate effects of each transaction, helping students understand the use of computers in a real-world accounting environment.
- GLS has the ability to modify the existing chart of accounts and beginning balances when creating new problems. This increases the instructor's flexibility in assigning alternate problems within the textbook. This feature also provides students with more opportunity to practice with computerized accounting systems.
- GLS is user-friendly and easy to use, with little start-up time. The Windows version is on two disks, plus a data disk.

Computerized Practice Sets.   The General Ledger Software is used to computerize University Bookstore, Inc.: A Corporate Practice Set.

Students receive the same materials as for the manual versions, but use GLS to input the transaction data. Screens for inputting data closely resemble those of general ledger packages that students will encounter in real-world business settings. The program will automatically post, close, and generate all financial statements.

Solving Financial Accounting Problems Using Excel for Windows.   These electronic spreadsheet templates allow students to complete selected end-of-chapter exercises and problems identified by a spreadsheet icon in the margin of the text. The manual, which includes the disks, guides students step-by-step from an introduction to computers and Excel, to completing preprogrammed spreadsheets, to designing their own spreadsheets. Prepared for students with a range of experience in spreadsheet applications, these templates and tutorials help students develop and hone their computer skills and expose them to software packages often used in real-world business environments.

Financial Accounting Tutor (FAcT).   FAcT is a self-paced CD-ROM tutorial designed to review financial accounting concepts. It uses simple examples that have been carefully crafted to introduce concepts gradually. Throughout, the program emphasizes the logic underlying the accounting process. FAcT uses interactive and graphical tools to enhance the learning process. Intuitive navigation and a powerful search mechanism allow you to easily follow the tutorial from start to finish or skip to the topics you want to complete. The discussions and examples are followed by brief, interactive problems that provide immediate feedback. Built-in tools, such as an on-line financial calculator, help solve the problems.

On-Line Business Survival Guide in Accounting. The journey of 1,000 Web sites begins with one click, and this practical guide gets you on the road. The On-Line Business Survival Guide is a brief, clear introduction to using the World Wide Web as a business research tool. Starting with the basics, this manual covers everything you need to know to become a master sleuth at finding critical information on the Internet. In addition, the guide provides a hands-on guide to using the Wall Street Journal Interactive Edition, as well as a discount offer for a subscription to the Wall Street Journal Interactive on-line.

Business Extra Web Site at http://www.wiley.com/ college/businessextra.   To complement the On-Line Business Survival Guide, the Business Extra Web Site gives you instant access to a wealth of current articles dealing with all aspects of financial accounting. The articles are organized by topic, and discussion questions follow each article. You will find a password inside the On-Line Business Survival Guide that will give you access to the Business Extra Web Site.

Jerry J. Weygandt
Madison, Wisconsin

Donald E. Kieso
DeKalb, Illinois

Paul D. Kimmel
Milwaukee, Wisconsin

ACKNOWLEDGMENTS

During the course of development of *Financial Accounting* the authors benefited greatly from manuscript reviewers and ancillary authors and proofers. The constructive suggestions and innovative ideas of the reviewers and the creativity and accuracy of the ancillary authors and checkers is greatly appreciated.

Reviewers and Focus Group Participants

Dawn Addington, Albuquerque TVI Community College
Laura Claus, Louisiana State University
Leslie Cohen, University of Arizona
Larry R. Falcetto, Emporia State University
Susan Kattelus, Eastern Michigan University
Mona Khaitan, Massachusetts Bay Community College
John Purisky, Salem State College
Ellen Sweat, Georgia Perimeter College
William Seltz, University of Massachusetts
Barbara Theisen, Oakland University
James Volpi, Rider University
Edward R. Walker, University of Texas-Pan American

Ancillary Authors, Contributors, and Proofers

Marianne Bradford (University of Tennessee, Knoxville)—PowerPoint Presentation Author
John C. Borke (University of Wisconsin, Platteville)—Solutions Manual Proofer and Technical Advisor
Larry Falcetto (Emporia State University)—Supplements Coordinator and Instructor's Manual and Test Bank Author
Jessica Frazier (Eastern Kentucky University)—Video Selector and Video Guide Author
Wayne Higley (Buena Vista University)—Content Proofer and Technical Advisor

Marilyn F. Hunt (University of Central Florida)—Self-Study Guide Author
Douglas W. Kieso (University of California, Irvine)—Study Guide Author
Jennifer Laudermilch (Coopers & Lybrand)—Self-Study Guide Proofer
Gary Lubin—General Ledger Software Programmer
Alice Sineath (Forsyth Technical Community College)—Test Bank and Study Guide Proofer
Dick Wasson (Southwestern College)—Working Papers Author and Solutions Manual Proofer

We appreciate the exemplary support and professional commitment given us by our solutions manual compositor Elm Street Publications (Ginger Yarrow and Barb Lange), our word processor Mary Ann Benson, our executive editor Susan Elbe, the vice president of college production and manufacturing Ann Berlin, our development editors Ann Torbert and Nancy Perry, our supplements editor Julie Kerr, and our production coordinator Suzanne Ingrao.

We thank Kellogg Company and General Mills, Inc. for permitting us the use of their 1998 Annual Reports for our specimen financial statements and accompanying notes.

Suggestions and comments from users are encouraged and appreciated. Please feel free to contact any one of us.

Jerry J. Weygandt

Donald E. Kieso

Paul D. Kimmel

HOW TO USE THE STUDY AIDS IN THIS BOOK

Concepts for Review, listed at the beginning of each chapter from Chapter 2 on, are the accounting concepts you learned in previous chapters that you will need to know in order to understand the topics you are about to learn. Page references are provided if you need to review before reading the chapter.

CONCEPTS FOR REVIEW

Before studying this chapter, you should know or, if necessary, review:

a. The cost principle (Ch. 1, p. 9) and matching principle of accounting. (Ch. 3, p. 94)
b. How to record purchases, sales, and cost of goods sold under a perpetual inventory system. (Ch. 5, pp. 191–199)
c. How to prepare financial statements for a merchandising company. (Ch. 5, pp. 199–203)

THE NAVIGATOR

The Navigator is a learning system designed to guide you through each chapter and help you succeed in learning the material. It consists of (1) a checklist at the beginning of the chapter, which outlines text features and study skills you will need, and (2) a series of check boxes that prompt you to use the learning aids in the chapter and set priorities as you study.

FEATURE STORY

Taking Stock— from Backpacks to Bicycles

Backpacks and jackets sporting the jagged peaks of the Mountain Equipment Co-op (MEC) logo are a familiar sight on hiking trails and campuses. Sales of these popular items help the Vancouver-based co-op to finance its primary goal: to

provide members with products and services for wilderness recreational activities, such as hiking and mounteering, at a reasonable cost.

MEC has five retail stores across Canada and a huge market in catalogue sales around the world. It ships everything from climbing ropes, kayaks, and bike helmets to destinations as far away as Japan and South America.

Keeping financial track of the flow of these items is a responsibility of Fara Jumani, a member of the inventory costing group at MEC and a part-time college student. "We have tens of thousands of items in inventory, and we are adding new ones all the time," says Ms. Jumani. "Because we make a lot of our own clothing goods, we [track] in-house inventory—plies that will be used [in our] products."

MEC tracks the [in]ventory using the av[erage cost method.] the various items in [inventory are] weighted by the nu[mber of units] at each different un[it cost. "The] average cost metho[d] tend to fluctuate," e[xplains Ms. Ju]mani, "that method [reduces] our overall costs."

Unlike most ret[ail stores,] MEC is not out to [maximize profit. As] a co-op, it exists to [serve its mem]bers. "But we have [to remain] healthy to do that," [explains Ms.] Jumani. "If we go b[ankrupt we] won't be serving an[yone. So car]ing for inventory— [from] backpacks to bicycle[s—is] an important part o[f] MEC's fiscal fitness regimen.

CHAPTER 6

INVENTORIES

THE NAVIGATOR ✓

- Understand *Concepts for Review* ☐
- Read *Feature Story* ☐
- Scan *Study Objectives* ☐
- Read *Preview* ☐
- Read text and answer *Before You Go On*
  p. 236 ☐ p. 242 ☐ p. 251 ☐ p. 255 ☐
- Work *Demonstration Problem* ☐
- Review *Summary of Study Objectives* ☐
- Answer *Self-Study Questions* ☐
- Complete assignments ☐

The **Feature Story** helps you picture how the chapter topic relates to the real world of accounting and business. You will find references to the story throughout the chapter and in the problem called **A Look Back at Our Feature Story** toward the end of the chapter.

STUDY OBJECTIVES

After studying this chapter, you should be able to:

1. Describe the steps in determining inventory quantities.
2. Prepare the entries for purchases and sales of inventory under a periodic inventory system.
3. Determine cost of goods sold under a periodic inventory system.
4. Identify the unique features of the income statement for a merchandising company using a periodic inventory system.
5. Explain the basis of accounting for inventories and describe the inventory cost flow methods.
6. Explain the financial statement and tax effects of each of the inventory cost flow methods.
7. Explain the lower of cost or market basis of accounting for inventories.
8. Indicate the effects of inventory errors on the financial statements.
9. Compute and interpret the inventory turnover ratio.

THE NAVIGATOR

231

Study Objectives at the beginning of each chapter give you a framework for learning the specific concepts and procedures covered in the chapter. You will also see each study objective in the margin where the concept is discussed. Finally, you can review all the study objectives in the **Summary** at the end of the chapter.

The Preview starts with an introductory paragraph linking the feature story with the major topics of the chapter. It is followed by a graphic outline of major topics and subtopics that will be discussed. This preview gives you a mental framework upon which to arrange the new information you are learning.

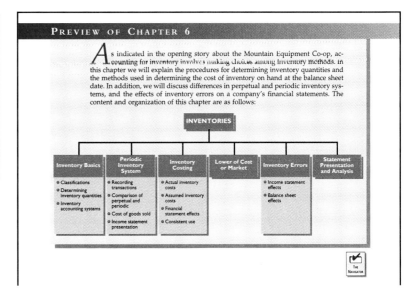

The Accounting Equation has been inserted in the margin next to key journal entries throughout the text. This new feature helps you understand the impact of an accounting transaction on the financial statements.

238   Chapter 6 • Inventories

A	=	L	+	SE
−3,430		−3,500		+70

May 14	Accounts Payable	3,500	
	Purchase Discounts		70
	Cash		3,430
	(To record payment to Highpoint Electronic within the discount period)		

Purchase Discounts is a temporary account whose normal balance is a credit.

Recording Sales of Merchandise

The sale of $3,800 of merchandise to Chelsea Video on May 4 (sales invoice No. 731, Illustration 5-4) is recorded by the seller, Highpoint Electronic, as follows:

A	=	L	+	SE
+3,800				+3,800

May 4	Accounts Receivable	3,800	
	Sales		3,800
	(To record credit sales per invoice #731 to Chelsea Video)		

Inventory Basics   233

Classifying Inventory

How a company classifies its inventory depends on whether the firm is a merchandiser or a manufacturer. In a **merchandising enterprise**, inventory consists of many different items. For example, in a grocery store, canned goods, dairy products, meats, and produce are just a few of the inventory items on hand. These items have two common characteristics: (1) they are owned by the company, and (2) they are in a form ready for sale to customers in the ordinary course of business. Thus, only one inventory classification, **merchandise inventory**, is needed to describe the many different items that make up the total inventory.

In a **manufacturing enterprise**, inventories are also owned by the company, but some goods may not yet be ready for sale. As a result, inventory is usually classified into three categories: finished goods, work in process, and raw materials. For example, General Motors classifies automobiles completed and ready for sale as **finished goods**. The automobiles on the assembly line in various stages of production are classified as **work in process**. The steel, glass, upholstery, and other components that are on hand waiting to be used in the production of automobiles are identified as **raw materials**.

The accounting principles and concepts discussed in this chapter apply to inventory classifications of both merchandising and manufacturing companies. In this chapter we will focus on merchandise inventory.

HELPFUL HINT
Regardless of the classification, all inventories are reported under Current Assets on the balance sheet.

Helpful Hints in the margins help clarify concepts being discussed.

Determining Inventory Quantities

Many businesses take a physical inventory count on the last day of the year. Businesses using the periodic inventory system are required to take an end-of-the-period physical inventory to determine the inventory on hand at the balance sheet date and to compute cost of goods sold. Even businesses using a perpetual inventory system must take a physical inventory at some time during the year.

Determining inventory quantities consists of two steps: (1) taking a physical inventory of goods on hand, and (2) determining the ownership of goods.

1
STUDY
OBJECTIVE

Describe the steps in determining inventory quantities.

Study Objectives reappear in the margins at the point where the topic is discussed. End-of-chapter assignments are keyed to study objectives.

ILLUSTRATION 6-1
Terms of sale

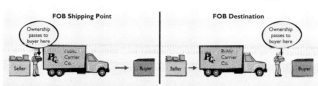

Infographics, a special type of illustration, pictorially link concepts to the real world and provide visual reminders of key concepts.

lowing goods in transit: (1) **sales** of 1,500 units shipped December 31 FOB destination, and (2) **purchases** of 2,500 units shipped FOB shipping point by the seller on December 31. Hargrove has legal title to both the units sold and the units purchased. Consequently, inventory quantities would be understated by 4,000 units (1,500 + 2,500) if units in transit are ignored.

TECHNOLOGY IN ACTION

Many companies have invested large amounts of time and money in automated inventory systems. One of the most sophisticated is Federal Express's Digitally Assisted Dispatch System (DADS). This system uses hand-held "SuperTrackers" to transmit data about the packages and documents to the firm's computer system. Based on bar codes, the system allows the firm to know where any package is at any time to prevent losses and to fulfill the firm's delivery commitments. More recently, FedEx's newly developed software enables customers to track shipments on their own PCs.

Technology in Action boxes, identified by a CD icon, show how computers are used by accountants and users of accounting information.

Accounting in Action boxes give you more glimpses into the real world. Each type of issue—business, ethics, and international—is identified by its own icon. Don't skip over the photos, figures, and tables.

ACCOUNTING IN ACTION
Business Insight

Most small firms use the FIFO method. But fears of rising inflation often cause many firms to switch to LIFO. For example, Chicago Heights Steel Co. in Illinois boosted cash "by 5% to 10% by lowering income taxes" when it switched to LIFO. Electronic games distributor Atlas Distributing Inc., Chicago, considered a switch "because the costs of our games, made in Japan, are rising 15% a year," says Joseph Serpico, treasurer. When inflation heats up, "the number of companies electing LIFO will rise dramatically," says William Spiro of BDO Seidman, New York.

Using Inventory Cost Flow Methods Consistently
Whatever cost flow method a company chooses, it should be used consistently from one accounting period to another. Consistent application enhances the comparability of financial statements over successive time periods. In contrast, using the FIFO method in one year and the LIFO method in the next year would make it difficult to compare the net incomes of the two years.

Although consistent application is preferred, it does not mean that a company may *never* change its method of inventory costing. When a company adopts a different method, the change and its effects on net income should be disclosed in the financial statements. A typical disclosure is shown in Illustration 6-22, using information from recent financial statements of the Quaker Oats Company.

Financial statements appear throughout the book. Those from real companies are identified by a logo or related photo. Often, numbers or categories are highlighted in colored type to draw your attention to key information.

ILLUSTRATION 6-22
Disclosure of change in cost flow method

QUAKER OATS COMPANY
Notes to the Financial Statements

Note 1 Effective July 1, the Company adopted the LIFO cost flow assumption for valuing the majority of U.S. Grocery Products inventories. The Company believes that the use of the LIFO method better matches current costs with current revenues. The effect of this change on the current year was to decrease net income by $16.0 million.

BEFORE YOU GO ON...
Review It

1. How do the cost and matching principles apply to inventoriable costs?
2. How are the three assumed cost flow methods applied in allocating inventoriable costs?
3. What factors should be considered by management in selecting an inventory cost flow method?
4. Which inventory cost flow method produces (a) the highest net income in a period of rising prices, and (b) the lowest income taxes?
5. What amount is reported by Kellogg Company in its 1998 Annual Report as inventories at December 31, 1998? Which inventory cost flow method does Kellogg Company use? The answer to this question is provided on p. 282.

Do It

The accounting records of Shumway Ag Implement show the following data:

Beginning inventory	4,000 units at $3	
Purchases	6,000 units at $4	
Sales	5,000 units at $12	

Determine the cost of goods sold during the period under a periodic inventory system using (a) the FIFO method, (b) the LIFO method, and (c) the average cost method.

Reasoning: Because the units of inventory on hand and available for sale may have been purchased at different prices, a systematic method must be adopted to allocate the costs between the goods sold and the goods on hand (ending inventory).

Solution:
(a) FIFO: (4,000 @ $3) + (1,000 @ $4) = $12,000 + $4,000 = $16,000.
(b) LIFO: 5,000 @ $4 = $20,000.
(c) Average cost: [(4,000 @ $3) + (6,000 @ $4)] ÷ 10,000 = ($12,000 + $24,000) ÷ 10,000 = $3.60 per unit; 5,000 @ $3.60 = $18,000.

Related exercise material: BE6–6, BE6–7, E6–5, E6–6, E6–7.

Before You Go On *Review It* questions serve as a learning check. If you cannot answer these questions, you should go back and read the section again.

Review It questions marked with the Tony the Tiger™ icon ask you to find information in Kellogg's 1998 Annual Report, which is packaged with this text and excerpted in Appendix A at the end of the text.

Brief *Do It* exercises help you apply what you are learning. They outline the *reasoning* necessary to complete the exercise, and their *solutions* help you see how the problem should be solved. (Keyed to homework exercises.)

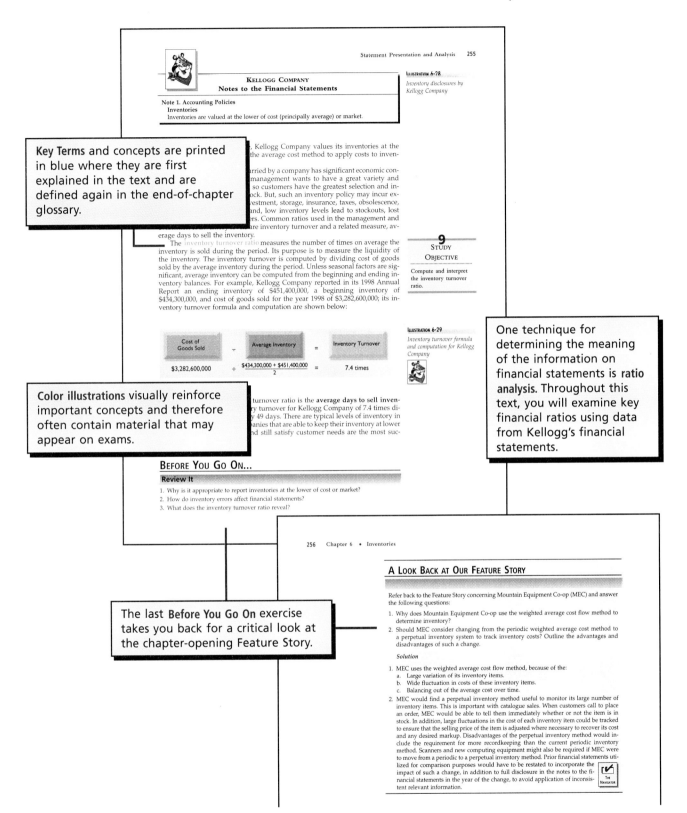

Statement Presentation and Analysis   255

KELLOGG COMPANY
Notes to the Financial Statements

Note 1. Accounting Policies
Inventories
Inventories are valued at the lower of cost (principally average) or market.

ILLUSTRATION 6-28
Inventory disclosures by Kellogg Company

Key Terms and concepts are printed in blue where they are first explained in the text and are defined again in the end-of-chapter glossary.

..., Kellogg Company values its inventories at the ... the average cost method to apply costs to inven-

... carried by a company has significant economic con-... management wants to have a great variety and ... so customers have the greatest selection and in-...ock. But, such an inventory policy may incur ex-...vestment, storage, insurance, taxes, obsolescence, ...and, low inventory levels lead to stockouts, lost ...ers. Common ratios used in the management and ...are inventory turnover and a related measure, av-erage days to sell the inventory.
The inventory turnover ratio measures the number of times on average the inventory is sold during the period. Its purpose is to measure the liquidity of the inventory. The inventory turnover is computed by dividing cost of goods sold by the average inventory during the period. Unless seasonal factors are sig-nificant, average inventory can be computed from the beginning and ending in-ventory balances. For example, Kellogg Company reported in its 1998 Annual Report an ending inventory of $451,400,000, a beginning inventory of $434,300,000, and cost of goods sold for the year 1998 of $3,282,600,000; its in-ventory turnover formula and computation are shown below:

9
STUDY OBJECTIVE

Compute and interpret the inventory turnover ratio.

ILLUSTRATION 6-29
Inventory turnover formula and computation for Kellogg Company

Cost of Goods Sold	÷	Average Inventory	=	Inventory Turnover
$3,282,600,000	÷	$\dfrac{\$434,300,000 + \$451,400,000}{2}$	=	7.4 times

One technique for determining the meaning of the information on financial statements is **ratio analysis**. Throughout this text, you will examine key financial ratios using data from Kellogg's financial statements.

Color illustrations visually reinforce important concepts and therefore often contain material that may appear on exams.

...turnover ratio is the **average days to sell inven-**...ry turnover for Kellogg Company of 7.4 times di-...y 49 days. There are typical levels of inventory in ...anies that are able to keep their inventory at lower ...nd still satisfy customer needs are the most suc-

BEFORE YOU GO ON...

Review It

1. Why is it appropriate to report inventories at the lower of cost or market?
2. How do inventory errors affect financial statements?
3. What does the inventory turnover ratio reveal?

256   Chapter 6 • Inventories

A LOOK BACK AT OUR FEATURE STORY

Refer back to the Feature Story concerning Mountain Equipment Co-op (MEC) and answer the following questions:

1. Why does Mountain Equipment Co-op use the weighted average cost flow method to determine inventory?
2. Should MEC consider changing from the periodic weighted average cost method to a perpetual inventory system to track inventory costs? Outline the advantages and disadvantages of such a change.

Solution

1. MEC uses the weighted average cost flow method, because of the:
   a. Large variation of its inventory items.
   b. Wide fluctuation in costs of these inventory items.
   c. Balancing out of the average cost over time.
2. MEC would find a perpetual inventory method useful to monitor its large number of inventory items. This is important with catalogue sales. When customers call to place an order, MEC would be able to tell them immediately whether or not the item is in stock. In addition, large fluctuations in the cost of each inventory item could be tracked to ensure that the selling price of the item is adjusted where necessary to recover its cost and any desired markup. Disadvantages of the perpetual inventory method would in-clude the requirement for more recordkeeping than the current periodic inventory method. Scanners and new computing equipment might also be required if MEC were to move from a periodic to a perpetual inventory method. Prior financial statements util-ized for comparison purposes would have to be restated to incorporate the impact of such a change, in addition to full disclosure in the notes to the fi-nancial statements in the year of the change, to avoid application of inconsis-tent relevant information.

THE NAVIGATOR

The last **Before You Go On** exercise takes you back for a critical look at the chapter-opening Feature Story.

DEMONSTRATION PROBLEM

Kenwear Company has the following inventory, purchases, and sales data for the month of March:

Inventory, March 1		200 units @ $4.00	$ 800
Purchases:			
	March 10	500 units @ $4.50	2,250
	March 20	400 units @ $4.75	1,900
	March 30	300 units @ $5.00	1,500
Sales:			
	March 15	500 units	
	March 25	400 units	

The physical inventory count on March 31 shows 500 units on hand.

Instructions

Under a **periodic inventory system**, determine the cost of inventory on hand at March 31 and the cost of goods sold for March under the (a) first-in, first-out (FIFO) method, (b) last-in, first-out (LIFO) method, and (c) average cost method.

Demonstration Problems review the chapter material. These sample problems provide you with *problem-solving strategies* and *solutions.*

SOLUTION TO DEMONSTRATION PROBLEM

The cost of goods available for sale is $6,450:

Inventory		200 units @ $4.00	$ 800
Purchases:			
	March 10	500 units @ $4.50	2,250
	March 20	400 units @ $4.75	1,900
	March 30	300 units @ $5.00	1,500
Total cost of goods available for sale			$6,450

Under a **periodic inventory system**, the cost of goods sold under each cost flow method is as follows:

FIFO Method

Ending Inventory:

Date	Units	Unit Cost	Total Cost	
March 30	300	$5.00	$1,500	
March 20	200	4.75	950	$2,450

Cost of goods sold: $6,450 − $2,450 = $4,000

LIFO Method

Ending Inventory:

Date	Units	Unit Cost	Total Cost	
March 1	200	$4.00	$ 800	
March 10	300	4.50	1,350	$2,150

Cost of goods sold: $6,450 − $2,150 = $4,300

Weighted Average Cost Method

Weighted average unit cost: $6,450 ÷ 1,400 = $4.607
Ending inventory: 500 × $4.607 = $2,303.50
Cost of goods sold: $6,450 − $2,303.50 = $4,146.50

PROBLEM-SOLVING STRATEGIES

1. For FIFO, the latest costs are allocated to inventory.
2. For LIFO, the earliest costs are allocated to inventory.
3. For average costs, use a weighted average for periodic.
4. Remember, the costs allocated to cost of goods sold can be proved.
5. Total purchases are the same under all three cost flow methods.

The Glossary defines all the terms and concepts introduced in the chapter. Page references help you find any terms you need to study further.

SUMMARY OF STUDY OBJECTIVES

1. *Describe the steps in determining inventory quantities.* The steps in determining inventory quantities are (1) taking a physical inventory of goods on hand and (2) determining the ownership of goods in transit.

2. *Prepare the entries for purchases and sales of inventory under a periodic inventory system.* In recording purchases, entries are required for (a) cash and credit purchases, (b) purchase returns and allowances, (c) purchase discounts, and (d) freight costs. In recording sales, entries are required for (a) cash and credit sales, (b) sales returns and allowances, and (c) sales discounts.

3. *Determine cost of goods sold under a periodic inventory system.* The steps in determining cost of goods sold are (a) recording the purchase of merchandise, (b) determining the cost of goods purchased, and (c) determining the cost of goods on hand at the beginning and end of the accounting period.

4. *Identify the unique features of the income statement for a merchandising company using a periodic inventory system.* The income statement for a merchandising company contains three sections: sales revenue, cost of goods sold, and operating expenses. The cost of goods sold section under a periodic inventory system generally shows more

---

The Summary of Study Questions relates the study objectives to the key points in the chapter. It gives you another opportunity to review as well as to see how all the key topics within the chapter are related.

GLOSSARY

Average cost method An inventory costing method that assumes that the goods available for sale have the same (average) cost per unit; generally the inventory items are similar in nature (i.e., homogeneous). (p. 247).

Consigned goods Goods shipped by a consignor, who retains ownership, to another party called the consignee. (p. 235).

Cost of goods available for sale The sum of the beginning merchandise inventory plus the cost of goods purchased. (p. 240).

Cost of goods purchased The sum of net purchases plus freight-in. (p. 240).

Cost of goods sold The total cost of merchandise sold during the period, determined by subtracting ending inventory from the cost of goods available for sale. (p. 240).

Current replacement cost The amount that would be paid at the present time to acquire an identical item. (p. 251).

First-in, first-out method (FIFO) An inventory costing method that assumes that the costs of the earliest goods acquired are the first to be recognized as cost of goods sold. (p. 245).

Inventoriable costs The pool of costs that consists of two elements: (1) the cost of the beginning inventory and (2) the cost of goods purchased during the period. (p. 242).

Inventory turnover ra... ber of times on averag... riod. It is computed by dividing cost of goods sold by the average inventory during the period. (p. 255).

Last-in, first-out method (LIFO) An inventory costing method that assumes that the costs of the latest units purchased are the first to be allocated to cost of goods sold. (p. 246).

Lower of cost or market basis (LCM) (inventories) A method of valuing inventory that recognizes the decline in the value when the current purchase price (market) is less than cost. (p. 251).

Net purchases Purchases less purchase returns and allowances and purchase discounts. (p. 240).

Periodic inventory system An inventory system in which inventoriable costs are allocated to ending inventory and cost of goods sold at the end of the period. Cost of goods sold is computed at the end of the period by subtracting the ending inventory (costs are assigned to a physical count of items on hand) from the cost of goods available for sale. (p. 236).

Specific identification method An actual physical flow costing method in which items still in inventory are specifically costed to arrive at the total cost of the ending inventory. (p. 243).

End-of-Chapter Appendixes address topics considered optional by some instructors.

APPENDIX 6A   ESTIMATING INVENTORIES

We have assumed throughout the chapter that a company would be able to do a physical count of its inventory. But what if it cannot, as in the example of the lumber inventory destroyed by fire? In that case, we would use an estimate.

Two circumstances explain the reasons for estimating rather than counting inventories. First, management may want monthly or quarterly financial statements but a physical inventory is taken only annually. Second, a casualty such as fire, flood, or earthquake may make it impossible to take a physical inventory. The need for estimating inventories is associated primarily with a periodic inventory system because of the absence of detailed inventory records.

There are two widely used methods of estimating inventories: (1) the gross profit method and (2) the retail inventory method.

10
STUDY
OBJECTIVE

Describe the two methods of estimating inventories.

Self-Study Questions, a practice test keyed to Study Objectives, give you an opportunity to check your knowledge of important topics. Answers appear on the last page of the chapter.

266   Chapter 6 • Inventories

*Note: All asterisked Questions, Exercises, and Problems relate to material in the appendixes to the chapter.

SELF-STUDY QUESTIONS

Answers are at the end of the chapter.

(SO 2) 1. When goods are purchased for resale by a company using a periodic inventory system:
  a. purchases on account are debited to Merchandise Inventory.
  b. purchases on account are debited to Purchases.
  c. purchase returns are debited to Purchase Returns and Allowances.
  d. freight costs are debited to Purchases.

(SO 3) 2. In determining cost of goods sold (periodic system):
  a. purchases discounts are deducted from net purchases.
  b. freight-out is added to net purchases.
  c. purchase returns and allowances are deducted from net purchases.
  d. freight-in is added to net purchases.

8. In periods of rising prices, LIFO will produce: (SO 6)
  a. higher net income than FIFO.
  b. the same net income as FIFO.
  c. lower net income than FIFO.
  d. higher net income than average costing.

9. Factors that affect the selection of an inventory costing   (SO 6)
  method do *not* include:
  a. tax effects.
  b. balance sheet effects.
  c. income statement effects.
  d. perpetual vs. periodic inventory system.

10. The lower of cost or market basis may be applied to: (SO 7)
  a. categories of inventories.
  b. individual items of inventories.
  c. total inventory.
  d. all of the above.

Questions allow you to explain your understanding of concepts and relationships covered in the chapter.

Questions   267

QUESTIONS

1. Goods costing $1,700 are purchased on account on July 15 with credit terms of 2/10, n/30. On July 18 a $200 credit memo is received from the supplier for damaged goods. Give the journal entry on July 24 to record payment of the balance due within the discount period.

2. Identify the accounts that are added to or deducted from purchases to determine the cost of goods purchased. For each account, indicate (a) whether it is added or deducted and (b) its normal balance.

Once a method has been selected, what accounting requirement applies?

14. Which assumed inventory cost flow method:
  (a) usually parallels the actual physical flow of merchandise?
  (b) assumes that goods available for sale during an accounting period are homogeneous?
  (c) assumes that the latest units purchased are the first to be sold?

---

268   Chapter 6 • Inventories

*26. John Ross Shoe Shop had goods available for sale in 2001 with a retail price of $120,000. The cost of these goods was $84,000. If sales during the period were $90,000, what is the ending inventory at cost using the retail inventory method?

*27. "When perpetual inventory records are kept, the results under the FIFO and LIFO methods are the same as they

would be in a periodic inventory system." Do you agree? Explain.

*28. How does the average method of inventory costing differ between a perpetual inventory system and a periodic inventory system?

BRIEF EXERCISES

Journalize purchase transactions.
(SO 2)

BE6–1 Prepare the journal entries to record the following transactions on Svenska Company's books using a periodic inventory system.
  (a) On March 2, Svenska Company purchased $900,000 of merchandise from Sing Tao Company, terms 2/10, n/30.
  (b) On March 6, Svenska Company returned $130,000 of the merchandise purchased on March 2 because it was defective.
  (c) On March 12, Svenska Company paid the balance due to Sing Tao Company.

Compute net purchases and cost of goods purchased.
(SO 3)

BE6–2 Assume that Shinhan Company uses a periodic inventory system and has the following account balances: Purchases $440,000, Purchase Returns and Allowances $11,000, Purchase Discounts $8,000, and Freight-in $16,000. Determine (a) net purchases and (b) cost of goods purchased.

Compute cost of goods sold and gross profit.
(SO 3)

BE6–3 Assume the same information as in BE6-2, and also that Shinhan Company has beginning inventory of $60,000, ending inventory of $90,000, and net sales of $650,000. Determine the amounts to be reported for cost of goods sold and gross profit.

Brief Exercises help you focus on one Study Objective at a time and thus help you build confidence in your basic skills and knowledge. (Keyed to Study Objectives.)

EXERCISES

E6–1 Presented below is the following information related to Brazil Co.

1. On April 5, purchased merchandise from Chile Company for $10,000 terms 2/10, net/30 FOB shipping point
2. On April 6, paid freight costs of $800 on merchandise purchased from Chile.
3. On April 7, purchased equipment on account for $26,000.
4. On April 8, returned damaged merchandise to Chile Company and was granted a $3,000 allowance.
5. On April 15, paid the amount due to Chile Company in full.

Instructions
(a) Prepare the journal entries to record these transactions on the books of Brazil Co. using a periodic inventory system.
(b) Assume that Brazil Co. paid the balance due to Chile Company on May 4 instead of April 15. Prepare the journal entry to record this payment.

Journalize purchases transactions.
(SO 2)

E6–2 The trial balance of Colombia Company at the end of its fiscal year, August 31, 2001, includes the following accounts: Merchandise Inventory $17,200, Purchases $142,400, Sales $190,000, Freight-in $4,000, Sales Returns and Allowances $3,000, Freight-out $1,000, and Purchase Returns and Allowances $2,000. The ending (August 31, 2001) merchandise inventory is $27,000.

Instructions
Prepare a cost of goods sold section for the year ending August 31 (periodic inventory).

Prepare cost of goods sold section.
(SO 3)

E6–3 Presented is information related to Mexico Co. for the month of January 2001.

Freight-in	$ 10,000	Rent expense	19,000
Freight-out	5,000	Salary expense	61,000
Insurance expense	12,000	Sales discounts	8,000
Purchases	200,000	Sales returns and allowances	13,000
Purchase discounts	3,000	Sales	312,000
Purchase returns and allowances	6,000		

Beginning merchandise inventory was $42,000 and ending inventory was $63,000.

Instructions
Prepare an income statement using the format presented on page 241 (Illustration 6-6). Operating expenses should not be segregated into selling and administrative expenses.

Prepare an income statement.
(SO 4)

E6–4 Yorkville Bank and Trust is considering giving Canada Company a loan. Before doing so, they decide that further discussions with Canada's accountant may be desirable. One area

Determine the correct inventory amount.
(SO 1)

> **Exercises**, which are more difficult than Brief Exercises, help you continue to build your confidence. (Keyed to Study Objectives.)

Determine ending inventory at cost using retail method.
(SO 10)

*E6–13 Swiss Shoe Store uses the retail inventory method for its two departments: Women's Shoes and Men's Shoes. The following information for each department is obtained:

Item	Women's Department	Men's Department
Beginning inventory at cost	$ 32,000	$ 46,450
Cost of goods purchased at cost	148,000	137,300
Net sales	187,000	195,000
Beginning inventory at retail		
Cost of goods purchased at retail		

Instructions
Compute the estimated cost of the ending inventory ... ventory method.

Apply cost flow methods to perpetual records.
(SO 11)

*E6–14 Morocco Appliance uses a perpetual inven... sets, the January 1 inventory was four sets at $600 ... chase was made: Jan. 10, 6 units at $640 each. Tha... sales: Jan. 8, 2 units and Jan. 15, 4 units.

Instructions
Compute the ending inventory under (1) FIFO, (2) ...

> **Spreadsheet Problems**, identified by , are selected exercises and problems that can be solved using the spreadsheet software *Solving Financial Accounting Problems Using Excel for Windows*.

PROBLEMS: SET A

Journalize, post, and prepare a trial balance and partial income statement.
(SO 2, 3, 4)

P6–1A Billy Jean Evert, a former professional tenn... Jackson Lake Resort. At the beginning of the current season, the ledger of B.J.'s Tennis Shop showed Cash $2,500, Merchandise Inventory $1,700, and Common Stock $4,200. The following transactions were completed during April 2001:

Apr. 4 Purchased racquets and balls from Robert Co. $640 FOB shipping point, terms 3/10, n/30.
  6 Paid freight on Robert purchase $40.
  8 Sold merchandise to members $900, terms n/30.
  10 Received credit of $40 from Robert Co. for a damaged racquet that was returned.
  11 Purchased tennis shoes from Niki Sports for cash, $300.
  13 Paid Robert Co. in full.
  14 Purchased tennis shirts and shorts from Martina's Sportswear $700, FOB shipping point, terms 2/10, n/60.
  15 Received cash refund of $50 from Niki Sports for damaged merchandise that was returned.
  17 Paid freight on Martina's Sportswear purchase $30.
  18 Sold merchandise to members, $800, terms n/30.
  20 Received $500 in cash from members in settlement of their accounts.
  21 Paid Martina's Sportswear in full.
  27 Granted credit of $30 to members for tennis clothing that did not fit.
  30 Sold merchandise to members $900, terms n/30.
  30 Received cash payments on account from members, $500.

The chart of accounts for the tennis shop includes the following: No. 101 Cash, No. 112 Accounts Receivable, No. 120 Merchandise Inventory, No. 201 Accounts Payable, No. 311 Common Stock, No. 401 Sales, No. 412 Sales Returns and Allowances, No. 510 Purchases, No. 512 Purchase Returns and Allowances, No. 514 Purchase Discounts, No. 516 Freight-in.

Instructions
(a) Journalize the April transactions using a periodic inventory system.
(b) Enter the beginning balances in the ledger accounts and post the April transactions. (Use J1 for the journal reference.)
(c) Prepare a trial balance on April 30, 2001.
(d) Prepare an income statement through gross profit, assuming merchandise inventory on hand at April 30 is $1,800.

> Two sets of **Problems—Sets A** and **B**—help you pull together and apply several concepts from the chapter. Included in these are problems that help you develop the writing skills that are so important in business. (Keyed to multiple Study Objectives.)

> **General Ledger Problems**, identified by , are selected problems that can be solved using the *General Ledger Software* package.

The Broadening Your Perspective section helps you pull together various concepts covered in the chapter and apply them to real-world business decisions.

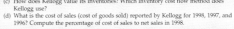

BROADENING YOUR PERSPECTIVE

FINANCIAL REPORTING AND ANALYSIS

FINANCIAL REPORTING PROBLEM: Kellogg Company

BYP6–1   The notes that accompany a company's financial statements provide informative details that would clutter the amounts and descriptions presented in the statements. Refer to the financial statements of Kellogg Company and the Notes to Consolidated Financial Statements in Appendix A.

Instructions

Answer the following questions. Complete the requirements in millions of dollars, as shown in Kellogg's annual report.

(a) What did Kellogg report for the amount of inventories in its Consolidated Balance Sheet at December 31, 1998? December 31, 1997?

(b) Compute the dollar amount of change and the percentage change in inventories between 1997 and 1998. Compute inventory as a percentage of current assets for 1998.

(c) How does Kellogg value its inventories? Which inventory cost flow method does Kellogg use?

(d) What is the cost of sales (cost of goods sold) reported by Kellogg for 1998, 1997, and 1996? Compute the percentage of cost of sales to net sales in 1998.

COMPARATIVE ANALYSIS PROBLEM: Kellogg Company vs. General Mills

BYP6–2   Kellogg's financial statements are presented in Appendix A; General Mills's financial statements are presented in Appendix B.

Instructions

(a) Based on the information contained in these financial statements, compute the following 1998 ratios for each company:
   1. Inventory
   2. Average d
(b) What conclus
   these data?

A Financial Reporting Problem directs you to study various aspects of the financial statements in Kellogg Company's 1998 Annual Report, which is packaged with the text and excerpted in Appendix A at the end of the text.

A Comparative Analysis Problem offers the opportunity to compare and contrast the financial reporting of Kellogg with that of a competitor, General Mills, whose financial statements are excerpted in Appendix B.

Financial Reporting and Analysis   279

RESEARCH ASSIGNMENT

BYP6-3   The March 5, 1999, issue of *Industry Week* contains an article by Doug Bartholomew entitled "What's Really Driving Apple's Recovery."

Instructions

Read the article and answer the following inventory-related questions.

(a) What were Timothy D. Cook's twin goals upon being hired as senior vice president at Apple Computer Inc.?

(b) What did Cook say was the primary cause of Apple Computer's huge $1 billion loss in 1997?

(c) What was Apple's inventory turnover in 1997, and what were its competitors' inventory turnover ratios?

(d) What improvements relative to inventory turnover did Cook accomplish by the end of 1998 at Apple Computer?

INTERPRETING FINANCIAL STATEMENTS: Nike and Reebok

BYP6-4   Nike and Reebok compete head-to-head in the sport shoe and sport apparel business. For both companies, inventory is a significant portion of their total assets. The following information was taken from each company's financial statements and notes to those financial statements.

Research Assignments lead you to reports and articles published in various popular business periodicals for further study and analysis of key topics.

NIKE, INC.

Inventory note
Inventories are stated at the lower of cost or market. Cost is determined using the last-in, first-out (LIFO) method for substantially all U.S. inventories. Non-U.S. inventories are valued on a first-in, first-out (FIFO) basis.

Inventories by major classification are as follows (in millions):

| | May 31 ||
	1998	1997
Finished goods	$1,303.8	$1,248.4
Work-in-process	34.7	50.2
Raw materials	58.1	40.0

Other information for Nike (in millions):

| | May 31 ||
	1998	1997
Inventory	$1,396.6	$1,338.6
Cost of goods sold	6,065.5	5,503.0

REEBOK INTERNATIONAL, LTD.

Inventory note
Inventory, substantially all finished goods, is recorded at the lower of cost (first-in, first-out method) or market.

Other information for Reebok (in millions):

| | December 31 ||
	1998	1997
Inventory	$ 535.5	$ 563.7
Cost of goods sold	2,037.5	2,294.0

Interpreting Financial Statements ask you to read parts of financial statements of actual companies and to interpret that information in light of concepts presented in the chapter.

REAL-WORLD FOCUS: General Motors Corporation

BYP6-5 **General Motors** is the largest producer of automobiles in the world, as well as the world's biggest industrial enterprise. After stumbling in the early 1990s, GM has enacted numerous cost-cutting measures, including downsizing and renegotiating contracts with suppliers. In addition, it has shifted more of its resources to the hot-selling truck market.

The annual report of General Motors Corporation disclosed the following information about its accounting for inventories:

GENERAL MOTORS CORPORATION
Notes to the Financial Statements

Note 5. Inventories
Automotive, Electronics and Other Operations' inventories included the following (in millions)

	December 31	
	1998	1997
Productive material, work in process, and supplies	$ 7,287	$ 7,023
Finished product, service parts, etc.	7,215	7,347
Total inventories at FIFO	14,502	14,370
Less LIFO allowance	2,295	2,268
Total inventories (less allowances)	$12,207	$12,102

Inventories are stated generally at cost, which is not in excess of market. The cost of substantially all U.S. inventories other than the inventories of Saturn Corporation (Saturn), Delco, and Hughes is determined by the last-in, first-out (LIFO) method. The cost of non-U.S., Saturn, Delco, and Hughes inventories is determined generally by the first-in, first-out (FIFO) or average cost methods.

Instructions
(a) What is meant by "inventories are stated generally at cost, which is not in excess of market"?
(b) The company uses LIFO for most of its inventory. What impact does this have on reported ending inventory if prices are increasing?
(c) General Motors uses different inventory methods for different types of inventory. Why might it do this?

> The **Real-World Focus** asks you to apply concepts presented in the chapter to specific situations faced by actual companies.

> The **Group Decision Case** helps you build decision-making skills by analyzing accounting information in a less structured situation. These cases require evaluation of a manager's decision or lead to a decision among alternative courses of action. As group activities, they prepare you for the business world, where you will be working with many people, by giving you practice in solving problems with colleagues.

CRITICAL THINKING

GROUP DECISION CASE

BYP6-6 Consider the case of a large company that reported inventories of $800 million at December 31, 2001, and $900 million at December 31, 2000. However, the ending inventory for 2000 had been overstated by $40 million as a result of errors in the physical counting process. This error was not discovered until after the financial statements for 2001 had been issued.

Instructions
Complete the table which follows. Indicate which items in the financial statements would be incorrect, and by how much. Use an income tax rate of 40% in your calculations, and assume that the tax is paid in cash immediately. For each item, indicate whether it would be **overstated, understated,** or **not affected.** Also, indicate the **amount** of the error (if any).

	Effect on Fiscal Year	
	2001	2000
Beginning inventory	_____	_____
Ending inventory	_____	_____
Cost of goods sold	_____	_____
Gross profit on sales	_____	_____
Income before tax	_____	_____
Income tax	_____	_____
Net income	_____	_____
Ending total assets	_____	_____
Ending shareholders' equity	_____	_____

COMMUNICATION ACTIVITY

BYP6-7 You are the controller of Small Toys Inc. Joe Paisley, the president, recently mentioned to you that he found an error in the 2000 financial statements which he believes has corrected itself. He determined, in discussions with the Purchasing Department, that 2000 ending inventory was overstated by $1 million. Joe says that the 2001 ending inventory is correct, thus he assumes that 2001 income is correct. Joe says to you, "What happened has happened—there's no point in worrying about it anymore."

Instructions
You conclude that Joe is incorrect. Write a brief, tactful memo to Joe, clarifying the situation.

> **Communication Activities** ask you to engage in real-world business situations using writing, speaking, or presentation skills.

ETHICS CASE

BYP6-8 Lonergan Wholesale Corp. uses the LIFO method of inventory costing. In the current year, profit at Lonergan is running unusually high. The corporate tax rate is also high this year, but it is scheduled to decline significantly next year. In an effort to lower current year's net income and to take advantage of the changing income tax rate, the president of Lonergan Wholesale instructs the plant accountant to recommend to the purchasing department a large purchase of inventory for delivery 3 days before the end of the year. The price of the inventory to be purchased has doubled during the year and the purchase will represent a major portion of the ending inventory value.

Instructions
(a) What is the effect of this transaction on this year's and next year's income statement and income tax expense? Why?
(b) If Lonergan Wholesale had been using the FIFO method of inventory costing, would the president give the same directive?
(c) Should the plant accountant order the inventory purchase to lower income? What are the ethical implications of this order?

> Through the **Ethics Cases,** you will reflect on typical ethical dilemmas and decide on an appropriate course of action.

Surfing the Net exercises guide you to Internet sites where you can find and analyze information related to the chapter topic.

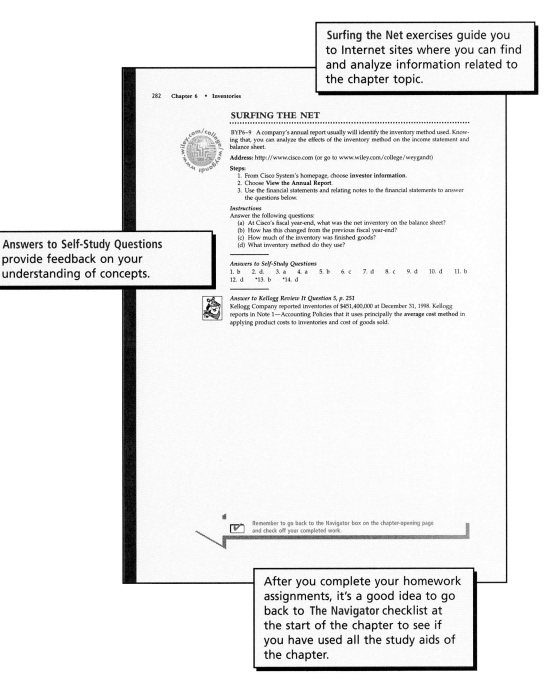

282   Chapter 6 • Inventories

SURFING THE NET

BYP6–9   A company's annual report usually will identify the inventory method used. Knowing that, you can analyze the effects of the inventory method on the income statement and balance sheet.

Address: http://www.cisco.com (or go to www.wiley.com/college/weygandt)

Steps:
1. From Cisco System's homepage, choose **investor information**.
2. Choose **View the Annual Report**.
3. Use the financial statements and relating notes to the financial statements to answer the questions below.

Instructions
Answer the following questions:
(a) At Cisco's fiscal year-end, what was the net inventory on the balance sheet?
(b) How has this changed from the previous fiscal year-end?
(c) How much of the inventory was finished goods?
(d) What inventory method do they use?

Answers to Self-Study Questions
1. b   2. d.   3. a   4. a   5. b   6. c   7. d   8. c   9. d   10. d   11. b
12. d   *13. b   *14. d

Answer to Kellogg Review It Question 5, p. 251
Kellogg Company reported inventories of $451,400,000 at December 31, 1998. Kellogg reports in Note 1—Accounting Policies that it uses principally the **average cost method** in applying product costs to inventories and cost of goods sold.

Remember to go back to the Navigator box on the chapter-opening page and check off your completed work.

Answers to Self-Study Questions provide feedback on your understanding of concepts.

After you complete your homework assignments, it's a good idea to go back to The Navigator checklist at the start of the chapter to see if you have used all the study aids of the chapter.

HOW DO YOU LEARN BEST?

Now that you have looked at your Owner's Manual, take time to find out how you learn best. This quiz was designed to help you find out something about your preferred learning method. Research on left brain/right brain differences and also on learning and personality differences suggests that each person has preferred ways to receive and communicate information. After you take the quiz, we will help you pinpoint the study aids in this text that will help you learn the material based on your learning style.

Circle the letter of the answer that best explains your preference. If a single answer does not match your perception, please circle two or more choices. Leave blank any question that does not apply.

1. You are about to give directions to a person. She is staying in a hotel in town and wants to visit your house. She has a rental car. Would you
   V) draw a map on paper?
   R) write down the directions (without a map)?
   A) tell her the directions?
   K) pick her up at the hotel in your car?

2. You are staying in a hotel and have a rental car. You would like to visit friends whose address/location you do not know. Would you like them to
   V) draw you a map on paper?
   R) write down the directions (without a map)?
   A) tell you the directions by phone?
   K) pick you up at the hotel in their car?

3. You have just received a copy of your itinerary for a world trip. This is of interest to a friend. Would you
   A) call her immediately and tell her about it?
   R) send her a copy of the printed itinerary?
   V) show her on a map of the world?

4. You are going to cook a dessert as a special treat for your family. Do you
   K) cook something familiar without need for instructions?
   V) thumb through the cookbook looking for ideas from the pictures?
   R) refer to a specific cookbook where there is a good recipe?
   A) ask for advice from others?

5. A group of tourists has been assigned to you to find out about national parks. Would you
   K) drive them to a national park?
   R) give them a book on national parks?
   V) show them slides and photographs?
   A) give them a talk on national parks?

6. You are about to purchase a new stereo. Other than price, what would most influence your decision?
   A) A friend talking about it.
   K) Listening to it.
   R) Reading the details about it.
   V) Its distinctive, upscale appearance.

7. Recall a time in your life when you learned how to do something like playing a new board game. (Try to avoid choosing a very physical skill, e.g., riding a bike.) How did you learn best? By
   V) visual clues—pictures, diagrams, charts?
   A) listening to somebody explaining it?
   R) written instructions?
   K) doing it?

8. Which of these games do you prefer?
   V) *Pictionary*
   R) *Scrabble*
   K) Charades

9. You are about to learn to use a new program on a computer. Would you
   K) ask a friend to show you?
   R) read the manual that comes with the program?
   A) telephone a friend and ask questions about it?

10. You are not sure whether a word should be spelled "dependent" or "dependant." Do you
    R) look it up in the dictionary?
    V) see the word in your mind and choose the best way it looks?
    A) sound it out in your mind?
    K) write both versions down?

11. Apart from price, what would most influence your decision to buy a particular textbook?
    K) Using a friend's copy.
    R) Skimming parts of it.
    A) A friend talking about it.
    V) It looks OK.

12. A new movie has arrived in town. What would most influence your decision to go or not to go?
    A) Friends talked about it.
    R) You read a review of it.
    V) You saw a preview of it.

13. Do you prefer a lecturer/teacher who likes to use
    R) handouts and/or a textbook?
    V) flow diagrams, charts, slides?
    K) field trips, labs, practical sessions?
    A) discussion, guest speakers?

Results: To determine your learning preference, add up the number of individual Vs, As, Rs, and Ks you have circled. Match the letter you have recorded most frequently to the same letter in the Learning Styles Chart. Next to each letter in the Chart are suggestions that will refer you to different learning aids throughout this text.

LEARNING STYLES CHART

VISUAL

WHAT TO DO IN CLASS	WHAT TO DO WHEN STUDYING	TEXT FEATURES THAT MAY HELP YOU THE MOST	WHAT TO DO PRIOR TO AND DURING EXAMS
Underline. Use different colors. Use symbols, charts, arrangements on the page.	Use the "In Class" strategies. Reconstruct images in different ways. Redraw pages from memory. Replace words with symbols and initials.	The Navigator Feature Story Preview Infographics/Illustrations Photos Accounting in Action Accounting Equation Analyses Key Terms in blue Words in bold Questions/Exercises/Problems Financial Reporting Problem Comparative Analysis Problem Interpreting Financial Statements Research Assignments Surfing the Net	Recall the "pictures of the pages." Draw, use diagrams where appropriate. Practice turning visuals back into words.

AURAL

WHAT TO DO IN CLASS	WHAT TO DO WHEN STUDYING	TEXT FEATURES THAT MAY HELP YOU THE MOST	WHAT TO DO PRIOR TO AND DURING EXAMS
Attend lectures and tutorials. Discuss topics with students. Explain new ideas to other people. Use a tape recorder. Describe overheads, pictures, and visuals to somebody not there. Leave space in your notes for later recall.	You may take poor notes because you prefer to listen. Therefore: Expand your notes. Put summarized notes on tape and listen. Read summarized notes out loud. Explain notes to another "aural" person.	Infographics/Illustrations Accounting in Action Review It/Do it Summary of Study Objectives Glossary Demonstration Problem Self-Study Questions Questions/Exercises/Problems Financial Reporting Problem Comparative Analysis Problem Real-World Focus Group Decision Case Communication Activity Ethics Case	Listen to your "voices" and write them down. Speak your answers. Practice writing answers to old exam questions.

Source: Adapted from Neil D. Fleming and Colleen Mills, "Not Another Inventory, Rather a Catalyst for Reflections," *To Improve the Academy,* Volume II (1992), pp. 137-155. Used by permission.

R READING/WRITING

WHAT TO DO IN CLASS	WHAT TO DO WHEN STUDYING	TEXT FEATURES THAT MAY HELP YOU THE MOST	WHAT TO DO PRIOR TO AND DURING EXAMS
Use lists, headings. Use dictionaries and definitions. Use handouts and textbooks. Read. Use lecture notes.	Write out words again and again. Reread notes silently. Rewrite ideas into other words. Organize diagrams into statements.	**The Navigator** **Feature Story** **Study Objectives** **Preview** **Review It/Do It** **Summary of Study Objectives** **Glossary** **Self-Study Questions** **Questions/Exercises/ Problems** **Writing Problems** **Financial Reporting Problem** **Comparative Analysis Problem** **Real-World Focus** **Group Decision Case** **Communication Activity** **Ethics Case** **Research Assignment**	Practice with multiple-choice questions. Write out lists. Write paragraphs, beginnings and endings.

K KINESTHETIC

WHAT TO DO IN CLASS	WHAT TO DO WHEN STUDYING	TEXT FEATURES THAT MAY HELP YOU THE MOST	WHAT TO DO PRIOR TO AND DURING EXAMS
Use all your senses. Go to labs, take field trips. Use trial-and-error methods. Listen to real-life examples. Use hands-on approach.	You may take notes poorly because topics do not seem relevant. Therefore: Put examples in note summaries. Use pictures and photos to illustrate. Talk about notes with another "kinesthetic" person.	**The Navigator** **Feature Story** **Preview** **Infographics/ Illustrations** **Review It/Do It** **Summary of Study Objectives** **Demonstration Problem** **Self-Study Questions** **Questions/Exercises/ Problems** **Financial Reporting Problem** **Comparative Analysis Problem** **Real-World Focus** **Group Decision Case** **Communication Activity** **Research Assignment** **Surfing the Net**	Write practice answers. Role-play the exam situation.

BRIEF CONTENTS

1 Accounting in Action   1
2 The Recording Process   45
3 Adjusting the Accounts   91
4 Completion of the Accounting Cycle   139
5 Accounting for Merchandising Operations   187
6 Inventories   231
7 Accounting Principles   285
8 Internal Control and Cash   329
9 Accounting for Receivables   373
10 Plant Assets, Natural Resources, and Intangible Assets   411
11 Liabilities   461
12 Corporations: Organization, Stock Transactions, Dividends, and Retained Earnings   511
13 Investments   567
14 The Statement of Cash Flows   607
15 Financial Statement Analysis   671

Appendixes

A Specimen Financial Statements: Kellogg Company   A2
B Specimen Financial Statements: General Mills, Inc.   B1
C Time Value of Money   C1
D Payroll Accounting   D1
E Subsidiary Ledgers and Special Journals   E1
F Other Significant Liabilities   F1

CONTENTS

CHAPTER 1

ACCOUNTING IN ACTION 1

Feature Story: The Best to You Each Morning   xxxiv

What Is Accounting?   2
Who Uses Accounting Data   3
Brief History of Accounting   5
Distinguishing between Bookkeeping and
    Accounting   6
Accounting and You   6

The Building Blocks of Accounting   8
Ethics—A Fundamental Business Concept   8
Generally Accepted Accounting Principles   9
Assumptions   10
Basic Accounting Equation   12

Using the Building Blocks   15
Transaction Analysis   16
Summary of Transactions   20

Financial Statements   22
Income Statement   22
Retained Earnings Statement   24
Balance Sheet   24
Statement of Cash Flows   24

CHAPTER 2

THE RECORDING PROCESS 45

Feature Story: No Such Thing as a Perfect World   44

The Account   46
Debits and Credits   47
Debit and Credit Procedures   48
Stockholders' Equity Relationships   51
Expansion of Basic Equation   51

Steps in the Recording Process   52
The Journal   53
The Ledger   55

The Recording Process Illustrated   59
Summary Illustration of Journalizing and Posting   65

The Trial Balance   66
Limitations of a Trial Balance   67
Locating Errors   67
Use of Dollar Signs   68

Electronic Data Processing   68
Comparative Advantages of Manual versus Computerized
    Systems   68
A Look into the Future   70

CHAPTER 3

ADJUSTING THE ACCOUNTS 91

Feature Story: Timing Is Everything   90

Timing Issues   92
Selecting an Accounting Time Period   93
Fiscal and Calendar Years   93
Recognizing Revenues and Expenses   93

The Basics of Adjusting Entries   95
Types of Adjusting Entries   95
Adjusting Entries for Prepayments   96
Adjusting Entries for Accruals   103
Summary of Basic Relationships   108

The Adjusted Trial Balance and Financial Statements   110
Preparing the Adjusted Trial Balance   110
Preparing Financial Statements   111

Accrual vs. Cash Basis of Accounting   112

Appendix 3A   *Alternative Treatment of Prepaid Expenses and Unearned Revenues*   115

Prepaid Expenses   116

Unearned Revenues   117

Summary of Additional Adjustment Relationships   118

CHAPTER 4

COMPLETION OF THE ACCOUNTING CYCLE 139

Feature Story: A Little Knowledge Brings a Lot of Profits   138

Using a Work Sheet   140
Steps in Preparing a Work Sheet   141
Preparing Financial Statements from a Work Sheet   143
Preparing Adjusting Entries from a Work Sheet   145

Closing the Books   145
Preparing Closing Entries   146
Closing Entries Illustration   148
Posting of Closing Entries   149
Preparing a Post-Closing Trial Balance   150

Summary of the Accounting Cycle   151
Reversing Entries—An Optional Step   154
Correcting Entries—An Avoidable Step   154

Classified Balance Sheet   157
Standard Classifications   157
Classified Balance Sheet Illustrated   161

Appendix   *Reversing Entries*   165

Illustration of Reversing Entries   166

CHAPTER 5

ACCOUNTING FOR MERCHANDISING OPERATIONS   187

Feature Story: Selling Dollars for 85 Cents   186

Merchandising Operations   188
Operating Cycles   189
Inventory Systems   190

Merchandising Transactions   191
Recording Purchases   192
Recording Sales   196

Measuring Net Income   199
Gross Profit   199
Operating Expenses   200
Income Statement   200

Completing the Accounting Cycle   201
Using a Work Sheet   201
Preparing Financial Statements   203
Adjusting and Closing Entries   204
Preparing the Post-Closing Trial Balance   205
Summary of Merchandising Entries   205

Forms of Income Statements   206
Multiple-Step Income Statement   206
Single-Step Income Statement   208

CHAPTER 6

INVENTORIES   231

Feature Story: Taking Stock—From Backpacks to Bicycles   230

Inventory Basics   232
Classifying Inventory   233
Determining Inventory Quantities   233
Inventory Accounting Systems   235

Periodic Inventory System   236
Recording Transactions   236
Recording Purchases of Merchandise   237
Recording Sales of Merchandise   238
Comparison of Entries—Perpetual vs. Periodic   238
Cost of Goods Sold   238
Income Statement Presentation   241

Inventory Costing Under a Periodic Inventory System   242
Using Actual Physical Flow Costing—Specific Identification   243
Using Assumed Cost Flow Methods—FIFO, LIFO, and Average Cost   244
Financial Statement Effects of Cost Flow Methods   248
Using Inventory Cost Flow Methods Consistently   250

Valuing Inventory at the Lower of Cost or Market (LCM)   251

Inventory Errors   252
Income Statement Effects   253
Balance Sheet Effects   253

Statement Presentation and Analysis   254

Appendix 6A   *Estimating Inventories*   259

Gross Profit Method   259

Retail Inventory Method   260

Appendix 6B   *Inventory Cost Flow Methods in Perpetual Inventory Systems*   262

First-In, First-Out (FIFO)   262

Last-In, Last-Out (LIFO)   263

Average Cost   263

CHAPTER 7

ACCOUNTING PRINCIPLES   285

Feature Story: Is Online "Off-Track"?   284

The Conceptual Framework of Accounting   286
Objectives of Financial Reporting   287
Qualitative Characteristics of Accounting Information   288
Elements of Financial Statements   289
Operating Guidelines   290

Assumptions   290
Monetary Unit Assumption   291
Economic Entity Assumption   291
Time Period Assumption   291
Going Concern Assumption   291

Principles   291
Revenue Recognition Principle   292
Matching Principle (Expense Recognition)   292
Full Disclosure Principle   294
Cost Principle   294

Constraints in Accounting   295
Materiality   295
Conservatism   296
Summary of Conceptual Framework   297

Financial Statement Presentation and Analysis   298
Classified Balance Sheet   298
Classified Income Statement   299
Analyzing Financial Statements   300
Financial Statement Presentation—An International Perspective   304

CHAPTER 8

INTERNAL CONTROL AND CASH   329

Feature Story: Minding the Money in Moose Jaw   328

Internal Control   330
Principles of Internal Control   331

Limitations of Internal Control   335

Cash Controls   336
Internal Control over Cash Receipts   337
Internal Control over Cash Disbursements   340

Use of a Bank   344
Making Bank Deposits   344
Writing Checks   345
Bank Statements   346
Reconciling the Bank Account   347

Reporting Cash   352

CHAPTER 9
ACCOUNTING FOR RECEIVABLES   373
Feature Story: How Do You Spell Relief?   372

Accounts Receivable   374
Types of Receivables   374
Recognizing Accounts Receivable   375
Valuing Accounts Receivable   376
Disposing of Accounts Receivable   382

Notes Receivable   385
Determining the Maturity Date   386
Computing Interest   387
Recognizing Notes Receivable   388
Valuing Notes Receivable   388
Disposing of Notes Receivable   388

Statement Presentation and Analysis of Receivables   391
Presentation   391
Analysis   391

CHAPTER 10
PLANT ASSETS, NATURAL RESOURCES, AND INTANGIBLE ASSETS   411
Feature Story: On the Books, Your Classroom May Be Worthless   410

Section 1   *Plant Assets*   412

Determining the Cost of Plant Assets   413
Land   413
Land Improvements   414
Buildings   414
Equipment   414

Depreciation   415
Factors in Computing Depreciation   416
Depreciation Methods   418
Depreciation and Income Taxes   423
Revising Periodic Depreciation   423

Expenditures during Useful Life   423

Plant Asset Disposals   424
Retirement of Plant Assets   424
Sale of Plant Assets   425

Exchange of Plant Assets   426

Section 2   *Natural Resources*   429

Acquisition Cost   429

Depletion   430

Section 3   *Intangible Assets*   432

Accounting for Intangible Assets   432
Patents   433
Copyrights   433
Trademarks and Trade Names   434
Franchises and Licenses   434
Goodwill   435

Research and Development Costs   435

Financial Statement Presentation and Analysis   436
Presentation   436
Analysis   437

CHAPTER 11
LIABILITIES   461
Feature Story: Financing His Dreams   460

Section 1   *Current Liabilities*   462

What Is a Current Liability?   462
Notes Payable   463
Sales Taxes Payable   464
Payroll and Payroll Taxes Payable   465
Unearned Revenues   466
Current Maturities of Long-Term Debt   467
Financial Statement Presentation and Analysis   467

Section 2   *Long-Term Liabilities*   469

Bond Basics   469
Why Issue Bonds?   470
Types of Bonds   471
Issuing Procedures   471
Bond Trading   473
Determining the Market Value of Bonds   473

Accounting for Bond Issues   474
Issuing Bonds at Face Value   474
Discount or Premium on Bonds   475
Issuing Bonds at a Discount   476
Issuing Bonds at a Premium   478
Issuing Bonds between Interest Dates   480

Accounting for Bond Retirements   481
Redeeming Bonds at Maturity   482
Redeeming Bonds before Maturity   482
Converting Bonds into Common Stock   482

Accounting for Long-Term Notes Payable   484

Financial Statement Presentation and Analysis of Long-Term Liabilties   485

Presentation   485
Analysis   485

Appendix   *Effective-Interest Amortization*   490

Amortizing Bond Discount   491

Amortizing Bond Premium   493

CHAPTER 12

CORPORATIONS: ORGANIZATION, STOCK TRANSACTIONS, DIVIDENDS, AND RETAINED EARNINGS   511

Feature Story: What's Cooking?   510

Section 1   *The Corporate Form of Organization*   512

Characteristics of a Corporation   513
Separate Legal Existence   513
Limited Liability of Stockholders   513
Transferable Ownership Rights   513
Ability to Acquire Capital   513
Continuous Life   514
Corporation Management   514
Government Regulations   515
Additional Taxes   515

Forming a Corporation   516

Corporate Capital   517
Ownership Rights of Stockholders   517
Stock Issue Considerations   519

Accounting for Common Stock Issues   522
Issuing Par Value Common Stock for Cash   522
Issuing No-Par Common Stock for Cash   523
Issuing Common Stock for Services or Noncash Assets   523

Accounting for Treasury Stock   525
Purchase of Treasury Stock   525
Disposal of Treasury Stock   527

Preferred Stock   528
Dividend Preferences   529
Liquidation Preference   530

Section 2   *Dividends*   530

Cash Dividends   531
Entries for Cash Dividends   532
Allocating Cash Dividends between Preferred and Common Stock   533

Stock Dividends   534
Entries for Stock Dividends   535
Effects of Stock Dividends   535

Stock Splits   536

Section 3   *Retained Earnings*   538

Retained Earnings Restrictions   539

Prior Period Adjustments   539

Retained Earnings Statement   540

Section 4   *Stockholders' Equity Presentation and Analysis*   542

Presentation   542

Analysis   543

Appendix 12A   *Stockholders' Equity Statement*   547

Appendix 12B   *Book Value—Another Per Share Amount*   547

Illustration   548

Book Value versus Market Value   549

CHAPTER 13
INVESTMENTS   567

Feature Story: Is There Anything Else We Can Buy?   566

Why Corporations Invest   568

Accounting for Debt Investments   570
Recording Acquisition of Bonds   570
Recording Bond Interest   570
Recording Sale of Bonds   570

Accounting for Stock Investments   572
Holdings of Less Than 20%   572
Holdings Between 20% and 50%   573
Holdings of More Than 50%   574

Valuing and Reporting Investments   577
Categories of Securities   577
Balance Sheet Presentation   578
Presentation of Realized and Unrealized Gain or Loss   580
Balance Sheet   581

Appendix   *Preparing Consolidated Financial Statements*   585

Preparing a Consolidated Balance Sheet   585
Use of a Work Sheet—Cost Equal to Book Value   587
Use of a Work Sheet—Cost Above Book Value   588
Content of a Consolidated Balance Sheet   588

Consolidated Income Statement   589

CHAPTER 14
THE STATEMENT OF CASH FLOWS   607

Feature Story: "Cash Is Cash, and Everything Else Is Accounting"   606

The Statement of Cash Flows: Purpose and Format   608
Purpose of the Statement of Cash Flows   609
Meaning of "Cash Flows"   609
Classification of Cash Flows   609

Significant Noncash Activities   611
Format of the Statement of Cash Flows   611
Usefulness of the Statement of Cash Flows   612
Preparing the Statement of Cash Flows   613
Indirect and Direct Methods   614

Section 1   Statement of Cash Flows— Indirect Method   615

First Year of Operations—2000   616

Determining the Net Increase/Decrease in Cash
(Step 1)   616
Determining Net Cash Provided/Used by Operating Activities
(Step 2)   617
Determining Net Cash Provided/Used by Investing and
Financing Activities (Step 3)   619
Statement of Cash Flows—2000   619

Second Year of Operations—2001   620

Determining the Net Increase/Decrease in Cash
(Step 1)   621
Determining Net Cash Provided/Used by Operating Activities
(Step 2)   621
Determining Net Cash Provided/Used by Investing and
Financing Activities (Step 3)   622
Statement of Cash Flows—2001   624
Summary of Conversion to Net Cash Provided by Operating
Activities—Indirect Method   624

Section 2   Statement of Cash Flows—Direct Method   627

First Year of Operations—2000   628

Determining the Net Increase/Decrease in Cash
(Step 1)   628
Determining Net Cash Provided/Used by Operating
Activities (Step 2)   629
Determining Net Cash Provided/Used by Investing and
Financing Activities (Step 3)   632
Statement of Cash Flows—2000   633

Second Year of Operations—2001   634

Determining the Net Increase/Decrease in Cash
(Step 1)   635
Determining Net Cash Provided/Used by Operating Activities
(Step 2)   635
Determining Net Cash Provided/Used by Investing and
Financing Activities (Step 3)   636
Statement of Cash Flows—2001   638

Analysis of the Statement of Cash Flows   640

Current Cash Debt Coverage Ratio   641
Cash Return on Sales Ratio   642
Cash Debt Coverage Ratio   642

Appendix   Using a Work Sheet for Preparing the Statement of Cash Flows—Indirect Method   646

Preparing the Work Sheet   647

Determining the Reconciling Items   648

Preparing the Statement   651

CHAPTER 15
FINANCIAL STATEMENT ANALYSIS   671

Feature Story: Just Fooling Around?   670

Basics of Financial Statement Analysis   672

Need for Comparative Analysis   673
Tools of Financial Statement Analysis   673

Horizontal Analysis   674

Balance Sheet   675
Income Statement   676
Retained Earnings Statement   676

Vertical Analysis   677

Balance Sheet   677
Income Statement   677

Ratio Analysis   680

Liquidity Ratios   681
Profitability Ratios   685
Solvency Ratios   692
Summary of Ratios   694

Earning Power and Irregular Items   696

Discontinued Operations   696
Extraordinary Items   697
Change in Accounting Principle   699
Comprehensive Income   700

Limitations of Financial Statement Analysis   700

Estimates   701
Cost   701
Alternative Accounting Methods   701
Atypical Data   701
Diversification of Firms   701

APPENDIXES

APPENDIX A
SPECIMEN FINANCIAL STATEMENTS: KELLOGG COMPANY   A2

The Annual Report   A2

Financial Highlights   A3

Auditor's Report   A8

Management Discussion and Analysis   A9

Financial Statements and Accompanying Notes   A15

APPENDIX B
SPECIMEN FINANCIAL STATEMENTS: GENERAL MILLS, INC.   B1

APPENDIX C
TIME VALUE OF MONEY   C1

Nature of Interest   C2
Simple Interest   C2
Compound Interest   C2

Section 1 *Future Value Concepts*   C3

Future Value of a Single Amount   C3

Future Value of an Annuity   C5

Section 2 *Present Value Concepts*   C8

Present Value Variables   C8

Present Value of a Single Amount   C8

Present Value of an Annuity   C10

Time Periods and Discounting   C12

Computing the Present Value of a Long-Term Note or Bond   C12

APPENDIX D
PAYROLL ACCOUNTING   D1

Payroll Defined   D2

Importance of Internal Control to Payroll   D2
Hiring Employees   D3
Timekeeping   D4
Preparing the Payroll   D4
Paying the Payroll   D5

Determining the Payroll   D5
Gross Earnings   D5
Payroll Deductions   D6
Net Pay   D8

Recording the Payroll   D9
Maintaining Payroll Department Records   D9
Recognizing Payroll Expenses and Liabilities   D10
Recording Payment of the Payroll   D11

Employer Payroll Taxes   D12
FICA Taxes   D12
Federal Unemployment Taxes   D13
State Unemployment Taxes   D13
Recording Employer Payroll Taxes   D13

Filing and Remitting Payroll Taxes   D14

APPENDIX E
SUBSIDIARY LEDGERS AND SPECIAL JOURNALS   E1

Section 1 *Expanding the Ledger—Subsidiary Ledgers*   E2

Nature and Purpose of Subsidiary Ledgers   E2

Illustration of Subsidiary Ledgers   E3

Advantages of Subsidiary Ledgers   E4

Section 2 *Expanding the Journal—Special Journals*   E5

Nature and Purpose of Special Journals   E5

Sales Journal   E6
Journalizing Credit Sales   E6
Posting the Sales Journal   E6
Proving the Ledgers   E7
Advantages of the Sales Journal   E8

Cash Receipts Journal   E8
Journalizing Cash Receipts Transactions   E10
Posting the Cash Receipts Journal   E11
Proving the Ledgers   E11

Purchases Journal   E12
Journalizing Credit Purchases of Merchandise   E13
Posting the Purchases Journal   E13
Expanding the Purchases Journal   E13

Cash Payments Journal   E14
Journalizing Cash Payments Transactions   E14
Posting the Cash Payments Journal   E15

Effects of Special Journals on General Journal   E16

APPENDIX F
OTHER SIGNIFICANT LIABILITIES   F1

Contingent Liabilities   F2
Recording a Contingent Liability   F2
Disclosure of Contingent Liabilities   F3

Lease Liabilities   F4
Operating Leases   F4
Capital Leases   F5

Additional Liabilities for Employee Fringe Benefits   F6
Paid Absences   F6
Postretirement Benefits   F7

Photo Credits   PC-1

Company Index   CI-1

Subject Index   SI-1

FEATURE STORY

The Best to You Each Morning

Sometimes it's better to be lucky than good. In 1894 two brothers were working on an experiment to introduce grain into the diet of sanitarium patients. Some of the grain got too wet, but they decided to roll it and toast it anyway. *Voilà*—the Kellogg brothers had just invented flaked cereal. At first they sold it by mail order, but in 1906 William Kellogg, believing he could serve a larger market, started his own company, the Battle Creek Toasted Corn Flake Company.

Today Kellogg produces 12 of the world's top 15 most popular cereals. It sells 40% of the cereal consumed in the world. How did it become so dominant? Kellogg's entrepreneurial vision was grounded in a clever marketing strategy. For example, one early promotion promised a box of cereal to any woman who winked at her grocer. Marketing has been a priority: Think about how many of Kellogg's products, slogans, or advertising jingles are ingrained in your memory, such as Tony the Tiger (Frosted Flakes) and Snap! Crackle! and Pop! (Rice Krispies). It is almost impossible to imagine growing up without

Rice Krispies bars—those gooey globs of rice are a rite of passage for nearly every American child.

But it takes more than marketing to build a dominant company. Kellogg's success has also come from careful planning. Management must make many decisions: where to locate, whether to buy or rent properties, how to finance current operations and expansion, and what new products to sell. Kellogg's 14,500 employees manufacture its products in 22 countries and distribute them in 160 countries. Managing such a colossal business requires vast amounts of accounting information.

As a business becomes large, its financial needs often exceed the resources of the original owners. When this happens, the company looks for financing from lenders or from additional owners. Kellogg has approximately 27,000 owners, called shareholders. In addition, lenders and creditors have provided it with $4.2 billion. Lenders and investors will not provide financing unless they feel confident about a company's future. In order to obtain additional financing, Kellogg communicates its past performance and its plans for the future to lenders and investors through accounting information.

THE NAVIGATOR

On the World Wide Web
http://www.kelloggs.com

CHAPTER 1

ACCOUNTING IN ACTION

THE NAVIGATOR ✔

- Understand *Concepts for Review* ☐
- Read *Feature Story* ☐
- Scan *Study Objectives* ☐
- Read *Preview* ☐
- Read text and answer *Before You Go On*
  p. 7 ☐ p. 14 ☐ p. 21 ☐ p. 25 ☐
- Work *Demonstration Problem* ☐
- Review *Summary of Study Objectives* ☐
- Answer *Self-Study Questions* ☐
- Complete assignments ☐

The Navigator is a learning system designed to prompt you to use the learning aids in the chapter and set priorities as you study.

STUDY OBJECTIVES

Study Objectives give you a framework for learning the specific concepts covered in the chapter.

After studying this chapter, you should be able to:
1. Explain the meaning of accounting.
2. Identify the users and uses of accounting.
3. Understand why ethics is a fundamental business concept.
4. Explain the meaning of generally accepted accounting principles and the cost principle.
5. Explain the meaning of the monetary unit assumption and the economic entity assumption.
6. State the basic accounting equation and explain the meaning of assets, liabilities, and stockholders' equity.
7. Analyze the effect of business transactions on the basic accounting equation.
8. Prepare an income statement, retained earnings statement, balance sheet, and statement of cash flows.

THE NAVIGATOR

1

*T*he opening story about the Kellogg Company highlights the need for accurate and sound reporting of financial information. It follows that regardless of one's pursuits or occupation, the need for financial information is inescapable. You cannot earn a living, spend money, buy on credit, make an investment, or pay taxes without receiving, using, or dispensing financial information. Good decision making depends on good information.

The purpose of this chapter is to show you that accounting is the system used to provide useful financial information. The content and organization of the chapter are as follows:

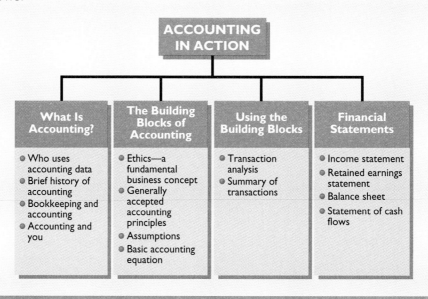

The **Preview** describes and outlines the major topics and subtopics you will see in the chapter.

THE NAVIGATOR

WHAT IS ACCOUNTING?

1
STUDY
OBJECTIVE
....
Explain the meaning of accounting.

Essential terms are printed in blue when they first appear, and are defined in the end-of-chapter glossary.

As a financial information system, accounting is a process of three activities: **identifying**, **recording**, and **communicating** the economic events of an organization (business or nonbusiness) to interested users of the information. Let's take a closer look at these three activities:

1. The first part of the process—**identifying**—involves selecting those events that are considered **evidence of economic activity relevant to a particular organization**. The sale of goods by Kellogg Company, the rendering of services by American Telephone & Telegraph, the payment of wages by Ford Motor Company, and the collection of ticket and broadcast money and the payment of expenses by major league baseball teams are examples of economic events.

2. Once identified and measured in dollars and cents, economic events are **recorded** to provide a permanent history of the financial activities of the organization. Recording consists of keeping a **chronological diary of measured events in an orderly and systematic manner**. In recording, economic events are also classified and summarized.

3. This identifying and recording activity is of little use unless the information is **communicated** to interested users. The information is communicated through the **preparation and distribution of accounting reports**, the most common of which are called **financial statements**. To make the reported financial information meaningful, accountants describe and report the recorded data in a standardized way. Information resulting from similar transactions is accumulated and totaled. Such data are said to be reported **in the aggregate**. For example, all sales transactions of Kellogg Company are accumulated over a certain period of time and reported as one amount in the financial statements of Kellogg. By presenting the recorded data in the aggregate, the accounting process simplifies a multitude of transactions and renders a series of activities understandable and meaningful.

References throughout the chapter tie the accounting concepts you are learning to the Feature Story that opened the chapter.

A vital element in communicating economic events is the accountant's ability and responsibility to **analyze** and **interpret** the reported information. Analysis involves the use of ratios, percentages, graphs, and charts to highlight significant financial trends and relationships. Interpretation involves **explaining the uses, meaning, and limitations of reported data**. Appendix A of this textbook illustrates the financial statements and accompanying notes and graphs from Kellogg Company; Appendix B illustrates the financial statements of General Mills. We refer to these statements at various places throughout the text. At this point, they probably strike you as complex and confusing. By the end of this course, you'll be surprised at how much about them you understand.

In summary, the accounting process may be diagrammed as follows:

Appendix A contains Kellogg Company's financial statements; Appendix B contains General Mills's financial statements.

ILLUSTRATION 1-1

Accounting process

Communication

Identification

Select economic events (transactions)

Recording

Record, classify, and summarize

Prepare accounting reports

Analyze and interpret for users

Accounting should consider the needs of the users of financial information. As a consequence, you should know who these users are and something about their needs for information.

Who Uses Accounting Data

Because it communicates financial information about a business enterprise, accounting is often called "the language of business." The information that a specific user of financial information needs depends upon the kinds of decisions

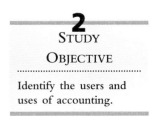

2
STUDY
OBJECTIVE

Identify the users and uses of accounting.

that user makes. The differences in the decisions divide the users of financial information into two broad groups: internal users and external users.

Internal Users

Internal users of accounting information are managers who plan, organize, and run a business. These include **marketing managers, production supervisors, finance directors, and company officers**. In running a business, managers must answer many important questions, as shown in Illustration 1-2.

ILLUSTRATION 1-2

Questions asked by internal users

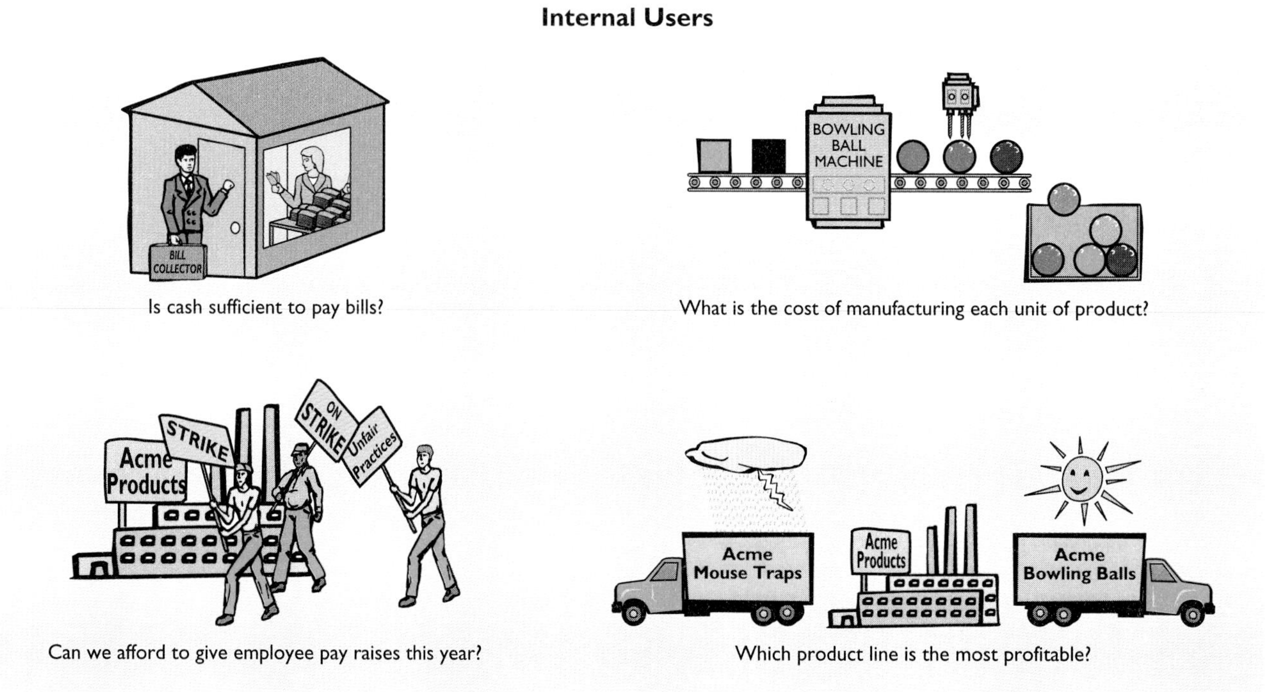
Internal Users
BILL COLLECTOR
Is cash sufficient to pay bills?
BOWLING BALL MACHINE
What is the cost of manufacturing each unit of product?
Acme Products
STRIKE
ON STRIKE
Unfair Practices
Can we afford to give employee pay raises this year?
Acme Mouse Traps
Acme Products
Acme Bowling Balls
Which product line is the most profitable?

To answer these and other questions, you need detailed information on a timely basis. For internal users, accounting provides internal reports, such as financial comparisons of operating alternatives, projections of income from new sales campaigns, and forecasts of cash needs for the next year. In addition, summarized financial information is presented in the form of financial statements.

External Users

There are several types of **external users** of accounting information. **Investors** (owners) use accounting information to make decisions to buy, hold, or sell stock. **Creditors** such as suppliers and bankers use accounting information to evaluate the risks of granting credit or lending money. Some questions that may be asked by investors and creditors about a company are shown in Illustration 1-3.

HELPFUL HINT
The IRS requires businesses to retain records that can be audited. Also, the Foreign Corrupt Practices Act requires public companies to keep records.

The information needs and questions of other external users vary considerably. **Taxing authorities**, such as the Internal Revenue Service, want to know whether the company complies with the tax laws. **Regulatory agencies**, such as the Securities and Exchange Commission or the Federal Trade Commission, want to know whether the company is operating within prescribed rules. **Customers**

ILLUSTRATION 1-3

Questions asked by external users

Questions Asked by External Users

Is the company earning satisfactory income?

How does the company compare in size and profitability with competitors?

Will the company be able to pay its debts as they come due?

are interested in whether a company will continue to honor product warranties and otherwise support its product lines. **Labor unions** want to know whether the owners have the ability to pay increased wages and benefits. **Economic planners** use accounting information to analyze and forecast economic activity.

ACCOUNTING IN ACTION

International Insight

When the chief engineer of Irkutsk Energo, a public utility in Moscow, addressed a gathering of international investors recently, he provided them with all kinds of financial information about the company. The reason: Russians are learning that corporate openness lures much-needed foreign investment. Foreign investors, however, have been reluctant to invest because Russian firms have been secretive (and sometimes deceptive) about their financial affairs. Now, however, things will probably change because firms such as Irkutsk Energo have enjoyed stock price surges after providing candid accounting information. In short, good accounting information may help Russia solve some of its economic problems.

Source: The Wall Street Journal, June 9, 1995, p. A-6.

Accounting in Action examples illustrate important and interesting accounting situations in business.

Brief History of Accounting

The **origins of accounting** are generally attributed to the work of Luca Pacioli, a famous Italian Renaissance mathematician. Pacioli was a close friend and tutor to Leonardo da Vinci and a contemporary of Christopher Columbus. In his text *Summa de Arithmetica, Geometria, Proportione et Proportionalite*, Pacioli described a system to ensure that financial information was recorded efficiently and accurately.

With the advent of the **industrial age** in the nineteenth century and, later, the emergence of large corporations, a separation of the owners from the managers of businesses took place. As a result, the need to report the status of the business enterprise took on increasing importance, to ensure that managers acted in accord with owners' wishes. In addition, transactions between businesses became more complex, making necessary improved approaches for reporting financial information.

Our economy has now evolved into a post-industrial age—**the information age**—in which the "products" are information services. The computer, as the information processor, has been the driver of the information age.

Distinguishing between Bookkeeping and Accounting

Many individuals mistakenly consider bookkeeping and accounting to be one and the same. This confusion is understandable because the accounting process **includes the bookkeeping function**. However, accounting also includes much more. Bookkeeping **usually involves only the recording of economic events** and is therefore just one part of the accounting process. In total, **accounting involves the entire process of identification, recording, and communication**.

The bookkeeping function is often performed by individuals with limited skills in accounting. As a result, it is not surprising that the increased use of computers by business enterprises has resulted in much of the detailed work that is part of the bookkeeping process being performed by machines.

Technology in Action

With the phenomenal growth in computers, more and more record keeping is being performed electronically. Businesses, small as well as large, are finding that through the use of the computer the entire recording process has become more efficient. However it is important to know the procedures used in a manual system to understand the operations a computer performs.

Technology in Action examples show how computer technology is used in accounting and business.

Accounting and You

One question frequently asked by students of accounting is, "How will the study of accounting help me?" It should help you a great deal, because a working knowledge of accounting is desirable for virtually every field of endeavor. Some illustrations of how accounting is used in other careers include:

General management: Imagine running General Motors, a major hospital, a school, a McDonald's franchise, a bike shop; all general managers need to understand and have access to accounting data in order to make wise business decisions.

Marketing/Advertising: A marketing specialist is someone who develops strategies to help the sales force be successful. But making a sale is meaningless unless it is a profitable sale. Marketing people must be sensitive to costs and benefits, which accounting helps them quantify and understand.

Marketing people are also involved in advertising. What would a flashy field such as advertising have to do with accounting? If you buy a commercial on a radio station, you'll want to know the cost per thousand listeners. You'll deal in ratings numbers and budgets all day. And ad agencies are always under pressure to cut costs, because their clients can be very fickle—particularly if the ad campaign doesn't work.

Finance: Do you want to be a banker, an investment analyst, a stock broker? These fields rely heavily on accounting. Suppose you decide to go into banking. You could become a lending officer, a money manager, a deal-maker, a foreign currency trader, or a retail branch supervisor. Whatever the situation, you will regularly examine and analyze financial statements. In fact, it is difficult to get a good job in a finance function without two or three courses in accounting.

Real estate: Perhaps the most prevalent career in real estate is that of a broker, a person who sells residential or commercial real estate. Because a third party—the bank—is almost always involved in financing a real estate transaction, brokers must understand the numbers involved: Can the buyer of the house afford to make the payments to the bank on a given salary? Does the cash flow from the industrial property justify the purchase price in this market? What are the tax benefits of making the purchase?

Accounting is useful even for occupations you might think completely unrelated. If you become a doctor, a lawyer, a social worker, a teacher, an engineer, an architect, or an entrepreneur—you name it—a working knowledge of accounting is relevant.

ACCOUNTING IN ACTION
Business Insight

Help Wanted: Forensic CPAs

Tom Taylor's job at the FBI has changed. He used to pack a .357 magnum; now he wields a No. 2 pencil. Taylor, age 37, for two years an FBI agent, is a forensic accountant, somebody who sniffs through company books to ferret out white-collar crime. Demand for this service has surged in the past few years. In one recent year, a recruiter for San Diego's Robert Half International, a headhunting firm, had requests for more than 1,000 such snoops.

Qualification: a CPA with FBI, IRS, or similar government experience. Interestingly, despite its macho image, the FBI has long hired mostly accountants and lawyers as agents.

BEFORE YOU GO ON . . .

Before You Go On questions at the end of major text sections offer an opportunity to stop and reexamine the key points you have studied.

Review It

1. What is accounting?
2. Who uses accounting information?
3. What is the difference between bookkeeping and accounting?
4. How can you use your accounting knowledge?

THE
NAVIGATOR

THE BUILDING BLOCKS OF ACCOUNTING

Every profession develops a body of theory consisting of principles, assumptions, and standards. Accounting is no exception. Just as a doctor follows certain standards in treating a patient's illness, an accountant follows certain standards in reporting financial information. For these standards to work, however, a fundamental business concept is followed—ethical behavior.

3

STUDY

OBJECTIVE

Understand why ethics is a fundamental business concept.

Ethics—A Fundamental Business Concept

Wherever you make your career—whether in accounting, marketing, management, finance, government, or elsewhere—your behavior and actions will affect other people and organizations. The standards of conduct by which one's actions are judged as right or wrong, honest or dishonest, fair or not fair, are ethics. Imagine trying to carry on a business, perform an audit, or invest money if you could not depend on the individuals you deal with to be honest. If managers, customers, investors, co-workers, and creditors all consistently lied, effective communication and economic activity would be impossible. Information would have no credibility.

Fortunately most individuals in business are ethical. Their actions are both legal and responsible, and they consider the organization's interests in their decision making. However, in some situations public officials, business executives, and respected leaders act unethically. For example, a former chief of the finance committee of the House of Representatives was indicted for possible illegal behavior; Sears was accused of widespread customer overcharging on car repairs; senior-most Archer Daniels Midland Co. executives were recently sentenced to prison in a historic price-fixing conspiracy. As one business leader noted: "We are all embarrassed by the events that make *The Wall Street Journal* read like the *Police Gazette.*"

Many companies have developed corporate mission statements. Some of these mission statements include discussion of the company's ethical values. In its statement of company philosophy, for example, Kellogg Company has the following statement regarding integrity and ethics.

ILLUSTRATION 1-4

Corporate ethics statement

KELLOGG COMPANY
Statement of Company Philosophy

Integrity and Ethics
Integrity is the cornerstone of our business practice. We will conduct our affairs in a manner consistent with the highest ethical standards.
   To meet this commitment, we will:

• Engage in fair and honest business practices.
• Show respect for each other, our consumers, customers, suppliers, shareholders and the communities in which we operate.
• Communicate in an honest, factual and accurate manner.

To sensitize you to ethical situations and to give you practice at solving ethical dilemmas, we have included in the book three types of ethics materials:

(1) marginal notes that provide helpful hints for developing ethical sensitivity, (2) ethics in accounting boxes that highlight ethics situations and issues, and (3) an ethics case simulating a business situation at the end of the chapter. In the process of analyzing these ethics cases, you should apply the steps outlined in Illustration 1-5.

ILLUSTRATION 1-5

Steps in analyzing ethics cases

Solving an Ethical Dilemma

1. Recognize an ethical situation and the ethical issues involved.	**2. Identify and analyze the principal elements in the situation.**	**3. Identify the alternatives, and weigh the impact of each alternative on various stakeholders.**
Use your personal ethics to identify ethical situations and issues. Some businesses and professional organizations provide written codes of ethics for guidance in some business situations.	Identify the *stakeholders*— persons or groups who may be harmed or benefited. Ask the question: What are the responsibilities and obligations of the parties involved?	Select the most ethical alternative, considering all the consequences. Sometimes there will be one right answer. Other situations involve more than one right solution; these situations require an evaluation of each and a selection of the best alternative.

Generally Accepted Accounting Principles

The accounting profession has attempted to develop a set of standards that is generally accepted and universally practiced. Its efforts have resulted in a common set of standards called generally accepted accounting principles (GAAP). These standards indicate how to report economic events.

Two organizations are primarily responsible for establishing generally accepted accounting principles. The first is the Financial Accounting Standards Board (FASB), a private organization that establishes broad reporting standards of general applicability as well as specific accounting rules. The second, the Securities and Exchange Commission (SEC), is a governmental agency that requires companies filing financial reports with it to follow generally accepted accounting principles. In situations where no principles exist, the SEC often mandates that certain guidelines be used. In general, the FASB and the SEC work hand in hand to assure that timely and useful accounting principles are developed.

One important principle is the cost principle, which states that assets should be recorded at their cost. **Cost is the value exchanged at the time something is acquired.** If you buy a house today, the cost is the amount you pay for it, say $100,000. If you sell the house in two years for $120,000, the sales price is its **market value**—the value determined by the market for homes at that time. At the time of acquisition, cost and fair market value are the same. In subsequent periods, cost and fair market value may vary, **but the cost amount continues to be used**.

For example, at one time, Greyhound Corporation had 128 bus stations nationwide that cost approximately $200 million. The current market value of the stations is approximately $1 billion. Under the cost principle, the bus stations are recorded and reported at $200 million, not $1 billion. Until the bus stations are actually sold, estimates of market values are considered too subjective.

4

STUDY

OBJECTIVE

Explain the meaning of generally accepted accounting principles and the cost principle.

INTERNATIONAL NOTE

The standard-setting processes in Canada, Mexico, and the United States are quite similar in most respects. All three have relatively open deliberations on new rules, and they support efforts to follow international standards. The use of similar accounting principles within North America has implications for the success of the North American Free Trade Agreement (NAFTA).

As the Greyhound example indicates, cost has an important advantage over other valuations: it is reliable. Cost is definite and verifiable. The values exchanged at the time something is acquired generally can be objectively measured. To rely on the information supplied, users must know that the information is based on fact. However, critics argue that cost is often not relevant and that market values provide more useful information. Despite its shortcomings, cost continues to be used in the financial statements because of its reliability.

ALTERNATIVE TERMINOLOGY
The cost principle is often referred to as the *historical cost principle.*

5
STUDY
OBJECTIVE
....
Explain the meaning of the monetary unit assumption and the economic entity assumption.

Assumptions

In developing generally accepted accounting principles, certain basic assumptions are made. These assumptions provide a foundation for the accounting process. Two main assumptions are the **monetary unit assumption** and the **economic entity assumption**.

Monetary Unit Assumption

The monetary unit assumption requires that only transaction data that can be expressed in terms of money be included in the accounting records of the economic entity. Because money is the commonly used medium of exchange, this assumption enables accounting to quantify (measure) the economic event. The monetary unit assumption is vital to applying the cost principle discussed earlier. This assumption prevents such relevant information as the health of the owner, the quality of service, and the morale of employees from being included in the accounting records because they cannot be quantified in terms of money.

An important corollary to the monetary unit assumption is the added assumption that the unit of measure remains sufficiently constant over time. However, the assumption of a stable monetary unit has been challenged because of the significant decline in the purchasing power of the dollar. For example, what used to cost $1.00 in 1960 costs over $4.00 in 1999. In such situations, adding, subtracting, or comparing 1960 dollars with 1999 dollars is highly questionable. The profession has recognized this problem and encourages companies to disclose the effects of changing prices.

Economic Entity Assumption

An economic entity can be any organization or unit in society. It may be a business enterprise (such as General Electric Company), a governmental unit (such as the state of Ohio), a municipality (such as Seattle), a school district (such as St. Louis District 48), or a church (Southern Baptist). The economic entity assumption states that economic events can be identified with a particular unit of accountability. This assumption requires that the activities of the entity be kept separate and distinct from (1) the activities of its owner and (2) all other economic entities. To illustrate, if Sally Rider, owner of Sally's Boutique, charges any of her personal living costs as expenses of the Boutique, the economic entity assumption is violated. Similarly, the economic entity assumption assumes that the activities of Kellogg, General Mills, and Quaker Oats can each be segregated into separate economic entities for accounting purposes.

Although the economic entity assumption can be applied to any unit of accountability, we will generally discuss it in relation to a business enterprise, which may be organized as a proprietorship, partnership, or corporation.

ACCOUNTING IN ACTION
Ethics Insight

A violation of the economic entity assumption contributed to the resignation by the chief executive of W.R. Grace and Company. Investors were angered to learn that company funds were used for personal medical care, a Manhattan apartment, and a personal chef for the company's chief. Funds were also used to support a hotel interest owned by the chief executive's son.

Proprietorship. A business owned by one person is generally a proprietorship. The owner is often the manager/operator of the business. Small service-type businesses (barber shops, law offices, plumbing companies, and auto repair shops), farms, and small retail stores (antique shops, clothing stores, and book stores) are often sole proprietorships. **Usually only a limited amount of money (capital) is necessary to start in business as a proprietorship, and the owner receives any profits, suffers any losses, and is personally liable for all debts of the business.** Although there is no legal distinction between the business as an economic unit and the owner, the records of the business activities are kept separate from the personal records and activities of the owner. Although sole proprietorships represent the largest number of businesses in the United States, they are typically the smallest in size and volume of business.

HELPFUL HINT
Approximately 70% of United States companies are proprietorships; however, they account for only 6.5% of gross revenues. Corporations, on the other hand, are approximately 19% of all companies, but account for 90% of the revenues.

Partnership. A business owned by two or more persons associated as partners is a partnership. In most respects a partnership is similar to a sole proprietorship except that more than one owner is involved. When a partnership is created, an agreement (written or oral) should set forth such terms as initial investment of each partner, duties of each partner, division of net income (or net loss), and settlement to be made upon death or withdrawal of a partner. Each partner generally has unlimited personal liability for the debts of the partnership. **Like a proprietorship, for accounting purposes the partnership affairs must be kept separate from the personal activities of the partners.** Partnerships are often used to organize retail and service-type businesses, including professional practices (lawyers, doctors, architects, and certified public accountants).

Corporation. A business organized as a separate legal entity under state corporation law and having ownership divided into transferable shares of stock is called a corporation. The holders of the shares (stockholders) **enjoy limited liability**; they are not personally liable for the debts of the corporate entity. Stockholders **may transfer all or part of their shares to other investors at any time** (i.e., sell their shares in the securities market). The ease with which ownership can change adds to the attractiveness of investing in a corporation. Because ownership can be transferred without dissolving the corporation, the corporation **enjoys an unlimited life**.

Although the combined number of proprietorships and partnerships in the United States is more than four times the number of corporations, the revenue produced by corporations is nine times greater. Most of the largest enterprises in the United States—for example, Exxon, General Motors, Sears Roebuck, Citicorp, and Kellogg Company—are corporations.

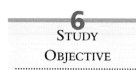

Basic Accounting Equation

Other essential building blocks of accounting are the categories into which economic events are classified. The two basic elements of a business are what it owns and what it owes. **Assets** are the resources owned by a business. For example, Kellogg's competitor, General Mills, has total assets of approximately $3.9 billion. Liabilities and stockholders' equity are the rights or claims against these resources. Thus, a company such as General Mills that has $3.9 billion of assets also has $3.9 billion of claims against those assets. Claims of creditors are called **liabilities**. Claims of owners are called **stockholders' equity**. For example, General Mills has liabilities of $3.7 billion and stockholders' equity of $.2 billion. This equation can be expressed as follows:

ILLUSTRATION 1-6

The basic accounting equation

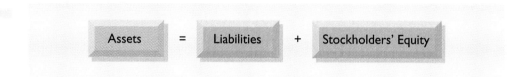

This equation is referred to as the basic accounting equation. Assets must equal the sum of liabilities and stockholders' equity. Because creditors' claims are paid before stockholders' claims if a business is liquidated, liabilities are shown before stockholders' equity in the basic accounting equation.

The accounting equation applies to all **economic entities** regardless of size, nature of business, or form of business organization. Thus, it applies to a small proprietorship such as a corner grocery store as well as to a giant corporation such as Kellogg or General Mills. The equation provides the underlying framework for recording and summarizing the economic events of a business enterprise.

Let's look in more detail at the categories in the basic accounting equation.

Assets

As indicated above, assets are resources owned by a business. Thus, they are the things of value used in carrying out such activities as production, consumption, and exchange. The common characteristic possessed by all assets is the capacity to provide future services or benefits to the entities that use them. In a business enterprise, that service potential or future economic benefit eventually results in cash inflows (receipts) to the enterprise.

For example, the enterprise Campus Pizza owns a delivery truck that provides economic benefits because it is used in delivering pizzas. Other assets of Campus Pizza are tables, chairs, jukebox, cash register, oven, mugs and silverware, and, of course, cash.

Liabilities

Liabilities are claims against assets. Put more simply, **liabilities are existing debts and obligations**. For example, businesses of all sizes and degrees of success usually find it necessary to borrow money and to purchase merchandise on credit. Campus Pizza, for instance, purchases cheese, sausage, flour, and beverages on credit from suppliers; these obligations are called **accounts payable**. Additionally, Campus Pizza has a **note payable** to First National

Bank for the money borrowed to purchase its delivery truck. Campus Pizza may also have **wages payable** to employees, and **sales and real estate taxes payable** to the local government. Persons or entities to whom Campus Pizza owes money are called **creditors**.

Most claims of creditors attach to **total** enterprise assets rather than to the specific assets provided by the creditor. In the event of nonpayment, creditors may legally force the liquidation of a business. In that case, the law requires that creditor claims be paid before stockholders' claims.

Stockholders' Equity

The ownership claim on total assets is known as stockholders' equity. It is equal to total assets minus total liabilities. Here is why: The assets of a business are supplied or claimed by either creditors or stockholders. To determine what belongs to stockholders, we therefore subtract creditors' claims—the liabilities—from assets. The remainder—stockholders' equity—is the stockholders' claim on the assets of the business. It is often referred to as residual equity. The stockholders' equity section of a corporation's balance sheet consists of (1) paid-in (contributed) capital and (2) retained earnings (earned capital).

Paid-in Capital.   **Paid-in capital** is the term used to describe the total amount paid in by stockholders. The principal source of paid-in capital is the investment of cash and other assets in the corporation by stockholders in exchange for capital stock. Corporations may issue several classes of stock, but the stock representing ownership interest is common stock.

Retained Earnings.   The **retained earnings** section of the balance sheet is determined by three items: revenues, expenses, and dividends.

Revenues.   Revenues are the gross increase in stockholders' equity resulting from business activities entered into for the purpose of earning income. Generally, revenues result from the sale of merchandise, the performance of services, the rental of property, and the lending of money.

Revenues usually result in an increase in an asset. They may arise from different sources and are identified by various names depending on the nature of the business. Campus Pizza, for instance, has two categories of sales revenues—pizza sales and beverage sales. Other titles for and sources of revenue common to many businesses are: sales, fees, services, commissions, interest, dividends, royalties, and rent.

Expenses.   Expenses are **the decreases in stockholders' equity that result from operating the business**. They are the cost of assets consumed or services used in the process of earning revenue. Expenses represent actual or expected cash outflows (payments). Like revenues, expenses take many forms and are identified by various names depending on the type of asset consumed or service used. For example, Campus Pizza recognizes the following types of expenses: cost of ingredients (meat, flour, cheese, tomato paste, mushrooms, etc.); cost of beverages; wages expense; utility expense (electric, gas, and water expense); telephone expense; delivery expense (gasoline, repairs, licenses, etc.); supplies expense (napkins, detergents, aprons, etc.); rent expense; interest expense; and property tax expense. When revenues exceed expenses, net income results. When expenses exceed revenues, a net loss results.

Dividends.   When a company is successful, it generates net income. **Net income** represents an increase in net assets which are then available to distribute

HELPFUL HINT
The effect of revenues is positive—an increase in stockholders' equity coupled with an increase in assets or a decrease in liabilities.

HELPFUL HINT
The effect of expenses is negative—a decrease in stockholders' equity coupled with a decrease in assets or an increase in liabilities.

to stockholders. The distribution of cash or other assets to stockholders is called a dividend. Dividends reduce retained earnings. However, dividends are not an expense of a corporation. A corporation first determines its revenues and expenses and then computes net income or net loss. At this point, a corporation may decide to distribute a dividend.

In summary, the principal sources (increases) of stockholders' equity are (1) investments by stockholders and (2) revenues from business' operations. In contrast, reductions (decreases) in stockholders' equity are a result of (1) expenses and (2) dividends. These relationships are shown in Illustration 1-7.

ILLUSTRATION 1-7

Increases and decreases in stockholders' equity

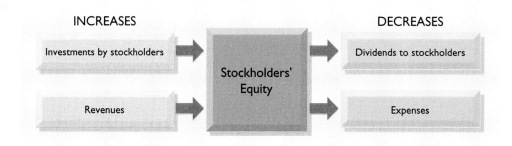

BEFORE YOU GO ON . . .

Review It

1. Why is ethics considered a fundamental business concept?
2. What are generally accepted accounting principles? Give an example of an accounting principle.
3. Explain the monetary unit and the economic entity assumptions.
4. What is the basic accounting equation? Replacing the words in that equation with dollar amounts, what is Kellogg's accounting equation at December 31, 1998? (The answer to this question is provided on page 43.)
5. What are assets, liabilities, and stockholders' equity?

Do It

Do It exercises give you immediate practice of the material just covered. These exercises outline the reasoning necessary to complete the exercise and a solution.

Classify the following items as issuance of stock (I), dividends (D), revenues (R), or expenses (E), and indicate whether these items increase or decrease stockholders' equity: (1) Rent Expense, (2) Service Revenue, (3) Dividends, and (4) Salaries Expense.

Reasoning: Both investments and service revenue increase stockholders' equity; however, service revenue arises from the sale of merchandise, the performance of services, the rental of property, or the lending of money. Investments are resources contributed to the business by the stockholders. Similarly, expenses and dividends decrease stockholders' equity; however, expenses arise from consuming assets or services. Dividends are distributions of cash or other assets to stockholders.

Solution:

1. Rent Expense is classified as an expense (E); it decreases stockholders' equity.
2. Service Revenue is classified as revenue (R); it increases stockholders' equity.
3. Dividends is classified as dividends (D); it decreases stockholders' equity.
4. Salaries Expense is classified as an expense (E); it decreases stockholders' equity.

Related exercise material: BE1–1, BE1–2, BE1–3, BE1–4, BE1–5, BE1–6, BE1–7, BE1–9, E1–1, E1–2, E1–3, E1–4, E1–6, and E1–7.

USING THE BUILDING BLOCKS

Transactions (often referred to as business transactions) are the economic events of the enterprise that are recorded. Transactions may be identified as external or internal. **External transactions involve economic events between the company and some outside enterprise or party.** For example, for Campus Pizza the purchase of cooking equipment from a supplier, the payment of monthly rent to the landlord, and the sale of pizzas to customers are external transactions. **Internal transactions are economic events that occur entirely within one company.** The use of office supplies illustrates this type of transaction for Campus Pizza.

A company may carry on many activities that do not in themselves represent business transactions. Hiring employees, answering the telephone, talking with customers, and placing an order for merchandise with a supplier are examples. Some of these activities, however, may lead to a business transaction: employees will earn wages, and merchandise will be delivered by the supplier. Each transaction must be analyzed in terms of its effect on the components of the basic accounting equation. This analysis must identify the specific items affected and the amount of the change in each item. Illustration 1-8 demonstrates the transaction identification process.

7
STUDY
OBJECTIVE
....
Analyze the effect of business transactions on the basic accounting● equation.

ILLUSTRATION 1-8
Transaction identification process

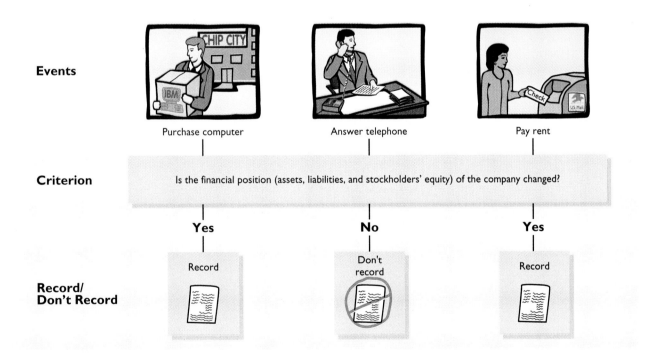

Events	Purchase computer	Answer telephone	Pay rent
Criterion	Is the financial position (assets, liabilities, and stockholders' equity) of the company changed?		
	Yes	**No**	**Yes**
Record/Don't Record	Record	Don't record	Record

The equality of the basic equation must be preserved. Therefore, each transaction must have a dual effect on the equation. For example, if an individual asset is increased, there must be a corresponding:

1. Decrease in another asset, or
2. Increase in a specific liability, or
3. Increase in stockholders' equity.

It follows that two or more items could be affected when an asset is increased. For example, as one asset is increased $10,000, another asset could decrease $6,000, and a specific liability could increase $4,000. Note also that any change in an individual liability or ownership claim is subject to similar analysis.

Transaction Analysis

The following examples are business transactions for a new computer programming business during its first month of operations. You will want to study these transactions until you are sure you understand them. They are not difficult, but they are important to your success in this course. The ability to analyze transactions in terms of the basic accounting equation is essential for an understanding of accounting.

Transaction (1). Investment by Stockholders. Ray and Barbara Neal decide to open a computer programming company that they incorporate as Softbyte, Inc. They invest $15,000 cash in the business in exchange for $15,000 of common stock. The common stock indicates the ownership interest that the Neals have in Softbyte, Inc. The transaction results in an equal increase in both assets and stockholders' equity. In this case, there is an increase in the asset Cash of $15,000, and an increase in Common Stock of $15,000.

The effect of this transaction on the basic equation is shown below. Recorded to the right of Common Stock is the reason why stockholders' equity changed, i.e., investment.

	Assets	=	Liabilities	+	Stockholders' Equity	
	Cash	=			Common Stock	
(1)	+ $15,000			=	+ $15,000	Investment

Observe that the equality of the basic equation has been maintained. Note also that the source of the increase in stockholders' equity is indicated, to make clear that the increase is an investment rather than revenue from operations. Why does this matter? Because investments by stockholders do not represent revenues, they are excluded in determining net income. Additional investments (i.e., investments made by stockholders after the corporation has been initially formed) have the same effect on stockholders' equity as the initial investment.

Transaction (2). Purchase of Equipment for Cash. Softbyte purchases computer equipment for $7,000 cash. This transaction results in an equal increase and decrease in total assets, though the composition of assets is changed: Cash is decreased $7,000, and the asset Equipment is increased $7,000. Both the specific effect of this transaction and the cumulative effect of the first two transactions are:

		Assets			=	Liabilities	+	Stockholders' Equity
		Cash	+	Equipment	=			Common Stock
	Old Bal.	$15,000						$15,000
(2)		−7,000		+$ 7,000				
	New Bal.	$ 8,000	+	$ 7,000	=			$15,000
			$15,000					

Observe that total assets are still $15,000 and stockholders' equity also remains at $15,000, the amount of the original investment.

Transaction (3). Purchase of Supplies on Credit. Softbyte, Inc. purchases computer paper and other supplies expected to last several months from Acme Supply Company for $1,600. Acme agrees to allow Softbyte to pay this bill in October, a month later. This transaction is often referred to as a purchase on account or a credit purchase. Assets are increased by this transaction because of the expected future benefits of using the paper and supplies, and liabilities are increased by the amount due Acme Company. The asset Supplies is increased $1,600, and the liability Accounts Payable is increased by the same amount. The effect on the equation is:

		Assets					=	Liabilities	+	Stockholders' Equity
		Cash	+	Supplies	+	Equipment	=	Accounts Payable	+	Common Stock
	Old Bal.	$8,000				$7,000				$15,000
(3)				+$1,600				+$1,600		
	New Bal.	$8,000	+	$1,600	+	$7,000	=	$1,600	+	$15,000

$16,600 $16,600

Total assets are now $16,600. This total is matched by a $1,600 creditor's claim and a $15,000 stockholders' claim.

Transaction (4). Services Rendered for Cash. Softbyte, Inc. receives $1,200 cash from customers for programming services. This transaction represents the principal revenue-producing activity of Softbyte. Recall that **revenue increases stockholders' equity**. Both assets and stockholders' equity are, therefore, increased. In this case, Cash is increased $1,200, and Retained Earnings is increased $1,200. The new balances in the equation are:

		Assets					=	Liabilities	+	Stockholders' Equity		
		Cash	+	Supplies	+	Equipment	=	Accounts Payable	+	Common Stock	+	Retained Earnings
	Old Bal.	$8,000		$1,600		$7,000		$1,600		$15,000		
(4)		+1,200										+1,200 Service Revenue
	New Bal.	$9,200	+	$1,600	+	$7,000	=	$1,600	+	$15,000	+	$1,200

$17,800 $17,800

The two sides of the equation balance at $17,800. Note that stockholders' equity is increased when revenues are earned. The source of the increase in stockholders' equity is indicated as service revenue. Service revenue is included in determining Softbyte, Inc's. net income.

Transaction (5). Purchase of Advertising on Credit. Softbyte, Inc. receives a bill for $250 from the *Daily News* for advertising the opening of its business but postpones payment of the bill until a later date. This transaction results in an increase in liabilities and a decrease in stockholders' equity. The specific items involved are Accounts Payable and Retained Earnings. The effect on the equation is:

		Assets			=	Liabilities	+		Stockholders' Equity		
						Accounts		Common	Retained		
	Cash	+ Supplies	+ Equipment	=		Payable	+	Stock	+ Earnings		
Old Bal.	$9,200	$1,600	$7,000			$1,600		$15,000	$1,200		
(5)						+250			−250	Advertising Expense
New Bal.	$9,200 +	$1,600 +	$7,000	=		$1,850	+	$15,000	+ $ 950		
		$17,800						$17,800			

The two sides of the equation still balance at $17,800. Observe that Retained Earnings is decreased when the expense is incurred, and the specific cause of the decrease is noted. Expenses do not have to be paid in cash at the time they are incurred. When payment is made at a later date, the liability Accounts Payable will be decreased and the asset Cash will be decreased [see Transaction (8)]. The cost of advertising is considered an expense as opposed to an asset because the benefits have been used. This expense is included in determining net income.

Transaction (6). Services Rendered for Cash and Credit. Softbyte provides programming services of $3,500 for customers. Cash amounting to $1,500 is received from customers, and the balance of $2,000 is billed to customers on account. This transaction results in an equal increase in assets and stockholders' equity. Three specific items are affected: Cash is increased $1,500; Accounts Receivable is increased $2,000; and Retained Earnings is increased $3,500. The new balances are as follows:

			Assets				=	Liabilities	+		Stockholders' Equity	
		Accounts						Accounts	Common	Retained		
	Cash	+ Receivable	+ Supplies	+ Equipment	=			Payable	+ Stock	+ Earnings		
Old Bal.	$ 9,200		$1,600	$7,000				$1,850	$15,000	$ 950		
(6)	+1,500	+$2,000								+3,500	Service Revenue
New Bal.	$10,700 +	$2,000 +	$1,600 +	$7,000	=			$1,850	+ $15,000	+ $4,450		
			$21,300						$21,300			

Why increase Retained Earnings by $3,500 when only $1,500 has been collected? Because the inflow of assets resulting from the earning of revenues does not have to be in the form of cash. Remember that stockholders' equity is increased when revenues are earned, and in Softbyte's case that is when the service is provided. When collections on account are received at a later date, Cash will be increased and Accounts Receivable will be decreased [see Transaction (9)].

Transaction (7). Payment of Expenses. Expenses paid in cash for September are store rent, $600, salaries of employees, $900, and utilities, $200. These payments result in an equal decrease in assets and stockholders' equity. Cash is decreased $1,700 and Retained Earnings is decreased by the same amount. The effect of these payments on the equation is:

	Assets				=	**Liabilities** +		**Stockholders' Equity**		
	Cash	+ Accounts Receivable	+ Supplies	+ Equipment =		Accounts Payable	+	Common Stock	+ Retained Earnings	
Old Bal.	$10,700	$2,000	$1,600	$7,000		$1,850		$15,000	$4,450	
(7)	−1,700								−600	Rent Expense
									−900	Salaries Expense
									−200	Utilities Expense
New Bal.	$ 9,000 +	$2,000 +	$1,600 +	$7,000 =		$1,850	+	$15,000 +	$2,750	

$19,600 $19,600

The two sides of the equation now balance at $19,600. Three lines are required in the analysis to indicate the different types of expenses that have been incurred.

Transaction (8).   Payment of Accounts Payable.   Softbyte, Inc. pays its *Daily News* advertising bill of $250 in cash. In analyzing the effect of this transaction, we must recall that the bill has previously been recorded in Transaction (5) as an increase in Accounts Payable and a decrease in Retained Earnings. Thus, this payment "on account" decreases both assets and liabilities. In this case, the asset Cash and the liability Accounts Payable are decreased by $250. The effect of this transaction on the equation is:

	Assets				=	**Liabilities** +		**Stockholders' Equity**	
	Cash	+ Accounts Receivable	+ Supplies	+ Equipment =		Accounts Payable	+	Common Stock	+ Retained Earnings
Old Bal.	$9,000	$2,000	$1,600	$7,000		$1,850		$15,000	$2,750
(8)	−250					−250			
New Bal.	$8,750 +	$2,000 +	$1,600	$7,000 =		$1,600	+	$15,000 +	$2,750

$19,350 $19,350

Observe that the payment of a liability related to an expense that has previously been incurred does not affect stockholders' equity. Neither Common Stock nor Retained Earnings changes as a result of this transaction.

Transaction (9).   Receipt of Cash on Account.   The sum of $600 in cash is received from customers who have previously been billed for services in Transaction (6). This transaction does not change total assets, but it changes the composition of Softbyte's assets. Cash is increased $600 and Accounts Receivable is decreased $600. The new balances are:

	Assets				=	**Liabilities** +		**Stockholders' Equity**	
	Cash	+ Accounts Receivable	+ Supplies	+ Equipment =		Accounts Payable	+	Common Stock	+ Retained Earnings
Old Bal.	$8,750	$2,000	$1,600	$7,000		$1,600		$15,000	$2,750
(9)	+600	−600							
New Bal.	$9,350 +	$1,400 +	$1,600 +	$7,000 =		$1,600	+	$15,000 +	$2,750

$19,350 $19,350

Note that a collection on account for services previously billed and recorded does not affect stockholders' equity. Revenue was already recorded in Transaction (6) and should not be recorded again.

Transaction (10).   Dividends.   The corporation pays a dividend of $1,300 in cash to Ray and Barbara Neal, the stockholders of Softbyte, Inc. The transaction results in an equal decrease in assets and stockholders' equity. Thus, both Cash and Retained Earnings are decreased $1,300 as shown below.

		Assets			= Liabilities +		Stockholders' Equity	
	Cash	+ Receivable	+ Supplies	+ Equipment =	Accounts Payable	Common + Stock	Retained + Earnings	
Old Bal.	$9,350	$1,400	$1,600	$7,000	$1,600	$15,000	$2,750	
(10)	−1,300						−1,300	Dividends
New Bal.	$8,050 +	$1,400 +	$1,600 +	$7,000 =	$1,600 +	$15,000 +	$1,450	

$$\underbrace{\qquad\qquad}_{\$18,050} \qquad\qquad \underbrace{\qquad\qquad}_{\$18,050}$$

Note that the dividend reduces retained earnings which is part of stockholders' equity. Dividends do not represent expenses. Like stockholders' investments, dividends are not included in determining net income.

Summary of Transactions

ILLUSTRATION 1-9

Tabular summary of Softbyte, Inc. transactions

The transactions of Softbyte, Inc. are summarized in Illustration 1-9 to show their cumulative effect on the basic accounting equation. The transaction num-

			Assets			= Liabilities +		Stockholders' Equity		
Transaction	Cash	+	Accounts Receivable +	Supplies +	Equipment =	Accounts Payable	+	Common Stock +	Retained Earnings	
(1)	+$15,000				=		+	$15,000		Investment
(2)	−7,000				+$7,000					
	8,000				+ 7,000 =			15,000		
(3)				+$1,600		+$1,600				
	8,000			+ 1,600 +	7,000 =	1,600	+	15,000		
(4)	+1,200								+1,200	Service Revenue
	9,200			+ 1,600 +	7,000 =	1,600	+	15,000 +	1,200	
(5)						+250			−250	Advert. Expense
	9,200			+ 1,600 +	7,000 =	1,850	+	15,000 +	950	
(6)	+1,500		+$2,000						+3,500	Service Revenue
	10,700	+	2,000 +	1,600 +	7,000 =	1,850	+	15,000 +	4,450	
(7)	−1,700								−600	Rent Expense
									−900	Salaries Expense
									−200	Utilities Expense
	9,000	+	2,000 +	1,600 +	7,000 =	1,850	+	15,000 +	2,750	
(8)	−250					−250				
	8,750	+	2,000 +	1,600 +	7,000 =	1,600	+	15,000 +	2,750	
(9)	+600		−600							
	9,350	+	1,400 +	1,600 +	7,000 =	1,600	+	15,000 +	2,750	
(10)	−1,300								−1,300	Dividends
	$ 8,050	+	$1,400 +	$1,600 +	$7,000 =	$1,600	+	$15,000 +	$1,450	

$$\underbrace{\qquad\qquad}_{\$18,050} \qquad\qquad \underbrace{\qquad\qquad}_{\$18,050}$$

ber, the specific effects of the transaction, and the balances after each transaction are indicated. The illustration demonstrates a number of significant facts:

1. Each transaction must be analyzed in terms of its effect on:
   (a) the three components of the basic accounting equation.
   (b) specific types (kinds) of items within each component.
2. The two sides of the equation must always be equal.
3. The causes of each change in the stockholders' claim on assets must be indicated in the Common Stock and Retained Earnings columns.

There! You made it through transaction analysis. If you feel a bit shaky on any of the transactions, it would probably be a good idea at this point to get up, take a short break, and come back again for a 10- to 15-minute review of the transactions, to make sure you understand them before you go on to the next section.

BEFORE YOU GO ON . . .

Review It

1. What is an example of an external transaction? What is an example of an internal transaction?
2. If an asset increases, what are the three possible effects on the basic accounting equation?

Do It

A tabular analysis of the transactions made by Roberta Mendez & Co., a business consulting firm, for the month of August is shown below. Each increase and decrease in stockholders' equity is explained.

	Assets		=	Liabilities +		Stockholders' Equity		
		Office		Accounts		Common	Retained	
	Cash	+ Equipment	=	Payable	+	Stock	+ Earnings	
1.	+25,000					+25,000		Investment
2.		+7,000		+7,000				
3.	+8,000						+8,000	Service Revenue
4.	− 850						− 850	Rent Expense

Describe each transaction that occurred for the month.

Reasoning: The accounting equation must always be in balance. A change in an asset requires a change in another asset, in a liability, or in stockholders' equity. By analyzing the tabular analysis we can determine each transaction.

Solution:

1. Stockholders purchased additional shares of stock for $25,000 cash.
2. The company purchased $7,000 of office equipment on credit.
3. The company received $8,000 of cash in exchange for services performed.
4. The company paid $850 for this month's rent.

THE NAVIGATOR

Related exercise material: BE1–4, BE1–5, BE1–6, BE1–7, E1–2, E1–3, E1–4, E1–6, and E1–7.

FINANCIAL STATEMENTS

8

STUDY

OBJECTIVE

Prepare an income
statement, retained
earnings statement,
balance sheet, and
statement of cash flows.

After transactions are identified, recorded, and summarized, four financial statements are prepared from the summarized accounting data:

1. An income statement presents the revenues and expenses and resulting net
   income or net loss of a company for a specific period of time.
2. A retained earnings statement summarizes the changes in retained earnings
   for a specific period of time.
3. A balance sheet reports the assets, liabilities, and stockholders' equity of a
   business enterprise at a specific date.
4. A statement of cash flows summarizes information concerning the cash inflows (receipts) and outflows (payments) for a specific period of time.

HELPFUL HINT
The income statement,
retained earnings statement,
and statement of cash flows are
all for a *period* of time, whereas
the balance sheet is for a *point*
in time.

Each statement provides management, stockholders, and other interested
parties with relevant financial data. The financial statements of Softbyte, Inc. and
their interrelationships are shown in Illustration 1-10. The statements are interrelated: **(1) Net income of $2,750 shown on the income statement is added to
the beginning balance of retained earnings in the retained earnings statement.
(2) Retained earnings of $1,450 at the end of the reporting period shown in
the retained earnings statement is reported on the balance sheet. (3) Cash of
$8,050 on the balance sheet is reported on the statement of cash flows.**

HELPFUL HINT
There is only one group of
notes for the whole set of
financial statements and not
separate sets of notes for each
financial statement.

Additionally, every set of financial statements is accompanied by explana-
tory notes and supporting schedules that are an integral part of the statements.
Examples of these notes and schedules are illustrated in later chapters of this
textbook.

Be sure to carefully examine the format and content of each statement. The
essential features of each are briefly described in the following sections.

ACCOUNTING IN ACTION
Business Insight

Why do companies choose the particular year-ends that they do? For example, why doesn't every company use December 31 as the accounting year-end?
Many companies choose to end their accounting year when inventory or operations are at a low. This is advantageous because compiling accounting information
requires much time and effort by managers, so they would rather do it when they
aren't as busy operating the business. Also, inventory is easier and less costly to count
when it is low. Some companies whose year-ends differ from December 31 are Delta
Air Lines, June 30; Walt Disney Productions, September 30; Kmart Corp., January 31;
Dunkin' Donuts, Inc., October 31; and General Mills, May 31.

Income Statement

ALTERNATIVE TERMINOLOGY
The income statement is
sometimes referred to as the
*statement of operations, earnings
statement,* or *profit and loss
statement.*

The income statement for Softbyte, Inc. is prepared from the data appearing in
the retained earnings column of Illustration 1-9. The heading of the statement
identifies the company, the type of statement, and the time period covered by
the statement. Note that the primary focus of the income statement is on reporting the success or profitability of the company's operations over a specified
period of time. To indicate that it applies for a period of time, the income statement is dated "For the Month Ended September 30, 2001."

ILLUSTRATION 1-10

Financial statements and their interrelationships

SOFTBYTE, INC.
Income Statement
For the Month Ended September 30, 2001

Revenues		
Service revenue		$4,700
Expenses		
Salaries expense	$900	
Rent expense	600	
Advertising expense	250	
Utilities expense	200	
Total expenses		1,950
Net income		$2,750

SOFTBYTE, INC.
Retained Earnings Statement
For the Month Ended September 30, 2001

Retained earnings, September 1	$ 0
Add: Net income	2,750
	2,750
Less: Dividends	1,300
Retained earnings, September 30	$1,450

①

HELPFUL HINT
The four financial statements are prepared in the sequence shown for the following reasons: Net income is computed first and is needed to determine the ending balance in retained earnings. The ending balance in retained earnings is needed in preparing the balance sheet. The cash shown on the balance sheet is needed in preparing the statement of cash flows.

SOFTBYTE, INC.
Balance Sheet
September 30, 2001

Assets

Cash		$ 8,050
Accounts receivable		1,400
Supplies		1,600
Equipment		7,000
Total assets		$18,050

Liabilities and Stockholders' Equity

Liabilities		
Accounts payable		$ 1,600
Stockholders' equity		
Common stock	$15,000	
Retained earnings	1,450	16,450
Total liabilities and stockholders' equity		$18,050

②

③

SOFTBYTE, INC.
Statement of Cash Flows
For the Month Ended September 30, 2001

Cash flows from operating activities		
Cash receipts from revenues		$ 3,300
Cash payments for expenses		(1,950)
Net cash provided by operating activities		1,350
Cash flows from investing activities		
Purchase of equipment		(7,000)
Cash flows from financing activities		
Sale of common stock	$15,000	
Payment of cash dividends	(1,300)	13,700
Net increase in cash		8,050
Cash at the beginning of the period		0
Cash at the end of the period		$ 8,050

Revenues are listed first, followed by expenses. Finally net income (or net loss) is determined. Although practice varies considerably on this matter, we have chosen in our illustrations and solutions to homework to list expenses in order of magnitude. Alternative formats for the income statement will be considered in later chapters.

Note that investment and dividend transactions between the stockholders and the business are not included in the measurement of net income. For example, the cash dividend from Softbyte, Inc. was not regarded as a business expense, as explained earlier. This type of transaction is considered a reduction of retained earnings which causes a decrease in stockholders' equity.

Retained Earnings Statement

Data for the preparation of the retained earnings statement are obtained from the retained earnings column of the tabular summary (Illustration 1-9) and from the income statement in Illustration 1-10. The heading of this statement identifies the company, the type of statement, and the time period covered by the statement. The time period is the same as that covered by the income statement and therefore is dated "For the Month Ended September 30, 2001." The beginning retained earnings amount is shown on the first line of the statement. Then, net income and dividends are identified in the statement. The retained earnings ending balance is the final amount on the statement. The information provided by this statement indicates the reasons why retained earnings increased or decreased during the period. If there is a net loss, it is deducted with dividends in the retained earnings statement.

Balance Sheet

The balance sheet for Softbyte, Inc. is prepared from the column headings and the month-end data shown in the last line of the tabular summary (Illustration 1-9). The heading of a balance sheet must identify the company, the statement, and the date. To indicate that the balance sheet is at a specific date, it is dated "September 30, 2001." Observe that the assets are listed at the top, followed by liabilities and stockholders' equity. Total assets must equal total liabilities and stockholders' equity. In the Softbyte illustration, only one liability, accounts payable, is reported on the balance sheet. In most cases, there will be more than one liability. When two or more liabilities are involved, a customary way of listing is as follows:

ILLUSTRATION 1-11

Presentation of liabilities

Liabilities	
Notes payable	$10,000
Accounts payable	63,000
Salaries payable	18,000
Total liabilities	$91,000

The balance sheet is like a snapshot of the company's financial condition at a specific moment in time (usually the month-end or year-end).

HELPFUL HINT
Investing activities pertain to investments made by the company, not investments made by the stockholders.

Statement of Cash Flows

The primary purpose of a statement of cash flows is to provide financial information about the cash receipts and cash payments of an enterprise for a specific period of time. To achieve this purpose and to aid investors, creditors, and others in their analysis of cash, **the statement of cash flows reports (1) the cash effects of a company's operations during a period, (2) its investing transactions, (3) its financing transactions, (4) the net increase or decrease in cash during the period, and (5) the cash amount at the end of the period**.

Reporting the sources, uses, and net increase or decrease in cash is useful because investors, creditors, and others want to know what is happening to a company's most liquid resource. The statement of cash flows, therefore, provides answers to the following simple but important questions:

1. Where did the cash come from during the period?
2. What was the cash used for during the period?
3. What was the change in the cash balance during the period?

A statement of cash flows for Softbyte, Inc., is provided in Illustration 1-10.

As shown in the statement, cash increased $8,050 during the year. This increase resulted because net cash flow provided from operating activities increased cash $1,350, cash flow from investing transactions decreased cash $7,000, and cash flow from financing transactions increased cash $13,700. At this time, you need not be concerned with how these amounts are determined. Chapter 14 will examine in detail how the statement is prepared.

HELPFUL HINT
The cash at the end of the period reported in the statement of cash flows equals the cash reported in the balance sheet.

BEFORE YOU GO ON . . .

Review It

1. What are the income statement, retained earnings statement, balance sheet, and statement of cash flows?
2. Indicate how the financial statements are interrelated.

A LOOK BACK AT OUR FEATURE STORY

Refer to the opening story about Kellogg Company, and answer the following questions:

1. If you were interested in investing in Kellogg Company, what would the balance sheet and income statement tell you?
2. When a business's financial needs exceed the resources of the original owners, to whom might the company turn for additional funds?
3. Will the financial statements show the market value of the company? Explain.

Solution:

1. The balance sheet reports the assets, liabilities, and stockholders' equity of the company. The income statement presents the revenues and expenses and resulting net income (or net loss) for a specific period of time. The balance sheet is like a snapshot of the company's financial condition at a point in time. The income statement should give you a good indication of the profitability of the company. Also, the sources of the company's revenues and a picture of its expenses are provided in the income statement.
2. A company can turn to lenders (banks, bond holders, creditors) or to investors (additional owners) for additional financing.
3. The financial statements will not show the market value of the company. As indicated, one important principle of accounting is the cost principle, which states that assets should be recorded at cost. Cost has an important advantage over other valuations: it is reliable.

THE NAVIGATOR

DEMONSTRATION PROBLEM

Legal Services, Inc. was incorporated on July 1, 2001. During the first month of operations, the following transactions occurred:

1. Stockholders invested $10,000 in cash in exchange for shares of stock.
2. Paid $800 for July rent on office space.
3. Purchased office equipment on account, $3,000.
4. Rendered legal services to clients for cash, $1,500 (use Service Revenue).
5. Borrowed $700 cash from a bank on a note payable.
6. Performed legal services for client on account, $2,000.
7. Paid monthly expenses: salaries, $500; utilities, $300; and telephone, $100.

Instructions
(a) Prepare a tabular summary of the transactions.
(b) Prepare the income statement, retained earnings statement, and balance sheet at July 31 for Legal Services, Inc.

PROBLEM-SOLVING STRATEGIES

1. Remember that assets must equal liabilities and stockholders' equity after each transaction.
2. Investments and revenues increase stockholders' equity.
3. Dividends and expenses decrease stockholders' equity.
4. The income statement shows revenues and expenses for a period of time.
5. The retained earnings statement shows the changes in retained earnings for a period of time.
6. The balance sheet reports assets, liabilities, and stockholders' equity at a specific date.

SOLUTION TO DEMONSTRATION PROBLEM

(a)

Trans-action	Assets			=	Liabilities		+	Stockholders' Equity		
	Cash	+ Accounts Receivable	+ Equipment	=	Notes Payable	+ Accounts Payable	+	Common Stock	+ Retained Earnings	
(1)	+$10,000							+$10,000		
(2)	−800								−$800	Rent Expense
	9,200			=				10,000 +	−800	
(3)			+$3,000			+$3,000				
	9,200	+	3,000	=		3,000 +		10,000 +	−800	
(4)	+1,500								+1,500	Service Revenue
	10,700	+	3,000	=		3,000 +		10,000 +	700	
(5)	+700				+$700					
	11,400	+	3,000	=	700 +	3,000 +		10,000 +	700	
(6)		+$2,000							+2,000	Service Revenue
	11,400 +	2,000	+ 3,000	=	700 +	3,000 +		10,000 +	2,700	
(7)	−900								−500	Salaries Expense
									−300	Utilities Expense
									−100	Telephone Expense
	$10,500 +	$2,000	+ $3,000	=	$700 +	$3,000 +		$10,000 +	$1,800	

$15,500 = $15,500

(b)

LEGAL SERVICES, INC.
Income Statement
For the Month Ended July 31, 2001

Revenues		
Service revenue		$3,500
Expenses		
Rent expense	$800	
Salaries expense	500	
Utilities expense	300	
Telephone expense	100	
Total expenses		1,700
Net income		$1,800

LEGAL SERVICES, INC.
Retained Earnings Statement
For the Month Ended July 31, 2001

Retained earnings, July 1	$ –0–
Add: Net income	1,800
Retained earnings, July 31	$1,800

LEGAL SERVICES, INC.
Balance Sheet
July 31, 2001

Assets

Cash	$10,500
Accounts receivable	2,000
Equipment	3,000
Total assets	$15,500

Liabilities and Stockholders' Equity

Liabilities		
Notes payable		$ 700
Accounts payable		3,000
Total liabilities		3,700
Stockholders' equity		
Common stock	$10,000	
Retained earnings	1,800	11,800
Total liabilities and stockholders' equity		$15,500

THE NAVIGATOR

This would be a good time to return to the Student Owner's Manual at the beginning of the book (or look at it for the first time if you skipped it before) to read about the various types of assignment materials that appear at the end of each chapter. Knowing the purpose of the different assignments will help you appreciate what each contributes to your accounting skills and competencies.

SUMMARY OF STUDY OBJECTIVES

1. *Explain the meaning of accounting.* Accounting is the process of identifying, recording, and communicating the economic events of an organization (business or nonbusiness) to interested users of the information.

2. *Identify the users and uses of accounting.* The major users and uses of accounting are: (a) Management uses accounting information in planning, controlling, and evaluating business operations. (b) Investors (owners) judge the wisdom of buying, holding, or selling their financial interests on the basis of accounting data. (c) Creditors (suppliers and bankers) evaluate the risks of granting credit or lending money to particular businesses on the basis of the accounting information obtained about those businesses.

Other groups with an indirect interest are taxing authorities, regulatory agencies, customers, labor unions, and economic planners.

3. *Understand why ethics is a fundamental business concept.* Ethics are the standards of conduct by which one's actions—both personal and business—are judged as right or wrong. If you cannot depend on the honesty of the individuals you deal with, effective communication and economic activity would be impossible and information would have no credibility.

4. *Explain the meaning of generally accepted accounting principles and the cost principle.* Generally accepted accounting principles are a common set of standards used by accountants. One important principle is the cost principle, which states that assets should be recorded at their cost.

5. Explain the meaning of the monetary unit assumption and the economic entity assumption. The monetary unit assumption requires that only transaction data capable of being expressed in terms of money be included in the accounting records of the economic entity. The economic entity assumption states that economic events can be identified with a particular unit of accountability.

6. State the basic accounting equation and explain the meaning of assets, liabilities, and stockholders' equity. The basic accounting equation is:

$$Assets = Liabilities + Stockholders' \; Equity$$

Assets are resources owned by a business. Liabilities are creditorship claims on total assets. Stockholders' equity is the ownership claim on total assets. It is often referred to as residual equity.

7. Analyze the effect of business transactions on the basic accounting equation. Each business transaction must have a dual effect on the accounting equation. For example, if an individual asset is increased, there must be a corresponding: (1) decrease in another asset, or (2) increase in a specific liability, or (3) increase in stockholders' equity.

8. Prepare an income statement, retained earnings statement, balance sheet, and statement of cash flows. An income statement presents the revenues and expenses of a company for a specified period of time. A retained earnings statement summarizes the changes in retained earnings that have occurred for a specific period of time. A balance sheet reports the assets, liabilities, and stockholders' equity of a business at a specific date. A statement of cash flows summarizes information concerning the cash inflows (receipts) and outflows (payments) for a specific period of time.

THE NAVIGATOR

GLOSSARY

Accounting The process of identifying, recording, and communicating the economic events of an organization to interested users of the information. (p. 2).

Assets Resources owned by a business. (p. 12).

Balance sheet A financial statement that reports the assets, liabilities, and stockholders' equity at a specific date. (p. 22).

Basic accounting equation Assets = Liabilities + Stockholders' Equity. (p. 12).

Bookkeeping A part of accounting that involves only the recording of economic events. (p. 6).

Corporation A business organized as a separate legal entity under state corporation law having ownership divided into transferable shares of stock. (p. 11).

Cost principle An accounting principle that states that assets should be recorded at their cost. (p. 9).

Dividend A distribution by a corporation to its stockholders on a pro rata (equal) basis. (p. 14).

Economic entity assumption An assumption that economic events can be identified with a particular unit of accountability. (p. 10).

Ethics The standards of conduct by which one's actions are judged as right or wrong, honest or dishonest, fair or not fair. (p. 8)

Expenses The cost of assets consumed or services used in the process of earning revenue. (p. 13).

Financial Accounting Standards Board (FASB) A private organization that establishes generally accepted accounting principles. (p. 9).

Generally accepted accounting principles (GAAP) A common set of standards that indicate how to report economic events. (p. 9).

Income statement A financial statement that presents the revenues and expenses and resulting net income or net loss of a company for a specific period of time. (p. 22).

Liabilities Creditorship claims on total assets. (p. 12).

Monetary unit assumption An assumption stating that only transaction data that can be expressed in terms of money be included in the accounting records of the economic entity. (p. 10).

Net income The amount by which revenues exceed expenses. (p. 13).

Net loss The amount by which expenses exceed revenues. (p. 13).

Partnership An association of two or more persons to carry on as co-owners of a business for profit. (p. 11).

Proprietorship A business owned by one person. (p. 11).

Retained earnings statement A financial statement that summarizes the changes in retained earnings for a specific period of time. (p. 22).

Revenues The gross increase in stockholders' equity resulting from business activities entered into for the purpose of earning income. (p. 13).

Securities and Exchange Commission (SEC) A governmental agency that requires companies to file financial reports in accordance with generally accepted accounting principles. (p. 9).

Statement of cash flows A financial statement that provides information about the cash inflows (receipts) and cash outflows (payments) of an entity for a specific period of time. (p. 22).

Stockholders' equity The ownership claim on total assets of a corporation. (p. 13).

Transactions The economic events of the enterprise recorded by accountants. (p. 15).

APPENDIX A THE ACCOUNTING PROFESSION

What would you do if you joined the accounting profession? You probably would apply your expertise in one of three major fields—public accounting, private accounting, or not-for-profit accounting.

PUBLIC ACCOUNTING

In public accounting, you would offer expert service to the general public in much the same way that a doctor serves patients and a lawyer serves clients. A major portion of public accounting practice is involved with auditing. In this area, a certified public accountant (CPA) examines the financial statements of companies and expresses an opinion as to the fairness of presentation. When the presentation is fair, users consider the statements to be **reliable**. For example, Kellogg's investors and creditors would demand audited financial statements before extending it financing.

Taxation is another major area of public accounting. The work performed by tax specialists includes tax advice and planning, preparing tax returns, and representing clients before governmental agencies such as the Internal Revenue Service.

A third area in public accounting is management consulting. Management consulting ranges from the installing of basic computerized accounting systems to helping companies determine whether they should use the space shuttle for high-tech research and development projects.

PRIVATE ACCOUNTING

Instead of working in public accounting, an accountant may be an employee of a business enterprise. In private (or managerial) accounting, you would be involved in one of the following activities:

1. **Cost accounting**—determining the cost of producing specific products.
2. **Budgeting**—assisting management in quantifying goals concerning revenues, costs of goods sold, and operating expenses.
3. **General accounting**—recording daily transactions and preparing financial statements and related information.
4. **Accounting information systems**—designing both manual and computerized data processing systems.
5. **Tax accounting**—preparing tax returns and engaging in tax planning for the company.
6. **Internal auditing**—reviewing the company's operations to determine compliance with management policies and evaluating the efficiency of operations.

From the above, you can see that within a specific company, private accountants perform as wide a variety of duties as the public accountant.

Illustration 1A-1 presents the general career paths in public and private accounting.

NOT-FOR-PROFIT ACCOUNTING

Like businesses that exist to make a profit, not-for-profit organizations also need sound financial reporting and control. Donors to such organizations as the United Way, the Ford Foundation, and the Red Cross want information about how well the organization has met its objectives and whether continued support is justified. Hospitals, colleges, and universities must make decisions about the allocation of funds. Local, state, and federal governmental units are continually

ILLUSTRATION 1A-1

Career paths in public and private accounting

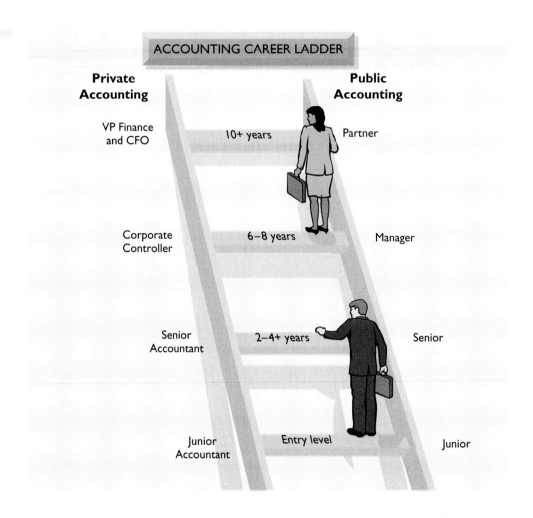

providing financial information to legislators, citizens, employees, and creditors. At the federal level, the largest employers of accountants are the Internal Revenue Service, the General Accounting Office, the Federal Bureau of Investigation, and the Securities and Exchange Commission.

SUMMARY OF STUDY OBJECTIVE FOR APPENDIX

9. Identify the three major fields of the accounting profession and potential accounting careers. The accounting profession is comprised of three major fields: public accounting, private accounting, and non-for-profit accounting. In public accounting one may pursue a career in auditing, taxation, or management consulting. In private or managerial accounting, one may pursue a career in cost accounting, budgeting, general accounting, accounting information systems, tax accounting, or internal auditing. In not-for-profit accounting one may pursue a career at hospitals, universities, and foundations, or in local, state, and federal governmental units.

GLOSSARY

Auditing The examination of financial statements by a certified public accountant in order to express an opinion as to the fairness of presentation. (p. 29).

Management consulting An area of public accounting involving financial planning and control and the development of accounting and computer systems. (p. 29).

Private (or managerial) accounting An area of accounting within a company that involves such activities as cost ac-

counting, budgeting, and accounting information systems. (p. 29).

Public accounting An area of accounting in which the accountant offers expert service to the general public. (p. 29).

Taxation An area of public accounting involving tax advice, tax planning, and preparing tax returns. (p. 29).

SELF-STUDY QUESTIONS

Answers are at the end of the chapter.

(SO 1) 1. The accounting process does *not* include:
 a. identification
 b. verification
 c. recording
 d. communication

(SO 2) 2. One of the following statements about users of accounting information is *incorrect*. The incorrect statement is:
 a. Management is considered an internal user.
 b. Taxing authorities are considered external users.
 c. Present creditors are considered external users.
 d. Regulatory authorities are considered internal users.

(SO 3) 3. Generally accepted accounting principles are:
 a. the guidelines used to resolve ethical dilemmas.
 b. established by the Internal Revenue Service.
 c. are primarily established by the Financial Accounting Standards Board and the Securities Exchange Commission.
 d. immutable truths derived from the laws of nature.

(SO 4) 4. The cost principle states that:
 a. assets should be recorded at cost and adjusted when the market value changes.
 b. activities of an entity be kept separate and distinct from its owner.
 c. assets should be recorded at their cost.
 d. only transaction data capable of being expressed in terms of money be included in the accounting records.

(SO 5) 5. Which of the following statements about basic assumptions is *incorrect*?
 a. Basic assumptions are the same as accounting principles.
 b. The economic entity assumption states that there should be a particular unit of accountability.

 c. The monetary unit assumption enables accounting to measure economic events.
 d. An important corollary to the monetary unit assumption is the stable monetary unit assumption.

6. Net income will result during a time period when: (SO 6)
 a. assets exceed liabilities.
 b. assets exceed revenues.
 c. expenses exceed revenues.
 d. revenues exceed expenses.

7. The effects on the basic accounting equation of per- (SO 7) forming services on account are:
 a. increase assets and decrease stockholders' equity.
 b. increase assets and increase stockholders' equity.
 c. increase assets and increase liabilities.
 d. increase liabilities and increase stockholders' equity.

8. As of December 31, 2001, Oswego Company has assets of (SO 7) $3,500 and stockholders' equity of $2,000. What are the liabilities for Oswego Company as of December 31, 2001?
 a. $1,500.
 b. $1,000.
 c. $2,500.
 d. $2,000.

9. On the last day of the period, Plano Company buys a (SO 8) $900 machine on credit. This transaction will affect the:
 a. income statement only.
 b. balance sheet only.
 c. income statement and retained earnings statement only.
 d. income statement, retained earnings statement, and balance sheet.

10. The financial statement that reports assets, liabilities, (SO 8) and stockholders' equity is the:
 a. income statement.
 b. retained earnings statement.
 c. balance sheet.
 d. statement of cash flows.

THE
NAVIGATOR

QUESTIONS

1. "Accounting is ingrained in our society and it is vital to our economic system." Do you agree? Explain.

2. Identify and describe the steps in the accounting process.

3. (a) Who are internal users of accounting data?
 (b) How does accounting provide relevant data to these users?

4. Distinguish between the two types of external users of accounting data and give examples of each.

5. "Bookkeeping and accounting are the same." Do you agree? Explain.

6. D. Wiley Inc. purchased land for $75,000 cash on December 10, 2001. At December 31, 2001, the land's value has increased to $93,000. What amount should be re-

ported for land on D. Wiley's balance sheet at December 31, 2001? Explain.

7. What is the monetary unit assumption? What impact does inflation have on the monetary unit assumption?

8. What is the economic entity assumption?

9. What are the three basic forms of business organizations for profit-oriented enterprises?

10. Mary Stone is the owner of a successful printing shop. Recently her business has been increasing, and Mary has been thinking about changing the organization of her business from a proprietorship to a corporation. Discuss some of the advantages Mary would enjoy if she were to incorporate her business.

11. What is the basic accounting equation?

12. (a) Define the terms assets, liabilities, and stockholders' equity. (b) What items affect stockholders' equity?

13. Which of the following items are liabilities of Glitz Jewelry Stores?
    (a) Cash.
    (b) Accounts payable.
    (c) Inventory.
    (d) Accounts receivable.
    (e) Supplies.
    (f) Equipment.
    (g) Salaries payable.
    (h) Service revenue.
    (i) Rent expense.

14. Can a business enter into a transaction in which only the left side of the basic accounting equation is affected? If so, give an example.

15. Are the following events recorded in the accounting records? Explain your answer in each case.
    (a) The president of a corporation dies.
    (b) Supplies are purchased on account.
    (c) An employee is fired.

16. Indicate how the following business transactions affect the basic accounting equation.
    (a) Paid cash for janitorial services.
    (b) Purchased equipment for cash.
    (c) Invested cash in the business for stock.
    (d) Paid an accounts payable in full.

17. Listed below are some items found in the financial statements of Frank Voris Inc. Indicate in which financial statement(s) the following items would appear.
    (a) Advertising expense.
    (b) Equipment.
    (c) Service revenue.
    (d) Cash.
    (e) Common stock.
    (f) Wages payable.

18. In February of 2000, John McKee invested $5,000 in Environs, Inc. Environ's accountant, Maggie Sharrer, recorded this receipt as an increase in cash and revenues. Is this treatment appropriate? Why or why not?

19. "A company's net income appears directly on the income statement and the retained earnings statement, and it is included indirectly in the company's balance sheet." Do you agree? Explain.

20. Hillary Brennan Inc. had a stockholders' equity balance of $138,000 at the beginning of the period. At the end of the accounting period, the stockholders' equity balance was $198,000.
    (a) Assuming no additional investment or distributions during the period, what is the net income for the period?
    (b) Assuming an additional investment of $13,000 but no distributions during the period, what is the net income for the period?

21. Summarized operations for the Linda Shumway Co. for the month of July are as follows:

    Revenues earned: for cash $45,000; on account $80,000.

    Expenses incurred: for cash $26,000; on account $40,000.

    Indicate for Linda Shumway Co. (a) the total revenues, (b) the total expenses, and (c) net income for the month of July.

BRIEF EXERCISES

Basic accounting equation.
(SO 6)

BE1–1 Presented below is the basic accounting equation. Determine the missing amounts:

Assets	=	Liabilities	+	Stockholders' Equity
(a) $80,000		$50,000		?
(b) ?		$45,000		$70,000
(c) $94,000		?		$62,000

Basic accounting equation.
(SO 6)

BE1–2 Given the accounting equation, answer each of the following questions:
1. The liabilities of Rosie Company are $90,000 and the stockholders' equity is $240,000. What is the amount of Rosie Company's total assets?
2. The total assets of O'Donnell Company are $170,000 and its stockholders' equity is $90,000. What is the amount of its total liabilities?
3. The total assets of Oprah Co. are $700,000 and its liabilities are equal to one half of its total assets. What is the amount of Oprah Co.'s stockholders' equity?

Basic accounting equation.
(SO 6)

BE1–3 At the beginning of the year, Montel Company had total assets of $700,000 and total liabilities of $500,000. Answer the following questions:
1. If total assets increased $150,000 during the year and total liabilities decreased $80,000, what is the amount of stockholders' equity at the end of the year?
2. During the year, total liabilities increased $100,000 and stockholders' equity decreased $70,000. What is the amount of total assets at the end of the year?
3. If total assets decreased $90,000 and stockholders' equity increased $110,000 during the year, what is the amount of total liabilities at the end of the year?

BE1–4   Presented below are three business transactions. On a sheet of paper, list the letters a, b, c with columns for assets, liabilities, and stockholders' equity. For each column, indicate whether the transactions increased (+), decreased (−) or had no effect (NE) on assets, liabilities, and stockholders' equity:

(a) Purchased supplies on account.
(b) Received cash for providing a service.
(c) Expenses paid in cash.

Determine effect of transactions on basic accounting equation.
(SO 7)

BE1–5   Follow the same format as BE1–4 above. Determine the effect on assets, liabilities, and stockholders' equity of the following three transactions:

(a) Invested cash in the business.
(b) Paid cash dividend.
(c) Received cash from a customer who had previously been billed for services provided.

Determine effect of transactions on basic accounting equation.
(SO 7)

BE1–6   Classify each of the following items as asset (A), liability (L), revenue (R), or expense (E).

Classify various items.
(SO 6, 7)

___ Advertising expense	___ Cash
___ Commission revenue	___ Rent revenue
___ Insurance expense	___ Utilities expense
___ Salaries expense	___ Accounts payable

BE1–7   Presented below are three transactions. Mark each transaction as affecting common stock (C), dividends (D), revenue (R), expense (E), or not affecting stockholders' equity (NSE):

___ Received cash for services performed
___ Paid cash to purchase equipment
___ Paid employee salaries

Determine effect of transactions on stockholders' equity.
(SO 7)

BE1–8   In alphabetical order below are balance sheet items for Sabrina Company at December 31, 2001. Prepare a balance sheet, following the format of Illustration 1-10.

Prepare a balance sheet.
(SO 8)

Accounts payable	$90,000
Accounts receivable	$81,000
Cash	$40,500
Common stock	$31,500

BE1–9   Indicate whether each of the following items is an asset (A), liability (L), or part of stockholders' equity (SE):

Identify assets, liabilities, and stockholders' equity.
(SO 6)

___ Accounts receivable	___ Office supplies
___ Salaries payable	___ Common stock
___ Equipment	___ Notes payable

BE1–10   Indicate whether the following items would appear on the income statement (IS), balance sheet (BS), or retained earnings statement (RE):

Determine where items appear on financial statements.
(SO 8)

___ Notes payable	___ Cash
___ Advertising expense	___ Fees earned
___ Common stock	

EXERCISES

E1–1   Fussey Cleaners has the following balance sheet items:

Classify accounts as assets, liabilities, and stockholders' equity.
(SO 6)

Accounts payable	Accounts receivable
Cash	Notes payable
Cleaning equipment	Salaries payable
Cleaning supplies	Common stock

Instructions
Classify each item as an asset, liability, or stockholders' equity.

E1–2   Selected transactions for Parched Lawn Care Company are listed below:

Analyze the effect of transactions.
(SO 6, 7)

1. Made cash investment to start business.
2. Paid monthly rent.

3. Purchased equipment on account.
4. Billed customers for services performed.
5. Paid dividends.
6. Received cash from customers billed in (4).
7. Incurred advertising expense on account.
8. Purchased additional equipment for cash.
9. Received cash from customers when service was rendered.

Instructions
List the numbers of the above transactions and describe the effect of each transaction on assets, liabilities, and stockholders' equity. For example, the first answer is: (1) Increase in assets and increase in stockholders' equity.

Analyze the effect of transactions on assets, liabilities, and stockholders' equity.
(SO 6, 7)

E1–3   Kap Shin Computer Timeshare Company entered into the following transactions during May 2001.

1. Purchased computer terminals for $19,000 from Digital Equipment on account.
2. Paid $4,000 cash for May rent on storage space.
3. Received $15,000 cash from customers for contracts billed in April.
4. Provided computer services to Brieske Construction Company for $3,000 cash.
5. Paid Southern States Power Co. $11,000 cash for energy usage in May.
6. Stockholders' invested an additional $32,000 in the business.
7. Paid Digital Equipment for the terminals purchased in (1) above.
8. Incurred advertising expense for May of $1,000 on account.

Instructions
Indicate with the appropriate letter whether each of the transactions above results in:

(a) an increase in assets and a decrease in assets.
(b) an increase in assets and an increase in stockholders' equity.
(c) an increase in assets and an increase in liabilities.
(d) a decrease in assets and a decrease in stockholders' equity.
(e) a decrease in assets and a decrease in liabilities.
(f) an increase in liabilities and a decrease in stockholders' equity.
(g) an increase in stockholders' equity and a decrease in liabilities.

Analyze transactions and compute net income.
(SO 7)

E1–4   A tabular analysis of the transactions made by Roberta Mendez & Co., a certified public accounting firm, for the month of August is shown below. Each increase and decrease in stockholders' equity is explained.

	Cash	+	Accounts Receivable	+	Supplies	+	Office Equipment	=	Accounts Payable	+	Stockholders' Equity
1.	+$15,000										+$15,000 Investment
2.	−2,000						+$5,000		+$3,000		
3.	−750				+$750						
4.	+4,600		+3,400								+8,000 Fees Earned
5.	−1,500								−1,500		
6.	−2,000										−2,000 Dividends
7.	−650										−650 Rent Expense
8.	+450		−450								
9.	−2,900										−2,900 Salaries Expense
10.									+500		−500 Utilities Expense

Instructions

(a) ▭▭▭▶ Describe each transaction that occurred for the month.
(b) Determine how much stockholders' equity increased for the month.
(c) Compute the amount of net income for the month.

Prepare an income statement, retained earnings statement, and a balance sheet.
(SO 8)

E1–5   The tabular analysis of transactions for Roberta Mendez & Co. is presented in E1–4.

Instructions
Prepare an income statement and a retained earnings statement for August and a balance sheet at August 31, 2001.

E1-6   Padre Company had the following assets and liabilities on the dates indicated:

Determine net income (or loss).
(SO 7)

December 31	Total Assets	Total Liabilities
1999	$380,000	$250,000
2000	$460,000	$310,000
2001	$590,000	$400,000

Padre began business on January 1, 1999, with an investment of $100,000.

Instructions

From an analysis of the change in stockholders' equity during the year, compute the net income (or loss) for:

(a) 1999, assuming Padre paid $15,000 in dividends for the year.

(b) 2000, assuming stockholders made an additional investment of $50,000 and Padre paid no dividends in 2000.

(c) 2001, assuming stockholders made an additional investment of $10,000 and Padre paid dividends of $20,000 in 2001.

E1-7   Two items are omitted from each of the following summaries of balance sheet and income statement data for two corporations for the year 2001, Neve Campbell, Inc., and Maxim Enterprises.

Analyze financial statements items.
(SO 6, 7)

	Neve Campbell, Inc.	Maxim Enterprises
Beginning of year:		
Total assets	$ 90,000	$130,000
Total liabilities	80,000	(c)
Total stockholders' equity	(a)	95,000
End of year:		
Total assets	160,000	180,000
Total liabilities	120,000	50,000
Total stockholders' equity	40,000	130,000
Changes during year in stockholders' equity:		
Additional investment	(b)	25,000
Dividends	24,000	(d)
Total revenues	215,000	100,000
Total expenses	165,000	80,000

Instructions

Determine the missing amounts.

E1-8   The following information relates to Stanley Tucci Co. for the year 2001.

Prepare income statement and retained earnings statement.
(SO 8)

Common stock, January 1, 2001	$45,000	Advertising expense	1,800
Dividends, during 2001	5,000	Rent expense	10,400
Service Revenue	50,000	Utilities expense	3,100
Salaries expense	28,000		

Instructions

After analyzing the data, prepare an income statement and a retained earnings statement for the year ending December 31, 2001. Beginning retained earnings was $5,000.

E1-9   Tahoe Inc. a public camping ground near the Lake Mead National Recreation Area, has compiled the following financial information as of December 31, 2001.

Compute net income and prepare a balance sheet.
(SO 8)

Revenues during 2001—camping fees	$147,000	Notes payable	60,000
Revenues during 2001—general store	40,000	Expenses during 2001	150,000
Accounts payable	11,000	Supplies on hand	2,500
Cash on hand	7,000	Common stock	50,000
Original cost of equipment	115,500	Retained earnings	?
Market value of equipment	140,000		

Instructions

(a) Determine Tahoe's net income for 2001.

(b) Prepare a balance sheet for Tahoe as of December 31, 2001.

E1-10   Presented below is financial information related to the 2001 operations of the Hockenberry Cruise Company, Inc.

Prepare an income statement.
(SO 8)

Boat rental expense	$ 90,000
Property tax expense (on dock facilities)	10,000
Salaries expense	142,000
Advertising expense	3,500
Ticket revenue	325,000

Instructions

Prepare the 2001 income statement for the Hockenberry Cruise Company.

Prepare a retained earnings statement.
(SO 8)

E1–11 Presented below is information related to Pocket Sprocket, Inc.

Retained earnings, January 1, 2001	$150,000
Legal fees earned—2001	380,000
Total expenses—2001	205,000
Dividends—2001	76,000

Instructions

Prepare the 2001 retained earnings statement for Pocket Sprocket, Inc.

PROBLEMS: SET A

Analyze transactions and compute net income.
(SO 6, 7)

P1–1A On April 1, Matrix Travel Agency, Inc. was established. The following transactions were completed during the month:

1. Stockholders invested $20,000 cash, receiving common stock in exchange.
2. Paid $400 cash for April office rent.
3. Purchased office equipment for $2,500 cash.
4. Incurred $300 of advertising costs in the Chicago Tribune, on account.
5. Paid $600 cash for office supplies.
6. Earned $9,000 for services rendered: Cash of $1,000 is received from customers, and the balance of $8,000 is billed to customers on account.
7. Paid $200 cash dividend.
8. Paid Chicago Tribune amount due in transaction (4).
9. Paid employees' salaries, $1,200.
10. Cash of $8,000 is received from customers who have previously been billed in transaction (6).

Instructions

(a) Prepare a tabular analysis of the transactions using the following column headings: Cash, Accounts Receivable, Supplies, Office Equipment, Accounts Payable, Common Stock and Retained Earnings.

(b) From an analysis of the column, Retained Earnings, compute the net income or net loss for April.

Analyze transactions and prepare income statement, balance sheet, and retained earnings statement.
(SO 6, 7, 8)

P1–2A Michelle Pfeiffer Corporation was formed on July 1, 2001. On July 31, the balance sheet showed Cash $4,000, Accounts Receivable $1,500, Supplies $500, Office Equipment $5,000, Accounts Payable $4,200, Common Stock $6,500, and Retained Earnings $300. During August the following transactions occurred:

1. Collected $1,400 of accounts receivable.
2. Paid $2,700 cash on accounts payable.
3. Earned fees of $6,400, of which $3,000 is collected in cash and the balance is due in September.
4. Purchased additional office equipment for $1,000, paying $400 in cash and the balance on account.
5. Paid salaries $1,500, rent for August $900, and advertising expenses $350.
6. Dividends of $550 were paid.
7. Received $1,000 from Standard Federal Bank—money borrowed on a note payable.
8. Incurred utility expenses for month on account, $250.

Instructions

(a) Prepare a tabular analysis of the August transactions beginning with July 31 balances. The column heading should be as follows: Cash + Accounts Receivable + Supplies + Office Equipment = Notes Payable + Accounts Payable + Common Stock + Retained Earnings.

(b) Prepare an income statement for August, a retained earnings statement for August, and a balance sheet at August 31

P1-3A Jessica Bell started her own consulting firm, Bell Consulting, Inc., on May 1, 2001. The following transactions occurred during the month of May:

Analyze transactions and prepare financial statements. (SO 7, 8)

May 1 Stockholders invested $10,000 cash in the business.
     2 Paid $800 for office rent for the month.
     3 Purchased $500 of supplies on account.
     5 Paid $50 to advertise in the County News.
     9 Received $1,000 cash for services provided.
    12 Paid $200 cash dividend.
    15 Performed $3,000 of services on account.
    17 Paid $2,500 for employee salaries.
    20 Paid for the supplies purchased on account on May 3.
    23 Received a cash payment of $2,000 for services provided on account on May 15.
    26 Borrowed $5,000 from the bank on a note payable.
    29 Purchased office equipment for $2,400 on account.
    30 Paid $150 for utilities.

Instructions
(a) Show the effects of the previous transactions on the accounting equation using the following format:

						Stockholders' Equity	
	Assets			**Liabilities**			
Date	Cash +	Accounts Receivable +	Supplies +	Office Equipment =	Notes Payable +	Accounts Payable +	Common Stock + Retained Earnings

Include explanations for any changes in the Retained Earnings account in your analysis.
(b) Prepare an income statement for the month of May.
(c) Prepare a balance sheet at May 31, 2001.

P1-4A Skyline Flying School, Inc. was started on May 1 with an investment of $45,000 cash. Following are the assets and liabilities of the company on May 31, 2001, and the revenues and expenses for the month of May.

Prepare income statement, retained earnings statement, and balance sheet. (SO 8)

Cash	$ 8,000	Notes Payable	$30,000
Accounts Receivable	7,000	Rent Expense	1,200
Equipment	64,000	Repair Expense	400
Service Revenue	9,600	Fuel Expense	2,200
Advertising Expense	500	Insurance Expense	400
		Accounts Payable	800

No additional investments were made by stockholders in May, but a dividend of $1,700 in cash was paid.

Instructions
(a) Prepare an income statement and retained earnings statement for the month of May and a balance sheet at May 31.
(b) Prepare an income statement and retained earnings statement for May assuming the following data are not included above: (1) $800 of fees were earned and billed but not collected at May 31, and (2) $5,300 of fuel expense was incurred but not paid.

P1-5A Financial statement information about four different companies is as follows:

Determine financial statement amounts and prepare retained earnings statements. (SO 7, 8)

	Yanni Company	Selena Company	Candlebox Company	Winans Company
January 1, 2001:				
Assets	$ 90,000	$110,000	(g)	$160,000
Liabilities	50,000	(d)	75,000	(j)
Stockholders' equity	(a)	60,000	55,000	90,000
December 31, 2001:				
Assets	(b)	150,000	200,000	(k)
Liabilities	55,000	65,000	(h)	80,000
Stockholders' equity	58,000	(e)	130,000	170,000

Stockholders' equity changes in year:

Additional investment	(c)	15,000	10,000	15,000
Dividends	25,000	(f)	14,000	20,000
Total revenues	350,000	420,000	(i)	520,000
Total expenses	320,000	385,000	350,000	(l)

Instructions

(a) Determine the missing amounts.

(b) Prepare the retained earnings statement for Selena Company. Assume that the beginning balance of retained earnings was zero.

(c) ▦▦▭▭▶ Write a memorandum explaining the sequence for preparing financial statements and the interrelationship of the retained earnings statement to the income statement and balance sheet.

PROBLEMS: SET B
••

Analyze transactions and compute net income.
(SO 6, 7)

P1–1B On May 1, Ben Affleck Inc. was started. A summary of May transactions is presented below.

1. Stockholders invested $15,000 cash in the Fox Valley Bank in the name of the business.
2. Purchased equipment for $5,000 cash.
3. Paid $400 cash for May rent.
4. Paid $500 cash for parts and supplies.
5. Incurred $250 of advertising costs in the Beacon News on account.
6. Received $4,100 in cash from customers for repair service.
7. Dividends of $500 were paid.
8. Paid part-time employee salaries $1,000.
9. Paid utility bills $140.
10. Provided repair service on account to customers, $200.
11. Collected cash of $150 for services billed in transaction (11).

Instructions

(a) Prepare a tabular analysis of the transactions, using the following column headings: Cash, Accounts Receivable, Supplies, Equipment, Accounts Payable, Common Stock and Retained Earnings. (Use the term service revenue to indicate revenue.)

(b) From an analysis of the column Retained Earnings compute the net income or net loss for May.

Analyze transactions and prepare income statement, balance sheet, and retained earnings statement.
(SO 6, 7, 8)

P1–2B On August 31, the balance sheet of Judi Dench Corporation showed Cash $9,000, Accounts Receivable $1,700, Supplies $600, Office Equipment $6,000, Accounts Payable $3,600, Common Stock $13,000, and Retained Earnings $700. During September the following transactions occurred:

1. Paid $3,100 cash on accounts payable.
2. Collected $1,300 of accounts receivable.
3. Purchased additional office equipment for $2,100, paying $800 in cash and the balance on account.
4. Earned fees of $5,900, of which $2,500 is paid in cash and the balance is due in October.
5. Dividends of $600 were paid.
6. Paid salaries $700, rent for September $900, and advertising expense $100.
7. Incurred utility expenses for month on account, $170.
8. Received $8,000 from Hilldale Bank—money borrowed on a note payable.

Instructions

(a) Prepare a tabular analysis of the September transactions beginning with August 31 balances. The column headings should be as follows: Cash + Accounts Receivable + Supplies + Office Equipment = Notes Payable + Accounts Payable + Common Stock + Retained Earnings.

(b) Prepare an income statement for September, a retained earnings statement for September, and a balance sheet at September 30.

P1–3B Peter Alex started his own delivery service, Alex Deliveries, Inc. on June 1, 2001. The following transactions occurred during the month of June:

Analyze transactions and prepare financial statements. (SO 7, 8)

June 1 Stockholders invested $15,000 cash in the business.
 2 Purchased a used van for deliveries for $10,000. Alex paid $2,000 cash and signed a note payable for the remaining balance.
 3 Paid $500 for office rent for the month.
 5 Performed $1,000 of services on account.
 9 Paid $200 in cash dividends.
 12 Purchased supplies for $150 on account.
 15 Received a cash payment of $750 for services provided on June 5.
 17 Purchased gasoline for $100 on account.
 20 Received a cash payment of $1,500 for services provided.
 23 Made a cash payment of $500 on the note payable.
 26 Paid $250 for utilities.
 29 Paid for the gasoline purchased on account on June 17.
 30 Paid $500 for employee salaries.

Instructions
(a) Show the effects of the previous transactions on the accounting equation using the following format:

| | | | | | | Stockholders' | |
	Assets			Liabilities		Equity	
		Accounts		Delivery	Notes	Accounts	Common	Retained
Date	Cash +	Receivable +	Supplies +	Van	= Payable +	Payable +	Stock	+ Earnings

Include explanations for any changes in the Retained Earnings account in your analysis.
(b) Prepare an income statement for the month of June.
(c) Prepare a balance sheet at June 30, 2001.

P1–4B On June 1, Cindy Crawford Cosmetics was started with an investment in the company of $26,200 in cash. Following are the assets and liabilities of the company at June 30 and the revenues and expenses for the month of June.

Prepare income statement, retained earnings statement, and balance sheet. (SO 8)

Cash	$12,000	Notes Payable	$13,000
Accounts Receivable	3,000	Accounts Payable	1,200
Service Revenue	6,500	Supplies Expense	1,200
Cosmetic Supplies on Hand	2,400	Gas and Oil Expense	800
Advertising Expense	500	Utilities Expense	300
Equipment	25,000		

No additional investments were made in June, but dividends of $1,700 were paid during the month.

Instructions
Prepare an income statement and retained earnings statement for the month of June and a balance sheet at June 30, 2001.

P1–5B Financial statement information about four different companies is as follows:

Determine financial statement amounts and prepare retained earnings statements. (SO 7, 8)

	Zarle Company	Wasicsko Company	McKane Company	Russe Company
January 1, 2001:				
Assets	$ 80,000	$100,000	(g)	$150,000
Liabilities	50,000	(d)	75,000	(j)
Stockholders' equity	(a)	60,000	45,000	90,000
December 31, 2001:				
Assets	(b)	130,000	180,000	(k)
Liabilities	55,000	62,000	(h)	80,000
Stockholders' equity	45,000	(e)	110,000	145,000

Stockholders' equity changes in year:				
Additional investment	(c)	8,000	10,000	15,000
Dividends	15,000	(f)	12,000	10,000
Total revenues	350,000	400,000	(i)	500,000
Total expenses	330,000	385,000	360,000	(l)

Instructions

(a) Determine the missing amounts.

(b) Prepare the retained earnings statement for Zarle Company. Assume that the beginning balance in retained earnings is zero.

(c) ▭▭▭▶ Write a memorandum explaining the sequence for preparing financial statements and the interrelationship of the retained earnings statement to the income statement and balance sheet.

BROADENING YOUR PERSPECTIVE

FINANCIAL REPORTING AND ANALYSIS

FINANCIAL REPORTING PROBLEM: Kellogg Company

BYP1-1   The actual financial statements of Kellogg Company, as presented in the company's 1998 Annual Report, are contained in Appendix A (at the back of the textbook).

Instructions

Refer to Kellogg's financial statements and answer the following questions:

(a) What were Kellogg's total assets at December 31, 1998? At December 31, 1997?

(b) How much cash (and cash equivalents) did Kellogg have on December 31, 1998?

(c) What amount of accounts payable did Kellogg report on December 31, 1998? On December 31, 1997?

(d) What were Kellogg's net sales in 1996? In 1997? In 1998?

(e) What is the amount of the change in Kellogg's net income from 1997 to 1998?

COMPARATIVE ANALYSIS PROBLEM: Kellogg Company vs. General Mills

BYP1-2   Kellogg's financial statements are presented in Appendix A; General Mills's financial statements are presented in Appendix B.

Instructions

(a) Based on the information contained in these financial statements, determine the following for each company:

   (1) Total assets at December 31, 1998, for Kellogg and at May 25, 1998, for General Mills.

   (2) Accounts (notes) receivable, less allowances at December 31, 1998, for Kellogg and at May 25, 1998, for General Mills.

   (3) Net sales for 1998.

   (4) Net income for 1998.

(b) What conclusions concerning the two companies can be drawn from these data?

RESEARCH ASSIGNMENT

BYP1-3   To do financial research, you need to know where to look. This assignment will familiarize you with two important resources. *The Wall Street Journal* (WSJ), published weekdays by Dow Jones & Company, Inc., is a premier source of business information.

Instructions

Examine a recent copy of the WSJ and answer the following questions.

(a) How many separate sections are included in the WSJ? What are the contents of each?

(b) An index of the companies referenced in each edition is included on page 2 of section B. Select a company from the index and read the associated article. What is the article about? Identify any accounting-related issues discussed in the article.

INTERPRETING FINANCIAL STATEMENTS: Lincoln Village Properties, Inc.

BYP1-4 Lincoln Village Properties, Inc. is a property management firm in Springfield, Missouri, that provides residential rental property management such as grounds maintenance, minor repair service, and trash collection for an annual fee. A portion of Lincoln Village's previous year's balance sheet follows:

LINCOLN VILLAGE PROPERTIES, INC. Balance Sheet (partial)	
Assets	
Cash	$ 10,000
Accounts receivable	2,000
Supplies inventory	8,000
Machinery and equipment, net	80,000
Other noncurrent assets	5,000
Total assets	$105,000

During the current year, the following events occurred:

1. $25,000 of machinery, net, was sold for cash.
2. $100,000 was received from cash sales.
3. $115,000 was paid for cash expenses.
4. Customers contracted for $150,000 in services on credit.
5. Lincoln Village Properties collected $148,000 from accounts receivable.

Instructions
Prepare the Assets portion of the current year's balance sheet for Lincoln Village Properties.

REAL-WORLD FOCUS: Air Transportation Holding Company Inc.

BYP1-5 Founded in 1980, **Air Transportation Holding Company** operates contract cargo shipping, specializing in small, overnight deliveries throughout the eastern United States. The company flies approximately 80 routes, as specified in its contracts with Federal Express. It has hangars and maintenance facilities in North Carolina, Michigan, and South Carolina.

The specific assets, liabilities, and subdivisions of stockholders' equity of any business depend on the type of business being operated. Management of Air Transportation Holding Company explained the year's results of operations as follows:

AIR TRANSPORTATION HOLDING COMPANY
Management Discussion

Operating expenses increased $5,498,000 (29.9%) to $23,904,000 in a recent year compared to the prior year. The increase in operating expenses consisted of the following changes: cost of flight operations increased $2,313,000 (25.7%) as a result of increases in pilot and flight personnel and costs associated with travel and landing fees which were partially offset by decreased aircraft lease and fuel costs; maintenance expense increased $2,850,000 (42.9%) primarily as a result of increases in aircraft parts purchases and mechanic and maintenance personnel costs (due to start-up of satellite maintenance facility and the operation of additional aircraft); the general and administrative expense increase of $470,000 (17.3%) resulted from increases in operational and clerical staffing related to expansion of the aircraft fleet operated.

Instructions
   (a) Recall the definition of an asset. Can you identify three specific types of assets owned by Air Transportation Holding Company?
   (b) The discussion above is largely about the operating expenses of the company. Identify five expenses of operations that Air Transportation incurs.
   (c) When this company renders service by providing air transportation, what account affecting stockholders' equity is increased?

CRITICAL THINKING

GROUP DECISION CASE

BYP1–6 Patsy and Perry Ross, local golf stars, opened the Long-Shot Driving Range on March 1, 2001, by investing $10,000 of their cash savings in the business. A caddy shack was constructed for cash at a cost of $4,000 and $800 was spent on golf balls and golf clubs. The Rosses leased five acres of land at a cost of $1,000 per month and paid the first month's rent. During the first month, advertising costs totaled $750 of which $150 was unpaid at March 31, and $400 was paid to members of the high school golf team for retrieving golf balls. All revenues from customers were deposited in the company's bank account. On March 15, dividends of $800 in cash were paid to stockholders. A $100 utility bill was received on March 31 but it was not paid. On March 31, the balance in the company's bank account was $7,550.

   Patsy and Perry thought they had a pretty good first month of operations. However, their estimates of profitability ranged from a loss of $2,450 to net income of $2,100.

Instructions
With the class divided into groups, answer the following:
   (a) How could the Rosses have concluded that the business operated at a loss of $2,450? Was this a valid basis on which to determine net income?
   (b) How could the Rosses have concluded that the business operated at a net income of $2,100? (*Hint:* Prepare a balance sheet at March 31.) Was this a valid basis on which to determine net income?
   (c) Without preparing an income statement, determine the actual net income for March.
   (d) What was the revenue earned in March?

COMMUNICATION ACTIVITY

BYP1–7 Lynn Bowen is the bookkeeper for Texas Company. Lynn has been trying to get the balance sheet of Texas Company to balance. The company's balance sheet is as follows:

TEXAS COMPANY
Balance Sheet
For the Month Ended December 31, 2001

Assets		Liabilities	
Equipment	$20,500	Common stock	$15,000
Cash	9,000	Retained Earnings	6,000
Supplies	2,000	Accounts receivable	(3,000)
Accounts payable	(5,000)	Dividends	(2,000)
	$26,500	Notes payable	10,500
			$26,500

Instructions
Explain to Lynn Bowen in a memo why the original balance sheet is incorrect, and what should be done to correct it.

ETHICS CASE

BYP1–8 After numerous campus interviews, Steve Pelli, a senior at Great Eastern College, received two office interview invitations from the Baltimore offices of two large firms. Both firms offered to cover his out-of-pocket expenses (travel, hotel, and meal). He scheduled the interviews for both firms on the same day, one in the morning and one in the afternoon. At the conclusion of each interview, he submitted to both firms his total out-of-pocket expenses for the trip to Baltimore, $244: mileage $70 (280 miles at $.25), hotel $120, meals $36, parking and tolls $18, for a total of $244. He believes this approach is appropriate. If he had made two trips, his cost would have been two times $244. He is also certain that neither firm knew he had visited the other on that same trip. Within ten days Steve received two checks in the mail, each in the amount of $244.

Instructions

    (a) Who are the stakeholders (affected parties) in this situation?
    (b) What are the ethical issues in this case?
    (c) What would you do in this situation?

SURFING THE NET
· ·

BYP1–9 This exercise will familiarize you with skill requirements, job descriptions, and salaries for accounting careers.

Address: http://www.cob.ohio-state.edu/dept/fin/jobs/account.htm (or go to www.wiley.com/college/weygandt

Instructions

Go to the site shown above. Answer the following questions:

    (a) What are the three broad areas of accounting?
    (b) List four skills required in these areas.
    (c) How do these areas differ in required skills?
    (d) Explain one of the key job functions in accounting.
    (e) Based on the *Smart Money* survey, what is the salary range for a junior staff accountant with Deloitte & Touche?

Answers to Self-Study Questions
1. b   2. d   3. c   4. c   5. a   6. d   7. b   8. a   9. b   10. c

---

Answer to Kellogg Review It Question 4, p. 14
Kellogg's accounting equation is:

Assets	=	Liabilities	+	Stockholders' Equity
$5,051,500,000	=	$4,161,700,000	+	$889,800,000

Remember to go back to the Navigator box on the chapter-opening page and check off your completed work.

Concepts for Review
highlight accounting
concepts that you need to
understand from earlier
chapters before starting
the new chapter.

Before studying this chapter, you should know or, if necessary, review:

a. What are assets, liabilities, common stock, retained earnings, dividends, revenues, and expenses. (Ch. 1, pp. 12–14)

b. Why assets equal liabilities plus stockholders' equity. (Ch. 1, p. 12)

c. What transactions are and how they affect the basic accounting equation. (Ch. 1, pp. 15–21)

THE NAVIGATOR

FEATURE STORY

No Such Thing As a Perfect World

When she got a job doing the accounting for Forster's Restaurants, Tanis Anderson had almost finished her business administration degree at Simon Fraser University. But even after Tanis completed her degree requirements, her education still continued—this time, in the real world.

Tanis's responsibilities include paying the bills, tracking food and labor costs, and managing the payroll for the Mug and Musket, a popular destination restaurant in Surrey, British Columbia. "My title is Director of Finance," she laughs, "but really that means I take care of whatever needs doing!"

The use of judgment is a big part of the job. As Tanis says, "I learned all the fundamentals in my business classes, but school prepares you for a perfect world, and there is no such thing."

She feels fortunate that her boss understands her job is a learning experience as well as a responsibility. "Sometimes he's let me do something he knew perfectly well was a mistake so I can learn something through experience," she admits.

To help others gain the benefits of her real-world learning, Tanis is always happy to help students in the area who want to use Forster's as the subject of a project or report. "It's the least I can do," she says.

THE NAVIGATOR

CHAPTER 2

THE NAVIGATOR ✔

- Understand *Concepts for Review* ☐
- Read *Feature Story* ☐
- Scan *Study Objectives* ☐
- Read *Preview* ☐
- Read text and answer *Before You Go On*
  p. 52 ☐ p. 55 ☐ p. 63 ☐ p. 70 ☐
- Work *Demonstration Problem* ☐
- Review *Summary of Study Objectives* ☐
- Answer *Self-Study Questions* ☐
- Complete assignments ☐

THE RECORDING PROCESS

STUDY OBJECTIVES

After studying this chapter, you should be able to:

1. Explain what an account is and how it helps in the recording process.
2. Define debits and credits and explain how they are used to record business transactions.
3. Identify the basic steps in the recording process.
4. Explain what a journal is and how it helps in the recording process.
5. Explain what a ledger is and how it helps in the recording process.
6. Explain what posting is and how it helps in the recording process.
7. Prepare a trial balance and explain its purposes.
8. Identify the key points in comparing manual and computerized accounting systems.

THE NAVIGATOR

*I*n Chapter 1, we analyzed business transactions in terms of the accounting equation and presented the cumulative effects of these transactions in tabular form. Imagine a restaurant and gift shop such as The Mug and Musket using the same tabular format as Softbyte Inc. to keep track of every one of its transactions. In a single day, this restaurant and gift shop engages in hundreds of business transactions. To record each transaction this way would be impractical, expensive, and unnecessary.

As a result, a set of procedures and records are used to make it possible to keep track of and accumulate transaction data more easily. In this chapter we will introduce and illustrate the basic procedures and records that are used. The content and organization of the chapter are as follows:

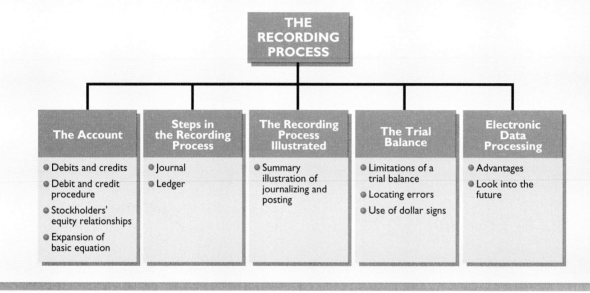

THE NAVIGATO

1
STUDY
OBJECTIVE

Explain what an account is and how it helps in the recording process.

ILLUSTRATION 2-1

Basic form of account

THE ACCOUNT

An account is an individual accounting record of increases and decreases in a specific asset, liability, or stockholders' equity item. For example, Softbyte Inc. (discussed in Chapter 1) would have separate accounts for Cash, Accounts Receivable, Accounts Payable, Service Revenue, Salaries Expense, and so on. In its simplest form, an account consists of three parts: (1) the title of the account, (2) a left or debit side, and (3) a right or credit side. Because the alignment of these parts of an account resembles the letter T, it is referred to as a T account. The basic form of an account is shown in Illustration 2-1.

Title of Account	
Left or debit side	Right or credit side
Debit balance	Credit balance

T Account

The T account is a standard shorthand in accounting that helps make clear the effects of transactions on individual accounts. This form of account will be used often throughout this book to explain basic accounting relationships.

TECHNOLOGY IN ACTION

Computerized and manual accounting systems basically parallel one another. Most of the procedures are handled by electronic circuitry in computerized systems. They seem to occur invisibly. Therefore, to fully comprehend how computerized systems operate, it is necessary to illustrate and understand manual approaches for processing accounting data.

Debits and Credits

The terms debit and credit mean left and right, respectively. They are commonly abbreviated as Dr. for debit and Cr. for credit.[1] These terms do not mean increase or decrease. The terms debit and credit are used repeatedly in the recording process. For example, the act of entering an amount on the left side of an account is called **debiting** the account, and making an entry on the right side is **crediting** the account. When the totals of the two sides are compared, an account will have a **debit balance** if the total of the debit amounts exceeds the credits. Conversely, an account will have a **credit balance** if the credit amounts exceed the debits.

The procedure of having debits on the left and credits on the right is an accounting custom, or rule. We could function just as well if debits and credits were reversed. However, the custom of having debits on the left side of an account and credits on the right side (like the custom of driving on the right-hand side of the road) has been adopted in the United States. **This rule applies to all accounts.**

The procedure of recording debits and credits in an account is shown in Illustration 2-2 for the cash transactions of Softbyte Inc. The data are taken from the cash column of the tabular summary in Illustration 1-9.

2

STUDY

OBJECTIVE

·····································

Define debits and credits and explain how they are used to record business transactions.

ILLUSTRATION 2-2

Tabular summary compared to account form

Tabular Summary	Account Form			
Cash		**Cash**		
$15,000	**(Debits)**	15,000	**(Credits)**	7,000
−7,000		1,200		1,700
1,200		1,500		250
1,500		600		1,300
−1,700	Balance	8,050		
−250	**(Debit)**			
600				
−1,300				
$ 8,050				

HELPFUL HINT
The word credit has a different meaning in accounting than it has in everyday life. For accounting purposes, think of the terms debit and credit solely as directional signals. Debit—use the left side of the account; credit—use the right side.

Every positive item in the tabular summary represents a receipt of cash; every negative amount constitutes a payment of cash. Notice that in the account form the increases in cash are recorded as debits, and the decreases in cash are recorded as credits. Having increases on one side and decreases on the other helps in determining the totals of each side of the account as well as the balance in the account. The account balance, a debit of $8,050, indicates that Softbyte Inc. has had $8,050 more increases than decreases in cash. That is, it has $8,050 in its Cash account.

---

[1] These abbreviations come from the Latin words *debere* (Dr.) and *credere* (Cr.).

Debit and Credit Procedure

In Chapter 1 you learned the effect of a transaction on the basic accounting equation. Remember that each transaction must affect two or more accounts to keep the basic accounting equation in balance. In other words, for each transaction **debits must equal credits** in the accounts. The equality of debits and credits provides the basis for the double-entry system of recording transactions (sometimes referred to as double-entry bookkeeping).

Under the universally used double-entry system, the dual (two-sided) effect of each transaction is recorded in appropriate accounts. This system provides a logical method for recording transactions. It also offers a means of proving the accuracy of the recorded amounts. If every transaction is recorded with equal debits and credits, then the sum of all the debits to the accounts must equal the sum of all the credits.

The double-entry system for determining the equality of the accounting equation is much more efficient than the plus/minus procedure used in Chapter 1. There, it was necessary after each transaction to compare total assets with total liabilities and stockholders' equity to determine the equality of the two sides of the accounting equation.

Assets and Liabilities

In the Softbyte Inc. illustration above, increases in cash—an asset—were entered on the left side, and decreases in cash were entered on the right side. We know that both sides of the basic equation (assets = liabilities + stockholders' equity) must be equal; it then follows that increases and decreases in liabilities will have to be recorded opposite from increases and decreases in assets. Thus, increases in liabilities must be entered on the right or credit side, and decreases in liabilities must be entered on the left or debit side. The effects that debits and credits have on assets and liabilities are summarized as follows:

ILLUSTRATION 2-3

Debit and credit effects— assets and liabilities

Debits	Credits
Increase assets	Decrease assets
Decrease liabilities	Increase liabilities

Debits to a specific asset account should exceed the credits to that account, and credits to a liability account should exceed debits to that account. Thus, asset accounts normally show debit balances, and liability accounts normally show credit balances. The normal balances may be diagrammed as follows:

ILLUSTRATION 2-4

Normal balances—assets and liabilities

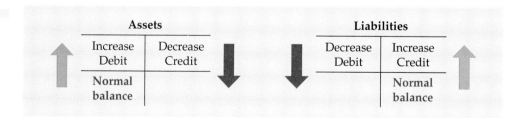

An awareness of the normal balance in an account may help you when you are trying to trace errors. For example, a credit balance in an asset account such as Land or a debit balance in a liability account such as Wages Payable would indicate errors in recording. Occasionally, however, an abnormal balance may be correct. The Cash account, for example, will have a credit balance when a company has overdrawn its bank balance (i.e., written a "bad" check).

Stockholders' Equity

As indicated in Chapter 1, there are five subdivisions of stockholders' equity: Common stock, retained earnings, dividends, revenues, and expenses. In a double-entry system, accounts are kept for each of these subdivisions as explained below.

Common Stock. Common stock is issued in exchange for the owners' investment paid in to the corporation. The Common Stock account is increased by credits and decreased by debits. When cash is invested in the business in exchange for shares of the corporation's stock, Cash is debited and Common Stock is credited.

The rules of debit and credit for the Common Stock account are stated as follows:

Debits	Credits
Decrease common stock	Increase common stock

ILLUSTRATION 2-5

Debit and credit effect—common stock

The normal balance in this account may be diagrammed as follows:

ILLUSTRATION 2-6

Normal balance—common stock

HELPFUL HINT
The rules for debit and credit and the normal balance of common stock are the same as for liabilities.

Retained Earnings. Retained earnings is net income that is retained in the business. It represents the portion of stockholders' equity which has been accumulated through the profitable operation of the business. Retained earnings is increased by credits (net income) and decreased by debits (dividends or net losses) as shown below.

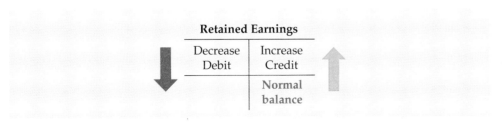

ILLUSTRATION 2-7

Debit and credit effect and normal balance—retained earnings

Dividends. A dividend is a distribution by a corporation to its stockholders on a pro rata (equal) basis. The most common form of a distribution is a cash dividend. Dividends can be declared (authorized) only by the board of directors and are a reduction of the stockholders' claims on retained earnings. The Dividends account is increased by debits and decreased by credits with a normal debit balance as shown in Illustration 2-8.

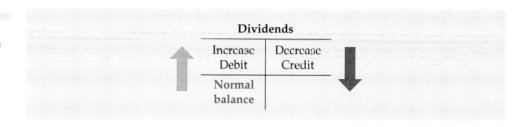

Revenues and Expenses

When revenues are earned, stockholders' equity is increased. Revenues are a subdivision of stockholders' equity that provides information as to why stockholders' equity increased. Revenue accounts are increased by credits and decreased by debits. Accordingly, **the effect of debits and credits on revenue accounts is identical to their effect on stockholders' equity**.

On the other hand, expenses decrease stockholders' equity. As a result, expenses are recorded by debits. Since expenses are the negative factor in the computation of net income, and revenues are the positive factor, it is logical that the increase and decrease sides of expense accounts should be the reverse of revenue accounts. Thus, expense accounts are increased by debits and decreased by credits. The effect of debits and credits on revenues and expenses may be stated as follows:

Debits	Credits
Decrease revenues	Increase revenues
Increase expenses	Decrease expenses

Credits to revenue accounts should exceed the debits, and debits to expense accounts should exceed credits. Thus, revenue accounts normally show credit balances and expense accounts normally show debit balances. The normal balances may be diagrammed as follows:

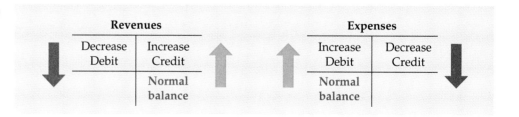

ACCOUNTING IN ACTION
Business Insight

The Chicago Cubs baseball team has the following major revenue and expense accounts:

Revenues	Expenses
Admissions (ticket sales)	Players' salaries
Concessions	Administrative salaries
Television and radio	Travel
Advertising	Ballpark maintenance

Stockholders' Equity Relationships

As indicated in Chapter 1, common stock and retained earnings are reported in the stockholders' equity section of the balance sheet. Dividends are reported on the retained earnings statement. Revenues and expenses are reported on the income statement. Dividends, revenues, and expenses are eventually transferred to retained earnings at the end of the period. As a result, changes in any one of these three items affects stockholders' equity. The relationships related to stockholders' equity are shown in Illustration 2-11.

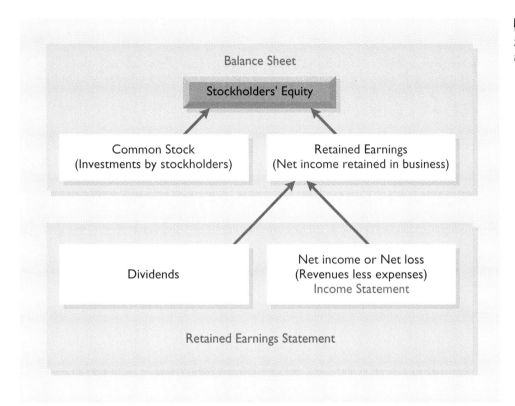

ILLUSTRATION 2-11

Stockholders' equity relationships

Expansion of Basic Equation

You have already learned the basic accounting equation. Illustration 2-12 expands this equation to show the accounts that comprise stockholders' equity. In addition, the debit/credit rules and effects on each type of account are illustrated. Study this diagram carefully. It will help you understand the fundamentals of the double-entry system. Like the basic equation, the expanded basic equation must be in balance (total debits equal total credits).

ILLUSTRATION 2-12

Expanded basic equation and debit/credit rules and effects

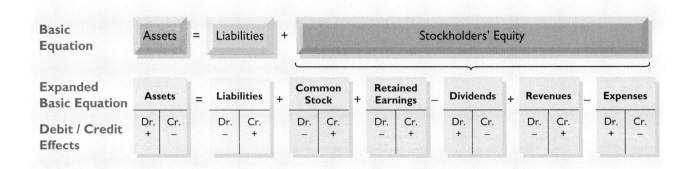

BEFORE YOU GO ON . . .

Review It

1. What do the terms debit and credit mean?
2. What are the debit and credit effects on assets, liabilities, and stockholders' equity?
3. What are the debit and credit effects on revenues, expenses, and dividends?
4. What are the normal balances for Kellogg Company's cash, accounts payable, and interest expense accounts? The answers to this question are provided on page 88.

Do It

Kate Browne, president of Hair It Is, Inc., has just rented space in a shopping mall for the purpose of opening and operating a beauty salon. Long before opening day and before purchasing equipment, hiring assistants, and remodeling the space, Kate is strongly advised to set up a double-entry set of accounting records in which to record all of her business transactions.

Identify the balance sheet accounts that Hair It Is, Inc., will likely need to record the transactions necessary to establish and open for business. Also, indicate whether the normal balance of each account is a debit or a credit.

Reasoning: To start the business, Hair It Is, Inc., will need to have asset accounts for each different type of asset invested in the business. In addition, the corporation will need liability accounts for debts incurred by the business. Hair It Is, Inc., will need only one stockholders' equity account for common stock when it begins the business. The other stockholders' equity accounts will be needed only after business has commenced.

Solution: Hair It Is, Inc., would likely need the following accounts in which to record the transactions necessary to establish and ready the beauty salon for opening day: Cash (debit balance); Equipment (debit balance); Supplies (debit balance); Accounts Payable (credit balance); Notes Payable (credit balance), if the business borrows money; and Common Stock (credit balance).

THE
NAVIGATOR

Related exercise material: BE2–1, BE2–2, E2–1, and E2–3.

3
STUDY

OBJECTIVE

Identify the basic steps
in the recording process.

STEPS IN THE RECORDING PROCESS

Although it is possible to enter transaction information directly into the accounts, few businesses do so. In practically every business, the basic steps in the recording process are:

1. Analyze each transaction in terms of its effect on the accounts.
2. Enter the transaction information in a journal (book of original entry).
3. Transfer the journal information to the appropriate accounts in the ledger (book of accounts).

The actual sequence of events begins with the transaction. Evidence of the transaction comes in the form of a **business document**, such as a sales slip, a check, a bill, or a cash register tape. This evidence is analyzed to determine the effect of the transaction on specific accounts. The transaction is then entered in the journal. Finally, the journal entry is transferred to the designated accounts in the ledger. The sequence of events in the recording process can be diagrammed as shown in Illustration 2-13.

The basic steps in the recording process occur repeatedly in every business enterprise. The analysis of transactions has already been illustrated, and further examples of this step will be given in this and later chapters. The other steps in the recording process are explained in the next sections.

ILLUSTRATION 2-13

The recording process

The Recording Process

Analyze each transaction   Enter transaction in a journal   Transfer journal information to ledger accounts

The Journal

Transactions are initially recorded in chronological order in a journal before being transferred to the accounts. Thus, the journal is referred to as the book of original entry. For each transaction the journal shows the debit and credit effects on specific accounts. Companies may use various kinds of journals, but every company has the most basic form of journal, a general journal. Typically, a general journal has spaces for dates, account titles and explanations, references, and two money columns. Whenever the term journal is used in this textbook without a modifying adjective, it will mean the general journal.

The journal makes several significant contributions to the recording process:

1. It discloses in one place the complete effect of a transaction.
2. It provides a chronological record of transactions.
3. It helps to prevent or locate errors because the debit and credit amounts for each entry can be readily compared.

Journalizing

Entering transaction data in the journal is known as journalizing. Separate journal entries are made for each transaction. A complete entry consists of: (1) the date of the transaction, (2) the accounts and amounts to be debited and credited, and (3) a brief explanation of the transaction.

To illustrate the technique of journalizing, the first two transactions of Softbyte Inc. are journalized in Illustration 2-14 using the first page (J1) of the general journal. These transactions were: September 1, stockholders invested $15,000 cash in the corporation in exchange for shares of stock, and computer equipment was purchased for $7,000 cash.

4
STUDY
OBJECTIVE

Explain what a journal is and how it helps in the recording process.

GENERAL JOURNAL				J1
Date	Account Titles and Explanation	Ref.	Debit	Credit
2001 Sept. 1	Cash		15,000	
	Common Stock			15,000
	(Issued shares of stock for cash)			
1	Computer Equipment		7,000	
	Cash			7,000
	(Purchased equipment for cash)			

ILLUSTRATION 2-14

Technique of journalizing

The standard form and content of journal entries are as follows:

1. The date of the transaction is entered in the Date column. The date recorded should include the year, month, and day of the transaction.
2. The debit account title (that is, the account to be debited) is entered first at the extreme left margin of the column headed "Account Titles and Explanation," and the amount of the debit is recorded in the Debit column.
3. The credit account title (that is, the account to be credited) is indented and entered on the next line in the column headed "Account Titles and Explanation," and the amount of the credit is recorded in the Credit column.
4. A brief explanation of the transaction is given.
5. A space is left between journal entries. The blank space separates individual journal entries and makes the entire journal easier to read.
6. The column entitled Ref. (which stands for reference) is left blank at the time the journal entry is made. The Reference column is used later when the journal entries are transferred to the ledger accounts. At that time, the ledger account number is placed in the Reference column to indicate where the amount in the journal entry was transferred.

It is important to use correct and specific account titles in journalizing. Since most accounts appear later in the financial statements, erroneous account titles lead to incorrect financial statements. Some flexibility exists initially in selecting account titles. The main criterion is that each title must appropriately describe the content of the account. For example, the account title used for the cost of delivery trucks may be Delivery Equipment, Delivery Trucks, or Trucks. Once a company chooses the specific title to use, all subsequent transactions involving the account should be recorded under that account title.[2]

If an entry involves only two accounts, one debit and one credit, it is considered a *simple entry*. For some transactions, however, it may be necessary to use more than two accounts in journalizing. Imagine, for example, the numerous accounts needed by Daimler Benz to record the acquisition of all the assets and liabilities of Chrysler in what was one of 1998's largest mergers. When three or more accounts are required in one journal entry, the entry is referred to as a *compound entry*. To illustrate, assume that on July 1, Butler Company purchases a delivery truck costing $14,000 by paying $8,000 cash and the balance on account (to be paid at a later date). The entry is as follows:

ILLUSTRATION 2-15

Compound journal entry

GENERAL JOURNAL				J1
Date	Account Titles and Explanation	Ref.	Debit	Credit
2001 July 1	Delivery Equipment		14,000	
	Cash			8,000
	Accounts Payable			6,000
	(Purchased truck for cash with balance on account)			

---

[2]In homework problems, when specific account titles are given, they should be used. When account titles are not given, you may select account titles that identify the nature and content of each account.

In a compound entry, it is important to determine that the total debit and credit amounts are equal. Also, the standard format requires that all debits be listed before the credits are listed.

BEFORE YOU GO ON . . .

Review It

1. What is the correct sequence of the steps in the recording process?
2. What contribution does the journal make to the recording process?
3. What is the standard form and content of a journal entry made in the general journal?

Do It

In establishing her beauty salon, Hair It Is, Inc., Kate Browne as president and sole stockholder engaged in the following activities:

1. Opened a bank account in the name of Hair It Is, Inc., and deposited $20,000 of her own money in this account in exchange for shares of common stock.
2. Purchased on account (to be paid in 30 days) equipment, for a total cost of $4,800.
3. Interviewed three persons for the position of beautician.

In what form (type of record) should Hair It Is, Inc., record these three activities? Prepare the entries to record the transactions.

Reasoning: Hair It Is, Inc., should record the transactions in a journal, which is a chronological record of the transactions. The record should be a complete and accurate representation of the transactions' effects on the business's assets, liabilities, and stockholders' equity.

Solution: Each transaction that is recorded is entered in the general journal. The three activities would be recorded as follows:

1. Cash	20,000	
Common Stock		20,000
(Issued shares of stock for cash)		
2. Equipment	4,800	
Accounts Payable		4,800
(Purchased equipment on account)		

3. No entry because no transaction has occurred.

Related exercise material: BE2–3, BE2–5, BE2–6, E2–2, E2–4, E2–6, E2–7, and E2–8.

The Ledger

The entire group of accounts maintained by a company is referred to collectively as the ledger. The ledger keeps in one place all the information about changes in specific account balances.

5
STUDY
OBJECTIVE

Explain what a ledger is and how it helps in the recording process.

Companies may use various kinds of ledgers, but every company has a general ledger. A general ledger contains all the assets, liabilities, and stockholders' equity accounts, as shown in Illustration 2-16. A business can use a looseleaf binder or card file for the ledger with each account kept on a separate sheet or card. Whenever the term ledger is used in this textbook without a modifying adjective, it will mean the general ledger.

The ledger should be arranged in statement order beginning with the balance sheet accounts. First in order are the asset accounts, followed by liability accounts, stockholders' equity accounts, revenues, and expenses. Each account is numbered for easier identification.

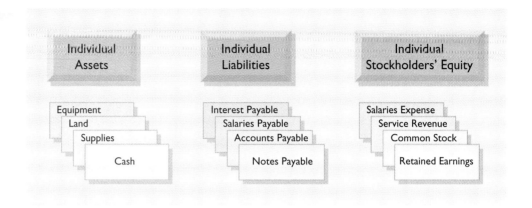

The information in the ledger provides management with the balances in various accounts. For example, the Cash account enables management to determine the amount of cash that is available to meet current obligations. Amounts due from customers and the amounts owed to creditors can be determined by examining the Accounts Receivable and Accounts Payable accounts, respectively.

ACCOUNTING IN ACTION
Business Insight

In his autobiography Sam Walton described the double-entry accounting system he began the Wal-Mart empire with: "We kept a little pigeonhole on the wall for the cash receipts and paperwork of each [Wal-Mart] store. I had a blue binder ledger book for each store. When we added a store, we added a pigeonhole. We did this at least up to twenty stores. Then once a month, the bookkeeper and I would enter the merchandise, enter the sales, enter the cash, and balance it."

Source: Sam Walton, *Made in America* (New York: Doubleday, 1992), p. 53.

Standard Form of Account
The simple T-account form of an account used in an accounting textbook is often very useful for illustration and analysis purposes. However, in practice, the account forms used in ledgers are much more structured. A form widely used in a manual system is shown in Illustration 2-17, using assumed data from a cash account.

	CASH				No. 10
Date	Explanation	Ref.	Debit	Credit	Balance
2001					
June 1			25,000		25,000
2				8,000	17,000
3			4,200		21,200
9			7,500		28,700
17				11,700	17,000
20				250	16,750
30				7,300	9,450

This form has three money columns—debit, credit, and balance. The balance in the account is determined after each transaction. Thus, this form is often called the three-column form of account. Note that the explanation space and reference columns are used to provide special information about the transaction.

Posting

The procedure of transferring journal entries to the ledger accounts is called posting. **This phase of the recording process accumulates the effects of journalized transactions in the individual accounts.**

Posting involves the following steps:

1. In the ledger, enter in the appropriate columns of the account(s) debited the date, journal page, and debit amount shown in the journal.
2. In the reference column of the journal, write the account number to which the debit amount was posted.
3. In the ledger, enter in the appropriate columns of the account(s) credited the date, journal page, and credit amount shown in the journal.
4. In the reference column of the journal, write the account number to which the credit amount was posted.

These four steps are diagrammed in Illustration 2-18 using the first journal entry of Softbyte Inc. The boxed numbers indicate the sequence of the steps.

HELPFUL HINT

When there is only one balance column, the amount shown is assumed to be the normal balance unless the balance is specifically identified as abnormal by putting it in parentheses or in red. Alternatively, there are forms that contain two balance columns.

6

STUDY

OBJECTIVE

···

Explain what posting is and how it helps in the recording process.

ILLUSTRATION 2-18

Posting a journal entry

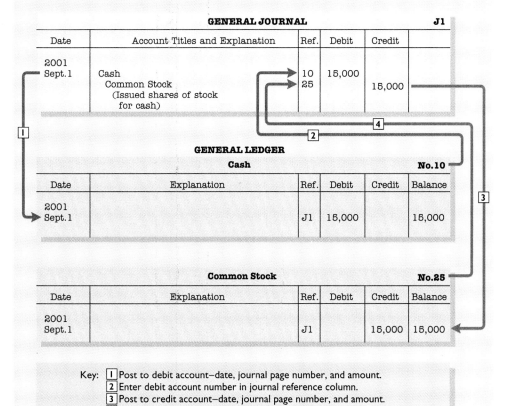

GENERAL JOURNAL   J1

Date	Account Titles and Explanation	Ref.	Debit	Credit	
2001 Sept. 1	Cash	10	15,000		
	Common Stock	25		15,000	
	(Issued shares of stock for cash)				

GENERAL LEDGER

Cash   No.10

Date	Explanation	Ref.	Debit	Credit	Balance
2001 Sept. 1		J1	15,000		15,000

Common Stock   No.25

Date	Explanation	Ref.	Debit	Credit	Balance
2001 Sept. 1		J1		15,000	15,000

Key: 1 Post to debit account—date, journal page number, and amount.
2 Enter debit account number in journal reference column.
3 Post to credit account—date, journal page number, and amount.
4 Enter credit account number in journal reference column.

HELPFUL HINT
Posting is essentially a copying procedure that should be done carefully if correct account balances are to be obtained.

Posting should be performed in chronological order. That is, all the debits and credits of one journal entry should be posted before proceeding to the next journal entry. Under the journalizing procedures described in this chapter, postings should be made on a timely basis to ensure that the ledger is up to date.[3]

The reference column **in the journal** serves several purposes. The numbers in this column indicate the entries that have been posted. After the last entry has been posted, the journal reference column should be scanned to see that all postings have been made.

The reference column **of a ledger** account indicates the journal page from which the transaction has been posted. The explanation space of the ledger account is used infrequently because an explanation already appears in the journal. It generally is used only when detailed analysis of account activity is required.

TECHNOLOGY IN ACTION

Determining what to record is the most critical (and for most businesses the most expensive) point in the accounting process. In computerized systems, after this phase is completed, your input and all further processing just boil down to file merging and report generation. Programmers and management information system types with good accounting backgrounds (such as they should gain from a good introductory accounting textbook) are better able to develop effective computerized systems.

Chart of Accounts

The number and type of accounts used differ for each enterprise, depending on the size, complexity, and type of business involved. For example, the number of accounts depends on the amount of detail desired by management. The management of one company may want one account for all types of utility expense. Another may keep separate expense accounts for each type of utility expenditure, such as gas, electricity, and water. Similarly, a small corporation like Softbyte Inc. will not have many accounts compared with a corporate giant like Ford Motor Company. Softbyte Inc. may be able to manage and report its activities in 20 to 30 accounts, while Ford requires thousands of accounts to keep track of its worldwide activities.

Most companies have a chart of accounts that lists the accounts and the account numbers which identify their location in the ledger. The numbering system used to identify the accounts usually starts with the balance sheet accounts and follows with the income statement accounts.

In this and the next two chapters, we will be explaining the accounting for Pioneer Advertising Agency Inc. (a service enterprise). Accounts 1–19 indicate asset accounts; 20–39 indicate liabilities; 40–49 indicate stockholders' equity accounts; 50–59, revenues; and 60–69, expenses.

The chart of accounts for Pioneer Advertising Agency Inc. is shown in Illustration 2-19. Accounts shown in red are used in this chapter; accounts shown in black are explained in later chapters.

---

[3]In homework problems, it will be permissible to journalize all transactions before posting any of the journal entries.

You will notice that there are gaps in the numbering system of the chart of accounts for Pioneer Advertising Agency Inc. Gaps are left to permit the insertion of new accounts as needed during the life of the business.

ILLUSTRATION 2-19

Chart of accounts

Chart of Accounts
Pioneer Advertising Agency Inc.

Assets	Stockholders' Equity
1. Cash	40. Common Stock
6. Accounts Receivable	41. Retained Earnings
8. Advertising Supplies	42. Dividends
10. Prepaid Insurance	49. Income Summary
15. Office Equipment	
16. Accumulated Depreciation—Office Equipment	**Revenues**
	50. Service Revenue
Liabilities	**Expenses**
25. Notes Payable	60. Salaries Expense
26. Accounts Payable	61. Advertising Supplies Expense
27. Interest Payable	62. Rent Expense
28. Unearned Revenue	63. Insurance Expense
29. Salaries Payable	64. Interest Expense
	65. Depreciation Expense

ACCOUNTING IN ACTION
Business Insight

The numbering system used to identify accounts can be quite sophisticated or relatively simple. For example, at Goodyear Tire & Rubber Company an 18-digit system is used. The first three digits identify the division or plant. The second set of three-digit numbers contains the following account classifications:

100–199 Assets	300–399 Revenues
200–299 Liabilities and Stockholders' Equity	400–599 Expenses

Other digits describe the location of a specific plant, product line, region of the country, and so on. In practice, account numbers are not the same from company to company. Therefore, to reflect the situation you would find in the real world, account numbers in the text and in the homework materials also vary from company to company.

THE RECORDING PROCESS ILLUSTRATED

Illustrations 2-20 through 2-29 show the basic steps in the recording process, using the October transactions of the Pioneer Advertising Agency Inc. Its accounting period is a month. A basic analysis and a debit-credit analysis precede the journalizing and posting of each transaction. Study these transaction analyses carefully. **The purpose of transaction analysis is first to identify the type of account involved, and then to determine whether a debit or a credit to the account is required.** You should always perform this type of analysis before preparing a journal entry. Doing so will help you understand the journal entries discussed in this chapter as well as more complex journal entries to be described in later chapters.

(text continues on page 65)

ILLUSTRATION 2-20

Investment of cash by stockholders

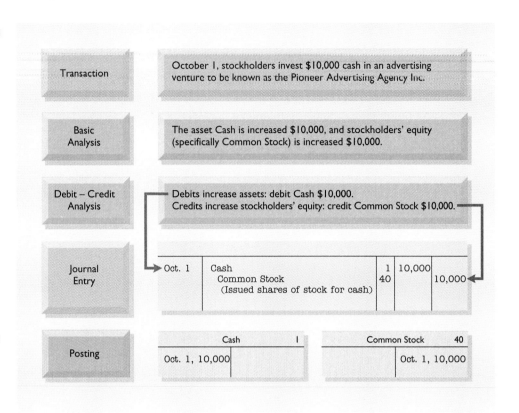

ILLUSTRATION 2-21

Purchase of office equipment

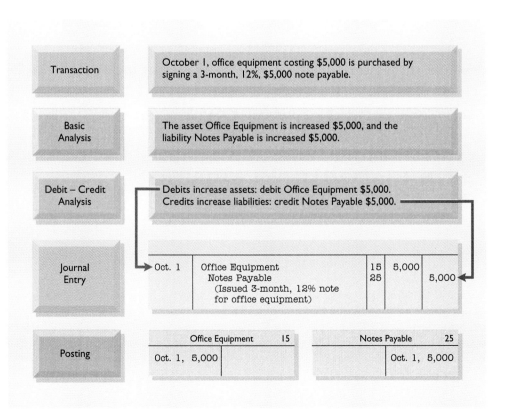

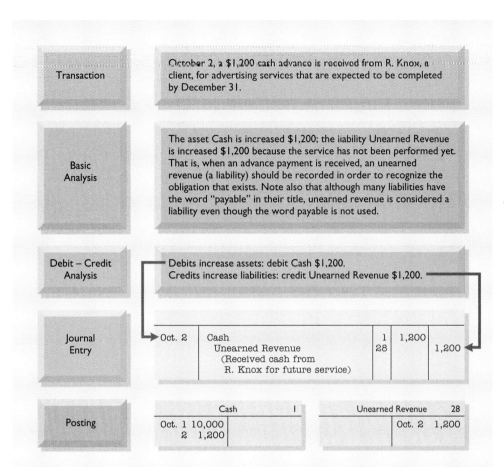

ILLUSTRATION 2-22

Receipt of cash for future service

Transaction	October 2, a $1,200 cash advance is received from R. Knox, a client, for advertising services that are expected to be completed by December 31.
Basic Analysis	The asset Cash is increased $1,200; the liability Unearned Revenue is increased $1,200 because the service has not been performed yet. That is, when an advance payment is received, an unearned revenue (a liability) should be recorded in order to recognize the obligation that exists. Note also that although many liabilities have the word "payable" in their title, unearned revenue is considered a liability even though the word payable is not used.
Debit – Credit Analysis	Debits increase assets: debit Cash $1,200. Credits increase liabilities: credit Unearned Revenue $1,200.

HELPFUL HINT
When the revenue is earned, the unearned revenue account is debited, and an earned revenue account is credited.

Journal Entry

Oct. 2	Cash	1	1,200	
	Unearned Revenue	28		1,200
	(Received cash from R. Knox for future service)			

Posting

Cash		1
Oct. 1	10,000	
2	1,200	

Unearned Revenue		28
	Oct. 2	1,200

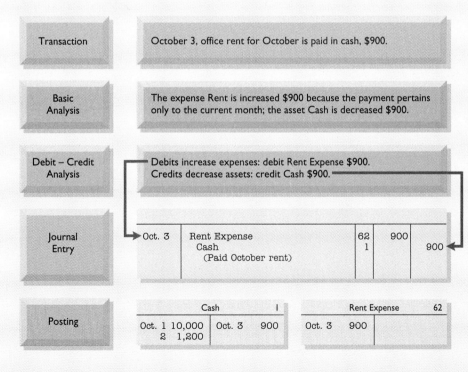

ILLUSTRATION 2-23

Payment of monthly rent

Transaction	October 3, office rent for October is paid in cash, $900.
Basic Analysis	The expense Rent is increased $900 because the payment pertains only to the current month; the asset Cash is decreased $900.
Debit – Credit Analysis	Debits increase expenses: debit Rent Expense $900. Credits decrease assets: credit Cash $900.

Journal Entry

Oct. 3	Rent Expense	62	900	
	Cash	1		900
	(Paid October rent)			

Posting

Cash		1
Oct. 1	10,000	Oct. 3 900
2	1,200	

Rent Expense		62
Oct. 3	900	

ILLUSTRATION 2-24

Payment for insurance

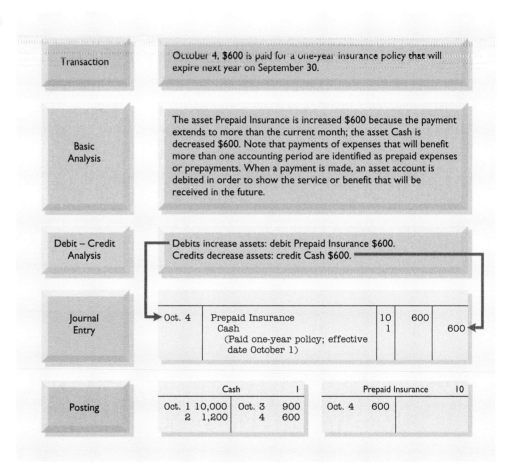

ILLUSTRATION 2-25

Purchase of supplies on credit

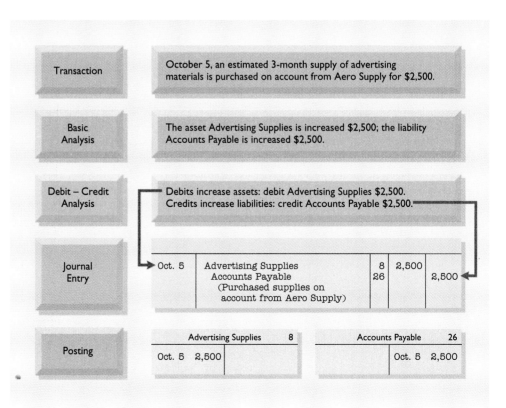

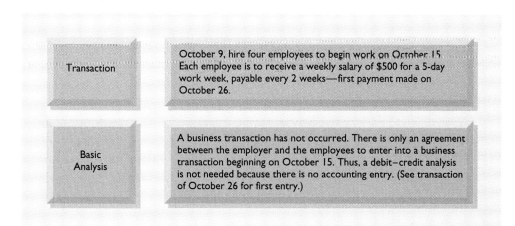

ILLUSTRATION 2-26

Hiring of employees

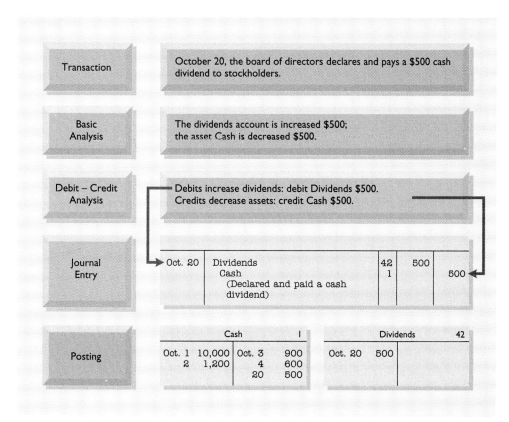

ILLUSTRATION 2-27

Declaration and payment of dividend by corporation

ILLUSTRATION 2-28

Payment of salaries

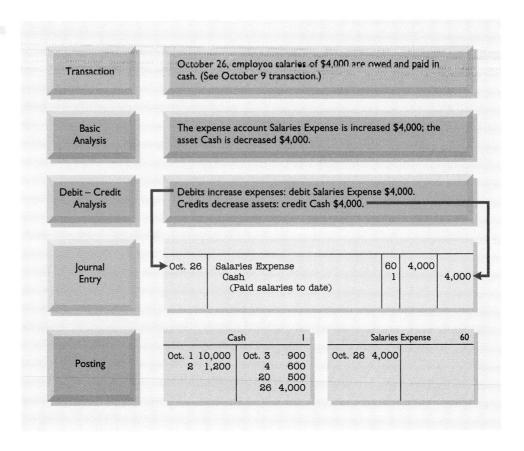

ILLUSTRATION 2-29

Receipt of cash for fees earned

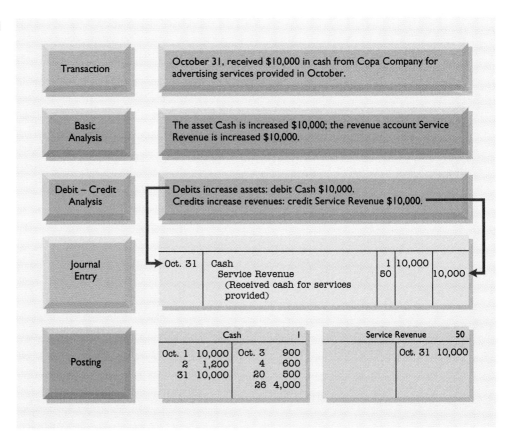

Keep in mind that every journal entry affects one or more of the following items: assets, liabilities, stockholders' equity, revenues, or expenses. By becoming skilled at transaction analysis, you will be able to recognize quickly the impact of any transaction on these five items. For simplicity, the T-account form is used in the illustrations instead of the standard account form.

BEFORE YOU GO ON ...

Review It

1. How does journalizing differ from posting?
2. What is the purpose of (a) the ledger and (b) a chart of accounts?

Summary Illustration of Journalizing and Posting

The journal for Pioneer Advertising Agency Inc. for the month of October is summarized in Illustration 2-30. The ledger is shown in Illustration 2-31, on page 66, with all balances in color.

ILLUSTRATION 2-30

General journal entries

GENERAL JOURNAL			PAGE J1	
Date	Account Titles and Explanation	Ref.	Debit	Credit
2001				
Oct. 1	Cash	1	10,000	
	Common Stock	40		10,000
	(Issued shares of stock for cash)			
1	Office Equipment	15	5,000	
	Notes Payable	25		5,000
	(Issued three-month, 12% note for office equipment)			
2	Cash	1	1,200	
	Unearned Revenue	28		1,200
	(Received cash from R. Knox for future services)			
3	Rent Expense	62	900	
	Cash	1		900
	(Paid October rent)			
4	Prepaid Insurance	10	600	
	Cash	1		600
	(Paid one-year policy; effective date, October 1)			
5	Advertising Supplies	8	2,500	
	Accounts Payable	26		2,500
	(Purchased supplies on account from Aero Supply)			
20	Dividends	42	500	
	Cash	1		500
	(Declared and paid a cash dividend)			
26	Salaries Expense	60	4,000	
	Cash	1		4,000
	(Paid salaries to date)			
31	Cash	1	10,000	
	Service Revenue	50		10,000
	(Received cash for services provided)			

ILLUSTRATION 2-31

General ledger

GENERAL LEDGER

Cash — No. 1

Date	Explanation	Ref.	Debit	Credit	Balance
2001					
Oct. 1		J1	10,000		10,000
2		J1	1,200		11,200
3		J1		900	10,300
4		J1		600	9,700
20		J1		500	9,200
26		J1		4,000	5,200
31		J1	10,000		15,200

Advertising Supplies — No. 8

Date	Explanation	Ref.	Debit	Credit	Balance
2001					
Oct. 5		J1	2,500		2,500

Prepaid Insurance — No. 10

Date	Explanation	Ref.	Debit	Credit	Balance
2001					
Oct. 4		J1	600		600

Office Equipment — No. 15

Date	Explanation	Ref.	Debit	Credit	Balance
2001					
Oct. 1		J1	5,000		5,000

Notes Payable — No. 25

Date	Explanation	Ref.	Debit	Credit	Balance
2001					
Oct. 1		J1		5,000	5,000

Accounts Payable — No. 26

Date	Explanation	Ref.	Debit	Credit	Balance
2001					
Oct. 5		J1		2,500	2,500

Unearned Revenue — No. 28

Date	Explanation	Ref.	Debit	Credit	Balance
2001					
Oct. 2		J1		1,200	1,200

Common Stock — No. 40

Date	Explanation	Ref.	Debit	Credit	Balance
2001					
Oct. 1		J1		10,000	10,000

Dividends — No. 42

Date	Explanation	Ref.	Debit	Credit	Balance
2001					
Oct. 20		J1	500		500

Service Revenue — No. 50

Date	Explanation	Ref.	Debit	Credit	Balance
2001					
Oct. 31		J1		10,000	10,000

Salaries Expense — No. 60

Date	Explanation	Ref.	Debit	Credit	Balance
2001					
Oct. 26		J1	4,000		4,000

Rent Expense — No. 62

Date	Explanation	Ref.	Debit	Credit	Balance
2001					
Oct. 3		J1	900		900

THE TRIAL BALANCE

7
STUDY
OBJECTIVE

Prepare a trial balance
and explain its purposes.

A trial balance is a list of accounts and their balances at a given time. Customarily, a trial balance is prepared at the end of an accounting period. The accounts are listed in the order in which they appear in the ledger, with debit balances listed in the left column and credit balances in the right column. The totals of the two columns must be in agreement.

The primary purpose of a trial balance is to prove the mathematical equality of debits and credits after posting. Under the double-entry system this equality will occur when the sum of the debit account balances equals the sum of the credit account balances. **A trial balance also uncovers errors in journalizing and posting. In addition, it is useful in the preparation of financial statements,** as will be explained in the next two chapters. The procedures for preparing a trial balance consist of:

HELPFUL HINT
A trial balance is so named because it is a test to determine if the sum of the debit balances equals the sum of the credit balances.

1. Listing the account titles and their balances.
2. Totaling the debit and credit columns.
3. Proving the equality of the two columns.

The trial balance prepared from the ledger of Pioneer Advertising Agency Inc. is presented below:

ILLUSTRATION 2-32
A trial balance

PIONEER ADVERTISING AGENCY INC. Trial Balance October 31, 2001		
	Debit	Credit
Cash	$15,200	
Advertising Supplies	2,500	
Prepaid Insurance	600	
Office Equipment	5,000	
Notes Payable		$ 5,000
Accounts Payable		2,500
Unearned Revenue		1,200
Common Stock		10,000
Dividends	500	
Service Revenue		10,000
Salaries Expense	4,000	
Rent Expense	900	
	$28,700	$28,700

HELPFUL HINT
To sum a column of figures is sometimes referred to as to foot the column. The column is then said to be footed.

Note that the total debits $28,700 equal the total credits $28,700. Account numbers are sometimes shown to the left of the account titles in the trial balance.

A trial balance is a necessary check point before proceeding to other steps in the accounting process. For example, if only the debit portion of a journal entry has been posted, the trial balance would bring this error to light.

Limitations of a Trial Balance
A trial balance does not prove that all transactions have been recorded or that the ledger is correct. Numerous errors may exist even though the trial balance columns agree. For example, the trial balance may balance even when (1) a transaction is not journalized, (2) a correct journal entry is not posted, (3) a journal entry is posted twice, (4) incorrect accounts are used in journalizing or posting, or (5) offsetting errors are made in recording the amount of a transaction. In other words, as long as equal debits and credits are posted, even to the wrong account or in the wrong amount, the total debits will equal the total credits.

Locating Errors
The procedure for preparing a trial balance is relatively simple. However, in manual systems if the trial balance does not balance, locating an error can be time-consuming, tedious, and frustrating. The error(s) generally results from

TECHNOLOGY IN ACTION

In a computerized system, the trial balance is often only one column (no debit or credit columns), and the accounts have plus and minus signs associated with them. The final balance therefore is zero. Any errors that develop in a computerized system will undoubtedly involve the initial recording rather than some error in the posting or preparation of a trial balance.

HELPFUL HINT

We have avoided the use of cents in the text to save you time and effort.

mathematical mistakes, incorrect postings, or simply transcribing the data incorrectly.

What happens if you are faced with a trial balance that does not balance? First determine the amount of the difference between the two columns of the trial balance. After this amount is known, the following steps are often helpful:

1. If the error is $1, $10, $100, or $1,000, re-add the trial balance columns and recompute the account balances.
2. If the error is divisible by two, scan the trial balance to see whether a balance equal to half the error has been entered in the wrong column.
3. If the error is divisible by nine, retrace the account balances on the trial balance to see whether they are incorrectly copied from the ledger. For example, if a balance was $12 and it was listed as $21, a $9 error has been made. Reversing the order of numbers is called a transposition error.
4. If the error is not divisible by two or nine (for example, $365), scan the ledger to see whether an account balance of $365 has been omitted from the trial balance, and scan the journal to see whether a $365 posting has been omitted.

Use of Dollar Signs

Note that dollar signs do not appear in the journals or ledgers. Dollar signs are usually used only in the trial balance and the financial statements. Generally, a dollar sign is shown only for the first item in the column and for the total of that column. A single line is placed under the column of figures to be added or subtracted; the total amount is double underlined to indicate the final sum.

ELECTRONIC DATA PROCESSING

Electronic data processing (also called computerized accounting information systems) encompasses all processing steps from the initial entry of data into the system to the preparation of financial reports for management.

Many students ask, "Why then study manual systems if the real world uses computerized systems?" The accounting concepts and principles do not change whether the system is manual or computerized. However, the concepts are more easily illustrated in a manual system than in a computerized system. In addition, the exact procedures in a computerized system depend on the computer hardware and software being used. Thus, manual systems have been used up to now in this textbook and will continue to be used in the remainder of the chapters.

8
STUDY
OBJECTIVE

Identify the key points in comparing manual and computerized accounting systems.

Comparative Advantages of Manual versus Computerized Systems

There are similarities and differences between manual and computerized systems. One should not conclude that computerized systems are always better. As with any selection, the costs and benefits of each alternative should be weighed before the choice is made. The following key points should be considered when evaluating and comparing manual and computerized systems.

Dollar Costs

The costs of bookkeepers' salaries and manual accounting records must be compared to the costs of computer hardware and software. Computer systems have some hidden costs that must be considered. Such costs include computer training of personnel and salary differences between bookkeepers and competent computer operators to run the system. Another consideration is the possibility that fewer individuals are needed to run a computer system. And, in general, with microcomputers widely available, as well as an abundance of user-friendly software packages, the manual system is losing its comparative advantage in even the smallest businesses.

Processing Speed

When the number of transactions is large, computerized systems offer real advantages. Thousands of transactions can be processed quickly by a computer, and high-speed printers can generate reports. However, delays in computer processing can occur. For example, if transactions are **batched** (grouped together into like categories and processed at a later time), records and balances may not contain the most up-to-date information. This delay can be avoided by processing transactions using **real-time** (on-line) processing systems in which data are processed as soon as received. In addition, if back-up hardware and software are not kept, malfunctions and breakdowns may bring the system to a standstill.

Processing Errors

Unless a hardware failure occurs, the computer will not make a processing error. Both hardware and software controls generally ensure accurate processing. Because humans perform the processing in a manual system, the potential for processing errors is greater in the manual system. However, humans may be involved with data entry in a computerized system, so some errors may creep into the system.

Responsiveness

Have you ever tried to call the computer to get your bill corrected? Errors and other problems are sometimes handled more swiftly and readily in a manual system than in a computerized system. For example, a bookkeeper may be more responsive to customer complaints. Also, an important psychological factor differentiates manual systems from computer systems. In computerized systems, customers too often become numbers, and customers generally prefer not to be treated as numbers; they like personalized relationships. However, recent innovations now permit computers to engage in conversation with the capabilities of asking questions, giving directions, taking orders, and recognizing words, voices, responses, and fingerprints, thus becoming more personalized.

Report Generation

A definite advantage of computerized systems is the ease with which reports can be prepared. Once the system contains the information, useful manipulations of the information can be performed and printed in a matter of minutes. These "demand" reports are also a result of the computer system's ability to bring together information from different parts of the system, such as sales transactions and the accounts receivable subsidiary ledger.

Although some trade-offs exist between the efficiencies of computers and the personal responsiveness of manual systems, computer systems are gaining so significantly in popularity that manual accounting systems are becoming an endangered species.

A Look into the Future

Initially, computer technology in business was used to automate the accounting system. Much of the clerical work involved in recording and summarizing accounting transaction data was eliminated. However, there was still a problem—a sales transaction was first processed by accountants. Then, this same sales information was reprocessed by production, marketing, and so on for use in their decision making.

Accountants are now beginning to use computer systems to capture all the organizational information and then provide this information to executives in the forms they desire. As one writer noted: Accountants are becoming organization historians by (a) recording complete histories of organizational events and (b) interpreting these histories for decision makers. Thus, an organizational data base of events is developed. This data base is then used to provide information for decision making for both internal and external purposes. These new developments will make accounting even more enjoyable and useful in the future.

BEFORE YOU GO ON . . .

Review It

1. What is a trial balance and how is it prepared?
2. What is the primary purpose of a trial balance?
3. What are the limitations of a trial balance?
4. Why study a manual system?
5. What are the advantages of using a computerized system to record business transactions?

A LOOK BACK AT OUR FEATURE STORY

Now that you have learned the details of the recording process, think back to the beginning of the chapter to Tanis Anderson and her position as Director of Finance at The Mug and Musket. Answer the following questions:

1. What accounting entries would Tanis likely make to record (a) the receipt of cash from a customer in payment of their bill, (b) payment of utility bill, and (c) payment of wages for the waiters?
2. How did Tanis's job as Director of Finance help in her studies as she finished her business administration degree?

Solution

1. Tanis would likely make the following entries:
   (a) Cash
           Food Sales Revenue
               (Receipt of payment for food services)
   (b) Utility Expense
           Cash
               (Payment of electric bill)
   (c) Salaries (or Wages) Expense
           Cash
               (Paid waiters' wages)

THE
NAVIGATOR

2. As a result of her accounting position, Tanis was able to relate the subject matter as well as much of the assignment material in her business courses to a real-world context. From her job, she knew how bills were paid, how supplies were determined, how employees were hired, managed, evaluated, and paid, and much more.

DEMONSTRATION PROBLEM

Bob Sample and other student investors opened the Campus Laundromat Inc. on September 1, 2001. During the first month of operations the following transactions occurred:

Sept. 1 Stockholders invested $20,000 cash in the business.

2 Paid $1,000 cash for store rent for the month of September.

3 Purchased washers and dryers for $25,000 paying $10,000 in cash and signing a $15,000 six-month 12% note payable.

4 Paid $1,200 for one-year accident insurance policy.

10 Received bill from the Daily News for advertising the opening of the laundromat, $200

20 Declared and paid a cash dividend to stockholders, $700.

30 Determined that cash receipts for laundry fees for the month were $6,200.

The chart of accounts for the company is the same as in Pioneer Advertising Agency Inc. except for the following: No. 15 Laundry Equipment and No. 61 Advertising Expense.

Instructions

(a) Journalize the September transactions. (Use J1 for the journal page number.)

(b) Open ledger accounts and post the September transactions.

(c) Prepare a trial balance at September 30, 2001.

SOLUTION TO DEMONSTRATION PROBLEM

(a)   **GENERAL JOURNAL**   **J1**

Date	Account Titles and Explanation	Ref.	Debit	Credit
2001				
Sept. 1	Cash	1	20,000	
	Common Stock	40		20,000
	(Stockholders invested cash in business)			
2	Rent Expense	62	1,000	
	Cash	1		1,000
	(Paid September rent)			
3	Laundry Equipment	15	25,000	
	Cash	1		10,000
	Notes Payable	25		15,000
	(Purchased laundry equipment for cash and six-month 12% note payable)			
4	Prepaid Insurance	10	1,200	
	Cash	1		1,200
	(Paid one-year insurance policy)			
10	Advertising Expense	61	200	
	Accounts Payable	26		200
	(Received bill from Daily News for advertising)			
20	Dividends	42	700	
	Cash	1		700
	(Declared and paid a cash dividend)			
30	Cash	1	6,200	
	Service Revenue	50		6,200
	(Received cash for laundry fees earned)			

PROBLEM-SOLVING STRATEGIES

1. Separate journal entries are made for each transaction.
2. In journalizing, make sure debits equal credits.
3. In journalizing, use specific account titles taken from the chart of accounts.
4. Provide appropriate description of journal entry.
5. Arrange ledger in statement order, beginning with the balance sheet accounts.
6. Post in chronological order.
7. Numbers in the reference column indicate the amount has been posted.
8. The trial balance lists accounts in the order in which they appear in the ledger.
9. Debit balances are listed in the left column, and credit balances in the right

(b)   **GENERAL LEDGER**

Cash					No. 1
Date	Explanation	Ref.	Debit	Credit	Balance
2001					
Sept. 1		J1	20,000		20,000
2		J1		1,000	19,000
3		J1		10,000	9,000
4		J1		1,200	7,800
20		J1		700	7,100
30		J1	6,200		13,300

Prepaid Insurance					No. 10
Date	Explanation	Ref.	Debit	Credit	Balance
2001					
Sept. 4		J1	1,200		1,200

Laundry Equipment					No. 15
Date	Explanation	Ref.	Debit	Credit	Balance
2001					
Sept. 3		J1	25,000		25,000

Notes Payable					No. 25
Date	Explanation	Ref.	Debit	Credit	Balance
2001					
Sept. 3		J1		15,000	15,000

Accounts Payable					No. 26
Date	Explanation	Ref.	Debit	Credit	Balance
2001					
Sept. 10		J1		200	200

Common Stock					No. 40
Date	Explanation	Ref.	Debit	Credit	Balance
2001					
Sept. 1		J1		20,000	20,000

Dividends					No. 42
Date	Explanation	Ref.	Debit	Credit	Balance
2001					
Sept. 1		J1	700		700

Service Revenue					No. 50
Date	Explanation	Ref.	Debit	Credit	Balance
2001					
Sept. 30		J1		6,200	6,200

Advertising Expense					No. 61
Date	Explanation	Ref.	Debit	Credit	Balance
2001					
Sept. 10		J1	200		200

Rent Expense					No. 62
Date	Explanation	Ref.	Debit	Credit	Balance
2001					
Sept. 2		J1	1,000		1,000

CAMPUS LAUNDROMAT INC.
Trial Balance
September 30, 2001

	Debit	Credit
Cash	$13,300	
Prepaid Insurance	1,200	
Laundry Equipment	25,000	
Notes Payable		$15,000
Accounts Payable		200
Common Stock		20,000
Dividends	700	
Service Revenue		6,200
Advertising Expense	200	
Rent Expense	1,000	
	$41,400	$41,400

THE
NAVIGATOR

SUMMARY OF STUDY OBJECTIVES

1. Explain what an account is and how it helps in the recording process. An account is an individual accounting record of increases and decreases in specific asset, liability, and stockholders' equity items.

2. Define debits and credits and explain how they are used to record business transactions. The terms debit and credit are synonymous with left and right. Assets, dividends, and expenses are increased by debits and decreased by credits. Liabilities, common stock, retained earnings, and revenues are increased by credits and decreased by debits.

3. Identify the basic steps in the recording process. The basic steps in the recording process are: (a) analyze each transaction in terms of its effect on the accounts, (b) enter the transaction information in a journal, (c) transfer the journal information to the appropriate accounts in the ledger.

4. Explain what a journal is and how it helps in the recording process. The initial accounting record of a transaction is entered in a journal before the data are entered in the accounts. A journal (a) discloses in one place the complete effect of a transaction, (b) provides a chronological record of transactions, and (c) prevents or locates errors because the debit and credit amounts for each entry can be readily compared.

5. Explain what a ledger is and how it helps in the recording process. The entire group of accounts maintained by a company is referred to collectively as a ledger. The ledger keeps in one place all the information about changes in specific account balances.

6. Explain what posting is and how it helps in the recording process. Posting is the procedure of transferring journal entries to the ledger accounts. This phase of the recording process accumulates the effects of journalized transactions in the individual accounts.

7. Prepare a trial balance and explain its purposes. A trial balance is a list of accounts and their balances at a given time. The primary purpose of the trial balance is to prove the mathematical equality of debits and credits after posting. A trial balance also uncovers errors in journalizing and posting and is useful in preparing financial statements.

8. Identify the key points in comparing manual and computerized accounting systems. The key points in comparing manual and computerized accounting systems are (a) cost considerations, (b) processing speed, (c) processing errors, (d) responsiveness, and (e) generation of reports on demand.

THE NAVIGATOR

GLOSSARY

Account An individual accounting record of increases and decreases in specific asset, liability, and stockholders' equity items. (p. 46).

Chart of accounts A list of accounts and the account numbers which identify their location in the ledger. (p. 58).

Common stock Issued in exchange for the owners' investment paid in to the corporation. (p. 49).

Compound entry An entry that involves three or more accounts. (p. 54).

Credit The right side of an account. (p. 47).

Debit The left side of an account. (p. 47).

Dividend A distribution by a corporation to its stockholders on a pro rata (equal) basis. (p. 49).

Double-entry system A system that records the dual effect of each transaction in appropriate accounts. (p. 48).

General journal The most basic form of journal. (p. 53).

General ledger A ledger that contains all asset, liability, and stockholders' equity accounts. (p. 55).

Journal An accounting record in which transactions are initially recorded in chronological order. (p. 53).

Journalizing The procedure of entering transaction data in the journal. (p. 53).

Ledger The entire group of accounts maintained by a company. (p. 55).

Posting The procedure of transferring journal entries to the ledger accounts. (p. 57).

Retained earnings Net income that is retained in the business. (p. 49).

Simple entry An entry that involves only two accounts. (p. 54).

T account The basic form of an account. (p. 46).

Three-column form of account A form containing money columns for debit, credit, and balance amounts in an account. (p. 57).

Trial balance A list of accounts and their balances at a given time. (p. 66).

SELF-STUDY QUESTIONS

Answers are at the end of the chapter.

(SO 1) 1. Which of the following statements about an account is true?
  a. In its simplest form, an account consists of two parts.
  b. An account is an individual accounting record of in-

creases and decreases in specific asset, liability, and stockholders' equity items.
  c. There are separate accounts for specific assets and liabilities but only one account for stockholders' equity items.
  d. The left side of an account is the credit or decrease side.

(SO 2) 2. Debits:
   a. increase both assets and liabilities.
   b. decrease both assets and liabilities.
   c. increase assets and decrease liabilities.
   d. decrease assets and increase liabilities.

(SO 2) 3. A revenue account:
   a. is increased by debits.
   b. is decreased by credits.
   c. has a normal balance of a debit.
   d. is increased by credits.

(SO 2) 4. Accounts that normally have debit balances are:
   a. assets, expenses, and revenues.
   b. assets, expenses, and common stock.
   c. assets, liabilities, and dividends.
   d. assets, dividends, and expenses.

(SO 3) 5. Which of the following is *not* part of the recording process?
   a. Analyzing transactions.
   b. Preparing a trial balance.
   c. Entering transactions in a journal.
   d. Posting transactions.

(SO 4) 6. Which of the following statements about a journal is false?
   a. It is not a book of original entry.
   b. It provides a chronological record of transactions.
   c. It helps to locate errors because the debit and credit amounts for each entry can be readily compared.
   d. It discloses in one place the complete effect of a transaction.

7. A ledger: (SO 5)
   a. contains only asset and liability accounts.
   b. should show accounts in alphabetical order.
   c. is a collection of the entire group of accounts maintained by a company.
   d. is a book of original entry.

8. Posting: (SO 6)
   a. normally occurs before journalizing.
   b. transfers ledger transaction data to the journal.
   c. is an optional step in the recording process.
   d. transfers journal entries to ledger accounts.

9. A trial balance: (SO 7)
   a. is a list of accounts with their balances at a given time.
   b. proves the mathematical accuracy of journalized transactions.
   c. will not balance if a correct journal entry is posted twice.
   d. proves that all transactions have been recorded.

10. A trial balance will not balance if: (SO 7)
   a. a correct journal entry is posted twice.
   b. the purchase of supplies on account is debited to Supplies and credited to Cash.
   c. a $100 cash dividend by the corporation is debited to Dividends for $1,000 and credited to Cash for $100.
   d. a $450 payment on account is debited to Accounts Payable for $45 and credited to Cash for $45.

QUESTIONS

1. Why is an account referred to as a T account?

2. The terms *debit* and *credit* mean increase and decrease, respectively. Do you agree? Explain.

3. Goldie Hawn, a fellow student, contends that the double-entry system means each transaction must be recorded twice. Is Goldie correct? Explain.

4. Kate Winslet, a beginning accounting student, believes debit balances are favorable and credit balances are unfavorable. Is Kate correct? Discuss.

5. State the rules of debit and credit as applied to (a) asset accounts, (b) liability accounts, and (c) stockholders' equity account.

6. What is the normal balance for each of the following accounts? (a) Accounts Receivable. (b) Cash. (c) Dividends. (d) Accounts Payable. (e) Service Revenue. (f) Salaries Expense. (g) Common Stock.

7. Indicate whether each of the following accounts is an asset, a liability, or a stockholders' equity account and whether it would have a debit or credit balance: (a) Accounts Receivable, (b) Accounts Payable, (c) Equipment, (d) Dividends, (e) Supplies.

8. For the following transactions, indicate the account debited and the account credited:
   (a) Supplies are purchased on account.
   (b) Cash is received on signing a note payable.
   (c) Employees are paid salaries in cash.

9. Presented below is a series of accounts. Indicate whether these accounts generally will have (a) debit entries only, (b) credit entries only, (c) both debit and credit entries.
   (1) Cash.
   (2) Accounts Receivable.
   (3) Dividends.
   (4) Accounts Payable.
   (5) Salaries Expense.
   (6) Service Revenue.

10. What are the basic steps in the recording process?

11. What are the advantages of using the journal in the recording process?

12. (a) When entering a transaction in the journal, should the debit or credit be written first?
    (b) Which should be indented, the debit or credit?

13. Give an example of a compound entry.

14. (a) Can business transaction debits and credits be recorded directly in the ledger accounts?
    (b) What are the advantages of first recording transactions in the journal and then posting to the ledger?

15. The account number is entered as the last step in posting the amounts from the journal to the ledger. What is the advantage of this step?

16. Journalize the following business transactions.
    (a) Dustin Hoffman invests $9,000 in the business in exchange for shares of common stock.
    (b) Insurance of $800 is paid for the year.
    (c) Supplies of $1,500 are purchased on account.
    (d) Cash of $7,500 is received for services rendered.

17. (a) What is a ledger? (b) Why is a chart of accounts important?

18. What is a trial balance and what are its purposes?

19. Kap Shin is confused about how accounting information flows through the accounting system. He believes the flow of information is as follows:
    (a) Debits and credits posted to the ledger.
    (b) Business transaction occurs.
    (c) Information entered in the journal.
    (d) Financial statements are prepared.
    (e) Trial balance is prepared.
    Indicate to Kap the proper flow of the information.

20. Two students are discussing the use of a trial balance. They wonder whether the following errors, each considered separately, would prevent the trial balance from balancing.
    (a) The bookkeeper debited Cash for $600 and credited Wages Expense for $600 for payment of wages.
    (b) Cash collected on account was debited to Cash for $900 and Service Revenue was credited for $90.
    What would you tell them?

21. What are the key points to be considered in evaluating and comparing manual and computerized systems?

22. What are the trade-offs between the efficiencies of computers and the personal responsiveness of manual systems?

BRIEF EXERCISES

BE2–1 For each of the following accounts indicate (a) the effect of a debit or a credit on the account and (b) the normal balance.

Indicate debit and credit effects and normal balance.
(SO 2)

1. Accounts Payable.
2. Advertising Expense.
3. Service Revenue.
4. Accounts Receivable.
5. Common Stock.
6. Dividends.

BE2–2 Transactions for the José Amaro Company for the month of June are presented below. Identify the accounts to be debited and credited for each transaction.

Identify accounts to be debited and credited.
(SO 2)

June 1 José Amaro invests $2,500 cash in exchange for shares of common stock in a small welding corporation.
     2 Buys equipment on account for $900.
     3 Pays $500 to landlord for June rent.
    12 Bills Teresa Alvarez $300 for welding work done.

BE2–3 Using the data in BE2–2, journalize the transactions. (You may omit explanations.)

Journalize transactions.
(SO 4)

BE2–4 ✏➤ Glenn Close, a fellow student, is unclear about the basic steps in the recording process. Identify and briefly explain the steps in the order in which they occur.

Identify and explain steps in recording process.
(SO 3)

BE2–5 Eddie Murphy Corporation has the following transactions during August of the current year. Indicate (a) the basic analysis and (b) the debit-credit analysis illustrated on pages 48–50 of the text.

Indicate basic and debit-credit analysis.
(SO 4)

Aug. 1 Opens an office as a financial advisor, investing $5,000 in cash in exchange for common stock.
     4 Pays insurance in advance for 6 months, $1,800.
    16 Receives $900 from clients for services rendered.
    27 Pays secretary $500 salary.

BE2–6 Using the data in BE2–5, journalize the transactions. (You may omit explanations.)

Journalize transactions.
(SO 4)

Post journal entries to T accounts.
(SO 6)

BE2–7 Selected transactions for the Fernandez Company are presented in journal form below. Post the transactions to T accounts.

J1

Date	Account Titles and Explanation	Ref.	Debit	Credit
May 5	Accounts Receivable		3,200	
	Service Revenue			3,200
12	Cash		2,400	
	Accounts Receivable			2,400
15	Cash		2,000	
	Service Revenue			2,000

Post journal entries to standard form of account.
(SO 6)
Prepare a trial balance.
(SO 7)

BE2–8 Selected journal entries for the Fernandez Company are presented in BE2–7. Post the transactions using the standard form of account.

BE2–9 From the ledger balances given below, prepare a trial balance for the Thailand Company at June 30, 2001. List the accounts in the order shown on page 00 of the text. All account balances are normal.

Accounts Payable $4,000, Cash $3,800, Common Stock $20,000, Dividends $1,200, Equipment $17,000, Service Revenue $6,000, Accounts Receivable $3,000, Salaries Expense $4,000, and Rent Expense $1,000.

Prepare a correct trial balance.
(SO 7)

BE2–10 An inexperienced bookkeeper prepared the following trial balance that does not balance. Prepare a correct trial balance, assuming all account balances are normal.

WANG COMPANY
Trial Balance
December 31, 2001

	Debit	Credit
Cash	$18,800	
Prepaid Insurance		$ 3,500
Accounts Payable		3,000
Unearned Fees	2,200	
Common Stock		17,000
Dividends		4,500
Service Revenue		25,600
Salaries Expense	18,600	
Rent Expense		2,400
	$39,600	$56,000

EXERCISES

Identify debits, credits, and normal balances.
(SO 2)

E2–1 Selected transactions for Existenz Inc., an interior decorating firm, in its first month of business, are as follows:

1. Invested $10,000 cash in business in exchange for common stock.
2. Purchased used car for $4,000 cash for use in business.
3. Purchased supplies on account for $500.
4. Billed customers $1,800 for services performed.
5. Paid $200 cash for advertising start of business.
6. Received $700 cash from customers billed in (4) above.
7. Paid creditor $300 cash on account.
8. Declared and paid a $500 cash dividend.

Instructions
For each transaction indicate (a) the basic type of account debited and credited (asset, liability, stockholders' equity); (b) the specific account debited and credited (cash, rent expense,

service revenue, etc.); (c) whether the specific account is increased or decreased; and (d) the normal balance of the specific account. Use the following format, in which transaction (1) is given as an example:

	Account Debited				Account Credited			
Trans-action	(a) Basic Type	(b) Specific Account	(c) Effect	(d) Normal Balance	(a) Basic Type	(b) Specific Account	(c) Effect	(d) Normal Balance
(1)	Asset	Cash	Increase	Debit	Stockholders' Equity	Common Stock	Increase	Credit

E2–2 Data for Existenz Inc., interior decorating, are presented in E2–1.

Journalize transactions (SO 4)

Instructions
Journalize the transactions using journal page J1.

E2–3 Presented below is information related to Cucaracha Real Estate Agency Inc.:

Analyze transactions and determine their effect on accounts. (SO 2)

Oct. 1 Lee Cucaracha begins business as a real estate agent with a cash investment of $13,000 in exchange for common stock.
      2 Hires an administrative assistant.
      3 Buys office furniture for $1,900, on account.
      6 Sells a house and lot for E. Roberts; revenue due from Roberts, $3,200 (not paid by Roberts at this time).
     10 Receives cash of $140 as fees for renting an apartment for the owner.
     27 Pays $700 on the balance indicated in the transaction of October 3.
     30 Pays the administrative assistant $960 in salary for October.

Instructions
Prepare the debit-credit analysis for each transaction as illustrated on pages 48–50.

E2–4 Transaction data for Cucaracha Real Estate Agency Inc., are presented in E2–3.

Journalize transactions. (SO 4)

Instructions
Journalize the transactions.

E2–5 Selected transactions from the journal of David Spade Inc., investment brokerage firm, are presented below.

Post journal entries and prepare a trial balance. (SO 6, 7)

Date	Account Titles and Explanation	Ref.	Debit	Credit
Aug. 1	Cash		1,600	
	Common Stock			1,600
	(Investment of cash for stock)			
10	Cash		2,400	
	Service Revenue			2,400
	(Received cash for services provided)			
12	Office Equipment		4,000	
	Cash			1,000
	Notes Payable			3,000
	(Purchased office equipment for cash and notes payable)			
25	Accounts Receivable		1,400	
	Service Revenue			1,400
	(Billed for services provided)			
31	Cash		900	
	Accounts Receivable			900
	(Receipt of cash on account)			

Instructions
(a) Post the transactions to T accounts.
(b) Prepare a trial balance at August 31, 2001.

Journalize transactions from account data and prepare a trial balance.
(SO 4, 7)

E2-6 The T accounts below summarize the ledger of Active Consulting Corporation at the end of the first month of operations:

	Cash		No. 101			Unearned Revenue		No. 205
4/1	8,000	4/15	600				4/30	800
4/12	900	4/25	1,500					
4/29	400							
4/30	800							

	Accounts Receivable		No. 112			Common Stock		No. 311
4/7	3,200	4/29	400				4/1	8,000

	Supplies		No. 126			Service Revenue		No. 400
4/4	1,800						4/7	3,200
							4/12	900

	Accounts Payable		No. 201			Salaries Expense		No. 726
4/25	1,500	4/4	1,800		4/15	600		

Instructions
(a) Prepare the complete general journal (including explanations) from which the postings to Cash were made.
(b) Prepare a trial balance at April 30, 2001.

Journalize transactions from account data and prepare a trial balance.
(SO 4, 7)

E2-7 Presented below is the ledger for Oriental Corp.

	Cash		No. 101			Common Stock		No. 311
10/1	4,000	10/4	400				10/1	4,000
10/10	650	10/12	1,500				10/25	2,000
10/10	5,000	10/15	250					
10/20	500	10/30	300			Dividends		No. 332
10/25	2,000	10/31	500		10/30	300		

	Accounts Receivable		No. 112			Service Revenue		No. 407
10/6	800	10/20	500				10/6	800
10/20	940						10/10	650
							10/20	940

	Supplies		No. 126			Store Wages Expense		No. 628
10/4	400				10/31	500		

	Furniture		No. 149			Rent Expense		No. 729
10/3	2,000				10/15	250		

	Notes Payable		No. 200
		10/10	5,000

	Accounts Payable		No. 201
10/12	1,500	10/3	2,000

Instructions
(a) Reproduce the journal entries for the transactions that occurred on October 1, 10, and 20 and provide explanations for each.
(b) Prepare a trial balance at October 31, 2001.

Prepare journal entries and post using standard account form.
(SO 4, 6)

E2-8 Selected transactions for Joan E. Robinson Corporation during its first month in business are presented below.

Sept. 1 Invested $15,000 cash in the business in exchange for common stock.
    5 Purchased equipment for $10,000 paying $5,000 in cash and the balance on account.
  25 Paid $3,000 cash on balance owed for equipment.
  30 Declared and paid a $500 cash dividend.

Robinson's chart of accounts shows: Cash, No. 101; Equipment, No. 157; and Accounts Payable, No. 201; Common Stock, No. 311; and Dividends, No. 332.

Instructions
   (a) Journalize the transactions on page J1 of the journal (omit explanations).
   (b) Post the transactions using the standard account form.

E2-9   The bookkeeper for Jackie Henning Corp. made a number of errors in journalizing and posting, as described below:

   1. A credit posting of $400 to Accounts Receivable was omitted.
   2. A debit posting of $750 for Prepaid Insurance was debited to Insurance Expense.
   3. A collection on account of $100 was journalized and posted as a debit to Cash $100 and a credit to Service Revenue $100.
   4. A credit posting of $300 to Property Taxes Payable was made twice.
   5. A cash purchase of supplies for $250 was journalized and posted as a debit to Supplies $25 and a credit to Cash $25.
   6. A debit of $465 to Advertising Expense was posted as $456.

Instructions
For each error, indicate (a) whether the trial balance will balance; if the trial balance will not balance, indicate (b) the amount of the difference, and (c) the trial balance column that will have the larger total. Consider each error separately. Use the following form, in which error (1) is given as an example.

Error	(a) In Balance	(b) Difference	(c) Larger Column
(1)	No	$400	debit

E2-10   The accounts in the ledger of On-Time Delivery Service contain the following balances on July 31, 2001:

Accounts Receivable	$ 7,642	Prepaid Insurance	$ 1,968
Accounts Payable	7,396	Repair Expense	961
Cash	?	Service Revenue	8,610
Delivery Equipment	49,360	Dividends	700
Gas and Oil Expense	758	Common Stock	40,000
Insurance Expense	523	Wages Expense	4,428
Notes Payable	18,450	Wages Payable	815
		Retained Earnings	4,636

Instructions
Prepare a trial balance with the accounts arranged as illustrated in the chapter and fill in the missing amount for Cash.

PROBLEMS: SET A

P2-1A   The Fantasy Miniature Golf and Driving Range Inc. was opened on March 1 by Tom Zarle. The following selected events and transactions occurred during March:

Mar. 1 Invested $60,000 cash in the business in exchange for common stock.
      3 Purchased Aurora's Golf Land for $38,000 cash. The price consists of land, $23,000, building, $9,000, and equipment, $6,000. (Make one compound entry.)
      5 Advertised the opening of the driving range and miniature golf course, paying advertising expenses of $1,600.
      6 Paid cash $1,480 for a one-year insurance policy.
     10 Purchased golf clubs and other equipment for $1,600 from Tiger Company payable in 30 days.
     18 Received $800 in cash for golf fees earned.
     19 Sold 100 coupon books for $15.00 each. Each book contains 10 coupons that enable the holder to one round of miniature golf or to hit one bucket of golf balls.
     25 Declared and paid a $500 cash dividend.
     30 Paid salaries of $600.
     30 Paid Tiger Company in full.
     31 Received $800 for golf fees earned.

The company uses the following accounts: Cash; Prepaid Insurance; Land; Buildings; Equipment; Accounts Payable; Unearned Revenue; Common Stock; Dividends; Golf Revenue; Advertising Expense; and Salaries Expense.

Instructions
Journalize the March transactions.

Journalize transactions, post, and prepare trial balance.
(SO 2, 4, 6, 7)

P2–2A   David Chambers incorporated as a licensed architect. During the first month of the operation of his business, the following events and transactions occurred.

April   1   Invested $13,000 cash in exchange for common stock.
         1   Hired a secretary-receptionist at a salary of $300 per week payable monthly.
         2   Paid office rent for the month, $800.
         3   Purchased architectural supplies on account from A. U. Company, $1,500.
        10   Completed blueprints on a carport and billed client $900 for services.
        11   Received $500 cash advance from Mike Dominick for the design of a new home.
        20   Received $1,500 cash for services completed and delivered to Nancy Zarle.
        30   Paid secretary-receptionist for the month, $1,200.
        30   Paid $600 to A. U. Company on account.

Chambers uses the following chart of accounts: No. 101 Cash, No. 112 Accounts Receivable, No. 126 Supplies, No. 201 Accounts Payable, No. 205 Unearned Revenue, No. 311 Common Stock, No. 400 Service Revenue, No. 726 Salaries Expense, and No. 729 Rent Expense.

Instructions
(a) Journalize the transactions.
(b) Post to the ledger accounts.
(c) Prepare a trial balance on April 30, 2001.

Journalize transactions, post, and prepare a trial balance.
(SO 2, 4, 6, 7)

P2–3A   The Egyptian Theater Corp. owned by Tim Michel, will begin operations in March. The Egyptian will be unique in that it will show only triple or quadruple features of sequential theme movies. As of February 28, the ledger of Egyptian showed: No. 101 Cash $16,000; No. 140 Land $42,000; No. 145 Buildings (concession stand, projection room, ticket booth, and screen) $18,000; No. 157 Equipment $16,000; No. 201 Accounts Payable $12,000; and No. 311 Common Stock $80,000. During the month of March the following events and transactions occurred:

Mar.   2   Acquired the four *Star Wars* movies (*Star Wars, The Empire Strikes Back, The Return of the Jedi,* and *The Phantom Menace*) to be shown for the first 3 weeks of March. The film rental was $12,000; $4,000 was paid in cash and $8,000 will be paid on March 10.
        3   Ordered the four *Star Trek* movies to be shown the last 10 days of March. It will cost $400 per night.
        9   Received $6,500 cash from admissions.
       10   Paid balance due on *Star Wars* movies rental and $3,000 on February 28 accounts payable.
       11   Hired Cathy Everen to operate concession stand. Everen to pay Egyptian Theater 15% of gross receipts payable monthly.
       12   Paid advertising expenses $800.
       20   Received $7,200 cash from admissions.
       20   Received the *Star Trek* movies and paid the rental fee of $4,000.
       31   Paid salaries of $3,800.
       31   Received statement from Cathy Everen showing gross receipts from concessions of $8,000 and the balance due to Egyptian Theater of $1,200 for March. Everen paid one-half the balance due and will remit the remainder on April 5.
       31   Received $12,500 cash from admissions.

In addition to the accounts identified above, the chart of accounts includes: No. 112 Accounts Receivable, No. 405 Admission Revenue, No. 406 Concession Revenue, No. 610 Advertising Expense, No. 632 Film Rental Expense, and No. 726 Salaries Expense.

Instructions
(a) Enter the beginning balances to the ledger. Insert a check mark (✓) in the reference column of the ledger for the beginning balance.
(b) Journalize the March transactions.

(c) Post the March journal entries to the ledger. Assume that all entries are posted from page 1 of the journal.

(d) Prepare a trial balance on March 31, 2001.

P2–4A Bablad Brokerage Services was formed on May 1, 2001. The following transactions took place during its first month:

Transactions on May 1:

1. Shareholders invested $120,000 cash in the company, in exchange for stock.
2. Hired two employees to work in the warehouse. They will each be paid a salary of $2,000 per month.
3. Signed a two-year rental agreement on a warehouse; paid $48,000 cash in advance for the first year. (*Hint:* The portion of the cost related to May 2001 is an expense for this month.)
4. Purchased furniture and equipment costing $70,000. A cash payment of $20,000 was made immediately; the remainder will be paid in six months.
5. Paid $3,000 cash for a one-year insurance policy on the furniture and equipment. (*Hint:* The portion of the cost related to May 2001 is an expense for this month.)

Transactions during the remainder of the month:

6. Purchased basic office supplies for $1,000 cash.
7. Purchased more office supplies for $2,000 on account.
8. Total revenues earned were $30,000—$10,000 cash and $20,000 on account.
9. Paid $800 to suppliers on account.
10. Collected $5,000 from customers on account.
11. Received utility bills in the amount of $400, to be paid next month.
12. Paid the monthly salaries of the two employees, totalling $4,000.

Instructions

(a) Prepare journal entries to record each of the events listed.

(b) Post the journal entries to T accounts.

(c) Prepare a trial balance as of May31, 2001.

(d) Prepare an income statement and a statement of retained earnings for Bablad Brokerage Services for the month ended May 31, 2001, and a balance sheet as of May 31, 2001.

P2–5A The owner of a small auto repair company prepared the following trial balance (in thousands of dollars):

Journalize transactions, post, prepare a trial balance and financial statements.
(SO 4, 6, 7)

Prepare a correct trial balance.
(SO 2, 7)

ALDOUS AUTOMOTIVE SERVICES
Trial Balance
For the Year Ended December 31, 2001

	Debit	Credit
Machinery and Equipment		$ 89
Accounts Payable	$ 38	
Prepaid Rent		5
Cash	24	
Common Stock	42	
Wages Expense	76	
Advertising Expense		30
Prepaid Insurance	3	
Miscellaneous Expenses	49	
Note Payable	45	
Service Revenues		202
Dividends	20	
Accounts Receivable		31
	$297	$357

Instructions

(a) Identify the errors in the trial balance presented above. Be specific.

(b) Prepare a corrected trial balance for Aldous Automotive Services.

PROBLEMS: SET B

••

Journalize a series of transactions (SO 2, 4)

P2–1B   Adventure Park Corp. was started on April 1 by George Lukas. The following selected events and transactions occurred during April.

Apr. 1 Invested $80,000 cash in the business in exchange for common stock.
       4 Purchased land costing $40,000 for cash.
       8 Incurred advertising expense of $1,800 on account.
      11 Paid salaries to employees $1,500.
      12 Hired park manager at a salary of $4,000 per month, effective May 1.
      13 Paid $1,500 for a one-year insurance policy.
      17 Declared and paid a $600 cash dividend.
      20 Received $5,700 in cash for admission fees.
      25 Sold 100 coupon books for $25 each. Each book contains 10 coupons that entitle the holder to one admission to the park.
      30 Received $5,900 in cash admission fees.
      30 Paid $700 on account for advertising incurred on April 8.

Adventure uses the following accounts: Cash; Prepaid Insurance; Land; Accounts Payable; Unearned Admissions; Common Stock; Dividends; Admission Revenue; Advertising Expense; and Salaries Expense.

Instructions
Journalize the April transactions.

Journalize transactions, post, and prepare a trial balance. (SO 2, 4, 6, 7)

P2–2B   Liam Neeson is a licensed incorporated CPA. During the first month of operations of the business, the following events and transactions occurred:

May 1 Invested $42,000 cash in exchange for common stock.
      2 Hired a secretary-receptionist at a salary of $1,500 per month.
      3 Purchased $1,200 of supplies on account from Jedi Supply Company.
      7 Paid office rent of $900 for the month.
     11 Completed a tax assignment and billed client $1,100 for services rendered.
     12 Received $3,500 advance on a management consulting engagement.
     17 Received cash of $1,200 for services completed for Nostalgia Co.
     31 Paid secretary-receptionist $1,500 salary for the month.
     31 Paid 40% of balance due Jedi Supply Company.

The company uses the following chart of accounts: No. 101 Cash, No. 112 Accounts Receivable, No. 126 Supplies, No. 201 Accounts Payable, No. 205 Unearned Revenue, No. 311 Common Stock, No. 400 Service Revenue, No. 726 Salaries Expense, and No. 729 Rent Expense.

Instructions
(a) Journalize the transactions.
(b) Post to the ledger accounts.
(c) Prepare a trial balance on May 31, 2001.

Journalize transactions, post, and prepare a trial balance. (SO 2, 4, 6, 7)

P2–3B   Chewbacca Theater Inc. opens on April 1. All facilities were completed on March 31. At this time, the ledger showed: No. 101 Cash $6,000; No. 140 Land $10,000; No. 145 Buildings (concession stand, projection room, ticket booth, and screen) $8,000; No. 157 Equipment $6,000; No. 201 Accounts Payable $2,000; No. 275 Mortgage Payable $8,000; and No. 311 Common Stock $20,000. During April, the following events and transactions occurred.

Apr. 2 Paid film rental of $800 on first movie.
       3 Ordered two additional films at $500 each.
       9 Received $1,800 cash from admissions.
      10 Made $2,000 payment on mortgage and $1,000 on accounts payable.
      11 Hired Jake Lloyd to operate concession stand. Jake Lloyd to pay Chewbacca Theater 17% of gross receipts payable monthly.
      12 Paid advertising expenses $300.
      20 Received one of the films ordered on April 3 and was billed $500. The film will be shown in April.
      25 Received $4,200 cash from admissions.
      29 Paid salaries $1,600.

30 Received statement from Jake Lloyd showing gross receipts of $1,000 and the balance due to Chewbacca Theater of $170 for April. Jake Lloyd paid one-half of the balance due and will remit the remainder on May 5.

30 Prepaid $700 rental on special film to be run in May.

In addition to the accounts identified above, the chart of accounts shows: No. 112 Accounts Receivable, No. 136 Prepaid Rentals, No. 405 Admission Revenue, No. 406 Concession Revenue, No. 610 Advertising Expense, No. 632 Film Rental Expense, and No. 726 Salaries Expense.

Instructions

(a) Enter the beginning balances in the ledger as of April 1. Insert a check mark (✓) in the reference column of the ledger for the beginning balance.

(b) Journalize the April transactions.

(c) Post the April journal entries to the ledger. Assume that all entries are posted from page 1 of the journal.

(d) Prepare a trial balance on April 30, 2001.

P2–4B Steven Jobe owns and manages a computer repair service, which had the following trial balance on December 31, 2000 (the end of its fiscal year):

BYTE REPAIR SERVICE
Trial Balance
December 31, 2000

	Debit	Credit
Cash	$ 8,000	
Accounts Receivable	15,000	
Parts Inventory	13,000	
Prepaid Rent	3,000	
Shop Equipment	21,000	
Accounts Payable		$19,000
Common Stock		40,000
Retained Earnings		1,000
	$60,000	$60,000

Summarized transactions for January 2001 were as follows:

1. Advertising costs, paid in cash, $1,000.
2. Additional repair parts inventory acquired on account, $3,000.
3. Miscellaneous expenses, paid in cash, $2,000.
4. Cash collected from customers on account, $13,000.
5. Cash paid to creditors on account, $15,000.
6. Repair parts used during January, $4,000. (*Hint:* Debit this to Repair Parts Expense.)
7. Repair services performed during January: for cash, $4,000; on account, $9,000.
8. Wages for January, paid in cash, $3,000.
9. Rent expense for January recorded. However, no cash was paid out for rent during January. A rent payment had been made for three months, in advance, on December 1, 2000, in the amount of $4,500.
10. Dividends paid during January were $2,000.

Instructions

(a) Explain why the December 31, 2000, balance in the Prepaid Rent account is $3,000. Refer to the trial balance and item (9) above.

(b) Open T accounts for each of the accounts listed in the trial balance, and enter the opening balances for 2001.

(c) Prepare journal entries to record each of the January transactions.

(d) Post the journal entries to the accounts in the ledger.

(e) Prepare a trial balance as of January 31, 2001.

(f) Determine the total assets as of January 31, 2001. (It is not nelcessary to prepare a balance sheet; simply list the relevant amounts from the trial balance, and calculate the total.)

(g) Determine the net income or loss for the month of January 2001. (It is not necessary to prepare an income statement; simply list the relevant amounts from the trial balance, and calculate the amount of the net income or loss.)

Prepare a correct trial balance.
(SO 7)

P2–5B The trial balance of the Pompeii Corporation shown below does not balance.

POMPEII CORPORATION
Trial Balance
May 31, 2001

	Debit	Credit
Cash	$ 5,850	
Accounts Receivable		$ 2,750
Prepaid Insurance	700	
Equipment	8,000	
Accounts Payable		4,500
Property Taxes Payable	560	
Common Stock		11,700
Service Revenue	6,690	
Salaries Expense	4,200	
Advertising Expense		1,100
Property Tax Expense	800	
	$26,800	$20,050

Your review of the ledger reveals that each account has a normal balance. You also discover the following errors.

1. The totals of the debit sides of Prepaid Insurance, Accounts Payable, and Property Tax Expense were each understated $100.
2. Transposition errors were made in Accounts Receivable and Service Revenue. Based on postings made, the correct balances were $2,570 and $6,960, respectively.
3. A debit posting to Salaries Expense of $200 was omitted.
4. A $700 cash dividend by the corporation was debited to Common Stock for $700 and credited to Cash for $700.
5. A $420 purchase of supplies on account was debited to Equipment for $420 and credited to Cash for $420.
6. A cash payment of $250 for advertising was debited to Advertising Expense for $25 and credited to Cash for $25.
7. A collection from a customer for $210 was debited to Cash for $210 and credited to Accounts Payable for $210.

Instructions
Prepare a correct trial balance. (Note: The chart of accounts includes the following: Dividends; Supplies; and Supplies Expense.)

BROADENING YOUR PERSPECTIVE

FINANCIAL REPORTING AND ANALYSIS

FINANCIAL REPORTING PROBLEM: Kellogg Company

BYP2–1 The financial statements and notes of Kellogg Company, presented in Appendix A, contain the following selected accounts, stated in millions of dollars:

Accounts Payable	$386.9	Notes Payable	$620.4
Accounts Receivable	693.0	Interest Expense	119.5
Property, net	2,888.8	Inventories	451.4

Instructions
(a) Answer the following questions:
   1. What is the increase and decrease side for each account?
   2. What is the normal balance for each account?
(b) Identify the probable other account in the transaction and the effect on that account when:
   1. Accounts Receivable is decreased.
   2. Accounts Payable is decreased.
   3. Inventories are increased.
(c) Identify the other account(s) that ordinarily would be involved when:
   1. Interest Expense is increased.
   2. Property is increased.

COMPARATIVE ANALYSIS PROBLEM: Kellogg Company vs. General Mills

BYP2–2 Kellogg's financial statements are presented in Appendix A; General Mills's financial statements are presented in Appendix B.

Instructions
(a) Based on the information contained in these financial statements, determine the normal balance of the listed account for each company:

Kellogg's	General Mills's
1. Inventories	1. Accounts receivable
2. Property, net	2. Land
3. Accounts payable	3. Depreciation expense
4. Interest expense	4. Sales (revenue)

(b) Identify the other account ordinarily involved when:
   1. Accounts receivable is increased.
   2. Accrued payroll is decreased.
   3. Property is increased.
   4. Interest expense is increased.

RESEARCH ASSIGNMENT

BYP2–3 Several commonly available indexes enable individuals to locate articles previously included in numerous business publications and periodicals. Articles can generally be searched for by company or by subject matter. Four common indexes are *The Wall Stret Journal Index, Business Abstracts* (formerly the *Business Periodical Index*), *Predicasts F&S Index,* and *ABI/Inform.* (*Note:* Your library may have hard copy or CD-ROM versions of these indexes.)

Instructions

Use one of these resources to find an article about a New York Stock Exchange company of your choosing. Read the article and answer the following questions.

(a) What is the article about?
(b) What company-specific information is included in the article?
(c) Is the article related to anything you read in Chapter 2 of your accounting textbook?
(d) Identify any accounting-related issues discussed in the article.

INTERPRETING FINANCIAL STATEMENTS: Bob Evans Farms, Inc.

BYP2-4   Bob Evans Farms, Inc. operates 354 restaurants and several food processing plants. The food processing plants primarily process pork into sausage, some of which is used in the restaurants, and some of which is sold to grocery stores. The food processing plants also produce "fast-food"-type frozen sandwiches, which are marketed to grocery stores.

   The balance sheet of Bob Evans Farms showed a cash balance of $10 million and trade accounts receivable of $16 million. The notes to the financial statements revealed that there was a line of credit available of $63 million, of which $26 million was then outstanding.

Instructions

(a) Explain why most of the trade accounts receivable would probably not pertain to the restaurant business.
(b) What kind of individuals or companies would you expect to find in the individual accounts receivable accounts?
(c) Why might Bob Evans Farms be keeping the $10 million in cash, instead of using most of it, for example $8 million, to help pay off the line of credit debt?

REAL-WORLD FOCUS: Automatic Security Holdings

BYP2-5   **Automated Security Holdings** operates multinationally, with principal markets in the United States and the United Kingdom. The company designs, produces, installs, and maintains security systems to safeguard life and property from a wide range of hazards. The markets for these security products include commercial, industrial, and residential customers.

   The following notes to the financial statements identify a few of the accounts found in the general ledger.

AUTOMATED SECURITY HOLDINGS
Notes to the Financial Statements

	November 30,	
	Previous Year	Current Year
	(in thousands)	
Income Tax Payable	$ 3,929	$ 3,919
Accounts Payable	6,499	9,620
Salaries Expense	16,353	9,213
Cash	4,749	2,869
Unearned Revenue	1,211	1,434
Notes Payable	52,000	40,000
Prepaid Insurance	1,333	2,000

Instructions

(a) Identify the accounts of Automated Security Holdings that have debit balances in the trial balance.
(b) What date has Automated Security Holdings adopted for its accounting year-end? Why might a company use some date other than December 31 as its year-end date?
(c) Are the accounts listed above in the order in which they would appear in Automated Security Holdings' general ledger? Explain.

CRITICAL THINKING

GROUP DECISION CASE

BYP2–6 A student works in the summer for a heating and air-conditioning installation company, while the staff accountant is on vacation. The student prepared the following financial statement:

HOT & COLD COMPANY
Statement of Revenues & Expenditures
December 31, 1999

Add Revenues:		
Installation fees		$700,000
Gain from increase in market value		
of the company's land during the year		30,000
		$730,000
Deduct Expenditures:		
Lease expense (building and vehicles)	$ 60,000	
Land purchased during the year	90,000	
Utilities expense	10,000	
Salaries and wages expense	215,000	
Parts and supplies on hand	95,000	
Parts and supplies used	80,000	
Dividends	50,000	
Advertising expense	20,000	
Miscellaneous expenses	40,000	
		660,000
Profit		$70,000

Instruction
With the class divided into groups, identify, and briefly explain any deficiencies in the above financial statement.

COMMUNICATION ACTIVITY

BYP2–7 Merlynn's Maid Company offers home cleaning service. Two recurring transactions for the company are billing customers for services rendered and paying employee salaries. For example, on March 15 bills totaling $6,000 were sent to customers and $2,000 was paid in salaries to employees.

Instructions
Write a memorandum to your instructor that explains and illustrates the steps in the recording process for each of the March 15 transactions. Use the format illustrated in the text under the heading, "The Recording Process Illustrated" (pp. 59–64).

ETHICS CASE

BYP2–8 Candy Mowinski is the assistant chief accountant at Galactic Company, a manufacturer of computer chips and cellular phones. The company presently has total sales of $20 million. It is the end of the first quarter and Candy is hurriedly trying to prepare a general ledger trial balance so that quarterly financial statements can be prepared and released to management and the regulatory agencies. The total credits on the trial balance exceed the debits by $1,000. In order to meet the 4 p.m. deadline, Candy decides to force the debits and credits to balance by adding the amount of the difference to the Equipment account. She chose Equipment because it is one of the larger account balances: percentage-wise it will be the least misstated. Candy plugs the difference! She believes that the difference is quite small and will not affect anyone's decisions. She wishes that she had another few days to find the error but realizes that the financial statements are already late.

Instructions
  (a) Who are the stakeholders in this situation?
  (b) What are the ethical issues involved in this case?
  (c) What are Candy's alternatives?

SURFING THE NET

BYP2–9   Much information about specific companies is available on the World Wide Web. This information includes basic descriptions of the company's location, activities, industry, financial health, and financial performance.

Address: http://biz.yahoo.com/i (or go to www.wiley.com/college/weygandt)

Steps:
  1. Type in a company name, or use index to find company name.
  2. Choose **Profile.** Perform instructions (a)–(c) below.
  3. Click on the company's specific industry to identify competitors. Perform instructions (d)–(g) below.

Instructions
Answer the following questions:

  (a) What was the company's net income?
  (b) What was the company's total sales?
  (c) What is the company's industry?
  (d) What are the names of four of the company's competitors?
  (e) Choose one of these competitors.
  (f) What is this competitor's name? What were its sales? What was its net income?
  (g) Which of these two companies is larger by size of sales? Which one reported higher net income?

Answers to Self-Study Questions
1. b   2. c   3. d   4. d   5. b   6. a   7. c   8. d   9. a   10. c

---

Answer to Kellogg Review It Question 4, p. 52
Cash—debit; accounts payable—credit; interest expense—debit.

   Remember to go back to the Navigator box on the chapter-opening page and check off your completed work.

CONCEPTS FOR REVIEW

Before studying this chapter, you should know, or, if necessary, review:

a. What a double-entry system is. (Ch. 2, p. 44)
b. How to increase or decrease assets, liabilities, and stockholders' equity using debit and credit procedures. (Ch. 2, pp. 48–50)
c. How to journalize a transaction. (Ch. 2, pp. 53–55)
d. How to post a transaction. (Ch. 2, pp. 57–58)
e. How to prepare a trial balance. (Ch. 2, pp. 66–67)

THE NAVIGATOR

FEATURE STORY

Timing is Everything

In Chapter 1 you learned a neat little formula: Net income = revenues − expenses. And in Chapter 2 you learned some nice, orderly rules for recording corporate revenue and expense transactions. Guess what? Things are not really that nice and neat. In fact, it is often difficult to determine in what time period some revenues and expenses should be reported. And, in measuring net income, timing is everything.

There are rules that give guidance on these issues, but occasionally these rules are overlooked, misinterpreted, or even intentionally ignored. Consider the following examples:

• McKesson HBOC, one of the largest prescription drug distributors, restated its first-quarter, 1999, earnings because $26.2 million included in healthcare software sales weren't final and should not have been recorded. This negative surprise caused McKesson's share price to plummet 48% overnight, from $65.75 to $34.50, wiping out $9 billion in the market value of its stock.

• Cambridge Biotech Corp., which develops vaccines and diagnostic tests for humans and animals, said that it reported revenue from transactions that "don't appear to be bona fide."

• Media Vision Technology Inc., a maker of sound and animation equipment for computers, was accused of operating a "phantom" warehouse to hide inventory for returned products already recorded as sales.

• Penguin USA, a book publisher, said that it understated expenses in a number of years because it failed to report expenses for discounts given to customers for paying early.

In each case, accrual accounting concepts were violated. That is, revenues or expenses were not recorded in the proper period, which had a substantial impact on reported income. Their timing was off!

THE NAVIGATOR

CHAPTER 3

ADJUSTING THE ACCOUNTS

THE NAVIGATOR ✔

- ■ Understand *Concepts for Review* ☐
- ■ Read *Feature Story* ☐
- ■ Scan *Study Objectives* ☐
- ■ Read *Preview* ☐
- ■ Read text and answer *Before You Go On*
  p. 95 ☐ p. 102 ☐ p. 107 ☐ p. 113 ☐
- ■ Work *Demonstration Problem* ☐
- ■ Review *Summary of Study Objectives* ☐
- ■ Answer *Self-Study Questions* ☐
- ■ Complete assignments ☐

STUDY OBJECTIVES

After studying this chapter, you should be able to:

1. *Explain the time period assumption.*
2. *Distinguish between the revenue recognition principle and the matching principle.*
3. *Explain why adjusting entries are needed.*
4. *Identify the major types of adjusting entries.*
5. *Prepare adjusting entries for prepayments.*
6. *Prepare adjusting entries for accruals.*
7. *Describe the nature and purpose of an adjusted trial balance.*
8. *Explain the accrual basis of accounting.*

THE NAVIGATOR

*I*n Chapter 2 we examined the basic steps in the recording process through the preparation of the trial balance. Before we will be ready to prepare financial statements from the trial balance, additional steps need to be taken. The timing mismatch between revenues and expenses of the four companies mentioned in our Feature Story illustrates the types of situations that make these additional steps necessary. For example, long-lived assets purchased or constructed in prior accounting years are being used to produce goods and provide services in the current year. What portion of these assets' costs, if any, should be recognized as an expense of the current period? Before financial statements can be prepared, this and other questions relating to the recognition of revenues and expenses must be answered. With the answers in hand, the relevant account balances can then be adjusted.

The content and organization of the chapter are as follows:

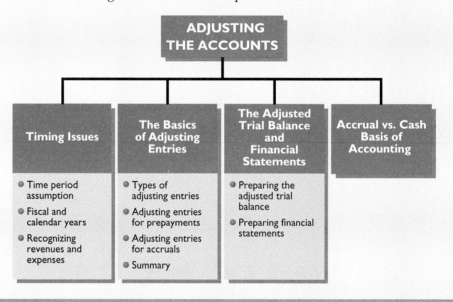

THE NAVIGATOR

TIMING ISSUES

1

STUDY

OBJECTIVE

Explain the time period assumption.

No adjustments would be necessary if we waited to prepare financial statements until a company ended its operations. At that point, we could readily determine its final balance sheet and the amount of lifetime income it earned. The following anecdote illustrates one way to compute lifetime income:

> A grocery store owner from the old country kept his accounts payable on a spindle, accounts receivable on a note pad, and cash in a cigar box. His daughter, having just passed the CPA exam, chided the father: "I don't understand how you can run your business this way. How do you know what your profits are?"
>
> "Well," the father replied, "when I got off the boat 40 years ago, I had nothing but the pants I was wearing. Today your brother is a doctor, your sister is a college professor, and you are a CPA. Your mother and I have a nice car, a well-furnished house, and a lake home. We have a good busi-

ness and everything is paid for. So, you add all that together, subtract the pants, and there's your profit."

Selecting an Accounting Time Period

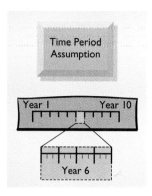

Although the old grocer may be correct in his evaluation, it is impractical to wait so long for the results of operations. All entities, from the corner grocery, to a global company like Kellogg, to your college or university, find it desirable and necessary to report the results of their activities more frequently. For example, management usually wants monthly financial statements, and the Internal Revenue Service requires all businesses to file annual tax returns. As a consequence, **accountants make the assumption that the economic life of a business can be divided into artificial time periods**. This assumption is referred to as the time period assumption.

Many business transactions affect more than one of these arbitrary time periods. For example, Farmer Brown's milking machine bought in 1998 and the airplanes purchased by Delta Air Lines 5 years ago are still in use today. Therefore it is necessary to determine the relevance of each business transaction to specific accounting periods. Doing so may involve subjective judgments and estimates. Generally, the shorter the time period (e.g., a month or a quarter of a year), the more difficult it becomes to determine the proper adjustments to be made.

ALTERNATIVE TERMINOLOGY
The time period assumption is also called the *periodicity assumption.*

Fiscal and Calendar Years

Both small and large companies prepare financial statements on a periodic basis in order to assess their financial condition and results of operations. **Accounting time periods are generally a month, a quarter, or a year.** Monthly and quarterly time periods are often referred to as interim periods. Most large companies are required to prepare both interim (quarterly) and annual financial statements.

An accounting time period that is one year in length is referred to as a fiscal year. A fiscal year usually begins with the first day of a month and ends 12 months later on the last day of a month. The accounting period used by most businesses coincides with the calendar year (January 1 to December 31). Companies whose fiscal year differs from the calendar year include Delta Air Lines, June 30; Walt Disney Productions, September 30; Kmart Corp., January 31; and Dunkin' Donuts, Inc., October 31. Your university's fiscal year is probably July 1 through June 30, which is typical of universities and governmental agencies.

Recognizing Revenues and Expenses

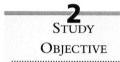

Determining the amount of revenues and expenses to be reported in a given accounting period can be difficult. Therefore, accountants have developed two principles as part of generally accepted accounting principles (GAAP) that help in this determination: the revenue recognition principle and the matching principle.

The revenue recognition principle dictates that revenue be recognized in the accounting period in which it is earned. **In a service enterprise, revenue is considered to be earned at the time the service is performed.** To illustrate, assume that a dry cleaning business cleans clothing on June 30 but customers do not claim and pay for their clothes until the first week of July. Under the revenue recognition principle, revenue is earned in June when the service is performed and not in July when the cash is received. At June 30, the dry cleaner would report a receivable on its balance sheet and revenue in its income statement for the service performed.

In recognizing expenses, accountants follow the approach of "let the expenses follow the revenues." Thus, expense recognition is tied to revenue recognition. In the preceding example, this principle means that the salary expense incurred

2
STUDY
OBJECTIVE
....
Distinguish between the revenue recognition principle and the matching principle.

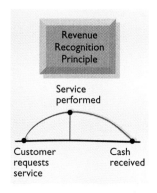

ACCOUNTING IN ACTION
Business Insight

Suppose you are a filmmaker like George Lucas and spend $11 million to produce a film such as *StarWars.* Over what period should the cost be expensed? It should be expensed over the economic life of the film. But what is its economic life? The filmmaker must estimate how much revenue will be earned from box office sales, video sales, television, and games and toys—a period that could be less than a year or more than 20 years, as is the case for Twentieth Century Fox's *StarWars.* Originally released in 1977, and rereleased in 1997, domestic revenues total nearly $500 million for *StarWars* and continue to grow. This situation demonstrates the difficulty of properly matching expenses to revenues.

Source: StarTrek Newsletter, 22.

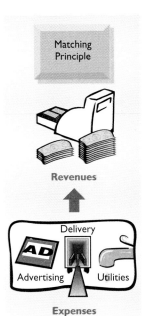

in performing the cleaning service on June 30 should be reported in the income statement for the same period in which the service revenue is recognized. The critical issue in expense recognition is when the expense makes its contribution to revenue. This may or may not be the same period in which the expense is paid. If the salary incurred on June 30 is not paid until July, the dry cleaner would report salaries payable on its June 30 balance sheet. The practice of expense recognition is referred to as the matching principle because it dictates that efforts (expenses) be matched with accomplishments (revenues).

Once the assumption is made that the economic life of a business can be divided into artificial time periods, it follows that the revenue recognition and matching principles can be applied. This one assumption and two principles thus provide guidelines as to when revenues and expenses should be reported. These relationships are shown in Illustration 3-1.

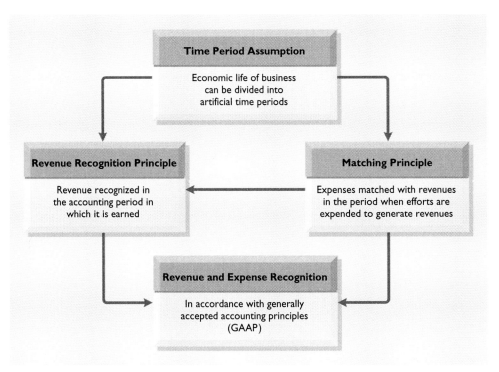

ILLUSTRATION 3-1

GAAP relationships in revenue and expense recognition

BEFORE YOU GO ON . . .

Review It

1. What is the relevance of the time period assumption to accounting?
2. What are the revenue recognition and matching principles?

....

THE BASICS OF ADJUSTING ENTRIES

In order for revenues to be recorded in the period in which they are earned, and for expenses to be recognized in the period in which they are incurred, adjusting entries are made at the end of the accounting period. In short, adjusting entries **are needed to ensure that the revenue recognition and matching principles are followed.**

The use of adjusting entries makes it possible to report on the balance sheet the appropriate assets, liabilities, and stockholders' equity at the statement date and to report on the income statement the proper net income (or loss) for the period. However, the trial balance—the first pulling together of the transaction data—may not contain up-to-date and complete data. This is true for the following reasons:

1. Some events are not journalized daily because it is inexpedient to do so. Examples are the consumption of supplies and the earning of wages by employees.
2. Some costs are not journalized during the accounting period because these costs expire with the passage of time rather than as a result of recurring daily transactions. Examples of such costs are building and equipment deterioration and rent and insurance.
3. Some items may be unrecorded. An example is a utility service bill that will not be received until the next accounting period.

Adjusting entries are required every time financial statements are prepared. An essential starting point is an analysis of each account in the trial balance to determine whether it is complete and up-to-date for financial statement purposes. The analysis requires a thorough understanding of the company's operations and the interrelationship of accounts. The preparation of adjusting entries is often an involved process. In accumulating the adjustment data, the company may need to make inventory counts of supplies and repair parts. Also it may be desirable to prepare supporting schedules of insurance policies, rental agreements, and other contractual commitments. Adjustments are often prepared after the balance sheet date. However, the adjusting entries are dated as of the balance sheet date.

Types of Adjusting Entries

Adjusting entries can be classified as either prepayments or accruals. Each of these classes has two subcategories as shown in Illustration 3-2:

3
STUDY
OBJECTIVE
....
Explain why adjusting entries are needed.

HELPFUL HINT
Adjusting entries are needed to enable financial statements to be in conformity with GAAP.

4
STUDY
OBJECTIVE
....
Identify the major types of adjusting entries.

ILLUSTRATION 3-2

*Categories of adjusting
entries*

Prepayments

1. **Prepaid Expenses.** Expenses paid in cash and recorded as assets before they are used or consumed.
2. **Unearned Revenues.** Cash received and recorded as liabilities before revenue is earned.

Accruals

1. **Accrued Revenues.** Revenues earned but not yet received in cash or recorded.
2. **Accrued Expenses.** Expenses incurred but not yet paid in cash or recorded.

Specific examples and explanations of each type of adjustment are given in subsequent sections. Each example is based on the October 31 trial balance of Pioneer Advertising Agency Inc. reproduced in Illustration 3-3 from the illustration in Chapter 2.

ILLUSTRATION 3-3

Trial balance

PIONEER ADVERTISING AGENCY INC.
Trial Balance
October 31, 2001

	Debit	Credit
Cash	$15,200	
Advertising Supplies	2,500	
Prepaid Insurance	600	
Office Equipment	5,000	
Notes Payable		$ 5,000
Accounts Payable		2,500
Unearned Revenue		1,200
Common Stock		10,000
Retained Earnings		–0–
Dividends	500	
Service Revenue		10,000
Salaries Expense	4,000	
Rent Expense	900	
	$28,700	$28,700

We assume that Pioneer Advertising uses an accounting period of one month. Thus, monthly adjusting entries will be made. The entries will be dated October 31.

Adjusting Entries for Prepayments

As indicated earlier, prepayments are either prepaid expenses or unearned revenues. Adjusting entries for prepayments are required at the statement date to record the portion of the prepayment that represents the **expense incurred or the revenue earned** in the current accounting period. Assuming an adjustment is needed for both types of prepayments, the asset and liability are overstated and the related expense and revenue are understated. For example, in the trial balance, the balance in the asset, Supplies, shows only supplies purchased. This balance is overstated; the related expense account, Supplies Expense, is understated because the cost of supplies used has not been recognized. Thus the adjusting entry for prepayments will decrease a balance sheet account and increase an income statement account. The effects of adjusting entries for prepayments are graphically depicted in Illustration 3-4.

5
STUDY
OBJECTIVE
....

Prepare adjusting entries for prepayments.

HELPFUL HINT
Remember that credits decrease assets and increase revenues. Debits increase expenses and decrease liabilities.

ILLUSTRATION 3-4

Adjusting entries for prepayments

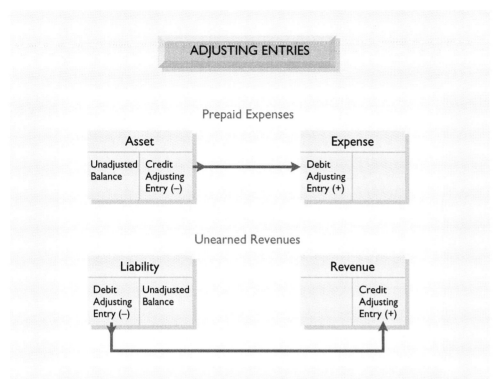

Illustration 3-4: ADJUSTING ENTRIES

Prepaid Expenses

Asset
| Unadjusted Balance | Credit Adjusting Entry (−) |

→ Expense
| Debit Adjusting Entry (+) | |

Unearned Revenues

Liability
| Debit Adjusting Entry (−) | Unadjusted Balance |

Revenue
| | Credit Adjusting Entry (+) |

Prepaid Expenses

As stated on page 96, expenses paid in cash and recorded as assets before they are used or consumed are identified as prepaid expenses. When a cost is prepaid, an asset account is debited to show the service or benefit that will be received in the future. Prepayments often occur in regard to insurance, supplies, advertising, and rent. In addition, prepayments are made when buildings and equipment are purchased.

Prepaid expenses expire either with the passage of time (e.g., rent and insurance) or through use and consumption (e.g., supplies). The expiration of these costs does not require daily recurring entries, which would be unnecessary and impractical. Accordingly, it is customary to postpone the recognition of such cost expirations until financial statements are prepared. At each statement date, adjusting entries are made to record the expenses that apply to the current accounting period and to show the unexpired costs in the asset accounts.

Prior to adjustment, assets are overstated and expenses are understated. **Thus, the prepaid expense adjusting entry results in a debit to an expense account and a credit to an asset account.**

Supplies.   Several different types of supplies are used in a business enterprise. For example, a CPA firm will have **office supplies** such as stationery, envelopes, and accounting paper. In contrast, an advertising firm will have **advertising supplies** such as graph paper, video film, and poster paper. Supplies are generally debited to an asset account when they are acquired. During the course of operations, supplies are depleted or entirely consumed. However, recognition of supplies used is deferred until the adjustment process when a physical inventory (count) of supplies is taken. The difference between the balance in the Supplies (asset) account and the cost of supplies on hand represents the supplies used (expense) for the period.

Supplies

Oct.5

Supplies purchased; record asset

Oct.31
Supplies used; record supplies expense

Pioneer Advertising Agency Inc. purchased advertising supplies costing $2,500 on October 5. The debit was made to the asset Advertising Supplies, and this account shows a balance of $2,500 in the October 31 trial balance. An inventory count at the close of business on October 31 reveals that $1,000 of supplies are still on hand. Thus, the cost of supplies used is $1,500 ($2,500 − $1,000), and the following adjusting entry is made:

Equation Analysis
A = L + SE
−1,500   −1,500

Oct. 31	Advertising Supplies Expense	1,500	
	Advertising Supplies		1,500
	(To record supplies used)		

ACCOUNTING IN ACTION
Business Insight

The costs of advertising on radio, television, and magazines for such products as burgers, bleaches, athletic shoes, and so on are sometimes considered prepayments. As a manager for Procter & Gamble noted, "If we run a long ad campaign for soap and bleach, we sometimes report the costs as prepayments if we think we'll receive sales benefits from the campaign down the road." Presently it is a judgment call whether these costs should be prepayments or expenses in the current period. Developing guidelines consistent with the matching principle is difficult because situations vary widely from company to company. The issue is important since the outlays for advertising can be substantial. Recent big spenders: Sears Roebuck spent $1.28 billion, Nike $978 million, Kellogg $695 million, and McDonald's $503 million.

After the adjusting entry is posted, the two supplies accounts in T-account form show:

ILLUSTRATION 3-5

Supplies accounts after adjustments

Advertising Supplies				Advertising Supplies Expense		
10/5	2,500	10/31 **Adj.**	1,500	10/31 **Adj.**	1,500	
10/31 **Bal.**	1,000					

The asset account Advertising Supplies now shows a balance of $1,000, which is equal to the cost of supplies on hand at the statement date. In addition, Advertising Supplies Expense shows a balance of $1,500, which equals the cost of supplies used in October. **If the adjusting entry is not made, October expenses will be understated and net income overstated by $1,500. Moreover, both assets and stockholders' equity will be overstated by $1,500 on the October 31 balance sheet.**

Insurance.   Most companies have fire and theft insurance on merchandise and equipment, personal liability insurance for accidents suffered by customers, and automobile insurance on company cars and trucks. The cost of insurance protection is determined by the payment of insurance premiums. The term and coverage are specified in the insurance policy. The minimum term is usually one year, but three- to five-year terms are available and offer lower annual premiums. Insurance premiums normally are charged to the asset account Prepaid Insurance when paid. At the financial statement date it is necessary to debit Insurance Expense and credit Prepaid Insurance for the cost that has expired during the period.

On October 4, Pioneer Advertising Agency Inc. paid $600 for a one-year fire insurance policy. The effective date of coverage was October 1. The pre-

Insurance

Oct.4

Insurance purchased; record asset

Insurance Policy			
Oct	Nov	Dec	Jan
$50	$50	$50	$50
Feb	March	April	May
$50	$50	$50	$50
June	July	Aug	Sept
$50	$50	$50	$50
I YEAR $600			

Oct.31

Insurance expired; record insurance expense

mium was charged to Prepaid Insurance when it was paid, and this account shows a balance of $600 in the October 31 trial balance. An analysis of the policy reveals that $50 ($600 ÷ 12) of insurance expires each month. Thus, the following adjusting entry is made:

Oct. 31	Insurance Expense	50	
	Prepaid Insurance		50
	(To record insurance expired)		

A	=	L	+	SE
−50				−50

After the adjusting entry is posted, the accounts show:

ILLUSTRATION 3-6

Insurance accounts after adjustment

Prepaid Insurance						Insurance Expense			
10/4		600	10/31 **Adj.**	50		10/31 **Adj.**	50		
10/31 Bal.		550							

The asset Prepaid Insurance shows a balance of $550, which represents the unexpired cost applicable to the remaining 11 months of coverage. At the same time, the balance in Insurance Expense is equal to the insurance cost that has expired in October. **If this adjustment is not made, October expenses will be understated by $50 and net income overstated by $50. Moreover, both assets and stockholders' equity also will be overstated by $50 on the October 31 balance sheet.**

Depreciation.   A business enterprise typically owns a variety of productive facilities such as buildings, equipment, and motor vehicles. These assets provide service for a number of years. The term of service is commonly referred to as the useful life of the asset. Because an asset such as a building is expected to provide service for many years, it is recorded as an asset, rather than an expense, in the year it is acquired. As explained in Chapter 1, such assets are recorded at cost, as required by the cost principle.

HELPFUL HINT
Depreciation is an estimate—one of many estimates inherent in accounting.

According to the matching principle, a portion of the cost of a long-lived asset should be reported as an expense during each period of the asset's useful life. Depreciation is the process of allocating the cost of an asset to expense over its useful life in a rational and systematic manner.

Need for Depreciation Adjustment.   From an accounting standpoint, the acquisition of productive facilities is viewed essentially as a long-term prepayment for services. The need for making periodic adjusting entries for depreciation is, therefore, the same as described before for other prepaid expenses; that is, to recognize the cost that has expired (expense) during the period and to report the unexpired cost (asset) at the end of the period.

In determining the useful life of a productive facility, the primary causes of depreciation are actual use, deterioration due to the elements, and obsolescence. At the time an asset is acquired, the effects of these factors cannot be known with certainty, so they must be estimated. Thus, you should recognize that depreciation is an estimate rather than a factual measurement of the cost that has expired. A common procedure in computing depreciation expense is to divide the cost of the asset by its useful life. For example, if cost is $10,000 and useful life is expected to be 10 years, annual depreciation is $1,000.[1]

Depreciation

Oct. 1

Office equipment purchased; record asset

Office Equipment			
Oct	Nov	Dec	Jan
$40	$40	$40	$40
Feb	March	April	May
$40	$40	$40	$40
June	July	Aug	Sept
$40	$40	$40	$40
Depreciation = $480/year			

Oct.31
  Depreciation recognized; record depreciation expense

---

[1]Additional consideration is given to computing depreciation expense in Chapter 10.

For Pioneer Advertising, depreciation on the office equipment is estimated to be $480 a year, or $40 per month. Accordingly, depreciation for October is recognized by the following adjusting entry:

Oct. 31	Depreciation Expense	40	
	Accumulated Depreciation—Office Equipment		40
	(To record monthly depreciation)		

After the adjusting entry is posted, the accounts show:

ILLUSTRATION 3-7

Accounts after adjustment for depreciation

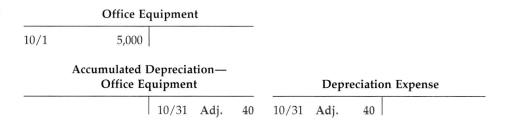

The balance in the accumulated depreciation account will increase $40 each month. Therefore, after journalizing and posting the adjusting entry at November 30, the balance will be $80.

Statement Presentation.   Accumulated Depreciation—Office Equipment is a contra asset account. A contra asset account is an account that is offset against an asset account on the balance sheet. This means that the accumulated depreciation account is offset against Office Equipment on the balance sheet and that its normal balance is a credit. This account is used instead of crediting Office Equipment in order to permit disclosure of **both the original cost** of the equipment **and the total cost that has expired to date**. In the balance sheet, Accumulated Depreciation—Office Equipment is deducted from the related asset account as follows:

HELPFUL HINT
All contra accounts have increases, decreases, and normal balances opposite to the account to which they relate.

ILLUSTRATION 3-8

Balance sheet presentation of accumulated depreciation

| Office equipment | $5,000 | |
| Less: Accumulated depreciation—office equipment | 40 | $4,960 |

The difference between the cost of any depreciable asset and its related accumulated depreciation is referred to as the book value of that asset. In Illustration 3-8, the book value of the equipment at the balance sheet date is $4,960. It is important to realize that the book value and the market value of the asset are generally two different values. The reason the two are different is that depreciation is not a matter of valuation but rather, a means of cost allocation.

ALTERNATIVE TERMINOLOGY
Book value is sometimes referred to as *carrying value* or *unexpired cost.*

Note also that depreciation expense identifies that portion of the asset's cost that has expired in October. As in the case of other prepaid adjustments, the omission of this adjusting entry would cause total assets, total stockholders' equity, and net income to be overstated and depreciation expense to be understated.

If additional equipment is involved, such as delivery or store equipment, or if the company has buildings, depreciation expense is recorded on each of these items. Related accumulated depreciation accounts also are established. These accumulated depreciation accounts would be described in the ledger as follows:

Accumulated Depreciation—Delivery Equipment; Accumulated Depreciation—Store Equipment; and Accumulated Depreciation—Buildings.

Unearned Revenues

As stated on page 96, cash received and recorded as liabilities before revenue is earned is called unearned revenues. Such items as rent, magazine subscriptions, and customer deposits for future service may result in unearned revenues. Airlines such as United, American, and Delta treat receipts from the sale of tickets as unearned revenue until the flight service is provided. Unearned revenues are the opposite of prepaid expenses. Indeed, unearned revenue on the books of one company is likely to be a prepayment on the books of the company that has made the advance payment. For example, if identical accounting periods are assumed, a landlord will have unearned rent revenue when a tenant has prepaid rent.

When the payment is received for services to be provided in a future accounting period, an unearned revenue (a liability) account should be credited to recognize the obligation that exists. Unearned revenues are subsequently earned through rendering service to a customer. During the accounting period it may not be practical to make daily recurring entries as the revenue is earned. In such cases, the recognition of earned revenue is delayed until the adjustment process. Then an adjusting entry is made to record the revenue that has been earned and to show the liability that remains. In the typical case, liabilities are overstated and revenues are understated prior to adjustment. Thus, **the adjusting entry for unearned revenues results in a debit (decrease) to a liability account and a credit (increase) to a revenue account**.

Pioneer Advertising Agency Inc. received $1,200 on October 2 from R. Knox for advertising services expected to be completed by December 31. The payment was credited to Unearned Revenue, and this account shows a balance of $1,200 in the October 31 trial balance. When analysis reveals that $400 of those fees has been earned in October, the following adjusting entry is made:

Unearned Revenues

Oct. 2

Cash is received in advance; liability is recorded

Oct. 31
Service is provided; revenue is recorded

ALTERNATIVE TERMINOLOGY
Unearned revenues is sometimes referred to as *deferred revenues.*

Oct. 31	Unearned Revenue	400	
	Service Revenue		400
	(To record revenue for services provided)		

A	=	L	+	SE
		−400		+400

After the adjusting entry is posted, the accounts show:

Unearned Revenue			
10/31 Adj. 400	10/2		1,200
	10/31 Bal.		800

Service Revenue			
	10/31 Bal.		10,000
	31 Adj.		400

ILLUSTRATION 3-9

Revenue accounts after prepayments adjustment

The liability Unearned Revenue now shows a balance of $800, which represents the remaining advertising services expected to be performed in the future. At the same time, Service Revenue shows total revenue earned in October of $10,400 ($10,000 + $400). **If this adjustment is not made, revenues and net income will be understated by $400 in the income statement. Moreover, liabilities will be overstated and stockholders' equity will be understated by $400 on the October 31 balance sheet.**

BEFORE YOU GO ON . . .

Review It

1. What are the four types of adjusting entries?
2. What is the effect on assets, stockholders' equity, expenses, and net income if a prepaid expense adjusting entry is not made?
3. What is the effect on liabilities, stockholders' equity, revenues, and net income if an unearned revenue adjusting entry is not made?

4. Using the Selected Financial Data section of Kellogg Company's financial statements what was the amount of depreciation and amortization expense for 1998 and 1997? The answer to this question is provided on page 136.

Do It

The ledger of Starwoids Inc. on March 31, 2001, includes the following selected accounts before adjusting entries are prepared:

	Debit	Credit
Prepaid Insurance	3,600	
Office Supplies	2,800	
Office Equipment	25,000	
Accumulated Depreciation—Office Equipment		5,000
Unearned Revenue		9,200

An analysis of the accounts shows the following:

1. Insurance expires at the rate of $100 per month.
2. Supplies on hand total $800.
3. The office equipment depreciates $200 a month.
4. One-half of the unearned revenue was earned in March.

Prepare the adjusting entries for the month of March.

Reasoning: In order for revenues to be recorded in the period in which they are earned, and for expenses to be recognized in the period in which they are incurred, adjusting entries are made at the end of the accounting period. Adjusting entries for prepayments are required at the statement date to record the portion of the prepayment that represents the expense incurred or the revenue earned in the current accounting period. The failure to adjust for the prepayment leads to overstatement of the asset or liability and a related understatement of the expense or revenue.

Solution:

1. Insurance Expense		100	
Prepaid Insurance			100
(To record insurance expired)			
2. Office Supplies Expense		2,000	
Office Supplies			2,000
(To record supplies used)			
3. Depreciation Expense		200	
Accumulated Depreciation—Office Equipment			200
(To record monthly depreciation)			
4. Unearned Revenue		4,600	
Service Revenue			4,600
(To record revenue for services provided)			

Related exercise material: BE3–3, BE3–4, BE3–5, BE3–6, E3–1, E3–2, E3–3, E3–4, E3–5, E3–6, E3–7, E3–8 and E3–9.

THE NAVIGATOR

Adjusting Entries for Accruals

The second category of adjusting entries is **accruals**. Adjusting entries for accruals are required to record revenues earned and expenses incurred in the current accounting period that have not been recognized through daily entries. If an accrual adjustment is needed, the revenue account (and the related asset account) and/or the expense account (and the related liability account) is understated. Thus, the adjusting entry for accruals will **increase both a balance sheet and an income statement account**. Adjusting entries for accruals are graphically depicted in Illustration 3-10.

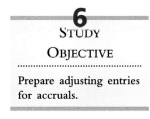

6
STUDY
OBJECTIVE
....
Prepare adjusting entries for accruals.

ILLUSTRATION 3-10

Adjusting entries for accruals

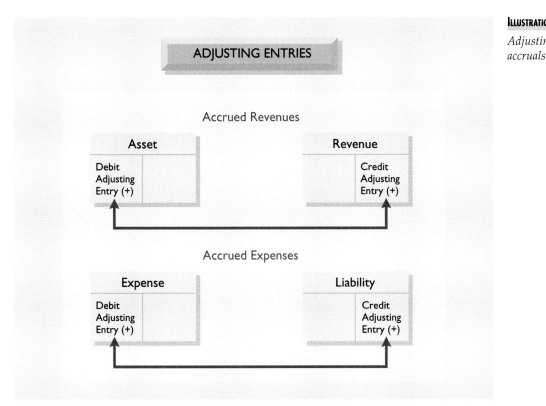

Accrued Revenues

As explained on page 96, revenues earned but not yet received in cash or recorded at the statement date are accrued revenues. Accrued revenues may accumulate (accrue) with the passing of time, as in the case of interest revenue and rent revenue. Or they may result from services that have been performed but neither billed nor collected, as in the case of commissions and fees. The former are unrecorded because the earning of interest and rent does not involve daily transactions; the latter may be unrecorded because only a portion of the total service has been provided.

An adjusting entry is required to show the receivable that exists at the balance sheet date and to record the revenue that has been earned during the period. Prior to adjustment both assets and revenues are understated. Accordingly, **an adjusting entry for accrued revenues results in a debit (increase) to an asset account and a credit (increase) to a revenue account**.

In October Pioneer Advertising Agency Inc. earned $200 for advertising services that were not billed to clients before October 31. Because these services have not been billed, they have not been recorded. Thus, the following adjusting entry is made:

Accrued Revenues

Oct.31

Revenue and receivable are recorded for unbilled services

Nov.

Cash is received; receivable is reduced

A	=	L	+	SE
+200				+200

Oct. 31	Accounts Receivable	200	
	Service Revenue		200
	(To record revenue for services provided)		

After the adjusting entry is posted, the accounts show:

ILLUSTRATION 3-11

Receivable and revenue accounts after accrual adjustment

Accounts Receivable		Service Revenue	
10/31 Adj. 200		10/31 10,000	
		31 400	
		31 Adj. 200	
		10/31 Bal. 10,600	

ALTERNATIVE TERMINOLOGY

Accrued revenues are also called *accrued receivables.*

The asset Accounts Receivable shows that $200 is owed by clients at the balance sheet date. The balance of $10,600 in Service Revenue represents the total revenue earned during the month ($10,000 + $400 + $200). **If the adjusting entry is not made, assets and stockholders' equity on the balance sheet, and revenues and net income on the income statement, will all be understated.**

In the next accounting period, the clients will be billed. When this occurs, the entry to record the billing should recognize that $200 of revenue earned in October has already been recorded in the October 31 adjusting entry. To illustrate, assume that bills totaling $3,000 are mailed to clients on November 10. Of this amount, $200 represents revenue earned in October and recorded as Service Revenue in the October 31 adjusting entry. The remaining $2,800 represents revenue earned in November. Thus, the following entry is made:

A	=	L	+	SE
+2,800				+2,800

Nov. 10	Accounts Receivable	2,800	
	Service Revenue		2,800
	(To record revenue for services provided)		

This entry records service revenue between November 1 and November 10. The subsequent collection of revenue from clients (including the $200 earned in October) will be recorded with a debit to Cash and a credit to Accounts Receivable.

Accrued Expenses

As indicated on page 96, expenses incurred but not yet paid or recorded at the statement date are called accrued expenses. Interest, rent, taxes, and salaries can be accrued expenses. Accrued expenses result from the same causes as accrued revenues. In fact, an accrued expense on the books of one company is an accrued revenue to another company. For example, the $200 accrual of fees by Pioneer is an accrued expense to the client that received the service.

ALTERNATIVE TERMINOLOGY

Accrued expenses are also called *accrued liabilities.*

Adjustments for accrued expenses are necessary to record the obligations that exist at the balance sheet date and to recognize the expenses that apply to the current accounting period. Prior to adjustment both liabilities and expenses are understated. Therefore, **the adjusting entry for accrued expenses results in a debit (increase) to an expense account and a credit (increase) to a liability account.**

Accrued Interest.   Pioneer Advertising Agency Inc. signed a 3-month note payable in the amount of $5,000 on October 1. The note requires interest at an annual rate of 12%. The amount of the interest accumulation is determined by three factors: (1) the face value of the note, (2) the interest rate, which is always expressed as an annual rate, and (3) the length of time the note is outstanding. In this instance, the total interest due on the $5,000 note at its due date 3 months hence is $150 ($5,000 × 12% × 3/12) or $50 for one month. The formula for computing interest and its application to Pioneer Advertising Agency Inc. for the month of October[2] are shown in Illustration 3-12.

HELPFUL HINT
Interest is a cost of borrowing money that accumulates with the passage of time.

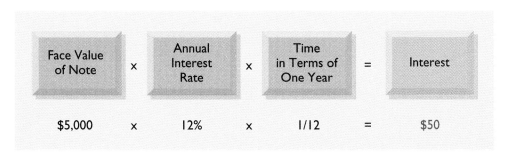

ILLUSTRATION 3-12

Formula for computing interest

Note that the time period is expressed as a fraction of a year. The accrued expense adjusting entry at October 31 is as follows:

Oct. 31	Interest Expense	50	
	Interest Payable		50
	(To record interest on notes payable)		

A	=	L	+	SE
		+50		−50

After this adjusting entry is posted, the accounts show:

Interest Expense	Interest Payable
10/31 **Adj.** 50	10/31 **Adj.** 50

ILLUSTRATION 3-13

Interest accounts after adjustment

Interest Expense shows the interest charges applicable to the month of October. The amount of interest owed at the statement date is shown in Interest Payable. It will not be paid until the note comes due at the end of three months. The Interest Payable account is used instead of crediting Notes Payable to disclose the two types of obligations (interest and principal) in the accounts and statements. **If this adjusting entry is not made, liabilities and interest expense will be understated, and net income and stockholders' equity will be overstated.**

Accrued Salaries.   Some types of expenses, such as employee salaries and commissions, are paid for after the services have been performed. At Pioneer Advertising Agency Inc., salaries were last paid on October 26; the next payment of salaries will not occur until November 9. As shown in the calendar on page 106, three working days remain in October (October 29–31).

---

[2]The computation of interest will be considered in more depth in later chapters.

At October 31, the salaries for these days represent an accrued expense and a related liability to Pioneer Advertising Agency Inc. As explained on page 63, the employees receive total salaries of $2,000 for a five-day work week, or $400 per day. Thus, accrued salaries at October 31 are $1,200 ($400 × 3), and the adjusting entry is:

A	=	L	+	SE
		+1,200		−1,200

Oct. 31	Salaries Expense	1,200	
	Salaries Payable		1,200
	(To record accrued salaries)		

After this adjusting entry is posted, the accounts show:

ILLUSTRATION 3-14

Salary accounts after adjustment

Salaries Expense			Salaries Payable	
10/26	4,000			10/31 **Adj.** **1,200**
31 **Adj.** **1,200**				
10/31 **Bal.** **5,200**				

After this adjustment, the balance in Salaries Expense of $5,200 (13 days × $400) is the actual salary expense for October. The balance in Salaries Payable of $1,200 is the amount of the liability for salaries owed as of October 31. **If the $1,200 adjustment for salaries is not recorded, Pioneer's expenses will be understated $1,200, and its liabilities will be understated $1,200.**

At Pioneer Advertising, salaries are payable every two weeks. Consequently, the next payday is November 9, when total salaries of $4,000 will again be paid. The payment consists of $1,200 of salaries payable at October 31 plus $2,800 of salaries expense for November (7 working days as shown in the November calendar × $400). Therefore, the following entry is made on November 9:

A	=	L	+	SE
−4,000		−1,200		−2,800

Nov. 9	Salaries Payable	1,200	
	Salaries Expense	2,800	
	Cash		4,000
	(To record November 9 payroll)		

This entry eliminates the liability for Salaries Payable that was recorded in the October 31 adjusting entry and records the proper amount of Salaries Expense for the period between November 1 and November 9.

TECHNOLOGY IN ACTION

In many computer systems, the adjusting process is handled like any other transaction, with the accountant inputting the adjustment at the time required. The main difference between adjusting entries and regular transactions is that with adjusting entries, one part of the computer system may perform the required calculation for such items as depreciation or interest and then "feed" these figures to the journalizing process.

Such systems are also able to display information before and after changes were made. Management may be interested in such information to highlight the impact that adjustments have on the various accounts and financial statements.

BEFORE YOU GO ON . . .

Review It

1. What is the effect on assets, stockholders' equity, revenues, and net income if an accrued revenue adjusting entry is not made?
2. What is the effect on liabilities, stockholders' equity, and interest expense if an accrued expense adjusting entry is not made?

Do It

Calvin and Hobbs are the new owners of Micro Computer Services. At the end of August 2001, their first month of operations, Calvin and Hobbs are trying to prepare a monthly financial statement. The following information relates to August:

1. At August 31, Micro Computer owed its employees $800 in salaries that will be paid on September 1.
2. On August 1, Micro Computer borrowed $30,000 from a local bank on a 15-year mortgage. The annual interest rate is 10%.
3. Service revenue unrecorded in August totaled $1,100.

Prepare the adjusting entries needed at August 31, 2001.

Reasoning: Adjusting entries for accruals are required to record revenues earned and expenses incurred in the current accounting period that have not been recognized through daily entries. An adjusting entry for accruals will increase both a balance sheet and an income statement account.

Solution:

1. Salaries Expense	800	
Salaries Payable		800
(To record accrued salaries)		
2. Interest Expense	250	
Interest Payable		250
(To record interest)		
($30,000 $\times$ 10% $\times$ 1/12 = $250)		
3. Accounts Receivable	1,100	
Service Revenue		1,100
(To record revenue for services provided)		

THE NAVIGATOR

Related exercise material: BE3–7, E3–1, E3–2, E3–3, E3–4, E3–5, E3–6, E3–7, E3–8, and E3–9.

Summary of Basic Relationships

The four basic types of adjusting entries are summarized in Illustration 3-15. Take some time to study and analyze the adjusting entries shown in the summary. Be sure to note that **each adjusting entry affects one balance sheet account and one income statement account**.

ILLUSTRATION 3-15

Summary of adjusting entries

Type of Adjustment	Reason for Adjustment	Accounts before Adjustment	Adjusting Entry
1. Prepaid expenses	(a) Prepaid expenses originally recorded in asset accounts have been used.	Assets overstated Expenses understated	Dr. Expenses Cr. Assets
2. Unearned revenues	(b) Unearned revenues initially recorded in liability accounts have been earned.	Liabilities overstated Revenues understated	Dr. Liabilities Cr. Revenues
3. Accrued revenues	(c) Revenues earned but not yet received in cash or recorded.	Assets understated Revenues understated	Dr. Assets Cr. Revenues
4. Accrued expenses	(d) Expenses incurred but not yet paid in cash or recorded.	Expenses understated Liabilities understated	Dr. Expenses Cr. Liabilities

The journalizing and posting of adjusting entries for Pioneer Advertising Agency Inc. on October 31 are shown in Illustrations 3-16 and 3-17. All adjustments are identified in the ledger by the reference J2 because they are journalized on page 2 of the general journal. A center caption entitled Adjusting Entries may be inserted between the last transaction entry and the first adjusting entry to identify these entries. When reviewing the general ledger in Illustration 3-17, note that the adjustments are highlighted in color.

ILLUSTRATION 3-16

General journal showing adjusting entries

HELPFUL HINT
(1) Remember that adjusting entries should not involve debits and credits to cash. (2) Evaluate whether the adjustment makes sense. For example, an adjustment to recognize supplies used should increase supplies expense. (3) Double-check all computations.

	GENERAL JOURNAL			**J2**
Date	**Account Titles and Explanation**	**Ref.**	**Debit**	**Credit**
2001	Adjusting Entries			
Oct. 31	Advertising Supplies Expense	61	1,500	
	Advertising Supplies	8		1,500
	(To record supplies used)			
31	Insurance Expense	63	50	
	Prepaid Insurance	10		50
	(To record insurance expired)			
31	Depreciation Expense	65	40	
	Accumulated Depreciation—Office Equipment	16		40
	(To record monthly depreciation)			
31	Unearned Revenue	28	400	
	Service Revenue	50		400
	(To record revenue for services provided)			
31	Accounts Receivable	6	200	
	Service Revenue	50		200
	(To record revenue for services provided)			
31	Interest Expense	64	50	
	Interest Payable	27		50
	(To record interest on notes payable)			
31	Salaries Expense	60	1,200	
	Salaries Payable	29		1,200
	(To record accrued salaries)			

GENERAL LEDGER

ILLUSTRATION 3-17

General ledger after adjustment

Cash   No. 1

Date	Explanation	Ref.	Debit	Credit	Balance
2001					
Oct. 1		J1	10,000		10,000
2		J1	1,200		11,200
3		J1		900	10,300
4		J1		600	9,700
20		J1		500	9,200
26		J1		4,000	5,200
31		J1	10,000		15,200

Accounts Receivable   No. 6

Date	Explanation	Ref.	Debit	Credit	Balance
2001					
Oct. 31	Adj. entry	J2	200		200

Advertising Supplies   No. 8

Date	Explanation	Ref.	Debit	Credit	Balance
2001					
Oct. 5		J1	2,500		2,500
31	Adj. entry	J2		1,500	1,000

Prepaid Insurance

Date	Explanation	Ref.	Debit	Credit	Balance
2001					
Oct. 4		J1	600		600
31	Adj. entry	J2		50	550

Office Equipment   No. 15

Date	Explanation	Ref.	Debit	Credit	Balance
2001					
Oct. 1		J1	5,000		5,000

Accumulated Depreciation — Office Equipment No. 16

Date	Explanation	Ref.	Debit	Credit	Balance
2001					
Oct. 31	Adj. entry	J2		40	40

Notes Payable

Date	Explanation	Ref.	Debit	Credit	Balance
2001					
Oct. 1		J1		5,000	5,000

Accounts Payable   No. 26

Date	Explanation	Ref.	Debit	Credit	Balance
2001					
Oct. 5		J1		2,500	2,500

Interest Payable   No. 27

Date	Explanation	Ref.	Debit	Credit	Balance
2001					
Oct. 31	Adj. entry	J2		50	50

Unearned Revenue   No. 28

Date	Explanation	Ref.	Debit	Credit	Balance
2001					
Oct. 2		J1		1,200	
31	Adj. entry	J2	400		800

Salaries Payable   No. 29

Date	Explanation	Ref.	Debit	Credit	Balance
2001					
Oct. 31	Adj. entry	J2		1,200	1,200

Common Stock   No. 40

Date	Explanation	Ref.	Debit	Credit	Balance
2001					
Oct. 1		J1		10,000	10,000

Retained Earnings   No. 41

Date	Explanation	Ref.	Debit	Credit	Balance
2001					

Dividends   No. 42

Date	Explanation	Ref.	Debit	Credit	Balance
2001					
Oct. 20		J1	500		500

Service Revenue   No. 50

Date	Explanation	Ref.	Debit	Credit	Balance
2001					
Oct. 31		J1		10,000	10,000
31	Adj. entry	J2		400	10,400
31	Adj. entry	J2		200	10,600

Salaries Expense   No. 60

Date	Explanation	Ref.	Debit	Credit	Balance
2001					
Oct. 26		J1	4,000		4,000
31	Adj. entry	J2	1,200		5,200

Advertising Supplies Expense   No. 61

Date	Explanation	Ref.	Debit	Credit	Balance
2001					
Oct. 31	Adj. entry	J2	1,500		1,500

Rent Expense   No. 62

Date	Explanation	Ref.	Debit	Credit	Balance
2001					
Oct. 3		J1	900		900

Insurance Expense   No. 63

Date	Explanation	Ref.	Debit	Credit	Balance
2001					
Oct. 31	Adj. entry	J2	50		50

Interest Expense   No. 64

Date	Explanation	Ref.	Debit	Credit	Balance
2001					
Oct. 31	Adj. entry	J2	50		50

Depreciation Expense   No. 65

Date	Explanation	Ref.	Debit	Credit	Balance
2001					
Oct. 31	Adj. entry	J2	40		40

STUDY

OBJECTIVE

Describe the nature and
purpose of an adjusted
trial balance.

THE ADJUSTED TRIAL BALANCE AND FINANCIAL STATEMENTS

After all adjusting entries have been journalized and posted, another trial balance is prepared from the ledger accounts. This trial balance is called an adjusted trial balance. It shows the balances of all accounts, including those that have been adjusted, at the end of the accounting period. The purpose of an adjusted trial balance is to **prove the equality** of the total debit balances and the total credit balances in the ledger after all adjustments have been made. Because the accounts contain all data that are needed for financial statements, the adjusted trial balance is the primary basis for the preparation of financial statements.

Preparing the Adjusted Trial Balance

The adjusted trial balance for Pioneer Advertising Agency Inc. shown in Illustration 3-18 has been prepared from the ledger accounts in Illustration 3-17. To facilitate the comparison of account balances, the trial balance data, labeled "Before Adjustment" (presented earlier in Illustration 3-3), are shown alongside the adjusted data, labeled "After Adjustment." In addition, the amounts affected by the adjusting entries are highlighted in color in the "After Adjustment" columns.

ILLUSTRATION 3-18

Trial balance and adjusted trial balance compared

	PIONEER ADVERTISING AGENCY INC. **Trial Balances** **October 31, 2001**			
	Before Adjustment		After Adjustment	
	Dr.	Cr.	Dr.	Cr.
Cash	$15,200		$15,200	
Accounts Receivable			200	
Advertising Supplies	2,500		1,000	
Prepaid Insurance	600		550	
Office Equipment	5,000		5,000	
Accumulated Depreciation— Office Equipment				$ 40
Notes Payable		$ 5,000		5,000
Accounts Payable		2,500		2,500
Interest Payable				50
Unearned Revenue		1,200		800
Salaries Payable				1,200
Common Stock		10,000		10,000
Retained Earnings		-0-		-0-
Dividends	500		500	
Service Revenue		10,000		10,600
Salaries Expense	4,000		5,200	
Advertising Supplies Expense			1,500	
Rent Expense	900		900	
Insurance Expense			50	
Interest Expense			50	
Depreciation Expense			40	
	$28,700	$28,700	$30,190	$30,190

Preparing Financial Statements

Financial statements can be prepared directly from an adjusted trial balance.
The preparation of financial statements from the adjusted trial balance of Pioneer Advertising Agency Inc. and the interrelationship of data are presented in Illustrations 3-19 and 3-20. As shown in Illustration 3-19 the income statement is prepared from the revenue and expense accounts; the retained earnings statement is derived from the retained earnings and dividends accounts and the net income (or net loss) shown in the income statement. As shown in Illustration 3-20 the balance sheet is then prepared from the asset and liability accounts, the common stock account, and the ending retained earnings balance as reported in the retained earnings statement.

ILLUSTRATION 3-19

Preparation of the income statement and retained earnings statement from the adjusted trial balance

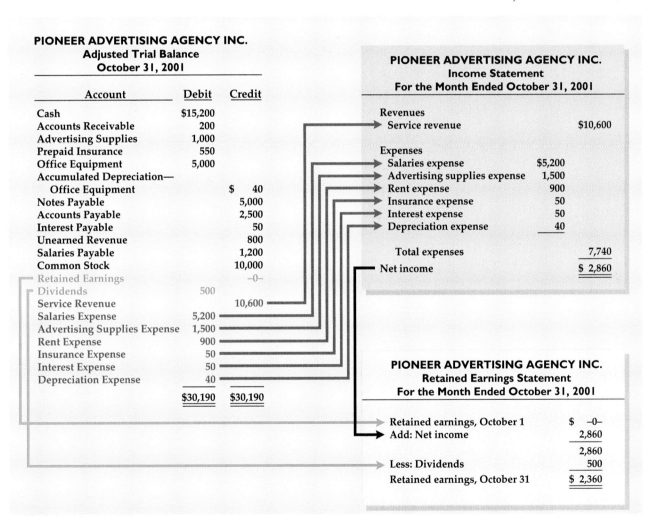

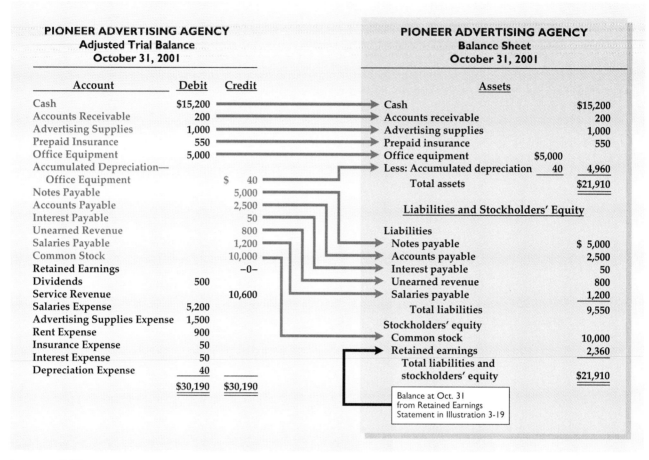

PIONEER ADVERTISING AGENCY
Adjusted Trial Balance
October 31, 2001

Account	Debit	Credit
Cash	$15,200	
Accounts Receivable	200	
Advertising Supplies	1,000	
Prepaid Insurance	550	
Office Equipment	5,000	
Accumulated Depreciation—		
Office Equipment		$ 40
Notes Payable		5,000
Accounts Payable		2,500
Interest Payable		50
Unearned Revenue		800
Salaries Payable		1,200
Common Stock		10,000
Retained Earnings		–0–
Dividends	500	
Service Revenue		10,600
Salaries Expense	5,200	
Advertising Supplies Expense	1,500	
Rent Expense	900	
Insurance Expense	50	
Interest Expense	50	
Depreciation Expense	40	
	$30,190	$30,190

PIONEER ADVERTISING AGENCY
Balance Sheet
October 31, 2001

Assets

Cash		$15,200
Accounts receivable		200
Advertising supplies		1,000
Prepaid insurance		550
Office equipment	$5,000	
Less: Accumulated depreciation	40	4,960
Total assets		$21,910

Liabilities and Stockholders' Equity

Liabilities		
Notes payable		$ 5,000
Accounts payable		2,500
Interest payable		50
Unearned revenue		800
Salaries payable		1,200
Total liabilities		9,550
Stockholders' equity		
Common stock		10,000
Retained earnings		2,360
Total liabilities and stockholders' equity		$21,910

Balance at Oct. 31
from Retained Earnings
Statement in Illustration 3-19

ILLUSTRATION 3-20

Preparation of the balance sheet from the adjusted trial balance

STUDY OBJECTIVE

Explain the accrual basis of accounting.

INTERNATIONAL NOTE

Although different accounting standards are often used in other major industrialized countries, the accrual basis of accounting is followed by all these countries.

ACCRUAL VS. CASH BASIS OF ACCOUNTING

What you have learned in this chapter is the accrual basis of accounting. Accrual basis accounting means that transactions that change a company's financial statements are recorded **in the periods in which the events occur**, rather than in the periods in which the company receives or pays cash. For example, using the accrual basis to determine net income means recognizing revenues when earned rather than when the cash is received, and recognizing expenses when incurred rather than when paid. Information presented on an accrual basis reveals relationships likely to be important in predicting future results. To illustrate, under accrual accounting, revenues are generally recognized when services are performed so they can be related to the economic environment in which they occur. Trends in revenues are thus more meaningful for decision-making purposes.

Under cash basis accounting, revenue is recorded only when the cash is received, and an expense is recorded only when cash is paid. As a result, the cash basis of accounting often leads to misleading financial statements. For example, it fails to record revenue which has been earned but for which the cash has not been received, violating the revenue recognition principle. In addition, expenses are also not matched with earned revenues and therefore the matching principle is not followed. Therefore, **the cash basis of accounting is not in accordance with generally accepted accounting principles.**

Although most companies use the accrual basis of accounting, some small companies use the cash basis of accounting. The cash basis of accounting is justified by these businesses because they often have few receivables and payables. Accountants are sometimes asked to convert cash basis records to the accrual basis. As you might expect, extensive adjusting entries are required for this task.

BEFORE YOU GO ON . . .

Review It

1. What is the purpose of an adjusted trial balance?
2. How is an adjusted trial balance prepared?
3. What are the differences between the cash and accrual bases of accounting?

A LOOK BACK AT OUR FEATURE STORY

Refer to the opening story about McKesson HBOC, Cambridge Biotech, Media Vision Technology, and Penguin USA, and answer the following questions.

1. What are the purposes of adjusting entries?
2. What do these four companies have in common relative to accrual accounting?
3. What adjusting entries should be made for long-lived productive assets purchased by these four companies in prior years?
4. What other types of adjusting entries do you believe these companies might make?

Solution:

1. Adjusting entries are necessary to make the financial statements complete and accurate. Adjusting entries are made to record revenues in the period in which they are earned and to recognize expenses in the period in which they are incurred. Therefore, adjustments ensure that the revenue recognition and matching principles are followed.
2. Each of the companies misstated net income by either overstating revenues (sales) or understating expenses. They failed to properly **time** the reporting of revenues or expenses.
3. The purchase and use of long-lived assets in the production of revenue require the systematic allocation of their cost over their useful lives by recording depreciation expense periodically.
4. (a) Accrued expenses: rent, salaries, utilities, interest, taxes.
   (b) Accrued revenues: interest earned, rent, commissions, fees.
   (c) Prepaid expenses: insurance, rent, supplies, advertising.
   (d) Unearned revenues: rent, subscriptions, customer deposits, and prepayments.

THE
NAVIGATOR

DEMONSTRATION PROBLEM

Luke Skywalker and a group of investors incorporates the Green Thumb Lawn Care Corporation on April 1. At April 30, the trial balance shows the following balances for selected accounts:

Prepaid Insurance	$ 3,600
Equipment	28,000
Notes Payable	20,000
Unearned Revenue	4,200
Service Revenue	1,800

Analysis reveals the following additional data pertaining to these accounts:

1. Prepaid insurance is the cost of a two-year insurance policy, effective April 1.
2. Depreciation on the equipment is $500 per month.
3. The note payable is dated April 1. It is a six-month, 12% note.
4. Seven customers paid for the company's six months' lawn service package of $600 beginning in April. These customers were serviced in April.
5. Lawn services rendered other customers but not billed at April 30 totaled $1,500.

Instructions
Prepare the adjusting entries for the month of April. Show computations.

SOLUTION TO DEMONSTRATION PROBLEM

<table>
<tr><td colspan="6" align="center">**GENERAL JOURNAL**</td><td>**J2**</td></tr>
<tr><td>**Date**</td><td colspan="3">**Account Titles and Explanation**</td><td>**Ref.**</td><td>**Debit**</td><td>**Credit**</td></tr>
<tr><td></td><td colspan="6" align="center">Adjusting Entries</td></tr>
<tr><td>Apr. 30</td><td colspan="3">Insurance Expense</td><td></td><td>150</td><td></td></tr>
<tr><td></td><td colspan="3">   Prepaid Insurance</td><td></td><td></td><td>150</td></tr>
<tr><td></td><td colspan="3">   (To record insurance expired:
    $3,600 ÷ 24 = $150 per month)</td><td></td><td></td><td></td></tr>
<tr><td>30</td><td colspan="3">Depreciation Expense</td><td></td><td>500</td><td></td></tr>
<tr><td></td><td colspan="3">   Accumulated Depreciation—Equipment</td><td></td><td></td><td>500</td></tr>
<tr><td></td><td colspan="3">   (To record monthly depreciation)</td><td></td><td></td><td></td></tr>
<tr><td>30</td><td colspan="3">Interest Expense</td><td></td><td>200</td><td></td></tr>
<tr><td></td><td colspan="3">   Interest Payable</td><td></td><td></td><td>200</td></tr>
<tr><td></td><td colspan="3">   (To record interest on notes payable:
    $20,000 × 12% × 1/12 = $200)</td><td></td><td></td><td></td></tr>
<tr><td>30</td><td colspan="3">Unearned Revenue</td><td></td><td>700</td><td></td></tr>
<tr><td></td><td colspan="3">   Service Revenue</td><td></td><td></td><td>700</td></tr>
<tr><td></td><td colspan="3">   (To record service revenue: $600 ÷ 6 = $100;
    $100 per month × 7 = $700)</td><td></td><td></td><td></td></tr>
<tr><td>30</td><td colspan="3">Accounts Receivable</td><td></td><td>1,500</td><td></td></tr>
<tr><td></td><td colspan="3">   Service Revenue</td><td></td><td></td><td>1,500</td></tr>
<tr><td></td><td colspan="3">   (To record revenue for services provided)</td><td></td><td></td><td></td></tr>
</table>

PROBLEM-SOLVING STRATEGIES

1. Note that adjustments are being made for one month.
2. Make computations carefully.
3. Select account titles carefully.
4. Make sure debits are made first and credits are indented.
5. Check that debits equal credits for each entry.

THE NAVIGATOR

SUMMARY OF STUDY OBJECTIVES

1. *Explain the time period assumption.* The time period assumption assumes that the economic life of a business can be divided into artificial time periods.

2. *Distinguish between the revenue recognition principle and the matching principle.* The revenue recognition principle dictates that revenue be recognized in the accounting period in which it is earned. The matching principle dictates that expenses be recognized when they make their contribution to revenues.

3. *Explain why adjusting entries are needed.* Adjusting entries are made at the end of an accounting period. They ensure that revenues are recorded in the period in which they are earned and that expenses are recognized in the period in which they are incurred.

4. *Identify the major types of adjusting entries.* The major types of adjusting entries are prepaid expenses, unearned revenues, accrued revenues, and accrued expenses.

5. *Prepare adjusting entries for prepayments.* Prepayments are either prepaid expenses or unearned revenues. Adjusting entries for prepayments are required at the statement date to record the portion of the prepayment that represents the expense incurred or the revenue earned in the current accounting period.

6. *Prepare adjusting entries for accruals.* Accruals are either accrued revenues or accrued expenses. Adjusting entries for accruals are required to record revenues earned and expenses incurred in the current accounting period that have not been recognized through daily entries.

7. *Describe the nature and purpose of an adjusted trial balance.* An adjusted trial balance is a trial balance that shows the balances of all accounts, including those that have been adjusted, at the end of an accounting period. The purpose of an adjusted trial balance is to show the effects of all financial events that have occurred during the accounting period.

8. *Explain the accrual basis of accounting.* Accrual basis accounting means that events that change a company's financial statements are recorded in the periods in which the events occur, rather than in the periods in which the company receives or pays cash.

GLOSSARY

Accrual basis of accounting Accounting basis in which transactions that change a company's financial statements are recorded in the periods in which the events occur, rather than in the periods in which the company receives or pays cash. (p. 112).

Accrued expenses Expenses incurred but not yet paid in cash or recorded. (p. 104).

Accrued revenues Revenues earned but not yet received in cash or recorded. (p. 103).

Adjusted trial balance A list of accounts and their balances after all adjustments have been made. (p. 110).

Adjusting entries Entries made at the end of an accounting period to ensure that the revenue recognition and matching principles are followed. (p. 95).

Book value The difference between the cost of a depreciable asset and its related accumulated depreciation. (p. 100).

Calendar year An accounting period that extends from January 1 to December 31. (p. 93).

Cash basis accounting Accounting basis in which revenue is recorded only when cash is received and an expense is recorded only when cash is paid. (p. 112).

Contra asset account An account that is offset against an asset account on the balance sheet. (p. 100).

Depreciation The process of allocating the cost of an asset to expense over its useful life in a rational and systematic manner. (p. 99).

Fiscal year An accounting period that is one year in length. (p. 93).

Interim periods Monthly or quarterly accounting time periods. (p. 93).

Matching principle The principle that efforts (expenses) be matched with accomplishments (revenues). (p. 94).

Prepaid expenses Expenses paid in cash and recorded as assets before they are used or consumed. (p. 97).

Revenue recognition principle The principle that revenue be recognized in the accounting period in which it is earned. (p. 93).

Time period assumption An assumption that the economic life of a business can be divided into artificial time periods. (p. 93).

Unearned revenues Cash received and recorded as liabilities before revenue is earned. (p. 101).

Useful life The length of service of a productive facility. (p. 99).

APPENDIX   ALTERNATIVE TREATMENT OF PREPAID EXPENSES AND UNEARNED REVENUES

In our discussion of adjusting entries for prepaid expenses and unearned revenues, we illustrated transactions for which the initial entries were made to balance sheet accounts. That is, in the case of prepaid expenses, the prepayment was debited to an asset account, and in the case of unearned revenue, the cash received was credited to a liability account. Some businesses use an alternative treatment: (1) At the time an expense is prepaid, it is debited to an expense account; (2) at the time of a receipt for future services, it is credited to a revenue account. The circumstances that justify such entries and the different adjusting entries that may be required are described below. The alternative treatment of prepaid expenses and unearned revenues has the same effect on the financial statements as the procedures described in the chapter.

9
STUDY
OBJECTIVE

Prepare adjusting entries for the alternative treatment of prepayments.

··

PREPAID EXPENSES

Prepaid expenses become expired costs either through the passage of time, as in the case of insurance, or through consumption, as in the case of advertising supplies. If, at the time of purchase, the company expects to consume the supplies before the next financial statement date, **it may be more convenient initially to debit (increase) an expense account rather than an asset account.** Assume, for example, that Pioneer Advertising expects that all of the supplies purchased on October 5 will be used before October 31. A debit of $2,500 to Advertising Supplies Expense rather than to the asset account, Advertising Supplies, on October 5 will eliminate the need for an adjusting entry on October 31, if all the supplies are used. At October 31, the Advertising Supplies Expense account will show a balance of $2,500, which is equal to the cost of supplies used between October 5 and October 31.

Assume, however, that the company does not use all the supplies, and an inventory of $1,000 of advertising supplies remains on October 31. What then? Obviously, in such a case an adjusting entry is needed. Prior to adjustment, the expense account, Advertising Supplies Expense, is overstated $1,000, and the asset account, Advertising Supplies, is understated $1,000. Thus the following adjusting entry is made:

A	=	L	+	SE
+1,000				+1,000

Oct. 31	Advertising Supplies	1,000	
	Advertising Supplies Expense		1,000
	(To record supplies inventory)		

After posting the adjusting entry, the accounts show:

*Prepaid expenses accounts
after adjustment*

Advertising Supplies

10/31	Adj.	1,000	

Advertising Supplies Expense

10/5		2,500	10/31	Adj.	1,000
10/31	Bal.	1,500			

After adjustment, the asset account, Advertising Supplies, shows a balance of $1,000, which is equal to the cost of supplies on hand at October 31. In addition, Advertising Supplies Expense shows a balance of $1,500, which is equal to the cost of supplies used between October 5 and October 31. If the adjusting entry is not made, expenses will be overstated and net income will be understated by $1,000 in the October income statement. Moreover, both assets and stockholders' equity will be understated by $1,000 on the October 31 balance sheet.

A comparative summary of the entries and accounts for advertising supplies is shown in Illustration 3A-2.

*Adjustment approaches—a
comparison*

	Prepayment Initially Debited to Asset Account (per chapter)			Prepayment Initially Debited to Expense Account (per appendix)	
Oct. 5	Advertising Supplies	2,500	Oct. 5	Advertising Supplies Expense	2,500
	Accounts Payable	2,500		Accounts Payable	2,500
Oct. 31	Advertising Supplies Expense	1,500	Oct. 31	Advertising Supplies	1,000
	Advertising Supplies	1,500		Advertising Supplies Expense	1,000

After posting the entries, the accounts appear as follows:

(per chapter) Advertising Supplies			(per appendix) Advertising Supplies		
10/5	2,500	10/31 Adj. 1,500	10/31 Adj. 1,000		
10/31 Bal. 1,000					

Advertising Supplies Expense			Advertising Supplies Expense		
10/31 Adj. 1,500			10/5	2,500	10/31 Adj. 1,000
			10/31 Bal. 1,500		

Note that the account balances under each alternative are the same at October 31; that is, Advertising Supplies $1,000, and Advertising Supplies Expense $1,500.

UNEARNED REVENUES

Unearned revenues become earned either through the passage of time, as in the case of unearned rent, or through rendering the service, as in the case of unearned fees. Like prepaid expenses, a revenue account may be credited when cash is received for future services and a different adjusting entry may be necessary.

To illustrate, assume that when Pioneer Advertising received $1,200 for future services on October 2 the services were expected to be performed before October 31.[3] In such a case, Service Revenue is credited. If revenue is in fact earned before October 31, no adjustment is needed. However, if, at the statement date, $800 of the services have not been performed, an adjusting entry is required. Prior to adjustment, the revenue account, Service Revenue, is overstated $800, and the liability account, Unearned Revenue, is understated $800. Thus, the following adjusting entry is made:

Oct. 31	Service Revenue		800	
	Unearned Revenue			800
	(To record unearned revenue)			

A	=	L	+	SE
		+800		−800

After posting the adjusting entry, the accounts show:

Unearned Revenue		Service Revenue		
10/31 Adj. 800		10/31 Adj. 800	10/2	1,200
			10/31 Bal.	400

---

[3]This example focuses only on the alternative treatment of unearned revenues. In the interest of simplicity, the entries to Service Revenue pertaining to the immediate earning of revenue ($10,000) and the adjusting entry for accrued revenue ($200) have been ignored.

The liability account, Unearned Revenue, shows a balance of $800, which is equal to the services that will be rendered in the future. In addition, the balance in Service Revenue equals the services rendered in October. If the adjusting entry is not made, both revenues and net income will be overstated by $800 in the October income statement. Moreover, liabilities will be understated by $800, and stockholders' equity will be overstated by $800 on the October 31 balance sheet.

A comparative summary of the entries and accounts for service revenue earned and unearned is presented in Illustration 3A-5:

ILLUSTRATION 3A-5

Adjustment approaches—a comparison

Unearned Revenue Initially Credited to Liability Account (per chapter)			Unearned Revenue Initially Credited to Revenue Account (per appendix)		
Oct. 2	Cash	1,200	Oct. 2	Cash	1,200
	Unearned Revenue	1,200		Service Revenue	1,200
Oct. 31	Unearned Revenue	400	Oct. 31	Service Revenue	800
	Service Revenue	400		Unearned Revenue	800

After posting the entries, the accounts will show:

ILLUSTRATION 3A-6

Comparison of accounts

(per chapter)
Unearned Revenue

10/31 Adj. 400	10/2 1,200
	10/31 Bal. 800

Service Revenue

	10/31 Adj. 400

(per appendix)
Unearned Revenue

	10/31 Adj. 800

Service Revenue

10/31 Adj. 800	10/2 1,200
	10/31 Bal. 400

Note that the balances in the accounts are the same under the two alternatives: Unearned Revenue $800, and Service Revenue $400.

SUMMARY OF ADDITIONAL ADJUSTMENT RELATIONSHIPS

The use of alternative adjusting entries requires additions to the summary of basic relationships presented earlier in Illustration 3-15. The additions are shown in color in Illustration 3A-7.

Alternative adjusting entries do not apply to accrued revenues and accrued expenses because **no entries occur before these types of adjusting entries are made**. Hence, the summary data shown in Illustration 3-15 for these two types of adjustments remains unchanged.

Type of Adjustment	Reason for Adjustment	Account Balances before Adjustment	Adjusting Entry
1. Prepaid Expenses	(a) Prepaid expenses initially recorded in asset accounts have been used.	Assets overstated Expenses understated	Dr. Expenses Cr. Assets
	(b) Prepaid expenses initially recorded in expense accounts have not been used.	Assets understated Expenses overstated	Dr. Assets Cr. Expenses
2. Unearned Revenues	(a) Unearned revenues initially recorded in liability accounts have been earned.	Liabilities overstated Revenues understated	Dr. Liabilities Cr. Revenues
	(b) Unearned revenues initially recorded in revenue accounts have not been earned.	Liabilities understated Revenues overstated	Dr. Revenues Cr. Liabilities

ILLUSTRATION 3A-7

Summary of basic relationships for prepayments

SUMMARY OF STUDY OBJECTIVES FOR APPENDIX

9. *Prepare adjusting entries for the alternative treatment of prepayments.* When prepayments are initially recorded in expense and revenue accounts, these accounts are overstated prior to adjustment. The adjusting entries for prepaid expenses are a debit to an asset account and a credit to an expense account. Adjusting entries for unearned revenues are a debit to a revenue account and a credit to a liability account.

*Note: All asterisked Questions, Exercises, and Problems relate to material in the appendix to the chapter.

SELF-STUDY QUESTIONS

Answers are at the end of the chapter.

(SO 1) 1. The time period assumption states that:
   a. revenue should be recognized in the accounting period in which it is earned.
   b. expenses should be matched with revenues.
   c. the economic life of a business can be divided into artificial time periods.
   d. the fiscal year should correspond with the calendar year.

(SO 2) 2. The principle which dictates that efforts (expenses) be matched with accomplishments (revenues) is the:
   a. matching principle.
   b. cost principle.
   c. periodicity principle.
   d. revenue recognition principle.

(SO 3) 3. Adjusting entries are made to ensure that:
   a. expenses are recognized in the period in which they are incurred.
   b. revenues are recorded in the period in which they are earned.

   c. balance sheet and income statement accounts have correct balances at the end of an accounting period.
   d. all of the above.

4. Each of the following is a major type (or category) of (SO 4) adjusting entries *except*:
   a. prepaid expenses.
   b. accrued revenues.
   c. accrued expenses.
   d. earned revenues.

5. The trial balance shows Supplies $1,350 and Supplies (SO 5) Expense $0. If $600 of supplies are on hand at the end of the period, the adjusting entry is:

a. Supplies	600	
Supplies Expense		600
b. Supplies	750	
Supplies Expense		750
c. Supplies Expense	750	
Supplies		750
d. Supplies Expense	600	
Supplies		600

(SO 5) 6. Adjustments for unearned revenues:
   a. decrease liabilities and increase revenues.
   b. have an assets and revenues account relationship.
   c. increase assets and increase revenues.
   d. decrease revenues and decrease assets.

(SO 6) 7. Adjustments for accrued revenues:
   a. have a liabilities and revenues account relationship.
   b. have an assets and revenues account relationship.
   c. decrease assets and revenues.
   d. decrease liabilities and increase revenues.

(SO 6) 8. Kathy Siska earned a salary of $400 for the last week of September. She will be paid on October 1. The adjusting entry for Kathy's employer at September 30 is:
   a. No entry is required

   b. Salaries Expense   400
         Salaries Payable   400
   c. Salaries Expense   400
         Cash   400
   d. Salaries Payable   400
         Cash   400

(SO 7) 9. Which of the following statements is *incorrect* concerning the adjusted trial balance?
   a. An adjusted trial balance proves the equality of the total debit balances and the total credit balances in the ledger after all adjustments are made.
   b. The adjusted trial balance provides the primary basis for the preparation of financial statements.

   c. The adjusted trial balance lists the account balances segregated by assets and liabilities.
   d. The adjusted trial balance is prepared after the adjusting entries have been journalized and posted.

10. One of the following statements about the accrual basis (SO 8) of accounting is *false*. That statement is:
   a. Events that change a company's financial statements are recorded in the periods in which the events occur.
   b. Revenue is recognized in the period in which it is earned.
   c. This basis is in accord with generally accepted accounting principles.
   d. Revenue is recorded only when cash is received, and expense is recorded only when cash is paid.

*11. The trial balance shows Supplies $0 and Supplies Ex- (SO 9) pense $1,500. If $800 of supplies are on hand at the end of the period, the adjusting entry is:
   a. debit Supplies $800 and credit Supplies Expense $800.
   b. debit Supplies Expense $800 and credit Supplies $800.
   c. debit Supplies $700 and credit Supplies Expense $700.
   d. debit Supplies Expense $700 and credit Supplies $700.

THE NAVIGATOR

QUESTIONS

1. (a) How does the time period assumption affect an accountant's analysis of business transactions?
   (b) Explain the terms *fiscal year*, *calendar year*, and *interim periods*

2. Identify and state two generally accepted accounting principles that relate to adjusting the accounts.

3. Bon Barone, a lawyer, accepts a legal engagement in March, performs the work in April, and is paid in May. If Barone's law firm prepares monthly financial statements, when should it recognize revenue from this engagement? Why?

4. In completing the engagement in (3) above, Barone incurs $4,500 of expenses in March, which are paid in April. How much expense should be deducted from revenues in the month the revenue is recognized? Why?

5. "Adjusting entries are required by the cost principle of accounting." Do you agree? Explain.

6. Why may a trial balance not contain up-to-date and complete financial information?

7. Distinguish between the two categories of adjusting entries and identify the types of adjustments applicable to each category.

8. What is the debit/credit effect of a prepaid expense adjusting entry?

9. "Depreciation is a process of valuation that results in the reporting of the fair market value of the asset." Do you agree? Explain.

10. Explain the differences between depreciation expense and accumulated depreciation.

11. Shen Company purchased equipment for $15,000. By the current balance sheet date, $7,000 had been depreciated. Indicate the balance sheet presentation of the data.

12. What is the debit/credit effect of an unearned revenue adjusting entry?

13. A company fails to recognize revenue earned but not yet received. Which of the following accounts are involved in the adjusting entry: (a) asset, (b) liability, (c) revenue, or (d) expense? For the accounts selected, indicate whether they would be debited or credited in the entry.

14. A company fails to recognize an expense incurred but not paid. Indicate which of the following accounts is debited and which is credited in the adjusting entry: (a) asset, (b) liability, (c) revenue, or (d) expense.

15. A company makes an accrued revenue adjusting entry for $800 and an accrued expense adjusting entry for $600. How much was net income understated prior to these entries? Explain.

16. On January 9, a company pays $5,000 for salaries of which $2,000 was reported as Salaries Payable on December 31. Give the entry to record the payment.

17. For each of the following items before adjustment, indicate the type of adjusting entry (prepaid expense, unearned revenue, accrued revenue, and accrued expense)

that is needed to correct the misstatement. If an item could result in more than one type of adjusting entry, indicate each of the types.

(a) Assets are understated.

(b) Liabilities are overstated.

(c) Liabilities are understated.

(d) Expenses are understated.

(e) Assets are overstated.

(f) Revenue is understated.

18. One-half of the adjusting entry is given below. Indicate the account title for the other half of the entry.

(a) Salaries Expense is debited.

(b) Depreciation Expense is debited.

(c) Interest Payable is credited.

(d) Supplies is credited.

(e) Accounts Receivable is debited.

(f) Unearned Service Revenue is debited.

19. "An adjusting entry may affect more than one balance sheet or income statement account." Do you agree? Why or why not?

20. Why is it possible to prepare financial statements directly from an adjusted trial balance?

21. Why do accrual basis financial statements provide more useful information than cash basis statements?

*22. The Alpha Company debits Supplies Expense for all purchases of supplies and credits Rent Revenue for all advanced rentals. For each type of adjustment, give the adjusting entry.

BRIEF EXERCISES

BE3–1   The ledger of the Hilo Company includes the following accounts. Explain why each account may require adjustment.

(a) Prepaid Insurance   (c) Unearned Revenue

(b) Depreciation Expense   (d) Interest Payable

Indicate why adjusting entries are needed.
(SO 3)

BE3–2   The Reno Company accumulates the following adjustment data at December 31. Indicate (a) the type of adjustment (prepaid expense, accrued revenues and so on), and (b) the accounts before adjustment (overstated or understated).

1. Supplies of $600 are on hand.
2. Services provided but unbilled total $900.
3. Interest of $200 has accumulated on a note payable.
4. Rent collected in advance totaling $800 has been earned.

Identify the major types of adjusting entries.
(SO 4)

BE3–3   The Spahn Advertising Company's trial balance at December 31 shows Advertising Supplies $8,700 and Advertising Supplies Expense $0. On December 31, there are $1,500 of supplies on hand. Prepare the adjusting entry at December 31 and, using T accounts, enter the balances in the accounts, post the adjusting entry, and indicate the adjusted balance in each account.

Prepare adjusting entry for supplies.
(SO 5)

BE3–4   At the end of its first year, the trial balance of Tabor Company shows Equipment $25,000 and zero balances in Accumulated Depreciation—Equipment and Depreciation Expense. Depreciation for the year is estimated to be $4,000. Prepare the adjusting entry for depreciation at December 31, post the adjustments to T accounts, and indicate the balance sheet presentation of the equipment at December 31.

Prepare adjusting entries for depreciation.
(SO 5)

BE3–5   On July 1, 2001, Blair Co. pays $18,000 to Hindi Insurance Co. for a three-year insurance contract. Both companies have fiscal years ending December 31. For Blair Co. journalize and post the entry on July 1 and the adjusting entry on December 31.

Prepare adjusting entries for prepaid expense.
(SO 5)

BE3–6   Using the data in BE3–5, journalize and post the entry on July 1 and the adjusting entry on December 31 for Hindi Insurance Co. Hindi uses the accounts Unearned Insurance Revenue and Insurance Revenue.

Prepare adjusting entry for unearned revenue.
(SO 5)

BE3–7   The bookkeeper for DeVoe Company asks you to prepare the following accrued adjusting entries at December 31.

1. Interest on notes payable of $300 is accrued.
2. Services provided but unbilled total $1,400.
3. Salaries earned by employees of $900 have not been recorded.

Use the following account titles: Service Revenue, Accounts Receivable, Interest Expense, Interest Payable, Salaries Expense, and Salaries Payable.

Prepare adjusting entries for accruals.
(SO 6)

BE3–8   The trial balance of Wilson Company includes the following balance sheet accounts. Identify the accounts that require adjustment. For each account that requires adjustment, in-

Analyze accounts in an adjusted trial balance.
(SO 7)

dicate (a) the type of adjusting entry (prepaid expenses, unearned revenues, accrued revenues, and accrued expenses) and (b) the related account in the adjusting entry.

Accounts Receivable	Notes Payable
Prepaid Insurance	Interest Payable
Equipment	Unearned Service Revenue
Accumulated Depreciation—Equipment	

Prepare an income statement from an adjusted trial balance. (SO 7)

BE3–9   The adjusted trial balance of Klar Company at December 31, 2001, includes the following accounts: Retained Earnings $15,600; Dividends $6,000; Service Revenue $38,400; Salaries Expense $13,000; Insurance Expense $2,000; Rent Expense $4,000; Supplies Expense $1,500; and Depreciation Expense $1,000. Prepare an income statement for the year.

Prepare a retained earnings statement from an adjusted trial balance. (SO 7)

BE3–10   Partial adjusted trial balance data for Klar Company is presented in BE3–9. The balance in Retained Earnings is the balance as of January 1. Prepare a retained earnings statement for the year assuming net income is $17,000 for the year.

Prepare adjusting entries under alternative treatment of prepayments. (SO 9)

*BE3–11**   Phelps Company records all prepayments in income statement accounts. At April 30, the trial balance shows Supplies Expense $2,800, Service Revenue $9,200, and zero balances in related balance sheet accounts. Prepare the adjusting entries at April 30 assuming (a) $1,500 of supplies on hand and (b) $800 of service revenue should be reported as unearned.

EXERCISES

Identify types of adjustments and account relationships. (SO 4, 5, 6)

E3–1   The McLain Company accumulates the following adjustment data at December 31.

1. Services provided but unbilled total $600.
2. Store supplies of $300 have been used.
3. Utility expenses of $225 are unpaid.
4. Unearned revenue of $260 has been earned.
5. Salaries of $800 are unpaid.
6. Prepaid insurance totaling $350 has expired.

Instructions
For each of the above items indicate:

(a) The type of adjustment (prepaid expense, unearned revenue, accrued revenue, or accrued expense).
(b) The accounts before adjustment (overstatement or understatement).

Prepare adjusting entries from selected account data. (SO 5, 6, 7)

E3–2   The ledger of Duggan Rental Agency on March 31 of the current year includes the following selected accounts before adjusting entries have been prepared.

	Debit	Credit
Prepaid Insurance	$ 3,600	
Supplies	2,800	
Equipment	25,000	
Accumulated Depreciation—Equipment		$ 8,400
Notes Payable		20,000
Unearned Rent Revenue		9,300
Rent Revenue		60,000
Interest Expense	–0–	
Wage Expense	14,000	

An analysis of the accounts shows the following:

1. The equipment depreciates $250 per month.
2. One-third of the unearned rent was earned during the quarter.
3. Interest of $500 is accrued on the notes payable.
4. Supplies on hand total $850.
5. Insurance expires at the rate of $300 per month.

Instructions
Prepare the adjusting entries at March 31, assuming that adjusting entries are made quarterly. Additional accounts are: Depreciation Expense, Insurance Expense, Interest Payable, and Supplies Expense.

E3–3 Jennifer Johnston, D.D.S., opened a dental practice on January 1, 2001. During the first month of operations the following transactions occurred.

Prepare adjusting entries.
(SO 5, 6, 7)

1. Performed services for patients who had dental plan insurance. At January 31, $750 of such services was earned but not yet billed to the insurance companies.
2. Utility expenses incurred but not paid prior to January 31 totaled $520.
3. Purchased dental equipment on January 1 for $80,000, paying $20,000 in cash and signing a $60,000, three-year-note payable. The equipment depreciates $400 per month. Interest is $500 per month.
4. Purchased a one-year malpractice insurance policy on January 1 for $12,000.
5. Purchased $1,600 of dental supplies. On January 31, determined that $500 of supplies were on hand.

Instructions
Prepare the adjusting entries on January 31. Account titles are: Accumulated Depreciation—Dental Equipment, Depreciation Expense, Service Revenue, Accounts Receivable, Insurance Expense, Interest Expense, Interest Payable, Prepaid Insurance, Supplies, Supplies Expense, Utilities Expense, and Utilities Payable.

E3–4 The trial balance for Pioneer Advertising Agency Inc. is shown in Illustration 3-3, p. 96. In lieu of the adjusting entries shown in the text at October 31, assume the following adjustment data:

Prepare adjusting entries.
(SO 5, 6, 7)

1. Advertising supplies on hand at October 31 total $1,400.
2. Expired insurance for the month is $100.
3. Depreciation for the month is $50.
4. Unearned revenue earned in October totals $600.
5. Services provided but unbilled at October 31 are $300.
6. Interest accrued at October 31 is $70.
7. Accrued salaries at October 31 are $1,500.

Instructions
Prepare the adjusting entries for the items above.

E3–5 The income statement of Ranier Co. for the month of July shows net income of $1,400 based on Service Revenue $5,500, Wages Expense $2,300, Supplies Expense $1,200, and Utilities Expense $600. In reviewing the statement, you discover the following:

Prepare correct income statement.
(SO 2, 5, 6, 7)

1. Insurance expired during July of $300 was omitted.
2. Supplies expense includes $500 of supplies that are still on hand at July 31.
3. Depreciation on equipment of $150 was omitted.
4. Accrued but unpaid wages at July 31 of $300 were not included.
5. Services provided but unrecorded totaled $900.

Instructions
Prepare a correct income statement for July, 2001.

E3–6 A partial adjusted trial balance of Piper Company at January 31, 2001, shows the following:

Analyze adjusted data.
(SO 2, 4, 5, 6, 7)

PIPER COMPANY
Adjusted Trial Balance
January 31, 2001

	Debit	Credit
Supplies	$ 700	
Prepaid Insurance	2,400	
Salaries Payable		800
Unearned Revenue		750
Supplies Expense	950	
Insurance Expense	400	
Salaries Expense	1,800	
Service Revenue		2,000

Instructions
Answer the following questions, assuming the year begins January 1:

(a) If the amount in Supplies Expense is the January 31 adjusting entry, and $850 of supplies was purchased in January, what was the balance in Supplies on January 1?

(b) If the amount in Insurance Expense is the January 31 adjusting entry, and the original insurance premium was for one year, what was the total premium and when was the policy purchased?

(c) If $2,500 of salaries was paid in January, what was the balance in Salaries Payable at December 31, 2000?

(d) If $1,600 was received in January for services performed in January, what was the balance in Unearned Revenue at December 31, 2000?

Journalize basic transactions and adjusting entries.
(SO 5, 6, 7)

E3–7   Selected accounts of Felipe Company are shown below:

Supplies Expense

7/31	500	

Supplies

7/1	Bal.	1,100	7/31	500
7/10		200		

Salaries Payable

	7/31	1,200

Accounts Receivable

7/31	500

Unearned Revenue

7/31	900	7/1	Bal.	1,500
		7/20		700

Salaries Expense

7/15	1,200
7/31	1,200

Service Revenue

	7/14	3,000
	7/31	500
	7/31	900

Instructions
After analyzing the accounts, journalize (a) the July transactions and (b) the adjusting entries that were made on July 31. (*Hint*: July transactions were for cash.)

Prepare adjusting entries from analysis of trial balances.
(SO 5, 6, 7)

E3–8   The trial balances before and after adjustment for Lund Company at the end of its fiscal year are presented below.

LUND COMPANY
Trial Balance
August 31, 2001

	Before Adjustment		After Adjustment	
	Dr.	Cr.	Dr.	Cr.
Cash	$10,400		$10,400	
Accounts Receivable	8,800		9,400	
Office Supplies	2,300		700	
Prepaid Insurance	4,000		2,500	
Office Equipment	14,000		14,000	
Accumulated Depreciation—Office Equipment		$ 3,600		$ 4,800
Accounts Payable		5,800		5,800
Salaries Payable		–0–		1,100
Unearned Rent Revenue		1,500		700
Common Stock		10,000		10,000
Retained Earnings		5,600		5,600
Service Revenue		34,000		34,600
Rent Revenue		11,000		11,800
Salaries Expense	17,000		18,100	
Office Supplies Expense	–0–		1,600	
Rent Expense	15,000		15,000	
Insurance Expense	–0–		1,500	
Depreciation Expense	–0–		1,200	
	$71,500	$71,500	$74,400	$74,400

Instructions

Prepare the adjusting entries that were made.

E3–9   The adjusted trial balance for the Lund Company is given in E3–8.

Prepare financial statements from adjusted trial balance.
(SO 5, 6, 7)

Instructions

Prepare the income statement and a retained earnings statement for the fiscal year 2001 and the balance sheet at August 31, 2001.

E3–10   On numerous occasions proposals have surfaced to put the federal government on the accrual basis of accounting. This is no small issue because if this basis were used, it would mean that billions in unrecorded liabilities would have to be booked and the federal deficit would increase substantially.

Distinguish between cash and accrual basis of accounting.
(SO 8)

Instructions
 (a) What is the difference between accrual basis accounting and cash basis accounting?
 (b) Comment on why politicians prefer a cash basis accounting system over an accrual basis system.
 (c) Write a letter to your senator explaining why you think the federal government should adopt the accrual basis of accounting.

E3–11   The following data are taken from the comparative balance sheets of Breakers Billiards Club, which prepares its financial statements using the accrual basis of accounting:

Record transactions on accrual basis; convert revenue to cash receipts.
(SO 5, 6)

December 31	2001	2000
Fees receivable from members	$12,000	$ 9,000
Unearned fees revenue	17,000	22,000

Fees are billed to members based upon their use of the club's facilities. Unearned fees arise from the sale of gift certificates, which members can apply to their future use of club facilities. The 2001 income statement for the club showed that fee revenue of $153,000 was earned during the year.

Instructions
(*Hint:* You will probably find it helpful to use T accounts to analyze this data.)

 (a) Prepare journal entries for each of the following events that took place during 2001:
   1. Fees receivable from 2000 were all collected.
   2. Gift certificates outstanding at the end of 2000 were all redeemed.
   3. An additional $30,000 worth of gift certificates were sold during 2001; a portion of these were used by the recipients during the year; the remainder were still outstanding at the end of 2001.
   4. Fees for 2001 were billed to members.
   5. Fees receivable for 2001 (i.e., those billed in item [4] above) were partially collected.
 (b) Determine the amount of cash received by the club, with respect to fees, during 2001.

*E3–12   At Harmony Company, prepayments are debited to expense when paid and unearned revenues are credited to revenue when received. During January of the current year, the following transactions occurred:

Journalize transactions and adjusting entries using appendix.
(SO 9)

Jan. 2   Paid $2,400 for fire insurance protection for the year.
    10   Paid $1,700 for supplies.
    15   Received $5,100 for services to be performed in the future.

On January 31, it is determined that $1,500 of the services fees have been earned and that there are $800 of supplies on hand.

Instructions
 (a) Journalize and post the January transactions. (Use T accounts.)
 (b) Journalize and post the adjusting entries at January 31.
 (c) Determine the ending balance in each of the accounts.

PROBLEMS: SET A

Prepare adjusting entries, post to ledger accounts, and prepare adjusted trial balance.
(SO 5, 6, 7)

P3–1A   Han Solo started his own consulting firm, Solo Company, on June 1, 2001. The trial balance at June 30 is as follows:

SOLO COMPANY
Trial Balance
June 30, 2001

Account Number		Debit	Credit
100	Cash	$ 7,750	
110	Accounts Receivable	6,000	
120	Prepaid Insurance	2,400	
130	Supplies	2,000	
135	Office Equipment	15,000	
200	Accounts Payable		$ 4,500
230	Unearned Service Revenue		4,000
300	Common Stock		21,750
400	Service Revenue		7,900
510	Salaries Expense	4,000	
520	Rent Expense	1,000	
		$38,150	$38,150

In addition those accounts listed on the trial balance, the chart of accounts for Solo Company also contains the following accounts and account numbers: No. 136 Accumulated Depreciation— Office Equipment, No. 210 Utilities Payable, No. 220 Salaries Payable, No. 530 Depreciation Expense, No. 540 Insurance Expense, No. 550 Utilities Expense, and No. 560 Supplies Expense.

Other data:

1. The balance in the supplies account at June 30 is $1,300.
2. A utility bill for $150 has not been recorded and will not be paid until next month.
3. The insurance policy is for a year.
4. $2,500 of unearned service revenue has been earned at the end of the month.
5. Salaries of $1,500 are accrued at June 30.
6. The office equipment has a 5-year life with no salvage value and is being depreciated at $250 per month for 60 months.
7. Invoices representing $3,000 of services performed during the month have not been recorded as of June 30.

Instructions
(a) Prepare the adjusting entries for the month of June. Use J3 as the page number for your journal.
(b) Post the adjusting entries to the ledger accounts. Enter the totals from the trial balance as beginning account balances and place a check mark in the posting reference column.
(c) Prepare an adjusted trial balance at June 30, 2001.

Prepare adjusting entries, post to ledger accounts, prepare adjusted trial balance and financial statements.
(SO 5, 6, 7)

P3–2A   Palpatine Hotel Inc. opened for business on May 1, 2001. Its trial balance before adjustment on May 31 is as follows:

PALPATINE HOTEL INC.
Trial Balance
May 31, 2001

	Debit	Credit
Cash	$ 2,500	
Prepaid Insurance	1,800	
Supplies	1,900	
Land	15,000	
Lodge	70,000	
Furniture	16,800	
Accounts Payable		$ 4,700
Unearned Rent Revenue		3,600
Mortgage Payable		35,000
Common Stock		60,000
Rent Revenue		9,200
Salaries Expense	3,000	
Utilities Expense	1,000	
Advertising Expense	500	
	$112,500	$112,500

Other data:

1. Insurance expires at the rate of $200 per month.
2. An inventory of supplies shows $1,200 of unused supplies on May 31.
3. Annual depreciation is $3,600 on the lodge and $3,000 on furniture.
4. The mortgage interest rate is 12%. (The mortgage was taken out on May 1.)
5. Unearned rent of $1,500 has been earned.
6. Salaries of $300 are accrued and unpaid at May 31.

Instructions
  (a) Journalize the adjusting entries on May 31.
  (b) Prepare a ledger using the three-column form of account. Enter the trial balance amounts and post the adjusting entries. (Use J1 as the posting reference.)
  (c) Prepare an adjusted trial balance on May 31.
  (d) Prepare an income statement and a retained earnings statement for the month of May and a balance sheet at May 31.

P3–3A Yoda Inc. was organized on July 1, 2001. Quarterly financial statements are prepared. The unadjusted and adjusted trial balances as of September 30 are shown below.

Prepare adjusting entries and financial statements.
(SO 5, 6, 7)

YODA INC.
Trial Balance
September 30, 2001

	Unadjusted		Adjusted	
	Dr.	Cr.	Dr.	Cr.
Cash	$ 6,700		$ 6,700	
Accounts Receivable	400		1,000	
Prepaid Rent	1,500		900	
Supplies	1,200		1,000	
Equipment	15,000		15,000	
Accumulated Depreciation—Equipment				$ 350
Notes Payable		$ 5,000		5,000
Accounts Payable		1,510		1,510
Salaries Payable				400
Interest Payable				50
Unearned Rent Revenue		900		600
Common Stock		14,000		14,000
Retained Earnings		–0–		–0–
Dividends	600		600	
Commission Revenue		14,000		14,600
Rent Revenue		400		700
Salaries Expense	9,000		9,400	
Rent Expense	900		1,500	
Depreciation Expense			350	
Supplies Expense			200	
Utilities Expense	510		510	
Interest Expense			50	
	$35,810	$35,810	$37,210	$37,210

Instructions
  (a) Journalize the adjusting entries that were made.
  (b) Prepare an income statement and a retained earnings statement for the 3 months ending September 30 and a balance sheet at September 30.
  (c) If the note bears interest at 12%, how many months has it been outstanding?

P3–4A A review of the ledger of Ewoks Company at December 31, 2001, produces the following data pertaining to the preparation of annual adjusting entries:

Prepare adjusting entries.
(SO 5, 6)

1. Prepaid Insurance $12,300. The company has separate insurance policies on its buildings and its motor vehicles. Policy B4564 on the building was purchased on July 1, 2000, for $9,000. The policy has a term of 3 years. Policy A2958 on the vehicles was purchased on January 1, 2001, for $4,800. This policy has a term of 2 years.

2. Unearned Subscription Revenue $49,000. The company began selling magazine subscriptions in 2001 on an annual basis. The selling price of a subscription is $50. A review of subscription contracts reveals the following:

Subscription Date	Number of Subscriptions
October 1	200
November 1	300
December 1	480
	980

3. Notes Payable, $40,000. This balance consists of a note for 6 months at an annual interest rate of 9%, dated September 1.
4. Salaries Payable $0. There are eight salaried employees. Salaries are paid every Friday for the current week. Five employees receive a salary of $600 each per week, and three employees earn $700 each per week. December 31 is a Wednesday. Employees do not work weekends. All employees worked the last 3 days of December.

Instructions
Prepare the adjusting entries at December 31, 2001.

Journalize transactions and follow through accounting cycle to preparation of financial statements.
(SO 5, 6, 7)

P3–5A On November 1, 2001, the account balances of Naboo Equipment Repair Corp. were as follows:

No.	Debits		No.	Credits	
101	Cash	$ 2,790	154	Accumulated Depreciation	$ 500
112	Accounts Receivable	2,510	201	Accounts Payable	2,100
126	Supplies	1,000	209	Unearned Service Revenue	400
153	Store Equipment	10,000	212	Salaries Payable	500
			311	Common Stock	10,000
			320	Retained Earnings	2,800
		$16,300			$16,300

During November the following summary transactions were completed.

Nov.   8 Paid $1,100 for salaries due employees, of which $600 is for November and $500 is for October.
   10 Received $1,200 cash from customers on account.
   12 Received $1,400 cash for services performed in November.
   15 Purchased store equipment on account $3,000.
   17 Purchased supplies on account $1,500.
   20 Paid creditors on account $2,500.
   22 Paid November rent $300.
   25 Paid salaries $1,000.
   27 Performed services on account and billed customers for services rendered $900.
   29 Received $550 from customers for future service.

Adjustment data consist of:
1. Supplies on hand $1,600.
2. Accrued salaries payable $500.
3. Depreciation for the month is $120.
4. Unearned service revenue of $300 is earned.

Instructions
(a) Enter the November 1 balances in the ledger accounts.
(b) Journalize the November transactions.
(c) Post to the ledger accounts. Use J1 for posting reference and No. 407 Service Revenue, No. 615 Depreciation Expense, No. 631 Supplies Expense, No. 726 Salaries Expense, and No. 729 Rent Expense.
(d) Prepare a trial balance at November 30.
(e) Journalize and post adjusting entries.
(f) Prepare an adjusted trial balance.
(g) Prepare an income statement and a retained earnings statement for November and a balance sheet at November 30.

*P3–6A   Leia Organa Graphics Company was organized on January 1, 2001, by Anakin Sky-walker. At the end of the first 6 months of operations, the trial balance contained the follow-ing accounts:

Prepare adjusting entries, adjusted trial balance, and financial statements using appendix. (SO 5, 6, 7, 9)

Debits		Credits	
Cash	$ 9,500	Notes Payable	$ 17,000
Accounts Receivable	14,000	Accounts Payable	9,000
Equipment	45,000	Common Stock	25,000
Insurance Expense	1,800	Graphic Revenue	52,100
Salaries Expense	30,000	Consulting Revenue	5,000
Supplies Expense	2,700		
Advertising Expense	1,900		
Rent Expense	1,500		
Utilities Expense	1,700		
	$108,100		$108,100

Analysis reveals the following additional data:

1. The $2,700 balance in Supplies Expense represents supplies purchased in January. At June 30, there was $1,500 of supplies on hand.
2. The note payable was issued on February 1. It is a 12%, 6-month note.
3. The balance in Insurance Expense is the premium on a one-year policy, dated March 1, 2001.
4. Consulting fees are credited to revenue when received. At June 30, consulting fees of $1,000 are unearned.
5. Graphic revenue earned but unbilled at June 30 totals $2,000.
5. Depreciation is $2,000 per year.

Instructions
(a) Journalize the adjusting entries at June 30. (Assume adjustments are recorded every 6 months.)
(b) Prepare an adjusted trial balance.
(c) Prepare an income statement and a retained earnings statement for the 6 months ended June 30 and a balance sheet at June 30.

PROBLEMS: SET B

P3–1B   Julie Brown started her own consulting firm, Astromech Consulting, on May 1, 2001. The trial balance at May 31 is as follows:

Prepare adjusting entries, post to ledger accounts, and prepare an adjusted trial balance. (SO 5, 6, 7)

ASTROMECH CONSULTING
Trial Balance
May 31, 2001

Account Number		Debit	Credit
100	Cash	$ 6,500	
110	Accounts Receivable	4,000	
120	Prepaid Insurance	3,600	
130	Supplies	1,500	
135	Office Equipment	12,000	
200	Accounts Payable		$ 3,500
230	Unearned Service Revenue		3,000
300	Common Stock		19,100
400	Service Revenue		6,000
510	Salaries Expense	3,000	
520	Rent Expense	1,000	
		$31,600	$31,600

In addition to those accounts listed on the trial balance, the chart of accounts for Astromech Con-sulting also contains the following accounts and account numbers: No. 136 Accumulated Depre-ciation—Office Furniture, No. 210 Travel Payable, No. 220 Salaries Payable, No. 530 Depreciation Expense, No. 540 Insurance Expense, No. 550 Travel Expense, and No. 560 Supplies Expense.

Other data:

1. $500 of supplies have been used during the month.
2. The insurance policy is for 2 years.
3. $1,000 of the balance in the unearned service revenue account remains unearned at the end of the month.
4. May 31 is a Wednesday and employees are paid on Fridays. Astromech Consulting has two employees that are paid $500 each for a 5-day work week.
5. The office furniture has a 5-year life with no salvage value and is being depreciated at $200 per month for 60 months.
6. Invoices representing $2,000 of services performed during the month have not been recorded as of May 31.

Instructions

(a) Prepare the adjusting entries for the month of May. Use J4 as the page number for your journal.
(b) Post the adjusting entries to the ledger accounts. Enter the totals from the trial balance as beginning account balances and place a check mark in the posting reference column.
(c) Prepare an adjusted trial balance at May 31, 2001.

Prepare adjusting entries, adjusted trial balance, and financial statements.
(SO 5, 6, 7)

P3–2B   Obi-Wan Resort opened for business on June 1 with eight air-conditioned units. Its trial balance before adjustment on August 31 is as follows:

OBI-WAN RESORT
Trial Balance
August 31, 2001

	Debit	Credit
Cash	$ 19,600	
Prepaid Insurance	5,400	
Supplies	3,300	
Land	25,000	
Cottages	125,000	
Furniture	26,000	
Accounts Payable		$ 6,500
Unearned Rent Revenue		6,800
Mortgage Payable		80,000
Common Stock		100,000
Dividends	5,000	
Rent Revenue		80,000
Salaries Expense	51,000	
Utilities Expense	9,400	
Repair Expense	3,600	
	$273,300	$273,300

Other data:

1. Insurance expires at the rate of $300 per month.
2. An inventory count on August 31 shows $900 of supplies on hand.
3. Annual depreciation is $4,800 on cottages and $2,400 on furniture.
4. Unearned rent of $5,000 was earned prior to August 31.
5. Salaries of $400 were unpaid at August 31.
6. Rentals of $800 were due from tenants at August 31. (Use Accounts Receivable.)
7. The mortgage interest rate is 12% per year. (The mortgage was taken out on August 1.)

Instructions

(a) Journalize the adjusting entries on August 31 for the 3-month period June 1–August 31.
(b) Prepare a ledger using the three-column form of account. Enter the trial balance amounts and post the adjusting entries. (Use J1 as the posting reference.)

(c) Prepare an adjusted trial balance on August 31.
(d) Prepare an income statement and a retained earnings statement for the 3 months ending August 31 and a balance sheet as of August 31.

P3-3B R2 D2 Advertising Agency Inc. was founded by Mace Windu in January 1997. Presented below are both the adjusted and unadjusted trial balances as of December 31, 2001.

Prepare adjusting entries and financial statements.
(SO 5, 6, 7)

R2–D2 ADVERTISING AGENCY INC.
Trial Balance
December 31, 2001

	Unadjusted		Adjusted	
	Dr.	Cr.	Dr.	Cr.
Cash	$ 11,000		$ 11,000	
Accounts Receivable	20,000		21,500	
Art Supplies	8,400		5,000	
Prepaid Insurance	3,350		2,500	
Printing Equipment	60,000		60,000	
Accumulated Depreciation		$ 28,000		$ 35,000
Accounts Payable		5,000		5,000
Interest Payable		0		150
Notes Payable		5,000		5,000
Unearned Advertising Revenue		7,000		5,600
Salaries Payable		0		1,300
Common Stock		20,000		20,000
Retained Earnings		5,500		5,500
Dividends	12,000		12,000	
Advertising Revenue		58,600		61,500
Salaries Expense	10,000		11,300	
Insurance Expense			850	
Interest Expense	350		500	
Depreciation Expense			7,000	
Art Supplies Expense			3,400	
Rent Expense	4,000		4,000	
	$129,100	$129,100	$139,050	$139,050

Instructions
(a) Journalize the annual adjusting entries that were made.
(b) Prepare an income statement and a retained earnings statement for the year ending December 31, 2001, and a balance sheet at December 31.
(c) Answer the following questions:
  (1) If the note has been outstanding 3 months, what is the annual interest rate on that note?
  (2) If the company paid $13,500 in salaries in 2001, what was the balance in Salaries Payable on December 31, 2000?

P3-4B A review of the ledger of Lott Dod Company at December 31, 2001, produces the following data pertaining to the preparation of annual adjusting entries.

Prepare adjusting entries.
(SO 5, 6)

1. Salaries Payable $0. There are eight salaried employees. Salaries are paid every Friday for the current week. Five employees receive a salary of $700 each per week, and three employees earn $500 each per week. December 31 is a Tuesday. Employees do not work weekends. All employees worked the last 2 days of December.
2. Unearned Rent Revenue $369,000. The company began subleasing office space in its new building on November 1. Each tenant is required to make a $5,000 security deposit that is not refundable until occupancy is terminated. At December 31, the company had the following rental contracts that are paid in full for the entire term of the lease.

Date	Term (in months)	Monthly Rent	Number of Leases
Nov. 1	6	$4,000	5
Dec. 1	6	$8,500	4

3. Prepaid Advertising $13,200. This balance consists of payments on two advertising contracts. The contracts provide for monthly advertising in two trade magazines. The terms of the contracts are as follows:

Contract	Date	Amount	Number of Magazine Issues
A650	May 1	$6,000	12
B974	Oct. 1	7,200	24

The first advertisement runs in the month in which the contract is signed.

4. Notes Payable $80,000. This balance consists of a note for one year at an annual interest rate of 12%, dated June 1.

Instructions
Prepare the adjusting entries at December 31, 2001. (Show all computations.)

Journalize transactions and follow through accounting cycle to preparation of financial statements.
(SO 5, 6, 7)

P3–5B On September 1, 2001, the account balances of Boba Fett Equipment Repair were as follows:

No.	Debits		No.	Credits	
101	Cash	$ 4,880	154	Accumulated Depreciation	$ 1,500
112	Accounts Receivable	3,520	201	Accounts Payable	3,400
126	Supplies	1,000	209	Unearned Service Revenue	400
153	Store Equipment	15,000	212	Salaries Payable	500
			311	Common Stock	10,000
			320	Retained Earnings	8,600
		$24,400			$24,400

During September the following summary transactions were completed.

Sept. 8 Paid $1,100 for salaries due employees, of which $600 is for September and $500 for August.
   10 Received $1,200 cash from customers on account.
   12 Received $3,400 cash for services performed in September.
   15 Purchased store equipment on account $3,000.
   17 Purchased supplies on account $1,500.
   20 Paid creditors $4,500 on account.
   22 Paid September rent $500.
   25 Paid salaries $1,050.
   27 Performed services on account and billed customers for services rendered $700.
   29 Received $650 from customers for future service.

Adjustment data consist of:
   1. Supplies on hand $1,800.
   2. Accrued salaries payable $400.
   3. Depreciation is $200 per month.
   4. Unearned service revenue of $350 is earned.

Instructions
(a) Enter the September 1 balances in the ledger accounts.
(b) Journalize the September transactions.
(c) Post to the ledger accounts. Use J1 for posting reference and No. 407 Service Revenue, No. 615 Depreciation Expense, No. 631 Supplies Expense, No. 726 Salaries Expense, and No. 729 Rent Expense.
(d) Prepare a trial balance at September 30.
(e) Journalize and post adjusting entries.
(f) Prepare an adjusted trial balance.
(g) Prepare an income statement and a retained earnings statement for September and a balance sheet at September 30.

*P3–6B   Your examination of the records of a company that follows the cash basis of accounting tells you that the company's reported cash basis income in 2001 is $35,190. If this firm had followed accrual basis accounting practices, it would have reported the following year-end balances:

Convert income from cash to accrual basis.
(SO 8)

	2000	2001
Accounts Receivable	$2,500	$3,400
Supplies on Hand	1,160	1,300
Wages Payable	2,400	1,200
Other Unpaid Amounts	1,600	1,440

Instructions
Determine the company's net income, on an accrual basis, for 2001. Show all your calculations, in an orderly fashion. (*Hint:* Start with cash basis income and adjust it to the accrual basis net income.)

BROADENING YOUR PERSPECTIVE

FINANCIAL REPORTING AND ANALYSIS
• •

FINANCIAL REPORTING PROBLEM: Kellogg Company

BYP3–1   The financial statements of Kellogg's are presented in Appendix A at the end of this textbook.

Instructions
(a) Using the consolidated financial statements and related information, identify items that may result in adjusting entries for prepayments.
(b) Using the consolidated financial statements and related information, identify items that may result in adjusting entries for accruals.
(c) Using the Selected Financial Data section, what has been the trend since 1988 for depreciation and amortization expense and for advertising expense?

COMPARATIVE ANALYSIS PROBLEM: Kellogg Company vs. General Mills

BYP3–2   Kellogg's financial statements are presented in Appendix A; General Mills's financial statements are presented in Appendix B.

Instructions
Based on information contained in these financial statements, determine the following for each company:

(a) Net increase (decrease) in property, plant, and equipment from 1997 to 1998.
(b) Increase (decrease) in selling, general, and administrative expenses from 1997 to 1998.
(c) Increase (decrease) in accounts payable from 1997 to 1998.
(d) Increase (decrease) in net income from 1997 to 1998.
(e) Increase (decrease) in cash and cash equivalents from 1997 to 1998.

RESEARCH ASSIGNMENT

BYP3–3   The Enterprise Standard Industrial Classification (SIC) coding scheme, a published classification of firms into separate industries, is commonly used in practice. SIC codes permit identification of company activities on three levels of detail. Two-digit codes designate a "major group," three-digit codes designate an "industry group," while four-digit codes identify a specific "industry."

Instructions
At your library, find the *Standard Industrial Classification Manual* (published by the U.S. Government's Office of Management and Budget in 1987) to answer the following questions:

(a) On what basis are SIC codes assigned to companies?

(b) Identify the major group/industry group/industry represented by the following codes: 12, 271, 3571, 7033, 75, and 872.

(c) Identify the SIC code for the following industries:
1. Golfing equipment—manufacturing
2. Worm farms
3. Felt tip markers—manufacturing
4. Household appliance stores, electric, or gas—retail
5. Advertising agencies

(d) You are interested in examining several companies in the passenger airline industry. Determine the appropriate two-, three-, and four-digit SIC codes. Use *Wards Business Directory of U.S. Private and Public Companies (Vol. 5)* to compile a list of the five largest parent companies (by total sales) in the industry. Note: If Wards is not available, alternative sources include *Standard & Poor's Register of Corporations, Directors, and Executives, Standard & Poor's Industry Surveys*, and the Dun & Bradstreet *Million Dollar Directory*.

INTERPRETING FINANCIAL STATEMENTS: Smith's Food and Drug Centers, Inc.

BYP3–4 Smith's Food and Drug Centers, Inc. is a supermarket and drug store chain that operates 137 stores in the Intermountain and Southwestern regions of the United States. Smith's competes using a strategy of providing one-stop shopping for customers. This requires large inventories and frequent restocking of inventories. To reduce these costs, Smith's owns and operates its own warehouse and distribution facilities. The Current Liabilities section of the company's balance sheet included the following (dollar amounts are in thousands):

SMITH'S FOOD AND DRUG CO. Balance Sheet (partial)	
Trade accounts payable	$235,843
Accrued sales and other taxes	44,379
Accrued payroll and related benefits	84,083

Instructions

(a) Why does the company have accrued payroll and related benefits? Does this mean that the company is behind in paying its employees? Explain.

(b) The company has state-of-the-art scanners at most of its registers. Even at older stores, each cash register computes daily totals for both sales and sales taxes. Why then does the company have accrued sales taxes?

REAL-WORLD FOCUS: Laser Recording Systems Incorporated

BYP3–5 **Laser Recording Systems,** founded in 1981, produces laser disks for use in the home market. Sales since 1985 have increased approximately 15 percent per year. The following is an excerpt from Laser Recording Systems' financial statements (all dollars in thousands):

LASER RECORDING SYSTEMS Management Discussion
Accrued liabilities increased to $1,642 at January 31, from $138 at the end of the previous fiscal year. Compensation and related accruals increased $195 due primarily to increases in accruals for severance, vacation, commissions, and relocation expenses. Accrued professional services increased by $137 primarily as a result of legal expenses related to several outstanding contractual disputes. Other expense increased $35, of which $18 was for interest payable.

Instructions
(a) Can you tell from the discussion whether Laser Recording has prepaid its legal expenses and is now making an adjustment to the asset account Prepaid Legal Expenses, or whether the company is handling the legal expense via an accrued expense adjustment?
(b) Identify each of the adjustments Laser Recording is discussing as one of the four types of possible adjustments discussed in the chapter. How is net income ultimately affected by each of the adjustments?
(c) What journal entry did Laser Recording make to record the accrued interest?

CRITICAL THINKING

GROUP DECISION CASE

BYP3–6 A partial adjusted trial balance of the Cordero Company at January 31, 2001, shows the following:

CORDERO COMPANY
Adjusted Trial Balance
January 31, 2001

	Debit	Credit
Supplies	$ 800	
Prepaid Insurance	2,400	
Salaries Payable		$ 700
Unearned Revenue		750
Supplies Expense	950	
Insurance Expense	400	
Salaries Expense	1,800	
Service Revenue		2,500

Instructions
With the class divided into groups, answer the following questions, assuming the company's fiscal year begins January 1:

(a) If the amount in Supplies Expense is the January 31 adjusting entry, and $850 of supplies were purchased in January, what was the balance in Supplies on January 1?
(b) If the amount in Insurance Expense is the January 31 adjusting entry, and the original insurance premium was for one year, what was the total premium, and when was the policy purchased?
(c) If $2,500 of salaries was paid in January, what was the balance in Salaries Payable at December 31, 2000?
(d) If $1,600 of fees was received in January for services performed in January, what was the balance in Unearned Revenue at December 31, 2000?

COMMUNICATION ACTIVITY

BYP3–7 In reviewing the accounts of the Marylee Co. at the end of the year, you discover that adjusting entries have not been made.

Instructions
Write a memorandum to Mary Lee Virgil, the owner of Marylee Co., that explains the following: the nature and purpose of adjusting entries, why adjusting entries are needed, and the types of adjusting entries that may be made.

ETHICS CASE

BYP3–8 Darth Maul Company is a pesticide manufacturer. Its sales declined greatly this year due to the passage of legislation outlawing the sale of several of Darth Maul's chemical pesticides. During the coming year, Darth Maul will have environmentally safe and competitive replacement chemicals to replace these discontinued products. Sales in the next year are expected to greatly exceed any prior year's. The decline in sales and profits appears to be a one-year aberration. But even so, the company president believes that a large dip in current year's profits could cause a significant drop in the market price of Darth Maul's stock and make it a takeover target.

To avoid this possibility, the company president urges Becky Freeman, controller, in making this period's year-end adjusting entries to accrue every possible revenue and to defer as many expenses as possible. The president says to Becky, "We need the revenues this year, and next year can easily absorb expenses deferred from this year. We can't let our stock price be hammered down!" Becky didn't get around to recording the adjusting entries until January 17, but she dated the entries December 31 as if they were recorded then. Becky also made every effort to comply with the president's request.

Instructions
(a) Who are the stakeholders in this situation?
(b) What are the ethical considerations of (1) the president's request and (2) Becky's dating the adjusting entries December 31?
(c) Can Becky accrue revenues and defer expenses and still be ethical?

SURFING THE NET

BYP3-9   A wealth of accounting-related information is available via the Internet. For example the Rutgers Accounting Web (http://www.rutgers.edu/accounting/raw.htm) offers access to a great variety of sources.

Instructions
Once in the Rutgers Accounting Web, click on "Accounting Resources" in the left margin, or click on "RAW's Features." (*Note:* Once on this page, you may have to click on the "text only" box to access the available information.)

(a) List the categories of information available through the "Accounting Resources on the Internet" page.
(b) Select any one of these categories and briefly describe the types of information available.

Answers to Self-Study Questions
1. c   2. a   3. d   4. d   5. c   6. a   7. b   8. b   9. c   10. d   11. a

Answer to Kellogg Review It Question 4, p. 102
1998 depreciation and amortization expense is $278.1 million; 1997 depreciation and amortization expense is $287.3 million.

Remember to go back to the Navigator box on the chapter-opening page and check off your completed work.

Before studying this chapter you should know or, if necessary, review:

a. How to apply the revenue recognition and matching principles. (Ch. 3, pp. 93–94)
b. How to make adjusting entries. (Ch. 3, pp. 95–107)
c. How to prepare an adjusted trial balance. (Ch. 3, p. 110)
d. How to prepare a balance sheet, income statement, and retained earnings statement. (Ch. 3, pp. 111–112)

THE NAVIGATOR

FEATURE STORY

A Little Knowledge Brings a Lot of Profits

Employee training in financial accounting has paid off for Jack Stack at SRC Corporation in Woodridge, Illinois, which rebuilds engines. President and owner of SRC, he was really concerned when his company lost $61,000 on sales of $16 million. He decided that the "only way to turn things around was to get employees to think like owners." But how to do it? He decided to "teach anyone who moved a broom or operated a grinder everything a bank lender would know. That way they would really understand how each nickel saved could make a difference."

Therefore, SRC spent $300,000 on financial accounting training for its employees. Each week the company stopped its operations for half an hour while its 800 employees broke into small groups to study the latest financial statements. "At first it wasn't easy for everyone to understand the numbers," concedes employee Craig Highbarger, "but we've been over the different figures enough times now, if you hand any one of us a financial statement and leave out a few numbers, we can fill them in." Employees now understand how much it costs to copy a document or turn on a light.

Has it made a difference? Recently SRC earned $6 million on sales of $100 million. As a result of this turnaround, SRC handed out $1.4 million in bonuses to its employees, who are now wealthier in both cash and knowledge.

THE NAVIGATOR

CHAPTER 4

THE NAVIGATOR ✔

- Understand *Concepts for Review* ☐
- Read *Feature Story* ☐
- Scan *Study Objectives* ☐
- Read *Preview* ☐
- Read text and answer *Before You Go On*
  p. 146 ☐   p. 156 ☐   p. 162 ☐
- Work *Demonstration Problem* ☐
- Review *Summary of Study Objectives* ☐
- Answer *Self-Study Questions* ☐
- Complete assignments ☐

COMPLETION OF THE ACCOUNTING CYCLE

STUDY OBJECTIVES

After studying this chapter, you should be able to:

1. *Prepare a work sheet.*
2. *Explain the process of closing the books.*
3. *Describe the content and purpose of a post-closing trial balance.*
4. *State the required steps in the accounting cycle.*
5. *Explain the approaches to preparing correcting entries.*
6. *Identify the sections of a classified balance sheet.*

THE NAVIGATOR

*A*s was true at SRC Corporation, financial statements can help employees understand what is happening in the business. In Chapter 3, we prepared financial statements directly from the adjusted trial balance. However, with so many details involved in the end-of-period accounting procedures, it is easy to make errors. Locating and correcting errors can cost much time and effort. One way to minimize errors in the records and to simplify the end-of-period procedures is to use a work sheet.

In this chapter we will explain the role of the work sheet in accounting as well as the remaining steps in the accounting cycle, most especially, the closing process, again using Pioneer Advertising Agency as an example. Then we will consider (1) correcting entries and (2) classified balance sheets. The content and organization of the chapter are as follows:

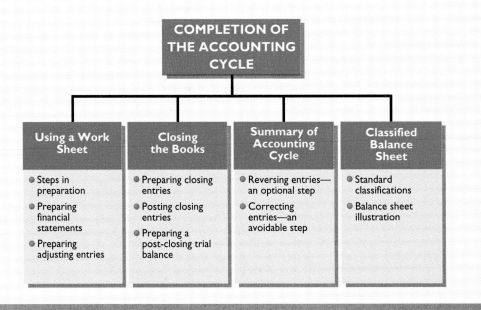

COMPLETION OF THE ACCOUNTING CYCLE

Using a Work Sheet	Closing the Books	Summary of Accounting Cycle	Classified Balance Sheet
• Steps in preparation	• Preparing closing entries	• Reversing entries—an optional step	• Standard classifications
• Preparing financial statements	• Posting closing entries	• Correcting entries—an avoidable step	• Balance sheet illustration
• Preparing adjusting entries	• Preparing a post-closing trial balance		

THE NAVIGATOR

USING A WORK SHEET

A work sheet is a multiple-column form that may be used in the adjustment process and in preparing financial statements. As its name suggests, the work sheet is a working tool or a supplementary device. **A work sheet is not a permanent accounting record**; it is neither a journal nor a part of the general ledger. The work sheet is merely a device used to make it easier to prepare adjusting entries and the financial statements. In small companies with relatively few accounts and adjustments, a work sheet may not be needed. In large companies with numerous accounts and many adjustments, it is almost indispensable.

The basic form of a work sheet and the procedure (5 steps) for preparing a work sheet are shown in Illustration 4-1. Each of the steps in preparing the work sheet must be performed in the prescribed sequence.

The use of a work sheet is optional. When a work sheet is used, financial statements are prepared from the work sheet. The adjustments are entered in the work sheet columns and are then journalized and posted after the financial state-

ILLUSTRATION 4-1

Form and procedure for a work sheet

Work Sheet

Account Titles	Trial Balance		Adjustments		Adjusted Trial Balance		Income Statement		Balance Sheet	
	Dr.	Cr.	Dr.	Cr.	Dr.	Cr.	Dr.	Cr.	Dr.	Cr.

1 Prepare a trial balance on the work sheet

2 Enter adjustment data

3 Enter adjusted balances

4 Extend adjusted balances to appropriate statement columns

5 Total the statement columns, compute net income (or net loss), and complete work sheet

ments have been prepared. Thus, management and other interested parties can receive the financial statements at an earlier date than without a work sheet.

Steps in Preparing a Work Sheet

We will use the October 31 trial balance and adjustment data of Pioneer Advertising in Chapter 3 to illustrate the preparation of a work sheet. Each step of the process is described below and demonstrated in Illustrations 4-2 and 4-3A, B, C, and D following page 143.

Step 1. Prepare a Trial Balance on the Work Sheet. The account title space and trial balance columns are used to prepare a trial balance. The data for the trial balance come directly from the ledger accounts. The trial balance for Pioneer Advertising Agency is entered in the trial balance columns of the work sheet as shown in Illustration 4-2.

Step 2. Enter the Adjustments in the Adjustment Columns. Turn over the first transparency, Illustration 4-3A. When a work sheet is used, all adjustments are entered in the adjustment columns. In entering the adjustments, applicable trial balance accounts should be used. If additional accounts are needed, they should be inserted on the lines immediately below the trial balance totals. Each adjustment is indexed and keyed to facilitate the journalizing of the adjusting entry in the general journal. **It is important to recognize that the adjustments are not journalized until after the work sheet is completed and the financial statements have been prepared.**

The adjustments for Pioneer Advertising Agency Inc. are the same as the adjustments illustrated on page 108. They are keyed in the adjustment columns of the work sheet as follows:

(a) An additional account, Advertising Supplies Expense, is debited $1,500 for the cost of supplies used, and Advertising Supplies is credited $1,500.

(b) An additional account, Insurance Expense, is debited $50 for the insurance that has expired, and Prepaid Insurance is credited $50.

(c) Two additional accounts are needed. Depreciation Expense is debited $40 for the month's depreciation, and Accumulated Depreciation—Office Equipment is credited $40.

(d) Unearned Revenue is debited $400 for services provided, and Service Revenue is credited $400.

(e) An additional account, Accounts Receivable, is debited $200 for services provided but not billed, and Service Revenue is credited $200.

(f) Two additional accounts are needed. Interest Expense is debited $50 for accrued interest, and Interest Payable is credited $50.

(g) Salaries Expense is debited $1,200 for accrued salaries, and an additional account, Salaries Payable, is credited $1,200.

Note in the illustration that after all the adjustments have been entered, the adjustment columns are totaled and the equality of the column totals is proved.

Step 3.   Enter Adjusted Balances in the Adjusted Trial Balance Columns. Turn over the second transparency, Illustration 4-3B. The adjusted balance of an account is obtained by combining the amounts entered in the first four columns of the work sheet for each account. For example, the Prepaid Insurance account in the trial balance columns has a $600 debit balance. When this is combined with the $50 credit in the adjustment columns, the result is a $550 debit balance recorded in the adjusted trial balance columns. **For each account on the work sheet, the amount in the adjusted trial balance columns is equal to the account balance that will appear in the ledger after the adjusting entries have been journalized and posted.** The balances in these columns are the same as those in the adjusted trial balance in Illustration 3-18 on page 110.

TECHNOLOGY IN ACTION

The work sheet can be computerized using an electronic spreadsheet program. The Excel and LOTUS 1-2-3 supplement for this textbook is one of the most popular versions of such spreadsheet packages. With a program like Excel or LOTUS 1-2-3, you can produce any type of work sheet (accounting or otherwise) that you could produce with paper and pencil on a columnar pad. The tremendous advantage of an electronic work sheet over the paper and pencil version is the ability to change selected data. When data are changed, the computer updates the balance of your computations instantly. More specific applications of electronic spreadsheets will be noted as we proceed.

Lotus
1·2·3 millennium edition
The Spreadsheet That's Revolutionizing the World... Again.

After the balances of all accounts have been entered in the adjusted trial balance columns, the columns are totaled and their equality is proved. The agreement of the column totals facilitates the completion of the work sheet. If these columns are not in agreement, the statement columns will not balance and the financial statements will be incorrect.

Step 4.   Extend Adjusted Trial Balance Amounts to Appropriate Financial Statement Columns. Turn over the third transparency, Illustration 4-3C. This step involves the extension of adjusted trial balance amounts to the last four columns of the work sheet. Balance sheet accounts such as Cash and Notes Payable are entered in the balance sheet debit and credit columns, respectively. The balance in accumulated depreciation is extended to the balance sheet credit column. This results because accumulated depreciation is a contra-asset account with a credit balance.

Because the work sheet does not have columns for the retained earnings statement, the balances in Common Stock and Retained Earnings, if any, are extended to the balance sheet credit column. In addition, the balance in Dividends is extended to the balance sheet debit column because it is a stockholders' equity account with a debit balance. The expense and revenue accounts such as Salaries Expense and Service Revenue are entered in the appropriate income statement columns. These extensions are shown in Illustration 4-3C.

Step 5.   Total the Statement Columns, Compute the Net Income (or Net Loss), and Complete the Work Sheet.   Turn over the fourth transparency, Illustration 4-3D. Each of the statement columns must be totaled. The net income or loss for the period is then found by computing the difference between the totals of the two income statement columns. If total credits exceed total debits, net income has resulted. In such a case, as shown in Illustration 4-3D, the words "net income" are inserted in the account title space. The amount then is entered in the income statement debit column and the balance sheet credit column. **The debit amount balances the income statement columns, and the credit amount balances the balance sheet columns.** In addition, the credit in the balance sheet column indicates the increase in stockholders' equity resulting from net income. Conversely, if total debits in the income statement columns exceed total credits, a net loss has occurred. The amount of the net loss is entered in the income statement credit column and the balance sheet debit column.

After the net income or net loss has been entered, new column totals are determined. The totals shown in the debit and credit income statement columns will be identical. The totals shown in the debit and credit balance sheet columns will also be identical. If either the income statement columns or the balance sheet columns are not equal after the net income or net loss has been entered, an error has been made in completing the work sheet. The completed work sheet for Pioneer Advertising Agency Inc. is shown in Illustration 4-3D.

Preparing Financial Statements from a Work Sheet

After a work sheet has been completed, the statement columns contain all the data that are required for the preparation of financial statements. The income statement is prepared from the income statement columns, and the balance sheet and retained earnings statement are prepared from the balance sheet columns. The financial statements prepared from the work sheet for Pioneer Advertising Agency Inc. are shown in Illustration 4-4. At this point, adjusting entries have not been journalized and posted. Therefore, the ledger does not support all financial statement amounts.

The amount shown for common stock on the work sheet does not change from the beginning to the end of the period unless additional stock is issued by the company during the period. Because there was no balance in Pioneer's retained earnings, the account is not listed on the work sheet. Only after dividends and net income (or loss) are posted to retained earnings does this account have a balance at the end of the first year of the business.

Using a work sheet, financial statements can be prepared before adjusting entries are journalized and posted. **However, the completed work sheet is not a substitute for formal financial statements.** Data in the financial statement columns are not properly arranged for statement purposes. Moreover, as noted above, the financial statement presentation for some accounts differs from their statement columns on the work sheet. **A work sheet is essentially a working tool of the accountant and is not distributed to management and other parties.**

HELPFUL HINT
Every adjusted trial balance amount must be extended to one of the four statement columns. Debit amounts go to debit columns and credit amounts go to credit columns.

HELPFUL HINT
All pairs of columns must balance for a work sheet to be complete.

(**Note:** Text continues on page 146, following acetate overlays.)

Illustration 4-2

Preparing a trial balance

PIONEER ADVERTISING AGENCY INC.
Work Sheet
For the Month Ended October 31, 2001

Account Titles	Trial Balance		Adjustments		Adjusted Trial Balance		Income Statement		Balance Sheet	
	Dr.	Cr.	Dr.	Cr.	Dr.	Cr.	Dr.	Cr.	Dr.	Cr.
Cash	15,200									
Advertising Supplies	2,500									
Prepaid Insurance	600									
Office Equipment	5,000									
Notes Payable		5,000								
Accounts Payable		2,500								
Unearned Revenue		1,200								
Common Stock		10,000								
Dividends	500									
Service Revenue		10,000								
Salaries Expense	4,000									
Rent Expense	900									
Totals	28,700	28,700								

Include all accounts from ledger with balances.

Trial balance amounts are taken directly from ledger accounts.

Illustration 4-4

Financial statements from a work sheet

PIONEER ADVERTISING AGENCY INC.
Income Statement
For the Month Ended October 31, 2001

Revenues		
Service revenue		$10,600
Expenses		
Salaries expense	$5,200	
Advertising supplies expense	1,500	
Rent expense	900	
Insurance expense	50	
Interest expense	50	
Depreciation expense	40	
Total expenses		7,740
Net income		$ 2,860

PIONEER ADVERTISING AGENCY INC.
Retained Earnings Statement
For the Month Ended October 31, 2001

Retained earnings, October 1	$ –0–
Add: Net income	2,860
	2,860
Less: Dividends	500
Retained earnings, October 31	$2,360

PIONEER ADVERTISING AGENCY INC.
Balance Sheet
October 31, 2001

Assets

Cash		$15,200
Accounts receivable		200
Advertising supplies		1,000
Prepaid insurance		550
Office equipment	$5,000	
Less: Accumulated depreciation	40	4,960
Total assets		$21,910

Liabilities and Stockholders' Equity

Liabilities	
Notes payable	$ 5,000
Accounts payable	2,500
Interest payable	50
Unearned revenue	800
Salaries payable	1,200
Total liabilities	9,550
Stockholders' equity	
Common stock	10,000
Retained earnings	2,360
Total liabilities and stockholders' equity	$21,910

Preparing Adjusting Entries from a Work Sheet

A work sheet is not a journal, and it cannot be used as a basis for posting to ledger accounts. To adjust the accounts, it is necessary to journalize and post the adjustments to the ledger. **The adjusting entries are prepared from the adjustment columns of the work sheet.** The reference letters in the adjustment columns and the explanation of the adjustments that appear at the bottom of the work sheet help identify entries. However, writing the explanation to the adjustments at the bottom of the work sheet is not required. As indicated previously, the journalizing and posting of adjusting entries **follows** the preparation of financial statements when a work sheet is used. The adjusting entries on October 31 for Pioneer Advertising Agency Inc. are the same as those shown in Illustration 3-16 (page 108).

BEFORE YOU GO ON...

Review It

1. What are the five steps in preparing a work sheet?
2. How is net income or net loss shown in a work sheet?
3. How does a work sheet relate to preparing financial statements and adjusting entries?

Do It

Melany Newby is preparing a work sheet. Explain to Melany how the following adjusted trial balance accounts should be extended to the financial statement columns of the work sheet: Cash; Accumulated Depreciation; Accounts Payable; Dividends; Service Revenue; and Salaries Expense.

Reasoning: Asset and liability balances are extended to the balance sheet debit and credit columns, respectively, except for accumulated depreciation which is extended to the balance sheet credit column. The dividends account is extended to the balance sheet debit column. Expenses are extended to the income statement debit column. Revenue accounts are extended to the income statement credit column.

Solution:

Income statement debit column — Salaries Expense
Income statement credit column — Service Revenue
Balance sheet debit column — Cash; Dividends
Balance sheet credit column — Accumulated Depreciation; Accounts Payable

As indicated in the Technology in Action box on page 142, the work sheet is an ideal application for electronic spreadsheet software like Microsoft Excel and LOTUS 1–2–3.

Related exercise material: BE4–1, BE4–2, BE4–3, E4–1, E4–2, E4–4, and E4–5.

CLOSING THE BOOKS

2
STUDY
OBJECTIVE
....
Explain the process of
closing the books.

In closing the books, it is necessary to distinguish between temporary and permanent accounts. Temporary or nominal accounts relate only to a given accounting period. They include all income statement accounts and Dividends. All temporary accounts are closed. In contrast, permanent or real accounts relate to one or more future accounting periods. They consist of all balance sheet accounts including Common Stock and Retained Earnings. Permanent accounts are not closed. Instead, their balances are carried forward into the next accounting period. Illustration 4-5 identifies the accounts in each category.

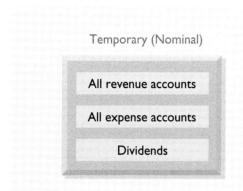
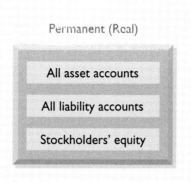

ILLUSTRATION 4-5
Temporary versus permanent accounts

HELPFUL HINT
A contra asset account, such as accumulated depreciation, is a real account also.

Preparing Closing Entries

At the end of the accounting period, the temporary account balances are transferred to the permanent stockholders' equity account, Retained Earnings, through the preparation of closing entries. Closing entries formally recognize in the ledger the transfer of net income or net loss and Dividends to Retained Earnings as shown in the retained earnings statement. **These entries also produce a zero balance in each temporary account so it can be used to accumulate data in the next accounting period separate from the data of prior periods.** Permanent accounts are not closed.

Journalizing and posting closing entries is a required step in the accounting cycle. This step is performed after financial statements have been prepared. In contrast to the steps in the cycle that you have already studied, closing entries are generally journalized and posted **only at the end of a company's annual accounting period.** This practice facilitates the preparation of annual financial statements because all temporary accounts will contain data for the entire year.

In preparing closing entries, each income statement account could be closed directly to Retained Earnings. However, to do so would result in excessive detail in the Retained Earnings account. Accordingly, the revenue and expense accounts are closed to another temporary account, Income Summary, and only the net income or net loss is transferred from this account to Retained Earnings.

Closing entries are journalized in the general journal. A center caption entitled Closing Entries may be inserted in the journal between the last adjusting entry and the first closing entry to identify these entries. Then the closing entries are posted to the ledger accounts. Closing entries may be prepared directly from the adjusted balances in the ledger, from the income statement and balance sheet columns of the work sheet, or from the income and retained earnings statements. Separate closing entries could be prepared for each nominal account, but the following four entries accomplish the desired result more efficiently:

HELPFUL HINT
When the work sheet is used, revenue and expense account data are found in the income statement columns, and Dividends is in the balance sheet debit column.

1. Debit each revenue account for its balance and credit Income Summary for total revenues.
2. Debit Income Summary for total expenses and credit each expense account for its balance.
3. Debit Income Summary and credit Retained Earnings for the amount of net income.
4. Debit Retained Earnings for the balance in the Dividends account and credit Dividends for the same amount.

The four entries are referenced in the diagram of the closing process shown in Illustration 4-6 and in the journal entries in Illustration 4-7. The posting of closing entries is shown in Illustration 4-8.

ILLUSTRATION 4-6

Diagram of closing process—corporation

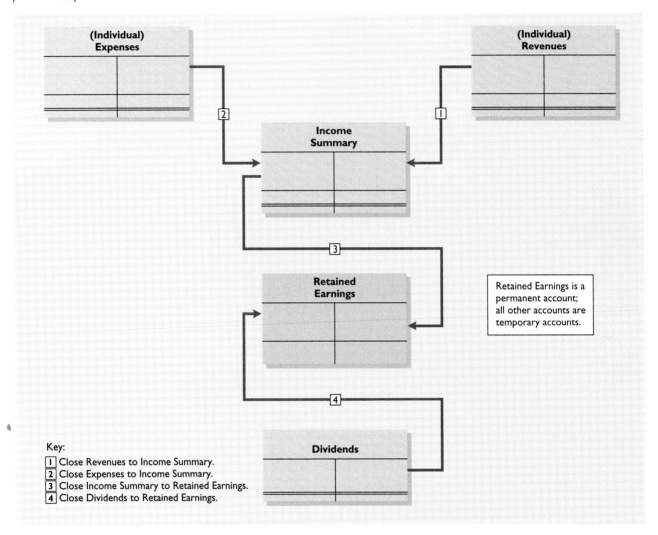

Key:
1 Close Revenues to Income Summary.
2 Close Expenses to Income Summary.
3 Close Income Summary to Retained Earnings.
4 Close Dividends to Retained Earnings.

If a net loss has occurred, entry (3) credits Income Summary and debits Retained Earnings.

ACCOUNTING IN ACTION
Business Insight

Until Sam Walton had opened twenty Wal-Mart stores, he used what he called the "ESP method" of closing the books. ESP was a pretty basic method: If the books didn't balance, Walton calculated the amount by which they were off and entered that amount under the heading ESP—which stood for "Error Some Place." As Walton noted, "It really sped things along when it came time to close those books."

Source: Sam Walton, *Made in America* (New York: Doubleday, 1992), p. 53.

Closing Entries Illustrated

As explained above, closing entries are generally prepared only at the end of a company's annual accounting period. However, to illustrate the journalizing and posting of closing entries, we will assume that Pioneer Advertising Agency Inc. closes its books monthly. The closing entries at October 31 are shown in Illustration 4-7.

Date	Account Titles and Explanation	Ref.	Debit	Credit
	General Journal			**J3**
	Closing Entries			
	(1)			
Oct. 31	Service Revenue	50	10,600	
	Income Summary	49		10,600
	(To close revenue account)			
	(2)			
31	Income Summary	49	7,740	
	Salaries Expense	60		5,200
	Advertising Supplies Expense	61		1,500
	Rent Expense	62		900
	Insurance Expense	63		50
	Interest Expense	64		50
	Depreciation Expense	65		40
	(To close expense accounts)			
	(3)			
31	Income Summary	49	2,860	
	Retained Earnings	40		2,860
	(To close net income to retained earnings)			
	(4)			
31	Retained Earnings	40	500	
	Dividends	41		500
	(To close dividends to retained earnings)			

ILLUSTRATION 4-7

Closing entries journalized

HELPFUL HINT
Income Summary is a very descriptive title: total revenues are closed to Income Summary, total expenses are closed to Income Summary, and the balance in the Income Summary is a net income or net loss.

Note that the amounts for Income Summary in entries (1) and (2) are the totals of the income statement credit and debit columns, respectively, in the work sheet.

A couple of cautions in preparing closing entries: (1) Avoid unintentionally doubling the revenue and expense balances rather than zeroing them. (2) Do not close Dividends through the Income Summary account. **Dividends are not expenses, and they are not a factor in determining net income.**

Posting of Closing Entries

The posting of the closing entries and the ruling of the accounts are shown in Illustration 4-8. Note that all temporary accounts have zero balances. In addition, you should realize that the balance in Retained Earnings represents the accumulated undistributed earnings of the corporation at the end of the accounting period. This balance is shown on the balance sheet and is the ending amount reported on the retained earnings statement, as shown in Illustration 4-4. **The Income Summary account is used only in closing.** No entries are journalized and posted to this account during the year.

As part of the closing process, the **temporary accounts** (revenues, expenses, and Dividends) in T-account form are totaled, balanced, and double ruled as shown in Illustration 4-8. The **permanent accounts**—assets, liabilities, and stockholders' equity (Common Stock and Retained Earnings)—are not closed. A single rule is drawn beneath the current-period entries, and the account balance carried forward to the next period is entered below the single rule (for example, see Retained Earnings).

HELPFUL HINT
The balance in Income Summary before it is closed must equal the net income or net loss for the period.

ILLUSTRATION 4-8

Posting of closing entries

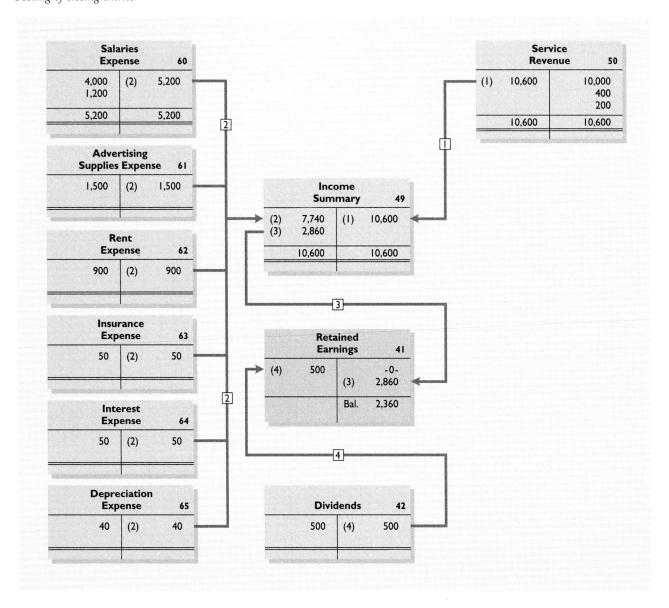

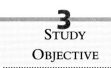

3
STUDY

OBJECTIVE
·····································
Describe the content
and purpose of a post-
closing trial balance.

Preparing a Post-Closing Trial Balance

After all closing entries have been journalized and posted, another trial balance, called a post-closing trial balance, is prepared from the ledger. A post-closing trial balance is a list of permanent accounts and their balances after closing entries have been journalized and posted. **The purpose of this trial balance is to prove the equality of the permanent account balances that are carried forward into the next accounting period.** Since all temporary accounts will have zero balances, the post-closing trial balance will contain only permanent—balance sheet—accounts.

The procedure for preparing a post-closing trial balance again consists entirely of listing the accounts and their balances. These balances are the same as those reported in the company's balance sheet in Illustration 4-4. The post-closing trial balance for Pioneer Advertising Agency Inc. is shown in Illustration 4-9.

ILLUSTRATION 4-9

Post-closing trial balance

PIONEER ADVERTISING AGENCY INC.
Post-Closing Trial Balance
October 31, 2001

	Debit	Credit
Cash	$15,200	
Accounts Receivable	200	
Advertising Supplies	1,000	
Prepaid Insurance	550	
Office Equipment	5,000	
Accumulated Depreciation—Office Equipment		$ 40
Notes Payable		5,000
Accounts Payable		2,500
Interest Payable		50
Unearned Revenue		800
Salaries Payable		1,200
Common Stock		10,000
Retained Earnings		2,360
	$21,950	$21,950

HELPFUL HINT
Will total debits in a post-closing trial balance equal total assets on the balance sheet? Answer: No. Accumulated depreciation is deducted from assets on the balance sheet but added to the credit balance total in a post-closing trial balance.

The post-closing trial balance is prepared from the permanent accounts in the ledger. The permanent accounts of Pioneer Advertising are shown in the general ledger in Illustration 4-10. Because the balance of each account is computed after every posting, no additional work on these accounts is needed as part of the closing process. The remaining accounts in the general ledger are temporary accounts (shown in Illustration 4-11). After the closing entries are posted, each temporary account has a zero balance. These accounts are double-ruled to finalize the closing process.

A post-closing trial balance provides evidence that the journalizing and posting of closing entries has been properly completed. In addition, it shows that the accounting equation is in balance at the end of the accounting period. However, as in the case of the trial balance, it does not prove that all transactions have been recorded or that the ledger is correct. For example, the post-closing trial balance will balance if a transaction is not journalized and posted or if a transaction is journalized and posted twice.

SUMMARY OF THE ACCOUNTING CYCLE

The required steps in the accounting cycle are shown graphically in Illustration 4-12 on page 154. From the graphic you can see that the cycle begins with the analysis of business transactions and ends with the preparation of a post-closing trial balance. The steps in the cycle are performed in sequence and are repeated in each accounting period.

Steps 1–3 may occur daily during the accounting period, as explained in Chapter 2. Steps 4–7 are performed on a periodic basis, such as monthly, quarterly, or annually. Steps 8 and 9, closing entries, and a post-closing trial balance, are usually prepared only at the end of a company's **annual** accounting period.

There are also two optional steps in the accounting cycle. As you have seen, a work sheet may be used in preparing adjusting entries and financial statements. In addition, reversing entries may be used, as explained in the following section.

4
STUDY
OBJECTIVE

State the required steps in the accounting cycle.

ILLUSTRATION 4-10

General ledger, permanent accounts

(Permanent Accounts Only)

GENERAL LEDGER

Cash   No. 1

Date	Explanation	Ref.	Debit	Credit	Balance
2001					
Oct. 1		J1	10,000		10,000
2		J1	1,200		11,200
3		J1		900	10,300
4		J1		600	9,700
20		J1		500	9,200
26		J1		4,000	5,200
31		J1	10,000		**15,200**

Accounts Receivable   No. 6

Date	Explanation	Ref.	Debit	Credit	Balance
2001					
Oct. 31	Adj. entry	J2	**200**		200

Advertising Supplies   No. 8

Date	Explanation	Ref.	Debit	Credit	Balance
2001					
Oct. 5		J1	2,500		2,500
31	Adj. entry	J2		**1,500**	1,000

Prepaid Insurance   No. 10

Date	Explanation	Ref.	Debit	Credit	Balance
2001					
Oct. 4		J1	600		600
31	Adj. entry	J2		50	550

Office Equipment   No. 15

Date	Explanation	Ref.	Debit	Credit	Balance
2001					
Oct. 1		J1	5,000		5,000

Accumulated Depreciation—Office Equipment   No. 16

Date	Explanation	Ref.	Debit	Credit	Balance
2001					
Oct. 31	Adj. entry	J2		40	40

Notes Payable   No. 25

Date	Explanation	Ref.	Debit	Credit	Balance
2001					
Oct. 1		J1		5,000	5,000

Accounts Payable   No. 26

Date	Explanation	Ref.	Debit	Credit	Balance
2001					
Oct. 5		J1		2,500	2,500

Interest Payable   No. 27

Date	Explanation	Ref.	Debit	Credit	Balance
2001					
Oct. 31	Adj. entry	J2		50	50

Unearned Revenue   No. 28

Date	Explanation	Ref.	Debit	Credit	Balance
2001					
Oct. 2		J1		1,200	1,200
31	Adj. entry	J2	400		800

Salaries Payable   No. 29

Date	Explanation	Ref.	Debit	Credit	Balance
2001					
Oct. 31	Adj. entry	J2		**1,200**	1,200

Common Stock   No. 40

Date	Explanation	Ref.	Debit	Credit	Balance
2001					
Oct. 1		J1		10,000	10,000

Retained Earnings   No. 41

Date	Explanation	Ref.	Debit	Credit	Balance
2001					
Oct. 1					-0-
31	Closing entry	J3		2,860	**2,860**
31	Closing entry	J3	500		**2,360**

> *Note:* The permanent accounts for Pioneer Advertising Agency Inc. are shown here; the temporary accounts are shown in Illustration 4-11. Both permanent and temporary accounts are part of the general ledger; they are segregated here to aid in learning.

ILLUSTRATION 4-11

General ledger, temporary accounts

(Temporary Accounts Only)

GENERAL LEDGER

Dividends   No. 42

Date	Explanation	Ref.	Debit	Credit	Balance
2001					
Oct. 20		J1	500		500
31	Closing entry	J3		500	–0–

Income Summary   No. 49

Date	Explanation	Ref.	Debit	Credit	Balance
2001					
Oct. 31	Closing entry	J3		10,600	10,600
31	Closing entry	J3	7,740		2,860
31	Closing entry	J3	2,860		–0–

Service Revenue   No. 50

Date	Explanation	Ref.	Debit	Credit	Balance
2001					
Oct. 31		J1		10,000	10,000
31	Adj. entry	J2		400	10,400
31	Adj. entry	J2		200	10,600
31	Closing entry	J3	10,600		–0–

Salaries Expense   No. 60

Date	Explanation	Ref.	Debit	Credit	Balance
2001					
Oct. 26		J1	4,000		4,000
31	Adj. entry	J2	1,200		5,200
31	Closing entry	J3		5,200	–0–

Advertising Supplies Expense   No. 61

Date	Explanation	Ref.	Debit	Credit	Balance
2001					
Oct. 31	Adj. entry	J2	1,500		1,500
31	Closing entry	J3		1,500	–0–

Rent Expense   No. 62

Date	Explanation	Ref.	Debit	Credit	Balance
2001					
Oct. 3		J1	900		900
31	Closing entry	J3		900	–0–

Insurance Expense   No. 63

Date	Explanation	Ref.	Debit	Credit	Balance
2001					
Oct. 31	Adj. entry	J2	50		50
31	Closing entry	J3		50	–0–

Interest Expense   No. 64

Date	Explanation	Ref.	Debit	Credit	Balance
2001					
Oct. 31	Adj. entry	J2	50		50
31	Closing entry	J3		50	–0–

Depreciation Expense   No. 65

Date	Explanation	Ref.	Debit	Credit	Balance
2001					
Oct. 31	Adj. entry	J2	40		40
31	Closing entry	J3		40	–0–

Note: The temporary accounts for Pioneer Advertising Agency Inc. are shown here; the permanent accounts are shown in Illustration 4-10. Both permanent and temporary accounts are part of the general ledger; they are segregated here to aid in learning.

ILLUSTRATION 4-12

Steps in the accounting cycle

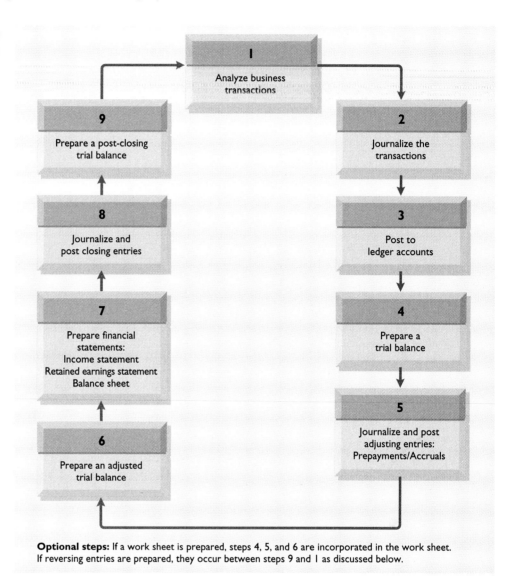

Optional steps: If a work sheet is prepared, steps 4, 5, and 6 are incorporated in the work sheet. If reversing entries are prepared, they occur between steps 9 and 1 as discussed below.

Reversing Entries—An Optional Step

Some accountants prefer to reverse certain adjusting entries at the beginning of a new accounting period. A reversing entry is made at the beginning of the next accounting period and is the exact opposite of the adjusting entry made in the previous period. **The preparation of reversing entries is an optional bookkeeping procedure that is not a required step in the accounting cycle.** Accordingly, we have chosen to cover this topic in an appendix at the end of the chapter.

Correcting Entries—An Avoidable Step

If the accounting records are free of errors, no correcting entries are necessary. Unfortunately, errors may occur in the recording process. Errors should be corrected **as soon as they are discovered** by journalizing and posting correcting entries. You should recognize several significant differences between correcting entries and adjusting entries. First, adjusting entries are an integral part of the accounting cycle, whereas correcting entries are unnecessary if the records are free of errors. Second, **adjustments are journalized and posted only at the end** of an accounting period; in contrast, correcting entries are made whenever an error is discovered. Finally, adjusting entries always affect at least one balance sheet account and one income statement account. In contrast, correcting entries may involve any combination of accounts in need of correction. Correcting entries must be posted before closing entries.

To determine the correcting entry, it is useful to compare the incorrect entry with the correct entry. Doing so helps identify the accounts and amounts that should—and should not—be corrected. After comparison, a correcting entry is made to correct the accounts. This approach is illustrated in the following two cases.

Case 1. On May 10, a $50 cash collection on account from a customer is journalized and posted as a debit to Cash $50 and a credit to Service Revenue $50. The error is discovered on May 20, when the customer pays the remaining balance in full.

Incorrect Entry (May 10)			**Correct Entry (May 10)**		
Cash	50		Cash	50	
Service Revenue		50	Accounts Receivable		50

ILLUSTRATION 4-13

Comparison of entries

A comparison of the incorrect entry with the correct entry reveals that the debit to Cash $50 is correct. However, the $50 credit to Service Revenue should have been credited to Accounts Receivable. As a result, both Service Revenue and Accounts Receivable are overstated in the ledger. The following correcting entry is required:

Correcting Entry

May 20	Service Revenue	50	
	Accounts Receivable		50
	(To correct entry of May 10)		

ILLUSTRATION 4-14

Correcting entry

A	=	L	+	SE
−50				−50

Case 2. On May 18, office equipment costing $450 is purchased on account. The transaction is journalized and posted as a debit to Delivery Equipment $45, and a credit to Accounts Payable $45. The error is discovered on June 3, when the monthly statement for May is received from the creditor.

Incorrect Entry (May 18)			**Correct Entry (May 18)**		
Delivery Equipment	45		Office Equipment	450	
Accounts Payable		45	Accounts Payable		450

ILLUSTRATION 4-15

Comparison of entries

A comparison of the two entries shows that three accounts are incorrect. Delivery Equipment is overstated $45; Office Equipment is understated $450; and Accounts Payable is understated $405. The correcting entry is:

Correcting Entry

June 3	Office Equipment	450	
	Delivery Equipment		45
	Accounts Payable		405
	(To correct May 18 entry)		

ILLUSTRATION 4-16

Correcting entry

A	=	L	+	SE
+450				
−45		+405		

Instead of preparing a correcting entry, **it is possible to reverse the incorrect entry and then prepare the correct entry**. This approach will result in more entries and postings than a correcting entry, but it will accomplish the desired result.

ACCOUNTING IN ACTION
Business Insight

Yale Express, a short-haul trucking firm, turned over much of its cargo to local truckers for delivery completion. Yale collected the entire delivery charge and, when billed by the local trucker, remitted payment for the final phase to the local trucker. Yale used a cutoff period of 20 days into the next accounting period in making its adjusting entries for accrued liabilities. That is, it waited 20 days to receive the local truckers' bills to determine the amount of the unpaid but incurred delivery charges as of the balance sheet date.

On the other hand, Republic Carloading, a nationwide, long-distance freight forwarder, frequently did not receive transportation bills from truckers to whom it passed on cargo until months after the year-end. In making its year-end adjusting entries, Republic waited for months in order to include all of these outstanding transportation bills.

When Yale Express merged with Republic Carloading, Yale's vice president employed the 20-day cutoff procedure for both firms. As a result, millions of dollars of Republic's accrued transportation bills went unrecorded. When the erroneous procedure was detected and correcting entries were made, these and other errors changed a reported profit of $1.14 million into a loss of $1.88 million!

BEFORE YOU GO ON...

Review It

1. How do permanent accounts differ from temporary accounts?
2. What four different types of entries are required in closing the books?
3. What is the content and purpose of a post-closing trial balance?
4. What are the required and optional steps in the accounting cycle?

Do It

The work sheet for Hancock Corporation shows the following in the financial statement columns: Common Stock $98,000, Dividends $15,000, Retained Earnings $42,000, and net income $18,000. Prepare the closing entries at December 31 that affect stockholders' equity.

Reasoning: Closing entries are made in sequence. The first two entries close revenues and expenses. The remaining two entries close net income and dividends to retained earnings.

Solution:

Dec. 31	Income Summary	18,000	
	Retained Earnings		18,000
	(To close net income to retained earnings)		
31	Retained Earnings	15,000	
	Dividends		15,000
	(To close dividends to retained earnings)		

THE
NAVIGATOR

Related exercise material: BE4–4, BE4–5, BE4–6, E4–3, E4–6, and E4–8.

CLASSIFIED BALANCE SHEET

The financial statements illustrated up to this point were purposely kept simple. We classified items as assets, liabilities, and stockholders' equity in the balance sheet, and as revenues and expenses in the income statement. **Financial statements, however, become more useful to management, creditors, and potential investors when the elements are classified into significant subgroups.** In the remainder of this chapter we will introduce you to the primary balance sheet classifications. The classified income statement will be presented in Chapter 5. The classified financial statements are what Jack Stack, the president of SRC Corporation, gave to his employees to understand what was happening in the business.

6
STUDY
OBJECTIVE
Identify the sections of a classified balance sheet.

Standard Classifications

A classified balance sheet usually contains these standard classifications:

Assets	Liabilities and Stockholders' Equity
Current assets	Current liabilities
Long-term investments	Long-term liabilities
Property, plant, and equipment	Stockholders' equity
Intangible assets	

ILLUSTRATION 4-17

Standard balance sheet classifications

These sections help the financial statement user to determine such matters as (1) the availability of assets to meet debts as they come due and (2) the claims of short- and long-term creditors on total assets. A classified balance sheet also makes it easier to compare companies in the same industry, such as GM, Ford, and Chrysler in the automobile industry. Each of the sections is explained below, except for stockholders' equity, which has already been discussed.

A complete set of specimen financial statements for Kellogg Company is shown in Appendix A at the back of the book.

Current Assets

Current assets are cash and other resources that are reasonably expected to be realized in cash or sold or consumed in the business within one year of the balance sheet date or the company's operating cycle, whichever is longer. For example, accounts receivable are included in current assets because they will be realized in cash through collection within one year. In contrast, a prepayment such as supplies is a current asset because of its expected use or consumption in the business within one year.

The operating cycle of a company is the average time that is required to go from cash to cash in producing revenues. The term "cycle" suggests a circular flow, which in this case, starts and ends with cash. For example, in municipal transit companies, the operating cycle would tend to be very short since services are rendered entirely on a cash basis. On the other hand, the operating cycle in public utility companies is longer: they bill customers for services rendered, and the collection period may extend for several months. Most companies have operating cycles of less than one year. More will be said about operating cycles in later chapters.

In a service enterprise, it is customary to recognize four types of current assets: (1) cash, (2) marketable securities such as U.S. government bonds held as a temporary (short-term) investment, (3) receivables (notes receivable, accounts

INTERNATIONAL NOTE

Other countries use a different format for the balance sheet. In Great Britain, for example, property, plant, and equipment are reported first on the balance sheet; assets and liabilities are netted and grouped into net current and net total assets.

receivable, and interest receivable), and (4) prepaid expenses (insurance and supplies). **These items are listed in the order of liquidity**, that is, in the order in
which they are expected to be converted into cash. This arrangement is illustrated below in the presentation of UAL, Inc. (United Airlines).

/// UNITED AIRLINES

UAL, INC. (UNITED AIRLINES)
Balance Sheet (partial)
(in thousands)

Current assets		
Cash		$ 52,368
Marketable securities		389,862
Receivables		721,479
Aircraft fuel, spare parts, and supplies		178,840
Prepaid expenses		83,662
Total current assets		$1,426,211

A company's current assets are important in assessing the company's short-term
debt-paying ability, as explained later in the chapter.

Long-Term Investments

Like current assets, long-term investments are resources that can be realized in
cash. However, the conversion into cash is not expected within one year or the
operating cycle, whichever is longer. In addition, long-term investments are not
intended for use or consumption within the business. This category, often just
called "investments," normally includes stocks and bonds of other corporations.
Deluxe Corporation reported the following in its balance sheet:

DELUXE CORPORATION
Balance Sheet (partial)

Long-term investments		
Investment in stock of Data Card Corporation	$20,468,000	
Other long-term investments	16,961,000	$37,429,000

Property, Plant, and Equipment

Property, plant, and equipment are tangible resources of a relatively permanent
nature that are used in the business and not intended for sale. This category includes land, buildings, machinery and equipment, delivery equipment, and furniture and fixtures. Assets subject to depreciation should be reported at cost less
accumulated depreciation. This practice is illustrated in the following presentation of Delta Air Lines:

DELTA AIR LINES, INC.
Balance Sheet (partial)
(in millions)

Property, plant, and equipment			
Flight equipment	$9,619		
Less: Accumulated depreciation	3,510	$6,109	
Ground property and equipment	3,032		
Less: Accumulated depreciation	1,758	1,274	$7,383

ILLUSTRATION 4-20

Property, plant, and equipment section

Intangible Assets

Intangible assets are noncurrent resources that do not have physical substance. Intangible assets are recorded at cost, and this cost is expensed over the useful life of the intangible asset. Intangible assets include patents, copyrights, and trademarks or trade names that give the holder **exclusive right** of use for a specified period of time. Their value to a company is generally derived from the rights or privileges granted by governmental authority.

In its balance sheet, Brunswick Corporation reported:

BRUNSWICK CORPORATION
Balance Sheet (partial)

Intangible assets	
Patents, trademarks, and other intangibles	$10,460,000

ILLUSTRATION 4-21

Intangible assets section

Current Liabilities

Listed first in the liabilities and stockholders' equity section of the balance sheet are current liabilities. Current liabilities are obligations that are reasonably expected to be paid from existing current assets or through the creation of other current liabilities. As in the case of current assets, the time period for payment is one year or the operating cycle, whichever is longer. Current liabilities include (1) debts related to the operating cycle, such as accounts payable and wages and salaries payable, and (2) other short-term debts, such as bank loans payable, interest payable, taxes payable, and current maturities of long-term obligations (payments to be made within the next year on long-term obligations).

The arrangement of items within the current liabilities section has evolved through custom rather than from a prescribed rule. Notes payable is usually listed first, followed by accounts payable. Other items are then listed in any order. The current liability section adapted from the balance sheet of UAL, Inc. (United Airlines) is as follows:

ILLUSTRATION 4-22

Current liabilities section

Liquidity

UAL, Inc. (United Airlines) Balance Sheet (partial) (in thousands)	
Current liabilities	
Notes payable	$ 297,518
Accounts payable	382,967
Current maturities of long-term obligations	81,525
Unearned ticket revenue	432,979
Salaries and wages payable	435,622
Taxes payable	80,390
Other current liabilities	240,652
Total current liabilities	$1,951,653

UNITED AIRLINES

Illiquidity

Users of financial statements look closely at the relationship between current assets and current liabilities. This relationship is important in evaluating a company's liquidity—its ability to pay obligations that are expected to become due within the next year or operating cycle. When current assets exceed current liabilities at the balance sheet date, the likelihood for paying the liabilities is favorable. When the reverse is true, short-term creditors may not be paid, and the company may ultimately be forced into bankruptcy.

Long-Term Liabilities

Obligations expected to be paid after one year or an operating cycle, whichever is longer, are classified as long-term liabilities (or long-term debt). Liabilities in this category include bonds payable, mortgages payable, long-term notes payable, lease liabilities, and obligations under employee pension plans. Many companies report long-term debt maturing after one year as a single amount in the balance sheet and show the details of the debt in the notes that accompany the financial statements. Others list the various sources of long-term liabilities. In its balance sheet, Consolidated Freightways, Inc. reported:

CONSOLIDATED FREIGHTWAYS, INC. Balance Sheet (partial) (in thousands)	
Long-term liabilities	
Bank notes payable	$10,000
Mortgage payable	2,900
Bonds payable	53,422
Other long-term debt	9,597
Total long-term liabilities	$75,919

CONSOLIDATED FREIGHTWAYS

ILLUSTRATION 4-23

Long-term liabilities section

Stockholders' (Owners') Equity

The content of the owner's equity section varies with the form of business organization. In a proprietorship, there is one capital account. In a partnership, there is a capital account for each partner. For a corporation, owners' (stockholders') equity is divided into two accounts—Common Stock and Retained Earnings. As previously indicated, investments of capital in the business by the stockholders are recorded in the Common Stock account. Income retained for use in the business is recorded in the Retained Earnings account. These two accounts are combined and reported as stockholders' equity on the balance sheet.

In its balance sheet, Dell Computer Corporation reported its stockholders' equity section in 1997 as follows:

DELL COMPUTER CORPORATION
(in millions)

ILLUSTRATION 4-24
Stockholders' equity section

Stockholders' equity:	
Common stock 173,047,420 shares	$195
Retained earnings	611
Total stockholders' equity	$806

Classified Balance Sheet Illustrated

An unclassified balance sheet of Pioneer Advertising Agency Inc. was presented in Illustration 3-20 on page 112. Using the same adjusted trial balance accounts for Pioneer at October 31, 2001, we can prepare the classified balance sheet shown in Illustration 4-25. For illustrative purposes, we have assumed that $1,000 of the notes payable is due currently and $4,000 is long-term.

The balance sheet is most often presented in **report form**, as in Illustration 4-25, with the assets shown above the liabilities and stockholders' equity. The balance sheet may also be presented in **account form** with the assets section placed on the left and the liabilities and stockholders' equity sections on the right.

HELPFUL HINT
A recent survey of 600 companies in *Accounting Trends & Techniques* showed that 77% use the report form and 23% use the account form balance sheet.

ILLUSTRATION 4-25
Classified balance sheet in report form

PIONEER ADVERTISING AGENCY INC.
Balance Sheet
October 31, 2001

Assets

Current assets		
Cash		$15,200
Accounts receivable		200
Advertising supplies		1,000
Prepaid insurance		550
Total current assets		16,950
Property, plant, and equipment		
Office equipment	$5,000	
Less: Accumulated depreciation	40	4,960
Total assets		$21,910

Liabilities and Stockholders' Equity

Current liabilities	
Notes payable	$ 1,000
Accounts payable	2,500
Interest payable	50
Unearned revenue	800
Salaries payable	1,200
Total current liabilities	5,550
Long-term liabilities	
Notes payable	4,000
Total liabilities	9,550
Stockholders' equity	
Common stock	10,000
Retained earnings	2,360
Total liabilities and stockholders' equity	$21,910

BEFORE YOU GO ON...

Review It

1. What are the major sections in a classified balance sheet?
2. Using the Kellogg Company annual report, determine its current liabilities at December 31, 1998, and December 31, 1997. Were current liabilities higher or lower than current assets in these two years? The answers to this question is provided on page 185.
3. What is the difference between the report form and the account form of the classified balance sheet?

A LOOK BACK AT OUR FEATURE STORY

Refer to the Feature Story about SRC Corporation, and answer the following questions:

1. What is the lesson of the SRC story and Jack Stack's innovations?
2. How did Craig Highbarger's knowledge of financial statements, especially the income statement, contribute to his effectiveness as an employee?

   Solution:

1. If you give employees equity in the company and provide them with the training and the information to understand the financial consequences of their decisions and actions, they will act more responsibly and make a greater contribution to the sales and income of the company. In other words, they begin to think like owners.
2. By understanding the income statement, he now recognizes the impact of revenues and expenses in arriving at net income—as well as how they affect his bonus.

THE NAVIGATOR

DEMONSTRATION PROBLEM

PROBLEM-SOLVING STRATEGIES

1. In completing the work sheet, be sure to (a) key the adjustments, (b) extend adjusted balances to the correct statement columns, and (c) enter net income (or net loss) in the proper columns.
2. In preparing a classified balance sheet, know the contents of each of the sections.
3. In journalizing closing entries, remember that there are only four entries and that Dividends is closed to Retained Earnings.

At the end of its first month of operations, Watson Answering Service, Inc. has the following unadjusted trial balance:

WATSON ANSWERING SERVICE, INC.
August 31, 2001
Trial Balance

	Debit	Credit
Cash	$ 5,400	
Accounts Receivable	8,800	
Prepaid Insurance	2,400	
Supplies	1,300	
Equipment	60,000	
Notes Payable		$40,000
Accounts Payable		2,400
Common Stock		30,000
Dividends	1,000	
Service Revenue		10,900
Salaries Expense	3,200	
Utilities Expense	800	
Advertising Expense	400	
	$83,300	$83,300

Other data consist of the following:

1. Insurance expires at the rate of $200 per month.
2. There are $1,000 of supplies on hand at August 31.
3. Monthly depreciation is $900 on the equipment.
4. Interest of $500 has accrued during August on the notes payable.

Instructions

(a) Prepare a work sheet.

(b) Prepare a classified balance sheet assuming $35,000 of the notes payable are long-term.

(c) Journalize the closing entries.

SOLUTION TO DEMONSTRATION PROBLEM

(a)

WATSON ANSWERING SERVICE, INC.
Work Sheet
For the Month Ended August 31, 2001

Account Titles	Trial Balance Dr.	Trial Balance Cr.	Adjustments Dr.	Adjustments Cr.	Adjusted Trial Balance Dr.	Adjusted Trial Balance Cr.	Income Statement Dr.	Income Statement Cr.	Balance Sheet Dr.	Balance Sheet Cr.
Cash	5,400				5,400				5,400	
Accounts Receivable	8,800				8,800				8,800	
Prepaid Insurance	2,400			(a) 200	2,200				2,200	
Supplies	1,300			(b) 300	1,000				1,000	
Equipment	60,000				60,000				60,000	
Notes Payable		40,000				40,000				40,000
Accounts Payable		2,400				2,400				2,400
Common Stock		30,000				30,000				30,000
Dividends	1,000				1,000				1,000	
Service Revenue		10,900				10,900		10,900		
Salaries Expense	3,200				3,200		3,200			
Utilities Expense	800				800		800			
Advertising Expense	400				400		400			
Totals	83,300	83,300								
Insurance Expense			(a) 200		200		200			
Supplies Expense			(b) 300		300		300			
Depreciation Expense			(c) 900		900		900			
Accumulated Depreciation—Equipment				(c) 900		900				900
Interest Expense			(d) 500		500		500			
Interest Payable				(d) 500		500				500
Totals			1,900	1,900	84,700	84,700	6,300	10,900	78,400	73,800
Net Income							4,600			4,600
Totals							10,900	10,900	78,400	78,400

Explanation: (a) Insurance expired, (b) Supplies used, (c) Depreciation expensed, (d) Interest accrued.

(b)

WATSON ANSWERING SERVICE, INC.
Balance Sheet
August 31, 2001

Assets

Current assets		
Cash		$ 5,400
Accounts receivable		8,800
Prepaid insurance		2,200
Supplies		1,000
Total current assets		17,400
Property, plant, and equipment		
Equipment	$60,000	
Less: Accumulated depreciation—equipment	900	59,100
Total assets		$76,500

Liabilities and Stockholders' Equity

Current liabilities	
Notes payable	$ 5,000
Accounts payable	2,400
Interest payable	500
Total current liabilities	7,900
Long-term liabilities	
Notes payable	35,000
Total liabilities	42,900
Stockholders' equity	
Common stock	30,000
Retained earnings	3,600*
Total liabilities and stockholders' equity	$76,500

*Net income of $4,600 less dividends of $1,000.

(c)

Aug. 31	Service Revenue		10,900	
	Income Summary			10,900
	(To close revenue account)			
31	Income Summary		6,300	
	Salaries Expense			3,200
	Depreciation Expense			900
	Utilities Expense			800
	Interest Expense			500
	Advertising Expense			400
	Supplies Expense			300
	Insurance Expense			200
	(To close expense accounts)			
31	Income Summary		4,600	
	Retained Earnings			4,600
	(To close net income to retained earnings)			
31	Retained Earnings		1,000	
	Dividends			1,000
	(To close dividends to retained earnings)			

THE
NAVIGATOR

SUMMARY OF STUDY OBJECTIVES

1. Prepare a work sheet. The steps in preparing a work sheet are: (a) prepare a trial balance on the work sheet, (b) enter the adjustments in the adjustment columns, (c) enter adjusted balances in the adjusted trial balance columns, (d) extend adjusted trial balance amounts to appropriate financial statement columns, and (e) total the statement columns, compute net income (or net loss), and complete the work sheet.

2. Explain the process of closing the books. Closing the books occurs at the end of an accounting period. The process is to journalize and post closing entries and then rule and balance all accounts. In closing the books, separate entries are made to close revenues and expenses to Income Summary, Income Summary to Retained Earnings, and Dividends to Retained Earnings. Only temporary accounts are closed.

3. Describe the content and purpose of a post-closing trial balance. A post-closing trial balance contains the balances in permanent accounts that are carried forward to the next accounting period. The purpose of this trial balance is to prove the equality of these balances.

4. State the required steps in the accounting cycle. The required steps in the accounting cycle are: (a) analyze business transactions, (b) journalize the transactions, (c) post to ledger accounts, (d) prepare a trial balance, (e) journalize and post adjusting entries, (f) prepare an adjusted trial balance, (g) prepare financial statements, (h) journalize and post closing entries, and (i) prepare a post-closing trial balance.

5. Explain the approaches to preparing correcting entries. One approach for determining the correcting entry is to compare the incorrect entry with the correct entry. After comparison, a correcting entry is made to correct the accounts. An alternative to a correcting entry is to reverse the incorrect entry and then prepare the correct entry.

6. *Identify the sections of a classified balance sheet.* In a classified balance sheet, assets are classified as current assets; long-term investments; property, plant, and equipment; or intangibles. Liabilities are classified as either current or long-term. There is also an owners' equity section, which varies with the form of business organization.

THE NAVIGATOR

GLOSSARY

Classified balance sheet   A balance sheet that contains a number of standard classifications or sections. (p. 157).

Closing entries   Entries at the end of an accounting period to transfer the balances of temporary accounts to a permanent stockholders' equity account, Retained Earnings. (p. 147).

Correcting entries   Entries to correct errors made in recording transactions. (p. 154).

Current assets   Cash and other resources that are reasonably expected to be realized in cash or sold or consumed in the business within one year or the operating cycle, whichever is longer. (p. 157).

Current liabilities   Obligations reasonably expected to be paid from existing current assets or through the creation of other current liabilities within the next year or operating cycle, whichever is longer. (p. 159).

Income Summary   A temporary account used in closing revenue and expense accounts. (p. 147).

Intangible assets   Noncurrent resources that do not have physical substance. (p. 159).

Liquidity   The ability of a company to pay obligations that are expected to become due within the next year or operating cycle. (p. 160).

Long-term investments   Resources not expected to be realized in cash within the next year or operating cycle. (p. 158).

Long-term liabilities (Long-term debt)   Obligations expected to be paid after one year. (p. 160).

Operating cycle   The average time required to go from cash to cash in producing revenues. (p. 157).

Permanent (real) accounts   Balance sheet accounts whose balances are carried forward to the next accounting period. (p. 146).

Post-closing trial balance   A list of permanent accounts and their balances after closing entries have been journalized and posted. (p. 150).

Property, plant, and equipment   Assets of a relatively permanent nature that are being used in the business and not intended for resale. (p. 158).

Reversing entry   An entry at the beginning of the next accounting period that is the exact opposite of the adjusting entry made in the previous period. (p. 154).

Stockholders' equity   The ownership claim of shareholders on total assets. (p. 160).

Temporary (nominal) accounts   Revenue, expense, and Dividends accounts whose balances are transferred to Retained Earnings at the end of an accounting period. (p. 146).

Work sheet   A multiple-column form that may be used in the adjustment process and in preparing financial statements. (p. 140).

APPENDIX   REVERSING ENTRIES

After the financial statements are prepared and the books are closed, it is often helpful to reverse some of the adjusting entries before recording the regular transactions of the next period. Such entries are called reversing entries. **A reversing entry is made at the beginning of the next accounting period and is the exact opposite of the adjusting entry made in the previous period.** The recording of reversing entries is an **optional** step in the accounting cycle.

The purpose of reversing entries is to simplify the recording of a subsequent transaction related to an adjusting entry. In Chapter 3, you may recall, the payment of salaries after an adjusting entry resulted in two debits: one to Salaries Payable and the other to Salaries Expense. With reversing entries, the entire subsequent payment can be debited to Salaries Expense. **The use of reversing entries does not change the amounts reported in the financial statements. It does, however, simplify the recording of subsequent transactions.**

7

STUDY

OBJECTIVE

Prepare reversing entries.

ILLUSTRATION OF REVERSING ENTRIES

Reversing entries are most often used to reverse two types of adjusting entries: accrued revenues and accrued expenses. They are seldom made for prepaid expenses and unearned revenues. To illustrate the optional use of reversing entries for accrued expenses, we will use the salaries expense transactions for Pioneer Advertising Agency Inc. The transaction and adjustment data are as follows:

1. October 26 (initial salary entry): $4,000 of salaries earned between October 15 and October 26 are paid.
2. October 31 (adjusting entry): Salaries earned between October 29 and October 31 are $1,200. These will be paid in the November 9 payroll.
3. November 9 (subsequent salary entry): Salaries paid are $4,000. Of this amount, $1,200 applied to accrued wages payable and $2,800 was earned between November 1 and November 9.

ILLUSTRATION 4A-1

Comparative entries—not reversing vs. reversing

The comparative entries with and without reversing entries are shown in Illustration 4A-1.

When Reversing Entries Are Not Used (per chapter)				When Reversing Entries Are Used (per appendix)			
Initial Salary Entry				**Initial Salary Entry**			
Oct. 26	Salaries Expense	4,000		Oct. 26	Salaries Expense	4,000	
	Cash		4,000		Cash		4,000
Adjusting Entry				**Adjusting Entry**			
Oct. 31	Salaries Expense	1,200		Oct. 31	Salaries Expense	1,200	
	Salaries Payable		1,200		Salaries Payable		1,200
Closing Entry				**Closing Entry**			
Oct. 31	Income Summary	5,200		Oct. 31	Income Summary	5,200	
	Salaries Expense		5,200		Salaries Expense		5,200
Reversing Entry				**Reversing Entry**			
Nov. 1	No reversing entry is made.			Nov. 1	Salaries Payable	1,200	
					Salaries Expense		1,200
Subsequent Salary Entry				**Subsequent Salary Entry**			
Nov. 9	Salaries Payable	1,200		Nov. 9	Salaries Expense	4,000	
	Salaries Expense	2,800			Cash		4,000
	Cash		4,000				

The comparative entries show that the first three entries are the same whether or not reversing entries are used. The last two entries, however, are different. The November 1 **reversing entry** eliminates the $1,200 balance in Salaries Payable that was created by the October 31 adjusting entry. The reversing entry also creates a $1,200 credit balance in the Salaries Expense account. As you know, it is unusual for an expense account to have a credit balance. The balance is correct in this instance, though, because it anticipates that the entire amount of the first salary payment in the new accounting period will be debited to Salaries Expense. This debit will eliminate the credit balance, and the resulting debit balance in the expense account will equal the salaries expense incurred in the new accounting period ($2,800 in this example).

TECHNOLOGY IN ACTION

Using reversing entries in a computerized accounting system is more efficient than in a manual system. The reversing entry saves writing a program to locate the amount accrued from the preceding period and making the more complicated entry in the current period. That is, the computer does not have to be programmed to determine whether any accrued items exist.

When reversing entries are made, all cash payments of expenses can be debited to the expense account. This means that on November 9 (and every payday) Salaries Expense can be debited for the amount paid without regard to the existence of any accrued salaries payable. Being able to make the same entry each time simplifies the recording process. Note that when reversing entries are used, the recording of subsequent transactions is simplified because they can be recorded as if the related adjusting entry had never been made.

The posting of the entries with reversing entries is shown in Illustration 4A-2.

ILLUSTRATION 4A-2

Postings with reversing entries

Salaries Expense					Salaries Payable				
10/26 Paid	4,000	10/31 Closing	5,200		11/1 Reversing	1,200	10/31 Adjusting	1,200	
31 Adjusting	1,200								
	5,200		5,200						
11/9 Paid	4,000	11/1 Reversing	1,200						

Reversing entries may also be made for accrued revenue adjusting entries. For Pioneer Advertising, the adjusting entry was: Accounts Receivable (Dr.) $200 and Service Revenue (Cr.) $200. Thus, the reversing entry on November 1 is:

Nov. 1	Service Revenue	200		A	=	L	+	SE
	Accounts Receivable		200	−200				−200
	(To reverse October 31 adjusting entry)							

When the accrued revenue is collected, Cash is debited and Service Revenue is credited.

SUMMARY OF STUDY OBJECTIVE FOR APPENDIX

7. *Prepare reversing entries.* Reversing entries are the direct opposite of the adjusting entry made in the preceding period. They are made at the beginning of a new accounting period to simplify the recording of later transactions related to the adjusting entry. In most cases, only accrued adjusting entries are reversed.

*Note: All asterisked Questions, Exercises, and Problems relate to material in the appendix to the chapter.

SELF-STUDY QUESTIONS

Answers are at the end of the chapter.

(SO 1) 1. Which of the following statements is *incorrect* concerning the work sheet?
  a. The work sheet is essentially a working tool of the accountant.
  b. The work sheet cannot be used as a basis for posting to ledger accounts.
  c. The work sheet is distributed to management and other interested parties.
  d. Financial statements can be prepared directly from the work sheet before journalizing and posting the adjusting entries.

(SO 1) 2. In a work sheet, net income is entered in the following columns:
  a. income statement (Dr) and balance sheet (Dr).
  b. income statement (Dr) and balance sheet (Cr).
  c. income statement (Cr) and balance sheet (Dr).
  d. income statement (Cr) and balance sheet (Cr).

(SO 2) 3. An account that will have a zero balance after closing entries have been journalized and posted is:
  a. Unearned Revenue.
  b. Advertising Supplies.
  c. Prepaid Insurance.
  d. Rent Expense.

(SO 2) 4. When a net loss has occurred, Income Summary is:
  a. credited and retained earnings is debited.
  b. debited and retained earnings is credited.
  c. debited and common stock is credited.
  d. credited and common stock is debited.

(SO 2) 5. The closing process involves separate entries to close (1) expenses, (2) dividends, (3) revenues and (4) net income (or loss). The correct sequencing of the entries is:
  a. (4), (3), (2), (1)
  b. (1), (2), (3), (4)
  c. (3), (2), (1), (4)
  d. (3), (1), (4), (2)

(SO 3) 6. Which types of accounts will appear in the post-closing trial balance?
  a. Temporary (nominal) accounts.
  b. Permanent (real) accounts.
  c. Accounts shown in the income statement columns of a work sheet.
  d. None of the above.

(SO 4) 7. All of the following are required steps in the accounting cycle *except*:
  a. preparing a work sheet.
  b. journalizing and posting closing entries.
  c. preparing an adjusted trial balance.
  d. preparing a post-closing trial balance.

(SO 5) 8. Cash of $100 received at the time the service was rendered was journalized and posted as a debit to Cash $100 and a credit to Accounts Receivable $100. Assuming the incorrect entry is not reversed, the correcting entry is:
  a. debit Service Revenue $100 and credit Accounts Receivable $100.
  b. debit Cash $100 and credit Service Revenue $100.
  c. debit Accounts Receivable $100 and credit Service Revenue $100.
  d. debit Accounts Receivable $100 and credit Cash $100.

(SO 6) 9. In a classified balance sheet, assets are usually classified as:
  a. current assets; long-term assets; property, plant, and equipment; and intangible assets.
  b. current assets; long-term investments; property, plant, and equipment; and other assets.
  c. current assets; long-term investments; property, plant, and equipment; and intangible assets.
  d. current assets; long-term investments; tangible assets; and intangible assets.

(SO 6) 10. Current assets are listed:
  a. by importance.
  b. by liquidity.
  c. by longevity.
  d. alphabetically.

(SO 7) *11. On December 31, the Scott Company correctly made an adjusting entry to recognize $2,000 of accrued salaries payable. On January 8 of the next year, total salaries of $3,500 were paid. Assuming the correct reversing entry was made on January 1, the entry on January 8 will result in a credit to Cash $3,500, and the following debit(s):
  a. Salaries Payable $3,500.
  b. Salaries Expense $3,500.
  c. Salaries Payable $2,000 and Salaries Expense $1,500.
  d. Salaries Payable $1,500 and Salaries Expense $2,000.

THE
NAVIGATOR

QUESTIONS

1. "A work sheet is a permanent accounting record and its use is required in the accounting cycle." Do you agree? Explain.

2. Explain the purpose of the work sheet.

3. What is the relationship, if any, between the amount shown in the adjusted trial balance column for an account and that account's ledger balance?

4. If a company's revenues are $125,000 and its expenses are $113,000, in which financial statement columns of the work sheet will the net income of $12,000 appear? When expenses exceed revenues, in which columns will the difference appear?

5. Why is it necessary to prepare formal financial statements when all of the data are in the statement columns of the work sheet?

6. Identify the account(s) debited and credited in each of the four closing entries, assuming the company has net income for the year.

7. Describe the nature of the Income Summary account and identify the types of summary data that may be posted to this account.

8. What are the content and purpose of a post-closing trial balance?

9. Which of the following accounts would not appear in the post-closing trial balance? Interest Payable; Equipment; Depreciation Expense; Dividends; Unearned Revenue; Accumulated Depreciation—Equipment; and Service Revenue.

10. Distinguish between a reversing entry and an adjusting entry. Are reversing entries required?

11. Indicate, in the sequence in which they are made, the three required steps in the accounting cycle that involve journalizing.

12. Identify, in the sequence in which they are prepared, the three trial balances that are often used to report financial information about a company.

13. How do correcting entries differ from adjusting entries?

14. What standard classifications are used in preparing a classified balance sheet?

15. What is meant by the term "operating cycle"?

16. Define current assets. What basis is used for arranging individual items within the current asset section?

17. Distinguish between long-term investments and property, plant, and equipment.

18. How do current liabilities differ from long-term liabilities?

19. (a) What is the term used to describe the owners' equity section of a corporation? (b) Identify the two owners' equity accounts in a corporation and indicate the purpose of each.

20. How does a report form balance sheet differ from an account form balance sheet?

*21. David Biel Company prepares reversing entries. If the adjusting entry for interest payable is reversed, what type of an account balance, if any, will there be in Interest Payable and Interest Expense after the reversing entry is posted?

*22. At December 31, accrued salaries payable totaled $4,500. On January 10, total salaries of $8,000 are paid. (a) Assume that reversing entries are made at January 1. Give the January 10 entry and indicate the Salaries Expense account balance after the entry is posted. (b) Repeat part (a) assuming reversing entries are not made.

BRIEF EXERCISES

BE4–1   The steps in using a work sheet are presented in random order below. List the steps in the proper order.

_____ Prepare a trial balance on the work sheet.
_____ Enter adjusted balances.
_____ Extend adjusted balances to appropriate statement columns.
_____ Total the statement columns, compute net income (loss), and complete the work sheet.
_____ Enter adjustment data.

List the steps in preparing a work sheet.
(SO 1)

BE4–2   The ledger of Warren Company includes the following unadjusted balances: Prepaid Insurance $4,000, Service Revenue $58,000, and Salaries Expense $25,000. Adjusting entries are required for (a) expired insurance $1,600, (b) services provided $900, but unbilled and uncollected, and (c) accrued salaries payable $800. Enter the unadjusted balances and adjustments into a work sheet and complete the work sheet for all accounts. Note: You will need to add the following accounts: Accounts Receivable, Salaries Payable, and Insurance Expense.

Prepare partial work sheet.
(SO 1)

BE4–3   The following selected accounts appear in the adjusted trial balance columns of the work sheet for the Falcetto Company: Accumulated Depreciation; Depreciation Expense; Common Stock; Dividends; Service Revenue; Supplies; and Accounts Payable. Indicate the financial statement column (income statement Dr., balance sheet Cr., etc.) to which each balance should be extended.

Identify work sheet columns for selected accounts.
(SO 1)

BE4–4   The ledger of the Perkins Company contains the following balances: Common Stock $30,000; Dividends $2,000; Service Revenue $45,000; Salaries Expense $26,000; and Supplies Expense $4,000. Prepare the closing entries at December 31.

Prepare closing entries from ledger balances.
(SO 2)

BE4–5   Using the data in BE4–4, enter the balances in T accounts, post the closing entries, and rule and balance the accounts.

Post closing entries and rule and balance T accounts.
(SO 2)

BE4–6   The income statement for Community Golf Club for the month ending July 31 shows Green Fee Revenue $14,000, Salaries Expense $6,200, Maintenance Expense $2,500, and Net Income $5,300. Prepare the entries to close the revenue and expense accounts. Post the entries to the revenue and expense accounts and complete the closing process for these accounts using the three-column form of account.

Journalize and post closing entries using the three-column form of account.
(SO 2)

Identify post-closing trial balance accounts.
(SO 3)

BE4–7 Using the data in BE4–3, identify the accounts that would be included in a post-closing trial balance.

List the required steps in the accounting cycle in sequence.
(SO 4)

BE4–8 The steps in the accounting cycle are listed in random order below. List the steps in proper sequence, assuming no work sheet is prepared.

___ Prepare a trial balance.
___ Journalize the transactions.
___ Journalize and post closing entries.
___ Prepare financial statements.
___ Journalize and post adjusting entries.
___ Post to ledger accounts.
___ Prepare a post-closing trial balance.
___ Prepare an adjusted trial balance.
___ Analyze business transactions.

Prepare correcting entries.
(SO 5)

BE4–9 At Ruhly Company, the following errors were discovered after the transactions had been journalized and posted. Prepare the correcting entries.

1. A collection on account from a customer for $780 was recorded as a debit to Cash $780 and a credit to Service Revenue $780.
2. The purchase of store supplies on account for $1,630 was recorded as a debit to Store Supplies $1,360 and a credit to Accounts Payable $1,360.

Prepare the current asset section of a balance sheet.
(SO 6)

BE4–10 The balance sheet debit column of the work sheet for Rueben Company includes the following accounts: Accounts Receivable $14,500; Prepaid Insurance $3,600; Cash $18,400; Supplies $5,200, and Marketable Securities $8,200. Prepare the current asset section of the balance sheet listing the accounts in proper sequence.

Prepare reversing entries.
(SO 7)

*BE4–11 At October 31, Julia Company made an accrued expense adjusting entry of $600 for salaries. Prepare the reversing entry on November 1 and indicate the balances in Salaries Payable and Salaries Expense after posting the reversing entry.

EXERCISES

Complete work sheet.
(SO 1)

E4–1 The adjusted trial balance columns of the work sheet for Jose Navarro Company are as follows:

JOSE NAVARRO COMPANY
Work Sheet (partial)
For the Month Ended April 30, 2001

Account Titles	Adjusted Trial Balance		Income Statement		Balance Sheet	
	Dr.	Cr.	Dr.	Cr.	Dr.	Cr.
Cash	17,052					
Accounts Receivable	7,840					
Prepaid Rent	2,280					
Equipment	23,050					
Accumulated Depreciation		4,921				
Notes Payable		5,700				
Accounts Payable		5,972				
Common Stock		30,000				
Retained Earnings		3,960				
Dividends	3,650					
Service Revenue		12,590				
Salaries Expense	7,840					
Rent Expense	760					
Depreciation Expense	671					
Interest Expense	57					
Interest Payable		57				
Totals	63,200	63,200				

Instructions
Complete the work sheet.

E4-2 Work sheet data for the Jose Navarro Company are presented in E4-1. The stockholders did not make any additional investments in the business in April.

Prepare financial statements from work sheet
(SO 1, 6)

Instructions
Prepare an income statement, a retained earnings statement, and a classified balance sheet.

E4-3 Work sheet data for the Jose Navarro Company are presented in E4-1.

Journalize and post closing entries and prepare a post-closing trial balance.
(SO 2, 3)

Instructions
(a) Journalize the closing entries at April 30.
(b) Post the closing entries to Income Summary and stockholders' equity. Use T accounts.
(c) Prepare a post-closing trial balance at April 30.

E4-4 The adjustments columns of the work sheet for Sorcerer Company are shown below.

Prepare adjusting entries from a work sheet and extend balances to work sheet columns.
(SO 1)

	Adjustments	
Account Titles	Debit	Credit
Accounts Receivable	800	
Prepaid Insurance		400
Accumulated Depreciation		1,000
Salaries Payable		500
Service Revenue		800
Salaries Expense	500	
Insurance Expense	400	
Depreciation Expense	1,000	
	2,700	2,700

Instructions
(a) Prepare the adjusting entries.
(b) Assuming the adjusted trial balance amount for each account is normal, indicate the financial statement column to which each balance should be extended.

E4-5 Selected work sheet data for Marinita Company are presented below.

Derive adjusting entries from work sheet data.
(SO 1)

Account Titles	Trial Balance		Adjusted Trial Balance	
	Dr.	Cr.	Dr.	Cr.
Accounts Receivable	?		34,000	
Prepaid Insurance	24,000		18,000	
Supplies	9,000		?	
Accumulated Depreciation		12,000		?
Salaries Payable		?		6,000
Service Revenue		90,000		95,000
Insurance Expense			?	
Depreciation Expense			10,000	
Supplies Expense			4,000	
Salaries Expense	?		49,000	

Instructions
(a) Fill in the missing amounts.
(b) Prepare the adjusting entries that were made.

E4-6 The adjusted trial balance of Rafael Company at the end of its fiscal year is:

Journalize and post closing entries and prepare a post-closing trial balance.
(SO 2, 3)

Rafael Company
Adjusted Trial Balance
July 31, 2001

No.	Account Titles	Debits	Credits
101	Cash	$ 11,940	
112	Accounts Receivable	8,780	
157	Equipment	15,900	
167	Accumulated Depreciation		$ 5,400
201	Accounts Payable		4,220
208	Unearned Rent Revenue		1,800
311	Common Stock		20,000
320	Retained Earnings		25,200
332	Dividends	14,000	
404	Commission Revenue		65,100
429	Rent Revenue		6,500
711	Depreciation Expense	4,000	
720	Salaries Expense	58,700	
732	Utilities Expense	14,900	
		$128,220	$128,220

Instructions
(a) Prepare the closing entries using page J15.
(b) Post to Retained Earnings and No. 350 Income Summary accounts. (Use the three-column form.)
(c) Prepare a post-closing trial balance at July 31.

Prepare financial statements.
(SO 6)

E4–7   The adjusted trial balance for Rafael Company is presented in E4–6.

Instructions
(a) Prepare an income statement and a retained earnings statement for the year. There was no issuance of stock during the year.
(b) Prepare a classified balance sheet at July 31.

Prepare closing entries.
(SO 2)

E4–8   Selected accounts for Comfort Zone Salon are presented below. All June 30 postings are from closing entries.

Salaries Expense				Service Revenue				Dividends			
6/10	3,200	6/30	8,800	6/30	15,600	6/15	7,200	6/15	1,300	6/30	1,300
6/28	5,600					6/24	8,400				

Supplies Expense				Common Stock			
6/12	800	6/30	1,500			6/1	12,000
6/24	700						

Rent Expense				Retained Earnings			
6/1	3,500	6/30	3,500	6/30	1,300	6/30	1,800
						Bal.	500

Instructions
(a) Prepare the closing entries that were made.
(b) Post the closing entries to Income Summary.

Prepare correcting entries.
(SO 5)

E4–9   The Kumar Company has an inexperienced accountant. During the first 2 weeks on the job, the following errors were made in journalizing transactions. All entries were posted as made.

1. A payment on account to a creditor of $630 was debited to Accounts Payable $360 and credited to Cash $360.
2. The purchase of supplies on account for $600 was debited to Equipment $60 and credited to Accounts Payable $60.
3. A $400 cash dividend was debited to Salaries Expense $400 and credited to Cash $400.

Instructions
Prepare the correcting entries.

E4–10 The adjusted trial balance for Bel-Air's Bowling Alley Inc. at December 31, 2001, contains the following accounts.

Prepare a classified balance sheet.
(SO 6)

Debits		Credits	
Building	$123,800	Common Stock	$100,000
Accounts Receivable	14,520	Retained Earnings	10,000
Prepaid Insurance	4,680	Accumulated Depreciation—Building	45,600
Cash	20,840	Accounts Payable	13,480
Equipment	62,400	Mortgage Payable	93,600
Land	61,200	Accumulated Depreciation—Equipment	18,720
Insurance Expense	780	Interest Payable	2,600
Depreciation Expense	7,360	Bowling Revenues	14,180
Interest Expense	2,600		$298,180
	$298,180		

Instructions
(a) Prepare a classified balance sheet; assume that $13,600 of the mortgage payable will be paid in 2002.
(b) ▭▭▭▷ Comment on the liquidity of the company.

*E4–11 On December 31, the adjusted trial balance of Garrett Employment Agency shows the following selected data:

Prepare closing and reversing entries.
(SO 2, 4, 7)

Accounts Receivable	$4,000	Commission Revenue	$96,000
Interest Expense	7,800	Interest Payable	2,000

Analysis shows that adjusting entries were made to (a) accrue $4,000 of commission revenue and (b) accrue $2,000 interest expense.

Instructions
(a) Prepare the closing entries for the temporary accounts at December 31.
(b) Prepare the reversing entries on January 1.
(c) Post the entries in (a) and (b). Rule and balance the accounts. (Use T accounts.)
(d) Prepare the entries to record (1) the collection of the accrued commissions on January 10 and (2) the payment of all interest due ($2,700) on January 15.
(e) Post the entries in (d) to the temporary accounts.

PROBLEMS: SET A

P4–1A The trial balance columns of the work sheet for Phantom Roofing Inc. at March 31, 2001, are as follows:

Prepare a work sheet, financial statements, and adjusting and closing entries.
(SO 1, 2, 3, 6)

PHANTOM ROOFING INC.
Work Sheet
For the Month Ended March 31, 2001

Account Titles	Trial Balance	
	Dr.	Cr.
Cash	$ 2,700	
Accounts Receivable	1,600	
Roofing Supplies	1,100	
Equipment	6,000	
Accumulated Depreciation—Equipment		$ 1,200
Accounts Payable		1,100
Unearned Revenue		300
Common Stock		5,000
Retained Earnings		2,000
Dividends	600	
Service Revenue		3,000
Salaries Expense	500	
Miscellaneous Expense	100	
	$12,600	$12,600

Other data:

1. A physical count reveals only $320 of roofing supplies on hand.
2. Depreciation for March is $200.
3. Unearned revenue amounted to $200 after adjustment on March 31.
4. Accrued salaries are $400.

Instructions

(a) Enter the trial balance on a work sheet and complete the work sheet.
(b) Prepare an income statement and retained earnings statement for the month of March and classified balance sheet at March 31. No additional shares of stock were issued in March.
(c) Journalize the adjusting entries from the adjustments columns of the work sheet.
(d) Journalize the closing entries from the financial statement columns of the work sheet.

Complete work sheet and prepare financial statements, closing entries, and post-closing trial balance.
(SO 1, 2, 3, 6)

P4–2A   The adjusted trial balance columns of the work sheet for Boss Nass Company are as follows:

BOSS NASS COMPANY
Work Sheet
For the Year Ended December 31, 2001

Account No.	Account Titles	Adjusted Trial Balance Dr.	Adjusted Trial Balance Cr.
101	Cash	16,600	
112	Accounts Receivable	15,400	
126	Supplies	1,500	
130	Prepaid Insurance	2,800	
151	Office Equipment	34,000	
152	Accumulated Depreciation—Office Equipment		8,000
200	Notes Payable		16,000
201	Accounts Payable		6,000
212	Salaries Payable		3,000
230	Interest Payable		500
311	Common Stock		20,000
320	Retained Earings		5,000
332	Dividends	10,000	
400	Service Revenue		88,000
610	Advertising Expense	12,000	
631	Supplies Expense	5,700	
711	Depreciation Expense	4,000	
722	Insurance Expense	5,000	
726	Salaries Expense	39,000	
905	Interest Expense	500	
		146,500	146,500

Instructions

(a) Complete the work sheet by extending the balances to the financial statement columns.

(b) Prepare an income statement, a retained earnings statement, and a classified balance sheet. (Note: $10,000 of the notes payable become due in 2002.) The company did not issue any additional shares of stock during the year.

(c) Prepare the closing entries. Use J14 for the journal page.

(d) Post the closing entries and rule and balance the accounts. Use the three-column form of account. Income Summary is No. 350.

(e) Prepare a post-closing trial balance.

P4-3A The completed financial statement columns of the work sheet for Nute Gunray Company are shown below.

Prepare financial statements, closing entries, and post-closing trial balance.
(SO 1, 2, 3, 6)

NUTE GUNRAY COMPANY
Work Sheet
For the Year Ended December 31, 2001

Account No.	Account Titles	Income Statement Dr.	Income Statement Cr.	Balance Sheet Dr.	Balance Sheet Cr.
101	Cash			13,600	
112	Accounts Receivable			13,500	
130	Prepaid Insurance			3,500	
157	Equipment			26,000	
167	Accumulated Depreciation				5,600
201	Accounts Payable				11,300
212	Salaries Payable				3,000
311	Common Stock				20,000
320	Retained Earnings				16,000
332	Dividends			12,000	
400	Service Revenue		56,000		
622	Repair Expense	1,800			
711	Depreciation Expense	2,600			
722	Insurance Expense	2,200			
726	Salaries Expense	35,000			
732	Utilities Expense	1,700			
	Totals	43,300	56,000	68,600	55,900
	Net Income	12,700			12,700
		56,000	56,000	68,600	68,600

Instructions

(a) Prepare an income statement, a retained earnings statement, and a classified balance sheet.

(b) Prepare the closing entries.

(c) Post the closing entries and rule and balance the accounts. Use T accounts. Income Summary is No. 350.

(d) Prepare a post-closing trial balance.

P4-4A Qui-Gon Jinn Management Services Inc. began business on January 1, 2001, with a capital investment of $90,000. The company manages condominiums for owners (Service Revenue) and rents space in its own office building (Rent Revenue). The trial and adjusted trial balance columns of the work sheet at the end of the first year are as follows:

Complete work sheet and prepare classified balance sheet, entries, and post-closing trial balance.
(SO 1, 2, 3, 6)

QUI-GON JINN MANAGEMENT SERVICES INC.
Work Sheet
For the Year Ended December 31, 2001

Account Titles	Trial Balance Dr.	Trial Balance Cr.	Adjusted Trial Balance Dr.	Adjusted Trial Balance Cr.
Cash	12,500		12,500	
Accounts Receivable	23,600		23,600	
Prepaid Insurance	3,100		1,600	
Land	56,000		56,000	
Building	106,000		106,000	
Equipment	48,000		48,000	
Accounts Payable		10,400		10,400
Unearned Rent Revenue		4,000		1,800
Mortgage Payable		100,000		100,000
Common Stock		90,000		90,000
Retained Earnings		30,000		30,000
Dividends	20,000		20,000	
Service Revenue		75,600		75,600
Rent Revenue		24,000		26,200
Salaries Expense	32,000		32,000	
Advertising Expense	17,000		17,000	
Utilities Expense	15,800		15,800	
Totals	334,000	334,000		
Insurance Expense			1,500	
Depreciation Expense—Building			2,500	
Accumulated Depreciation—Building				2,500
Depreciation Expense—Equipment			3,900	
Accumulated Depreciation—Equipment				3,900
Interest Expense			10,000	
Interest Payable				10,000
Totals			350,400	350,400

Instructions
(a) Prepare a complete work sheet.
(b) Prepare a classified balance sheet. (Note: $10,000 of the mortgage payable is due for payment next year.)
(c) Journalize the adjusting entries.
(d) Journalize the closing entries.
(e) Prepare a post-closing trial balance.

Complete all steps in accounting cycle.
(SO 1, 2, 3, 4, 6)

P4–5A Terry Duffy opened Corellian Window Washing Inc. on July 1, 2001. During July the following transactions were completed.

July 1	Issued $9,000 of common stock for $9,000 cash.
1	Purchased used truck for $6,000, paying $3,000 cash and the balance on account.
3	Purchased cleaning supplies for $900 on account.
5	Paid $1,200 cash on one-year insurance policy effective July 1.
12	Billed customers $2,500 for cleaning services.
18	Paid $1,000 cash on amount owed on truck and $500 on amount owed on cleaning supplies.
20	Paid $1,200 cash for employee salaries.
21	Collected $1,400 cash from customers billed on July 12.
25	Billed customers $2,000 for cleaning services.
31	Paid gas and oil for month on truck $200.
31	Declared and paid $600 cash dividend.

The chart of accounts for Corellian Window Washing contains the following accounts: No. 101 Cash, No. 112 Accounts Receivable, No. 128 Cleaning Supplies, No. 130 Prepaid Insurance, No. 157 Equipment, No. 158 Accumulated Depreciation—Equipment, No. 201 Accounts Payable, No. 212 Salaries Payable, No. 311 Common Stock, No. 320 Retained Earnings, No. 332 Dividends, No. 350 Income Summary, No. 400 Service Revenue, No. 633 Gas & Oil Expense, No. 634 Cleaning Supplies Expense, No. 711 Depreciation Expense, No. 722 Insurance Expense, No. 726 Salaries Expense.

Instructions
(a) Journalize and post the July transactions. Use page J1 for the journal and the three-column form of account.
(b) Prepare a trial balance at July 31 on a work sheet.
(c) Enter the following adjustments on the work sheet and complete the work sheet.
   (1) Services provided but unbilled and uncollected at July 31 were $1,100.
   (2) Depreciation on equipment for the month was $200.
   (3) One-twelfth of the insurance expired.
   (4) An inventory count shows $600 of cleaning supplies on hand at July 31.
   (5) Accrued but unpaid employee salaries were $400.
(d) Journalize and post adjusting entries. Use page J2 for the journal.
(e) Prepare the income statement and a retained earnings statement for July and a classified balance sheet at July 31.
(f) Journalize and post closing entries and complete the closing process. Use page J3 for the journal.
(g) Prepare a post-closing trial balance at July 31.

P4–6A Queen Amidala, CPA, was retained by Hutts TV Repair Corp. to prepare financial statements for April 2001. Amidala accumulated all the ledger balances per Hutts' records and found the following:

Analyze errors and prepare correcting entries.
(SO 5)

HUTTS TV REPAIR CORP.
Trial Balance
April 30, 2001

	Debit	Credit
Cash	$ 5,100	
Accounts Receivable	3,200	
Supplies	800	
Equipment	10,600	
Accumulated Depreciation		$ 1,350
Accounts Payable		2,100
Salaries Payable		500
Unearned Revenue		890
Common Stock		10,000
Retained Earnings		3,900
Service Revenue		5,450
Salaries Expense	3,300	
Advertising Expense	400	
Miscellaneous Expense	290	
Depreciation Expense	500	
	$24,190	$24,190

Queen Amidala reviewed the records and found the following errors:

1. Cash received from a customer on account was recorded as $750 instead of $570.
2. A payment of $30 for advertising expense was entered as a debit to Miscellaneous Expense $30 and a credit to Cash $30.
3. The first salary payment this month was for $1,900, which included $500 of salaries payable on March 31. The payment was recorded as a debit to Salaries Expense $1,900 and a credit to Cash $1,900. (No reversing entries were made on April 1.)
4. The purchase, on account, of a typewriter costing $340 was recorded as a debit to Supplies and a credit to Accounts Payable for $340.
5. A cash payment of repair expense on equipment for $86 was recorded as a debit to Equipment $68 and a credit to Cash $68.

Instructions

    (a) Prepare an analysis of each error showing (1) the incorrect entry, (2) the correct entry, and (3) the correcting entry. Items 4 and 5 occurred on April 30, 2001.

    (b) Prepare a correct trial balance.

PROBLEMS: SET B

Prepare work sheet, financial statements, and adjusting and closing entries.
(SO 1, 2, 3, 6)

P4–1B   Darth Vader began operations as a private investigator on January 1, 2001. The trial balance columns of the work sheet for Vader P.I., Inc., at March 31 are as follows:

VADER P.I., INC.
Work Sheet
For the Quarter Ended March 31, 2001

Account Titles	Trial Balance	
	Dr.	Cr.
Cash	$12,400	
Accounts Receivable	5,620	
Supplies	1,050	
Prepaid Insurance	2,400	
Equipment	30,000	
Notes Payable		$10,000
Accounts Payable		12,350
Common Stock		20,000
Dividends	600	
Service Revenue		13,620
Salaries Expense	1,200	
Travel Expense	1,300	
Rent Expense	1,200	
Miscellaneous Expense	200	
	$55,970	$55,970

Other data:

    1. Supplies on hand total $750.
    2. Depreciation is $400 per quarter.
    3. Interest accrued on 6-month note payable, issued January 1, $300.
    4. Insurance expires at the rate of $150 per month.
    5. Services provided but unbilled at March 31 total $750.

Instructions

    (a) Enter the trial balance on a work sheet and complete the work sheet.

    (b) Prepare an income statement and a retained earnings statement for the quarter and a classified balance sheet at March 31. Stockholders did not make any additional investments in the business during the quarter ended March 31, 2001.

    (c) Journalize the adjusting entries from the adjustments columns of the work sheet.

    (d) Journalize the closing entries from the financial statement columns of the work sheet.

P4–2B   The adjusted trial balance columns of the work sheet for Shmi Skywalker Company is as follows:

Complete work sheet and
prepare financial statements,
closing entries, and post-
closing trial balance.
(SO 1, 2, 3, 6)

SHMI SKYWALKER COMPANY
Work Sheet
For the Year Ended December 31, 2001

Account No.	Account Titles	Adjusted Trial Balance Dr.	Cr.
101	Cash	22,800	
112	Accounts Receivable	15,400	
126	Supplies	2,300	
130	Prepaid Insurance	4,800	
151	Office Equipment	44,000	
152	Accumulated Depreciation—Office Equipment		18,000
200	Notes Payable		20,000
201	Accounts Payable		8,000
212	Salaries Payable		3,000
230	Interest Payable		1,000
311	Common Stock		20,000
320	Retained Earnings		16,000
332	Dividends	12,000	
400	Service Revenue		79,000
610	Advertising Expense	12,000	
631	Supplies Expense	3,700	
711	Depreciation Expense	6,000	
722	Insurance Expense	4,000	
726	Salaries Expense	37,000	
905	Interest Expense	1,000	
		165,000	165,000

Instructions
(a) Complete the work sheet by extending the balances to the financial statement columns.
(b) Prepare an income statement, a retained earnings statement, and a classified balance sheet. $10,000 of the notes payable become due in 2002. Shareholders did not make any additional investments in the business during 2001.
(c) Prepare the closing entries. Use J14 for the journal page.
(d) Post the closing entries and rule and balance the accounts. Use the three-column form of account. Income Summary is No. 350.
(e) Prepare a post-closing trial balance.

P4–3B   The completed financial statement columns of the work sheet for Panaka Company are shown below.

Prepare financial statements,
closing entries, and post-
closing trial balance.
(SO 1, 2, 3, 6)

PANAKA COMPANY
Work Sheet
For the Year Ended December 31, 2001

Account No.	Account Titles	Income Statement Dr.	Cr.	Balance Sheet Dr.	Cr.
101	Cash			8,200	
112	Accounts Receivable			7,500	
130	Prepaid Insurance			1,800	
157	Equipment			28,000	
167	Accumulated Depreciation				8,600
201	Accounts Payable				12,000

Account No.	Account Titles	Income Statement Dr.	Income Statement Cr.	Balance Sheet Dr.	Balance Sheet Cr.
212	Salaries Payable				3,000
311	Common Stock				20,000
320	Retained Earnings				14,000
332	Dividends			7,200	
400	Service Revenue		42,000		
622	Repair Expense	3,200			
711	Depreciation Expense	2,800			
722	Insurance Expense	1,200			
726	Salaries Expense	36,000			
732	Utilities Expense	3,700			
	Totals	46,900	42,000	52,700	57,600
	Net Loss		4,900	4,900	
		46,900	46,900	57,600	57,600

Instructions

(a) Prepare an income statement, retained earnings statement, and a classified balance sheet. Stockholders made additional investments in the business of $4,000 during 2001.

(b) Prepare the closing entries.

(c) Post the closing entries and rule and balance the accounts. Use T accounts. Income Summary is No. 350.

(d) Prepare a post-closing trial balance.

Complete work sheet and prepare classified balance sheet, entries, and post-closing trial balance.
(SO 1, 2, 3, 6)

P4–4B Wookie Amusement Park Inc. has a fiscal year ending on September 30. Selected data from the September 30 work sheet are presented below:

WOOKIE AMUSEMENT PARK INC.
Work Sheet
For the Year Ended September 30, 2001

	Trial Balance Dr.	Trial Balance Cr.	Adjusted Trial Balance Dr.	Adjusted Trial Balance Cr.
Cash	37,400		37,400	
Supplies	18,600		1,200	
Prepaid Insurance	31,900		3,900	
Land	80,000		80,000	
Equipment	120,000		120,000	
Accumulated Depreciation		36,200		43,000
Accounts Payable		14,600		14,600
Unearned Admissions Revenue		2,700		1,700
Mortgage Payable		50,000		50,000
Common Stock		100,000		100,000
Retained Earnings		9,700		9,700
Dividends	14,000		14,000	
Admissions Revenue		278,500		279,500
Salaries Expense	109,000		109,000	
Repair Expense	30,500		30,500	
Advertising Expense	9,400		9,400	
Utilities Expense	16,900		16,900	
Property Taxes Expense	18,000		21,000	
Interest Expense	6,000		12,000	
Totals	491,700	491,700		
Insurance Expense			28,000	
Supplies Expense			17,400	
Interest Payable				6,000
Depreciation Expense			6,800	
Property Taxes Payable				3,000
Totals			507,500	507,500

Instructions
(a) Prepare a complete work sheet.
(b) Prepare a classified balance sheet. (Note: $10,000 of the mortgage payable is due for payment in the next fiscal year.)
(c) Journalize the adjusting entries using the work sheet as a basis.
(d) Journalize the closing entries using the work sheet as a basis.
(e) Prepare a post-closing trial balance.

P4–5B Ewok-Ackbar opened Ewok's Carpet Cleaners on March 1. During March, the following transactions were completed.

Complete all steps in accounting cycle.
(SO 1, 2, 3, 4, 6)

Mar. 1   Issued $10,000 of common stock for $10,000 cash.
     1   Purchased used truck for $6,000, paying $4,000 cash and the balance on account.
     3   Purchased cleaning supplies for $1,200 on account.
     5   Paid $1,800 cash on one-year insurance policy effective March 1.
    14   Billed customers $2,800 for cleaning services.
    18   Paid $1,500 cash on amount owed on truck and $500 on amount owed on cleaning supplies.
    20   Paid $1,500 cash for employee salaries.
    21   Collected $1,600 cash from customers billed on July 14.
    28   Billed customers $3,500 for cleaning services.
    31   Paid gas and oil for month on truck $200.
    31   Declared and paid a $900 cash dividend.

The chart of accounts for Ewok's Carpet Cleaners contains the following accounts: No. 101 Cash, No. 112 Accounts Receivable, No. 128 Cleaning Supplies, No. 130 Prepaid Insurance, No. 157 Equipment, No. 158 Accumulated Depreciation—Equipment, No. 201 Accounts Payable, No. 212 Salaries Payable, No. 311 Common Stock, No. 320 Retained Earnings, No. 332 Dividends, No. 350 Income Summary, No. 400 Service Revenue, No. 633 Gas & Oil Expense, No. 634 Cleaning Supplies Expense, No. 711 Depreciation Expense, No. 722 Insurance Expense, No. 726 Salaries Expense.

Instructions
(a) Journalize and post the March transactions. Use page J1 for the journal and the three-column form of account.
(b) Prepare a trial balance at March 31 on a work sheet.
(c) Enter the following adjustments on the work sheet and complete the work sheet.
    (1) Earned but unbilled revenue at March 31 was $600.
    (2) Depreciation on equipment for the month was $250.
    (3) One-twelfth of the insurance expired.
    (4) An inventory count shows $400 of cleaning supplies on hand at March 31.
    (5) Accrued but unpaid employee salaries were $500.
(d) Journalize and post adjusting entries. Use page J2 for the journal.
(e) Prepare the income statement and a retained earnings statement for March and a classified balance sheet at March 31.
(f) Journalize and post closing entries and complete the closing process. Use page J3 for the journal.
(g) Prepare a post-closing trial balance at March 31.

BROADENING YOUR PERSPECTIVE

FINANCIAL REPORTING AND ANALYSIS

FINANCIAL REPORTING PROBLEM: Kellogg Company

BYP4–1 The financial statements of Kellogg Company are presented in Appendix A at the end of this textbook.

Instructions
Answer the following questions using the Consolidated Balance Sheet and the Notes to Consolidated Financial Statements section.

(a) What were Kellogg's total current assets at December 31, 1998, and 1997?
(h) Are assets that Kellogg included under current assets listed in proper order? Explain.
(c) How are Kellogg's assets classified?
(d) What are "cash equivalents"?
(e) What were Kellogg's total current liabilities at December 31, 1998, and 1997?

COMPARATIVE ANALYSIS PROBLEM: Kellogg Company vs. General Mills

BYP4–2   Kellogg's financial statements are presented in Appendix A; General Mills's financial statements are presented in Appendix B.

Instructions
(a) Based on the information contained in these financial statements, determine the following for Kellogg at December 31, 1998, and for General Mills at May 31, 1998.
   1. Total current assets.
   2. Net amount of property, plant, and equipment (land, buildings, and equipment).
   3. Total current liabilities.
   4. Total stockholders' (shareholders') equity.
(b) What conclusions about the companies' financial positions can be drawn?

RESEARCH ASSIGNMENT

BYP4–3   The March 1995 issue of *Management Review* includes an article by Barbara Ettorre, entitled "How Motorola Closes Its Books in Two Days."

Instructions
Read the article and answer the following questions.

(a) How often does Motorola close its books? How long did the process used to take?
(b) What was the major change Motorola initiated to shorten the closing process?
(c) What incentive does Motorola offer to ensure accurate and timely information?
(d) In a given year, how many journal entry lines does Motorola process?
(e) Provide an example of an external force that prevents Motorola from closing faster than a day-and-a-half.
(f) According to Motorola's corporate vice president and controller, how do external financial statement users perceive companies that release information early?

INTERPRETING FINANCIAL STATEMENTS: Case Corporation

BYP4–4   Case Corporation, based in Racine, Wisconsin, manufactures farm tractors, farm equipment, and light- and medium-sized construction equipment. The company's products are distributed through both independent and company-owned distributing companies, which are located throughout the world. Case Corporation's partial income statement is shown below.

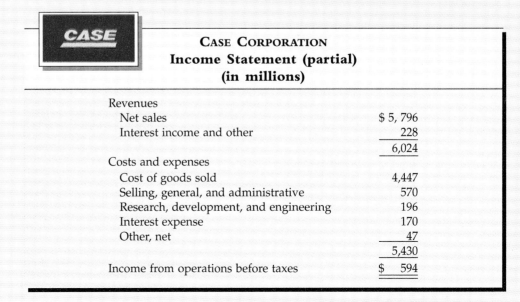

CASE CORPORATION
Income Statement (partial)
(in millions)

Revenues	
Net sales	$ 5,796
Interest income and other	228
	6,024
Costs and expenses	
Cost of goods sold	4,447
Selling, general, and administrative	570
Research, development, and engineering	196
Interest expense	170
Other, net	47
	5,430
Income from operations before taxes	$ 594

The internal audit staff identified the following items that require adjustments:

1. Depreciation on the administrative offices of $13 million needs to be recorded.
2. A physical inventory determined that $1 million in office supplies had been used during the year.
3. $4 million in salaries have been earned but not recorded, and half this amount is for the salaries of the engineering staff; the other half is for the administrative staff.
4. $2 million of prepaid insurance expired during the period.
5. $7 million in prepaid rent has expired at year-end.
6. Cost of goods sold of $2 million was recorded in error as interest expense.

Assume that the partial income statement above was prepared before all adjusting entries had been made.

Instructions
(a) Make the adjusting journal entries required. Use standard account titles, with prepayments having been recorded as assets.
(b) Which of the entries is not a routine adjusting entry? Explain your answer.
(c) For each of the accounts in these adjusting entries that will be posted to Case's general ledger, tell which item on the income statement will be increased or decreased.
(d) Recast the partial income statement based on the adjusting entries prepared.

REAL-WORLD FOCUS: Bethlehem Corporation

BYP4–5 Located in Easton, Pennsylvania, **Bethlehem Corporation** was established in 1856. Today it offers contract services for industrial products, rebuilding and remanufacturing industrial and military equipment per customer specifications and designs. The company also manufactures and sells a line of equipment used in the chemical, environmental, and food industries.

Bethlehem Corporation had a net loss for the year of $239,251. One reason for the loss is that Bethlehem established an accrual to provide for expenses and costs associated with certain legal proceedings against Bethlehem.

Instructions
(a) Indicate how the net loss would be shown in Bethlehem's work sheet.
(b) Where in the general ledger would you expect to find the two accounts related to the accrual for expenses and costs associated with legal proceedings?
(c) Identify the financial statement columns to which the balances of the two accounts in part (b) would be extended on the work sheet.

CRITICAL THINKING
. . . .

GROUP DECISION CASE

BYP4–6 Cleanfast Janitorial Service Inc. was started 2 years ago by Pat Hardy. Because business has been exceptionally good, Pat decided on July 1, 1999, to expand operations by acquiring an additional truck and hiring two more assistants. To finance the expansion, Pat obtained on July 1, 1999, a $25,000, 10% bank loan, payable $10,000 on July 1, 2000, and the balance on July 1, 2001. The terms of the loan require the borrower to have $10,000 more current assets than current liabilities at December 31, 1999. If these terms are not met, the bank loan will be refinanced at 15% interest. At December 31, 1999, the accountant for Cleanfast Janitorial Service Inc. prepared the following balance sheet:

CLEANFAST JANITORIAL SERVICE INC.
Balance Sheet
December 31, 1999

Assets

Current assets		
Cash		$ 6,500
Accounts receivable		9,000
Janitorial supplies		5,200
Prepaid insurance		4,800
Total current assets		25,500
Property, plant, and equipment		
Cleaning equipment (net)	$22,000	
Delivery trucks (net)	34,000	56,000
Total assets		$81,500

Liabilities and Stockholders' Equity

Current liabilities		
Notes payable		$10,000
Accounts payable		2,500
Total current liabilities		12,500
Long-term liability		
Notes payable		15,000
Total liabilities		27,500
Stockholders' equity		
Common stock		40,000
Retained earnings		14,000
Total liabilities and stockholders' equity		$81,500

Pat presented the balance sheet to the bank's loan office on January 2, 2000, confident that the company had met the terms of the loan. The loan officer was not impressed. She said, "We need financial statements audited by a CPA." A CPA was hired and immediately realized that the balance sheet had been prepared from a trial balance and not from an adjusted trial balance. The adjustment data at the balance sheet date consisted of the following:

1. Earned but unbilled janitorial services were $3,000.
2. Janitorial supplies on hand were $3,500.
3. Prepaid insurance was a 3-year policy dated January 1, 1999.
4. December expenses incurred but unpaid at December 31, $300.
5. Interest on the bank loan was not recorded.
6. The amounts for plant assets were net of accumulated depreciation of $4,000 for cleaning equipment and $5,000 for delivery trucks as of January 1, 1999. Depreciation for 1999 was $2,000 for cleaning equipment and $5,000 for delivery trucks.

Instructions
With the class divided into groups, answer the following:

(a) Prepare a correct balance sheet.
(b) Were the terms of the bank loan met? Explain.

COMMUNICATION ACTIVITY

BYP4–7   The accounting cycle is important in understanding the accounting process.

Instructions
Write a memorandum to your instructor which lists the steps of the accounting cycle in the order in which they should be completed. Complete your memorandum with a paragraph that explains the optional steps in the cycle.

ETHICS CASE

BYP4–8 As the controller of Magnus Perfume Company, you discover a misstatement that overstated net income in the prior year's financial statements. The misleading financial statements appear in the company's annual report which was issued to banks and other creditors less than a month ago. After much thought about the consequences of telling the president, David Rudman, about this misstatement, you gather your courage to inform him. David says, "Hey! What they don't know won't hurt them. But, just so we set the record straight, we'll adjust this year's financial statements for last year's misstatement. We can absorb that misstatement better in this year than in last year anyway! Just don't make such a mistake again."

Instructions
- (a) Who are the stakeholders in this situation?
- (b) What are the ethical issues in this situation?
- (c) What would you do as a controller in this situation?

SURFING THE NET

BYP4–9 Numerous companies have established home pages on the Internet, e.g., Boston Beer Company (http://www.samadams.com), Ford Motor Company (http://www.ford.com), and Kodak (http://www.kodak.com). You may have noticed company Internet addresses in television commercials or magazine advertisements.

Instructions
Examine the home pages of any two companies and answer the following questions.

- (a) What type of information is available?
- (b) Is any accounting-related information presented?
- (c) Would you describe the home page as informative, promotional, or both? Why?

Answers to Self-Study Questions
1. c   2. b   3. d   4. a   5. d   6. b   7. a   8. c   9. c   10. b   11. b

Answer to Kellogg Review It Question 2, p. 162
Current liabilities in 1998 were $1,718.5 million, and current liabilities in 1997 were $1,657.3 million. In both 1998 and 1997, current liabilities were greater than current assets.

  Remember to go back to the Navigator box on the chapter-opening page and check off your completed work.

Before studying this chapter, you should know or, if necessary, review:

a. How to prepare a work sheet. (Ch. 4, pp. 141–44)
b. How to close revenue, expense, and dividend accounts. (Ch. 4, pp. 146–50)
c. The steps in the accounting cycle. (Ch. 4, p. 154)

THE NAVIGATOR

FEATURE STORY

Selling Dollars for 85 Cents

Entrepreneur Scott Blum, CEO of Buy.com, is selling consumer products at or below cost, and trying to create an outlet synonymous with low prices—with the hope of becoming the leading E-commerce portal on the Internet. He plans to make up the losses from sales by selling advertising on the company's Website.

As if the idea of selling below cost weren't unusual enough, Blum has added another twist to merchandising: Since he doesn't want to touch inventory, he has wholesalers

and distributors ship the products directly to his Website customers.

Buy.com's slogan, "The lowest prices on earth," may be the most eye-catching sales pitch ever. The company is ruthlessly committed to being the price leader—even if it means losing money on every sale. Its own computers search competitors' Websites to make sure that Buy.com has the lowest prices on the Internet.

The amount of available capital (cash) is the natural limit to a business model in which money is lost on every sale. Buy.com has raised $60 million from Softbank, the Japanese conglomerate that backed

Yahoo! and E-Trade. Based on its employee size of about 100 people, the company should have operating expenses of about $12 million. Even if it loses money on each sale and spends marginally on advertising, Buy.com should be able to run for a while.

Consider the implications if Buy.com is successful. First, it will prove that it is possible to build a brand and a business completely and exclusively on price. Second, Buy.com's success could change the very way wholesalers and distributors view their businesses. Third, Buy.com's success may have an impact on all kinds of retailers—starting with Buy.com itself. If Buy.com proves that the ad space on a product order form—its Website—is almost as valuable as the product being ordered, another virtual reseller is sure to enter the market with even lower prices. That kind of pricing could intensify competition between wholesalers and Internet retailers. And, manufacturers may be increasingly pressured to drop-ship directly to the consumer.

Of course, there is one big winner if Buy.com succeeds: you. It has never been a better time to be a customer.

Source: J. William Gurley, "Buy.com May Fail, But If It Succeeds, Retailing May Never Be the Same," *Fortune*, January 11, 1999, pp. 150–52.

THE NAVIGATOR

On the World Wide Web
www.buy.com

CHAPTER 5

ACCOUNTING FOR MERCHANDISING OPERATIONS

THE NAVIGATOR ✔

- Understand *Concepts for Review* ☐
- Read *Feature Story* ☐
- Scan *Study Objectives* ☐
- Read *Preview* ☐
- Read text and answer *Before You Go On*
  p. 196 ☐ p. 201 ☐ p. 206 ☐ p. 209 ☐
- Work *Demonstration Problem* ☐
- Review *Summary of Study Objectives* ☐
- Answer *Self-Study Questions* ☐
- Complete assignments ☐

STUDY OBJECTIVES

After studying this chapter, you should be able to:

1. *Identify the differences between a service enterprise and a merchandising company.*
2. *Explain the entries for purchases under a perpetual inventory system.*
3. *Explain the entries for sales revenues under a perpetual inventory system.*
4. *Explain the computation and importance of gross profit.*
5. *Identify the features of the income statement for a merchandising company.*
6. *Explain the steps in the accounting cycle for a merchandising company.*
7. *Distinguish between a multiple-step and a single-step income statement.*

THE NAVIGATOR

*A*s indicated in the opening story, Buy.com is an unusual merchandiser in that it does not have its own inventory. Like other merchandisers, though, it generates revenues by selling goods to customers rather than performing services. Merchandising companies that purchase and sell directly to consumers—such as Wal-Mart, Kmart, Safeway, and Toys "R" Us—are called **retailers**. In contrast, merchandising companies that sell to retailers are known as **wholesalers**. For example, retailer Walgreens might buy goods from wholesaler McKessonHBOC; Office Depot might buy office supplies from wholesaler United Stationers.

The steps in the accounting cycle for a merchandising company are the same as the steps for a service enterprise. However, merchandising companies use additional accounts and entries which are required in recording merchandising transactions. The content and organization of this chapter are as follows:

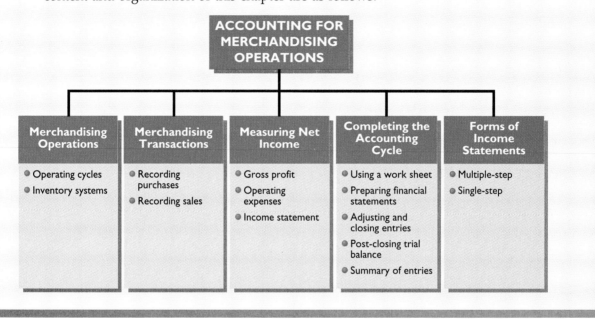

THE
NAVIGATOR

MERCHANDISING OPERATIONS

1
STUDY
OBJECTIVE

Identify the differences between a service enterprise and a merchandising company.

Measuring net income for a merchandising company is conceptually the same as for a service enterprise. That is, net income (or loss) results from the matching of expenses with revenues. In a merchandising company, the primary source of revenues is the sale of merchandise, often referred to as sales revenue or sales. Unlike expenses for a service company, expenses for a merchandising company are divided into two categories: (1) the cost of goods sold and (2) operating expenses.

The cost of goods sold is the total cost of merchandise sold during the period. This expense is directly related to the revenue recognized from the sale of the goods. Sales revenue less cost of goods sold is called gross profit on sales. For example, when a calculator costing $15 is sold for $25, the gross profit is $10. Merchandising companies report gross profit on sales in the income statement.

After gross profit is calculated, operating expenses are deducted to determine net income (or loss). Operating expenses are expenses incurred in the process of earning sales revenue. Examples of operating expenses are sales salaries, advertising expense, and insurance expense. The operating expenses of a merchandising company include many of the expenses found in a service enterprise.

The income measurement process for a merchandiser may be diagrammed as shown in Illustration 5-1. The items in the three blue boxes are peculiar to a merchandising company; they are not used by a service company.

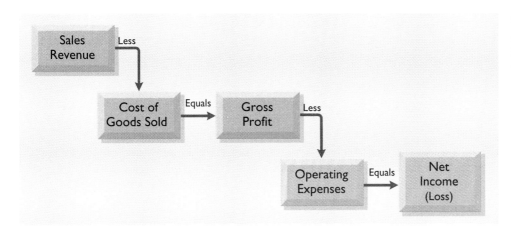

ILLUSTRATION 5-1

Income measurement process for a merchandising company

Operating Cycles

While measuring income for a merchandising company is conceptually the same as for a service company, their operating cycles differ, as shown in Illustration 5-2. The operating cycle of a merchandising company ordinarily is longer than that of a service company. The purchase of merchandise inventory and its eventual

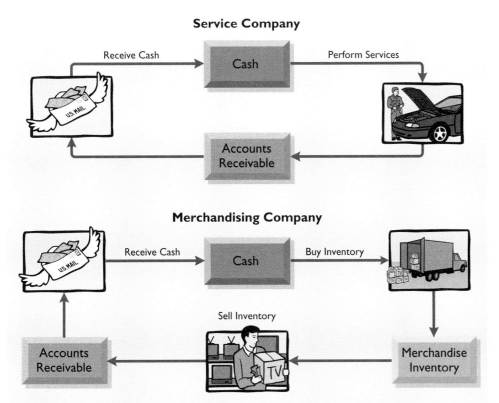

ILLUSTRATION 5-2

Operating cycles for a service company and a merchandising company

sale lengthens the cycle. Note that the added asset account for a merchandising company is an **inventory** account (usually entitled Merchandise Inventory). Merchandise inventory is reported as a current asset on the balance sheet.

Inventory Systems

Either of two systems may be used in accounting for merchandising transactions: (1) a **perpetual inventory system** or (2) a **periodic inventory system**.

In a perpetual inventory system, detailed records of the cost of each inventory purchase and sale are maintained and continuously (perpetually) show the inventory that should be on hand for every item. A perpetual inventory keeps track of both **quantities and costs**. For example, a Ford dealership will have separate inventory records for each automobile, truck, and van on its lot and showroom floor. With the use of bar codes and optical scanners, a grocery store can keep a daily running record of every box of cereal and every jar of jelly that it buys and sells. **Under a perpetual inventory system the cost of goods sold is determined and recorded each time a sale occurs.**

In a periodic inventory system, no attempt is made to keep detailed inventory records of the goods on hand throughout the period. **The cost of goods sold is determined only at the end of the accounting period when a physical inventory count is taken to determine the cost of goods on hand.**

To determine the cost of goods sold under a periodic inventory system, it is necessary to (1) record purchases of merchandise, (2) determine the cost of goods purchased, and (3) determine the cost of goods on hand at the beginning and end of the accounting period.

Illustration 5-3 graphically compares the sequence of activities and the timing of the cost of goods sold computation under the two inventory systems.

Some businesses employ the periodic system because they can control merchandise and manage day-to-day operations without detailed inventory records. In addition, perpetual systems are in many cases more expensive.

Under a perpetual inventory system, inventory shrinkage and lost or stolen goods are more readily determined. Also, reorder decisions are more accurately made under a perpetual system because exact inventory levels are known constantly. Because the perpetual inventory system is growing in popularity, we illustrate it in this chapter. The periodic system is described in Chapter 6.

ILLUSTRATION 5-3

Comparing perpetual to periodic inventory

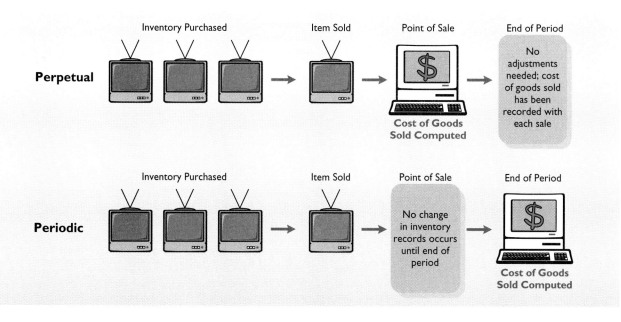

ACCOUNTING IN ACTION
Business Insight

Perpetual inventory systems, combined with high-tech advances, have enabled many manufacturers, wholesalers, and retailers to use integrated *just-in-time* inventory management systems. Business consultant S. El-Raheb explains:"If you buy a mattress at Leon's Stores, it won't be in stock. The store will place an electronic order with the manufacturer, who makes it and ships it to their dock. Another truck is right there to pick up and deliver the piece, and all this takes place in less than 24 hours." Within the company, ordering, inventory control, billing, and accounting is seamless. The computer determines when and how many items to buy, prepares and submits the purchase order, issues the bill, and updates the inventory and accounting records.

Source: Financial Post, April 26, 1997, p. 58.

MERCHANDISING TRANSACTIONS

Recording merchandising transactions requires the analysis of purchases and sales of merchandise. Related to both purchases and sales are returns and allowances, discounts, and transportation costs.

Recording Purchases

2
STUDY
OBJECTIVE

Explain the entries for purchases under a perpetual inventory system.

Purchases may be made for cash or on account (credit). Purchases are normally recorded when the goods are received from the supplier. Every purchase should be supported by business documents that provide written evidence of the transaction. Cash purchases should be supported by canceled checks or cash register receipts indicating the items purchased and amounts paid. Credit purchases should be supported by an invoice, like the one shown in Illustration 5-4, that indicates the items purchased and the total purchase price. An invoice is a document prepared by the seller that shows the relevant information about a sale. From the seller's perspective this document is a sales invoice, and from the buyer's perspective it is a purchase invoice.

Illustration 5-4 shows a sales invoice prepared by Highpoint Electronic, Inc. to document a sale to Chelsea Video. Chelsea Video will use this as a purchase invoice to document the purchase from Highpoint. Chelsea will make the following entry to record the purchase of merchandise from Highpoint:

May 4	Merchandise Inventory	3,800	
	Accounts Payable		3,800
	(To record goods purchased on account, terms 2/10, n/30, from Highpoint Electronic)		

A   =   L   +   SE
+3,800   +3,800

Under the perpetual inventory system, purchases of merchandise for sale are recorded in the Merchandise Inventory account. Thus, Sears, Kmart, and Wal-Mart **debit Merchandise Inventory for goods purchased for resale to customers.** However, not all purchases are debited to Merchandise Inventory. Purchases of assets acquired for use and not for resale, such as supplies, equipment, and similar items, should be **debited to specific asset accounts rather than to Merchandise Inventory.** For example, Wal-Mart would debit Supplies for the supplies purchased to make shelf signs, banners, tags, and labels that identify which goods are on special sale.

Purchase Returns and Allowances

A purchaser may be dissatisfied with the merchandise received because the goods are damaged or defective, of inferior quality, or not in accord with the

HELPFUL HINT
To better understand the
contents of this invoice,
identify the:
(1) Seller.
(2) Invoice date.
(3) Purchaser.
(4) Salesperson.
(5) Credit terms.
(6) Freight terms.
(7) Goods sold: Catalogue no.,
description, quantity, price
per unit.
(8) Total invoice amount.

purchaser's specifications. In such cases, the purchaser may return the goods to the supplier for credit if the sale was made on credit, or for a cash refund if the purchase was originally for cash. This transaction is known as a **purchase return**. Alternatively, the purchaser may choose to keep the merchandise if the supplier is willing to grant an allowance (deduction) from the purchase price. This transaction is known as a **purchase allowance**.

The purchaser initiates the request for a reduction of the balance due through the issuance of a debit memorandum. A debit memorandum is a document issued by a purchaser to inform a supplier that a debit has been made to the supplier's account on the purchaser's books. The original copy of the memorandum is sent to the supplier, and one copy is retained by the purchaser. The information contained in a debit memorandum is shown in Illustration 5-5; it relates to the sales invoice shown in Illustration 5-4.

The entry by Chelsea Video for the merchandise returned to Highpoint Electronic on May 8 is:

A	=	L	+	SE
−300		−300		

May 8	Accounts Payable	300	
	Merchandise Inventory		300
	(To record return of inoperable goods received from Highpoint Electronic, DM No. 126)		

ILLUSTRATION 5-5

Debit memorandum

DEBIT-DM126

Chelsea Video

125 Main Street
Chelsea, IL 60915

Purchased
From:

Firm Name _____Highpoint Electronic, Inc._____

Attention of _____Susan Malone, Sales Representative_____

Address _____27 Circle Drive_____

Harding	MI	48281
City	State	Zip

Date 5/8/01	Salesperson Malone	Invoice No. 731	Invoice Date 5/4/01	Approved Reid

Catalogue No.	Description	Quantity	Price	Amount
A2547Z45	Production Model Circuits (Inoperative)	1	300	$300

Cash Refund ☐   Debit Account ☒   Other ☐

Because Merchandise Inventory was debited when the goods were received, Merchandise Inventory is credited when the goods are returned.

Purchase Discounts

The credit terms of a purchase on account may permit the purchaser to claim a cash discount for the prompt payment of a balance due. The purchaser calls this cash discount a purchase discount. This incentive offers advantages to both parties: The purchaser saves money, and the supplier is able to convert the accounts receivable into cash earlier.

The **credit terms** specify the amount and time period for the cash discount. They also indicate the length of time in which the purchaser is expected to pay the full invoice price. In the sales invoice in Illustration 5-4, credit terms are 2/10, n/30, which is read "two-ten, net thirty." This means that a 2% cash discount may be taken on the invoice price (less any returns or allowances) if payment is made within 10 days of the invoice date (the **discount period**); otherwise, the invoice price less any returns or allowances is due 30 days from the invoice date. Alternatively, the discount period may extend to a specified number of days following the month in which the sale occurs. For example, 1/10 EOM (end-of-month) means that a 1% discount is available if the invoice is paid within the first 10 days of the next month.

Purchase Discount

"Get that check in the mail this week so we can save 2%."

Merchandise Inventory	
	XXX

HELPFUL HINT
Assume goods were sold on June 1, terms 1/10, net 30. Question: What is the due date for taking the discount? Answer: June 11. Question: If the terms were 2/10 EOM, what is the due date for taking the discount? Answer: July 10.

When the supplier elects not to offer a cash discount for prompt payment, credit terms will specify only the maximum time period for paying the balance due. For example, the time period may be stated as n/30, n/60, or n/10 EOM.

When an invoice is paid within the discount period, the amount of the discount is credited to Merchandise Inventory. To illustrate, assume Chelsea Video pays the balance due of $3,500 (gross invoice price of $3,800 less purchase returns and allowances of $300) on May 14, the last day of the discount period. The cash discount is $70 ($3,500 × 2%) and the amount of cash paid by Chelsea Video is $3,430 ($3,500 − $70) The entry to record the May 14 payment by Chelsea Video is as follows:

A	=	L	+	SE
−3,430		−3,500		
−		70		

May 14	Accounts Payable	3,500	
	Cash		3,430
	Merchandise Inventory		70
	(To record payment within discount period)		

If Chelsea Video had failed to take the discount and full payment is made on June 3, Chelsea would have made the following entry:

A	=	L	+	SE
		−3,500		−3,500

June 3	Accounts Payable	3,500	
	Cash		3,500
	(To record payment with no discount taken)		

ACCOUNTING IN ACTION
Business Insight

In the early 1990s, Sears wielded its retail clout by telling its suppliers that, rather than pay its obligations in the standard 30-day period, it would now pay in 60 days. This practice is often adopted by firms that are experiencing financial distress from a shortage of cash. A Sears spokesperson insisted, however, that Sears did not have cash problems, but, rather, was simply utilizing "vendor-financed inventory methods to improve its return on investment." Supplier trade groups criticized Sears' policy, and pointed out that consumers would be the ultimate victims, because the financing costs would eventually be passed on to them.

HELPFUL HINT
So as not to miss purchase discounts, unpaid invoices should be filed (electronically or manually) by due dates. This procedure helps the purchaser remember the discount date, prevents early payment of bills, and maximizes the time that cash can be used for other purposes.

A buyer usually should take all available discounts. For example, if Chelsea Video takes the discount, it pays $3,430 instead of $3,500, thus saving $70. If it does not take the discount and invests the $3,430 in a bank savings account for 20 days (30 − 10) at 10% interest, it will earn only $19.06 in interest.[1] The savings obtained by taking the discount is computed as follows:

---

[1]If Chelsea Video does not pay at the end of 10 days, it has the use of $3,430 for an additional 20 days at a cost (lost discount) of $70. For the 20-day period, the interest rate on the $3,430 is effectively 2.04% ($70 ÷ $3,430). Interest rates are generally expressed on an annualized basis of 360 days; thus Highpoint Electronic's discount terms are equivalent to 36.72% (360/20 × 2.04%). In view of this high interest rate, it would be better for Chelsea Video to take the discount.

Discount of 2% on $3,500	$70.00
Interest received on $3,130	
(for 20 days at 10%)	19.06
Savings by taking the discount	**$50.94**

ILLUSTRATION 5-6
Savings obtained by taking purchase discount

Freight Costs

The sales agreement should indicate whether the seller or the buyer is to pay the cost of transporting the goods to the buyer's place of business. When a common carrier such as a railroad, trucking company, or airline is used, the transportation company prepares a freight bill (often called a bill of lading) in accordance with the sales agreement. Freight terms are expressed as either **FOB shipping point** or **FOB destination**. The letters FOB mean **free on board**. Thus, FOB shipping point means that goods are placed free on board the carrier by the seller, and the buyer pays the freight costs. Conversely, FOB destination means that the goods are placed free on board to the buyer's place of business, and the seller pays the freight. For example, the sales invoice in Illustration 5-4 on page 192 indicates that freight is FOB shipping point. Thus, the buyer (Chelsea Video) pays the freight charges.

When the purchaser directly incurs the freight costs, the account Merchandise Inventory is debited. For example, if upon delivery of the goods on May 6, Chelsea Video pays Acme Freight Company $150 for freight charges, the entry on Chelsea's books is:

May 6	Merchandise Inventory	150	
	Cash		150
	(To record payment of freight, terms FOB shipping point)		

HELPFUL HINT
Freight terms may be stated by location. A Chicago seller may use "FOB Chicago" for FOB shipping point and the buyer's city for FOB destination.

A	=	L	+	SE
+150				
−150				

In contrast, **freight costs incurred by the seller on outgoing merchandise are an operating expense to the seller**. These costs are debited to Freight-out or Delivery Expense. For example, if the freight terms on invoice No. 731 in Illustration 5-4 had specified FOB destination and Highpoint Electronic paid the $150 freight charges, the entry by Highpoint would be:

May 4	Freight-out (Delivery Expense)	150	
	Cash		150
	(To record payment of freight on goods sold FOB destination)		

HELPFUL HINT
The freight cost under the terms FOB shipping point and paid by Chelsea does not enter into the computation of the discount shown above.

| A | = | L | + | SE |
| −150 | | | | −150 |

When the freight charges are paid by the seller, the seller will usually establish a higher invoice price for the goods, to cover the expense of shipping.

Alternative Accounting for Returns and Allowances, Discounts, and Freight Costs

A business manager may want to keep detailed records of returns and allowances, discounts, and freight costs related to purchases of merchandise. For example, if management wishes to know the amount saved through cash discounts on purchases of merchandise, the amount of discounts taken can be accumulated in a separate Purchase Discounts account. Or, if management wishes to keep track of the purchase returns and allowances due to defective, inferior quality, or damaged goods, a special account, Purchase Returns and Allowances, may be credited to serve as a running record of such transactions. And, Freight-in could be debited for transportation costs on purchased merchandise. In order to report Merchandise Inventory at total cost in the financial statements, these separate accounts may be combined with the amount in Merchandise Inventory as follows:

Merchandise inventory		$XXXX
Less: Purchase returns and allowances	$XXX	
Purchase discounts	XXX	XXX
Net purchases of merchandise inventory		XXXX
Add: Freight-in		XXX
Total cost of merchandise inventory		$XXXX

BEFORE YOU GO ON ...

Review It

1. How do the components used in measuring net income in a merchandising company differ from those in a service enterprise?
2. In what ways is a perpetual inventory system different from a periodic inventory system?
3. What entries are made to record purchases of inventory, purchase returns and allowances, purchase discounts, and freight-in under a perpetual inventory system?
4. What is an alternative method of accounting for purchase returns and allowances, discounts, and freight costs?

Recording Sales

Sales revenues, like service revenues, are recorded when earned. This is in accordance with the revenue recognition principle. Typically, sales revenues are earned when the goods are transferred from the seller to the buyer. At this point, the sales transaction is completed and the sales price is established.

Sales may be made on credit or for cash. Every sales transaction should be supported by a **business document** that provides written evidence of the sale. **Cash register tapes** provide evidence of cash sales. A sales invoice, like the one shown in Illustration 5-4, provides support for a credit sale. The original copy of the invoice goes to the customer, and a copy is kept by the seller for use in recording the sale. The invoice shows the date of sale, customer name, total sales price, and other relevant information.

For cash sales, the Cash account is debited and the Sales account is credited; and, under the perpetual inventory system, the **cost of the merchandise sold** and the **reduction in merchandise inventory** are also recorded. Therefore, two entries are made for each sale, one at the selling price of the goods and the other at the cost of the goods sold. For example, assume that on May 4 Highpoint Electronic has cash sales of $2,200 from merchandise having a cost of $1,400. The entries to record the day's cash sales are as follows:

A	=	L	+	SE
+2,200				+2,200

May 4	Cash		2,200	
	Sales			2,220
	(To record daily cash sales)			

A	=	L	+	SE
−1,400				−1,400

4	Cost of Goods Sold		1,400	
	Merchandise Inventory			1,400
	(To record cost of merchandise sold			
	for cash)			

For credit sales, Accounts Receivable is debited and Sales is credited; and, Cost of Goods Sold is debited and Merchandise Inventory is credited. In this way, under a perpetual inventory system, the Merchandise Inventory account will show at all times the amount of inventory that should be on hand. To illustrate a credit sales transaction, Highpoint Electronic's sales of $3,800 per invoice No. 731 (Illustration 5-4) of May 4 to Chelsea Video would be recorded as follows (assume the merchandise cost Highpoint $2,400):

May 4	Accounts Receivable	3,800	
	Sales		3,800
	(To record credit sale to Chelsea Video per invoice #731)		

A	=	L	+	SE
+3,800				+3,800

4	Cost of Goods Sold	2,400	
	Merchandise Inventory		2,400
	(To record cost of merchandise sold on invoice #731 to Chelsea Video)		

A	=	L	+	SE
−2,400				−2,400

Merchandising companies may use more than one sales account. For example, Highpoint Electronic may decide to keep separate sales accounts for its sales of television sets, videocassette recorders, and microwave ovens. Because sales are the principal source of revenue for a merchandising company, the amount and trend of sales are of critical importance. For example, an increase in sales from the preceding year signifies a growing business and often leads to higher net income. A decrease in sales may suggest an unfavorable trend, and, therefore, lower future earnings.

ACCOUNTING IN ACTION
Ethics Insight

Inventory losses can be substantial. Shoplifting is a big crime in the United States, with a cost of more than $18 billion annually, or 5% of retail sales, not including thefts by store employees. Shoplifting losses have led to the demise of many companies. For example, Dayton-Hudson closed its landmark store in downtown Detroit, in part, because of excessive shoplifting losses. Many department stores are trying to reduce shoplifting losses by use of electronic tags on merchandise and by continuous surveillance of customers on closed circuit television.

Sales Returns and Allowances

A purchase return and allowance on the purchaser's books is recorded as a **sales return and allowance** on the books of the seller. To grant the customer a sales return or allowance, the seller normally prepares a credit memorandum. This document informs a customer that a credit has been made to the customer's account receivable for a sales return or allowance. The information contained in a credit memorandum is similar to the information found in the debit memorandum in Illustration 5-5 (p. 193). The original copy of the credit memorandum is sent to the customer, and a copy is kept by the seller as evidence of the transaction. Highpoint's entries to record a credit memorandum for returned goods involve (1) a debit to Sales Returns and Allowances and a credit to Accounts Receivable at the $300 selling price, and (2) a debit to Merchandise Inventory (assume a $140 cost) and a credit to Cost of Goods Sold as follows:

A	=	L	+	SE	
300				−300	

May 8	Sales Returns and Allowances		300	
	Accounts Receivable			300
	(To record return of inoperable goods delivered to Chelsea Video, per credit memorandum)			

A	=	L	+	SE	
+140				+140	

8	Merchandise Inventory		140	
	Cost of Goods Sold			140
	(To record cost of goods returned per credit memorandum)			

When a sales allowance for damaged goods is granted on a **credit sale**, no entry to inventory and cost of goods sold is necessary because the supplier receives no returned goods from the customer. As shown in the first entry above, the supplier debits Sales Returns and Allowances and credits Accounts Receivable for the damaged goods allowance.

When goods are returned or an allowance is made on a **cash sale**, the supplier normally provides a cash refund and debits Sales Returns and Allowances and credits Cash. If the supplier **receives returned merchandise** in good condition, a second entry is made debiting Merchandise Inventory and crediting Cost of Goods Sold at cost. If the supplier grants an allowance and the **merchandise is not returned**, no entry affecting inventory and cost of goods sold is necessary by the supplier.

Sales Returns and Allowances is a contra revenue account to Sales with a normal debit balance. A contra account is used, instead of debiting Sales, to disclose the amount of sales returns and allowances in the accounts and in the income statement because disclosure of this information is important to management. Excessive returns and allowances suggest inferior merchandise, inefficiencies in filling orders, errors in billing customers, and mistakes in delivery or shipment of the goods. Moreover, a debit directly to Sales would obscure the relative importance of sales returns and allowances as a percentage of sales and could distort comparisons between total sales in different accounting periods.

ETHICS NOTE

Large retailers of electronics often have generous return policies, allowing returns for any reason within the first 30 days. Unfortunately, unscrupulous customers will "buy" video cameras or large stereos for special events such as weddings, use them, and then return them after the event. The retailer suffers a loss because they must then sell the item as returned merchandise.

ACCOUNTING IN ACTION
Business Insight

How high is too high? Returns can become so high that it is questionable whether sales revenue should have been recognized in the first place. An example of high returns is Florafax International Inc., a floral supply company, which was alleged to have shipped its product without customer authorization on 10 holiday occasions, including 8,562 shipments of its product to customers for Mother's Day and 6,575 for Secretary's Day. The return rate on these shipments went as high as 69% of sales. As one employee noted: "Products went out the front door and came in the back door."

An offshoot of high returns is "channel stuffing." In channel stuffing, the seller "sells" its product by providing substantial inducements to buy. Although this helps the seller's revenue in the short run, the long term can be devastating when the merchandise bought remains on the purchasers' shelves for a long period of time.

Sales Discounts

As mentioned in our discussion of purchase transactions, the seller may offer the customer a cash discount, called by the seller a sales discount, for the prompt payment of the balance due. Like a purchase discount, a sales discount is based on the invoice price less returns and allowances, if any. Sales Discounts is debited for the cash discounts that are taken. The entry by Highpoint to record the cash receipt on May 14 from Chelsea Video within the discount period is as follows:

May 14	Cash	3,430	
	Sales Discounts	70	
	Accounts Receivable		3,500
	(To record collection within 2/10, n/30		
	discount period from Chelsea Video)		

A	=	L	+	SE
+3,430				−70
−3,500				

Sales Discount

"That's right, pay within 10 days and you'll get a 2% discount."

Sales Discounts	
XXX	

Like Sales Returns and Allowances, Sales Discounts is a **contra revenue account** to Sales. Its normal balance is a debit. This account is used, instead of debiting sales, to accumulate the amount of cash discounts taken by customers. If the discount is not taken, Highpoint Electronic debits Cash for $3,500 and credits Accounts Receivable for $3,500 at the date of the collection.

Statement Presentation of Sales

As contra revenue accounts, sales returns and allowances and sales discounts are deducted from sales in the income statement to arrive at net sales. The sales revenues section of the income statement based on assumed data for Highpoint Electronic is as follows:

ILLUSTRATION 5-7

Statement presentation of sales revenues section

HIGHPOINT ELECTRONIC, INC.		
Income Statement (partial)		
Sales revenues		
Sales		$480,000
Less: Sales returns and allowances	$12,000	
Sales discounts	8,000	20,000
Net sales		$460,000

This presentation discloses the significant aspects of the company's principal revenue producing activities.

MEASURING NET INCOME

Gross Profit

From Illustration 5-1, you learned that cost of goods sold is deducted from sales revenue to determine **gross profit**. Sales revenue used for this computation is **net sales** (which takes into account sales returns and allowances and sales discounts). On the basis of the sales data presented in Illustration 5-7 (net sales of $460,000) and the cost of goods sold, accumulated under the perpetual inventory system (assume a balance of $316,000), the gross profit for Highpoint Electronic is $144,000, computed as follows:

Net sales	$460,000
Cost of goods sold	316,000
Gross profit	**$144,000**

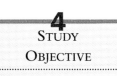

4
STUDY
OBJECTIVE

Explain the computation and importance of gross profit.

ILLUSTRATION 5-8

Computation of gross profit

A company's gross profit may also be expressed as a percentage by dividing the amount of gross profit by net sales. For Highpoint Electronic the gross profit rate is 31.3% ($144,000 ÷ $460,000). The gross profit rate is generally

ALTERNATIVE TERMINOLOGY
Gross profit is sometimes referred to as *merchandising profit* or *gross margin.*

considered to be more useful than the gross profit amount because it expresses a more meaningful relationship between net sales and gross profit. For example, a gross profit of $1,000,000 may be impressive. But, if it is the result of a gross profit rate of only 7%, it is not so impressive. The gross profit rate tells how many cents of each sales dollar go to gross profit.

Gross profit represents the **merchandising profit** of a company. It is not a measure of the overall profitability of a company, because operating expenses have not been deducted. Nevertheless, the amount and trend of gross profit is closely watched by management and other interested parties. Comparisons of current gross profit with amounts reported in past periods, and comparisons of gross profit rates of competitors and with industry averages provide information about the effectiveness of a company's purchasing function and the soundness of its pricing policies.

Operating Expenses

Operating expenses are the third component in measuring net income for a merchandising company. As indicated earlier, these expenses are similar in merchandising and service enterprises. At Highpoint Electronic, operating expenses were $114,000. The firm's net income is determined by subtracting operating expenses from gross profit. Thus, net income is $30,000 as shown below:

ILLUSTRATION 5-9

Operating expenses in computing net income

Gross profit	$144,000
Operating expenses	**114,000**
Net income	$ 30,000

5
STUDY
OBJECTIVE

Identify the features of the income statement for a merchandising company.

The net income amount is the "bottom line" of a company's income statement.

Income Statement

The income statement for retailers and wholesalers contains three features not found in the income statement of a service enterprise. These features are: (1) a sales revenue section, (2) a cost of goods sold section, and (3) gross profit. Using assumed data for specific operating expenses, the income statement for Highpoint Electronic, Inc., is shown in Illustration 5-10.

ILLUSTRATION 5-10

Income statement for a merchandising company

HIGHPOINT ELECTRONIC, INC. Income Statement For the Year Ended December 31, 2001			
Sales revenues			
Sales			$480,000
Less: Sales returns and allowances		$ 12,000	
Sales discounts		8,000	20,000
Net sales			460,000
Cost of goods sold			316,000
Gross profit			144,000
Operating expenses			
Store salaries expense		45,000	
Rent expense		19,000	
Utilities expense		17,000	
Advertising expense		16,000	
Depreciation expense—store equipment		8,000	
Freight-out		7,000	
Insurance expense		2,000	
Total operating expenses			114,000
Net income			$ 30,000

Before You Go On ...

1. What entries are made to record sales, sales returns and allowances, and sales discounts?
2. How are sales and contra revenue accounts reported in the income statement?
3. What is the significance of gross profit?
4. Determine Kellogg Company's gross profit rate for 1998 and 1997. Indicate whether it increased or decreased from 1997 to 1998. The answer to this question is provided on page 228.

COMPLETING THE ACCOUNTING CYCLE

6
STUDY
OBJECTIVE
....
Explain the steps in the accounting cycle for a merchandising company.

Up to this point, we have been primarily concerned with measuring net income in a merchandising company. We have also illustrated the basic entries in recording transactions relating to purchases and sales in a perpetual inventory system. Now it is time to consider the remaining steps in the accounting cycle that were identified in Chapter 4.

Each of the required steps in the cycle applies to a merchandising company. Again, a work sheet is an optional step. To illustrate the steps in the cycle, we will assume that Highpoint Electronic uses a work sheet.

Using a Work Sheet

As indicated in Chapter 4, a work sheet enables financial statements to be prepared before the adjusting entries are journalized and posted. The steps in preparing a work sheet for a merchandising company are the same as they are for a service enterprise (see pp. 141–143). The work sheet for Highpoint Electronic, Inc. is shown in Illustration 5-11 (on the next page). The unique accounts for a merchandising company, using a perpetual inventory system, are shown in capital letters in red.

Trial Balance Columns

Data for the trial balance are obtained from the ledger balances of Highpoint Electronic at December 31. The amount shown for Merchandise Inventory, $40,000, is the year-end inventory amount which results from the application of a perpetual inventory system.

Adjustments Columns

A merchandising company generally has the same types of adjustments as a service company. As you see in the work sheet, adjustments (a), (b), and (c) are for insurance, depreciation, and salaries. These adjustments were also required for Pioneer Advertising Agency, as illustrated in Chapters 3 and 4.

After all adjustment data are entered on the work sheet, the equality of the adjustment column totals is established. The balances in all accounts are then extended to the adjusted trial balance columns.

Adjusted Trial Balance

The adjusted trial balance shows the balance of all accounts after adjustment at the end of the accounting period.

Income Statement Columns

The accounts and balances that affect the income statement are transferred from the adjusted trial balance columns to the income statement columns. For Highpoint

ILLUSTRATION 5-11

Work sheet for merchandising company

HIGHPOINT ELECTRONIC, INC.
Work Sheet
For the Year Ended December 31, 2001

Account Titles	Trial Balance Dr.	Cr.	Adjustments Dr.	Cr.	Adjusted Trial Balance Dr.	Cr.	Income Statement Dr.	Cr.	Balance Sheet Dr.	Cr.
Cash	9,500				9,500				9,500	
Accounts Receivable	16,100				16,100				16,100	
MERCHANDISE INVENTORY	40,000				40,000				40,000	
Prepaid Insurance	3,800			(a) 2,000	1,800				1,800	
Store Equipment	80,000				80,000				80,000	
Accumulated Depreciation		16,000		(b) 8,000		24,000				24,000
Accounts Payable		20,400				20,400				20,400
Common Stock		50,000				50,000				50,000
Retained Earnings		33,000				33,000				33,000
Dividends	15,000				15,000				15,000	
SALES		480,000				480,000		480,000		
SALES RETURNS AND ALLOWANCES	12,000				12,000		12,000			
SALES DISCOUNTS	8,000				8,000		8,000			
COST OF GOODS SOLD	316,000				316,000		316,000			
Freight-out	7,000				7,000		7,000			
Advertising Expense	16,000				16,000		16,000			
Rent Expense	19,000				19,000		19,000			
Store Salaries Expense	40,000		(c) 5,000		45,000		45,000			
Utilities Expense	17,000				17,000		17,000			
Totals	599,400	599,400								
Insurance Expense			(a) 2,000		2,000		2,000			
Depreciation Expense			(b) 8,000		8,000		8,000			
Salaries Payable				(c) 5,000		5,000				5,000
Totals			15,000	15,000	612,400	612,400	450,000	480,000	162,400	132,400
Net income							30,000			30,000
Totals							480,000	480,000	162,400	162,400

Key: (a) Insurance expired, (b) Depreciation expensed, (c) Salaries accrued.

Electronic, Sales of $480,000 is shown in the credit column, whereas the contra revenue accounts, Sales Returns and Allowances of $12,000 and Sales Discounts of $8,000, are shown in the debit column. Thus, the difference of $460,000 is the net sales shown on the income statement (Illustration 5-10).

Finally, all the credits in the income statement column should be totaled and compared to the total of all the debits in the income statement column. If the credits exceed the debits, then the company has net income. In Highpoint Electronic's case there was net income of $30,000. Conversely if the debits exceed the credits, the company would report a net loss.

Balance Sheet Columns

The major difference between the balance sheets of a service company and a merchandising company is inventory. For Highpoint Electronic, the ending inventory amount of $40,000 is shown in the balance sheet debit column. Note also that the information to prepare the retained earnings statement is also found in these columns. That is, the retained earnings account beginning balance is

$33,000. The dividends are $15,000. The total of the debit column exceeds the total of the credit column in the balance sheet columns of the work sheet because net income was earned. Conversely, the total of the credits exceeds the total of the debit balances because a net loss occurred. These three amounts comprise the contents of the retained earnings statement.

Preparing Financial Statements

As is true in a service enterprise, financial statements for a merchandising company are prepared from the financial statement columns of the work sheet. The income statement for Highpoint Electronic has already been illustrated (see Illustration 5-10).

The retained earnings statement is as follows:

ILLUSTRATION 5-12

Retained earnings statement

HIGHPOINT ELECTRONIC, INC.
Retained Earnings Statement
For the Year Ended December 31, 2001

Retained earnings, January 1	$33,000
Add: Net income	30,000
	63,000
Less: Dividends	15,000
Retained earnings, December 31	$48,000

The classified balance sheet, then, is as follows:

ILLUSTRATION 5-13

Classified balance sheet

HIGHPOINT ELECTRONIC, INC.
Balance Sheet
December 31, 2001

Assets

Current assets		
Cash		$ 9,500
Accounts receivable		16,100
Merchandise inventory		40,000
Prepaid insurance		1,800
Total current assets		67,400
Property, plant, and equipment		
Store equipment	$80,000	
Less: Accumulated depreciation—store equipment	24,000	56,000
Total assets		$123,400

Liabilities and Stockholders' Equity

Current liabilities	
Accounts payable	$20,400
Salaries payable	5,000
Total current liabilities	25,400
Stockholders' equity	
Common stock	50,000
Retained earnings	48,000
Total liabilities and stockholders' equity	$123,400

HELPFUL HINT
The $40,000 is the cost of the inventory on hand, not its expected selling price.

In the balance sheet, merchandise inventory is reported as a current asset immediately below accounts receivable. Recall that items are listed under current assets in the order of liquidity. Merchandise inventory is less liquid than accounts receivable because the goods must first be sold and then collection must be made from the customer.

HELPFUL HINT
Merchandise inventory is a current asset because it is expected to be sold within one year or the operating cycle, whichever is longer.

ACCOUNTING IN ACTION
Ethics Insight

Phar Mor was one of the largest and fastest growing retail dry goods and pharmacy chains in the United States until a massive fraud was discovered by the company's auditors, Coopers and Lybrand. Dry goods were Phar Mor's business, but some of its executives had a taste for "raisin cookies." Schemers in Phar Mor's executive suite kept two sets of records, an official ledger that they sometimes manipulated with false entries, and another, nicknamed the "cookies," where they kept track of the false entries, called "raisins." They would refer to their ledger domain as "putting raisins in the cookies."

Based on reports in *The Wall Street Journal*, the assets of the company were overstated by more than $400 million, or about one-third of Phar Mor's gross revenue. Most of this overstatement pertained to fake or overvalued merchandise inventories at various store locations, and was perpetrated by the company's top financial managers.

Adjusting and Closing Entries

Adjusting entries are journalized from the adjustment columns of the work sheet. Because the journalizing and posting of the entries are the same as they are for a service enterprise, they are not illustrated here.

For a merchandising company, like a service enterprise, all accounts that affect the determination of net income are closed to Income Summary. Data for the preparation of closing entries may be obtained from the income statement columns of the work sheet. In journalizing, all debit column amounts are credited, and all credit column amounts are debited, as shown below for Highpoint Electronic. Cost of Goods Sold is a new account that must be closed to Income Summary.

HELPFUL HINT

The easiest way to prepare the first two closing entries is to identify the temporary accounts by their balances and then prepare one entry for the credits and one for the debits.

Date	Account	Debit	Credit
Dec. 31	Sales	480,000	
	Income Summary		480,000
	(To close income statement accounts with credit balances)		
31	Income Summary	450,000	
	Sales Returns and Allowances		12,000
	Sales Discounts		8,000
	Cost of Goods Sold		316,000
	Store Salaries Expense		45,000
	Rent Expense		19,000
	Freight-out		7,000
	Advertising Expense		16,000
	Utilities Expense		17,000
	Depreciation Expense		8,000
	Insurance Expense		2,000
	(To close income statement accounts with debit balances)		
31	Income Summary	30,000	
	Retained Earnings		30,000
	(To close net income to retained earnings)		
31	Retained Earnings	15,000	
	Dividends		15,000
	(To close dividends to retained earnings)		

After the closing entries are posted, all temporary accounts have zero balances. In addition, Retained Earnings has a credit balance of $48,000: beginning balance + net income − dividends ($33,000 + $30,000 − $15,000).

Preparing the Post-Closing Trial Balance

After the closing entries are posted, the post-closing trial balance is prepared. The only new account in the post-closing trial balance is Merchandise Inventory. The post-closing trial balance for Highpoint Electronic, Inc. at December 31, 2001, is shown in Illustration 5-14.

ILLUSTRATION **5-14**

Post-closing trial balance

HIGHPOINT ELECTRONIC, INC.
Post-Closing Trial Balance
December 31, 2001

	Debit	Credit
Cash	$ 9,500	
Accounts receivable	16,100	
Merchandise inventory	**40,000**	
Prepaid insurance	1,800	
Store equipment	80,000	
Accumulated depreciation		$ 24,000
Accounts payable		20,400
Salaries payable		5,000
Common stock		50,000
Retained earnings		48,000
	$147,400	$147,400

Summary of Merchandising Entries

The entries for the merchandising accounts using a perpetual inventory system are summarized in Illustration 5-15.

ILLUSTRATION **5-15**

Daily recurring and closing entries

Transactions	Daily Recurring Entries	Dr.	Cr.
Selling merchandise to customers	Cash or Accounts Receivable	XX	
	Sales		XX
	Cost of Goods Sold	XX	
	Merchandise Inventory		XX
Granting sales returns or allowances to customers	Sales Returns and Allowances	XX	
	Cash or Accounts Receivable		XX
	Merchandise Inventory	XX	
	Cost of Goods Sold		XX
Paying freight costs on sales; FOB destination	Freight-out	XX	
	Cash		XX
Receiving payment from customers within discount period	Cash	XX	
	Sales Discounts	XX	
	Accounts Receivable		XX
Purchasing merchandise for resale	Merchandise Inventory	XX	
	Cash or Accounts Payable		XX
Paying freight costs on merchandise purchased; FOB shipping point	Merchandise Inventory	XX	
	Cash		XX
Receiving purchase returns or allowances from suppliers	Cash or Accounts Payable	XX	
	Merchandise Inventory		XX
Paying suppliers within discount period	Accounts Payable	XX	
	Merchandise Inventory		XX
	Cash		XX

ILLUSTRATION 5-15

Closing entries (Continued)

Events	Closing Entries	Dr.	Cr.
Closing accounts with credit balances	Sales	XX	
	Income Summary		XX
Closing accounts with debit balances	Income Summary	XX	
	Sales Returns and Allowances		XX
	Sales Discounts		XX
	Cost of Goods Sold		XX
	Freight-out		XX
	Expenses		XX

BEFORE YOU GO ON ...

Review It

1. How does a work sheet for a merchandising company differ from a work sheet for a service company? In what ways are the work sheet similar for a merchandising company and a service company?
2. In what columns of the work sheet will (a) merchandise inventory and (b) cost of goods sold be shown?
3. What merchandising account(s) will appear in the post-closing trial balance?

Do It

The trial balance of Revere Clothing Company at December 31 shows Merchandise Inventory $25,000, Sales $162,400, Sales Returns and Allowances $4,800, Sales Discounts $3,600, Cost of Goods Sold $110,000, Rental Revenue $6,000, Freight-out $1,800, Rent Expense $8,800, and Salaries and Wages Expense $22,000. Prepare the closing entries for the above accounts.

Reasoning: The first closing entry for a merchandising company closes temporary accounts with credit balances to Income Summary. The second closing entry closes temporary accounts with debit balances to Income Summary.

Solution: The two closing entries are:

Dec. 31	Sales	162,400	
	Rental Revenue	6,000	
	Income Summary		168,400
	(To close accounts with credit balances)		
Dec. 31	Income Summary	151,000	
	Cost of Goods Sold		110,000
	Sales Returns and Allowances		4,800
	Sales Discounts		3,600
	Freight-out		1,800
	Rent Expense		8,800
	Salaries and Wages Expense		22,000
	(To close accounts with debit balances)		

THE NAVIGATOR

Related exercise material: BE5–8, E5–6, and E5–7.

FORMS OF INCOME STATEMENTS

7

STUDY OBJECTIVE

Distinguish between a multiple-step and a single-step income statement.

Two forms of the income statement are widely used by merchandising companies. These income statements are explained below.

Multiple-Step Income Statement

The multiple-step income statement is so named because it shows the numerous steps in determining net income (or net loss). The Highpoint Electronic income statement in Illustration 5-10 is an example. It shows two steps: (1) cost of goods sold was subtracted from net sales, and (2) operating expenses were deducted from gross profit. These steps pertain to the company's principal operating activities. A multiple-step statement provides users with more information about a company's income performance by distinguishing between **operating** and **nonoperating activities**. The statement also highlights intermediate components of income and shows subgroupings of expenses.

Nonoperating Activities

Nonoperating activities consist of (1) revenues and expenses that result from secondary or auxiliary operations and (2) gains and losses that are unrelated to the company's operations. The results of nonoperating activities are shown in two sections: Other revenues and gains and Other expenses and losses. For a merchandising company, these sections will typically include the following items:

Other Revenues and Gains	Other Expenses and Losses
Interest revenue from notes receivable and investment securities	Interest expense on notes and loans payable
Dividend revenue from investments in capital stock	Casualty losses from recurring causes such as vandalism and accidents
Rent revenue from subleasing a portion of the store	Loss from the sale or abandonment of property, plant, and equipment
Gain from the sale of property, plant, and equipment	Loss from strikes by employees and suppliers

ILLUSTRATION 5-16

Items reported in nonoperating sections

The nonoperating sections are reported in the income statement immediately after the sections that pertain to the company's primary operating activities. These sections are shown in Illustration 5-17 using assumed data for Highpoint Electronic.

ILLUSTRATION 5-17

Multiple-step income statement—nonoperating sections and subgroupings of operating expenses

HIGHPOINT ELECTRONIC, INC.
Income Statement
For the Year Ended December 31, 2001

Sales revenues			
Sales			$480,000
Less: Sales returns and allowances		$ 12,000	
Sales discounts		8,000	20,000
Net sales			460,000
Cost of goods sold			316,000
Gross profit			144,000
Operating expenses			
Selling expenses			
Store salaries expense	$ 45,000		
Advertising expense	16,000		
Depreciation expense—store equipment	8,000		
Freight-out	7,000		
Total selling expenses		76,000	
Administrative expenses			
Rent expense	19,000		
Utilities expense	17,000		
Insurance expense	2,000		
Total administrative expenses		38,000	
Total operating expenses			114,000
Income from operations			30,000
Other revenues and gains			
Interest revenue	3,000		
Gain on sale of equipment	600	3,600	
Other expenses and losses			
Interest expense	1,800		
Casualty loss from vandalism	200	2,000	1,600
Net income			$ 31,600

HELPFUL HINT
What are the steps in arriving at each of the three profit (income) amounts reported in the statement?
Answer:
1. Gross profit—Net sales less cost of goods sold.
2. Income from operations—Gross profit less operating expenses.
3. Net income—Income from operations plus other revenues and gains and less other expenses and losses.

When the two nonoperating sections are included, the label Income from operations (or Operating income) precedes them. It clearly identifies the results of the company's normal operations. Income from operations is determined by subtracting cost of goods sold and operating expenses from net sales.

Observe that the results of the two nonoperating sections are netted. The difference is added to or subtracted from income from operations to determine net income. Finally, within the nonoperating sections, items are generally reported at the net amount. Thus, if a company received a $2,500 insurance settlement on vandalism losses of $2,700, the loss is reported at $200. It is not uncommon for companies to combine these two nonoperating sections into a single "Other Revenues and Expenses" section.

ACCOUNTING IN ACTION
Business Insight

The distinction between operating and nonoperating activities is crucial to many external users of financial data. The reason is that operating income is viewed as sustainable and therefore long-term, and nonoperating is viewed as nonrecurring and therefore short-term. For example, it was reported that a large cinema chain in North America was selling some of its assets and counting the gains as part of operating income. As a result, operating losses were being offset by these gains. Because of unfavorable press reaction to this practice, the company revised its financial statements. By not counting its nonrecurring items as part of operating income, its first quarter results changed from $24.9 million operating income to a $22.6 million loss. Although the net income figure didn't change, investors were able to see that income was derived from selling assets rather than from selling movie tickets. Thus, with this new information, investors were able to make a more informed decision about the company's earnings.

Subgrouping of Operating Expenses

In larger companies, operating expenses are often subdivided into selling expenses and administrative expenses, as illustrated in the income statement in Illustration 5-17. Selling expenses are those associated with making sales. They include sales promotional expenses as well as expenses of completing the sale, such as delivery and shipping expenses. Administrative expenses (sometimes called general expenses) relate to general operating activities such as personnel management, accounting, and store security.

When subgroupings are made, some expenses may have to be prorated, e.g., 70% to selling and 30% to administrative expenses. For example, if a store building is used for both selling and general functions, building expenses such as depreciation, utilities, and property taxes will need to be allocated.

Any reasonable classification of expenses that serves to inform those who use the statement is satisfactory. For example, the present tendency in statements prepared for management is to present in considerable detail expense data grouped along lines of responsibility.

Single-Step Income Statement

Another format for income statement presentation is the single-step income statement. The statement is so named because only one step, subtracting total expenses from total revenues, is required in determining net income (or net loss).

In a single-step statement, all data are classified under two categories: (1) **Revenues**, which includes both operating revenues and other revenues and gains, or (2) **Expenses**, which includes cost of goods sold, operating expenses, and other expenses and losses. A condensed single-step statement for Highpoint Electronic is illustrated in Illustration 5-18.

ILLUSTRATION 5-18

Single-step income statement

HIGHPOINT ELECTRONIC, INC.
Income Statement
For the Year Ended December 31, 2001

Revenues		
Net sales		$460,000
Interest revenue		3,000
Gain on sale of equipment		600
Total revenues		463,600
Expenses		
Cost of goods sold	$316,000	
Selling expenses	76,000	
Administrative expenses	38,000	
Interest expense	1,800	
Casualty loss from vandalism	200	
Total expenses		432,000
Net income		$ 31,600

There are two primary reasons for using the single-step form: (1) A company does not realize any type of profit or income until total revenues exceed total expenses, so it makes sense to divide the statement into these two categories. (2) The form is simpler and easier to read than the multiple-step form. However, for homework problems, the single-step form of income statement should be used only when it is specifically requested.

BEFORE YOU GO ON ...

Review It

1. What are nonoperating activities and how are they reported in the income statement?
2. How does a single-step income statement differ from a multiple-step income statement?

A LOOK BACK AT OUR FEATURE STORY

Refer to the opening story concerning Buy.com's unique merchandising methods, and answer the following questions:

1. What is the business of Buy.com? What makes it attractive to consumers?
2. How much of an inventory does Buy.com carry?
3. How does Buy.com's operating cycle differ from those of other retailers because of its unique merchandising system?
4. In what way might Buy.com's unique method of merchandising affect the general ledger accounts used?
5. How does Buy.com expect to sell products below its costs and still remain in business long term?

Solution

1. Buy.com is a Web site retailer that sells and delivers goods directly from wholesalers to consumers. Buy.com's slogan is "The lowest prices on earth." The company is ruthlessly committed to being the price leader—even if it means losing money on every sale.
2. Buy.com has no inventory. It is a *virtual* corporation of 100 employees that advertises on a Web site and places orders with wholesalers who deliver direct to customers from whom Buy.com has taken orders.

3. Buy.com's operating cycle is more like that of a service company than a merchandising company because it carries no inventory. Therefore, the operating cycle is abbreviated—cash to accounts receivable to cash.

4. Buy.com's general ledger will contain no Merchandise Inventory account and may or may not contain the following accounts: Freight-in, Freight-out, Purchase Returns and Allowances, Sales Returns and Allowances, Purchase Discounts, and Sales Discounts. The use of these accounts depends on the agreement Buy.com has with it suppliers (the wholesalers and distributors who deliver direct to customers) and with its customers.

5. Buy.com is trying to create a brand synonymous with low price—with the hope of becoming the leading E-commerce portal. If it becomes the leading commercial Web site, its site becomes valuable ad space. Buy.com hopes to make up its deficit through advertising revenues.

DEMONSTRATION PROBLEM

The adjusted trial balance columns of the work sheet for the year ended December 31, 2001, for Dykstra Company are as follows:

Debit		Credit	
Cash	$ 14,500	Accumulated Depreciation	$ 18,000
Accounts Receivable	11,100	Notes Payable	25,000
Merchandise Inventory	29,000	Accounts Payable	10,600
Prepaid Insurance	2,500	Common Stock	50,000
Store Equipment	95,000	Retained Earnings	31,000
Dividends	12,000	Sales	536,800
Sales Returns and Allowances	6,700	Interest Revenue	2,500
Sales Discounts	5,000		$673,900
Cost of Goods Sold	363,400		
Freight-out	7,600		
Advertising Expense	12,000		
Store Salaries Expense	56,000		
Utilities Expense	18,000		
Rent Expense	24,000		
Depreciation Expense	9,000		
Insurance Expense	4,500		
Interest Expense	3,600		
	$673,900		

Instructions
(a) Enter the adjusted trial balance data on a work sheet. Complete the work sheet.
(b) Prepare a multiple-step income statement assuming Dykstra Company does not use subgroupings for operating expenses.

SOLUTION TO DEMONSTRATION PROBLEM

(a)   **DYKSTRA COMPANY**
Work Sheet
For the Year Ended December 31, 2001

Account Titles	Adjusted Trial Balance		Income Statement		Balance Sheet	
	Dr.	Cr.	Dr.	Cr.	Dr.	Cr.
Cash	14,500				14,500	
Accounts Receivable	11,100				11,100	
Merchandise Inventory	29,000				29,000	
Prepaid Insurance	2,500				2,500	

Account Titles (continued)	Adjusted Trial Balance		Income Statement		Balance Sheet	
	Dr.	**Cr.**	**Dr.**	**Cr.**	**Dr.**	**Cr.**
Store Equipment	95,000				95,000	
Accumulated Depreciation		18,000				18,000
Notes Payable		25,000				25,000
Accounts Payable		10,600				10,600
Common Stock		50,000				50,000
Retained Earnings		31,000				31,000
Dividends	12,000				12,000	
Sales		536,800		536,800		
Sales Returns and Allowances	6,700		6,700			
Sales Discounts	5,000		5,000			
Cost of Goods Sold	363,400		363,400			
Freight-out	7,600		7,600			
Advertising Expense	12,000		12,000			
Store Salaries Expense	56,000		56,000			
Utilities Expense	18,000		18,000			
Rent Expense	24,000		24,000			
Depreciation Expense	9,000		9,000			
Insurance Expense	4,500		4,500			
Interest Expense	3,600		3,600			
Interest Revenue		2,500		2,500		
Totals	673,900	673,900	509,800	539,300	164,100	134,600
Net Income			29,500			29,500
Totals			539,300	539,300	164,100	164,100

PROBLEM-SOLVING STRATEGIES

1. Make sure in the adjusted trial balance that debits and credits are equal before transferring amounts to the income statement and balance sheet columns.
2. Transfer all amounts in the adjusted trial balance to either the income statement or balance sheet columns.
3. The net income or net loss is the reconciling item in both the income statement and the balance sheet columns.

(b)

DYKSTRA COMPANY
Income Statement
For the Year Ended December 31, 2001

Sales revenues			
Sales			$536,800
Less: Sales returns and allowances		$ 6,700	
Sales discounts		5,000	11,700
Net sales			525,100
Cost of goods sold			363,400
Gross profit			161,700
Operating expenses			
Store salaries expense		56,000	
Rent expense		24,000	
Utilities expense		18,000	
Advertising expense		12,000	
Depreciation expense		9,000	
Freight-out		7,600	
Insurance expense		4,500	
Total operating expenses			131,100
Income from operations			30,600
Other revenues and gains			
Interest revenue		2,500	
Other expenses and losses			
Interest expense		3,600	1,100
Net income			$29,500

PROBLEM-SOLVING STRATEGIES

1. In preparing the income statement, remember that the key components are net sales, cost of goods sold, gross profit, total operating expenses, and net income (or net loss). These components are reported in the right-hand column of the income statement.
2. Nonoperating items follow income from operations.

THE NAVIGATOR

SUMMARY OF STUDY OBJECTIVES

1. Identify the differences between a service enterprise and a merchandising company. Because of the presence of inventory, a merchandising company has sales revenue, cost of goods sold, and gross profit. To account for inventory, a merchandising company must choose between a perpetual inventory system and a periodic inventory system.

2. Explain the entries for purchases under a perpetual inventory system. The Merchandise Inventory account is debited for all purchases of merchandise, for freight-in and other costs, and it is credited for purchase discounts and purchase returns and allowances.

3. Explain the entries for sales revenues under a perpetual inventory system. When inventory is sold, Accounts Receivable (or Cash) is debited and Sales is credited for the **selling price** of the merchandise. At the same time, Cost of Goods Sold is debited and Merchandise Inventory is credited for the **cost** of the inventory items sold.

4. Explain the computation and importance of gross profit. Gross profit is computed by subtracting cost of goods sold from net sales. Gross profit represents the merchandising profit of a company, and the amount and trend of gross profit is closely watched by management and other interested parties.

5. Identify the features of the income statement for a merchandising company. The income statement for a merchandising company contains three sections: sales revenues, cost of goods sold, and operating expenses.

6. Explain the steps in the accounting cycle for a merchandising company. Each of the required steps in the accounting cycle for a service enterprise applies to a merchandising company. A work sheet is again an optional step.

7. Distinguish between a multiple-step and a single-step income statement. A multiple-step income statement shows numerous steps in determining net income including nonoperating sections. In a single-step income statement all data are classified under two categories, revenues or expenses, and net income is determined by one step.

THE NAVIGATOR

GLOSSARY

Administrative expenses   Expenses relating to general operating activities such as personnel management, accounting, and store security. (p. 208).

Contra revenue account   An account that is offset against a revenue account on the income statement. (p. 198).

Cost of goods sold   The total cost of merchandise sold during the period. (p. 188).

Credit memorandum   A document issued by a seller to inform a customer that a credit has been made to the customer's account receivable for a sales return or allowance. (p. 197).

Debit memorandum   A document issued by a buyer to inform a seller that a debit has been made to the seller's account because of unsatisfactory merchandise. (p. 192).

FOB destination   Freight terms indicating that the goods will be placed free on board at the buyer's place of business, and the seller pays the freight costs. (p. 195).

FOB shipping point   Freight terms indicating that goods are placed free on board the carrier by the seller, and the buyer pays the freight costs. (p. 195).

Gross profit   The excess of net sales over the cost of goods sold. (p. 188).

Income from operations   Income from a company's principal operating activity determined by subtracting cost of goods sold and operating expenses from net sales. (p. 208).

Invoice   A document that provides support for a credit purchase. (p. 191).

Multiple-step income statement   An income statement that shows numerous steps in determining net income (or net loss). (p. 206).

Net sales   Sales less sales returns and allowances and sales discounts. (p. 199).

Operating expenses   Expenses incurred in the process of earning sales revenues that are deducted from gross profit in the income statement. (p. 188).

Other expenses and losses   A nonoperating section of the income statement that shows expenses from auxiliary operations and losses unrelated to the company's operations. (p. 207).

Other revenues and gains   A nonoperating section of the income statement that shows revenues from auxiliary operations and gains unrelated to the company's operations. (p. 207).

Periodic inventory system   An inventory system in which detailed records are not maintained throughout the accounting period and the cost of goods sold is determined only at the end of an accounting period. (p. 190).

Perpetual inventory system   A detailed inventory system in which the cost of each inventory item is maintained throughout the accounting period and the records continuously show the inventory that should be on hand. (p. 190).

Purchase discount   A cash discount claimed by a buyer for prompt payment of a balance due. (p. 193).

Sales discount   A reduction given by a seller for prompt payment of a credit sale. (p. 198).

Sales invoice   A document that provides support for credit sales. (p. 196).

Sales revenue (sales)   Primary source of revenue in a merchandising company. (p. 188).

Selling expenses   Expenses associated with the making of sales. (p. 208).

Single-step income statement   An income statement that shows only one step in determining net income (or net loss). (p. 208).

SELF-STUDY QUESTIONS

Answers are at the end of the chapter.

(SO 1) 1. Gross profit will result if:
 a. operating expenses are less than net income.
 b. sales revenues are greater than operating expenses.
 c. sales revenues are greater than cost of goods sold.
 d. operating expenses are greater than cost of goods sold.

(SO 2) 2. Under a perpetual inventory system, when goods are purchased for resale by a company:
 a. purchases on account are debited to Merchandise Inventory.
 b. purchases on account are debited to Purchases.
 c. purchase returns are debited to Purchase Returns and Allowances.
 d. freight costs are debited to Freight-out.

(SO 3) 3. The sales accounts that normally have a debit balance are:
 a. Sales Discounts.
 b. Sales Returns and Allowances.
 c. both (a) and (b).
 d. neither (a) nor (b).

(SO 3) 4. A credit sale of $750 is made on June 13, terms 2/10, net/30, on which a return of $50 is granted on June 16. The amount received as payment in full on June 23 is:
 a. $700.
 b. $686.
 c. $685.
 d. $650.

(SO 3) 5. Which of the following accounts will normally appear in the ledger of a merchandising company that uses a perpetual inventory system?
 a. Purchases.
 b. Freight-in.
 c. Cost of Goods Sold.
 d. Purchase Discounts.

(SO 4) 6. If sales revenues are $400,000, cost of goods sold is $310,000, and operating expenses are $60,000, the gross profit is:
 a. $30,000.
 b. $90,000.
 c. $340,000.
 d. $400,000.

(SO 5) 7. The multiple-step income statement for a merchandising company shows each of the following features *except*:
 a. gross profit.
 b. cost of goods sold.
 c. a sales revenue section.
 d. investing activities section.

(SO 6) 8. In a work sheet, Merchandise Inventory is shown in the following columns:
 a. Adjusted trial balance debit and balance sheet debit.
 b. Income statement debit and balance sheet debit.
 c. Income statement credit and balance sheet debit.
 d. Income statement credit and adjusted trial balance debit.

(SO 7) 9. In a single-step income statement:
 a. gross profit is reported.
 b. cost of goods sold is not reported.
 c. sales revenues and other revenues and gains are reported in the revenues section of the income statement.
 d. operating income is separately reported.

(SO 7) 10. Which of the following appears on both a single-step and multiple-step income statement?
 a. sales.
 b. gross profit.
 c. income from operations.
 d. cost of goods sold.

THE
NAVIGATOR

QUESTIONS

1. (a) "The steps in the accounting cycle for a merchandising company are different from the accounting cycle for a service enterprise." Do you agree or disagree? (b) Is the measurement of net income in a merchandising company conceptually the same as in a service enterprise? Explain.

2. (a) How do the components of revenues and expenses differ between a merchandising company and a service enterprise? (b) Explain the income measurement process in a merchandising company.

3. How does income measurement differ between a merchandising company and a service company?

4. When is cost of goods sold determined in a perpetual inventory system?

5. Distinguish between FOB shipping point and FOB destination. Identify the freight terms that will result in a debit to Merchandise Inventory by the purchaser and a debit to Freight-out by the seller.

6. Explain the meaning of the credit terms 2/10, n/30.

7. Goods costing $2,000 are purchased on account on July 15 with credit terms of 2/10, n/30. On July 18 a $100 credit memo is received from the supplier for damaged goods. Give the journal entry on July 24 to record payment of the balance due within the discount period using a perpetual inventory system.

8. Patty Loveless believes revenues from credit sales may be earned before they are collected in cash. Do you agree? Explain.

9. (a) What is the primary source document for recording (1) cash sales, (2) credit sales, and (3) sales returns and allowances? (b) Using XXs for amounts, give the journal entry for each of the transactions in part (a).

10. A credit sale is made on July 10 for $800, terms 2/10, n/30. On July 12, $100 of goods are returned for credit. Give the journal entry on July 19 to record the receipt of the balance due within the discount period.

11. Randy Travis Co. has sales revenue of $110,000, cost of goods sold of $70,000, and operating expenses of $20,000. What is its gross profit?

12. Lionel Richie Company reports net sales of $800,000, gross profit of $580,000, and net income of $200,000. What are its operating expenses?

13. Identify the distinguishing features of an income statement for a merchandising company.

14. Indicate the columns of the work sheet in which (a) merchandise inventory, and (b) cost of goods sold will be shown.

15. Why is the normal operating cycle for a merchandising company likely to be longer than for a service company?

16. Prepare the closing entries for the Sales account, assuming a balance of $200,000 and the Cost of Goods Sold account which has a $120,000 balance.

17. What merchandising account(s) will appear in the post-closing trial balance?

18. Identify the sections of a multiple-step income statement that relate to (a) operating activities, and (b) nonoperating activities.

19. Distinguish between the types of functional groupings of operating expenses. What problem is created by these groupings?

20. How does the single-step form of income statement differ from the multiple-step form?

21. What types of businesses do you think are most likely to use a perpetual inventory system?

THE NAVIGATOR

BRIEF EXERCISES

Compute missing amounts in determining net income.
(SO 1)

BE5–1   Presented below are the components in Nacho Cano Company's income statement. Determine the missing amounts.

	Sales	Cost of Goods Sold	Gross Profit	Operating Expenses	Net Income
(a)	$75,000	?	$33,500	?	$10,800
(b)	$108,000	$70,000	?	?	29,500
(c)	?	$71,900	$99,600	$39,500	?

Journalize perpetual inventory entries.
(SO 2,3)

BE5–2   Chico Company buys merchandise on account from Cesar Company. The selling price of the goods is $800, and the cost of the goods is $600. Both companies use perpetual inventory systems. Journalize the transaction on the books of both companies.

Journalize perpetual inventory entries.
(SO 2, 3)

BE5–3   Wayne Gretzky Company uses a perpetual inventory system. In March, its first month of operations, it has the following transactions: March 3, purchased on account 20 units of Product X at $25 per unit; March 6, returned 3 units for credit; March 21, sold on account 10 units at $45 per unit. Journalize the three transactions.

Journalize sales transactions.
(SO 3)

BE5–4   Prepare the journal entries to record the following transactions on Ednita Company's books using a perpetual inventory system.

(a) On March 2, Ednita Company sold $800,000 of merchandise to Nazario Company, terms 2/10, n/30. The cost of the merchandise sold was $600,000.

(b) On March 6, Nazario Company returned $120,000 of the merchandise purchased on March 2 because it was defective. The cost of the returned merchandise was $90,000.

(c) On March 12, Ednita Company received the balance due from Nazario Company.

Journalize purchases transactions
(SO 2)

BE5–5   From the information in BE5–4, prepare the journal entries to record these transactions on Nazario Company's books under a perpetual inventory system.

Prepare sales revenues section of income statement.
(SO 3)

BE5–6   Matt Damon Company provides the following information for the month ended October 31, 2001: Sales on credit $280,000, Cash sales $100,000, Sales discounts $5,000, Sales returns and allowances $20,000. Prepare the sales revenues section of the income statement based on this information.

Identify work sheet columns for selected accounts.
(SO 6)

BE5–7   Presented below is the format of the work sheet presented in the chapter.

Trial Balance		Adjustments		Adjusted Trial Balance		Income Statement		Balance Sheet	
Dr.	Cr.	Dr.	Cr.	Dr.	Cr.	Dr.	Cr.	Dr.	Cr.

Indicate where the following items will appear on the work sheet: (a) Cash, (b) Merchandise Inventory, (c) Sales, (d) Cost of goods sold.

Example:

    Cash: Trial balance debit column; Adjusted trial balance debit column; and Balance sheet debit column.

BE5–8 Cajon Company has the following merchandise account balances: Sales $180,000, Sales Discounts $2,000, Cost of Goods Sold $100,000, and Merchandise Inventory $40,000. Prepare the entries to record the closing of these items to Income Summary.

Prepare closing entries for merchandise accounts.
(SO 6)

BE5–9 ▭▭▭▷ Explain where each of the following items would appear on (1) a multiple-step income statement and on (2) a single-step income statement: (a) gain on sale of equipment, (b) casualty loss from vandalism, and (c) cost of goods sold.

Contrast presentation in multiple-step and single-step income statements.
(SO 7)

BE5–10 Assume Bayou Company has the following account balances: Sales $500,000, Sales Returns and Allowances $15,000, Cost of Goods Sold $340,000, Selling Expenses $70,000, and Administrative Expenses $40,000. Compute (a) net sales, (b) gross profit, and (c) income from operations.

Compute net sales, gross profit, and income from operations.
(SO 3, 4, 7)

BE5–11 Motorola, Inc., reported 1998 net sales of $29,398 million, cost of goods sold of $20,886 million, operating expenses of $9,886 million, and income tax benefit (refund) of $412 million. Compute (a) gross profit, (b) gross profit rate, (c) income (loss) from operations, and (d) net income (loss).

Compute gross profit, income (loss) from operations, and net income (loss).
(SO 4, 7)

EXERCISES

E5–1 Information related to Esplande Co. is presented below.

1. On April 5, purchased merchandise from Dumaine Company for $16,000 terms 2/10, net/30, FOB shipping point.
2. On April 6 paid freight costs of $900 on merchandise purchased from Dumaine.
3. On April 7, purchased equipment on account for $26,000.
4. On April 8, returned damaged merchandise to Dumaine Company and was granted a $3,000 allowance.
5. On April 15 paid the amount due to Dumaine Company in full.

Journalize purchases transactions
(SO 2)

Instructions

(a) Prepare the journal entries to record these transactions on the books of Esplande Co. under a perpetual inventory system.
(b) Assume that Esplande Co. paid the balance due to Dumaine Company on May 4 instead of April 15. Prepare the journal entry to record this payment.

E5–2 On September 1, College Office Supply had an inventory of 30 deluxe pocket calculators at a cost of $20 each. The company uses a perpetual inventory system. During September, the following transactions occurred.

Journalize perpetual inventory entries
(SO 2, 3)

Sept. 6 Purchased 80 calculators at $19 each from Digital Co. for cash.
     9 Paid freight of $80 on calculators purchased from Digital Co.
   10 Returned 2 calculators to Digital Co. for $40 cash (including refund of freight costs) because they did not meet specifications.
   12 Sold 26 calculators costing $20 (including freight-in) for $30 each to Campus Book Store, terms, n/30.
   14 Granted credit of $30 to Campus Book Store for the return of one calculator that was not ordered.
   20 Sold 30 calculators costing $20 for $30 each to Varsity Card Shop, terms, n/30.

Instructions
Journalize the September transactions.

E5–3 On June 10, Arcadian Company purchased $6,000 of merchandise from R. Duvall Company FOB shipping point, terms 2/10, n/30. Arcadian pays the freight costs of $300 on June 11. Damaged goods totaling $300 are returned to R. Duvall for credit on June 12. On June 19, Arcadian pays R. Duvall Company in full, less the purchase discount. Both companies use a perpetual inventory system.

Prepare purchase and sale entries.
(SO 2, 3)

Instructions
(a) Prepare separate entries for each transaction on the books of Arcadian Company.
(b) Prepare separate entries for each transaction for Duvall Company. The merchandise purchased by Arcadian on June 10 had cost Duvall $3,000.

Journalize sales transactions.
(SO 3)

E5–4   Presented below are transactions related to S. Pippen Company.

1. On December 3, S. Pippen Company sold $480,000 of merchandise to Barkley Co., terms 2/10, n/30, FOB shipping point. The cost of the merchandise sold was $320,000.
2. On December 8, Barkley Co. was granted an allowance of $20,000 for merchandise purchased on December 3.
3. On December 13, S. Pippen Company received the balance due from Barkley Co.

Instructions
(a) Prepare the journal entries to record these transactions on the books of S. Pippen Company using a perpetual inventory system.
(b) Assume that S. Pippen Company received the balance due from Barkley Co. on January 2 of the following year instead of December 13. Prepare the journal entry to record the receipt of payment on January 2.

Prepare correcting entries for
sales and purchases.
(SO 2, 3)

E5–5   An inexperienced accountant for Salvador Company made the following errors in recording merchandising transactions:

1. A $150 refund to a customer for faulty merchandise was debited to Sales $150 and credited to Cash $150.
2. A $200 credit purchase of supplies was debited to Merchandise Inventory $200 and credited to Cash $200.
3. An $80 sales discount was debited to Sales.
4. A cash payment of $30 for freight on merchandise purchases was debited to Freight-out $300 and credited to Cash $300.

Instructions
Prepare separate correcting entries for each error, assuming that the incorrect entry is not reversed. (Omit explanations.)

Prepare sales revenues section
and closing entries.
(SO 3, 5, 6)

E5–6   The adjusted trial balance of Lopez Company shows the following data pertaining to sales at the end of its fiscal year October 31, 2001: Sales $800,000, Freight-out $12,000, Sales Returns and Allowances $24,000, and Sales Discounts $15,000.

Instructions
(a) Prepare the sales revenues section of the income statement.
(b) Prepare separate closing entries for (1) sales, and (2) the contra accounts to sales.

Prepare closing entries.
(SO 6)

E5–7   Presented is information related to Gonzales Co. for the month of January 2001.

Cost of Goods Sold	208,000	Salary expense	61,000
Freight-out	7,000	Sales discounts	8,000
Insurance expense	12,000	Sales returns and allowances	13,000
Rent expense	20,000	Sales	350,000

Instructions
Prepare the necessary closing entries.

Complete work sheet.
(SO 6)

E5–8   Presented below are selected accounts for Alvarez Company as reported in the work sheet at the end of May 2001.

Accounts	Adjusted Trial Balance		Income Statement		Balance Sheet	
	Dr.	Cr.	Dr.	Cr.	Dr.	Cr.
Cash	9,000					
Merchandise Inventory	80,000					
Sales		450,000				
Sales Returns and Allowances	10,000					
Sales Discounts	5,000					
Cost of Goods Sold	250,000					

Instructions
Complete the work sheet by extending amounts reported in the adjusted trial balance to the appropriate columns in the work sheet. Do not total individual columns.

E5–9 Presented below is financial information for two different companies:

	Alatorre Company	Eduardo Company
Sales	$90,000	$ (d)
Sales returns	(a)	5,000
Net sales	81,000	95,000
Cost of goods sold	56,000	(e)
Gross profit	(b)	38,000
Operating expenses	15,000	(f)
Net income	(c)	15,000

Instructions
Determine the missing amounts.

E5–10 In its income statement for the year ended December 31, 2001, Acevedo Company reported the following condensed data:

Administrative expenses	$435,000	Selling expenses	$ 690,000
Cost of goods sold	989,000	Loss on sale of equipment	10,000
Interest expense	70,000	Net sales	2,350,000
Interest revenue	45,000		

Instructions
(a) Prepare a multiple-step income statement.
(b) Prepare a single-step income statement.

E5–11 In its income statement for the year ended December 31, 1998, Microdynamics, Inc., reported the following condensed data (in millions):

Gain on sale of real estate	$ 91	Interest expense	$ 55
Interest revenue	13	Selling expenses	162
Administrative expenses	320	Cost of goods sold	708
Sales revenues	1,412	Sales returns and allowances	3
Sales discounts	11	Income tax expenses	72

Instructions
Prepare a multiple-step income statement.

PROBLEMS: SET A

P5–1A Dazzle Book Warehouse distributes hardback books to retail stores and extends credit terms of 2/10, n/30 to all of its customers. At the end of May, Dazzle's inventory consisted of 240 books purchased at $600. During the month of June the following merchandising transactions occurred.

June 1 Purchased 130 books on account for $5 each from Reader's World Publishers, FOB shipping point, terms 1/10, n/30. The appropriate party also made a cash payment of $50 for the freight on this date.

   3 Sold 140 books on account to the Book Nook for $10 each.

   6 Received $50 credit for 10 books returned to Reader's World Publishers.

   9 Paid Reader's World Publishers in full.

  15 Received payment in full from the Book Nook.

  17 Sold 120 books on account to Read-A-Lot Bookstore for $10 each.

  20 Purchased 120 books on account for $5 each from Read More Publishers, FOB destination, terms 2/15, n/30. The appropriate party also made a cash payment of $50 for the freight on this date.

  24 Received payment in full from Read-A-Lot Bookstore.

  26 Paid Read More Publishers in full.

  28 Sold 110 books on account to Readers Bookstore for $10 each.

  30 Granted Readers Bookstore $150 credit for 15 books returned costing $75.

Instructions
Journalize the transactions for the month of June for Dazzle Book Warehouse using a perpetual inventory system.

Journalize, post, and prepare partial income statement.
(SO 2, 3, 4, 5)

P5–2A Carlos Hardware Store Inc. completed the following merchandising transactions in the month of May. At the beginning of May, the ledger of Carlos showed Cash of $5,000 and Common Stock of $5,000.

May	1	Purchased merchandise on account from Depot Wholesale Supply $6,000, terms 2/10, n/30.
	2	Sold merchandise on account $4,500, terms 2/10, n/30. The cost of the merchandise sold was $3,000.
	5	Received credit from Depot Wholesale Supply for merchandise returned $200.
	9	Received collections in full, less discounts, from customers billed on sales of $4,500 on May 2.
	10	Paid Depot Wholesale Supply in full, less discount.
	11	Purchased supplies for cash $900.
	12	Purchased merchandise for cash $2,400. ✓
	15	Received refund for poor quality merchandise from supplier on cash purchase $230.
	17	Purchased merchandise from Harlow Distributors $1,900, FOB shipping point, terms 2/10, n/30.
	19	Paid freight on May 17 purchase $250.
	24	Sold merchandise for cash $6,200. The merchandise sold had a cost of $4,340.
	25	Purchased merchandise from Horicon Inc. $1,000, FOB destination, terms 2/10, n/30.
	27	Paid Harlow Distributors in full, less discount.
	29	Made refunds to cash customers for defective merchandise $100. The returned merchandise had a cost of $70.
	31	Sold merchandise on account $1,600, terms n/30. The cost of the merchandise sold was $1,120.

Carlos Hardware's chart of accounts includes the following: No. 101 Cash, No. 112 Accounts Receivable, No. 120 Merchandise Inventory, No. 126 Supplies, No. 201 Accounts Payable, No. 311 Common Stock, No. 401 Sales, No. 412 Sales Returns and Allowances, No. 414 Sales Discounts, No. 505 Cost of Goods Sold.

Instructions
(a) Journalize the transactions using a perpetual inventory system.
(b) Enter the beginning cash and common stock balances and post the transactions. (Use J1 for the journal reference.)
(c) Prepare an income statement through gross profit for the month of May 2001.

Complete accounting cycle beginning with a work sheet.
(SO 5, 6, 7)

P5–3A The trial balance of Monty Zuma Wholesale Company contained the following accounts at December 31, the end of the company's fiscal year:

MONTY ZUMA WHOLESALE COMPANY
Trial Balance
December 31, 2001

	Debit	Credit
Cash	$ 23,400	
Accounts Receivable	37,600	
Merchandise Inventory	90,000	
Land	92,000	
Buildings	197,000	
Accumulated Depreciation—Buildings		$ 54,000
Equipment	83,500	
Accumulated Depreciation—Equipment		42,400
Notes Payable		50,000
Accounts Payable		37,500
Common Stock		200,000
Retained Earnings		67,800

	Debit	Credit
Dividends	$ 10,000	
Sales		$ 902,100
Sales Discounts	4,600	
Cost of Goods Sold	709,900	
Salaries Expense	69,800	
Utilities Expense	19,400	
Repair Expense	5,900	
Gas and Oil Expense	7,200	
Insurance Expense	3,500	
	$1,353,800	$1,353,800

Adjustment data:

1. Depreciation is $10,000 on buildings and $9,000 on equipment. (Both are administrative expenses.)
2. Interest of $7,000 is due and unpaid on notes payable at December 31.

Other data:

1. Salaries are 80% selling and 20% administrative.
2. Utilities expense, repair expense, and insurance expense are 100% administrative.
3. $15,000 of the notes payable are payable next year.
4. Gas and oil expense is a selling expense.

Instructions
(a) Enter the trial balance on a work sheet and complete the work sheet.
(b) Prepare a multiple-step income statement and retained earnings statement for the year, and a classified balance sheet at December 31, 2001.
(c) Journalize the adjusting entries.
(d) Journalize the closing entries.
(e) Prepare a post-closing trial balance.

P5–4A Rowbuck Department Store is located in midtown Metropolis. During the past several years, net income has been declining because of suburban shopping centers. At the end of the company's fiscal year on November 30, 2001, the following accounts appeared in two of its trial balances:

Prepare financial statements and adjusting and closing entries.
(SO 5, 6, 7)

	Unadjusted	Adjusted
Accounts Payable	$ 47,310	$ 47,310
Accounts Receivable	11,770	11,770
Accumulated Depreciation—Delivery Equipment	15,680	19,680
Accumulated Depreciation—Store Equipment	32,300	41,800
Cash	8,000	8,000
Common Stock	70,000	70,000
Cost of Goods Sold	633,220	633,220
Delivery Expense	8,200	8,200
Delivery Equipment	57,000	57,000
Depreciation Expense—Delivery Equipment		4,000
Depreciation Expense—Store Equipment		9,500
Dividends	12,000	12,000
Insurance Expense		9,000
Interest Expense	8,000	8,000
Interest Revenue	5,000	5,000
Merchandise Inventory	36,200	36,200
Notes Payable	46,000	46,000
Prepaid Insurance	13,500	4,500
Property Tax Expense		3,500
Property Taxes Payable		3,500
Rent Expense	19,000	19,000
Retained Earnings	14,200	14,200
Salaries Expense	120,000	120,000

	Unadjusted	Adjusted
Sales	$850,000	$850,000
Sales Commissions Expense	8,000	14,000
Sales Commissions Payable		6,000
Sales Returns and Allowances	10,000	10,000
Store Equipment	125,000	125,000
Utilities Expense	10,600	10,600

Analysis reveals the following additional data:

1. Salaries expense is 70% selling and 30% administrative.
2. Insurance expense is 50% selling and 50% administrative.
3. Rent expense, utilities expense, and property tax expense are administrative expenses.
4. Notes payable are due in 2003.

Instructions

(a) Prepare a multiple-step income statement, a retained earnings statement, and a classified balance sheet.
(b) Journalize the adjusting entries that were made.
(c) Journalize the closing entries that are necessary.

P5–5A   Chi Chi Garcia, a former professional golf star, operates Chi Chi's Pro Shop at Bay Golf Course. At the beginning of the current season on April 1, the ledger of Chi Chi's Pro Shop showed Cash $2,500, Merchandise Inventory $3,500, and Common Stock $6,000. The following transactions were completed during April 2001.

Apr. 5   Purchased golf bags, clubs, and balls on account from Balata Co. $1,600, FOB shipping point, terms 2/10, n/60.
     7   Paid freight on Balata purchase $80.
     9   Received credit from Balata Co. for merchandise returned $100.
    10   Sold merchandise on account to members $900, terms n/30. The merchandise sold had a cost of $630.
    12   Purchased golf shoes, sweaters, and other accessories on account from Titleist Sportswear $660, terms 1/10, n/30.
    14   Paid Balata Co. in full.
    17   Received credit from Titleist Sportswear for merchandise returned $60.
    20   Made sales on account to members $700, terms n/30. The cost of the merchandise sold was $490.
    21   Paid Titleist Sportswear in full.
    27   Granted an allowance to members for clothing that did not fit properly $30.
    30   Received payments on account from members $1,100.

The chart of accounts for the pro shop includes the following: No. 101 Cash, No. 112 Accounts Receivable, No. 120 Merchandise Inventory, No. 201 Accounts Payable, No. 311 Common Stock, No. 401 Sales, No. 412 Sales Returns and Allowances, No. 505 Cost of Goods Sold.

Instructions

(a) Journalize the April transactions using a perpetual inventory system.
(b) Enter the beginning balances in the ledger accounts and post the April transactions. (Use J1 for the journal reference.)
(c) Prepare a trial balance on April 30, 2001.

PROBLEMS: SET B
••

P5–1B   Travel Warehouse distributes suitcases to retail stores and extends credit terms of 1/10, n/30 to all of its customers. At the end of July, Travel's inventory consisted of 40 suitcases purchased at $30 each. During the month of July the following merchandising transactions occurred.

July 1   Purchased 50 suitcases on account for $30 each from Suitcase Manufacturers, FOB destination, terms 1/15, n/30. The appropriate party also made a cash payment of $100 for freight on this date.
      3   Sold 40 suitcases on account to Luggage World for $50 each.
      9   Paid Suitcase Manufacturers in full.
     12   Received payment in full from Luggage World.
     17   Sold 30 suitcases on account to The Travel Spot for $50 each.
     18   Purchased 60 suitcases on account for $1,700 from Vacation Manufacturers, FOB shipping point, terms 2/10, n/30. The appropriate party also made a cash payment of $100 for freight on this date.
     20   Received $300 credit for 10 suitcases returned to Vacation Manufacturers.
     21   Received payment in full from The Travel Spot.
     22   Sold 40 suitcases on account to Vacations-Are-Us for $50 each.
     30   Paid Vacation Manufacturers in full.
     31   Granted Vacations-Are-Us $250 credit for 5 suitcases returned costing $150.

Instructions
  Journalize the transactions for the month of July for Travel Warehouse using a perpetual inventory system.

P5–2B The Maggie Zine Distributing Company completed the following merchandising transactions in the month of April. At the beginning of April, the ledger of Maggie Zine showed Cash of $9,000 and Common Stock of $9,000.

Journalize, post, and prepare a partial income statement.
(SO 2, 3, 4, 5)

Apr. 2   Purchased merchandise on account from Ken Tuckee Supply Co. $5,900, terms 2/10, n/30.
      4   Sold merchandise on account $5,000, FOB destination, terms 2/10, n/30. The cost of the merchandise sold was $4,000.
      5   Paid $200 freight on April 4 sale.
      6   Received credit from Ken Tuckee Supply Co. for merchandise returned $300.
     11   Paid Ken Tuckee Supply Co. in full, less discount.
     13   Received collections in full, less discounts, from customers billed on April 4.
     14   Purchased merchandise for cash $4,400.
     16   Received refund from supplier on cash purchase of April 14, $500.
     18   Purchased merchandise from Ida Hoe Distributors $4,200, FOB shipping point, terms 2/10, n/30.
     20   Paid freight on April 18 purchase $100.
     23   Sold merchandise for cash $6,400. The merchandise sold had a cost of $5,120.
     26   Purchased merchandise for cash $2,300.
     27   Paid Ida Hoe Distributors in full, less discount.
     29   Made refunds to cash customers for defective merchandise $90. The returned merchandise had a cost of $70.
     30   Sold merchandise on account $3,700, terms n/30. The cost of the merchandise sold was $3,000.

Maggie Zine Company's chart of accounts includes the following: No. 101 Cash, No. 112 Accounts Receivable, No. 120 Merchandise Inventory, No. 201 Accounts Payable, No. 311 Common Stock, No. 401 Sales, No. 412 Sales Returns and Allowances, No. 414 Sales Discounts, No. 505 Cost of Goods Sold, and No. 644 Freight-out.

Instructions
  (a) Journalize the transactions using a perpetual inventory system.
  (b) Enter the beginning cash and common stock balances, and post the transactions. (Use J1 for the journal reference.)
  (c) Prepare the income statement through gross profit for the month of April 2001.

P5–3B The trial balance of Cal A. Fornia Fashion Center contained the following accounts at November 30, the end of the company's fiscal year.

Complete accounting cycle beginning with a work sheet.
(SO 5, 6, 7)

CAL A. FORNIA FASHION CENTER
Trial Balance
November 30, 2001

	Debit	Credit
Cash	$ 26,700	
Accounts Receivable	33,700	
Merchandise Inventory	45,000	
Store Supplies	5,500	
Store Equipment	85,000	
Accumulated Depreciation—Store Equipment		$ 18,000
Delivery Equipment	48,000	
Accumulated Depreciation—Delivery Equipment		6,000
Notes Payable		51,000
Accounts Payable		48,500
Common Stock		80,000
Retained Earnings		30,000
Dividends	12,000	
Sales		757,200
Sales Returns and Allowances	4,200	
Cost of Goods Sold	497,400	
Salaries Expense	140,000	
Advertising Expense	26,400	
Utilities Expense	14,000	
Repair Expense	12,100	
Delivery Expense	16,700	
Rent Expense	24,000	
	$990,700	$990,700

Adjustment data:

1. Store supplies on hand totaled $3,500.
2. Depreciation is $9,000 on the store equipment and $7,000 on the delivery equipment (both are selling expenses).
3. Interest of $11,000 is accrued on notes payable at November 30.

Other data:

1. Salaries expense is 70% selling and 30% administrative.
2. Rent expense and utilities expense are 80% selling and 20% administrative.
3. $30,000 of notes payable are due for payment next year.
4. Repair expense is 100% administrative.

Instructions
(a) Enter the trial balance on a work sheet and complete the work sheet.
(b) Prepare a multiple-step income statement and retained earnings statement for the year and a classified balance sheet as of November 30, 2001.
(c) Journalize the adjusting entries.
(d) Journalize the closing entries.
(e) Prepare a post-closing trial balance.

Prepare financial statements and adjusting and closing entries.
(SO 5, 6, 7)

P5–4B   The Al Falfa Department Store is located near the Village shopping mall. At the end of the company's fiscal year on December 31, 2001, the following accounts appeared in two of its trial balances.

	Unadjusted	Adjusted
Accounts Payable	$ 79,300	$ 79,300
Accounts Receivable	50,300	50,300
Accumulated Depreciation—Building	42,100	52,500
Accumulated Depreciation—Equipment	29,600	42,900
Building	190,000	190,000
Cash	23,000	23,000
Common Stock	150,000	150,000
Cost of Goods Sold	412,700	412,700

	Unadjusted	Adjusted
Depreciation Expense—Building	$	$ 10,400
Depreciation Expense—Equipment		13,300
Dividends	28,000	28,000
Equipment	110,000	110,000
Insurance Expense		7,200
Interest Expense	3,000	11,000
Interest Payable		8,000
Interest Revenue	4,000	4,000
Merchandise Inventory	75,000	75,000
Mortgage Payable	80,000	80,000
Office Salaries Expense	32,000	32,000
Prepaid Insurance	9,600	2,400
Property Taxes Expense		4,800
Property Taxes Payable		4,800
Retained Earnings	26,600	26,600
Sales	628,000	628,000
Sales Commissions Expense	11,000	14,500
Sales Commissions Payable		3,500
Sales Returns and Allowances	8,000	8,000
Sales Salaries Expense	76,000	76,000
Utilities Expense	11,000	11,000

Analysis reveals the following additional data:

1. Insurance expense and utilities expense are 60% selling and 40% administrative.
2. $20,000 of the mortgage payable is due for payment next year.
3. Depreciation on the building and property tax expense are administrative expenses; depreciation on the equipment is a selling expense.

Instructions
(a) Prepare a multiple-step income statement, a retained earnings statement, and a classified balance sheet.
(b) Journalize the adjusting entries that were made.
(c) Journalize the closing entries that are necessary.

P5–5B Bobby Jo Evans, a former professional tennis star, operates B.J.'s Tennis Shop at the Jackson Lake Resort. At the beginning of the current season, the ledger of B.J.'s Tennis Shop showed Cash $2,500, Merchandise Inventory $1,700, and Common Stock $4,200. The following transactions were completed during April 2001.

Journalize, post, and prepare a trial balance.
(SO 2, 3, 6)

Apr. 4 Purchased racquets and balls from Sampras Co. $640 FOB shipping point, terms 3/10, n/30.
6 Paid freight on Sampras's purchase $40.
8 Sold merchandise to members $900, terms n/30. The merchandise sold had a cost of $600.
10 Received credit of $40 from Sampras Co. for a damaged racquet that was returned.
11 Purchased tennis shoes from Niki Sports for cash, $300.
13 Paid Sampras Co. in full.
14 Purchased tennis shirts and shorts from Martina's Sportswear $700, FOB shipping point, terms 2/10, n/60.
15 Received cash refund of $50 from Niki Sports for damaged merchandise that was returned.
17 Paid freight on Martina's Sportswear purchase $30.
18 Sold merchandise to members, $800, terms n/30. The cost of the merchandise sold was $530.
20 Received $500 in cash from members in settlement of their accounts.
21 Paid Martina's Sportswear in full.
27 Granted an allowance of $30 to members for tennis clothing that was of the wrong color.
30 Received cash payments on account from members, $500.

The chart of accounts for the tennis shop includes the following: No. 101 Cash, No. 112 Accounts Receivable, No. 120 Merchandise Inventory, No. 201 Accounts Payable, No. 311 Common Stock, No. 401 Sales, No. 412 Sales Returns and Allowances, No. 505 Cost of Goods Sold.

Instructions
(a) Journalize the April transactions using a perpetual inventory system.
(b) Enter the beginning balances in the ledger accounts and post the April transactions. (Use J1 for the journal reference.)
(c) Prepare a trial balance on April 30, 2001.

BROADENING YOUR PERSPECTIVE

FINANCIAL REPORTING AND ANALYSIS
....

FINANCIAL REPORTING PROBLEM: Kellogg Company

BYP5–1 The financial statements of Kellogg Company are presented in Appendix A at the end of this textbook.

Instructions
Answer the following questions using the Consolidated Statement of Earnings.

(a) What was the percentage change in (1) sales and in (2) net income from 1996 to 1997 and from 1997 to 1998?
(b) What was Kellogg's gross profit rate in 1996, 1997, and 1998?
(c) What was Kellogg's percentage of net income to net sales in 1996, 1997, and 1998? Comment on any trend in this percentage.

COMPARATIVE ANALYSIS PROBLEM: Kellogg Company vs. General Mills

BYP5–2 Kellogg's financial statements are presented in Appendix A; General Mills's financial statements are presented in Appendix B.

Instructions
(a) Based on the information contained in these financial statements, determine each of the following for each company:
(1) Gross profit for 1998.
(2) Gross profit rate for 1998.
(3) Operating income for 1998 (exclude interest expense and nonrecurring or unusual items).
(4) Percent change in operating income from 1997 to 1998.
(b) What conclusions concerning the relative profitability of the two companies can be drawn from these data?

RESEARCH ASSIGNMENT

BYP5–3 The May 1998 issue of the *Journal of Accountancy* includes an article by Randall W. Luecke and David T. Meeting entitled "How Companies Report Income."

Instructions
Read the article and answer the following questions:

(a) What two major income reporting concepts have been used by business accountants at different times over the years? Define and differentiate these two income reporting concepts.
(b) The article states, "The pendulum of income reporting is again changing direction." Which way is the pendulum swinging?
(c) What recent pronouncement pushed income reporting in the new direction?

(d) What items are included in Other Comprehensive Income?

(e) What are three ways companies have to display comprehensive income?

INTERPRETING FINANCIAL STATEMENTS: McDonnell Douglas

BYP5-4   Before being purchased by Boeing Co. in 1997, McDonnell Douglas, based in St. Louis, Missouri, described itself in its Annual Report as the world's largest builder of fighter and military transport aircraft, the third largest commercial aircraft maker, and a leading producer of helicopters, missiles, and satellite launch vehicles. The company's strategy for future growth might have been described as "cautiously aggressive," because it aggressively competed in markets in which it believed that it had a competitive advantage, while it evaluated other markets carefully, and then expanded its product line or divested, depending upon whether it believed that it could remain or become a leading competitor.

A recent pre-merger McDonnell Douglas income statement is reproduced below. Dollar amounts are in millions.

McDONNELL DOUGLAS
Income Statement (partial)

Revenues	$13,176
Costs and expenses:	
Cost of products, services, and rentals	11,026
General and administrative expenses	684
Research and development	297
Interest expense	249
Total costs and expenses	12,256
Earnings before income taxes	920
Income taxes	322
Net earnings	$ 598

Instructions

(a) What account name appears to represent McDonnell Douglas's cost of goods sold account? Why do you think the company chose the account name that it did? Using that account as cost of goods sold, what is gross profit?

(b) The income statement shown is in summary form. This means that each account title listed is a summary of several other accounts. For example, the Revenue account includes such things as Commercial Aircraft Revenue, Defense Contract Revenue, and so forth, as well as any offsetting accounts such as Sales Discounts. Indicate in which summary account from the income statement the following merchandising accounts would be located:
1. Sales returns and allowances.
2. Freight-in.
3. Merchandise inventory increases and decreases.
4. Sales discounts.

(c) The company was evaluating a divisional plant that would build satellite launch vehicles. The product line consisted of a single vehicle, which was the only one of its kind, but competitors had built vehicles that could launch smaller satellites. The company was confident that it could produce an expanded product line, which would include both larger and smaller vehicles than the one currently made. The two choices being evaluated were: First, spend approximately $17 million in research and development to expand the product line. This cost would be considered an expense immediately. Revenue of about $100 million would be generated each year, beginning two years after development; it would continue at least five years, but possibly more. Second, sell the assets of the existing business to a competitor. This would generate a gain of $315 million next year.

If the choice had been made at the end of this year, how would net income be affected under each alternative? How would gross profit change? Which alternative would you have recommended? Give reasons for your answer.

REAL-WORLD FOCUS: A.L. Laboratories

BYP5–5   **A.L. Laboratories** is headquartered in Ft. Lee, N.J., and also has operations in Scandinavia and Indonesia. The company develops and produces generic pharmaceuticals, specializing in both over-the-counter and prescription creams and ointments, aerosol inhalants, and liquids such as cough syrups. A significant share of its income is also derived from the development and distribution of animal health products such as food additives for poultry. The company was founded in 1975 and today has over 2,700 employees.

Gross profit at A.L. Laboratories declined in both dollars and as a percentage of revenues. The decline was attributed to lower sales volume, customer credits associated with product recalls, inventory disposals, and the impact of higher inventory costs. In addition to the above, the gross profit percentage declined as a result of lower production volumes.

Instructions
- (a) What account is affected when A.L. Laboratories has a product recall?
- (b) What factors caused gross profit to decline?
- (c) What factors could cause this company to have to dispose of inventory?

CRITICAL THINKING

GROUP DECISION CASE

BYP5–6   Three years ago, Kathy Webb and her brother-in-law John Utley opened FedCo Department Store. For the first 2 years, business was good, but the following condensed income results for 2000 were disappointing.

FEDCO DEPARTMENT STORE
Income Statement
For the Year Ended December 31, 2000

Net sales		$700,000
Cost of goods sold		546,000
Gross profit		154,000
Operating expenses		
Selling expenses	$100,000	
Administrative expenses	25,000	125,000
Net income		$ 29,000

Kathy believes the problem lies in the relatively low gross profit rate (gross profit divided by net sales) of 22%. John believes the problem is that operating expenses are too high.

Kathy thinks the gross profit rate can be improved by making both of the following changes: (1) Increase average selling prices by 17%; this increase is expected to lower sales volume so that total sales will increase only 6%. (2) Buy merchandise in larger quantities and take all purchase discounts; these changes are expected to increase the gross profit rate to 25%. Kathy does not anticipate that these changes will have any effect on operating expenses.

John thinks expenses can be cut by making both of the following changes: (1) Cut 2000 sales salaries of $60,000 in half and give sales personnel a commission of 2% of net sales. (2) Reduce store deliveries to one day per week rather than twice a week; this change will reduce 2000 delivery expenses of $30,000 by 40%. John feels that these changes will not have any effect on net sales.

Kathy and John come to you for help in deciding the best way to improve net income.

Instructions
With the class divided into groups, answer the following:
- (a) Prepare a condensed income statement for 2001 assuming (1) Kathy's changes are implemented and (2) John's ideas are adopted.

(b) What is your recommendation to Kathy and John?
(c) Prepare a condensed income statement for 2001 assuming both sets of proposed changes are made.

COMMUNICATION ACTIVITY

BYP5–7 The following situation is in chronological order:

1. Dexter decides to buy a surfboard.
2. He calls Surfing USA Co. to inquire about their surfboards.
3. Two days later he requests Surfing USA Co. to make him a surfboard.
4. Three days later, Surfing USA Co. sends him a purchase order to fill out.
5. He sends back the purchase order.
6. Surfing USA Co. receives the completed purchase order.
7. Surfing USA Co. completes the surfboard.
8. Dexter picks up the surfboard.
9. Surfing USA Co. bills Dexter.
10. Surfing USA Co. receives payment from Dexter.

Instructions
In a memo to the president of Surfing USA Co., explain the following:

(a) When should Surfing USA Co. record the sale?
(b) Suppose that with his purchase order, Dexter is required to make a down payment. Would that change your answer?

ETHICS CASE

BYP5–8 Rita Pelzer was just hired as the assistant treasurer of Yorkshire Stores, a specialty chain store company consisting of nine retail stores concentrated in one metropolitan area. Among other things, the payment of all invoices is centralized in one of the departments Rita will manage. Her primary responsibility is to maintain the company's high credit rating by paying all bills when due and to take advantage of all cash discounts. Jamie Caterino, the former assistant treasurer who has been promoted to treasurer, is training Rita in her new duties. He instructs Rita that she is to continue the practice of preparing all checks "net of discount" and dating the checks the last day of the discount period. "But," Jamie continues, "we always hold the checks at least four days beyond the discount period before mailing them. That way we get another four days of interest on our money. Most of our creditors need our business and don't complain. And, if they scream about our missing the discount period, we blame it on the mail room or the post office. We've only lost one discount out of every hundred we take that way. I think everybody does it. By the way, welcome to our team!"

Instructions
(a) What are the ethical considerations in this case?
(b) Who are the stakeholders that are harmed or benefitted in this situation?
(c) Should Rita continue the practice started by Jamie? Does she have any choice?

SURFING THE NET

BYP5–9 No financial decision maker should ever rely solely on the financial information reported in the annual report to make decisions. It is important to keep abreast of financial news. This activity demonstrates how to search for financial news on the Web.

Address: http://biz.yahoo.com/i (or go to www.wiley.com/college/weygandt)

Steps:
1. Type in either Kellogg Company or General Mills, Inc.
2. Choose **News**.
3. Select an article that sounds interesting to you.

Instructions
(a) What was the source of the article? (For example, Reuters, Businesswire, Prenewswire.)

(b) Pretend that you are a personal financial planner and that one of your clients owns stock in the company. Write a brief memo to your client summarizing the article and explaining the implications of the article for their investment.

Answers to Self-Study Questions
1. c   2. a   3. c   4. b   5. c   6. b   7. d   8. a   9. c   10. d

Answer to Kellogg Review It Question 4, p. 201
The 1998 gross profit rate is 51.5% ($3,479.5 ÷ $6,762.1), and the 1997 gross profit rate is 52.1% ($3,560 ÷ $6,830.1). The rate therefore decreased by 0.6% from 1997 to 1998. All this information was provided in the Kellogg Company's management discussion and analysis section. It also could be computed from the income statement presented.

Remember to go back to the Navigator box on the chapter-opening page and check off your completed work.

Before studying this chapter, you should know or, if necessary, review:

a. The cost principle (Ch. 1, p. 9) and matching principle of accounting. (Ch. 3, p. 94)

b. How to record purchases, sales, and cost of goods sold under a perpetual inventory system. (Ch. 5, pp. 191–199)

c. How to prepare financial statements for a merchandising company. (Ch. 5, pp. 199–203)

THE NAVIGATOR

FEATURE STORY

Taking Stock— from Backpacks to Bicycles

Backpacks and jackets sporting the jagged peaks of the Mountain Equipment Co-op (MEC) logo are a familiar sight on hiking trails and campuses. Sales of these popular items help the Vancouver-based co-op to finance its primary goal: to provide members with products and services for wilderness recreational activities, such as hiking and mounteering, at a reasonable cost.

MEC has five retail stores across Canada and a huge market in catalogue sales around the world. It ships everything from climbing ropes, kayaks, and bike helmets to destinations as far away as Japan and South America.

Keeping financial track of the flow of these items is a responsibility of Fara Jumani, a member of the inventory costing group at MEC and a part-time college student. "We have tens of thousands of items in inventory, and we are adding new ones all the time," says Ms. Jumani. "Because we make a lot of our own clothing goods, we also have a lot of in-house inventory—fabric and supplies that will be used to make products."

MEC tracks the cost of its inventory using the average cost of the various items in inventory, weighted by the number purchased at each different unit cost (weighted average cost method). "Because costs tend to fluctuate," explains Ms. Jumani, "that method best captures our overall costs."

Unlike most retail operations, MEC is not out to make a profit; as a co-op, it exists to serve its members. "But we have to stay fiscally healthy to do that," points out Ms. Jumani. "If we go bankrupt, we won't be serving anyone." Accounting for inventory—from backpacks to bicycles—is an important part of MEC's fiscal fitness regimen.

THE NAVIGATOR

CHAPTER 6

INVENTORIES

THE NAVIGATOR ✔

- Understand *Concepts for Review* ☐
- Read *Feature Story* ☐
- Scan *Study Objectives* ☐
- Read *Preview* ☐
- Read text and answer *Before You Go On*
  p. 236 ☐ p. 242 ☐ p. 251 ☐ p. 255 ☐
- Work *Demonstration Problem* ☐
- Review *Summary of Study Objectives* ☐
- Answer *Self-Study Questions* ☐
- Complete assignments ☐

STUDY OBJECTIVES

After studying this chapter, you should be able to:

1. Describe the steps in determining inventory quantities.
2. Prepare the entries for purchases and sales of inventory under a periodic inventory system.
3. Determine cost of goods sold under a periodic inventory system.
4. Identify the unique features of the income statement for a merchandising company using a periodic inventory system.
5. Explain the basis of accounting for inventories and describe the inventory cost flow methods.
6. Explain the financial statement and tax effects of each of the inventory cost flow methods.
7. Explain the lower of cost or market basis of accounting for inventories.
8. Indicate the effects of inventory errors on the financial statements.
9. Compute and interpret the inventory turnover ratio.

THE NAVIGATOR

*A*s indicated in the opening story about the Mountain Equipment Co-op, accounting for inventory involves making choices among inventory methods. In this chapter we will explain the procedures for determining inventory quantities and the methods used in determining the cost of inventory on hand at the balance sheet date. In addition, we will discuss differences in perpetual and periodic inventory systems, and the effects of inventory errors on a company's financial statements. The content and organization of this chapter are as follows:

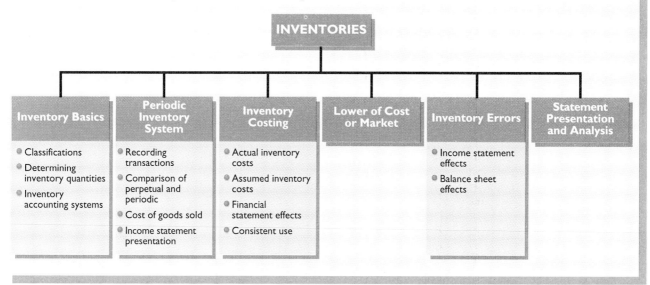

THE NAVIGATOR

INVENTORY BASICS

In our economy, inventories are an important barometer of business activity. The U.S. Commerce Department, for example, publishes monthly combined inventory data for retailers, wholesalers, and manufacturers. The amount of inventories and the time required to sell the goods on hand are two indicators that are closely watched. During downturns in the economy, there is an initial buildup of inventories, as the length of time needed to sell existing quantities increases. The reverse effects are generally associated with an upturn in business activity. A delicate balance must be maintained between too little inventory and too much. A merchandiser or manufacturer with too little inventory to meet demand will have dissatisfied customers and sales personnel. One with too much inventory will be burdened with unnecessary carrying costs.

Inventories affect both the balance sheet and the income statement. In the **balance sheet** of merchandising companies, inventory is frequently the most significant current asset. Of course, its amount and relative importance can vary, even for enterprises in the same industry. For example, Wal-Mart reported inventory of $17 billion, representing 81% of total current assets, whereas for the same period, J.C. Penney Company reported $6 billion of inventory, representing 54% of total current assets. In the **income statement**, inventory is vital in determining the results of operations for a particular period. Moreover, gross profit (net sales less cost of goods sold) is closely watched by management, owners, and other interested parties (as explained in Chapter 5).

Classifying Inventory

How a company classifies its inventory depends on whether the firm is a merchandiser or a manufacturer. In a **merchandising enterprise**, inventory consists of many different items. For example, in a grocery store, canned goods, dairy products, meats, and produce are just a few of the inventory items on hand. These items have two common characteristics: (1) they are owned by the company, and (2) they are in a form ready for sale to customers in the ordinary course of business. Thus, only one inventory classification, **merchandise inventory**, is needed to describe the many different items that make up the total inventory.

In a **manufacturing enterprise**, inventories are also owned by the company, but some goods may not yet be ready for sale. As a result, inventory is usually classified into three categories: finished goods, work in process, and raw materials. For example, General Motors classifies automobiles completed and ready for sale as **finished goods**. The automobiles on the assembly line in various stages of production are classified as **work in process**. The steel, glass, upholstery, and other components that are on hand waiting to be used in the production of automobiles are identified as **raw materials**.

The accounting principles and concepts discussed in this chapter apply to inventory classifications of both merchandising and manufacturing companies. In this chapter we will focus on merchandise inventory.

HELPFUL HINT
Regardless of the classification, all inventories are reported under Current Assets on the balance sheet.

Determining Inventory Quantities

Many businesses take a physical inventory count on the last day of the year. Businesses using the periodic inventory system are required to take an end-of-the-period physical inventory to determine the inventory on hand at the balance sheet date and to compute cost of goods sold. Even businesses using a perpetual inventory system must take a physical inventory at some time during the year.

Determining inventory quantities consists of two steps: (1) taking a physical inventory of goods on hand, and (2) determining the ownership of goods.

1
STUDY
OBJECTIVE
Describe the steps in determining inventory quantities.

Taking a Physical Inventory

Taking a physical inventory involves actually counting, weighing, or measuring each kind of inventory on hand. In many companies, taking an inventory is a formidable task. Retailers, such as Kmart, True Value Hardware, or your favorite music store have thousands of different inventory items. An inventory count is generally more accurate when goods are not being sold or received during the counting. Consequently, companies often "take inventory" when the business is closed or when business is slow. Many retailers, for example, close early on a chosen day in January—after the holiday sales and returns—to count their inventory.

To minimize errors in taking the inventory, a company should adopt the following procedures to insure the accuracy of the count and to safeguard inventory:

1. The counting should be done by employees who do not have custodial responsibility for the inventory.
2. Each counter should establish the authenticity of each inventory item, e.g., each box does contain a 25-inch television set, and each storage tank does contain gasoline.
3. There should be a second count by another employee.
4. Prenumbered inventory tags should be used, and all inventory tags should be accounted for.

5. A designated supervisor should ascertain at the conclusion of the count that all inventory items are tagged and that no items have more than one tag.

After the physical inventory is taken, the quantity of each kind of inventory is listed on **inventory summary sheets**. To assure the accuracy of the summary sheets, the listing should be verified by a second employee or supervisor. Subsequently, unit costs will be applied to the quantities in order to determine a total cost of the inventory—which is the topic of later sections.[1]

ACCOUNTING IN ACTION
Business Insight

Failure to observe the foregoing internal control procedures contributed to the Great Salad Oil Swindle. In this case, management intentionally overstated its salad oil inventory, which was stored in large holding tanks. Three procedures contributed to overstating the oil inventory: (1) Water added to the bottom of the holding tanks caused the oil to float to the top. Inventory-taking crews who viewed the holding tanks from the top observed only salad oil, when, in fact, as much as 37 out of 40 feet of many of the holding tanks contained water. (2) The company's inventory records listed more holding tanks than it actually had. The company repainted numbers on the tanks after inventory crews examined them, so the crews counted the same tanks twice. (3) Underground pipes pumped oil from one holding tank to another during the inventory taking; therefore, the same salad oil was counted more than once. Although the salad oil swindle was unusual, it demonstrates the complexities involved in assuring that inventory is properly counted.

Determining Ownership of Goods

Before we can begin to calculate the cost of inventory, we need to consider the ownership of goods: specifically, we need to be sure that we have not included in the inventory any goods that do not belong to the company.

Goods in Transit.   Goods are considered to be **in transit** when they are in the hands of a public carrier, such as a railroad, trucking, or airline company at the statement date. Goods in transit should be included in the inventory of the party that has legal title to the goods. Legal title is determined by the terms of sale, as shown in Illustration 6-1 and described below:

1. When the terms are **FOB (free on board) shipping point**, ownership of the goods passes to the buyer when the public carrier accepts the goods from the seller.
2. When the terms are **FOB destination**, legal title to the goods remains with the seller until the goods reach the buyer.

Significant errors may occur in determining inventory quantities if goods in transit at the statement date are ignored. Assume, for example, that Hargrove Company has 20,000 units of inventory on hand on December 31 and the fol-

HELPFUL HINT
AMICO Co.'s goods in transit at December 31 consist of sales made (1) FOB destination and (2) FOB shipping point, and purchases made (3) FOB destination and (4) FOB shipping point. Which items should be included in AMICO's inventory at December 31? Answer: Items (1) and (4).

---

[1]To arrive at an estimate of the cost of inventory when a physical inventory cannot be taken (the inventory is destroyed) or when it is inconvenient (during interim periods), estimating methods are applied. These methods (gross profit method and retail inventory method) are discussed in Appendix 6A.

ILLUSTRATION 6-1

Terms of sale

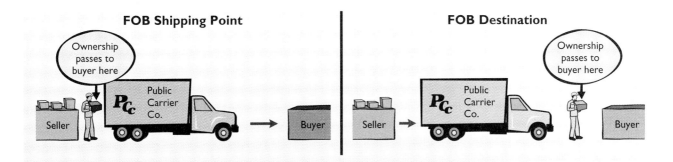

lowing goods in transit: (1) **sales** of 1,500 units shipped December 31 FOB destination, and (2) **purchases** of 2,500 units shipped FOB shipping point by the seller on December 31. Hargrove has legal title to both the units sold and the units purchased. Consequently, inventory quantities would be understated by 4,000 units (1,500 + 2,500) if units in transit are ignored.

TECHNOLOGY IN ACTION

Many companies have invested large amounts of time and money in automated inventory systems. One of the most sophisticated is Federal Express's Digitally Assisted Dispatch System (DADS). This system uses hand-held "SuperTrackers" to transmit data about the packages and documents to the firm's computer system. Based on bar codes, the system allows the firm to know where any package is at any time to prevent losses and to fulfill the firm's delivery commitments. More recently, FedEx's newly developed software enables customers to track shipments on their own PCs.

Consigned Goods. In some lines of business, it is customary to acquire merchandise on consignment. Under a consignment arrangement, the holder of the goods (called the *consignee*) does not own the goods. Ownership remains with the shipper of the goods (called the *consignor*) until the goods are actually sold to a customer. Because consigned goods are not owned by the consignee, they should not be included in the consignee's physical inventory count. Conversely, the consignor should include merchandise held by the consignee as part of its inventory.

Inventory Accounting Systems

One of two basic systems of accounting for inventories may be used: **(1) the perpetual inventory system, or (2) the periodic inventory system.** Chapter 5 of this textbook discussed and illustrated the characteristics of the perpetual inventory system. This chapter discusses and illustrates the periodic inventory system and provides a comparison of it with the perpetual inventory system; Appendix B to this chapter continues coverage of the perpetual inventory system.

Some businesses find it either unnecessary or uneconomical to invest in a computerized perpetual inventory system that maintains up-to-date records of merchandise on hand and cost of goods sold. Many small merchandising business managers, especially, still feel a perpetual inventory system costs more than it is worth. These managers can control merchandise and manage day-to-day operations without detailed inventory records. They use a periodic inventory system.

BEFORE YOU GO ON . . .

Review It

1. What steps are involved in determining inventory quantities?
2. How is ownership determined for goods in transit at the balance sheet date?
3. Who has title to consigned goods?
4. Name two basic systems of accounting for inventories.

Do It

Hasbeen Corporation completed its inventory count, arriving at a total value for inventory of $200,000. You have been informed of the information listed below. Discuss how this information affects the reported cost of inventory.

1. Goods held on consignment for Falls Corp., costing $15,000, were included in the inventory.
2. Purchased goods of $10,000 which were in transit (terms: FOB shipping point) were not included in the count.
3. Sold inventory with a cost of $12,000 which was in transit (terms: FOB shipping point) was not included in the count.

Reasoning: For goods in transit, ownership is determined by the freight terms. For consigned goods, ownership rests with the consignor until the goods are sold by the consignee.

Solution: The goods held on consignment of $15,000 should be deducted from the inventory count. The goods of $10,000 purchased FOB shipping point should be added to the inventory count. Sold goods of $12,000 which were in transit FOB shipping point should not be included in the ending inventory.

THE
NAVIGATOR

Related exercise material: BE6–4, E6–1, E6–4

PERIODIC INVENTORY SYSTEM

2
STUDY
OBJECTIVE

Prepare the entries for purchases and sales of inventory under a periodic inventory system.

In a periodic inventory system, revenues from the sale of merchandise are recorded when sales are made, in the same way as in a perpetual system. But, no attempt is made on the date of sale to record the cost of the merchandise sold. Instead, a physical inventory count is taken at the end of the period to determine (1) the cost of the merchandise then on hand and (2) the cost of the goods sold during the period. And, under a periodic system, purchases of merchandise are recorded in a Purchases account rather than a Merchandise Inventory account. Also, under a periodic system, it is customary to record purchase returns and allowances, purchase discounts, and freight-in on purchases in separate accounts so that the accumulated amounts for each are known.

Recording Transactions

To illustrate the recording of merchandise transactions under a periodic inventory system, we will use the purchase/sale transactions between Highpoint Electronic, Inc. and Chelsea Video discussed in Chapter 5.

Recording Purchases of Merchandise

On the basis of the sales invoice (Illustration 5-4) shown on page 192 and receipt of the merchandise ordered from Highpoint Electronic, Chelsea Video records the $3,800 purchase as follows:

May 4	Purchases	3,800	
	Accounts Payable		3,800
	(To record goods purchased on account, terms 2/10, n/30)		

A	=	L	+	SE
		+3,800		−3,800

Purchases is a temporary account whose normal balance is a debit.

HELPFUL HINT
Be careful not to fall into the trap of debiting purchases of equipment or supplies to Purchases.

Purchase Returns and Allowances

Because $300 of merchandise received from Highpoint Electronic is inoperable, Chelsea Video returns the goods, issues the debit memorandum (Illustration 5-5) shown on page 193, and prepares the following entry to recognize the purchase return:

May 8	Accounts Payable	300	
	Purchase Returns and Allowances		300
	(To record return of inoperable goods purchased from Highpoint Electronic)		

A	=	L	+	SE
		−300		+300

Purchases Returns and Allowances is a temporary account whose normal balance is a credit.

Freight Costs

When the purchaser directly incurs the freight costs, the account Freight-in (or Transportation-in) is debited. For example, if upon delivery of the goods on May 6, Chelsea pays Acme Freight Company $150 for freight charges on its purchase from Highpoint Electronic, the entry on Chelsea's books is:

May 9	Freight-in (Transportation-in)	150	
	Cash		150
	(To record payment of freight, terms FOB shipping point)		

A	=	L	+	SE
−150				−150

Like Purchases, Freight-in is a temporary account whose normal balance is a debit. **Freight-in is part of cost of goods purchased.** The reason is that cost of goods purchased should include any freight charges necessary to bring the goods to the purchaser. Freight costs are not subject to a purchase discount. Purchase discounts apply on the invoice cost of the merchandise.

Purchase Discounts

On May 14 Chelsea Video pays the balance due on account to Highpoint Electronic taking the 2% cash discount allowed by Highpoint for payment within 10 days. The payment and discount are recorded by Chelsea Video as follows:

A	=	L	+	SE
−3,430		−3,500		+70

May 14	Accounts Payable	3,500	
	Purchase Discounts		70
	Cash		3,430
	(To record payment to Highpoint Electronic within the discount period)		

Purchase Discounts is a temporary account whose normal balance is a credit.

Recording Sales of Merchandise

The sale of $3,800 of merchandise to Chelsea Video on May 4 (sales invoice No. 731, Illustration 5-4) is recorded by the seller, Highpoint Electronic, as follows:

A	=	L	+	SE
+3,800				+3,800

May 4	Accounts Receivable	3,800	
	Sales		3,800
	(To record credit sales per invoice #731 to Chelsea Video)		

Sales Returns and Allowances

Based on the debit memorandum (Illustration 5-5, page 193) received from Chelsea Video on May 8 for returned goods, Highpoint Electronic records the $300 sales return as follows:

A	=	L	+	SE
−300				−300

May 8	Sales Returns and Allowances	300	
	Accounts Receivable		300
	(To record return of goods from Chelsea Video)		

Sales Discounts

On May 15, Highpoint Electronic receives payment of $3,430 on account from Chelsea Video. Highpoint honors the 2% cash discount and records the payment of Chelsea's account receivable in full as follows:

A	=	L	+	SE
+3,430				−70
−3,500				

May 15	Cash	3,430	
	Sales Discounts	70	
	Accounts Receivable		3,500
	(To record collection from Chelsea Video within 2/10, n/30 discount period)		

Comparison of Entries—Perpetual vs. Periodic

The periodic inventory system entries above are shown in Illustration 6-2 on page 239 next to those that were illustrated in Chapter 5 (pages 191–99) under the perpetual inventory system for both Highpoint Electronic and Chelsea Video.

3
STUDY
OBJECTIVE
....
Determine cost of goods sold under a periodic inventory system.

Cost of Goods Sold

As noted from the entries in Illustration 6-2, under a periodic inventory system, a running account of the changes in inventory is not recorded as either purchases or sales transactions occur. Neither the daily amount of inventory of merchandise on hand is known nor is the cost of goods sold. To determine the cost of goods sold under a periodic inventory system, it is necessary to (1) record purchases of merchandise (as shown above), (2) determine the cost of goods purchased, and (3) determine the cost of goods on hand at the beginning and end of the accounting period. The cost of goods on hand must be determined by a physical inventory count and application of the cost to the items counted in the inventory.

ENTRIES ON CHELSEA VIDEO'S BOOKS

Transaction		Perpetual Inventory System			Periodic Inventory System		
May 4	Purchase of merchandise on credit.	Merchandise Inventory Accounts Payable	3,800	3,800	Purchases Accounts Payable	3,800	3,800
May 8	Purchase returns and allowances.	Accounts Payable Merchandise Inventory	300	300	Accounts Payable Purchase Returns and Allowances	300	300
May 9	Freight costs on purchases.	Merchandise Inventory Cash	150	150	Freight-in Cash	150	150
May 14	Payment on account with a discount.	Accounts Payable Cash Merchandise Inventory	3,500	3,430 70	Accounts Payable Cash Purchase Discounts	3,500	3,430 70

ENTRIES ON HIGHPOINT ELECTRONIC'S BOOKS

Transaction		Perpetual Inventory System			Periodic Inventory System		
May 4	Sale of merchandise on credit.	Accounts Receivable Sales	3,800	3,800	Accounts Receivable Sales	3,800	3,800
		Cost of Goods Sold Merchandise Inventory	2,400	2,400	No entry for cost of goods sold		
May 8	Return of merchandise sold.	Sales Returns and Allowances Accounts Receivable	300	300	Sales Returns and Allowances Accounts Receivable	300	300
		Merchandise Inventory Cost of Goods Sold	140	140	No entry		
May 15	Cash received on account with a discount.	Cash Sales Discounts Accounts Receivable	3,430 70	3,500	Cash Sales Discounts Accounts Receivable	3,430 70	3,500

ILLUSTRATION 6-2

Comparison of journal entries under perpetual and periodic inventory systems

Determining Cost of Goods Purchased

We used four accounts to record the purchase of inventory under a periodic inventory system. These accounts are:

Account	Normal Balance
Purchases	Debit
Purchase Returns and Allowances	Credit
Purchase Discounts	Credit
Freight-in	Debit

ILLUSTRATION 6-3

Normal balances: cost of goods purchased accounts

All of these accounts are temporary accounts because they are used to determine the cost of goods sold which is an expense disclosed on the income statement. Therefore, the balances in these accounts must be reduced to zero at the end of each accounting period so that information about cost of goods sold can be accumulated in the next accounting period. The procedure for determining the cost of goods purchased is as follows:

1. The accounts with credit balances (Purchase Returns and Allowances and Purchase Discounts) are subtracted from Purchases to produce net purchases.
2. Freight-in is then added to net purchases to produce cost of goods purchased.

To illustrate, assume that Highpoint Electronic shows the following balances for the accounts above: Purchases $325,000; Purchase Returns and Allowances $10,400; Purchase Discounts $6,800; and Freight-in $12,200. Net purchases and cost of goods purchased are $307,800 and $320,000, respectively, as computed in Illustration 6-4:

Purchases		$325,000
(1) Less: Purchase returns and allowances	$10,400	
Purchase discounts	6,800	17,200
Net purchases		307,800
(2) Add: Freight-in		12,200
Cost of goods purchased		$320,000

Determining Cost of Goods on Hand

To **determine the cost of inventory on hand, it is necessary to take a physical inventory.** As explained earlier in this chapter, taking a physical inventory involves:

1. Counting the units on hand for each item of inventory.
2. Applying unit costs to the total units on hand for each item of inventory.
3. Aggregating the costs for each item of inventory to determine the total cost of goods on hand.

A physical inventory should be taken at or near the balance sheet date. To improve the accuracy of the count, many businesses suspend operations while inventory is being taken.

The account Merchandise Inventory is used to record the cost of inventory on hand at the balance sheet date. This amount becomes the beginning inventory for the next accounting period. For Highpoint Electronic, the balance in Merchandise Inventory at December 31, 2000, is $36,000. This amount is also the January 1, 2001, balance in Merchandise Inventory. During 2001, **no entries are made to Merchandise Inventory.** At December 31, 2001, entries are made to eliminate the beginning inventory and to record the ending inventory, which we will assume is $40,000.

Computing Cost of Goods Sold

We have now reached the point where we can compute cost of goods sold. Doing so involves two steps:

1. Add the cost of goods purchased to the cost of goods on hand at the beginning of the period (beginning inventory) to obtain the cost of goods available for sale.

ALTERNATIVE TERMINOLOGY

Some use the term *cost of sales* instead of *cost of goods sold.*

2. Subtract the cost of goods on hand at the end of the period (ending inventory) from the cost of goods available for sale to arrive at the cost of goods sold.

For Highpoint Electronic the cost of goods available for sale and the cost of goods sold are $356,000 and $316,000, respectively, as shown below.

ILLUSTRATION 6-5

Computation of cost of goods available for sale and cost of goods sold

Beginning inventory	$ 36,000
(1) Add: Cost of goods purchased	320,000
Cost of goods available for sale	**356,000**
(2) Less: Ending inventory	40,000
Cost of goods sold	**$316,000**

Gross profit, operating expenses, and net income are computed and reported in a periodic inventory system in the same manner as under a perpetual inventory system as shown in Illustration 6-6.

Income Statement Presentation

As under a perpetual inventory system, the income statement for retailers and wholesalers under a periodic inventory system contains three features not found in the income statement of a service enterprise. These features are: (1) a sales revenue section, (2) a cost of goods sold section, and (3) gross profit. But, under a periodic inventory system, the cost of goods sold section generally will

4
STUDY
OBJECTIVE

Identify the unique features of the income statement for a merchandising company using a periodic inventory system.

HIGHPOINT ELECTRONIC, INC.
Income Statement
For the Year Ended December 31, 2001

Sales revenues				
Sales				$480,000
Less: Sales returns and allowances			$ 12,000	
Sales discounts			8,000	20,000
Net sales				460,000
Cost of goods sold				
Inventory, January 1			36,000	
Purchases		$325,000		
Less: Purchases returns and allowances	$10,400			
Purchase discounts	6,800	17,200		
Net purchases		307,800		
Add: Freight-in		12,200		
Cost of goods purchased			320,000	
Cost of goods available for sale			356,000	
Inventory, December 31			40,000	
Cost of goods sold				316,000
Gross profit				144,000
Operating expenses				
Store salaries expense			45,000	
Rent expense			19,000	
Utilities expense			17,000	
Advertising expense			16,000	
Depreciation expense—store equipment			8,000	
Freight-out			7,000	
Insurance expense			2,000	
Total operating expenses				114,000
Net income				$ 30,000

HELPFUL HINT
The far right column identifies the major subdivisions of the income statement. The next column identifies the primary items comprising cost of goods sold of $316,000 and operating expenses of $114,000; in addition, contra revenue items of $20,000 are reported. The third column explains cost of goods purchased of $320,000. The fourth column reports contra purchase items of $17,200.

ILLUSTRATION 6-6

Income statement for a merchandising company using a periodic inventory system

ALTERNATIVE TERMINOLOGY
Gross profit is sometimes referred to as *merchandising profit* or *gross margin*.

contain more detail. Using assumed data for specific operating expenses, the income statement for Highpoint Electronic using a periodic inventory system is shown in Illustration 6-6. Whether the periodic or the perpetual inventory system is used, merchandise inventory is reported at the same amount in the current assets section of the balance sheet.

BEFORE YOU GO ON . . .

Review It

1. Identify the three steps in determining cost of goods sold.
2. What accounts are used in determining the cost of goods purchased?
3. What is included in cost of goods available for sale?

Do It

Aerosmith Company's accounting records show the following at year-end: Purchase Discounts $3,400; Freight-in $6,100; Sales $240,000; Purchases $162,500; Beginning Inventory $18,000; Ending Inventory $20,000; Sales Discounts $10,000; Purchase Returns $5,200; and Operating Expenses $57,000. Compute the following amounts for Aerosmith Company: net sales, cost of goods purchased, cost of goods sold, gross profit, and net income.

Reasoning: To compute the required amounts, it is important to know the relationships in measuring net income for a merchandising company. For example, it is necessary to know the difference between the following: sales and net sales, goods available for sale and cost of goods sold, and gross profit and net income.

Solution:
Net sales: $240,000 − $10,000 = $230,000.
Cost of goods purchased: $162,500 − $5,200 − $3,400 + $6,100 = $160,000.
Cost of goods sold: $18,000 + $160,000 − $20,000 = $158,000.
Gross profit: $230,000 − $158,000 = $72,000.
Net income: $72,000 − $57,000 = $15,000.

THE NAVIGATOR

Related exercise material: BE6–2, BE6–3, E6–2, E6–3

INVENTORY COSTING UNDER A PERIODIC INVENTORY SYSTEM

5
STUDY
OBJECTIVE

Explain the basis of accounting for inventories and describe the inventory cost flow methods.

All expenditures necessary to acquire the goods and to make them ready for sale are included as inventoriable costs. Inventoriable costs may be regarded as a pool of costs that consists of two elements: (1) the cost of the beginning inventory and (2) the cost of goods purchased during the year. The sum of these two elements equals the cost of goods available for sale. Conceptually, the costs of the purchasing, receiving, and warehousing departments (whose efforts make the goods available for sale) should also be included in inventoriable costs. However, because of the practical difficulties in allocating these costs to inventory, they are generally accounted for as **operating expenses** in the period in which they are incurred.

HELPFUL HINT
Under a perpetual inventory system, described in Chapter 5, the allocation is continuously recognized as purchases and sales are made.

Inventoriable costs are allocated to ending inventory and to cost of goods sold. Under a periodic inventory system, the allocation is made at the end of the accounting period. First, the costs assignable to the ending inventory are determined. Second, the cost of the ending inventory is subtracted from the cost of goods available for sale to determine the cost of goods sold. Cost of goods sold is then deducted from sales revenues in accordance with the matching principle.

To illustrate, assume that General Suppliers has a cost of goods available for sale of $120,000, based on a beginning inventory of $20,000 and cost of goods purchased of $100,000. The physical inventory indicates that 5,000 units are on hand. The costs applicable to the units are $3.00 per unit. The allocation of the pool of costs is shown in Illustration 6-7. As shown, the $120,000 of goods available for sale are allocated $15,000 to ending inventory and $105,000 to cost of goods sold.

ILLUSTRATION 6-7

Allocation (matching) of pool of costs

Pool of Costs
Cost of Goods Available for Sale

Beginning inventory	$ 20,000
Cost of goods purchased	100,000
Cost of goods available for sale	**$120,000**

Step 1			**Step 2**	
Ending Inventory			**Cost of Goods Sold**	
Units	Unit Cost	Total Cost	Cost of goods available for sale	$120,000
			Less: Ending inventory	15,000
5,000	$3.00	**$15,000**	Cost of goods sold	**$105,000**

Using Actual Physical Flow Costing—Specific Identification

Costing of the inventory is complicated because the units on hand for a specific item of inventory may have been purchased at different prices. For example, in a period of rising prices, a company may experience several increases in the cost of identical goods within a given year. Alternatively, unit costs may decline. Under such circumstances, how should the different unit costs in the cost of goods available for sale be allocated between the ending inventory and cost of goods sold?

One answer is to use specific identification of the units purchased. This method tracks the **actual physical flow** of the goods. **Each item of inventory is marked, tagged, or coded with its "specific" unit cost.** Items still in inventory at the end of the year are specifically costed to arrive at the total cost of the ending inventory. Assume, for example, that Southland Music Company purchases three 46-inch television sets at costs of $700, $750, and $800, respectively. During the year, two sets are sold at $1,200 each. At December 31, the company determines that the $750 set is still on hand. Accordingly, the ending inventory is $750 and the cost of goods sold is $1,500 ($700 + $800). This is shown graphically in Illustration 6-8.

HELPFUL HINT

What gross profit will Southland Music report? Answer: $900 (Sales $2,400 − CGS $1,500).

ILLUSTRATION 6-8

Specific identification

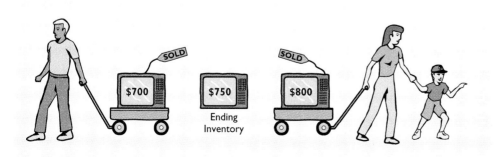

Specific identification is possible when a company sells a limited variety of high unit-cost items that can be clearly identified from the time of purchase through the time of sale. Examples of such companies are automobile dealerships (cars, trucks, and vans), music stores (pianos and organs), and antique shops (tables and cabinets).

Ordinarily, however, the identity of goods purchased at a specific cost is lost between the date of purchase and the date of sale. For example, drug, grocery, and hardware stores sell thousands of relatively low unit-cost items of inventory. These items are often indistinguishable from one another, making it impossible or impractical to track each item's cost.

When feasible, specific identification seems to be the ideal method of allocating cost of goods available for sale. Under this method, the ending inventory is reported at actual cost and the actual cost of goods sold is matched against sales revenue. This method, however, may enable management to manipulate net income. For example, assume that a music store has three identical Steinway grand pianos that were purchased at different costs. When selling one piano, management could maximize its net income by selecting the piano with the lowest cost to match with revenues. Alternatively, it could minimize net income by selecting the highest-cost piano.

Using Assumed Cost Flow Methods— FIFO, LIFO, and Average Cost

Because specific identification is often impractical, other cost flow methods are allowed. These differ from specific identification in that they assume flows of costs that may be unrelated to the physical flow of goods. For this reason we call them **assumed cost flow methods** or **cost flow assumptions**. They are:

1. First-in, first-out (FIFO).
2. Last-in, first-out (LIFO).
3. Average cost.

INTERNATIONAL NOTE

A survey of accounting standards in 21 major industrial countries found that all three methods were permissible. In Ireland and the U.K., LIFO is permitted only in extreme circumstances.

There is no accounting requirement that the cost flow assumption be consistent with the physical movement of the goods. The selection of the appropriate cost flow assumption (method) is made by management. The management of companies in the same industry may reach different conclusions as to the most appropriate method.

To illustrate these three inventory cost flow methods, we will assume that Bow Valley Electronics uses a **periodic inventory system** and has the information shown in Illustration 6-9 for its Z202 Astro condenser.

ILLUSTRATION 6-9

Inventoriable units and costs

BOW VALLEY ELECTRONICS
Z202 Astro Condensers

Date	Explanation	Units	Unit Cost	Total Cost
1/1	Beginning inventory	100	$10	$ 1,000
4/15	Purchase	200	11	2,200
8/24	Purchase	300	12	3,600
11/27	Purchase	400	13	5,200
	Total	1,000		$12,000

During the year, 550 units were sold and 450 units are on hand at December 31.

First-in, First-out (FIFO)

The FIFO method assumes that the **earliest goods** purchased are the first to be sold. FIFO often parallels the actual physical flow of merchandise because it generally is good business practice to sell the oldest units first. Under the FIFO method, therefore, the **costs** of the earliest goods purchased are the first to be recognized as cost of goods sold. The allocation of the cost of goods available for sale at Bow Valley Electronics under FIFO is shown in Illustrations 6-10 and 6-11.

ILLUSTRATION 6-10

Allocation of costs—FIFO method

Pool of Costs
Cost of Goods Available for Sale

Date	Explanation	Units	Unit Cost	Total Cost
1/1	Beginning inventory	100	$10	$ 1,000
4/15	Purchase	200	11	2,200
8/24	Purchase	300	12	3,600
11/27	Purchase	400	13	5,200
	Total	1,000		$12,000

HELPFUL HINT
Note the sequencing of the allocation: (1) compute ending inventory and (2) determine cost of goods sold.

Step 1 — Ending Inventory

Date	Units	Unit Cost	Total Cost
11/27	400	$13	$5,200
8/24	50	12	600
Total	450		$5,800

Step 2 — Cost of Goods Sold

Cost of goods available for sale	$12,000
Less: Ending inventory	5,800
Cost of goods sold	$ 6,200

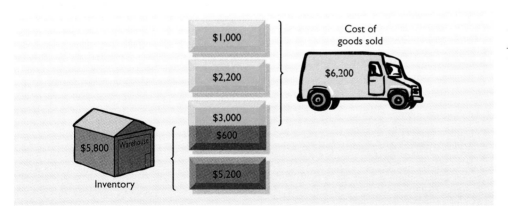

ILLUSTRATION 6-11

FIFO—First costs in are first costs out in computing cost of goods sold

Note that the ending inventory is based on the latest units purchased. That is, **the cost of the ending inventory is obtained by taking the unit cost of the most recent purchase and working backward until all units of inventory have been costed**.

We can verify the accuracy of the cost of goods sold by recognizing that the **first units acquired are the first units sold**. The computations for the 550 units sold are shown in Illustration 6-12.

ILLUSTRATION 6-12

Proof of cost of goods sold

Date	Units		Unit Cost		Total Cost
1/1	100	×	$10	=	$1,000
4/15	200	×	11	=	2,200
8/24	250	×	12	=	3,000
Total	550				$6,200

Last-in, First-out (LIFO)

The LIFO method assumes that the **latest goods** purchased are the first to be sold. LIFO seldom coincides with the actual physical flow of inventory. Under the LIFO method, the **costs** of the latest goods purchased are the first to be recognized as cost of goods sold. The allocation of the cost of goods available for sale at Bow Valley Electronics under LIFO is shown in Illustration 6-13.

ILLUSTRATION 6-13

Allocation of costs—LIFO method

Pool of Costs
Cost of Goods Available for Sale

Date	Explanation	Units	Unit Cost	Total Cost
1/1	Beginning inventory	100	$10	$ 1,000
4/15	Purchase	200	11	2,200
8/24	Purchase	300	12	3,600
11/27	Purchase	400	13	5,200
	Total	1,000		$12,000

Step 1	Step 2
Ending Inventory	**Cost of Goods Sold**

HELPFUL HINT

The costs allocated to ending inventory ($5,000) plus the costs allocated to CGS ($7,000) must equal CGAS ($12,000).

Date	Units	Unit Cost	Total Cost		
1/1	100	$10	$1,000	Cost of goods available for sale	$12,000
4/15	200	11	2,200	Less: Ending inventory	5,000
8/24	150	12	1,800	Cost of goods sold	$ 7,000
Total	450		$5,000		

Illustration 6-14 graphically displays the LIFO cost flow.

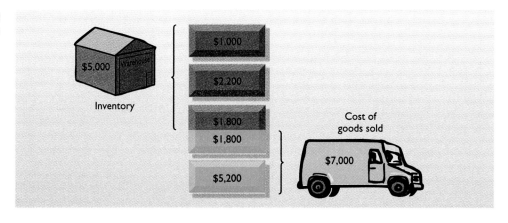

Under the LIFO method, **the cost of the ending inventory is obtained by taking the unit cost of the earliest goods available for sale and working forward until all units of inventory are costed**. As a result, the first costs assigned to ending inventory are the costs of the beginning inventory. Proof of the costs allocated to cost of goods sold is shown in Illustration 6-15.

ILLUSTRATION 6-15

Proof of cost of goods sold

Date	Units		Unit Cost		Total Cost
11/27	400	×	$13	=	$5,200
8/24	150	×	12	=	1,800
Total	550				$7,000

Note that the cost of the **last** goods in is the **first** to be assigned to cost of goods sold. Under a periodic inventory system, which we are using here, **all goods purchased during the period are assumed to be available for the first sale, regardless of the date of purchase**.

Average Cost

The average cost method assumes that the goods available for sale have the same (average) cost per unit; generally the goods are similar in nature (i.e., homogeneous). Under this method, the allocation of the cost of goods available for sale is made on the basis of the **weighted average unit cost** incurred. The formula and a sample computation of the weighted average unit cost are:

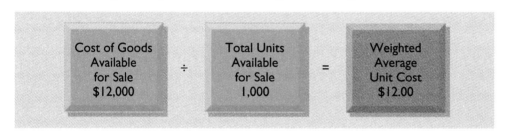

ILLUSTRATION 6-16

Formula for weighted average unit cost

The weighted average unit cost is then applied to the units on hand to determine the cost of the ending inventory. The allocation of the cost of goods available for sale at Bow Valley Electronics using average cost is shown in Illustrations 6-17 and 6-18.

ILLUSTRATION 6-17

Allocation of costs—average cost method

Pool of Costs
Cost of Goods Available for Sale

Date	Explanation	Units	Unit Cost	Total Cost
1/1	Beginning inventory	100	$10	$ 1,000
4/15	Purchase	200	11	2,200
8/24	Purchase	300	12	3,600
11/27	Purchase	400	13	5,200
	Total	1,000		$12,000

Step 1	Step 2
Ending Inventory	**Cost of Goods Sold**

				Cost of goods available for sale	$12,000
$12,000	÷	1,000	= $12.00	Less: Ending inventory	5,400
	Unit	**Total**		Cost of goods sold	$ 6,600
Units	**Cost**	**Cost**			
450	× $12.00	= $5,400			

We can verify the cost of goods sold data presented in Illustration 6-17 under this method by multiplying the units sold by the weighted average unit cost (550 × $12 = $6,600). Note that this method does not use the average of the unit costs. That average is $11.50 ($10 + $11 + $12 + $13 = $46; $46 ÷ 4). The average cost method instead uses the average **weighted** by the quantities purchased at each unit cost.

ILLUSTRATION 6-18

Average cost—The average cost of the goods available for sale during the period is the cost used to compute cost of goods sold

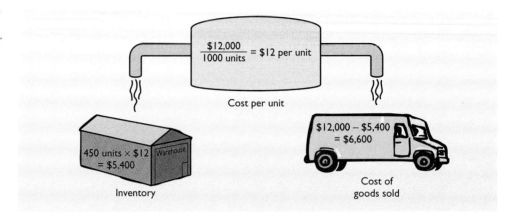

As the Feature Story described, the periodic weighted average cost method is the cost flow assumption used by Mountain Equipment.

Financial Statement Effects of Cost Flow Methods

6

STUDY

OBJECTIVE

Explain the financial statement and tax effects of each of the inventory cost flow methods.

Each of the three cost flow methods is acceptable. For example, Black and Decker Manufacturing Company and Wendy's International currently use the FIFO method of inventory costing. Campbell Soup Company, Krogers, and Walgreen Drugs use LIFO for part or all of their inventory. Bristol-Myers-Squibb Co. and Motorola, Inc. use the average cost method. A company may also use more than one cost flow method at the same time. Del Monte Corporation, for example, uses LIFO for domestic inventories and FIFO for foreign inventories. Illustration 6-19 shows the use of the three cost flow methods in the 600 largest companies in the U.S. The reasons why companies adopt different inventory cost flow methods are varied, but they usually involve one of the following factors:

1. Income statement effects
2. Balance sheet effects
3. Tax effects

ILLUSTRATION 6-19

Use of cost flow methods in major U.S. companies

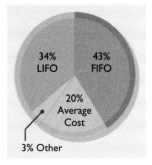

Income Statement Effects

To understand why companies might choose a particular cost flow method, let's examine the effects of the different flow assumptions on the financial statements of Bow Valley Electronics. The condensed income statements in Illustration 6-20 on page 249 assume that Bow Valley sold its 550 units for $11,500, its operating expenses were $2,000, and its income tax rate is 30%.

Although the cost of goods available for sale ($12,000) is the same under each of the three inventory cost flow methods, both the ending inventories and cost of goods sold are different. This difference is due to the unit costs that are allocated to cost of goods sold and to ending inventory. Each dollar of difference in ending inventory results in a corresponding dollar difference in income before income taxes. For Bow Valley, there is an $800 difference between FIFO and LIFO. In a period of inflation, FIFO produced a higher net income because the lower unit costs of the first units purchased are matched against revenues. In a period of rising prices (as is the case here), FIFO reports the highest net income ($2,310) and LIFO the lowest ($1,750); average cost falls in the middle ($2,030). If prices are falling, the results from the use of FIFO and LIFO are reversed. FIFO will report the lowest net income and LIFO the highest. To man-

BOW VALLEY ELECTRONICS **Condensed Income Statements**			
	FIFO	**LIFO**	**Average Cost**
Sales	$11,500	$11,500	$11,500
Beginning inventory	1,000	1,000	1,000
Purchases	11,000	11,000	11,000
Cost of goods available for sale	12,000	12,000	12,000
Ending inventory	5,800	5,000	5,400
Cost of goods sold	6,200	7,000	6,600
Gross profit	5,300	4,500	4,900
Operating expenses	2,000	2,000	2,000
Income before income taxes[2]	3,300	2,500	2,900
Income tax expense (30%)	990	750	870
Net income	$ 2,310	$ 1,750	$ 2,030

ILLUSTRATION 6-20

Comparative effects of cost flow methods

agement, higher net income is an advantage: it causes external users to view the company more favorably. In addition, if management bonuses are based on net income, FIFO will provide the basis for higher bonuses.

Some argue that the use of LIFO in a period of inflation enables the company to avoid reporting **paper or phantom profit** as economic gain. To illustrate, assume that Kralik Company buys 200 XR492s at $20 per unit on January 10 and 200 more on December 31 at $24 each. During the year, 200 units are sold at $30 each. The results under FIFO and LIFO are shown in Illustration 6-21.

	FIFO	**LIFO**
Sales (200 × $30)	$6,000	$6,000
Cost of goods sold	4,000 (200 × $20)	4,800 (200 × $24)
Gross profit	$2,000	$1,200

ILLUSTRATION 6-21

Income statement effects compared

Under LIFO, the company has recovered the current replacement cost ($4,800) of the units sold. Thus, the gross profit in economic terms is real. However, under FIFO, the company has recovered only the January 10 cost ($4,000). To replace the units sold, it must reinvest $800 (200 x $4) of the gross profit. Thus, $800 of the gross profit is said to be phantom or illusory. As a result, reported net income is also overstated in real terms.

Balance Sheet Effects
A major advantage of the FIFO method is that in a period of inflation, the costs allocated to ending inventory will approximate their current cost. For example, for Bow Valley, 400 of the 450 units in the ending inventory are costed at the November 27 unit cost of $13.

Conversely, a major shortcoming of the LIFO method is that in a period of inflation, the costs allocated to ending inventory may be significantly understated in terms of current cost. This is true for Bow Valley, where the cost of the

---

[2]It is assumed that Bow Valley is a corporation, and corporations are required to pay income taxes.

ending inventory includes the $10 unit cost of the beginning inventory. The understatement becomes greater over prolonged periods of inflation if the inventory includes goods purchased in one or more prior accounting periods.

Tax Effects

We have seen that both inventory on the balance sheet and net income on the income statement are higher when FIFO is used in a period of inflation. Yet, many companies have switched to LIFO. The reason is that LIFO results in the lowest income taxes (because of lower net income) during times of rising prices. For example, at Bow Valley Electronics, income taxes are $750 under LIFO, compared to $990 under FIFO. The tax saving of $240 makes more cash available for use in the business.

ACCOUNTING IN ACTION
Business Insight

Most small firms use the FIFO method. But fears of rising inflation often cause many firms to switch to LIFO. For example, Chicago Heights Steel Co. in Illinois boosted cash "by 5% to 10% by lowering income taxes" when it switched to LIFO. Electronic games distributor Atlas Distributing Inc., Chicago, considered a switch "because the costs of our games, made in Japan, are rising 15% a year," says Joseph Serpico, treasurer. When inflation heats up, "the number of companies electing LIFO will rise dramatically," says William Spiro of BDO Seidman, New York.

Using Inventory Cost Flow Methods Consistently

Whatever cost flow method a company chooses, it should be used consistently from one accounting period to another. Consistent application enhances the comparability of financial statements over successive time periods. In contrast, using the FIFO method in one year and the LIFO method in the next year would make it difficult to compare the net incomes of the two years.

Although consistent application is preferred, it does not mean that a company may *never* change its method of inventory costing. When a company adopts a different method, the change and its effects on net income should be disclosed in the financial statements. A typical disclosure is shown in Illustration 6-22, using information from recent financial statements of the Quaker Oats Company.

ILLUSTRATION 6-22

Disclosure of change in cost flow method

QUAKER OATS COMPANY
Notes to the Financial Statements

Note 1   Effective July 1, the Company adopted the LIFO cost flow assumption for valuing the majority of U.S. Grocery Products inventories. The Company believes that the use of the LIFO method better matches current costs with current revenues. The effect of this change on the current year was to decrease net income by $16.0 million.

ACCOUNTING IN ACTION
International Insight

U.S. companies typically choose between LIFO and FIFO. Many choose LIFO because it reduces inventory profits and taxes. However, the international community recently considered rules that would ban LIFO entirely and force companies to use FIFO. This proposal was defeated, but the issue will not go away.

The issue is sensitive. As John Wulff, controller for Union Carbide noted, "We were in support of the international effort up until the proposal to eliminate LIFO." Wulff says that if Union Carbide had been suddenly forced to switch from LIFO to FIFO, its reported $632 million pretax income would have jumped by $300 million. That would have increased Carbide's income tax bill by as much as $120 million. Given this, do you believe that accounting principles and rules should be the same around the world?

BEFORE YOU GO ON...

Review It

1. How do the cost and matching principles apply to inventoriable costs?
2. How are the three assumed cost flow methods applied in allocating inventoriable costs?
3. What factors should be considered by management in selecting an inventory cost flow method?
4. Which inventory cost flow method produces (a) the highest net income in a period of rising prices, and (b) the lowest income taxes?
5. What amount is reported by Kellogg Company in its 1998 Annual Report as inventories at December 31, 1998? Which inventory cost flow method does Kellogg Company use? The answer to this question is provided on p. 282.

Do It

The accounting records of Shumway Ag Implement show the following data:

Beginning inventory	4,000 units at $3
Purchases	6,000 units at $4
Sales	5,000 units at $12

Determine the cost of goods sold during the period under a periodic inventory system using (a) the FIFO method, (b) the LIFO method, and (c) the average cost method.

Reasoning: Because the units of inventory on hand and available for sale may have been purchased at different prices, a systematic method must be adopted to allocate the costs between the goods sold and the goods on hand (ending inventory).

Solution:
(a) FIFO: (4,000 @ $3) + (1,000 @ $4) = $12,000 + $4,000 = $16,000.
(b) LIFO: 5,000 @ $4 = $20,000.
(c) Average cost: [(4,000 @ $3) + (6,000 @ $4)] ÷ 10,000 = ($12,000 + $24,000) ÷
      10,000 = $3.60 per unit; 5,000 @ $3.60 = $18,000.

THE
NAVIGATOR

Related exercise material: BE6–6, BE6–7, E6–5, E6–6, E6–7.

VALUING INVENTORY AT THE LOWER OF COST OR MARKET (LCM)

When the value of inventory is lower than its cost, the inventory is written down to its market value. This is accomplished by valuing the inventory at the lower of cost or market (LCM) in the period in which the price decline occurs. LCM is an example of the accounting concept of conservatism. **Conservatism** means that when choosing among accounting alternatives, the best choice is to select the method that is least likely to overstate assets and net income.

Under the LCM basis, market is defined as current replacement cost, not selling price. For a merchandising company, market is the cost of purchasing the same goods at the present time from the usual suppliers in the usual quantities.

7
STUDY
OBJECTIVE

Explain the lower of cost or market basis of accounting for inventories.

Current replacement cost is used because a decline in the replacement cost of an item usually leads to a decline in the selling price of the item.

The lower of cost or market basis may be applied to individual items of inventory, major categories of inventory, or total inventory. For example, assume that Len's TV has the following lines of merchandise with costs and market values as indicated. LCM produces the following three results:

ILLUSTRATION 6-23

Alternative lower of cost or market results

| | | | Lower of Cost or Market by: | | |
	Cost	Market	Individual Items	Major Categories	Total Inventory
Television sets					
Consoles	$ 60,000	$ 55,000	$ 55,000		
Portables	45,000	52,000	45,000		
Total	105,000	107,000		$105,000	
Video equipment					
Recorders	48,000	45,000	45,000		
Movies	15,000	14,000	14,000		
Total	63,000	59,000		59,000	
Total inventory	$168,000	$166,000	$159,000	$164,000	$166,000

The amount entered in the individual items column is the lower of the cost or market amount for **each item**. For the major categories column, the amount is the lower of the total cost or total market for **each category**. Finally, the amount for the total inventory column is the lower of the cost or market for the **entire inventory**. The common practice is to use individual items in determining the LCM valuation. This approach gives the most conservative valuation for balance sheet purposes and also the lowest net income. LCM should be applied consistently from period to period.

LCM is applied to the items in inventory after one of the costing methods (specific identification, FIFO, LIFO, or average cost) has been applied to determine cost.

8

STUDY

OBJECTIVE

Indicate the effects of inventory errors on the financial statements.

INVENTORY ERRORS

Unfortunately, errors occasionally occur in taking or costing inventory. In some cases, errors are caused by failure to count or price the inventory correctly. In other cases, errors occur because proper recognition is not given to the transfer of legal title to goods that are in transit. When errors occur, they affect both the income statement and the balance sheet.

ACCOUNTING IN ACTION
Ethics Insight

 Sometimes a line of goods doesn't sell very well, then allegedly disappears or is destroyed by fire. Forensic accountants are increasingly called in by insurance companies to investigate staged theft or suspected arson cases. These accountants look at the degree of financial motivation for theft or arson, sales figures, obligations, profitability, and cash flow of the firm, in addition to various financial ratios such as the ones computed later in this chapter, to uncover fraud. Many forsenic accounting firms employ former police officers and criminologists with expertise in everything from surveillance to undercover work.

Income Statement Effects

Remember that both the beginning and ending inventories are used to determine cost of goods sold in a periodic system. The ending inventory of one period automatically becomes the beginning inventory of the next period. Inventory errors affect the determination of cost of goods sold and net income.

The effects on cost of goods sold can be determined by entering the incorrect data in the following formula and then substituting the correct data.

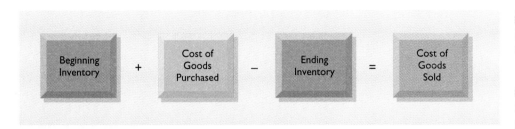

ILLUSTRATION 6-24

Formula for cost of goods sold

ETHICS NOTE

Inventory fraud includes pricing inventory at amounts in excess of their actual value, or claiming to have inventory when no inventory exists. Inventory fraud is usually done to overstate ending inventory, and so understate cost of goods sold and create higher income.

If beginning inventory is understated, cost of goods sold will be understated. On the other hand, an understatement of ending inventory will overstate cost of goods sold. The effects of inventory errors on the current year's income statement are shown in Illustration 6-25.

Inventory Error	Cost of Goods Sold	Net Income
Understate beginning inventory	Understated	Overstated
Overstate beginning inventory	Overstated	Understated
Understate ending inventory	Overstated	Understated
Overstate ending inventory	Understated	Overstated

ILLUSTRATION 6-25

Effects of inventory errors on current year's income statement

An error in ending inventory of the current period will have a **reverse effect on net income of the next accounting period**. This is shown in Illustration 6-26 on the next page. Note that the understatement of ending inventory in 2001 results in an understatement of beginning inventory in 2002 and an overstatement of net income in 2002.

Over the 2 years, total net income is correct because the errors offset one another. Notice that total income using incorrect data is $35,000 ($22,000 + $13,000), which is the same as the total income of $35,000 ($25,000 + $10,000) using correct data. Also note in this example that an error in the beginning inventory does not result in a corresponding error in the ending inventory for that period. The correctness of the ending inventory depends entirely on the accuracy of taking and costing the inventory at the balance sheet date.

Balance Sheet Effects

The effect of ending inventory errors on the balance sheet can be determined by using the basic accounting equation: assets equal liabilities plus stockholders' equity. The effects on these balance sheet elements of errors in the ending inventory are shown in Illustration 6-27 on page 254.

ILLUSTRATION 6-26

*Effects of inventory errors on
2 years' income statements*

Condensed Income Statement

	2001				2002			
	Incorrect		Correct		Incorrect		Correct	
Sales		$80,000		$80,000		$90,000		$90,000
Beginning inventory	$20,000		$20,000		$12,000		$15,000	
Cost of goods purchased	40,000		40,000		68,000		68,000	
Cost of goods available for sale	60,000		60,000		80,000		83,000	
Ending inventory	12,000		15,000		23,000		23,000	
Cost of goods sold		48,000		45,000		57,000		60,000
Gross profit		32,000		35,000		33,000		30,000
Operating expenses		10,000		10,000		20,000		20,000
Net income		$22,000		$25,000		$13,000		$10,000

($3,000)
Net income
understated

$3,000
Net income
overstated

Total income for
2 years is correct

ILLUSTRATION 6-27

*Ending inventory error—
balance sheet effects*

Ending Inventory Error	Assets	Liabilities	Stockholders' Equity
Overstated	Overstated	None	Overstated
Understated	Understated	None	Understated

The effect of an error in ending inventory on the subsequent period was shown in Illustration 6-26. Recall that if the error is not corrected, total net income for the two periods would be correct. Thus, total stockholders' equity reported on the balance sheet at the end of 2002 will also be correct.

STATEMENT PRESENTATION AND ANALYSIS

As indicated in an earlier chapter, inventory is classified as a current asset after receivables in the balance sheet, and cost of goods sold is subtracted from sales in a multiple-step income statement. In addition, there should be disclosure of (1) the major inventory classifications, (2) the basis of accounting (cost or lower of cost or market), and (3) the costing method (FIFO, LIFO, or average).

Kellogg Company, for example, in its December 31, 1998, balance sheet reported inventory of $451,400,000 under current assets. The accompanying notes to the financial statements, as shown in Illustration 6-28, disclosed the following information:

ILLUSTRATION 6-28

Inventory disclosures by Kellogg Company

KELLOGG COMPANY
Notes to the Financial Statements

Note 1. Accounting Policies
Inventories
Inventories are valued at the lower of cost (principally average) or market.

As indicated in this brief note, Kellogg Company values its inventories at the lower of cost or market using the average cost method to apply costs to inventory and cost of goods sold.

The amount of inventory carried by a company has significant economic consequences. On the one hand, management wants to have a great variety and quantity of inventory on hand so customers have the greatest selection and inventory items are always in stock. But, such an inventory policy may incur excessive carrying costs (e.g., investment, storage, insurance, taxes, obsolescence, and damage). On the other hand, low inventory levels lead to stockouts, lost sales, and disgruntled customers. Common ratios used in the management and evaluation of inventory levels are inventory turnover and a related measure, average days to sell the inventory.

The inventory turnover ratio measures the number of times on average the inventory is sold during the period. Its purpose is to measure the liquidity of the inventory. The inventory turnover is computed by dividing cost of goods sold by the average inventory during the period. Unless seasonal factors are significant, average inventory can be computed from the beginning and ending inventory balances. For example, Kellogg Company reported in its 1998 Annual Report an ending inventory of $451,400,000, a beginning inventory of $434,300,000, and cost of goods sold for the year 1998 of $3,282,600,000; its inventory turnover formula and computation are shown below:

STUDY
OBJECTIVE
Compute and interpret the inventory turnover ratio.

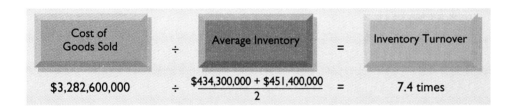

$$\text{Cost of Goods Sold} \div \text{Average Inventory} = \text{Inventory Turnover}$$

$$\$3,282,600,000 \div \frac{\$434,300,000 + \$451,400,000}{2} = 7.4 \text{ times}$$

A variant of the inventory turnover ratio is the **average days to sell inventory**. For example, the inventory turnover for Kellogg Company of 7.4 times divided into 365 is approximately 49 days. There are typical levels of inventory in every industry. However, companies that are able to keep their inventory at lower levels and higher turnovers and still satisfy customer needs are the most successful.

BEFORE YOU GO ON...

Review It

1. Why is it appropriate to report inventories at the lower of cost or market?
2. How do inventory errors affect financial statements?
3. What does the inventory turnover ratio reveal?

A LOOK BACK AT OUR FEATURE STORY

Refer back to the Feature Story concerning Mountain Equipment Co-op (MEC) and answer the following questions:

1. Why does Mountain Equipment Co-op use the weighted average cost flow method to determine inventory?
2. Should MEC consider changing from the periodic weighted average cost method to a perpetual inventory system to track inventory costs? Outline the advantages and disadvantages of such a change.

Solution

1. MEC uses the weighted average cost flow method, because of the:
   a. Large variation of its inventory items.
   b. Wide fluctuation in costs of these inventory items.
   c. Balancing out of the average cost over time.
2. MEC would find a perpetual inventory method useful to monitor its large number of inventory items. This is important with catalogue sales. When customers call to place an order, MEC would be able to tell them immediately whether or not the item is in stock. In addition, large fluctuations in the cost of each inventory item could be tracked to ensure that the selling price of the item is adjusted where necessary to recover its cost and any desired markup. Disadvantages of the perpetual inventory method would include the requirement for more recordkeeping than the current periodic inventory method. Scanners and new computing equipment might also be required if MEC were to move from a periodic to a perpetual inventory method. Prior financial statements utilized for comparison purposes would have to be restated to incorporate the impact of such a change, in addition to full disclosure in the notes to the financial statements in the year of the change, to avoid application of inconsistent relevant information.

THE NAVIGATOR

DEMONSTRATION PROBLEM

Kemwear Company has the following inventory, purchases, and sales data for the month of March:

Inventory, March 1		200 units @ $4.00	$ 800
Purchases:			
	March 10	500 units @ $4.50	2,250
	March 20	400 units @ $4.75	1,900
	March 30	300 units @ $5.00	1,500
Sales:			
	March 15	500 units	
	March 25	400 units	

The physical inventory count on March 31 shows 500 units on hand.

Instructions

Under a **periodic inventory system**, determine the cost of inventory on hand at March 31 and the cost of goods sold for March under the (a) first-in, first-out (FIFO) method, (b) last-in, first-out (LIFO) method, and (c) average cost method.

SOLUTION TO DEMONSTRATION PROBLEM

The cost of goods available for sale is $6,450:

Inventory		200 units @ $4.00	$ 800
Purchases:			
	March 10	500 units @ $4.50	2,250
	March 20	400 units @ $4.75	1,900
	March 30	300 units @ $5.00	1,500
	Total cost of goods available for sale		$6,450

Under a **periodic inventory system**, the cost of goods sold under each cost flow method is as follows:

FIFO Method

Ending Inventory:

Date	Units	Unit Cost	Total Cost	
March 30	300	$5.00	$1,500	
March 20	200	4.75	950	$2,450

Cost of goods sold: $6,450 − $2,450 = $4,000

LIFO Method

Ending Inventory:

Date	Units	Unit Cost	Total Cost	
March 1	200	$4.00	$ 800	
March 10	300	4.50	1,350	$2,150

Cost of goods sold: $6,450 − $2,150 = $4,300

Weighted Average Cost Method

Weighted average unit cost: $6,450 ÷ 1,400 = $4.607
Ending inventory: 500 × $4.607 = $2,303.50

Cost of goods sold: $6,450 − $2,303.50 = $4,146.50

PROBLEM-SOLVING STRATEGIES

1. For FIFO, the latest costs are allocated to inventory.
2. For LIFO, the earliest costs are allocated to inventory.
3. For average costs, use a weighted average for periodic.
4. Remember, the costs allocated to cost of goods sold can be proved.
5. Total purchases are the same under all three cost flow methods.

THE NAVIGATOR

SUMMARY OF STUDY OBJECTIVES

1. *Describe the steps in determining inventory quantities.* The steps in determining inventory quantities are (1) taking a physical inventory of goods on hand and (2) determining the ownership of goods in transit.

2. *Prepare the entries for purchases and sales of inventory under a periodic inventory system.* In recording purchases, entries are required for (a) cash and credit purchases, (b) purchase returns and allowances, (c) purchase discounts, and (d) freight costs. In recording sales, entries are required for (a) cash and credit sales, (b) sales returns and allowances, and (c) sales discounts.

3. *Determine cost of goods sold under a periodic inventory system.* The steps in determining cost of goods sold are (a) recording the purchase of merchandise, (b) determining the cost of goods purchased, and (c) determining the cost of goods on hand at the beginning and end of the accounting period.

4. *Identify the unique features of the income statement for a merchandising company using a periodic inventory system.* The income statement for a merchandising company contains three sections: sales revenue, cost of goods sold, and operating expenses. The cost of goods sold section under a periodic inventory system generally shows more detail by reporting beginning and ending inventory, net purchases, and total goods available for sale.

5. Explain the basis of accounting for inventories and describe the inventory cost flow methods. The primary basis of accounting for inventories is cost. Cost includes all expenditures necessary to acquire goods and place them in condition ready for sale. Inventoriable costs include (1) cost of beginning inventory and (2) the cost of goods purchased. The inventory cost flow methods are: specific identification, FIFO, LIFO, and average cost.

6. Explain the financial statement and tax effects of each of the inventory cost flow methods. The cost of goods available for sale may be allocated to cost of goods sold and ending inventory by specific identification or by a method based on an assumed cost flow. These methods have different effects on financial statements during periods of changing prices. When prices are rising, the first-in, first-out method (FIFO) results in lower cost of goods sold and higher net income than the average and the last-in, first-out (LIFO) methods. LIFO results in the lowest income taxes (because of lower net income). The reverse is true when prices are falling. In the balance sheet, FIFO results in an ending inventory that is closest to current value, whereas the inventory under LIFO is the farthest from current value.

7. Explain the lower of cost or market basis of accounting for inventories. The lower of cost or market basis (LCM) is used when the current replacement cost (market) is less than cost. Under LCM, the loss is recognized in the period in which the price decline occurs. LCM may be applied to individual inventory items, major categories of inventory, or to total inventory.

8. Indicate the effects of inventory errors on the financial statements. In the income statement of the current year: (a) an error in beginning inventory will have a reverse effect on net income (overstatement of inventory results in understatement of net income) and (b) an error in ending inventory will have a similar effect on net income (overstatement of inventory results in overstatement of net income). If ending inventory errors are not corrected in the following period, their effect on net income for that period is reversed, and total net income for the two years will be correct. In the balance sheet, ending inventory errors will have the same effect on total assets and total stockholders' equity and no effect on liabilities.

9. Compute and interpret the inventory turnover ratio. The inventory turnover ratio is calculated as cost of goods sold divided by average inventory. It can be converted to average days in inventory by dividing 365 days by the inventory turnover ratio. A higher turnover ratio or lower average days in inventory suggests that management is trying to keep inventory levels low relative to its sales level.

GLOSSARY
••

Average cost method An inventory costing method that assumes that the goods available for sale have the same (average) cost per unit; generally the inventory items are similar in nature (i.e., homogeneous). (p. 247).

Consigned goods Goods shipped by a consignor, who retains ownership, to another party called the consignee. (p. 235).

Cost of goods available for sale The sum of the beginning merchandise inventory plus the cost of goods purchased. (p. 240).

Cost of goods purchased The sum of net purchases plus freight-in. (p. 240).

Cost of goods sold The total cost of merchandise sold during the period, determined by subtracting ending inventory from the cost of goods available for sale. (p. 240).

Current replacement cost The amount that would be paid at the present time to acquire an identical item. (p. 251).

First-in, first-out method (FIFO) An inventory costing method that assumes that the costs of the earliest goods acquired are the first to be recognized as cost of goods sold. (p. 245).

Inventoriable costs The pool of costs that consists of two elements: (1) the cost of the beginning inventory and (2) the cost of goods purchased during the period. (p. 242).

Inventory turnover ratio A ratio that measures the number of times on average the inventory is sold during the period. It is computed by dividing cost of goods sold by the average inventory during the period. (p. 255).

Last-in, first-out method (LIFO) An inventory costing method that assumes that the costs of the latest units purchased are the first to be allocated to cost of goods sold. (p. 246).

Lower of cost or market basis (LCM) (inventories) A method of valuing inventory that recognizes the decline in the value when the current purchase price (market) is less than cost. (p. 251).

Net purchases Purchases less purchase returns and allowances and purchase discounts. (p. 240).

Periodic inventory system An inventory system in which inventoriable costs are allocated to ending inventory and cost of goods sold at the end of the period. Cost of goods sold is computed at the end of the period by subtracting the ending inventory (costs are assigned to a physical count of items on hand) from the cost of goods available for sale. (p. 236).

Specific identification method An actual physical flow costing method in which items still in inventory are specifically costed to arrive at the total cost of the ending inventory. (p. 243).

APPENDIX 6A ESTIMATING INVENTORIES

We have assumed throughout the chapter that a company would be able to do a physical count of its inventory. But what if it cannot, as in the example of the lumber inventory destroyed by fire? In that case, we would use an estimate.

Two circumstances explain the reasons for estimating rather than counting inventories. First, management may want monthly or quarterly financial statements but a physical inventory is taken only annually. Second, a casualty such as fire, flood, or earthquake may make it impossible to take a physical inventory. The need for estimating inventories is associated primarily with a periodic inventory system because of the absence of detailed inventory records.

There are two widely used methods of estimating inventories: (1) the gross profit method and (2) the retail inventory method.

10
STUDY
OBJECTIVE

Describe the two methods of estimating inventories.

GROSS PROFIT METHOD

The gross profit method estimates the cost of ending inventory by applying a gross profit rate to net sales. It is used in preparing monthly financial statements under a periodic system when physical inventories are not taken. This method is a relatively simple but effective estimation technique. Accountants, auditors, and managers frequently use the gross profit method to test the reasonableness of the ending inventory amount. This method will detect large errors. To use this method, a company needs to know its net sales, cost of goods available for sale, and gross profit rate. The company then uses the gross profit rate to estimate its gross profit for the accounting period. The formulas for using the gross profit method are given in Illustration 6A-1.

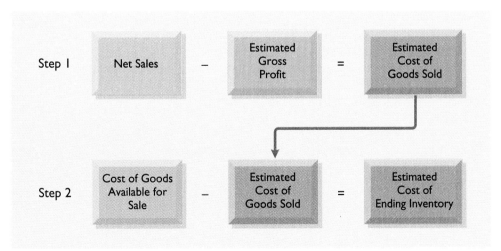

ILLUSTRATION 6A-1

Gross profit method formulas

To illustrate, assume that Williams Company wishes to prepare an income statement for the month of January, when its records show net sales $200,000; beginning inventory $40,000; and cost of goods purchased $120,000. In the preceding year, the company realized a 30% gross profit rate, and it expects to earn the same rate this year. Given these facts and assumptions, the estimated cost of the ending inventory at January 31 under the gross profit method is $20,000, computed as shown in Illustration 6A-2 on page 260.

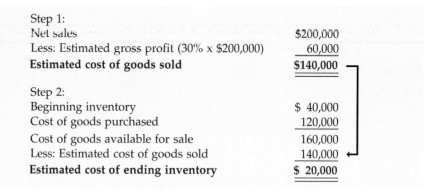

Step 1:	
Net sales	$200,000
Less: Estimated gross profit (30% x $200,000)	60,000
Estimated cost of goods sold	**$140,000**
Step 2:	
Beginning inventory	$ 40,000
Cost of goods purchased	120,000
Cost of goods available for sale	160,000
Less: Estimated cost of goods sold	140,000
Estimated cost of ending inventory	**$ 20,000**

The gross profit method is based on the assumption that the rate of gross profit will remain constant from one year to the next. It may not remain constant, though, because of a change either in merchandising policies or in market conditions. In such cases, the rate of the prior period should be adjusted to reflect current operating conditions. In some cases, a more accurate estimate may be obtained by applying this method on a department or product-line basis.

The gross profit method should not be used in preparing a company's financial statements at the end of the year. These statements should be based on a physical inventory count.

RETAIL INVENTORY METHOD

A retail store such as Kmart, Ace Hardware, or Wal-Mart has thousands of different types of merchandise at low unit costs. In such cases the application of unit costs to inventory quantities is difficult and time-consuming. An alternative is to use the retail inventory method to estimate the cost of inventory. In most retail concerns, a relationship between cost and sales price can be established. Under the retail inventory method, the cost to retail percentage is then applied to the ending inventory at retail prices to determine inventory at cost.

To use the retail inventory method, a company must maintain records that show both the cost and retail value of the goods available for sale. Under the retail inventory method, the estimated cost of the ending inventory is derived from the formulas presented in Illustration 6A-3.

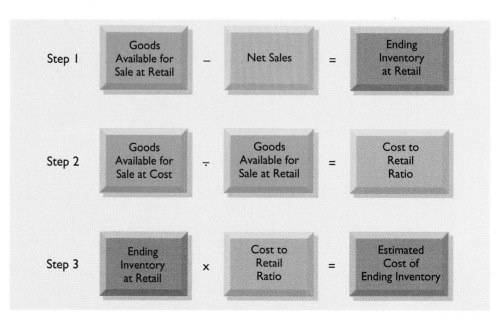

The logic of the retail method can be demonstrated by using unit cost data. Assume that 10 units purchased at $7.00 each are marked to sell for $10 per unit. Thus, the cost to retail ratio is 70% ($70 : $100). If 4 units remain unsold, their retail value is $40 and their cost is $28 ($40 × 70%), which agrees with the total cost of goods on hand on a per unit basis (4 × $7).

The application of the retail method based on the accounting records and supplementary data for Lacy Co. is shown in Illustration 6A-4. Note that it is not necessary to take a physical inventory to determine the estimated cost of goods on hand at any given time.

	At Cost	At Retail
Beginning inventory	$14,000	$ 21,500
Goods purchased	61,000	78,500
Goods available for sale	$75,000	100,000
Net sales		70,000
(1) Ending inventory at retail		$ 30,000

ILLUSTRATION 6A-4

Example of retail inventory method

(2) Cost to retail ratio = ($75,000 ÷ $100,000) = 75%
(3) Estimated cost of ending inventory = ($30,000 × 75%) $22,500

The retail inventory method also facilitates taking a physical inventory at the end of year. With this method, the goods on hand can be valued at the prices marked on the merchandise. The cost to retail ratio is then applied to the goods actually on hand at retail to determine the ending inventory at cost.

HELPFUL HINT

In determining inventory at retail, selling prices on the units are used, and tracing actual unit costs to invoices is unnecessary.

The major disadvantage of the retail method is that it is an averaging technique. It may produce an incorrect inventory valuation if the mix of the ending inventory is not representative of the mix in the goods available for sale. Assume, for example, that the cost to retail ratio of 75% in the Lacy Co. consists of equal proportions of inventory items that have cost to retail ratios of 70%, 75%, and 80%, respectively. If the ending inventory contains only items with a 70% ratio, an incorrect inventory cost will result. This problem can be minimized by applying the retail method on a departmental or product-line basis.

SUMMARY OF STUDY OBJECTIVES FOR APPENDIX 6A

10. *Describe the two methods of estimating inventories.* The two methods of estimating inventories are the gross profit method and the retail inventory method. Under the gross profit method, a gross profit rate is applied to net sales to determine estimated cost of goods sold. Estimated cost of goods sold is then subtracted from cost of goods available for sale to determine the estimated cost of the ending inventory. Under the retail inventory method, a cost to retail ratio is computed by dividing the cost of goods available for sale by the retail value of the goods available for sale. This ratio is then applied to the ending inventory at retail to determine the estimated cost of the ending inventory.

GLOSSARY FOR APPENDIX 6A

Gross profit method A method for estimating the cost of the ending inventory by applying a gross profit rate to net sales. (p. 259).

Retail inventory method A method used to estimate the cost of the ending inventory by applying a cost to retail ratio to the ending inventory at retail. (p. 260).

APPENDIX 6B   INVENTORY COST FLOW METHODS IN PERPETUAL INVENTORY SYSTEMS

11

STUDY

OBJECTIVE

Apply the inventory cost flow methods to perpetual inventory records.

Each of the inventory cost flow methods described in the chapter for a periodic inventory system may be used in a perpetual inventory system. To illustrate the application of the three assumed cost flow methods (FIFO, LIFO, and average cost), we will use the data shown below and in this chapter for Bow Valley Electronics' product Z202 Astro Condenser.

BOW VALLEY ELECTRONICS
Z202 Astro Condensers

Date	Explanation	Units	Unit Cost	Total Cost	Balance in Units
1/1	Beginning inventory	100	$10	$ 1,000	100
4/15	Purchases	200	11	2,200	300
8/24	Purchases	300	12	3,600	600
9/10	Sales	550			50
11/27	Purchases	400	13	5,200	450
				$12,000	

ILLUSTRATION 6B-1

Inventoriable units and costs

FIRST-IN, FIRST-OUT (FIFO)

Under FIFO, the cost of the earliest goods on hand prior to each sale is charged to cost of goods sold. Therefore, the cost of goods sold on September 10 consists of the units on hand January 1 and the units purchased April 15 and August 24. The inventory on a FIFO method perpetual system is shown in Illustration 6B-2.

ILLUSTRATION 6B-2

Perpetual system—FIFO

Date	Purchases	Sales	Balance
January 1			(100 @ $10) $1,000
April 15	(200 @ $11) $2,200		(100 @ $10) ⎱ $3,200 (200 @ $11) ⎰
August 24	(300 @ $12) $3,600		(100 @ $10) ⎫ (200 @ $11) ⎬ $6,800 (300 @ $12) ⎭
September 10		(100 @ $10) (200 @ $11) (250 @ $12) ‾‾‾‾‾‾ $6,200	(50 @ $12) $ 600
November 27	(400 @ $13) $5,200		(50 @ $12) ⎱ $5,800 (400 @ $13) ⎰

The ending inventory in this situation is $5,800 and the cost of goods sold is $6,200 [(100 @ $10) + (200 @ $11) + (250 @ $12)].

The results under FIFO in a perpetual system are the **same as in a periodic system** (see Illustration 6-10 on page 245 where, similarly, the ending inventory is $5,800 and cost of goods sold is $6,200). Regardless of the system, the first costs in are the costs assigned to cost of goods sold.

LAST-IN, FIRST-OUT (LIFO)

Under the LIFO method using a perpetual system, the cost of the most recent purchase prior to sale is allocated to the units sold. Therefore, the cost of the goods sold on September 10 consists of all the units from the August 24 and April 15 purchases and 50 of the units in beginning inventory. The ending inventory on a LIFO method is computed in Illustration 6B-3.

ILLUSTRATION 6B-3

Perpetual system—LIFO

Date	Purchases		Sales	Balance	
January 1				(100 @ $10)	$1,000
April 15	(200 @ $11)	$2,200		(100 @ $10) (200 @ $11)	$3,200
August 24	(300 @ $12)	$3,600		(100 @ $10) (200 @ $11) (300 @ $12)	$6,800
September 10			(300 @ $12) (200 @ $11) (50 @ $10)	(50 @ $10)	$ 500
			$6,300		
November 27	(400 @ $13)	$5,200		(50 @ $10) (400 @ $13)	$5,700

The use of LIFO in a perpetual system will usually produce cost allocations that differ from using LIFO in a periodic system. In a perpetual system, the latest units incurred prior to each sale are allocated to cost of goods sold. In contrast, in a periodic system, the latest units incurred during the period are allocated to cost of goods sold. Thus, when a purchase is made after the last sale, the LIFO periodic system will apply this purchase to the previous sale. See Illustration 6-15 on page 247 where the proof shows the 400 units @ $13 purchased on November 27 applied to the sale of 550 units on September 10.

As shown above under the LIFO perpetual system, the 400 units @ $13 purchased on November 27 are all applied to the ending inventory.

The ending inventory in this LIFO perpetual illustration is $5,700 and cost of goods sold is $6,300, as compared to the LIFO periodic illustration where the ending inventory is $5,000 and cost of goods sold is $7,000.

AVERAGE COST

The average cost method in a perpetual inventory system is called the moving average method. Under this method a new average is computed **after each purchase**. The average cost is computed by dividing the cost of goods available for sale by the units on hand. The average cost is then applied to: (1) the units sold, to determine the cost of goods sold, and (2) the remaining units on hand, to determine the ending inventory amount. The application of the average cost method by Bow Valley Electronics is shown in Illustration 6B-4.

ILLUSTRATION 6B-4

Perpetual system—average cost method

Date	Purchases	Sales	Balance	
January 1			(100 @ $10)	$1,000
April 15	(200 @ $11) $2,200		(300 @ $10.667)	$3,200
August 24	(300 @ $12) $3,600		(600 @ $11.333)	$6,800
September 10		(550 @ $11.333) ($6,233)	(50 @ $11.333)	$ 567
November 27	(400 @ $13) $5,200		(450 @ $12.816)	$5,767

As indicated above, **a new average is computed each time a purchase is made**. On April 15, after 200 units are purchased for $2,200, a total of 300 units costing $3,200 ($1,000 + $2,200) are on hand. The average unit cost is $10.667 ($3,200 ÷ 300). On August 24, after 300 units are purchased for $3,600, a total of 600 units costing $6,800 ($1,000 + $2,200 + $3,600) are on hand at an average cost per unit of $11.333 ($6,800 ÷ 600). This unit cost of $11.333 is used in costing sales until another purchase is made, when a new unit cost is computed. Accordingly, the unit cost of the 550 units sold on September 10 is $11.333, and the total cost of goods sold is $6,233. On November 27, following the purchase of 400 units for $5,200, there are 450 units on hand costing $5,767 ($567 + $5,200) with a new average cost of $12.816 ($5,767 ÷ 450).

This moving average cost under the perpetual inventory system should be compared to Illustration 6-17 on page 247 showing the weighted average method under a periodic inventory system.

DEMONSTRATION PROBLEM

The Demonstration Problem on pages 256–57 showed cost of goods sold computations under a periodic inventory system. Now let's assume that Kemwear Company uses a perpetual inventory system and has the same inventory, purchases, and sales data for the month of March as shown earlier:

Inventory, March 1	200 units @ $4.00	$ 800
Purchases:		
March 10	500 units @ $4.50	2,250
March 20	400 units @ $4.75	1,900
March 30	300 units @ $5.00	1,500
Sales:		
March 15	500 units	
March 25	400 units	

The physical inventory count on March 31 shows 500 units on hand.

PROBLEM-SOLVING STRATEGIES

1. For FIFO, the latest costs are allocated to inventory.
2. For LIFO, the earliest costs are allocated to inventory.
3. For average costs, use a weighted average for periodic and a moving average for perpetual.
4. Remember, the costs allocated to cost of goods sold can be proved.
5. Total purchases are the same under all three cost flow methods.

Insturctions

Under a **perpetual inventory system**, determine the cost of inventory on hand at March 31 and the cost of goods sold for March under the (a) first-in, first-out (FIFO) method, (b) last-in, first-out (LIFO) method, and (c) average cost method.

SOLUTION TO DEMONSTRATION PROBLEM

The cost of goods available for sale is $6,450:

Inventory	200 units @ $4.00	$ 800
Purchases:		
March 10	500 units @ $4.50	2,250
March 20	400 units @ $4.75	1,900
March 30	300 units @ $5.00	1,500
Total cost of goods available for sale		$6,450

Under a **perpetual inventory system**, the cost of goods sold under each cost flow method is as follows:

FIFO Method

Date	Purchases		Sales		Balance	
March 1					(200 @ $4.00)	$ 800
March 10	(500 @ $4.50)	$2,250			(200 @ $4.00) ⎱ (500 @ $4.50) ⎰	$3,050
March 15			(200 @ $4.00) (300 @ $4.50) ——— $2,150		(200 @ $4.50)	$ 900
March 20	(400 @ $4.75)	$1,900			(200 @ $4.50) ⎱ (400 @ $4.75) ⎰	$2,800
March 25			(200 @ $4.50) (200 @ $4.75) ——— $1,850		(200 @ $4.75)	$ 950
March 30	(300 @ $5.00)	$1,500			(200 @ $4.75) ⎱ (300 @ $5.00) ⎰	$2,450

Ending inventory $2,450. Cost of goods sold: $6,450 − $2,450 = $4,000

LIFO Method

Date	Purchases		Sales		Balance	
March 1					(200 @ $4.00)	$ 800
March 10	(500 @ $4.50)	$2,250			(200 @ $4.00) ⎱ (500 @ $4.50) ⎰	$3,050
March 15			(500 @ $4.50)	$2,250	(200 @ $4.00)	$ 800
March 20	(400 @ $4.75)	$1,900			(200 @ $4.00) ⎱ (400 @ $4.75) ⎰	$2,700
March 25			(400 @ $4.75)	$1,900	(200 @ $4.00)	$ 800
March 30	(300 @ $5.00)	$1,500			(200 @ $4.00) ⎱ (300 @ $5.00) ⎰	$2,300

Ending inventory $2,300. Cost of goods sold: $6,450 − $2,300 = $4,150

Moving Average Cost Method

Date	Purchases		Sales		Balance	
March 1					(200 @ $4.00)	$ 800
March 10	(500 @ $4.50)	$2,250			(700 @ $4.357)	$3,050
March 15			(500 @ $4.357)	$2,179	(200 @ $4.357)	$ 871
March 20	(400 @ $4.75)	$1,900			(600 @ $4.618)	$2,771
March 25			(400 @ $4.618)	$1,847	(200 @ $4.618)	$ 924
March 30	(300 @ $5.00)	$1,500			(500 @ $4.848)	$2,424

Ending inventory $2,424. Cost of goods sold: $6,450 − $2,424 = $4,026

SUMMARY OF STUDY OBJECTIVES FOR APPENDIX 6B

11. *Apply the inventory cost flow methods to perpetual inventory records.* Under FIFO, the cost of the earliest goods on hand prior to each sale is charged to cost of goods sold. Under LIFO, the cost of the most recent purchase prior to sale is charged to cost of goods sold. Under the average cost method, a new average cost is computed after each purchase.

GLOSSARY FOR APPENDIX 6B

Moving average method The average cost method used in a perpetual inventory system; computes a new average after each purchase, and this new average is applied to the units sold and the remaining units on hand. (p. 263).

*Note: All asterisked Questions, Exercises, and Problems relate to material in the appendixes to the chapter.

SELF-STUDY QUESTIONS

Answers are at the end of the chapter.

(SO 2) 1. When goods are purchased for resale by a company using a periodic inventory system:
  a. purchases on account are debited to Merchandise Inventory.
  b. purchases on account are debited to Purchases.
  c. purchase returns are debited to Purchase Returns and Allowances.
  d. freight costs are debited to Purchases.

(SO 3) 2. In determining cost of goods sold (periodic system):
  a. purchases discounts are deducted from net purchases.
  b. freight-out is added to net purchases.
  c. purchase returns and allowances are deducted from net purchases.
  d. freight-in is added to net purchases.

(SO 3) 3. If beginning inventory is $60,000, cost of goods purchased is $380,000, and ending inventory is $50,000, cost of goods sold is:
  a. $390,000.   c. $330,000.
  b. $370,000.   d. $420,000.

(SO 1) 4. Which of the following should *not* be included in the physical inventory of a company?
  a. Goods held on consignment from another company.
  b. Goods shipped on consignment to another company.
  c. Goods in transit from another company shipped FOB shipping point.
  d. None of the above.

(SO 5) 5. Inventoriable costs consist of two elements: beginning inventory and
  a. ending inventory.
  b. cost of goods purchased.
  c. cost of goods sold.
  d. cost of goods available for sale.

(SO 5) 6. Electrolux Company has the following:

	Units	Unit Cost
Inventory, Jan. 1	8,000	$11
Purchase, June 19	13,000	12
Purchase, Nov. 8	5,000	13

If 9,000 units are on hand at December 31, the cost of the ending inventory under FIFO is:
  a. $99,000.   c. $113,000.
  b. $108,000.   d. $117,000.

(SO 5) 7. Using the data in (6) above, the cost of the ending inventory under LIFO is:
  a. $113,000.   c. $99,000.
  b. $108,000.   d. $100,000.

(SO 6) 8. In periods of rising prices, LIFO will produce:
  a. higher net income than FIFO.
  b. the same net income as FIFO.
  c. lower net income than FIFO.
  d. higher net income than average costing.

(SO 6) 9. Factors that affect the selection of an inventory costing method do *not* include:
  a. tax effects.
  b. balance sheet effects.
  c. income statement effects.
  d. perpetual vs. periodic inventory system.

(SO 7) 10. The lower of cost or market basis may be applied to:
  a. categories of inventories.
  b. individual items of inventories.
  c. total inventory.
  d. all of the above.

(SO 8) 11. Peugeot Company's ending inventory is understated $4,000. The effects of this error on the current year's cost of goods sold and net income, respectively, are:
  a. understated, overstated.
  b. overstated, understated.
  c. overstated, overstated.
  d. understated, understated.

(SO 9) 12. Which of these would cause the inventory turnover ratio to increase the most?
  a. Increasing the amount of inventory on hand.
  b. Keeping the amount of inventory on hand constant but increasing sales.
  c. Keeping the amount of inventory on hand constant but decreasing sales.
  d. Decreasing the amount of inventory on hand and increasing sales.

*13. Volvo Company has sales of $150,000 and cost of goods (SO 9) available for sale of $135,000. If the gross profit rate is 30%, the estimated cost of the ending inventory under the gross profit method is:
  a. $15,000.
  b. $30,000.
  c. $45,000.
  d. $75,000.

*14. In a perpetual inventory system, (SO
  a. LIFO cost of goods sold will be the same as in a periodic inventory system.
  b. average costs are based entirely on unit cost averages.
  c. a new average is computed under the average cost method after each sale.
  d. FIFO cost of goods sold will be the same as in a periodic inventory system.

THE
NAVIGATOR

QUESTIONS

1. Goods costing $1,700 are purchased on account on July 15 with credit terms of 2/10, n/30. On July 18 a $200 credit memo is received from the supplier for damaged goods. Give the journal entry on July 24 to record payment of the balance due within the discount period.

2. Identify the accounts that are added to or deducted from purchases to determine the cost of goods purchased. For each account, indicate (a) whether it is added or deducted and (b) its normal balance.

3. In the following separate mini cases, using a periodic inventory system, identify the item(s) designated by letter.
   (a) Purchases − X − Y = Net purchases.
   (b) Cost of goods purchased − Net purchases = X.
   (c) Beginning inventory + X = Cost of goods available for sale.
   (d) Cost of goods available for sale − Cost of goods sold = X.

4. "The key to successful business operations is effective inventory management." Do you agree? Explain.

5. An item must possess two characteristics to be classified as inventory by a merchandiser. What are these two characteristics?

6. Your friend Tom Wetzel has been hired to help take the physical inventory in Hitachi Hardware Store. Explain to Tom Wetzel what this job will entail.

7. (a) Janine Company ships merchandise to Laura Company on December 30. The merchandise reaches the buyer on January 6. Indicate the terms of sale that will result in the goods being included in (1) Janine's December 31 inventory, and (2) Laura's December 31 inventory.
   (b) Under what circumstances should Janine Company include consigned goods in its inventory?

8. Mary Ann's Hat Shop received a shipment of hats for which it paid the wholesaler $2,940. The price of the hats was $3,000, but Mary Ann's was given a $60 cash discount and required to pay freight charges of $80. In addition, Mary Ann's paid $130 to cover the travel expenses of an employee who negotiated the purchase of the hats. What amount will Mary Ann record for inventory? Why?

9. What is the primary basis of accounting for inventories? What is the major objective in accounting for inventories? What accounting principles are involved here?

10. Identify the distinguishing features of an income statement for a merchandising company.

11. Roland Carlson believes that the allocation of inventoriable costs should be based on the actual physical flow of the goods. Explain to Roland why this may be both impractical and inappropriate.

12. What is a major advantage and a major disadvantage of the specific identification method of inventory costing?

13. "The selection of an inventory cost flow method is a decision made by accountants." Do you agree? Explain. Once a method has been selected, what accounting requirement applies?

14. Which assumed inventory cost flow method:
    (a) usually parallels the actual physical flow of merchandise?
    (b) assumes that goods available for sale during an accounting period are homogeneous?
    (c) assumes that the latest units purchased are the first to be sold?

15. In a period of rising prices, the inventory reported in Jim Groat Company's balance sheet is close to the current cost of the inventory, whereas Greg Hanson Company's inventory is considerably below its current cost. Identify the inventory cost flow method being used by each company. Which company has probably been reporting the higher gross profit?

16. Char Lewis Company has been using the FIFO cost flow method during a prolonged period of inflation. During the same time period, Char Lewis has been paying out all of its net income as dividends. What adverse effects may result from this policy?

17. Bob Thebeau is studying for the next accounting midterm examination. What should Bob know about (a) departing from the cost basis of accounting for inventories and (b) the meaning of "market" in the lower of cost or market method?

18. John Hohenberger Music Center has 5 CD players on hand at the balance sheet date that cost $400 each. The current replacement cost is $320 per unit. Under the lower of cost or market basis of accounting for inventories, what value should be reported for the CD players on the balance sheet? Why?

19. What methods may be used under the lower of cost or market basis of accounting for inventories? Which method will produce the lowest inventory value?

20. Elaine Stahl Company discovers in 2001 that its ending inventory at December 31, 2000, was $5,000 understated. What effect will this error have on (a) 2000 net income, (b) 2001 net income, and (c) the combined net income for the 2 years?

21. Maureen & Nathan Company's balance sheet shows Inventories $162,800. What additional disclosures should be made?

22. Under what circumstances might the inventory turnover ratio be too high; that is, what possible negative consequences might occur?

*23. When is it necessary to estimate inventories?

*24. Both the gross profit method and the retail inventory method are based on averages. For each method, indicate the average used, how it is determined, and how it is applied.

*25. Jana Kingston Company has net sales of $400,000 and cost of goods available for sale of $300,000. If the gross profit rate is 30%, what is the estimated cost of the ending inventory? Show computations.

*26. John Ross Shoe Shop had goods available for sale in 2001 with a retail price of $120,000. The cost of these goods was $84,000. If sales during the period were $90,000, what is the ending inventory at cost using the retail inventory method?

*27. "When perpetual inventory records are kept, the results under the FIFO and LIFO methods are the same as they would be in a periodic inventory system." Do you agree? Explain.

*28. How does the average method of inventory costing differ between a perpetual inventory system and a periodic inventory system?

BRIEF EXERCISES

Journalize purchase transactions.
(SO 2)

BE6–1 Prepare the journal entries to record the following transactions on Svenska Company's books using a periodic inventory system.

(a) On March 2, Svenska Company purchased $900,000 of merchandise from Sing Tao Company, terms 2/10, n/30.

(b) On March 6, Svenska Company returned $130,000 of the merchandise purchased on March 2 because it was defective.

(c) On March 12, Svenska Company paid the balance due to Sing Tao Company.

Compute net purchases and cost of goods purchased.
(SO 3)

BE6–2 Assume that Shinhan Company uses a periodic inventory system and has the following account balances: Purchases $440,000, Purchase Returns and Allowances $11,000, Purchase Discounts $8,000, and Freight-in $16,000. Determine (a) net purchases and (b) cost of goods purchased.

Compute cost of goods sold and gross profit.
(SO 3)

BE6–3 Assume the same information as in BE6-2, and also that Shinhan Company has beginning inventory of $60,000, ending inventory of $90,000, and net sales of $650,000. Determine the amounts to be reported for cost of goods sold and gross profit.

Identify items to be included in taking a physical inventory.
(SO 1)

BE6–4 Oriental Press Company identifies the following items for possible inclusion in the taking of a physical inventory. Indicate whether each item should be included or excluded from the inventory taking.

1. Goods shipped on consignment by Oriental Press to another company.
2. Goods in transit from a supplier shipped FOB destination.
3. Goods sold but being held for customer pickup.
4. Goods held on consignment from another company.

Identify the components of inventoriable costs.
(SO 5)

BE6–5 The ledger of Norway Company includes the following items: (1) Freight-in, (2) Purchase Returns and Allowances, (3) Purchases, (4) Sales Discounts, (5) Purchase Discounts. Identify which items are included in inventoriable costs.

Compute ending inventory using FIFO and LIFO.
(SO 5)

BE6–6 In its first month of operations, Finlandia Company made three purchases of merchandise in the following sequence: (1) 300 units at $6, (2) 400 units at $7, and (3) 300 units at $8. Assuming there are 400 units on hand, compute the cost of the ending inventory under the (1) FIFO method and (2) LIFO method. Finlandia uses a periodic inventory system.

Compute the ending inventory using average costs.
(SO 5)

BE6–7 Data for Finlandia Company are presented in BE6-6. Compute the cost of the ending inventory under the average cost method, assuming there are 400 units on hand.

Determine the LCM valuation using inventory categories.
(SO 7)

BE6–8 Germania Appliance Center accumulates the following cost and market data at December 31:

Inventory Categories	Cost Data	Market Data
Cameras	$12,000	$10,200
Camcorders	9,000	9,700
VCRs	14,000	12,800

Compute the lower of cost or market valuation using categories.

Determine correct income statement amounts.
(SO 8)

BE6–9 Italy Company reports net income of $90,000 in 2001. However, ending inventory was understated $7,000. What is the correct net income for 2001? What effect, if any, will this error have on total assets as reported in the balance sheet at December 31, 2001?

Compute inventory turnover ratio and days in inventory.
(SO 9)

BE6–10 At December 31, 2001, the following information was available for Aurora Company: ending inventory $80,000; beginning inventory $60,000; cost of goods sold $210,000; and sales revenue $280,000. Calculate the inventory turnover ratio and days in inventory for Au rora Company.

Apply the gross profit method. (SO 10)

*BE6–11 At May 31, Poland Company has net sales of $300,000 and cost of goods available for sale of $230,000. Compute the estimated cost of the ending inventory assuming the gross profit rate is 40%.

Apply the retail inventory method. (SO 10)

*BE6–12 On June 30, French Fabrics has the following data pertaining to the retail inventory method: Goods available for sale: at cost $35,000, at retail $50,000; net sales $30,000, and ending inventory at retail $20,000. Compute the estimated cost of the ending inventory using the retail inventory method.

Apply cost flow methods to records. (SO 11)

*BE6–13 Spain Department Store uses a perpetual inventory system. Data for product E2–D2 include the following purchases:

Date	Number of Units	Unit Price
May 7	50	$10
July 28	30	15

On June 1 Spain sold 30 units, and on August 27, 33 more units. Prepare the perpetual inventory card for the above transactions using (1) FIFO, (2) LIFO, and (3) average cost.

EXERCISES

Journalize purchases transactions. (SO 2)

E6–1 Presented below is the following information related to Brazil Co.

1. On April 5, purchased merchandise from Chile Company for $18,000 terms 2/10, net/30, FOB shipping point.
2. On April 6, paid freight costs of $800 on merchandise purchased from Chile.
3. On April 7, purchased equipment on account for $26,000.
4. On April 8, returned damaged merchandise to Chile Company and was granted a $3,000 allowance.
5. On April 15, paid the amount due to Chile Company in full.

Instructions
(a) Prepare the journal entries to record these transactions on the books of Brazil Co. using a periodic inventory system.
(b) Assume that Brazil Co. paid the balance due to Chile Company on May 4 instead of April 15. Prepare the journal entry to record this payment.

Prepare cost of goods sold section. (SO 3)

E6–2 The trial balance of Colombia Company at the end of its fiscal year, August 31, 2001, includes the following accounts: Merchandise Inventory $17,200, Purchases $142,400, Sales $190,000, Freight-in $4,000, Sales Returns and Allowances $3,000, Freight-out $1,000, and Purchase Returns and Allowances $2,000. The ending (August 31, 2001) merchandise inventory is $27,000.

Instructions
Prepare a cost of goods sold section for the year ending August 31 (periodic inventory).

Prepare an income statement. (SO 4)

E6–3 Presented is information related to Mexico Co. for the month of January 2001.

Freight-in	$ 10,000	Rent expense	19,000
Freight-out	5,000	Salary expense	61,000
Insurance expense	12,000	Sales discounts	8,000
Purchases	200,000	Sales returns and allowances	13,000
Purchase discounts	3,000	Sales	312,000
Purchase returns and allowances	6,000		

Beginning merchandise inventory was $42,000 and ending inventory was $63,000.

Instructions
Prepare an income statement using the format presented on page 241 (Illustration 6-6). Operating expenses should not be segregated into selling and administrative expenses.

Determine the correct inventory amount. (SO 1)

E6–4 Yorkville Bank and Trust is considering giving Canada Company a loan. Before doing so, they decide that further discussions with Canada's accountant may be desirable. One area of particular concern is the inventory account, which has a year-end balance of $297,000. Discussions with the accountant reveal the following:

1. Canada sold goods costing $38,000 to Moghul Company FOB shipping point on December 28. The goods are not expected to arrive in India until January 12. The goods were not included in the physical inventory because they were not in the warehouse.

2. The physical count of the inventory did not include goods costing $95,000 that were shipped to Canada FOB destination on December 27, and were still in transit at year-end.

3. Canada received goods costing $25,000 on January 2. The goods were shipped FOB shipping point on December 26 by Cellar Co. The goods were not included in the physical count.

4. Canada sold goods costing $40,000 to Sterling of Mexico FOB destination on December 30. The goods were received in Mexico on January 8. They were not included in Canada's physical inventory.

5. Canada received goods costing $44,000 on January 2 that were shipped FOB destination on December 29. The shipment was a rush order that was supposed to arrive December 31. This purchase was included in the ending inventory of $297,000.

Instructions
Determine the correct inventory amount on December 31.

Compute inventory and cost of goods sold using FIFO and LIFO.
(SO 5)

E6–5   Egypt Co. uses a periodic inventory system. Its records show the following for the month of May, in which 78 units were sold.

		Units	Unit Cost	Total Cost
May 1	Inventory	30	$ 8	$240
15	Purchases	25	10	250
24	Purchases	35	13	455
	Totals	90		$945

Instructions
Compute the ending inventory at May 31 using the FIFO and LIFO methods. Prove the amount allocated to cost of goods sold under each method.

Compute inventory and cost of goods sold using FIFO and LIFO.
(SO 5, 6)

E6–6   In June, Luxemburg Company reports the following for the month of June.

		Units	Unit Cost	Total Cost
June 1	Inventory	200	$5	$1,000
12	Purchases	300	6	1,800
23	Purchases	500	7	3,500
30	Inventory	180		

Instructions
(a) Compute the cost of the ending inventory and the cost of goods sold under (1) FIFO and (2) LIFO.
(b) Which costing method gives the higher ending inventory? Why?
(c) Which method results in the higher cost of goods sold? Why?

Compute inventory and cost of goods sold using average costs.
(SO 5, 6)

E6–7   Inventory data for Luxemburg Company are presented in E6–6.

Instructions
(a) Compute the cost of the ending inventory and the cost of goods sold using the average cost method.
(b) Will the results in (a) be higher or lower than the results under (1) FIFO and (2) LIFO?
(c) Why is the average unit cost not $6?

Determine ending inventory under lower of cost or market inventory method.
(SO 7)

E6–8   China Camera Shop uses the lower of cost or market basis for its inventory. The following data are available at December 31:

Item	Units	Unit Cost	Unit Market
Cameras			
Minolta	5	$170	$160
Canon	7	150	152
Light Meters			
Vivitar	12	125	110
Kodak	10	115	135

Instructions
Determine the amount of the ending inventory by applying the lower of cost or market basis to (a) individual items, (b) inventory categories, and (c) the total inventory.

E6–9   Korea Hardware reported cost of goods sold as follows:

Determine effects of inventory errors.
(SO 8)

	2001	2002
Beginning inventory	$ 20,000	$ 30,000
Cost of goods purchased	150,000	175,000
Cost of goods available for sale	170,000	205,000
Ending inventory	30,000	35,000
Cost of goods sold	$140,000	$170,000

Korea made two errors: (1) 2001 ending inventory was overstated $4,000, and (2) 2002 ending inventory was understated $3,000.

Instructions
Compute the correct cost of goods sold for each year.

E6–10   Zurich Watch Company reported the following income statement data for a 2-year period.

Prepare correct income statements.
(SO 8)

	2001	2002
Sales	$210,000	$250,000
Cost of goods sold		
Beginning inventory	32,000	40,000
Cost of goods purchased	173,000	202,000
Cost of goods available for sale	205,000	242,000
Ending inventory	40,000	52,000
Cost of goods sold	165,000	190,000
Gross profit	$ 45,000	$ 60,000

Zurich uses a periodic inventory system. The inventories at January 1, 2001, and December 31, 2002, are correct. However, the ending inventory at December 31, 2001, was overstated $6,000.

Instructions
(a) Prepare correct income statement data for the 2 years.
(b) What is the cumulative effect of the inventory error on total gross profit for the 2 years?
(c) ▪▪▪▪▪➤ Explain in a letter to the president of Zurich Watch Company what has happened—i.e., the nature of the error and its effect on the financial statements.

E6–11   This information is available for Linda Wasicsko Corporation for 1999, 2000, and 2001.

Compute inventory turnover ratio, days in inventory, and gross profit rate.
(SO 9, 10)

	1999	2000	2001
Beginning inventory	$ 200,000	$ 300,000	$ 400,000
Ending inventory	300,000	400,000	500,000
Cost of goods sold	900,000	1,120,000	1,250,000
Sales	1,200,000	1,600,000	1,900,000

Instructions
Calculate the inventory turnover ratio, days in inventory, and gross profit rate (from Chapter 5) for Linda Wasicsko Corporation for 1999, 2000, 2001. Comment on any trends.

*E6–12   The inventory of DeBeers Company was destroyed by fire on March 1. From an examination of the accounting records, the following data for the first 2 months of the year are obtained: Sales $51,000, Sales Returns and Allowances $1,000, Purchases $28,200, Freight-in $1,200, and Purchase Returns and Allowances $1,400.

Determine merchandise lost using the gross profit method of estimating inventory.
(SO 10)

Instructions
Determine the merchandise lost by fire, assuming:

(a) A beginning inventory of $20,000 and a gross profit rate of 30% on net sales.
(b) A beginning inventory of $25,000 and a gross profit rate of 25% on net sales.

Determine ending inventory at cost using retail method.
(SO 10)

*E6–13   Swiss Shoe Store uses the retail inventory method for its two departments: Women's Shoes and Men's Shoes. The following information for each department is obtained:

Item	Women's Department	Men's Department
Beginning inventory at cost	$ 32,000	$ 46,450
Cost of goods purchased at cost	148,000	137,300
Net sales	187,000	195,000
Beginning inventory at retail	45,000	60,000
Cost of goods purchased at retail	182,000	185,000

Instructions
Compute the estimated cost of the ending inventory for each department under the retail inventory method.

Apply cost flow methods to perpetual records.
(SO 11)

*E6–14   Morocco Appliance uses a perpetual inventory system. For its model B47 television sets, the January 1 inventory was four sets at $600 each. During January, the following purchase was made: Jan. 10, 6 units at $640 each. That month, the company had the following sales: Jan. 8, 2 units and Jan. 15, 4 units.

Instructions
Compute the ending inventory under (1) FIFO, (2) LIFO, and (3) average cost.

PROBLEMS: SET A

Journalize, post, and prepare a trial balance and partial income statement.
(SO 2, 3, 4)

P6–1A   Billy Jean Evert, a former professional tennis star, operates B.J.'s Tennis Shop at the Jackson Lake Resort. At the beginning of the current season, the ledger of B.J.'s Tennis Shop showed Cash $2,500, Merchandise Inventory $1,700, and Common Stock $4,200. The following transactions were completed during April 2001:

Apr. 4   Purchased racquets and balls from Robert Co. $640 FOB shipping point, terms 3/10, n/30.
      6   Paid freight on Robert purchase $40.
      8   Sold merchandise to members $900, terms n/30.
     10   Received credit of $40 from Robert Co. for a damaged racquet that was returned.
     11   Purchased tennis shoes from Niki Sports for cash, $300.
     13   Paid Robert Co. in full.
     14   Purchased tennis shirts and shorts from Martina's Sportswear $700, FOB shipping point, terms 2/10, n/60.
     15   Received cash refund of $50 from Niki Sports for damaged merchandise that was returned.
     17   Paid freight on Martina's Sportswear purchase $30.
     18   Sold merchandise to members, $800, terms n/30.
     20   Received $500 in cash from members in settlement of their accounts.
     21   Paid Martina's Sportswear in full.
     27   Granted credit of $30 to members for tennis clothing that did not fit.
     30   Sold merchandise to members $900, terms n/30.
     30   Received cash payments on account from members, $500.

The chart of accounts for the tennis shop includes the following: No. 101 Cash, No. 112 Accounts Receivable, No. 120 Merchandise Inventory, No. 201 Accounts Payable, No. 311 Common Stock, No. 401 Sales, No. 412 Sales Returns and Allowances, No. 510 Purchases, No. 512 Purchase Returns and Allowances, No. 514 Purchase Discounts, No. 516 Freight-in.

Instructions
(a) Journalize the April transactions using a periodic inventory system.
(b) Enter the beginning balances in the ledger accounts and post the April transactions. (Use J1 for the journal reference.)
(c) Prepare a trial balance on April 30, 2001.
(d) Prepare an income statement through gross profit, assuming merchandise inventory on hand at April 30 is $1,800.

P6-2A   Austrian Department Store is located near the Village shopping mall. At the end of the company's fiscal year on December 31, 2001, the following accounts appeared in its adjusted trial balance:

Prepare an income statement.
(SO 3, 4)

Accounts Payable	$ 89,300
Accounts Receivable	50,300
Accumulated Depreciation—Building	52,500
Accumulated Depreciation—Equipment	42,900
Building	190,000
Cash	23,000
Depreciation Expense—Building	10,400
Depreciation Expense—Equipment	13,300
Equipment	110,000
Freight-in	3,600
Insurance Expense	7,200
Merchandise Inventory	40,500
Mortgage Payable	80,000
Office Salaries Expense	32,000
Prepaid Insurance	2,400
Property Taxes Payable	4,300
Purchases	462,000
Purchase Discounts	12,000
Purchase Returns and Allowances	6,400
Sales	618,000
Sales Commissions Expense	14,500
Sales Commissions Payable	4,000
Sales Returns and Allowances	8,000
Sales Salaries Expense	74,000
Common Stock	150,000
Retained Earnings	27,600
Dividends	28,000
Property Taxes Expense	4,800
Utilities Expense	11,000

Analysis reveals the following additional data:

1. Merchandise inventory on December 31, 2001, is $75,000.
2. Insurance expense and utilities expense are 60% selling and 40% administrative.
3. Depreciation on the building and property tax expense are administrative expenses; depreciation on the equipment is a selling expense.

Instructions
Prepare an income statement for the year ended December 31, 2001.

P6-3A   Russia Company had a beginning inventory of 400 units of Product USSR at a cost of $8.00 per unit. During the year, purchases were:

Determine cost of goods sold and ending inventory, using FIFO, LIFO, and average cost.
(SO 5, 6)

Feb. 20	700 units at $9.00	Aug. 12	300 units at $11.00
May 5	500 units at $10.00	Dec. 8	100 units at $12.00

Russia Company uses a periodic inventory system. Sales totaled 1,550 units.

Instructions
(a) Determine the cost of goods available for sale.
(b) Determine (1) the ending inventory, and (2) the cost of goods sold under each of the assumed cost flow methods (FIFO, LIFO, and average). Prove the accuracy of the cost of goods sold under the FIFO and LIFO methods.
(c) Which cost flow method results in (1) the lowest inventory amount for the balance sheet, and (2) the lowest cost of goods sold for the income statement?

P6-4A   The management of India Co. is reevaluating the appropriateness of using its present inventory cost flow method, which is average cost. They request your help in determining the results of operations for 2001 if either the FIFO method or the LIFO method had been used. For 2001, the accounting records show the following data:

Compute ending inventory, prepare income statements, and answer questions using FIFO and LIFO.
(SO 5, 6)

Inventories		Purchases and Sales	
Beginning (15,000 units)	$34,000	Total net sales (225,000 units)	$865,000
Ending (20,000 units)		Total cost of goods purchased (230,000 units)	578,500

Purchases were made quarterly as follows:

Quarter	Units	Unit Cost	Total Cost
1	60,000	$2.30	$138,000
2	50,000	2.50	125,000
3	50,000	2.60	130,000
4	70,000	2.65	185,500
	230,000		$578,500

Operating expenses were $147,000, and the company's income tax rate is 32%.

Instructions

(a) Prepare comparative condensed income statements for 2001 under FIFO and LIFO. (Show computations of ending inventory.)

(b) ▭▭▭▭▷ Answer the following questions for management:

    (1) Which cost flow method (FIFO or LIFO) produces the more meaningful inventory amount for the balance sheet? Why?

    (2) Which cost flow method (FIFO or LIFO) produces the more meaningful net income? Why?

    (3) Which cost flow method (FIFO or LIFO) is more likely to approximate actual physical flow of the goods? Why?

    (4) How much additional cash will be available for management under LIFO than under FIFO? Why?

    (5) Will gross profit under the average cost method be higher or lower than (a) FIFO and (b) LIFO? (*Note:* It is not necessary to quantify your answer.)

Estimate inventory loss using gross profit method.
(SO 10)

*P6–5A Tibet Company lost 80% of its inventory in a fire on March 25, 2001. The accounting records showed the following gross profit data for February and March.

	February	March (to 3/25)
Net sales	$270,000	$260,000
Net purchases	200,800	191,000
Freight-in	2,900	4,000
Beginning inventory	16,500	20,400
Ending inventory	20,400	?

Tibet Company is fully insured for fire losses but must prepare a report for the insurance company.

Instructions

(a) Compute the gross profit rate for the month of February.

(b) Using the gross profit rate for February, determine both the estimated total inventory and inventory lost in the fire in March.

Compute ending inventory and cost of inventory lost using retail method.
(SO 10)

*P6–6A Japanese Department Store uses the retail inventory method to estimate its monthly ending inventories. The following information is available for two of its departments at August 31, 2001.

	Sporting Goods		Jewelry and Cosmetics	
	Cost	Retail	Cost	Retail
Net sales		$1,020,000		$1,160,000
Purchases	$670,000	1,066,000	$733,000	1,158,000
Purchase returns	(26,000)	(40,000)	(12,000)	(20,000)
Purchase discounts	(15,360)	—	(9,440)	—
Freight-in	6,000	—	8,000	—
Beginning inventory	47,360	74,000	36,440	62,000

At December 31, Japanese Department Store takes a physical inventory at retail. The actual retail values of the inventories in each department are: Sporting Goods $75,000, and Jewelry and Cosmetics $44,000.

Instructions

(a) Determine the estimated cost of the ending inventory for each department on August 31, 2001, using the retail inventory method.

(b) Compute the ending inventory at cost for each department at December 31, assuming the cost-to-retail ratios are 60% for Sporting Goods and 65% for Jewelry and Cosmetics using the actual retail values given above.

*P6–7A The Family Home Appliance Mart begins operations on May 1. It uses a perpetual inventory system. During May the company had the following purchases and sales for its Model 25 Sureshot camera.

Determine ending inventory under a perpetual inventory system.
(SO 11)

	Purchases		Sales
Date	Units	Unit Cost	Units
May 1	7	$150	
4			5
8	8	$170	
12			5
15	5	$180	
20			4
25			3

Instructions

(a) Determine the ending inventory under a perpetual inventory system using (1) FIFO, (2) average cost, and (3) LIFO.

(b) Which costing method produces (1) the highest ending inventory valuation and (2) the lowest ending inventory valuation?

PROBLEMS: SET B

P6–1B Chi Chi Lopez, a former professional golf star, operates Chi Chi's Pro Shop at Bay Golf Course. At the beginning of the current season on April 1, 2001, the ledger of Chi Chi's Pro Shop showed Cash $2,500, Merchandise Inventory $3,500, and Common Stock $6,000. The following transactions were completed during April.

Journalize, post, and prepare trial balance and partial income statement.
(SO 2, 3, 4)

Apr. 5 Purchased golf bags, clubs, and balls on account from Balata Co. $1,600, FOB shipping point, terms 2/10, n/60.
    7 Paid freight on Balata purchase $80.
    9 Received credit from Balata Co. for merchandise returned $100.
  10 Sold merchandise on account to members $900, terms n/30.
  12 Purchased golf shoes, sweaters, and other accessories on account from Arrow Sportswear $660, terms 1/10, n/30.
  14 Paid Balata Co. in full.
  17 Received credit from Arrow Sportswear for merchandise returned $60.
  20 Made sales on account to members $700, terms n/30.
  21 Paid Arrow Sportswear in full.
  27 Granted credit to members for clothing that did not fit $30.
  30 Made cash sales $600.
  30 Received payments on account from members $1,100.

The chart of accounts for the pro shop includes the following: No. 101 Cash, No. 112 Accounts Receivable, No. 120 Merchandise Inventory, No. 201 Accounts Payable, No. 311 Common Stock, No. 401 Sales, No. 412 Sales Returns and Allowances, No. 510 Purchases, No. 512 Purchase Returns and Allowances, No. 514 Purchase Discounts, No. 516 Freight-in.

Instructions

(a) Journalize the April transactions using a periodic inventory system.

(b) Enter the beginning balances in the ledger accounts and post the April transactions. (Use J1 for the journal reference.)

(c) Prepare a trial balance on April 30, 2001

(d) Prepare an income statement through gross profit, assuming merchandise inventory on hand at April 30 is $4,200.

Prepare an income statement.
(SO 3, 4)

P6–2B Asian Department Store is located in midtown Metropolis. During the past several years, net income has been declining because of suburban shopping centers. At the end of the company's fiscal year on November 30, 2001, the following accounts appeared in its adjusted trial balance:

Accounts Payable	$ 35,310
Accounts Receivable	11,770
Accumulated Depreciation—Delivery Equipment	19,680
Accumulated Depreciation—Store Equipment	41,800
Cash	8,000
Delivery Equipment	57,000
Delivery Expense	8,200
Depreciation Expense—Delivery Equipment	4,000
Depreciation Expense—Store Equipment	9,500
Freight-in	5,060
Common Stock	70,000
Retained Earnings	17,200
Dividends	12,000
Insurance Expense	9,000
Merchandise Inventory	34,360
Notes Payable	46,000
Prepaid Insurance	4,500
Property Tax Expense	3,500
Purchases	640,000
Purchase Discounts	7,000
Purchase Returns and Allowances	3,000
Rent Expense	19,000
Salaries Expense	120,000
Sales	860,000
Sales Commissions Expense	12,000
Sales Commissions Payable	8,000
Sales Returns and Allowances	10,000
Store Equipment	125,000
Property Taxes Payable	3,500
Utilities Expense	10,600

Analysis reveals the following additional data:

1. Salaries expense is 70% selling and 30% administrative.
2. Insurance expense is 50% selling and 50% administrative.
3. Merchandise inventory at November 30, 2001, is $36,200.
4. Rent expense, utilities expense, and property tax expense are administrative expenses.

Instructions
Prepare an income statement for the year ended November 30, 2001.

Determine cost of goods sold and ending inventory, using FIFO, LIFO, and average cost with analysis.
(SO 5, 6)

P6–3B Europe Company had a beginning inventory on January 1 of 100 units of Product WD-44 at a cost of $20 per unit. During the year, the following purchases were made.

Mar.	15	300 units at $24	Sept.	4	300 units at $28
July	20	200 units at 25	Dec.	2	100 units at 30

850 units were sold. Europe Company uses a periodic inventory system.

Instructions

(a) Determine the cost of goods available for sale.

(b) Determine (1) the ending inventory, and (2) the cost of goods sold under each of the assumed cost flow methods (FIFO, LIFO, and average). Prove the accuracy of the cost of goods sold under the FIFO and LIFO methods.

(c) Which cost flow method results in (1) the highest inventory amount for the balance sheet and (2) the highest cost of goods sold for the income statement?

P6–4B The management of African Co. asks your help in determining the comparative effects of the FIFO and LIFO inventory cost flow methods. For 2001, the accounting records show the following data.

Compute ending inventory, prepare income statements, and answer questions using FIFO and LIFO.
(SO 5, 6)

Inventory, January 1 (10,000 units)	$ 35,000
Cost of 110,000 units purchased	460,000
Selling price of 95,000 units sold	665,000
Operating expenses	120,000

Units purchased consisted of 40,000 units at $4.00 on May 10; 50,000 units at $4.20 on August 15; and 20,000 units at $4.50 on November 20. Income taxes are 28%.

Instructions
  (a) Prepare comparative condensed income statements for 2001 under FIFO and LIFO. (Show computations of ending inventory.)
  (b) ▯▭▭▭▭▷ Answer the following questions for management in the form of a business letter:
    (1) Which inventory cost flow method produces the most meaningful inventory amount for the balance sheet? Why?
    (2) Which inventory cost flow method produces the most meaningful net income? Why?
    (3) Which inventory cost flow method is most likely to approximate actual physical flow of the goods? Why?
    (4) How much additional cash will be available for management under LIFO than under FIFO? Why?
    (5) How much of the gross profit under FIFO is illusionary in comparison with the gross profit under LIFO?

*P6–5B Australia Company lost all of its inventory in a fire on December 26, 2001. The accounting records showed the following gross profit data for November and December.

Compute gross profit rate and inventory loss using gross profit method.
(SO 10)

	November	December (to 12/26)
Net sales	$400,000	$300,000
Beginning inventory	22,100	29,100
Purchases	314,975	236,000
Purchase returns and allowances	11,800	5,000
Purchase discounts	8,577	6,000
Freight-in	4,402	3,700
Ending inventory	29,100	?

Australia is fully insured for fire losses but must prepare a report for the insurance company.

Instructions
  (a) Compute the gross profit rate for November.
  (b) Using the gross profit rate for November, determine the estimated cost of the inventory lost in the fire.

*P6–6B French's Book Store uses the retail inventory method to estimate its monthly ending inventories. The following information is available for two of its departments at October 31, 2001.

Compute ending inventory using retail method.
(SO 10)

	Hardcovers		Paperbacks	
	Cost	Retail	Cost	Retail
Beginning inventory	$ 260,000	$ 400,000	$ 65,000	$ 90,000
Purchases	1,180,000	1,800,000	266,000	380,000
Freight-in	5,000		2,000	
Purchase discounts	15,000		4,000	
Net sales		1,810,000		363,000

At December 31, French's Book Store takes a physical inventory at retail. The actual retail values of the inventories in each department are: Hardcovers $400,000 and Paperbacks $100,000.

Instructions
  (a) Determine the estimated cost of the ending inventory for each department at October 31, 2001, using the retail inventory method.

(b) Compute the ending inventory at cost for each department at **December 31**, assuming the cost to retail ratios for the year are 65% for hardcovers and 70% for paperbacks (using the actual retail values given above).

Determine ending inventory under a perpetual inventory system.
(SO 11)

*P6–7B   Save-Mart Center began operations on July 1. It uses a perpetual inventory system. During July the company had the following purchases and sales:

Date	Purchases Units	Purchases Unit Cost	Sales Units
July 1	5	$90	
July 6			3
July 11	4	$99	
July 14			3
July 21	3	$106	
July 27			4

Instructions
(a) Determine the ending inventory under a perpetual inventory system using (1) FIFO, (2) average cost, and (3) LIFO.
(b) Which costing method produces the highest ending inventory valuation?

BROADENING YOUR PERSPECTIVE

FINANCIAL REPORTING AND ANALYSIS
....

FINANCIAL REPORTING PROBLEM: Kellogg Company

BYP6–1   The notes that accompany a company's financial statements provide informative details that would clutter the amounts and descriptions presented in the statements. Refer to the financial statements of Kellogg Company and the Notes to Consolidated Financial Statements in Appendix A.

Instructions
Answer the following questions. Complete the requirements in millions of dollars, as shown in Kellogg's annual report.

(a) What did Kellogg report for the amount of inventories in its Consolidated Balance Sheet at December 31, 1998? December 31, 1997?
(b) Compute the dollar amount of change and the percentage change in inventories between 1997 and 1998. Compute inventory as a percentage of current assets for 1998.
(c) How does Kellogg value its inventories? Which inventory cost flow method does Kellogg use?
(d) What is the cost of sales (cost of goods sold) reported by Kellogg for 1998, 1997, and 1996? Compute the percentage of cost of sales to net sales in 1998.

COMPARATIVE ANALYSIS PROBLEM: Kellogg Company vs. General Mills

BYP6–2   Kellogg's financial statements are presented in Appendix A; General Mills's financial statements are presented in Appendix B.

Instructions
(a) Based on the information contained in these financial statements, compute the following 1998 ratios for each company:
    1. Inventory turnover ratio
    2. Average days to sell inventory
(b) What conclusions concerning the management of the inventory can be drawn from these data?

RESEARCH ASSIGNMENT

BYP6-3   The March 5, 1999, issue of *Industry Week* contains an article by Doug Bartholomew entitled "What's Really Driving Apple's Recovery."

Instructions
Read the article and answer the following inventory-related questions.

    (a) What were Timothy D. Cook's twin goals upon being hired as senior vice president at Apple Computer Inc.?

    (b) What did Cook say was the primary cause of Apple Computer's huge $1 billion loss in 1997?

    (c) What was Apple's inventory turnover in 1997, and what were its competitors' inventory turnover ratios?

    (d) What improvements relative to inventory turnover did Cook accomplish by the end of 1998 at Apple Computer?

INTERPRETING FINANCIAL STATEMENTS: Nike and Reebok

BYP6-4   Nike and Reebok compete head-to-head in the sport shoe and sport apparel business. For both companies, inventory is a significant portion of their total assets. The following information was taken from each company's financial statements and notes to those financial statements.

NIKE, INC.

Inventory note
Inventories are stated at the lower of cost or market. Cost is determined using the last-in, first-out (LIFO) method for substantially all U.S. inventories. Non-U.S. inventories are valued on a first-in, first-out (FIFO) basis.

Inventories by major classification are as follows (in millions):

	May 31	
	1998	1997
Finished goods	$1,303.8	$1,248.4
Work-in-process	34.7	50.2
Raw materials	58.1	40.0

Other information for Nike (in millions):

	May 31	
	1998	1997
Inventory	$1,396.6	$1,338.6
Cost of goods sold	6,065.5	5,503.0

REEBOK INTERNATIONAL, LTD.

Inventory note
Inventory, substantially all finished goods, is recorded at the lower of cost (first-in, first-out method) or market.

Other information for Reebok (in millions):

	December 31	
	1998	1997
Inventory	$ 535.5	$ 563.7
Cost of goods sold	2,037.5	2,294.0

Instructions

Address each of the following questions which deal with how these two companies manage their inventory.

(a) What problems of inventory management face Nike and Reebok in the international sport apparel industry?

(b) What inventory cost flow assumptions does each company use? Why might Nike use a different approach for U.S. operations versus international operations? What are the implications of their respective cost flow assumptions for their financial statements?

(c) Nike provides more detail regarding the nature of its inventory (e.g., raw materials, work-in-process, and finished goods) than does Reebok. How might this additional information be useful in evaluating Nike?

(d) Calculate and interpret the inventory turnover ratio and average days to sell inventory for each company. Comment on how the use of different inventory methods by the two companies impacts your ability to compare their ratios.

REAL-WORLD FOCUS: General Motors Corporation

BYP6–5   General Motors is the largest producer of automobiles in the world, as well as the world's biggest industrial enterprise. After stumbling in the early 1990s, GM has enacted numerous cost-cutting measures, including downsizing and renegotiating contracts with suppliers. In addition, it has shifted more of its resources to the hot-selling truck market.

The annual report of General Motors Corporation disclosed the following information about its accounting for inventories:

GENERAL MOTORS CORPORATION
Notes to the Financial Statements

Note 5. Inventories

Automotive, Electronics and Other Operations' inventories included the following (in millions)

| | December 31 | |
	1998	1997
Productive material, work in process, and supplies	$ 7,287	$ 7,023
Finished product, service parts, etc.	7,215	7,347
Total inventories at FIFO	14,502	14,370
Less LIFO allowance	2,295	2,268
Total inventories (less allowances)	$12,207	$12,102

Inventories are stated generally at cost, which is not in excess of market. The cost of substantially all U.S. inventories other than the inventories of Saturn Corporation (Saturn), Delco, and Hughes is determined by the last-in, first-out (LIFO) method. The cost of non-U.S., Saturn, Delco, and Hughes inventories is determined generally by the first-in, first-out (FIFO) or average cost methods.

Instructions

(a) What is meant by "inventories are stated generally at cost, which is not in excess of market'"?

(b) The company uses LIFO for most of its inventory. What impact does this have on reported ending inventory if prices are increasing?

(c) General Motors uses different inventory methods for different types of inventory. Why might it do this?

CRITICAL THINKING

GROUP DECISION CASE

BYP6–6   Consider the case of a large company that reported inventories of $800 million at December 31, 2001, and $900 million at December 31, 2000. However, the ending inventory for 2000 had been overstated by $40 million as a result of errors in the physical counting process. This error was not discovered until after the financial statements for 2001 had been issued.

Instructions
Complete the table which follows. Indicate which items in the financial statements would be incorrect, and by how much. Use an income tax rate of 40% in your calculations, and assume that the tax is paid in cash immediately. For each item, indicate whether it would be **overstated**, **understated**, or **not affected**. Also, indicate the **amount** of the error (if any).

	Effect on Fiscal Year	
	2001	**2000**
Beginning inventory	_____	_____
Ending inventory	_____	_____
Cost of goods sold	_____	_____
Gross profit on sales	_____	_____
Income before tax	_____	_____
Income tax	_____	_____
Net income	_____	_____
Ending total assets	_____	_____
Ending shareholders' equity	_____	_____

COMMUNICATION ACTIVITY

BYP6–7   You are the controller of Small Toys Inc. Joe Paisley, the president, recently mentioned to you that he found an error in the 2000 financial statements which he believes has corrected itself. He determined, in discussions with the Purchasing Department, that 2000 ending inventory was overstated by $1 million. Joe says that the 2001 ending inventory is correct, thus he assumes that 2001 income is correct. Joe says to you, "What happened has happened—there's no point in worrying about it anymore."

Instructions
You conclude that Joe is incorrect. Write a brief, tactful memo to Joe, clarifying the situation.

ETHICS CASE

BYP6–8   Lonergan Wholesale Corp. uses the LIFO method of inventory costing. In the current year, profit at Lonergan is running unusually high. The corporate tax rate is also high this year, but it is scheduled to decline significantly next year. In an effort to lower current year's net income and to take advantage of the changing income tax rate, the president of Lonergan Wholesale instructs the plant accountant to recommend to the purchasing department a large purchase of inventory for delivery 3 days before the end of the year. The price of the inventory to be purchased has doubled during the year and the purchase will represent a major portion of the ending inventory value.

Instructions
(a) What is the effect of this transaction on this year's and next year's income statement and income tax expense? Why?
(b) If Lonergan Wholesale had been using the FIFO method of inventory costing, would the president give the same directive?
(c) Should the plant accountant order the inventory purchase to lower income? What are the ethical implications of this order?

SURFING THE NET

BYP6–9 A company's annual report usually will identify the inventory method used. Knowing that, you can analyze the effects of the inventory method on the income statement and balance sheet.

Address: http://www.cisco.com (or go to www.wiley.com/college/weygandt)

Steps:
1. From Cisco System's homepage, choose **investor information**.
2. Choose **View the Annual Report**.
3. Use the financial statements and relating notes to the financial statements to answer the questions below.

Instructions
Answer the following questions:
   (a) At Cisco's fiscal year-end, what was the net inventory on the balance sheet?
   (b) How has this changed from the previous fiscal year-end?
   (c) How much of the inventory was finished goods?
   (d) What inventory method do they use?

Answers to Self-Study Questions
1. b   2. d   3. a   4. a   5. b   6. c   7. d   8. c   9. d   10. d   11. b
12. d   *13. b   *14. d

Answer to Kellogg Review It Question 5, p. 251
Kellogg Company reported inventories of $451,400,000 at December 31, 1998. Kellogg reports in Note 1—Accounting Policies that it uses principally the **average cost method** in applying product costs to inventories and cost of goods sold.

Remember to go back to the Navigator box on the chapter-opening page and check off your completed work.

Before studying this chapter, you should know or, if necessary, review:

a. The two organizations primarily responsible for setting accounting standards. (Ch. 1, p. 9)

b. The monetary unit assumption, the economic entity assumption, and the time period assumption. (Chs. 1 and 3, pp. 10, 93)

c. The cost principle, the revenue recognition principle, and the matching principle. (Chs. 1 and 3, pp. 9, 93, 94)

d. The presentation of classified balance sheets (Ch. 4, p. 161) and classified (multiple-step) income statements. (Ch. 5, p. 207)

THE NAVIGATOR

FEATURE STORY

Is Online "Off-Track"?

In the world of interactive media, subscribers pay a monthly fee ($19.95 or so) for limited access to electronic data systems. America Online (AOL) is one of the success stories in this industry.

AOL's biggest expenditure is the cost of attracting subscribers. The company sends out millions of mail solicitations and gives away trial subscriptions. Such promotion is expensive; in a recent year, subscription-acquisition costs totaled $54 million. Are those an expense to be charged against revenue? Or are they an investment undertaken to create an asset?

AOL believes they are the latter. The company capitalizes the costs and amortizes them over 18 months. The other treatment would reduce earnings more: If it had expensed the $54 million as incurred, AOL would have reported a net loss rather than a net income. AOL's practice has the FASB's blessing: the FASB considers the cost of obtaining the subscriptions from direct-mail campaigns to be assets. Magazine publishers, similarly, often capitalize such costs.

However, many of AOL's competitors take a more conservative approach by expensing subscriber-acquisition costs as they occur. The controller of one of AOL's competitors noted, "We didn't want to taint [our earnings] or dilute them by following [AOL's] accounting." And, Loretta Hoi, accounting manager at Internet Direct, says emphatically, "We expense all such costs right now."

AOL defends its accounting as a policy of matching expenses with revenues. As its CFO notes, "We're writing these costs off much more rapidly than the ongoing revenue stream." One test of the wisdom of AOL's accounting practice may be the long-term loyalty of subscribers: If they stay with AOL in the face of increasing competition, the subscription-acquisition costs will indeed have created long-term assets.

THE NAVIGATOR

CHAPTER 7

ACCOUNTING PRINCIPLES

THE NAVIGATOR ✔

- Understand *Concepts for Review* ☐
- Read *Feature Story* ☐
- Scan *Study Objectives* ☐
- Read *Preview* ☐
- Read text and answer *Before You Go On*
  p. 290 ☐ p. 297 ☐ p. 306 ☐
- Work *Demonstration Problems* ☐
- Review *Summary of Study Objectives* ☐
- Answer *Self-Study Questions* ☐
- Complete assignments ☐

STUDY OBJECTIVES

After studying this chapter, you should be able to:

1. *Explain the meaning of generally accepted accounting principles and identify the key items of the conceptual framework.*
2. *Describe the basic objectives of financial reporting.*
3. *Discuss the qualitative characteristics of accounting information and elements of financial statements.*
4. *Identify the basic assumptions used by accountants.*
5. *Identify the basic principles of accounting.*
6. *Identify the two constraints in accounting.*
7. *Understand and analyze classified financial statements.*
8. *Explain the accounting principles used in international operations.*

THE NAVIGATOR

*A*s indicated in the opening story, it is important that general guidelines be available to resolve accounting issues such as that faced by America Online. Without these basic guidelines, each enterprise would have to develop its own set of accounting practices. If this happened, we would have to become familiar with every company's peculiar accounting and reporting rules in order to understand their financial statements. Thus, it would be difficult, if not impossible, to compare the financial statements of different companies.

This chapter explores the basic accounting principles followed in developing specific accounting guidelines. The content and organization of the chapter are as follows:

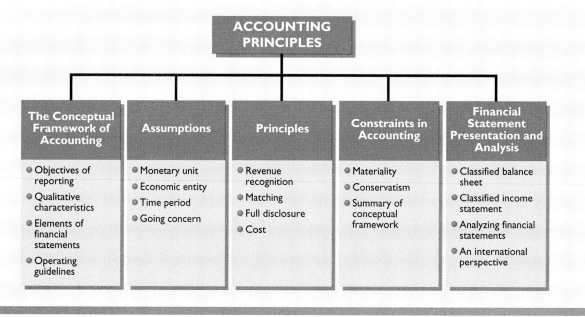

THE
NAVIGATOR

THE CONCEPTUAL FRAMEWORK OF ACCOUNTING

1

STUDY

OBJECTIVE

Explain the meaning of generally accepted accounting principles and identify the key items of the conceptual framework.

The accounting profession has established a set of standards and rules that are recognized as a general guide for financial reporting purposes. This recognized set of standards is called generally accepted accounting principles (GAAP). "Generally accepted" means that these principles must have "substantial authoritative support." Such support usually comes from two standard-setting bodies: the Financial Accounting Standards Board (FASB) and the Securities and Exchange Commission (SEC).[1]

Since the early 1970s the business and governmental communities have given the FASB the responsibility for developing accounting principles in this country.

---

[1]The SEC is an agency of the U.S. government that was established in 1933 to administer laws and regulations relating to the exchange of securities and the publication of financial information by U.S. businesses. The agency has the authority to mandate generally accepted accounting principles for companies under its jurisdiction. However, throughout its history, the SEC has been willing to accept the principles set forth by the FASB and similar bodies.

This job is an ongoing process in which accounting principles change to reflect changes in the business environment and in the needs of users of accounting information.

Prior to the establishment of the FASB, accounting principles were developed on a problem-by-problem basis. Thus, rule-making bodies developed and issued accounting rules and methods to solve specific problems. Critics charged that the problem-by-problem approach led to inconsistent rules and practices over time. Unfortunately, no clearly developed conceptual framework of accounting existed for the accounting rule makers to refer to in solving problems.

In response to these criticisms, the FASB developed a conceptual framework to serve as the basis for resolving accounting and reporting problems. The FASB spent considerable time and effort on this project. The Board views its conceptual framework as "... a constitution, a coherent system of interrelated objectives and fundamentals."[2]

The FASB's conceptual framework consists of the following four items:

1. Objectives of financial reporting.
2. Qualitative characteristics of accounting information.
3. Elements of financial statements.
4. Operating guidelines (assumptions, principles, and constraints).

We will discuss each of these items on the following pages.

ACCOUNTING IN ACTION
International Insight

You should recognize that different political and cultural influences affect the accounting that occurs in foreign countries. For example, in Sweden, accounting is considered an instrument to be used to shape fiscal policy. In Europe generally, more emphasis is given to social reporting (more information on employment statistics, health of workers, and so on) because employees and their labor organizations are strong and demand that type of information from management.

Objectives of Financial Reporting

In developing the conceptual framework, the FASB concluded that the first level of study was to determine the objectives of financial reporting. Determining these objectives required answers to such basic questions as: Who uses financial statements? Why? What information do they need? How knowledgeable about business and accounting are the users of financial statements? How should financial information be reported so that it is best understood?

In answering these questions, the FASB concluded that the objectives of financial reporting are to provide information that:

1. Is useful to those making investment and credit decisions.
2. Is helpful in assessing future cash flows.
3. Identifies the economic resources (assets), the claims to those resources (liabilities), and the changes in those resources and claims.

2
STUDY
OBJECTIVE
....
Describe the basic objectives of financial reporting.

---

[2]"Conceptual Framework for Financial Accounting and Reporting: Elements of Financial Statements and Their Measurement," *FASB Discussion Memorandum* (Stamford, Conn.: 1976), p. 1.

The FASB then undertook to describe the characteristics that make accounting information useful.

Qualitative Characteristics of Accounting Information

How does a company like Microsoft decide on the amount of financial information to disclose? In what format should its financial information be presented? How should assets, liabilities, revenues, and expenses be measured? **The FASB concluded that the overriding criterion by which such accounting choices should be judged is decision usefulness.** The accounting practice selected or the policy adopted should be the one that generates the most useful financial information for making a decision. To be useful, information should possess the following qualitative characteristics: relevance, reliability, comparability, and consistency.

Relevance

Accounting information is relevant if it makes a difference in a decision. Relevant information has either predictive or feedback value or both. **Predictive value** helps users forecast future events. For example, when Exxon issues financial statements, the information in the statements is considered relevant because it provides a basis for forecasting (predicting) future earnings. **Feedback value** confirms or corrects prior expectations. When Exxon issues financial statements, in addition to helping predict future events, it confirms or corrects prior expectations about the financial health of the company.

In addition, for accounting information to be relevant it must be **timely**. That is, it must be available to decision makers before it loses its capacity to influence decisions. If Exxon reported its financial information only every 5 years, the information would have limited usefulness for decision-making purposes.

Reliability

Reliability of information means that the information is free of error and bias; it can be depended on. To be reliable, accounting information must be **verifiable**—we must be able to prove that it is free of error and bias. The information must be a **faithful representation** of what it purports to be—it must be factual. If Sears, Roebuck's income statement reports sales of $100 billion when it had sales of $51 billion, then the statement is not a faithful representation. Finally, accounting information must be **neutral**—it cannot be selected, prepared, or presented to favor one set of interested users over another. To ensure reliability, certified public accountants audit financial statements, just as the Internal Revenue Service audits tax returns for the same purpose.

Comparability and Consistency

Accounting information about an enterprise is most useful when it can be compared with accounting information about other enterprises. Comparability results when different companies use the same accounting principles. For example, Sears, Roebuck, Montgomery Ward, and J.C. Penney all use the cost principle in reporting plant assets on the balance sheet. Moreover, each company uses the revenue recognition and matching principles in determining its net income.

Conceptually, comparability should also extend to the methods used by companies in complying with an accounting principle. Accounting methods include the FIFO and LIFO methods of inventory costing, and various depreciation methods. At this point, comparability of methods is not required, even for companies in the same industry. Thus, Ford, General Motors, and DaimlerChrysler may use different inventory costing and depreciation methods in their financial statements. The only accounting requirement is that each company **must disclose** the accounting methods used. From the disclosures, the external user can determine whether the financial information is comparable.

Consistency means that a company uses the same accounting principles and methods from year to year. Thus, if a company selects FIFO as the inventory costing method in the first year of operations, it is expected to continue to use FIFO in succeeding years. When financial information has been reported on a consistent basis, the financial statements permit meaningful analysis of trends within a company.

A company can change to a new method of accounting if management can justify that the new method results in more meaningful financial information. In the year in which the change occurs, the change must be disclosed in the notes to the financial statements so that users of the financial statements are aware of the lack of consistency.

ACCOUNTING IN ACTION
Business Insight

There is an old story that professors often tell students about a company looking for an accountant. The company approached the first accountant and asked: "What do you believe our net income will be this year?" The accountant said $4 million dollars. The company asked the second accountant the same question, and the answer was "What would you like it to be?" Guess who got the job? The reason we tell the story here is that, because accounting principles offer flexibility, it is important that a consistent treatment be provided from period to period. Otherwise it would be very difficult to interpret financial statements. Perhaps *no* alternative methods should be permitted in accounting. What do you think?

The qualitative characteristics of accounting information are summarized in Illustration 7-1.

ILLUSTRATION 7-1

Qualitative characteristics of accounting information

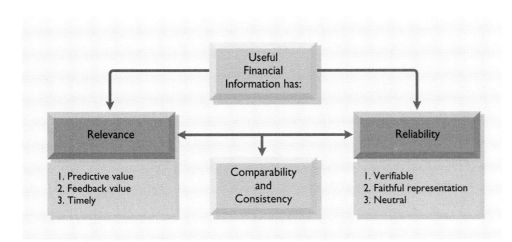

Elements of Financial Statements

An important part of an accounting conceptual framework is a set of definitions that describe the basic terms used in accounting. The FASB refers to this set of definitions as the elements of financial statements. They include such terms as assets, liabilities, equity, revenues, and expenses.

Because these elements are so important, it is imperative that they be precisely defined and universally understood and applied. Finding the appropriate definition for many of these elements is not easy. For example, how should an asset be defined? Should the value of a company's employees be reported as an asset on a balance sheet? Should the death of the company's president be reported as a loss? A good set of definitions should provide answers to these types of questions. Because you have already encountered most of these definitions in earlier chapters, they are not repeated here.

Operating Guidelines

The objectives of financial statements, the qualitative characteristics of accounting information, and the elements of financial statements are very broad. However, because practicing accountants and standard-setting bodies must solve practical problems, more detailed guidelines are needed. In its conceptual framework, the FASB recognized the need for operating guidelines. We have chosen to classify these guidelines as assumptions, principles, and constraints. These guidelines are well-established and accepted in accounting.

Assumptions provide a foundation for the accounting process. **Principles** are specific rules that indicate how economic events should be reported in the accounting process. **Constraints** on the accounting process allow for a relaxation of the principles under certain circumstances. Illustration 7-2 provides a roadmap of the operating guidelines of accounting. These guidelines are discussed in more detail in the following sections.

ILLUSTRATION 7-2

The operating guidelines of accounting

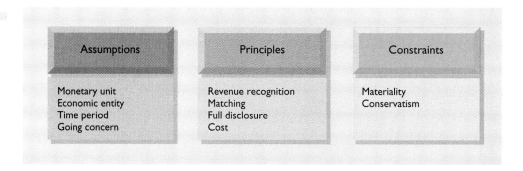

Assumptions	Principles	Constraints
Monetary unit Economic entity Time period Going concern	Revenue recognition Matching Full disclosure Cost	Materiality Conservatism

BEFORE YOU GO ON . . .

Review It

1. What are generally accepted accounting principles?
2. What is stated about generally accepted accounting principles in the Report of Independent Accountants for Kellogg? The answer to this question appears on page 327.
3. What are the basic objectives of financial information?
4. What are the qualitative characteristics that make accounting information useful? Identify two elements of the financial statements.

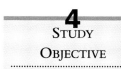

STUDY OBJECTIVE

Identify the basic assumptions used by accountants.

ASSUMPTIONS

As noted above, assumptions provide a foundation for the accounting process. You have already studied three of the major assumptions in preceding chapters—the monetary unit, economic entity, and time period assumptions. The fourth is called the going concern assumption.

Monetary Unit Assumption

The monetary unit assumption states that only transaction data capable of being expressed in terms of money should be included in the accounting records of the economic entity. For example, the value of a company president is not reported in a company's financial records because it cannot be expressed easily in dollars.

An important corollary to the monetary unit assumption is the added assumption that the unit of measure remains sufficiently constant over time. This point will be discussed in more detail later in this chapter.

Economic Entity Assumption

The economic entity assumption states that economic events can be identified with a particular unit of accountability. For example, it is assumed that the activities of IBM can be distinguished from those of other computer companies such as Apple, Compaq, and Hewlett-Packard.

Time Period Assumption

The time period assumption states that the economic life of a business can be divided into artificial time periods. Thus, it is assumed that the activities of business enterprises such as General Electric, America Online, Exxon, or any enterprise can be subdivided into months, quarters, or a year for meaningful financial reporting purposes.

Going Concern Assumption

The going concern assumption states that the enterprise will continue in operation long enough to carry out its existing objectives. Experience indicates that, in spite of numerous business failures, companies have a fairly high continuance rate, and it has proved useful to adopt a going concern assumption for accounting purposes.

The accounting implications of adopting this assumption are critical. If a going concern assumption is not used, then plant assets should be stated at their liquidation value (selling price less cost of disposal)—not at their cost. As a result, depreciation and amortization of these assets would not be needed. Each period these assets would simply be reported at their liquidation value. Also, without this assumption, the current–noncurrent classification of assets and liabilities would have little significance. Labeling anything as fixed or long-term would be difficult to justify.

Acceptance of the going concern assumption gives credibility to the cost principle. If, instead, liquidation were assumed, assets would be better stated at liquidation value than at cost. Only when liquidation appears imminent is the going concern assumption inapplicable.

These basic accounting assumptions are illustrated graphically in Illustration 7-3 on the next page.

HELPFUL HINT
(1) Which accounting assumption assumes that an enterprise will remain in business long enough to recover the cost of its assets? (2) Which accounting assumption is justification for the cost principle? Answers: (1) and (2) Going concern assumption.

PRINCIPLES

On the basis of these fundamental assumptions of accounting, the accounting profession has developed principles that dictate how transactions and other economic events should be recorded and reported. In earlier chapters we discussed the cost principle (Chapter 1) and the revenue recognition and matching principles (Chapter 3). We now examine a number of reporting issues related to these principles. In addition, another principle, the full disclosure principle, is discussed.

5
STUDY
OBJECTIVE

Identify the basic principles of accounting.

ILLUSTRATION 7-3

Assumptions used in accounting

Economic Entity

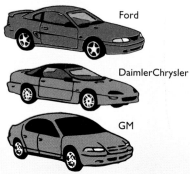

Ford

DaimlerChrysler

GM

Economic events can be identified with a particular unit of accountability.

Monetary Unit

| Measure of employee satisfaction | Salaries paid |
| Total number of employees | Percent of international employees |

- Acct. Records
-Salaries paid

Only transaction data capable of being expressed in terms of money should be included in the accounting records of the economic entity.

Time Period

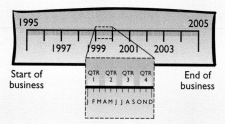

| 1995 | | | | 2005 |
| 1997 | 1999 | 2001 | 2003 | |

Start of business

QTR 1 QTR 2 QTR 3 QTR 4

J F M A M J J A S O N D

End of business

The economic life of a business can be divided into artificial time periods.

Going Concern

Now   Future

The enterprise will continue in operation long enough to carry out its existing objectives.

Revenue Recognition Principle

The revenue recognition principle dictates that revenue should be recognized in the accounting period in which it is earned. Applying this general principle in practice, however, can be difficult. For example, it was reported that Automatic Inc. was improperly recognizing revenue on goods that had not been shipped to customers. Similarly, many questioned the revenue recognition practices of financial institutions, which until recently recorded a large portion of their fees for granting a loan as revenue immediately rather than spreading those fees over the life of the loan.

When a sale is involved, revenue is recognized at the point of sale. The **sales basis** involves an exchange transaction between the seller and buyer, and the sales price provides an objective measure of the amount of revenue realized. There are, however, alternative methods to the sales basis for revenue recognition that have become generally accepted in special circumstances. These methods are left for more advanced courses.

Matching Principle (Expense Recognition)

Expense recognition is traditionally tied to revenue recognition: "Let the expense follow the revenue." This practice is referred to as the matching principle: it dictates that expenses be matched with revenues in the period in which efforts are expended to generate revenues. Expenses are not recognized when cash is paid, or when the work is performed, or when the product is produced; they are recognized when the labor (service) or the product actually makes its contribution to revenue.

The problem is that it is sometimes difficult to determine the accounting period in which the expense contributed to the generation of revenues. Several ap-

HELPFUL HINT

Revenue should be recognized in the accounting period in which it is earned, which may not be the period in which the related cash is received. In a retail establishment the point of sale is often the critical point in the process of earning revenue.

proaches have therefore been devised for matching expenses and revenues on the income statement.

To understand these approaches, it is necessary to examine the nature of expenses. Costs that will generate revenues only in the current accounting period are expensed immediately. They are reported as operating expenses in the income statement. Examples include such costs as advertising, sales salaries, and repairs. These expenses are often called **expired costs**.

Costs that will generate revenues in future accounting periods are recognized as assets. Examples include merchandise inventory, prepaid expenses, and plant assets. These costs represent **unexpired costs**. Unexpired costs become expenses in two ways:

1. **Cost of goods sold.** Costs carried as merchandise inventory are expensed as cost of goods sold in the period when the sale occurs. Thus, there is a direct matching of expenses with revenues.
2. **Operating expenses.** Unexpired costs become operating expenses through use or consumption (as in the case of store supplies) or through the passage of time (as in the case of prepaid insurance and prepaid rent). The cost of plant assets and other long-lived productive resources is expensed through rational and systematic allocation methods which result in periodic depreciation and amortization. Operating expenses contribute to the revenues of the period but their association with revenues is less direct than for cost of goods sold.

These points about expense recognition are illustrated in Illustration 7-4.

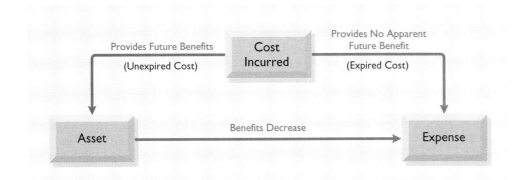

ILLUSTRATION 7-4

Expense recognition pattern

ACCOUNTING IN ACTION
Business Insight

Implementing expense recognition guidelines can be difficult. Consider, for example, Harold's Club (a gambling casino) in Reno, Nevada. How should it report expenses related to the payoff of its progressive slot machines? Progressive slot machines, which generally have no ceiling on their jackpots, are capable of providing a lucky winner with all the money that many losers had previously put in. Payoffs tend to be huge, but infrequent; at Harold's, the progressive slots pay off on average every $4\frac{1}{2}$ months. The basic accounting question is: Can Harold's deduct the millions of dollars sitting in its progressive slot machines from the revenue recognized at the end of the accounting period? One might argue that no, you cannot deduct the money until the "winning handle pull." However, a winning handle pull might not occur for many months or even years. Although admittedly an estimate would have to be used, the better answer is to match these costs with the revenue recognized, assuming that an average $4\frac{1}{2}$ months' payout is well documented. This example demonstrates that the matching principle can be difficult to apply in practice.

Full Disclosure Principle

The full disclosure principle requires that circumstances and events that make a difference to financial statement users be disclosed. For example, most accountants would agree that the tobacco companies Phillip Morris and RJR should disclose the numerous liability suits pending against them so that interested parties were made aware of this contingent loss. Similarly, it is generally agreed that companies should disclose the major provisions of employee pension plans and long-term lease contracts.

Compliance with the full disclosure principle occurs through the data contained in the financial statements and the information in the notes that accompany the statements. The first note in most cases is a **summary of significant accounting policies**. The summary includes, among others, the methods used by the company for inventory costing, depreciation of plant assets, and amortization of intangible assets.

Deciding how much disclosure is enough can be difficult. Accountants could disclose every financial event that occurs and every contingency that exists. However, accounting information must be condensed and combined to make it understandable. Providing additional information entails a cost, and the benefits of providing this information in some cases may be less than the costs. Many companies complain of an accounting standards overload. In addition, they object to requirements that force them to disclose confidential information. Determining where to draw the line on disclosure is not easy.

One thing is certain: financial reporting was much simpler years ago, when many companies provided little additional information regarding the financial statements. In 1930, General Electric had no notes to the financial statements; today it has over 10 pages of notes! Why this change? A major reason is that the objectives of financial reporting have changed. In the past, information was generally presented on what the business had done. Today the objectives of financial reporting are more future-oriented; accounting is trying to provide information that makes it possible to predict the amount, timing, and uncertainty of future cash flows.

TECHNOLOGY IN ACTION

Some accountants are reconsidering the current means of financial reporting. These accountants propose a database concept of financial reporting. In such a system, all the information from transactions would be stored in a computerized database to be accessed by various user groups. The main benefit of such a system is the ability to tailor the information requested to the needs of each user.

What makes it controversial? The debate revolves around access and aggregation issues. Questions such as "Who should be allowed to make inquiries of the system?" "What is the lowest/smallest level of information to be provided?" and "Will such a system necessarily improve on the current means of disclosure?" must be answered before such a system can be implemented on a large scale.

Cost Principle

As you know, the cost principle dictates that assets are recorded at their cost. Cost is used because it is both relevant and reliable. Cost is **relevant** because it represents the price paid, the assets sacrificed, or the commitment made at the date of acquisition. Cost is **reliable** because it is objectively measurable, factual, and verifiable. It is the result of an exchange transaction. Cost is the basis used in preparing financial statements.

The cost principle, however, has come under much criticism. It is criticized by some as irrelevant. Subsequent to acquisition, the argument goes, cost is not equivalent to market value or current value. For that matter, as the purchasing power of the dollar changes, so also does the meaning associated with the dollar that is used as the basis of measurement. Consider the classic story about the individual who went to sleep and woke up 10 years later. Hurrying to a telephone, he got through to his broker and asked what his formerly modest stock portfolio was worth. He was told that he was a multi-millionaire—his General Motors stock was worth $5 million and his AT&T stock was up to $10 million. Elated, he was about to inquire about his other holdings, when the telephone operator cut in with "Your time is up. Please deposit $100,000 for the next 3 minutes."[3]

This story demonstrates that prices can and do change over a period of time, and that one is not necessarily better off when they do. Although the numbers in the story are extreme, consider some more realistic data that compare prices in 1980 with what would have been expected in 2000, assuming average price increases of 6% and 12% per year.

ILLUSTRATION 7-5

Example of changing prices

	1980	2000	
Assumed average price increase		6%	12%
Public college, yearly average cost	$ 3,350.00	$ 10,743.92	$ 32,315.07
Average taxi ride, New York City (before tip)	2.95	9.46	28.46
Slice of pizza	.65	2.08	6.27
First-class postage stamp	.15	.48	1.45
Suburban house, New York City area	150,000.00	481,071.00	1,446,943.50
McDonald's milk shake	.75	2.41	7.23

HELPFUL HINT
Are you a winner or loser when you hold cash in a period of inflation? Answer: A loser, because the value of the cash declines as inflation climbs.

Despite the inevitability of changing prices during a period of inflation, the accounting profession still follows the stable monetary unit assumption in preparing a company's primary financial statements. While admitting that some changes in prices do occur, the profession believes the unit of measure—the dollar—has remained sufficiently constant over time to provide meaningful financial information. If presented, the **disclosure of price-level adjusted data is in the form of supplemental information** that accompanies the financial statements.

The basic principles of accounting are summarized in Illustration 7-6 on page 296.

CONSTRAINTS IN ACCOUNTING

Constraints permit a company to modify generally accepted accounting principles without reducing the usefulness of the reported information. The constraints are materiality and conservatism.

STUDY OBJECTIVE

Identify the two constraints in accounting.

Materiality
Materiality relates to an item's impact on a firm's overall financial condition and operations. An item is material when it is likely to influence the decision of a reasonably prudent investor or creditor. It is immaterial if its inclusion or omission has no impact on a decision maker. In short, if the item does not make a difference, GAAP does not have to be followed. To determine the materiality of an amount—that is, to determine its financial significance, the accountant usually compares it with such items as total assets, total liabilities, and net income.

---

[3]Adapted from *Barron's*, January 28, 1980, p. 27.

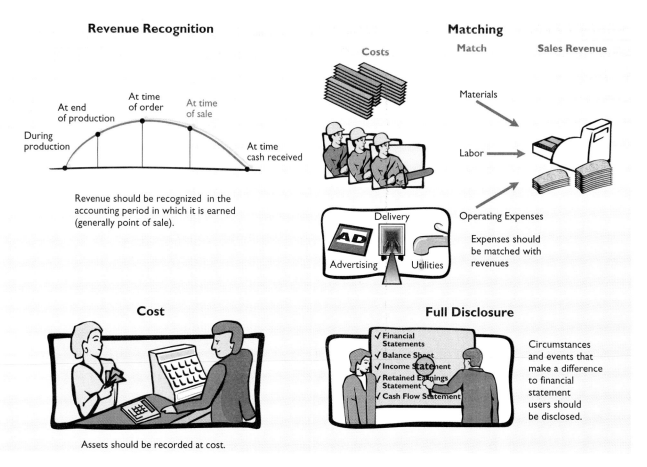

Revenue Recognition

During production · At end of production · At time of order · At time of sale · At time cash received

Revenue should be recognized in the accounting period in which it is earned (generally point of sale).

Matching

Costs · Match · Sales Revenue

Materials

Labor

Delivery · AD · Advertising · Utilities

Operating Expenses

Expenses should be matched with revenues

Cost

Assets should be recorded at cost.

Full Disclosure

✓ Financial Statements
✓ Balance Sheet
✓ Income Statement
✓ Retained Earnings Statement
✓ Cash Flow Statement

Circumstances and events that make a difference to financial statement users should be disclosed.

ILLUSTRATION 7-6

Basic principles used in accounting

To illustrate how the constraint of materiality is applied, assume that Rodriguez Co. purchases a number of low-cost plant assets, such as wastepaper baskets. Although the proper accounting would appear to be to depreciate these wastepaper baskets over their useful life, they are usually expensed immediately. This practice is justified because these costs are considered immaterial. Establishing depreciation schedules for these assets is costly and time-consuming and will not make a material difference on total assets and net income. Other applications of the materiality constraint are the expensing of small tools or the expensing of any plant assets under a certain dollar amount.

Conservatism

HELPFUL HINT

In other words, if two methods are otherwise equally appropriate, choose the one that will least likely overstate assets and income.

Conservatism in accounting means that when in doubt choose the method that will be least likely to overstate assets and income. It does **not** mean **understating** assets or income. Conservatism provides a guide in difficult situations, and the guide is a reasonable one: do not overstate assets and income.

A common application of the conservatism constraint is the use of the lower of cost or market method for inventories. As indicated in Chapter 6, inventories are reported at market value if market value is below cost. This practice results in a higher cost of goods sold and lower net income. In addition, inventory on the balance sheet is stated at a lower amount when market value is below cost. Other examples of conservatism in accounting are the use of the LIFO method for inventory valuation when prices are rising and the use of accelerated depreciation methods for plant assets. Both of these methods result in lower asset carrying values and lower net income than alternative methods.

The two constraints are graphically depicted in Illustration 7-7.

Materiality

For small amounts, GAAP
does not have to be followed.

Conservatism

When in doubt, choose the solution that will
be least likely to overstate assets and income.

ILLUSTRATION 7-7

Constraints in accounting

Summary of Conceptual Framework

As we have seen, the conceptual framework for developing sound reporting practices starts with a set of objectives for financial reporting and follows with the development of qualities that make information useful. In addition, elements of financial statements are defined. Operating guidelines in the form of assumptions and principles are then provided. The conceptual framework also recognizes that important constraints exist on the reporting environment. These points are illustrated graphically in Illustration 7-8:

ILLUSTRATION 7-8

Conceptual framework

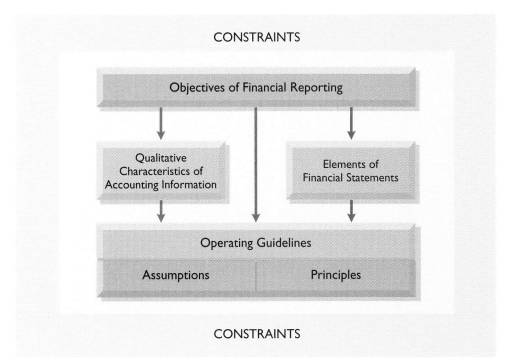

CONSTRAINTS

Objectives of Financial Reporting

Qualitative Characteristics of Accounting Information

Elements of Financial Statements

Operating Guidelines

Assumptions

Principles

CONSTRAINTS

BEFORE YOU GO ON. . . .

Review It

1. What are the monetary unit assumption, the economic entity assumption, the time period assumption, and the going concern assumption?
2. What are the revenue recognition principle, the matching principle, the full disclosure principle, and the cost principle?
3. What are the materiality constraint and the conservatism constraint?

THE
NAVIGATOR

FINANCIAL STATEMENT PRESENTATION AND ANALYSIS

7
STUDY
OBJECTIVE

Understand and analyze
classified financial
statements.

Financial statements play an important role in attempting to meet the objectives of financial reporting. "Bottom line" information such as total assets and net income are useful to investors, but these single numbers lack sufficient detail for serious analysis. Investors and creditors generally find the parts of a financial statement more useful than the whole. Proper classification within the financial statements is therefore extremely important.

Classified Balance Sheet

The balance sheet is composed of three major elements: assets, liabilities, and stockholders' equity. Additional segregation within these groups, however, is considered useful to financial statement readers. As indicated in Chapter 4, the following classification is generally found.

ILLUSTRATION **7-9**

*Standard classification of
balance sheet*

Assets	Liabilities and Stockholders' Equity
Current assets	Current liabilities
Long-term investments	Long-term liabilities
Property, plant, and equipment	Stockholders' equity
Intangible assets	

If the form of organization is a proprietorship, the term "owner's equity" instead of stockholders' equity is used to describe that section of the balance sheet. An account called capital is reported in the owner's equity section of the balance sheet for a proprietorship. **Capital** is the owner's investment in the business.

To illustrate, assume that Sally Field invests $90,000 on July 10, 2001, to start up Med/Waste Company. The company's balance sheet immediately after the investment is as follows:

ILLUSTRATION **7-10**

Proprietorship balance sheet

		MED/WASTE COMPANY	
		Balance Sheet	
		July 10, 2001	
Cash	$90,000	Sally Field, Capital	$90,000

Because Sally Field owns the business and has chosen not to incorporate, common stock is not issued and net income (net loss) belongs to her. Therefore, common stock and retained earnings accounts are not needed. Instead, her capital account is increased by investments and net income and is decreased by withdrawals of assets for personal use and net losses. The capital account represents Sally Field's claim to the net assets (assets less liabilities) of the company.

If the form of organization is a partnership, each partner has a separate capital account and the owners' equity section shows the capital accounts of all the partners. For example, assume that A. Roy and B. Siegfried form a partnership on December 11, 2001, at which time Roy and Siegfried each invest $60,000. The balance sheet immediately after their investments is as follows:

ROY AND SIEGFRIED Balance Sheet December 11, 2001			
Cash	$120,000	A. Roy, Capital	$ 60,000
		B. Siegfried, Capital	60,000
			$120,000

ILLUSTRATION 7-11
Partnership balance sheet

Classified Income Statement

Chapter 5 presented a multiple-step income statement for Highpoint Electronic, Inc. The multiple-step income statement included the following:

Sales revenue section—Presents the sales, discounts, allowances, and other related information to arrive at the net amount of sales revenue.

Cost of goods sold—Indicates the cost of goods sold to produce sales.

Operating expenses—Provides information on both selling and administrative expenses.

Other revenues and gains—Indicates revenues earned or gains resulting from nonoperating transactions.

Other expenses and losses—Indicates expenses or losses incurred from nonoperating transactions.

Two additional items are income tax expense and earnings per share.

Income Tax Expense

Income taxes must be paid and therefore reported for a corporation because a corporation is a legal entity separate and distinct from its owners. Proprietorships and partnerships are not separate legal entities; owners are therefore taxed directly on their business income. Stockholders are taxed only on the dividends they receive.

Corporate **income taxes (or income tax expense)** are reported in a separate section of the income statement before net income. The condensed income statement for Leads Inc. in Illustration 7-12 shows a typical presentation. Note that income before income taxes is reported before income tax expense.

LEADS INC. Income Statement For the Year Ended December 31, 2001	
Sales	$800,000
Cost of goods sold	600,000
Gross profit	200,000
Operating expenses	50,000
Income from operations	150,000
Other revenues and gains	10,000
Other expenses and losses	4,000
Income before income taxes	**156,000**
Income tax expense	**46,800**
Net income	$109,200

ILLUSTRATION 7-12
Income statement with income taxes

HELPFUL HINT
Corporations may also use the single-step form of income statements discussed in Chapter 5.

Income tax expense and the related liability for income taxes payable are recorded as part of the adjusting process preceding financial statement preparation. Using the data above for Leads Inc., the adjusting entry for income tax expense at December 31, 2001, would be as follows:

A	=	L	+	SE
		+46,800		−46,800

Income Tax Expense	46,800	
Income Taxes Payable		46,800
(To record income taxes for 2001)		

Other examples of income tax presentation appear in the demonstration problem income statement of Chapter 15 and the income statement of Kellogg's in Appendix A.

Earnings Per Share

Earnings per share data are frequently reported in the financial press and are widely used by stockholders and potential investors in evaluating the profitability of a company. Investors, especially, attempt to link earnings per share to the market price per share.[4] **Earnings per share (EPS)** indicates the net income earned by each share of outstanding common stock. Thus, **earnings per share is reported only for common stock**. The formula for computing earnings per share when there has been no change in outstanding shares during the year is as follows:

ILLUSTRATION 7-13

Earnings per share formula—no change in outstanding shares

For example, Leads Inc. (Illustration 7-12) has net income of $109,200. Assuming that it has 54,600 shares of common stock outstanding for the year, earnings per share is $2 ($109,200 ÷ 54,600).[5]

Because of the importance of earnings per share (EPS), most companies are required to report it on the face of the income statement. Generally this amount is simply reported below net income on the statement. For Leads Inc. the presentation would be:

ILLUSTRATION 7-14

Basic earnings per share disclosure

LEADS INC.
Income Statement (partial)
For the Year Ended December 31, 2001

Net income	$109,200
Earnings per share	$2.00

---

[4]The ratio of the market price per share to the earnings per share is referred to as the *price-earnings ratio*. This ratio is reported in *The Wall Street Journal* and other newspapers for common stocks listed on major stock exchanges.
[5]Whenever the number of outstanding shares changes during the year the calculation of EPS becomes more complicated. These computations are covered later in Chapter 15.

Analyzing Financial Statements

The financial statements should provide financial information that is useful for helping make sound investment and credit decisions. Presented below are the condensed balance sheet and income statement of Genlyte Inc. for 2001:

ILLUSTRATION 7-15

Financial statements—Genlyte Inc.

GENLYTE INC.
Balance Sheet
December 31, 2001

Assets		Liabilities and Stockholders' Equity	
Current assets	$156,000	Current liabilities	$ 70,000
Plant and equipment (net)	74,000	Long-term liabilities	114,000
Intangible assets	14,000	Stockholders' equity	60,000
Total assets	$244,000	Total liabilities and stockholders' equity	$244,000

GENLYTE INC.
Income Statement
For the Year Ended December 31, 2001

Net sales	$430,000
Cost of sales	295,000
Gross profit	135,000
Selling and administrative expenses	109,000
Income from operations	26,000
Other expenses and losses	5,000
Income before income taxes	21,000
Income tax expense	7,000
Net income	$ 14,000
Earnings per share	$0.35

In analyzing and interpreting financial statement information, three major characteristics are generally evaluated: **liquidity, profitability**, and **solvency**. A **short-term debt holder**, for example, is primarily interested in the ability of a borrower to pay obligations when they become due. The liquidity of the borrower in such a case is extremely important in assessing the safety of a loan. A **long-term debt holder**, however, looks to indicators such as profitability and solvency that point to the firm's ability to survive over a long period of time. Long-term debt holders analyze earnings per share, the relationship of income to total assets invested, and the amount of debt in relation to total assets to determine whether money should be lent and at what interest rate. Similarly, **stockholders** are interested in the profitability and solvency of a company when assessing the likelihood of dividends and the growth potential of the common stock.

Liquidity

What is Genlyte's ability to pay its maturing obligations and meet unexpected needs for cash? The relationship between current assets and current liabilities is critical to helping answer this question. These relationships are expressed as a ratio, called the **current ratio**, and as a dollar amount, called **working capital**.

Current Ratio.   The current ratio is current assets divided by current liabilities. For Genlyte Inc., the ratio is 2.23:1, computed as follows:

ILLUSTRATION 7-16

Current ratio formula and computation

This ratio means that current assets are more than two times greater than current liabilities. Bankers, other creditors, and agencies such as Dun & Bradstreet use this ratio to determine whether the company is a good credit risk. Traditionally, a ratio of 2:1 is considered to be the standard for a good credit rating. Today, however, many sound companies have current ratios of less than 2:1. With its 2.23:1 ratio, Genlyte's short-term debt-paying ability appears to be very favorable.

From the foregoing, you might at first assume that the higher the current ratio, the better. This is not necessarily true. A very high current ratio may indicate that the company is holding more current assets than it currently needs in the business. It is possible, therefore, that the excess resources might be directed to more profitable investment opportunities.

Working Capital. The excess of current assets over current liabilities is called **working capital**. For Genlyte Inc., working capital is $86,000, as shown below:

ILLUSTRATION 7-17

Working capital formula and computation

The amount of working capital provides some indication of the company's ability to meet its existing current obligations. A large amount of working capital generally means a company can meet its current liabilities as they fall due and pay dividends, if desired. Although no set standards exist for the level of working capital a company should maintain, the general adequacy of a company's working capital is often determined by comparing data from prior periods and from similar companies of comparable size. Genlyte's working capital appears adequate.

Profitability

Profitability ratios measure the income or operating success of an enterprise for a given period of time. Income, or the lack of it, affects the company's ability to obtain debt or equity financing and the company's ability to grow.

Profit Margin Percentage. One important ratio used to measure profitability is the **profit margin percentage** (or rate of return on sales). It measures the percentage of each dollar of sales that results in net income. It is calculated by dividing net income by net sales for the period. Genlyte Inc.'s profit margin percentage is 3.3 percent, computed as follows:

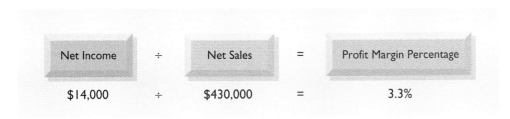

ILLUSTRATION 7-18
Profit margin formula and computation

This ratio seems low. Much, however, depends on the type of industry. High-volume retailers, such as grocery stores (Safeway or Kroger) or discount stores (Wal-Mart or Kmart), generally have a low profit margin. They make a small profit on each sale but have many sales.

ACCOUNTING IN ACTION
Business Insight

The type of industry can make a difference in the profit margin percentage investors and creditors expect. Profit margins among service companies—from airlines and banks to telecommunication companies and utilities—have traditionally been lower than those among manufacturers. MCI Communications, for example, showed a profit margin percentage of 4.9 percent which is high for a telecommunications company. Sprint's profit margin percentage was only 0.5 percent, and AT&T posted a loss. By contrast, the top three pharmaceutical firms—Johnson & Johnson, Bristol-Meyers Squibb, and Merck—had a profit margin percentage of 12.6 percent, 17.2 percent, and 20.6 percent, respectively. Before using a ratio like the profit margin percentage to evaluate company performance, you need to know what is reasonable performance for the industry.

Return on Assets.   In making an investment, an investor wants to know what rate of return to expect and what risks are associated with that rate of return. The greater the risk, the higher the rate of return the investor will demand on the investment.

One overall measure of profitability of a company is its **rate of return on assets**. It is calculated by dividing net income by total assets.[6] Genlyte Inc.'s rate of return is 5.7 percent, computed as follows:

ILLUSTRATION 7-19
Return on assets formula and computation

The rate of return on assets is relatively low, which suggests that Genlyte may not be using its assets effectively.

Return on Common Stockholders' Equity.   Another widely used rate that measures profitability from the common stockholders' viewpoint is **return on com-**

---

[6]For simplicity, the rate of return calculations are based on end-of-year total amounts. The more conceptually correct *average* total assets and *average* common stockholders' equity are used in later chapters.

mon stockholders' equity. This rate shows how many dollars of net income were earned for each dollar of owner investment. It is calculated by dividing net income by common stockholders' equity. In Genlyte Inc.'s case, the rate of return is 23.3 percent, computed as follows:

ILLUSTRATION **7-20**

Return on common stockholders' equity formula and computation

Genlyte's return on common stockholders' equity is quite good. The reason for this high rate of return is that Genlyte's assets are earning a return higher than the borrowing costs the company incurs.

Solvency

Solvency measures the ability of an enterprise to survive over a long period of time. Long-term debt holders and stockholders are interested in a company's ability to pay periodic interest and to repay the face value of the debt at maturity.

Debt to Total Assets.   One useful measure of solvency is the **debt to total assets ratio**. It measures the percentage of total assets that creditors, as opposed to stockholders, provide. It is calculated by dividing total debt (liabilities) by total assets, normally expressed as a percentage. Genlyte Inc.'s debt to total assets ratio is 75.4 percent, computed as follows:

ILLUSTRATION **7-21**

Debt to total assets formula and computation

Debt to total assets of 75.4 percent means that Genlyte's creditors have provided approximately three-quarters of its total assets. The higher the percentage of debt to total assets, the greater the risk that the company may be unable to meet its maturing obligations; the lower the percentage, the greater the "buffer" available to creditors should the company become insolvent. In Genlyte Inc.'s case, unless earnings are positive and very stable, the company may have too much debt.

These percentage and ratio relationships are often used in comparison with (1) expected results, (2) prior year results, and (3) published results of other companies in the same line of business. Conclusions based on a single year's results are hazardous at best. Chapter 15 provides more detailed consideration of the analysis of financial statements.

Financial Statement Presentation— An International Perspective

World markets are becoming increasingly intertwined. Foreigners use American computers, eat American breakfast cereals, read American magazines, listen to

American rock music, watch American movies and TV shows, and drink American soda. And, Americans drive Japanese cars, wear Italian shoes and Scottish woolens, drink Brazilian coffee and Indian tea, eat Swiss chocolate bars, sit on Danish furniture, and use Arabian oil. The tremendous variety and volume of both exported and imported goods indicates the extensive involvement of U.S. business in international trade. For many U.S. companies, the world is their market.

The following table illustrates the magnitude of foreign sales and type of product sold by U.S. companies.

8
STUDY
OBJECTIVE
····································

Explain the accounting principles used in international operations.

Company	Foreign Sales as a % of Total	Product
Reebok	44.3	Sport clothing
Coca-Cola	67.0	Beverages
Disney	23.0	Entertainment
E.I. duPont de Nemours	42.1	Specialty chemicals
General Electric	27.7	Diversified
Ford Motor	32.7	Motor vehicles and parts
Campbell Soup	31.0	Prepared foods
Sears, Roebuck & Co.	8.9	Retail and diversified
Phillip Morris	53.8	Tobacco, beverages, food products
RJR Nabisco	37.0	Tobacco, beverages, food products

ILLUSTRATION 7-22

Foreign sales and type of product

Firms that conduct their operations in more than one country through subsidiaries, divisions, or branches in foreign countries are referred to as **multinational corporations**. The accounting for multinational corporations is complicated because foreign currencies are involved. These international transactions and operations must be translated into U.S. dollars.

HELPFUL HINT
Accounting and auditing in the free world is dominated by the large international American public accounting firms and their affiliates. These firms audit companies everywhere in the world.

Differences in Standards
As the "world economy" is becoming globalized, many investment and credit decisions require the analysis and interpretation of foreign financial statements. Unfortunately, there is a lack of uniformity in accounting standards from country to country. This lack of uniformity is the result of different legal systems, different processes for developing accounting standards, different governmental requirements, and different economic environments.

ACCOUNTING IN ACTION
International Insight

Research and development costs are an example of different international accounting standards. Compare how four countries account for research and development costs:

Country	Accounting Treatment
United States	Expenditures are expensed.
United Kingdom	Certain expenditures may be capitalized.
Germany	Expenditures are expensed.
Japan	Expenditures may be capitalized and amortized over 5 years.

Thus, a research and development expenditure of $100 million is charged totally to expense in the current period in the United States and Germany. The accounting treatment of this same expense could range from zero to $100 million in the United Kingdom and from $20 million to $100 million in Japan!

Do you think that accounting principles should be comparable across countries?

Uniformity in Standards

Efforts to obtain uniformity in international accounting practices are taking place. In 1973 the International Accounting Standards Committee (IASC) was formed by agreement of accounting organizations in the United States, the United Kingdom, Canada, Australia, France, Germany, Japan, Mexico, and the Netherlands. The purpose of the IASC is to formulate and publish international accounting standards and to promote their acceptance worldwide.

To date, numerous International Accounting Standards have been issued for IASC members to introduce to their respective countries. But, because the IASC has no enforcement powers, these standards are by no means universally applied. They are, however, generally followed by the large multinational companies that are audited by international public accounting firms. Thus, the foundation has been laid for considerable progress toward greater uniformity in international accounting.

BEFORE YOU GO ON . . .

Review It

1. What is the major difference in the equity section of the balance sheet between a corporation and proprietorship?
2. Where are income tax expense and earnings per share reported on the income statement? How is earnings per share computed?
3. How are the current ratio, working capital, profit margin percentage, return on assets, return on common stockholders' equity, and debt to total assets computed?
4. Explain how these ratios are useful in financial statement analysis.
5. What is the purpose of the International Accounting Standards Committee?

A LOOK BACK AT OUR FEATURE STORY

Refer back to the opening story and answer the following questions.
1. Competitors of America Online expense their subscriber acquisition costs as incurred; AOL capitalizes these costs and amortizes them over 18 months. Are the concepts of comparability or consistency violated in this situation? Explain.
2. The controller of one of AOL's competitors stated, "We consider our earnings strong. We didn't want to taint them or dilute them by following [AOL's] accounting." Explain this statement.

Solution:
1. Comparability results when different companies use the same accounting principles. In this case, comparability does not occur because the companies use different practices to account for subscriber acquisition costs. Consistency means that a company uses the same accounting principles and methods from year to year. All of the companies are consistent in that they continue to use the same accounting method from year to year.
2. Competitors of AOL expense their subscriber acquisition costs as incurred. Their earnings are therefore conservatively reported (often referred to as "high-quality earnings"). That is, earnings may be understated because of the expensing of subscriber acquisition costs.

DEMONSTRATION PROBLEM 1

Presented below are a number of operational guidelines and practices that have developed over time. Identify the accounting assumption, accounting principle, or reporting constraint that most appropriately justifies these procedures and practices. Use only one item per description.

1. The first note, "Summary of Significant Accounting Policies," presents information on the subclassification of plant assets and discusses the company's depreciation methods.

PROBLEM-SOLVING
STRATEGIES
1. The four principles are cost, revenue recognition, matching, and full disclosure.
2. The two constraints are materiality and conservatism.
3. Full disclosure relates generally to the item; materiality to the amount. Thus the better answer for 5 is full disclosure.
4. Try to find the concept that best describes the situation.

2. The local hamburger restaurant expenses all spatulas, french fry baskets, and other cooking utensils when purchased.

3. Retailers recognize revenue at the point of sale.

4. Green-Grow Lawn Mowers, Inc., includes an estimate of warranty expense in the year in which it sells its lawn mowers, which carry a two-year warranty.

5. Companies present sufficient financial information so that creditors and reasonably prudent investors will not be misled.

6. Companies listed on U.S. stock exchanges report audited financial information annually and report unaudited information quarterly.

7. Beach Resorts, Inc., does not record the 2001 value of $1.5 million for a piece of beachfront property it purchased in 1979 for $500,000.

8. Office Systems, Inc., takes a $32,000 loss on a number of older microcomputers in its inventory; it paid the manufacturer $107,000 for them but can sell them for only $75,000.

9. Frito Lay is a wholly owned subsidiary of PepsiCo, Inc., and Frito Lay's operating results and financial condition are included in the consolidated financial statements of PepsiCo. (Do not use full disclosure.)

SOLUTION TO DEMONSTRATION PROBLEM 1

1. Full disclosure principle
2. Materiality constraint
3. Revenue recognition principle
4. Matching principle
5. Full disclosure principle

6. Time period assumption
7. Cost principle
8. Conservatism constraint
9. Economic entity assumption

THE
NAVIGATOR

DEMONSTRATION PROBLEM 2

Presented below is financial information related to Notting Hill Corporation for the year 2001. All balances are ending balances unless stated otherwise.

Accounts payable	$ 868,000
Accounts receivable	700,000
Accumulated depreciation—equipment	100,000
Administrative expenses	280,000
Bonds payable	1,600,000
Cash	800,000
Common stock	500,000
Cost of goods sold	1,600,000
Dividends	60,000
Equipment	1,100,000
Income tax expense	83,000
Interest expense	60,000
Interest revenue	120,000
Inventories	500,000
Loss on the sale of equipment	35,000
Marketable (trading) securities	400,000
Net sales	2,400,000
Notes payable (short-term)	800,000
Other long-term debt	387,000
Patents and other intangibles	900,000
Prepaid expenses	200,000
Retained earnings (January 1, 2001)	80,000
Selling expenses	220,000
Taxes payable	83,000

Notting Hill Corporation had 88,000 shares of common stock outstanding for the entire year.

PROBLEM-SOLVING
STRATEGIES
1. Review the format in Chapter 5, page 207 for a multiple-step income statement. Note the multiple-step income statement reports gross profit and income from operations. A single-step income statement does not report these items.
2. Income tax expense is reported immediately after Income before income taxes for both a multiple-step and single-step income statement.
3. Earnings per share must be reported on both a multiple-step and a single-step income statement.
4. A retained earnings statement reports net income and dividends.
5. Refer to Chapter 4, p. 163 for an example of a classified balance sheet.

Instructions:

(a) Prepare a multiple-step income statement.

(b) Prepare a single-step income statement.

(c) Prepare a retained earnings statement.

(d) Prepare a classified balance sheet.

(e) Compute the following balance sheet relationships:
   (1) current ratio,
   (2) the amount of working capital, and
   (3) debt to total assets ratio.
   What insights do these relationships provide to the reader of the financial statements?

(f) Compute three measures of profitability from the income statement and balance sheet information. What insights do these relationships provide to the reader of the financial statements?

SOLUTION TO DEMONSTRATION PROBLEM 2

(a) Multiple-step income statement

NOTTING HILL CORPORATION
Income Statement
For the Year Ended December 31, 2001

Net sales		$2,400,000
Cost of goods sold		1,600,000
Gross profit		800,000
Selling expenses	$220,000	
Administrative expenses	280,000	500,000
Income from operations		300,000
Other revenues and gains		
Interest revenue		120,000
Other expenses and losses		
Loss on sale of equipment	35,000	
Interest expense	60,000	95,000
Income before income taxes		325,000
Income tax expense		83,000
Net income		$ 242,000
Earnings per share		$2.75

(b) Single-step income statement

NOTTING HILL CORPORATION
Income Statement
For the Year Ended December 31, 2001

Revenues		
Net sales		$2,400,000
Interest revenue		120,000
Total revenues		2,520,000
Expenses		
Cost of goods sold	$1,600,000	
Selling expenses	220,000	
Administrative expenses	280,000	
Interest expense	60,000	
Loss on the sale of equipment	35,000	2,195,000
Income before income taxes		325,000
Income tax expense		83,000
Net income		$ 242,000
Earnings per share		$2.75

(c) Retained earnings statement

NOTTING HILL CORPORATION
Retained Earnings Statement
For the Year Ended December 31, 2001

Retained earnings, January 1	$ 80,000
Add: Net income	242,000
	322,000
Less: Dividends	60,000
Retained earnings, December 31	$262,000

(d) Classified balance sheet

NOTTING HILL CORPORATION
Balance Sheet
December 31, 2001

Current assets		
Cash		$ 800,000
Marketable (trading) securities		400,000
Accounts receivable		700,000
Inventories		500,000
Prepaid expenses		200,000
Total current assets		2,600,000
Property, plant, and equipment		
Equipment	$1,100,000	
Less: Accumulated depreciation	100,000	1,000,000
Intangible assets		
Patents and other intangible assets		900,000
Total assets		$4,500,000
Current liabilities		
Notes payable		$ 800,000
Accounts payable		868,000
Taxes payable		83,000
Total current liabilities		1,751,000
Long-term liabilities		
Bonds payable	$1,600,000	
Other long-term debt	387,000	1,987,000
Total liabilities		3,738,000
Stockholders' equity		
Common stock	500,000	
Retained earnings	262,000	762,000
Total liabilities and stockholders' equity		$4,500,000

(e) Balance sheet relationships

(1) Current ratio $= \dfrac{\text{Current assets}}{\text{Current liabilities}} = \dfrac{\$2,600,000}{\$1,751,000} = 1.48{:}1$

(2) Working capital = Current assets − Current liabilities

Current assets	$2,600,000
Current liabilities	1,751,000
Working capital	$ 849,000

(3) Debt to total assets $= \dfrac{\text{Debt}}{\text{Total assets}} = \dfrac{\$3,738,000}{\$4,500,000} = 83.07\%$

Notting Hill's liquidity does not look good. The current ratio is not substantial. Its working capital looks healthy, with current assets well in excess of current liabilities; and its debt to total assets, at well over 80%, is too high. Given the company's relatively low profitability (see below), its creditors should be concerned.

(f) Profitability relationships

$$\text{Profit margin} = \frac{\text{Net income}}{\text{Net sales}} = \frac{\$242,000}{\$2,400,000} = 10.08\%$$

$$\text{Return on assets} = \frac{\text{Net income}}{\text{Total assets}} = \frac{\$242,000}{\$4,500,000} = 5.38\%$$

$$\text{Return on common stockholders' equity} = \frac{\text{Net income}}{\text{Common stockholders' equity}} = \frac{\$242,000}{\$762,000} = 31.76\%$$

The profit margin percentage (return on sales) for Notting Hill seems adequate. Given the company's large asset base, however, it should probably generate a higher profit. The company's overall financial picture, then, could be better.

THE NAVIGATOR

SUMMARY OF STUDY OBJECTIVES

1. Explain the meaning of generally accepted accounting principles and identify the key items of the conceptual framework. Generally accepted accounting principles are a set of rules and practices that are recognized as a general guide for financial reporting purposes. Generally accepted means that these principles must have "substantial authoritative support." The key items of the conceptual framework are: (1) objectives of financial reporting; (2) qualitative characteristics of accounting information; (3) elements of financial statements; and (4) operating guidelines (assumptions, principles, and constraints).

2. Describe the basic objectives of financial reporting. The basic objectives of financial reporting are to provide information that is (1) useful to those making investment and credit decisions; (2) helpful in assessing future cash flows; and (3) helpful in identifying economic resources (assets), the claims to those resources (liabilities), and the changes in those resources and claims.

3. Discuss the qualitative characteristics of accounting information and elements of financial statements. To be judged useful, information should possess the following qualitative characteristics: relevance, reliability, comparability, and consistency. The elements of financial statements are a set of definitions that can be used to describe the basic terms used in accounting.

4. Identify the basic assumptions used by accountants. The major assumptions are: monetary unit, economic entity, time period, and going concern.

5. Identify the basic principles of accounting. The major principles are revenue recognition, matching, full disclosure, and cost.

6. Identify the two constraints in accounting. The major constraints are materiality and conservatism.

7. Understand and analyze classified financial statements. We presented classified balance sheets and classified (multiple-step) income statements in Chapters 4 and 5, respectively. Two new items added to the classified income statement in this chapter are income taxes and earnings per share. Three items used to analyze the balance sheet are the current ratio, working capital, and debt to total assets. Earnings per share, profit margin percentage (return on sales), return on assets, and return on common stockholders' equity are used to analyze profitability.

8. Explain the accounting principles used in international operations. There are few recognized worldwide accounting standards. The International Accounting Standards Committee (IASC), of which the United States is a member, is making efforts to obtain conformity in international accounting practices.

THE NAVIGATOR

GLOSSARY

Comparability Ability to compare accounting information of different companies because they use the same accounting principles. (p. 288).

Conceptual framework A coherent system of interrelated objectives and fundamentals that can lead to consistent standards. (p. 287).

Conservatism The approach of choosing an accounting method when in doubt that will least likely overstate assets and net income. (p. 296).

Consistency Use of the same accounting principles and methods from year to year within a company. (p. 289).

Cost principle   Accounting principle that assets should be recorded at their historical cost. (p. 294).

Current ratio   A measure that expresses the relationship of current assets to current liabilities by dividing current assets by current liabilities. (p. 301).

Earnings per share (EPS)   The net income earned by each share of outstanding common stock. (p. 300).

Economic entity assumption   Accounting assumption that economic events can be identified with a particular unit of accountability. (p. 291).

Elements of financial statements   Definitions of basic terms used in accounting. (p. 289).

Full disclosure principle   Accounting principle that circumstances and events that make a difference to financial statement users should be disclosed. (p. 294).

Generally accepted accounting principles (GAAP)   A set of rules and practices, having substantial authoritative support, that are recognized as a general guide for financial reporting purposes. (p. 286).

Going concern assumption   The assumption that the enterprise will continue in operation long enough to carry out its existing objectives and commitments. (p. 291).

International Accounting Standards Committee (IASC)   An accounting organization whose purpose is to formulate and publish international accounting standards and to promote their acceptance worldwide. (p. 306).

Matching principle   Accounting principle that expenses should be matched with revenues in the period when efforts are expended to generate revenues. (p. 292).

Materiality   The constraint of determining if an item is important enough to likely influence the decision of a reasonably prudent investor or creditor. (p. 295).

Monetary unit assumption   Accounting assumption that only transaction data capable of being expressed in monetary terms should be included in accounting records. (p. 291).

Relevance   The quality of information that indicates the information makes a difference in a decision (p. 288).

Reliability   The quality of information that gives assurance that it is free of error and bias. (p. 288).

Revenue recognition principle   Accounting principle that revenue should be recognized in the accounting period in which it is earned (generally at the point of sale). (p. 292).

Time period assumption   Accounting assumption that the economic life of a business can be divided into artificial time periods. (p. 291).

SELF-STUDY QUESTIONS

Answers are at the end of the chapter.

(SO 1) 1. Generally accepted accounting principles are:
   a. a set of standards and rules that are recognized as a general guide for financial reporting.
   b. usually established by the Internal Revenue Service.
   c. the guidelines used to resolve ethical dilemmas.
   d. fundamental truths that can be derived from the laws of nature.

(SO 2) 2. Which of the following is *not* an objective of financial reporting?
   a. Provide information that is useful in investment and credit decisions.
   b. Provide information about economic resources, claims to those resources, and changes in them.
   c. Provide information that is useful in assessing future cash flows.
   d. Provide information on the liquidation value of a business.

(SO 3) 3. The primary criterion by which accounting information can be judged is:
   a. consistency.
   b. predictive value.
   c. decision-usefulness.
   d. comparability.

(SO 3) 4. Verifiable is an ingredient of:

	Reliability	Relevance
a.	Yes	Yes
b.	No	No
c.	Yes	No
d.	No	Yes

(SO 4, 5, 6) 5. Valuing assets at their liquidation value rather than their cost is *inconsistent* with the:
   a. time period assumption.
   b. matching principle.
   c. going concern assumption.
   d. materiality constraint.

(SO 4, 5, 6) 6. The accounting constraint that refers to the tendency of accountants to resolve uncertainty in favor of understating assets and revenues is known as (the):
   a. matching principle.
   b. materiality.
   c. conservatism.
   d. monetary unit assumption.

(SO 7) 7. Naboo Enterprises has current assets of $80,000 and current liabilities of $20,000. Its current ratio and working capital are:
   a. .25:1; $60,000.
   b. 4:1; $60,000.
   c. .25:1; $80,000.
   d. 4:1; $80,000.

(SO 7) 8. Hernandez Company has a retained earnings balance of $162,000 at the beginning of the period. At the end of the period, the retained earnings balance was $220,000. Assuming a dividend of $25,000 was declared and paid during the period, the net income for the period was:
   a. $33,000.
   b. $58,000.
   c. $83,000.
   d. $187,000.

(SO 7) 9. The basic formula for computing earnings per share is net income divided by:
   a. common shares authorized.
   b. common shares issued.
   c. common shares outstanding.
   d. common stock purchased.

10. Jar Jar Corp. has total liabilities of $1,400,000, total stock- (SO 7) holders' equity of $2,800,000, current assets of $600,000, and current liabilities of $400,000. Jar Jar's total debt to total assets ratio is:
   a. 50%.
   b. 41.2%.
   c. 33.3%.
   d. 28.6%.

THE NAVIGATOR

QUESTIONS

1. (a) What are generally accepted accounting principles (GAAP)? (b) What bodies provide authoritative support for GAAP?

2. What elements comprise the FASB's conceptual framework?

3. (a) What are the objectives of financial reporting? (b) Identify the qualitative characteristics of accounting information.

4. Amy Dala, the president of Edenic Company, is pleased. Edenic substantially increased its net income in 2000 while keeping the number of **units** in its inventory relatively the same. Han Solo, chief accountant, cautions Dala, however. Solo says that since Edenic changed its method of inventory **valuation**, there is a consistency problem and it would be difficult to determine if Edenic is better off. Is Solo correct? Why?

5. What is the distinction between comparability and consistency?

6. Why is it necessary for accountants to assume that an economic entity will remain a going concern?

7. When should revenue be recognized? Why has the date of sale been chosen as the point at which to recognize the revenue resulting from the entire producing and selling process?

8. Distinguish between expired costs and unexpired costs.

9. (a) Where does the accountant disclose information about an entity's financial position, operations, and cash flows? (b) The full disclosure principle recognizes that the nature and amount of information included in financial reports reflects a series of judgmental trade-offs. What are the objectives of these trade-offs?

10. Sue Leonard is the president of Better Books. She has no accounting background. Leonard cannot understand why current cost is not used as the basis for accounting measurement and reporting. Explain what basis is used and why.

11. Describe the two constraints inherent in the presentation of accounting information.

12. In February 2000, Richard Holland invested an additional $5,000 in his business, Holland's Pharmacy, which is organized as a corporation. Holland's accountant, Louisa Newton, recorded this receipt as an increase in cash and revenues. Is this treatment appropriate? Why or why not?

13. Identify three financial relationships that are useful in analyzing the profitability of a company. Why might we want more than one measure of profitability?

14. Ann Schmitt Company has current assets of $50,000 and current liabilities of $20,000. What is its (a) working capital and (b) current ratio?

15. If current assets are less than current liabilities, will working capital be positive or negative? Will the current ratio be greater than or less than 1:1?

16. Smiley Inc.'s debt to total assets stands at 62 percent. If you were a banker, would you be comfortable about extending additional credit to Smiley? Why or why not?

17. Your roommate believes that international accounting standards are uniform throughout the world. Is your roommate correct? Explain.

18. What organization establishes international accounting standards?

BRIEF EXERCISES

Identify generally accepted accounting principles.
(SO 1)

BE7–1 Indicate whether each of the following statements is true or false.

   1. ____ GAAP is a set of rules and practices established by the accounting profession to serve as a general guide for financial reporting purposes.

   2. ____ Substantial authoritative support for GAAP usually comes from two standard-setting bodies: the FASB and the IRS.

   3. ____ *"Generally accepted"* means that these principles must have "substantial authoritative support."

BE7–2 Indicate which of the following items is(are) included in the FASB's conceptual framework. (Use "Yes" or "No" to answer this question.) *Identify items included in conceptual framework.*
(SO 1)

1. ____ Analysis of financial statement ratios.
2. ____ Objectives of financial reporting.
3. ____ Qualitative characteristics of accounting information.

BE7–3 According to the FASB's conceptual framework, which of the following are objectives of financial reporting? (Use "Yes" or "No" to answer this question.) *Identify objectives of financial reporting.*
(SO 2)

1. ____ Provide information that is helpful in assessing past cash flows and stock prices.
2. ____ Provide information that is useful to those making investment and credit decisions.
3. ____ Provide information that identifies the economic resources (assets), the claims to those resources (liabilities), and the changes in those resources and claims.

BE7–4 Presented below is a chart of the qualitative characteristics of accounting information. Fill in the blanks from (a) to (e). *Identify qualitative characteristics.*
(SO 3)

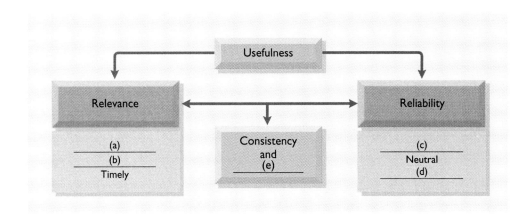

BE7–5 Given the *qualitative characteristics* of accounting established by the FASB's conceptual framework, complete each of the following statements: *Identify qualitative characteristics.*
(SO 3)

1. For information to be ____, it should have predictive or feedback value, and it must be presented on a timely basis.
2. ____ is the quality of information that gives assurance that it is free of error and bias; it can be depended on.
3. ____ means using the same accounting principles and methods from year to year within a company.

BE7–6 Presented below is a set of qualitative characteristics of accounting information. *Identify qualitative characteristics.*
(SO 3)

(a) Predictive value   (c) Verifiable
(b) Neutral   (d) Timely

Match these qualitative characteristics to the following statements, using letters a through d.

1. ____ Accounting information should help users make predictions about the outcome of past, present, and future events.
2. ____ Accounting information cannot be selected, prepared, or presented to favor one set of interested users over another.
3. ____ Accounting information must be proved to be free of error and bias.
4. ____ Accounting information must be available to decision makers before it loses its capacity to influence their decisions.

BE7–7 Presented below are four concepts discussed in this chapter. *Identify operating guidelines.*
(SO 4, 5, 6)

(a) Time period assumption   (c) Full disclosure principle
(b) Cost principle   (d) Conservatism

Match these concepts to the following accounting practices. Each letter can be used only once.

1. ____ Recording inventory at its purchase price.
2. ____ Using notes and supplementary schedules in the financial statements.
3. ____ Preparing financial statements on an annual basis.
4. ____ Using the lower of cost or market method for inventory valuation.

Identify the constraints that have been violated.
(SO 6)

BE7–8   The Lightsaber Company uses the following accounting practices:

1. Inventory is reported at cost when market value is lower.
2. The alternative accounting methods are selected in order to avoid reporting a higher net income.
3. Small tools are recorded as plant assets and depreciated.
4. The income statement shows paper clips expense of $10.

Indicate the accounting constraint, if any, that has been violated by each practice.

Perform balance sheet analysis.
(SO 7)

BE7–9   The following data are taken from the balance sheet of Nike, Inc. The data are arranged in alphabetical order (in millions).

Accounts payable	$ 584,600	Other current liabilities	$ 608,500
Accounts receivable	1,674,400	Retained earnings	3,043,400
Cash	108,600	Income taxes payable	28,900

Compute Nike's (a) current ratio and (b) working capital.

Compute income statement relationships.
(SO 7)

BE7–10   The following information, presented in alphabetical order, is taken from the financial statements of Palpatine Inc.:

Gross profit	$895,000	Other revenues and gains	$ 36,000
Income before income taxes	276,000	Net income	179,400
Income from operations	240,000	Net sales	1,652,000

Compute Palpatine's (a) operating expenses and (b) income tax expense for the period.

Compute earnings per share.
(SO 7)

BE7–11   Additional information for Palpatine Inc. (BE7–10) is as follows:

Common shares outstanding		Dividends on common stock	
for the entire year	46,000	paid during the year	$34,500

Given the information above and in BE7–10, compute Palpatine's earnings per share.

EXERCISES

Identify the assumption, principle, or constraint that has been violated.
(SO 4, 5, 6)

E7–1   A number of accounting reporting situations are described below.

1. Mowinski Company recognizes revenue at the end of the production cycle, but before sale. The price of the product, as well as the amount that can be sold, is not certain.
2. In preparing its financial statements, Thebeau Company omitted information concerning its method of accounting for inventories.
3. Jan Way Corp. charges the entire premium on a two-year insurance policy to the first year.
4. Rowland Hospital Supply Corporation reports only current assets and current liabilities on its balance sheet. Property, plant, and equipment and bonds payable are reported as current assets and current liabilities, respectively. Liquidation of the company is unlikely.
5. Barton Inc. is carrying inventory at its current market value of $100,000. Inventory had an original cost of $110,000.
6. Karen Allman Company is in its fifth year of operation and has yet to issue financial statements. (Do not use full disclosure principle.)
7. Watts Company has inventory on hand that cost $400,000. Watts reports inventory on its balance sheet at its current market value of $425,000.
8. Susan Elbe, president of the Classic Music Company, bought a computer for her personal use. She paid for the computer by using company funds and debited the "computers" account.

Instructions

For each of the above, list the assumption, principle, or constraint that has been violated, if any. List only one term for each case.

E7–2 Presented below are some business transactions that occurred during 2000 for S. Sosa Company.

Identify the assumption, principle, or constraint that has been violated and prepare correct entries.
(SO 4, 5, 6)

(a) Merchandise inventory with a cost of $208,000 is reported at its market value of $260,000. The following entry was made:

Merchandise Inventory	52,000	
Gain		52,000

(b) Equipment worth $90,000 was acquired at a cost of $72,000 from a company that had water damage in a flood. The following entry was made:

Equipment	90,000	
Cash		72,000
Gain		18,000

(c) The president of S. Sosa Company, George Winston, purchased a truck for personal use and charged it to his expense account. The following entry was made:

Travel Expense	18,000	
Cash		18,000

(d) An electric pencil sharpener costing $50 is being depreciated over 5 years. The following entry was made:

Depreciation Expense—Pencil Sharpener	10	
Accumulated Depreciation—Pencil Sharpener		10

Instructions
In each of the situations above, identify the assumption, principle, or constraint that has been violated, if any, and discuss the appropriateness of the journal entries. Give the correct journal entry, if necessary.

E7–3 Presented below are the assumptions, principles, and constraints discussed in this chapter:

Identify accounting assumptions, principles, and constraints.
(SO 4, 5, 6)

(a) Economic entity assumption
(b) Going concern assumption
(c) Monetary unit assumption
(d) Time period assumption
(e) Cost principle

(f) Matching principle
(g) Full disclosure principle
(h) Revenue recognition principle
(i) Materiality
(j) Conservatism

Instructions
Identify by letter the accounting assumption, principle, or constraint that describes each situation below. Do not use a letter more than once.

1. Is the rationale for why plant assets are not reported at liquidation value. (Do not use historical cost principle.)
2. Indicates that personal and business record-keeping should be separately maintained.
3. Ensures that all relevant financial information is reported.
4. Assumes that the dollar is the "measuring stick" used to report on financial performance.
5. Requires that the operational guidelines be followed for all significant items.
6. Separates financial information into time periods for reporting purpose.
7. Requires recognition of expenses in the same period as related revenues.
8. Indicates that market value changes subsequent to purchase are not recorded in the accounts.

E7–4 Consider the following transactions of Kokomo Company for 2000.

Determine the amount of revenue to be recognized.
(SO 5)

1. Sold a 6-month insurance policy to Taylor Corporation for $9,000 on March 1.
2. Leased office space to Excel Supplies for a 1-year period beginning September 1. The rent of $36,000 was paid in advance.
3. A sales order for merchandise costing $9,000 that had a sales price of $12,000 was received on December 28 from Warfield Company. The goods were shipped FOB shipping point on December 31 and Warfield received them on January 3, 2001.
4. Merchandise inventory on hand at year-end amounted to $160,000. Kokomo expects to sell the inventory in 2001 for $180,000.

Instructions

For each item above, indicate the amount of revenue Kokomo should recognize in calendar year 2000. Explain.

E7-5   The ledger of Batavia Corporation at December 31, 2000, contains the following summary information:

Administrative expenses	$112,000	Other expenses and losses	$34,700
Cost of goods sold	409,200	Other revenues and gains	17,500
Net sales	682,000	Selling expenses	98,600

The income tax rate for all items is 30%. Batavia had 10,000 shares of common stock outstanding throughout the year, and the company paid $15,000 in dividends during 2000.

Instructions

Compute earnings per share for 2000.

E7-6   Presented below, in alphabetical order, is information related to the Pritt Corporation for the year 2000:

Cost of goods sold	$1,499,900
Dividends on common stock	140,000
Gain on the sale of equipment	110,000
Income tax expense	150,000
Interest expense	90,000
Interest revenue	300,000
Net sales	2,142,800
Selling and administrative expenses	340,750

Pritt had 35,000 shares outstanding for the entire year.

Instructions

(a) Prepare in good form a single-step income statement for Pritt Corporation for 2000.
(b) Assuming a multiple-step income statement was prepared instead, compute
   (1) gross profit,
   (2) income from operations, and
   (3) net income.
(c) Calculate Pritt Corporation's profit margin percentage (return on sales).

E7-7   Net sales, net income, total assets, and total common stockholders' equity information is available for the following three companies:

Company	Net Sales (in millions)	Net Income (in millions)	Total Assets (in millions)	Total Common Equity (in millions)
Intel	$ 8,782.0	$2,295.0	$11,344.0	$7,500.0
MCI Communications	11,921.0	582.0	11,276.0	4,713.0
Pacific Gas & Electric	10,582.4	1,065.5	27,165.5	9,254.0

Instructions

(a) Compute the following relationships for each company:
   (1) Debt to total assets ratio.
   (2) Return on sales (profit margin percentage).
   (3) Return on assets.
   (4) Return on common stockholders' equity.
(b) What reasons might there be for the differing relationships among these three companies? In your answer, consider the different kinds of industries these companies represent. Do any similarities or differences in the type of business help account for the differences you see?

E7-8   Net sales, net income, total assets, and total common stockholders' equity information is available for the following three companies:

Company	Net Sales (in millions)	Net Income (in millions)	Total Assets (in millions)	Total Common Equity (in millions)
Ford Motor Company	$108,521.0	$2,529.0	$198,938.0	$15,574.0
Exxon	97,825.0	5,280.0	84,145.0	34,792.0
Sears, Roebuck	54,873.4	2,374.4	90,807.8	11,664.1

Instructions

(a) Compute the following relationships for each company:

(1) Debt to total assets ratio.

(2) Return on sales (profit margin percentage).

(3) Return on assets.

(4) Return on common stockholders' equity.

(b) What reasons might there be for the differing relationships among these three companies? In your answer, consider the different kinds of industries these companies represent. Do any similarities or differences in the type of business help account for the differences you see?

E7–9 As of December 31, 2000, Yosemite Corporation has a current ratio of 2.6:1 and working capital of $600,000. Yosemite's total debt is 60% of its total assets. All of Yosemite's long-term assets, which are exactly half of total assets, are properly categorized as property, plant, and equipment.

Use balance sheet relationships to prepare a balance sheet. (SO 7)

Instructions

Prepare a summary classified balance sheet for Yosemite Corporation at year-end 2000. (*Hint:* First calculate Yosemite's current asset and current liability amounts.)

E7–10 Presented below is partial balance sheet information related to Batten Ltd., a United Kingdom company. All financial information has been translated from pounds to dollars.

Restate foreign financial statements. (SO 8)

BATTEN LTD.
Balance Sheet (partial)
December 31, 2000
(in thousands)

Fixed assets		
Tangible assets		$1,200,000
Current assets		
Stocks (inventory)	$300,000	
Debtors	121,000	
Investments	53,000	
Cash	62,000	
	536,000	
Creditors		
Amount falling due within one year	110,000	
Net current assets		426,000
Total assets less current liabilities		1,626,000
Creditors		
Amounts falling due after one year		230,000
Total net assets		$1,396,000

Instructions

(a) Restate the asset side of the balance sheet in accordance with generally accepted accounting principles in the United States.

(b) What is the amount of total stockholders' equity?

PROBLEMS: SET A

P7–1A Carson and McMann are accountants for Desktop Computers. They are having disagreements concerning the following transactions that occurred during the calendar year 2001.

Analyze transactions to identify accounting principle or assumption violated and prepare correct entries. (SO 4, 5)

1. Desktop purchased equipment for $35,000 at a going-out-of-business sale. The equipment was worth $45,000. Carson believes that the following entry should be made:

Equipment	45,000	
Cash		35,000
Gain		10,000

2. Land costing $60,000 was appraised at $90,000. Carson suggests the following journal entry:

Land	30,000	
Gain on Appreciation of Land		30,000

3. Depreciation on vehicles for the year was $18,000. Since net income is expected to be lower this year, Carson suggests deferring depreciation to a year when there is more net income.

4. Desktop bought a custom-made piece of equipment for $18,000. This equipment has a useful life of 6 years. Desktop depreciates equipment at the rate of $3,000 per year. "Since the equipment is custom-made, it will have no resale value and, therefore, shouldn't be depreciated but instead expensed immediately," argues Carson. "Besides, it provides for lower net income."

5. Carson suggests that equipment should be reported on the balance sheet at its liquidation value, which is $15,000 less than its cost.

McMann disagrees with Carson on each of the above situations.

Instructions

For each transaction, indicate why McMann disagrees. Identify the accounting principle or assumption that Carson would be violating if his suggestions were used. Prepare the correct journal entry for each transaction, if any.

Determine the appropriateness of journal entries in terms of generally accepted accounting principles or assumptions.
(SO 4, 5)

P7–2A   Presented below are a number of business transactions that occurred during the current year for Jose, Inc.

1. Materials were purchased on March 31 for $65,000 and this amount was entered in the Materials account. On December 31, the materials would have cost $85,000, so the following entry was made:

Inventory	20,000	
Gain on Inventories		20,000

2. An order for $30,000 has been received from a customer for products on hand. This order is to be shipped on January 9 next year. The following entry was made:

Accounts Receivable	30,000	
Sales		30,000

3. The president of Jose, Inc. used his expense account to purchase a new Buick Park Avenue solely for personal use. The following entry was made:

Miscellaneous Expense	34,000	
Cash		34,000

4. Because of a "flood sale," equipment obviously worth $230,000 was acquired at a cost of $150,000. The following entry was made:

Equipment	230,000	
Cash		150,000
Gain on Purchase of Equipment		80,000

5. Because the general level of prices increased during the current year, Jose, Inc. determined that there was a $10,000 understatement of depreciation expense on its equipment and decided to record it in its accounts. The following entry was made:

Depreciation Expense	10,000	
Accumulated Depreciation		10,000

Instructions

▓▓▓▓▶ In each of the situations above, discuss the appropriateness of the journal entries in terms of generally accepted accounting principles.

Identify accounting assumptions, principles, and constraints.
(SO 4, 5, 6)

P7–3A   Presented below are the assumptions, principles, and constraints used in this chapter.

(a) Economic entity assumption
(b) Going concern assumption
(c) Monetary unit assumption
(d) Time period assumption
(e) Full disclosure principle
(f) Revenue recognition principle
(g) Matching principle
(h) Cost principle
(i) Materiality
(j) Conservatism

Identify by letter the accounting assumption, principle, or constraint that matches each description below. Do not use a letter more than once.

1. Assets are not stated at their liquidation value. (Do not use cost principle.)
2. The death of the president is not recorded in the accounts.
3. Pencil sharpeners are expensed when purchased.
4. Depreciation is recorded in the accounts over the life of an asset. (Do not use the going concern assumption.)
5. Each entity is kept as a unit distinct from its owner or owners.
6. Reporting must be done at defined intervals.
7. Revenue is recorded at the point of sale.
8. When in doubt, it is better to understate rather than overstate net income.
9. All important information related to inventories is presented in the footnotes or in the financial statements.

P7–4A   The adjusted trial balance of Inder Outfitters Inc. as of October 31, 2001 (its year-end) contains the following information:

Prepare a classified balance sheet and analyze financial position.
(SO 7)

Accounts payable	$162,000
Accounts receivable	15,000
Accumulated depreciation—Buildings	144,000
Accumulated depreciation—Equipment	715,000
Bonds payable	600,000
Buildings—Offices and cabins	660,000
Cash	36,000
Common stock	300,000
Equipment	840,000
Income taxes payable	56,250
Interest payable	30,000
Inventories	480,000
Investment in the Superior Trading Post, Inc. (trading—short-term)	140,000
Land	650,000
Mortgage payable (on fishing cabins—long-term)	247,750
Notes payable (short-term)	160,000
Prepaid advertising	17,000
Prepaid insurance	9,000
Retained earnings (October 31, 2001)	444,000
Supplies	12,000

Instructions
(a) Prepare in good form a classified balance sheet for Inder Outfitters.
(b) Calculate the following balance sheet relationships: current ratio, debt to total assets ratio, and working capital.
(c) Assume that Inder Outfitters has come to you, as the senior loan officer of Lake Shore Credit Union, seeking a $500,000 loan to help defray the costs of replacing much of its rental camping gear and canoes. Would you be willing to approve the loan? Is there any additional information you would like to have before making your decision?

P7–5A   The ledgers of Ginny Brown Galleries Inc. contain the following balances as of December 31, 2001:

Prepare a multiple-step income statement and analyze profitability
(SO 7)

Advertising expense	$ 126,000
Commissions expense on art sales	1,200,000
Depreciation expense (administrative)	98,000
Dividend revenue	44,000
Insurance expense	600,000
Interest expense	98,000
Inventory, January 1	1,650,000
Inventory, December 31	1,424,000
Loss on the sale of office equipment	23,300
Miscellaneous administrative expenses	53,200
Miscellaneous selling expenses	39,000

Net purchases	3,500,000
Net sales	9,675,000
Rent expense	805,000
Freight-in	232,000
Freight-out	82,500
Utilities expense	117,000
Wages and salaries	1,264,000

Income taxes are calculated at 30 percent of income; the galleries had 90,000 shares of common stock outstanding for the entire year. Total assets amounted to $7,509,000, and common stockholder's equity was $3,975,400.

Instructions
(a) Prepare in good form a multiple income statement for Ginny Brown Galleries.
(b) Calculate three measures of profitability and one ratio of solvency.
(c) Assume that you are considering supplying Ginny Brown Galleries with a line of miniature replicas of fine arts sculptures for sale in its gift shops. Is this a company for which you would like to be a supplier? What additional information would you like to have before deciding to become a major supplier for Ginny Brown Galleries?

PROBLEMS: SET B
....

Analyze transactions to identify accounting principle or assumption violated and prepare correct entries.
(SO 4, 5)

P7–1B Check and Doublecheck are accountants for Elbert Printers. They are having disagreements concerning the following transactions that occurred during the year.

1. Elbert purchased equipment at a fire sale for $21,000. The equipment was worth $26,000. Check believes that the following entry should be made:

Equipment	26,000	
Cash		21,000
Gain		5,000

2. Check suggests that Elbert should carry equipment on the balance sheet at its liquidation value, which is $20,000 less than its cost.

3. Elbert rented office space for one year starting October 1, 2001. The total amount of $30,000 was paid in advance. Check believes that the following entry should be made on October 1:

Rent Expense	30,000	
Cash		30,000

4. Land costing $41,000 was appraised at $49,000. Check suggests the following journal entry:

Land	8,000	
Gain on Appreciation of Land		8,000

5. Elbert bought equipment for $40,000, including installation costs. The equipment has a useful life of 5 years. Elbert depreciates equipment at the rate of $8,000 per year. "Since the equipment as installed into the system cannot be removed without considerable damage, it will have no resale value, and therefore should not be depreciated but instead expensed immediately," argues Check. "Besides, it lowers net income."

6. Depreciation for the year was $26,000. Since net income is expected to be lower this year, Check suggests deferring depreciation to a year when there is more net income.

Doublecheck disagrees with Check on each of the situations above.

Instructions
For each transaction, indicate why Doublecheck disagrees. Identify the accounting principle or assumption that Check would be violating if his suggestions were used. Prepare the correct journal entry for each transaction, if any.

P7-2B Presented below are a number of business transactions that occurred during the current year for Quester, Inc.

Determine the appropriateness of journal entries in terms of generally accepted accounting principles or assumptions.
(SO 4, 5)

1. The president of Quester, Inc., used his expense account to purchase a pre-owned Mercedes-Benz E420 solely for personal use. The following entry was made:

Miscellaneous Expense	54,000	
Cash		54,000

2. Land was purchased on April 30 for $200,000 and this amount was entered in the Land account. On December 31, the land would have cost $230,000, so the following entry was made:

Land	30,000	
Gain on Land		30,000

3. An order for $60,000 has been received from a customer for products on hand. This order is to be shipped on January 9 next year. The following entry was made:

Accounts Receivable	60,000	
Sales		60,000

4. Because of a "flood sale," equipment obviously worth $300,000 was acquired at a cost of $250,000. The following entry was made:

Equipment	300,000	
Cash		250,000
Gain on Purchase of Equipment		50,000

5. Because the general level of prices increased during the current year, Quester, Inc., determined that there was a $40,000 understatement of depreciation expense on its equipment and decided to record it in its accounts. The following entry was made:

Depreciation Expense	40,000	
Accumulated Depreciation		40,000

Instructions

In each of the situations above, discuss the appropriateness of the journal entries in terms of generally accepted accounting principles.

P7-3B Presented below are the assumptions, principles, and constraints used in this chapter.

Identify accounting assumptions, principles, and constraints.
(SO 4, 5, 6)

(a) Economic entity assumption
(b) Going concern assumption
(c) Monetary unit assumption
(d) Time period assumption
(e) Full disclosure principle
(f) Revenue recognition principle
(g) Matching principle
(h) Cost principle
(i) Materiality
(j) Conservatism

Identify by letter the accounting assumption, principle, or constraint that matches each description below. Do not use a letter more than once.

1. Repair tools are expensed when purchased. (Do not use conservatism)
2. Allocates expenses to revenues in proper period.
3. Assumes that the dollar is the measuring stick used to report financial information.
4. Separates financial information into time periods for reporting purposes.
5. Market value changes subsequent to purchase are not recorded in the accounts. (Do not use revenue recognition principle.)
6. Indicates that personal and business record keeping should be separately maintained.
7. Ensures that all relevant financial information is reported.
8. Lower of cost or market is used to value inventories.

P7-4B The adjusted trial balance of Dagobah Bottle and Glass, Inc., as of June 30, 2001 (its year-end) contains the following information:

Prepare a classified balance sheet and analyze financial position.
(SO 7)

Accounts payable	$ 478,000
Accounts receivable	420,000
Accumulated depreciation—Buildings	180,000

Accumulated depreciation—Equipment	577,500
Bonds payable	1,750,000
Buildings—Manufacturing plant and offices	680,000
Cash	79,000
Common stock	500,000
Equipment	1,650,000
Income taxes payable	45,000
Interest payable	70,000
Interest receivable	21,000
Inventories	845,000
Investment in Zarle, Inc., bonds (held-to-maturity—long-term)	600,000
Land	200,000
Mortgage payable (on manufacturing plant—long-term)	310,000
Notes payable (short-term)	200,000
Prepaid advertising	9,500
Prepaid insurance	19,000
Retained earnings (June 30, 2001)	447,000
Supplies	34,000

Instructions

(a) Prepare in good form a classified balance sheet for Dagobah Bottle & Glass.

(b) Calculate the following balance sheet relationships: current ratio, debt-to-total assets ratio, and working capital.

(c) Assume that Dagobah has come to you, as vice president of Neighborhood National Bank, seeking a $450,000 loan to help defray the costs of upgrading some of its bottling machinery. Would you be willing to approve the loan? Is there any additional information you would like to have before making your decision?

Prepare a multiple-step income statement and analyze profitability.
(SO 7)

P7–5B   The ledgers of Lovely Leathers Inc. contain the following balances as of January 31, 2000 (its year-end):

Advertising expense	$ 126,000
Depreciation expense (administrative)	53,000
Freight-in	27,900
Freight-out	6,800
Gain on the sale of equipment	8,500
Insurance expense	54,000
Interest expense	13,900
Interest revenue	7,300
Inventory, February 1, 1999	296,400
Inventory, January 31, 2000	303,400
Managerial salaries	129,800
Miscellaneous administrative expenses	22,200
Miscellaneous selling expenses	39,000
Net purchases	1,697,000
Net sales	2,647,000
Rent expense	84,000
Sales staff wages	159,000
Utilities expense	30,300

Income taxes are calculated at 30 percent of income; Lovely had 84,000 shares of common stock outstanding for the entire year. Total assets amounted to $5,460,000, and common stockholders' equity was $1,966,200 at year end.

Instructions

(a) Prepare in good form a multiple-step income statement for Lovely Leathers Inc.

(b) Calculate three measures of profitability and one ratio of solvency.

(c) Assume that you are considering supplying Lovely Leathers with a line of wallets, key holders, and other small leather goods for sale in its two stores. Is this a company for which you would like to be a supplier? What additional information would you like to have before deciding to become a supplier for Lovely Leathers?

COMPREHENSIVE PROBLEM

Presented below is financial information related to Tatis Corporation for the year 2000. Unless otherwise stated, all balances are ending balances.

Accounts payable	$ 874,200
Accounts receivable	1,000,800
Accumulated depreciation—Equipment	1,560,000
Administrative expenses	420,000
Bonds payable	3,400,000
Cash	125,000
Common stock	2,200,000
Cost of goods sold	2,285,000
Dividends	290,000
Equipment	5,894,000
Gain on the sale of land	87,000
Interest expense	108,000
Interest revenue	94,000
Inventories	984,000
Marketable securities (short-term)	1,175,000
Net sales	3,670,000
Notes payable (short-term)	1,136,500
Other long-term debt	401,300
Patents and other intangibles	1,250,100
Prepaid expenses	356,100
Retained earnings (January 1, 2000)	833,000
Selling expenses	368,000

Tatis Corporation had 88,000 shares of common stock outstanding for the entire year. Its effective income tax rate for state and federal income taxes combined is 35 percent.

Instructions
(a) Prepare a multiple-step income statement.
(b) Prepare a single-step income statement.
(c) Prepare a retained earnings statement.
(d) Prepare a classified balance sheet.
(e) Compute the following balance sheet relationships:
   (1) current ratio.
   (2) the amount of working capital.
   (3) debt to total assets ratio.
   What insights do these relationships provide to the reader of the financial statements?
(f) Compute three measures of profitability. What insights do these relationships provide to the reader of the financial statements?
(g) Compare the results for Tatis Corporation, calculated here, and the results for Notting Hill Corporation in Demonstration Problem 2. As an investor, which corporation seems more attractive to you? Why?

BROADENING YOUR PERSPECTIVE

FINANCIAL REPORTING AND ANALYSIS

Financial Reporting Problem

BYP7–1 Suzanne Wessels has successfully completed her first accounting course during the spring semester and is now working as a management trainee for First Arizona Bank during the summer. One of her fellow management trainees, Wade Greaton, is taking the same accounting course this summer and has been having a "lot of trouble." On the second examination, for example, Wade became confused about inventory valuation methods and completely missed all the points on a problem involving LIFO and FIFO.

Wade's instructor recently indicated that the third examination will probably have a number of essay questions dealing with accounting principle issues. Wade is quite concerned about the third examination for two reasons. First, he has never taken an accounting examination where essay answers were required. Second, Wade feels he has to do well on this examination to get an acceptable grade in the course.

Wade has therefore asked Suzanne to help him prepare for the next examination. She agrees, and suggests that Wade develop a set of possible questions on the accounting principles material that they might discuss.

Instructions
Answer the following questions that were developed by Wade.

(a) What is a conceptual framework?
(b) Why is there a need for a conceptual framework?
(c) What are the objectives of financial reporting?
(d) If you had to explain generally accepted accounting principles to a nonaccountant, what essential characteristics would you include in your explanation?
(e) What are the qualitative characteristics of accounting? Explain each one.
(f) Identify the basic assumptions used in accounting.
(g) What are two major constraints involved in financial reporting? Explain both of them.

COMPARATIVE ANALYSIS PROBLEM: Kellogg Company vs. General Mills

BYP7-2   Kellogg's financial statements are presented in Appendix A; General Mill's financial statements are presented in Appendix B.

Instructions
(a) Based on the information contained in these financial statements, compute the following 1998 ratios for each company:
(1) Current ratio.   (4) Return on assets.
(2) Working capital.   (5) Return on common stockholders' equity.
(3) Profit margin percentage.   (6) Debt to total assets ratio.
(b) Compare the liquidity, profitability, and solvency of the two companies.

RESEARCH ASSIGNMENT

BYP7-3   During the years 1978–85, the Financial Accounting Standards Board (FASB) issued six *Statements of Financial Accounting Concepts* (SFACs). From the library, obtain copies of SFAC No. 2 (*Qualitative Characteristics of Accounting Information*) and SFAC No. 3 (*Elements of Financial Statements of Business Enterprises*).

Instructions
Use these statements to answer the following questions:

(a) Your textbook indicates that "an item is material when it is likely to influence the decision of a reasonably prudent investor or creditor." SFAC No. 2 identifies a number of examples in which specific quantitative guidelines are provided to accountants and auditors. Identify two of these examples. Do you think that materiality guidelines should be quantified? Why or why not?
(b) SFAC No. 3 discusses the concept of "articulation" between financial statement elements. Briefly summarize the meaning of this term and how it relates to an entity's financial statements.

INTERPRETING FINANCIAL STATEMENTS: Weyerhaeuser Company

BYP7-4   Weyerhaeuser Company is one of the world's largest growers and producers of forest and lumber products. It has assets of $14 billion and annual sales of over $12 billion. Weyerhaeuser employs over 38,000 workers and has as its most significant assets its many acres of prime timberland.

Presented below is a statement that appeared about Weyerhaeuser Company in a financial magazine.

The land and timber holdings are now carried on the company's books at a mere $422 million. The value of the timber alone is variously estimated at $3 billion to $7 billion and is rising all the time. "The understatement of the company is pretty severe," conceded Charles W. Bingham, a senior vice-president. Adds Robert L. Schuyler, another senior vice-president: "We have a whole stream of profit nobody sees and there is no way to show it on our books."

Instructions
(a) What does Schuyler mean when he says that "we have a whole stream of profit nobody sees and there is no way to show it on our books"?
(b) If the understatement of the company's assets is severe, why doesn't accounting report this information?

REAL-WORLD FOCUS: RJR Nabisco and Phillip Morris

BYP7–5 The results of RJR Nabisco and Phillip Morris Companies, Inc., are frequently compared since the two are fierce competitors. RJR Nabisco makes Winston, Camel, and Salem cigarettes, while Phillip Morris makes Marlboro and L&M cigarettes. Both companies also have significant operations in other product lines—RJR Nabisco makes Oreo cookies, Ritz crackers, and Planters nuts, while Phillip Morris makes Post cereals, Maxwell House coffee, and Miller beer. The following information is provided in order to compare the profitability of these two companies in 1998.

(all dollars in millions)	RJR Nabisco	Phillip Morris
Net sales	$17,037	$74,391
Net income	(516)	5,372
Total assets	15,545	59,920
Common stockholders' equity	9,886	16,197

Instructions
(a) Compare the profitability of these two companies using each of the following measures. In each case describe what the ratio is intended to measure.
   (1) Profit margin percentage.
   (2) Return on assets.
   (3) Return on common stockholders' equity.
(b) Comment on any problems or challenges incurred by comparing the two companies in this fashion.

CRITICAL THINKING

GROUP DECISION CASE

BYP7–6 Presented below are key figures and relationships from the financial statements of a prominent company in each of three different industries for two recent fiscal years:

	Manfacturing		Mining/Oil		Merchandising	
	2000	2001	2000	2001	2000	2001
From the balance sheets:						
Total assets (millions)	$11,079	$11,083	$33,884	$35,089	$ 8,524	$ 9,485
Current ratio	1.72	1.73	1.14	1.12	1.51	1.56
Working capital (millions)	$ 2,390	$ 2,349	$ 1,037	$ 1,072	$ 1,236	$ 1,452
Debt to total assets ratio	0.45	0.43	0.59	0.58	0.72	0.72
Profitability:						
Total sales (millions)	$13,021	$13,340	$31,916	$41,540	$14,739	$16,115
Profit margin percentage	10.0%	8.7%	0.8%	5.2%	2.8%	1.9%
Return on assets	11.8%	10.4%	0.7%	6.1%	4.8%	3.2%
Return on common equity	21.4%	18.3%	1.8%	15.0%	20.1%	13.5%
Earnings per common share	$5.91	$5.26	$0.73	$6.10	$5.20	$3.72
From the annual reports:						
End-of-year stock price	$67.75	$72.63	$85.75	$95.25	$56.50	$62.00

Instructions

With the class divided into groups, answer the following:

(a) The benchmark for the current ratio is generally 2:1. None of these companies has a ratio that high, yet all three are well regarded firms. Why might a current ratio less than 2:1 *not* signal a problem?

(b) The merchandising company acquired a chain of well-known department stores just prior to 2000. Apart from such major acquisitions, what else might contribute to differing debt to total asset ratios? Consider industry-specific as well as company-specific considerations.

(c) For all three companies, the ratio of debt to total assets changed little from 2000 to 2001, yet for two of the three companies return on common stockholders' equity decreased. What might cause this pattern?

(d) The profitability relationships and earnings per share for both the manufacturing and the merchandising companies decreased from 2000 to 2001, yet the price per share of stock for each company increased. Why might investors be willing to pay more for these companies in 2001?

COMMUNICATION ACTIVITY

BYP7–7 If you go on to advanced accounting courses, you'll study the differences between accounting in the business world and university accounting. You'll find that there's one major similarity: both depend heavily on the matching principle.

At Long Beach City College, a two-year community college with 30,000 students, most of the revenues come from the state of California and the federal government. As a condition of receiving these grants, "we must match expenses against revenues in the right fiscal year," says the school's accounting manager.

For example, the college receives federal funding under the Job Training Partnership Act. "We receive funding from the federal government, which allows us to offer classes to students for job preparation. The government specifies the grant periods, for instance, from July 1 to June 30. We therefore have to ensure that all transactions for that project are completed within that fiscal year." Another project is the amnesty program, the federal government's legalization of foreign nationals. Expenses to offset the grant money are mostly teaching salaries and instructional materials.

By year-end, the goal is to break even. Excess funds, if any, have to be returned. But program managers do not want a deficit, either, because these projects are accountable to the college administration and any overspending will come from the college's general fund.

Instructions

Write a letter to your instructor covering the following points:

1. Why is the matching principle important in accounting for government grants?
2. Give some examples of grant or special programs to which the matching principle might be applied at your college or university.
3. What are some examples of costs that Long Beach Community College might properly charge to its grant or special programs?

ETHICS CASE

BYP7–8 When the Financial Accounting Standards Board issues new standards, the required implementation date is usually 12 months or more from the date of issuance, with early implementation encouraged. Sarah Lane, accountant at Mintur Corporation, discusses with her financial vice president the need for early implementation of a recently issued standard that would result in a much fairer presentation of the company's financial condition and earnings. When the financial vice president determines that early implementation of the standard will adversely affect reported net income for the year, he strongly discourages Sarah from implementing the standard until it is required.

Instructions

(a) Who are the stakeholders in this situation?
(b) What, if any, are the ethical considerations in this situation?
(c) What does Sarah have to gain by advocating early implementation? Who might be affected by the decision against early implementation?

SURFING THE NET

BYP7–9   The Financial Accounting Standards Board (FASB) is a private organization established to improve accounting standards and financial reporting. The FASB conducts extensive research before issuing a "Statement of Financial Accounting Standards," which represents an authoritative expression of generally accepted accounting principles.

Address: http://www.rutgers.edu/accounting/raw (or go to www.wiley.com/college/weygandt).

Steps: 1. Choose FASB.
　　　　 2. Choose FASB Facts.

Instructions
Answer the following questions;

 (a) What is the mission of the FASB?
 (b) How are topics added to the FASB technical agenda?
 (c) What characteristics make the FASB's procedures an "open" decision-making process?

Answers to Self-Study Questions
1. a   2. d   3. c   4. c   5. c   6. c   7. b   8. c   9. c   10. c

Answer to Kellogg Review It Question 2, p. 290
The Report of Independent Accountants indicates that the financial statements (balance sheet, income statement, shareholders' equity, and cash flows) are presented fairly, in accordance with generally accepted accounting principles.

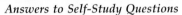

Remember to go back to the Navigator box on the chapter-opening page and check off your completed work.

Before studying this chapter, you should know or, if necessary, review:

a. How cash transactions are recorded. (Ch. 2, pp. 53–55, 60–64)

b. How cash is classified on a balance sheet. (Ch. 4, p. 157–158, 161)

c. The role ethics plays in proper financial reporting. (Ch. 1, p. 8)

THE
NAVIGATOR

FEATURE STORY

Minding the Money in Moose Jaw

If you're ever looking for a cappuccino in Moose Jaw, Saskatchewan, stop by Stephanie's Gourmet Coffee and More, located on Main Street. Staff there serve, on average, 646 cups of coffee a day—including both regular and specialty coffees—not to mention soups, Italian sandwiches, and a wide assortment of gourmet cheesecakes.

"We've got high school students who come here, and students from the community college," says owner/manager Stephanie Mintenko, who has run the place since opening it in 1995. "We have customers who are retired, and others who are working people and have only 30 minutes for lunch. We have to be pretty quick."

That means that the cashiers have to be efficient. Like most businesses where purchases are low-cost and high-volume, cash control has to be simple.

"We have an electronic cash register, but it's not the fancy new kind where you just punch in the item," explains Ms. Mintenko. "You have to punch in the prices." The machine does keep track of sales in several categories, however—cashiers punch a button to indicate whether each item is a beverage, a meal, or a charge for the café's Internet connections. All transactions are recorded on an internal tape in the machine; the customer receives a receipt only upon request.

There is only one cash register; "up to three of us might operate it on any given shift, including myself," says Ms. Mintenko.

She and her staff do two "cashouts" each day—one with the shift change at 5:00, and one when the shop closes at 10:00. "The machine gives the total for the shift, and we count what's left in the float, and hopefully they match!" If there's a discrepancy, there's another count; then, if necessary, "we go through the whole tape to find the mistake," she explains. "It usually turns out to be someone who punched in $18 instead of $1.80, or something like that."

Ms. Mintenko sends all the cash tapes and float totals to a bookkeeper, who double checks everything and provides regular reports. "We try to keep the accounting simple, so we can concentrate on making great coffee and food."

THE
NAVIGATOR

CHAPTER 8

INTERNAL CONTROL AND CASH

THE NAVIGATOR ✔

- Understand *Concepts for Review* ☐
- Read *Feature Story* ☐
- Scan *Study Objectives* ☐
- Read *Preview* ☐
- Read text and answer *Before You Go On*
  p. 336 ☐ p. 343 ☐ p. 352 ☐ p. 353 ☐
- Work *Demonstration Problem* ☐
- Review *Summary of Study Objectives* ☐
- Answer *Self-Study Questions* ☐
- Complete assignments ☐

STUDY OBJECTIVES

After studying this chapter, you should be able to:

1. *Define internal control.*
2. *Identify the principles of internal control.*
3. *Explain the applications of internal control principles to cash receipts.*
4. *Describe the applications of internal control principles to cash disbursements.*
5. *Explain the operation of a petty cash fund.*
6. *Indicate the control features of a bank account.*
7. *Prepare a bank reconciliation.*
8. *Explain the reporting of cash.*

THE
NAVIGATOR

*A*s the story about recording sales at Stephanie's Gourmet Coffee and More indicates, control of cash is important. Similarly, controls are needed to safeguard other types of assets. For example, Stephanie's undoubtedly has controls to prevent the theft of food and supplies inventories and controls to prevent the theft of silverware and dishes from its kitchen.

In this chapter, we explain the essential features of an internal control system and then describe how those controls apply to cash. The applications include some controls with which you may be already familiar. Toward the end of the chapter, we describe the use of a bank and explain how cash is reported on the balance sheet. The content and organization of Chapter 8 are as follows:

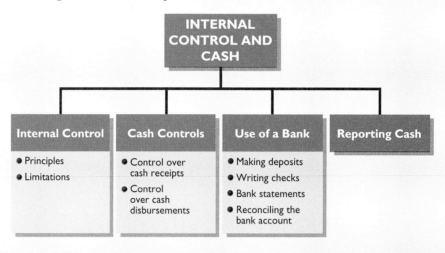

THE
NAVIGATOR

INTERNAL CONTROL

STUDY
OBJECTIVE

1

Define internal control.

Could there be dishonest employees in the business that you own or manage? Unfortunately, the answer sometimes is Yes. For example, the financial press recently reported the following:

A bookkeeper in a small company diverted $750,000 of bill payments to a personal bank account over a 3-year period.

A shipping clerk with 28 years of service shipped $125,000 of merchandise to himself.

A computer operator embezzled $21 million from Wells Fargo Bank over a 2-year period.

A church treasurer "borrowed" $150,000 of church funds to finance a friend's business dealings.

These situations emphasize the need for a good system of internal control.

Internal control consists of the plan of organization and all the related methods and measures adopted within a business to:

1. Safeguard its assets from employee theft, robbery, and unauthorized use.

2. **Enhance the accuracy and reliability of its accounting records** by reducing the risk of **errors** (unintentional mistakes) and **irregularities** (intentional mistakes and misrepresentations) in the accounting process.

Under the Foreign Corrupt Practices Act of 1977, all major U.S. corporations are required to maintain an adequate system of internal control. Companies that fail to comply are subject to fines, and company officers may be imprisoned. Also, the National Commission on Fraudulent Financial Reporting concluded that all companies whose stock is publicly traded should maintain internal controls that can provide reasonable assurance that fraudulent financial reporting will be prevented or be subject to early detection.[1]

Principles of Internal Control

To safeguard its assets and enhance the accuracy and reliability of its accounting records, a company follows specific control principles. Of course, internal control measures vary with the size and nature of the business and with management's control philosophy. However, the six principles listed in Illustration 8-1 apply to most enterprises. Each principle is explained in the following sections.

INTERNATIONAL NOTE

U.S. companies also adopt model business codes that guide their international operations to provide for a safe and healthy workplace, avoid child and forced labor, abstain from bribes, and follow sound environmental practices.

2
STUDY
OBJECTIVE

Identify the principles of internal control.

ILLUSTRATION 8-1

Principles of internal control

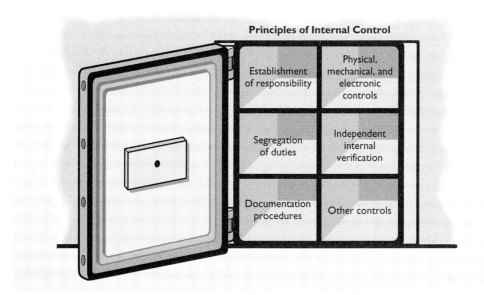

Establishment of Responsibility

An essential characteristic of internal control is the assignment of responsibility to specific individuals. **Control is most effective when only one person is responsible for a given task.** To illustrate, assume that the cash on hand at the end of the day in a Safeway supermarket is $10 short of the cash rung up on the cash register. If only one person has operated the register, responsibility for the shortage can be assessed quickly. However, if two or more individuals have worked the register, it may be impossible to determine who is responsible for the error unless each person is assigned a separate cash drawer and register key. The principle of establishing responsibility was not followed by Stephanie's Gourmet Coffee and More (in the Feature Story) where three cashiers operated out of one cash register drawer.

Transfer of cash drawers

---

[1]Report of the National Commission on Fraudulent Financial Reporting, October 1987, p. 11.

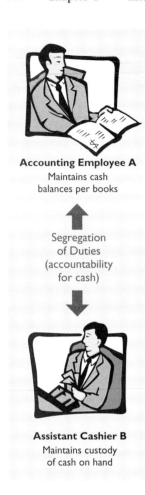

Accounting Employee A
Maintains cash
balances per books

Segregation
of Duties
(accountability
for cash)

Assistant Cashier B
Maintains custody
of cash on hand

Establishing responsibility includes the authorization and approval of transactions. For example, the vice president of sales should have the authority to establish policies for making credit sales. The policies ordinarily will require written credit department approval of credit sales.

Segregation of Duties

This principle (also identified as separation of functions or division of work) is indispensable in a system of internal control. There are two common applications of this principle:

1. The responsibility for related activities should be assigned to different individuals.
2. The responsibility for establishing the accountability (keeping the records) for an asset should be separate from the physical custody of that asset.

The rationale for segregation of duties is that the work of one employee should, without a duplication of effort, provide a reliable basis for evaluating the work of another employee.

Related Activities.   Related activities that should be assigned to different individuals arise in both the purchasing and selling areas. **When one individual is responsible for all of the related activities, the potential for errors and irregularities is increased.** Related purchasing activities include ordering the merchandise, receiving the goods, and paying (or authorizing payment) for the merchandise. In purchasing, for example, orders could be placed with friends or with suppliers who give kickbacks. Similarly, only a cursory count and inspection could be made upon receiving the goods, which could lead to errors and poor quality merchandise. In addition, payment might be authorized without a careful review of the invoice, or even worse, fictitious invoices might be approved for payment. When the responsibility for ordering, receiving, and paying are assigned to different individuals or departments, the risk of such abuses is minimized.

Similarly, related sales activities should be assigned to different individuals. Related selling activities include making a sale, shipping (or delivering) the goods to the customer, billing the customer, and receiving payment. When one person is responsible for related sales transactions, a salesperson could make sales at unauthorized prices to increase sales commissions; a shipping clerk could ship goods to himself, as indicated at the beginning of the chapter; a billing clerk could understate the amount billed for sales made to friends and relatives. These abuses are reduced when salespersons make the sale, shipping department employees ship the goods on the basis of the sales order, and billing department employees prepare the sales invoice after comparing the sales order with the report of goods shipped.

Accountability for Assets.   If accounting is to provide a valid basis of accountability for an asset, the accountant should have neither physical custody of the asset nor access to it. Moreover, the custodian of the asset should not maintain or have access to the accounting records. **When one employee maintains the record of the asset that should be on hand, and a different employee has physical custody of the asset, the custodian of the asset is not likely to convert the asset to personal use.** The separation of accounting responsibility from the custody of assets is especially important for cash and inventories because these assets are very vulnerable to unauthorized use or misappropriation.

Documentation Procedures

Documents provide evidence that transactions and events have occurred. In Stephanie's Gourmet Coffee and More, the cash register tape was the cafés doc-

ACCOUNTING IN ACTION
International Insight

Recently Sumitomo Corporation became the fifth Japanese company to announce a huge loss, this time $1.8 billion, due to a single copper trader. Some are blaming Japanese culture because it encourages group harmony over confrontation and thus may contribute to poor internal controls. For example, good controls require that both parties to a copper trade send a confirmation slip to management to verify all trades. In Japan the counterparty to the trade often sends the confirmation slip to the trader, who then forwards it to management. Thus, it is possible for the trader to change the confirmation slip. An unethical trader could create fictitious trades to hide losses for an extended period of time or to conceal trades that are larger than allowed limits.

Source: Sheryl Wudunn, "Big New Loss Makes Japan Look Inward," *New York Times,* June 17, 1996, p. D1.

umentation for the sale and the amount of cash received. Similarly, shipping documents indicate that the goods have been shipped, and sales invoices indicate that customers have been billed for the goods. By adding signatures (or initials) to the documents, the individual(s) responsible for the transaction or event can be identified. Documentation of transactions should be made when the transaction occurs. Documentation of events, such as those leading to adjusting entries, is generally developed when the adjustments are made.

Several procedures should be established for documents. First, whenever possible, **documents should be prenumbered and all documents should be accounted for**. Prenumbering helps to prevent a transaction from being recorded more than once, or conversely, to prevent the transactions from not being recorded. Second, documents that are **source documents for accounting entries should be promptly forwarded to the accounting department to help ensure timely recording of the transaction and event**. Thus, this control measure contributes directly to the accuracy and reliability of the accounting records.

Prenumbered invoices

Physical, Mechanical, and Electronic Controls
Use of physical, mechanical, and electronic controls is essential. Physical controls relate primarily to the safeguarding of assets. Mechanical and electronic controls safeguard assets and enhance the accuracy and reliability of the accounting records. Examples of these controls are shown in Illustration 8-2.

HELPFUL HINT

An important corollary to prenumbering is that voided documents be kept until all documents are accounted for.

ACCOUNTING IN ACTION
Business Insight

John Patterson, a young Ohio merchant, couldn't understand why his retail business didn't show a profit. There were lots of customers, but the money just seemed to disappear. Patterson suspected pilferage and sloppy bookkeeping by store clerks. Frustrated, he placed an order with a Dayton, Ohio, company for two rudimentary cash registers. A year later, Patterson's store was in the black.

"What is a good thing for this little store is a good thing for every retail store in the world," he observed. A few months later, in 1884, John Patterson and his brother, Frank, bought the tiny cash register maker for $6,500. The word around Dayton was that the Patterson boys got stung.

In the following 37 years, John Patterson built National Cash Register Co. into a corporate giant. Patterson died in 1922, the year in which NCR sold its two millionth cash register.

Source: The Wall Street Journal, January 28, 1989.

ILLUSTRATION 8-2

Physical, mechanical, and electronic controls

Physical Controls

Safes, vaults, and safety
deposit boxes for cash
and business papers

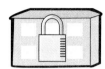

Locked warehouses
and storage cabinets for
inventories and records

Computer facilities
with pass key access

Mechanical and Electronic Controls

Alarms to
prevent break-ins

Television monitors
and garment sensors
to deter theft

Time clocks for
recording time worked

Independent Internal Verification

Most systems of internal control provide for independent internal verification. This principle involves the review, comparison, and reconciliation of data prepared by one or several employees. To obtain maximum benefit from independent internal verification:

1. The verification should be made periodically or on a surprise basis.
2. The verification should be done by an employee who is independent of the personnel responsible for the information.
3. Discrepancies and exceptions should be reported to a management level that can take appropriate corrective action.

Independent internal verification is especially useful in comparing recorded accountability with existing assets. The reconciliation of the cash register tape with the cash in the register at Stephanie's Gourmet Coffee and More is an example of this internal control principle. Another common example is the reconciliation by an independent person of the cash balance per books with the cash balance per bank. The relationship between this principle and the segregation of duties principle is shown graphically in Illustration 8-3.

In large companies, independent internal verification is often assigned to internal auditors. Internal auditors are employees of the company who evaluate on a continuous basis the effectiveness of the company's system of internal control. They periodically review the activities of departments and individuals to determine whether prescribed internal controls are being followed and to make recommendations for improvement. The importance of this function is illustrated by the number of internal auditors employed by companies. In a recent year, AT&T had 350 internal auditors, Exxon had 395, and IBM had 142.

ILLUSTRATION 8-3

Comparison of segregation of duties principle with independent internal verification principle

Other Controls

Other control measures include the following:

1. **Bonding of employees who handle cash.** Bonding involves obtaining insurance protection against misappropriation of assets by dishonest employees. This measure contributes to the safeguarding of cash in two ways: First, the insurance company carefully screens all individuals before adding them to the policy and may reject risky applicants. Second, bonded employees know that the insurance company will vigorously prosecute all offenders.

2. **Rotating employees' duties and requiring employees to take vacations.** These measures are designed to deter employees from attempting any thefts since they will not be able to permanently conceal their improper actions. Many bank embezzlements, for example, have been discovered when the perpetrator has been on vacation or assigned to a new position.

Limitations of Internal Control

A company's system of internal control is generally designed to provide reasonable assurance that assets are properly safeguarded and that the accounting records are reliable. **The concept of reasonable assurance rests on the premise that the costs of establishing control procedures should not exceed their expected benefit.** To illustrate, consider shoplifting losses in retail stores. Such losses could be completely eliminated by having a security guard stop and search customers as they leave the store. Store managers have concluded, however, that the negative effects of adopting such a procedure cannot be justified. Instead, stores have attempted to "control" shoplifting losses by less costly procedures such as: (1) posting signs saying, "We reserve the right to inspect all packages," and "All shoplifters will be prosecuted," (2) using hidden TV cameras and store detectives to monitor customer activity, and (3) using sensoring equipment at exits.

The **human element** is also an important factor in every system of internal control. A good system can become ineffective as a result of employee fatigue, carelessness, or indifference. For example, a receiving clerk may not bother to count goods received or may just "fudge" the counts. Occasionally, two or more individuals may work together to get around prescribed controls. Such **collusion** can significantly impair the effectiveness of a system, because it eliminates

HELPFUL HINT
The extensiveness of controls may vary with the risk level of the activity. For example, management may consider cash to be high risk and maintaining inventories in the stock room as low risk and thus have stricter controls for cash.

the protection anticipated from segregation of duties. If a supervisor and a cashier collaborate to understate cash receipts, the system of internal control may be negated (at least in the short run). No system of internal control is perfect.

The size of the business may impose limitations on internal control. In a small company, for example, it may be difficult to apply the principles of segregation of duties and independent internal verification.

TECHNOLOGY IN ACTION

Unfortunately, computer-related frauds have become a major concern. The average computer fraud loss is $650,000, compared with an average loss of only $19,000 resulting from other types of white-collar crime.

Computer fraud can be perpetrated almost invisibly and done with electronic speed. Psychologically, stealing with impersonal computer tools can seem far less criminal. Therefore, the moral threshold to commit computer fraud is far lower than fraud involving person-to-person contact.

Preventing and detecting computer fraud represents a major challenge. One of the best ways for a company to minimize the likelihood of computer fraud is to have a good system of internal control that allows the benefits of computerization to be gained without opening the possibility for rampant fraud.

BEFORE YOU GO ON . . .

Review It

1. What are the two primary objectives of internal control?
2. Identify and describe the principles of internal control.
3. What are the limitations of internal control?

Do It

Li Song owns a small retail store. Li wants to establish good internal control procedures but is confused about the difference between segregation of duties and independent internal verification. Explain the differences to Li.

Reasoning: In order to help Li, you need to thoroughly understand each principle. From this knowledge, and a study of Illustration 8-3, it should be possible to explain the differences between the two principles.

Solution: Segregation of duties pertains to the assignment of responsibility so that the work of one employee will permit the evaluation of the work of another employee. Segregation of duties occurs daily in executing and recording transactions. In contrast, independent internal verification involves reviewing, comparing, and reconciling data prepared by one or several employees. Independent internal verification occurs after the fact, as in the case of reconciling cash register totals at the end of the day with cash on hand.

THE NAVIGATOR

Related exercise material: BE8–1, BE8–2, E8–1, and E8–2.

CASH CONTROLS

Just as cash is the beginning of a company's operating cycle, it is usually the starting point for a company's system of internal control. Cash is the one asset that is readily convertible into any other type of asset; it is easily concealed and transported; and it is highly desired. Because of these characteristics, **cash is the asset most susceptible to improper diversion and use**. Moreover, because of the large volume of cash transactions, numerous errors may occur in executing and recording cash transactions. To safeguard cash and to assure the accuracy of the accounting records for cash, effective internal control over cash is imperative.

Cash consists of coins, currency (paper money), checks, money orders, and money on hand or on deposit in a bank or similar depository. The general rule is that if the bank will accept it for deposit, it is cash. Items such as postage stamps and postdated checks (checks payable in the future) are not cash. Stamps are a prepaid expense; the postdated checks are accounts receivable. The application of internal control principles to cash receipts and cash disbursements is explained in the following sections.

Internal Control over Cash Receipts

Cash receipts may result from a variety of sources: cash sales; collections on account from customers; the receipt of interest, rents, and dividends; investments by owners; bank loans; and proceeds from the sale of noncurrent assets. The internal control principles explained earlier apply to cash receipts transactions as shown in Illustration 8-4.

INTERNATIONAL NOTE

Other countries also have control problems. For example, a judge in France has issued a 36-page "book" detailing many of the scams that are widespread, such as kickbacks in public-works contracts, the skimming of development aid money to Africa, and bribes on arms sales.

ILLUSTRATION 8-4

Application of internal control principles to cash receipts

Internal Control over Cash Receipts

Establishment of Responsibility

Only designated personnel authorized to handle cash receipts (cashiers)

Physical, Mechanical, and Electronic Controls

Store cash in safes and bank vaults; limit access to storage areas; use cash registers

Segregation of Duties

Different individuals receive cash, record cash receipts, and hold the cash

Independent Internal Verification

Supervisors count cash receipts daily; treasurer compares total receipts to bank deposits daily

Documentation Procedures

Use remittance advice (mail receipts), cash register tapes, and deposit slips

Other Controls

Bond personnel who handle cash; require vacations; all cash deposited in bank daily

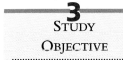

STUDY OBJECTIVE

Explain the applications of internal control principles to cash receipts.

As might be expected, companies vary considerably in how they apply these principles. To illustrate internal control over cash receipts, we will examine control measures for a retail store with both over-the-counter and mail receipts.

Over-the-Counter Receipts

Control of over-the-counter receipts in retail businesses is centered on cash registers that are visible to customers. In supermarkets and variety stores such as Kmart, cash registers are placed in check-out lines near the exit(s). In Sears, Roebuck & Co. and J. C. Penney stores each department has its own cash register. When a cash sale occurs, the sale is "rung up" on a cash register **with the amount clearly visible to the customer**. This measure prevents the cashier from ringing up a lower amount and pocketing the difference. The customer receives an itemized cash register receipt slip and is expected to count the change received. A cash register tape, which is locked into the register until removed by a supervisor or manager, accumulates the daily transactions and totals. When the tape is removed, the supervisor compares the total with the amount of cash in the register. It should show all registered receipts accounted for. The supervisor's findings are reported on a cash count sheet that is signed by both the cashier and supervisor. The cash count sheet used by Alrite Food Mart is shown in Illustration 8-5.

ILLUSTRATION 8-5

Cash count sheet

Store No. ___8___	Date March 8, 2001
1. Opening cash balance	$ 50.00
2. Cash sales per tape (attached)	6,956.20
3. Total cash to be accounted for	7,006.20
4. Cash on hand (see list)	6,996.10
5. Cash (short) or over	$ (10.10)
6. Ending cash balance	$ 50.00
7. Cash for deposit (Line 4 — Line 6)	$6,946.10

Cashier *J. Cruse*   Supervisor *M. Braun*

The count sheets, register tapes, and cash are then given to the head cashier. This individual prepares a daily cash summary showing the total cash received and the amount from each source, such as cash sales and collections on account. The head cashier sends one copy of the summary to the accounting department for entry into the cash receipts journal. The other copy goes to the treasurer's office for subsequent comparison with the daily bank deposit. Next, the head cashier prepares a deposit slip (see Illustration 8-9 on page 345) and makes the bank deposit. The total amount deposited should be equal to the total receipts on the daily cash summary. This will assure that all receipts have been placed in the custody of the bank. In accepting the bank deposit, the bank stamps (authenticates) the duplicate deposit slip and sends it to the company treasurer, who makes the comparison with the daily cash summary. The foregoing measures for cash sales are graphically presented in Illustration 8-6. The activities of the sales department are shown separate from those of the cashier's department to indicate the segregation of duties in handling cash.

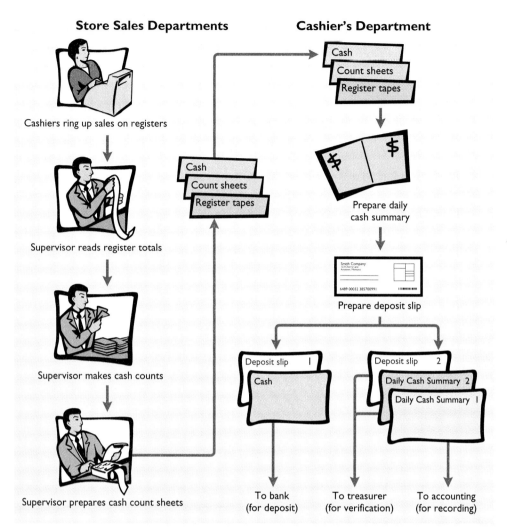

Store Sales Departments

Cashiers ring up sales on registers

Supervisor reads register totals

Supervisor makes cash counts

Supervisor prepares cash count sheets

Cashier's Department

Cash
Count sheets
Register tapes

Cash
Count sheets
Register tapes

Prepare daily
cash summary

Smith Company
123 Cherry Lane
Anytown, Montana

6489 00032 385700991

Prepare deposit slip

Deposit slip   1
Cash

Deposit slip   2
Daily Cash Summary 2
Daily Cash Summary 1

To bank
(for deposit)

To treasurer
(for verification)

To accounting
(for recording)

ILLUSTRATION 8-6

*Executing over-the-counter
cash sales*

HELPFUL HINT
Flowcharts enhance the
understanding of the flow of
documents, the processing
steps, and the internal control
procedures.

Mail Receipts

Because of your experience as an individual customer, you may be more familiar with over-the-counter receipts than with mail receipts. However, mail receipts resulting from billings and credit sales are by far the most common way cash is received by the greatest variety of businesses. Think, for example, of the number of checks received through the mail daily by a national retailer such as Land's End or L.L. Bean.

All mail receipts should be received in the presence of two mail clerks. These receipts are generally in the form of checks or money orders and frequently are accompanied by a remittance advice stating the purpose of the check. Each check should be promptly endorsed "For Deposit Only" by use of a company stamp. This **restrictive endorsement** reduces the likelihood that the check will be diverted to personal use because banks will not give an individual any cash under this type of endorsement.

A list of the checks received each day should be prepared in duplicate showing the name of the issuer of the check, the purpose of the payment, and the amount of the check. Each mail clerk should sign the list to establish responsibility for the data. The original copy of the list, along with the checks and remittance advices, are then sent to the cashier's department, where they are added to over-the-counter receipts (if any) in preparing the daily cash summary and in making the daily bank deposit. In addition, a copy of the list is sent to the treasurer's office for comparison with the total mail receipts shown on the daily cash summary, to assure that all mail receipts have been included.

STUDY

OBJECTIVE

....

Describe the applications of internal control principles to cash disbursements.

Internal Control over Cash Disbursements

Cash may be disbursed for a variety of reasons, such as to pay expenses and liabilities, or to purchase assets. **Generally, internal control over cash disbursements is more effective when payments are made by check, rather than by cash, except for incidental amounts that are paid out of petty cash.**[2] Payment by check generally occurs only after specified control procedures have been followed. In addition, the "paid" check provides proof of payment. Principles of internal control apply to cash disbursements as shown in Illustration 8-7.

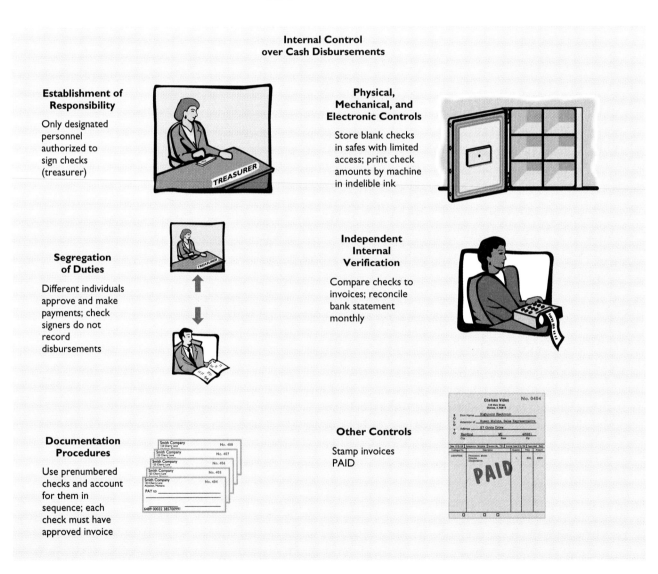

**Internal Control
over Cash Disbursements**

**Establishment of
Responsibility**

Only designated personnel authorized to sign checks (treasurer)

**Physical,
Mechanical, and
Electronic Controls**

Store blank checks in safes with limited access; print check amounts by machine in indelible ink

**Segregation
of Duties**

Different individuals approve and make payments; check signers do not record disbursements

**Independent
Internal
Verification**

Compare checks to invoices; reconcile bank statement monthly

**Documentation
Procedures**

Use prenumbered checks and account for them in sequence; each check must have approved invoice

Other Controls

Stamp invoices PAID

ILLUSTRATION 8-7

Application of internal control principles to cash disbursements

Voucher System

Most medium and large companies use a voucher system as part of their internal control over cash disbursements. A voucher system is an extensive network of approvals by authorized individuals acting independently to ensure that all disbursements by check are proper.

---

[2]The operation of a petty cash fund is explained on pages 341–343.

The system begins with the authorization to incur the cost or expense and ends with the issuance of a check for the liability incurred. A voucher is an authorization form prepared for each expenditure in a voucher system. Vouchers are required for all types of cash disbursements except those from petty cash. The voucher is prepared in the accounts payable department.

The starting point in preparing a voucher is to fill in the appropriate information about the liability on the face of the voucher from the vendor's invoice. Then, the voucher must be recorded (in the journal called a **voucher register**) and filed according to the date on which it is to be paid. A check is sent on that date, the voucher is stamped "paid," and the paid voucher is sent to the accounting department for recording (in a journal called the **check register**).

Electronic Funds Transfer (EFT) System

To account for and control cash is an expensive and time-consuming process. For example, it was estimated recently that the cost to process a check through a bank system ranges from $0.55 to $1.00 and is increasing. It is not surprising, therefore, that new approaches are being developed to transfer funds among parties without the use of paper (deposit tickets, checks, etc.). Such a procedure is called an electronic funds transfer (EFT). EFT is a disbursement system that uses wire, telephone, telegraph, or computer to transfer cash from one location to another. Use of EFT is quite common. For example, the authors receive no formal payroll checks from their universities, which simply send magnetic tapes to the appropriate banks for deposit. Regular payments such as those for house, car, or utilities are frequently made by EFT.

TECHNOLOGY IN ACTION

The development of EFT will continue. Already it is estimated that over 80% of the total volume of bank transactions in the United States is performed using EFT. The computer technology is available to create a "checkless" society. The only major barriers appear to be the individual's concern for privacy and protection and certain legislative constraints. It should be noted that numerous safeguards have been built into EFT systems. However, the possibility of errors and fraud still exists because only a limited number of individuals are involved in the transfers, which may prevent appropriate segregation of duties.

Petty Cash Fund

As you learned earlier in the chapter, better internal control over cash disbursements is possible when payments are made by check. However, using checks to pay such small amounts as those for postage due, employee lunches, and taxi fares is both impractical and a nuisance. A common way of handling such payments, while maintaining satisfactory control, is to use a petty cash fund. A petty cash fund is a cash fund used to pay relatively small amounts. The operation of a petty cash fund, often called an **imprest system**, involves (1) establishing the fund, (2) making payments from the fund, and (3) replenishing the fund.[3]

5
STUDY
OBJECTIVE
....
Explain the operation of
a petty cash fund.

Establishing the Fund.   Two essential steps in establishing a petty cash fund are (1) appointing a petty cash custodian who will be responsible for the fund and (2) determining the size of the fund. Ordinarily, the amount is expected to cover anticipated disbursements for a 3- to 4-week period. When the fund is established,

---

[3]The term "imprest" means an advance of money for a designated purpose.

a check payable to the petty cash custodian is issued for the stipulated amount. If the Laird Company decides to establish a $100 fund on March 1, the entry in general journal form is:

A	=	L	+	SE
+100				
−100				

Mar. 1	Petty Cash	100	
	Cash		100
	(To establish a petty cash fund)		

The check is then cashed and the proceeds are placed in a locked petty cash box or drawer. Most petty cash funds are established on a fixed amount basis. Moreover, no additional entries will be made to the Petty Cash account unless the stipulated amount of the fund is changed. For example, if Laird Company decides on July 1 to increase the size of the fund to $250, it would debit Petty Cash $150 and credit Cash $150.

Making Payments from the Fund.   The custodian of the petty cash fund has the authority to make payments from the fund that conform to prescribed management policies. Usually, management limits the size of expenditures that may be made and does not permit use of the fund for certain types of transactions (such as making short-term loans to employees). Each payment from the fund must be documented on a prenumbered petty cash receipt (or petty cash voucher), as shown in Illustration 8-8. Note that the signatures of both the custodian and the individual receiving payment are required on the receipt. If other supporting documents such as a freight bill or invoice are available, they should be attached to the petty cash receipt.

ILLUSTRATION 8-8

Petty cash receipt

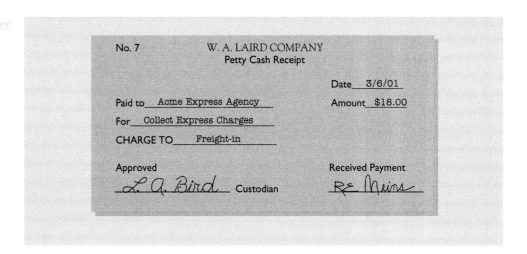

The receipts are kept in the petty cash box until the fund is replenished. As a result, the sum of the petty cash receipts and money in the fund should equal the established total at all times. This means that surprise counts can be made at any time by an independent person, such as an internal auditor, to determine whether the fund is being maintained intact.

No accounting entry is made to record a payment at the time it is made from petty cash. It is considered to be both inexpedient and unnecessary to do so. Instead, the accounting effects of each payment are recognized when the fund is replenished.

Replenishing the Fund.   When the money in the petty cash fund reaches a minimum level, the fund is replenished. The request for reimbursement is initiated by the petty cash custodian. This individual prepares a schedule (or summary) of the payments that have been made and sends the schedule, supported by petty cash receipts and other documentation, to the treasurer's office. The receipts and supporting documents are examined in the treasurer's office to verify that they were proper payments from the fund. The treasurer then approves the request and a check is prepared to restore the fund to its established amount. At the same time, all supporting documentation is stamped "paid" so that it cannot be submitted again for payment.

To illustrate, assume that on March 15 the petty cash custodian requests a check for $87. The fund contains $13 cash and petty cash receipts for postage $44, freight-out $38, and miscellaneous expenses $5. The entry, in general journal form, to record the check is:

Mar. 15	Postage Expense	44	
	Freight-out	38	
	Miscellaneous Expense	5	
	Cash		87
	(To replenish petty cash fund)		

A	=	L	+	SE
−87				−44
				−38
				−5

Note that the Petty Cash account is not affected by the reimbursement entry. Replenishment changes the composition of the fund by replacing the petty cash receipts with cash, but it does not change the balance in the fund.

It may be necessary in replenishing a petty cash fund to recognize a cash shortage or overage. This results when the cash plus receipts in the petty cash box do not equal the established amount of the petty cash fund. To illustrate, assume in the example above that the custodian had only $12 in cash in the fund plus the receipts as listed. The request for reimbursement would, therefore, have been for $88, and the following entry would be made:

HELPFUL HINT
Cash over and short situations result from mathematical errors or from failure to keep accurate records.

Mar. 15	Postage Expense	44	
	Freight-out	38	
	Miscellaneous Expense	5	
	Cash Over and Short	1	
	Cash		88
	(To replenish petty cash fund)		

A	=	L	+	SE
−88				−44
				−38
				−5
				−1

Conversely, if the custodian had $14 in cash, the reimbursement request would have been for $86 and Cash Over and Short would have been credited for $1. A debit balance in Cash Over and Short is reported in the income statement as miscellaneous expense; a credit balance is reported as miscellaneous revenue. Cash Over and Short is closed to Income Summary at the end of the year.

A petty cash fund should be replenished at the end of the accounting period regardless of the cash in the fund. Replenishment at this time is necessary in order to recognize the effects of the petty cash payments on the financial statements.

Internal control over a petty cash fund is strengthened by (1) having a supervisor make surprise counts of the fund to ascertain whether the paid vouchers and fund cash equal the imprest amount and (2) canceling or mutilating the paid vouchers so they cannot be resubmitted for reimbursement.

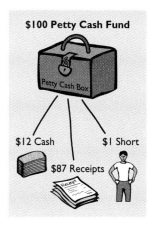

$100 Petty Cash Fund

$12 Cash $1 Short

$87 Receipts

BEFORE YOU GO ON ...

Review It

1. How do the principles of internal control apply to cash receipts?
2. How do the principles of internal control apply to cash disbursements?
3. When are entries required in a petty cash system?

Do It

L. R. Cortez is concerned about the control over cash receipts in his fast-food restaurant, Big Cheese. The restaurant has two cash registers. At no time do more than two employees take customer orders and ring up sales. Work shifts for employees range from 4 to 8 hours. Cortez asks your help in installing a good system of internal control over cash receipts.

Reasoning: Cortez needs to understand the principles of internal control, especially the principles of establishing responsibility, the use of electronic controls, and independent internal verification. Using this knowledge, an effective system of control over cash receipts can be designed and implemented.

Solution: Cortez should assign a cash register to each employee at the start of each work shift, with register totals set at zero. Each employee should be instructed to use only the assigned register and to ring up all sales. At the end of each work shift, Cortez or a supervisor/manager should total the register and make a cash count to see whether all cash is accounted for.

Related exercise material: BE8–3 and E8–1.

THE NAVIGATOR

USE OF A BANK

6
STUDY
OBJECTIVE

Indicate the control features of a bank account.

The use of a bank contributes significantly to good internal control over cash. A company can safeguard its cash by using a bank as a depository and clearing house for checks received and checks written. Use of a bank minimizes the amount of currency that must be kept on hand. In addition, the use of a bank facilitates the control of cash because a double record is maintained of all bank transactions—one by the business and the other by the bank. The asset account Cash, maintained by the depositor, is the reciprocal of the bank's liability account for each depositor. It should be possible to **reconcile these accounts** (make them agree) at any time.

Opening a bank checking account is a relatively simple procedure. Typically, the bank makes a credit check on the new customer and the depositor is required to sign a **signature card**. The card should contain the signatures of each person authorized to sign checks on the account. The signature card is used by bank employees to validate signatures on the checks.

As soon as possible after an account is opened, the bank will provide the depositor with a book of serially numbered checks and deposit slips imprinted with the depositor's name and address. Each check and deposit slip is imprinted with both a bank and a depositor identification number in magnetic ink to permit computer processing of the transaction.

Many companies have more than one bank account. For efficiency of operations and better control, national retailers like Wal-Mart Stores and Kmart may have regional bank accounts. Similarly, a company such as Exxon with more than 150,000 employees may have a payroll bank account, as well as one or more general bank accounts. In addition, a company may maintain several bank accounts in order to have more than one source for obtaining short-term loans when needed.

Making Bank Deposits

Bank deposits should be made by an authorized employee, such as the head cashier. Each deposit must be documented by a deposit slip (ticket), as shown in Illustration 8-9 on page 345.

Deposit slips are prepared in duplicate. The original is retained by the bank; the duplicate, machine stamped by the bank to establish its authenticity, is retained by the depositor.

ILLUSTRATION 8-9

Deposit slip

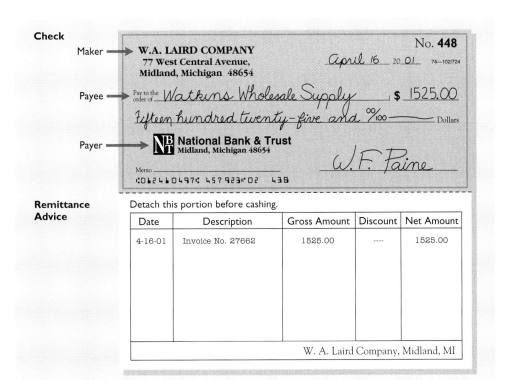

CHECKS	LIST SINGLY	DOLLARS	CENTS
1	74 – 331/724	175	40
2	61 – 157/220	292	60
3	19 – 401/710	337	55
4	22 – 815/666	165	72
5	15 – 360/011	145	53
6			
7			
8			
9			
10			
11			
12			
13			
14			
15			
16			
17			
18			
19			
TOTAL		1116	80

ENTER TOTAL ON THE FRONT OF THIS TICKET

Bank code numbers

DEPOSIT TICKET

W.A. LAIRD COMPANY
77 West Central Avenue,
Midland, Michigan 48654

DATE _____ April 19 __ 20 _ 01_

CASH	CURRENCY	462	10
	COIN		
LIST CHECKS SINGLY			
TOTAL FROM OTHER SIDE		1116	80
TOTAL		1578	90
TOTAL FROM OTHER SIDE			
NET DEPOSIT		1578	90

74—102/724

USE OTHER SIDE FOR
ADDITIONAL LISTINGS

BE SURE EACH ITEM IS
PROPERLY ENDORSED

N B T National Bank & Trust
Midland, Michigan 48654

⑆0124⑆0497⑆ 457 923⑈ 02   75

CHECKS AND OTHER ITEMS ARE RECEIVED FOR DEPOSIT SUBJECT TO THE PROVISIONS OF THE UNIFORM COMMERCIAL CODE OR ANY APPLICABLE COLLECTION AGREEMENT

Front side

Reverse side

Writing Checks

A check is a written order signed by the depositor directing the bank to pay a specified sum of money to a designated recipient. Thus, there are three parties to a check: the **maker** (or drawer) who issues the check, the **bank** (or payer) on which the check is drawn, and the **payee** to whom the check is payable. A check is a negotiable instrument that can be transferred to another party by endorsement. Each check should be accompanied by an explanation of its purposes. In many businesses, this is done by attaching a remittance advice to the check, as shown in Illustration 8-10.

ILLUSTRATION 8-10

Check with remittance advice

Check

Maker

W.A. LAIRD COMPANY
77 West Central Avenue,
Midland, Michigan 48654

No. **448**

April 16 20 01   74—102/724

Payee

Pay to the order of _Watkins Wholesale Supply_ $ _1525.00_

Fifteen hundred twenty-five and 00/100 _____ Dollars

Payer

N B T National Bank & Trust
Midland, Michigan 48654

W. F. Paine

Memo _____

⑆0124⑆0497⑆ 457 923⑈ 02   438

Remittance Advice

Detach this portion before cashing.

Date	Description	Gross Amount	Discount	Net Amount
4-16-01	Invoice No. 27662	1525.00	----	1525.00

W. A. Laird Company, Midland, MI

For both individuals and businesses, it is important to know the balance in the checking account at all times. To keep the balance current, each deposit and check should be entered on running balance memorandum forms provided by the bank or on the check stubs contained in the checkbook.

TECHNOLOGY IN ACTION

One big consumer business on the information highway is a set of financial household chores: balancing the checkbook, paying bills, and saving for retirement. Many U.S. banks now offer electronic home banking. For customers, the new capabilities mean more convenient service, more up-to-date information about their finances, and more control over their money. Millions of households now do a substantial amount of their money management electronically from home, and this number is expected to increase significantly in the near future.

Bank Statements

HELPFUL HINT

Essentially, the bank statement is a copy of the bank's records sent to the customer for periodic review.

Each month, the depositor receives a bank statement from the bank. A **bank statement** shows the depositor's bank transactions and balances. For example, the statement, like the one in Illustration 8-11, shows (1) checks paid and other debits that reduce the balance in the depositor's account, (2) deposits and other credits that increase the balance in the depositor's account, and (3) the account balance after each day's transactions.

ILLUSTRATION 8-11

Bank statement

HELPFUL HINT

Every deposit received by the bank is *credited* to the customer's account. The reverse occurs when the bank "pays" a check issued by a company on its checking account balance: Payment reduces the bank's liability and is therefore *debited* to the customer's account with the bank.

NBT National Bank & Trust
Midland, Michigan 48654   Member FDIC

ACCOUNT STATEMENT

W. A. LAIRD COMPANY
77 WEST CENTRAL AVENUE
MIDLAND, MICHIGAN 48654

Statement Date/Credit
Line Closing Date

April 30, 2001

457923

ACCOUNT NUMBER

Balance Last Statement	Deposits and Credits		Checks and Debits		Balance This Statement
	No.	Total Amount	No.	Total Amount	
13,256.90	20	34,805.10	26	32,154.55	15,907.45

CHECKS AND DEBITS			DEPOSITS AND CREDITS		DAILY BALANCE	
Date	No.	Amount	Date	Amount	Date	Amount
4–2	435	644.95	4–2	4,276.85	4–2	16,888.80
4–5	436	3,260.00	4–3	2,137.50	4–3	18,249.65
4–4	437	1,185.79	4–5	1,350.47	4–4	17,063.86
4–3	438	776.65	4–7	982.46	4–5	15,154.33
4–8	439	1,781.70	4–8	1,320.28	4–7	14,648.89
4–7	440	1,487.90	4–9 CM	1,035.00	4–8	11,767.47
4–8	441	2,420.00	4–11	2,720.00	4–9	12,802.47
4–11	442	1,585.60	4–12	757.41	4–11	13,936.87
4–12	443	1,226.00	4–13	1,218.56	4–12	13,468.28
4–29	NSF	425.60	4–27	1,545.57	4–27	13,005.45
4–29	459	1,080.30	4–29	2,929.45	4–29	14,429.00
4–30	DM	30.00	4–30	2,128.60	4–30	15,907.45
4–30	461	620.15				

Symbols: **CM** Credit Memo   **EC** Error Correction   **NSF** Not Sufficient Funds   Reconcile Your Account Promptly
          DM Debit Memo   **INT** Interest Earned   **SC** Service Charge

Most banks offer depositors the option of receiving "paid" checks with their bank statements. For those who decline, the bank keeps a record of each check on microfilm. Irrespective of the depositor's choice, all "paid" checks are listed in numerical sequence on the bank statement along with the date the check was paid and its amount. Upon paying a check, the bank stamps the check "paid"; a paid check is sometimes referred to as a **canceled** check. In addition, the bank includes with the bank statement memoranda explaining other debits and credits made by the bank to the depositor's account.

Debit Memorandum

Banks charge a monthly fee for the use of their services. Often the fee is charged only when the average monthly balance in a checking account falls below a specified amount. The fee, called a bank service charge, is often identified on the bank statement by a code symbol such as SC. A debit memorandum explaining the charge is included with the bank statement. Separate debit memoranda may also be issued for other bank services such as the cost of printing checks, issuing traveler's checks, and wiring funds to other locations. The symbol DM is often used for such charges.

A debit memorandum is used by the bank when a previously deposited customer's check "bounces" because of insufficient funds. In such a case, the check is marked NSF (not sufficient funds) by the customer's bank and is returned to the depositor's bank. The bank then debits the depositor's account, as shown by the symbol NSF on the bank statement in Illustration 8-11, and sends the NSF check and debit memorandum to the depositor as notification of the charge. The NSF check creates an account receivable for the depositor and reduces cash in the bank account.

ACCOUNTING IN ACTION
Business Insight

As copying machines have become ever more sophisticated, check counterfeiting has flourished. For example, in just one quarter of a recent fiscal year, the Woolworth Corporation had a $5 million loss from bad checks. Most of the total occurred in the Foot Locker division of the company, a spokesperson said. In the U.S. business community as a whole, some $10 billion worth of bad checks are written every year.

Checkmate Electronic Inc. thinks it has at least a partial answer to this problem. It makes electronic devices that read the magnetic ink used to print account and routing numbers on checks. By identifying the magnetic frequencies as well as the precise shape and size of the numbers, the machine can determine if a check is a fake. Checkmate has a machine small enough to be installed beside cash registers, and it is now in use by such retailers as J.C. Penney, Neiman-Marcus, and Pier 1 Imports.

Source: The Wall Street Journal, March 31, 1994, p. C2; and Business Week, May 23, 1994, p. 9.

Credit Memorandum

A depositor may ask the bank to collect its notes receivable. In such a case, the bank will credit the depositor's account for the cash proceeds of the note, as illustrated on the bank statement by the symbol CM. It will issue a credit memorandum which is sent with the statement to explain the entry. Many banks also offer interest on checking accounts. The interest earned may be indicated on the bank statement by the symbol CM or INT.

Reconciling the Bank Account

Because the bank and the depositor maintain independent records of the depositor's checking account, you might assume that the respective balances will always agree. In fact, the two balances are seldom the same at any given time,

7
STUDY
OBJECTIVE
Prepare a bank reconciliation.

and it is necessary to make the balance per books agree with the balance per bank—a process called **reconciling the bank account**. The lack of agreement between the two balances is due to:

1. **Time lags** that prevent one of the parties from recording the transaction in the same period.
2. **Errors** by either party in recording transactions.

Time lags occur frequently. For example, several days may elapse between the time a check is mailed to a payee and the date the check is paid by the bank.

ACCOUNTING IN ACTION
Ethics Insight

Some companies use time lags to their—illegal—advantage. An Alberta financier once wrote checks that totalled nearly $850 million over a period of five years on a Citibank account in New York. The bank's check-clearing procedures were manual and took about six business days to clear. He deposited these checks in his companies' Canadian bank accounts and received immediate credit for the funds, even though the money wasn't withdrawn from the U.S. bank account to cover the deposit for the six business days. This is known as kiting, which allows cash shortages to be concealed. Eventually, bank officials grew suspicious when the daily checks exceeded the yearly income of the companies. The swindler has since been convicted of fraud and theft for this elaborate check kiting scheme.

Source: The Bottom Line, June 1997, p. 19.

Similarly, when the depositor uses the bank's night depository to make its deposits, there will be a difference of at least one day between the time the receipts are recorded by the depositor and the time they are recorded by the bank. A time lag also occurs whenever the bank mails a debit or credit memorandum to the depositor.

The incidence of errors depends on the effectiveness of the internal controls maintained by the depositor and the bank. Bank errors are infrequent. However, either party could inadvertently record a $450 check as $45 or $540. In addition, the bank might mistakenly charge a check drawn by C. D. Berg to the account of C. D. Burg.

TECHNOLOGY IN ACTION

A malfunctioning computer software program doubled all withdrawals and transfers made at Chemical Bank automatic teller machines (ATMs) in New York state for about 12 hours. The printed record of transactions spit out by the ATM was accurate, but the computerized posting of the transactions was automatically doubled. The bank corrected all errors, which in the aggregate may have been $15 million.

Source: Denver Post, February 19, 1994.

Reconciliation Procedure

To obtain maximum benefit from a bank reconciliation, the reconciliation should be prepared by an employee who has no other responsibilities pertaining to cash. When the internal control principle of independent internal verification is not followed in preparing the reconciliation, cash embezzlements may escape unnoticed. For example, a cashier who prepares the reconciliation can embezzle cash and conceal the embezzlement by misstating the reconciliation. Thus, the bank accounts would reconcile and the embezzlement would not be detected.

In reconciling the bank account, it is customary to reconcile the balance per books and balance per bank to their adjusted (correct or true) cash balances. The reconciliation schedule is divided into two sections, as shown in Illustration 8-12. The starting point in preparing the reconciliation is to enter the balance per bank statement and balance per books on the schedule. The following steps should reveal all the reconciling items that cause the difference between the two balances.

1. Compare the individual deposits on the bank statement with deposits in transit from the preceding bank reconciliation and with the deposits per company records or copies of duplicate deposit slips. Deposits recorded by the depositor that have not been recorded by the bank represent deposits in transit and are added to the balance per bank.

2. Compare the paid checks shown on the bank statement or the paid checks returned with the bank statement with (a) checks outstanding from the preceding bank reconciliation and (b) checks issued by the company as recorded in the cash payments journal. Issued checks recorded by the company that have not been paid by the bank represent outstanding checks that are deducted from the balance per the bank.

HELPFUL HINT
Deposits in transit and outstanding checks are reconciling items because of time lags.

ILLUSTRATION 8-12
Bank reconciliation procedures

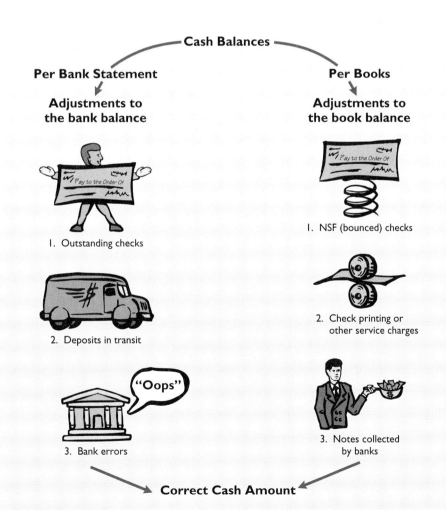

Cash Balances

Per Bank Statement

Adjustments to the bank balance

1. Outstanding checks

2. Deposits in transit

"Oops"

3. Bank errors

Per Books

Adjustments to the book balance

1. NSF (bounced) checks

2. Check printing or other service charges

3. Notes collected by banks

Correct Cash Amount

3. Note any **errors** discovered in the foregoing steps and list them in the appropriate section of the reconciliation schedule. For example, if a paid check correctly written by the company for $195 was mistakenly recorded by the company for $159, the error of $36 is deducted from the balance per books. All errors made by the depositor are reconciling items in determining the adjusted cash balance per books. In contrast, all errors made by the bank are reconciling items in determining the adjusted cash balance per the bank.

4. Trace **bank memoranda** to the depositor's records. Any unrecorded memoranda should be listed in the appropriate section of the reconciliation schedule. For example, a $5 debit memorandum for bank service charges is deducted from the balance per books, and $32 of interest earned is added to the balance per books.

Bank Reconciliation Illustrated

The bank statement for the Laird Company is shown in Illustration 8-11. It shows a balance per bank of $15,907.45 on April 30, 2001. On this date the balance of cash per books is $11,589.45. From the foregoing steps, the following reconciling items are determined.

<table>
<tr><td>1. Deposits in transit: April 30 deposit (received by bank on May 1).</td><td>$2,201.40</td></tr>
<tr><td>2. Outstanding checks: No. 453 $3,000.00; No. 457 $1,401.30; No. 460 $1,502.70.</td><td>5,904.00</td></tr>
<tr><td>3. Errors: Check No. 443 was correctly written by Laird for $1,226.00 and was correctly paid by the bank. However, it was recorded for $1,262.00 by Laird Company.</td><td>36.00</td></tr>
<tr><td>4. Bank memoranda:</td><td></td></tr>
<tr><td>   **a.** Debit—NSF check from J. R. Baron for $425.60</td><td>425.60</td></tr>
<tr><td>   **b.** Debit—Printing company checks charge, $30.00</td><td>30.00</td></tr>
<tr><td>   **c.** Credit—Collection of note receivable for $1,000 plus interest earned $50, less bank collection fee $15.00</td><td>1,035.00</td></tr>
</table>

The bank reconciliation is shown in Illustration 8-13.

HELPFUL HINT

Note in the bank statement that checks No. 459 and 461 have been paid but check No. 460 is not listed. Thus, this check is outstanding. If a complete bank statement were provided, checks No. 453 and 457 would also not be listed. The amounts for these three checks are obtained from the company's cash payments records.

ILLUSTRATION 8-13

Bank reconciliation

ALTERNATIVE TERMINOLOGY

The terms *adjusted balance*, *true cash balance*, and *correct cash balance* may be used interchangeably.

<table>
<tr><td colspan="3" align="center">**LAIRD COMPANY**
Bank Reconciliation
April 30, 2001</td></tr>
<tr><td>Cash balance per bank statement</td><td></td><td>$15,907.45</td></tr>
<tr><td>Add: Deposits in transit</td><td></td><td>2,201.40</td></tr>
<tr><td></td><td></td><td>18,108.85</td></tr>
<tr><td>Less: Outstanding checks</td><td></td><td></td></tr>
<tr><td>   No. 453</td><td>$3,000.00</td><td></td></tr>
<tr><td>   No. 457</td><td>1,401.30</td><td></td></tr>
<tr><td>   No. 460</td><td>1,502.70</td><td>5,904.00</td></tr>
<tr><td>**Adjusted cash balance per bank**</td><td></td><td>**$12,204.85**</td></tr>
<tr><td>Cash balance per books</td><td></td><td>$11,589.45</td></tr>
<tr><td>Add: Collection of note receivable, $1,000 plus interest</td><td></td><td></td></tr>
<tr><td>   earned $50, less collection fee $15</td><td>$1,035.00</td><td></td></tr>
<tr><td>   Error in recording check No. 443</td><td>36.00</td><td>1,071.00</td></tr>
<tr><td></td><td></td><td>12,660.45</td></tr>
<tr><td>Less: NSF check</td><td>425.60</td><td></td></tr>
<tr><td>   Bank service charge</td><td>30.00</td><td>455.60</td></tr>
<tr><td>**Adjusted cash balance per books**</td><td></td><td>**$12,204.85**</td></tr>
</table>

Entries from Bank Reconciliation

Each reconciling item in determining the **adjusted cash balance per books** should be recorded by the depositor. **If these items are not journalized and posted, the Cash account will not show the correct balance**. The entries for the Laird Company on April 30 are as follows:

Collection of Note Receivable. This entry involves four accounts. Assuming that the interest of $50 has not been accrued and the collection fee is charged to Miscellaneous Expense, the entry is:

Apr. 30	Cash	1,035.00	
	Miscellaneous Expense	15.00	
	Notes Receivable		1,000.00
	Interest Revenue		50.00
	(To record collection of notes receivable by bank)		

```
A       =   L   +   SE
+1,035              -15
-1,000              +50
```

Book Error. An examination of the cash disbursements journal shows that check No. 443 was a payment on account to Andrea Company, a supplier. The correcting entry is:

Apr. 30	Cash	36.00	
	Accounts Payable—Andrea Company		36.00
	(To correct error in recording check No. 443)		

```
A    =   L   +   SE
+36     +36
```

NSF Check. As indicated earlier, an NSF check becomes an accounts receivable to the depositor. The entry is:

Apr. 30	Accounts Receivable—J. R. Baron	425.60	
	Cash		425.60
	(To record NSF check)		

```
A         =   L   +   SE
+425.60
-425.60
```

Bank Service Charges. Check printing charges (DM) and other bank service charges (SC) are debited to Miscellaneous Expense because they are usually nominal in amount. The entry is:

Apr. 30	Miscellaneous Expense	30.00	
	Cash		30.00
	(To record charge for printing company checks)		

```
A    =   L   +   SE
-30              -30
```

The foregoing entries could also be combined into one compound entry. After the entries are posted, the cash account will show the following:

Cash

Apr. 30 Bal.	11,589.45	Apr. 30	425.60
30	1,035.00	30	30.00
30	36.00		
Apr. 30 Bal.	**12,204.85**		

The adjusted cash balance in the ledger should agree with the adjusted cash balance per books in the bank reconciliation in Illustration 8-13.

What entries does the bank make? If any bank errors are discovered in preparing the reconciliation, the bank should be notified so it can make the necessary corrections on its records. The bank does not make any entries for deposits in transit or outstanding checks. Only when these items reach the bank will the bank record these items.

BEFORE YOU GO ON ...

Review It

1. Why is it necessary to reconcile a bank account?
2. What steps are involved in the reconciliation procedure?
3. What information is included in a bank reconciliation?

Do It

Sally Kist owns Linen Kist Fabrics. Sally asks you to explain how the following reconciling items should be treated in reconciling the bank account at December 31: (1) a debit memorandum for an NSF check, (2) a credit memorandum for a note collected by the bank, (3) outstanding checks, and (4) a deposit in transit.

Reasoning: Sally needs to understand that one cause of a reconciling item is time lags. Items (1) and (2) are reconciling items because Linen Kist Fabrics has not yet recorded the memoranda. Items (3) and (4) are reconciling items because the bank has not recorded the transactions.

Solution: In reconciling the bank account, the reconciling items are treated as follows:

NSF check: Deducted from balance per books.
Collection of note: Added to balance per books.
Outstanding checks: Deducted from balance per bank.
Deposit in transit: Added to balance per bank.

Related exercise material: BE8–6, BE8–7, BE8–8, BE8–9, E8–5, E8–6, E8–7, and E8–8.

THE NAVIGATOR

REPORTING CASH

8
STUDY
OBJECTIVE

Explain the reporting of cash.

Cash on hand, cash in banks, and petty cash are often combined and reported simply as **Cash**. Because it is the most liquid asset owned by a company, cash is listed first in the current assets, section of the balance sheet. Some companies use the designation "cash and cash equivalents" in reporting cash, as illustrated by the following:

ILLUSTRATION 8-15

Presentation of cash and cash equivalents

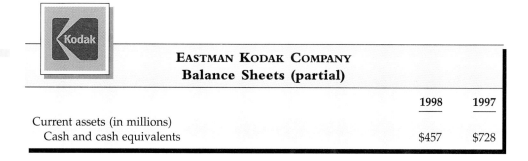

EASTMAN KODAK COMPANY
Balance Sheets (partial)

	1998	1997
Current assets (in millions)		
Cash and cash equivalents	$457	$728

Cash equivalents are highly liquid investments, with maturities of 3 months or less when purchased, that can be converted into a specific amount of cash. They include money market funds, money market savings certificates, bank certificates of deposit, and U.S. Treasury bills and notes.

A company may have cash that is restricted for a special purpose. Examples include a payroll bank account for paying salaries and wages, and plant expansion fund cash for financing new construction. If the restricted cash is expected to be used within the next year, the amount should be reported as a current asset. However, when this is not the case, the restricted funds should be reported as a noncurrent asset. Since a payroll bank account will be used as early as the next payday for employees, it is reported as a current asset. In contrast, unless the new construction will begin within the next year, plant expansion fund cash is classified as a noncurrent asset.

In making loans to depositors, it is common for banks to require the borrowers to maintain minimum cash balances. These minimum balances, called compensating balances, provide the bank with support for the loans. Compensating balances are a restriction on the use of cash that may affect a company's liquidity. Accordingly, compensating balances should be disclosed in the financial statements.

BEFORE YOU GO ON . . .

Review It

1. What is generally reported as cash on a company's balance sheet?
2. What is meant by cash equivalents and compensating balances?
3. At what amount does Kellogg Company report cash and cash equivalents in its 1998 consolidated balance sheet? The answer to this question is provided on page 371.

A LOOK BACK AT OUR FEATURE STORY

Refer to the Feature Story about Stephanie's Gourmet Coffee and More café in Moose Jaw, and answer the following questions:

1. Does Stephanie Mintenko have a valid basis for establishing responsibility for overages or shortages? Why or why not?
2. What internal control principles are applicable to reconciling the cash register tape and the amount of cash in the cash drawer at the end of each shift?
3. What internal control principle is violated by not printing a receipt for each customer who purchases beverages, a meal, or uses the café's computer?
4. Do you think cashiers are, or should be, bonded (insured against misappropriation of assets)?
5. What adjusting entry would the bookkeeper likely make to record a cash shortage of $5?

Solution
1. Establishing responsibility for overages or shortages occurs twice a day: at the end of the 5:00 pm shift, and at closing. This procedure provides a valid basis for evaluation only if one person worked an assigned register since the last reconciliation. Since up to three people work a single register during a shift, there is no valid basis for establishing who is responsible for any overage or shortage.
2. Internal control principles are: (a) Authorization—not applicable since cashiers are not assigned to a specific cash register for their shift. (b) Segregation of duties—cashiers (other than the owner/manager) are not involved in performing the reconciliation. (c) Documentation—the cash register tape provides the documentation for total receipts for the shift. (d) Safeguard assets—an electronic cash register is used with an internal tape whose access presumably is restricted. (e) Independent verification—a bookkeeper, in addition to Stephanie Mintenko, performs the reconciliation regularly.

3. The internal control principle of documentation procedures is involved. If a customer making a purchase sees that a sale isn't rung up or if the customer doesn't request a receipt, there is a possibility that the transaction has not been recorded. However, the internal control does not reside in the receipt itself. The control is forcing the cashier to ring up each sale so that a receipt is produced. Each receipt is recorded on an internal cash register tape. At the end of the day, the tape is used in determining overages or shortages.

4. It is doubtful that Stephanie's café would bond part-time employees. From the employer's standpoint, bonding is protection against major embezzlements by dishonest employees. The risk of this occurring in a small café, with the active participation of the owner/manager, is relatively low.

THE NAVIGATOR

5. Cash Over and Short (miscellaneous expense account)   5
   Cash   5

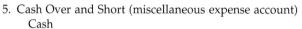

DEMONSTRATION PROBLEM

Trillo Company's bank statement for May 2001 shows the following data:

Balance 5/1	$12,650	Balance 5/31	$14,280
Debit memorandum:		Credit memorandum:	
NSF check	$175	Collection of note receivable	$505

The cash balance per books at May 31 is $13,319. Your review of the data reveals the following:

1. The NSF check was from Hup Co., a customer.
2. The note collected by the bank was a $500, three-month, 12% note. The bank charged a $10 collection fee. No interest has been accrued.
3. Outstanding checks at May 31 total $2,410.
4. Deposits in transit at May 31 total $1,752.
5. A Trillo Company check for $352 dated May 10 cleared the bank on May 25. This check, which was a payment on account, was journalized for $325.

Instructions
(a) Prepare a bank reconciliation at May 31.
(b) Journalize the entries required by the reconciliation.

SOLUTION TO DEMONSTRATION PROBLEM

PROBLEM-SOLVING STRATEGIES
1. Follow the four steps used in reconciling items (p. 349–350).
2. Work carefully to minimize mathematical errors in the reconciliation.
3. All entries are based on reconciling items per books.
4. Make sure the cash ledger balance after posting the reconciling entries agrees with the adjusted cash balance per books.

(a)

TRILLO COMPANY
Bank Reconciliation
May 31, 2001

Cash balance per bank statement		$14,280
Add: Deposits in transit		1,752
		16,032
Less: Outstanding checks		2,410
Adjusted cash balance per bank		$13,622
Cash balance per books		$13,319
Add: Collection of note receivable $500, plus $15 interest less		
collection fee $10		505
		13,824
Less: NSF check	$175	
Error in recording check	27	202
Adjusted cash balance per books		$13,622

(b)

May 31	Cash		505	
	Miscellaneous Expense		10	
	Notes Receivable			500
	Interest Revenue			15
	(To record collection of note by bank)			
31	Accounts Receivable—Hup Co.		175	
	Cash			175
	(To record NSF check from Hup Co.)			
31	Accounts Payable		27	
	Cash			27
	(To correct error in recording check)			

SUMMARY OF STUDY OBJECTIVES

1. Define internal control. Internal control is the plan of organization and related methods and procedures adopted within a business to safeguard its assets and to enhance the accuracy and reliability of its accounting records.

2. Identify the principles of internal control. The principles of internal control are: establishment of responsibility; segregation of duties; documentation procedures; physical, mechanical, and electronic controls; independent internal verification; and other controls.

3. Explain the applications of internal control principles to cash receipts. Internal controls over cash receipts include: (a) designating only personnel such as cashiers to handle cash; (b) assigning the duties of receiving cash, recording cash, and custody of cash to different individuals; (c) obtaining remittance advices for mail receipts, cash register tapes for over-the-counter receipts, and deposit slips for bank deposits; (d) using company safes and bank vaults to store cash with access limited to authorized personnel, and using cash registers in executing over-the-counter receipts; (e) making independent daily counts of register receipts and daily comparisons of total receipts with total deposits; and (f) bonding personnel who handle cash and requiring them to take vacations.

4. Describe the applications of internal control principles to cash disbursements. Internal controls over cash disbursements include: (a) having only specified individuals such as the treasurer authorized to sign checks; (b) assigning the duties of approving items for payment, paying the items, and recording the payment to different individuals;

(c) using prenumbered checks and accounting for all checks, with each check supported by an approved invoice; (d) storing blank checks in a safe or vault with access restricted to authorized personnel, and using a checkwriter to imprint amounts on checks; (e) comparing each check with the approved invoice before issuing the check, and making monthly reconciliations of bank and book balances; and (f) after payment, stamping each approved invoice "paid."

5. Explain the operation of a petty cash fund. In operating a petty cash fund, it is necessary to establish the fund, make payments from the fund, and replenish the fund.

6. Indicate the control features of a bank account. A bank account contributes to good internal control by providing physical controls for the storage of cash, minimizing the amount of currency that must be kept on hand, and creating a double record of a depositor's bank transactions.

7. Prepare a bank reconciliation. In reconciling the bank account, it is customary to reconcile the balance per books and balance per bank to their adjusted balances. The steps in determining the reconciling items are to ascertain deposits in transit, outstanding checks, errors by the depositor or the bank, and unrecorded bank memoranda.

8. Explain the reporting of cash. Cash is listed first in the current assets section of the balance sheet. In some cases, cash is reported together with cash equivalents. Cash restricted for a special purpose is reported separately as a current asset or as a noncurrent asset depending on when the cash is expected to be used.

GLOSSARY

Bank service charge A fee charged by a bank for the use of its services. (p. 347).

Bank statement A statement received monthly from the bank that shows the depositor's bank transactions and balances. (p. 346).

Cash Resources that consist of coins, currency, checks, money orders, and money on hand or on deposit in a bank or similar depository. (p. 337).

Cash equivalents Highly liquid investments, with maturities of three months or less when purchased, that can be converted to a specific amount of cash. (p. 352).

Check   A written order signed by the depositor directing the bank to pay a specified sum of money to a designated recipient (p. 345).

Compensating balances   Minimum cash balances required by a bank in support of bank loans. (p. 353).

Deposits in transit   Deposits recorded by the depositor that have not been recorded by the bank. (p. 349).

Electronic funds transfer (EFT)   A disbursement system that uses wire, telephone, telegraph, or computer to transfer cash from one location to another. (p. 341).

Internal auditors   Company employees who evaluate on a continuous basis the effectiveness of the company's system of internal control. (p. 334).

Internal control   The plan of organization and all the related methods and measures adopted within a business to safeguard its assets and enhance the accuracy and reliability of its accounting records. (p. 330).

NSF check   A check that is not paid by a bank because of insufficient funds in a customer's bank account. (p. 347).

Outstanding checks   Checks issued and recorded by a company that have not been paid by the bank. (p. 349).

Petty cash fund   A cash fund used to pay relatively small amounts. (p. 341).

Voucher   An authorization form prepared for each payment by check in a voucher system. (p. 341).

Voucher system   An extensive network of approvals by authorized individuals acting independently to ensure that all disbursements by check are proper. (p. 340).

SELF-STUDY QUESTIONS

Answers are at the end of the chapter.

(SO 1) 1. Internal control is used in a business to enhance the accuracy and reliability of its accounting records and to:
  a. safeguard its assets.
  b. prevent fraud.
  c. produce correct financial statements.
  d. deter employee dishonesty.

(SO 2) 2. The principles of internal control do *not* include:
  a. establishment of responsibility.
  b. documentation procedures.
  c. management responsibility.
  d. independent internal verification.

(SO 2) 3. Physical controls do *not* include:
  a. safes and vaults to store cash.
  b. independent bank reconciliations.
  c. locked warehouses for inventories.
  d. bank safety deposit boxes for important papers.

(SO 3) 4. Which of the following items in a cash drawer at November 30 is *not* cash?
  a. Money orders.
  b. Coins and currency.
  c. A customer check dated December 1.
  d. A customer check dated November 28.

(SO 3) 5. Permitting only designated personnel such as cashiers to handle cash receipts is an application of the principle of:
  a. segregation of duties.
  b. establishment of responsibility.
  c. independent check.
  d. other controls.

(SO 4) 6. The use of prenumbered checks in disbursing cash is an application of the principle of:
  a. establishment of responsibility.
  b. segregation of duties.
  c. physical, mechanical, and electronic controls.
  d. documentation procedures.

(SO 5) 7. A check is written to replenish a $100 petty cash fund when the fund contains receipts of $94 and $3 in cash. In recording the check,
  a. Cash Over and Short should be debited for $3.
  b. Petty Cash should be debited for $94.
  c. Cash should be credited for $94.
  d. Petty Cash should be credited for $3.

(SO 6) 8. The control features of a bank account do *not* include:
  a. having bank auditors verify the correctness of the bank balance per books.
  b. minimizing the amount of cash that must be kept on hand.
  c. providing a double record of all bank transactions.
  d. safeguarding cash by using a bank as a depository.

(SO 7) 9. In a bank reconciliation, deposits in transit are:
  a. deducted from the book balance.
  b. added to the book balance
  c. added to the bank balance.
  d. deducted from the bank balance.

(SO 7) 10. The reconciling item in a bank reconciliation that will result in an adjusting entry by the depositor is:
  a. outstanding checks.
  b. deposit in transit.
  c. a bank error.
  d. bank service charges.

(SO 8) 11. The statement that correctly describes the reporting of cash is:
  a. Cash cannot be combined with cash equivalents.
  b. Restricted cash funds may be combined with Cash.
  c. Cash is listed first in the current asset section.
  d. Restricted cash funds cannot be reported as a current asset.

THE
NAVIGATOR

QUESTIONS

1. "Internal control is concerned only with enhancing the accuracy of the accounting records." Do you agree? Explain.

2. What principles of internal control apply to most business enterprises?

3. In the corner grocery store, all sales clerks make change out of one cash register drawer. Is this a violation of internal control? Why?

4. W. Mozart is reviewing the principle of segregation of duties. What are the two common applications of this principle?

5. How do documentation procedures contribute to good internal control?

6. What internal control objectives are met by physical, mechanical, and electronic controls?

7. (a) Explain the control principle of independent internal verification. (b) What practices are important in applying this principle?

8. The management of Cobo Company asks you, as the company accountant, to explain (a) the concept of reasonable assurance in internal control and (b) the importance of the human factor in internal control.

9. Fauji Fertilizer Co. owns the following assets at the balance sheet date:

Cash in bank savings account	$ 6,000
Cash on hand	850
Cash refund due from the IRS	1,000
Checking account balance	12,000
Postdated checks	500

What amount should be reported as cash in the balance sheet?

10. What principle(s) of internal control is (are) involved in making daily cash counts of over-the-counter receipts?

11. Metro Department Stores has just installed new electronic cash registers in its stores. How do cash registers improve internal control over cash receipts?

12. In Bangkok Wholesale Company, two mail clerks open all mail receipts. How does this strengthen internal control?

13. "To have maximum effective internal control over cash disbursements, all payments should be made by check." Is this true? Explain.

14. Mardi Gras Company's internal controls over cash disbursements provide for the treasurer to sign checks imprinted by a checkwriter after comparing the check with the approved invoice. Identify the internal control principles that are present in these controls.

15. How do the principles of (a) physical, mechanical, and electronic controls and (b) other controls apply to cash disbursements?

16. (a) What is a voucher system? (b) What principles of internal control apply to a voucher system?

17. What is the essential feature of an electronic funds transfer (EFT) procedure?

18. (a) Identify the three activities that pertain to a petty cash fund, and indicate an internal control principle that is applicable to each activity. (b) When are journal entries required in the operation of a petty cash fund?

19. "The use of a bank contributes significantly to good internal control over cash." Is this true? Why?

20. Lou Reid is confused about the lack of agreement between the cash balance per books and the balance per the bank. Explain the causes for the lack of agreement to Lou, and give an example of each cause.

21. What are the four steps involved in finding differences between the balance per books and balance per banks?

22. Anne Warin asks your help concerning an NSF check. Explain to Anne (a) what an NSF check is, (b) how it is treated in a bank reconciliation, and (c) whether it will require an adjusting entry per bank.

23. (a) "Cash equivalents are the same as cash." Do you agree? Explain. (b) How should restricted cash funds be reported on the balance sheet?

BRIEF EXERCISES

BE8-1 Sarah McLachlan is the new owner of Galaxy Parking. She has heard about internal control but is not clear about its importance for her business. Explain to Sarah the two purposes of internal control and give her one application of each purpose for Galaxy Parking.

Explain the importance of internal control.
(SO 1)

BE8-2 The internal control procedures in The Wallflowers Company provide that:

(a) Employees who have physical custody of assets do not have access to the accounting records.

(b) Each month the assets on hand are compared to the accounting records by an internal auditor.

(c) A prenumbered shipping document is prepared for each shipment of goods to customers.

Identify the principles of internal control that are being followed.

Identify internal control principles.
(SO 2)

Identify the internal control principles applicable to cash receipts.
(SO 3)

BE8–3 Fresno Company has the following internal control procedures over cash receipts. Identify the internal control principle that is applicable to each procedure.

1. All over-the-counter receipts are registered on cash registers.
2. All cashiers are bonded.
3. Daily cash counts are made by cashier department supervisors.
4. The duties of receiving cash, recording cash, and custody of cash are assigned to different individuals.
5. Only cashiers may operate cash registers.

Identify the internal control principles applicable to cash disbursements.
(SO 4)

BE8–4 Romez Company has the following internal control procedures over cash disbursements. Identify the internal control principle that is applicable to each procedure.

1. Company checks are prenumbered.
2. The bank statement is reconciled monthly by an internal auditor.
3. Blank checks are stored in a safe in the treasurer's office.
4. Only the treasurer or assistant treasurer may sign checks.
5. Check signers are not allowed to record cash disbursement transactions.

Prepare entry to replenish a petty cash fund.
(SO 5)

BE8–5 On March 20, Grandy's petty cash fund of $100 is replenished when the fund contains $9 in cash and receipts for postage $52, freight-out $26, and travel expense $10. Prepare the journal entry to record the replenishment of the petty cash fund.

Identify the control features of a bank account.
(SO 6)

BE8–6 Olga C. Boad is uncertain about the control features of a bank account. Explain the control benefits of (a) a signature card, (b) a check, and (c) a bank statement.

Indicate location of reconciling items in a bank reconciliation.
(SO 7)

BE8–7 The following reconciling items are applicable to the bank reconciliation for Cindy Crawford Company: (1) outstanding checks, (2) bank debit memorandum for service charge, (3) bank credit memorandum for collecting a note for the depositor, (4) deposit in transit. Indicate how each item should be shown on a bank reconciliation.

Identify reconciling items that require adjusting entries.
(SO 7)

BE8–8 Using the data in BE8–7, indicate (a) the items that will result in an adjustment to the depositor's records and (b) why the other items do not require adjustment.

Prepare partial bank reconciliation.
(SO 7)

BE8–9 At August 31, Rolex Company has a cash balance per books of $9,500 and the following additional data from the bank statement: charge for printing Rolex Company checks $35, interest earned on checking account balance $40, and outstanding checks $800. Determine the adjusted cash balance per books at August 31.

Explain the statement presentation of cash balances.
(SO 8)

BE8–10 Dupre Company has the following cash balances: Cash in Bank $15,742, Payroll Bank Account $6,000, and Plant Expansion Fund Cash $25,000. Explain how each balance should be reported on the balance sheet.

EXERCISES

List internal control weaknesses over cash receipts and suggest improvements.
(SO 2, 3)

E8–1 The following control procedures are used in the Seymor Company for over-the-counter cash receipts.

1. To minimize the risk of robbery, cash in excess of $100 is stored in an unlocked attaché case in the stock room until it is deposited in the bank.
2. All over-the-counter receipts are registered by three clerks who use a cash register with a single cash drawer.
3. The company accountant makes the bank deposit and then records the day's receipts.
4. At the end of each day, the total receipts are counted by the cashier on duty and reconciled to the cash register total.
5. Cashiers are experienced; thus they are not bonded.

Instructions
(a) For each procedure, explain the weakness in internal control and identify the control principle that is violated.
(b) For each weakness, suggest a change in procedure that will result in good internal control.

List internal control weaknesses over cash disbursements and suggest improvements.
(SO 2, 4)

E8–2 The following control procedures are used in Hilga's Botique Shoppe for cash disbursements.

1. The company accountant prepares the bank reconciliation and reports any discrepancies to the owner.

2. The store manager personally approves all payments before signing and issuing checks.
3. Each week, Hilga leaves 100 company checks in an unmarked envelope on a shelf behind the cash register.
4. After payment, bills are "filed" in a paid invoice folder.
5. The company checks are unnumbered.

Instructions

(a) For each procedure, explain the weakness in internal control and identify the internal control principle that is violated.

(b) For each weakness, suggest a change in the procedure that will result in good internal control.

E8–3 At Vermont Company, checks are not prenumbered because both the purchasing agent and the treasurer are authorized to issue checks. Each signer has access to unissued checks kept in an unlocked file cabinet. The purchasing agent pays all bills pertaining to goods purchased for resale. Prior to payment, the purchasing agent determines that the goods have been received and verifies the mathematical accuracy of the vendor's invoice. After payment, the invoice is filed by vendor, and the purchasing agent records the payment in the cash disbursements journal. The treasurer pays all other bills following approval by authorized employees. After payment, the treasurer stamps all bills PAID, files them by payment date, and records the checks in the cash disbursements journal. Vermont Company maintains one checking account that is reconciled by the treasurer.

Identify internal control weaknesses for cash disbursements and make recommendations for improvement.
(SO 4)

Instructions

(a) List the weaknesses in internal control over cash disbursements.

(b) ▐▐▐▐═══▶ Write a memo to your boss indicating your recommendations for improvement.

E8–4 During October, Kadloc Company experiences the following transactions in establishing a petty cash fund.

Prepare journal entries for a petty cash fund.
(SO 5)

10/1   An imprest fund is established with a check for $100 issued to the petty cash custodian.

31   A count of the petty cash fund disclosed the following items:

Currency	$6.00
Coins	.40
Expenditure receipts (vouchers):	

Office supplies	$28.10
Telephone and FAX	16.40
Postage	41.30
Freight-out	6.80

31   A check was written to reimburse the fund and increase the fund to $200.

Instructions

Journalize the entries in October that pertain to the petty cash fund.

E8–5 Alana Davis is unable to reconcile the bank balance at January 31. Alana's reconciliation is as follows:

Prepare bank reconciliation and adjusting entries.
(SO 7)

Cash balance per bank	$3,660.20
Add: NSF check	430.00
Less: Bank service charge	25.00
Adjusted balance per bank	$4,065.20
Cash balance per books	$3,875.20
Less: Deposits in transit	490.00
Add: Outstanding checks	730.00
Adjusted balance per books	$4,115.20

Instructions

(a) Prepare a correct bank reconciliation.

(b) Journalize the entries required by the reconciliation.

E8–6 On April 30, the bank reconciliation of Bossa Nova Company shows three outstanding checks: No. 254 $650, No. 255 $720, and No. 257 $410. The May bank statement and the May cash payments journal show the following:

Determine outstanding checks.
(SO 7)

Bank Statement			Cash Payments Journal		
Checks Paid			Checks Issued		
Date	Check No.	Amount	Date	Check No.	Amount
5/4	254	$650	5/2	258	$159
5/2	257	410	5/5	259	275
5/17	258	159	5/10	260	925
5/12	259	275	5/15	261	500
5/20	261	500	5/22	262	750
5/29	263	480	5/24	263	480
5/30	262	750	5/29	264	360

Instructions
Using step 2 in the reconciliation procedure, list the outstanding checks at May 31.

Prepare bank reconciliation and adjusting entries.
(SO 7)

E8–7 The information below relates to the Cash account in the ledger of Mawmeg Company.

Balance September 1—$17,150; Cash deposited—$64,000.
Balance September 30—$17,404; Checks written—$63,746.

The September bank statement shows a balance of $16,422 on September 30 and the following memorandum:

Credits		Debits	
Collection of $1,800 note plus interest $30	$1,830	NSF check: J. Hower	$410
Interest earned on checking account	45	Safety deposit box rent	30

At September 30, deposits in transit were $4,800 and outstanding checks totaled $2,383.

Instructions
(a) Prepare the bank reconciliation at September 30.
(b) Prepare the adjusting entries at September 30, assuming (1) the NSF check was from a customer on account, and (2) no interest had been accrued on the note.

Compute deposits in transit and outstanding checks for two bank reconciliations.
(SO 7)

E8–8 The cash records of Chi Chi Company show the following:

1. The June 30 bank reconciliation indicated that deposits in transit total $750. During July the general ledger account Cash shows deposits of $15,750, but the bank statement indicates that only $15,600 in deposits were received during the month.
2. The June 30 bank reconciliation also reported outstanding checks of $920. During the month of July, Chi Chi Company books show that $17,200 of checks were issued, yet the bank statement showed that $16,400 of checks cleared the bank in July.
3. In September, deposits per the bank statement totaled $26,700, deposits per books were $25,400, and deposits in transit at September 30 were $2,400.
4. In September, cash disbursements per books were $23,700, checks clearing the bank were $24,000, and outstanding checks at September 30 were $2,100.

There were no bank debit or credit memoranda, and no errors were made by either the bank or Chi Chi Company.

Instructions
Answer the following questions:

(a) In situation (1), what were the deposits in transit at July 31?
(b) In situation (2), what were the outstanding checks at July 31?
(c) In situation (3), what were the deposits in transit at August 31?
(d) In situation (4), what were the outstanding checks at August 31?

PROBLEMS: SET A

Identify internal control weaknesses over cash receipts.
(SO 2, 3)

P8–1A Burlington Theater is located in the Burlington Mall. A cashier's booth is located near the entrance to the theater. Two cashiers are employed. One works from 1–5 P.M., the other from 5–9 P.M. Each cashier is bonded. The cashiers receive cash from customers and operate a machine that ejects serially numbered tickets. The rolls of tickets are inserted and locked into the machine by the theater manager at the beginning of each cashier's shift.

After purchasing a ticket, the customer takes the ticket to a doorperson stationed at the entrance of the theater lobby some 60 feet from the cashier's booth. The doorperson tears the ticket in half, admits the customer, and returns the ticket stub to the customer. The other half of the ticket is dropped into a locked box by the doorperson.

At the end of each cashier's shift, the theater manager removes the ticket rolls from the machine and makes a cash count. The cash count sheet is initialed by the cashier. At the end of the day, the manager deposits the receipts in total in a bank night deposit vault located in the mall. In addition, the manager sends copies of the deposit slip and the initialed cash count sheets to the theater company treasurer for verification and to the company's accounting department. Receipts from the first shift are stored in a safe located in the manager's office.

Instructions
(a) Identify the internal control principles and their application to the cash receipts transactions of the Burlington Theater.
(b) If the doorperson and cashier decide to collaborate to misappropriate cash, what actions might they take?

P8–2A ABM Company maintains a petty cash fund for small expenditures. The following transactions occurred over a 2-month period:

Journalize and post petty cash fund transactions.
(SO 2, 5)

July   1   Established petty cash fund by writing a check on Metro Bank for $200.
      15   Replenished the petty cash fund by writing a check for $194.30. On this date the fund consisted of $5.70 in cash and the following petty cash receipts: Freight-out $94.00, postage expense $42.40, entertainment expense $46.60, and miscellaneous expense $10.70.
      31   Replenished the petty cash fund by writing a check for $192.00. At this date, the fund consisted of $8.00 in cash and the following petty cash receipts: Freight-out $82.10, charitable contributions expense $30.00, postage expense $47.80, and miscellaneous expense $32.10.
Aug. 15   Replenished the petty cash fund by writing a check for $188.00. On this date, the fund consisted of $12.00 in cash and the following petty cash receipts: Freight-out $74.40, entertainment expense $43.00, postage expense $33.00, and miscellaneous expense $38.00.
      16   Increased the amount of the petty cash fund to $400 by writing a check for $200.
      31   Replenished petty cash fund by writing a check for $283.00. On this date, the fund consisted of $117 in cash and the following petty cash receipts: Postage expense $145.00, entertainment expense $90.60, and freight-out $45.40.

Instructions
(a) Journalize the petty cash transactions.
(b) Post to the Petty Cash account.
(c) What internal control features exist in a petty cash fund?

P8–3A Agricultural Genetics Company of Emporia, Kansas, spreads herbicides and applies liquid fertilizer for local farmers. On May 31, 2001, the company's cash account per its general ledger showed the following balance:

Prepare a bank reconciliation and adjusting entries.
(SO 7)

CASH						No. 101
Date	Explanation	Ref.	Debit	Credit	Balance	
May 31	Balance				6,781.50	

The bank statement from Emporia State Bank on that date showed the following balance:

EMPORIA STATE BANK

Checks and Debits	Deposits and Credits	Daily Balance
XXX	XXX	5-31 6,804.60

A comparison of the details on the bank statement with the details in the cash account revealed the following facts:

1. The statement included a debit memo of $40 for the printing of additional company checks.
2. Cash sales of $836.15 on May 12 were deposited in the bank. The cash receipts journal entry and the deposit slip were incorrectly made for $846.15. The bank credited Agricultural Genetics Company for the correct amount.
3. Outstanding checks at May 31 totaled $276.25, and deposits in transit were $936.15.
4. On May 18, the company issued check No. 1181 for $685 to L. Kingston, on account. The check, which cleared the bank in May, was incorrectly journalized and posted by Agricultural Genetics Company for $658.
5. A $2,000 note receivable was collected by the bank for Agricultural Genetics Company on May 31 plus $80 interest. The bank charged a collection fee of $20. No interest has been accrued on the note.
6. Included with the cancelled checks was a check issued by Teller Company to P. Jonet for $600 that was incorrectly charged to Agricultural Genetics Company by the bank.
7. On May 31, the bank statement showed an NSF charge of $700 for a check issued by Pete Dell, a customer, to Agricultural Genetics Company on account.

Instructions
(a) Prepare the bank reconciliation at May 31, 2001.
(b) Prepare the necessary adjusting entries for Agricultural Genetics Company at May 31, 2001.

Prepare a bank reconciliation and adjusting entries from detailed data.
(SO 7)

P8–4A The bank portion of the bank reconciliation for Zurich Company at October 31, 2001, was as follows:

ZURICH COMPANY
Bank Reconciliation
October 31, 2001

Cash balance per bank		$12,367.90
Add: Deposits in transit		1,530.20
		13,898.10
Less: Outstanding checks		

Check Number	Check Amount	
2451	$1,260.40	
2470	720.10	
2471	844.50	
2472	426.80	
2474	1,050.00	4,301.80

Adjusted cash balance per bank	$9,596.30

The adjusted cash balance per bank agreed with the cash balance per books at October 31. The November bank statement showed the following checks and deposits:

Bank Statement					
Checks			**Deposits**		
Date	Number	Amount	Date	Amount	
11-1	2470	$ 720.10	11-1	$ 1,530.20	
11-2	2471	844.50	11-4	1,211.60	
11-5	2474	1,050.00	11-8	990.10	
11-4	2475	1,640.70	11-13	2,575.00	
11-8	2476	2,830.00	11-18	1,472.70	
11-10	2477	600.00	11-21	2,945.00	
11-15	2479	1,750.00	11-25	2,567.30	
11-18	2480	1,330.00	11-28	1,650.00	
11-27	2481	695.40	11-30	1,186.00	
11-30	2483	575.50	Total	$16,127.90	
11-29	2486	900.00			
	Total	$12,936.20			

The cash records per books for November showed the following:

Cash Payments Journal							Cash Receipts Journal	
Date	Number	Amount	Date	Number	Amount		Date	Amount
11-1	2475	$1,640.70	11-20	2483	$ 575.50		11-3	$ 1,211.60
11-2	2476	2,830.00	11-22	2484	829.50		11-7	990.10
11-2	2477	600.00	11-23	2485	974.80		11-12	2,575.00
11-4	2478	538.20	11-24	2486	900.00		11-17	1,472.70
11-8	2479	1,570.00	11-29	2487	398.00		11-20	2,954.00
11-10	2480	1,330.00	11-30	2488	800.00		11-24	2,567.30
11-15	2481	695.40	Total		$14,294.10		11-27	1,650.00
11-18	2482	612.00					11-29	1,186.00
							11-30	1,225.00
							Total	$15,831.70

The bank statement contained two bank memoranda:

1. A credit of $1,905.00 for the collection of an $1,800 note for Zurich Company plus interest of $120 and less a collection fee of $15. Zurich Company has not accrued any interest on the note.
2. A debit for the printing of additional company checks, $50.00.

At November 30 the cash balance per books was $11,133.90, and the cash balance per the bank statement was $17,414.60. The bank did not make any errors, but two errors were made by Zurich Company.

Instructions

(a) Using the four steps in the reconciliation procedure described on pages 349–350, prepare a bank reconciliation at November 30.
(b) Prepare the adjusting entries based on the reconciliation. (*Hint:* The correction of any errors pertaining to recording checks should be made to Accounts Payable. The correction of any errors relating to recording cash receipts should be made to Accounts Receivable.)

P8–5A Melo Company's bank statement from First National Bank at August 31, 2001, shows the following information:

Prepare a bank reconciliation and adjusting entries.
(SO 7)

Balance, August 1	$17,400	Bank credit memorandum:		
August deposits	72,000	Collection of note		
Checks cleared in August	68,660	receivable plus $90		
Balance, August 31	24,850	interest	$4,090	
		Interest earned	45	
		Bank debit memorandum:		
		Safety deposit box rent	25	

A summary of the Cash account in the ledger for August shows: Balance, August 1, $16,900; receipts $77,000; disbursements $73,570; and balance, August 31, $20,330. Analysis reveals that the only reconciling items on the July 31 bank reconciliation were a deposit in transit for $4,000 and outstanding checks of $4,500. The deposit in transit was the first deposit recorded by the bank in August. In addition, you determine that there were two errors involving company checks drawn in August: (1) a check for $400 to a creditor on account that cleared the bank in August was journalized and posted for $420, and (2) a salary check to an employee for $275 was recorded by the bank for $285.

Instructions

(a) Prepare a bank reconciliation at August 31.
(b) Journalize the adjusting entries to be made by Melo Company at August 31. Assume the interest on the note has been accrued by the company.

P8–6A Cedar Grove Middle School wants to raise money for a new sound system for its auditorium. The primary fund raising event is a dance at which the famous disc jockey Obnoxious Al will play classic and not-so-classic dance tunes. Roger DeMaster, the music and theater instructor, has been given the responsibility for coordinating the fund raising efforts. This is Roger's first experience with fund raising. He decides to put the eighth grade choir in charge of the event; he will be a relatively passive observer.

Identify internal control weaknesses in cash receipts and cash disbursements.
(SO 2, 3, 4, 5, 6)

Roger had 500 unnumbered tickets printed for the dance. He left the tickets in a box on his desk and told the choir students to take as many tickets as they thought they could sell for $5 each. In order to ensure that no extra tickets would be floating around, he told them to dispose of any unsold tickets. When the students received payment for the tickets, they were to bring the cash back to Roger, and he would put it in a locked box in his desk drawer.

Some of the students were responsible for decorating the gymnasium for the dance. Roger gave each of them a key to the money box and told them that if they took money out to purchase materials, they should put a note in the box saying how much they took and what it was used for. After two weeks the money box appeared to be getting full, so Roger asked Steve Stevens to count the money, prepare a deposit slip, and deposit the money in a bank account Roger had opened.

The day of the dance, Roger wrote a check from the account to pay the DJ. Obnoxious Al, however, said that he accepted only cash and did not give receipts. So Roger took $200 out of the cash box and gave it to Al. At the dance Roger had Sara Billings working at the entrance to the gymnasium, collecting tickets from students and selling tickets to those who had not pre-purchased them. Roger estimated that 400 students attended the dance.

The following day Roger closed out the bank account, which had $250 in it, and gave that amount plus the $180 in the cash box to Principal Skinner. Principal Skinner seemed surprised that, after generating roughly $2,000 in sales, the dance netted only $430 in cash. Roger did not know how to respond.

Instructions
Identify as many internal control weaknesses as you can in this scenario, and suggest how each could be addressed.

PROBLEMS: SET B

Identify internal control principles over cash disbursements.
(SO 2, 4)

P8–1B Talley Office Supply Company recently changed its system of internal control over cash disbursements. The system includes the following features.

Instead of being unnumbered and manually prepared, all checks must now be prenumbered and written by using the new checkwriter purchased by the company. Before a check can be issued, each invoice must have the approval of Lois Bedient, the purchasing agent, and Sara Power, the receiving department supervisor. Checks must be signed by either Amy Rochford, the treasurer, or Joel Reid, the assistant treasurer. Before signing a check, the signer is expected to compare the amounts of the check with the amounts on the invoice.

After signing a check, the signer stamps the invoice PAID and inserts within the stamp, the date, check number, and amount of the check. The "paid" invoice is then sent to the accounting department for recording.

Blank checks are stored in a safe in the treasurer's office. The combination to the safe is known only by the treasurer and assistant treasurer. Each month, the bank statement is reconciled with the bank balance per books by the assistant chief accountant.

Instructions
Identify the internal control principles and their application to cash disbursements of Talley Office Supply Company.

Journalize and post petty cash fund transactions.
(SO 2, 5)

P8–2B Vickers Company maintains a petty cash fund for small expenditures. The following transactions occurred over a 2-month period:

July 1   Established petty cash fund by writing a check on Metro Bank for $200.
     15   Replenished the petty cash fund by writing a check for $195.00. On this date the fund consisted of $5.00 in cash and the following petty cash receipts: Freight-out $94.00, postage expense $42.40, entertainment expense $46.60, and miscellaneous expense $11.90.
     31   Replenished the petty cash fund by writing a check for $192.00. At this date, the fund consisted of $8.00 in cash and the following petty cash receipts: Freight-out $82.10, charitable contributions expense $40.00, postage expense $27.80, and miscellaneous expense $42.10.
Aug. 15   Replenished the petty cash fund by writing a check for $187.00. On this date, the fund consisted of $13.00 in cash and the following petty cash receipts: Freight-out $74.60, entertainment expense $43.00, postage expense $33.00, and miscellaneous expense $37.00.

16 Increased the amount of the petty cash fund to $400 by writing a check for $200.
31 Replenished petty cash fund by writing a check for $283.00. On this date, the fund consisted of $117 in cash and the following petty cash receipts: Postage expense $140.00, travel expense $95.60, and freight-out $46.40.

Instructions
(a) Journalize the petty cash transactions.
(b) Post to the Petty Cash account.
(c) What internal control features exist in a petty cash fund?

P8–3B Ag-Tech Company of Peoria, Illinois, provides liquid fertilizer and herbicides to regional farmers. On July 31, 2001, the company's cash account per its general ledger showed the following balance:

Prepare a bank reconciliation and adjusting entries.
(SO 7)

	CASH				No. 101
Date	Explanation	Ref.	Debit	Credit	Balance
July 31	Balance				5,815.30

The bank statement from Castle National Bank on that date showed the following balance:

CASTLE NATIONAL BANK

Checks and Debits	Deposits and Credits	Daily Balance
XXX	XXX	7-31 7,075.80

A comparison of the details on the bank statement with the details in the cash account revealed the following facts:

1. The bank service charge for July was $25.
2. The bank collected a note receivable of $1,200 for Ag-Tech Company on July 15, plus $48 of interest. The bank made a $10 charge for the collection. Ag-Tech has not accrued any interest on the note.
3. The July 31 receipts of $1,819.60 were not included in the bank deposits for July. These receipts were deposited by the company in a night deposit vault on July 31.
4. Company check No. 2480 issued to G. Shumway, a creditor, for $492 that cleared the bank in July was incorrectly entered in the cash payments journal on July 10 for $429.
5. Checks outstanding on July 31 totaled $2,480.10.
6. On July 31, the bank statement showed an NSF charge of $550 for a check received by the company from B.N. Dette, a customer, on account.

Instructions
(a) Prepare the bank reconciliation as of July 31, 2001.
(b) Prepare the necessary adjusting entries at July 31, 2001.

P8–4B The bank portion of the bank reconciliation for Kona Company at November 30, 2001, was as follows:

Prepare a bank reconciliation and adjusting entries from detailed data.
(SO 7)

KONA COMPANY
Bank Reconciliation
November 30, 2001

Cash balance per bank			$14,367.90
Add: Deposits in transit			2,530.20
			16,898.10
Less: Outstanding checks			
	Check Number	Check Amount	
	3451	$2,260.40	
	3470	720.10	
	3471	844.50	
	3472	1,426.80	
	3474	1,050.00	6,301.80
Adjusted cash balance per bank			$10,596.30

The adjusted cash balance per bank agreed with the cash balance per books at November 30.

The December bank statement showed the following checks and deposits:

Bank Statement				
Checks			**Deposits**	
Date	Number	Amount	Date	Amount
12-1	3451	$ 2,260.40	12-1	$ 2,530.20
12-2	3471	844.50	12-4	1,211.60
12-7	3472	1,426.80	12-8	2,365.10
12-4	3475	1,640.70	12-16	2,672.70
12-8	3476	1,300.00	12-21	2,945.00
12-10	3477	2,130.00	12-26	2,567.30
12-15	3479	3,080.00	12-29	2,836.00
12-27	3480	600.00	12-30	1,025.00
12-30	3482	475.50	Total	$18,152.90
12-29	3483	1,140.00		
12 31	3485	540.80		
	Total	$15,438.70		

The cash records per books for November showed the following:

Cash Payments Journal							Cash Receipts Journal	
Date	Number	Amount	Date	Number	Amount		Date	Amount
12-1	3475	$1,640.70	12-20	3482	$ 475.50		12-3	$ 1,211.60
12-2	3476	1,300.00	12-22	3483	1,140.00		12-7	2,365.10
12-2	3477	2,130.00	12-23	3484	832.00		12-15	2,672.70
12-4	3478	538.20	12-24	3485	450.80		12-20	2,954.00
12-8	3479	3,080.00	12-30	3486	1,389.50		12-25	2,567.30
12-10	3480	600.00	Total		$14,384.10		12-28	2,836.00
12-17	3481	807.40					12-20	1,025.00
							12-31	1,190.40
							Total	$16,822.10

The bank statement contained two bank memoranda:

1. A credit of $3,145 for the collection of a $3,000 note for Kona Company plus interest of $160 and less a collection fee of $15.00. Kona Company has not accrued any interest on the note.
2. A debit of $547.10 for an NSF check written by D. Lu, a customer. At December 31, the check had not been redeposited in the bank.

At December 31 the cash balance per books was $13,034.30, and the cash balance per the bank statement was $19,680. The bank did not make any errors, but two errors were made by Kona Company.

Instructions
(a) Using the four steps in the reconciliation procedure, prepare a bank reconciliation at December 31.
(b) Prepare the adjusting entries based on the reconciliation. (*Hint:* The correction of any errors pertaining to recording checks should be made to Accounts Payable. The correction of any errors relating to recording cash receipts should be made to Accounts Receivable.)

Prepare a bank reconciliation and adjusting entries.
(SO 7)

P8–5B Aluminum Company maintains a checking account at the Port City Bank. At July 31, selected data from the ledger balance and the bank statement are as follows:

Cash in Bank		
	Per Books	Per Bank
Balance, July 1	$17,600	$19,200
July receipts	82,000	
July credits		79,000
July disbursements	76,900	
July debits		74,700
Balance, July 31	$22,700	$23,500

Analysis of the bank data reveals that the credits consist of $79,000 of July deposits and a credit memorandum of $1,070 for the collection of a $1,000 note plus interest revenue of $70. The July debits per bank consist of checks cleared, $74,700 and a debit memorandum of $40 for printing additional company checks.

You also discover the following errors involving July checks: (1) a check for $230 to a creditor on account that cleared the bank in July was journalized and posted as $320, and (2) a salary check to an employee for $255 was recorded by the bank for $155.

The June 30 bank reconciliation contained only two reconciling items: deposits in transit $5,000 and outstanding checks of $6,600.

Instructions
(a) Prepare a bank reconciliation at July 31.
(b) Journalize the adjusting entries to be made by Aluminum Company at July 31, 2001. Assume that the interest on the note has been accrued.

P8–6B   Giant Company is a very profitable small business. It has not, however, given much consideration to internal control. For example, in an attempt to keep clerical and office expenses to a minimum, the company has combined the jobs of cashier and bookkeeper. As a result, K. Kilgora handles all cash receipts, keeps the accounting records, and prepares the monthly bank reconciliations.

Prepare comprehensive bank reconciliation with theft and internal control deficiencies.
(SO 2, 3, 4, 7)

The balance per the bank statement on October 31, 2001, was $18,180. Outstanding checks were: No. 62 for $126.75, No. 183 for $150, No. 284 for $253.25, No. 862 for $190.71, No. 863 for $226.80, and No. 864 for $165.28. Included with the statement was a credit memorandum of $400 indicating the collection of a note receivable for the Giant Company by the bank on October 25. This memorandum has not been recorded by Giant Company.

The company's ledger showed one cash account with a balance of $21,892.72. The balance included undeposited cash on hand. Because of the lack of internal controls, Kilgora took for personal use all of the undeposited receipts in excess of $3,795.51. He then prepared the following bank reconciliation in an effort to conceal his theft of cash.

BANK RECONCILIATION

Cash balance per books, October 31		$21,892.72
Add: Outstanding checks		
No. 862	$190.71	
No. 863	226.80	
No. 864	165.28	482.79
		22,375.51
Less: Undeposited receipts		3,795.51
Unadjusted balance per bank, October 31		18,580.00
Less: Bank credit memorandum		400.00
Cash balance per bank statement, October 31		$18,180.00

Instructions
(a) Prepare a correct bank reconciliation. (*Hint:* Deduct the amount of the theft from the adjusted balance per books.)
(b) Indicate the three ways that Kilgora attempted to conceal the theft and the dollar amount pertaining to each method.
(c) What principles of internal control were violated in this case?

BROADENING YOUR PERSPECTIVE

FINANCIAL REPORTING AND ANALYSIS

FINANCIAL REPORTING PROBLEM: Kellogg Company

BYP8–1   The financial statements of Kellogg Company are presented in Appendix A at the end of this textbook.

Instructions
- (a) What comments, if any, are made about cash and cash flows in the "Report of the Independent Accountants," Pricewaterhouse Coopers?
- (b) What data about cash and cash equivalents are shown in the consolidated balance sheet (statement of financial condition)?
- (c) What are the major activities identified in the consolidated statement of cash flows as being responsible for the changes in cash during 1998?
- (d) How are cash equivalents defined under the Notes to Consolidated Financial Statements?

COMPARATIVE ANALYSIS PROBLEM: Kellogg Company vs. General Mills

BYP8–2   Kellogg's financial statements are presented in Appendix A; General Mills's financial statements are presented in Appendix B.

Instructions
- (a) Based on the information contained in these financial statements, determine each of the following for each company:
  1. Cash and cash equivalents balance at December 31, 1998, for Kellogg, and May 31, 1998, for General Mills.
  2. Increase (decrease) in cash and cash equivalents from 1997 to 1998.
  3. Cash provided by operating activities during 1998 (from Statement of Cash Flows).
- (b) What conclusions concerning the management of cash can be drawn from these data?

RESEARCH ASSIGNMENT

BYP8–3   The March 31, 1999, issue of *The Wall Street Journal* includes an article by Mark Maremont entitled "Store Markdowns: Leaning on Suppliers, Rite Aid Deducts Cash at Bill-Paying Time."

Instructions
Read the article and answer the following questions:
- (a) What reasons does Rite Aid give for reducing the amount it paid its suppliers?
- (b) Other than its stated reason for reducing its payments, what other incentives might Rite Aid have for reducing the amount paid to its suppliers?
- (c) What are the implications of Rite Aid's actions for the suppliers? What are the suppliers' possible courses of action?

INTERPRETING FINANCIAL STATEMENTS: Microsoft, Inc. and Oracle

BYP8–4   Microsoft is the leading developer of software in the world. To continue to be successful Microsoft must generate new products. Generating new products requires significant amounts of cash. Shown below is the current assets section of Microsoft's June 30, 1998, balance sheet and excerpts from a footnote describing the first item listed in the balance sheet, "cash, cash equivalents, and short-term investments." Below Microsoft is the current assets section of Oracle, another major software developer. (All dollar amounts are in millions.)

Microsoft

MICROSOFT, INC.
Balance Sheets (partial)
As of June 30

	1997	1998
Current assets		
Cash, cash equivalents, and short-term investments	$ 8,966	$13,927
Accounts receivable	980	1,460
Other	427	502
Total current assets	10,373	15,889
Total current liabilities	3,610	5,730

ORACLE

ORACLE
Balance Sheets (partial)
As of May 31

	1997	1998
Current assets		
Cash and cash equivalents	$ 890	$1,274
Short-term cash investments	323	646
Receivables	1,540	1,857
Other current assets	518	546
Total current assets	3,271	4,323
Current liabilities	1,922	2,484

Instructions
(a) What is the definition of a cash equivalent? Give some examples of cash equivalents. How do cash equivalents differ from other types of short-term investments?
(b) Comment on Microsoft's presentation of cash in its balance sheet.
(c) What problems might this presentation of cash pose for a user of Microsoft's financial statements?
(d) Compare the liquidity of Microsoft and Oracle for 1998.
(e) Is it possible to have too many liquid assets?

REAL-WORLD FOCUS: Alternative Distributor Corp.

BYP8-5 Alternative Distributor Corp., a distributor of groceries and related products, is headquartered in Medford, Massachusetts. It was founded in 1980 and today has seven employees, with a total sales of $7 million.

During its audit, the Alternative Distributor Corp. was advised that previously existing internal controls necessary for the company to develop reliable financial statements were inadequate. The audit report stated that the current system of accounting for sales, receivables, and cash receipts constituted a material weakness.

Among other items, the report focused on non-timely deposit of cash receipts, exposing Alternative Distributor to potential loss or misappropriation; excessive past due accounts receivable due to lack of collection efforts; disregard of advantages offered by vendors for prompt payment of invoices; absence of appropriate segregation of duties by personnel consistent with appropriate control objectives; inadequate procedures for applying accounting principles; lack of qualified management personnel; lack of supervision by an outside board of directors; and overall poor record keeping.

Instructions
Identify the principles of internal control violated by Alternative Distributor Corp.

CRITICAL THINKING
....
GROUP DECISION CASE

BYP8–6 The board of trustees of a local church is concerned about the internal accounting controls pertaining to the offering collections made at weekly services. The trustees ask you to serve on a three-person audit team with the internal auditor of the university and a CPA who has just joined the church.

At a meeting of the audit team and the board of trustees you learn the following:

1. The church's board of trustees has delegated responsibility for the financial management and audit of the financial records to the finance committee. This group prepares the annual budget and approves major disbursements but is not involved in collections or record keeping. No audit has been made in recent years because the same trusted employee has kept church records and served as financial secretary for 15 years. The church does not carry any fidelity insurance.
2. The collection at the weekly service is taken by a team of ushers who volunteer to serve one month. The ushers take the collection plates to a basement office at the rear of the church. They hand their plates to the head usher and return to the church service. After all plates have been turned in, the head usher counts the cash received. The head usher then places the cash in the church safe along with a notation of the amount counted. The head usher volunteers to serve for 3 months.
3. The next morning the financial secretary opens the safe and recounts the collection. The secretary withholds $150–$200 in cash, depending on the cash expenditures expected for the week, and deposits the remainder of the collections in the bank. To facilitate the deposit, church members who contribute by check are asked to make their checks payable to "cash."
4. Each month, the financial secretary reconciles the bank statement and submits a copy of the reconciliation to the board of trustees. The reconciliations have rarely contained any bank errors and have never shown any errors per books.

Instructions
With the class divided into groups, answer the following:

(a) Indicate the weaknesses in internal accounting control over the handling of collections.
(b) List the improvements in internal control procedures that you plan to make at the next meeting of the audit team for (1) the ushers, (2) the head usher, (3) the financial secretary, and (4) the finance committee.
(c) What church policies should be changed to improve internal control?

COMMUNICATION ACTIVITY

BYP8–7   As a new auditor for the CPA firm of Kennedy, Maison, and Davis you have been assigned to review the internal controls over mail cash receipts of Emerik Company. Your review reveals the following: Checks are promptly endorsed "For Deposit Only," but no list of the checks is prepared by the person opening the mail. The mail is opened either by the cashier or by the employee who maintains the accounts receivable records. Mail receipts are deposited in the bank weekly by the cashier.

Instructions
Write a letter to L. S. Croix, owner of the Emerik Company, explaining the weaknesses in internal control and your recommendations for improving the system.

ETHICS CASE

BYP8–8   You are the assistant controller in charge of general ledger accounting at Bad Water Bottling Company. Your company has a large loan from an insurance company. The loan agreement requires that the company's cash account balance be maintained at $200,000 or more as reported monthly. At June 30 the cash balance is $80,000, which you report to Marais Thompson, the financial vice president. Marais excitedly instructs you to keep the cash receipts book open for one additional day for purposes of the June 30 report to the insurance company. Marais says, "If we don't get that cash balance over $200,000, we'll default on our loan agreement. They could close us down, put us all out of our jobs!" Marais continues, "I talked to Grochum Distributors (one of Bad Water's largest customers) this morning and they said they sent us a check for $150,000 yesterday. We should receive it tomorrow. If we include just that one check in our cash balance, we'll be in the clear. It's in the mail!"

Instructions
- (a) Who will suffer negative effects if you do not comply with Marais Thompson's instructions? Who will suffer if you do comply?
- (b) What are the ethical considerations in this case?
- (c) What alternatives do you have?

SURFING THE NET

BYP8–9   All organizations should have systems of internal control. Universities are no exception. This site discusses the basics of internal control in a university setting.

Address: http://www.bc.edu/bc_org/fvp/ia/ic/intro.html (or go to www.wiley.com/college/weygandt)

Steps: Go to the site shown above.

Instructions
The front page of this site provides links to pages that answer six critical questions. Use these links to answer the following questions:
- (a) In a university setting who has responsibility for evaluating the adequacy of the system of internal control?
- (b) What do reconciliations ensure in the university setting? Who should review the reconciliation?
- (c) What are some examples of physical controls?
- (d) What are two ways to accomplish inventory counts?

Answers to Self-Study Questions
1. a   2. c   3. b   4. c   5. b   6. d   7. a   8. a   9. c   10. d   11. c

---

Answer to Kellogg Review It Question 3, p. 353
Kellogg reports cash and cash equivalents on its balance sheet for 1998 of $136.4 million.

Remember to go back to the Navigator box on the chapter-opening page and check off your completed work.

Before studying this chapter, you should know or, if necessary, review:

a. How to record sales transactions. (Ch. 5, pp. 196–199)

b. Why adjusting entries are made. (Ch. 3, p. 95)

c. How to compute interest. (Ch. 3, pp. 104–105)

THE NAVIGATOR

FEATURE STORY

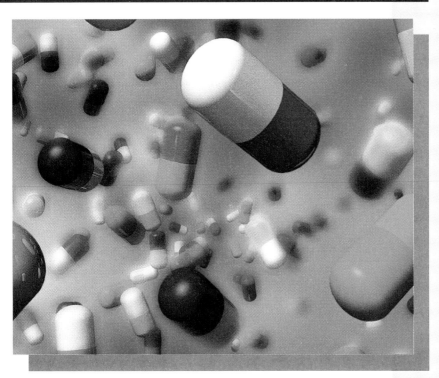

How Do You Spell Relief?

Fred Tarter believes that in every problem lies an opportunity—and sometimes that opportunity can mean a big profit. For example, today fewer people pay cash for their prescriptions; instead, pharmacies bill a customer's health plan for some or all of the prescription's cost. Consequently pharmacies must spend a lot of time and energy collecting cash from these health plans. This procedure is a headache for pharmacies because there are 4,500 different health plans that create 770 million third-party receivables each week.

Also, it often leaves pharmacies with too many receivables and not enough cash. Their suppliers want to be paid within 15 days, but 70% of their receivables are outstanding for 30 and often 60 days. And, it is estimated that credit losses equal 3% of the $40 billion of prescriptions purchased through health care plans.

Enter Fred Tarter. While reading a pharmacy trade journal, he learned of the pharmacies' headache. To Fred this problem spelled opportunity.

Fred found out that 56,000 pharmacies are connected by computer to a claims processing business. Fred's idea was this: Taking advantage of this network, he would

purchase pharmacy receivables, charging a fee of 1.4% to 2%. Pharmacies would be willing to pay this because they would get their cash sooner and save the headache of having to collect the accounts.

Based on this idea, Fred started a company called the Pharmacy Fund in 1993. By 1996 over 500 small pharmacies were selling their receivables to his company. The Pharmacy Fund establishes a computer link with each pharmacy, which allows it to buy the receivables at the end of each day and credit the pharmacy's account immediately. Thus, rather than having to wait weeks to receive its cash from insurance companies, the pharmacy gets its cash the same day as the sale. The Pharmacy Fund's customers say that this has solved their cash-flow problems, reduced their overhead costs, and allowed them to automate their billing and record-keeping. Using these receivables as backing, the Pharmacy Fund raised additional financing of $80 million in 1996 and an even larger amount in 1997.

Other investors are interested in getting in on this action. Nursing home receivables or home health care receivables have been mentioned as other possibilities. Fred Tarter has already identified his next opportunity—a target some would say is a "natural" for him: dentistry receivables. (Get it? Tarter—dentistry. We'll stick to accounting jokes from now on!)

THE NAVIGATOR

CHAPTER 9

ACCOUNTING FOR RECEIVABLES

THE NAVIGATOR ✔

- Understand *Concepts for Review* ☐
- Read *Feature Story* ☐
- Scan *Study Objectives* ☐
- Read *Preview* ☐
- Read text and answer *Before You Go On*
  p. 385 ☐ p. 390 ☐ p. 392 ☐
- Work *Demonstration Problem* ☐
- Review *Summary of Study Objectives* ☐
- Answer *Self-Study Questions* ☐
- Complete assignments ☐

STUDY OBJECTIVES

After studying this chapter, you should be able to:

1. *Identify the different types of receivables.*
2. *Explain how accounts receivable are recognized in the accounts.*
3. *Distinguish between the methods and bases used to value accounts receivable.*
4. *Describe the entries to record the disposition of accounts receivable.*
5. *Compute the maturity date of, and interest on, notes receivable.*
6. *Explain how notes receivable are recognized in the accounts.*
7. *Describe how notes receivable are valued.*
8. *Describe the entries to record the disposition of notes receivable.*
9. *Explain the statement presentation and analysis of receivables.*

THE NAVIGATOR

*I*n this chapter you will learn what journal entries companies make when products are sold, when cash is collected from those sales, and when uncollectible accounts are written off. As indicated in the Feature Story, receivables are a significant asset on the books of many pharmacies. The same situation also occurs for many other companies, because a significant portion of sales are done on credit in the United States. As a consequence, companies must pay close attention to their receivables balances and manage them carefully.

The content and organization of the chapter are as follows:

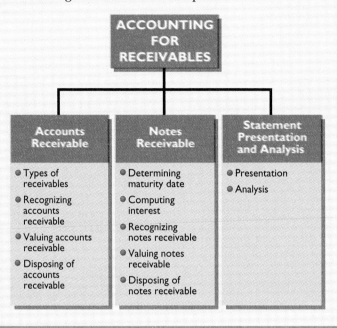

THE
NAVIGATOR

ACCOUNTS RECEIVABLE

Types of Receivables

1
STUDY
OBJECTIVE

Identify the different
types of receivables.

The term "receivables" refers to amounts due from individuals and other companies. Receivables are claims that are expected to be collected in cash. Receivables are frequently classified as (1) accounts, (2) notes, and (3) other.

Accounts receivable are amounts owed by customers on account. They result from the sale of goods and services. These receivables generally are expected to be collected within 30 to 60 days. They are usually the most significant type of claim held by a company.

Notes receivable represent claims for which formal instruments of credit are issued as evidence of the debt. The credit instrument normally requires the debtor to pay interest and extends for time periods of 60–90 days or longer. Notes and accounts receivable that result from sales transactions are often called trade receivables.

Other receivables include nontrade receivables such as interest receivable, loans to company officers, advances to employees, and income taxes refundable. These are unusual; therefore, they are generally classified and reported as separate items in the balance sheet.

The three primary accounting problems associated with accounts receivable are:

1. **Recognizing** accounts receivable.
2. **Valuing** accounts receivable.
3. **Disposing of** accounts receivable.

Recognizing Accounts Receivable

Recognizing accounts receivable is relatively straightforward. In Chapter 5 we saw how accounts receivable are affected by the sale of merchandise. To illustrate, assume that Jordache Co. on July 1, 2001, sells merchandise on account to Polo Company for $1,000 terms 2/10, n/30. On July 5, merchandise worth $100 is returned to Jordache Co. On July 11, payment is received from Polo Company for the balance due. The journal entries to record these transactions on the books of Jordache Co. are as follows:

July 1	Accounts Receivable—Polo Company	1,000	
	Sales		1,000
	(To record sales on account)		
July 5	Sales Returns and Allowances	100	
	Accounts Receivable—Polo Company		100
	(To record merchandise returned)		
July 11	Cash ($900 − $18)	882	
	Sales Discounts ($900 × .02)	18	
	Accounts Receivable—Polo Company		900
	(To record collection of accounts receivable)		

The opportunity to receive a cash discount usually occurs when a manufacturer sells to a wholesaler or a wholesaler sells to a retailer. A discount is given in these situations either to encourage prompt payment or for competitive reasons.

On the other hand, retailers rarely grant cash discounts to customers. For example, we would be surprised if you ever received a cash discount in purchasing goods from any well-known retailer, such as Kmart, Sears, Wal-Mart, and so on. In these situations, most sales are either cash or credit card sales. In fact, when you use a retailer's credit card (J. C. Penney or Sears, for example), instead of giving a discount, the retailer charges interest on the balance due if not paid within a specified period (usually 25–30 days).

To illustrate, assume that you charge on your J. C. Penney account an outfit that costs $300. J. C. Penney will make the following entry at the date of sale:

Accounts Receivable		300	
Sales			300
(To record sale of merchandise)			

J. C. Penney will then send you a monthly statement of this transaction and any others that have occurred during the month. If you fail to pay in full within 30 days, J. C. Penney adds an interest (financing) charge to the balance due. Although interest rates vary from state to state and from time to time (depending in part on federal monetary policy), rates for retailers run as high as 18% per year or 1.5% per month for first-time card holders.

ETHICS NOTE

Receivables from employees and officers of a company are reported separately in the financial statements. The reason: Sometimes those assets are valued inappropriately or are not based on an "arm's length" transaction.

2
STUDY OBJECTIVE

Explain how accounts receivable are recognized in the accounts.

A	=	L	+	SE
+1,000				+1,000

A	=	L	+	SE
−100				−100

A	=	L	+	SE
+882				−18
−900				

HELPFUL HINT
These entries are the same as those described in Chapter 5. For simplicity, inventory and cost of goods sold are omitted from this set of journal entries.

A	+	L	+	SE
+300				+300

When financing charges are added, the seller recognizes interest revenue. Assuming that you owe $300 at the end of the month, and J. C. Penney charges 1.5% per month on the balance due, the adjusting entry to record interest revenue of $4.50 ($300 × 1.5%) is as follows:

A	=	L	+	SE
+4.50				+4.50

Accounts Receivable		4.50	
Interest Revenue			4.50
(To record interest on amount due)			

Interest revenue is often substantial for many retailers. Sears Roebuck in 1998, for example, earned interest of $4.9 billion on credit transactions.

ACCOUNTING IN ACTION
Business Insight

Interest rates on most credit cards are quite high, averaging approximately 18.8%. As a result, consumers are often looking for companies that charge lower rates. But be careful—some companies offer lower interest rates but have eliminated the standard 25-day grace period before finance charges are incurred. Other companies encourage consumers to get more in debt by advertising that only a $1 minimum payment is due on a $1,000 account balance! They, of course, earn more interest! Chase Manhattan Corp. markets a credit card that allows cardholders to skip a payment twice a year. However, the outstanding balance continues to incur interest. Other credit card companies calculate finance charges initially on two-month, rather than one-month averages, a practice which often translates into higher interest charges. In short, read the fine print.

Valuing Accounts Receivable

3

Once receivables are recorded in the accounts, the next question is: How should these receivables be reported on the balance sheet? Determining the amount to report as an asset is important because some receivables will become uncollectible. To ensure that receivables are not overstated on the balance sheet, they are stated at their cash (net) realizable value. Cash (net) realizable value is the net amount expected to be received in cash. The cash realizable value excludes amounts that the company estimates it will not be able to collect. Receivables are therefore reduced by estimated uncollectible receivables on the balance sheet.

The income statement also is affected by the amount of uncollectibles. An expense for estimated uncollectibles is recorded to make certain that expenses are not understated and are matched with related sales revenue. This expense is reported as **bad debts expense** on the income statement.

Uncollectible Accounts Receivable

Although each customer must satisfy the credit requirements of the seller before the credit sale is approved, inevitably some accounts receivable become uncollectible. For example, a company may experience a decline in sales because of a downturn in the economy, and as a result, the wholesaler may be unable to collect its accounts receivable from the retailer. Similarly, individuals may be laid off from their jobs or be faced with unexpected hospital bills.

In accounting, credit losses are debited to Bad Debts Expense (or Uncollectible Accounts Expense). Such losses are considered a normal and necessary risk of doing business on a credit basis. In fact, from a management point of view, a reasonable amount of uncollectible accounts is evidence of a sound credit policy. When bad debts are abnormally low, the company may be losing profitable business by following a credit policy that is too strict. Of course, abnormally high bad debts indicate a credit policy that is too lenient.

Two methods are used in accounting for uncollectible accounts: (1) the allowance method and (2) the direct write-off method. Each of these methods is explained in the following sections.

Allowance Method.   The allowance method is required for financial reporting purposes when bad debts are material in amount. Its essential features are:

1. Uncollectible accounts are estimated and the expense for the uncollectible accounts is matched against sales in the same accounting period in which the sales occurred.
2. Estimated uncollectibles are debited to Bad Debts Expense and credited to Allowance for Doubtful Accounts through an adjusting entry at the end of each period.
3. Actual uncollectibles are debited to Allowance for Doubtful Accounts and credited to Accounts Receivable at the time the specific account is written off.

Recording Estimated Uncollectibles.   To illustrate the allowance method, assume that Hampson Furniture has credit sales of $1,200,000 in the year 2000, of which $200,000 remain uncollected at December 31. The credit manager estimates that $12,000 of these sales will prove uncollectible. The adjusting entry to record the estimated uncollectibles is:

Dec. 31	Bad Debts Expense	12,000	
	Allowance for Doubtful Accounts		12,000
	(To record estimate of uncollectible accounts)		

A	=	L	+	SE
−12,000				−12,000

Bad Debts Expense is reported in the income statement as an operating expense (usually as a selling expense). Thus, the estimated uncollectibles are **matched** with sales in 2000 because the expense is recorded in the same year the sales are made.

Allowance for Doubtful Accounts is a contra asset account that shows the claims on customers that are expected to become uncollectible in the future. A contra account is used instead of a direct credit to Accounts Receivable because we do not know which customers will not pay. The credit balance in this account will absorb the specific write-offs when they occur. **Allowance for Doubtful Accounts is not closed at the end of the fiscal year.** It is deducted from Accounts Receivable in the current asset section of the balance sheet as follows:

ALTERNATIVE TERMINOLOGY

Bad debts expense is also called *uncollectible accounts expense.* Allowance for doubtful accounts is also called *allowance for uncollectibles* or *allowance for bad debts.*

ILLUSTRATION 9-1

Presentation of allowance for doubtful accounts

HAMPSON FURNITURE Balance Sheet (partial)		
Current assets		
Cash		$ 14,800
Accounts receivable	$200,000	
Less: Allowance for doubtful accounts	12,000	188,000
Merchandise inventory		310,000
Prepaid expense		25,000
Total current assets		$537,800

The amount of $188,000 represents the expected **cash realizable value** of the accounts receivable at the statement date.

Recording the Write-off of an Uncollectible Account.   Companies use various methods of collecting past-due accounts, such as a sequence of letters, calls, and legal action. When all means of collecting a past-due account have been exhausted and collection appears impossible, the account should be written off. To prevent premature write-offs, each write-off should be formally approved in writing by authorized management personnel.

Assume, for example, that the vice president of finance of Hampson Furniture authorizes the write-off of the $500 balance owed by R. A. Ware on March 1, 2001. The entry to record the write-off is:

A	=	L	+	SE
+500				
−500				

Mar. 1	Allowance for Doubtful Accounts		500	
	Accounts Receivable—R. A. Ware			500
	(Write-off of R. A. Ware account)			

Bad Debts Expense is not debited when the write-off occurs. **Under the allowance method, every bad debt write-off is debited to the allowance account and not to Bad Debts Expense.** A debit to Bad Debts Expense would be incorrect, because the expense is recognized when the adjusting entry is made for estimated bad debts. After posting, the general ledger accounts will show:

ILLUSTRATION 9-2

General ledger balances after write-off

Accounts Receivable						Allowance for Doubtful Accounts					
1/1/01	Bal.	200,000	3/1/01	500		3/1/01	500	1/1/01	Bal.	12,000
3/1/01	Bal.	199,500						3/1/01		11,500

A write-off affects only balance sheet accounts. The write-off of the account reduces both Accounts Receivable and the Allowance for Doubtful Accounts. Cash realizable value in the balance sheet, therefore, remains the same as illustrated below.

ILLUSTRATION 9-3

Cash realizable value comparison

	Before Write-off	After Write-off
Accounts receivable	$200,000	$199,500
Allowance for doubtful accounts	12,000	11,500
Cash realizable value	**$188,000**	**$188,000**

ACCOUNTING IN ACTION
Business Insight

Nearly half of the goods sold by Sears are purchased with a Sears credit card. This makes interest earned by Sears on its credit cards a very important part of its business plan. It also means that how Sears accounts for its bad debts can have a significant impact on Sears's net income. In one recent quarter Sears reduced its loan loss provision by 61% compared to the same quarter in the previous year. In so doing, Sears was able to report earnings that slightly exceeded analysts' forecasts. Some analysts expressed concern that, because the number of delinquent accounts receivable had actually increased, Sears should probably have *increased* its loan loss provision, rather than reducing it. Although Sears's management defended its actions, analysts appeared to be unimpressed, and Sears's stock price declined on the news.

Recovery of an Uncollectible Account. Occasionally, a company collects from a customer after the account has been written off as uncollectible. Two entries are required to record the recovery of a bad debt: (1) The entry made in writing off the account is reversed to reinstate the customer's account. (2) The collection is journalized in the usual manner. To illustrate, assume that on July 1, R. A. Ware pays the $500 amount that had been written off on March 1. The entries are:

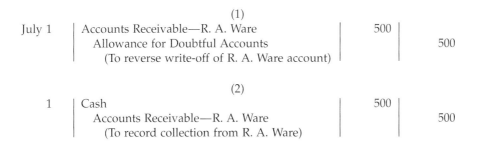

		(1)		
July 1	Accounts Receivable—R. A. Ware		500	
	Allowance for Doubtful Accounts			500
	(To reverse write-off of R. A. Ware account)			

A	=	L	+	SE
+500				
−500				

		(2)		
1	Cash		500	
	Accounts Receivable—R. A. Ware			500
	(To record collection from R. A. Ware)			

A	=	L	+	SE
+500				
−500				

Note that the recovery of a bad debt, like the write-off of a bad debt, affects only balance sheet accounts. The net effect of the two entries above is a debit to Cash and a credit to Allowance for Doubtful Accounts for $500. Accounts Receivable is debited and the Allowance for Doubtful Accounts is credited for two reasons: First, the company made an error in judgment when it wrote off the account receivable. Second, R. A. Ware did pay, and therefore the Accounts Receivable account in the general ledger and Ware's account in the subsidiary accounts receivable ledger should show this collection for possible future credit purposes.

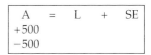

HELPFUL HINT

Like the write-off, a recovery does not involve the income statement.

Bases Used for Allowance Method. To simplify the preceding explanation, the amount of the expected uncollectibles was given. However, in "real life" companies must estimate that amount if they use the allowance method. Two bases are used to determine this amount: **(1) percentage of sales**, and **(2) percentage of receivables**. Both bases are generally accepted in accounting. The choice is a management decision. It depends on the relative emphasis that management wishes to give to expenses and revenues on the one hand or to cash realizable value of the accounts receivable on the other. The choice is whether to emphasize income statement or balance sheet relationships. Illustration 9-4 compares the two bases.

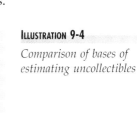

ILLUSTRATION 9-4

Comparison of bases of estimating uncollectibles

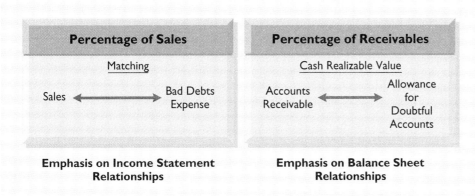

The percentage of sales basis results in a better matching of expenses with revenues—an income statement viewpoint. In contrast, the percentage of receivables basis produces the better estimate of cash realizable value—a balance sheet viewpoint. Under both bases, it is necessary to determine the company's past experience with bad debt losses.

Percentage of Sales. In the percentage of sales basis, management establishes a percentage relationship between the amount of credit sales and expected losses from uncollectible accounts. The percentage is based on past experience and anticipated credit policy.

The percentage is usually applied to either total credit sales or net credit sales of the current year. To illustrate, assume that Gonzalez Company elects to use the percentage of sales basis and concludes that 1% of net credit sales will become uncollectible. If net credit sales for 2001 are $800,000, the estimated bad debts expense is $8,000 (1% × $800,000). The adjusting entry is:

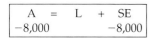

A	=	L	+	SE
−8,000				−8,000

Dec. 31	Bad Debts Expense		8,000	
	Allowance for Doubtful Accounts			8,000
	(To record estimated bad debts for year)			

After the adjusting entry is posted, assuming the allowance account already has a credit balance of $1,723, the accounts of Gonzalez Company will show:

ILLUSTRATION 9-5

Bad debts accounts after posting

Bad Debts Expense		Allowance for Doubtful Accounts	
12/31 Adj. 8,000			Bal. 1,723
			12/31 Adj. 8,000
			Bal. 9,723

This basis of estimating uncollectibles emphasizes the matching of expenses with revenues. As a result, Bad Debts Expense will show a direct percentage relationship to the sales base on which it is computed. **When the adjusting entry is made, the existing balance in the Allowance for Doubtful Accounts is disregarded.** The adjusted balance in this account should result in a reasonable approximation of the realizable value of the receivables. If actual write-offs differ significantly from the amount estimated, the percentage for future years should be modified.

Percentage of Receivables. Under the percentage of receivables basis, management establishes a percentage relationship between the amount of receivables and expected losses from uncollectible accounts. A schedule (often called an **aging schedule**) is prepared, in which customer balances are classified by the length of time they have been unpaid. Because of its emphasis on time, the analysis is often called aging the accounts receivable.

TECHNOLOGY IN ACTION

The aging schedule is another example of output that can be obtained from a computerized accounts receivable system. Manually, preparation of this schedule is an onerous and time-consuming task. However, the schedule can be done in minutes on computer systems.

After the accounts are aged, the expected bad debt losses are determined by applying percentages based on past experience to the totals of each category. The longer a receivable is past due, the less likely it is to be collected. As a result, the estimated percentage of uncollectible debts increases as the number of days past due increases. An aging schedule for Dart Company is shown in Illustration 9-6. Note the increasing percentages from 2% to 40% as the likelihood of collection diminishes.

ILLUSTRATION 9-6

Aging schedule

Customer	Total	Not Yet Due	Number of Days Past Due			
			1–30	31–60	61–90	Over 90
T. E. Adert	$ 600		$ 300		$ 200	$ 100
R. C. Bortz	300	$ 300				
B. A. Carl	450		200	$ 250		
O. L. Diker	700	500			200	
T. O. Ebbet	600			300		300
Others	36,950	26,200	5,200	2,450	1,600	1,500
	$39,600	$27,000	$5,700	$3,000	$2,000	$1,900
Estimated Percentage Uncollectible		2%	4%	10%	20%	40%
Total Estimated Bad Debts	$ 2,228	$ 540	$ 228	$ 300	$ 400	$ 760

HELPFUL HINT
The higher percentages are used for the older categories because the longer an account is past due, the less likely it is to be collected.

Total uncollectibles for Dart Company ($2,228) represent the amount of existing customer claims expected to become uncollectible in the future. Thus, this amount represents the **required balance** in Allowance for Doubtful Accounts at the balance sheet date. Accordingly, **the amount of the bad debt adjusting entry is the difference between the required balance and the existing balance in the allowance account**. If the trial balance shows Allowance for Doubtful Accounts with a credit balance of $528, an adjusting entry for $1,700 ($2,228 − $528) is necessary, as shown below:

Dec. 31	Bad Debts Expense	1,700	
	Allowance for Doubtful Accounts		1,700
	(To adjust allowance account to total estimated uncollectibles)		

A	=	L	+	SE
−1,700				−1,700

After the adjusting entry is posted, the accounts of the Dart Company will show:

ILLUSTRATION 9-7

Bad debt accounts after posting

Bad Debts Expense

12/31 Adj. 1,700	

Allowance for Doubtful Accounts

	Bal.	528
	12/31 Adj.	1,700
	Bal.	2,228

Occasionally the allowance account will have a **debit balance** prior to adjustment, because write-offs during the year have exceeded previous provisions for bad debts. In such a case **the debit balance is added to the required balance** when the adjusting entry is made. Thus, if there had been a $500 debit balance in the allowance account before adjustment, the adjusting entry would have been for $2,728 ($2,228 + $500) to arrive at a credit balance of $2,228.

The percentage of receivables method will normally result in the better approximation of cash realizable value. This method, however, will not result in the better matching of expenses with revenues if some customers' accounts are more than one year past due. In such a case, bad debts expense for the current period would include amounts applicable to the sales of a prior period.

Direct Write-off Method.   Under the direct write-off method, bad debt losses are not estimated and no allowance account is used. When an account is determined to be uncollectible, the loss is charged to Bad Debts Expense. Assume, for example, that Warden Co. writes off M. E. Doran's $200 balance as uncollectible on December 12. The entry is:

A	=	L	+	SE
−200				−200

Dec. 12	Bad Debts Expense	200	
	Accounts Receivable—M. E. Doran		200
	(To record write-off of M. E. Doran account)		

When this method is used, bad debts expense will show only actual losses from uncollectibles. Accounts receivable will be reported at its gross amount.

Under the direct write-off method, bad debts expense is often recorded in a period different from the period in which the revenue was recorded. Thus, no attempt is made to match bad debts expense to sales revenues in the income statement or to show the cash realizable value of the accounts receivable in the balance sheet. **Consequently, unless bad debt losses are insignificant, the direct write-off method is not acceptable for financial reporting purposes.** The direct write-off method is, however, used for tax purposes. The Internal Revenue Service allows a tax deduction for uncollectible accounts only when specific accounts receivable are deemed uncollectible.

Disposing of Accounts Receivable

STUDY OBJECTIVE

Describe the entries to record the disposition of accounts receivable.

HELPFUL HINT
Two common expressions apply here:
1. Time is money; i.e., waiting for the normal collection process costs money.
2. A bird in the hand is worth two in the bush; i.e., getting the cash now is better than getting it later.

In the normal course of events, accounts receivable are collected in cash and removed from the books. However, as credit sales and receivables have grown in size and significance, the "normal course of events" has changed. In order to accelerate the receipt of cash from receivables, companies frequently sell the receivables to another company for cash, thereby shortening the cash-to-cash operating cycle.

There are several reasons for the sale of receivables. **First, for competitive reasons, sellers** (retailers, wholesalers, and manufacturers) **often must provide financing to purchasers of their goods.** For example, in the sale of durable goods, such as automobiles, trucks, industrial and farm equipment, computers, and appliances, a majority of the sales are on a credit basis. Many major companies in these industries have therefore created companies that accept responsibility for accounts receivable financing. General Motors has General Motors Acceptance Corp. (GMAC), Sears has Sears Roebuck Acceptance Corp. (SRAC), Ford has Ford Motor Credit Corp. (FMCC), and General Electric has GE Capital Services (GECS). These companies are referred to as captive finance companies because they are wholly owned by the company making the product. The purpose of captive financing companies is to encourage the sale of their product by assuring financing to buyers.

Second, receivables may be sold because they may be the only reasonable source of cash. When money is tight, companies may not be able to borrow money in the usual credit markets. If money is available, the cost of borrowing may be prohibitive. A final reason for selling receivables is that **billing and collection are often time consuming and costly**. As a result, it is often easier for a retailer to sell the receivable to another party with expertise in billing and collection matters. Credit card companies such as MasterCard, VISA, American Express, and Diners Club specialize in billing and collecting accounts receivable.

Sale of Receivables

A common sale of receivables is a sale to a factor. A *factor* is a finance company or bank that buys receivables from businesses for a fee and then collects the payments directly from the customers. Factoring was traditionally associated with the textiles, apparel, footwear, furniture, and home furnishing industries. It has now spread to many other types of businesses and is a multibillion dollar business. For example, Sears, Roebuck and Co. in 1998 sold $6.6 billion of customer accounts receivable.

Factoring arrangements vary widely, but typically the factor (purchaser of the receivables) charges a commission. It ranges from 1% to 3% of the amount of receivables purchased. To illustrate, assume that Hendredon Furniture factors $600,000 of receivables to Federal Factors, Inc. Federal Factors assesses a service charge of 2% of the amount of receivables sold. The journal entry to record the sale by Hendredon Furniture is as follows:

HELPFUL HINT
The seller can usually earn more than the commission by (1) taking advantage of 2–3% purchase discounts, (2) investing in short-term securities, or (3) reinvesting the money in productive assets.

Cash	588,000	
Service Charge Expense (2% × $600,000)	12,000	
Accounts Receivable		600,000
(To record the sale of accounts receivable)		

A	=	L	+	SE
+588,000				−12,000
−600,000				

If the company usually sells its receivables, the service charge expense incurred by Hendredon Furniture is recorded as selling expense. If receivables are sold infrequently, this amount may be reported in the Other Expenses and Losses section of the income statement.

ACCOUNTING IN ACTION
Business Insight

"They're the devil in disguise," is how CEO Barry Weinstein described factors. Unable to raise capital from bankers or outside investors, Weinstein turned to factoring receivables. The arrangement was pricey: the factor charged interest of 5% a month, to a maximum of 13% of the total invoice, on any uncollected invoices that were factored. The deal became an endless cycle. Soon Weinstein was factoring all new invoices to get the cash to pay the interest on the older factored invoices.

Source: Inc., July 1994, p. 97.

Credit Card Sales

Approximately 1 billion credit cards were estimated to be in use recently—more than three credit cards for every man, woman, and child in this country. A common type of credit card is a national credit card such as VISA, MasterCard, and American Express. Three parties are involved when national credit cards are used in making retail sales: (1) the credit card issuer, who is independent of the retailer, (2) the retailer, and (3) the customer. A retailer's acceptance of a national credit card is another form of selling (factoring) the receivable.

The major advantages of these national credit cards to the retailer are shown in Illustration 9-8. In exchange for these advantages, the retailer pays the credit card issuer a fee of 2–6% of the invoice price for its services.

HELPFUL HINT
Having millions of cards in use translates to more sales with zero bad debts. Both are powerful reasons for a retailer to accept national credit cards.

ILLUSTRATION 9-8

Advantages of credit cards to the retailer

VISA and MasterCard Sales.   Sales resulting from the use of VISA and Master-Card are considered cash sales by the retailer. These cards are issued by banks. Upon receipt of credit card sales slips from a retailer, the bank immediately adds the amount to the seller's bank balance. These credit card sales slips are there-fore recorded in the same manner as checks deposited from a cash sale. Banks generally charge a fee of 2–4% of the credit card sales slips for this service. To illustrate, Anita Ferreri purchases a number of compact discs for her restaurant from Karen Kerr Music Co. for $1,000 using her VISA First Bank Card. The ser-vice fee that First Bank charges is 3%. The entry to record this transaction by Karen Kerr Music is as follows:

A	=	L	+	SE
+970				−30
				+1,000

Cash	970	
Service Charge Expense	30	
Sales		1,000
(To record Visa credit card sales)		

American Express Sales.   Sales using American Express cards are reported as credit sales, not cash sales. Conversion into cash does not occur until American Express remits the net amount to the seller. To illustrate, assume that Four Sea-sons restaurant accepts an American Express card for a $300 bill. The entry for the sale by Four Seasons (assuming a 5% fee) is:

A	=	L	+	SE
+285				−15
				+300

Accounts Receivable—American Express	285	
Service Charge Expense	15	
Sales		300
(To record American Express credit card sales)		

Thus American Express will subsequently pay the restaurant $285 which the restaurant will record as follows:

Cash	285	
Accounts Receivable—American Express		285
(To record redemption of credit card billings)		

A	=	L	+	SE
+285				
−285				

Service Charge Expense is reported as a selling expense in the income statement by the restaurant.

BEFORE YOU GO ON . . .

Review It

1. How are accounts receivable recognized in the accounts?
2. What are the essential features of the allowance method?
3. Explain the difference between the percentage of sales and the percentage of receivables methods.
4. Why do companies sell their receivables?
5. What is the journal entry when a company sells its receivables to a factor?
6. What factors indicate that Kellogg Company has limited its risks related to concentrations of credit? (*Hint:* See "Credit Risk Concentration" paragraph of Note 11 in Kellogg's 1998 Annual Report.) The answer to this question is provided on page 408.

Do It

Peter M. Dell Wholesalers Co. has been expanding faster than it can raise capital and, according to its local banker, the company has reached its debt ceiling. Dell's customers are slow in paying (60–90 days), but its suppliers (creditors) are demanding 30-day payment. Dell has a cash flow problem.

Dell needs to raise $120,000 in cash to safely cover next Friday's employee payroll. Dell's present balance of outstanding receivables totals $750,000. What might Dell do to alleviate this cash crunch? Record the entry that Dell would make when it raises the needed cash.

Reasoning: One source of immediate cash at a competitive cost is the sale of receivables to a factor. Rather than waiting until it can collect receivables, Dell may raise immediate cash by selling its receivables. The last thing Dell (or any employer) wants to do is miss a payroll.

Solution: Assuming that Dell Co. factors $125,000 of its accounts receivable at a 1% service charge, the following entry would be made:

Cash	123,750	
Service Charge Expense	1,250	
Accounts Receivable		125,000
(To record sale of receivables to factor)		

Related exercise material: BE9–9 and E9–5.

THE
NAVIGATOR

NOTES RECEIVABLE

Credit may also be granted in exchange for a formal credit instrument known as a promissory note. A promissory note is a written promise to pay a specified amount of money on demand or at a definite time. Promissory notes may be used (1) when individuals and companies lend or borrow money, (2) when the amount of the transaction and the credit period exceed normal limits, and (3) in settlement of accounts receivable.

In a promissory note, the party making the promise to pay is called the maker; the party to whom payment is to be made is called the payee. The payee may be specifically identified by name or may be designated simply as the bearer of the note. In the note shown in Illustration 9-9, Brent Company is the maker and Wilma Company is the payee. To the Wilma Company, the promissory note is a note receivable; to the Brent Company, the note is a note payable.

ILLUSTRATION 9-9

Promissory note

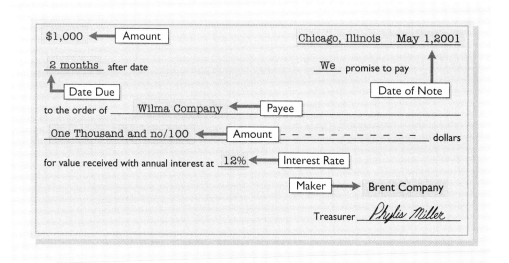

HELPFUL HINT

Who are the two key parties to a note, and what entry does each party make when the note is issued?

Answer:

1. The maker, Brent Company, credits Notes Payable.

2. The payee, Wilma Company, debits Notes Receivable.

Notes receivable give the holder a stronger legal claim to assets than accounts receivable. Like accounts receivable, notes receivable can be readily sold to another party. Promissory notes are negotiable instruments (as are checks), which means that they can be transferred to another party by endorsement.

Notes receivable are frequently accepted from customers who need to extend the payment of an outstanding account receivable and are often required from high-risk customers. In some industries (e.g., the pleasure and sport boat industry) all credit sales are supported by notes. The majority of notes, however, originate from lending transactions. The basic issues in accounting for notes receivable are the same as those for accounts receivable.

1. **Recognizing** notes receivable.
2. **Valuing** notes receivable.
3. **Disposing of** notes receivable.

On the following pages, we will look at each of these issues. Before we do, though, we need to consider two issues that did not apply to accounts receivable: the maturity date and the computation of interest.

Determining the Maturity Date

5

STUDY

OBJECTIVE

Compute the maturity date of, and interest on, notes receivable.

When the life of a note is expressed in terms of months, the due date is found by counting the months from the date of issue. For example, the maturity date of a 3-month note dated May 1 is August 1. A note drawn on the last day of a month matures on the last day of a subsequent month; that is, a July 31 note due in 2 months matures on September 30. When the due date is stated in terms of days, it is necessary to count the exact number of days to determine the maturity date. In counting, **the date the note is issued is omitted but the due date is included**. For example, the maturity date of a 60-day note dated July 17 is September 15, computed as follows:

ILLUSTRATION 9-10

Computation of maturity date

Term of note		60
July (31 − 17)	14	
August	31	45
Maturity date, September		**15**

The due date (maturity date) of a promissory note may be stated in one of three ways, as shown in Illustration 9-11.

ILLUSTRATION 9-11

Maturity date of different notes

Computing Interest

As indicated in Chapter 3, the basic formula for computing interest on an interest-bearing note is:

ILLUSTRATION 9-12

Formula for computing interest

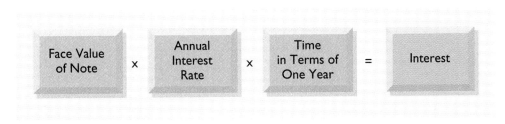

The interest rate specified on the note is an **annual** rate of interest. The time factor in the computation above expresses the fraction of a year that the note is outstanding. When the maturity date is stated in days, the time factor is frequently the number of days divided by 360. When the due date is stated in months, the time factor is the number of months divided by 12. The computation of interest is shown in Illustration 9-13.

ILLUSTRATION 9-13

Computation of interest

Terms of Note	Interest Computation				
	Face	× Rate ×	Time	=	Interest
$ 730, 18%, 120 days	$ 730	× 18% ×	120/360	=	$ 43.80
$1,000, 15%, 6 months	$1,000	× 15% ×	6/12	=	$ 75.00
$2,000, 12%, 1 year	$2,000	× 12% ×	1/1	=	$240.00

STUDY

OBJECTIVE

....

Explain how notes
receivable are
recognized in the
accounts.

There are many different ways to calculate interest. For example, the computation above assumed the total days to be used for the year are 360. Many financial institutions use 365 days to compute interest. It is more profitable, though, to use 360 days because the holder of the note receives more interest than if 365 days are used. For homework problems, assume 360 days.

Recognizing Notes Receivable

To illustrate the basic entry for notes receivable, we will use the $1,000, 2-month, 12% promissory note on page 386. Assuming that the note was written to settle an open account, the entry for the receipt of the note by Wilma Company is:

A	=	L	+	SE
+1,000				
−1,000				

May 1	Notes Receivable	1,000	
	Accounts Receivable—Brent Company		1,000
	(To record acceptance of Brent Company note)		

Observe that the note receivable is recorded at its **face value**, the value shown on the face of the note. No interest revenue is reported when the note is accepted because the revenue recognition principle does not recognize revenue until earned. Interest is earned (accrued) as time passes.

If a note is exchanged for cash, the entry is a debit to Notes Receivable and a credit to Cash in the amount of the loan.

Valuing Notes Receivable

Like accounts receivable, short-term notes receivable are reported at their **cash (net) realizable value**. The notes receivable allowance account is Allowance for Doubtful Accounts. Valuing short-term notes receivable is the same as valuing accounts receivable. The computations and estimations involved in determining cash realizable value and in recording the proper amount of bad debt expense and related allowance are similar.

Long-term notes receivable, however, pose additional estimation problems. As an example, we need only look at the problems a number of large U.S. banks have had in collecting their receivables. Loans to less-developed countries are particularly worrisome. Developing countries need loans for development but often find repayment difficult. U.S. loans (notes) to less-developed countries at one time totaled approximately $135 billion. In Brazil alone, Citibank at one time had loans equivalent to 80% of its stockholders' equity; Chemical Bank had 77% of its equity lent out in Mexico. Determining the proper allowance is understandably difficult for these types of long-term receivables.

ACCOUNTING IN ACTION
International Insight

Varied plans have been proposed to alleviate international debt problems. These plans range from encouraging more lending to reducing or forgiving the debt. At one time, this debt burden to banks worldwide exceeded $1.3 trillion. (As an aside, a trillion is a lot of money—enough money to give every man, woman, and child in the world approximately $250 each.) Why were these loans made in the first place? The reasons are numerous, but the three major ones are: (1) to provide stability to these governments and thereby increase trade, (2) the belief that governments would never default on payment, and (3) the desire by banks to increase their income by lending to these countries.

Disposing of Notes Receivable

Notes may be held to their maturity date, at which time the face value plus accrued interest is due. In some situations, the maker of the note defaults and appropriate adjustment must be made. In other situations, similar to accounts receivable, the holder of the note speeds up the conversion to cash by selling the receivables. The entries for honoring and dishonoring notes are illustrated below.

8
STUDY
OBJECTIVE
....

Describe the entries to record the disposition of notes receivable.

Honor of Notes Receivable

A note is **honored** when it is paid in full at its maturity date. For each interest-bearing note, the amount due at maturity is the face value of the note plus interest for the length of time specified on the note.

To illustrate, assume that Betty Co. lends Wayne Higley Inc. $10,000 on June 1, accepting a 4-month, 9% interest note. In this situation, interest is $300 ($10,000 × 9% × 4/12); the amount due, the maturity value, is $10,300. To obtain payment, Betty Co. (the payee) must present the note either to Wayne Higley Inc. (the maker) or to the maker's duly appointed agent, such as a bank. Assuming that Betty Co. presents the note to Wayne Higley Inc. on October 1, the maturity date, the entry by Betty Co. to record the collection is:

Oct. 1	Cash	10,300	
	Notes Receivable		10,000
	Interest Revenue		300
	(To record collection of Higley Inc. note)		

$$\begin{array}{lcl} A & = L + & SE \\ +10,300 & & +300 \\ -10,000 & & \end{array}$$

If Betty Co. prepares financial statements as of September 30, it would be necessary to accrue interest. In this case, the adjusting entry by Betty Co. would be for 4 months, or $300, as shown below.

Sept. 30	Interest Receivable	300	
	Interest Revenue		300
	(To accrue 4 months' interest)		

$$\begin{array}{lcl} A & = L + & SE \\ +300 & & +300 \end{array}$$

When interest has been accrued, it is necessary to credit Interest Receivable at maturity. The entry by Betty Co. to record the honoring of the Wayne Higley Inc. note on October 1 is:

Oct. 1	Cash	10,300	
	Notes Receivable		10,000
	Interest Receivable		300
	(To record collection of note at maturity)		

$$\begin{array}{lcl} A & = L + & SE \\ +10,300 & & \\ -10,000 & & \\ -300 & & \end{array}$$

In this case, Interest Receivable is credited because the receivable was established in the adjusting entry.

Dishonor of Notes Receivable

A dishonored note is a note that is not paid in full at maturity. A dishonored note receivable is no longer negotiable. However, the payee still has a claim against the maker of the note. Therefore the Notes Receivable account is usually transferred to an Account Receivable.

To illustrate, assume that Wayne Higley Inc. on October 1 indicates that it cannot pay at the present time. The entry to record the dishonor of the note depends on whether eventual collection is expected. If Betty Co. expects eventual collection, the amount due (face value and interest) on the note is debited to Accounts Receivable. Betty Co. would make the following entry at the time the note is dishonored (assuming no previous accrual of interest):

Oct. 1	Accounts Receivable	10,300	
	Notes Receivable		10,000
	Interest Revenue		300
	(To record the dishonor of the note)		

$$\begin{array}{lcl} A & = L + & SE \\ +10,300 & & +300 \\ -10,000 & & \end{array}$$

If there is no hope of collection, the face value of the note should be written off by debiting the Allowance for Doubtful Accounts. No interest revenue would be recorded because collection will not occur.

Sale of Notes Receivable

The accounting for the sales of notes receivable is recorded in a manner similar to the sale of accounts receivable. The accounting entries for the sale of notes receivable are left for a more advanced course.

BEFORE YOU GO ON . . .

Review It

1. What is the basic formula for computing interest?
2. At what value are notes receivable reported on the balance sheet?
3. Explain the difference between honoring and dishonoring a note receivable.

Do It

Gambit Stores accepts from Leonard Co. a $3,400, 90-day, 12% note dated May 10 in settlement of Leonard's overdue open account. What is the maturity date of the note? What is the entry made by Gambit at the maturity date, assuming Leonard pays the note and interest in full at that time?

Reasoning: When the due date is stated in terms of days, it is necessary to count the exact number of days to determine the maturity date. In counting, the date the note is issued is omitted, but the due date is included. The entry to record interest at maturity in this solution assumes that no interest is accrued on this note.

Solution: The maturity date is August 8, computed as follows:

Term of note:		90 days
May (31 − 10)	21	
June	30	
July	31	82
Maturity date, August		8

The interest payable at maturity date is $102, computed as follows:

$$\text{Face} \times \text{Rate} \times \text{Time} = \text{Interest}$$
$$\$3,400 \times 12\% \times 90/360 = \$102$$

The entry recorded by Gambit Stores at the maturity date is:

Cash	3,502	
Notes Receivable		3,400
Interest Revenue		102
(To record collection of Leonard note)		

THE NAVIGATOR

Related exercise material: BE9–8, BE9–10, E9–8, and E9–9.

ACCOUNTING IN ACTION
Business Insight

Give the man credit. Like most of us, John Galbreath receives piles of unsolicited, "preapproved" credit card applications in the mail. Galbreath doesn't just toss them out, though. In April he filled out a credit card application on which he stated he was 97 years old and had no income, no telephone, and no Social Security number. In a space inviting him to let the credit card company pay off his other credit card balances, Galbreath said he owed money to the Mafia.

Back came a credit card and a letter welcoming John to the fold with a $1,500 credit limit. Galbreath had requested the card under a false name, John C. Reath, an alias under which he had received two other credit cards—earning exemplary credit. John C. Reath might be a bit "long in the tooth," but it seems he paid his bills on time.

Source: "Forbes Informer," edited by Kate Bohner Lewis, *Forbes*, August 14, 1995, p. 19. Reprinted by permission of FORBES Magazine; © Forbes Inc., 1995

STATEMENT PRESENTATION AND ANALYSIS

Presentation

Each of the major types of receivables should be identified in the balance sheet or in the notes to the financial statements. Short-term receivables are reported within the current assets section of the balance sheet below temporary investments. Temporary investments appear before short-term receivables, because these investments are more liquid, or nearer to cash. Both the gross amount of receivables and the allowance for doubtful accounts should be reported. Illustration 9-14 shows the current asset presentation of receivables for Kellogg Company, at December 31, 1998.

STUDY OBJECTIVE

Explain the statement presentation and analysis of receivables.

KELLOGG COMPANY
Balance Sheet (partial)
December 31, 1998

Accounts receivables (in millions)	$705.9
Less: Allowance for doubtful accounts	12.9
Net receivables	$693.0

ILLUSTRATION 9-14

Balance sheet presentation of receivables

In a multiple-step income statement, Bad Debts Expense and Service Charge Expense are reported as selling expenses in the Operating Expenses section. Interest Revenue is shown under Other Revenues and Gains in the nonoperating section of the income statement.

Analysis

Financial ratios are frequently computed to evaluate the liquidity of a company's accounts receivable. The ratio used to assess the liquidity of the receivables is the accounts receivables turnover ratio. This ratio measures the number of times, on average, accounts receivable are collected during the period. The accounts receivable turnover ratio is computed by dividing net credit sales (net sales less cash sales) by the average net accounts receivable during the year. Unless seasonal factors are significant, average net accounts receivable outstanding can be computed from the beginning and ending balance of the net accounts receivable.

For example, in 1998 Kellogg had net sales of $6,762.1 million for the year and a beginning net accounts receivable balance of $587.5 million. Assuming that Kellogg's sales were all on credit, its accounts receivable turnover ratio is computed as follows:

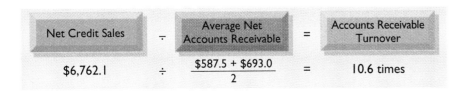

ILLUSTRATION 9-15

Accounts receivable turnover ratio and computation

The result indicates an accounts receivable turnover ratio of 10.6 times per year. The higher the turnover ratio the more liquid the company's receivables.

Another variant of the accounts receivable turnover ratio that makes the liquidity even more evident is the conversion of it into an average collection period in terms of days. This is done by dividing the turnover ratio into 365 days. For example, Kellogg's turnover of 10.6 times is divided into 365 days, as follows, to obtain approximately 34.4 days:

ILLUSTRATION 9-16

Average collection period for receivables formula and computation

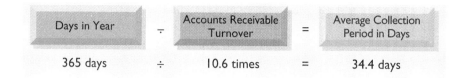

Days in Year	÷	Accounts Receivable Turnover	=	Average Collection Period in Days
365 days	÷	10.6 times	=	34.4 days

This means that Kellogg's average collection period for accounts receivable is 34.4 days. The average collection period is frequently used to assess the effectiveness of a company's credit and collection policies. The general rule is that the collection period should not greatly exceed the credit term period (i.e., the time allowed for payment).

BEFORE YOU GO ON . . .

Review It

1. Explain where accounts and notes receivable are reported on the balance sheet.
2. Where are bad debts expense, service charge expense, and interest revenue reported on the multiple-step income statement?

A LOOK BACK AT OUR FEATURE STORY

Refer back to the Feature Story about Fred Tarter and his Pharmacy Fund company at the beginning of the chapter, and answer the following questions:

1. Why has the pharmacy business moved from a cash-based business to a receivables-based business?
2. What is the economic motivation for pharmacies to sell their receivables?
3. What is the economic motivation for the Pharmacy Fund to purchase the receivables?

Solution:
1. Due to the proliferation of health plans, pharmacists now deal with many small receivables from third-party payers instead of cash payments from customers. There are 4,500 health plans combining to create $770 million of third-party receivables each week.
2. It is estimated that credit losses equal 3% of the $40 billion of prescriptions purchased through health care plans. In addition, pharmacists must wait between 30 and 60 days to receive about 70% of their receivables. Selling the receivables provides cash within 24 hours and relieves pharmacists of collection responsibilities.
3. The Pharmacy Fund maintains credit files on health plan sponsors and other third-party payers. Thus, it can minimize credit losses. The fund receives a 1.4% to 2% discount on receivables purchased. As the volume of business expands, it is expected that this discount will cover expenses and provide a profit.

THE NAVIGATOR

DEMONSTRATION PROBLEM

Presented below are selected transactions related to Falcetto Company.

Mar. 1   Sold $20,000 of merchandise to Potter Company, terms 2/10, n/30.
11   Received payment in full from Potter Company for balance due.
12   Accepted Juno Company's $20,000 6-month, 12% note for balance due.
13   Made Falcetto Company credit card sales for $13,200.

15   Made American Express credit sales totaling $6,700. A 5% service fee is charged by American Express.

30   Received payment in full from American Express Company less the 5% service charge.

Apr. 11   Sold accounts receivable of $8,000 to Harcot Factor. Harcot Factor assesses a service charge of 2% of the amount of receivables sold.

13   Received collections of $8,200 on Falcetto Company credit card sales and added finance charges of 1.5% to the remaining balances.

May 10   Wrote off as uncollectible $16,000 of accounts receivable. Falcetto uses the percentage of sales basis to estimate bad debts.

June 30   Credit sales for the first six months total $2,000,000 and the bad debt percentage is 1% of credit sales. At June 30, the balance in the allowance account is $3,500.

July 16   One of the accounts receivable written off in May pays the amount due, $4,000, in full.

Instructions
Prepare the journal entries for the transactions.

SOLUTION TO DEMONSTRATION PROBLEM

Date	Account	Debit	Credit
Mar. 1	Accounts Receivable—Potter	20,000	
	Sales		20,000
	(To record sales on account)		
Mar. 11	Cash	19,600	
	Sales Discounts (2% × $20,000)	400	
	Accounts Receivable—Potter		20,000
	(To record collection of accounts receivable)		
Mar. 12	Notes Receivable	20,000	
	Accounts Receivable—Juno		20,000
	(To record acceptance of Juno Company note)		
Mar. 13	Accounts Receivable	13,200	
	Sales		13,200
	(To record company credit card sales)		
Mar. 15	Accounts Receivable—American Express	6,365	
	Service Charge Expense (5% × $6,700)	335	
	Sales		6,700
	(To record credit card sales)		
Mar. 30	Cash	6,365	
	Accounts Receivable—American Express		6,365
	(To record redemption of credit card billings)		
Apr. 11	Cash	7,840	
	Service Charge Expense (2% × $8,000)	160	
	Accounts Receivable		8,000
	(To record sale of receivables to factor)		
Apr. 13	Cash	8,200	
	Accounts Receivable		8,200
	(To record collection of accounts receivable)		
	Accounts Receivable [($13,200 − $8,200) × 1.5%]	75	
	Interest Revenue		75
	(To record interest on amount due)		

May 10	Allowance for Doubtful Accounts		16,000	
	Accounts Receivable			16,000
	(To record write-off of accounts receivable)			
June 30	Bad Debts Expense ($2,000,000 × 1%)		20,000	
	Allowance for Doubtful Accounts			20,000
	(To record estimate of uncollectible accounts)			
July 16	Accounts Receivable		4,000	
	Allowance for Doubtful Accounts			4,000
	(To reverse write-off of accounts receivable)			
	Cash		4,000	
	Accounts Receivable			4,000
	(To record collection of accounts receivable)			

THE NAVIGATOR

SUMMARY OF STUDY OBJECTIVES

1. Identify the different types of receivables. Receivables are frequently classified as (1) accounts, (2) notes, and (3) other. Accounts receivable are amounts owed by customers on account. Notes receivable represent claims that are evidenced by formal instruments of credit. Other receivables include nontrade receivables such as interest receivable, loans to company officers, advances to employees, and income taxes refundable.

2. Explain how accounts receivable are recognized in the accounts. Accounts receivable are recorded at invoice price. They are reduced by Sales Returns and Allowances. Cash discounts reduce the amount received on accounts receivable. When interest is charged on a past due receivable, this interest is added to the accounts receivable balance and is recognized as interest revenue.

3. Distinguish between the methods and bases used to value accounts receivable. There are two methods of accounting for uncollectible accounts: (1) the allowance method and (2) the direct write-off method. Either the percentage of sales or the percentage of receivables basis may be used to estimate uncollectible accounts using the allowance method. The percentage of sales basis emphasizes the matching principle. The percentage of receivables basis emphasizes the cash realizable value of the accounts receivable. An aging schedule is frequently used with this basis.

4. Describe the entries to record the disposition of accounts receivable. When an account receivable is collected, Accounts Receivable is credited. When an account receivable is sold, a service charge expense is charged which reduces the amount collected.

5. Compute the maturity date of, and interest on, notes receivable. The maturity date of a note must be computed unless the due date is specified or the note is payable on demand. For a note stated in months, the maturity date is found by counting the months from the date of issue. For a note stated in days, the number of days is counted, omitting the issue date and counting the due date. The formula for computing interest is face value × interest rate × time.

6. Explain how notes receivable are recognized in the accounts. Notes receivable are recorded at face value. In some cases, it is necessary to accrue interest prior to maturity. In this case, Interest Receivable is debited and Interest Revenue is credited.

7. Describe how notes receivable are valued. Like accounts receivable, notes receivable are reported at their cash (net) realizable value. The notes receivable allowance account is the Allowance for Doubtful Accounts. The computation and estimations involved in valuing notes receivable at cash realizable value, and in recording the proper amount of bad debt expense and related allowance are similar to accounts receivable.

8. Describe the entries to record the disposition of notes receivable. Notes can be held to maturity, at which time the face value plus accrued interest is due and the note is removed from the accounts. However, in many cases, similar to accounts receivable, the holder of the note speeds up the conversion by selling the receivable to another party. In some situations, the maker of the note dishonors the note (defaults), and the note is written off.

9. Explain the statement presentation and analysis of receivables. Each major type of receivable should be identified in the balance sheet or in the notes to the financial statements. Short-term receivables are considered current assets. The gross amount of receivables and allowance for doubtful accounts should be reported. Bad debts and service charge expenses are reported in the multiple-step income statement as operating (selling) expenses, and interest revenue is shown as other revenues and gains in the nonoperating section of the statement. Accounts receivables may be evaluated for liquidity by computing a turnover ratio and an average collection period.

THE NAVIGATOR

GLOSSARY

Accounts receivable turnover ratio A measure of the liquidity of accounts receivable, computed by dividing net credit sales by average net accounts receivable. (p. 391).

Aging of accounts receivable The analysis of customer balances by the length of time they have been unpaid. (p. 380).

Average collection period The average amount of time that a receivable is outstanding, calculated by dividing 365 days by the receivables turnover ratio. (p. 391).

Cash (net) realizable value The net amount expected to be received in cash. (p. 376).

Dishonored note A note that is not paid in full at maturity. (p. 389).

Factor A finance company or bank that buys receivables from businesses for a fee and then collects the payments directly from the customers. (p. 383).

Maker The party in a promissory note who is making the promise to pay. (p. 385).

Payee The party to whom payment of a promissory note is to be made. (p. 385).

Percentage of receivables basis Management establishes a percentage relationship between the amount of receivables and the expected losses from uncollectible accounts. (p. 380).

Percentage of sales basis Management establishes a percentage relationship between the amount of credit sales and expected losses from uncollectible accounts. (p. 380).

Promissory note A written promise to pay a specified amount of money on demand or at a definite time. (p. 385).

Trade receivables Notes and accounts receivable that result from sales transactions. (p. 374).

SELF-STUDY QUESTIONS

Answers are at the end of the chapter.

(SO 2) 1. Remmers Company on June 15 sells merchandise on account to Tucci Co. for $1,000 terms 2/10, n/30. On June 20, Tucci Co. returns merchandise worth $300 to Remmers Company. On June 24, payment is received from Tucci Co. for the balance due. What is the amount of cash received?
   a. $700.
   b. $680.
   c. $686.
   d. None of the above.

(SO 3) 2. Which of the following approaches for bad debts is best described as a balance sheet method?
   a. Percentage of receivables basis.
   b. Direct write-off method.
   c. Percentage of sales basis.
   d. Both a and b.

(SO 3) 3. Net sales for the month are $800,000 and bad debts are expected to be 1.5% of net sales. The company uses the percentage of sales basis. If the Allowance for Doubtful Accounts has a credit balance of $15,000 before adjustment, what is the balance after adjustment?
   a. $15,000.
   b. $27,000.
   c. $23,000.
   d. $31,000.

(SO 3) 4. In 2001, Roland Carlson Company had net credit sales of $750,000. On January 1, 2001, Allowance for Doubtful Accounts had a credit balance of $18,000. During 2001, $30,000 of uncollectible accounts receivable were written off. Past experience indicates that 3% of net credit sales become uncollectible. What should be the adjusted balance of Allowance for Doubtful Accounts at December 31, 2001?
   a. $10,050.

   b. $10,500.
   c. $22,500.
   d. $40,500.

5. An analysis and aging of the accounts receivable of (SO 3) Machiavelli Company at December 31 reveals the following data:

Accounts Receivable	$800,000
Allowance for Doubtful Accounts per books before adjustment	50,000
Amounts expected to become uncollectible	65,000

The cash realizable value of the accounts receivable at December 31, after adjustment, is:
   a. $685,000.
   b. $750,000.
   c. $800,000.
   d. $735,000.

6. One of the following statements about promissory notes (SO 6) is incorrect. The *incorrect* statement is:
   a. The party making the promise to pay is called the maker.
   b. The party to whom payment is to be made is called the payee.
   c. A promissory note is not a negotiable instrument.
   d. A promissory note is more liquid than an accounts receivable.

7. Which of the following statements about VISA credit (SO 4) card sales is incorrect?
   a. The credit card issuer makes the credit investigation of the customer.
   b. The retailer is not involved in the collection process.
   c. Two parties are involved.
   d. The retailer receives cash more quickly than it would from individual customers on account.

(SO 4) 8. Morgan Retailers accepted $50,000 of Citibank VISA credit card charges for merchandise sold on July 1. Citibank charges 4% for its credit card use. The entry to record this transaction by Morgan Retailers will include a credit to Sales of $50,000 and a debit(s) to:

a. Cash $48,000
    and Service Charge Expense $2,000
b. Accounts Receivable $48,000
    and Service Charge Expense $2,000
c. Cash $50,000
d. Accounts Receivable $50,000

(SO 6) 9. Bickner Co. accepts a $1,000, 3-month, 12% promissory note in settlement of an account with Streisand Co. The entry to record this transaction is as follows:

a. Notes Receivable   1,030
    Accounts Receivable   1,030
b. Notes Receivable   1,000
    Accounts Receivable   1,000

c. Notes Receivable   1,000
    Sales   1,000
d. Notes Receivable   1,020
    Accounts Receivable   1,020

10. Schlicht Co. holds Osgrove Inc.'s $10,000, 120-day, 9% (SO 8) note. The entry made by Schlicht Co. when the note is collected, assuming no interest has been accrued, is

a. Cash   10,300
    Notes Receivable   10,300
b. Cash   10,000
    Notes Receivable   10,000
c. Accounts Receivable   10,300
    Notes Receivable   10,000
    Interest Revenue   300
d. Cash   10,300
    Notes Receivable   10,000
    Interest Revenue   300

THE NAVIGATOR

QUESTIONS

1. What is the difference between an account receivable and a note receivable?

2. What are some common types of receivables other than accounts receivable or notes receivable?

3. Texaco Oil Company issues its own credit cards. Assume that Texaco charges you $40 on an unpaid balance. Prepare the journal entry that Texaco makes to record this revenue.

4. What are the essential features of the allowance method of accounting for bad debts?

5. Dorothy Fleming cannot understand why cash realizable value does not decrease when an uncollectible account is written off under the allowance method. Clarify this point for Dorothy Fleming.

6. Distinguish between the two bases that may be used in estimating uncollectible accounts.

7. Kosinsky Company has a credit balance of $3,500 in Allowance for Doubtful Accounts. The estimated bad debts expense under the percentage of sales basis is $4,100, and the total estimated uncollectibles under the percentage of receivables basis is $5,800. Prepare the adjusting entry under each basis.

8. How are bad debts accounted for under the direct write-off method? What are the disadvantages of this method?

9. Elbe Company accepts both its own credit cards and national credit cards. What are the advantages of accepting both types of cards?

10. An article recently appeared in *The Wall Street Journal* indicating that companies are selling their receivables at a record rate. Why are companies selling their receivables?

11. Southern Textiles decides to sell $800,000 of its accounts receivable to First Central Factors Inc. First Central Factors assesses a service charge of 2% of the amount of receivables sold. Prepare the journal entry that Southern Textiles makes to record this sale.

12. Your roommate is uncertain about the advantages of a promissory note. Compare the advantages of a note receivable with those of an accounts receivable.

13. How may the maturity date of a promissory note be stated?

14. Indicate the maturity date of each of the following promissory notes:

Date of Note	Terms
(a) March 13	one year after date of note
(b) May 4	3 months after date
(c) June 20	30 days after date
(d) July 1	60 days after date

15. Compute the missing amounts for each of the following notes:

	Principal	Annual Interest Rate	Time	Total Interest
(a)	?	9%	120 days	$ 450
(b)	$30,000	10%	3 years	?
(c)	$60,000	?	5 months	$3,000
(d)	$50,000	11%	?	$1,375

16. In determining interest revenue, some financial institutions use 365 days per year whereas others use 360 days. Why might a financial institution use 360 days?

17. Nick Coffin Company dishonors a note at maturity. What actions by Coffin may occur with the dishonoring of the note?

18. Paula Company has accounts receivable and notes receivable. How should the receivables be reported on the balance sheet?

19. If the accounts receivables turnover ratio is 7.15 and average net receivables during the period are $210,000, what is the amount of net credit sales for the period?

BRIEF EXERCISES

• •

BE9–1 Presented below are three receivable transactions. Indicate whether these receivables are reported as accounts receivable, notes receivable, or other receivables on a balance sheet.

1. Sold merchandise on account for $60,000 to a customer.
2. Received a promissory note of $57,000 for services performed.
3. Advanced $10,000 to an employee.

BE9–2 Record the following transactions on the books of Jose Co.

1. On July 1, Jose Co. sold merchandise on account to Cambridge Inc. for $15,000, terms 2/10, n/30.
2. On July 8, Cambridge Inc. returned merchandise worth $3,800 to Jose Co.
3. On July 11, Cambridge Inc. paid for the merchandise.

BE9–3 During its first year of operations, Alvarado Company had credit sales of $3,000,000, of which $600,000 remained uncollected at year-end. The credit manager estimates that $30,000 of these receivables will become uncollectible. (a) Prepare the journal entry to record the estimated uncollectibles. (b) Prepare the current asset section of the balance sheet for Alvarado Company, assuming that in addition to the receivables it has cash of $90,000, merchandise inventory of $130,000, and prepaid expenses of $13,000.

BE9–4 At the end of 2001, Delacruz Co. has accounts receivable of $700,000 and an allowance for doubtful accounts of $54,000. On January 24, 2002, it is learned that the company's receivable from Hutley Inc. is not collectible and therefore management authorizes a write-off of $6,000. (a) Prepare the journal entry to record the write-off. (b) What is the cash realizable value of the accounts receivable (1) before the write-off and (2) after the write-off?

BE9–5 Assume the same information as BE9–4 and that on March 4, 2002, Delacruz Co. receives payment of $6,000 in full from Hutley Co. Prepare the journal entries to record this transaction.

BE9–6 Einhause Co. elects to use the percentage of sales basis in 2001 to record bad debts expense and concludes that 2% of net credit sales will become uncollectible. Sales are $800,000 for 2001, sales returns and allowances are $50,000, and the allowance for doubtful accounts has a credit balance of $12,000. Prepare the adjusting entry to record bad debts expense in 2001.

BE9–7 Grolesky Co. uses the percentage of accounts receivable basis to record bad debt expense, and concludes that 1% of accounts receivable will become uncollectible. Accounts receivable are $400,000 at the end of the year, and the allowance for doubtful accounts has a credit balance of $3,000. (a) Prepare the adjusting journal entry to record bad debt expense for the year. (b) If the allowance for doubtful accounts had a debit balance of $800 instead of credit balance of $3,000, determine the amount to be reported for bad debt expense.

BE9–8 Presented below are three promissory notes. Determine the missing amounts.

Date of Note	Terms	Maturity Date	Principal	Annual Interest Rate	Total Interest
(a) April 1	60 days	?	$900,000	9%	?
(b) July 2	30 days	?	90,000	?	$600
(c) March 7	6 months	?	60,000	12%	?

BE9–9 Presented below are the following transactions.

1. Castle Restaurant accepted a Visa card in payment of a $100 lunch bill. The bank charges a 3% fee. What entry should Castle make?
2. Mayfield Company sold its accounts receivable of $80,000. What entry should Mayfield make, given a service charge of 3% on the amount of receivables sold?

BE9–10 On January 10, 2001, Raja Co. sold merchandise on account to Dewey Yeager for $9,000, n/30. On February 9, Dewey Yeager gave Raja Co. a 10% promissory note in settlement of this account. Prepare the journal entry to record the sale and the settlement of the accounts receivable.

BE9–11 The financial statements of Minnesota Mining and Manufacturing Company (3M) report net sales of $9.4 billion. Accounts receivable are $1.6 billion at the beginning of the year and $1.4 billion at the end of the year. Compute 3M's receivable's turnover ratio. Compute 3M's average collection period for accounts receivable in days.

EXERCISES

••

Journalize entries for recognizing accounts receivable.
(SO 2)

E9-1   Presented below are two independent situations that occurred during the year.

1. On January 6, Herzog Co. sells merchandise on account to Watson Inc. for $3,000, terms 2/10, n/30. On January 16, Watson pays the amount due. Prepare the entries on Herzog's books to record the sale and related collection.
2. On January 10, Diane Leto uses her Salizar Co. credit card to purchase merchandise from Salizar Co. for $11,000. On February 10, Leto is billed for the amount due of $11,000. On February 12, Leto pays $6,000 on the balance due. On March 10, Leto is billed for the amount due, including interest at 2% per month on the unpaid balance as of February 12. Prepare the entries on Salizar Co.'s books related to the transactions that occurred on January 10, February 12, and March 10.

Journalize entries to record allowance for doubtful accounts using two different bases.
(SO 3)

E9-2   The ledger of the Kadlec Company at the end of the current year shows Accounts Receivable $90,000, Sales $840,000, and Sales Returns and Allowances $40,000.

Instructions
(a) If Allowance for Doubtful Accounts has a credit balance of $800 in the trial balance, journalize the adjusting entry at December 31, assuming bad debts are expected to be (1) 1% of net sales, and (2) 10% of accounts receivable.
(b) If Allowance for Doubtful Accounts has a debit balance of $500 in the trial balance, journalize the adjusting entry at December 31, assuming bad debts are expected to be (1) .75% of net sales and (2) 8% of accounts receivable.

Determine bad debts expense and prepare the adjusting entry for bad debts expense.
(SO 3)

E9-3   Garcia Company has accounts receivable of $92,500 at March 31. An analysis of the accounts shows the following:

Month of Sale	Balance, March 31
March	$65,000
February	12,600
December and January	8,500
November and October	6,400
	$92,500

Credit terms are 2/10, n/30. At March 31, there is a $1,600 credit balance in Allowance for Doubtful Accounts prior to adjustment. The company uses the percentage of receivables basis for estimating uncollectible accounts. The company's estimate of bad debts is as follows:

Age of Accounts	Estimated Percentage Uncollectible
1–30 days past due	2.0%
30–60 days past due	5.0%
60–90 days past due	30.0%
Over 90 days	50.0%

Instructions
(a) Determine the total estimated uncollectibles.
(b) Prepare the adjusting entry at March 31 to record bad debts expense.

Journalize percentage of sales basis, write-off, recovery.
(SO 3)

E9-4   On December 31, 2001, Jana Co. estimates that 2% of its net sales of $400,000 will become uncollectible and records this amount as an addition to Allowance for Doubtful Accounts. On May 11, 2002, Jana Co. determined that Bob Knight's account was uncollectible and wrote off $900. On June 12, 2002, Knight paid the amount previously written off.

Instructions
Prepare the journal entries on December 31, 2001, May 11, 2002, and June 12, 2002.

Journalize entries for the sale of accounts receivable.
(SO 4)

E9-5   Presented below are two independent situations:

1. On March 3, Dennis Stoia Appliances sells $800,000 of its receivables to Potter Factors Inc. Potter Factors Inc. assesses a finance charge of 3% of the amount of receivables sold. Prepare the entry on Dennis Stoia Appliances' books to record the sale of the receivables.
2. On May 10, Monee Company sold merchandise for $4,000 and accepted the customer's First Business Bank MasterCard. At the end of the day, the First Business Bank MasterCard receipts were deposited in the company's bank account. First Business Bank charges a 4% service charge for credit card sales. Prepare the entry on Monee Company's books to record the sale of merchandise.

E9–6   Presented below are two independent situations that occurred during the year.

Journalize entries for credit card sales.
(SO 4)

1. On April 2, Elaine Stahl uses her J. C. Penney credit card to purchase merchandise from a J. C. Penney store for $1,300. On May 1, Stahl is billed for the $1,300 amount due. Stahl pays $800 on the balance due on May 3. On June 1, Stahl receives a bill for the amount due, including interest at 1.0% per month on the unpaid balance as of May 3. Prepare the entries on J. C. Penney Co.'s books related to the transactions that occurred on April 2, May 3, and June 1.

2. On July 4, Robyn's Restaurant accepts an American Express card for a $300 dinner bill. American Express charges a 4% service fee. On July 10, American Express pays Robyn $288. Prepare the entries on Robyn's books related to the transactions.

E9–7   Sapaniak Stores accepts both its own and national credit cards. During the year the following selected summary transactions occurred.

Journalize credit card sales and indicate the statement presentation of financing charges and service charge expense.
(SO 4)

Jan. 15   Made Sapaniak credit card sales totaling $15,000. (There were no balances prior to 1/15.)

   20   Made American Express credit card sales (service charge fee, 5%) totaling $2,600.

   30   Received payment in full from American Express.

Feb. 10   Collected $12,000 on Sapaniak credit card sales.

   15   Added finance charges of 1.5% to Sapaniak credit card balance.

Instructions

(a) Journalize the transactions for Sapaniak Stores.

(b) Indicate the statement presentation of the financing charges and the credit card service expense for Sapaniak Stores.

E9–8   Marv Tice Supply Co. has the following transactions related to notes receivable during the last 2 months of the year.

Journalize entries for notes receivable transactions.
(SO 5, 6)

Nov. 1   Loaned $18,000 cash to Sheila Skinner on a 1-year, 10% note.

Dec. 11   Sold goods to Lucinda Higdon, Inc., receiving a $3,600, 90-day, 12% note.

   16   Received a $4,000, 6-month, 12% note in exchange for existing $4,000 receivable from Deanna Prentice.

   31   Accrued interest revenue on all notes receivable.

Instructions

Journalize the transactions for Marv Tice Supply Co.

E9–9   Record the following transactions for the Plano Molding Co. in the general journal:

Journalize entries for notes receivable.
(SO 5, 6)

2001

May 1   Received a $9,000, 1-year, 10% note in exchange for existing $9,000 receivable from John Lewis.

Dec. 31   Accrued interest on the Lewis note.

Dec. 31   Closed the interest revenue account.

2002

May 1   Received principal plus interest on the Lewis note. (No interest has been accrued in 2000.)

E9–10   On May 2, Cynthia Taylor Company lends $6,000 to Nancy Barnes Inc., issuing a 6-month, 10% note. At the maturity date, November 2, Barnes indicates that it cannot pay.

Journalize entries for dishonor of notes receivable.
(SO 5, 8)

Instructions

(a) Prepare the entry to record the dishonor of the note, assuming that Taylor Company expects collection will occur.

(b) Prepare the entry to record the dishonor of the note, assuming that Taylor Company does not expect collection in the future.

E9–11   The following information pertains to the Moosa Merchandising Company:

Determine missing amounts related to sales and accounts receivable.
(SO 2, 4, 9)

Merchandise inventory at end of year	$33,000
Accounts receivable at beginning of year	24,000
Cash sales made during the year	15,000
Gross profit (margin) on sales	27,000
Accounts receivable written off during the year	1,000
Purchases made during the year	60,000
Accounts receivable collected during the year	78,000
Merchandise inventory at beginning of year	36,000

Instructions

(a) Calculate the amount of credit sales made during the year. (*Hint:* You will need to use income statement relationships—introduced in Chapter 5—in order to determine this.)

(b) Calculate the balance of accounts receivable at the end of the year.

PROBLEMS: SET A

Prepare journal entries related to bad debt expenses.
(SO 2, 3, 9)

P9–1A At December 31, 2001, Mike Muzzillo Imports reported the following information on its balance sheet:

Accounts receivable	$1,000,000
Less: Allowance for doubtful accounts	60,000

During 2002, the company had the following transactions related to receivables.

1. Sales on account	$2,600,000
2. Sales returns and allowances	40,000
3. Collections of accounts receivable	2,300,000
4. Write-offs of accounts receivable deemed uncollectible	65,000
5. Recovery of bad debts previously written off as uncollectible	25,000

Instructions

(a) Prepare the journal entries to record each of these five transactions. Assume that no cash discounts were taken on the collections of accounts receivable.

(b) Enter the January 1, 2002, balances in Accounts Receivable and Allowance for Doubtful Accounts, post the entries to the two accounts (use T accounts), and determine the balances.

(c) Prepare the journal entry to record bad debts expense for 2002, assuming that an aging of accounts receivable indicates that estimated bad debts are $70,000.

(d) Compute the accounts receivable turnover ratio for the year 2002.

Compute bad debts amounts.
(SO 3)

P9–2A Information related to Tisinai Company for 2001 is summarized below:

Total credit sales	$1,500,000
Accounts receivable at December 31	600,000
Bad debts written off	24,000

Instructions

(a) What amount of bad debts expense will Tisinai Company report if it uses the direct write-off method of accounting for bad debts?

(b) Assume that Tisinai Company decides to estimate its bad debts expense to be 3% of credit sales. What amount of bad debts expense will Tisinai Company record if Allowance for Doubtful Accounts has a credit balance of $3,000?

(c) Assume that Tisinai Company decides to estimate its bad debts expense based on 5% of accounts receivable. What amount of bad debts expense will Tisinai Company record if Allowance for Doubtful Accounts balance has a credit balance of $4,000?

(d) Assume the same facts as in (c), except that there is a $2,000 debit balance in Allowance for Doubtful Accounts. What amount of bad debts expense will Tisinai record?

(e) What is the weakness of the direct write-off method of reporting bad debts expense?

Journalize entries to record transactions related to bad debts.
(SO 2, 3)

P9–3A Presented below is an aging schedule for Chris Cain Company.

Customer	Total	Not Yet Due	Number of Days Past Due			
			1–30	31–60	61–90	Over 90
Sandy Freewalt	$ 20,000		$ 9,000	$11,000		
Joni Schnabel	30,000	$ 30,000				
Kay Nelson	50,000	15,000	5,000		$30,000	
Ken Mason	38,000					$38,000
Others	120,000	92,000	15,000	13,000		
	$258,000	$137,000	$29,000	$24,000	$30,000	$38,000
Estimated Percentage Uncollectible		3%	6%	12%	24%	50%
Total Estimated Bad Debts	$ 34,930	$ 4,110	$ 1,740	$ 2,880	$ 7,200	$19,000

At December 31, 2001, the unadjusted balance in Allowance for Doubtful Accounts is a credit of $10,000.

Instructions

(a) Journalize and post the adjusting entry for bad debts at December 31, 2001.

(b) Journalize and post to the allowance account the following events and transactions in the year 2002:

    (1) March 1, an $800 customer balance originating in 2001 is judged uncollectible.

    (2) May 1, a check for $800 is received from the customer whose account was written off as uncollectible on March 1.

(c) Journalize the adjusting entry for bad debts on December 31, 2002, assuming that the unadjusted balance in Allowance for Doubtful Accounts is a debit of $1,100 and the aging schedule indicates that total estimated bad debts will be $29,100.

P9–4A At December 31, 2001, the trial balance of John Gleason Company contained the following amounts before adjustment:

Journalize entries to record transactions related to bad debts.
(SO 3)

	Debits	Credits
Accounts Receivable	$350,000	
Allowance for Doubtful Accounts		$ 1,500
Sales		875,000

Instructions

(a) Prepare the adjusting entry at December 31, 2001, to record bad debt expense under each of the following independent assumptions:

    (1) An aging schedule indicates that $16,750 of accounts receivable will be uncollectible.

    (2) It is estimated that 2% of sales will be uncollectible.

(b) Repeat part (a) assuming that instead of a credit balance there is a $1,500 debit balance in the Allowance for Doubtful Accounts.

(c) During the next month, January 2002, a $4,500 account receivable is written off as uncollectible. Prepare the journal entry to record the write-off.

(d) Repeat part (c) assuming that John Gleason Company uses the direct write-off method instead of the allowance method in accounting for uncollectible accounts receivable.

(e) ▯▭▭▭▷ What are the advantages of using the allowance method in accounting for uncollectible accounts as compared to the direct write-off method?

P9–5A Connie Kolzow Co. closes its books monthly. On June 30, selected ledger account balances are:

Prepare entries for various note receivable transactions.
(SO 2, 4, 5, 8, 9)

Notes Receivable	$20,800
Interest Receivable	$132.80

Notes Receivable include the following:

Date	Maker	Face	Term	Interest
May 21	Don Inc.	$6,000	60 days	12%
May 25	John Co.	4,800	60 days	11%
June 30	Pete Corp.	10,000	6 months	9%

During July, the following transactions were completed.

July 5 Made sales of $6,200 on Connie Kolzow Co. credit cards.

    14 Made sales of $700 on VISA credit cards. The credit card service charge is 3%.

    16 Added $415 to Connie Kolzow Co. charge customer balances for finance charges on unpaid balances.

    20 Received payment in full from Don Inc. on the amount due.

    25 Received notice that John Co. note has been dishonored. (Assume that John Co. is expected to pay in the future.)

Instructions

(a) Journalize the July transactions and the July 31 adjusting entry for accrued interest receivable. (Interest is computed using 360 days.)

(b) Enter the balances at July 1 in the receivable accounts and post the entries to all of the receivable accounts.

(c) Show the balance sheet presentation of the receivable accounts at July 31.

Prepare entries for various receivables transactions.
(SO 2, 4, 5, 6, 7, 8)

P9–6A   On January 1, 2001, Judy Elam Company had Accounts Receivable $54,200 and Allowance for Doubtful Accounts $4,700. Judy Elam Company prepares financial statements annually. During the year the following selected transactions occurred.

Jan. 5 Sold $6,000 of merchandise to Garth Brooks Company, terms n/30.
Feb. 2 Accepted a $6,000, 4-month, 12% promissory note from Garth Brooks Company for balance due.
     12 Sold $7,800 of merchandise to Lynn Easton Company and accepted Easton's $7,800, 2-month, 10% note for the balance due.
     26 Sold $4,000 of merchandise to Mathias Co., terms n/10.
Apr. 5 Accepted a $4,000, 3-month, 8% note from Mathias Co. for balance due.
     12 Collected Lynne Easton Company note in full.
June 2 Collected Garth Brooks Company note in full.
July 5 Mathias Co. dishonors its note of April 5. It is expected that Mathias will eventually pay the amount owed.
     15 Sold $3,000 of merchandise to John Ross Co. and accepted Ross's $3,000, 3-month, 12% note for the amount due.
Oct. 15 John Ross Co. note was dishonored. John Ross Co. is bankrupt, and there is no hope of future settlement.

Instructions
Journalize the transactions.

Prepare journal entries for receivables and bad debts.
(SO 3, 4)

P9–7A   The balance sheets of Morgan Sondgeroth Corporation on December 31, 2001 and 2002, showed gross accounts receivable of $8,300,000 and $9,500,000 respectively. The balances in the Allowance for Doubtful Accounts at the end of 2001 and 2002—after adjusting entries—were $750,000 and $930,000, respectively.

   The income statements for 2001 and 2002 showed bad debts expense of $250,000 and $300,000, respectively, which was equal to 1% of sales. All sales were on account.

Instructions
Prepare summary journal entries for 2002 to record the sales, collections, write-offs, and bad debts expense. (*Hint:* You may find the use of T accounts helpful in determining the amounts involved.)

PROBLEMS: SET B
• •

Prepare journal entries related to bad debts expense.
(SO 2, 3, 9)

P9–1B   At December 31, 2001, Cellular Ten Co. reported the following information on its balance sheet.

Accounts receivable	$960,000
Less: Allowance for doubtful accounts	70,000

During 2002, the company had the following transactions related to receivables.

1. Sales on account	$3,200,000
2. Sales returns and allowances	50,000
3. Collections of accounts receivable	2,800,000
4. Write-offs of accounts receivable deemed uncollectible	90,000
5. Recovery of bad debts previously written off as uncollectible	25,000

Instructions
   (a) Prepare the journal entries to record each of these five transactions. Assume that no cash discounts were taken on the collections of accounts receivable.
   (b) Enter the January 1, 2002, balances in Accounts Receivable and Allowance for Doubtful Accounts, post the entries to the two accounts (use T accounts), and determine the balances.
   (c) Prepare the journal entry to record bad debts expense for 2002, assuming that an aging of accounts receivable indicates that expected bad debts are $100,000.
   (d) Compute the accounts receivable turnover ratio for 2002.

Compute bad debts amounts.
(SO 3)

P9–2B   Information related to Sue Hohenberger Company for 2001 is summarized below:

Total credit sales	$2,000,000
Accounts receivable at December 31	800,000
Bad debts written off	36,000

Instructions

(a) What amount of bad debts expense will Hohenberger Company report if it uses the direct write-off method of accounting for bad debts?

(b) Assume that Hohenberger Company decides to estimate its bad debts expense to be 3% of credit sales. What amount of bad debts expense will Hohenberger Company record if it has an Allowance for Doubtful Accounts credit balance of $4,000?

(c) Assume that Hohenberger Company decides to estimate its bad debts expense based on 6% of accounts receivable. What amount of bad debts expense will Hohenberger Company record if it has an Allowance for Doubtful Accounts credit balance of $3,000?

(d) Assume the same facts as in (c), except that there is a $3,000 debit balance in Allowance for Doubtful Accounts. What amount of bad debts expense will Hohenberger record?

(e) What is the weakness of the direct write-off method of reporting bad debts expense?

P9–3B Presented below is an aging schedule for Sandy Hake Company.

Journalize entries to record transactions related to bad debts.

(SO 2, 3)

Customer	Total	Not Yet Due	1–30	31–60	61–90	Over 90
			Number of Days Past Due			
Ruth Benson	$ 22,000		$10,000	$12,000		
Jean Ripper	40,000	$ 40,000				
Mary Ann Bilek	57,000	16,000	6,000		$35,000	
Sherri Freeland	34,000					$34,000
Others	126,000	96,000	16,000	14,000		
	$279,000	$152,000	$32,000	$26,000	$35,000	$34,000
Estimated Percentage Uncollectible		4%	7%	13%	25%	50%
Total Estimated Bad Debts	$ 37,450	$ 6,080	$ 2,240	$ 3,380	$ 8,750	$17,000

At December 31, 2001, the unadjusted balance in Allowance for Doubtful Accounts is a credit of $12,000.

Instructions

(a) Journalize and post the adjusting entry for bad debts at December 31, 2001.

(b) Journalize and post to the allowance account the following events and transactions in the year 2002.

(1) March 31, an $800 customer balance originating in 2001 is judged uncollectible.

(2) May 31, a check for $800 is received from the customer whose account was written off as uncollectible on March 31.

(c) Journalize the adjusting entry for bad debts on December 31, 2002, assuming that the unadjusted balance in Allowance for Doubtful Accounts is a debit of $800 and the aging schedule indicates that total estimated bad debts will be $30,300.

P9–4B At December 31, 2001, the trial balance of Lexington Company contained the following amounts before adjustment:

Journalize entries to record transactions related to bad debts.

(SO 3)

	Debits	Credits
Accounts Receivable	$400,000	
Allowance for Doubtful Accounts		$ 1,000
Sales		950,000

Instructions

(a) Based on the information given, which method of accounting for bad debts is Lexington Company using—the direct write-off method or the allowance method? How can you tell?

(b) Prepare the adjusting entry at December 31, 2001, for bad debt expense under each of the following independent assumptions:
   (1) An aging schedule indicates that $11,750 of accounts receivable will be uncollectible.
   (2) It is estimated that 1% of sales will be uncollectible.
(c) Repeat part (b) assuming that instead of a credit balance there is a $1,000 debit balance in the Allowance of Doubtful Accounts.
(d) During the next month, January 2002, a $5,000 account receivable is written off as uncollectible. Prepare the journal entry to record the write-off.
(e) Repeat part (d) assuming that Lexington uses the direct write-off method instead of the allowance method in accounting for uncollectible accounts receivable.
(f) ▨▧▧▧▷ What type of account is the allowance for doubtful accounts? How does it affect how accounts receivable is reported on the balance sheet at the end of the accounting period?

Prepare entries for various note receivable transactions.
(SO 2, 4, 5, 8, 9)

P9–5B   Cheryl French Company closes its books monthly. On September 30, selected ledger account balances are:

Notes Receivable	$23,200
Interest Receivable	$182.40

Notes Receivable include the following:

Date	Maker	Face	Term	Interest
Aug. 16	Valaitis Co.	$ 8,000	60 days	12%
Aug. 25	Jenelle Co.	5,200	60 days	12%
Sept. 30	Grumieaux Corp.	12,000	6 months	9%

Interest is computed using a 360-day year. During October, the following transactions were completed.

Oct. 7 Made sales of $6,900 on Cheryl French credit cards.
    12 Made sales of $750 on VISA credit cards. The credit card service charge is 4%.
    15 Added $485 to Cheryl French charge customer balance for finance charges on unpaid balances.
    15 Received payment in full from Valaitis Co. on the amount due.
    24 Received notice that Jenelle note has been dishonored. (Assume that Jenelle is expected to pay in future.)

Instructions
(a) Journalize the October transactions and the October 31 adjusting entry for accrued interest receivable.
(b) Enter the balances at October 1 in the receivable accounts and post the entries to all of the receivable accounts.
(c) Show the balance sheet presentation of the receivable accounts at October 31.

Prepare entries for various receivable transactions.
(SO 2, 4, 5, 6, 7, 8)

P9–6B   On January 1, 2001, Paul Gleason Company had Accounts Receivable $146,000, Notes Receivable $15,000, and Allowance for Doubtful Accounts $13,200. The note receivable is from the Linda Johnson Company. It is a 4-month, 12% note dated December 31, 2000. Paul Gleason Company prepares financial statements annually. During the year the following selected transactions occurred.

Jan.   5 Sold $16,000 of merchandise to George Company, terms n/15.
    20 Accepted George Company's $16,000, 3-month, 9% note for balance due.
Feb. 18 Sold $8,000 of merchandise to Swaim Company and accepted Swaim's $8,000, 6-month, 10% note for the amount due.
Apr. 20 Collected George Company note in full.
    30 Received payment in full from Linda Johnson Company on the amount due.
May   25 Accepted Avery Inc.'s $6,000, 3-month, 8% note in settlement of a past-due balance on account.
Aug. 18 Received payment in full from Swaim Company on note due.
    25 The Avery Inc. note was dishonored. Avery Inc. is not bankrupt and future payment is anticipated.
Sept. 1 Sold $10,000 of merchandise to Jose Trevino Company and accepted a $10,000, 6-month, 10% note for the amount due.

Instructions
Journalize the transactions.

P9–7B The balance sheets of Jonathan Elbert Corporation on December 31, 2001 and 2002, showed gross accounts receivable of $4,100,000 and $4,800,000, respectively. The balances in the Allowance for Doubtful Accounts at the end of 2001 and 2002—after adjusting entries— were $350,000 and $425,000, respectively. Accounts receivable written off amounted to $125,000 during 2001 and $150,000 during 2002.

Prepare journal entries for receivables and bad debts.
(SO 2, 3, 4)

All sales were made on account. Bad debts expense for each year was estimated as *one-half of 1% of sales.*

Instructions
Show (in summary form) all the journal entries made during 2002 that had an effect on Accounts Receivable or the Allowance for Doubtful Accounts. (*Hint:* You may find the use of T accounts helpful in analyzing this problem.)

BROADENING YOUR PERSPECTIVE

FINANCIAL REPORTING AND ANALYSIS
···

FINANCIAL REPORTING PROBLEM: Kellogg Company

BYP9–1 The receivables turnover ratio and the average collection period for receivables for Kellogg Company were computed in this chapter, based upon the company's financial statements for the year 1998. The 1998 financial statements (along with the 1997 financials) are presented in Kellogg's Annual Report and in Appendix A.

Instructions
(a) Compute Kellogg's receivables turnover ratio and average collection period for receivables for the year 1997. (Kellogg's accounts receivable at the end of 1996 amounted to $592.3 million.)
(b) Comment on any significant differences that you observe between the ratios for 1998 (as computed in the chapter) and those for 1997, as computed in part (a).

COMPARATIVE ANALYSIS PROBLEM: Kellogg Company vs. General Mills

BYP9–2 Kellogg's financial statements are presented in Appendix A; General Mills's financial statements are presented in Appendix B.

Instructions
(a) Based on the information contained in these financial statements, compute the following 1998 ratios for each company:
   1. Accounts receivable turnover ratio.
   2. Average collection period for receivables.
(b) What conclusions concerning the management of accounts receivable can be drawn from these data?

RESEARCH ASSIGNMENT

BYP9–3 The "Fortune 500" issue of *Fortune* magazine can serve as a useful reference. This annual issue of *Fortune*, generally appearing in late April or early May, contains a great deal of information regarding the largest U.S. industrial and service companies.

Instructions
Examine the most recent edition and answer the following questions.
(a) Identify the four largest U.S. corporations in terms of revenues, profits, assets, market value, and employees.
(b) Identify the largest corporation headquartered (or operating, if needed) in your state (by total revenue). How does this corporation rank in terms of revenues, profits, assets, market value, and number of employees?

INTERPRETING FINANCIAL STATEMENTS: Sears, Roebuck & Co.

BYP9–4   Sears is one of the world's largest retailers. It is also a huge provider of credit through its Sears credit card. Revenue generated from credit operations was $4.6 billion in 1998 from 30 million Sears cardholders. The rate of interest Sears earns on outstanding receivables varies from 10 to 21 percent in the United States to up to 28 percent in Canada. Managing these receivables is critical to the performance of the corporation. One aspect of receivables management is that in some instances, to acquire cash when needed, the company will sell its receivables. At December 31, 1998, Sears had sold $6.63 billion of its receivables.

The following information was available in Sears's 1998 financial statements (in millions of dollars).

SEARS

SEARS, ROEBUCK AND CO.
Data from 1998 Financial Statements

	1998	1997	1996
Accounts receivable (gross)	$18,946	$20,956	$22,371
Allowance for doubtful accounts	974	1,113	808
Merchandise sales	36,704	36,371	33,751
Credit revenues	4,618	4,925	4,313
Bad debts expense	1,287	1,532	971

Instructions
 (a) Discuss whether the sale of receivables by Sears represents a significant portion of its receivables. Why might Sears have sold these receivables? As an investor, what concerns might you have about these sales?
 (b) Calculate and discuss the accounts receivable turnover ratio and average collection period for Sears for 1998 and 1997.
 (c) Do you think Sears provides credit as a revenue-generating activity, or as a convenience for its customers?
 (d) Compute the ratio of Bad Debt Expense to Merchandise sales for 1998 and 1997. Did this ratio improve or get worse? What considerations should Sears make in deciding whether it wants to have liberal or conservative policies?

REAL-WORLD FOCUS: Art World Industries, Inc.

BYP9–5   **Art World Industries, Inc.** was incorporated in 1986 in Delaware, though it is located in Los Angeles. The company employs 25 people to print, publish, and sell limited edition graphics and reproductive prints in the wholesale market.

The operating expenses for the fiscal year for Art World Industries, Inc., include bad debts expense of $6,715.50. The balance sheet shows an allowance for doubtful accounts of $175,477. The allowance was set up against certain Japanese accounts receivable which average over one year in age. The Japanese acknowledge the amount due, but with the slow economy in Japan lack the resources to pay at this time.

Instructions
 (a) Which basis for estimating uncollectible accounts does Art World Industries use?
 (b) When Art World makes its adjusting entry to record bad debts expense must it consider a previous existing balance in the Allowance for Doubtful Accounts?
 (c) Explain the difference between the percentage of sales and percentage of receivables methods. In applying either of these methods, based on Art World's disclosure above, what important factor would you have to consider in arriving at appropriate percentages to apply?

CRITICAL THINKING

GROUP DECISION CASE

BYP9-6   Linda and Gene Shumway own Somonauk Fashions. From its inception Somonauk Fashions has sold merchandise on either a cash or credit basis, but no credit cards have been accepted. During the past several months, the Shumways have begun to question their sales policies. First, they have lost some sales because of refusing to accept credit cards. Second, representatives of two metropolitan banks have been persuasive in convincing them to accept their national credit cards. One bank, City National Bank, has stated that (1) its credit card fee is 4%, and (2) it pays the retailer 96 cents on each $1 of sales within 3 days of receiving the credit card billings.

The Shumways decide that they should determine the cost of carrying their own credit sales. From the accounting records of the past three years they accumulate the following data:

	1999	1998	1997
Net credit sales	$500,000	$600,000	$400,000
Collection agency fees for slow paying customers	2,450	2,500	2,400
Salary of part-time accounts receivable clerk	3,800	3,800	3,800

Credit and collection expenses as a percentage of net credit sales: uncollectible accounts 1.6%, billing and mailing costs 0.5%, and credit investigation fee on new customers 0.15%.

Linda and Gene also determine that the average accounts receivable balance outstanding during the year is 5% of net credit sales. The Shumways estimate that they could earn an average of 10% annually on cash invested in other business opportunities.

Instructions
With the class divided into groups, answer the following:

(a) Prepare a tabulation showing for each year total credit and collection expenses in dollars and as a percentage of net credit sales.
(b) Determine the net credit and collection expense in dollars and as a percentage of sales after considering the revenue not earned from other investment opportunities. (*Note:* The income lost on the cash held by the bank for 3 days is considered to be immaterial.)
(c) Discuss both the financial and nonfinancial factors that are relevant to the decision.

COMMUNICATION ACTIVITY

BYP9-7   Jackie Henning, a friend of yours who knows little about accounting, asks you to help make sense of a discussion she overheard at work about changes her employer wants to make in accounting for uncollectible accounts. Specifically, she asks you to explain the differences between the percentage of sales, percentage of receivables, and the direct write-off methods for uncollectible accounts.

Instructions
In a letter of one page (or less), explain to Jackie the three methods of accounting for uncollectibles. Be sure to discuss differences among these methods.

ETHICS CASE

BYP9-8   Jacket Co. is a subsidiary of Suit Corp. The controller believes that the yearly allowance for doubtful accounts for Jacket Co. should be 2% of net credit sales. The president of Jacket Co., nervous that the parent company might expect the subsidiary to sustain its 10% growth rate, suggests that the controller increase the allowance for doubtful accounts to 4%. The president thinks that the lower net income, which reflects a 6% growth rate, will be a more sustainable rate for Jacket Co.

Instructions
(a) Who are the stakeholders in this case?
(b) Does the president's request pose an ethical dilemma for the controller?
(c) Should the controller be concerned with Jacket Co.'s growth rate in estimating the allowance? Explain your answer.

SURFING THE NET

BYP9–9   The Security Exchange Act of 1934 requires any firm that is listed on one of the national exchanges to file annual reports (form 10-K), financial statements, and quarterly reports (form 10-Q) with the SEC. This exercise demonstrates how to search and access available SEC filings through the Internet.

Address: http://biz.yahoo.com/i (May use SEC address instead.)

Steps:
1. Type in a company's name, or use index to find a company name.
2. Choose **profile**.
3. Choose **SEC Filings**.

Instructions
Answer the following questions:

(a) Which SEC filings were available for the company you selected?
(b) In the company's quarterly report (SEC Form 10Q), what was one key point discussed in the "Management's Discussion and Analysis of Results of Operations and Financial Condition"?
(c) What was the net income for the period selected?

Answers to Self-Study Questions
1. c   2. a   3. b   4. b   5. d   6. c   7. c   8. a   9. b   10. d

---

Answer to Kellogg Review It Question 6, p. 385
Concentrations of credit risk with respect to accounts receivable are limited due to (1) the large number of customers, (2) generally short payment terms, and (3) their dispersion across geographic areas.

Remember to go back to the Navigator box on the chapter-opening page and check off your completed work.

Before studying this chapter, you should know or, if necessary, review:

a. The time period assumption. (Ch. 3, pp. 92–93)
b. The cost principle. (Ch. 1, p. 9) and the matching principle. (Ch. 3, pp. 93–94)
c. What is depreciation? (Ch. 3, p. 99)
d. How to make adjustments for depreciation. (Ch. 3, pp. 99–100)

THE NAVIGATOR

FEATURE STORY

On the Books, Your Classroom May Be Worthless

Take a stroll around your campus. Some of those buildings were built before you were born. How much do you think they cost to build? Are they depreciating? Are they appreciating?

These questions are not merely academic. It costs millions of dollars to construct, maintain, and sometimes demolish these campus buildings. Where does the money come from? Partly your tuition, perhaps tax dollars, perhaps from contributions of wealthy alumni, or from long-term borrowing. How these dollars are allocated can depend upon a reasonable estimate of a building's condition, its remaining life—and of course, how much it would cost to replace (its replacement cost).

At Westbrook College in Portland, Maine, Ms. Betty-Ann Doucette, the school's controller, recently researched the age of certain buildings on campus. The reason: a recent Financial Accounting Standards Board rule mandates that private colleges report fixed assets and depreciate them. Ms. Doucette found that some of the college's buildings go back to the nineteenth century. In order to value each building, she tried to find original construction costs and periodic renovations costs, as well as current replacement costs.

"For example, the building I'm in, Goddard Hall, was built in the early part of this century," says Ms. Doucette. "It's now being depreciated over 40 years, and because it's over eighty years old, I show it as fully depreciated." If it is fully depreciated, does that mean it has a zero value? "On the books it says it does," she says. Of course, that doesn't mean it's worthless. An asset can have a zero value on the books yet have a substantial market value.

THE NAVIGATOR

CHAPTER 10

THE NAVIGATOR ✔

- Understand *Concepts for Review* ☐
- Read *Feature Story* ☐
- Scan *Study Objectives* ☐
- Read *Preview* ☐
- Read text and answer *Before You Go On*
  p. 417 ☐ p. 428 ☐ p. 431 ☐ p. 438 ☐
- Work *Demonstration Problems* ☐
- Review *Summary of Study Objectives* ☐
- Answer *Self-Study Questions* ☐
- Complete assignments ☐

PLANT ASSETS, NATURAL RESOURCES, AND INTANGIBLE ASSETS

STUDY OBJECTIVES

After studying this chapter, you should be able to:

1. Describe the application of the cost principle to plant assets.
2. Explain the concept of depreciation.
3. Compute periodic depreciation using different methods.
4. Describe the procedure for revising periodic depreciation.
5. Distinguish between revenue and capital expenditures and explain the entries for these expenditures.
6. Explain how to account for the disposal of a plant asset through retirement, sale, or exchange.
7. Identify the basic accounting issues related to natural resources.
8. Contrast the accounting for intangible assets with the accounting for plant assets.
9. Indicate how plant assets, natural resources, and intangible assets are reported and analyzed.

THE NAVIGATOR

*A*s you can see, the accounting for campus buildings at Westbrook College is complex. In this chapter, we explain the application of the cost principle of accounting to buildings like those at Westbrook, as well as to natural resources and intangible assets such as Westbrook's school logo. We also describe the methods that may be used to allocate an asset's cost over its useful life. In addition, the accounting for expenditures incurred during the useful life of assets is discussed. The content and organization of this chapter are as follows:

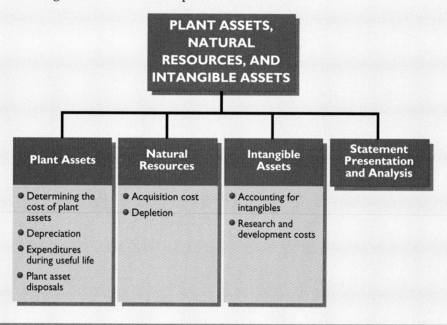

THE NAVIGATOR

SECTION 1 PLANT ASSETS

Plant assets are tangible resources that are used in the operations of the business and are not intended for sale to customers. They are also called **property, plant, and equipment; plant and equipment**; or **fixed assets**. These assets are generally long-lived and are expected to provide services to the company for a number of years. Except for land, plant assets decline in service potential over their useful lives.

Many companies have substantial investments in plant assets. In public utility companies, for example, net plant assets (plant assets less accumulated depreciation) often represent more than 70% of total assets. Recently net plant assets were 88% of American Water Works Company's total assets and 73% of Northern Illinois Gas Company's total assets. In other types of companies the percentages of plant assets to total assets were:

ILLUSTRATION 10-1

Percentages of plant assets to total assets

Burlington Northern Santa Fe Corporation	91%	General Motors Corporation	37%
McDonald's	86%	Delta Airlines	82%
Sears, Roebuck	17%	Compaq Computer	13%

In the income statement, the relationship of depreciation expense and maintenance expense to total operating expenses was 12.3% for Burlington Northern Santa Fe Corporation (railway), 9.6% for Delta Airlines, and 6.2% for General Motors.

Plant assets are often subdivided into four classes:

1. **Land**, such as a building site.
2. **Land improvements**, such as driveways, parking lots, fences, and underground sprinkler systems.
3. **Buildings**, such as stores, offices, factories, and warehouses.
4. **Equipment**, such as store check-out counters, cash registers, coolers, office furniture, factory machinery, and delivery equipment.

Like the purchase of a home by an individual, the acquisition of plant assets is an important decision for a business enterprise. It is also important for a business enterprise to (1) keep the asset in good operating condition, (2) replace worn-out or outdated facilities, and (3) expand its productive resources as needed. The decline of rail travel in the United States can be traced in part to the failure of railroad companies to meet the first two conditions. Conversely, the growth of air travel in this country can be attributed in part to the general willingness of airline companies to observe these essential conditions.

DETERMINING THE COST OF PLANT ASSETS

Plant assets are recorded at cost in accordance with the **cost principle** of accounting. Thus the buildings at Westbrook College are recorded at cost. Cost consists of all expenditures necessary to acquire the asset and make it ready for its intended use. For example, the purchase price, freight costs paid by the purchaser, and installation costs are all considered part of the cost of factory machinery.

Cost is measured by the cash paid in a cash transaction or by the cash equivalent price paid when noncash assets are used in payment. **The cash equivalent price is equal to the fair market value of the asset given up or the fair market value of the asset received, whichever is more clearly determinable.** Once cost is established, it becomes the basis of accounting for the plant asset over its useful life. Current market or replacement values are not used after acquisition. The application of the cost principle to each of the major classes of plant assets is explained in the following sections.

Land

The cost of land includes (1) the cash purchase price, (2) closing costs such as title and attorney's fees, (3) real estate brokers' commissions, and (4) accrued property taxes and other liens on the land assumed by the purchaser. For example, if the cash price is $50,000 and the purchaser agrees to pay accrued taxes of $5,000, the cost of the land is $55,000.

All necessary costs incurred in making land **ready for its intended use** are debited to the Land account. When vacant land is acquired, these costs include expenditures for clearing, draining, filling, and grading. Sometimes the land has a building on it that must be removed to make the site suitable for construction of a new building. In this case, all demolition and removal costs less any proceeds from salvaged materials are chargeable to the Land account. To illustrate,

1
STUDY
OBJECTIVE

Describe the application of the cost principle to plant assets.

INTERNATIONAL NOTE

The United Kingdom (UK) is more flexible regarding asset valuation. Most companies in the UK make occasional revaluations to fair value when they believe this information is more relevant. Other examples of countries that permit revaluations are Switzerland and the Netherlands.

HELPFUL HINT

Management's intended use is important in applying the cost principle.

assume that Hayes Manufacturing Company acquires real estate at a cash cost of $100,000. The property contains an old warehouse that is razed at a net cost of $6,000 ($7,500 in costs less $1,500 proceeds from salvaged materials). Additional expenditures consist of the attorney's fee, $1,000, and the real estate broker's commission, $8,000. Given these factors, the cost of the land is $115,000, computed as follows:

ILLUSTRATION 10-2

Computation of cost of land

Land	
Cash price of property	$100,000
Net removal cost of warehouse	6,000
Attorney's fee	1,000
Real estate broker's commission	8,000
Cost of land	**$115,000**

In recording the acquisition, Land is debited for $115,000 and Cash is credited for $115,000.

Land Improvements

The cost of land improvements includes all expenditures necessary to make the improvements ready for their intended use. For example, the cost of a new company parking lot will include the amount paid for paving, fencing, and lighting. These improvements have limited useful lives and their maintenance and replacement are the responsibility of the company. Thus, these costs are debited to Land Improvements and are depreciated over the useful lives of the improvements.

Buildings

All necessary expenditures relating to the purchase or construction of a building are charged to the Buildings account. When a building is purchased, such costs include the **purchase price, closing costs (attorney's fees, title insurance, etc.), and real estate broker's commission**. Costs to make the building ready for its intended use consist of **expenditures for remodeling rooms and offices and replacing or repairing the roof, floors, electrical wiring, and plumbing**.

When a new building is constructed, such as a new science building by Westbrook College, cost consists of the contract price plus payments made by the owner for architects' fees, building permits, and excavation costs. In addition, interest costs incurred to finance the project are included in the cost of the asset when a significant period of time is required to get the asset ready for use. In these circumstances, interest costs are considered as necessary as materials and labor. The inclusion of interest costs in the cost of a constructed building is **limited to the construction period**. When construction has been completed, subsequent interest payments on funds borrowed to finance the construction are debited to Interest Expense.

Equipment

HELPFUL HINT
Two criteria apply in determining cost here: (1) the frequency of the cost—one-time or recurring, and (2) the benefit period—life of asset or one year.

The cost of equipment consists of the **cash purchase price, sales taxes, freight charges, and insurance during transit paid by the purchaser**. It also includes **expenditures required in assembling, installing, and testing the unit**. However, motor vehicle licenses and accident insurance on company trucks and cars are expensed as incurred, because they represent annual recurring expenditures and do not benefit future periods.

To illustrate, assume that the Lenard Company purchases a delivery truck at a cash price of $22,000. Related expenditures consist of sales taxes $1,320, painting and lettering $500, motor vehicle license $80, and a 3-year accident insurance policy $1,600. The cost of the delivery truck is $23,820, computed as follows:

Delivery Truck

Cash price	$22,000
Sales taxes	1,320
Painting and lettering	500
Cost of delivery truck	**$23,820**

ILLUSTRATION 10-3

Computation of cost of delivery truck

The motor vehicle license is expensed when incurred, and the insurance policy is a prepaid asset. Thus, the summary entry to record the purchase of the truck and related expenditures is:

Delivery Truck	23,820	
License Expense	80	
Prepaid Insurance	1,600	
Cash		25,500
(To record purchase of delivery truck and related expenditures)		

A	=	L	+	SE
+ 23,820				−80
+ 1,600				
−25,500				

For another example, assume the Merten Company purchases factory machinery at a cash price of $50,000. Related expenditures consist of sales taxes $3,000, insurance during shipping $500, and installation and testing $1,000. The cost of the factory machinery is $54,500 computed as follows:

Factory Machinery

Cash price	$50,000
Sales taxes	3,000
Insurance during shipping	500
Installation and testing	1,000
Cost of factory machinery	**$54,500**

ILLUSTRATION 10-4

Computation of cost of factory machinery

The summary entry to record the purchase and related expenditures is:

Factory Machinery	54,500	
Cash		54,500
(To record purchase of factory machine)		

A	=	L	+	SE
+54,500				
−54,500				

DEPRECIATION

As explained in Chapter 3, **depreciation is the process of allocating to expense the cost of a plant asset over its useful (service) life in a rational and systematic manner.** Cost allocation is designed to provide for the proper matching of expenses with revenues in accordance with the matching principle (see Illustration 10-5).

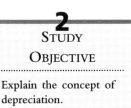

2

STUDY

OBJECTIVE

Explain the concept of depreciation.

ILLUSTRATION 10-5

Depreciation as an allocation concept

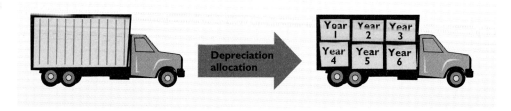

Depreciation is a process of cost allocation, not a process of asset valuation. Accountants make no attempt to measure the change in an asset's market value during ownership, because plant assets are not held for resale. Thus, the **book value** (cost less accumulated depreciation) of a plant asset may differ significantly from its market value. This is why Goddard Hall, in the Feature Story, can have zero book value and still have substantial market value.

Depreciation applies to three classes of plant assets: land improvements, buildings, and equipment. Each of these classes is considered to be a **depreciable asset**, because the usefulness to the company and revenue-producing ability of each class will decline over the asset's useful life. Depreciation does not apply to land because its usefulness and revenue-producing ability generally remain intact as long as the asset is owned. In fact, in many cases, the usefulness of land is greater over time because of the scarcity of good land sites. Thus, **land is not a depreciable asset**.

During a depreciable asset's useful life its revenue-producing ability will decline because of **wear and tear**. A delivery truck that has been driven 100,000 miles will be less useful to a company than one driven only 800 miles. Similarly, trucks and planes exposed to snow and salt will deteriorate faster than equipment that is not exposed to these elements.

A decline in revenue-producing ability may also occur because of **obsolescence**. Obsolescence is the process of becoming out of date before the asset physically wears out. The rerouting of major airlines from Chicago's Midway Airport to Chicago-O'Hare International Airport because Midway's runways were too short for jumbo jets is an example. Likewise, diesel train engines made coal-burning locomotives obsolete, and municipal buses sent streetcars to the scrap heap.

Recognition of depreciation does not result in the accumulation of cash for the replacement of the asset. The balance in Accumulated Depreciation represents the total cost that has been charged to expense; it is not a cash fund.

Factors in Computing Depreciation

Three factors affect the computation of depreciation, as shown in Illustration 10-6.

1. **Cost.** Considerations affecting the cost of a depreciable asset have been explained earlier in this chapter. You will recall that plant assets are recorded at cost, in accordance with the cost principle of accounting.

ILLUSTRATION 10-6

Three factors in computing depreciation

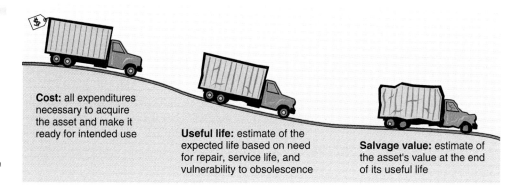

Cost: all expenditures necessary to acquire the asset and make it ready for intended use

Useful life: estimate of the expected life based on need for repair, service life, and vulnerability to obsolescence

Salvage value: estimate of the asset's value at the end of its useful life

2. **Useful life.** Useful life is an estimate of the expected productive life, also called service life, of the asset. Useful life may be expressed in terms of time, units of activity such as machine hours, or in units of output. Like salvage value, useful life is an estimate. In making the estimate, management should consider such factors as the intended use of the asset, its expected repair and maintenance policies, and its vulnerability to obsolescence. The company's past experience with similar assets is often helpful in deciding on expected useful life.

3. **Salvage value.** Salvage value is an estimate of the asset's value at the end of its useful life. The value may be based on the asset's worth as scrap or salvage or on its expected trade-in value. Salvage value is an estimate. In making the estimate, management should consider how it plans to dispose of the asset and its experience with similar assets.

ALTERNATIVE TERMINOLOGY
Another term sometimes used for salvage value is *residual value*.

ACCOUNTING IN ACTION
Business Insight

Willamette Industries, Inc., of Portland, Oregon, said in March 1999 that it would change its accounting estimates relating to depreciation of certain assets, beginning with the first quarter of 1999. The vertically integrated forest products company said the changes were due to advances in technology that have increased the service life on its equipment an extra 5 years. Willamette expected the accounting changes to increase its 1999 full-year earnings by about $57 million, or $0.52 a share. Its 1998 earnings were $89 million, or $0.80 a share. Imagine a 65% improvement in earnings per share from a mere change in the estimated life of equipment!

BEFORE YOU GO ON . . .
Review It

1. What are plant assets? What are the major classes of plant assets? How is the cost principle applied to accounting for plant assets?
2. What is the relationship, if any, of depreciation to (a) cost allocation, (b) asset valuation, and (c) cash accumulation?
3. Explain the factors that affect the computation of depreciation.
4. Where does Kellogg report the detail about its "Property, net" of $2,888.8 million? What classifications and amounts does Kellogg report in the details of its "Property, net" for 1998? The answer to this question is provided on page 458.

Do It

Assume that a delivery truck is purchased for $15,000 cash, plus sales taxes of $900 and delivery costs to the dealer of $500. The buyer also pays $200 for painting and lettering, $600 for an annual insurance policy, and $80 for a motor vehicle license. Explain how each of these costs would be accounted for.

Reasoning: The cost principle applies to all expenditures made in order to get delivery equipment ready for its intended use. The principle does not apply to operating costs incurred during the useful life of the equipment, such as gas and oil, motor tune-ups, and insurance.

Solution: The first four payments ($15,000, $900, $500, and $200) are considered to be expenditures necessary to make the truck ready for its intended use. Thus, the cost of the truck is $16,600. The payments for insurance and the license are considered to be operating expenses incurred during the useful life of the asset.

Related exercise material: BE10–1, BE10–2, E10–1, and E10–2.

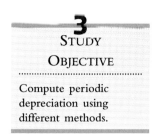

3
STUDY
OBJECTIVE

Compute periodic
depreciation using
different methods.

Depreciation Methods

Depreciation is generally computed using one of the following methods:

1. Straight-line
2. Units-of-activity
3. Declining-balance

Like the inventory methods discussed in Chapter 6, each depreciation method is acceptable under generally accepted accounting principles. Management selects the method or methods it believes to be appropriate in the circumstances. The objective is to select the method that best measures the asset's contribution to revenue over its useful life. Once a method is chosen, it should be applied consistently over the useful life of the asset. Consistency enhances the comparability of financial statements.

To facilitate the comparison of the three depreciation methods, we will base all computations on the following data applicable to a small delivery truck purchased by Barb's Florists on January 1, 2001:

ILLUSTRATION 10-7

Delivery truck data

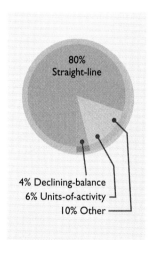

ILLUSTRATION 10-8

Use of depreciation methods

ILLUSTRATION 10-9

Formula for straight-line method

Cost	$13,000
Expected salvage value	$ 1,000
Estimated useful life in years	5
Estimated useful life in miles	100,000

Depreciation affects the balance sheet through accumulated depreciation and the income statement through depreciation expense. Illustration 10-8 shows the use of the different depreciation methods in 600 of the largest companies in the United States.

Straight-Line

Under the straight-line method, depreciation is the same for each year of the asset's useful life. It is measured solely by the passage of time. In order to compute depreciation expense, it is necessary to determine depreciable cost. Depreciable cost is the cost of the asset less its salvage value. It is the total amount subject to depreciation. Depreciable cost is then divided by the asset's useful life to determine depreciation expense. The formula and computation of depreciation expense in the first year for Barb's Florists are shown in Illustration 10-9.

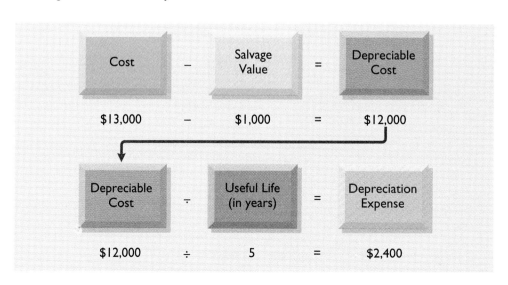

Alternatively, we also can compute an annual rate at which the delivery truck is being depreciated. In this case, the rate is 20% (100% ÷ 5 years). When an annual rate is used under the straight-line method, the percentage rate is applied to the depreciable cost of the asset, as shown in the following **depreciation schedule**:

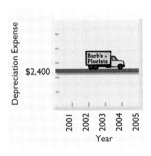

ILLUSTRATION 10-10

Straight-line depreciation schedule

	BARB'S FLORISTS				
	Computation		Annual	End of Year	
Year	Depreciable Cost	× Depreciation Rate	= Depreciation Expense	Accumulated Depreciation	Book Value
2001	$12,000	20%	**$2,400**	$ 2,400	$10,600*
2002	12,000	20	**2,400**	4,800	8,200
2003	12,000	20	**2,400**	7,200	5,800
2004	12,000	20	**2,400**	9,600	3,400
2005	12,000	20	**2,400**	12,000	**1,000**

*($13,000 – $2,400).

Note that the depreciation expense of $2,400 is the same each year, and that the book value at the end of the useful life is equal to the estimated $1,000 salvage value.

What happens when an asset is purchased **during** the year, rather than on January 1, as in our example? In that case, it is necessary to **prorate the annual depreciation** for the proportion of time used. If Barb's Florists had purchased the delivery truck on April 1, 2001, the depreciation for 2001 would be $1,800 ($12,000 × 20% × 9/12 of a year).

The straight-line method predominates in practice, as shown in Illustration 10-8. For example, such large companies as Campbell Soup, Marriott Corporation, and General Mills use the straight-line method. It is simple to apply, and it matches expenses with revenues appropriately when the use of the asset is reasonably uniform throughout the service life. In the opening story, Westbrook College is probably using the straight-line method of depreciation for its buildings.

HELPFUL HINT

Depreciation stops when the asset's book value equals expected salvage value.

Units-of-Activity

Under the units-of-activity method, instead of expressing the life as a time period, useful life is expressed in terms of the total units of production or use expected from the asset. The units-of-activity method is ideally suited to factory machinery: production can be measured in terms of units of output or in terms of machine hours used in operating the machinery. It is also possible to use this method for such items as delivery equipment (miles driven) and airplanes (hours in use). The units-of-activity method is generally not suitable for such assets as buildings or furniture, because depreciation for these assets is more a function of time than of use.

To use this method, the total units of activity for the entire useful life are estimated, the amount is divided into depreciable cost to determine the depreciation cost per unit. The depreciation cost per unit is then applied to the units of activity during the year to determine the annual depreciation. To illustrate, assume that the delivery truck of Barb's Florists is driven 15,000 miles in the first year. The formula and computation of depreciation expense in the first year are:

ALTERNATIVE TERMINOLOGY

Another term often used is the *units-of-production method.*

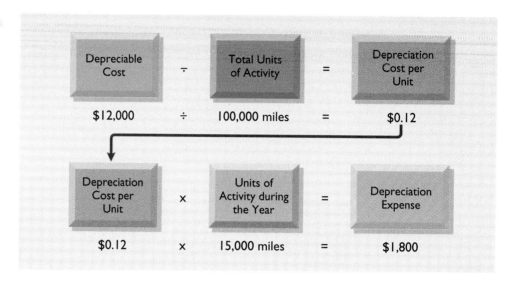

The depreciation schedule, using assumed mileage data, is as follows:

ILLUSTRATION 10-12

Units-of-activity depreciation schedule

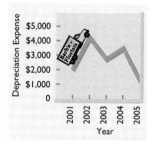

	Computation			Annual	End of Year	
Year	Units of Activity	× Depreciation Cost/Unit	=	Depreciation Expense	Accumulated Depreciation	Book Value
2001	15,000	$.12		**$1,800**	$ 1,800	$11,200*
2002	30,000	.12		**3,600**	5,400	7,600
2003	20,000	.12		**2,400**	7,800	5,200
2004	25,000	.12		**3,000**	10,800	2,200
2005	10,000	.12		**1,200**	12,000	**1,000**

BARB'S FLORISTS

*($13,000 – $1,800).

The units-of-activity method is not nearly as popular as the straight-line method (see Illustration 10-8), primarily because it is often difficult to make a reasonable estimate of total activity. However, this method is used by some very large companies, such as Standard Oil Company of California and Boise Cascade Corporation. When the productivity of the asset varies significantly from one period to another, the units-of-activity method results in the best matching of expenses with revenues. This method is easy to apply when assets are purchased during the year. In such a case, the productivity of the asset for the partial year is used in computing the depreciation.

Declining-Balance

The declining-balance method produces a decreasing annual depreciation expense over the useful life of the asset. The method is so named because the computation of periodic depreciation is based on a **declining book value** (cost less accumulated depreciation) of the asset. Annual depreciation expense is computed by multiplying the book value at the beginning of the year by the declining-balance depreciation rate. **The depreciation rate remains constant from year to year, but the book value to which the rate is applied declines each year.**

Book value for the first year is the cost of the asset, because the balance in accumulated depreciation at the beginning of the asset's useful life is zero. In subsequent years, book value is the difference between cost and accumulated

HELPFUL HINT

Book value is variable and the depreciation rate is constant for this method.

depreciation at the beginning of the year. **Unlike the other depreciation methods, salvage value is ignored in determining the amount to which the declining balance rate is applied.** Salvage value, however, does limit the total depreciation that can be taken. Depreciation stops when the asset's book value equals expected salvage value.

A common declining-balance rate is double the straight-line rate. As a result, the method is often referred to as the **double-declining-balance method**. If Barb's Florists uses the double-declining-balance method, the depreciation rate is 40% (2 × the straight-line rate of 20%). The formula and computation of depreciation for the first year on the delivery truck are:

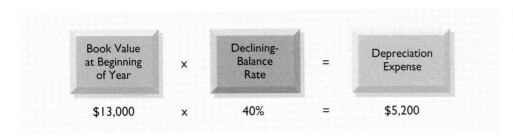

ILLUSTRATION 10-13

Formula for declining-balance method

The depreciation schedule under this method is as follows:

ILLUSTRATION 10-14

Double-declining-balance depreciation schedule

BARB'S FLORISTS

Year	Book Value Beginning of Year	× Depreciation Rate =	Annual Depreciation Expense	Accumulated Depreciation	Book Value
2001	$13,000	40%	**5,200**	$ 5,200	$7,800
2002	7,800	40	**3,120**	8,320	4,680
2003	4,680	40	**1,872**	10,192	2,808
2004	2,808	40	**1,123**	11,315	1,685
2005	1,685	40	685*	12,000	**1,000**

The "Computation" heading spans Book Value Beginning of Year and Depreciation Rate. "End of Year" spans Accumulated Depreciation and Book Value.

*Computation of $674 ($1,685 x 40%) is adjusted to $685 in order for book value to equal salvage value.

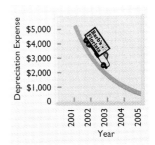

You can see that the delivery equipment is 69% depreciated ($8,320 ÷ $12,000) at the end of the second year. Under the straight-line method it would be depreciated 40% ($4,800 ÷ $12,000) at that time. Because the declining-balance method produces higher depreciation expense in the early years than in the later years, it is considered an accelerated-depreciation method. The declining balance method is compatible with the matching principle. The higher depreciation expense in early years is matched with the higher benefits received in these years. Conversely, lower depreciation expense is recognized in later years when the asset's contribution to revenue is less. Also, some assets lose usefulness rapidly because of obsolescence. In these cases, the declining-balance method provides a more appropriate depreciation amount.

When an asset is purchased during the year, it is necessary to prorate the declining-balance depreciation in the first year on a time basis. For example, if Barb's Florists had purchased the delivery equipment on April 1, 2001, depreciation for 2001 would become $3,900 ($13,000 × 40% × 9/12). The book value for computing depreciation in 2002 then becomes $9,100 ($13,000 − $3,900), and the 2002 depreciation is $3,640 ($9,100 × 40%).

HELPFUL HINT

The method designed for an asset that is expected to be more productive in the first half of its useful life is the declining-balance method.

ACCOUNTING IN ACTION
Business Insight

Why does Gingiss Formal Wear have 70 depreciation accounts and use the units-of-activity method for its tuxedos? The reason is that Gingiss wants to track wear and tear on each of its 16,000 dinner jackets individually. So each tuxedo has a bar code, like a box of cereal at the supermarket. When a tux is rented, a clerk runs its code across an electronic scanner. At year-end, the computer adds up the total rentals for each of 15 styles, then divides by expected total use to compute the rate. For instance, on one dolphin-gray tux, Gingiss expects a life of 30 rentals. In a recent year the tux was rented 13 times. So depreciation that period was 43% ($13 \div 30$) of the total cost.

Comparison of Methods

A comparison of annual and total depreciation expense under each of the three methods is shown for Barb's Florists in Illustration 10-15.

ILLUSTRATION 10-15

Comparison of depreciation methods

Year	Straight-Line	Units-of-Activity	Declining-Balance
2001	$ 2,400	$ 1,800	$ 5,200
2002	2,400	3,600	3,120
2003	2,400	2,400	1,872
2004	2,400	3,000	1,123
2005	2,400	1,200	685
	$12,000	$12,000	$12,000

Observe that periodic depreciation varies considerably among the methods, but total depreciation is the same for the 5-year period. Each method is acceptable in accounting, because each recognizes the decline in service potential of the asset in a rational and systematic manner. The depreciation expense pattern under each method is presented graphically in Illustration 10-16.

ILLUSTRATION 10-16

Patterns of depreciation

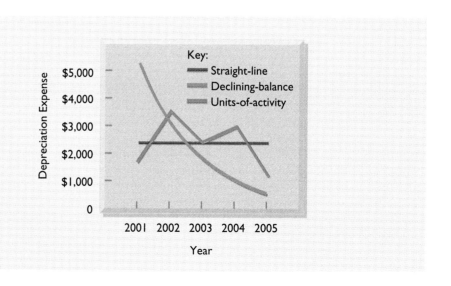

Depreciation and Income Taxes

The Internal Revenue Service (IRS) allows corporate taxpayers to deduct depreciation expense when computing taxable income. However, the IRS does not require the taxpayer to use the same depreciation method on the tax return that is used in preparing financial statements. Consequently, many corporations use straight-line in their financial statements to maximize net income, and at the same time, a special accelerated-depreciation method is generally used on their tax returns to minimize their income taxes. Taxpayers must use on their tax returns either the straight-line method or a special accelerated-depreciation method called **Modified Accelerated Cost Recovery System** (MACRS).

INTERNATIONAL NOTE

In Germany, tax laws have a strong influence on financial accounting. Depreciation expense determined by the tax code must also be used for preparing financial statements.

Revising Periodic Depreciation

Depreciation is one example of the estimation procedures that are part of the accounting process. Annual depreciation expense should be reviewed periodically by management. If wear and tear or obsolescence indicate that annual depreciation is inadequate or excessive, a change in the amount should be made.

When a change in an estimate is required, the change is made in **current and future years but not to prior periods**. Thus, (1) there is no correction of previously recorded depreciation expense, and (2) depreciation expense for current and future years is revised. The rationale: continual restatement of prior periods would adversely affect the reader's confidence in financial statements.

To determine the new annual depreciation expense, we compute the asset's depreciable cost at the time of the revision and allocate it to the remaining useful life. To illustrate, assume that Barb's Florists decides on January 1, 2004, to extend the useful life of the truck one year because of its excellent condition. The company has used the straight-line method to depreciate the asset to date, and book value is $5,800 ($13,000 − $7,200). The new annual depreciation is $1,600, computed as follows:

4
STUDY
OBJECTIVE

Describe the procedure for revising periodic depreciation.

Book value, 1/1/04	$5,800	
Less: Salvage value	1,000	
Depreciable cost	$4,800	
Remaining useful life	3 years	(2004–2006)
Revised annual depreciation ($4,800 ÷ 3)	**$1,600**	

ILLUSTRATION 10-17

Revised depreciation computation

On January 1, 2004, or at any other time, Barb's Florists makes no entry for the change in estimate. On December 31, 2004, during the preparation of adjusting entries, it would record depreciation expense of $1,600. Significant changes in estimates must be described in the financial statements.

HELPFUL HINT

Use a step-by-step approach: (1) determine new depreciable cost; (2) divide by remaining useful life.

EXPENDITURES DURING USEFUL LIFE

During the useful life of a plant asset a company may incur costs for ordinary repairs, additions, and improvements. Ordinary repairs are expenditures to maintain the operating efficiency and expected productive life of the unit. They usually are fairly small amounts that occur frequently throughout the asset's service life. Motor tune-ups and oil changes, the painting of buildings, and the replacing of worn-out gears on factory machinery are examples. They are debited to Repair (or Maintenance) Expense as incurred. Because they are

5
STUDY
OBJECTIVE

Distinguish between revenue and capital expenditures and explain the entries for these expenditures.

immediately charged against revenues as an expense, these costs are often referred to as revenue expenditures.

Additions and improvements are costs incurred to increase the operating efficiency, productive capacity, or expected useful life of the plant asset. These expenditures are usually material in amount and occur infrequently during the period of ownership. Expenditures for additions and improvements increase the company's investment in productive facilities and are generally debited to the plant asset affected. Accordingly, they are often referred to as capital expenditures. Most major U.S. corporations disclose the amount of their annual capital expenditures. In a recent year, both IBM and General Motors reported capital expenditures slightly in excess of $6 billion. The accounting for capital expenditures varies depending on the nature of the expenditure.

PLANT ASSET DISPOSALS

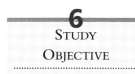

6
STUDY
OBJECTIVE

Explain how to account for the disposal of a plant asset through retirement, sale, or exchange.

Plant assets of various types may be disposed of in three ways, as shown in Illustration 10-18. Whatever the method of disposal, at the time of disposal it is necessary to determine the book value of the plant asset. The book value is the difference between the cost of the plant asset and the accumulated depreciation to date. If the disposal occurs at any time during the year, depreciation for the fraction of the year to the date of disposal must be recorded. The book value is then eliminated by debiting Accumulated Depreciation for the total depreciation to the date of disposal and crediting the asset account for the cost of the asset. In this section we will examine the accounting for each of the three methods of plant asset disposal.

Retirement
Equipment is scrapped or discarded.

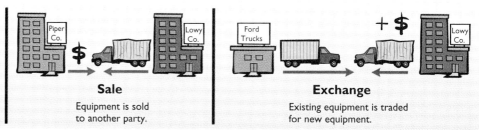

Sale
Equipment is sold to another party.

Exchange
Existing equipment is traded for new equipment.

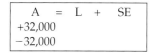

ILLUSTRATION 10-18

Methods of plant asset disposal

Retirement of Plant Assets

To illustrate the accounting for a retirement of plant assets, assume that Hobart Enterprises retires its computer printers, which cost $32,000. The accumulated depreciation on these printers is also $32,000; the equipment, therefore, is fully depreciated (zero book value). The entry to record this retirement is as follows:

A = L + SE
+32,000
−32,000

Accumulated Depreciation—Printing Equipment	32,000	
Printing Equipment		32,000
(To record retirement of fully depreciated equipment)		

What happens if a fully depreciated plant asset is still useful to the company? In this case, the plant asset and the related accumulated depreciation continue to be reported on the balance sheet without further depreciation or adjustment until the asset is retired. Reporting the asset and related accumulated depreciation on the balance sheet informs the reader of the financial statements that the asset is still being used by the company. However, once an asset is fully depreciated, even if it is still being used, no additional depreciation should be taken. In no situation can the accumulated depreciation on the plant asset exceed its cost.

If a plant asset is retired before it is fully depreciated, and no scrap or salvage value is received, a loss on disposal occurs. For example, assume that Sunset Company discards delivery equipment that cost $18,000 and has accumulated depreciation of $14,000 at the date of retirement. The entry is as follows:

Accumulated Depreciation—Delivery Equipment	14,000		
Loss on Disposal	4,000		
Delivery Equipment		18,000	
(To record retirement of delivery equipment at a loss)			

A	=	L	+	SE
+14,000				−4,000
−18,000				

The loss on disposal is reported in the Other Expenses and Losses section of the income statement.

Sale of Plant Assets

In a disposal by sale, the book value of the asset is compared with the proceeds received from the sale. **If the proceeds of the sale exceed the book value of the plant asset, a gain on disposal occurs. If the proceeds of the sale are less than the book value of the plant asset sold, a loss on disposal occurs.**

Only by coincidence will the book value and the fair market value of the asset be the same at the time the asset is sold. Gains and losses on sales of plant assets are, therefore, quite common. As an example, Delta Airlines, Inc. recently reported a $94,343,000 gain on the sale of five Boeing B-727-200 aircraft and five Lockheed L-1011-1 aircraft.

HELPFUL HINT

When a plant asset is disposed of, all amounts related to the asset must be removed from the accounts. This includes the original cost in the asset account and the total depreciation to date in the accumulated depreciation account.

Gain on Disposal

To illustrate a gain, assume that on July 1, 2001, Wright Company sells office furniture for $16,000 cash. The office furniture originally cost $60,000 and as of January 1, 2001, had accumulated depreciation of $41,000. Depreciation for the first six months of 2001 is $8,000. The entry to record depreciation expense and update accumulated depreciation to July 1 is as follows:

July 1	Depreciation Expense	8,000		
	Accumulated Depreciation—Office Furniture		8,000	
	(To record depreciation expense for the first six months of 2001)			

A	=	L	+	SE
−8,000				−8,000

After the accumulated depreciation balance is updated, a gain on disposal of $5,000 is computed:

ILLUSTRATION 10-19

Computation of gain on disposal

Cost of office furniture	$60,000
Less: Accumulated depreciation ($41,000 + $8,000)	49,000
Book value at date of disposal	11,000
Proceeds from sale	16,000
Gain on disposal	**$ 5,000**

The entry to record the sale and the gain on disposal is as follows:

July 1	Cash	16,000		
	Accumulated Depreciation—Office Furniture	49,000		
	Office Furniture		60,000	
	Gain on Disposal		5,000	
	(To record sale of office furniture at a gain)			

A	=	L	+	SE
+16,000				+5,000
+49,000				
−60,000				

The gain on disposal is reported in the Other Revenues and Gains section of the income statement.

Loss on Disposal

Assume that instead of selling the office furniture for $16,000, Wright sells it for $9,000. In this case, a loss of $2,000 is computed:

ILLUSTRATION 10-20

Computation of loss on disposal

Cost of office furniture	$60,000
Less: Accumulated depreciation	49,000
Book value at date of disposal	11,000
Proceeds from sale	9,000
Loss on disposal	**$ 2,000**

The entry to record the sale and the loss on disposal is as follows:

A	=	L	+	SE
+9,000				−2,000
+49,000				
−60,000				

July 1	Cash	9,000	
	Accumulated Depreciation—Office Furniture	49,000	
	Loss on Disposal	2,000	
	Office Furniture		60,000
	(To record sale of office furniture at a loss)		

The loss on disposal is reported in the Other Expenses and Losses section of the income statement.

Exchange of Plant Assets

HELPFUL HINT

A building costing $200,000 was destroyed by fire. At the date of the fire, accumulated depreciation was $150,000. Insurance based on replacement value was $325,000. Prepare the entry to record the insurance proceeds and disposition of building. Answer: Debit Cash $325,000; debit Accumulated Depreciation $150,000; Credit Building $200,000; and Credit Gain on Disposal $275,000. (Or a more descriptive Gain account title might be used.)

Plant assets may also be disposed of through exchange. Exchanges can be for either similar or dissimilar assets. Because exchanges of similar assets are more common, they are discussed here.

An exchange of similar assets involves assets of the same type. This occurs, for example, when old delivery equipment is exchanged for new delivery equipment or when old office furniture is exchanged for new office furniture. In an exchange of similar assets, the new asset performs the **same function** as the old asset.

In exchanges of similar plant assets, it is necessary to determine (1) the cost of the asset acquired and (2) the gain or loss on the asset given up. Because a noncash asset is given up in the exchange, cost is equal to the **cash equivalent price** paid. Cost, therefore, is the fair market value of the asset given up plus the cash paid. The gain or loss on disposal is the **difference between the fair market value and the book value of the asset given up**. These determinations and the resulting accounting entries are explained and illustrated below.

Loss Treatment

When a loss occurs on the exchange of similar assets, it is recognized immediately. To illustrate the accounting for a loss, assume that Roland Company exchanged old office equipment for similar new office equipment. The **book value** of the old office equipment is $26,000 (cost $70,000 less accumulated depreciation $44,000), its **fair market value** is $10,000, and cash of $81,000 is paid. The cost of the new office equipment, $91,000, is computed as follows:

ILLUSTRATION 10-21

Computation of cost of new office equipment

Fair market value of old office equipment	$10,000
Cash	81,000
Cost of new office equipment	**$91,000**

Through this exchange, a loss on disposal of $16,000 is incurred. A loss results when the book value is greater than the fair market value of the asset given up. The computation is as follows:

Book value of old office equipment ($70,000 − $44,000)	$26,000
Fair market value of old office equipment	10,000
Loss on disposal	**$16,000**

ILLUSTRATION 10-22

Computation of loss on disposal

In recording an exchange at a loss it is necessary to (1) eliminate the book value of the asset given up, (2) record the cost of the asset acquired, and (3) recognize the loss on disposal. The entry for the Roland Company is as follows:

Office Equipment (new)	91,000	
Accumulated Depreciation—Office Equipment (old)	44,000	
Loss on Disposal	16,000	
Office Equipment (old)		70,000
Cash		81,000
(To record exchange of old office equipment for similar new equipment)		

A	=	L	+	SE
+91,000				−16,000
+44,000				
−70,000				
−81,000				

Gain Treatment

When a gain occurs on the exchange of similar assets, it is not recognized immediately. Instead, the gain is deferred by reducing the cost basis of the new asset. Thus, in determining the cost of the asset acquired, it is necessary to compute the **cost before deferral of the gain** and then the **cost after deferral of the gain**.

To illustrate the accounting for similar assets, assume that Mark's Express Delivery decides to exchange its old delivery equipment plus cash of $3,000 for new delivery equipment. At this time, the **book value** of the old delivery equipment is $12,000 (cost $40,000 less accumulated depreciation $28,000). In addition, it is determined that the **fair market value** of the old delivery equipment is $19,000.

The cost of the new asset received (before deferral of the gain) is equal to the **fair market value of the old asset exchanged plus any cash or other consideration given up**. The cost of the new delivery equipment (before deferral of the gain) is $22,000, computed as follows:

HELPFUL HINT

Gains on the exchange of similar assets are not recognized because the earnings process is not considered completed. Losses, however, are recognized, to be conservative.

Fair market value of old delivery equipment	$19,000
Cash	3,000
Cost of new delivery equipment (before deferral of gain)	**$22,000**

ILLUSTRATION 10-23

Cost of new equipment (before deferral of gain)

A gain results when the fair market value is greater than the book value of the asset given up. For Mark's Express, there is a gain of $7,000, computed as follows, on the disposal:

Fair market value of old delivery equipment	$19,000
Book value of old delivery equipment ($40,000 − $28,000)	12,000
Gain on disposal	**$7,000**

ILLUSTRATION 10-24

Computation of gain on disposal

The $7,000 gain on disposal is then offset against the $22,000 cost of the new delivery equipment. The result is a $15,000 cost of the new delivery equipment, after deferral of the gain, as shown in Illustration 10-25.

ILLUSTRATION 10-25

Cost of new equipment (after deferral of gain)

Cost of new delivery equipment (before deferral of gain)	$22,000
Less: Gain on disposal	7,000
Cost of new delivery equipment (after deferral of gain)	**$15,000**

The entry to record the exchange is as follows:

A = L + SE
+15,000
+28,000
−40,000
−3,000

Delivery Equipment (new)	15,000	
Accumulated Depreciation—Delivery Equipment (old)	28,000	
Delivery Equipment (old)		40,000
Cash		3,000
(To record exchange of old delivery equipment for similar new delivery equipment)		

This entry does not eliminate the gain; it just postpones or defers it to future periods. The deferred gain of $7,000 reduces the $22,000 cost to $15,000. As a result, net income in future periods increases because depreciation expense on the newly acquired delivery equipment is less by $7,000.

Summarizing, the rules for accounting for exchanges of similar assets are as follows:

ILLUSTRATION 10-26

Accounting rules for plant asset exchanges

Type of Event	Recognition
Loss	Recognize immediately by debiting Loss on Disposal
Gain	Defer and reduce cost of new asset

BEFORE YOU GO ON ...

Review It

1. What are the formulas for computing annual depreciation under each of the depreciation methods?
2. How do the methods differ in terms of their effects on annual depreciation over the useful life of the asset?
3. Are revisions of periodic depreciation made to prior periods? Explain.
4. How does a capital expenditure differ from a revenue expenditure?
5. What is the proper accounting for the retirement and sale of plant assets?
6. What is the proper accounting for the exchange of similar plant assets?

Do It

Overland Trucking has an old truck that cost $30,000, has accumulated depreciation of $16,000, and a fair value of $17,000. It has a choice of either selling the truck for cash of $17,000 or exchanging the old truck and $3,000 cash for a new truck. What is the entry that Overland Trucking would record under each option?

Reasoning: Gains and losses on the sale or exchange of plant assets are determined by the difference between the book value and the fair value of the company's asset. Gains on the exchange of similar assets are deferred. Losses are recognized immediately.

Solution:
Sale of truck for cash:

Cash	17,000	
Accumulated Depreciation—Truck (old)	16,000	
Truck (old)		30,000
Gain on Disposal [$17,000 − ($30,000 − $16,000)]		3,000
(To record sale of truck at a gain)		

Exchange of old truck and cash for new truck:

Truck (new)*	17,000	
Accumulated Depreciation—Truck (old)	16,000	
Truck (old)		30,000
Cash		3,000
(To record exchange of old truck for similar new truck)		

*[($17,000 + $3,000) − $3,000]

If the old truck is exchanged for the new truck, the $3,000 gain is deferred, and the recorded cost of the new truck is reduced by $3,000.

THE
NAVIGATOR

Related exercise material: BE10–8, BE10–9, BE10–10, BE10–11, E10–6, E10–7, E10–8, and E10–9.

SECTION 2   NATURAL RESOURCES

Natural resources consist of standing timber and underground deposits of oil, gas, and minerals. Such resources include the much-publicized offshore oil deposits of major petroleum companies and the oil deposits for which the Alaskan pipeline was built. These long-lived productive assets have two distinguishing characteristics: (1) they are physically extracted in operations (such as mining, cutting, or pumping), and (2) they are replaceable only by an act of nature. Because of these characteristics, natural resources are frequently called **wasting assets.**

HELPFUL HINT
On a balance sheet, natural resources may be described as Timberlands, Mineral Deposits, Oil Reserves, and so on.

ACQUISITION COST

The acquisition cost of a natural resource is the cash or cash equivalent price necessary to acquire the resource and prepare it for its intended use. For an already discovered resource, such as an existing coal mine, cost is the price paid for the property.

    Determining acquisition cost becomes a problem when exploration is involved. For example, some argue that the costs of unsuccessful exploration as well as successful exploration should be capitalized. They believe that, using an oil well as an example, the cost of drilling the dry holes is a cost that is needed to find the commercially profitable wells. As a result, both successful and unsuccessful explorations are capitalized, and the costs are written off to expense over the useful life of the successful wells. This method is often referred to as the full-cost approach.

    Others disagree, arguing that the costs of only successful projects should be capitalized and unsuccessful projects should be expensed. They maintain that if only one of ten exploratory wells becomes commercially viable, it is inappropriate to assign the costs of the nine unsuccessful wells to the cost of the successful well. This method is referred to as the successful efforts approach. At present, both approaches are used in accounting for natural resources. For example, such companies as American Petrofina, DuPont, Callahan Mining, and Copperweld use full costing, whereas Texaco, Mobil, and Imperial Oil use successful efforts.

7
STUDY
OBJECTIVE

Identify the basic accounting issues related to natural resources.

ACCOUNTING IN ACTION
Business Insight

Should both full cost and successful efforts be permitted in accounting? Views are particularly strong on this subject. As one financial expert, commenting on the full-cost method, noted: "It lets them call a dry hole an asset, and as far as I am concerned, any company that uses full-cost accounting is guilty until proven innocent." On the other hand, companies using the full-cost method argue that "it enables us to undertake risky exploration projects without having sharp swings in reported earnings." Or as one writer noted: "Forcing companies to use successful efforts accounting would retard domestic oil and gas exploration and imperil national security." The debate raises some interesting questions: Does the choice of accounting method actually affect a company's exploration activities? If it does, should accounting be concerned with national security, or should it "tell it like it is"?

DEPLETION

The process of allocating the cost of natural resources to expense in a rational and systematic manner over the resource's useful life is called depletion. **The units-of-activity method is generally used to compute depletion, because periodic depletion generally is a function of the units extracted during the year.** Under this method, the total cost of the natural resource minus salvage value, if any, is divided by the number of units estimated to be in the resource. The result is a depletion cost per unit of product. The depletion cost per unit is then multiplied by the number of units extracted and sold, to compute the depletion expense. The formula is as follows:

ILLUSTRATION 10-27

Formula to compute depletion expense

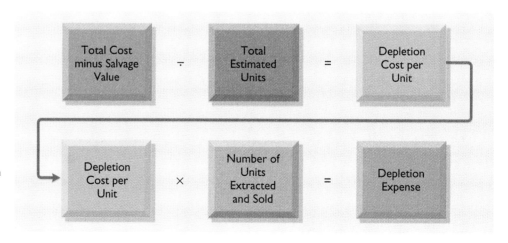

HELPFUL HINT

The computation for depletion is similar to the computation for depreciation using the units-of-activity method of depreciation.

To illustrate, assume that the Lane Coal Company invests $5 million in a mine estimated to have 10 million tons of coal and no salvage value. In the first year, 800,000 tons of coal are extracted and sold. Using the formulas above, the computations are as follows:

$$\$5,000,000 \div 10,000,000 = \$.50 \text{ depletion cost per ton}$$

$$\$.50 \times 800,000 = \$400,000 \text{ depletion expense}$$

The entry to record depletion expense for the first year of operation is as follows:

Dec. 31	Depletion Expense	400,000	
	Accumulated Depletion		400,000
	(To record depletion expense on coal		
	deposits)		

A	=	L	+	SE
−400,000				−400,000

The account Depletion Expense is reported as a part of the cost of producing the product. Accumulated Depletion, a contra asset account similar to accumulated depreciation, is deducted from the cost of the natural resource in the balance sheet as follows:

HELPFUL HINT

Natural resources are generally reported as part of Property, Plant, and Equipment on the balance sheet.

LANE COAL COMPANY
Balance Sheet (partial)

Coal mine	$5,000,000	
Less: Accumulated depletion	400,000	$4,600,000

ILLUSTRATION 10-28

Statement presentation of accumulated depletion

However, in many companies an Accumulated Depletion account is not used, and the amount of depletion is credited directly to the natural resource account.

Sometimes, natural resources extracted in one accounting period will not be sold until a later period. In this case, depletion is not expensed until the resource is sold. The amount not sold is reported in the Current Assets section as inventory.

BEFORE YOU GO ON ...

Review It

1. What is the difference between the full-cost and successful efforts methods in accounting for natural resources?
2. How is depletion expense computed?

Do It

Explain the method used in computing depletion and show the computation, assuming Hard Rock Mining Corporation invests $12 million in a mine estimated to have 10 million tons of ore and a $2 million salvage value. In the first year 40,000 tons of ore are mined and sold.

Reasoning: There are many similarities between depreciation and depletion. In computing depletion expense, the units-of-activity method is generally used.

Solution: Under the units-of-activity method, a depletion cost per unit is determined by dividing total cost minus salvage value by the total estimated units. The computation is as follows:

$$(\$12{,}000{,}000 - \$2{,}000{,}000) \div 10{,}000{,}000 = \$1 \text{ depletion cost per ton}$$

The cost per unit is then multiplied by the number of units extracted and sold to determine depletion expense. Depletion expense for Hard Rock is $40,000 ($1 x 40,000).

THE NAVIGATOR

Related exercise material: BE10–12, BE10–13, and E10–10.

SECTION 3 INTANGIBLE ASSETS

Intangible assets are rights, privileges, and competitive advantages that result from the ownership of long-lived assets that do not possess physical substance. Evidence of intangibles may exist in the form of contracts, licenses, and other documents. Intangibles may arise from:

1. Government grants such as patents, copyrights, franchises, trademarks, and trade names.
2. Acquisition of another business in which the purchase price includes a payment for goodwill.
3. Private monopolistic arrangements arising from contractual agreements, such as franchises and leases.

Some widely known intangibles are the patents of Polaroid, the franchises of McDonald's, the trade name of Col. Sander's Kentucky Fried Chicken, and the trademark 3M of Minnesota Mining and Manufacturing Company.

ACCOUNTING FOR INTANGIBLE ASSETS

8
STUDY
OBJECTIVE
Contrast the accounting for intangible assets with the accounting for plant assets.

In general, accounting for intangible assets parallels the accounting for plant assets. That is, **intangible assets are recorded at cost**, and this cost is expensed **over the useful life of the intangible asset in a rational and systematic manner**. At disposal, the book value of the intangible asset is eliminated, and a gain or loss, if any, is recorded.

There are, however, differences between accounting for intangible assets and accounting for plant assets. First, the term used to describe the allocation of the cost of an intangible asset to expense is amortization, rather than depreciation. To record amortization of an intangible, an amortization expense is debited and the specific intangible asset is credited. An alternative is to credit an accumulated amortization account, similar to accumulated depreciation. Most companies, however, choose simply to reduce the cost of the intangible asset.

There is also a difference in determining cost. For plant assets, cost includes both the purchase price of an asset and the costs incurred by a company in designing and constructing the plant asset. In contrast, cost for an intangible asset includes only the purchase price. Costs incurred in developing an intangible asset are expensed as incurred.

A third difference is that **the amortization period of an intangible asset cannot be longer than 40 years**. For example, even if the useful life of an intangible asset is 60 years, it must be written off over 40 years. Conversely, if the useful life is less than 40 years, the useful life is used. This rule ensures that all intangibles, especially those with indeterminable lives, will be written off in a reasonable period of time.[1]

---

[1]The FASB has recently *proposed* a maximum 20-year amortization period for certain intangible assets.

ACCOUNTING IN ACTION
Business Insight

Three Canadians founded Imax and pioneered the giant-screen, large-format projection technology, first introduced at Expo '70 in Osaka. Imax was subsequently sold in 1994 to two entrepreneur/venture capitalists with the backing of a U.S. investment bank for $54.3 million. Although the carrying value of the invention was much smaller on the prior owner's books—essentially the cost of registering the patent—it now sits at a substantially higher amount on its new owner's books as part of the **$48.6 million of intangible assets** arising from the acquisition of Imax.

Intangible assets are typically amortized on a straight-line basis. The widespread use of this method adds comparability in accounting for intangible assets.

Patents

A patent is an exclusive right issued by the United States Patent Office that enables the recipient to manufacture, sell, or otherwise control an invention for a period of 17 years from the date of the grant. A patent is nonrenewable, but the legal life of a patent may be extended beyond its original term by obtaining new patents for improvements and other changes in the basic design.

The initial cost of a patent is the cash or cash equivalent price paid to acquire the patent. It should be noted that the saying, "A patent is only as good as the money you're prepared to spend defending it," is very true. Most patents are subject to some type of litigation by competitors. A well-known example is the patent infringement suit won by Polaroid against Eastman Kodak in protecting its patent on instant cameras. If the owner incurs legal costs in successfully defending the patent in an infringement suit, such costs are considered necessary to establish the validity of the patent. Thus, **they are added to the Patents account and amortized over the remaining life of the patent**.

The cost of a patent should be amortized over its 17-year legal life or its useful life, whichever is shorter. In determining useful life, obsolescence, inadequacy, and other factors should be considered; these may cause a patent to become economically ineffective before the end of its legal life. To illustrate the computation of patent expense, assume that National Labs purchases a patent at a cost of $60,000. If the useful life of the patent is 8 years, the annual amortization expense is $7,500 ($60,000 ÷ 8). The entry to record the annual amortization is:

Dec. 31	Amortization Expense—Patents	7,500	
	Patents		7,500
	(To record patent amortization)		

A	=	L	+	SE
−7,500				−7,500

Amortization Expense—Patents is classified as an **operating expense** in the income statement.

Copyrights

Copyrights are granted by the federal government, giving the owner the exclusive right to reproduce and sell an artistic or published work. Copyrights extend for the life of the creator plus 50 years. The cost of the copyright consists of the **cost of acquiring and defending it**. The cost may be only the $10 fee paid to the U.S. Copyright office, or it may amount to a great deal more if a copyright infringement suit is involved.

The useful life of a copyright generally is significantly shorter than its legal life. Similar to other intangible assets, the maximum write-off is 40 years. However, because of the difficulties of determining the period over which benefits are to be received, copyrights usually are amortized over a relatively short period of time.

ACCOUNTING IN ACTION
International Insight

One of the significant new items copyrighted today is computer software. Lotus 1-2-3, Microsoft Office, Netscape, and WordPerfect are some examples. These intangible assets—copyrights, in this case—are one of the most valuable assets of these corporations. To illustrate how important copyrights are, consider that software piracy is estimated to cost the software industry $17 billion worldwide each year.

Copyright laws are being revised and developed to discourage bootlegging and provide protection against unlicensed copying of copyright material, but nowhere more vigorously than in cyberspace. Copyright laws based on national boundaries have been made irrelevant by the Internet. Representatives from more than 120 countries are currently working on this problem under the auspices of the World Intellectual Property Organization—a specialized UN coordinating body for international patents, trademarks, and copyrights.

Trademarks and Trade Names

A trademark or trade name is a word, phrase, jingle, or symbol that distinguishes or identifies a particular enterprise or product. Trade names like Wheaties, Jacuzzi, Sunkist, Kleenex, Windows, Coca-Cola, Big Mac, and Cadillac create immediate product identification and generally enhance the sale of the product. The creator or original user may obtain exclusive legal right to the trademark or trade name by registering it with the U.S. Patent Office. Such registration provides 20 years' protection and may be renewed indefinitely as long as the trademark or trade name is in use.

If the trademark or trade name is purchased, the cost is the purchase price. If it is developed by the enterprise itself, the cost includes attorney's fees, registration fees, design costs, successful legal defense costs, and other expenditures directly related to securing it.

As with other intangibles, the cost of trademarks and trade names must be amortized over the shorter of its useful life or 40 years. Because of the uncertainty involved in estimating the useful life, the cost is frequently amortized over a much shorter period.

ETHICS NOTE

A pharmaceutical company was growing rapidly by buying unwanted drug licensing rights. These licensing rights, reported as intangible assets, represented over 70% of the company's total assets. The company experienced a 50% drop in value when the market realized the rights were being amortized over 40 years. If a more reasonable life had been used to amortize the rights, the company's reported profits would, instead, have been huge losses.

Franchises and Licenses

When you drive down the street in your Blazer purchased from a General Motors dealer, fill up your tank at the corner Standard Oil station, eat lunch at Wendy's, and vacation at a Club Med resort, you are dealing with franchises. A franchise is a contractual arrangement under which the franchisor grants the franchisee the right to sell certain products, to render specific services, or to use certain trademarks or trade names, usually within a designated geographical area.

Another type of franchise is that entered into between a governmental body (commonly municipalities) and a business enterprise. This type of franchise permits the enterprise to use public property in performing its services. Examples are the use of city streets for a bus line or taxi service, use of public land for telephone and electric lines, and the use of airwaves for radio or TV broadcasting. Such operating rights are referred to as licenses.

Franchises and licenses may be granted for a definite period of time, an indefinite period, or perpetual. **When costs can be identified with the acquisition of the franchise or license, an intangible asset should be recognized.** In the case of a limited life, the cost of a franchise (or license) should be amortized as operating expense over the useful life. If the life is indefinite or perpetual, the cost may be amortized over a reasonable period not to exceed 40 years. Annual payments made under a franchise agreement should be recorded as **operating expenses** in the period in which they are incurred.

Goodwill

Usually, the largest intangible asset that appears on a company's balance sheet is goodwill. Goodwill is the value of all favorable attributes that relate to a business enterprise. These include exceptional management, desirable location, good customer relations, skilled employees, high-quality products, fair pricing policies, and harmonious relations with labor unions. Some view goodwill as expected earnings in excess of normal earnings. Goodwill is, therefore, unusual: unlike other assets such as investments, plant assets, and other intangibles that can be sold individually in the marketplace, goodwill can be identified only with the business as a whole.

If goodwill can be identified only with the business as a whole, how can it be determined? Certainly, many of the factors above (exceptional management, desirable location, and so on) are present in many business enterprises. However, to determine the amount of goodwill in these types of situations would be too difficult and very subjective. In other words, to recognize goodwill without an exchange transaction would lead to subjective valuations that do not contribute to the reliability of financial statements. **Therefore, goodwill is recorded only when there is an exchange transaction that involves the purchase of an entire business. When an entire business is purchased, goodwill is the excess of cost over the fair market value of the net assets (assets less liabilities) acquired.**

In recording the purchase of a business, the net assets are shown at their fair market values, goodwill is recorded at its cost, and cash is credited for the purchase price. Subsequently, goodwill is written off over its useful life, not to exceed 40 years. The amortization entry generally results in a debit to Goodwill Expense and a credit to Goodwill. Goodwill is reported in the balance sheet under Intangible Assets.

HELPFUL HINT
Goodwill is recorded only when it has been purchased along with tangible and identifiable intangible assets of a business.

RESEARCH AND DEVELOPMENT COSTS

Research and development costs are not intangible costs, but because these expenditures may lead to patents and copyrights, they are discussed in this section. Many companies spend considerable sums of money on research and development in an ongoing effort to develop new products or processes. For example, in a recent year IBM spent over $2.5 billion on research and development, an amount greater than the total expenditure budget of some state governments.

Research and development costs present accounting problems: (1) it is sometimes difficult to assign the costs to specific projects, and (2) there are uncertainties in identifying the extent and timing of future benefits. As a result, research and development costs are **usually recorded as an expense when incurred**, whether the research and development is successful or not.

To illustrate, assume that Laser Scanner Company spent $3 million on research and development. Those research and development costs resulted in the development of two highly successful patents. The R&D costs, however, cannot be included in the cost of the patent. Rather, they are recorded as an expense when incurred.

Many disagree with this accounting approach. They argue that to expense these costs leads to understated assets and net income. Others, however, argue that capitalizing these costs will lead only to highly speculative assets on the balance sheet. Who is right is difficult to determine. The controversy, however, illustrates how difficult it is to establish proper guidelines for financial reporting.

··

STATEMENT PRESENTATION AND ANALYSIS

Presentation

Usually plant assets and natural resources are combined under Property, Plant, and Equipment, and intangibles are shown separately under Intangible Assets. Either within the balance sheet or in the notes, there should be disclosure of the balances of the major classes of assets, such as land, buildings, and equipment, and accumulated depreciation by major classes or in total. In addition, the depreciation and amortization methods used should be described and the amount of depreciation and amortization expense for the period disclosed.

The financial statement presentation of property, plant, and equipment by Kellogg Company in its 1998 balance sheet is quite brief, as shown in Illustration 10-29.

ILLUSTRATION 10-29

Kellogg's presentation of property, plant, and equipment, and intangible assets

	KELLOGG COMPANY			
	Balance Sheet (partial)			
	December 31 (in millions)			
			1998	1997
	Property, net		$2,888.8	$2,773.3
	Other assets		666.2	636.6

The notes to Kellogg's financial statements present greater details, namely, that "Other assets" contains goodwill of $185.5 million and other intangibles of $194 million.

A more comprehensive presentation of property, plant, and equipment is excerpted from the balance sheet of Owens-Illinois and shown in Illustration 10-30. The notes to the financial statements of Owens-Illinois identify the major classes of property, plant, and equipment. They also indicate that depreciation is by the straight-line method, depletion is by the units-of-activity method, and amortization is by the straight-line method.

OWENS-ILLINOIS, INC. Balance Sheet (partial) (in millions of dollars)			
Property, plant, and equipment			
Timberlands, at cost, less accumulated depletion		$ 95.4	
Buildings and equipment, at cost	$2,207.1		
Less: Accumulated depreciation	1,229.0	978.1	
Total property, plant, and equipment			$1,073.5
Intangibles			
Patents			410.0
Total			$1,483.5

ILLUSTRATION 10-30

Statement presentation of property, plant, and equipment and intangible assets

Analysis

Because the original cost ($5,246.8 million), the accumulated depreciation ($2,358 million), and the current period's depreciation expense for property, plant, and equipment ($278.1 million), are reported in the notes to Kellogg's 1998 financial statements, it is possible to analyze the lives and ages of these assets (especially for companies, like Kellogg, that use the straight-line method of depreciation). A measure of the average life and the average age of these assets can be computed using the following formulas and the data above from Kellogg Company:

ILLUSTRATION 10-31

Average life and average age formulas and computations

Cost of Property, Plant and Equipment	÷	Depreciation Expense	=	Average Life
$5,246.8	÷	$278.1	=	18.9 years

Accumulated Depreciation	÷	Depreciation Expense	=	Average Age
$2,358	÷	$278.1	=	8.48 years

These averages are only rough estimates and possess all the weaknesses of averages. The actual lives of the individual assets that are contained in these averages range from 3 years (tools and office machines) to 35 years (buildings). However, the usefulness of these averages may come from a comparison with averages of other companies in the same industry.

The turnover of assets may be used in analyzing the productivity of a company's assets. That is, the asset turnover ratio is computed to measure how efficiently a company uses its assets to generate sales. This ratio is computed by dividing net sales by average total assets for the period, as shown in the formula in Illustration 10-32. (Kellogg's net sales for 1998 are $6,762.1 million, and total ending assets are $5,051.5 million and beginning are $4,877.6 million.)

ILLUSTRATION 10-32

Asset turnover formula and computation

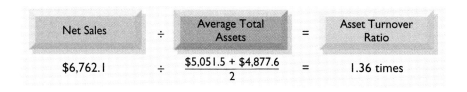

Net Sales	÷	Average Total Assets	=	Asset Turnover Ratio
$6,762.1	÷	$\dfrac{\$5,051.5 + \$4,877.6}{2}$	=	1.36 times

This ratio shows the dollars of sales produced for each dollar invested in average total assets. If a company is using its assets efficiently, each dollar of assets will create a high amount of sales. This ratio varies greatly among different industries—from those that are asset intensive (utility) to those that are not (services).

BEFORE YOU GO ON . . .

Review It

1. What are the main differences between accounting for intangible assets and plant assets?
2. Identify the major types of intangibles and the proper accounting for them.
3. Explain the accounting for research and development costs.
4. What ratios may be computed to analyze property, plant, and equipment?

A LOOK BACK AT OUR FEATURE STORY

Refer back to the Feature Story about Westbrook College, and answer the following questions:

1. Why should Westbrook College depreciate its buildings?
2. How can Westbrook College have a building with a zero book value yet a substantial market value?
3. Give some examples of intangibles other than a trademark that you might find on your college campus.
4. Give some examples of company or product trademarks or trade names. Are trade names and trademarks reported on a company's balance sheet? Explain.

Solution

1. Westbrook College should depreciate its buildings because depreciation is necessary in order to allocate the cost of the buildings to the periods in which they are used.
2. A building can have a zero book value if it has no salvage value and it is fully depreciated—that is, if it has been used for a period longer than its expected life. Because depreciation is used to allocate cost rather than to reflect actual value, it is not at all unlikely that a building could have a low or zero book value, but a positive market value.
3. Examples of other intangibles that might be found on a college campus are franchise of a bookstore chain, license to operate a radio station, patents developed by professors, and a permit to operate a bus service.
4. Typical company or product trade names are:
   Clothes—Gap, Gitano, Dockers, Calvin Klein, Polo, Guess.
   Perfume—Passion, Tommy Girl, Chanel No. 5, Diamonds.
   Cars—TransAm, Saturn, Prelude, Jeep Cherokee, Eclipse.
   Shoes—Nike, Florsheim, Doc Martens, Adidas.
   Breakfast cereals—Frosted Flakes, Rice Krispies, Cheerios, Wheaties.

   Trade names and trademarks are reported on a balance sheet, if there is a cost attached to them, as the last item in the assets section.

THE NAVIGATOR

DEMONSTRATION PROBLEM 1

DuPage Company purchases a factory machine at a cost of $18,000 on January 1, 2001. The machine is expected to have a salvage value of $2,000 at the end of its 4-year useful life.

During its useful life, the machine is expected to be used 160,000 hours. Actual annual hourly use was: Year 1, 40,000; Year 2, 60,000; Year 3, 35,000; and Year 4, 25,000.

Instructions

Prepare depreciation schedules for the following methods: (a) the straight-line, (b) units-of-activity, and (c) declining-balance using double the straight-line rate.

SOLUTION TO DEMONSTRATION PROBLEM 1

(a)

Straight-Line Method

Year	Computation Depreciable Cost	×	Depreciation Rate	=	Annual Depreciation Expense	End of Year Accumulated Depreciation	Book Value
2001	$16,000		25%		$4,000	$ 4,000	$14,000*
2002	16,000		25%		4,000	8,000	10,000
2003	16,000		25%		4,000	12,000	6,000
2004	16,000		25%		4,000	16,000	2,000

*$18,000 − $4,000.

(b)

Units-of-Activity Method

Year	Computation Units of Activity	×	Depreciation Cost/Unit	=	Annual Depreciation Expense	End of Year Accumulated Depreciation	Book Value
2001	40,000		$.10		$4,000	$ 4,000	$14,000
2002	60,000		.10		6,000	10,000	8,000
2003	35,000		.10		3,500	13,500	4,500
2004	25,000		.10		2,500	16,000	2,000

(c)

Declining-Balance Method

Year	Book Value Beginning of Year	×	Depreciation Rate	=	Annual Depreciation Expense	End of Year Accumulated Depreciation	Book Value
2001	$18,000		50%		$9,000	$ 9,000	$9,000
2002	9,000		50%		4,500	13,500	4,500
2003	4,500		50%		2,250	15,750	2,250
2004	2,250		50%		250*	16,000	2,000

*Adjusted to $250 because ending book value should not be less than expected salvage value.

THE NAVIGATOR

PROBLEM-SOLVING STRATEGIES

1. Under the straight-line method, the depreciation rate is applied to depreciable cost.
2. Under the units-of-activity method, depreciation cost per unit is computed by dividing depreciable cost by total units of activity.
3. Under the declining-balance method, the depreciation rate is applied to **book value** at the beginning of the year.

DEMONSTRATION PROBLEM 2

On January 1, 1999, the Skyline Limousine Co. purchased a limousine at an acquisition cost of $28,000. The vehicle has been depreciated by the straight-line method using a 4-year service life and a $4,000 salvage value. The company's fiscal year ends on December 31.

Instructions

Prepare the journal entry or entries to record the disposal of the limousine assuming that it was:

(1) Retired and scrapped with no salvage value on January 1, 2003.
(2) Sold for $5,000 on July 1, 2002.

(3) Traded in on a new limousine on January 1, 2002. The fair market value of the old vehicle was $9,000 and $22,000 was paid in cash.

(4) Traded in on a new limousine on January 1, 2002. The fair market value of the old vehicle was $11,000 and $2,000 was paid in cash.

SOLUTION TO DEMONSTRATION PROBLEM 2

(1)	1/1/03	Accumulated Depreciation—Limousine	24,000	
		Loss on Disposal	4,000	
		Limousine		28,000
		(To record retirement of limousine)		
(2)	7/1/02	Depreciation Expense	3,000	
		Accumulated Depreciation—Limousine		3,000
		(To record depreciation to date of disposal)		
		Cash	5,000	
		Accumulated Depreciation—Limousine	21,000	
		Loss on Disposal	2,000	
		Limousine		28,000
		(To record sale of limousine)		
(3)	1/1/02	Limousine (new)	31,000	
		Accumulated Depreciation—Limousine	18,000	
		Loss on Disposal	1,000	
		Limousine		28,000
		Cash		22,000
		(To record exchange of limousines)		
(4)	1/1/02	Limousine (new)*	12,000	
		Accumulated Depreciation—Limousine (old)	18,000	
		Limousine (old)		28,000
		Cash		2,000
		(To record exchange of limousines)		

*($11,000 + $2,000 - $1,000)

THE
NAVIGATOR

SUMMARY OF STUDY OBJECTIVES

1. Describe the application of the cost principle to plant assets. The cost of plant assets includes all expenditures necessary to acquire the asset and make it ready for its intended use. Cost is measured by the cash or cash equivalent price paid.

2. Explain the concept of depreciation. Depreciation is the process of allocating to expense the cost of a plant asset over its useful (service) life in a rational and systematic manner. Depreciation is not a process of valuation, and it is not a process that results in an accumulation of cash. Depreciation is caused by wear and tear and by obsolescence.

3. Compute periodic depreciation using different methods. There are three depreciation methods:

Method	Effect on Annual Depreciation	Formula
Straight-line	Constant amount	Depreciable cost ÷ useful life (in years)
Units-of-activity	Varying amount	Depreciation cost per unit × units of activity during the year
Declining-balance	Decreasing amount	Book value at beginning of year × declining-balance rate

4. *Describe the procedure for revising periodic depreciation.* Revisions of periodic depreciation are made in present and future periods, not retroactively. The new annual depreciation is determined by dividing the depreciable cost at the time of the revision by the remaining useful life.

5. *Distinguish between revenue and capital expenditures and explain the entries for these expenditures.* Revenue expenditures are incurred to maintain the operating efficiency and expected productive life of the asset. These expenditures are debited to Repair Expense as incurred. Capital expenditures increase the operating efficiency, productive capacity, or expected useful life of the asset. These expenditures are generally debited to the plant asset affected.

6. *Explain how to account for the disposal of a plant asset through retirement, sale, or exchange.* The accounting for disposal of a plant asset through retirement or sale is as follows:
(a) Eliminate the book value of the plant asset at the date of disposal.
(b) Record cash proceeds, if any.
(c) Account for the difference between the book value and the cash proceeds as a gain or loss on disposal.

In accounting for exchanges of similar assets:
(a) Eliminate the book value of the old asset at the date of the exchange.
(b) Record the acquisition cost of the new asset.
(c) Account for the loss or gain, if any, on the old asset.
  1. If a loss, recognize it immediately.
  2. If a gain, defer and reduce the cost of the new asset.

7. *Identify the basic accounting issues related to natural resources.* The basic accounting issues related to natural resources are whether exploration costs on unsuccessful explorations should be capitalized or expensed. Under the full-cost approach, both successful and unsuccessful explorations are capitalized and the costs amortized to expense over the useful life of the successful efforts. The other approach is to capitalize only the costs of successful explorations. This is referred to as the successful efforts approach.

8. *Contrast the accounting for intangible assets with the accounting for plant assets.* The accounting for intangible assets and plant assets is much the same. One difference is that the term used to describe the write-off of an intangible asset is amortization, rather than depreciation. In addition, the amortization of the intangible asset cannot be longer than 40 years. The straight-line method is normally used for amortizing intangible assets.

9. *Indicate how plant assets, natural resources, and intangible assets are reported and analyzed.* Usually plant assets and natural resources are combined under Property, Plant, and Equipment; intangibles are shown separately under Intangible Assets. Either within the balance sheet or in the notes, the balances of the major classes of assets, such as land, buildings, and equipment, and accumulated depreciation by major classes or in total should be disclosed. Also, the depreciation and amortization methods used should be described, and the amount of depreciation and amortization expense for the period should be disclosed. Assets may be analyzed to measure average life, average age, and asset turnover.

THE NAVIGATOR

GLOSSARY

Accelerated-depreciation method A depreciation method that produces higher depreciation expense in the early years than in the later years. (p. 421).

Additions and improvements Costs incurred to increase the operating efficiency, productive capacity, or expected useful life of a plant asset. (p. 424).

Amortization The allocation of the cost of an intangible asset to expense over its useful life in a systematic and rational manner. (p. 432).

Asset turnover ratio A measure of how efficiently a company uses its assets to generate sales, calculated as net sales divided by average assets. (p. 437).

Average age of plant assets A comparative measure of the age of a company's plant assets, calculated as accumulated depreciation divided by depreciation expense. (p. 437).

Average life of plant assets A comparative measure of a company's plant assets, calculated as cost of plant assets divided by depreciation expense. (p. 437).

Capital expenditures Expenditures that increase the company's investment in productive facilities. (p. 424).

Cash equivalent price An amount equal to the fair market value of the asset given up or the fair market value of the asset received, whichever is more clearly determinable. (p. 413).

Copyright An exclusive right granted by the federal government allowing the owner to reproduce and sell an artistic or published work. (p. 433).

Declining-balance method A depreciation method that applies a constant rate to the declining book value of the asset and produces a decreasing annual depreciation expense over the useful life of the asset. (p. 420).

Depletion The process of allocating the cost of a natural resource to expense in a rational and systematic manner over the resource's useful life. (p. 430).

Depreciable cost The cost of a plant asset less its salvage value. (p. 418).

Franchise (license)   A contractual arrangement under which the franchisor grants the franchisee the right to sell certain products, to render specific services, or to use certain trademarks or trade names, usually within a designated geographical area. (p. 434).

Full-cost approach   Method in which both successful and unsuccessful exploration costs are included in the cost of a natural resource and the costs are written off to expense over the useful life of the successful wells. (p. 429).

Goodwill   The value of all favorable attributes that relate to a business enterprise. (p. 435).

Intangible assets   Rights, privileges, and competitive advantages that result from the ownership of long-lived assets that do not possess physical substance. (p. 432).

Licenses   Operating rights to use public property, granted to a business enterprise by a governmental agency. (p. 434).

Natural resources   Assets that consist of standing timber and underground deposits of oil, gas, and minerals. Also called *wasting assets*. (p. 429).

Ordinary repairs   Expenditures to maintain the operating efficiency and expected productive life of the unit. (p. 423).

Patent   An exclusive right issued by the U.S. Patent Office that enables the recipient to manufacture, sell, or otherwise control an invention for a period of 17 years from the date of the grant. (p. 433).

Plant assets   Tangible resources that are used in the operations of the business and are not intended for sale to customers. (p. 412).

Research and development costs   Expenditures that may lead to patents, copyrights, new processes, and products. (p. 435).

Revenue expenditures   Expenditures that are immediately charged against revenues as an expense. (p. 424).

Straight-line method   A depreciation method in which periodic depreciation is the same for each year of the asset's useful life. (p. 418).

Successful efforts approach   Method in which only the costs of successful exploration are included in the cost of a natural resource. (p. 429).

Trademark (trade name)   A word, phrase, jingle, or symbol that distinguishes or identifies a particular enterprise or product. (p. 434).

Units-of-activity method   A depreciation method in which useful life is expressed in terms of the total units of production or use expected from the asset. (p. 419).

SELF-STUDY QUESTIONS

Answers are at the end of the chapter.

(SO 1) 1. Erin Danielle Company purchased equipment and the following costs were incurred:

Cash price	$24,000
Sales taxes	1,200
Insurance during transit	200
Installation and testing	400
Total costs	$25,800

What amount should be recorded as the cost of the equipment?
a. $24,000.
b. $25,200.
c. $25,400.
d. $25,800.

(SO 2) 2. Depreciation is a process of:
a. valuation.
b. cost allocation.
c. cash accumulation.
d. appraisal.

(SO 3) 3. Micah Bartlett Company purchased equipment on January 1, 2000, at a total invoice cost of $400,000. The equipment has an estimated salvage value of $10,000 and an estimated useful life of 5 years. The amount of accumulated depreciation at December 31, 2001, if the straight-line method of depreciation is used, is:
a. $80,000.
b. $160,000.
c. $78,000.
d. $156,000.

4. Ann Torbert purchased a truck for $11,000 on January   (SO 3) 1, 2000. The truck will have an estimated salvage value of $1,000 at the end of 5 years. Using the units-of-activity method, the balance in accumulated depreciation at December 31, 2001, can be computed by the following formula:
a. ($11,000 ÷ Total estimated activity) × Units of activity for 2001.
b. ($10,000 ÷ Total estimated activity) × Units of activity for 2001.
c. ($11,000 ÷ Total estimated activity) × Units of activity for 2000 and 2001.
d. ($10,000 ÷ Total estimated activity) × Units of activity for 2000 and 2001.

5. When there is a change in estimated depreciation: (SO 4)
a. previous depreciation should be corrected.
b. current and future years' depreciation should be revised.
c. only future years' depreciation should be revised.
d. None of the above.

6. Additions to plant assets are: (SO 5)
a. revenue expenditures.
b. debited to a Repair Expense account.
c. debited to a Purchases account.
d. capital expenditures.

7. Schopenhauer Company exchanged an old machine,   (SO 6) with a book value of $39,000 and a fair market value of $35,000, and paid $10,000 cash for a similar new machine. At what amount should the machine acquired in

the exchange be recorded on the books of Schopenhauer?
a. $45,000.
b. $46,000.
c. $49,000.
d. $50,000.

(SO 6) 8. In exchanges of similar assets:
a. neither gains nor losses are recognized immediately.
b. gains, but not losses, are recognized immediately.
c. losses, but not gains, are recognized immediately.
d. both gains and losses are recognized immediately.

(SO 7) 9. Maggie Sharrer Company expects to extract 20 million tons of coal from a mine that cost $12 million. If no salvage value is expected, and 2 million tons are mined and sold in the first year, the entry to record depletion will include a:
a. debit to Accumulated Depletion of $2,000,000.
b. credit to Depletion Expense of $1,200,000.
c. debit to Depletion Expense of $1,200,000.
d. credit to Accumulated Depletion of $2,000,000.

SO 8, 9) 10. Ingrid Mount Company incurred $150,000 of research and development costs in its laboratory to develop a patent granted on January 2, 2001. On July 31, 2001, Mount paid $35,000 for legal fees in a successful defense of the patent. The total amount debited to Patents through July 31, 2001, should be:
a. $150,000.
b. $35,000.
c. $185,000.
d. some other amount.

11. Indicate which of the following statements is *true*.   (SO 9)
a. Since intangible assets lack physical substance they need be disclosed only in the notes to the financial statements.
b. Goodwill should be reported as a contra-account in the Stockholders' Equity section.
c. Totals of major classes of assets can be shown in the balance sheet, with asset details disclosed in the notes to the financial statements.
d. Intangible assets are typically combined with plant assets and natural resources and then shown in the Property, Plant, and Equipment section.

QUESTIONS

1. Phil Collins is uncertain about the applicability of the cost principle to plant assets. Explain the principle to Phil.

2. How is cost for a plant asset measured in (a) a cash transaction, and (b) a noncash transaction?

3. Winans Company acquires the land and building owned by Corrs Company. What types of costs may be incurred to make the asset ready for its intended use if Winans Company wants to use (a) only the land, and (b) both the land and the building?

4. In a recent newspaper release, the president of Smashing Pumpkins Company asserted that something has to be done about depreciation. The president said, "Depreciation does not come close to accumulating the cash needed to replace the asset at the end of its useful life." What is your response to the president?

5. Michael is studying for the next accounting examination. He asks your help on two questions: (a) What is salvage value? (b) Is salvage value used in determining depreciable cost under each depreciation method? Answer Michael's questions.

6. Contrast the straight-line method and the units-of-activity method as to (a) useful life, and (b) the pattern of periodic depreciation over useful life.

7. Contrast the effects of the three depreciation methods on annual depreciation expense.

8. In the fourth year of an asset's 5-year useful life, the company decides that the asset will have a 6-year service life. How should the revision of depreciation be recorded? Why?

9. Distinguish between revenue expenditures and capital expenditures during useful life.

10. How is a gain or loss on the sale of a plant asset computed?

11. Bimini Corporation owns a machine that is fully depreciated but is still being used. How should Bimini account for this asset and report it in the financial statements?

12. When similar assets are exchanged, how is the gain or loss on disposal computed?

13. Batman Refrigeration Company trades in an old machine on a new model when the fair market value of the old machine is greater than its book value. Should Batman recognize a gain on disposal? If the fair market value of the old machine is less than its book value, should Batmam recognize a loss on disposal?

14. Moon Company experienced a gain on disposal when exchanging similar machines. In accordance with generally accepted accounting principles, the gain was not recognized. How will Moon's future financial statements be affected by not recognizing the gain?

15. What are natural resources, and what are their distinguishing characteristics?

16. Van Amos and Benedict Arnold are arguing about the full-cost approach and the successful efforts approach. Amos says that the full-cost approach will provide a greater reported asset value, while Arnold says that the successful efforts approach would. Who is correct?

17. What are the similarities and differences between the terms depreciation, depletion, and amortization?

18. Mitra Company hires an accounting intern who says that intangible assets should always be amortized over their legal lives. Is the intern correct? Explain.

19. Goodwill has been defined as the value of all favorable attributes that relate to a business enterprise. What types of attributes could result in goodwill?

20. Clint Eastwood, a business major, is working on a case problem for one of his classes. In this case problem, the company needs to raise cash to market a new product it developed. Jack Gleason, an engineering major, takes one look at the company's balance sheet and says, "This company has an awful lot of goodwill. Why don't you recommend that they sell some of it to raise cash?" How should Clint respond to Jack?

21. Under what conditions is goodwill recorded?

22. Often research and development costs provide companies with benefits that last a number of years. (For example, these costs can lead to the development of a patent that will increase the company's income for many years.) However, generally accepted accounting principles require that such costs be recorded as an expense when incurred. Why?

23. McDonald's Corporation reports total average assets of $14.5 billion and net sales of $9.8 billion. What is the company's asset turnover ratio?

24. Morgan Corporation and Fairchild Corporation both operate in the same industry. Morgan uses the straight-line method to account for depreciation, whereas Fairchild uses an accelerated method. Explain what complications might arise in trying to compare the results of these two companies.

25. Lucille Corporation uses straight-line depreciation for financial reporting purposes but an accelerated method for tax purposes. Is it acceptable to use different methods for the two purposes? What is Lucille Corporation's motivation for doing this?

26. You are comparing two companies in the same industry. You have determined that Betty Corp. depreciates its plant assets over a 40-year life, whereas Veronica Corp. depreciates its plant assets over a 20-year life. Discuss the implications this has for comparing the results of the two companies.

27. Pizner Company is doing significant work to revitalize its warehouses. It is not sure whether it should capitalize these costs or expense them. What are the implications for current year net income and future net income of expensing verses capitalizing these costs?

BRIEF EXERCISES

Determine the cost of land.
(SO 1)

BE10–1 The following expenditures were incurred by JFK Company in purchasing land. Cash price $40,000, accrued taxes $3,000, attorneys' fees $2,500, real estate broker's commission $2,000, and clearing and grading $3,500. What is the cost of the land?

Determine the cost of a truck.
(SO 1)

BE10–2 Housman Company incurs the following expenditures in purchasing a truck: cash price $20,000, accident insurance $2,000, sales taxes $900, motor vehicle license $100, and painting and lettering $400. What is the cost of the truck?

Compute straight-line depreciation.
(SO 3)

BE10–3 Graig Ehlo Company acquires a delivery truck at a cost of $26,000. The truck is expected to have a salvage value of $2,000 at the end of its 4-year useful life. Compute annual depreciation for the first and second years using the straight-line method.

Compute depreciation and evaluate treatment.
(SO 3)

BE10–4 Olympic Company purchased land and a building on January 1, 2001. Management's best estimate of the value of the land was $100,000 and of the building $200,000, but management told the accounting department to record the land at $250,000 and the building at $50,000. The building is being depreciated on a straight-line basis over 20 years with no salvage value. Why do you suppose management requested this accounting treatment? Is it ethical?

Compute declining-balance depreciation.
(SO 3)

BE10–5 Depreciation information for Graig Ehlo Company is given in BE10–3. Assuming the declining-balance depreciation rate is double the straight-line rate, compute annual depreciation for the first and second years under the declining-balance method.

Compute depreciation using the units-of-activity method.
(SO 3)

BE10–6 Spud Webb Taxi Service uses the units-of-activity method in computing depreciation on its taxicabs. Each cab is expected to be driven 120,000 miles. Taxi No. 10 cost $36,500 and is expected to have a salvage value of $500. Taxi No. 10 is driven 30,000 miles in Year 1 and 20,000 miles in Year 2. Compute the depreciation for each year.

Compute revised depreciation.
(SO 4)

BE10–7 On January 1, 2001, the Wilkins Company ledger shows Equipment $32,000 and Accumulated Depreciation $9,000. The depreciation resulted from using the straight-line method with a useful life of 10 years and salvage value of $2,000. On this date, the company concludes that the equipment has a remaining useful life of only 4 years with the same salvage value. Compute the revised annual depreciation.

BE10–8 Prepare journal entries to record the following:

(a) Arna Company retires its delivery equipment, which cost $41,000. Accumulated depreciation is also $41,000 on this delivery equipment. No salvage value is received.

(b) Assume the same information as (a), except that accumulated depreciation for Arna Company is $38,000, instead of $41,000.

Prepare entries for disposal by retirement.
(SO 6)

BE10–9 Garrison Company sells office equipment on September 30, 2001, for $20,000 cash. The office equipment originally cost $72,000 and as of January 1, 2001, had accumulated depreciation of $42,000. Depreciation for the first 9 months of 2001 is $6,250. Prepare the journal entries to (a) update depreciation to September 30, 2001, and (b) record the sale of the equipment.

Prepare entries for disposal by sale.
(SO 6)

BE10–10 Keillor Company exchanges old delivery equipment for similar new delivery equipment. The book value of the old delivery equipment is $31,000 (cost $61,000 less accumulated depreciation $30,000), its fair market value is $19,000, and cash of $5,000 is paid. Prepare the entry to record the exchange.

Prepare entry for disposal by exchange.
(SO 6)

BE10–11 Assume the same information as BE10–10, except that the fair market value of the old delivery equipment is $42,000. Prepare the entry to record the exchange.

Prepare entry for disposal by exchange.
(SO 6)

BE10–12 Adamson Mining Co. purchased for $7 million a mine which is estimated to have 28 million tons of ore and no salvage value. In the first year, 6 million tons of ore are extracted and sold. (a) Prepare the journal entry to record depletion expense for the first year. (b) Show how this mine is reported on the balance sheet at the end of the first year.

Prepare depletion expense entry and balance sheet presentation for natural resources.
(SO 7)

BE10–13 Fayne Company purchases a patent for $160,000 on January 2, 2001. Its estimated useful life is 10 years. (a) Prepare the journal entry to record patent expense for the first year. (b) Show how this patent is reported on the balance sheet at the end of the first year.

Prepare patent expense entry and balance sheet presentation for intangibles.
(SO 8, 9)

BE10–14 Information related to plant assets, natural resources and intangibles at the end of 2001 for Riddler Company is as follows: buildings $900,000; accumulated depreciation—buildings $650,000; goodwill $410,000; coal mine $200,000; accumulated depletion—coal mine $108,000. Prepare a partial balance sheet of Riddler Company for these items.

Classify long-lived assets on balance sheet.
(SO 9)

BE10–15 In its 1998 annual report McDonald's Corporation reported beginning total assets of $18.2 billion; ending total assets of $19.8 billion; property, plant, and equipment (at cost) of $21.8 billion; accumulated depreciation of $5.7 billion; depreciation expense of $881.1 million; and net sales of $12.4 billion. (a) Compute the average life of McDonald's property, plant, and equipment. (b) Compute the average age of McDonald's property, plant, and equipment. (c) Compute McDonald's asset turnover ratio.

Analyze long-lived assets.
(SO 9)

EXERCISES

E10–1 The following expenditures relating to plant assets were made by Salvador Company during the first 2 months of 2001.

1. Paid $5,000 of accrued taxes at time plant site was acquired.
2. Paid $200 insurance to cover possible accident loss on new factory machinery while the machinery was in transit.
3. Paid $850 sales taxes on new delivery truck.
4. Paid $17,500 for parking lots and driveways on new plant site.
5. Paid $250 to have company name and advertising slogan painted on new delivery truck.
6. Paid $8,000 for installation of new factory machinery.
7. Paid $900 for one-year accident insurance policy on new delivery truck.
8. Paid $75 motor vehicle license fee on the new truck.

Determine cost of plant acquisitions.
(SO 1)

Instructions

(a) ⬛▶ Explain the application of the cost principle in determining the acquisition cost of plant assets.

(b) List the numbers of the foregoing transactions, and opposite each indicate the account title to which each expenditure should be debited.

E10–2 On March 1, 2001, Neil Young Company acquired real estate, on which it planned to construct a small office building, by paying $90,000 in cash. An old warehouse on the prop-

Determine acquisition costs on land.
(SO 1)

erty was razed at a cost of $6,600; the salvaged materials were sold for $1,700. Additional expenditures before construction began included $1,100 attorney's fee for work concerning the land purchase, $4,000 real estate broker's fee, $7,800 architect's fee, and $14,000 to put in driveways and a parking lot.

Instructions
(a) Determine the amount to be reported as the cost of the land.
(b) For each cost not used in part (a), indicate the account to be debited.

Compute depreciation under units-of-activity method.
(SO 3)

E10–3   Galactic Bus Lines uses the units-of-activity method in depreciating its buses. One bus was purchased on January 1, 2001, at a cost of $108,000. Over its 4-year useful life, the bus is expected to be driven 100,000 miles. Salvage value is expected to be $8,000.

Instructions
(a) Compute the depreciation cost per unit.
(b) Prepare a depreciation schedule assuming actual mileage was: 2001, 26,000; 2002, 32,000; 2003, 25,000; and 2004, 17,000.

Determine depreciation for partial periods.
(SO 3)

E10–4   Tory Amos Company purchased a new machine on October 1, 2001, at a cost of $96,000. The company estimated that the machine will have a salvage value of $12,000. The machine is expected to be used for 70,000 working hours during its 5-year life.

Instructions
Compute the depreciation expense under the following methods for the year indicated: (a) straight-line for 2001, (b) units-of-activity for 2001, assuming machine usage was 1,700 hours, and (c) declining-balance using double the straight-line rate for 2001 and 2002.

Compute revised annual depreciation.
(SO 3, 4)

E10–5   Bill Simpson, the new controller of the Bellingham Company, has reviewed the expected useful lives and salvage values of selected depreciable assets at the beginning of 2001. His findings are as follows:

Type of Asset	Date Acquired	Cost	Accumulated Depreciation 1/1/01	Useful Life in Years		Salvage Value	
				Old	Proposed	Old	Proposed
Building	1/1/95	$800,000	$114,000	40	50	$40,000	$48,000
Warehouse	1/1/98	100,000	11,400	25	20	5,000	3,600

All assets are depreciated by the straight-line method. Bellingham Company uses a calendar year in preparing annual financial statements. After discussion, management has agreed to accept Bill's proposed changes.

Instructions
(a) Compute the revised annual depreciation on each asset in 2001. (Show computations.)
(b) Prepare the entry (or entries) to record depreciation on the building in 2001.

Journalize entries for disposal of plant assets.
(SO 6)

E10–6   Presented below are selected transactions at Chen Company for 2001.

Jan. 1   Retired a piece of machinery that was purchased on January 1, 1991. The machine cost $62,000 on that date, and had a useful life of 10 years with no salvage value.

June 30   Sold a computer that was purchased on January 1, 1998. The computer cost $35,000, and had a useful life of 7 years with no salvage value. The computer was sold for $25,000.

Dec. 31   Discarded a delivery truck that was purchased on January 1, 1997. The truck cost $27,000 and was depreciated based on a 6-year useful life with a $3,000 salvage value.

Instructions
Journalize all entries required on the above dates, including entries to update depreciation, where applicable, on assets disposed of. Chen Company uses straight-line depreciation. (Assume depreciation is up to date as of December 31, 2000.)

Journalize entries for exchange of similar assets.
(SO 6)

E10–7   Presented below are two independent transactions:

1. White Cloud Co. exchanged trucks (cost $64,000 less $22,000 accumulated depreciation) plus cash of $17,000 for new trucks. The old trucks had a fair market value of $38,000. Prepare the entry to record the exchange of similar assets by White Cloud Co.

2. Nelle Inc. trades its used machine (cost $10,000 less $4,000 accumulated depreciation) for a new machine. In addition to exchanging the old machine (which had a fair market value of $9,000), Nelle also paid cash of $2,000.

Instructions
Prepare the entry to record the exchange of similar assets by Nelle Inc.

E10–8   Wind Company exchanges similar equipment with the Earth Company. Also Sun Company exchanges similar equipment with Moon Company. The following information pertains to these two exchanges:

Journalize entries for the exchange of similar plant assets.
(SO 6)

	Wind Co.	Sun Co.
Equipment (cost)	$28,000	$22,000
Accumulated depreciation	20,000	5,000
Fair market value of equipment	12,000	14,000
Cash paid	2,000	–0–

Instructions
Prepare the journal entries to record the exchange on the books of Wind Company and Sun Company.

E10–9   Peru's Delivery Company and Brazil's Express Delivery exchanged similar delivery trucks on January 1, 2001. Peru's truck cost $20,000, had accumulated depreciation of $13,000, and has a fair market value of $3,000. Brazil's truck cost $10,000, had accumulated depreciation of $8,000, and has a fair market value of $3,000.

Journalize entries for the exchange of similar plant assets.
(SO 6)

Instructions
(a) Journalize the exchange for Peru's Delivery Company.
(b) Journalize the exchange for Brazil's Express Delivery.

E10–10   On July 1, 2001, Reggie Inc. invested $360,000 in a mine estimated to have 800,000 tons of ore of uniform grade. During the last 6 months of 2001, 100,000 tons of ore were mined and sold.

Journalize entries for natural resources depletion.
(SO 7)

Instructions
(a) Prepare the journal entry to record depletion expense.
(b) Assume that the 100,000 tons of ore were mined, but only 80,000 units were sold. How are the costs applicable to the 20,000 unsold units reported?

E10–11   The following are selected 2001 transactions of McGillis Corporation.

Prepare adjusting entries for amortization.
(SO 8)

Jan. 1   Purchased a small company and recorded goodwill of $140,000. The goodwill has a useful life of 55 years.
May 1   Purchased a patent with an estimated useful life of 5 years and a legal life of 17 years for $30,000.

Instructions
Prepare all adjusting entries at December 31 to record amortization required by the events above.

E10–12   Vail Company, organized in 2001, has the following transactions related to intangible assets.

Prepare entries to set up appropriate accounts for different intangibles; amortize intangible assets.
(SO 8)

1/2/01	Purchased patent (7-year life)	$420,000
4/1/01	Goodwill purchased (indefinite life)	360,000
7/1/01	10-year franchise; expiration date 7/1/2011	450,000
9/1/01	Research and development costs	185,000

Instructions
Prepare the necessary entries to record these intangibles. All costs incurred were for cash. Make the entries as of December 31, 2001, recording any necessary amortization and reflecting all balances accurately as of that date.

E10–13   During 2000 Kettle Corporation reported net sales of $2,500,000, net income of $1,500,000, and depreciation expense of $150,000. Its balance sheet reported total assets of $1,400,000, plant assets of $800,000, and accumulated depreciation on plant assets of $300,000.

Calculate average useful life, average age of plant assets, and asset turnover ratio.
(SO 9)

Instructions
Calculate (a) average useful life of plant assets, (b) average age of plant assets, and (c) asset turnover ratio.

PROBLEMS: SET A

*Determine acquisition costs of
land and building.*
(SO 1)

P10–1A Hootie and the Blow Fish Company was organized on January 1. During the first year of operations, the following plant asset expenditures and receipts were recorded in random order.

Debits

1. Cost of real estate purchased as a plant site (land $200,000 and building $60,000)	$260,000
2. Installation cost of fences around property	6,750
3. Cost of demolishing building to make land suitable for construction of new building	19,000
4. Excavation costs for new building	23,000
5. Accrued real estate taxes paid at time of purchase of real estate	2,179
6. Cost of parking lots and driveways	29,000
7. Architect's fees on building plans	40,000
8. Real estate taxes paid for the current year on land	6,500
9. Full payment to building contractor	600,000
	$986,429

Credits

10. Proceeds from salvage of demolished building	$5,000

Instructions
Analyze the foregoing transactions using the following tabular arrangement. Insert the number of each transaction in the Item space and insert the amounts in the appropriate columns. For amounts entered in the Other Accounts column also indicate the account title.

Item	Land	Building	Other Accounts

*Compute depreciation under
different methods.*
(SO 3)

P10–2A In recent years, Erie Company has purchased three machines. Because of heavy turnover in the accounting department, a different accountant was in charge of selecting the depreciation method for each machine, and various methods have been selected. Information concerning the machines is summarized below:

Machine	Acquired	Cost	Salvage Value	Useful Life in Years	Depreciation Method
1	1/1/98	$96,000	$ 6,000	10	Straight-line
2	1/1/99	80,000	10,000	8	Declining-balance
3	11/1/01	78,000	6,000	6	Units-of-activity

For the declining-balance method, Erie Company uses the double-declining rate. For the units-of-activity method, total machine hours are expected to be 24,000. Actual hours of use in the first 3 years were: 2001, 4,000; 2002, 4,500; and 2003, 5,000.

Instructions
(a) Compute the amount of accumulated depreciation on each machine at December 31, 2001.
(b) If machine 2 was purchased on April 1 instead of January 1, what is the depreciation expense for this machine in (1) 1999 and (2) 2000?

*Compute depreciation under
different methods.*
(SO 3)

P10–3A On January 1, 2001, Rose Company purchased the following two machines for use in its production process:

Machine A: The cash price of this machine was $30,000. Related expenditures included: sales tax $1,800, shipping costs $175, insurance during shipping $75, installation and testing costs $50, and $90 of oil and lubricants to be used with the machinery during its first year of operation. Rose estimates that the useful life of the machine is 4 years with a $5,000 salvage value remaining at the end of that time period.

Machine B: The recorded cost of this machine was $60,000. Rose estimates that the useful life of the machine is 4 years with a $5,000 salvage value remaining at the end of that time period.

Instructions

(a) Prepare the following for Machine A:
   (1) The journal entry to record its purchase on January 1, 2001.
   (2) The journal entry to record annual depreciation at December 31, 2001, assuming the straight-line method of depreciation is used.

(b) Calculate the amount of depreciation expense that Rose should record for Machine B each year of its useful life assuming:
   (1) Rose uses the straight-line method of depreciation.
   (2) Rose uses the declining-balance method. The rate used is twice the straight-line rate.
   (3) Rose uses the units-of-activity method and estimates that the useful life of the machine is 27,500 units. Actual usage is as follows: 2001, 9,000 units; 2002, 7,500 units; 2003, 6,000 units; 2004, 5,000 units.

(c) Which method used to calculate depreciation on Machine B reports the lowest amount of depreciation expense in year 1 (2001)? The lowest amount in year 4 (2004)? The lowest total amount over the 4-year period?

P10–4A At December 31, 2001, Wallace Company reported the following as plant assets:

Journalize a series of equipment transactions related to purchase, sale, retirement, and depreciation.
(SO 3, 6, 9)

Land		$ 3,000,000
Buildings	$26,500,000	
Less: Accumulated depreciation—buildings	12,100,000	14,400,000
Equipment	40,000,000	
Less: Accumulated depreciation—equipment	5,000,000	35,000,000
Total plant assets		$52,400,000

During 2002, the following selected cash transactions occurred:

April 1 Purchased land for $2,200,000.
May 1 Sold equipment that cost $600,000 when purchased on January 1, 1998. The equipment was sold for $360,000.
June 1 Sold land purchased on June 1, 1992, for $1,800,000. The land cost $500,000.
July 1 Purchased equipment for $1,400,000.
Dec. 31 Retired equipment that cost $500,000 when purchased on December 31, 1992. No salvage value was received.

Instructions

(a) Journalize the above transactions. Wallace uses straight-line depreciation for buildings and equipment. The buildings are estimated to have a 40-year useful life and no salvage value; the equipment is estimated to have a 10-year useful life and no salvage value. Update depreciation on assets disposed of at the time of sale or retirement.

(b) Record adjusting entries for depreciation for 2002.

(c) Prepare the plant assets section of Wallace's balance sheet at December 31, 2002.

P10–5A Ghani Co. has delivery equipment that cost $50,000 and that has been depreciated $20,000. Record the disposal under the following assumptions:

Record disposals.
(SO 6)

(a) It was scrapped as having no value.
(b) It was sold for $31,000.
(c) It was sold for $18,000.
(d) It was exchanged for similar delivery equipment. The old delivery equipment has a fair market value of $12,000 and $32,000 was paid.
(e) It was exchanged for similar delivery equipment. The old delivery equipment has a fair market value of $35,000 and $9,000 was paid.

P10–6A The intangible assets section of El-Gazzar Company at December 31, 2001, is presented below:

Prepare entries to record transactions related to acquisition and amortization of intangibles; prepare the intangible assets section.
(SO 8, 9)

Patent ($60,000 cost less $6,000 amortization)	$54,000
Copyright ($36,000 cost less $14,400 amortization)	21,600
Total	$75,600

The patent was acquired in January 2001 and has a useful life of 10 years. The copyright was acquired in January 1998 and also has a useful life of 10 years. The following cash transactions may have affected intangible assets during 2002:

Jan. 2   Paid $18,000 legal costs to successfully defend the patent against infringement by another company.

Jan.–June   Developed a new product incurring $140,000 in research and development costs. A patent was granted for the product on July 1, and its useful life is equal to its legal life.

Sept. 1   Paid $60,000 to a quarterback to appear in commercials advertising the company's products. The commercials will air in September and October.

Oct. 1   Acquired a copyright for $80,000. The copyright has a useful life of 50 years.

Instructions

(a) Prepare journal entries to record the transactions above.
(b) Prepare journal entries to record the 2002 amortization expense for intangible assets.
(c) Prepare the intangible assets section of the balance sheet at December 31, 2002.
(d) ▓▓═▷ Prepare the note to the financials on El-Gazzar's intangibles as of December 31, 2002.

Prepare entries to correct errors made in recording and amortizing intangible assets.
(SO 8)

P10–7A   Due to rapid turnover in the accounting department, a number of transactions involving intangible assets were improperly recorded by Baird Company in 2001.

1. Baird developed a new manufacturing process, incurring research and development costs of $85,000. The company also purchased a patent for $37,400. In early January, Baird capitalized $122,400 as the cost of the patents. Patent amortization expense of $7,200 was recorded based on a 17-year useful life.

2. On July 1, 2001, Baird purchased a small company and as a result acquired goodwill of $60,000. Baird recorded a half-year's amortization in 2001, based on a 50-year life ($600 amortization).

Instructions

Prepare all journal entries necessary to correct any errors made during 2001. Assume the books have not yet been closed for 2001.

Calculate and comment on average age, average useful life of plant assets, and asset turnover ratio.
(SO 9)

P10–8A   Croix Corporation and Rye Corporation, two corporations of roughly the same size, are both involved in the manufacture of canoes and sea kayaks. Each company depreciates its plant assets using the straight-line approach. An investigation of their financial statements reveals this information:

	Croix Corp.	Rye Corp.
Net income	$ 400,000	$ 600,000
Sales	1,400,000	1,200,000
Total assets	2,000,000	1,500,000
Plant assets	1,500,000	800,000
Accumulated depreciation	300,000	625,000
Depreciation expense	75,000	25,000
Intangible assets (goodwill)	300,000	0
Amortization expense	60,000	0

Instructions

(a) For each company, calculate these values:
    (1) Average age of plant assets.
    (2) Average useful life.
    (3) Asset turnover ratio.
(b) ▓▓═▷ Based on your calculations in part (a), comment on the relative effectiveness of the two companies in using their assets to generate sales and produce net income. What factors complicate your ability to compare the two companies?

PROBLEMS: SET B

* *

Determine acquisition costs of land and building.
(SO 1)

P10–1B   Earth, Wind, and Fire Company was organized on January 1. During the first year of operations, the following plant asset expenditures and receipts were recorded in random order.

Debits

1. Cost of real estate purchased as a plant site (land $180,000 and building $70,000)		$ 250,000
2. Accrued real estate taxes paid at time of purchase of real estate		3,123
3. Cost of demolishing building to make land suitable for construction of new building		21,000
4. Cost of filling and grading the land		7,270
5. Excavation costs for new building		21,900
6. Architect's fees on building plans		55,000
7. Full payment to building contractor		629,500
8. Cost of parking lots and driveways		31,800
9. Real estate taxes paid for the current year on land		5,320
		$1,024,913

Credits

10. Proceeds for salvage of demolished building		$ 12,700

Instructions

Analyze the foregoing transactions using the following tabular arrangement. Insert the number of each transaction in the Item space and insert the amounts in the appropriate columns. For amounts entered in the Other Accounts column, also indicate the account titles.

Item	Land	Building	Other Accounts

P10–2B   In recent years, Lakeshore Transportation purchased three used buses. Because of frequent turnover in the accounting department, a different accountant selected the depreciation method for each bus, and various methods have been selected. Information concerning the buses is summarized below:

Compute depreciation under different methods.
(SO 3)

Bus	Acquired	Cost	Salvage Value	Useful Life in Years	Depreciation Method
1	1/1/99	$ 86,000	$ 6,000	5	Straight-line
2	1/1/99	140,000	10,000	4	Declining-balance
3	1/1/00	80,000	8,000	5	Units-of-activity

For the declining balance method, Lakeshore Transportation uses the double-declining rate. For the units-of-activity method, total miles are expected to be 120,000. Actual miles of use in the first 3 years were: 2000, 24,000; 2001, 34,000; and 2002, 30,000.

Instructions

(a) Compute the amount of accumulated depreciation on each bus at December 31, 2001.

(b) If Bus No. 2 was purchased on April 1 instead of January 1, what is the depreciation expense for this bus in (1) 1999 and (2) 2000?

P10–3B   On January 1, 2001, Axel Company purchased the following two machines for use in its production process:

Compute depreciation under different methods.
(SO 3)

Machine A: The cash price of this machine was $25,000. Related expenditures included: sales tax $1,500, shipping costs $150, insurance during shipping $80, installation and testing costs $70, and $100 of oil and lubricants to be used with the machinery during its first year of operations. Axel estimates that the useful life of the machine is 5 years with a $5,000 salvage value remaining at the end of that time period. Assume that the straight-line method of depreciation is used.

Machine B: The recorded cost of this machine was $50,000. Axel estimates that the useful life of the machine is 4 years with a $5,000 salvage value remaining at the end of that time period.

Instructions

(a) Prepare the following for Machine A:
   (1) The journal entry to record its purchase on January 1, 2001.
   (2) The journal entry to record annual depreciation at December 31, 2001.

(b) Calculate the amount of depreciation expense that Axel should record for Machine B each year of its useful life assuming:
   (1) Axel uses the straight-line method of depreciation.
   (2) Axel uses the declining-balance method. The rate used is twice the straight-line rate.
   (3) Axel uses the units-of-activity method and estimates that the useful life of the machine is 125,000 units. Actual usage is as follows: 2001, 45,000 units; 2002, 35,000 units; 2003, 25,000 units; 2004, 20,000 units.

(c) Which method used to calculate depreciation on Machine B reports the highest amount of depreciation expense in year 1 (2001)? The highest amount in year 4 (2004)? The highest total amount over the 4-year period?

Journalize a series of equipment transactions related to purchase, sale, retirement, and depreciation.
(SO 3, 6, 9)

P10–4B At December 31, 2001, Los Alamos Company reported the following as plant assets:

Land		$4,000,000
Buildings	$28,500,000	
Less: Accumulated depreciation—buildings	12,100,000	16,400,000
Equipment	48,000,000	
Less: Accumulated depreciation—equipment	5,000,000	43,000,000
Total plant assets		$63,400,000

During 2002, the following selected cash transactions occurred:

April 1 Purchased land for $2,630,000.
May 1 Sold equipment that cost $600,000 when purchased on January 1, 1998. The equipment was sold for $350,000.
June 1 Sold land purchased on June 1, 1992, for $1,800,000. The land cost $200,000.
July 1 Purchased equipment for $1,000,000.
Dec. 31 Retired equipment that cost $500,000 when purchased on December 31, 1992. No salvage value was received.

Instructions
(a) Journalize the above transactions. Los Alamos uses straight-line depreciation for buildings and equipment. The buildings are estimated to have a 40-year life and no salvage value; the equipment is estimated to have a 10-year useful life and no salvage value. Update depreciation on assets disposed of at the time of sale or retirement.
(b) Record adjusting entries for depreciation for 2002.
(c) Prepare the plant assets section of Los Alamos's balance sheet at December 31, 2002.

Record disposals.
(SO 6)

P10–5B Chon Co. has office furniture that cost $80,000 and that has been depreciated $48,000. Record the disposal under the following assumptions:

(a) It was scrapped as having no value.
(b) It was sold for $21,000.
(c) It was sold for $61,000.
(d) It was exchanged for similar office furniture. The old office furniture has a fair market value of $46,000 and $8,000 was paid.
(e) It was exchanged for similar office furniture. The old office furniture has a fair market value of $25,000 and $29,000 was paid.

Prepare entries to record transactions related to acquisition and amortization of intangibles; prepare the intangible assets section.
(SO 8, 9)

P10–6B The intangible assets section of De Paul Company at December 31, 2001, is presented below:

Patent ($70,000 cost less $7,000 amortization)	$63,000
Copyright ($48,000 cost less $19,200 amortization)	28,800
Total	$91,800

The patent was acquired in January 2001 and has a useful life of 10 years. The copyright was acquired in January 1998 and also has a useful life of 10 years. The following cash transactions may have affected intangible assets during 2002:

Jan. 2 Paid $18,000 legal costs to successfully defend the patent against infringement by another company.
Jan.–June Developed a new product incurring $140,000 in research and development costs. A patent was granted for the product on July 1, and its useful life is equal to its legal life.

Sept. 1   Paid $80,000 to an extremely large defensive lineman to appear in commercials advertising the company's products. The commercials will air in September and October.

Oct. 1   Acquired a copyright for $160,000. The copyright has a useful life of 50 years.

Instructions

(a) Prepare journal entries to record the transactions above.

(b) Prepare journal entries to record the 2002 amortization expense.

(c) Prepare the intangible assets section of the balance sheet at December 31, 2002.

P10–7B   Due to rapid turnover in the accounting department, a number of transactions involving intangible assets were improperly recorded by the Coker Company in 2001.

Prepare entries to correct for errors made in recording and amortizing intangible assets.
(SO 8)

1. Coker developed a new manufacturing process, incurring research and development costs of $153,000. The company also purchased a patent for $39,100. In early January, Coker capitalized $192,100 as the cost of the patents. Patent amortization expense of $11,300 was recorded based on a 17-year useful life.

2. On July 1, 2001, Coker purchased a small company and as a result acquired goodwill of $76,000. Coker recorded a half-year's amortization in 2001, based on a 50-year life ($760 amortization).

Instructions

Prepare all journal entries necessary to correct any errors made during 2001. Assume the books have not yet been closed for 2001.

P10–8B   Reggie Company and Newman Corporation, two corporations of roughly the same size, are both involved in the manufacture of in-line skates. Each company depreciates its plant assets using the straight-line approach. An investigation of their financial statements reveals the information:

Calculate and comment on average age, average useful life of plant assets, and asset turnover ratio.
(SO 9)

	Reggie Co.	Newman Corp.
Net income	$ 800,000	$1,000,000
Sales	1,600,000	1,300,000
Total assets	2,500,000	1,700,000
Plant assets	1,800,000	1,000,000
Accumulated depreciation	500,000	825,000
Depreciation expense	120,000	31,250
Intangible assets (goodwill)	300,000	0
Amortization expense	60,000	0

Instructions

(a) For each company, calculate these values:
   (1) Average age of plant assets.
   (2) Average useful life.
   (3) Asset turnover ratio.

(b) ▭▭▭▭▷ Based on your calculations in part (a), comment on the relative effectiveness of the two companies in using their assets to generate sales and produce income. What factors complicate your ability to compare the two companies?

BROADENING YOUR PERSPECTIVE

FINANCIAL REPORTING AND ANALYSIS

•••

FINANCIAL REPORTING AND ANALYSIS: Kellogg Company

BYP10–1   The financial statements and the Notes to Consolidated Financial Statements of Kellogg Company are presented in Appendix A.

Instructions

Refer to Kellogg's financial statements and answer the following questions:

(a) What was the total cost and book value of property, plant, and equipment at December 31, 1998?

(b) What method or methods of depreciation are used by Kellogg for financial reporting purposes?

(c) What was the amount of depreciation and amortization expense for each of the three years 1996–1998?

(d) Using the Statement of Cash Flows, what is the amount of additions to properties in 1998 and 1997?

(e) Where does Kellogg disclose its intangible assets, and what are the classifications and amounts of its intangibles at December 31, 1998?

(f) In December 1996, Kellogg acquired Lender's Bagel's business for $466 million in cash. Name the three components and the amounts of the intangible assets included in the acquisition price. What useful life is used to amortize these intangibles?

(g) What was the amount of research and development expenses Kellogg had in 1998?

COMPARATIVE ANALYSIS PROBLEM: Kellogg Company vs. General Mills

BYP10–2   Kellogg's financial statements are presented in Appendix A; General Mills's financial statements are presented in Appendix B.

Instructions

(a) The cost of General Mills's plant assets was $2,489 and its accumulated depreciation was $1,302.7. Based on the information contained in these financial statements, compute the following 1998 ratios for each company (use "Depreciation and amortization expense" amount for both Kellogg and General Mills):

1. Average life of plant assets.
2. Average age of plant assets.
3. Asset turnover ratio.

(b) What conclusions concerning the management of assets can be drawn from these data?

RESEARCH ASSIGNMENT

BYP10–3   The April 5, 1999, issue of *The Wall Street Journal* includes an article by Tara Parker-Pope entitled "Stopping Diaper Leaks Can Be Nasty Business, P&G Shows Its Rivals."

Instructions

Read the article and answer the following questions:

(a) How much money does the article say that Procter & Gamble and Kimberly-Clark receive in royalty payments from the sale of every package of diapers sold by competitors?

(b) How many patents are held on diaper-related inventions?

(c) How did Kimberly-Clark and Procter & Gamble resolve their long-running patent lawsuit? Why do you suppose they chose to resolve it this way?

(d) What were the results of Paragon Trade Brands' decision to fight Procter & Gamble, rather than pay a royalty payment? What impact do royalty payments have on the profit margins of small diaper manufacturers?

(e) What would have been the accounting implications had Procter & Gamble lost its patent infringement lawsuit with Paragon? That is, what accounting entry or adjustments might have been required?

INTERPRETING FINANCIAL STATEMENTS
Boeing and McDonnell Douglas

BYP10–4   Boeing and McDonnell Douglas were two leaders in the manufacture of aircraft. In 1996 Boeing announced intentions to acquire McDonnell Douglas and create one huge corporation. Its competitors, primarily Airbus of Europe, were very concerned that they would not be able to compete with such a huge rival. In addition, customers are concerned that this will reduce the number of suppliers to a point where Boeing would be able to dictate prices. Provided below are figures taken from the financial statements of Boeing and McDonnell Douglas which allow a comparison of the operations of the two corporations prior to their merger.

(in millions of dollars)	Boeing	McDonnell Douglas
Total revenue	$19,515	$14,322
Net income (loss)	393	(416)
Total assets	22,098	10,466
Land	404	91
Buildings and fixtures	5,791	1,647
Machinery and equipment	7,251	2,161
Total property, plant, and equipment (at cost)	13,744	3,899
Accumulated depreciation	7,288	2,541
Depreciation expense	976	196

Instructions
(a) Which company had older assets?
(b) Which company used a longer average estimated useful life for its assets?
(c) Based on the total asset turnover ratio, which company used its assets more effectively to generate sales?
(d) Besides an increase in size, what other factors might have motivated this merger?

Merck and Johnson & Johnson

BYP10–5 Merck Co., Inc. and Johnson & Johnson are two leading producers of health care products. Each has considerable assets, as well as expending considerable funds each year toward the development of new products. The development of a new health care product is often very expensive, and risky. New products frequently must undergo considerable testing before approval for distribution to the public. For example, it took Johnson & Johnson 4 years and $200 million to develop its 1-DAY ACUVUE contact lenses. Below are some basic data compiled from the financial statements of these two companies.

(all dollars in millions)	Johnson & Johnson	Merck
Total assets	$15,668	$21,857
Total revenue	15,734	14,970
Net income	2,006	2,997
Research and development expense	1,278	1,230
Intangible assets	2,403	7,212

Instructions
(a) What kinds of intangible assets might a health care products company have? Does the composition of these intangibles matter to investors—that is, would it be perceived differently if all of Merck's intangibles were goodwill, than if all of its intangibles were patents?
(b) By employing the asset turnover ratio, determine which company is using its assets more effectively. (*Note:* The previous year's total assets were $19,928 million for Merck and $12,242 million for Johnson & Johnson.)
(c) Suppose the president of Merck has come to you for advice. He has noted that by eliminating research and development expenditures the company could have reported $1.3 billion more in net income in the current year. He is frustrated because much of the research never results in a product, or the products take years to develop. He says shareholders are eager for higher returns, so he is considering eliminating research and development expenditures for at least a couple of years. What would you advise?
(d) The notes to Merck's financial statements indicate that Merck has goodwill of $4.1 billion. Where does recorded goodwill come from? Is it necessarily a good thing to have a lot of goodwill on your books?

REAL-WORLD FOCUS: Clark Equipment Company

BYP10–6 **Clark Equipment Company** was originally formed in 1902 as a general manufacturing company. During its history it has specialized in the manufacture of drills, gears, towing tractors, lift trucks, and truck transmissions. At the time of the example presented below, Clark operated throughout the U.S. and Europe in the design, manufacture, and sale of skid steer loaders and mini-excavators, golf carts and utility vehicles, axles and transmissions for off-highway vehicles, and asphalt paving equipment. In 1995, Ingersoll-Rand Company acquired Clark and combined its operating units with existing I-R businesses.

The following information relates to the plant assets of Clark Equipment:

CLARK EQUIPMENT COMPANY Balance Sheet (partial) (in millions)		
	Previous Year	Current Year
Land	$ 7.4	$ 13.2
Land improvements	5.9	8.8
Buildings	77.3	126.0
Machinery and equipment	398.4	451.7
Totals	489.0	599.7
Accumulated depreciation	272.8	315.9
Total plant assets	$216.2	$283.8

Instructions
- (a) What type of costs would Clark Equipment capitalize in the land category of plant assets?
- (b) Cite several possible types of land improvements that Clark Equipment might have made.
- *(c) What is the book value of Clark Equipment's plant assets for the current year?

CRITICAL THINKING

GROUP DECISION CASE

BYP10–7 Fresno Company and Auburn Company are two proprietorships that are similar in many respects except that Fresno Company uses the straight-line method and Auburn Company uses the declining-balance method at double the straight-line rate. On January 2, 1999, both companies acquired the following depreciable assets.

Asset	Cost	Salvage Value	Useful Life
Building	$320,000	$20,000	40 years
Equipment	110,000	10,000	10 years

Including the appropriate depreciation charges, annual net income for the companies in the years 1999, 2000, and 2001 and total income for the 3 years were as follows:

	1999	2000	2001	Total
Fresno Company	$84,000	$88,400	$90,000	$262,400
Auburn Company	68,000	76,000	85,000	229,000

At December 31, 2001, the balance sheets of the two companies are similar except that Auburn Company has more cash than Fresno Company.

Mary Flaherty is interested in buying one of the companies, and she comes to you for advice.

Instructions
With the class divided into groups, answer the following:

- (a) Determine the annual and total depreciation recorded by each company during the 3 years.

(b) Assuming that Auburn Company also uses the straight-line method of depreciation instead of the declining-balance method as in (a), prepare comparative income data for the 3 years.

(c) Which company should Mrs. Flaherty buy? Why?

COMMUNICATION ACTIVITY

BYP10–8   The following was published with the financial statements to American Exploration Company:

AMERICAN EXPLORATION COMPANY
Notes to the Financial Statements

Property, Plant, and Equipment—The Company accounts for its oil and gas exploration and production activities using the successful efforts method of accounting. Under this method, acquisition costs for proved and unproved properties are capitalized when incurred . . . . The costs of drilling exploratory wells are capitalized pending determination of whether each well has discovered proved reserves. If proved reserves are not discovered, such drilling costs are charged to expense . . . . Depletion of the cost of producing oil and gas properties is computed on the units-of-activity method.

Instructions
Write a brief memo to your instructor discussing American Exploration Company's note regarding property, plant, and equipment. Your memo should address what is meant by the "successful efforts method" and "units-of-activity method."

ETHICS CASE

BYP10–9   Henning Plastic Molding Company is suffering declining sales of its principal product, nonbiodegradeable plastic cartons. The president, Philip Shapeero, instructs his controller, Sharon Fetters, to lengthen asset lives to reduce depreciation expense. A processing line of automated plastic extruding equipment, purchased for $2.7 million in January 1999 was originally estimated to have a useful life of 8 years and a salvage value of $300,000. Depreciation has been recorded for 2 years on that basis. Philip wants the estimated life changed to 12 years total, and the straight-line method continued. Sharon is hesitant to make the change, believing it is unethical to increase net income in this manner. Philip says, "Hey, the life is only an estimate, and I've heard that our competition uses a 12-year life on their production equipment."

Instructions
(a) Who are the stakeholders in this situation?
(b) Is the change in asset life unethical or simply a good business practice by an astute president?
(c) What is the effect of Philip Shapeero's proposed change on income before taxes in the year of change?

SURFING THE NET

BYP10–10   A company's annual report identifies the amount of its plant assets and the depreciation method used.

Address: http://www.reportgallery.com (or go to www.wiley.com/college/weygandt)

Steps:
1. From Report Gallery Homepage, choose **Viewing Library**.
2. Select a particular company.
3. Choose **Annual Report**.
4. Follow instructions below.

Instructions
Answer the following questions:

   (a) What is the name of the company?
   (b) What is the Internet address of the annual report?
   (c) At fiscal year-end, what is the net amount of its plant assets?
   (d) What is the accumulated depreciation?
   (e) Which method of depreciation does the company use?

Answers to Self-Study Questions
1. d   2. b   3. d   4. d   5. b   6. d   7. a   8. c   9. c   10. b   11. c

Answer to Kellogg Review It Question 4, p. 417
Kellogg reports the detail about its "Property, net" in Note 14 "Supplemental financial statement data." The classifications and amounts constituting the detail for "Property, net" are reported by Kellogg as (in millions) land $49.3; buildings $1,247.9; machinery and equipment $3,608.2; construction in progress $341.4; and accumulated depreciation $2,358.

 Remember to go back to the Navigator box on the chapter-opening page and check off your completed work.

Before studying this chapter, you should know or, if necessary, review:

a. What is a current liability? a long-term liability? (Ch. 4, pp. 159–160)

b. The importance of liquidity in evaluating the financial position of a company. (Ch. 4, p. 160)

c. How to make adjusting entries related to unearned revenue (Ch. 3, p. 101) and accrued expenses. (Ch. 3, pp. 104–106)

d. How to record adjusting entries for interest expense and interest payable. (Ch. 3, pp. 104–105)

THE NAVIGATOR

FEATURE STORY

Financing His Dreams

What would you do if you had a great idea for a new product, but you couldn't come up with the cash you needed to get the business off the ground? Small businesses often can't attract common stock investors, nor can they obtain traditional debt financing through bank loans or bond issuances. Instead, they often resort to unusual, and costly, forms of nontraditional financing. Such was the case for Wilbert Murdock. Although Mur-

dock grew up in a New York housing project, he always had great ambitions. This ambitious spirit led him to a number of business ventures that failed: a medical diagnostic tool, a device to eliminate carpal-tunnel syndrome, custom sneakers, and a device to keep people from falling asleep while driving.

His latest idea is computerized golf clubs that analyze a golfer's swing and provide immediate feedback. Murdock believes that the idea has great potential: many golfers are willing to shell out considerable sums of money for devices that might im-

prove their game. But Murdock had no cash to develop his product, and banks and other lenders have shied away. Rather than giving up because he couldn't get outside financing, Murdock resorted to credit cards—in a big way. He quickly owed $25,000 to credit card companies.

While funding a business with credit cards might sound unusual, it isn't. A recent study found that one-third of businesses with fewer than 20 employees financed at least part of their operations with credit cards. As Murdock explains, credit cards are an appealing way to finance a start-up because "credit-card companies don't care how the money is spent." But they do care how they are paid. And so Murdock endures high interest charges and a barrage of credit card collection letters. The debt that hangs over his head has forced him to sacrifice nearly everything in order to keep his business afloat. His car doesn't work, he barely has enough money to buy food, and he lives and works out of a dimly lit apartment in his mother's basement. Through it all he tries to maintain a positive spirit, joking that, if he becomes successful, he might some day get to appear in an American Express commercial.

Source: Rodney Ho, "Banking on Plastic: To Finance a Dream, Many Entrepreneurs Binge on Credit Cards," *The Wall Street Journal*, March 9, 1998, p. A1.

THE NAVIGATOR

CHAPTER **11**

LIABILITIES

THE NAVIGATOR ✔

■ Understand *Concepts for Review* ☐

■ Read *Feature Story* ☐

■ Scan *Study Objectives* ☐

■ Read *Preview* ☐

■ Read text and answer *Before You Go On*
p. 469 ☐ p. 474 ☐ p. 481 ☐ p. 483 ☐

■ Work *Demonstration Problem* ☐

■ Review *Summary of Study Objectives* ☐

■ Answer *Self-Study Questions* ☐

■ Complete assignments ☐

STUDY OBJECTIVES

After studying this chapter, you should be able to:

1. *Explain a current liability and identify the major types of current liabilities.*
2. *Describe the accounting for notes payable.*
3. *Explain the accounting for other current liabilities.*
4. *Explain why bonds are issued and identify the types of bonds.*
5. *Prepare the entries for the issuance of bonds and interest expense.*
6. *Describe the entries when bonds are redeemed or converted.*
7. *Describe the accounting for long-term notes payable.*
8. *Identify the methods for the financial statement presentation and analysis of long-term liabilities.*

THE
NAVIGATOR

*I*n Chapter 4, we defined liabilities as "creditors' claims on total assets" and as "existing debts and obligations." These claims, debts, and obligations must be settled or paid at some time in the **future** by the transfer of assets or services. The future date on which they are due or payable (maturity date) is a significant feature of liabilities. This "future date" feature gives rise to two basic classifications of liabilities: (1) current liabilities and (2) long-term liabilities. Thus, our discussion of liabilities in this chapter is divided into these two classifications.

Inventor-entrepreneur Wilbert Murdock, as you can tell from the Feature Story, has been forced for lack of other sources to use multiple credit cards to finance his business ventures. Murdock's credit card debts would be classified as *current liabilities* because they are due every month. Yet Murdock, by making minimal payments and paying high interest each month, uses this credit source long-term. Some credit card balances remain outstanding for years as they accumulate interest. The content and organization of the chapter are as follows:

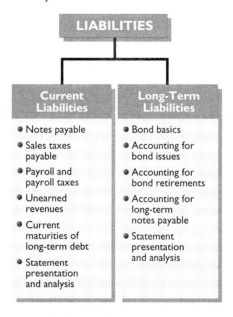

THE NAVIGATOR

SECTION 1 CURRENT LIABILITIES

WHAT IS A CURRENT LIABILITY?

1

STUDY
OBJECTIVE

Explain a current liability and identify the major types of current liabilities.

As explained in Chapter 4, a **current liability** is a debt that can reasonably be expected to be paid (1) from existing current assets or through the creation of other current liabilities, and (2) within one year or the operating cycle, whichever is longer. Debts that do not meet both criteria are classified as long-term liabilities. In most companies, current liabilities are paid within one year out of current assets, rather than through the creation of other liabilities.

Companies must carefully monitor the relationship of current liabilities to current assets. This relationship is critical in evaluating a company's liquidity, or short-term debt paying ability. A company that has more current liabilities than current assets is usually the subject of some concern because the company may not be able to meet its current obligations when they become due.

Current liabilities include notes payable, accounts payable, unearned revenues, and accrued liabilities such as taxes, salaries and wages, and interest payable. The entries for accounts payable and adjusting entries for some current liabilities have been explained in previous chapters. Other types of current liabilities that are frequently encountered in practice are discussed in the following sections.

Notes Payable

Obligations in the form of written promissory notes are recorded as notes payable. Notes payable are often used instead of accounts payable. Doing so gives the lender written documentation of the obligation in case legal remedies are needed to collect the debt. Notes payable usually require the borrower to pay interest and frequently are issued to meet short-term financing needs.

Notes are issued for varying periods. **Those due for payment within one year of the balance sheet date are usually classified as current liabilities.** Most notes are interest-bearing. To illustrate the accounting for notes payable, assume that First National Bank agrees to lend $100,000 on March 1, 2001, if Cole Williams Co. signs a $100,000, 12%, 4-month note. With an interest-bearing promissory note, the amount of assets received upon issuance of the note generally equals the note's face value. Cole Williams Co. therefore will receive $100,000 cash and will make the following journal entry:

Mar. 1	Cash	100,000	
	Notes Payable		100,000
	(To record issuance of 12%, 4-month note to		
	First National Bank)		

A	=	L	+	SE
+100,000		+100,000		

Interest accrues over the life of the note and must be recorded periodically. If Cole Williams Co. prepares financial statements semiannually, an adjusting entry is required to recognize interest expense and interest payable of $4,000 ($100,000 × 12% × 4/12) at June 30. The formula for computing interest and its application to Cole Williams Co. are shown in Illustration 11-1.

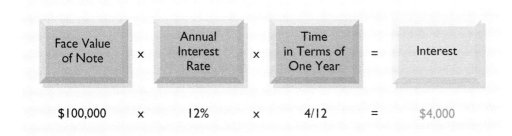

The adjusting entry is:

June 30	Interest Expense	4,000	
	Interest Payable		4,000
	(To accrue interest for 4 months on First		
	National Bank note)		

A	=	L	+	SE
		+4,000		−4,000

In the June 30 financial statements, the current liability section of the balance sheet will show notes payable $100,000 and interest payable $4,000. In addition, interest expense of $4,000 will be reported under Other Expenses and Losses in the income statement. If Cole Williams Co. prepared financial statements monthly, the adjusting entry at the end of each month would have been $1,000 ($100,000 × 12% × 1/12).

HELPFUL HINT
The current liability section gives creditors a good idea of what obligations are coming due.

STUDY
OBJECTIVE

Describe the accounting for notes payable.

ILLUSTRATION 11-1

Formula for computing interest

At maturity (July 1), Cole Williams Co. must pay the face value of the note ($100,000) plus $4,000 interest ($100,000 × 12% × 4/12). The entry to record payment of the note and accrued interest is as follows:

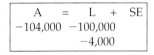

July 1	Notes Payable	100,000	
	Interest Payable	4,000	
	Cash		104,000
	(To record payment of First National Bank interest-bearing note and accrued interest at maturity)		

Sales Taxes Payable

As consumers, we are well aware that many of the products we purchase at retail stores are subject to sales taxes. The tax is expressed as a stated percentage of the sales price. The retailer (or selling company) collects the tax from the customer when the sale occurs, and periodically (usually monthly) remits the collections to the state's department of revenue.

Under most state sales tax laws, the amount of the sale and the amount of the sales tax collected must be rung up separately on the cash register. (Gasoline sales are a major exception.) The cash register readings are then used to credit Sales and Sales Taxes Payable. For example, assuming that the March 25 cash register readings for Cooley Grocery show sales of $10,000 and sales taxes of $600 (sales tax rate of 6%), the entry is:

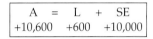

Mar. 25	Cash	10,600	
	Sales		10,000
	Sales Taxes Payable		600
	(To record daily sales and sales taxes)		

When the taxes are remitted to the taxing agency, Sales Taxes Payable is debited and Cash is credited. The company does not report sales taxes as an expense; it simply forwards the amount paid by the customer to the government. Thus, Cooley Grocery serves only as a **collection agent** for the taxing authority.

ACCOUNTING IN ACTION
Business Insight

Sales taxes do not apply exclusively to retail companies. They also apply to manufacturing companies, service companies, and public utilities, and the extent of the taxes is increasing. There are now over 9,000 state and local sales taxes. "Compliance is becoming much more complex as states expand their sales taxes," says an American Telephone and Telegraph (AT&T) tax attorney. They are also becoming more costly. AT&T employs a staff just to file the company's sales tax returns and handle the sales tax audits.

When sales taxes are not rung up separately on the cash register, total receipts are divided by 100% plus the sales tax percentage to determine sales. To illustrate, assume in the above example that Cooley Grocery "rings up" total receipts, which are $10,600. Because the amount received from the sale is equal to the sales price, 100%, plus 6% of sales, or 1.06 times the sales total, we can compute sales as follows:

$$\$10,600 \div 1.06 = \$10,000$$

Thus, the sales tax amount of $600 is found either by (1) subtracting sales from total receipts ($10,600 − $10,000) or (2) multiplying sales by the sales tax rate ($10,000 × 6%).

Payroll and Payroll Taxes Payable

Every employer incurs liabilities relating to employees' salaries and wages. One is the amount of wages and salaries owed to employees—**wages and salaries payable**. Another is the amount required by law to be withheld from employees' gross pay. Until these **withholding taxes** (federal and state income taxes, and Social Security taxes) are remitted to the governmental taxing authorities, they are credited to appropriate liability accounts. For example, if a corporation withholds taxes from its employees' wages and salaries, accrual and payment of a $100,000 payroll would be recorded as follows:

March 7	Salaries and Wages Expense	100,000	
	FICA Taxes Payable[1]		7,250
	Federal Income Taxes Payable		21,864
	State Income Taxes Payable		2,922
	Salaries and Wages Payable		67,964
	(To record payroll and withholding taxes for the week ending March 7)		

A	=	L	+	SE
		+7,250		−100,000
		+21,864		
		+2,922		
		+67,964		

March 11	Salaries and Wages Payable	67,964	
	Cash		67,964
	(To record payment of the March 7 payroll)		

A	=	L	+	SE
−67,964		−67,964		

Illustration 11-2 summarizes the types of payroll deductions.

ILLUSTRATION 11-2

Payroll deductions

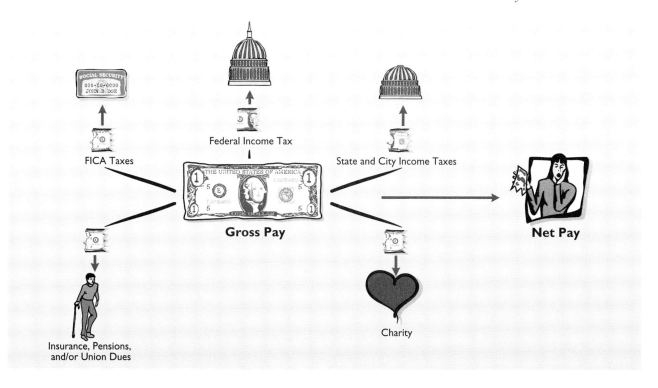

Also, with every payroll, the employer incurs liabilities to pay various **payroll taxes** levied upon the employer. These payroll taxes include the employer's share of Social Security taxes and the state and federal unemployment taxes.

---

[1]Social Security taxes are commonly referred to as FICA taxes. In 1937, Congress enacted the Federal Insurance Contribution Act (FICA). This act and other payroll issues are discussed in greater detail in Appendix D.

Based on the $100,000 payroll in the previous example, the following entry would be made to record the employer's expense and liability for these payroll taxes.

A	=	L	+	SE
		+7,250		−13,450
		+800		
		+5,400		

March 7	Payroll Tax Expense	13,450	
	FICA Taxes Payable		7,250
	Federal Unemployment Taxes Payable		800
	State Unemployment Taxes Payable		5,400
	(To record employer's payroll taxes on March 7 payroll)		

ILLUSTRATION 11-3

Employer payroll taxes

Illustration 11-3 shows the types of taxes levied on employers.

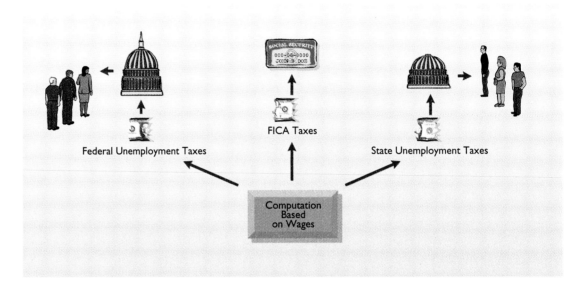

The payroll and payroll tax liability accounts are classified as current liabilities because they must be paid to employees or remitted to taxing authorities periodically and near term. Taxing authorities impose substantial fines and penalties on employers if the withholding and payroll taxes are not computed correctly and paid on time.

Unearned Revenues

A magazine publisher such as Sports Illustrated may receive a customer's check when magazines are ordered, and an airline company, such as American Airlines, often receives cash when it sells tickets for future flights. How do these companies account for unearned revenues that are received before goods are delivered or services are rendered?

1. When the advance is received, Cash is debited, and a current liability account identifying the source of the unearned revenue is credited.
2. When the revenue is earned, the unearned revenue account is debited, and an earned revenue account is credited.

To illustrate, assume that Superior University sells 10,000 season football tickets at $50 each for its five-game home schedule. The entry for the sales of season tickets is:

A	=	L	+	SE
+500,000		+500,000		

Aug. 6	Cash	500,000	
	Unearned Football Ticket Revenue		500,000
	(To record sale of 10,000 season tickets)		

As each game is completed, the following entry is made:

Sept. 7	Unearned Football Ticket Revenue	100,000	
	Football Ticket Revenue		100,000
	(To record football ticket revenues earned)		

A	=	L	+	SE
		−100,000		+100,000

Unearned Football Ticket Revenue is, therefore, unearned revenue and is reported as a current liability in the balance sheet. As revenue is earned, a transfer from unearned revenue to earned revenue occurs. Unearned revenue is material for some companies: In the airline industry, for example, tickets sold for future flights represent almost 50% of total current liabilities. At United Air Lines, unearned ticket revenue is the largest current liability, recently amounting to over $1 billion.

Illustration 11-4 shows specific unearned and earned revenue accounts used in selected types of businesses.

Type of Business	Account Title	
	Unearned Revenue	**Earned Revenue**
Airline	Unearned Passenger Ticket Revenue	Passenger Revenue
Magazine publisher	Unearned Subscription Revenue	Subscription Revenue
Hotel	Unearned Rental Revenue	Rental Revenue

ILLUSTRATION 11-4

Unearned and earned revenue accounts

Current Maturities of Long-Term Debt

Companies often have a portion of long-term debt that comes due in the current year. For example, assume that Wendy Construction issues a 5-year interest-bearing $25,000 note on January 1, 2000. This note specifies that each January 1, starting January 1, 2001, $5,000 of the note should be paid. When financial statements are prepared on December 31, 2000, $5,000 should be reported as a current liability and $20,000 as a long-term liability. Current maturities of long-term debt are often identified on the balance sheet as **long-term debt due within one year**.

It is not necessary to prepare an adjusting entry to recognize the current maturity of long-term debt. The proper statement classification of each balance sheet account is recognized when the balance sheet is prepared.

Financial Statement Presentation and Analysis

Presentation

As indicated in Chapter 4, current liabilities are the first category under liabilities on the balance sheet. Each of the principal types of current liabilities is listed separately within the category. In addition, the terms of notes payable and other pertinent information concerning the individual items are disclosed in the notes to the financial statements.

Current liabilities are seldom listed in the order of maturity because of the varying maturity dates that may exist for specific obligations such as notes payable. A more common, and entirely satisfactory, method of presenting current liabilities is to list them by **order of magnitude**, with the largest obligations first. Many companies, as a matter of custom, show notes payable and accounts payable first, regardless of amount. Illustration 11-5 presents the current liabilities section of Kellogg Company.

Analysis

Classifying assets and liabilities into current and noncurrent allows a company's liquidity to be analyzed and evaluated. Liquidity refers to the ability of a company to pay its maturing obligations and meet unexpected needs for cash. The

KELLOGG COMPANY
Balance Sheet
December 31, 1998
(in millions)

Assets

Current assets	$1,496.5
Property, plant, and equipment (net)	2,888.8
Identifiable intangible assets and goodwill	666.2
Total assets	$5,051.5

Liabilities and Stockholders' Equity

Current liabilities	
Current maturities of long-term debt	$ 1.1
Notes payable	620.4
Accounts payable	386.9
Other current liabilities	710.1
Total current liabilities	1,718.5
Noncurrent liabilities	2,443.2
Stockholders' equity	889.8
Total liabilities and stockholders' equity	$5,051.5

HELPFUL HINT

For another example of a current liability section refer to the General Mills balance sheet in Appendix B.

relationship of current assets and current liabilities is critical in analyzing liquidity. This relationship is expressed as a dollar amount called working capital and as a ratio called the current ratio.

The difference between current assets and current liabilities is working capital. The formula for the computation of Kellogg's working capital is shown in Illustration 11-6 (dollar amounts in millions).

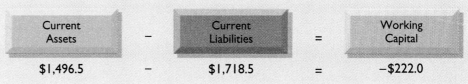

Current Assets	−	Current Liabilities	=	Working Capital
$1,496.5	−	$1,718.5	=	−$222.0

As an absolute dollar amount, working capital is limited in its informational value. For example $1 million of working capital may be far more than needed for a small company but be inadequate for a large corporation. And, $1 million of working capital may be adequate for a company at one time but be inadequate at another time. The current ratio permits us to compare the liquidity of different sized companies and of a single company at different times. The current ratio is current assets divided by current liabilities. The formula for this ratio is illustrated below, along with its computation using Kellogg's current asset and current liability data:

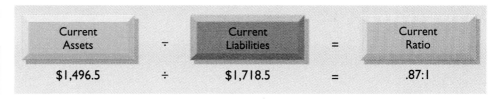

Current Assets	÷	Current Liabilities	=	Current Ratio
$1,496.5	÷	$1,718.5	=	.87:1

Historically, a ratio of 2:1 was considered to be the standard for a good credit rating. In recent years, however, many healthy companies have maintained ratios well below 2:1. This is exemplified by Kellogg, which is considered a healthy company even though its current ratio is below 1:1.

BEFORE YOU GO ON ...

Review It

1. What are the two criteria for classifying a debt as a current liability?
2. Identify three liabilities classified as current by Kellogg. The answer to this question is provided on page 509.
3. What entries are made for an interest-bearing note payable?
4. How are sales taxes recorded by a retailer? Identify three examples of unearned revenues.
5. What are the three taxes generally withheld from employees' wages or salaries?
6. How may the liquidity of a company be analyzed?

Do It

You and several classmates are studying for the next accounting examination. They ask you to answer the following questions: (1) How is the sales tax amount determined when the cash register total includes sales taxes? (2) What is the amount of taxes to be withheld from an employee's payroll check?

Reasoning: To answer the first question, you must remove the sales taxes from the total sales. To answer the second question, you need to know the employee's gross pay, the number of exemptions claimed by the employee, the maximum taxable earnings, the employee's accumulated earnings, and the tax rates.

Solution:

(1) First, divide the total proceeds by 100% plus the sales tax percentage to find the sales amount; second, subtract the sales amount from the total proceeds to determine the sales taxes.

(2) The taxable FICA earnings are multiplied by the FICA tax rate. Both the federal and state income tax withheld are determined by multiplying the applicable tax rate times the amount of current earnings.

THE
NAVIGATOR

Related exercise material: BE11–3, BE11–4, E11–1, E11–2, E11–3.

SECTION 2 LONG-TERM LIABILITIES

Long-term liabilities are obligations that are expected to be paid after one year. In this section we will explain the accounting for the principal types of obligations reported in the long-term liability section of the balance sheet. These obligations often are in the form of bonds or long-term notes.

BOND BASICS

Bonds are a form of interest-bearing notes payable issued by corporations, universities, and governmental agencies. Bonds, like common stock, are sold in small denominations (usually a thousand dollars or multiples of a thousand dollars). As a result, bonds attract many investors.

STUDY

OBJECTIVE

Explain why bonds are issued and identify the types of bonds.

Why Issue Bonds?

A corporation may use long-term financing other than bonds, such as notes payable and leasing. However, these other forms of financing involve one individual, one company, or a financial institution. Notes payable and leasing are therefore seldom sufficient to furnish the funds needed for plant expansion and major projects like new buildings. To obtain **large amounts of long-term capital,** corporate management usually must decide whether to issue bonds or to use equity financing (common stock).

From the standpoint of the corporation seeking long-term financing, bonds offer the following advantages over common stock:

ILLUSTRATION 11-8

Advantages of bond financing over common stock

Bond Financing	Advantages
	1. **Stockholder control is not affected.** Bondholders do not have voting rights, so current owners (stockholders) retain full control of the company.
	2. **Tax savings result.** Bond interest is deductible for tax purposes; dividends on stock are not.
	3. **Earnings per share on common stock may be higher.** Although bond interest expense reduces net income, earnings per share on common stock often is higher under bond financing because no additional shares of common stock are issued.

To illustrate the potential effect on earnings per share, assume that Microsystems, Inc., is considering two plans for financing the construction of a new $5 million plant: Plan A involves issuance of 200,000 shares of common stock at the current market price of $25 per share. Plan B involves issuance of $5 million, 12% bonds at face value. Income before interest and taxes on the new plant will be $1.5 million; income taxes are expected to be 30%. Microsystems currently has 100,000 shares of common stock outstanding. The alternative effects on earnings per share are shown in Illustration 11-9.

ILLUSTRATION 11-9

Effects on earnings per share—stocks vs. bonds

	Plan A Issue Stock	Plan B Issue Bonds
Income before interest and taxes	$1,500,000	$1,500,000
Interest (12% × $5,000,000)	—	600,000
Income before income taxes	1,500,000	900,000
Income tax expense (30%)	450,000	270,000
Net income	$1,050,000	$ 630,000
Outstanding shares	300,000	100,000
Earnings per share	$ 3.50	$ 6.30

INTERNATIONAL NOTE

The priority of bondholders' versus stockholders' rights varies across countries. In Japan, Germany, and France stockholders and employees are given priority, with liquidation of the firm to pay creditors seen as a last resort. In Britain creditors' interests are put first—the courts are quick to give control of the firm to creditors.

Note that net income is $420,000 ($1,050,000 − $630,000) less with long-term debt financing (bonds). However, earnings per share is higher because there are 200,000 fewer shares of common stock outstanding.

The major disadvantages resulting from the use of bonds are that interest must be paid on a periodic basis and the principal (face value) of the bonds must be paid at maturity. A company with fluctuating earnings and a relatively weak cash position may experience great difficulty in meeting interest requirements in periods of low earnings.

Types of Bonds

Bonds may have many different features. Some types of bonds commonly issued are described in the following sections:

Secured and Unsecured Bonds

Secured bonds have specific assets of the issuer pledged as collateral for the bonds. A bond secured by real estate, for example, is called a mortgage bond. A bond secured by specific assets set aside to retire the bonds is called a sinking fund bond. Unsecured bonds are issued against the general credit of the borrower. These bonds, called debenture bonds, are used extensively by large corporations with good credit ratings. For example, in a recent annual report, DuPont reported over $2 billion of debenture bonds outstanding.

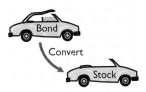

Secured Bonds

Unsecured Bonds

Term and Serial Bonds

Bonds that are due for payment (mature) at a single specified future date are called term bonds. In contrast, bonds that mature in installments are called serial bonds. For example, Caterpillar Inc. debentures due in 2007 are term bonds, and their debentures due between 2000 and 2007 are serial bonds.

Registered and Bearer Bonds

Bonds issued in the name of the owner are called registered bonds; interest payments on registered bonds are made by check to bondholders of record. Bonds not registered are called bearer (or coupon) bonds; holders are required to send in coupons to receive interest payments. Coupon bonds may be transferred directly to another party. In contrast, the transfer of registered bonds requires cancellation of the bonds by the corporation and the issuance of new bonds. With minor exceptions, most bonds issued today are registered bonds.

Convertible Bonds

Convertible and Callable Bonds

Bonds that can be converted into common stock at the bondholder's option are called convertible bonds. Bonds subject to retirement at a stated dollar amount prior to maturity at the option of the issuer are known as callable bonds.

Callable Bonds

Issuing Procedures

State laws grant corporations the power to issue bonds. Within the corporation, formal approval by both the board of directors and stockholders is usually required before bonds can be issued. **In authorizing the bond issue, the board of directors must stipulate the total number of bonds to be authorized, total face value, and the contractual interest rate.** The total bond authorization often exceeds the number of bonds originally issued. This is done intentionally to help ensure that the corporation will have the flexibility it needs to meet future cash requirements.

The face value is the amount of principal due at the maturity date. The contractual interest rate, often referred to as the **stated rate**, is the rate used to determine the amount of cash interest the borrower pays and the investor receives. Usually the contractual rate is stated as an annual rate, and interest is generally paid semiannually.

The terms of the bond issue are set forth in a legal document called a bond indenture. In addition to the terms, the indenture summarizes the respective rights and privileges of the bondholders and their trustees, as well as the obligations and commitments of the issuing company. The **trustee** (usually a financial institution) keeps records of each bondholder, maintains custody of unissued bonds, and holds conditional title to pledged property.

HELPFUL HINT
Do not confuse the terms *indenture* and *debenture*. Indenture refers to the formal bond document (contract). Debenture bonds are unsecured bonds.

ACCOUNTING IN ACTION
Business Insight

Although bonds are generally secured by solid, substantial assets like land, buildings, and equipment, exceptions occur. For example, Trans World Airlines Inc. (TWA) at one time decided to issue $300 million of high-yielding 5-year bonds. TWA's bonds would be secured by a grab bag of assets, including some durable spare parts, but also a lot of disposable items that TWA had in its warehouses, such as light bulbs and gaskets. Some called the planned TWA bonds "light bulb bonds." As one financial expert noted: "You've got to admit that some security is better than none." However, another noted, "They're digging pretty far down the barrel."

After the bond indenture is prepared, **bond certificates** are printed. The indenture and the certificate are separate documents. As shown in Illustration 11-10, a bond certificate provides information such as the following: name of the issuer, the face value of the bonds, the contractual interest rate, and the maturity date of the bonds. Bonds are generally sold through an investment company that specializes in selling securities. In most cases, the issue is underwritten by the investment company. Under an underwriting arrangement, the company sells the bonds to the investment company, which, in turn, sells the bonds to individual investors.

ILLUSTRATION 11-10

Bond certificate

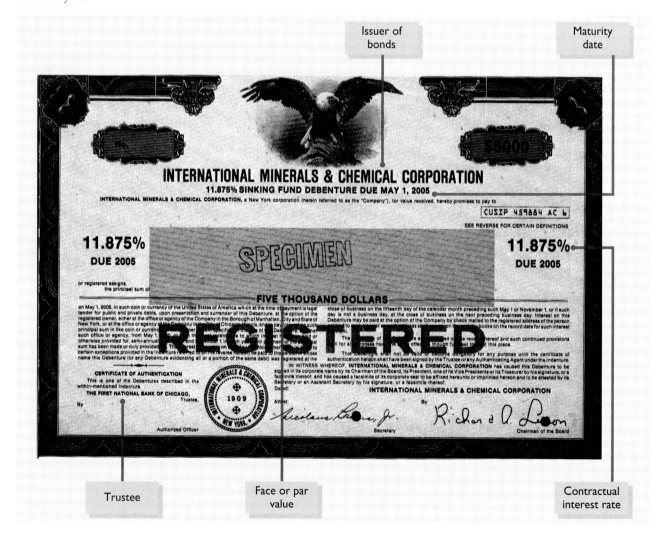

Bond Trading

Corporate bonds, like capital stock, are traded on national securities markets. Thus, bondholders have the opportunity to convert their holdings into cash at any time by selling the bonds at the current market price.

Bond prices are quoted as a percentage of the face value of the bond, which is usually $1,000. Thus, a $1,000 bond with a quoted price of 97 means that the selling price of the bond is 97% of face value, or $970 in this case. Bond prices and trading activity are published daily in newspapers and the financial press, as illustrated by the following:

Bonds	Current Yield	Volume	Close	Net Change
IBM $8\frac{3}{8}$ 19	7.5	50	$112\frac{1}{8}$	$+\frac{3}{8}$

The information in Illustration 11-11 indicates that IBM has outstanding $8\frac{3}{8}\%$ $1,000 bonds maturing in 2019 and currently yielding a 7.5% return. In addition, 50 bonds were traded on this day; and at the close of trading, the price was $112\frac{1}{8}\%$ of face value, or $1,121.25. The net change column indicates the difference between the day's closing price and the previous day's closing price.

Transactions between a bondholder and other investors **are not journalized by the issuing corporation**. If Tom Smith sells bonds that are bought by Faith Jones, the issuing corporation does not journalize the transaction (although it does keep records of the names of bondholders in the case of registered bonds). A corporation makes journal entries only when it issues or buys back bonds, and when bondholders convert bonds into common stock.

HELPFUL HINT
(1) What is the price of a $1,000 bond trading at $95\frac{1}{4}$?
(2) What is the price of a $1,000 bond trading at $101\frac{7}{8}$?
Answers: (1) $952.50 and (2) $1,018.75.

Determining the Market Value of Bonds

If you were an investor interested in purchasing a bond, how would you determine how much to pay? To be more specific, assume that Coronet, Inc., issues a zero-interest bond (pays no interest) with a face value of $1,000,000 due in 20 years. For this bond, the only cash you receive is a million dollars at the end of 20 years. Would you pay a million dollars for this bond? We hope not, because a million dollars received 20 years from now is not worth as much as a million dollars received today. The reason you would not pay a million dollars relates to what is called the **time value of money**. If you had a million dollars today, you would invest it and earn interest such that at the end of 20 years, your investment would be worth much more than a million dollars. Thus, if someone is going to pay you a million dollars 20 years from now, you would want to find its equivalent today, or its **present value**. In other words, you would want to determine how much must be invested today at current interest rates to have a million dollars in 20 years.

The market value (present value) of a bond is, therefore, a function of three factors: (1) the dollar amounts to be received, (2) the length of time until the amounts are received, and (3) the market rate of interest. The market interest rate is the rate investors demand for loaning funds to the corporation. The process of finding the present value is referred to as **discounting** the future amounts.

To illustrate, assume that Kell Company on January 1, 2000, issues $100,000 of 9% bonds, due in 5 years, with interest payable annually at year-end. The purchaser of the bonds would receive the following two cash payments: (1) **principal** $100,000 to be paid at maturity, and (2) five $9,000 **interest payments** ($100,000 × 9%) over the term of the bonds. The time diagram depicting both cash flows is shown below:

2001

2021

Same dollars at different times are not equal.

ILLUSTRATION 11-12

Time diagram depicting cash flows

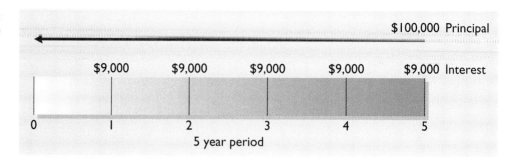

The present values of these amounts are as shown in Illustration 11-13.

ILLUSTRATION 11-13

Computing the market price of bonds

Present value of $100,000 received in 5 years	$ 64,993
Present value of $9,000 received annually for 5 years	35,007
Market price of bonds	**$100,000**

Tables are available to provide the present value numbers to be used, or these values can be determined mathematically.[2] Further discussion of time value of money computations is provided in Appendix C near the end of the book.

BEFORE YOU GO ON . . .

Review It

1. What are the advantages of bond versus stock financing?
2. What are secured versus unsecured bonds, term versus serial bonds, registered versus bearer bonds, and callable versus convertible bonds?
3. Explain the terms face value, contractual interest rate, and bond indenture.
4. Explain why you would prefer to receive $1 million today rather than 5 years from now.

THE NAVIGATOR

ACCOUNTING FOR BOND ISSUES

5

STUDY OBJECTIVE

Prepare the entries for the issuance of bonds and interest expense.

Bonds may be issued at face value, below face value (discount), or above face value (premium). They also are sometimes issued between interest dates.

Issuing Bonds at Face Value

To illustrate the accounting for bonds, assume that Devor Corporation issues 1,000, 10-year, 9%, $1,000 bonds dated January 1, 2000, at 100 (100% of face value). The entry to record the sale is:

A	=	L	+ SE
+1,000,000		+1,000,000	

Jan. 1	Cash		1,000,000	
	Bonds Payable			1,000,000
	(To record sale of bonds at face value)			

---

[2]For those knowledgeable in the use of present value tables, the computations in this example are: $100,000 × .64993 = $64,993, and $9,000 × 3.88965 = $35,007 (rounded).

Bonds payable are reported in the long-term liabilities section of the balance sheet because the maturity date is January 1, 2010 (more than one year away).

Over the term (life) of the bonds, entries are required for bond interest. Interest on bonds payable is computed in the same manner as interest on notes payable, as explained earlier in the chapter. Assuming that interest is payable semiannually on January 1 and July 1 on the bonds described above, interest of $45,000 ($1,000,000 $\times$ 9% $\times$ 6/12) must be paid on July 1, 2000. The entry for the payment, assuming no previous accrual of interest, is:

July 1	Bond Interest Expense	45,000	
	Cash		45,000
	(To record payment of bond interest)		

A	=	L	+	SE
−45,000				−45,000

At December 31, an adjusting entry is required to recognize the $45,000 of interest expense incurred since July 1. The entry is:

Dec. 31	Bond Interest Expense	45,000	
	Bond Interest Payable		45,000
	(To accrue bond interest)		

A	=	L	+	SE
		+45,000		−45,000

Bond interest payable is classified as a current liability, because it is scheduled for payment within the next year. When the interest is paid on January 1, 2001, Bond Interest Payable is debited and Cash is credited for $45,000.

Discount or Premium on Bonds

The previous illustrations assumed that the interest rate paid on bonds, often referred to as the contractual (stated) interest rate and the market (effective) interest rate were the same. The contractual interest rate is the rate applied to the face (par) value to arrive at the interest paid in a year. The market interest rate is the rate investors demand for loaning funds to the corporation. When the contractual interest rate and the market interest rate are the same, bonds sell at face value.

However, market interest rates change daily. They are influenced by the type of bond issued, the state of the economy, current industry conditions, and the company's individual performance. As a result, the contractual and market interest rates often differ and therefore bonds sell below or above face value.

To illustrate, suppose that investors have one of two options: purchase bonds that have a market rate of interest of 10% or purchase bonds that have a contractual rate of interest of 8%. Assuming that the bonds are of equal risk, investors will select the 10% investment. To make the investments equal, investors will demand a rate of interest higher than the contractual interest rate on the 8% bonds. Because investors cannot change the contractual interest rate, they will pay less than the face value for the bonds. By paying less for the bonds, they can obtain the market rate of interest. In these cases, **bonds sell at a discount**.

Conversely, if the market rate of interest is **lower** than the contractual interest rate, investors will have to pay more than face value for the bonds. That is, if the market rate of interest is 8%, but the contractual interest rate is 9%, the issuer will require more funds from the investor. In these cases, **bonds sell at a premium**. These relationships are shown graphically in Illustration 11-14.

HELPFUL HINT
Bond prices vary inversely with changes in the market interest rate. As the market interest rate declines, bond prices will increase. When a bond is issued, if the market interest rate is below the contractual rate, the price will be higher than the face value. In the Candlestick example on the next page, the market rate is greater than the 10% and therefore the bonds sell at a discount.

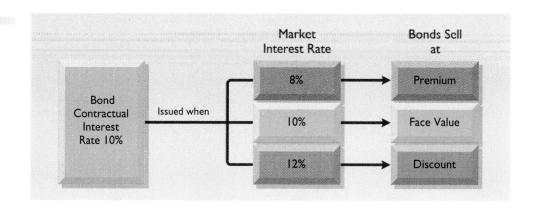

Issuance of bonds at an amount different from face value is quite common. By the time a company prints the bond certificates and markets the bonds, it will be a coincidence if the market rate and the contractual rate are the same. Thus, the issuance of bonds at a discount does not mean that the financial strength of the issuer is suspect. Conversely, the sale of bonds at a premium does not indicate that the financial strength of the issuer is exceptional.

Issuing Bonds at a Discount

To illustrate the issuance of bonds at a discount, assume that on January 1, 2000, Candlestick, Inc., sells $1 million, 5-year, 10% bonds at 98 (98% of face value) with interest payable on July 1 and January 1. The entry to record the issuance is:

HELPFUL HINT

Discount on Bonds Payable

Increase Debit ↓ Normal Balance	Decrease Credit

A	=	L	+	SE
+980,000		−20,000		
		+1,000,000		

Jan. 1	Cash	980,000	
	Discount on Bonds Payable	20,000	
	Bonds Payable		1,000,000
	(To record sale of bonds at a discount)		

Although Discount on Bonds Payable has a debit balance, **it is not an asset**. Rather it is a **contra account**, which is **deducted from bonds payable** on the balance sheet, as illustrated below:

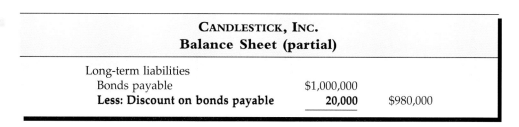

CANDLESTICK, INC.
Balance Sheet (partial)

Long-term liabilities		
Bonds payable	$1,000,000	
Less: Discount on bonds payable	**20,000**	$980,000

The $980,000 represents the **carrying (or book) value** of the bonds. On the date of issue this amount equals the market price of the bonds.

The issuance of bonds below face value causes the total cost of borrowing to differ from the bond interest paid. That is, at maturity the issuing corporation must pay not only the contractual interest rate over the term of the bonds, but also the face value (rather than the issuance price). Therefore, the difference between the issuance price and face value of the bonds—the discount—is an **additional cost of borrowing that should be recorded as bond interest expense over the life of the bonds**. The total cost of borrowing $980,000 for Candlestick, Inc., is $520,000, computed as follows:

HELPFUL HINT

Carrying value (book value) of bonds issued at a discount is determined by subtracting the balance of the discount account from the balance of the Bonds Payable account.

ILLUSTRATION 11-16

Total cost of borrowing—bonds issued at a discount

Bonds Issued at a Discount

Semiannual interest payments	
$1,000,000 × 10% × ½ = $50,000; $50,000 × 10)	$500,000
Add: Bond discount ($1,000,000 − $980,000)	20,000
Total cost of borrowing	$520,000

Alternatively, the total cost of borrowing can be determined as follows:

ILLUSTRATION 11-17

Alternative computation of total cost of borrowing—bonds issued at a discount

Bonds Issued at a Discount

Principal at maturity	$1,000,000
Semiannual interest payments ($50,000 × 10)	500,000
Cash to be paid to bondholders	1,500,000
Cash received from bondholders	980,000
Total cost of borrowing	$ 520,000

Amortizing Bond Discount

To comply with the matching principle, it follows that bond discount should be allocated systematically to each accounting period benefiting from the use of the cash proceeds.

One method, the straight-line method of amortization, allocates the same amount to interest expense in each interest period.[3] The amount is determined as shown in Illustration 11-18:

ILLUSTRATION 11-18

Formula for straight-line method of bond discount amortization

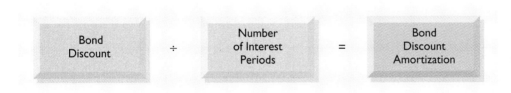

In this example, the bond discount amortization is $2,000 ($20,000 ÷ 10). The entry to record the payment of bond interest and the amortization of bond discount on the first interest date (July 1, 2000) is:

July 1	Bond Interest Expense	52,000	
	Discount on Bonds Payable		2,000
	Cash		50,000
	(To record payment of bond interest and amortization of bond discount)		

A	=	L	+	SE
−50,000		+2,000		−52,000

At December 31, the adjusting entry is:

Dec. 31	Bond Interest Expense	52,000	
	Discount on Bonds Payable		2,000
	Bond Interest Payable		50,000
	(To record accrued bond interest and amortization of bond discount)		

A	=	L	+	SE
		+2,000		−52,000
		+50,000		

---

[3]Another method, the effective-interest method, is discussed in the appendix at the end of this chapter.

Over the term of the bonds, the balance in Discount on Bonds Payable will decrease annually by the same amount until it has a zero balance at the maturity date of the bonds. Thus, the carrying value of the bonds at maturity will be equal to the face value of the bonds.

Preparing a bond discount amortization schedule as shown in Illustration 11-19 is useful to determine interest expense, discount amortization, and the carrying value of the bond. As indicated, the interest expense recorded each period is $52,000. Also note that the carrying value of the bond increases $2,000 each period until it reaches its face value $1,000,000 at the end of period 10.

ILLUSTRATION 11-19

Bond discount amortization schedule

Semiannual Interest Periods	(A) Interest to Be Paid (5% × $1,000,000)	(B) Interest Expense to Be Recorded (A) + (C)	(C) Discount Amortization ($20,000 ÷ 10)	(D) Unamortized Discount (D) − (C)	(E) Bond Carrying Value ($1,000,000 − D)
Issue date				$20,000	$ 980,000
1	$ 50,000	$ 52,000	$ 2,000	18,000	982,000
2	50,000	52,000	2,000	16,000	984,000
3	50,000	52,000	2,000	14,000	986,000
4	50,000	52,000	2,000	12,000	988,000
5	50,000	52,000	2,000	10,000	990,000
6	50,000	52,000	2,000	8,000	992,000
7	50,000	52,000	2,000	6,000	994,000
8	50,000	52,000	2,000	4,000	996,000
9	50,000	52,000	2,000	2,000	998,000
10	50,000	52,000	2,000	–0–	1,000,000
	$500,000	$520,000	$20,000		

Column **(A)** remains constant because the face value of the bonds ($1,000,000) is multiplied by the semiannual contractual interest rate (5%) each period.

Column **(B)** is computed as the interest paid (Column A) plus the discount amortization (Column C).

Column **(C)** indicates the discount amortization each period.

Column **(D)** decreases each period by the same amount until it reaches zero at maturity.

Column **(E)** increases each period by the amount of discount amortization until it equals the face value at maturity.

Issuing Bonds at a Premium

The issuance of bonds at a premium can be illustrated by assuming the Candlestick, Inc., bonds described above are sold at 102 (102% of face value) rather than at 98.

The entry to record the sale is:

```
A   =   L  +  SE
+1,020,000 +1,000,000
          +20,000
```

Jan. 1	Cash	1,020,000	
	Bonds Payable		1,000,000
	Premium on Bonds Payable		20,000
	(To record sale of bonds at a premium)		

Premium on bonds payable is **added to bonds payable** on the balance sheet, as shown below:

ILLUSTRATION 11-20

Statement presentation of bond premium

CANDLESTICK, INC.
Balance Sheet (partial)

Long-term liabilities		
Bonds payable	$1,000,000	
Add: Premium on bonds payable	**20,000**	$1,020,000

The sale of bonds above face value causes the total cost of borrowing to be **less than the bond interest paid**, because the borrower is not required to pay the bond premium at the maturity date of the bonds. Thus, the premium is considered to be **a reduction in the cost of borrowing** that should be credited to Bond Interest Expense over the life of the bonds. The total cost of borrowing $1,020,000 for Candlestick, Inc., is $480,000, computed as follows:

HELPFUL HINT

Premium on Bonds Payable

Decrease Debit	Increase Credit
	↓
	Normal Balance

ILLUSTRATION 11-21

Total cost of borrowing—bonds issued at a premium

Bonds Issued at a Premium

Semiannual interest payments	
($1,000,000 × 10% × ½ = $50,000; $50,000 × 10)	$500,000
Less: Bond premium ($1,020,000 − $1,000,000)	20,000
Total cost of borrowing	$480,000

Alternatively, the cost of borrowing can be computed as follows:

ILLUSTRATION 11-22

Alternative computation of total cost of borrowing—bonds issued at a premium

Bonds Issued at a Premium

Principal at maturity	$1,000,000
Semiannual interest payments ($50,000 × 10)	500,000
Cash to be paid to bondholders	1,500,000
Cash received from bondholders	1,020,000
Total cost of borrowing	$ 480,000

Amortizing Bond Premium

The formula for determining bond premium amortization under the straight-line method is presented in Illustration 11-23.

ILLUSTRATION 11-23

Formula for straight-line method of bond premium amortization

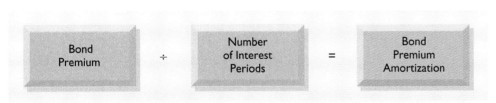

Thus, in our example, the premium amortization for each interest period is $2,000 ($20,000 ÷ 10). The entry to record the first payment of interest on July 1 is:

July 1	Bond Interest Expense	48,000	
	Premium on Bonds Payable	2,000	
	Cash		50,000
	(To record payment of bond interest and		
	amortization of bond premium)		

A	=	L	+	SE
−50,000		−2,000		−48,000

At December 31, the adjusting entry is:

Dec. 31	Bond Interest Expense	48,000	
	Premium on Bonds Payable	2,000	
	Bond Interest Payable		50,000
	(To record accrued bond interest and		
	amortization of bond premium)		

A	=	L	+	SE
		− 2,000		−48,000
		+50,000		

Over the term of the bonds, the balance in Premium on Bonds Payable will decrease annually by the same amount until it has a zero balance at maturity.

Preparing a bond premium amortization schedule as shown in Illustration 11-24 is useful to determine interest expense, premium amortized, and the carrying value of the bond. As indicated, the interest expense recorded each period is $48,000. Also note that the carrying value of the bond decreases $2,000 each period until it reaches its face value $1,000,000 at the end of period 10.

ILLUSTRATION 11-24

Bond premium amortization schedule

Semiannual Interest Periods	(A) Interest to Be Paid (5% × $1,000,000)	(B) Interest Expense to Be Recorded (A) − (C)	(C) Premium Amortization ($20,000 ÷ 10)	(D) Unamortized Premium (D) − (C)	(E) Bond Carrying Value ($1,000,000 +D)
Issue date				$20,000	$1,020,000
1	$ 50,000	$ 48,000	$ 2,000	18,000	1,018,000
2	50,000	48,000	2,000	16,000	1,016,000
3	50,000	48,000	2,000	14,000	1,014,000
4	50,000	48,000	2,000	12,000	1,012,000
5	50,000	48,000	2,000	10,000	1,010,000
6	50,000	48,000	2,000	8,000	1,008,000
7	50,000	48,000	2,000	6,000	1,006,000
8	50,000	48,000	2,000	4,000	1,004,000
9	50,000	48,000	2,000	2,000	1,002,000
10	50,000	48,000	2,000	–0–	1,000,000
	$500,000	$480,000	$20,000		

Column **(A)** remains constant because the face value of the bonds ($1,000,000) is multiplied by the semiannual contractual interest rate (5%) each period.

Column **(B)** is computed as the interest paid (Column A) less the premium amortization (Column C).

Column **(C)** indicates the premium amortization each period.

Column **(D)** decreases each period by the same amount until it reaches zero at maturity.

Column **(E)** decreases each period by the amount of premium amortization until it equals the face value at maturity.

Issuing Bonds between Interest Dates

Bonds are often issued between interest payment dates. **When this occurs, the issuer requires the investor to pay the market price for the bonds plus accrued interest since the last interest date.** At the next interest date, the corporation will return the accrued interest to the investor by paying the full amount of interest due on outstanding bonds.

To illustrate, assume that Deer Corporation sells $1,000,000, 9% bonds at face value plus accrued interest on March 1. Interest is payable semiannually on July 1 and January 1. The accrued interest is $15,000 ($1,000,000 × 9% × 2/12). The total proceeds on the sale of the bonds, therefore, are $1,015,000, and the entry to record the sale is:

A	=	L	+	SE
+1,015,000		+1,000,000		
		+15,000		

Mar. 1	Cash	1,015,000	
	Bonds Payable		1,000,000
	Bond Interest Payable		15,000
	(To record sale of bonds at face value plus accrued interest)		

At the first interest date, it is necessary to eliminate the bond interest payable balance and to recognize interest expense for the 4 months (March 1–June 30) the bonds have been outstanding. Interest expense in this example is, therefore, $30,000 ($1,000,000 × 9% × 4/12). The entry on July 1 for the $45,000 interest payment is:

July 1	Bond Interest Payable	15,000	
	Bond Interest Expense	30,000	
	Cash		45,000
	(To record payment of bond interest)		

A	=	L	+	SE
−45,000		−15,000		−30,000

Why does Deer Corporation collect interest at the time of issuance and then return this interest at the time of payment? The rationale: Collection of accrued interest at the issuance date allows the company to pay a full period's interest to all bondholders at the next interest payment date. Deer Corporation does not have to determine the individual amount of interest due each holder based on the time each bond has been outstanding during the interest period.

In other words, if bonds are not sold "with accrued interest," Deer Corporation would have to keep track of the purchaser and the dates that the bonds were purchased. This procedure would be necessary to ensure that each bondholder received the correct amount of interest. By selling the bonds "with accrued interest," Deer does not have to maintain detailed records, and cost savings occur.

BEFORE YOU GO ON ...

Review It

1. What entry is made to record the issuance of bonds payable of $1 million at 100? at 96? at 102?
2. Why do bonds sell at a discount? at a premium? at face value?
3. Explain the accounting for bonds sold between interest dates.

Do It

A bond amortization table shows (a) interest to be paid $50,000, (b) interest expense to be recorded $52,000, and (c) amortization $2,000. Answer the following questions: (1) Were the bonds sold at a premium or a discount? (2) After recording the interest expense, will the bond carrying value increase or decrease?

Reasoning: To answer the questions you need to know the effects that the amortization of bond discount and bond premium have on bond interest expense and on the carrying value of the bonds. Bond discount amortization increases both bond interest expense and the carrying value of the bonds. Bond premium amortization has the reverse effect.

Solution: The bond amortization table indicates that interest expense is $2,000 greater than the interest paid. This difference is equal to the amortization amount. Thus, the bonds were sold at a discount. The interest entry will decrease Discount on Bonds Payable and increase the carrying value of the bonds.

Related exercise material: BE11–2, BE11–3, BE11–5, E11–2, E11–3, E11–4, and E11–5.

ACCOUNTING FOR BOND RETIREMENTS

6
STUDY
OBJECTIVE

Describe the entries when bonds are redeemed or converted.

Bonds may be retired either when they are purchased (redeemed) by the issuing corporation or when they are converted into common stock by bondholders. The appropriate entries for these transactions are explained in the following sections.

Redeeming Bonds at Maturity

Regardless of the issue price of bonds, the book value of the bonds at maturity will equal their face value. This can be seen in Illustrations 11-19 and 11-24 where the carrying value of the bonds at the end of their 10-year life ($1 million) is equal to the face value of the bonds.

Assuming that the interest for the last interest period is paid and recorded separately, the entry to record the redemption of the Candlestick bonds at maturity is:

A	=	L	+ SE
−1,000,000		−1,000,000	

Bonds Payable	1,000,000	
Cash		1,000,000
(To record redemption of bonds at maturity)		

Redeeming Bonds before Maturity

Bonds may be redeemed before maturity. A company may decide to retire bonds before maturity to reduce interest cost and remove debt from its balance sheet. A company should retire debt early only if it has sufficient cash resources. When bonds are retired before maturity, it is necessary to: (1) eliminate the carrying value of the bonds at the redemption date, (2) record the cash paid, and (3) recognize the gain or loss on redemption. The carrying value of the bonds is the face value of the bonds less unamortized bond discount or plus unamortized bond premium at the redemption date.

To illustrate, assume at the end of the eighth period Candlestick, Inc. (having sold its bonds at a premium, per Illustration 11-24) retires its bonds at 103 after paying the semiannual interest. The carrying value of the bonds at the redemption date, as shown in the bond premium amortization schedule, is $1,004,000. The entry to record the redemption at the end of the eighth interest period (January 1, 2004) is:

HELPFUL HINT
Question: If a bond is redeemed prior to its maturity date and its carrying value exceeds its redemption price, will the retirement result in a gain or a loss on redemption? Answer: Gain.

A	=	L	+	SE
−1,030,000		−1,000,000		−26,000
		−4,000		

Jan. 1			
	Bonds Payable	1,000,000	
	Premium on Bonds Payable	4,000	
	Loss on Bond Redemption	26,000	
	Cash		1,030,000
	(To record redemption of bonds at 103)		

Note that the loss of $26,000 is the difference between the cash paid of $1,030,000 and the carrying value of the bonds of $1,004,000. Losses (gains) on bond redemption are reported in the income statement as extraordinary items, as required by the accounting profession.

Converting Bonds into Common Stock

Convertible bonds have features that are attractive both to bondholders and to the issuer. The conversion often gives bondholders an opportunity to benefit if the market price of the common stock increases substantially. Furthermore, until conversion, the bondholder receives interest on the bond. For the issuer, the bonds sell at a higher price and pay a lower rate of interest than comparable debt securities that do not have a conversion option. Many corporations, such as USAir, USX Corp., and Daimler-Chrysler Corporation, have convertible bonds outstanding.

When bonds are converted into common stock and the conversion is recorded, the current market prices of the bonds and the stock are ignored. Instead, the **carrying value** of the bonds is transferred to paid-in capital accounts, and **no gain or loss is recognized**. To illustrate, assume that on July 1 Saunders Associates converts $100,000 bonds sold at face value into 10,000 shares of $10 par value common stock. Both the bonds and the common stock have a market value of $130,000. The entry to record the conversion is:

HELPFUL HINT
The method of recording this conversion of bonds to stock is called the *book value method* because the amount of the book value of the bonds is removed from the liability accounts and recorded as common stock.

July 1	Bonds Payable	100,000	
	Common Stock		100,000
	(To record bond conversion)		

A =	L	+	SE
	−100,000		+100,000

Note that the current market price of the bonds and stock ($130,000) is not considered in making the entry. This method of recording the bond conversion is often referred to as the **carrying (or book) value method**.

ACCOUNTING IN ACTION
International Insight

Now that you have read about bonds, you may be beginning to realize how significant bond financing can be. A dramatic example of bond financing—which literally changed the course of history—is seen in Britain's struggle for supremacy in the eighteenth and nineteenth centuries. With only a fraction of the population and wealth of France, Britain ultimately humbled its mightier foe through the use of bonds. Because of its effective central bank and a fair system of collecting taxes, Britain developed the capital markets that enabled its government to issue bonds. Britain was able to borrow money at almost half the cost paid by France, and was able to incur more debt as a proportion of the economy than could France. Britain thus could more than match the French navy, raise an army of its own, and lavishly subsidize other armies, eventually destroying Napoleon and his threat to Europe.

Source: "How British Bonds Beat Back Bigger France," *Forbes*, March 13, 1995.

BEFORE YOU GO ON . . .

Review It

1. Explain the accounting for redemption of bonds at maturity; before maturity by payment in cash; and before maturity by conversion into common stock.
2. Did Kellogg Company redeem any of its debt during 1998? (*Hint:* To find information related to this question, examine Kellogg Company's statement of cash flows. The answer to this question is provided on page 509.)

Do It

R & B Inc. issued $500,000, 10-year bonds at a premium. Prior to maturity, when the carrying value of the bonds is $508,000, the company retires the bonds at 102. Prepare the entry to record the redemption of the bonds.

Reasoning: In recording the redemption of bonds before maturity, it is necessary to (1) eliminate the carrying value of the bonds, (2) recognize the cash paid, and (3) recognize the gain or loss equal to the difference between (1) and (2).

Solution: There is a loss on redemption because the cash paid, $510,000 ($500,000 × 102%), is greater than the carrying value of $508,000. The entry is:

Bonds Payable	500,000	
Premium on Bonds Payable	8,000	
Loss on Bond Redemption	2,000	
Cash		510,000
(To record redemption of bonds at 102)		

THE NAVIGATOR

Related exercise material: BE11–6, E11–3, E11–4, and E11–6.

ACCOUNTING FOR LONG-TERM NOTES PAYABLE

7

STUDY OBJECTIVE

Describe the accounting for long-term notes payable.

The use of notes payable in long-term debt financing is quite common. Long-term notes payable are similar to short-term interest-bearing notes payable except that the terms of the notes exceed one year. In periods of unstable interest rates, the interest rate on long-term notes may be tied to changes in the market rate for comparable loans. Examples are the 8.03% adjustable rate notes issued by General Motors and the floating rate notes issued by American Express Company.

A long-term note may be secured by a document called a **mortgage** that pledges title to specific assets as security for a loan. Mortgage notes payable are widely used in the purchase of homes by individuals and in the acquisition of plant assets by many small and some large companies. For example, approximately 18% of McDonald's long-term debt relates to mortgage notes on land, buildings, and improvements. Like other long-term notes payable, the mortgage loan terms may stipulate either a fixed or an adjustable interest rate. Typically, the terms require the borrower to make installment payments over the term of the loan. Each payment consists of (1) interest on the unpaid balance of the loan, and (2) a reduction of loan principal. The interest decreases each period, while the portion applied to the loan principal increases.

HELPFUL HINT

Electronic spreadsheet programs can create a schedule of installment loan payments. This allows you to put in the data for your own mortgage loan and get an illustration that really hits home.

Mortgage notes payable are recorded initially at face value, and entries are required subsequently for each installment payment. To illustrate, assume that Porter Technology Inc. issues a $500,000, 12%, 20-year mortgage note on December 31, 2000, to obtain needed financing for the construction of a new research laboratory. The terms provide for semiannual installment payments of $33,231 (not including real estate taxes and insurance). The installment payment schedule for the first 2 years is as follows:

ILLUSTRATION 11-25

Mortgage installment payment schedule

Semiannual Interest Period	(A) Cash Payment	(B) Interest Expense (D) × 6%	(C) Reduction of Principal (A) − (B)	(D) Principal Balance (D) − (C)
Issue date				$500,000
1	$33,231	$30,000	$3,231	496,769
2	33,231	29,806	3,425	493,344
3	33,231	29,601	3,630	489,714
4	33,231	29,383	3,848	485,866

The entries to record the mortgage loan and first installment payment are as follows:

A	=	L	+ SE
+500,000		+500,000	

Dec. 31	Cash		500,000	
	Mortgage Notes Payable			500,000
	(To record mortgage loan)			

A	=	L	+	SE
−33,231		−3,231		−30,000

June 30	Interest Expense		30,000	
	Mortgage Notes Payable		3,231	
	Cash			33,231
	(To record semiannual payment on mortgage)			

In the balance sheet, the reduction in principal for the next year is reported as a current liability, and the remaining unpaid principal balance is classified as a long-term liability. At December 31, 2001, the total liability is $493,344 of which $7,478 ($3,630 + $3,848) is current, and $485,866 ($493,344 − $7,478) is long-term.

FINANCIAL STATEMENT PRESENTATION AND ANALYSIS OF LONG-TERM LIABILITIES

8
STUDY OBJECTIVE

Identify the methods for the financial statement presentation and analysis of long-term liabilities.

Presentation

Long-term liabilities are reported in a separate section of the balance sheet immediately following current liabilities, as shown below.

ILLUSTRATION 11-26

Balance sheet presentation of long-term liabilities

LAX CORPORATION Balance Sheet (partial)		
Long-term liabilities		
Bonds payable 10% due in 2009	$1,000,000	
Less: Discount on bonds payable	80,000	$ 920,000
Mortgage notes payable, 11%, due in 2015		
and secured by plant assets		500,000
Total long-term liabilities		$1,420,000

Alternatively, summary data may be presented in the balance sheet with detailed data (such as interest rates, maturity dates, conversion privileges, and assets pledged as collateral) shown in a supporting schedule in the notes. The current maturities of long-term debt should be reported under current liabilities if they are to be paid from current assets (see Kellogg's balance sheet in Appendix A).

Analysis

Long-term creditors and stockholders are interested in a company's long-run solvency, particularly its ability to pay interest as it comes due and to repay the face value of the debt at maturity. Debt to total assets and times interest earned are two ratios that provide information about debt-paying ability and long-run solvency.

The debt to total assets ratio measures the percentage of the total assets provided by creditors. It is computed, as shown in the formula in Illustration 11-27, by dividing total debt (both current and long-term liabilities) by total assets. The higher the percentage of debt to total assets, the greater the risk that the company may be unable to meet its maturing obligations.

The times interest earned ratio provides an indication of the company's ability to meet interest payments as they come due. It is computed by dividing income before interest expense and income taxes by interest expense.

To illustrate these ratios, we will use data from Kellogg Company's annual report which disclosed total liabilities of $4,161.7 million, total assets of $5,051.5 million, interest expense of $119.5 million, income taxes of $279.9 million, and net income of $502.6 million. Kellogg's debt to total assets ratio and times interest earned ratio are shown graphically below, along with their computations.

ILLUSTRATION 11-27

Debt to total assets and times interest earned ratios, with computations

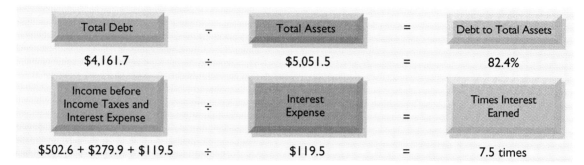

Total Debt	÷	Total Assets	=	Debt to Total Assets
$4,161.7	÷	$5,051.5	=	82.4%
Income before Income Taxes and Interest Expense	÷	Interest Expense	=	Times Interest Earned
$502.6 + $279.9 + $119.5	÷	$119.5	=	7.5 times

Even though Kellogg Company has a relatively high debt to total assets percentage of 82.4%, its interest coverage of 7.5 times appears very safe.

BEFORE YOU GO ON . . .

Review It

1. Explain the accounting for long-term mortgage notes payable.
2. Where are current maturities of long-term debt reported in the financial statements?
3. What ratios may be computed to analyze a company's long-run solvency?

A LOOK BACK AT OUR FEATURE STORY

Refer to the Feature Story and answer the following questions:

1. Why do entrepreneurs like Wilbert Murdock and other small businesses have difficulty obtaining traditional debt financing?
2. What type of financing did Wilbert Murdock resort to, as did one-third of businesses with fewer than 20 employees? Why is Murdock's method of financing at all appealing?
3. What are the disadvantages of using credit cards as a means of debt financing?

Solution:

1. Traditional debt financing is generally not available to entrepreneurs and other small businesses because bank loans and bond issuances require established credit ratings, earnings records, positive cash flow, and collateral—none of which are usually possessed by new, emerging small businesses.
2. Wilbert Murdock resorted to using credit cards to finance his business ventures. Credit cards are appealing because they are readily available (new card applications appear in mailboxes weekly) and because credit card companies don't moniter how the money is spent.
3. Credit card financing is generally expensive, with interest ranging between 14% and 21% (except for special introductory offers, which are temporary in nature), and the amounts per individual credit card are generally small ($2,000–$10,000).

THE NAVIGATOR

DEMONSTRATION PROBLEM

Techynecky Inc. has successfully developed a new spreadsheet program. However, to produce and market the program, the company needed $2.0 million of additional financing. On December 31, 1999, Techynecky borrowed money as follows:

1. Techynecky issued $500,000, 11%, 10-year convertible bonds. The bonds sold at face value and pay semiannual interest on January 1 and July 1. Each $1,000 bond is convertible into 40 shares of Techynecky's $25 par value common stock.

2. Techynecky issued $1.0 million, 10%, 10-year bonds for $885,301. Interest is payable semiannually on January 1 and July 1. Techynecky uses the straight-line method of amortization.

3. Techynecky also issued a $500,000, 12%, 15-year mortgage note payable. The terms provide for semiannual installment payments of $36,324 on June 30 and December 31.

Instructions

1. For the convertible bonds, prepare journal entries for:
   (a) the issuance of the bonds on January 1, 2000.
   (b) interest expense on July 1 and December 31, 2000.
   (c) the payment of interest on January 1, 2001.
   (d) the conversion of all bonds into common stock on January 1, 2001, when the market value of the common stock was $67 per share.

2. For the 10-year, 10% bonds:
   (a) journalize the issuance of the bonds on January 1, 2000.
   (b) prepare a bond discount amortization schedule for the first six interest periods.
   (c) prepare the journal entries for interest expense and amortization of bond discount in 2000.
   (d) prepare the entry for the redemption of the bonds at 101 on January 1, 2003, after paying the interest due on this date.

3. For the mortgage note payable:
   (a) prepare the entry for the issuance of the note on December 31, 1999.
   (b) prepare a payment schedule for the first four installment payments.
   (c) indicate the current and noncurrent amounts for the mortgage note payable at December 31, 2000.

SOLUTION TO DEMONSTRATION PROBLEM

1. (a) 2000

Jan. 1	Cash	500,000	
	Bonds Payable		500,000
	(To record issue of 11%, 10-year convertible bonds at face value)		

   (b) 2000

July 1	Bond Interest Expense	27,500	
	Cash ($500,000 x 0.055)		27,500
	(To record payment of semiannual interest)		
Dec. 31	Bond Interest Expense	27,500	
	Bond Interest Payable		27,500
	(To record accrual of semiannual bond interest)		

(c) 2001

Jan. 1	Bond Interest Payable		27,500	
	Cash			27,500
	(To record payment of accrued interest)			

(d)   **Jan. 1**

	Bonds Payable		500,000	
	Common Stock			500,000*
	(To record conversion of bonds into common stock)			
	*($500,000 ÷ $1,000 = 500 bonds; 500 × 40 = 20,000 shares; 20,000 × $25 = $500,000)			

2. (a) 2000

Jan. 1	Cash		885,301	
	Discount on Bonds Payable		114,699	
	Bonds Payable			1,000,000
	(To record issuance of bonds at a discount)			

(b)

Semiannual Interest Period	Interest to Be Paid	Interest Expense to Be Recorded	Discount Amortization	Unamortized Discount	Bond Carrying Value
Issue date				$114,699	$885,301
1	$50,000	$55,735	$5,735	108,964	891,036
2	50,000	55,735	5,735	103,229	896,771
3	50,000	55,735	5,735	97,494	902,506
4	50,000	55,735	5,735	91,759	908,241
5	50,000	55,735	5,735	86,024	913,976
6	50,000	55,735	5,735	80,289	919,711

(c) 2000

July 1	Bond Interest Expense		55,735	
	Discount on Bonds Payable			5,735
	Cash			50,000
	(To record payment of semiannual interest and amortization of bond discount)			
Dec. 31	Bond Interest Expense		55,735	
	Discount on Bonds Payable			5,735
	Bond Interest Payable			50,000
	(To record accrual of semiannual interest and amortization of bond discount)			

(d) 2003

Jan. 1	Bonds Payable		1,000,000	
	Loss on Bond Redemption		90,289*	
	Discount on Bonds Payable			80,289
	Cash			1,010,000
	(To record redemption of bonds at 101)			
	*($1,010,000 − $919,711)			

3. (a) 1999

Dec. 31	Cash		500,000	
	Mortgage Notes Payable			500,000
	(To record issuance of mortgage note payable)			

(b)

Semiannual Interest Period	Cash Payment	Interest Expense	Reduction of Principal	Principal Balance
Issue date				$500,000
1	$36,324	$30,000	$6,324	493,676
2	36,324	29,621	6,703	486,973
3	36,324	29,218	7,106	479,867
4	36,324	28,792	7,532	472,335

(c) Current liability $14,638 ($7,106 + $7,532)
    Long-term liability $472,335

THE NAVIGATOR

PROBLEM-SOLVING STRATEGIES

1. Interest expense decreases each period because the principal is decreasing each period.
2. Each payment consists of (1) interest on the unpaid loan balance and (2) a reduction of the loan principal.

SUMMARY OF STUDY OBJECTIVES

1. Explain a current liability and identify the major types of current liabilities. A current liability is a debt that can reasonably be expected to be paid (1) from existing current assets or through the creation of other current liabilities, and (2) within one year or the operating cycle, whichever is longer. The major types of current liabilities are notes payable, accounts payable, sales taxes payable, unearned revenues, and accrued liabilities such as taxes, salaries and wages, and interest payable.

2. Describe the accounting for notes payable. When a promissory note is interest-bearing, the amount of assets received upon the issuance of the note is generally equal to the face value of the note, and interest expense is accrued over the life of the note. At maturity, the amount paid is equal to the face value of the note plus accrued interest.

3. Explain the accounting for other current liabilities. Sales taxes payable are recorded at the time the related sales occur. The company serves as a collection agent for the taxing authority. Sales taxes are not an expense to the company. Until employee withholding taxes are remitted to governmental taxing authorities, they are credited to appropriate liability accounts. Unearned revenues are initially recorded in an unearned revenue account. As the revenue is earned, a transfer from unearned revenue to earned revenue occurs. The current maturities of long-term debt should be reported as a current liability in the balance sheet.

4. Explain why bonds are issued and identify the types of bonds. Bonds may be sold to many investors, and they offer the following advantages over common stock: (a) stockholder control is not affected, (b) tax savings result, and (c) earnings per share of common stock may be higher. The following different types of bonds may be issued: secured and

unsecured bonds, term and serial bonds, registered and bearer bonds, convertible and callable bonds.

5. Prepare the entries for the issuance of bonds and interest expense. When bonds are issued, Cash is debited for the cash proceeds and Bonds Payable is credited for the face value of the bonds. In addition, Bond Interest Payable is credited if there is accrued interest, and the accounts Premium on Bonds Payable or Discount on Bonds Payable are used to show the bond premium or bond discount. Bond discount and bond premium are amortized by the straight-line method.

6. Describe the entries when bonds are redeemed or converted. When bonds are redeemed at maturity, Cash is credited and Bonds Payable is debited for the face value of the bonds. When bonds are redeemed before maturity, it is necessary to (a) eliminate the carrying value of the bonds at the redemption date, (b) record the cash paid, and (c) recognize the gain or loss on redemption. When bonds are converted to common stock, the carrying (or book) value of the bonds is transferred to appropriate paid-in capital accounts, and no gain or loss is recognized.

7. Describe the accounting for long-term notes payable. Each payment consists of (1) interest on the unpaid balance of the loan, and (2) a reduction of loan principal. The interest decreases each period, while the portion applied to the loan principal increases each period.

8. Identify the methods for the financial statement presentation and analysis of long-term liabilities. The nature and amount of each long-term debt should be reported in the balance sheet or in schedules in the notes accompanying the statements. The long-run solvency of a company may be analyzed by computing the debt to total assets and the times interest earned ratios.

THE NAVIGATOR

GLOSSARY

Bearer (coupon) bonds Bonds not registered. (p. 471)

Bond certificate A legal document that indicates the name of the issuer, the face value of the bonds, and such other data as the contractual interest rate and maturity date of the bonds. (p. 472)

Bond indenture A legal document that sets forth the terms of the bond issue. (p. 471)

Bonds A form of interest-bearing notes payable issued by corporations, universities, and governmental entities. (p. 469)

Callable bonds Bonds that are subject to retirement at a stated dollar amount prior to maturity at the option of the issuer. (p. 471)

Convertible bonds Bonds that permit bondholders to convert them into common stock at their option. (p. 471)

Contractual interest rate Rate used to determine the amount of interest the borrower pays and the investor receives (p. 471)

Current ratio A measure of a company's liquidity, computed as current assets divided by current liabilities. (p. 468)

Debenture bonds Bonds issued against the general credit of the borrower. Also called unsecured bonds. (p. 471)

Debt to total assets ratio A solvency measure that indicates the percentage of total assets provided by creditors, computed as total debt divided by total assets. (p. 485)

Face value Amount of principal due at the maturity date of the bond. (p. 471)

Long-term liabilities Obligations expected to be paid after one year. (p. 469)

Market interest rate The rate investors demand for loaning funds to the corporation. (p. 473)

Mortgage bond A bond secured by real estate. (p. 471)

Mortgage note payable A long-term note secured by a mortgage that pledges title to specific units of property as security for the loan. (p. 484)

Registered bonds Bonds issued in the name of the owner. (p. 471)

Secured bonds Bonds that have specific assets of the issuer pledged as collateral. (p. 471)

Serial bonds Bonds that mature in installments. (p. 471)

Sinking fund bonds Bonds secured by specific assets set aside to retire them. (p. 471)

Straight-line method of amortization A method of amortizing bond discount or bond premium that allocates the same amount to interest expense in each interest period. (p. 477)

Term bonds Bonds that mature at a single specified future date. (p. 471)

Times interest earned ratio A solvency measure that indicates a company's ability to meet interest payments, computed by dividing income before interest expense and income taxes by interest expense. (p. 485)

Unsecured bonds Bonds issued against the general credit of the borrower. Also called debenture bonds. (p. 471)

Working capital A measure of a company's liquidity, computed as the difference between current assets and current liabilities. (p. 468)

APPENDIX EFFECTIVE-INTEREST AMORTIZATION

The straight-line method of amortization that you studied in the chapter has a conceptual deficiency: It does not completely satisfy the matching principle. Under the straight-line method, interest expense as a percentage of the carrying value of the bonds varies each interest period. This can be seen by using data from the first three interest periods of the bond amortization schedule that was shown in Illustration 11-19:

ILLUSTRATION 11A-1

Interest percentage rates under straight-line method

Semiannual Interest Period	Interest Expense to be Recorded (A)	Bond Carrying Value (B)	Interest Expense as a Percentage of Carrying Value (A) ÷ (B)
1	$52,000	$980,000	5.31%
2	52,000	982,000	5.29%
3	52,000	984,000	5.27%
10	52,000	998,000	5.21%

Note that interest expense as a percentage of carrying value declines in each interest period. However, to completely comply with the matching principle, interest expense as a percentage of carrying value should not change over the life of the bonds. This percentage, referred to as the effective-interest rate, is established when the bonds are issued and remains constant in each interest period. The effective-interest method of amortization accomplishes this result.

Under the effective-interest method, the amortization of bond discount or bond premium results in periodic interest expense equal to a constant percentage of the carrying value of the bonds. The effective-interest method results in varying amounts of amortization and interest expense per period but a constant percentage rate; the straight-line method results in constant amounts of amortization and interest expense per period but a varying percentage rate.

The following steps are required under the effective-interest method:

1. Compute the **bond interest expense** by multiplying the carrying value of the bonds at the beginning of the interest period by the effective-interest rate.
2. Compute the **bond interest paid** (or accrued) by multiplying the face value of the bonds by the contractual interest rate.
3. Compute the **amortization amount** by determining the difference between the amounts computed in steps (1) and (2).

These steps are graphically depicted in Illustration 11A-2.

Contrast the effects of the straight-line and effective-interest methods of amortizing bond discount and bond premium.

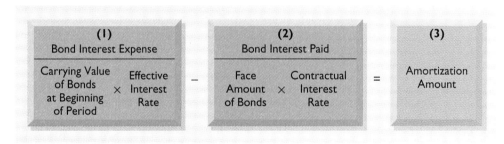

ILLUSTRATION 11A-2

Computation of amortization—effective-interest method

Both the straight-line and effective-interest methods of amortization result in the same total amount of interest expense over the term of the bonds. Furthermore, interest expense each interest period is generally comparable in amount. However, **when the amounts are materially different, the effective-interest method is required under generally accepted accounting principles (GAAP)**.

AMORTIZING BOND DISCOUNT

To illustrate the effective-interest method of bond discount amortization, assume that Wrightway Corporation issues $100,000 of 10%, 5-year bonds on January 1, 2001, with interest payable each July 1 and January 1. The bonds sell for $92,639 (92.639% of face value), which results in bond discount of $7,361 ($100,000 − $92,639) and an effective-interest rate of 12%. (Note that the $92,639 can be proven as shown in Appendix C at the end of this book.) Preparing a bond discount amortization schedule as shown in Illustration 11A-3 on the next page facilitates the recording of interest expense and the discount amortization. Note that interest expense as a percentage of carrying value remains constant at 6%.

ILLUSTRATION 11A-3

Bond discount amortization schedule

WRIGHTWAY CORPORATION
Bond Discount Amortization
Effective-Interest Method—Semiannual Interest Payments
10% Bonds Issued at 12%

Semiannual Interest Periods	(A) Interest to Be Paid (5% × $100,000)	(B) Interest Expense to Be Recorded (6% × Preceding Bond Carrying Value)	(C) Discount Amortization (B) − (A)	(D) Unamortized Discount (D) − (C)	(E) Bond Carrying Value ($100,000 − D)
Issue date				$7,361	$ 92,639
1	$ 5,000	$ 5,558 (6% × $92,639)	$ 558	6,803	93,197
2	5,000	5,592 (6% × $93,197)	592	6,211	93,789
3	5,000	5,627 (6% × $93,789)	627	5,584	94,416
4	5,000	5,665 (6% × $94,416)	665	4,919	95,081
5	5,000	5,705 (6% × $95,081)	705	4,214	95,786
6	5,000	5,747 (6% × $95,786)	747	3,467	96,533
7	5,000	5,792 (6% × $96,533)	792	2,675	97,325
8	5,000	5,840 (6% × $97,325)	840	1,835	98,165
9	5,000	5,890 (6% × $98,165)	890	945	99,055
10	5,000	5,945* (6% × $99,055)	945	–0–	100,000
	$50,000	$57,361	$7,361		

Column **(A)** remains constant because the face value of the bonds ($100,000) is multiplied by the semiannual contractual interest rate (5%) each period.

Column **(B)** is computed as the preceeding bond carrying value times the semiannual effective-interest rate (6%).

Column **(C)** indicates the discount amortization each period.

Column **(D)** decreases each period until it reaches zero at maturity.

Column **(E)** increases each period until it equals face value at maturity.

*$2 difference due to rounding.

For the first interest period, the computations of bond interest expense and the bond discount amortization are as follows:

ILLUSTRATION 11A-4

Computation of bond discount amortization

Bond interest expense ($92,639 × 6%)	$5,558
Contractual interest ($100,000 × 5%)	5,000
Bond discount amortization	**$ 558**

As a result, the entry to record the payment of interest and amortization of bond discount by Wrightway Corporation on July 1, 2001, is:

A	=	L	+	SE
−5,000		+558		−5,558

July 1	Bond Interest Expense	5,558	
	Discount on Bonds Payable		558
	Cash		5,000
	(To record payment of bond interest and amortization of bond discount)		

For the second interest period, bond interest expense will be $5,592 ($93,197 × 6%), and the discount amortization will be $592. At December 31, the following adjusting entry is made:

Dec. 31	Bond Interest Expense	5,592	
	Discount on Bonds Payable		592
	Bond Interest Payable		5,000
	(To record accrued interest and		
	amortization of bond discount)		

$$A = L + SE$$
$$+592 \quad -5,592$$
$$+5,000$$

Total bond interest expense for 2001 is $11,150 ($5,558 + $5,592). On January 1, payment of the interest is recorded by a debit to Bond Interest Payable and a credit to Cash.

AMORTIZING BOND PREMIUM

The amortization of bond premium by the effective-interest method is similar to the procedures described for bond discount. As an example, assume that Wrightway Corporation issues $100,000, 10%, 5-year bonds on January 1, 2001, with interest payable on July 1 and January 1. In this case, the bonds sell for $108,111, which results in bond premium of $8,111 and an effective-interest rate of 8%. The bond premium amortization schedule is shown in Illustration 11A-5.

HELPFUL HINT
When a bond sells for $108,111, it is quoted as 108.111% of face value. Note that $108,111 can be proven as shown in Appendix C.

ILLUSTRATION 11A-5

Bond premium amortization schedule

WRIGHTWAY CORPORATION
Bond Premium Amortization
Effective-Interest Method—Semiannual Interest Payments
10% Bonds Issued at 8%

Semiannual Interest Periods	(A) Interest to Be Paid (5% × $100,000)	(B) Interest Expense to Be Recorded (4% × Preceding Bond Carry Value)	(C) Premium Amortization (A) − (B)	(D) Unamortized Premium (D) − (C)	(E) Bond Carrying Value ($100,000 + D)
Issue date				$8,111	$108,111
1	$ 5,000	$ 4,324 (4% × $108,111)	$ 676	7,435	107,435
2	5,000	4,297 (4% × $107,435)	703	6,732	106,732
3	5,000	4,269 (4% × $106,732)	731	6,001	106,001
4	5,000	4,240 (4% × $106,001)	760	5,241	105,241
5	5,000	4,210 (4% × $105,241)	790	4,451	104,451
6	5,000	4,178 (4% × $104,451)	822	3,629	103,629
7	5,000	4,145 (4% × $103,629)	855	2,774	102,774
8	5,000	4,111 (4% × $102,774)	889	1,885	101,885
9	5,000	4,075 (4% × $101,885)	925	960	100,960
10	5,000	4,040* (4% × $100,960)	960	—0—	100,000
	$50,000	$41,889	$8,111		

Column (A) remains constant because the face value of the bonds ($100,000) is multiplied by the semiannual contractual interest rate (5%) each period.

Column (B) is computed as the carrying value of the bonds times the semiannual effective-interest rate (4%).

Column (C) indicates the premium amortization each period.

Column (D) decreases each period until it reaches zero at maturity.

Column (E) decreases each period until it equals face value at maturity.

*$2 difference due to rounding.

For the first interest period, the computations of bond interest expense and the bond premium amortization are:

ILLUSTRATION 11A-6

Computation of bond premium amortization

Bond interest expense ($108,111 × 4%)	$4,324
Contractual interest ($100,000 × 5%)	5,000
Bond premium amortization	**$ 676**

The entry on the first interest date is:

A	=	L	+	SE
−5,000		−676		−4,324

July 1	Bond Interest Expense	4,324	
	Premium on Bonds Payable	676	
	Cash		5,000
	(To record payment of bond interest and		
	amortization of bond premium)		

For the second interest period, interest expense will be $4,297, and the premium amortization will be $703. Total bond interest expense for 2001 is $8,621 ($4,324 + $4,297).

TECHNOLOGY IN ACTION

The amortization schedule is an excellent example of an accounting computation efficiently and effectively performed by an electronic spreadsheet. Once the selling price, face amount, contractual rate of interest, effective rate of interest, and number of interest periods are determined and entered into the spreadsheet, all of the computations until maturity can be performed by the computer. Note that all data needed for the adjusting entries can be taken directly from the amortization schedule.

PROBLEM-SOLVING STRATEGIES

1. Bond carrying value at beginning of period times effective-interest rate equals interest expense.
2. Credit to cash (or bond interest payable) is computed by multiplying the face value of the bonds by the contractual interest rate.
3. Bond premium or discount amortization is the difference between (1) and (2).
4. Interest expense increases when the effective-interest method is used for bonds issued at a discount. The reason is that a constant percentage is applied to an increasing book value to compute interest expense.

DEMONSTRATION PROBLEM

Gardner Corporation issues $1,750,000, 10-year, 12% bonds on January 1, 2001, at $1,970,000 to yield 10%. The bonds pay semiannual interest July 1 and January 1. Gardner uses the effective-interest method of amortization.

Instructions
(a) Prepare the journal entry to record the issuance of the bonds.
(b) Prepare the journal entry to record the payment of interest on July 1, 2001.

SOLUTION TO DEMONSTRATION PROBLEM

(a) 2001

Jan. 1	Cash	1,970,000	
	Bonds Payable		1,750,000
	Premium on Bonds Payable		220,000
	(To record issuance of bonds at a premium)		

(b) 2001

July 1	Bond Interest Expense	98,500*	
	Premium on Bonds Payable	6,500**	
	Cash		105,000
	(To record payment of semiannual interest		
	and amortization of bond premium)		
	*($1,970,000 × 5%)		
	**($105,000 − $98,500)		

SUMMARY OF STUDY OBJECTIVES FOR APPENDIX

9. *Contrast the effects of the straight-line and effective-interest methods of amortizing bond discount and bond premium.* The straight-line method of amortization results in a constant amount of amortization and interest expense per period but a varying percentage rate. In contrast, the effective-interest method results in varying amounts of amorti-zation and interest expense per period but a constant percentage rate of interest. The effective-interest method generally results in a better matching of expenses with revenues. When the difference between the straight-line and effective-interest method is material, the use of the effective-interest method is required under GAAP.

GLOSSARY FOR APPENDIX

Effective-interest method of amortization A method of amortizing bond discount or bond premium that results in periodic interest expense equal to a constant percentage of the carrying value of the bonds. (p. 491).

Effective-interest rate Rate established when bonds are issued that remains constant in each interest period. (p. 491).

*****Note:** All asterisked Questions, Exercises, and Problems relate to material in the appendix to the chapter.

SELF-STUDY QUESTIONS

Answers are at the end of the chapter.

(SO 1) 1. The time period for classifying a liability as current is one year or the operating cycle, whichever is:
   a. longer.
   b. shorter.
   c. probable.
   d. possible.

(SO 1) 2. To be classified as a current liability, a debt must be expected to be paid:
   a. out of existing current assets.
   b. by creating other current liabilities.
   c. within two years.
   d. both (a) and (b).

(SO 2) 3. Shumway Company borrows $88,500 on September 1, 2000, from the Sandwich State Bank by signing an $88,500 12%, one-year note. What is the accrued interest at December 31, 2000?
   a. $2,655.
   b. $3,540.
   c. $4,425.
   d. $10,620.

(SO 3) 4. L. Elbert Company has total proceeds from sales of $4,515. If the proceeds include sales taxes of 5%, the amount to be credited to Sales is:
   a. $4,000.
   b. $4,300.
   c. $4,289.25.
   d. No correct answer given.

(SO 4) 5. The term used for bonds that are unsecured is:
   a. callable bonds.
   b. indenture bonds.
   c. debenture bonds.
   d. bearer bonds.

(SO 5) 6. Norton Inc. issues 10-year bonds with a maturity value of $200,000. If the bonds are issued at a premium, this indicates that:

   a. the contractual interest rate exceeds the market interest rate.
   b. the market interest rate exceeds the contractual interest rate.
   c. the contractual interest rate and the market interest rate are the same.
   d. no relationship exists between the two rates.

(SO 5) 7. On January 1, Hurley Corporation issues $500,000, 5-year, 12% bonds at 96 with interest payable on July 1 and January 1. The entry on July 1 to record payment of bond interest and the amortization of bond discount using the straight-line method will include a:
   a. debit to Interest Expense, $30,000.
   b. debit to Interest Expense, $60,000.
   c. credit to Discount on Bonds Payable, $4,000.
   d. credit to Discount on Bonds Payable, $2,000.

(SO 5) 8. For the bonds issued in question 7, above, what is the carrying value of the bonds at the end of the third interest period?
   a. $486,000.
   b. $488,000.
   c. $472,000.
   d. $464,000.

(SO 5) 9. Lahey Corporation retires its $100,000 face value bonds at 105 on January 1, following the payment of semiannual interest. The carrying value of the bonds at the redemption date is $103,745. The entry to record the redemption will include a:
   a. credit of $3,745 to Loss on Bond Redemption.
   b. debit of $3,745 to Premium on Bonds Payable.
   c. credit of $1,255 to Gain on Bond Redemption.
   d. debit of $5,000 to Premium on Bonds Payable.

(SO 6) 10. Engstrom Inc. converts $600,000 of bonds sold at face value into 10,000 shares of common stock, par value $1. Both the bonds and the stock have a market value of $760,000. What amount should be credited to Paid-

in Capital in Excess of Par as a result of the conversion?
a. $10,000.
b. $160,000.
c. $600,000.
d. $590,000.

(SO 5) 11. Wieseman Inc. issues a $497,000, 10% 3-year mortgage
note on January 1. The note will be paid in three annual
installments of $200,000, each payable at the end of the
year. What is the amount of interest expense that should
be recognized by Wieseman Inc. in the second year?
a. $16,567.
b. $49,740.
c. $34,670.
d. $347,600.

(SO 9) *12. On January 1, Jean Loptein Inc. issued $1,000,000, 9%
bonds for $939,000. The market rate of interest for these
bonds is 10%. Interest is payable annually on December

31. Jean Loptein uses the effective interest method of
amortizing bond discount. At the end of the first year,
Jean Loptein should report unamortized bond discount
of:
a. $54,900.
b. $57,100.
c. $51,610.
d. $51,000.

*13. On January 1, Cleopatra Corporation issued $1,000,000, (SO 9)
14%, 5-year bonds with interest payable on July 1 and
January 1. The bonds sold for $1,098,540. The market
rate of interest for these bonds was 12%. On the first interest date, using the effective-interest method, the debit
entry to Bond Interest Expense is for:
a. $60,000.
b. $76,898.
c. $65,912.
d. $131,825.

QUESTIONS

1. David Spade believes a current liability is a debt that
can be expected to be paid in one year. Is David correct?
Explain.

2. Rio Grande Company obtains $25,000 in cash by sign-
ing a 9%, 6-month, $25,000 note payable to First Bank
on July 1. Rio Grande's fiscal year ends on September
30. What information should be reported for the note
payable in the annual financial statements?

3. (a) Your roommate says, "Sales taxes are reported as an
expense in the income statement." Do you agree? Explain.
   (b) Rock Hard Cafe has cash proceeds from sales of
$10,400. This amount includes $400 of sales taxes.
Give the entry to record the proceeds.

4. Aurora University sold 10,000 season football tickets at
$90 each for its five-game home schedule. What entries
should be made (a) when the tickets were sold and (b)
after each game?

5. Identify three taxes commonly withheld by the employer from an employee's gross pay.

6. Identify three taxes commonly paid by employers on
employee's salaries and wages. Where in the financial
statements does the employer report taxes withheld
from employee's pay?

7. (a) What are long-term liabilities? Give three examples.
   (b) What is a bond?

8. (a) As a source of long-term financing, what are the major advantages of bonds over common stock? (b) What
are the major disadvantages in using bonds for long-
term financing?

9. Contrast the following types of bonds: (a) secured and
unsecured, (b) term and serial, (c) registered and bearer,
and (d) convertible and callable.

10. The following terms are important in issuing bonds: (a)
face value, (b) contractual interest rate, (c) bond indenture, and (d) bond certificate. Explain each of these
terms.

11. Describe the two major obligations incurred by a company when bonds are issued.

12. Assume that Spartans Inc. sold bonds with a par value
of $100,000 for $104,000. Was the market interest rate
equal to, less than, or greater than the bonds' contractual interest rate? Explain.

13. Andy Manion and Linda O'Neill are discussing how the
market price of a bond is determined. Linda believes
that the market price of a bond is solely a function of
the amount of the principal payment at the end of the
term of a bond. Is she right? Discuss.

14. If a 10%, 10-year, $600,000 bond is issued at par and in-
terest is paid semiannually, what is the amount of the
interest payment at the end of the first semiannual period?

15. If the Bonds Payable account has a balance of $900,000
and the Discount on Bonds Payable account has a balance of $40,000, what is the carrying value of the bonds?

16. Explain the straight-line method of amortizing discount
and premium on bonds payable.

17. Jennifer Brent Corporation issues $200,000 of 8%, 5-year
bonds on January 1, 2001, at 104. Assuming that the

straight-line method is used to amortize the premium, what is the total amount of interest expense for 2001?

18. Which accounts are debited and which are credited if a bond issue originally sold at a premium is redeemed before maturity at 97 immediately following the payment of interest?

19. Li Feng Corporation is considering issuing a convertible bond. What is a convertible bond? Discuss the advantages of a convertible bond from the standpoint of (a) the bondholders and (b) the issuing corporation.

20. Jude Law, a friend of yours, has recently purchased a home for $125,000, paying $25,000 down and the remainder financed by a 10.5%, 20-year mortgage, payable at $998.38 per month. At the end of the first month, Jude receives a statement from the bank indicating that only $123.38 of principal was paid during the month. At this rate, he calculates that it will take over 67 years to pay off the mortgage. Is he right? Discuss.

21. In general, what are the requirements for the financial statement presentation of long-term liabilities? What ratios may be computed to evaluate a company's liquidity and solvency?

*22. Kate Winslet is discussing the advantages of the effective-interest method of bond amortization with her accounting staff. What do you think Kate is saying?

*23. Summit Corporation issues $400,000 of 9%, 5-year bonds on January 1, 2001, at 104. If Summit uses the effective-interest method in amortizing the premium, will the annual interest expense increase or decrease over the life of the bonds? Explain.

BRIEF EXERCISES

BE11–1 Existenz Company has the following obligations at December 31: (a) a note payable for $100,000 due in 2 years, (b) a 10-year mortgage payable of $200,000 payable in 10 $20,000 annual payments, (c) interest payable of $15,000 on the mortgage, and (d) accounts payable of $60,000. For each obligation, indicate whether it should be classified as a current liability.

Identify whether obligations are current liabilities.
(SO 1)

BE11–2 J.J. Leigh Company borrows $60,000 on July 1 from the bank by signing a $60,000 10%, one-year note payable. Prepare the journal entries to record (a) the proceeds of the note and (b) accrued interest at December 31, assuming adjusting entries are made only at the end of the year.

Prepare entries for an interest-bearing note payable.
(SO 2)

BE11–3 Cronenberg Auto Supply does not segregate sales and sales taxes at the time of sale. The register total for March 16 is $9,975. All sales are subject to a 5% sales tax. Compute sales taxes payable and make the entry to record sales taxes payable and sales.

Compute and record sales taxes payable.
(SO 3)

BE11–4 Grambling University sells 3,000 season basketball tickets at $60 each for its 12-game home schedule. Give the entry to record (a) the sale of the season tickets and (b) the revenue earned by playing the first home game.

Prepare entries for unearned revenues.
(SO 3)

BE11–5 J. Cusack Inc. is considering two alternatives to finance its construction of a new $2 million plant:

(a) Issuance of 200,000 shares of common stock at the market price of $10 per share.
(b) Issuance of $2 million, 8% bonds at par.

Compare bond versus stock financing.
(SO 4)

Complete the following table and indicate which alternative is preferable.

	Issue Stock	Issue Bond
Income before interest and taxes	$1,000,000	$1,000,000
Interest expense from bonds	_____	_____
Income before income taxes	$	$
Income tax expense (30%)	_____	_____
Net income	$_____	$_____
Outstanding shares	_____	700,000
Earnings per share	_____	_____

BE11–6 F. Voris Corporation issued 1,000, 9%, 5-year, $1,000 bonds dated January 1, 2001, at 100. (a) Prepare the journal entry to record the sale of these bonds on January 1, 2001. (b) Prepare the journal entry to record the first interest payment on July 1, 2001 (interest payable semiannually), assuming no previous accrual of interest. (c) Prepare the adjusting journal entry on December 31, 2001, to record interest expense.

Prepare journal entries for bonds issued at face value.
(SO 5)

Prepare journal entries for bonds issued at a discount. (SO 5)

BE11–7   J. McKee Company issues $2 million, 10 year, 9% bonds at 98, with interest payable on July 1 and January 1. The straight-line method is used to amortize bond discount. (a) Prepare the journal entry to record the sale of these bonds on January 1, 2001. (b) Prepare the journal entry to record interest expense and bond discount amortization on July 1, 2001, assuming no previous accrual of interest.

Prepare journal entries for bonds issued at a premium. (SO 5)

BE11–8   Billie Bob Inc. issues $5 million, 5-year, 10% bonds at 103, with interest payable on July 1 and January 1. The straight-line method is used to amortize bond premium. (a) Prepare the journal entry to record the sale of these bonds on January 1, 2001. (b) Prepare the journal entry to record interest expense and bond premium amortization on July 1, 2001, assuming no previous accrual of interest.

Prepare journal entries for bonds issued between interest dates. (SO 5)

BE11–9   Pushing Tin Inc. has outstanding $1 million, 10-year, 12% bonds with interest payable on July 1 and January 1. The bonds were dated January 1, 2001, but were issued on May 1, 2001, at face value plus accrued interest. (a) Prepare the journal entry to record the sale of the bonds on May 1, 2001. (b) Prepare the journal entry to record the interest payment on July 1, 2001.

Record redemption of bonds. (SO 6)

BE11–10   The balance sheet for S. Marceau Company reports the following information on July 1, 2001:

Long-term liabilities		
Bonds payable	$1,000,000	
Less: Discount on bonds payable	60,000	$940,000

Marceau decides to redeem these bonds at 102 after paying semiannual interest. Prepare the journal entry to record the redemption on July 1, 2001.

Account for long-term notes payable. (SO 7)

BE11–11   Escobar Inc. issues a $300,000, 10%, 10-year mortgage note on December 31, 2001, to obtain financing for a new building. The terms provide for semiannual installment payments of $24,073. Prepare the entry to record the mortgage loan on December 31, 2001, and the first installment payment.

Prepare financial statement presentation of long-term liabilities. (SO 8)

BE 11–12   Presented below are long-term liability items for Cate Blanchett Company at December 31, 2001. Prepare the long-term liabilities section of the balance sheet for Cate Blanchett Company.

Bonds payable, due 2006	$900,000
Notes payable, due 2008	80,000
Discount on bonds payable	45,000

Analyze liquidity and solvency. (SO 8)

BE 11–13   Motorola's financial statements recently contained the following selected data (in millions):

Current assets	$10,510	Interest expense	$ 149
Total assets	22,801	Income taxes	1,001
Current liabilities	7,791	Net income	1,781
Total liabilities	11,753		

Compute the following ratios:

(a) Working capital.   (c) Debt to total assets ratio.
(b) Current ratio.   (d) Times interest earned ratio.

Use effective interest method of bond amortization. (SO 9)

*BE11–14   Presented below is the partial bond discount amortization schedule for Closet Corp. Closet Corp. uses the effective-interest method of amortization.

Semiannual Interest Periods	Interest to Be Paid	Interest Expense to Be Recorded	Discount Amortization	Unamortized Discount	Bond Carrying Value
Issue date				$62,311	$937,689
1	$45,000	$46,884	$1,884	60,427	939,573
2	45,000	46,979	1,979	58,448	941,552

Instructions

(a) Prepare the journal entry to record the payment of interest and the discount amortization at the end of period 1.

(b) ▨▨▨▶ Explain why interest expense is greater than interest paid.

(c) ▨▨▨▶ Explain why interest expense will increase each period.

EXERCISES

••

E11–1 Nathan K. Company on June 1 borrows $50,000 from Corner Bank on a 6-month, $50,000, 12% note.

Prepare entries for interest-bearing notes.
(SO 2)

Instructions
  (a) Prepare the entry on June 1.
  (b) Prepare the adjusting entry on June 30.
  (c) Prepare the entry at maturity (December 1), assuming monthly adjusting entries have been made through November 30.
  (d) What was the total financing cost (interest expense)?

E11–2 In providing accounting services to small businesses, you encounter the following situations pertaining to cash sales:

Journalize sales and related taxes.
(SO 3)

  1. Chan Company rings up sales and sales taxes separately on its cash register. On April 10, the register totals are sales $25,000 and sales taxes $1,500.
  2. Dragon Company does not segregate sales and sales taxes. Its register total for April 15 is $13,780, which includes a 6% sales tax.

Instructions
Prepare the entry to record the sales transactions and related taxes for each client.

E11–3 Outdoor Company publishes a monthly sports magazine, *Fishing Preview*. Subscriptions to the magazine cost $24 per year. During November 2000, Outdoor sells 6,000 subscriptions beginning with the December issue. Outdoor prepares financial statements quarterly and recognizes subscription revenue earned at the end of the quarter. The company uses the accounts Unearned Subscription Revenue and Subscription Revenue.

Journalize unearned subscription revenue.
(SO 3)

Instructions
  (a) Prepare the entry in November for the receipt of the subscriptions.
  (b) Prepare the adjusting entry at December 31, 2000, to record subscription revenue earned in December of 2000.
  (c) Prepare the adjusting entry at March 31, 2001, to record subscription revenue earned in the first quarter of 2001.

E11–4 Flypaper Airlines is considering two alternatives for the financing of a purchase of a fleet of airplanes. These two alternatives are:

Compare two alternatives of financing—issuance of common stock vs. issuance of bonds.
(SO 4)

  1. Issue 60,000 shares of common stock at $45 per share. (Cash dividends have not been paid nor is the payment of any contemplated.)
  2. Issue 13%, 10-year bonds at face value for $2,700,000.

It is estimated that the company will earn $900,000 before interest and taxes as a result of this purchase. The company has an estimated tax rate of 30% and has 90,000 shares of common stock outstanding prior to the new financing.

Instructions
Determine the effect on net income and earnings per share for these two methods of financing.

E11–5 On January 1, Montana Company issued $90,000, 10%, 10-year bonds at face value. Interest is payable semiannually on July 1 and January 1. Interest is not accrued on June 30.

Prepare journal entries for issuance of bonds and payment and accrual of bond interest.
(SO 5)

Instructions
Present journal entries to record:
  (a) The issuance of the bonds.
  (b) The payment of interest on July 1.
  (c) The accrual of interest on December 31.

E11–6 Pueblo Company issued $240,000, 9%, 20-year bonds on January 1, 2001, at 103. Interest is payable semiannually on July 1 and January 1. Pueblo uses straight-line amortization for bond premium or discount. Interest is not accrued on June 30.

Prepare journal entries to record issuance of bonds, payment of interest, amortization of premium, and redemption at maturity.
(SO 5, 6)

Instructions
Prepare the journal entries to record:
  (a) The issuance of the bonds.

(b) The payment of interest and the premium amortization on July 1, 2001.
(c) The accrual of interest and the premium amortization on December 31, 2001.
(d) The redemption of the bonds at maturity, assuming interest for the last interest period has been paid and recorded.

Prepare journal entries to record issuance of bonds, payment of interest, amortization of discount, and redemption at maturity.
(SO 5, 6)

E11–7   Teacher Company issued $180,000, 11%, 10-year bonds on December 31, 2000, for $172,000. Interest is payable semiannually on June 30 and December 31. Teacher uses the straight-line method to amortize bond premium or discount.

Instructions
Prepare the journal entries to record:

(a) The issuance of the bonds.
(b) The payment of interest and the discount amortization on June 30, 2001.
(c) The payment of interest and the discount amortization on December 31, 2001.
(d) The redemption of the bonds at maturity, assuming interest for the last interest period has been paid and recorded.

Prepare journal entries to record issuance of bonds between interest dates, and payment and accrual of interest.
(SO 5)

E11–8   On April 1, Shirley Company issued $72,000, 10%, 10-year bonds dated January 1 at face value plus accrued interest. Interest is payable semiannually on July 1 and January 1.

Instructions
Present journal entries to record:

(a) The issuance of the bonds.
(b) The payment of interest on July 1. Interest is not accrued on June 30.
(c) The accrual of interest on December 31.

Prepare journal entries for redemption of bonds and conversion of bonds into common stock.
(SO 6)

E11–9   Presented below are three independent situations:

1. Price Corporation retired $120,000 face value, 12% bonds on June 30, 2001, at 102. The carrying value of the bonds at the redemption date was $107,500. The bonds pay semiannual interest and the interest payment due on June 30, 2001, has been made and recorded.
2. Waterhouse, Inc. retired $150,000 face value, 12.5% bonds on June 30, 2001, at 98. The carrying value of the bonds at the redemption date was $151,000. The bonds pay semiannual interest and the interest payment due on June 30, 2001, has been made and recorded.
3. Jefferson Company has $80,000, 8%, 12-year convertible bonds outstanding. These bonds were sold at face value and pay semiannual interest on June 30 and December 31 of each year. The bonds are convertible into 30 shares of Jefferson $2 par value common stock for each $1,000 worth of bonds. On December 31, 2001, after the bond interest has been paid, $20,000 face value bonds were converted. The market value of Jefferson common stock was $44 per share on December 31, 2001.

Instructions
For each independent situation above, prepare the appropriate journal entry for the redemption or conversion of the bonds.

Prepare journal entries to record mortgage note and installment payments.
(SO 7)

E11–10   Walter Payton Co. receives $110,000 when it issues a $110,000, 10%, mortgage note payable to finance the construction of a building at December 31, 2001. The terms provide for semiannual installment payments of $7,500 on June 30 and December 31.

Instructions
Prepare the journal entries to record the mortgage loan and the first two installment payments.

Prepare statement presentation of long-term liabilities.
(SO 8)

E11–11   The adjusted trial balance for Montreal Corporation at the end of the current year contained the following accounts:

Bond interest payable	$ 9,000
Mortgage note payable	59,500
Bonds payable, due 2007	120,000
Premium on bonds payable	32,000

Instructions
(a) Prepare the long-term liabilities section of the balance sheet.
(b) Indicate the proper balance sheet classification for the account(s) listed above that do not belong in the long-term liabilities section.

E11–12   Quebec Corporation issued $260,000, 9%, 10-year bonds on January 1, 2001, for $243,799. This price resulted in an effective interest rate of 10% on the bonds. Interest is payable semiannually on July 1 and January 1. Quebec uses the effective-interest method to amortize bond premium or discount. Interest is not accrued on June 30.

Instructions
Prepare the journal entries to record (round to the nearest dollar):
(a) The issuance of the bonds.
(b) The payment of interest and the discount amortization on July 1, 2001.
(c) The accrual of interest and the discount amortization on December 31, 2001.

E11–13   Detroit Company issued $180,000, 11%, 10-year bonds on January 1, 2001, for $191,216. This price resulted in an effective interest rate of 10% on the bonds. Interest is payable semiannually on July 1 and January 1. Detroit uses the effective-interest method to amortize bond premium or discount. Interest is not accrued on June 30.

Instructions
Prepare the journal entries (rounded to the nearest dollar) to record:
(a) The issuance of the bonds.
(b) The payment of interest and the premium amortization on July 1, 2001.
(c) The accrual of interest and the premium amortization on December 31, 2001.

PROBLEMS: SET A

P11–1A   On January 1, 2001, the ledger of Malaga Company contains the following liability accounts.

Accounts Payable	$42,500
Sales Taxes Payable	5,600
Unearned Service Revenue	15,000

During January the following selected transactions occurred:

Jan. 1   Borrowed $15,000 in cash from Midland Bank on a 4-month, 10%, $15,000 note.
    5   Sold merchandise for cash totaling $7,800 which includes 4% sales taxes.
   12   Provided services for customers who had made advance payments of $8,000. (Credit Service Revenue.)
   14   Paid state treasurer's department for sales taxes collected in December 2000 $5,600.
   20   Sold 500 units of a new product on credit at $52 per unit, plus 4% sales tax.
   25   Sold merchandise for cash totaling $11,440, which includes 4% sales taxes.

Instructions
(a) Journalize the January transactions.
(b) Journalize the adjusting entries at January 31 for the outstanding note payable.
(c) Prepare the current liabilities section of the balance sheet at January 31, 2001. Assume no change in Accounts Payable.

P11–2A   The following are selected transactions of Rockford Company. Rockford prepares financial statements *quarterly* (a perpetual inventory system is used).

Jan. 2   Purchased merchandise on account from Dick Wasson Company, $15,000, terms 2/10, n/30.
Feb. 1   Issued a 10%, 2-month, $15,000 note to Dick Wasson in payment of account.
Mar. 31   Accrued interest for 2 months on Dick Wasson note.
Apr. 1   Paid face value and interest on Dick Wasson note.
July 1   Purchased equipment from Scottie Equipment paying $11,000 in cash and signing a 10%, 3-month, $24,000 note.

Sept. 30   Accrued interest for 3 months on Scottie note.
  Oct. 1   Paid face value and interest on Scottie note.
  Dec. 1   Borrowed $10,000 from the Federation Bank by issuing a 3-month, 9%-interest-bearing note with a face value of $10,000.
  Dec. 31   Recognized interest expense for 1 month on Federation Bank note.

Instructions

(a) Prepare journal entries for the above transactions and events.
(b) Post to the accounts Notes Payable, Interest Payable, and Interest Expense.
(c) Show the balance sheet presentation of notes payable at December 31.
(d) What is total interest expense for the year?

Prepare journal entries to record issuance of bonds, interest accrual, and amortization for 2 years.
(SO 5, 8)

P11–3A   Moriarity Company sold $4,000,000, 9%, 20-year bonds on January 1, 2001. The bonds were dated January 1, 2001, and pay interest on January 1 and July 1. Moriarity Company uses the straight-line method to amortize bond premium or discount. The bonds were sold at 97. Assume no interest is accrued on June 30.

Instructions

(a) Prepare the journal entry to record the issuance of the bonds on January 1, 2001.
(b) Prepare a bond discount amortization schedule for the first four interest periods.
(c) Prepare the journal entries for interest and the amortization of the discount in 2001 and 2002.
(d) Show the balance sheet presentation of the bond liability at December 31, 2002.

Prepare journal entries to record issuance of bonds, interest, and amortization of bond premium and discount.
(SO 5, 8)

11–4A   J. Downey Co. sold $5,000,000, 9%, 5-year bonds on January 1, 2000. The bonds were dated January 1, 2000, and pay interest on July 1 and January 1. The company uses straight-line amortization on bond premiums and discounts. Financial statements are prepared annually.

Instructions

(a) Prepare the journal entries to record the issuance of the bonds assuming they sold at:
(1) 103.
(2) 98.
(b) Prepare amortization tables for both assumed sales for the first three interest payments.
(c) Prepare the journal entries to record interest expense for 2000 under both assumed sales.
(d) Show the balance sheet presentation for both assumed sales at December 31, 2000.

Prepare journal entries to record interest payments, discount amortization, and redemption of bonds.
(SO 5, 8)

P11–5A   The following is taken from Jamaica Corp. balance sheet at December 31, 2001:

Current liabilities
  Bond interest payable (for 6 months)
    from July 1 to December 31) $132,000
Long-term liabilities
  Bonds payable, 11%, due
  January 1, 2012 $2,400,000
  Less: Discount on bonds payable   84,000 $2,316,000

Interest is payable semiannually on January 1 and July 1. The bonds are callable on any semiannual interest date. Jamaica uses straight-line amortization for any bond premium or discount. From December 31, 2001, the bonds will be outstanding for an additional 10 years or 120 months. Assume no interest is accrued on June 30.

Instructions

(Round all computations to the nearest dollar.)

(a) Journalize the payment of bond interest on January 1, 2002.
(b) Prepare the entry to amortize bond discount and to pay the interest due on July 1, 2002.
(c) Assume on July 1, 2002, after paying interest that Jamaica Corp. calls bonds having a face value of $800,000. The call price is 102. Record the redemption of the bonds.
(d) Prepare the adjusting entry at December 31, 2002, to amortize bond discount and to accrue interest on the remaining bonds.

P11–6A Atwater Corporation is building a new, state-of-the-art production and assembly facility for $10,000,000. To finance the facility it is using $2,000,000 it received from the issuance of shares of common stock, and the balance is being funded from the issuance of bonds. The $8,000,000, 11%, 5-year bonds were sold on August 1, 2001. They were dated August 1, 2001, and pay interest August 1 and February 1. Atwater uses the straight-line method to amortize bond premium or discount. Assume no interest is accrued on January 31 or July 31.

Atwater also purchased a new piece of equipment to be used in its new facility. The $550,000 piece of equipment was purchased with a $50,000 down payment and with cash received through the issuance of a $500,000, 8%, 3-year mortgage note payable issued on October 1, 2001. The terms provide for quarterly installment payments of $47,280 on December 31, March 31, June 30, and September 30.

Instructions
(Round all computations to the nearest dollar.)

(a) Prepare all necessary journal entries to record the issuance of the bonds and bond interest expense for 2001, assuming the bonds sold at 101.
(b) Prepare an installment payments schedule for the first five payments of the notes payable.
(c) Prepare all necessary journal entries related to the notes payable for 2001.
(d) Show balance sheet presentation for these obligations for December 31, 2001. (*Hint:* Be sure to distinguish between the current and long-term portions of the note.)

*P11–7A On July 1, 2001, Global Satellites Corporation issued $1,200,000 face value, 9%, 10-year bonds at $1,125,227. This price resulted in an effective-interest rate of 10% on the bonds. Global uses the effective-interest method to amortize bond premium or discount. The bonds pay semi-annual interest July 1 and January 1.

Instructions
(Round all computations to the nearest dollar.)

(a) Prepare the journal entry to record the issuance of the bonds on July 1, 2001.
(b) Prepare an amortization table through December 31, 2002 (three interest periods) for this bond issue.
(c) Prepare the journal entry to record the accrual of interest and the amortization of the discount on December 31, 2001.
(d) Prepare the journal entry to record the payment of interest and the amortization of the discount on July 1, 2002.
(e) Prepare the journal entry to record the accrual of interest and the amortization of the discount on December 31, 2002.

*P11–8A On July 1, 2001, Amoco Imperial Company issued $2,000,000 face value, 12%, 10-year bonds at $2,249,245. This price resulted in a 10% effective-interest rate on the bonds. Amoco Imperial uses the effective-interest method to amortize bond premium or discount. The bonds pay semiannual interest on each July 1 and January 1.

Instructions

(a) Prepare the journal entries to record the following transactions:
   (1) The issuance of the bonds on July 1, 2001.
   (2) The accrual of interest and the amortization of the premium on December 31, 2001.
   (3) The payment of interest and the amortization of the premium on July 1, 2002.
   (4) The accrual of interest and the amortization of the premium on December 31, 2002.
(b) Show the proper balance sheet presentation for the liability for bonds payable on the December 31, 2002, balance sheet.
(c) Provide the answers to the following questions in letter form.
   (1) What amount of interest expense is reported for 2002?
   (2) Would the bond interest expense reported in 2002 be the same as, greater than, or less than the amount that would be reported if the straight-line method of amortization were used?

(3) Determine the total cost of borrowing over the life of the bond.
(4) Would the total bond interest expense be greater than, the same as, or less than the total interest expense if the straight-line method of amortization were used?

PROBLEMS: SET B

Prepare current liability entries, adjusting entries, and current liability section.
(SO 1, 2, 3)

P11–1B   On January 1, 2001, the ledger of Burlington Company contains the following liability accounts:

Accounts Payable	$52,000
Sales Taxes Payable	7,500
Unearned Service Revenue	16,000

During January the following selected transactions occurred:

Jan. 5   Sold merchandise for cash totaling $16,632, which includes 8% sales taxes.
  12   Provided services for customers who had made advance payments of $9,000. (Credit Service Revenue)
  14   Paid state revenue department for sales taxes collected in December 2000 ($7,500).
  20   Sold 500 units of a new product on credit at $50 per unit, plus 8% sales tax.
  21   Borrowed $18,000 from Castle Bank on a 3-month, 10%, $18,000 note.
  25   Sold merchandise for cash totaling $11,340, which includes 8% sales taxes.

Instructions
(a) Journalize the January transactions.
(b) Journalize the adjusting entries at January 31 for the outstanding notes payable.
(c) Prepare the current liability section of the balance sheet at January 31, 2001. Assume no change in accounts payable.

Prepare journal entries to record issuance of bonds, interest accrual, and amortization for 2 years.
(SO 5, 8)

P11–2B   Pompeii Corp. sold $3,000,000, 10%, 10-year bonds on January 1, 2001. The bonds were dated January 1 and pay interest July 1 and January 1. Pompeii Corp. uses the straight-line method to amortize bond premium or discount. The bonds were sold at 104. Assume no interest is accrued on June 30.

Instructions
(a) Prepare the journal entry to record the issuance of the bonds on January 1, 2001.
(b) Prepare a bond premium amortization schedule for the first four interest periods.
(c) Prepare the journal entries for interest and the amortization of the premium in 2001 and 2002.
(d) Show the balance sheet presentation of the bond liability at December 31, 2002.

Prepare journal entries to record issuance of bonds, interest, and amortization of bond premium and discount.
(SO 5, 8)

P11–3B   Gwynn Company sold $1,500,000, 12%, 10-year bonds on July 1, 2001. The bonds were dated July 1, 2001, and pay interest July 1 and January 1. Gwynn Company uses the straight-line method to amortize bond premium or discount. Assume no interest is accrued on June 30.

Instructions
(a) Prepare all necessary journal entries to record the issuance of the bonds and bond interest expense for 2001, assuming that the bonds sold at 102.
(b) Prepare journal entries as in part (a) assuming that the bonds sold at 94.
(c) Show balance sheet presentation for each bond issue at December 31, 2001.

Prepare journal entries to record issuance of bonds, interest, and amortization of bond premium and discount.
(SO 5, 8)

P11–4B   Chula Vista Corporation sold $3,500,000, 7%, 20-year bonds on June 30, 2000. The bonds were dated June 30, 2000, and pay interest on June 30 and December 31. The company uses straight-line amortization for premiums and discounts. Financial statements are prepared annually.

Instructions
(a) Prepare the journal entry to record the issuance of the bonds assuming they sold at:
  (1) 96 1/2.
  (2) 104.
(b) Prepare amortization tables for both of the assumed sales for the first three interest payments.

(c) Prepare the journal entries to record the first two interest payments under both assumed sales.

(d) Show the balance sheet presentation for both assumed sales at December 31, 2000.

P11–5B   Elite Electronics Corporation issues an $800,000, 12%, 10-year mortgage note on December 31, 2000. The proceeds from the note are to be used in financing a new research laboratory. The terms of the note provide for semiannual installment payments, exclusive of real estate taxes and insurance, of $69,748. Payments are due June 30 and December 31.

Prepare installment schedule and journal entries for a mortgage note payable.
(SO 7)

Instructions
(a) Prepare an installment payments schedule for the first 2 years.
(b) Prepare the entries for (1) the loan and (2) the first two installment payments.
(c) Show how the total mortgage liability should be reported on the balance sheet at December 31, 2001.

P11–6B   Myron Corporation is building a new, state-of-the-art production and assembly facility for $15,000,000. To finance the facility it is using $3,000,000 it received from the issuance of shares of common stock, and the balance is being funded from the issuance of bonds. The $12,000,000, 9%, 10-year bonds were sold on August 1, 2001. They were dated August 1, 2001, and pay interest August 1 and February 1. Myron uses the straight-line method to amortize bond premium or discount. Assume no interest is accrued on January 31 or July 31.

Prepare journal entries for issuance of bonds and interest; prepare installment payments schedule and journal entries for a mortgage note payable.
(SO 5, 7, 8)

Myron also purchased a new piece of equipment to be used in its new facility. The $750,000 piece of equipment was purchased with a $50,000 down payment and with cash received through the issuance of a $700,000, 6%, 4-year mortgage note payable issued on October 1, 2001. The terms provide for quarterly installment payments of $49,536 on December 31, March 31, June 30, and September 30.

Instructions
(Round all computations to the nearest dollar.)

(a) Prepare all necessary journal entries to record the issuance of the bonds and bond interest expense for 2001, assuming the bonds sold at 98.
(b) Prepare an installment payments schedule for the first five payments of the notes payable.
(c) Prepare all necessary journal entries related to the notes payable for 2001.
(d) Show balance sheet presentation for these obligations for December 31, 2001. (*Hint:* Be sure to distinguish between the current and long-term portions of the note.)

*P11–7B   On July 1, 2001, Cleopatra Corporation issued $1,500,000 face value, 12%, 10-year bonds at $1,686,934. This price resulted in an effective-interest rate of 10% on the bonds. Cleopatra uses the effective-interest method to amortize bond premium or discount. The bonds pay semiannual interest July 1 and January 1.

Prepare journal entries to record issuance of bonds, payment of interest, and amortization of bond premium using effective-interest method.
(SO 5, 9)

Instructions
(Round all computations to the nearest dollar.)

(a) Prepare the journal entry to record the issuance of the bonds on July 1, 2001.
(b) Prepare an amortization table through December 31, 2002 (three interest periods) for this bond issue.
(c) Prepare the journal entry to record the accrual of interest and the amortization of the premium on December 31, 2001.
(d) Prepare the journal entry to record the payment of interest and the amortization of the premium on July 1, 2002.
(e) Prepare the journal entry to record the accrual of interest and the amortization of the premium on December 31, 2002.

*P11–8B   On July 1, 2001, Waubonsee Company issued $2,200,000 face value, 10%, 10-year bonds at $1,947,651. This price resulted in an effective-interest rate of 12% on the bonds. Waubonsee uses the effective-interest method to amortize bond premium or discount. The bonds pay semiannual interest July 1 and January 1.

Prepare journal entries to record issuance of bonds, payment of interest, and amortization of discount using effective-interest method. In addition, answer questions.
(SO 5, 9)

Instructions

(a) Prepare the journal entries to record the following transactions.
  (1) The issuance of the bonds on July 1, 2001.
  (2) The accrual of interest and the amortization of the discount on December 31, 2001.
  (3) The payment of interest and the amortization of the discount on July 1, 2002.
  (4) The accrual of interest and the amortization of the discount on December 31, 2002.
(b) Show the proper balance sheet presentation for the liability for bonds payable on the December 31, 2002, balance sheet.
(c) ▥▤▤▤▷ Provide the answers to the following questions in letter form.
  (1) What amount of interest expense is reported for 2002?
  (2) Would the bond interest expense reported in 2002 be the same as, greater than, or less than the amount that would be reported if the straight-line method of amortization were used?
  (3) Determine the total cost of borrowing over the life of the bond.
  (4) Would the total bond interest expense be greater than, the same as, or less than the total interest expense that would be reported if the straight-line method of amortization were used?

BROADENING YOUR PERSPECTIVE

FINANCIAL REPORTING AND ANALYSIS

FINANCIAL REPORTING PROBLEM: Kellogg Company

BYP11–1 Refer to the financial statements of Kellogg Company and the Notes to Consolidated Financial Statements in Appendix A.

Instructions
Answer the following questions:

(a) What was Kellogg's total long-term debt at December 31, 1998? What was the increase/decrease in Kellogg's total long-term debt (excluding other liabilities) from the prior year?
(b) What were the components of total long-term debt (excluding other liabilities) on December 31, 1998?
(c) What is the amount of leases that are reported as part of long-term debt?

COMPARATIVE ANALYSIS PROBLEM: Kellogg Company vs. General Mills

BYP11–2 Kellogg's financial statements are presented in Appendix A; General Mills's financial statements are presented in Appendix B.

Instructions
(a) Based on the information contained in these financial statements, compute the following 1998 ratios for each company:
  (1) Debt to total assets.
  (2) Times interest earned.
(b) What conclusions concerning the companies' long-run solvency can be drawn from these ratios?

RESEARCH ASSIGNMENT

BYP11–3 The November 6, 1995, edition of *The Wall Street Journal* contains an article by Linda Sandler entitled "Kmart Is Pressured Over Obscure Bond 'Puts,' Which Stir Worries Amid Tough Retail Times."

Instructions

Read the article and answer these questions.

(a) What is the total dollar amount of the bond issue in question? Who purchased these bonds?

(b) What right does the "put option" give to bondholders?

(c) What amount is available under Kmart's bank lines? Why can't Kmart borrow under these lines to purchase the bonds? What is the most likely solution to the problem?

(d) Were the terms of the put bonds adequately disclosed?

INTERPRETING FINANCIAL STATEMENTS: Texas Instruments

BYP11–4   Texas Instruments designs and produces devices that use semiconductor technology. You may have one of its calculators on your desk. Because it is in a high-tech industry, the company must constantly invest in new technology, which requires considerable financing. Information (in millions) from Texas Instruments' 1998 annual report is shown below:

	1998	1997
Current assets	$ 4,846	$ 6,103
Total assets	11,250	10,849
Current liabilities	2,196	2,496
Total liabilities	4,723	4,935
Stockholders' equity	6,527	5,914
Sales revenue	8,460	9,750
Income taxes	210	411
Interest expense	75	94
Net income	407	354

Maturities (in millions) of long-term debt due during the 4 years subsequent to December 31, 1998, are:

1999	$267	2001	$135
2000	312	2002	27

Instructions

Address each of these questions related to the liabilities of Texas Instruments:

(a) Using both working capital and the current ratio as indicators, evaluate the change in the company's liquidity from 1997 to 1998.

(b) Using both the debt to total assets ratio and the times interest earned ratio, evaluate the change in the company's solvency from 1997 to 1998.

(c) What are the implications of the information provided about the maturities of the company's long-term debt?

REAL-WORLD FOCUS: Apache Corporation

BYP11–5   **Apache Corporation** is an international, independent energy enterprise engaged in the exploration, development, production, gathering, processing, and marketing of natural gas and crude oil. Its corporate headquarters are located in Houston, Texas, and it has operations in North America, Australia, Egypt, Poland, People's Republic of China, Indonesia, and the Ivory Coast.

The 1994 annual report of Apache Corporation disclosed the information shown at the top of the next page in its management discussion section.

Instructions

(a) Identify the face amount, contractual interest rate, and selling price of the newly issued bonds due in 2002. Explain whether the bonds sold at a premium or a discount.

(b) For what purposes has Apache Corporation been incurring more debt?

APACHE CORPORATION
Management Discussion

In May 1994, Apache issued 9.25% bonds due 2002 in the principal amount of $100 million. The proceeds of $99 million from the offering were used to reduce bank debt, to pay off the 9.5% convertible debentures due 1996, and for general corporate purposes. In December 1994, the company privately placed 3.93% convertible notes due 1997 in the principal amount of $75 million. The notes are not redeemable before maturity and are convertible into Apache common stock at the option of the holders at any time prior to maturity, at a conversion price of $27 per share. Proceeds from the sale of the notes were used for the repayment of bank debt.

CRITICAL THINKING

GROUP DECISION CASE

BYP11–6   On January 1, 1999, Marsh Corporation issued $1,200,000 of 5-year, 8% bonds at 96; the bonds pay interest semiannually on July 1 and January 1. By January 1, 2001, the market rate of interest for bonds of risk similar to those of Marsh Corporation had risen. As a result the market value of these bonds was $1,000,000 on January 1, 2001—below their carrying value. Tom Marsh, president of the company, suggests repurchasing all of these bonds in the open market at the $1,000,000 price. To do so the company will have to issue $1,000,000 (face value) of new 10-year, 12% bonds at par. The president asks you, as controller, "What is the feasibility of my proposed repurchase plan?"

Instructions
With the class divided into groups, answer the following:

   (a) What is the carrying value of the outstanding Marsh Corporation 5-year bonds on January 1, 2001? (Assume straight-line amortization.)
   (b) Prepare the journal entry to retire the 5-year bonds on January 1, 2001. Prepare the journal entry to issue the new 10-year bonds.
   (c) Prepare a short memo to the president in response to his request for advice. List the economic factors that you believe should be considered for his repurchase proposal.

COMMUNICATION ACTIVITY

BYP11–7   Dane Ely, president of the Briley Corporation, is considering the issuance of bonds to finance an expansion of his business. He has asked you to (1) discuss the advantages of bonds over common stock financing, (2) indicate the type of bonds he might issue, and (3) explain the issuing procedures used in bond transactions.

Instructions
Write a memorandum to the president, answering his request.

ETHICS CASE

BYP11–8   Ron Grandgeorge is the president, founder, and majority owner of Newman Medical Corporation, an emerging medical technology products company. Newman is in dire need of additional capital to keep operating and to bring several promising products to final development, testing, and production. Ron, as owner of 51% of the outstanding stock, manages the company's operations. He places heavy emphasis on research and development and on long-term growth. The other principal stockholder is Judy Costello who, as a nonemployee investor, owns 40% of the stock. Judy would like to deemphasize the R&D functions and emphasize the marketing function, to maximize short-run sales and profits from existing products. She believes this strategy would raise the market price of Newman's stock.

All of Ron's personal capital and borrowing power is tied up in his 51% stock owner-ship. He knows that any offering of additional shares of stock will dilute his controlling in-terest because he won't be able to participate in such an issuance. But, Judy has money and would likely buy enough shares to gain control of Newman. She then would dictate the com-pany's future direction, even if it meant replacing Ron as president and CEO.

The company already has considerable debt. Raising additional debt will be costly, will adversely affect Newman's credit rating, and will increase the company's reported losses due to the growth in interest expense. Judy and the other minority stockholders express opposi-tion to the assumption of additional debt, fearing the company will be pushed to the brink of bankruptcy. Wanting to maintain his control and to preserve the direction of "his" com-pany, Ron is doing everything to avoid a stock issuance and is contemplating a large issuance of bonds, even if it means the bonds are issued with a high effective-interest rate.

Instructions
   (a) Who are the stakeholders in this situation?
   (b) What are the ethical issues in this case?
   (c) What would you do if you were Ron?

SURFING THE NET

BYP11–9   Bond or debt securities pay a stated rate of interest. This rate of interest is de-pendent on the risk associated with the investment. Moody's Investment Service provides rat-ings for companies that issue debt securities.

Address: http://www.moodys.com/index.shtml (or go to
              www.wiley.com/college/weygandt)

Steps: From Moody's homepage choose **SiteMap.**

Instructions
Answer the following questions:

   (a) What year did Moody's introduce the first bond rating?
   (b) List three basic principles Moody's uses in rating bonds.
   (c) What is the definition of Moody's Aaa rating on long-term taxable debt?

Answers to Self-Study Questions
1. a   2. d   3. b   4. b   5. c   6. a   7. d   8. a   9. b   10. d   11. c
*12. b   *13. c

Answer to Kellogg Review It Question 2, p. 469
Under the heading of current liabilities, Kellogg has listed current maturities of long-term debt, notes payable, and accounts payable.

Answer to Kellogg Review It Question 2, p. 483
An examination of Kellogg Company's statement of cash flows indicates the following reductions of debt: reductions of notes payable, with maturities less than or equal to 90 days ($152.9 million); reductions of notes payable, with maturities greater than 90 days ($800 thousand), and reductions of long-term debt ($210.3 million).

     Remember to go back to the Navigator box on the chapter-opening page
          and check off your completed work.

Before studying this chapter, you should know or, if necessary, review:

a. The content of the stockholders' equity section of a balance sheet. (Ch. 4, pp. 160–161)
b. How to prepare closing entries for a corporation. (Ch. 4, pp. 147–149)
c. What is the difference between paid-in capital and retained earnings. (Ch. 1, p. 13)

THE NAVIGATOR

FEATURE STORY

What's Cooking?

What major U.S. corporation got its start 29 years ago with a waffle iron? Hint: It doesn't sell food. Another hint: Swoosh. Another hint: "just do it." That's right, Nike. In 1971 Nike cofounder, Bill Bowerman, put a piece of rubber into a kitchen waffle iron, and the trademark waffle sole was born.

Nike was cofounded by Bowerman and Phil Knight, a member of Bowerman's University of Oregon track team. Each began in the shoe business independently during the early 1960s. Bowerman got his start by making hand-crafted running shoes for his university track team. Knight, after completing graduate school, started a small business importing low-cost, high-quality shoes from Japan. In 1964 the two joined forces, each contributing $500, and formed Blue Ribbon Sports, a partnership. At first they marketed Japanese shoes. It wasn't until 1971 that the company began manufacturing its own line of shoes. With the new shoes came a new corporate name—Nike—the Greek goddess of victory. It is hard to imagine that the company that now boasts a stable full of world-class athletes as promoters at one time had part-time employees selling shoes out of car trunks at track meets.

By 1980 Nike was sufficiently established that it was able to issue its first stock to the public. In that same year it also created a stock ownership program for its employees, allowing them to share in the company's success. Since then Nike has enjoyed phenomenal growth, with 1998 sales reaching $9.5 billion—fully double its 1995 $4.7 billion in sales. Its dividend per share to shareholders has increased every year for the last 11 years.

Nike is not alone in its quest for the top of the sport shoe world. Reebok pushes Nike every step of the way. It's a race to see who will dominate the sports shoe industry. Currently, Nike is outpacing Reebok. But, is the race over? Probably not. The shoe market is fickle, with new styles becoming popular almost daily. Reebok's unwillingness to give up the race was boldly stated in its recent ad campaign: "This is my planet." Whether one of these two giants does eventually take control of the planet remains to be seen. Meanwhile the shareholders sit anxiously in the stands as this Olympic-size drama unfolds.

THE NAVIGATOR

On the World Wide Web
http://www.nike.com
http://www.reebok.com

CHAPTER 12

THE NAVIGATOR ✓

- Understand *Concepts for Review* ☐
- Read *Feature Story* ☐
- Scan *Study Objectives* ☐
- Read *Preview* ☐
- Read text and answer *Before You Go On*
  p. 519 ☐ p. 521 ☐ p. 524 ☐ p. 528 ☐
  p. 530 ☐ p. 537 ☐ p. 541 ☐ p. 544 ☐
- Work *Demonstration Problem* ☐
- Review *Summary of Study Objectives* ☐
- Answer *Self-Study Questions* ☐
- Complete assignments ☐

CORPORATIONS: ORGANIZATION, STOCK TRANSACTIONS, DIVIDENDS, AND RETAINED EARNINGS

STUDY OBJECTIVES

After studying this chapter, you should be able to:

1. *Identify and discuss the major characteristics of a corporation.*
2. *Record the issuance of common stock.*
3. *Explain the accounting for treasury stock.*
4. *Differentiate preferred stock from common stock.*
5. *Prepare the entries for cash dividends and stock dividends.*
6. *Identify the items that are reported in a retained earnings statement.*
7. *Prepare and analyze a comprehensive stockholders' equity section.*

THE NAVIGATOR

Corporations like Nike, Inc. have substantial resources. In fact, the corporation is the dominant form of business organization in the United States in terms of dollar volume of sales, earnings, and employees. All of the 500 largest companies in the United States are corporations. In this chapter we will explain the essential features of a corporation, the accounting for a corporation's capital stock transactions, dividends and retained earnings. The content and organization of this chapter are as follows:

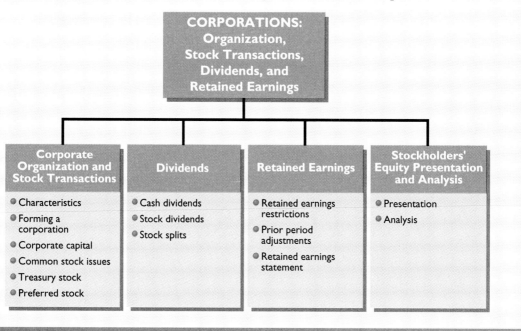

SECTION 1 THE CORPORATE FORM OF ORGANIZATION AND STOCK TRANSACTIONS

A corporation is created by law, and its continued existence depends upon the corporate statutes of the state in which it is incorporated. As a legal entity, a corporation has most of the rights and privileges of a person. The major exceptions relate to privileges that can be exercised only by a living person, such as the right to vote or to hold public office. Similarly, a corporation is subject to the same duties and responsibilities as a person, e.g., it must abide by the laws and it must pay taxes.

Corporations may be classified in a variety of ways. Two common bases are by purpose and by ownership. A corporation may be organized for the **purpose** of making a **profit**, or it may be **nonprofit**. Corporations for profit include such well-known companies as McDonald's, General Motors, Kellogg, and Apple Computer. Nonprofit corporations are organized for charitable, medical, and educational purposes and include the Salvation Army, the American Cancer Society, and the Ford Foundation.

Classification by **ownership** distinguishes between publicly held and privately held corporations. A publicly held corporation may have thousands of stockholders, and its stock is regularly traded on a national securities market such as the New York Stock Exchange. Most of the largest U.S. corporations are publicly held. Examples of publicly held corporations are International Business Machines, Caterpillar Inc., and General Electric. In contrast, a privately held corporation, often referred to as a closely held corporation, usually has only a few stockholders, and does not offer its stock for sale to the general public. Privately held companies are generally much smaller than publicly held companies.

CHARACTERISTICS OF A CORPORATION

A number of characteristics distinguish a corporation from proprietorships and partnerships. The most important of these characteristics are explained below.

Separate Legal Existence

As an entity separate and distinct from its owners, the corporation acts under its own name rather than in the name of its stockholders. A corporation may buy, own, and sell property, borrow money, and enter into legally binding contracts in its own name. It may also sue or be sued, and it pays its own taxes.

In contrast to a partnership, in which the acts of the owners (partners) bind the partnership, the acts of the owners (stockholders) do not bind the corporation unless such owners are appointed agents of the corporation. For example, if you owned shares of Nike, Inc. stock, you would not have the right to purchase shoes or materials for the company unless you were appointed as an agent of the corporation.

Limited Liability of Stockholders

Since a corporation is a separate legal entity, creditors ordinarily have recourse only to corporate assets to satisfy their claims. The liability of stockholders is normally limited to their investment in the corporation, and creditors have no legal claim on the personal assets of the owners unless fraud has occurred. Thus, even in the event of bankruptcy of the corporation, stockholders' losses are generally limited to their capital investment in the corporation.

Transferable Ownership Rights

Ownership of a corporation is shown in shares of capital stock, which are transferable units. Stockholders may dispose of part or all of their interest in a corporation simply by selling their stock. In contrast to the transfer of an ownership interest in a partnership, which requires the consent of each owner, the transfer of stock is entirely at the discretion of the stockholder. It does not require the approval of either the corporation or other stockholders. The transfer of ownership rights between stockholders normally has no effect on the operating activities of the corporation or on a corporation's assets, liabilities, and total ownership equity. That is, the enterprise does not participate in the transfer of these ownership rights after it issues the capital stock.

Ability to Acquire Capital

It generally is relatively easy for a corporation to obtain capital through the issuance of stock. Buying stock in a corporation is often more attractive to an investor than investing in a partnership because a stockholder has limited liability and shares of stock are readily transferable. Moreover, many individuals can become stockholders by investing small amounts of money. In sum, the ability of a successful corporation to obtain capital is virtually unlimited.

STUDY
OBJECTIVE

Identify and discuss the major characteristics of a corporation.

Legal existence separate from owners

Limited liability of stockholders

Transferable ownership rights

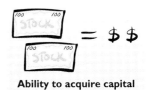

Ability to acquire capital

Continuous life

Continuous Life

The life of a corporation is stated in its charter; it may be perpetual or it may be limited to a specific number of years. If it is limited, the period of existence can be extended through renewal of the charter. Since a corporation is a separate legal entity, the life of a corporation and its continuance as a going concern are not affected by the withdrawal, death, or incapacity of a stockholder, employee, or officer. As a result, a successful enterprise can have a continuous and perpetual life.

Corporation Management

Although stockholders legally own the corporation, as in Nike, Inc., they manage the corporation indirectly through a board of directors they elect. The board, in turn, formulates the operating policies for the company and selects officers, such as a president and one or more vice presidents, to execute policy and to perform daily management functions.

A typical organization chart showing the delegation of responsibility is shown in Illustration 12-1. The **president** is the chief executive officer with direct responsibility for managing the business. As the organization chart shows, the president delegates responsibility to other officers. The chief accounting officer is the **controller**. The controller's responsibilities include (1) maintaining the accounting records, (2) maintaining an adequate system of internal control, and (3) preparing financial statements, tax returns, and internal reports. The **treasurer** has custody of the corporation's funds and is responsible for maintaining the company's cash position.

ILLUSTRATION 12-1

Corporation organization chart

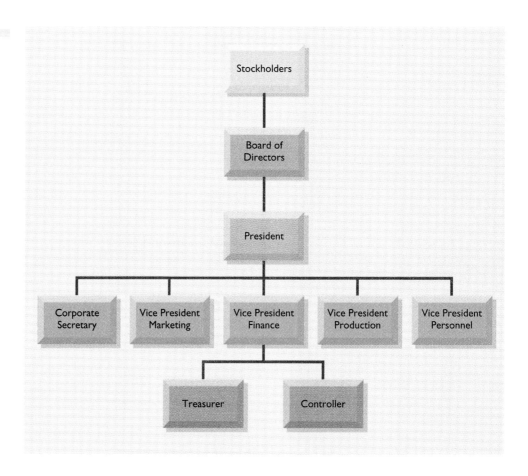

The organizational structure of a corporation enables a company to hire professional managers to run the business. On the other hand, the separation of ownership and management prevents owners from having an active role in managing the company, which some owners like to have.

ACCOUNTING IN ACTION
Business Insight

An interesting question is: Who runs a corporation—the stockholders or the board of directors? This issue has taken on increased importance because stockholders and boards of directors are often on the opposite sides of the fence these days when potential takeovers occur.

A classic example is the unfriendly takeover bid made by Paramount Communication Inc. for Time Inc. Paramount bid up Time's stock price substantially; many stockholders said sell—but Time's board of directors had other plans. They were in the process of trying to make a friendly deal with Warner Communications. Some stockholders said, "Let's vote on what we should do." But Time decided to proceed without a stockholders' vote, even though the board of directors knew the Warner deal would depress Time's stock price. They figured that many stockholders would prefer to accept the Paramount bid. The stockholders sued to overturn the deal with Warner Communications but lost. The judge wrote: "Corporation law does not operate on the theory that directors, in exercising their powers to manage the firm, are obligated to follow the wishes of a majority of stockholders. In fact, the directors, not the stockholders, are charged with the duty to manage the firm."

Government Regulations

A corporation is subject to numerous state and federal regulations. For example, state laws usually prescribe the requirements for issuing stock, the distributions of earnings permitted to stockholders, and the effects of retiring stock, as well as other procedures and restrictions. Similarly, federal securities laws govern the sale of capital stock to the general public. Also, most publicly held corporations are required to make extensive disclosure of their financial affairs to the Securities and Exchange Commission through quarterly and annual reports. In addition, when a corporate stock is listed and traded on organized securities markets, the corporation must comply with the reporting requirements of these exchanges.

Government regulations are designed to protect the owners of the corporation. Unlike the owners of most proprietorships and partnerships, most stockholders do not participate in the day-to-day management of the company.

State laws / SEC laws / WKK Corp. / Stock exchange requirements / Federal regulations

Government regulations

Additional Taxes

Neither proprietorships nor partnerships pay income taxes. The owner's share of these organizations' earnings is reported on his or her personal income tax return. Taxes are then paid by the individual on this amount. Corporations, on the other hand, must pay federal and state income taxes as a separate legal entity. These taxes are substantial: they can amount to as much as 40% of taxable income.

In addition, stockholders are required to pay taxes on cash dividends, which are pro rata distributions of net income. Thus, many argue that corporate income is **taxed twice (double taxation)**, once at the corporate level, and again at the individual level.

Additional taxes

From the foregoing, we can identify the following advantages and disadvantages of a corporation compared to a proprietorship and partnership:

ILLUSTRATION 12-2

*Advantages and
disadvantages of a
corporation*

Advantages	Disadvantages
Separate legal existence	Corporation management—separation of
Limited liability of stockholders	ownership and management
Transferable ownership rights	Government regulations
Ability to acquire capital	Additional taxes
Continuous life	
Corporation management—professional	
managers	

FORMING A CORPORATION

The initial step in the formation of a corporation is to file an application with the Secretary of State in the state in which incorporation is desired. The application contains the following types of information: (1) the name, purpose, and duration of the proposed corporation; (2) amounts, kinds, and number of shares of capital stock to be authorized; (3) the address of the corporation's principal office; (4) the names and addresses of the incorporators; and (5) the shares of stock to which each has subscribed.

After the incorporation fee is paid and the application approved, a **charter** is granted. The charter may be an approved copy of the application form or it may be a separate document containing the same basic data. The issuance of the charter, often referred to as the **articles of incorporation**, creates the corporation. Upon receipt of the charter, the corporation develops its by-laws. The **by-laws** establish the internal rules and procedures for conducting the affairs of the corporation and indicate the powers and relationships of the stockholders, directors, and officers of the enterprise.[1]

ACCOUNTING IN ACTION
Business Insight

It is not necessary for a corporation to have an office in the state in which it incorporates. In fact, more than 50% of the Fortune 500 corporations are incorporated in Delaware. A primary reason is the Delaware courts' long-standing "business judgment rule." The rule provides that as long as directors exercise "due care" in the interests of stockholders, their actions will not be second-guessed by the courts. The rule has enabled directors to reject hostile takeover offers, even with hefty premiums, or to spurn takeovers simply because they did not want to sell the company. However, new interpretations are emerging. In a recent case, the state court ruled for the company that made a hostile takeover bid. On appeal, the Delaware Supreme Court ruled for the directors but gave the following guideline to the state courts: "Was the board's response reasonable in the light of the threat posed?"

Regardless of the number of states in which a corporation has operating divisions, it is incorporated in only one state. It is to the company's advantage to incorporate in a state whose laws are favorable to the corporate form of business organization. General Motors, for example, is incorporated in Delaware, whereas USX Corp. is a New Jersey corporation. In fact, many corporations choose to incorporate in states with rules favorable to existing management. For

---

[1]Following approval by two-thirds of the stockholders, the by-laws become binding upon all stockholders, directors, and officers. Legally, a corporation is regulated first by the laws of the state, second by its charter, and third by its by-laws. Care must be exercised to ensure that the provisions of the by-laws are not in conflict with either state laws or the charter.

example, Gulf Oil changed its state of incorporation to Delaware to thwart possible unfriendly takeovers. There, certain defensive tactics against takeovers can be approved by the board of directors alone, without a vote by shareholders.

Corporations engaged in interstate commerce must obtain a license from each state in which they do business. The license subjects the corporation's operating activities to the general corporation laws of the state. Costs incurred in the formation of a corporation are called organization costs. These costs include fees to underwriters for handling stock and bond issues, legal fees, state incorporation fees, and promotional expenditures involved in the organization of the business.

In the past, organization costs were capitalized as an intangible asset and amortized over some arbitrary time period not to exceed 40 years. A recent change in the accounting standards, however, now requires organization costs to be charged to expense as incurred. Conceptually, these costs are an intangible asset that benefits the corporation over its entire life. But, as a practical matter, such costs are expensed immediately, even though they are usually amortized over a five-year period for income tax purposes.

INTERNATIONAL NOTE

U.S. corporations are identified by *Inc.*, which stands for *incorporated*. In Italy the letters used are *SpA* (Societa per Azioni); in Sweden *AB* (Aktiebolag); in France *SA* (Sociedad Anonima); and in the Netherlands *NV* (Naamloze Vennootschap).

In the United Kingdom public limited corporations are identified by *PLC*, while private corporations are denoted by *LTD*. The parallel designations in Germany are *AG* for public corporations and *GmbH* for private corporations.

CORPORATE CAPITAL

Owners' equity in a corporation is identified as **stockholders' equity, shareholders' equity**, or **corporate capital**. The stockholders' equity section of a corporation's balance sheet consists of: (1) paid-in (contributed) capital, and (2) retained earnings (earned capital). The distinction between paid-in capital and retained earnings is important from both a legal and an economic point of view. Legally, dividends can be declared out of retained earning in all states, but in many states dividends cannot be declared out of paid-in capital. Economically, management, stockholders, and others look to earnings for the continued existence and growth of the corporation.

Ownership Rights of Stockholders

When chartered, the corporation may begin selling ownership rights in the form of shares of stock. When a corporation has only one class of stock, it is identified as **common stock**. Each share of common stock gives the stockholder the ownership rights pictured in Illustration 12-3 on page 518. The ownership rights of a share of stock are stated in the articles of incorporation or in the by-laws.

ACCOUNTING IN ACTION
International Insight

In Japan, stockholders are considered to be far less important to a corporation than employees, customers, and suppliers. Stockholders are rarely asked to vote on an issue, and the notion of bending corporate policy to favor stockholders borders on the heretical in Japan. This attitude toward stockholders appears to be slowly changing, however, as influential Japanese are advocating listening to investors, raising the extremely low dividends paid by Japanese corporations, and improving disclosure of financial information.

Proof of stock ownership is evidenced by a printed or engraved form known as a **stock certificate**. As shown in Illustration 12-4, the face of the certificate shows the name of the corporation, the stockholder's name, the class

ILLUSTRATION 12-3

Ownership rights of stockholders

Stockholders have the right:

1. To vote in election of board of directors at annual meeting. To vote on actions that require stockholder approval.

2. To share the corporate earnings through receipt of dividends.

3. To keep same percentage ownership when new shares of stock are issued (**preemptive right**[2]).

4. To share in assets upon liquidation, in proportion to their holdings. Called a **residual claim** because owners are paid with assets remaining after all claims have been paid.

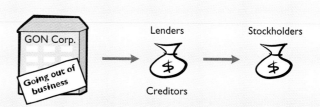

ILLUSTRATION 12-4

A stock certificate

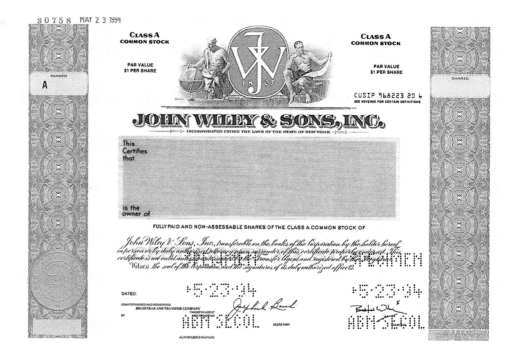

---

[2]A number of companies have eliminated the preemptive right, because they believe it makes an unnecessary and cumbersome demand on management. For example, IBM, by stockholder approval, has dropped its preemptive right for stockholders.

and special features of the stock, the number of shares owned, and the signatures of authorized corporate officials. Certificates are prenumbered to facilitate their accountability; they may be issued for any quantity of shares.

BEFORE YOU GO ON ...

Review It

1. What are the advantages and disadvantages of a corporation compared to a proprietorship and a partnership?
2. Identify the principal steps in forming a corporation.
3. What rights are inherent in owning a share of stock in a corporation?

THE NAVIGATOR

Stock Issue Considerations

In considering the issuance (or sale) of stock, a corporation must resolve a number of basic questions: How many shares should be authorized for sale? How should the stock be issued? At what price should the shares be issued? What value should be assigned to the stock? These questions are answered in the following sections.

Authorized Stock

The amount of stock that a corporation is **authorized** to sell is indicated in its charter. The total amount of authorized stock at the time of incorporation normally anticipates both initial and subsequent capital needs of a company. As a result, the number of total shares authorized generally exceeds the number of shares initially sold. If all authorized stock is sold, a corporation must obtain consent of the state to amend its charter before it can issue additional shares.

The authorization of capital stock does not result in a formal accounting entry, since the event has no immediate effect on either corporate assets or stockholders' equity. However, disclosure of the number of shares of authorized stock is required in the stockholders' equity section. To determine the number of unissued shares that can be issued without amending the charter, the total shares issued are subtracted from the total authorized. For example, if Advanced Macro Inc. was authorized to sell 100,000 shares of common stock and issued 80,000 shares, 20,000 shares would remain unissued.

Issuance of Stock

A corporation has the choice of issuing common stock **directly** to investors or **indirectly** through an investment banking firm (brokerage house) that specializes in bringing securities to the attention of prospective investors. Direct issue is typical in closely held companies, whereas indirect issue is customary for a publicly held corporation.

In an indirect issue, the investment banking firm may agree to **underwrite** the entire stock issue. Under this arrangement, the investment banker buys the stock from the corporation at a stipulated price and resells the shares to investors. The corporation avoids any risk of being unable to sell the shares, and it obtains immediate use of the cash received from the underwriter. The investment banking firm, in turn, assumes the risk of reselling the shares in return for an underwriting fee—the profits expected to be realized from a sales price to the public higher than the price paid to the corporation.[3] For example, Kolff Medical,

INTERNATIONAL NOTE

U.S. and U.K. corporations raise most of their capital through millions of outside shareholders and bondholders. In contrast, companies in Germany, France, and Japan acquire financing from large banks or other institutions. Consequently, in the latter environment, shareholders are less important, and external reporting and auditing receive less emphasis.

Indirect Issuance

---

[3]Alternatively, the investment banking firm may agree only to enter into a **best efforts** contract with the corporation. In such cases, the banker agrees to sell as many shares as possible at a specified price, and the corporation bears the risk of unsold stock. Under a best efforts arrangement, the banking firm is paid a fee or commission for its services.

maker of the Jarvik artificial heart, used an underwriter to help it issue common stock to the public. The underwriter charged a 6.6% underwriting fee on Kolff Medical's approximate $20 million public offering.

How does a corporation set the price for a new issue of stock? Among the factors to be considered are (1) the company's anticipated future earnings, (2) its expected dividend rate per share, (3) its current financial position, (4) the current state of the economy, and (5) the current state of the securities market. The calculation can be complex and is properly the subject of a finance course.

Market Value of Stock

The stock of publicly held companies is traded on organized exchanges at dollar prices per share established by the interaction between buyers and sellers. In general, the prices set by the marketplace tend to follow the trend of a company's earnings and dividends. However, factors beyond a company's control, such as the imposition of an oil embargo, changes in interest rates, and the outcome of a presidential election, may cause day-to-day fluctuations in market prices.

The volume of trading on national and international exchanges is heavy. Shares in excess of 600 million are often traded daily on the New York Stock Exchange alone. For each listed security the financial press reports the highs and lows of the stock during the year, the total volume of stock traded for a given day, the high and low price for the day, and the closing market price, with the net change for the day. A recent listing for Kellogg is shown below:

ILLUSTRATION 12-5

Stock market price information

| Stock | 52 Weeks | | Volume | High | Low | Close | Net Change |
	High	Low					
Kellogg	$42\frac{1}{4}$	$28\frac{1}{2}$	4333	$35\frac{9}{16}$	$34\frac{7}{16}$	$34\frac{5}{8}$	$-\frac{13}{16}$

These numbers indicate that Kellogg's high and low market prices for the last 52 weeks have been $42\frac{1}{4}$ and $28\frac{1}{2}$; the trading volume on that one day was 433,000 shares; the high, low, and closing prices for that date were $35\frac{9}{16}$, $34\frac{7}{16}$, and $34\frac{5}{8}$, respectively; and the net change for the day was a decrease of $-\frac{13}{16}$, or $.8125 per share.

The trading of capital stock on securities exchanges involves the transfer of **already issued shares** from an existing stockholder to another investor. Consequently, these transactions have no impact on a corporation's stockholders' equity section.

TECHNOLOGY IN ACTION

Giant, publicly held corporations could not exist without organized stock markets, and the stock markets could not exist without massive computerization. Not too many years ago, the NYSE "ticker" would run behind, or trading would even be halted, when sales exceeded 30 million shares or so. Now, with sales sometimes in excess of 800 million shares, the NYSE and its companion exchanges throughout the country operate efficiently with computer technology. Technology has also made possible extended trading hours. An investor in New York, for example, can trade electronically at 3:30 A.M., which is the time in New York when the London Stock Exchange opens. It appears that 24-hour-trading is not far off.

Par and No-Par Value Stocks

Par value stock is capital stock that has been assigned a value per share in the corporate charter. The par value may be any amount selected by the corporation. Generally, the amount of par value is quite low, because states often levy a tax on the corporation based on par value. For example, International Business Machines has a par of $1.25, Ford Motor Company, $1 par, General Motors Corporation, $1.67, and PepsiCo has $1\frac{2}{3}$ cents.

Par value is not indicative of the worth or market value of the stock. As indicated above, IBM has a par value of $1.25, but its recent market price was $120 per share. **The significance of par value is a legal matter.** Par value represents the legal capital per share that must be retained in the business for the protection of corporate creditors. That is, it is not available for withdrawal by stockholders. Thus, most states require the corporation to sell its shares at par or above.

No-par value stock is capital stock that has not been assigned a value in the corporate charter. No-par value stock is often issued because some confusion still exists concerning par value and fair market value. If shares have no par value, the questionable treatment of using par value as a basis for fair market value never arises. The major disadvantage of no-par stock is that some states levy a high tax on the shares issued.

No-par value stock is quite common today. For example, Procter & Gamble and North American Van Lines both have no-par stock. In many states the board of directors is permitted to assign a stated value to the no-par shares, which becomes the legal capital per share. The stated value of no-par stock may be changed at any time by action of the directors. Stated value, like par value, is not indicative of the market value of the stock. When there is no assigned stated value, the entire proceeds received upon issuance of the stock is considered to be legal capital.

The relationship of par and no-par value to legal capital is shown below.

Stock	Legal Capital per Share
Par value	→ Par value
No-par value with stated value	→ Stated value
No-par value without stated value	→ Entire proceeds

ILLUSTRATION 12-6

Relationship of par and no-par value stock to legal capital

As will be explained later, a common stock account is credited for the legal capital per share each time stock is issued.

BEFORE YOU GO ON ...

Review It

1. Of what significance to a corporation is the amount of authorized stock?
2. What alternative approaches may a corporation use in issuing stock?
3. Distinguish between par value and fair market value.

Do It

At the end of its first year of operation, Doral Corporation has $750,000 of common stock and net income of $122,000. Prepare (a) the closing entry for net income (as shown in Chapter 4) and (b) the stockholders' equity section at year-end.

Reasoning: Net income is recorded in Retained Earnings by a closing entry in which Income Summary is debited and Retained Earnings is credited. The stockholders' equity section consists of (1) paid-in capital and (2) retained earnings.

Solution:

(a) Income Summary	122,000	
Retained Earnings		122,000
(To close income summary and transfer net income to retained earnings)		

(b) Stockholders' equity		
Paid-in capital		
Common stock	$750,000	
Retained earnings	122,000	
Total stockholders' equity		$872,000

Related exercise material: BE12–12, E12–6, E12–13, E12–14, and E12–15.

ACCOUNTING FOR COMMON STOCK ISSUES

2
STUDY
OBJECTIVE

Record the issuance of common stock.

Let's now look at how to account for issues of common stock. The primary objectives in accounting for the issuance of common stock are to (1) identify the specific sources of paid-in capital and (2) maintain the distinction between paid-in capital and retained earnings. As shown below, **the issue of common stock affects only paid-in capital accounts.**

Issuing Par Value Common Stock for Cash

As discussed earlier, par value does not indicate a stock's market value. Therefore, the cash proceeds from issuing par value stock may be equal to, greater than, or less than par value. When the issuance of common stock for cash is recorded, the par value of the shares is credited to Common Stock, and the portion of the proceeds that is above or below par value is recorded in a separate paid-in capital account.

To illustrate, assume that Hydro-Slide, Inc. issues 1,000 shares of $1 par value common stock at par for cash. The entry to record this transaction is:

A = L + SE
+1,000   +1,000

Cash	1,000	
Common Stock		1,000
(To record issuance of 1,000 shares of $1 par common stock at par)		

ALTERNATIVE TERMINOLOGY
Paid-in Capital in Excess of Par is also called *Premium on Stock* or *Additional Paid-in Capital.*

If Hydro-Slide, Inc. issues an additional 1,000 shares of the $1 par value common stock for cash at $5 per share, the entry is:

A = L + SE
+5,000   +1,000
+4,000

Cash	5,000	
Common Stock		1,000
Paid-in Capital in Excess of Par Value		4,000
(To record issuance of 1,000 shares of common stock in excess of par)		

The total paid-in capital from these two transactions is $6,000, and the legal capital is $2,000. If Hydro-Slide, Inc. has retained earnings of $27,000, the stockholders' equity section is as follows:

HYDRO-SLIDE, INC. Balance Sheet (partial)	
Stockholders' equity	
Paid-in capital	
Common stock	$ 2,000
Paid-in capital in excess of par value	4,000
Total paid-in capital	6,000
Retained earnings	27,000
Total stockholders' equity	$33,000

ILLUSTRATION 12-7

Stockholders' equity—paid-in capital in excess of par value

When stock is issued for less than par value, the account Paid-in Capital in Excess of Par Value is debited, if a credit balance exists in this account. If a credit balance does not exist, then the amount less than par is debited to Retained Earnings. This situation occurs only rarely: The sale of common stock below par value is not permitted in most states because stockholders may be held personally liable for the difference between the price paid upon original sale and par value.

Issuing No-Par Common Stock for Cash

When no-par common stock has a stated value, the entries are similar to those illustrated for par value stock. The stated value represents legal capital and therefore is credited to Common Stock. In addition, when the selling price of no-par stock exceeds stated value, the excess is credited to Paid-in Capital in Excess of Stated Value. For example, assume that instead of $1 par value stock, Hydro-Slide, Inc. has $5 stated value no-par stock and that it issues 5,000 shares at $8 per share for cash. The entry is:

Cash	40,000	
Common Stock		25,000
Paid-in Capital in Excess of Stated Value		15,000
(To record issue of 5,000 shares of $5 stated value no-par stock)		

A	=	L	+	SE
+40,000				+25,000
				+15,000

Paid-in Capital in Excess of Stated Value is reported as part of paid-in capital in the stockholders' equity section.

When no-par stock does not have a stated value, the entire proceeds from the issue become legal capital and are credited to Common Stock. Thus, if Hydro-Slide does not assign a stated value to its no-par stock, the issuance of the 5,000 shares at $8 per share for cash is recorded as follows:

Cash	40,000	
Common Stock		40,000
(To record issue of 5,000 shares of no-par stock)		

A	=	L	+	SE
+40,000				+40,000

The amount of legal capital for Hydro-Slide with a $5 stated value is $25,000; without a stated value, it is $40,000.

Issuing Common Stock for Services or Noncash Assets

Stock may be issued for services (compensation to attorneys, consultants, and others) or for noncash assets (land, buildings, and equipment). In such cases, a question arises as to the cost that should be recognized in the exchange transaction.

To comply with the **cost principle** in a noncash transaction, **cost is the cash equivalent price.** Thus, **cost is either the fair market value of the consideration given up or the fair market value of the consideration received,** whichever is more clearly determinable.

To illustrate, assume that the attorneys for The Jordan Company agree to accept 4,000 shares of $1 par value common stock in payment of their bill of $5,000 for services performed in helping the company to incorporate. At the time of the exchange, there is no established market price for the stock. In this case, the market value of the consideration received, $5,000, is more clearly evident. Accordingly, the entry is:

A	=	L	+	SE
+5,000				+4,000
				+1,000

Organization Expense	5,000	
Common Stock		4,000
Paid-in Capital in Excess of Par Value		1,000
(To record issuance of 4,000 shares of $1 par value		
stock to attorneys)		

As explained on page 517, organization costs are expensed in the period incurred.

In contrast, assume that Athletic Research Inc. is a publicly held corporation whose $5 par value stock is actively traded at $8 per share. The company issues 10,000 shares of stock to acquire land recently advertised for sale at $90,000. On the basis of these facts the most clearly evident value is the market price of the consideration given, $80,000. Thus, the transaction is recorded as follows:

A	=	L	+	SE
+80,000				+50,000
				+30,000

Land	80,000	
Common Stock		50,000
Paid-in Capital in Excess of Par Value		30,000
(To record issuance of 10,000 shares of $5 par value		
stock for land)		

As illustrated in these examples, **the par value of the stock is never a factor in determining the cost of the assets received.** This is also true of the stated value of no-par stock.

BEFORE YOU GO ON ...

Review It

1. Explain the accounting for par and no-par common stock issued for cash.
2. Explain the accounting for the issuance of stock for services or noncash assets.

3. What is the par or stated value per share of Kellogg's common stock? How many shares of common stock is Kellogg authorized to issue? How many shares are issued at December 31, 1998? The answers to these questions are provided on page 565.

Do It

Cayman Corporation begins operations on March 1 by issuing 100,000 shares of $10 par value common stock for cash at $12 per share. On March 15, it issues 5,000 shares of common stock to attorneys in settlement of their bill of $50,000 for organization expenses. Journalize the issuance of the shares assuming the stock is not publicly traded.

Reasoning: In issuing shares for cash, common stock is credited for par value per share and any additional proceeds are credited to a separate paid-in capital account. When stock is issued for services, the cash equivalent price should be used. In this case, this price is the value of the attorneys' services.

Solution:

Mar. 1	Cash	1,200,000	
	Common Stock		1,000,000
	Paid-in Capital in Excess of Par Value		200,000
	(To record issuance of 100,000 shares at $12 per share)		
Mar. 15	Organization Expense	50,000	
	Common Stock		50,000
	(To record issuance of 5,000 shares for attorneys' fees)		

THE NAVIGATOR

Related exercise material: BE12–2, BE12–3, BE12–4, E12–1, E12–2, E12–3, and E12–7.

ACCOUNTING FOR TREASURY STOCK

3
STUDY
OBJECTIVE

Explain the accounting for treasury stock.

Treasury stock is a corporation's own stock that has been issued, fully paid for, and reacquired by the corporation but not retired. A corporation may acquire treasury stock for the reasons listed below.

1. Reissue the shares to officers and employees under bonus and stock compensation plans.
2. Increase trading of the company's stock in the securities market in the hopes of enhancing its market value.
3. Have additional shares available for use in the acquisition of other companies.
4. Reduce the number of shares outstanding and thereby increase earnings per share.
5. Rid the company of disgruntled investors, perhaps to avoid a takeover.

HELPFUL HINT
Treasury stock is so named because the company often holds the shares in its treasury for safekeeping.

Many corporations have treasury stock. For example, one survey of 600 companies in the United States found that 64% have treasury stock.[4] Specifically, Campbell Soup Company recently reported 84 million treasury shares, The Coca-Cola Company 459.5 million, and McDonald's Corporation 135.7 million.

Purchase of Treasury Stock

The cost method is generally used in accounting for treasury stock. This method derives its name from the fact that the Treasury Stock account is maintained at the cost of shares purchased. Under the cost method, **Treasury Stock is debited at the price paid to reacquire the shares, and the same amount is credited to Treasury Stock when the shares are sold.** To illustrate, assume that on January 1, 2001, the stockholders' equity section of Mead, Inc., has 100,000 shares of $5 par value common stock outstanding (all issued at par value) and Retained Earnings of $200,000.

[4]*Accounting Trends & Techniques 1998* (New York: American Institute of Certified Public Accountants).

The stockholders' equity section before purchase of treasury stock is as follows:

ILLUSTRATION 12-8

Stockholders' equity with no treasury stock

MEAD, INC.
Balance Sheet (partial)

Stockholders' equity	
Paid-in capital	
Common stock, $5 par value, 100,000 shares issued and outstanding	$500,000
Retained earnings	200,000
Total stockholders' equity	$700,000

On February 1, 2001, Mead acquires 4,000 shares of its stock at $8 per share. The entry is:

A = L + SE
−32,000   −32,000

Feb. 1	Treasury Stock		32,000	
	Cash			32,000
	(To record purchase of 4,000 shares of treasury stock at $8 per share)			

HELPFUL HINT

Treasury shares do not have dividend rights or voting rights.

Note that Treasury Stock is debited for the cost of the shares purchased. The original paid-in capital account, Common Stock, is not affected because the number of issued shares does not change. Treasury stock is deducted from total paid-in capital and retained earnings in the stockholders' equity section. Treasury Stock is a contra stockholders' equity account.

The stockholders' equity section of Mead, Inc., after purchase of treasury stock is as follows:

ILLUSTRATION 12-9

Stockholders' equity with treasury stock

MEAD, INC.
Balance Sheet (partial)

Stockholders' equity	
Paid-in capital	
Common stock, $5 par value, 100,000 shares issued and 96,000 shares outstanding	$500,000
Retained earnings	200,000
Total paid-in capital and retained earnings	700,000
Less: Treasury stock (4,000 shares)	**32,000**
Total stockholders' equity	$668,000

Thus, the acquisition of treasury stock reduces stockholders' equity.

Both the number of shares issued (100,000) and the number in the treasury (4,000) are disclosed. The difference is the number of shares of stock outstanding (96,000). The term outstanding stock means the number of shares of issued stock that are being held by stockholders.

Some maintain that treasury stock should be reported as an asset because it can be sold for cash. Under this reasoning, unissued stock should also be shown as an asset, clearly an erroneous conclusion. Rather than being an asset, treasury stock reduces stockholder claims on corporate assets. This effect is correctly shown by reporting treasury stock as a deduction from total paid-in capital and retained earnings.

Disposal of Treasury Stock

Treasury stock is usually sold or retired. The accounting for its sale is different when treasury stock is sold above cost than when it is sold below cost.

Sale of Treasury Stock above Cost

If the selling price of the treasury shares is equal to cost, the sale of the shares is recorded by a debit to Cash and a credit to Treasury Stock. When the selling price of the shares is greater than cost, the difference is credited to Paid-in Capital from Treasury Stock. To illustrate, assume that 1,000 shares of treasury stock of Mead, Inc., previously acquired at $8 per share, are sold at $10 per share on July 1. The entry is as follows:

July 1	Cash	10,000	
	Treasury Stock		8,000
	Paid-in Capital from Treasury Stock		2,000
	(To record sale of 1,000 shares of treasury		
	stock above cost)		

A	=	L	+	SE
+10,000				+8,000
				+2,000

The $2,000 credit in the entry is **not** made to Gain on Sale of Treasury Stock for two reasons: (1) Gains on sales occur when assets are sold and treasury stock is not an asset. (2) A corporation does not realize a gain or suffer a loss from stock transactions with its own stockholders. Thus, paid-in capital arising from the sale of treasury stock should not be included in the measurement of net income. Paid-in Capital from Treasury Stock is listed separately on the balance sheet as a part of paid-in capital.

Sale of Treasury Stock below Cost

When treasury stock is sold below its cost, the excess of cost over selling price is usually debited to Paid-in Capital from Treasury Stock. Thus, if Mead, Inc. sells an additional 800 shares of treasury stock on October 1 at $7 per share, the entry is as follows:

Oct. 1	Cash	5,600	
	Paid-in Capital from Treasury Stock	800	
	Treasury Stock		6,400
	(To record sale of 800 shares of treasury		
	stock below cost)		

A	=	L	+	SE
+5,600				−800
				+6,400

Observe from the two sales entries that (1) Treasury Stock is credited at cost in each entry, (2) Paid-in Capital from Treasury Stock is used for the difference between the cost and resale price of the shares, and (3) the original paid-in capital account, Common Stock, again is not affected. **The sale of treasury stock increases both total assets and total stockholders' equity.**

After posting the foregoing entries, the treasury stock accounts will show the following balances on October 1:

Treasury Stock				Paid-in Capital from Treasury Stock			
Feb. 1	32,000	July 1	8,000	Oct. 1	800	July 1	2,000
		Oct. 1	6,400				
						Oct. 1 Bal.	1,200
Oct. 1 Bal.	17,600						

When the credit balance in Paid-in Capital from Treasury Stock is eliminated, any additional excess of cost over selling price is debited to Retained Earnings.

To illustrate, assume that Mead, Inc., sells its remaining 2,200 shares at $7 per share on December 1. The excess of cost over selling price is $2,200 [2,200 × ($8 − $7)]. In this case, $1,200 of the excess is debited to Paid-in Capital from Treasury Stock, and the remainder is debited to Retained Earnings. The entry is:

A	=	L	+	SE
+15,400				−1,200
				−1,000
				+17,600

Dec. 1	Cash	15,400	
	Paid-in Capital from Treasury Stock	1,200	
	Retained Earnings	1,000	
	Treasury Stock		17,600
	(To record sale of 2,200 shares of treasury stock at $7 per share)		

BEFORE YOU GO ON ...

Review It

1. What is treasury stock, and why do companies acquire it?
2. How is treasury stock recorded?
3. Where is treasury stock reported in the financial statements? Does a company record gains and losses on treasury stock transactions? Explain.

4. How many shares of treasury stock did Kellogg have outstanding at December 31, 1997 and at December 31, 1998? Why the huge difference between 1997 and 1998? The answers to these questions are provided on page 565.

Do It

Santa Anita Inc. purchases 3,000 shares of its $50 par value common stock for $180,000 cash on July 1. The shares are to be held in the treasury until resold. On November 1, the corporation sells 1,000 shares of treasury stock for cash at $70 per share. Journalize the treasury stock transactions.

Reasoning: The purchase of treasury stock is recorded at cost. When treasury stock is sold, the excess of the selling price over cost is credited to Paid-in Capital from Treasury Stock.

Solution:

July 1	Treasury Stock	180,000	
	Cash		180,000
	(To record the purchase of 3,000 shares at $60 per share)		
Nov. 1	Cash	70,000	
	Treasury Stock		60,000
	Paid-in Capital from Treasury Stock		10,000
	(To record the sale of 1,000 shares at $70 per share)		

THE
NAVIGATOR

Related exercise material: BE12–5, E12–2, E12–4, E12–7, and E12–13.

PREFERRED STOCK

4
STUDY
OBJECTIVE

Differentiate preferred stock from common stock.

To appeal to a larger segment of potential investors, a corporation may issue a class of stock in addition to common stock, called preferred stock. Preferred stock has contractual provisions that give it a preference or priority over common stock in certain areas. Typically, preferred stockholders have a priority as to (1) dividends and (2) assets in the event of liquidation. However, they generally do not have voting rights.

Like common stock, preferred stock may be issued for cash or for noncash assets. The entries for these transactions are similar to the entries for common stock. When a corporation has more than one class of stock, each paid-in capital account title should identify the stock to which it relates (e.g., Preferred Stock, Common Stock, Paid-in Capital in Excess of Par Value—Preferred Stock, and Paid-in Capital in Excess of Par Value—Common Stock). Assume that Stine Corporation issues 10,000 shares of $10 par value preferred stock for $12 cash per share. The entry to record the issuance is:

Cash	120,000	
Preferred Stock		100,000
Paid-in Capital in Excess of Par Value—Preferred Stock		20,000
(To record the issuance of 10,000 shares of $10 par		
value preferred stock)		

A	=	L	+	SE
+120,000				+100,000
				+20,000

Preferred stock may have either a par value or no-par value. For example, Walgreen Drug Co. has $0.50 par value preferred and General Motors has three classes of no-par preferred stock, each with a stated value of $100. In the stockholders' equity section, preferred stock is shown first because of its dividend and liquidation preferences over common stock.

The discussion that follows reflects features associated with the issuance of preferred stock, including dividend preferences, liquidation preferences, convertibility, and callability.

Dividend Preferences

As indicated before, **preferred stockholders have the right to share in the distribution of corporate income before common stockholders.** For example, if the dividend rate on preferred stock is $5 per share, common shareholders will not receive any dividends in the current year until preferred stockholders have received $5 per share. The first claim to dividends does not, however, guarantee dividends. Dividends depend on many factors, such as adequate retained earnings and availability of cash.

The per share dividend amount is stated as a percentage of the par value of preferred stock or as a specified amount. For example, the Crane Company specifies $3\frac{3}{4}$% dividend on its $100 par value preferred ($100 \times 3\frac{3}{4}$% = $3.75 per share), whereas DuPont has both a $4.50 and a $3.50 series of no-par preferred stock.

I hope there is some money left when it's my turn.

Preferred   Common
stockholders stockholders

Dividend Preference

Cumulative Dividend

Preferred stock contracts often contain a cumulative dividend feature. This right means that preferred stockholders must be paid both current-year dividends and any unpaid prior-year dividends before common stockholders receive dividends. When preferred stock is cumulative, preferred dividends not declared in a given period are called **dividends in arrears**. To illustrate, assume that Scientific Leasing has 5,000 shares of 7%, $100 par value cumulative preferred stock outstanding. The annual dividend is $35,000 (5,000 × $7 per share). If dividends are 2 years in arrears, preferred stockholders are entitled to receive the following dividends in the current year before any distribution is made to common stockholders:

Dividends in arrears ($35,000 × 2)	$ 70,000
Current-year dividends	35,000
Total preferred dividends	**$105,000**

ILLUSTRATION 12-11

Computation of total dividends to preferred stock

ACCOUNTING IN ACTION
Business Insight

Dividends in arrears can extend for fairly long periods of time. Long Island Lighting Company's directors voted at one time to make up some $390 million in preferred dividends that had been in arrears nearly ten years and to resume normal quarterly preferred payments. The announcement resulted from an agreement between the company and New York State to abandon a nuclear power plant in exchange for sizable rate increases over the next 10 years.

Dividends in arrears are not considered a liability. No obligation exists until a dividend is declared by the board of directors. However, the amount of dividends in arrears should be disclosed in the notes to the financial statements. Doing so enables investors to assess the potential impact of this commitment on the corporation's financial position.

Dividends cannot be paid on common stock while any dividend on preferred stock is in arrears. The cumulative feature is often critical in investor acceptance of a preferred stock issue. When preferred stock is noncumulative, a dividend passed in any year is lost forever. Companies that are unable to meet their dividend obligations are not looked upon favorably by the investment community. As a financial officer noted in discussing one company's failure to pay its cumulative preferred dividend for a period of time, "Not meeting your obligations on something like that is a major black mark on your record."

**Payment of a
Cumulative Dividend**

Dividend
in
arrears

Current
dividend

Preferred
stockholders

Liquidation Preference

Most preferred stocks have a preference on corporate assets if the corporation fails. This feature provides security for the preferred stockholder. The preference to assets may be for the par value of the shares or for a specified liquidating value. For example, Commonwealth Edison issued preferred stock that entitles the holders to receive $31.80 per share, plus accrued and unpaid dividends, in the event of involuntary liquidation. The liquidation preference is used in litigation pertaining to bankruptcy lawsuits involving the respective claims of creditors and preferred stockholders.

BEFORE YOU GO ON ...

Review It

1. Preferred stock has what preferences over common stock?
2. Why are dividends in arrears on preferred stock not considered a liability?
3. Of what value is the preference in liquidation to preferred stockholders?

THE
NAVIGATOR

SECTION 2 DIVIDENDS

5
STUDY
OBJECTIVE

Prepare the entries for cash dividends and stock dividends.

A dividend **is a distribution by a corporation to its stockholders on a pro rata (proportional) basis.** Potential buyers and sellers of a corporation's stock are very interested in a company's dividend policies and practices. Dividends can take four forms: cash, property, scrip (promissory note to pay cash), or (capital) stock. Cash dividends, which predominate in practice, and stock dividends, which are declared with some frequency, will be the focus of discussion in this chapter.

Dividends may be expressed as a percentage of the par or stated value of the stock or as a dollar amount per share. In the financial press, **dividends are generally reported quarterly as a dollar amount per share**. For example, Boeing Company's quarterly dividend rate recently was 28 cents a share, Ford Motor Company's was 38.5 cents, and Nike's was 9.5 cents.

....

CASH DIVIDENDS

A cash dividend is a pro rata distribution of cash to stockholders. For a cash dividend to occur, a corporation must have:

1. **Retained earnings.** The legality of a cash dividend depends on the laws of the state in which the company is incorporated. In general, cash dividends based on retained earnings are legal, and distributions based on common stock (legal capital) are illegal. Statutory provisions vary considerably with respect to cash dividends based on paid-in capital in excess of par or stated value. Many states permit such dividends. A dividend declared out of paid-in capital is termed a liquidating dividend, because the amount originally paid in by stockholders is being reduced or "liquidated."

2. **Adequate cash.** The legality of a dividend does not indicate a company's ability to pay a dividend. For example, a company such as Nike, with a cash balance of $108.6 million and retained earnings of $3,043.4 million, could legally declare a dividend of $3,043.3 million. However, if it attempted to pay the dividend, it would need to raise additional cash through the sale of other assets or through additional financing. It follows that before declaring a cash dividend, the board of directors must carefully consider both current and future demands on the company's cash resources. In some cases, current liabilities may make a cash dividend inappropriate; in other cases, a major plant expansion program may warrant only a relatively small dividend.

3. **Declared dividends.** The board of directors has full authority to determine the amount of income to be distributed in the form of a dividend and the amount to be retained in the business. Dividends do not accrue like interest on a note payable, and they are not a liability until declared.

> **HELPFUL HINT**
> A corporation does not have a contractual obligation to pay dividends.

The amount and timing of a dividend are important issues for management to consider. The payment of a large cash dividend could lead to liquidity problems for the enterprise. Conversely, a small dividend or a missed dividend may cause unhappiness among stockholders who expect to receive a reasonable cash payment from the company on a periodic basis. Many companies declare and pay cash dividends quarterly.

ACCOUNTING IN ACTION
Business Insight

In order to remain in business, companies must honor their interest payments to creditors, bankers, and bondholders. But the payment of dividends to stockholders is another matter. Many companies can survive, even thrive, without such payouts. In fact, managements might consider dividend payments unnecessary, even harmful to the company. Pay your creditors, by all means. But, fork over perfectly good cash to stockholders as dividends? "Why give money to those strangers?" is the response of one company president.

Investors must keep an eye on the company's dividend policy. For most companies, regular boosts in the face of irregular earnings can be a warning signal. So can the

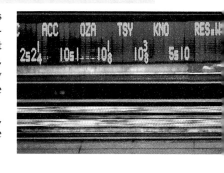

refusal of management to lower dividends when earnings fall or capital requirements rise. Companies with high dividends and rising debt may be borrowing money to pay shareholders. For investors who are seeking high returns on their stock investments, low dividends may mean high returns through market appreciation.

Entries for Cash Dividends

Three dates are important in connection with dividends: (1) the declaration date, (2) the record date, and (3) the payment date. Normally, there is a time span of two to four weeks between each date. Accounting entries are required on two of the dates—the declaration date and the payment date.

On the declaration date, the board of directors formally declares (authorizes) the cash dividend and announces it to stockholders. The declaration of a cash dividend **commits the corporation to a binding legal obligation** that cannot be rescinded. Thus, an entry is required to recognize the decrease in retained earnings and the increase in the liability Dividends Payable. To illustrate, assume that on December 1, 2001, the directors of Media General declare a 50¢ per share cash dividend on 100,000 shares of $10 par value common stock. The dividend is $50,000 (100,000 × 50¢), and the entry to record the declaration is:

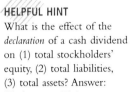

HELPFUL HINT
What is the effect of the *declaration* of a cash dividend on (1) total stockholders' equity, (2) total liabilities, (3) total assets? Answer: (1) decrease, (2) increase, (3) no effect.

		Declaration Date		
Dec. 1	Retained Earnings (or Dividends)		50,000	
	Dividends Payable			50,000
	(To record declaration of cash dividend)			

Dividends Payable is a current liability because it will normally be paid within the next several months. Instead of debiting Retained Earnings, the account Dividends may be debited. This account provides additional information in the ledger. For example, a company may have separate dividend accounts for each class of stock. When a dividend account is used, its balance is transferred to Retained Earnings at the end of the year by a closing entry. Consequently, the effect of the declaration is the same: retained earnings is decreased and a current liability is increased. For homework problems, you should use the Retained Earnings account for recording dividend declarations.

The record date marks the time when ownership of the outstanding shares is determined for dividend purposes. The stockholders' records maintained by the corporation supply this information. The time interval between the declaration date and the record date enables the corporation to update its stock ownership records. Between the declaration date and record date, the number of shares outstanding should remain the same. Thus, the purpose of the record date is to identify the persons or entities that will receive the dividend, not to determine the amount of the dividend liability. For Media General, the record date is December 22. No entry is required on this date because the corporation's liability recognized on the declaration date is unchanged:

	Record Date		
Dec. 22	No entry necessary		

On the payment date, dividend checks are mailed to the stockholders and the payment of the dividend is recorded. Assuming that the payment date is January 20 for Media General, the entry on that date is:

		Payment Date		
Jan. 20	Dividends Payable		50,000	
	Cash			50,000
	(To record payment of cash dividend)			

Note that payment of the dividend reduces both current assets and current liabilities but has no effect on stockholders' equity. The cumulative effect of the **declaration and payment** of a cash dividend on a company's financial statements is to **decrease both stockholders' equity and total assets**. Illustration 12-12 summarizes the three important dates associated with dividends.

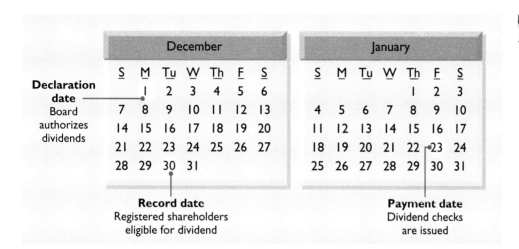

ILLUSTRATION 12-12

Key dividend dates

Allocating Cash Dividends between Preferred and Common Stock

As explained on page 529, preferred stock has priority over common stock in regard to dividends. That is, cash dividends must be paid to preferred stockholders before common stockholders are paid any dividends.

To illustrate, assume that IBR Inc. has 1,000 shares of 8%, $100 par value cumulative preferred stock and 50,000 shares of $10 par value common stock outstanding at December 31, 2001. The dividend per share for preferred stock is $8 ($100 par value × 8%), and the required annual dividend for preferred stock is $8,000 (1,000 × $8). At December 31, 2001, the directors declare a $6,000 cash dividend. In this case, the entire dividend amount goes to preferred stockholders because of their dividend preference. The entry to record the declaration of the dividend is:

Dec. 31	Retained Earnings (or Dividends)	6,000	
	Dividends Payable		6,000
	(To record $6 per share cash dividend to preferred stockholders)		

A	=	L	+	SE
		+6,000		−6,000

Because of the cumulative feature, dividends of $2 per share are in arrears on preferred stock for 2001. These dividends must be paid to preferred stockholders before any future dividends can be paid to common stockholders. As explained on page 530, dividends in arrears should be disclosed in the financial statements.

At December 31, 2002, IBR declares a $50,000 cash dividend. The allocation of the dividend to the two classes of stock is as follows:

Total dividend		$50,000
Allocated to preferred stock		
Dividends in arrears, 2001 (1,000 × $2)	$2,000	
2002 dividend (1,000 × $8)	8,000	10,000
Remainder allocated to common stock		$40,000

ILLUSTRATION 12-13

Allocating dividends to preferred and common stock

The entry to record the declaration of the dividend is:

A	=	L	+	SE
		+50,000		−50,000

Dec. 31	Retained Earnings (or Dividends)	50,000	
	Dividends Payable		50,000
	(To record declaration of cash dividends of $10,000 to preferred stock and $40,000 to common stock)		

If the preferred stock were not cumulative, preferred stockholders would have received only $8,000 in dividends in 2002, and common stockholders would have received $42,000.

STOCK DIVIDENDS

A stock dividend is a pro rata distribution of the corporation's own stock to stockholders. Whereas a cash dividend is paid in cash, a stock dividend is paid in stock. **A stock dividend results in a decrease in retained earnings and an increase in paid-in capital.** Unlike a cash dividend, a stock dividend does not decrease total stockholders' equity or total assets.

To illustrate a stock dividend, assume that you have a 2% ownership interest in Cetus Inc. by virtue of owning 20 of its 1,000 shares of common stock. In a 10% stock dividend, 100 shares (1,000 × 10%) of stock would be issued. You would receive two shares (2% × 100), but your ownership interest would remain at 2% (22 ÷ 1,100). **You now own more shares of stock but your ownership interest has not changed.** Moreover, no cash is disbursed, and no liabilities have been assumed by the corporation. Illustration 12-14 shows the effect of a stock dividend.

ILLUSTRATION 12-14

Effect of stock dividend

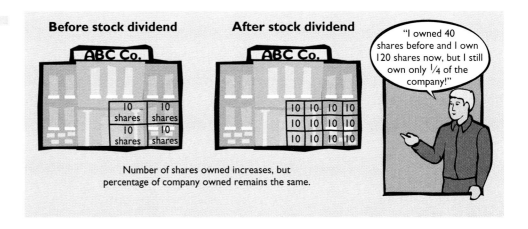

What then are the purposes and benefits of a stock dividend? Corporations issue stock dividends generally for one or more of the following reasons:

1. To satisfy stockholders' dividend expectations without spending cash.
2. To increase the marketability of its stock by increasing the number of shares outstanding and thereby decreasing the market price per share. Decreasing the market price of the stock makes it easier for smaller investors to purchase the shares.
3. To emphasize that a portion of stockholders' equity has been permanently reinvested in the business and therefore is unavailable for cash dividends.

The size of the stock dividend and the value to be assigned to each dividend share are determined by the board of directors when the dividend is declared. The per share amount must be at least equal to the par or stated value in order to meet legal requirements.

The accounting profession distinguishes between a **small stock dividend** (less than 20–25% of the corporation's issued stock) and a **large stock dividend** (greater than 20–25%). It recommends that the directors assign the **fair market value per share** for small stock dividends. The recommendation is based on the assumption that a small stock dividend will have little effect on the market price of the shares previously outstanding. Thus, many stockholders consider small stock dividends to be distributions of earnings equal to the fair market value of the shares distributed. The amount to be assigned for a large stock dividend is not specified by the accounting profession. However, **par or stated value per share** is normally assigned. Small stock dividends predominate in practice. Thus, we will illustrate only the entries for small stock dividends.

Entries for Stock Dividends

To illustrate the accounting for stock dividends, assume that Medland Corporation has a balance of $300,000 in retained earnings and declares a 10% stock dividend on its 50,000 shares of $10 par value common stock. The current fair market value of its stock is $15 per share. The number of shares to be issued is 5,000 (10% × 50,000) and the total amount to be debited to Retained Earnings is $75,000 (5,000 × $15). The entry to record this transaction at the declaration date is as follows:

Retained Earnings	75,000	
Common Stock Dividends Distributable		50,000
Paid-in Capital in Excess of Par Value		25,000
(To record declaration of 10% stock dividend)		

A	=	L	+	SE
				−75,000
				+50,000
				+25,000

Note that Retained Earnings is debited for the fair market value of the stock issued; Common Stock Dividends Distributable is credited for the par value of the dividend shares (5,000 × $10); and the excess over par (5,000 × $5) is credited to an additional paid-in capital account.

Common Stock Dividends Distributable is a stockholders' equity account; it is not a liability because assets will not be used to pay the dividend. If a balance sheet is prepared before the dividend shares are issued, the distributable account is reported in paid-in capital as an addition to common stock issued, as shown below:

Paid-in capital		
Common stock	$500,000	
Common stock dividends distributable	**50,000**	$550,000

ILLUSTRATION 12-15

Statement presentation of common stock dividends distributable

When the dividend shares are issued, Common Stock Dividends Distributable is debited and Common Stock is credited as follows:

Common Stock Dividends Distributable	50,000	
Common Stock		50,000
(To record issuance of 5,000 shares in a stock dividend)		

A	=	L	+	SE
				−50,000
				+50,000

Effects of Stock Dividends

How do stock dividends affect stockholders' equity? They **change the composition of stockholders' equity** because a portion of retained earnings is transferred to paid-in capital. However, **total stockholders' equity remains the same**. Stock dividends also have no effect on the par or stated value per share, but the number of shares outstanding increases. These effects are shown for Medland Corporation in Illustration 12-16.

ILLUSTRATION 12-16

Stock dividend effects

	Before Dividend	After Dividend
Stockholders' equity		
Paid-in capital		
Common stock, $10 par	$500,000	$550,000
Paid-in capital in excess of par value	—	25,000
Total paid-in capital	500,000	575,000
Retained earnings	300,000	225,000
Total stockholders' equity	$800,000	$800,000
Outstanding shares	50,000	55,000

In this example, total paid-in capital is increased by $75,000 and retained earnings is decreased by the same amount. Note also that total stockholders' equity remains unchanged at $800,000.

STOCK SPLITS

A stock split, like a stock dividend, involves the issuance of additional shares of stock to stockholders according to their percentage ownership. However, **a stock split results in a reduction in the par or stated value per share.** The purpose of a stock split is to increase the marketability of the stock by lowering its market value per share. This, in turn, makes it easier for the corporation to issue additional stock. The effect of a split on market value is generally inversely proportional to the size of the split. For example, after a recent 2-for-1 stock split, the market value of Nike's stock fell from $111 to approximately $55.

In a stock split, the number of shares is increased in the same proportion that par or stated value per share is decreased. For example, in a 2-for-1 split, one share of $10 par value stock is exchanged for two shares of $5 par value stock. **A stock split does not have any effect on total paid-in capital, retained earnings, and total stockholders' equity.** However, the number of shares outstanding increases. These effects are shown in Illustration 12-17 for Medland Corporation, assuming that it splits its 50,000 shares of common stock on a 2-for-1 basis.

HELPFUL HINT
A stock split changes the par value per share but does not affect any balances in stockholders' equity.

ILLUSTRATION 12-17

Stock split effects

	Before Stock Split	After Stock Split
Stockholders' equity		
Paid-in capital		
Common stock	$500,000	$500,000
Paid-in capital in excess of par value	–0–	–0–
Total paid-in capital	500,000	500,000
Retained earnings	300,000	300,000
Total stockholders' equity	$800,000	$800,000
Outstanding shares	50,000	100,000

Because a stock split does not affect the balances in any stockholders' equity accounts, **it is not necessary to journalize a stock split**. Significant differences between stock splits and stock dividends are shown in Illustration 12-18:

Item	Stock Split	Stock Dividend
Total paid-in capital	No change	Increase
Total retained earnings	No change	Decrease
Total par value (common stock)	No change	Increase
Par value per share	Decrease	No change

ILLUSTRATION 12-18

Differences between the effects of stock splits and stock dividends

ACCOUNTING IN ACTION
Business Insight

A handful of U.S. companies have no intention of keeping their stock trading in a range accessible to mere mortals. These companies never split their stock, no matter how high their stock price gets. The king of these is investment company Berkshire Hathaway's Class A stock, which goes for a pricey $72,000—per share! The company's Class B stock is a relative bargain at roughly $2,350 per share. Other "premium" stocks are A.D. Makepeace at $9,000 and Mechanics Bank of Richmond, California, at $9,600.

BEFORE YOU GO ON . . .

Review It

1. What entries are made for cash dividends on (a) the declaration date, (b) the record date, and (c) the payment date?
2. Distinguish between a small and large stock dividend and indicate the basis for valuing each kind of dividend.
3. Contrast the effects of a small stock dividend and a 2-for-1 stock split on (a) stockholders' equity, and (b) outstanding shares.
4. How are stock dividends distributable reported in the stockholders' equity section?

Do It

Due to 5 years of record earnings at Sing CD Corporation, the market price of its 500,000 shares of $2 par value common stock tripled from $15 per share to $45. During this period, paid-in capital remained the same at $2,000,000, but retained earnings increased from $1,500,000 to $10,000,000. President Joan Elbert is considering either (1) a 10% stock dividend or (2) a 2-for-1 stock split. She asks you to show the before and after effects of each option on (a) retained earnings and (b) total stockholders' equity and the total shares outstanding.

Reasoning: A stock dividend decreases retained earnings and increases paid-in capital, but total stockholders' equity remains the same. Because additional shares of stock are issued in the dividend, book value per share is decreased. A stock split only changes par value per share and the number of shares outstanding. Thus, this event has no effect on the retained earnings balance.

Solution:
(a) (1) The stock dividend amount is $2,250,000 [(500,000 × 10%) × $45]. The new balance in retained earnings is $7,750,000 ($10,000,000 − $2,250,000).
   (2) The retained earnings balance after the stock split is the same as it was before the split: $10,000,000.

(b) The book value effects are as follows:

	Original Balances	After Dividend	After Split
Paid-in capital	$ 2,000,000	$ 4,250,000	$ 2,000,000
Retained earnings	10,000,000	7,750,000	10,000,000
Total stockholders' equity	$12,000,000	$12,000,000	$12,000,000
Shares outstanding	500,000	550,000	1,000,000

Related exercise material: BE12–8, BE12–9, *BE12–13, E12–9, E12–10, E12–11, E12–12, *E12–15, *E12–16 and *E12–17.

THE NAVIGATOR

SECTION 3   RETAINED EARNINGS

6

STUDY

OBJECTIVE

Identify the items that are reported in a retained earnings statement.

Retained earnings is net income that is retained in the business. The balance in retained earnings is part of the stockholders' claim on the total assets of the corporation. It does not, however, represent a claim on any specific asset. Nor can the amount of retained earnings be associated with the balance of any asset account. For example, a $100,000 balance in retained earnings does not mean that there should be $100,000 in cash. The reason is that the cash resulting from the excess of revenues over expenses may have been used to purchase buildings, equipment, and other assets. Illustration 12-19 shows the relationship of cash to retained earnings in selected companies.

ILLUSTRATION 12-19

Retained earnings and cash balances

	(in millions)	
Company	**Retained Earnings**	**Cash**
Walt Disney Co.	$1,278	$7,933
Sears, Roebuck and Co.	4,848	495
The Home Depot	146	2,173
Netscape	(2)	88

When expenses exceed revenues, a **net loss** results. In contrast to net income, a net loss is debited to Retained Earnings in preparing closing entries. This is done even if a debit balance results in Retained Earnings. **Net losses are not debited to paid-in capital accounts.** To do so would destroy the distinction between paid-in and earned capital. A debit balance in retained earnings is identified as a deficit and is reported as a deduction in the stockholders' equity section, as shown below:

ILLUSTRATION 12-20

Stockholders' equity with deficit

Stockholders' equity	
Paid-in capital	
Common stock	$800,000
Retained earnings (deficit)	**(50,000)**
Total stockholders' equity	$750,000

RETAINED EARNINGS RESTRICTIONS

The balance in retained earnings is generally available for dividend declarations. Some companies state this fact. For example, in the notes to its financial statements, Martin Lockheed Corporation states:

MARTIN LOCKHEED CORPORATION
Notes to the Financial Statements

At December 31, retained earnings were unrestricted and available for dividend payments.

ILLUSTRATION 12-21

Disclosure of unrestricted retained earnings

In some cases, however, there may be retained earnings restrictions that make a portion of the balance currently unavailable for dividends. Restrictions result from one or more of the following causes: legal, contractual, or voluntary.

1. **Legal restrictions.** Many states require a corporation to restrict retained earnings for the cost of treasury stock purchased. The restriction serves to keep intact the corporation's legal capital that is temporarily being held as treasury stock. When the treasury stock is sold, the restriction is lifted.
2. **Contractual restrictions.** Long-term debt contracts may impose a restriction on retained earnings as a condition for the loan. The restriction limits the use of corporate assets for the payment of dividends. Thus, it enhances the likelihood that the corporation will be able to meet required loan payments.
3. **Voluntary restrictions.** The board of directors of a corporation may voluntarily create retained earnings restrictions for specific purposes. For example, the board may authorize a restriction for the purpose of future plant expansion. By reducing the amount of retained earnings available for dividends, more cash may be available for the planned expansion.

Retained earnings restrictions are generally disclosed in the notes to the financial statements. For example, Pratt & Lambert, a leading producer of architectural finishes (paint) has the following note in a recent financial statement:

PRATT & LAMBERT
Notes to the Financial Statements

Note D: Long-term Debt and Retained Earnings Loan agreements contain, among other covenants, a restriction on the payment of dividends, which limits future dividend payments to $20,565,000 plus 75% of future net income.

ILLUSTRATION 12-22

Disclosure of restriction

PRIOR PERIOD ADJUSTMENTS

Suppose that after the books have been closed and the financial statements have been issued, a corporation discovers that a material error has been made in reporting net income of a prior year. How should this situation be recorded in the accounts and reported in the financial statements? The correction of an error in previously issued financial statements is known as a prior period adjustment. The correction is made directly to Retained Earnings because the effect of the error is now in this account; the net income for the prior period has been recorded in retained earnings through the journalizing and posting of closing entries.

To illustrate, assume that General Microwave discovers in 2001 that it understated depreciation expense in 2000 by $300,000 as a result of computational errors. These errors overstated net income for 2000, and the current balance in retained earnings is also overstated. The entry for the prior period adjustment, assuming all tax effects are ignored, is as follows:

A	=	L	+	SE
−300,000				−300,000

Retained Earnings	300,000	
Accumulated Depreciation		300,000
(To adjust for understatement of depreciation in a prior period)		

A debit to an income statement account in 2001 would be incorrect because the error pertains to a prior year.

Prior period adjustments are reported in the retained earnings statement.[5] They are added (or deducted) from the beginning retained earnings balance to show the adjusted beginning balance. Assuming General Microwave has a beginning balance of $800,000 in retained earnings, the prior period adjustment is reported as follows:

ILLUSTRATION 12-23

Statement presentation of prior period adjustments

GENERAL MICROWAVE	
Retained Earnings Statement (partial)	
Balance, January 1, as reported	$800,000
Correction for overstatement of net income in prior period (depreciation error)	300,000
Balance, January 1, as adjusted	$500,000

Reporting the correction in the current year's income statement would be incorrect because it applies to a prior year's income statement.

RETAINED EARNINGS STATEMENT

The retained earnings statement shows the changes in retained earnings during the year. The statement is prepared from the Retained Earnings account. Transactions and events that affect retained earnings are tabulated in account form as shown in Illustration 12-24.

ILLUSTRATION 12-24

Debits and credits to retained earnings

Retained Earnings	
1. Net loss	1. Net income
2. Prior period adjustments for overstatement of net income	2. Prior period adjustments for understatement of net income
3. Cash and stock dividends	
4. Some disposals of treasury stock	

---

[5]A complete retained earnings statement is shown in Illustration 12-25 on the next page.

As indicated, net income increases retained earnings, and a net loss decreases retained earnings. Prior period adjustments may either increase or decrease retained earnings, whereas both cash and stock dividends decrease retained earnings. The circumstances when treasury stock transactions decrease retained earnings are explained on page 528. The retained earnings statement for Graber Inc., based on assumed data, is as follows:

ILLUSTRATION 12-25

Retained earnings statement

GRABER INC.
Retained Earnings Statement
For the Year Ended December 31, 2001

Balance, January 1, as reported		$1,050,000
Correction for understatement of net income in prior period (inventory error)		50,000
Balance, January 1, as adjusted		1,100,000
Add: Net income		360,000
		1,460,000
Less: Cash dividends	$100,000	
Stock dividends	200,000	300,000
Balance, December 31		$1,160,000

BEFORE YOU GO ON ...

Review It

1. How are retained earnings restrictions generally reported?
2. What is a prior period adjustment and how is it reported?
3. What are the principal sources of debits and credits to Retained Earnings?

Do It

Vega Corporation has retained earnings of $5,130,000 on January 1, 2001. During the year, the company earns $2,000,000 of net income and it declares and pays a $250,000 cash dividend. In 2001, Vega records an adjustment of $180,000 that pertains to the understatement of 2000 depreciation expense due to a mathematical error. Prepare a retained earnings statement for 2001.

Reasoning: The $180,000 correction of 2000 depreciation is a prior period adjustment. It should be reported as a deduction from the beginning retained earnings balance. Net income is shown as an addition in the statement and dividends are deducted in the statement.

Solution:

VEGA CORPORATION
Retained Earnings Statement
For the Year Ended December 31, 2001

Balance, January 1, as reported	$5,130,000
Correction for overstatement of net income in prior period (depreciation error)	180,000
Balance, January 1, as adjusted	4,950,000
Add: Net income	2,000,000
	6,950,000
Less: Cash dividends	250,000
Balance, December 31	$6,700,000

*Related exercise material: BE12–10, BE12–11, E12–12, and *E12–15.*

THE NAVIGATOR

SECTION 4   STOCKHOLDERS' EQUITY PRESENTATION AND ANALYSIS

7
STUDY
OBJECTIVE

Prepare and analyze a comprehensive stockholders' equity section.

In the stockholders' equity section of the balance sheet, paid-in capital and retained earnings are reported, and the specific sources of paid-in capital are identified.

Within paid-in capital, two classifications are recognized:

1. **Capital stock**, which consists of preferred and common stock. Preferred stock is shown before common stock because of its preferential rights. Information as to the par value, shares authorized, shares issued, and shares outstanding is reported for each class of stock.
2. **Additional paid-in capital**, which includes the excess of amounts paid in over par or stated value and paid-in capital from treasury stock.

PRESENTATION

The stockholders' equity section of the balance sheet of Graber Inc. is presented in Illustration 12-26. Note that (1) Common Stock Dividends Distributable is shown under capital stock in paid-in capital, and (2) a retained earnings restriction is disclosed in the notes.

ILLUSTRATION 12-26

Comprehensive stockholders' equity section

INTERNATIONAL NOTE

In Switzerland, there are no specific disclosure requirements for shareholders' equity. However, companies typically disclose separate categories of capital on the balance sheet.

GRABER INC. Balance Sheet (partial)		
Stockholders' equity		
Paid-in capital		
Capital stock		
9% preferred stock, $100 par value, cumulative, callable at $120, 10,000 shares authorized, 6,000 shares issued and outstanding		$ 600,000
Common stock, no par, $5 stated value, 500,000 shares authorized, 400,000 shares issued and 390,000 outstanding	$2,000,000	
Common stock dividends distributable	**50,000**	2,050,000
Total capital stock		2,650,000
Additional paid-in capital		
In excess of par value—preferred stock	30,000	
In excess of stated value—common stock	1,050,000	
Total additional paid-in capital		1,080,000
Total paid-in capital		3,730,000
Retained earnings **(see Note R)**		1,160,000
Total paid-in capital and retained earnings		4,890,000
Less: Treasury stock—common (10,000 shares)		80,000
Total stockholders' equity		$4,810,000

Note R: Retained earnings is restricted for the cost of treasury stock, $80,000.

The stockholders' equity section of Graber Inc. shown in Illustration 12-26 includes most of the accounts discussed in this chapter. The disclosures pertaining to Graber's common stock indicate that 400,000 shares are issued, 100,000 shares are unissued (500,000 authorized less 400,000 issued), and 390,000 shares are outstanding (400,000 issued less 10,000 shares in treasury).

In published annual reports, subclassifications within the stockholders' equity section are seldom presented. Moreover, the individual sources of additional paid-in capital are often combined and reported as a single amount as shown in Illustration 12-27.

>KNIGHT RIDDER>

KNIGHT-RIDDER INC.
Balance Sheet (partial)

Stockholders' equity (in millions)

Common stock, $.02½ par value; shares authorized—250,000,000; shares issued—45,720,000	$ 1,143
Additional paid-in capital	342,201
Retained earnings	899,825
Total stockholders' equity	$1,243,169

ILLUSTRATION 12-27

Published stockholders' equity section

In practice, the term "capital surplus" is sometimes used in place of additional paid-in capital and "earned surplus" in place of retained earnings. The use of the term "surplus" suggests that an excess amount of funds is available. Such is not necessarily the case, which is why **the term surplus should not be employed in accounting**. Unfortunately, a number of financial statements still include these terms.

Instead of presenting a detailed stockholders' equity section in the balance sheet and a retained earnings statement, many companies prepare a stockholders' equity statement. This statement shows the changes in each stockholders' equity account and in total stockholders' equity that have occurred during the year. An example of a stockholders' equity statement is illustrated in an appendix to this chapter and in Kellogg's financial statements in Appendix A.

HELPFUL HINT

Accounting Trends & Techniques reported in 1998 that 87% of the 600 companies prepare a stockholders' equity statement.

ANALYSIS

A widely used ratio that measures profitability from the common stockholder's viewpoint is return on common stockholders' equity. This ratio shows how many dollars of net income were earned for each dollar invested by the owners. It is computed by dividing net income available to common stockholders (which is Net income − Preferred stock dividends) by average common stockholders' equity. For example, assuming that Kellogg's beginning-of-the-year and end-of-the-year common stockholders' equity were $997.5 and $889.8 million respectively, net income was $502.6 million, and no preferred stock was outstanding, the return on common stockholders' equity ratio is shown graphically and computed as follows:

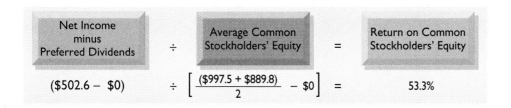

ILLUSTRATION 12-28

Return on common stockholders' equity ratio and computation

As shown above, if preferred stock is present, **preferred dividend** requirements are deducted from net income to compute income available to common stockholders. Similarly, the par value of preferred stock is deducted from total average stockholders' equity to arrive at the amount of common stockholders' equity used in this ratio.

BEFORE YOU GO ON . . .

Review It

1. Identify the classifications within the paid-in capital section and the totals that are stated in the stockholders' equity section of a balance sheet.
2. Explain the return on common stockholders' equity ratio.

A LOOK BACK AT OUR FEATURE STORY

To answer the following questions, refer to the Feature Story.

1. Nike's stock has split numerous times in recent years. What is the likely reason for these splits?
2. Prepare the quarterly journal entry (accounts and amount) recorded by a Nike shareholder when he or she receives a dividend of $1,000 from Nike.
3. Nike has increased its cash dividend per share every year for the past 10 years. What issues must it consider when deciding the level of the dividend payment?

Solution:

1. In recent years Nike's stock has experienced a rapid increase in value. To keep the stock in an affordable price range for the average investor, management has split the stock a number of times.
2. The entry to record receipt of a dividend each quarter is:

Cash	1,000	
Dividend Revenue		1,000
(To record quarterly dividend revenue)		

THE NAVIGATOR

3. Nike should consider the adequacy of its cash, the adequacy of its retained earnings, the level of its future earnings, and its ability to maintain the dividend level in the future.

DEMONSTRATION PROBLEM

Rolman Corporation is authorized to issue 1,000,000 shares of $5 par value common stock. In its first year, the company has the following stock transactions:

Jan. 10 Issued 400,000 shares of stock at $8 per share.
July 1 Issued 100,000 shares of stock for land. The land had an asking price of $900,000. The stock is currently selling on a national exchange at $8.25 per share.
Sept. 1 Purchased 10,000 shares of common stock for the treasury at $9.00 per share.
Dec. 1 Sold 4,000 shares of the treasury stock at $10 per share.
Dec. 24 Declared a cash dividend of 10¢ per share.

Instructions
(a) Journalize the transactions.
(b) Prepare the stockholders' equity section assuming the company had retained earnings of $150,600 at December 31.

SOLUTION TO DEMONSTRATION PROBLEM

(a) Jan. 10	Cash	3,200,000	
	Common Stock		2,000,000
	Paid-in Capital in Excess of Par Value		1,200,000
	(To record issuance of 400,000 shares of $5 par value stock)		
July 1	Land	825,000	
	Common Stock		500,000
	Paid-in Capital in Excess of Par Value		325,000
	(To record issuance of 100,000 shares of $5 par value stock for land)		
Sept. 1	Treasury Stock	90,000	
	Cash		90,000
	(To record purchase of 10,000 shares of treasury stock at cost)		
Dec. 1	Cash	40,000	
	Treasury Stock		36,000
	Paid-in Capital from Treasury Stock		4,000
	(To record sale of 4,000 shares of treasury stock above cost)		
Dec. 24	Retained Earnings	49,400	
	Dividends Payable		49,400
	(To record declaration of 10¢ per share cash dividends)		

(b) Stockholders' equity
    Paid-in capital
      Capital stock
        Common stock, $5 par value, 1,000,000 shares
          authorized, 500,000 shares issued, 494,000 shares
          outstanding $2,500,000
      Additional paid-in capital
        In excess of par value $1,525,000
        From treasury stock   4,000
          Total additional paid-in capital   1,529,000
        Total paid-in capital   4,029,000
    Retained earnings   150,600
        Total paid-in capital and retained earnings   4,179,600
      Less: Treasury stock (6,000 shares)   54,000
        Total stockholders' equity $4,125,600

PROBLEM-SOLVING STRATEGIES

1. When common stock has a par value, Common Stock is always credited for par value.
2. In a noncash transaction, fair market value should be used.
3. The Treasury Stock account is debited and credited at cost.
4. Differences between the cost and selling price of treasury stock are recorded in stockholders' equity accounts, not as gains or losses.

THE NAVIGATOR

SUMMARY OF STUDY OBJECTIVES

1. Identify and discuss the major characteristics of a corporation. The major characteristics of a corporation are separate legal existence, limited liability of stockholders, transferable ownership rights, ability to acquire capital, continuous life, corporation management, government regulations, and additional taxes.

2. Record the issuance of common stock. When the issuance of common stock for cash is recorded, the par value of the shares is credited to Common Stock and the portion of the proceeds that is above or below par value is recorded

in a separate paid-in capital account. When no-par common stock has a stated value, the entries are similar to those for par value stock. When no-par does not have a stated value, the entire proceeds from the issue become legal capital and are credited to Common Stock.

3. Explain the accounting for treasury stock. The cost method is generally used in accounting for treasury stock. Under this approach, Treasury Stock is debited at the price paid to reacquire the shares, and the same amount is credited to Treasury Stock when the shares are sold. The difference between the sales price and cost is recorded in stockholders' equity accounts, not in income statement accounts.

4. *Differentiate preferred stock from common stock.* Preferred stock has contractual provisions that give it priority over common stock in certain areas. Typically, preferred stockholders have a preference as to (1) dividends and (2) assets in the event of liquidation. However, they usually do not have voting rights.

5. *Prepare the entries for cash dividends and stock dividends.* Entries for both cash and stock dividends are required at the declaration date and the payment date. At the declaration date the entries are: Cash dividend—debit Retained Earnings and credit Dividends Payable; small stock dividend—debit Retained Earnings, credit Paid-in Capital in Excess of Par (or Stated) Value, and credit Common Stock Dividends Distributable. At the payment date, the entries for cash and stock dividends, respectively, are debit Dividends Payable and credit Cash, and debit Common Stock Dividends Distributable and credit Common Stock.

6. *Identify the items that are reported in a retained earnings statement.* Each of the individual debits and credits to retained earnings should be reported in the retained earnings statement. Additions consist of net income and prior period adjustments to correct understatements of prior years' net income. Deductions consist of net loss, adjustments to correct overstatements of prior years' net income, cash and stock dividends, and some disposals of treasury stock.

7. *Prepare and analyze a comprehensive stockholders' equity section.* In the stockholders' equity section, paid-in capital and retained earnings are reported and specific sources of paid-in capital are identified. Within paid-in capital, two classifications are shown: capital stock and additional paid-in capital. If a corporation has treasury stock, the cost of treasury stock is deducted from total paid-in capital and retained earnings to obtain total stockholders' equity. One measure of profitability is the return on common stockholders' equity ratio, calculated as income available to common stockholders divided by average common stockholders' equity.

GLOSSARY

Authorized stock The amount of stock that a corporation is authorized to sell as indicated in its charter. (p. 519)

Cash dividend A pro rata distribution of cash to stockholders. (p. 531)

Cumulative dividend A feature of preferred stock entitling the stockholder to receive current and unpaid prior-year dividends before common stockholders receive any dividends. (p. 529)

Declaration date The date the board of directors formally declares the dividend and announces it to stockholders. (p. 532)

Deficit A debit balance in retained earnings. (p. 538)

Dividend A distribution by a corporation to its stockholders on a pro rata (equal) basis. (p. 530)

Legal capital The amount per share of stock that must be retained in the business for the protection of corporate creditors. (p. 521)

Liquidating dividend A dividend declared out of paid-in capital. (p. 531)

No-par value stock Capital stock that has not been assigned a value in the corporate charter. (p. 521)

Organization costs Costs incurred in the formation of a corporation. (p. 517)

Outstanding stock Capital stock that has been issued and is being held by stockholders. (p. 526)

Par value stock Capital stock that has been assigned a value per share in the corporate charter. (p. 521)

Payment date The date dividend checks are mailed to stockholders. (p. 532)

Preferred stock Capital stock that has contractual preferences over common stock in certain areas. (p. 528)

Prior period adjustment The correction of an error in previously issued financial statements. (p. 540)

Privately held corporation A corporation that has only a few stockholders and whose stock is not available for sale to the general public. (p. 513)

Publicly held corporation A corporation that may have thousands of stockholders and whose stock is regularly traded on a national securities market. (p. 512)

Record date The date when ownership of outstanding shares is determined for dividend purposes. (p. 532)

Retained earnings Net income that is retained in the business. (p. 538)

Retained earnings restrictions Circumstances that make a portion of retained earnings currently unavailable for dividends. (p. 539)

Retained earnings statement A financial statement that shows the changes in retained earnings during the year. (p. 540)

Return on common stockholders' equity ratio A ratio that measures profitability from the stockholders' point of view. It is computed by dividing net income by average common stockholders' equity. (p. 543)

Stated value The amount per share assigned by the board of directors to no-par stock that becomes legal capital per share. (p. 521)

Stock dividend A pro rata distribution of the corporation's own stock to stockholders. (p. 534)

Stock split The issuance of additional shares of stock to stockholders accompanied by a reduction in the par or stated value per share. (p. 536)

Stockholders' equity statement A statement that shows the changes in each stockholders' equity account and in total stockholders' equity during the year. (p. 543)

Treasury stock A corporation's own stock that has been issued, fully paid for, and reacquired by the corporation but not retired. (p. 525)

APPENDIX 12A STOCKHOLDERS' EQUITY STATEMENT

When balance sheets and income statements are presented by a corporation, changes in the separate accounts comprising stockholders' equity should also be disclosed. Disclosure of such changes is necessary to make the financial statements sufficiently informative for users. The disclosures may be made in an additional statement or in the notes to the financial statements.

Many corporations make the disclosures in a stockholders' equity statement. The statement shows the changes in **each** stockholders' equity account and in **total** stockholders' equity during the year. As shown in Illustration 12A-1 the stockholders' equity statement is prepared in columnar form, with columns for each account and for total stockholders' equity. The transactions are then identified and their effects are shown in the appropriate columns.

In practice, additional columns are usually provided to show the number of shares of issued stock and treasury stock. The stockholders' equity statement for Kellogg Company, for a three-year period, is shown in Appendix A. **When this statement is presented, a retained earnings statement is not necessary** because the retained earnings column explains the changes in this account.

8
STUDY
OBJECTIVE

Describe the use and content of the stockholders' equity statement.

ILLUSTRATION 12A-1

Stockholders' equity statement

HAMPTON CORPORATION
Stockholders' Equity Statement
For the Year Ended December 31, 2001

	Common Stock ($5 Par)	Paid-in Capital in Excess of Par	Retained Earnings	Treasury Stock	Total
Balance January 1	$300,000	$200,000	$650,000	$(34,000)	$1,116,000
Issued 5,000 shares of common stock at $15	25,000	50,000			75,000
Declared a $40,000 cash dividend			(40,000)		(40,000)
Purchased 2,000 shares for treasury at $16				(32,000)	(32,000)
Net income for year			240,000		240,000
Balance December 31	$325,000	$250,000	$850,000	$(66,000)	$1,359,000

SUMMARY OF STUDY OBJECTIVES FOR APPENDIX 12A

8. *Describe the use and content of the stockholders' equity statement.* Corporations must disclose changes in stockholders' equity accounts and may choose to do so by issuing a separate stockholders' equity statement. This statement, prepared in columnar form, shows changes in each stockholders' equity account and in total stockholders' equity during the accounting period. When this statement is presented, a retained earnings statement is not necessary.

APPENDIX 12B BOOK VALUE—ANOTHER PER SHARE AMOUNT

You have learned about a number of per share amounts in this chapter. Another per share amount of some importance is book value per share. This per share amount represents **the equity a common stockholder has in the net assets of the**

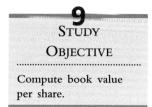

9
STUDY
OBJECTIVE

Compute book value
per share.

corporation from owning one share of stock. Since the net assets of a corporation must be equal to total stockholders' equity, the formula for computing book value per share when a company has only one class of stock outstanding is:

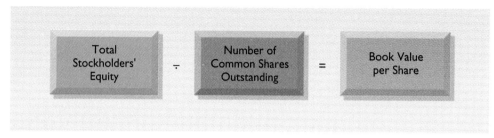

ILLUSTRATION 12B-1

Book value per share formula

Thus, if the Marlo Corporation has total stockholders' equity of $1,500,000 (Common Stock $1,000,000 and Retained Earnings $500,000) and 50,000 shares of common stock outstanding, book value per share is $30 ($1,500,000 ÷ 50,000).

When a company has both preferred and common stock, the computation of book value is more complex. Since preferred stockholders have a prior claim on net assets over common stockholders, their equity must be deducted from total stockholders' equity to determine the stockholders' equity that applies to the common stock. The computation of book value per share involves the following steps:

1. Compute the preferred stock equity. This equity is equal to the sum of the call price of preferred stock plus any cumulative dividends in arrears. If the preferred stock does not have a call price, the par value of the stock is used.
2. Determine the common stock equity by subtracting the preferred stock equity from total stockholders' equity.
3. Divide common stock equity by shares of common stock outstanding to determine book value per share.

Illustration

We will use the stockholders' equity section of Graber Inc. shown in Illustration 12-26. Graber's preferred stock is callable at $120 per share and cumulative. Assume that dividends on Graber's preferred stock were in arrears for one year, $54,000 (6,000 × $9). The computation of preferred stock equity is:

ILLUSTRATION 12B-2

Computation of preferred stock equity (Step 1)

Call price (6,000 shares × $120)	$720,000
Dividends in arrears (6,000 shares × $9)	54,000
Preferred stock equity	**$774,000**

The computation of book value is as follows:

ILLUSTRATION 12B-3

Computation of book value per share with preferred stock (Steps 2 and 3)

Total stockholders' equity	$4,810,000
Less: Preferred stock equity	774,000
Common stock equity	**$4,036,000**
Shares of common stock outstanding	390,000
Book value per share ($4,036,000 ÷ 390,000)	$10.35

The call price of $120 was used instead of the par value of $100. Note also that the paid-in capital in excess of par value of preferred stock, $30,000, **is not assigned to the preferred stock equity**. Preferred stockholders ordinarily do not have a right to amounts paid-in in excess of par value. Accordingly, such amounts are assigned to the common stock equity in computing book value.

BOOK VALUE VERSUS MARKET VALUE

Book value per share may not equal market value. Book value is based on recorded costs; market value reflects the subjective judgment of thousands of stockholders and prospective investors about a company's potential for future earnings and dividends. Market value per share may exceed book value per share, but that fact does not necessarily mean that the stock is overpriced. The correlation between book value and the annual range of a company's market value per share is often remote, as indicated by the following recent data:

HELPFUL HINT
Book value can obscure real value. Companies that have real estate, brand names, licenses, or other properties worth more than the GAAP numbers are closely watched; therefore, the market value of the stock often reflects these "hidden" values.

ILLUSTRATION 12B-4
Book and market values compared

Company	Book Value (year-end)	Market Range (for year)
Sears, Roebuck	$15.82	$39.06–$65.00
Callaway Golf	$ 6.90	$17.19–$65.25
Eastman Kodak	$ 8.85	$40.38–$64.75

Book value per share **is** useful in determining the trend of a stockholder's per share equity in a corporation. It is also significant in many contracts and in court cases where the rights of individual parties are based on cost information.

SUMMARY OF STUDY OBJECTIVES FOR APPENDIX 12B

9. *Compute book value per share.* Book value per share represents the equity a common stockholder has in the net assets of a corporation from owning one share of stock. When there is only common stock outstanding, the formula for computing book value is: Total Stockholders' Equity ÷ Number of Common Shares Outstanding = Book Value per Share.

GLOSSARY FOR APPENDIX 12B

Book value per share The equity a common stockholder has in the net assets of the corporation from owning one share of stock. (p. 547)

***Note:** All asterisked Questions, Exercises, and Problems relate to material in the appendixes to the chapter.

SELF-STUDY QUESTIONS

Answers are at the end of the chapter.

(SO 1) 1. Which of the following is *not* a major advantage of a corporation?
   a. Separate legal existence.
   b. Continuous life.
   c. Government regulations.
   d. Transferable ownership rights.

2. A major disadvantage of a corporation is: (SO 1)
   a. limited liability of stockholders.
   b. additional taxes.

c. transferable ownership rights.

d. none of the above.

(SO 2) 3. Which of the following statements is *false*?

a. Ownership of common stock gives the owner a voting right.

b. The stockholders' equity section begins with paid-in capital.

c. The authorization of capital stock does not result in a formal accounting entry.

d. Legal capital per share applies to par value stock but not to no-par value stock.

(SO 2) 4. Lemon Corporation issues 1,000 shares of $10 par value common stock at $12 per share. In recording the transaction, credits are made to:

a. Common Stock $10,000 and Paid-in Capital in Excess of Stated Value, $2,000.

b. Common Stock $12,000.

c. Common Stock $10,000 and Paid-in Capital in Excess of Par Value $2,000.

d. Common Stock $10,000 and Retained Earnings $2,000.

(SO 3) 5. Buggert Inc. sells 100 shares of $5 par value treasury stock at $13 per share. If the cost of acquiring the shares was $10 per share, the entry for the sale should include credits to:

a. Treasury Stock $1,000 and Paid-in Capital from Treasury Stock $300.

b. Treasury Stock $500 and Paid-in Capital from Treasury Stock $800.

c. Treasury Stock $1,000 and Retained Earnings $300.

d. Treasury Stock $500 and Paid-in Capital in Excess of Par Value $800.

(SO 3) 6. In the stockholders' equity section, the cost of treasury stock is deducted from:

a. Total paid-in capital and retained earnings.

b. Retained earnings.

c. Total stockholders' equity.

d. Common stock.

(SO 4) 7. Preferred stock may have priority over common stock *except* in:

a. dividends.

b. assets in the event of liquidation.

c. conversion.

d. voting.

(SO 5) 8. Entries for cash dividends are required on the:

a. declaration date and the record date.

b. record date and the payment date.

c. declaration date, record date, and payment date.

d. declaration date and the payment date.

9. Which of the following statements about small stock (SO 5) dividends is *true*?

a. A debit to Retained Earnings for the par value of the shares issued should be made.

b. Market value per share should be assigned to the dividend shares.

c. A stock dividend decreases total stockholders' equity.

d. A stock dividend ordinarily will have no effect on book value per share of stock.

10. All *but one* of the following is reported in a retained earn- (SO 6) ings statement. The exception is:

a. cash and stock dividends.

b. net income and net loss.

c. some disposals of treasury stock below cost.

d. sales of treasury stock above cost.

11. A prior period adjustment is: (SO 6)

a. reported in the income statement as a nontypical item.

b. a correction of an error that is made directly to retained earnings.

c. reported directly in the stockholders' equity section.

d. reported in the retained earnings statement as an adjustment of the ending balance of retained earnings.

*12. When a stockholders' equity statement is presented, it (SO 8) is not necessary to prepare a(an):

a. retained earnings statement.

b. balance sheet.

c. income statement.

d. none of the above.

*13. The ledger of TSW, Inc., shows common stock, common (SO 9) treasury stock, and no preferred stock. For this company, the formula for computing book value per share is:

a. Total paid-in capital and retained earnings divided by the number of shares of common stock issued.

b. Common stock divided by the number of shares of common stock issued.

c. Total stockholders' equity divided by the number of shares of common stock outstanding.

d. Total stockholders' equity divided by the number of shares of common stock issued.

THE NAVIGATOR

QUESTIONS

1. Morgan Sondgeroth, a student, asks your help in understanding the following characteristics of a corporation: (a) separate legal existence, (b) limited liability of stockholders, and (c) transferable ownership rights. Explain these characteristics to Morgan.

2. (a) Your friend Jack Borke cannot understand how the characteristic of corporation management is both an advantage and a disadvantage. Clarify this problem for Jack.

   (b) Identify and explain two other disadvantages of a corporation.

3. Ann Torbert believes a corporation must be incorporated in the state in which its headquarters office is located. Is Ann correct? Explain.

4. What are the basic ownership rights of common stockholders in the absence of restrictive provisions?

5. A corporation has been defined as an entity separate and distinct from its owners. In what ways is a corporation a separate legal entity?

6. What are the two principal components of stockholders' equity?

7. The corporate charter of J. Leno Corporation allows the issuance of a maximum of 100,000 shares of common stock. During its first two years of operations, J. Leno sold 60,000 shares to shareholders and reacquired 7,000 of these shares. After these transactions, how many shares are authorized, issued, and outstanding?

8. Which is the better investment—common stock with a par value of $5 per share or common stock with a par value of $20 per share?

9. What factors help determine the market value of stock?

10. Why is common stock usually not issued at a price that is less than par value?

11. Land appraised at $80,000 is purchased by issuing 1,000 shares of $20 par value common stock. The market price of the shares at the time of the exchange, based on active trading in the securities market, is $90 per share. Should the land be recorded at $20,000, $80,000, or $90,000? Explain.

12. For what reasons might a company like IBM repurchase some of its stock (treasury stock)?

13. Earlville Inc. purchases 1,000 shares of its own previously issued $5 par common stock for $11,000. Assuming the shares are held in the treasury, what effect does this transaction have on (a) net income, (b) total assets, (c) total paid-in capital, and (d) total stockholders' equity?

14. The treasury stock purchased in question 13, above, is resold by Earlville Inc. for $12,500. What effect does this transaction have on (a) net income, (b) total assets, (c) total paid-in capital, and (d) total stockholders' equity?

15. (a) What are the principal differences between common stock and preferred stock?
    (b) Preferred stock may be cumulative. Discuss this feature.
    (c) How are dividends in arrears presented in the financial statements?

16. Identify the events that result in credits and debits to retained earnings.

17. Indicate how each of the following accounts should be classified in the stockholders' equity section.
    (a) Common stock.
    (b) Paid-in capital in excess of par value.
    (c) Retained earnings.
    (d) Treasury stock.
    (e) Paid-in capital from treasury stock.
    (f) Paid-in capital in excess of stated value.
    (g) Preferred stock.

18. What are the three conditions that must exist before a cash dividend is paid?

19. Three dates associated with Leland Company's cash dividend are May 1, May 15, and May 31. Discuss the significance of each date and give the entry at each date.

20. Contrast the effects of a cash dividend and a stock dividend on a corporation's balance sheet.

21. Dawna Remmers asks, "Since stock dividends don't change anything, why declare them?" What is your answer to Dawna?

22. Prado Corporation has 10,000 shares of $15 par value common stock outstanding when they announce a 2-for-1 split. Before the split, the stock had a market price of $140 per share. After the split, how many shares of stock will be outstanding, and what will be the approximate market price per share?

23. The board of directors is considering a stock split or a stock dividend. They understand that total stockholders' equity will remain the same under either action. However, they are not sure of the different effects of the two types of actions on other aspects of stockholders' equity. Explain the differences to the directors.

24. What is a prior period adjustment, and how is it reported in the financial statements?

25. What is the purpose of a retained earnings restriction? Identify the possible causes of retained earnings restrictions.

*26. Perez Inc.'s common stock has a par value of $1, a book value of $29, and a current market value of $15. Explain why these amounts are all different.

*27. What is the formula for computing book value per share when a corporation has only common stock?

BRIEF EXERCISES

BE12–1 Sally Diehl is studying for her accounting midterm examination. Identify for Sally the advantages and disadvantages of the corporate form of business organization.

Cite advantages and disadvantages of a corporation.
(SO 1)

BE12–2 On May 10, Armada Corporation issues 1,000 shares of $10 par value common stock for cash at $14 per share. Journalize the issuance of the stock.

Journalize issuance of par value common stock.
(SO 2)

BE12–3 On June 1, Sparrow Inc. issues 2,000 shares of no-par common stock at a cash price of $7 per share. Journalize the issuance of the shares assuming the stock has a stated value of $1 per share.

Journalize issuance of no-par value common stock.
(SO 2)

Journalize issuance of stock in a noncash transaction.
(SO 2)

BE12–4   Kleckner Inc.'s $10 par value common stock is actively traded at a market value of $14 per share. Kleckner issues 5,000 shares to purchase land advertised for sale at $80,000. Journalize the issuance of the stock in acquiring the land.

Journalize treasury stock transactions.
(SO 3)

BE12–5   On July 1, Alice Corporation purchases 500 shares of its $5 par value common stock for the treasury at a cash price of $7 per share. On September 1, it sells 300 shares of the treasury stock for cash at $10 per share. Journalize the two treasury stock transactions.

Journalize issuance of preferred stock.
(SO 4)

BE12–6   Kansas Inc. issues 5,000 shares of $100 par value preferred stock for cash at $112 per share. Journalize the issuance of the preferred stock.

Prepare entries for a cash dividend.
(SO 5)

BE12–7   The Seabee Corporation has 10,000 shares of common stock outstanding. It declares a $1 per share cash dividend on November 1 to stockholders of record on December 1. The dividend is paid on December 31. Prepare the entries on the appropriate dates to record the declaration and payment of the cash dividend.

Prepare entries for a stock dividend.
(SO 5)

BE12–8   Satina Corporation has 100,000 shares of $10 par value common stock outstanding. It declares a 10% stock dividend on December 1 when the market value per share is $12. The dividend shares are issued on December 31. Prepare the entries for the declaration and payment of the stock dividend.

Show before and after effects of a stock dividend.
(SO 5)

BE12–9   The stockholders' equity section of the Desi Corporation consists of common stock ($10 par) $1,000,000 and retained earnings $400,000. A 10% stock dividend (10,000 shares) is declared when the market value per share is $12. Show the before and after effects of the dividend on (a) the components of stockholders' equity, and (b) shares outstanding.

Prepare a retained earnings statement.
(SO 6)

BE12–10   For the year ending December 31, 2001, Carlson Inc. reports net income $182,000 and dividends $85,000. Prepare the retained earnings statement for the year assuming the balance in retained earnings on January 1, 2001 was $220,000.

Prepare a retained earnings statement.
(SO 6)

BE12–11   The balance in retained earnings on January 1, 2001, for Julio Cortez Inc. was $800,000. During the year, the corporation paid cash dividends of $90,000 and distributed a stock dividend of $8,000. In addition, the company determined that it had understated its depreciation expense in prior years by $50,000. Net income for 2001 was $150,000. Prepare the retained earnings statement for 2001.

Prepare a stockholders' equity section.
(SO 7)

BE12–12   Mexico Corporation has the following accounts at December 31: Common Stock, $10 par, 5,000 shares issued $50,000; Paid-in Capital in Excess of Par Value $10,000; Retained Earnings $29,000; and Treasury Stock—Common, 500 shares, $7,000. Prepare the stockholders' equity section of the balance sheet.

Compute book value per share.
(SO 9)

*BE12–13   The balance sheet for Roland Inc. shows the following: total paid-in capital and retained earnings $860,000, total stockholders' equity $840,000, common stock issued 44,000 shares, and common stock outstanding 40,000 shares. Compute the book value per share.

EXERCISES

Journalize issuance of common stock.
(SO 2)

E12–1   During its first year of operations, Hispanic Corporation had the following transactions pertaining to its common stock.

Jan. 10   Issued 80,000 shares for cash at $5 per share.
July 1   Issued 30,000 shares for cash at $7 per share.

Instructions
   (a) Journalize the transactions, assuming that the common stock has a par value of $5 per share.
   (b) Journalize the transactions, assuming that the common stock is no-par with a stated value of $1 per share.

Prepare entries for issuance of common and preferred stock and purchase of treasury stock.
(SO 2, 3, 4)

E12–2   Santiago Co. had the following transactions during the current period:

Mar. 2   Issued 5,000 shares of $1 par value common stock to attorneys in payment of a bill for $27,000 for services rendered in helping the company to incorporate.
June 12   Issued 60,000 shares of $1 par value common stock for cash of $375,000.
July 11   Issued 1,000 shares of $100 par value preferred stock for cash at $105 per share.
Nov. 28   Purchased 2,000 shares of treasury stock for $80,000.

Instructions
Journalize the transactions.

E12-3 As an auditor for the CPA firm of Ketchum and Jailum, you encounter the following situations in auditing different clients:

Journalize noncash common stock transactions.
(SO 2)

1. Cheng Corporation is a closely held corporation whose stock is not publicly traded. On December 5, the corporation acquired land by issuing 5,000 shares of its $20 par value common stock. The owners' asking price for the land was $120,000, and the fair market value of the land was $110,000.
2. Jamamoto Corporation is a publicly held corporation whose common stock is traded on the securities markets. On June 1, it acquired land by issuing 20,000 shares of its $10 par value stock. At the time of the exchange, the land was advertised for sale at $250,000, and the stock was selling at $12 per share.

Instructions
Prepare the journal entries for each of the situations above.

E12-4 On January 1, 2001, the stockholders' equity section of Linda O'Neil Corporation shows: Common stock ($5 par value) $1,500,000; Paid-in capital in excess of par value $1,000,000; and Retained earnings $1,200,000. During the year, the following treasury stock transactions occurred:

Journalize treasury stock transactions.
(SO 3)

Mar. 1   Purchased 50,000 shares for cash at $14 per share.
July 1   Sold 10,000 treasury shares for cash at $16 per share.
Sept. 1   Sold 8,000 treasury shares for cash at $13 per share.

Instructions
(a) Journalize the treasury stock transactions.
(b) Restate the entry for September 1, assuming the treasury shares were sold at $11 per share.

E12-5 Steinway Corporation is authorized to issue both preferred and common stock. The par value of the preferred is $50. During the first year of operations, the company had the following events and transactions pertaining to its preferred stock:

Journalize preferred stock transactions and indicate statement presentation.
(SO 4, 7)

Feb. 1   Issued 30,000 shares for cash at $53 per share.
July 1   Issued 10,000 shares for cash at $57 per share.

Instructions
(a) Journalize the transactions.
(b) Post to the stockholders' equity accounts.
(c) Indicate the statement presentation of the accounts.

E12-6 The stockholders' equity section of Louis Henning Corporation at December 31 is as follows:

Answer questions about stockholders' equity section.
(SO 2, 3, 4, 7)

Paid-in capital
  Preferred stock, cumulative, 10,000 shares authorized, 6,000 shares issued
    and outstanding .... $ 600,000
  Common stock, no par, 750,000 shares authorized, 600,000 shares issued ... 1,800,000
      Total paid-in capital 2,400,000
Retained earnings 1,158,000
      Total paid-in capital and retained earnings 3,558,000
Less: Treasury stock (10,000 common shares) .... (64,000)
      Total stockholders' equity $3,494,000

Instructions
From a review of the stockholders' equity section, answer the following questions.

(a) How many shares of common stock are outstanding?
(b) Assuming there is a stated value, what is the stated value of the common stock?
(c) What is the par value of the preferred stock?
(d) If the annual dividend on preferred stock is $48,000, what is the dividend rate on preferred stock?
(e) If dividends of $96,000 were in arrears on preferred stock, what would be the balance reported for Retained Earnings?

Prepare correct entries for capital stock transactions.
(SO 2, 3, 4)

E12–7   Castle Corporation recently hired a new accountant with extensive experience in accounting for partnerships. Because of the pressure of the new job, the accountant was unable to review what he had learned earlier about corporation accounting. During the first month, the accountant made the following entries for the corporation's capital stock:

May 2	Cash	144,000	
	Capital Stock		144,000
	(Issued 12,000 shares of $5 par value common stock at $12 per share)		
10	Cash	600,000	
	Capital Stock		600,000
	(Issued 10,000 shares of $50 par value preferred stock at $60 per share)		
15	Capital Stock	14,000	
	Cash		14,000
	(Purchased 1,000 shares of common stock for the treasury at $14 per share)		
31	Cash	7,500	
	Capital Stock		2,500
	Gain on Sale of Stock		5,000
	(Sold 500 shares of treasury stock at $15 per share)		

Instructions
On the basis of the explanation for each entry, prepare the entry that should have been made for the capital stock transactions.

Journalize cash dividends and indicate statement presentation.
(SO 5)

E12–8   On January 1, Hinckley Corporation had 75,000 shares of no-par common stock issued and outstanding. The stock has a stated value of $5 per share. During the year, the following occurred:

Apr. 1   Issued 5,000 additional shares of common stock.
June 15   Declared a cash dividend of $1 per share to stockholders of record on June 30.
July 10   Paid the $1 cash dividend.
Dec. 1   Issued 2,000 additional shares of common stock.
15   Declared a cash dividend on outstanding shares of $1.20 per share to stockholders of record on December 31.

Instructions
(a) Prepare the entries, if any, on each of the three dividend dates.
(b) How are dividends and dividends payable reported in the financial statements prepared at December 31?

Journalize stock dividends.
(SO 5)

E12–9   On January 1, 2001, Tyler Remmers Corporation had $1,500,000 of common stock outstanding that was issued at par and retained earnings of $750,000. The company issued 50,000 shares of common stock at par on July 1 and earned net income of $400,000 for the year.

Instructions
Journalize the declaration of a 10% stock dividend on December 10, 2001, for the following independent assumptions:

1. Par value is $10 and market value is $15.
2. Par value is $5 and market value is $20.

Compare effects of a stock dividend and a stock split.
(SO 5)

E12–10   On October 31, the stockholders' equity section of Plano Company consists of common stock $800,000 and retained earnings $400,000. Plano is considering the following two courses of action: (1) declaring a 10% stock dividend on the 80,000 $10 par value shares outstanding or (2) effecting a 2-for-1 stock split that will reduce par value to $5 per share. The current market price is $15 per share.

Instructions
Prepare a tabular summary of the effects of the alternative actions on the components of stockholders' equity, outstanding shares, and book value per share. Use the following column headings: Before Action, After Stock Dividend, and After Stock Split.

E12–11 Before preparing financial statements for the current year, the chief accountant for Tanner Tucci Company discovered the following errors in the accounts:

Prepare correcting entries for dividends and a stock split.
(SO 5)

1. The declaration and payment of $25,000 cash dividend was recorded as a debit to Interest Expense $25,000 and a credit to Cash $25,000.
2. A 10% stock dividend (1,000 shares) was declared on the $10 par value stock when the market value per share was $17. The only entry made was: Retained Earnings (Dr.) $10,000 and Dividend Payable (Cr.) $10,000. The shares have not been issued.
3. A 4-for-1 stock split involving the issue of 400,000 shares of $5 par value common stock for 100,000 shares of $20 par value common stock was recorded as a debit to Retained Earnings $2,000,000 and a credit to Common Stock $2,000,000.

Instructions
Prepare the correcting entries at December 31.

E12–12 On January 1, 2001, Waikiki Corporation had Retained Earnings of $580,000. During the year, Waikiki had the following selected transactions:

Prepare a retained earnings statement.
(SO 6)

1. Declared cash dividends $120,000.
2. Corrected overstatement of 2000 net income because of depreciation error $20,000.
3. Earned net income $310,000.
4. Declared stock dividends $60,000.

Instructions
Prepare a retained earnings statement for the year.

E12–13 The ledger of Yorkville Corporation contains the following accounts: Common Stock, Preferred Stock, Treasury Stock—Common, Paid-in Capital in Excess of Par Value—Preferred Stock, Paid-in Capital in Excess of Stated Value—Common Stock, Paid-in Capital from Treasury Stock, and Retained Earnings.

Classify stockholders' equity accounts.
(SO 7)

Instructions
Classify each account using the following tabular alignment:

	Paid-in Capital			
Account	Capital Stock	Additional	Retained Earnings	Other

E12–14 The following accounts appear in the ledger of David Chambers Inc. after the books are closed at December 31.

Prepare a stockholders' equity section.
(SO 7)

Common Stock, no par, $1 stated value, 400,000 shares authorized; 300,000 shares issued	$ 300,000
Common Stock Dividends Distributable	75,000
Paid-in Capital in Excess of Stated Value—Common Stock	1,200,000
Preferred Stock, $5 par value, 8%, 40,000 shares authorized; 30,000 shares issued	150,000
Retained Earnings	900,000
Treasury Stock (10,000 common shares)	60,000
Paid-in Capital in Excess of Par Value—Preferred Stock	244,000

Instructions
Prepare the stockholders' equity section at December 31, assuming retained earnings is restricted for plant expansion in the amount of $100,000.

*E12–15 In a recent year, the stockholders' equity section of the Aluminum Company of America (Alcoa) showed the following (in alphabetical order): Additional (Paid-in) capital $680.5, Common stock $88.3, Preferred stock $66.0, and Retained earnings $3,750.2. All dollar data are in millions.

Prepare a stockholders' equity section and compute book value.
(SO 7, 9)

The preferred stock has 660,000 shares authorized with a par value of $100 and an annual $3.75 per share cumulative dividend preference. At December 31, all authorized preferred stock is issued and outstanding. There are 300 million shares of $1 par value common stock authorized, of which 88.3 million are outstanding at December 31.

Instructions
(a) Prepare the stockholders' equity section, including disclosure of all relevant data.
(b) Compute the book value per share of common stock, assuming there are no preferred dividends in arrears. (Round to two decimals.)

Compute book value per share with preferred stock.
(SO 4, 9)

*E12–16 At December 31, Oswego Corporation has total stockholders' equity of $3,000,000. Included in this total are Preferred stock $500,000 and Paid-in capital in excess of par value—Preferred stock $50,000. There are 10,000 shares of $50 par value 10% cumulative preferred stock outstanding. At year-end, 200,000 shares of common stock are outstanding.

Instructions
Compute the book value per share of common stock, under each of the following assumptions:

(a) There are no preferred dividends in arrears, and the preferred stock does not have a call price.

(b) Preferred dividends are one year in arrears, and the preferred stock has a call price of $60 per share.

Compute book value per share and indicate account balances after a stock dividend.
(SO 5, 7, 9)

*E12–17 On October 1, 2001, Manchester Corporation's stockholders' equity is as follows:

Common stock $10 par value	$200,000
Paid-in capital in excess of par value	25,000
Retained earnings	175,000
Total stockholders' equity	$400,000

On October 1, Manchester declares and distributes a 10% stock dividend when the market value of the stock is $15 per share.

Instructions

(a) Compute the book value per share (1) before the stock dividend and (2) after the stock dividend. (Round to two decimals.)

(b) Indicate the balances in the three stockholders' equity accounts after the stock dividend shares have been distributed.

PROBLEMS: SET A

Journalize stock transactions, post, and prepare paid-in capital section.
(SO 2, 4, 7)

P12–1A Jennifer Johnston Corporation was organized on January 1, 2001. It is authorized to issue 20,000 shares of 6%, $50 par value preferred stock, and 500,000 shares of no-par common stock with a stated value of $1 per share. The following stock transactions were completed during the first year:

Jan. 10 Issued 100,000 shares of common stock for cash at $3 per share.
Mar. 1 Issued 10,000 shares of preferred stock for cash at $51 per share.
Apr. 1 Issued 25,000 shares of common stock for land. The asking price of the land was $90,000; fair market value of the land was $85,000.
May 1 Issued 75,000 shares of common stock for cash at $4 per share.
Aug. 1 Issued 10,000 shares of common stock to attorneys in payment of their bill for $50,000 pertaining to services rendered in helping the company organize.
Sept. 1 Issued 5,000 shares of common stock for cash at $6 per share.
Nov. 1 Issued 2,000 shares of preferred stock for cash at $53 per share.

Instructions

(a) Journalize the transactions.

(b) Post to the stockholders' equity accounts. (Use J1 as the posting reference.)

(c) Prepare the paid-in capital section of stockholders' equity at December 31, 2001.

Journalize treasury stock transactions and prepare stockholders' equity section.
(SO 3, 7)

P12–2A S. Ayala Corporation had the following stockholders' equity account balances at June 30, 2000: Common Stock ($2 par) $600,000; Paid-in Capital in Excess of Stated Value $900,000; and Retained Earnings $250,000. During the next 9 months, the company had the following treasury stock transactions:

Aug. 1, 2000 Purchased 10,000 shares at $10 a share.
Oct. 1, 2000 Sold 3,000 shares at $11 a share.
Dec. 1, 2000 Sold 2,000 shares at $9 a share.
Apr. 1, 2001 Sold 4,000 shares at $8 a share.

The corporation uses the cost method of accounting for treasury stock. In 2000, the company earned $70,000; in 2001, it lost $10,000.

Instructions

   (a) Journalize the treasury stock transactions and the closing entry for the year 2000.
   (b) Prepare the stockholders' equity section of the balance sheet as of December 31, 2000.
   (c) Journalize the treasury stock transaction and the closing entry for the year 2001.
   (d) Prepare the stockholders' equity section of the balance sheet as of December 31, 2001.

P12–3A   The stockholders' equity accounts of Oslo Corporation on January 1, 2001, were as follows:

Preferred Stock (10%, $100 par noncumulative, 5,000 shares authorized)	$ 300,000
Common Stock ($5 stated value, 300,000 shares authorized)	1,000,000
Paid-in Capital in Excess of Par Value—Preferred Stock	15,000
Paid-in Capital in Excess of Stated Value—Common Stock	400,000
Retained Earnings	488,000
Treasury Stock—Common (5,000 shares)	40,000

Journalize and post transactions, prepare stockholders' equity section, and compute book value.
(SO 2, 3, 4, 7, 9)

During 2001, the corporation had the following transactions and events pertaining to its stockholders' equity:

Feb. 1	Issued 4,000 shares of common stock for $25,000.
Mar. 20	Purchased 1,000 additional shares of common treasury stock at $8 per share.
June 14	Sold 4,000 shares of treasury stock—common for $34,000.
Sept. 3	Issued 2,000 shares of common stock for a patent valued at $13,000.
Dec. 31	Determined that net income for the year was $215,000.

Instructions

   (a) Journalize the transactions and the closing entry for net income.
   (b) Enter the beginning balances in the accounts and post the journal entries to the stockholders' equity accounts. (Use J1 as the posting reference.)
   (c) Prepare a stockholders' equity section at December 31, 2001.
  *(d) Compute the book value per share of common stock at December 31, 2001, assuming the preferred stock does not have a call price.

P12–4A   On December 31, 2000, Dan Steffan Company had 1,500,000 shares of $10 par common stock issued and outstanding. The stockholders' equity accounts at December 31, 2000, had the following balances.

Prepare a retained earnings statement and the stockholders' equity section.
(SO 6, 7)

Common Stock	$15,000,000
Additional Paid-in Capital	1,500,000
Retained Earnings	900,000

Transactions during 2001 and other information related to stockholders' equity accounts were as follows:

   1. On January 10, 2001, Steffan issues at $110 per share 100,000 shares of $100 par value, 8% cumulative preferred stock.
   2. On February 8, 2001, Steffan reacquired 10,000 shares of its common stock for $16 per share.
   3. On June 8, 2001, Steffan declared a cash dividend of $1 per share on the common stock outstanding, payable on July 10, 2001, to stockholders of record on July 1, 2001.
   4. On December 15, 2001, Steffan declared the yearly cash dividend on preferred stock, payable January 10, 2002, to stockholders of record on December 15, 2001.
   5. Net income for the year is $3,600,000.
   6. It was discovered that depreciation expense has been overstated in 2000 by $100,000.

Instructions

   (a) Prepare a retained earnings statement for the year ended December 31, 2001.
   (b) Prepare the stockholders' equity section of Steffan's balance sheet at December 31, 2001.

P12–5A   The ledger of Pedro Corporation at December 31, 2001, after the books have been closed, contains the following stockholders' equity accounts:

Prepare retained earnings statement and stockholders' equity section.
(SO 5, 6, 7)

Preferred Stock (10,000 shares issued)	$1,000,000
Common Stock (400,000 shares issued)	2,000,000
Paid-in Capital in Excess of Par Value—Preferred	200,000
Paid-in Capital in Excess of Par Value—Common	1,200,000
Common Stock Dividends Distributable	100,000
Retained Earnings	2,540,000

A review of the accounting records reveals the following:

1. No errors have been made in recording 2001 transactions or in preparing the closing entry for net income.
2. Preferred stock is 10% $100 par value, noncumulative, and callable at $125. Since January 1, 2000, 10,000 shares have been outstanding; 20,000 shares are authorized.
3. Common stock is no-par with a stated value of $5 per share; 600,000 shares are authorized.
4. The January 1 balance in Retained Earnings was $2,200,000.
5. On October 1, 100,000 shares of common stock were sold for cash at $8 per share.
6. A cash dividend of $400,000 was declared and properly allocated to preferred and common stock on November 1. No dividends were paid to preferred stockholders in 2000.
7. On December 31, a 5% common stock dividend was declared out of retained earnings on common stock when the market price per share was $7.
8. Net income for the year was $880,000.
9. On December 31, 2001, the directors authorized disclosure of a $100,000 restriction of retained earnings for plant expansion. (Use Note A.)

Instructions
(a) Reproduce the retained earnings account (T-account) for the year.
(b) Prepare a retained earnings statement for the year.
(c) Prepare a stockholders' equity section at December 31.

Prepare entries for stock transactions and stockholders' equity section.
(SO 2, 3, 4, 7)

P12–6A Kishwaukee Corporation has been authorized to issue 20,000 shares of $100 par value, 10%, noncumulative preferred stock and 1,000,000 shares of no-par common stock. The corporation assigned a $2.50 stated value to the common stock. At December 31, 2001, the ledger contained the following balances pertaining to stockholders' equity:

Preferred Stock	$ 120,000
Paid-in Capital in Excess of Par Value—Preferred	24,000
Common Stock	1,000,000
Paid-in Capital in Excess of Stated Value—Common	2,850,000
Treasury Stock—Common (1,000 shares)	12,000
Paid-in Capital from Treasury Stock	1,000
Retained Earnings	82,000

The preferred stock was issued for land having a fair market value of $144,000. All common stock issued was for cash. In November, 1,500 shares of common stock were purchased for the treasury at a per share cost of $12. In December, 500 shares of treasury stock were sold for $14 per share. No dividends were declared in 2001.

Instructions
(a) Prepare the journal entries for the:
  (1) Issuance of preferred stock for land.
  (2) Issuance of common stock for cash.
  (3) Purchase of common treasury stock for cash.
  (4) Sale of treasury stock for cash.
(b) Prepare the stockholders' equity section at December 31, 2001.

Prepare dividend entries and stockholders' equity section.
(SO 5, 7)

P12–7A On January 1, 2001, Danish Corporation had the following stockholders' equity accounts:

Common Stock ($10 par value, 80,000 shares issued and outstanding)	$800,000
Paid-in Capital in Excess of Par Value	200,000
Retained Earnings	540,000

During the year, the following transactions occurred:

Jan. 15 Declared a $1 cash dividend per share to stockholders of record on January 31, payable February 15.
Feb. 15 Paid the dividend declared in January.
Apr. 15 Declared a 10% stock dividend to stockholders of record on April 30, distributable May 15. On April 15, the market price of the stock was $13 per share.
May 15 Issued the shares for the stock dividend.
July 1 Announced a 2-for-1 stock split. The market price per share prior to the announcement was $15. (The new par value is $5.)

Dec. 1   Declared a $0.50 per share cash dividend to stockholders of record on December 15, payable January 10, 2002.

    31   Determined that net income for the year was $220,000.

Instructions

(a) Journalize the transactions and the closing entry for net income.

(b) Enter the beginning balances and post the entries to the stockholders' equity accounts. (*Note:* Open additional stockholders' equity accounts as needed.)

(c) Prepare a stockholders' equity section at December 31, 2001.

*P12–8A   The following stockholders' equity accounts arranged alphabetically are in the ledger of Kilarny Corporation at December 31, 2001:

Prepare stockholders' equity section and compute book value.
(SO 7, 9)

Common Stock ($10 stated value)	$1,500,000
Paid-in Capital from Treasury Stock	6,000
Paid-in Capital in Excess of Par Value—Preferred Stock	280,000
Paid-in Capital in Excess of Stated Value—Common Stock	900,000
Preferred Stock (8%, $100 par, noncumulative)	400,000
Retained Earnings	1,134,000
Treasury Stock—Common (8,000 shares)	88,000

Instructions

(a) Prepare a stockholders' equity section at December 31, 2001.

(b) Compute the book value per share of the common stock, assuming the preferred stock has a call price of $110 per share.

*P12–9A   On January 1, 2001, Aurora Inc. had the following stockholders' equity balances:

Prepare stockholders' equity statement.
(SO 8)

Common Stock (500,000 shares issued)	$1,000,000
Paid-in Capital in Excess of Par Value	500,000
Stock Dividends Distributable	100,000
Retained Earnings	600,000

During 2001, the following transactions and events occurred:

1. Issued 50,000 shares of $2 par value common stock as a result of 10% stock dividend declared on December 15, 1995.
2. Issued 30,000 shares of common stock for cash at $5 per share.
3. Purchased 20,000 shares of common stock for the treasury at $6 per share.
4. Declared and paid a cash dividend of $100,000.
5. Sold 5,000 shares of treasury stock for cash at $6 per share.
6. Earned net income of $300,000.

Instructions

Prepare a stockholders' equity statement for the year.

PROBLEMS: SET B

P12–1B   D. Ramos Corporation was organized on January 1, 2001. It is authorized to issue 10,000 shares of 8%, $100 par value preferred stock, and 500,000 shares of no-par common stock with a stated value of $2 per share. The following stock transactions were completed during the first year:

Journalize stock transactions, post, and prepare paid-in capital section.
(SO 2, 4, 7)

Jan. 10   Issued 80,000 shares of common stock for cash at $3 per share.

Mar. 1   Issued 5,000 shares of preferred stock for cash at $104 per share.

Apr. 1   Issued 24,000 shares of common stock for land. The asking price of the land was $90,000; the fair market value of the land was $80,000.

May 1   Issued 80,000 shares of common stock for cash at $4 per share.

Aug. 1   Issued 10,000 shares of common stock to attorneys in payment of their bill of $50,000 for services rendered in helping the company organize.

Sept. 1   Issued 10,000 shares of common stock for cash at $5 per share.

Nov. 1   Issued 1,000 shares of preferred stock for cash at $108 per share.

Instructions

(a) Journalize the transactions.

(b) Post to the stockholders' equity accounts. (Use J5 as the posting reference.)

(c) Prepare the paid-in capital section of stockholders' equity at December 31, 2001.

Journalize treasury stock transactions and prepare stockholders' equity section.
(SO 3, 7)

P12–2B   F. Mendez Corporation had the following stockholders' equity account balances at June 30, 2000: Common Stock ($2 par) $300,000; Paid-in Capital in Excess of Par Value $450,000; and Retained Earnings $200,000. During the next 9 months, the company had the following treasury stock transactions:

Aug. 1, 2000   Purchased 8,000 shares at $8 a share.
Oct. 1, 2000   Sold 2,000 shares at $10 a share.
Dec. 1, 2000   Sold 3,000 shares at $7 a share.
Apr. 1, 2001   Sold 2,000 shares at $6 a share.

The corporation uses the cost method of accounting for treasury stock. In 2000, the company earned $50,000; in 2001, it lost $5,000.

Instructions

(a) Journalize the treasury stock transactions and the closing entry for the year 2000.

(b) Prepare the stockholders' equity section of the balance sheet as of December 31, 2000.

(c) Journalize the treasury stock transaction and the closing entry for the year 2001.

(d) Prepare the stockholders' equity section of the balance sheet as of December 31, 2001.

Journalize and post transactions, prepare stockholders' equity section, and compute book value.
(SO 2, 3, 4, 7, 9)

P12–3B   The stockholders' equity accounts of Sorrento Corporation on January 1, 2001, were as follows:

Preferred Stock (12%, $50 par cumulative, 10,000 shares authorized)	$ 400,000
Common Stock ($1 stated value, 2,000,000 shares authorized)	1,000,000
Paid-in Capital in Excess of Par Value—Preferred Stock	80,000
Paid-in Capital in Excess of Stated Value—Common Stock	1,400,000
Retained Earnings	1,816,000
Treasury Stock—Common (10,000 shares)	40,000

During 2001, the corporation had the following transactions and events pertaining to its stockholders' equity:

Feb. 1   Issued 20,000 shares of common stock for $100,000.
Apr. 14   Sold 6,000 shares of treasury stock—common for $28,000.
Sept. 3   Issued 5,000 shares of common stock for a patent valued at $25,000.
Nov. 10   Purchased 1,000 shares of common stock for the treasury at a cost of $6,000.
Dec. 31   Determined that net income for the year was $377,000.

No dividends were declared during the year.

Instructions

(a) Journalize the transactions and the closing entry for net income.

(b) Enter the beginning balances in the accounts and post the journal entries to the stockholders' equity accounts. (Use J5 for the posting reference.)

(c) Prepare a stockholders' equity section at December 31, 2001, including the disclosure of the preferred dividends in arrears.

*(d) Compute the book value per share of common stock at December 31, 2001. (Round to two decimals.)

Prepare dividend entries and stockholders' equity section.
(SO 5, 7)

P12–4B   On January 1, 2001, Skywalker Corporation had the following stockholders' equity accounts:

Common Stock ($20 par value, 60,000 shares issued and outstanding)	$1,200,000
Paid-in Capital in Excess of Par Value	200,000
Retained Earnings	500,000

During the year, the following transactions occurred:

Feb. 1   Declared a $1 cash dividend per share to stockholders of record on February 15, payable March 1.
Mar. 1   Paid the dividend declared in February.
Apr. 1   Announced a 4-for-1 stock split. Prior to the split, the market price per share was $36.
July 1   Declared a 5% stock dividend to stockholders of record on July 15, distributable July 31. On July 1, the market price of the stock was $10 per share.

July 31 Issued the shares for the stock dividend.

Dec. 1 Declared a $.50 per share dividend to stockholders of record on December 15, payable January 5, 2002.

31 Determined that net income for the year was $325,000.

Instructions

(a) Journalize the transactions and closing entries.

(b) Enter the beginning balances and post the entries to the stockholders' equity accounts. (*Note:* Open additional stockholders' equity accounts as needed.)

(c) Prepare a stockholders' equity section at December 31.

P12–5B On December 31, 2001, K. Schipper Company had 1,000,000 shares of $1 par common stock issued and outstanding. The stockholders' equity accounts at December 31, 2001, had the following balances:

Prepare a retained earnings statement and the stockholders' equity section. (SO 6, 7)

Common Stock	1,000,000
Additional Paid-in Capital	500,000
Retained Earnings	700,000

Transactions during 2002 and other information related to stockholders' equity accounts were as follows:

1. On January 9, 2002, Schipper issues at $6 per share 100,000 shares of $5 par value, 8% cumulative preferred stock.

2. On February 8, 2002, Schipper reacquired 10,000 shares of its common stock for $12 per share.

3. On June 10, 2002, Schipper declared a cash dividend of $1 per share on the common stock outstanding, payable on July 10, 2002, to stockholders of record on July 1, 2002.

4. On December 15, 2002, Schipper declared the yearly cash dividend on preferred stock, payable January 10, 2003, to stockholders of record on December 15, 2002.

5. Net income for the year is $2,400,000.

6. It was discovered that depreciation expense had been overstated in 2001 by $100,000.

Instructions

(a) Prepare a retained earnings statement for the year ended December 31, 2002.

(b) Prepare the stockholders' equity section of Schipper's balance sheet at December 31, 2002.

P12–6B The post-closing trial balance of Shmi Corporation at December 31, 2001, contains the following stockholders' equity accounts:

Prepare retained earnings statement and stockholders' equity section. (SO 5, 6, 7)

Preferred Stock (15,000 shares issued)	$ 750,000
Common Stock (250,000 shares issued)	2,500,000
Paid-in Capital in Excess of Par Value—Preferred	250,000
Paid-in Capital in Excess of Par Value—Common	500,000
Common Stock Dividends Distributable	200,000
Retained Earnings	743,000

A review of the accounting records reveals the following:

1. No errors have been made in recording 2001 transactions or in preparing the closing entry for net income.

2. Preferred stock is $50 par, 10%, and cumulative. 15,000 shares have been outstanding since January 1, 2000.

3. Authorized stock is 20,000 shares of preferred, 500,000 shares of common with a $10 par value.

4. The January 1 balance in Retained Earnings was $920,000.

5. On July 1, 20,000 shares of common stock were sold for cash at $16 per share.

6. On September 1, the company discovered an understatement error of $60,000 in computing depreciation in 2000. The net of tax effect of $42,000 was properly debited directly to Retained Earnings.

7. A cash dividend of $250,000 was declared and properly allocated to preferred and common stock on October 1. No dividends were paid to preferred stockholders in 2000.

8. On December 31, an 8% common stock dividend was declared out of retained earnings on common stock when the market price per share was $16.

9. Net income for the year was $435,000.

10. On December 31, 2001, the directors authorized disclosure of a $200,000 restriction of retained earnings for plant expansion. (Use Note X.)

Instructions

(a) Reproduce the retained earnings account for the year 2001.

(b) Prepare a retained earnings statement for the year 2001.

(c) Prepare a stockholders' equity section at December 31, 2001.

Prepare stockholders' equity section and compute book value.

(SO 7, 9)

*P12–7B The following stockholders' equity accounts arranged alphabetically are in the ledger of Clara Miller Corporation at December 31, 2001:

Common Stock ($5 stated value)	$2,500,000
Paid-in Capital from Treasury Stock	10,000
Paid-in Capital in Excess of Par Value—Preferred Stock	692,000
Paid-in Capital in Excess of Stated Value—Common Stock	1,500,000
Preferred Stock (8%, $50 par, noncumulative)	800,000
Retained Earnings	1,958,000
Treasury Stock—Common (10,000 shares)	130,000

Instructions

(a) Prepare a stockholders' equity section at December 31, 2001.

(b) Compute the book value per share of the common stock, assuming the preferred stock has a call price of $60 per share.

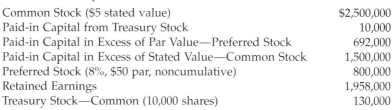

BROADENING YOUR PERSPECTIVE

FINANCIAL REPORTING AND ANALYSIS

FINANCIAL REPORTING PROBLEM: Kellogg Company

BYP12–1 The stockholders' equity section for Kellogg Company is shown in Appendix A. You will also find data relative to this problem on other pages of the appendix.

Instructions

Answer the following questions.

(a) What is the par or stated value per share of Kellogg's common stock?

(b) What percentage of Kellogg's authorized common stock was issued at December 31, 1998? (Round to the nearest full percentage.)

(c) How many shares of common stock were outstanding at December 31, 1998, and at December 31, 1997?

*(d) What was book value per share at December 31, 1998, and at December 31, 1997? (*Note:* The currency translation adjustment is part of stockholders' equity.)

(e) What was the closing market price per share at December 31, 1998, as reported under Note 12?

(f) What were the low and high quarterly cash dividends per share during the two-year period 1998 and 1997? What information concerning Kellogg's dividends is reported in the financial highlights section?

COMPARATIVE ANALYSIS PROBLEM: Kellogg Company vs. General Mills

BYP12–2 Kellogg's financial statements are presented in Appendix A; General Mill's financial statements are presented in Appendix B.

Instructions

(a) Compute return on common stockholders' equity for both companies for 1998. Assume Kellogg's weighted average shares were 407,800,000 and General Mill's weighted average shares were 158,100,000. Can these measures be used to compare the profitability of the two companies? Why or why not?

(b) What was the total amount of dividends paid by each company in 1998? What fraction of net income did the dividend represent for each company?

RESEARCH ASSIGNMENT

BYP12–3 The June 1999 issue of *Money* includes an article by David Futrelle entitled "Stock Splits: How the Dumb Get Rich."

Instructions

Read the article and answer the following questions:

(a) What is a stock split?

(b) How do anxious traders and investors obtain timely information about stock splits?

(c) What are the statistics relative to market price reactions for stocks of companies that have split their stocks?

(d) Is there a downside to buying the stock of companies that announce stock splits?

INTERPRETING FINANCIAL STATEMENTS: Kellogg Company

BYP12–4   In a recent three-year period, Kellogg Company took numerous steps aimed at improving its profitability and earnings per share. Included in these steps was the layoff of 2,000 employees, roughly 13% of Kellogg's workforce. In addition, in 1995, 1994, and 1993 the company repurchased 5,684,864, 6,194,500, and 9,487,508 of its own shares, and announced plans for significant additional repurchases in the coming years. During 1995, 1994, and 1993 amounts expended for share repurchases were $380 million, $327 million, and $548 million—nearly $1.3 billion over a three-year period. Total amounts expended for new property during this same period was $1.1 billion. Thus the company spent more money repurchasing stock than building the company. Also during this period the company issued $400 million in new debt. Presented below are some basic facts for Kellogg.

(all dollars in millions)	1995	1994
Net sales	$7,003	$6,562
Net income	490	705
Common stock, $25 par value	78	78
Capital in excess of par value	105	69
Retained earnings	3,963	3,801
Treasury stock, at cost	2,361	1,981
Preferred stock	0	0
Number of shares outstanding (in millions)	217	222

Instructions

(a) What are some of the reasons that management purchases its own stock?

(b) What was the approximate impact on earnings per share of the common stock repurchases during this three-year period? (That is, calculate 1995 earnings per share with the share repurchases and without the repurchases. Use the total repurchases during the three-year period—21,366,872 shares—rounded to 21 million.) If necessary, refer to EPS material on page 300.

REAL-WORLD FOCUS: Barrister Information Systems Corporation

BYP12–5   Barrister Information Systems Corp. develops, assembles, markets, and services computer systems and local area networks for law firms. Headquartered in Buffalo, N.Y., it has offices in 19 U.S. cities. The company has two classes of preferred stock—A and C—in addition to its common stock. The 1,300 shares of Series A preferred stock are nonvoting, have a 12% cumulative dividend, have liquidation preference rights over the Series C preferred stock and the common stock, and are callable by the company at any time for $1,000 per share plus cumulative unpaid dividends. Each share of Series A preferred stock is convertible into 500 shares of common stock. The cumulative unpaid dividends on the Series A preferred stock recently totaled $254,000.

Instructions

(a) Should the $254,000 in dividends not paid be reported as a liability on the balance sheet?

(b) If the par value of the Class A preferred stock is $100 per share, what dollar amount in dividends can the shareholders expect annually on the Class A preferred stock?

CRITICAL THINKING

GROUP DECISION CASE

BYP12–6   The stockholders' meeting for McGwire Corporation has been in progress for some time. The chief financial officer for McGwire is presently reviewing the company's financial statements and is explaining the items that comprise the stockholders' equity section of the balance sheet for the current year. The stockholders' equity section of McGwire Corporation at December 31, 2001, is as follows:

McGWIRE CORPORATION
Balance Sheet (partial)
December 31, 2001

Paid-in capital		
Capital stock		
Preferred stock, authorized 1,000,000		
shares cumulative, $100 par value, $8 per share, 6,000		
shares issued and outstanding		$ 600,000
Common stock, authorized 5,000,000 shares, $1 par		
value, 3,000,000 shares issued, and 2,700,000		
outstanding		3,000,000
Total capital stock		3,600,000
Additional paid-in capital		
In excess of par value–preferred stock	$ 50,000	
In excess of par value–common stock	25,000,000	
Total additional paid-in capital		25,050,000
Total paid-in capital		28,650,000
Retained earnings		900,000
Total paid-in capital and retained earnings		29,550,000
Less: Common treasury stock (300,000 shares)		9,300,000
Total stockholders' equity		$20,250,000

A number of questions regarding the stockholders' equity section of McGwire Corporation's balance sheet have been raised at the meeting.

Instructions
With the class divided into groups, answer the following questions as if you were the chief financial officer for McGwire Corporation.

(a) "What does the cumulative provision related to the preferred stock mean?"
(b) "I thought the common stock was presently selling at $29.75, and yet the company has the stock stated at $1 per share. How can that be?"
(c) "Why is the company buying back its common stock? Furthermore, the treasury stock has a debit balance because it is subtracted from stockholders' equity. Why is treasury stock not reported as an asset if it has a debit balance?"
(d) "Why is it necessary to show additional paid-in capital? Why not just show common stock at the total amount paid in?"

COMMUNICATION ACTIVITY

BYP12–7   Tony Baden, your uncle, is an inventor who has decided to incorporate. Uncle Tony knows that you are an accounting major at U.N.O. In a recent letter to you, he ends with the question, "I'm filling out a state incorporation application. Can you tell me the difference in the following terms: (1) authorized stock, (2) issued stock, (3) outstanding stock, (4) preferred stock?"

Instructions
In a brief note, differentiate for Uncle Tony among the four different stock terms. Write the letter to be friendly, yet professional.

ETHICS CASE

BYP12-8 The R & D division of Spencer Chemical Corp. has just developed a chemical for sterilizing the vicious Brazilian "killer bees" which are invading Mexico and the southern states of the United States. The president of Spencer is anxious to get the chemical on the market because Spencer's profits need a boost—his job is in jeopardy because of decreasing sales and profits. Spencer has an opportunity to sell this chemical in Central American countries, where the laws are much more relaxed than in the United States.

The director of Spencer's R & D division strongly recommends further testing in the laboratory for side effects of this chemical on other insects, birds, animals, plants, and even humans. He cautions the president, "We could be sued from all sides if the chemical has tragic side effects that we didn't even test for in the labs." The president answers, "We can't wait an additional year for your lab tests. We can avoid losses from such lawsuits by establishing a separate wholly owned corporation to shield Spencer Corp. from such lawsuits. We can't lose any more than our investment in the new corporation, and we'll invest just the patent covering this chemical. We'll reap the benefits if the chemical works and is safe, and avoid the losses from lawsuits if it's a disaster." The following week Spencer creates a new wholly owned corporation called Zarle Inc., sells the chemical patent to it for $10, and watches the spraying begin.

Instructions
(a) Who are the stakeholders in this situation?
(b) Are the president's motives and actions ethical?
(c) Can Spencer shield itself against losses of Zarle Inc.?

SURFING THE NET

BYP12-9 SEC filings of publicly-traded companies are available to view online.

Address: http://finance.yahoo.com/i (or go to www.wiley.com/college/weygandt)

Steps:
1. Enter stock symbol or use "Symbol Lookup."
2. Choose **Get Quotes**.

Instructions
Answer the following questions:

(a) What company did you select?
(b) What is its stock symbol?
(c) What was the stock's trading range today?
(d) What was the stock's trading range for the year?

Answers to Self-Study Questions
1. c   2. b   3. d   4. c   5. a   6. a   7. d   8. d   9. b   10. d   11. b
12. a   13. c

Answers to Kellogg Review It Question 3, p. 524 and Question 4, p. 528
3. The par value of Kellogg's common stock is $0.25 per share. Kellogg is authorized to issue 500,000,000 shares of common stock. On December 31, 1998, 415,343,626 shares had been issued.
4. Treasury shares outstanding on December 31, 1997, at Kellogg Company were 4,143,124 and on December 31, 1998, were 10,346,524. The huge difference in treasury shares is due to Kellogg's repurchases of 6.3 million common shares during 1998.

 Remember to go back to the Navigator box on the chapter-opening page and check off your completed work.

Before studying this chapter, you should know or, if necessary, review:

a. How to record the issuance of bonds. (Ch. 11, pp. 474–481)
b. How to compute and record interest. (Ch. 3, p. 105, Ch. 9, p. 387, and Ch. 11, p. 463)
c. How to record amortization of bond discount and bond premium using the straight-line method. (Ch. 11, pp. 477–480)
d. Where temporary and long-term investments are classified on a balance sheet. (Ch. 4, pp. 157–158)

THE NAVIGATOR

FEATURE STORY

Is There Anything Else We Can Buy?

In a rapidly changing world you must change rapidly or suffer the consequences. In business, to change means to invest. A case in point is found in the entertainment industry. Technology is bringing about new innovations so quickly that it is nearly impossible to guess which technologies will last and which will soon fade away. For example, consider the publishing industry. Will paper newspapers and magazines be

replaced by online news via the World Wide Web? If you are a publisher, you have to make your best guess about what the future holds and invest accordingly.

Time Warner Corporation lives at the center of this arena. It is not an environment for the timid, and Time Warner's philosophy is anything but timid. It might be characterized as "If we can't beat you, we will buy you." Its mantra is "invest, invest, invest." An abbreviated list of Time Warner's holdings gives an idea of its reach. Magazines: *People,*

Time, Life, Sports Illustrated, Fortune. Book publishers: Time-Life Books, Book-of-the-Month Club, Little, Brown & Co. Music: Warner Bros., Reprise, Atlantic, Rhino. Television and movies: Warner Bros. ("ER" and "Friends"), HBO, and movies like *Batman Forever.* And, in 1996 Time Warner merged with Turner Broadcasting, so it now owns TNT, CNN, and Turner's library of thousands of classic movies. Even before the Turner merger, Time Warner owned more information and entertainment copyrights and brands than any other company in the world.

So what has Time Warner's aggressive acquisition spree meant for the bottom line? It has left Time Warner with huge debt and massive interest costs. In addition, some of the acquisitions have not come cheap, resulting in large amounts of reported goodwill and goodwill amortization. As a consequence, since the merger of Time and Warner in 1988, the combined corporation has reported net losses in all but two years through 1998, and many analysts expect losses for some time longer. With so much investing by Time Warner and so little profit to show for it, one is reminded of one more of its companies, Looney Tunes cartoons—"That's all, folks."

THE NAVIGATOR

On the World Wide Web
http://www.timewarner.com

CHAPTER 13

THE NAVIGATOR ✓

- Understand *Concepts for Review* ☐
- Read *Feature Story* ☐
- Scan *Study Objectives* ☐
- Read *Preview* ☐
- Read text and answer *Before You Go On*
  p. 571 ☐ p. 576 ☐ p. 583 ☐
- Work *Demonstration Problems* ☐
- Review *Summary of Study Objectives* ☐
- Answer *Self-Study Questions* ☐
- Complete assignments ☐

INVESTMENTS

STUDY OBJECTIVES

After studying this chapter, you should be able to:

1. *Identify the reasons corporations invest in stocks and debt securities.*
2. *Explain the accounting for debt investments.*
3. *Explain the accounting for stock investments.*
4. *Describe the purpose and usefulness of consolidated financial statements.*
5. *Indicate how debt and stock investments are valued and reported on the financial statements.*
6. *Distinguish between temporary and long-term investments.*

THE NAVIGATOR

*T*ime Warner's management believes in a policy of aggressive growth through investing in the stock of existing companies. In addition to purchasing stock, companies also purchase other securities such as debt securities issued by corporations or by governments. Investments can be purchased for a short or long period of time, as a passive investment, or with the intent to control another company. As you will see later in the chapter, the way in which a company accounts for its investments is determined by a number of factors.

The content and organization of this chapter are as follows:

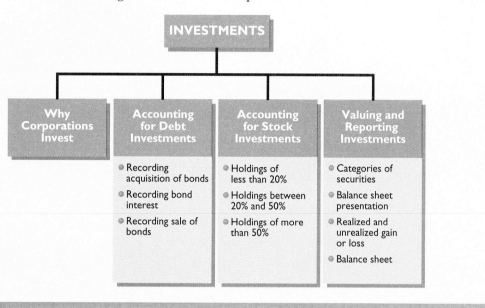

THE NAVIGATOR

WHY CORPORATIONS INVEST

1
STUDY
OBJECTIVE

Identify the reasons corporations invest in stocks and debt securities.

Corporations purchase investments in debt or equity securities generally for one of three reasons. First, a corporation may **have excess cash** that it does not need for the immediate purchase of operating assets. For example, many companies experience seasonal fluctuations in sales. A Cape Cod marina has more sales in the spring and summer than in the fall and winter, whereas the reverse is true for an Aspen ski shop. Thus, at the end of an operating cycle, many companies may have cash on hand that is temporarily idle pending the start of another operating cycle. Until the cash is needed, these companies may invest the excess funds to earn, through interest and dividends, a greater return than they would get by just holding the funds in the bank. The role played by such temporary investments in the operating cycle is depicted in Illustration 13-1.

A second reason some companies purchase investments is that they generate a **significant portion of their earnings from investment income.** Although banks make most of their earnings by lending money, they also generate earnings by investing in debt and equity securities. Banks purchase investment securities because loan demand varies both seasonally and with changes in the economic climate. Thus, when loan demand is low, a bank must find other uses for its cash. Investing in securities also allows banks to diversify some of their

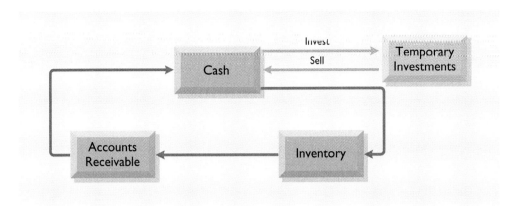

ILLUSTRATION 13-1

Temporary investments and the operating cycle

risk. Bank regulators severely limit the ability of banks to invest in common stock; therefore, most investments held by banks are debt securities.

Pension funds and mutual funds are corporations that also regularly invest to generate earnings. However, they do so for **speculative reasons**; that is, they are speculating that the investment will increase in value and thus result in positive returns. Therefore, they invest primarily in the common stock of other corporations. These investments are passive in nature; the pension fund or mutual fund does not usually take an active role in controlling the affairs of the companies in which they invest.

A third reason why companies invest is for **strategic reasons**. A company may purchase a noncontrolling interest in another firm in a related industry in which it wishes to establish a presence. For example, Time Warner initially purchased an interest of less than 20% in Turner Broadcasting to have a stake in Turner's expanding business opportunities. Similarly, Canadian giant Seagram purchased a significant interest in Time Warner. (Thus, not even a huge corporation like Time Warner is at the top of the corporate "food chain.") Alternatively, a company can exercise some influence over one of its customers or suppliers by purchasing a significant, but not controlling, interest in that company.

In summary, businesses invest in other companies for the reasons shown in Illustration 13-2.

ILLUSTRATION 13-2

Why corporations invest

Reason	Typical Investment
To house excess cash until needed	Low-risk, high-liquidity, short-term securities such as government-issued securities
To generate earnings I need 1,000 Treasury bills by tonight. BANK	Debt securities (banks and other financial institutions); and stock securities (mutual funds and pension funds)
To meet strategic goals	Stocks of companies in a related industry or in an unrelated industry that the company wishes to enter

ACCOUNTING FOR DEBT INVESTMENTS

2
STUDY
OBJECTIVE

Explain the accounting for debt investments.

Debt investments are investments in government and corporation bonds. In accounting for debt investments, entries are required to record (1) the acquisition, (2) the interest revenue, and (3) the sale.

Recording Acquisition of Bonds

At acquisition, the cost principle applies. Cost includes all expenditures necessary to acquire these investments, such as the price paid plus brokerage fees (commissions), if any. Assume, for example, that Kuhl Corporation acquires 50 Doan Inc. 12%, 10-year, $1,000 bonds on January 1, 2001, for $54,000, including brokerage fees of $1,000. The entry to record the investment is:

```
A    =  L  +  SE
+54,000
-54,000
```

Jan. 1	Debt Investments	54,000	
	Cash		54,000
	(To record purchase of 50 Doan Inc. bonds)		

Recording Bond Interest

The bonds pay interest of $3,000 semiannually on July 1 and January 1 ($50,000 × 12% × ½). The entry for the receipt of interest on July 1 is:

```
A    =  L  +  SE
+3,000       +3,000
```

July 1	Cash	3,000	
	Interest Revenue		3,000
	(To record receipt of interest on Doan Inc. bonds)		

If Kuhl Corporation's fiscal year ends on December 31, it is necessary to accrue the interest of $3,000 earned since July 1. The adjusting entry is:

```
A    =  L  +  SE
+3,000       +3,000
```

Dec. 31	Interest Receivable	3,000	
	Interest Revenue		3,000
	(To accrue interest on Doan Inc. bonds)		

Interest Receivable is reported as a current asset in the balance sheet; Interest Revenue is reported under Other Revenues and Gains in the income statement. When the interest is received on January 1, the entry is:

```
A    =  L  +  SE
+3,000
-3,000
```

Jan. 1	Cash	3,000	
	Interest Receivable		3,000
	(To record receipt of accrued interest)		

A credit to Interest Revenue at this time is incorrect because the interest revenue was earned and accrued in the preceding accounting period.

Recording Sale of Bonds

When the bonds are sold, it is necessary to credit the investment account for the cost of the bonds. Any difference between the net proceeds (sales price less brokerage fees) from sale and the cost of the bonds is recorded as a gain or loss. Assume, for example, that Kuhl Corporation receives net proceeds of $58,000 on the sale of the Doan Inc. bonds on January 1, 2002, after receiving the interest due. Since the securities cost $54,000, a gain of $4,000 has been realized. The entry to record the sale is:

Jan. 1	Cash	58,000	
	Debt Investments		54,000
	Gain on Sale of Debt Investments		4,000
	(To record sale of Doan Inc. bonds)		

A	=	L	+	SE
+ 58,000				
−54,000				+4,000

The gain on sale of debt investments is reported under Other Revenues and Gains in the income statement.

The accounting for temporary debt investments and for long-term debt investments is similar. The major exception is when bonds are purchased at a premium or discount. For temporary investments, the bond premium or discount is not amortized to interest revenue because the bonds are held for a short period of time and a misstatement of interest revenue for such a period is not considered material. For long-term investments, however, any bond premium or discount is amortized to interest revenue over the remaining term of the bonds. Like the issuer of the bonds, the investor uses either the straight-line or the effective-interest method of amortization. The effective-interest method is required under generally accepted accounting principles when the annual amounts of the two amortization methods are materially different.

BEFORE YOU GO ON . . .

Review It

1. Why might a company purchase debt or equity investments?
2. What entries are required in accounting for debt investments?
3. How does the accounting for a temporary debt investment differ from that for a long-term debt investment?

Do It

The Waldo Corporation had the following transactions pertaining to debt investments:

Jan. 1   Purchased 30 10%, $1,000 Hillary Co. bonds for $30,000 plus brokerage fees of $900. Interest is payable semiannually on July 1 and January 1.

July 1   Received semiannual interest on Hillary Co. bonds.

July 1   Sold 15 Hillary Co. bonds for $15,000 less $400 brokerage fees.

(a) Journalize the transactions, and (b) prepare the adjusting entry for the accrual of interest on December 31.

Reasoning: Bond investments are recorded at cost. Interest is recorded when received and/or accrued. When bonds are sold, the investment account is credited for the cost of the bonds. Any difference between the cost and the net proceeds is recorded as a gain or loss.

Solution:

(a) Jan. 1	Debt Investments	30,900	
	Cash		30,900
	(To record purchase of 30 Hillary Co. bonds)		
July 1	Cash	1,500	
	Interest Revenue ($30,000 × .10 × 6/12)		1,500
	(To record receipt of interest on Hillary Co. bonds)		
July 1	Cash	14,600	
	Loss on Sale of Debt Investments	850	
	Debt Investments ($30,900 ÷ 15/30)		15,450
	(To record sale of 15 Hillary Co. bonds)		
(b) Dec. 31	Interest Receivable	750	
	Interest Revenue ($15,000 × .10 × 6/12)		750
	(To accrue interest on Hillary Co. bonds)		

Related exercise material: BE13–1 and E13–1.

THE NAVIGATOR

ACCOUNTING FOR STOCK INVESTMENTS

3
STUDY
OBJECTIVE

Explain the accounting for stock investments.

Stock investments are investments in the capital stock of corporations. When a company holds stock (and/or debt) of several different corporations, the group of securities is identified as an investment portfolio. The accounting for investments in common stock is based on the extent of the investor's influence over the operating and financial affairs of the issuing corporation (commonly called the **investee**) as shown in Illustration 13-3. In some cases, depending on the degree of investor influence, net income of the investee is considered to be income to the investor.

ILLUSTRATION 13-3

Accounting guidelines for stock investments

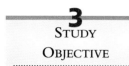

Investor's Ownership Interest in Investee's Common Stock	Presumed Influence on Investee	Accounting Guidelines
Less than 20%	Insignificant	Cost method
Between 20% and 50%	Significant	Equity method
More than 50%	Controlling	Consolidated financial statements

INTERNATIONAL NOTE

A recent study demonstrated the peril of investing overseas. For the same company under different reporting systems, income was $84,600, $260,600, $240,600, and $10,402 in the United States, the United Kingdom, Australia, and West Germany, respectively.

The presumed influence may be negated by extenuating circumstances. For example, a company that acquires a 25% interest in another company in a "hostile" takeover may not have any significant influence over the investee.[1] In other words, companies are required to use judgment instead of blindly following the guidelines. On the following pages we will explain and illustrate the application of each guideline.

Holdings of Less Than 20%

In accounting for stock investments of less than 20%, the cost method is used. Under the cost method, the investment is recorded at cost and revenue is recognized only when cash dividends are received.

Recording Acquisition of Stock Investments

At acquisition, the cost principle applies. Cost includes all expenditures necessary to acquire these investments, such as the price paid plus brokerage fees (commissions), if any. Assume, for example, that on July 1, 2001, Sanchez Corporation acquires 1,000 shares (10% ownership) of Beal Corporation common stock at $40 per share plus brokerage fees of $500. The entry for the purchase is:

---

[1]Among the factors that should be considered in determining an investor's influence are whether (1) the investor has representation on the investee's board of directors, (2) the investor participates in the investee's policy-making process, (3) there are material transactions between the investor and investee, and (4) the common stock held by other stockholders is concentrated or dispersed.

July 1	Stock Investments	40,500	
	Cash		40,500
	(To record purchase of 1,000 shares of Beal		
	Corporation common stock)		

A = L + SE
+40,500
40,500

Recording Dividends

During the time the stock is held, entries are required for any cash dividends received. Thus, if a $2.00 per share dividend is received by Sanchez Corporation on December 31, the entry is:

Dec. 31	Cash (1,000 × $2)	2,000	
	Dividend Revenue		2,000
	(To record receipt of a cash dividend)		

A = L + SE
+2,000   +2,000

Dividend Revenue is reported under Other Revenues and Gains in the income statement. Unlike interest on notes and bonds, dividends do not accrue. Therefore, adjusting entries are not made to accrue dividends.

Recording Sale of Stock

When stock is sold, the difference between the net proceeds (sales price less brokerage fees) from the sale and the cost of the stock is recognized as a gain or a loss. Assume, for instance, that Sanchez Corporation receives net proceeds of $39,500 on the sale of its Beal stock on February 10, 2002. Because the stock cost $40,500, a loss of $1,000 has been incurred. The entry to record the sale is:

Feb. 10	Cash	39,500	
	Loss on Sale of Stock Investments	1,000	
	Stock Investments		40,500
	(To record sale of Beal common stock)		

A = L + SE
+39,500   −1,000
−40,500

The loss account is reported under Other Expenses and Losses in the income statement, whereas a gain on sale is shown under Other Revenues and Gains.

HELPFUL HINT
The entries for investments in common stock also apply to investments in preferred stock.

Holdings between 20% and 50%

When an investor company owns only a small portion of the shares of stock of another company (the investee), the investor cannot exercise control over the company. When an investor owns between 20% and 50% of the common stock of a corporation, however, it is generally presumed that the investor has significant influence over the financial and operating activities of the investee. The investor probably has a representative on the investee's board of directors. With a representative on the board, the investor begins to exercise some control over the investee—and the investee company in some sense really becomes part of the investor company.

For example, even prior to purchasing all of Turner Broadcasting, Time Warner owned 20% of Turner. Because it exercised significant control over major decisions made by Turner, Time Warner used an approach called the equity method. Under the equity method, **the investor records its share of the net income of the investee in the year when it is earned.** To delay recognizing the investor's share of net income until a cash dividend is declared ignores the fact that the investor and investee are, in some sense, one company, so the investor is better off by the investee's earned income.

Under the equity method, the investment in common stock is initially recorded at cost, and the investment account is **adjusted annually** to show the investor's equity in the investee. Each year, the investor (1) increases (debits) the investment account and increases (credits) revenue for its share of the investee's net income[2]

HELPFUL HINT
Revenue is recognized under the equity method on the accrual basis—i.e., when it is earned by the investee.

---

[2]Conversely, the investor increases (debits) a loss account and decreases (credits) the investment account for its share of the investee's net loss.

and (2) decreases (credits) the investment account for the amount of dividends received. The investment account is reduced for dividends received because the net assets of the investee are decreased when a dividend is paid.

Recording Acquisition of Stock Investments

Assume that Milar Corporation acquires 30% of the common stock of Beck Company for $120,000 on January 1, 2001. The entry to record this transaction is:

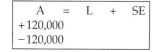

Jan. 1	Stock Investments	120,000	
	Cash		120,000
	(To record purchase of Beck common stock)		

Recording Revenue and Dividends

For 2001, Beck reports net income of $100,000 and declares and pays a $40,000 cash dividend. Milar is required to record (1) its share of Beck's income, $30,000 (30% × $100,000) and (2) the reduction in the investment account for the dividends received, $12,000 ($40,000 × 30%). The entries are:

(1)

Dec. 31	Stock Investments	30,000	
	Revenue from Investment in Beck Company		30,000
	(To record 30% equity in Beck's 2001 net income)		

(2)

Dec. 31	Cash	12,000	
	Stock Investments		12,000
	(To record dividends received)		

After posting the transactions for the year, the investment and revenue accounts will show the following:

ILLUSTRATION 13-4

Investment and revenue accounts after posting

	Stock Investments				Revenue from Investment in Beck Company	
Jan. 1	120,000	Dec. 31	12,000		Dec. 31	30,000
Dec. 31	30,000					
Dec. 31 Bal.	138,000					

During the year, the investment account has increased by $18,000. This $18,000 is Milar's 30% equity in the $60,000 increase in Beck's retained earnings ($100,000 − $40,000). In addition, Milar will report $30,000 of revenue from its investment, which is 30% of Beck's net income of $100,000. Note that the difference between reported income under the cost method and reported revenue under the equity method can be significant. For example, Milar would report only $12,000 of dividend revenue (30% × $40,000) if the cost method were used.

Holdings of More Than 50%

A company that owns more than 50% of the common stock of another entity is known as the parent company. The entity whose stock is owned by the parent company is called the subsidiary (affiliated) company. Because of its stock ownership, the parent company has a controlling interest in the subsidiary company.

When a company owns more than 50% of the common stock of another company, consolidated financial statements are usually prepared. Consolidated fi-

4
STUDY OBJECTIVE

Describe the purpose and usefulness of consolidated financial statements.

nancial statements present the assets and liabilities controlled by the parent company and the aggregate profitability of the subsidiary companies. They are prepared **in addition to** the financial statements for each of the individual parent and subsidiary companies. As noted earlier, prior to acquiring all of Turner Broadcasting, Time Warner accounted for its investment in Turner using the equity method. Time Warner's net investment in Turner was reported in a single line item—Other Investments. After the merger, Time Warner instead consolidated Turner's results with its own. Under this approach, the individual assets and liabilities of Turner are included with those of Time Warner; its plant and equipment are added to Time Warner's plant and equipment, its receivables are added to Time Warner's receivables, and so on.

Consolidated statements are especially useful to the stockholders, board of directors, and management of the parent company. Moreover, consolidated statements inform creditors, prospective investors, and regulatory agencies as to the magnitude and scope of operations of the companies under common control. For example, regulators and the courts undoubtedly used the consolidated statements of AT&T to determine whether a breakup of AT&T was in the public interest. Listed below are three companies that prepare consolidated statements and some of the companies they have owned. Note that one, Disney, is Time Warner's arch rival.

HELPFUL HINT
If parent (A) has three wholly owned subsidiaries (B, C, & D), there are four separate legal entities, but only one economic entity from the viewpoint of the shareholders of the parent company.

Beatrice Foods	American Brands, Inc.	The Walt Disney Company
Tropicana Frozen Juices	American Tobacco Company	Capital Cities/ABC, Inc.
Switzer Candy Company	Master Lock Company	Disneyland, Disney World
Samsonite Corporation	Pinkerton's Security Service	Mighty Ducks
Dannon Yogurt Company	Titleist Golf Company	Anaheim Angels
		ESPN

The preparation of consolidated financial statements is discussed in the appendix to this chapter.

ACCOUNTING IN ACTION
Business Insight

Time Warner, Inc., owns 100% of the common stock of Home Box Office (HBO) Corporation. The common stockholders of Time Warner elect the board of directors of the company, who, in turn, select the officers and managers of the company. The board of directors controls the property owned by the corporation, which includes the common stock of HBO. Thus, they are in a position to elect the board of directors of HBO and, in effect, control its operations. These relationships are graphically illustrated here:

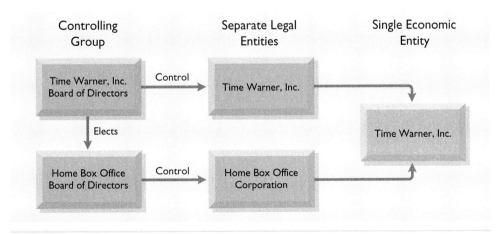

BEFORE YOU GO ON . . .

Review It

1. What are the accounting entries for investments in stock for which ownership is less than 20%?
2. What entries are made under the equity method when (a) the investor receives a cash dividend from the investee and (b) the investee reports net income for the year?
3. What is the purpose of consolidated financial statements?
4. What does Kellogg Company state regarding its accounting policy involving consolidated financial statements? The answer to this question is provided on page 604.

Do It

Presented below are two independent situations:

1. Rho Jean Inc. acquired 5% of the 400,000 shares of common stock of Stillwater Corp. at a total cost of $6 per share on May 18, 2001. On August 30, Stillwater declared and paid a $75,000 dividend. On December 31, Stillwater reported net income of $244,000 for the year.
2. Debbie, Inc., obtained significant influence over North Sails by buying 40% of North Sails' 60,000 outstanding shares of common stock at a cost of $12 per share on January 1, 2001. On April 15, North Sails declared and paid a cash dividend of $45,000. On December 31, North Sails reported a net income of $120,000 for the year.

Prepare all necessary journal entries for 2001 for (1) Rho Jean Inc. and (2) Debbie, Inc.

Reasoning: When an investor owns less than 20% of the common stock of another corporation, it is presumed that the investor has relatively little influence over the investee. As a result, net income earned by the investee is not considered a proper basis for recognizing income from the investment by the investor. For investments of 20%–50%, significant influence is presumed, and, therefore, the investor's share of the net income of the investee should be recorded.

Solution:

(1) May 18	Stock Investments (20,000 × $6)
	    Cash
	        (To record purchase of 20,000 shares of
	        Stillwater Corp. stock)
		120,000		120,000

Aug. 30	Cash
	    Dividend Revenue ($75,000 × 5%)
	        (To record receipt of cash dividend)
		3,750		3,750

(2) Jan. 1	Stock Investments (60,000 × 40% × $12)
	    Cash
	        (To record purchase of 24,000 shares of
	        North Sails' stock)
		288,000		288,000

Apr. 15	Cash
	    Stock Investments ($45,000 × 40%)
	        (To record receipt of cash dividend)
		18,000		18,000

Dec. 31	Stock Investments ($120,000 × 40%)
	    Revenue from Investment in North Sails
	        (To record 40% equity in North Sails' net
	        income)
		48,000		48,000

Related exercise material: BE13–2, BE13–3, E13–1, E13–2, E13–3, E13–4, and E13–5.

THE
NAVIGATOR

VALUING AND REPORTING INVESTMENTS

The value of debt and stock investments may fluctuate greatly during the time they are held. For example, in one 12-month period, the stock of Digital Equipment Corporation hit a high of $76\frac{1}{2}$ and a low of $28\frac{3}{8}$. In light of such price fluctuations, how should investments be valued at the balance sheet date? Valuation could be at cost, at fair value (market value), or at the lower of cost or market value. Many people argue that fair value offers the best approach because it represents the expected cash realizable value of securities. Fair value is the amount for which a security could be sold in a normal market. Others counter that, unless a security is going to be sold soon, the fair value is not relevant because the price of the security will likely change again.

5
STUDY
OBJECTIVE

Indicate how debt and stock investments are valued and reported on the financial statements.

Categories of Securities

For purposes of valuation and reporting at a financial statement date, debt and stock investments are classified into three categories of securities:

1. Trading securities are securities bought and held primarily for sale in the near term to generate income on short-term price differences.
2. Available-for-sale securities are securities that may be sold in the future.
3. Held-to-maturity securities are debt securities that the investor has the intent and ability to hold to maturity.

The valuation guidelines for these securities are shown in Illustration 13-5. These guidelines apply to all debt securities and all stock investments where the holdings are less than 20%.

ILLUSTRATION 13-5

Valuation guidelines

Trading

At fair value with changes reported in net income

Available-for-sale

At fair value with changes reported in the stockholders' equity section

Held-to-maturity

At amortized cost[3]

Trading Securities

Trading securities are held with the intention of selling them in a short period of time (generally less than a month). Trading means frequent buying and selling. As indicated in Illustration 13-5, trading securities are reported at fair value, and changes from cost are reported as part of net income. The changes are reported as **unrealized gains or losses** because the securities have not been sold.

---

[3]This category is provided for completeness. The accounting and valuation issues related to held-to-maturity securities are discussed in more advanced accounting courses.

The unrealized gain or loss is the difference between the **total cost** of the securities in the category and their **total fair value.**

As an example, Illustration 13-6 shows the cost and fair values for investments classified as trading securities for Pace Corporation on December 31, 2001. Pace Corporation has an unrealized gain of $7,000 because total fair value ($147,000) is $7,000 greater than total cost ($140,000).

ILLUSTRATION 13-6

Valuation of trading securities

Trading Securities, December 31, 2001

Investments	Cost	Fair Value	Unrealized Gain (Loss)
Yorkville Company bonds	$ 50,000	$ 48,000	$(2,000)
Kodak Company stock	90,000	99,000	9,000
Total	$140,000	$147,000	$ 7,000

HELPFUL HINT

An unrealized gain or loss is reported in the income statement because of the likelihood that the securities will be sold at fair value since they are a short-term investment.

A	=	L	+	SE
+7,000				+7,000

The fact that trading securities are a short-term investment increases the likelihood that they will be sold at fair value (the company may not be able to time their sale) and the likelihood that there will be an unrealized gain or loss. Fair value and unrealized gain or loss are recorded through an adjusting entry at the time financial statements are prepared. In the entry, a valuation allowance account, Market Adjustment—Trading, is used to record the difference between the total cost and the total fair value of the securities. The adjusting entry for Pace Corporation is:

Dec. 31	Market Adjustment—Trading	7,000	
	Unrealized Gain—Income		7,000
	(To record unrealized gain on trading securities)		

The use of a Market Adjustment—Trading account enables the company to maintain a record of the investment cost. Actual cost is needed to determine the gain or loss realized when the securities are sold. The Market Adjustment—Trading balance is added to the cost of the investments to arrive at a fair value for the trading securities.

The fair value of the securities is the amount reported on the balance sheet. The unrealized gain is reported on the income statement in the Other Revenues and Gains section. The term income is used in the account title to indicate that the gain affects net income. When the total cost of the trading securities is greater than total fair value, an unrealized loss has occurred. In such a case, the adjusting entry is a debit to Unrealized Loss—Income and a credit to Market Adjustment—Trading. The unrealized loss is reported under Other Expenses and Losses in the income statement.

The market adjustment account is carried forward into future accounting periods. No entries are made to this account during the period. At the end of each reporting period, the balance in the account is adjusted to the difference between cost and fair value. The Unrealized Gain or Loss—Income account is closed at the end of the reporting period.

Available-for-Sale Securities

As indicated earlier, available-for-sale securities are held with the intent of selling them sometime in the future. If the intent is to sell the securities within the next year or operating cycle, the securities are classified as current assets in the balance sheet. Otherwise, they are classified as long-term assets in the investments section of the balance sheet.

ETHICS NOTE

Some managers appear to manage their reported earnings by holding their available-for-sale securities that have experienced losses, while selling those that have gains, thus increasing income. Do you think this is ethical?

Available-for-sale securities are also reported at fair value. The procedure for determining fair value and the unrealized gain or loss for these securities is the same as for trading securities. To illustrate, assume that Elbert Corporation has two securities that are classified as available-for-sale. Illustration 13-7 provides information on cost, fair value, and the amount of the unrealized gain or loss. For Elbert Corporation, there is an unrealized loss of $9,537 because total cost ($293,537) is $9,537 more than total fair value ($284,000).

Available-for-Sale Securities, December 31, 2001

Investments	Cost	Fair Value	Unrealized Gain (Loss)
Campbell Soup Corporation 8% bonds	$ 93,537	$103,600	$ 10,063
Hershey Foods Corp. stock	200,000	180,400	(19,600)
Total	$293,537	$284,000	$ (9,537)

ILLUSTRATION 13-7

Valuation of available-for-sale securities

Both the adjusting entry and the reporting of the unrealized gain or loss from available-for-sale securities differ from those illustrated for trading securities. The differences result because these securities are not going to be sold in the near term. Thus, prior to actual sale there is a much greater likelihood of changes in fair value that may reverse either unrealized gains or losses. Accordingly, an unrealized gain or loss is not reported in the income statement. Instead, it is reported as a **separate component of stockholders' equity.** In the adjusting entry, the market adjustment account is identified with the label "available-for-sale" securities, and the unrealized gain or loss account is identified with the label "equity". The adjusting entry for Elbert Corporation to record the unrealized loss of $9,537 is as follows:

Dec. 31	Unrealized Loss—Equity	9,537	
	Market Adjustment—Available-for-Sale		9,537
	(To record unrealized loss on available-for-sale securities)		

A	=	L	+	SE
−9,537				−9,537

If total fair value exceeds total cost, the adjusting entry would have a debit to the market adjustment account and a credit to an unrealized gain account.

For available-for-sale securities, the unrealized gain or loss account is carried forward to future periods. At each future balance sheet date, it is adjusted with the market adjustment account to show the difference between cost and fair value at that time.

Balance Sheet Presentation

For balance sheet presentation, investments are classified as either temporary or long-term.

Temporary Investments

Temporary investments are securities held by a company that are (1) **readily marketable** and (2) **intended to be converted into cash** within the next year or operating cycle, whichever is longer. Investments that do not meet **both criteria** are classified as long-term investments. In a recent survey of 600 large U.S. companies, over 400 reported temporary investments.

6
STUDY
OBJECTIVE

Distinguish between temporary and long-term investments.

Readily Marketable.   An investment is readily marketable when it can be sold easily whenever the need for cash arises. Short-term paper[4] meets this criterion because it can be sold readily to other investors. Stocks and bonds traded on organized securities markets, such as the New York Stock Exchange, are readily marketable because they can be bought and sold daily. In contrast, there may be only a limited market for the securities issued by small corporations and no market for the securities of a privately held company.

HELPFUL HINT

Trading securities are always classified as temporary. Available-for-sale securities can be either temporary or long-term.

Intent to Convert.   Intent to convert means that management intends to sell the investment within the next year or operating cycle, whichever is longer. Generally, this criterion is satisfied when the investment is considered a resource that will be used whenever the need for cash arises. For example, a ski resort may invest idle cash during the summer months with the intent to sell the securities to buy supplies and equipment shortly before the next winter season. This investment is considered temporary even if lack of snow cancels the next ski season and eliminates the need to convert the securities into cash as intended.

Because of their high liquidity, temporary investments are listed immediately below Cash in the current assets section of the balance sheet. Temporary investments are reported at fair value. For example, Pace Corporation would report its trading securities as shown in Illustration 13-8.

ILLUSTRATION 13-8

Presentation of temporary investments

PACE CORPORATION	
Balance Sheet (partial)	
Current assets	
Cash	$ 21,000
Temporary investments, at fair value	147,000

Long-Term Investments

Long-term investments are generally reported in a separate section of the balance sheet immediately below Current assets, as shown later in Illustration 13-11. Long-term investments in available-for-sale securities are reported at fair value, and investments in common stock accounted for under the equity method are reported at equity.

Presentation of Realized and Unrealized Gain or Loss

Gains and losses on investments, whether realized or unrealized, must be presented in the financial statements. In the income statement, gains and losses, as well as interest and dividend revenue, are reported in the nonoperating section under the categories listed in Illustration 13-9.

---

[4]Short-term paper includes (1) certificates of deposits (CDs) issued by banks, (2) money market certificates issued by banks and savings and loan associations, (3) Treasury bills issued by the U.S. government, and (4) commercial paper issued by corporations with good credit ratings.

Other Revenue and Gains	Other Expenses and Losses
Interest Revenue	Loss on Sales of Investments
Dividend Revenue	Unrealized Loss—Income
Gain on Sale of Investments	
Unrealized Gain—Income	

ILLUSTRATION 13-9

Nonoperating items related to investments

As indicated earlier, an unrealized gain or loss on available-for-sale securities is reported as a separate component of stockholders' equity. To illustrate, assume that Dawson Inc. has common stock of $3,000,000, retained earnings of $1,500,000, and an unrealized loss on available-for-sale securities of $100,000. The statement presentation of the unrealized loss is shown in Illustration 13-10.

ILLUSTRATION 13-10

Unrealized loss in stockholders' equity section

DAWSON INC. Balance Sheet (partial)	
Stockholders' equity	
Common stock	$3,000,000
Retained earnings	1,500,000
Total paid-in capital and retained earnings	4,500,000
Less: **Unrealized loss on available-for-sale securities**	(100,000)
Total stockholders' equity	$4,400,000

Note that the presentation of the loss is similar to the presentation of the cost of treasury stock in the stockholders' equity section. An unrealized gain is added in this section. Reporting the unrealized gain or loss in the stockholders' equity section serves two important purposes: (1) It reduces the volatility of net income due to fluctuations in fair value, and (2) it informs the financial statement user of the gain or loss that would occur if the securities were sold at fair value.

A new accounting standard requires that items such as this, which affect stockholders' equity but are not included in the calculation of net income, must be reported as part of a more inclusive measure called *comprehensive income*. Comprehensive income is discussed in Chapter 15.

Balance Sheet

Many sections of classified balance sheets have been presented in this and preceding chapters. The comprehensive balance sheet in Illustration 13-11 on page 582 includes such topics from previous chapters as the issuance of par value common stock, restrictions of retained earnings, and issuance of long-term bonds. From this chapter, the statement includes (highlighted in red) temporary and long-term investments. The investments in temporary securities are considered trading securities; the long-term investments in stock of less than 20% owned companies are considered available-for-sale securities. Illustration 13-11 also includes a long-term investment reported at equity and descriptive notations within the statement, such as the basis for valuing merchandise and two notes to the statement.

ILLUSTRATION 13-11

Comprehensive balance sheet

PACE CORPORATION
Balance Sheet
December 31, 2001

Assets

Current assets
Cash			$ 21,000
Temporary investments, at fair value			147,000
Accounts receivable		$ 84,000	
Less: Allowance for doubtful accounts		4,000	80,000
Merchandise inventory, at FIFO cost			43,000
Prepaid insurance			23,000
Total current assets			314,000

Investments
Investment in bonds		100,000	
Investments in stock of less than 20% owned companies, at fair value		50,000	
Investment in stock of 20–50% owned company, at equity		150,000	
Total investments			300,000

Property, plant, and equipment
Land		200,000	
Buildings	$800,000		
Less: Accumulated depreciation	200,000	600,000	
Equipment	180,000		
Less: Accumulated depreciation	54,000	126,000	
Total property, plant, and equipment			926,000

Intangible assets
Goodwill (Note 1)		100,000	
Patents		70,000	
Total intangible assets			170,000
Total assets			$1,710,000

Liabilities and Stockholders' Equity

Current liabilities
Accounts payable			$ 185,000
Bond interest payable			10,000
Federal income taxes payable			60,000
Total current liabilities			255,000

Long-term liabilities
Bonds payable, 10%, due 2010		$ 300,000	
Less: Discount on bonds		10,000	
Total long-term liabilities			290,000
Total liabilities			545,000

Stockholders' equity
Paid-in capital
Common stock, $10 par value, 200,000 shares authorized, 80,000 shares issued and outstanding		800,000	
Paid-in capital in excess of par value		100,000	
Total paid-in capital		900,000	
Retained earnings (Note 2)		255,000	
Total paid-in capital and retained earnings		1,155,000	
Add: Unrealized gain on available-for-sale securities		10,000	
Total stockholders' equity			1,165,000
Total liabilities and stockholders' equity			$1,710,000

Note 1. Goodwill is amortized by the straight-line method over 40 years.

Note 2. Retained earnings of $100,000 is restricted for plant expansion.

BEFORE YOU GO ON ...

Review It

1. What is the proper valuation and reporting of trading and available-for-sale securities on a balance sheet?
2. Explain how the unrealized gain or loss for both trading and available-for-sale securities is reported.
3. Explain where temporary and long-term investments are reported on a balance sheet.

A LOOK BACK AT OUR FEATURE STORY

Refer back to the Feature Story about Time Warner Corporation, and answer the following questions:

1. For what reason(s) is Time Warner investing in equity securities?
2. Would you expect Time Warner to prepare consolidated financial statements for the many companies it owns? Explain your answer.
3. What has Time Warner's aggressive acquisition spree meant for its bottom line?

Solution
1. Time Warner is investing for strategic reasons. As indicated in the Feature Story, the company's attitude is "If we can't beat you, we will buy you." Time Warner is diversifying because it is not sure what industry or set of industries will be successful in the future. As a result, Time Warner now owns more information and entertainment copyrights and brands than any other company in the world.
2. When a company owns more than 50% of the common stock of another company, consolidated financial statements are usually prepared. Because Time Warner owns over 50% of the outstanding common stock of the companies mentioned in the Feature Story, Time Warner would consolidate these subsidiary companies with its own.
3. To date, Time Warner's acquisition spree has left it with huge debt and massive interest costs. In addition, some of the acquisitions have not come cheap, resulting in large amounts of reported goodwill and goodwill amortization. As a result, Time Warner has reported net losses in all but two years from 1989 through 1998.

DEMONSTRATION PROBLEM

In its first year of operations, the DeMarco Company had the following selected transactions in stock investments which are considered trading securities:

June 1   Purchased for cash 600 shares of Sanburg common stock at $24 per share plus $300 brokerage fees.
July 1   Purchased for cash 800 shares of Cey common stock at $33 per share plus $600 brokerage fees.
Sept. 1   Received a $1 per share cash dividend from Cey Corporation.
Nov. 1   Sold 200 shares of Sanburg common stock for cash at $27 per share less $150 brokerage fees.
Dec. 15   Received a $.50 per share cash dividend on Sanburg common stock.

At December 31, the fair values per share were: Sanburg $25 and Cey $30.

Instructions

(a) Journalize the transactions.

(b) Prepare the adjusting entry at December 31 to report the securities at fair value.

PROBLEM-SOLVING STRATEGIES

1. Cost includes the price paid plus brokerage fees.
2. Gain or loss on sales is determined by the difference between net selling price and the cost of the securities.
3. The adjustment to fair value is based on the total difference between cost and fair value of the securities.

SOLUTION TO DEMONSTRATION PROBLEM

(a)	June 1	Stock Investments	14,700	
		Cash		14,700
		(To record purchase of 600 shares of Sanburg common stock)		
	July 1	Stock Investments	27,000	
		Cash		27,000
		(To record purchase of 800 shares of Cey common stock)		
	Sept. 1	Cash	800	
		Dividend Revenue		800
		(To record receipt of $1 per share cash dividend from Cey Corporation)		
	Nov. 1	Cash	5,250	
		Stock Investments		4,900
		Gain on Sale of Stock Investments		350
		(To record sale of 200 shares of Sanburg common stock)		
	Dec.15	Cash	200	
		Dividend Revenue		200
		(To record receipt of $.50 per share dividend from Sanburg Corporation)		
(b)	Dec. 31	Unrealized Loss—Income	2,800	
		Market Adjustment—Trading		2,800
		(To record unrealized loss on trading securities)		

Investment	Cost	Fair Value	Unrealized Gain (Loss)
Sanburg common stock	$ 9,800	$10,000	$ 200
Cey common stock	27,000	24,000	(3,000)
Totals	$36,800	$34,000	$(2,800)

THE NAVIGATOR

SUMMARY OF STUDY OBJECTIVES

1. *Identify the reasons corporations invest in stocks and debt securities.* Corporations invest for three primary reasons: (a) They have excess cash; (b) they view investments as a significant revenue source; or (c) they have strategic goals such as gaining control of a competitor or moving into a new line of business.

2. *Explain the accounting for debt investments.* Entries for investments in debt securities are required when the bonds are purchased, interest is received or accrued, and the bonds are sold. The accounting for long-term investments in bonds is the same as for temporary investments in bonds, except that bond premium and bond discount must be amortized.

3. *Explain the accounting for stock investments.* Entries for investments in common stock are required when the stock is purchased, dividends are received, and stock is sold. When ownership is less than 20%, the cost method is used. When ownership is between 20% and 50%, the equity method should be used. When ownership is more than 50%, consolidated financial statements should be prepared.

4. *Describe the purpose and usefulness of consolidated financial statements.* When a company owns more than 50% of the common stock of another company, consolidated financial statements are usually prepared. These statements are especially useful to the stockholders, board of directors, and management of the parent company.

5. Indicate how debt and stock investments are valued and reported on the financial statements. Investments in debt and stock securities are classified as trading, available-for-sale, or held-to-maturity securities for valuation and reporting purposes. Trading securities are reported in current assets at fair value with changes from cost reported in net income. Available-for-sale securities are also reported at fair value with the changes from cost reported in stockholders'

equity. Available-for-sale securities are classified as temporary or long-term depending on their expected realization.

6. Distinguish between temporary and long-term investments. Temporary investments are securities, held by a company, that are readily marketable and intended to be converted to cash within the next year or operating cycle, whichever is longer. Investments that do not meet both criteria are classified as long-term investments.

THE NAVIGATOR

GLOSSARY

Available-for-sale securities Securities that may be sold in the future. (p. 577)

Consolidated financial statements Financial statements that present the assets and liabilities controlled by the parent company and the aggregate profitability of the affiliated companies. (p. 574)

Controlling interest Ownership of more than 50% of the common stock of another entity. (p. 574)

Cost method An accounting method in which the investment in common stock is recorded at cost and revenue is recognized only when cash dividends are received. (p. 572)

Debt investments Investments in government and corporation bonds. (p. 570)

Equity method An accounting method in which the investment in common stock is initially recorded at cost, and the investment account is then adjusted annually to show the investor's equity in the investee. (p. 573)

Fair value Amount for which a security could be sold in a normal market. (p. 577)

Held-to-maturity securities Debt securities which the investor has the intent and ability to hold to their maturity date. (p. 577)

Investment portfolio A group of stocks in different corporations held for investment purposes. (p. 572)

Long-term investments Investments that are not readily marketable or that management does not intend to convert into cash within the next year or operating cycle, whichever is longer. (p. 579)

Parent company A company that owns more than 50% of the common stock of another entity. (p. 574)

Stock investments Investments in the capital stock of corporations. (p. 572)

Subsidiary (affiliated) company A company in which more than 50% of its stock is owned by another company. (p. 574)

Temporary investments Investments that are readily marketable and intended to be converted into cash within the next year or operating cycle, whichever is longer. (p. 579)

Trading securities Securities bought and held primarily for sale in the near term to generate income on short-term price differences. (p. 577)

APPENDIX PREPARING CONSOLIDATED FINANCIAL STATEMENTS

Most of the large U.S. corporations are holding companies that own other corporations and, therefore, prepare consolidated financial statements that combine the separate companies.

CONSOLIDATED BALANCE SHEET

Consolidated balance sheets are prepared from the individual balance sheets of the affiliated companies. They are not prepared from ledger accounts kept by the consolidated entity because only the separate legal entities maintain accounting records.

All items in the individual balance sheets are included in the consolidated balance sheet except amounts that pertain to transactions between the affiliated companies. Transactions between the affiliated companies are identified as intercompany transactions. The process of excluding these transactions in preparing consolidated statements is referred to as intercompany eliminations. These eliminations are necessary to avoid overstating assets, liabilities, and stockholders' equity in the consolidated balance sheet. For example, amounts owed by a subsidiary to a parent company and the related receivable reported by the parent company would be eliminated. The objective in a consolidated balance sheet is to show only obligations to and receivables from parties who are not part of the affiliated group of companies.

To illustrate, assume that on January 1, 2001, Powers Construction Company pays $150,000 in cash for 100% of Serto Brick Company's common stock. Powers Company records the investment at cost, as required by the cost principle. The separate balance sheets of the two companies immediately after the purchase, together with combined and consolidated data, are presented in Illustration 13A-1.[5] The balances in the "combined" column are obtained by adding the items in the separate balance sheets of the affiliated companies. The combined totals do not represent a consolidated balance sheet, because there has been a double counting of assets and owners' equity in the amount of $150,000.

ILLUSTRATION 13A-1

Combined and consolidated data

	POWERS COMPANY AND SERTO COMPANY **Balance Sheets** **January 1, 2001**			
Assets	Powers Company	Serto Company	Combined Data	Consolidated Data
Current assets	$ 50,000	$ 80,000	$130,000	$130,000
Investment in Serto Company common stock	150,000		150,000	–0–
Plant and equipment (net)	325,000	145,000	470,000	470,000
Total assets	$525,000	$225,000	$750,000	$600,000
Liabilities and Stockholders' Equity				
Current liabilities	$ 50,000	$ 75,000	$125,000	$125,000
Common stock	300,000	100,000	400,000	300,000
Retained earnings	175,000	50,000	225,000	175,000
Total liabilities and stockholders' equity	$525,000	$225,000	$750,000	$600,000

The Investment in Serto Company common stock that appears on the balance sheet of Powers Company represents an interest in the net assets of Serto. As a result, there has been a double counting of assets. Similarly, there has been a double counting in stockholders' equity, because the common stock of Serto Company is completely owned by the stockholders of Powers Company.

The balances in the consolidated data column are the amounts that should appear in the consolidated balance sheet. The double counting has been eliminated by showing Investment in Serto Company at zero and by reporting only the common stock and retained earnings of Powers Company as stockholders' equity.

---

[5]Condensed data will be used throughout this material to keep details at a minimum.

Use of a Work Sheet—Cost Equal to Book Value

The preparation of consolidated balance sheets is usually facilitated by the use of a work sheet. As shown in Illustration 13A-2, the work sheet for a consolidated balance sheet contains columns for (1) the balance sheet data for the separate legal entities, (2) intercompany eliminations, and (3) consolidated data. All data in the work sheet relate to the preceding example in which Powers Company acquires 100% ownership of Serto Company for $150,000. In this case, the cost of the investment, $150,000, is equal to the book value $150,000 ($225,000 − $75,000) of the subsidiary's net assets. The intercompany elimination results in a credit to the Investment account maintained by Powers Company for its balance, $150,000, and debits to the Common Stock and Retained Earnings accounts of Serto Company for their respective balances, $100,000 and $50,000.

7

STUDY

OBJECTIVE

Describe the content of a work sheet for a consolidated balance sheet.

ILLUSTRATION 13A-2

Work sheet—Cost equals book value

POWERS COMPANY AND SUBSIDIARY
Work Sheet—Consolidated Balance Sheet
January 1, 2001 (Acquisition Data)

Assets	Powers Company	Serto Company	Eliminations Dr.	Eliminations Cr.	Consolidated Data
Current assets	50,000	80,000			130,000
Investment in Serto Company common stock	150,000			150,000	–0–
Plant and equipment (net)	325,000	145,000			470,000
Totals	525,000	225,000			600,000
Liabilities and Stockholders' Equity					
Current liabilities	50,000	75,000			125,000
Common stock—Powers Company	300,000				300,000
Common stock—Serto Company		100,000	100,000		–0–
Retained earnings—Powers Company	175,000				175,000
Retained earnings—Serto Company		50,000	50,000		–0–
Totals	525,000	225,000	150,000	150,000	600,000

It is important to recognize that intercompany eliminations are made solely on the work sheet to present correct consolidated data. **They are not journalized or posted by either of the affiliated companies, and, therefore, do not affect the ledger accounts.** Powers Company's investment account and Serto Company's common stock and retained earnings accounts are reported by the separate entities in preparing their own financial statements.

HELPFUL HINT

As in the case of the work sheets explained earlier in this textbook, consolidated work sheets are also optional.

TECHNOLOGY IN ACTION

The consolidated work sheet is another good spreadsheet application. At this stage in the course, we hope you have familiarized yourself enough with electronic spreadsheets to be able to create your own templates. If not, this is a good work sheet to attempt since the required instructions are very straightforward.

However, computer programs are available that can merge multiple general ledgers for consolidated entities. All you need to do is supply the eliminating information, enter a few command keystrokes, and the consolidated financial statements will come off the printer, ready for distribution.

Use of a Work Sheet—Cost Above Book Value

The cost of acquiring the common stock of another company may be above or below its book value. The management of the parent company may pay more than book value because it believes (1) the fair market values of identifiable assets such as land, buildings, and equipment are higher than their recorded book values, or (2) the subsidiary's future earnings prospects warrant a payment for goodwill.

To illustrate, assume the same data used above, except that Powers Company pays $165,000 in cash for 100% of Serto's common stock. The excess of cost over book value is $15,000 ($165,000 − $150,000). This amount is separately recognized in eliminating the parent company's investment account, as shown in Illustration 13A-3.

Total assets and total liabilities and stockholders' equity are the same as in the preceding example ($600,000). However, in this case, total assets include $15,000 of Excess of Cost Over Book Value of Subsidiary. The disposition of the excess is explained in the next section.

ILLUSTRATION 13A-3

Work sheet—Cost above book value

POWERS COMPANY AND SUBSIDIARY
Work Sheet—Consolidated Balance Sheet
January 1, 2001 (Acquisition Date)

Assets	Powers Company	Serto Company	Eliminations Dr.	Eliminations Cr.	Consolidated Data
Current assets	35,000	80,000			115,000
Investment in Serto Company common stock	165,000			165,000	–0–
Plant and equipment (net)	325,000	145,000			470,000
EXCESS OF COST OVER BOOK VALUE OF SUBSIDIARY			15,000		15,000
Totals	525,000	225,000			600,000
Liabilities and Stockholders' Equity					
Current liabilities	50,000	75,000			125,000
Common stock — Powers Company	300,000				300,000
Common stock — Serto Company		100,000	100,000		–0–
Retained earnings — Powers Company	175,000				175,000
Retained earnings — Serto Company		50,000	50,000		–0–
Totals	525,000	225,000	165,000	165,000	600,000

Note that a separate line is added to the work sheet for the excess of cost over book value of subsidiary.

Content of a Consolidated Balance Sheet

STUDY
OBJECTIVE

Explain the form and content of consolidated financial statements.

To illustrate a consolidated balance sheet, we will use the work sheet shown in Illustration 13A-3. This work sheet shows an excess of cost over book value of $15,000. In the consolidated balance sheet, this amount is first allocated to specific assets, such as inventory and plant equipment, if their fair market values on the acquisition date exceed their book values. Any remainder is considered to be goodwill. For Serto Company, assume that the fair market value of property and equipment is $155,000. Thus, $10,000 of the excess of cost over book value is allocated to property and equipment, and the remainder, $5,000, is allocated to goodwill.

The condensed consolidated balance sheet of Powers Company is shown in Illustration 13A-4. As explained in Chapter 10, goodwill would be amortized by the straight-line method over the period benefited, but not in excess of 40 years.

POWERS COMPANY Consolidated Balance Sheet January 1, 2001		
Assets		
Current assets		$115,000
Plant and equipment (net)		480,000
Goodwill		5,000
Total assets		$600,000
Liabilities and Stockholders' Equity		
Current liabilities		$125,000
Stockholders' equity		
Common stock	$300,000	
Retained earnings	175,000	475,000
Total liabilities and stockholders' equity		$600,000

ACCOUNTING IN ACTION
Business Insight

Through innovative financial restructuring, the Coca-Cola Company at one time eliminated a substantial amount of non-intercompany debt. It sold to the public 51% of two bottling companies. The "49% solution," as insiders call the strategy, enabled Coca-Cola to keep effective control over the businesses and it swept $3 billion of debt from its consolidated balance sheet. (It no longer consolidated the two bottling companies.) At the same time the new companies obtained independent access to equity markets to satisfy their own voracious appetites for capital.

CONSOLIDATED INCOME STATEMENT

A consolidated income statement is also prepared for affiliated companies. This statement shows the results of operations of affiliated companies as though they are one economic unit. This means that the statement shows only revenue and expense transactions between the consolidated entity and companies and individuals who are outside the affiliated group. Consequently, all intercompany revenue and expense transactions must be eliminated. Intercompany transactions such as sales between affiliates and interest on loans charged by one affiliate to another must be eliminated. A work sheet facilitates the preparation of consolidated income statements in the same manner as it does for the balance sheet.

BEFORE YOU GO ON ...

Review It

1. Why are eliminations needed in preparing consolidated financial statements?
2. What eliminations are made for the parent company's investment in the common stock of a subsidiary company?
3. How may the excess of cost over book value be reported in a consolidated balance sheet?

SUMMARY OF STUDY OBJECTIVES FOR APPENDIX

7. Describe the content of a work sheet for a consolidated balance sheet. The work sheet for a consolidated balance sheet contains columns for (a) the balance sheet data for the separate entities, (b) intercompany eliminations, and (c) consolidated data.

8. Explain the form and content of consolidated financial statements. Consolidated financial statements are similar in form and content to the financial statements of an individual corporation. A consolidated balance sheet shows the assets and liabilities controlled by the parent company. A consolidated income statement shows the results of operations of affiliated companies as though they are one economic unit.

GLOSSARY FOR APPENDIX

Intercompany eliminations Eliminations made to exclude the effects of intercompany transactions in preparing consolidated statements. (p. 586).

Intercompany transactions Transactions between affiliated companies. (p. 586).

*Note: All asterisked Questions, Exercises, and Problems relate to material in the appendix to the chapter.

SELF-STUDY QUESTIONS

Answers are at the end of the chapter.

(SO 2) 1. Debt investments are initially recorded at:
   a. cost.
   b. cost plus accrued interest.
   c. fair value.
   d. None of the above.

(SO 2) 2. Hanes Company sells debt investments costing $26,000 for $28,000 plus accrued interest that has been recorded. In journalizing the sale, credits are:
   a. Debt Investments and Loss on Sale of Debt Investments.
   b. Debt Investments, Gain on Sale of Debt Investments, and Bond Interest Receivable.
   c. Stock Investments and Bond Interest Receivable.
   d. No correct answer given.

(SO 3) 3. Pryor Company receives net proceeds of $42,000 on the sale of stock investments that cost $39,500. This transaction will result in reporting in the income statement a:
   a. loss of $2,500 under Other Expenses and Losses.
   b. loss of $2,500 under Operating Expenses.
   c. gain of $2,500 under Other Revenues and Gains.
   d. gain of $2,500 under Operating Revenues.

(SO 3) 4. The equity method of accounting for long-term investments in stock should be used when the investor has significant influence over an investee and owns:
   a. between 20% and 50% of the investee's common stock.
   b. 20% or more of the investee's common stock.
   c. more than 50% of the investee's common stock.
   d. less than 20% of the investee's common stock.

(SO 4) 5. Which of the following statements is *not true*? Consolidated financial statements are useful to:
   a. determine the profitability of specific subsidiaries.
   b. determine the aggregate profitability of enterprises under common control.

   c. determine the breadth of a parent company's operations.
   d. determine the full extent of aggregate obligations of enterprises under common control.

6. At the end of the first year of operations, the total cost of (SO 5) the trading securities portfolio is $120,000, and total fair value is $115,000. The financial statements should show:
   a. a reduction of an asset of $5,000 and a realized loss of $5,000.
   b. a reduction of an asset of $5,000 and an unrealized loss of $5,000 in the stockholders' equity section.
   c. a reduction of an asset of $5,000 in the current assets section and an unrealized loss in Other Expenses and Losses of $5,000.
   d. a reduction of an asset of $5,000 in the current assets section and a realized loss of $5,000 in Other Expenses and Losses.

7. In the balance sheet, Unrealized Loss—Equity is re- (SO 5) ported as a:
   a. contra asset account.
   b. contra stockholders' equity account.
   c. loss in the income statement.
   d. loss in the retained earnings statement.

8. Temporary debt investments must be readily mar- (SO 6) ketable and be expected to be sold within:
   a. 3 months from the date of purchase.
   b. the next year or operating cycle, whichever is shorter.
   c. the next year or operating cycle, whichever is longer.
   d. the operating cycle.

*9. Pate Company pays $175,000 for 100% of Sinko's com- (SO 7) mon stock when Sinko's stockholders' equity consists of Common Stock $100,000 and Retained Earnings $60,000. In the work sheet for the consolidated balance sheet, the eliminations will include a:
   a. credit to Investment in Sinko Common Stock $160,000.

b. credit to Excess of Book Value over Cost of Subsidiary $15,000.

c. debit to Retained Earnings $75,000.

d. debit to Excess of Cost over Book Value of Subsidiary $15,000.

(SO 7) *10. Which of the following statements about intercompany eliminations is *true*?

a. They are not journalized or posted by any of the subsidiaries.

b. They do not affect the ledger accounts of any of the subsidiaries.

c. Intercompany eliminations are made solely on the work sheet to arrive at correct consolidated data.

d. All of these statements are true.

*11. Which one of the following statements about consolidated income statements is *false*?

a. A work sheet facilitates the preparation of the statement.

b. The consolidated income statement shows the results of operations of affiliated companies as a single economic unit.

c. All revenue and expense transactions between parent and subsidiary companies are eliminated.

d. When a subsidiary is wholly owned, the form and content of the statement will differ from the income statement of an individual corporation.

QUESTIONS

1. What are the reasons that corporations invest in securities?

2. (a) What is the cost of an investment in bonds?
   (b) When is interest on bonds recorded?

3. Sara Stine is confused about losses and gains on the sale of debt investments. Explain to Sara (a) how the gain or loss is computed, and (b) the statement presentation of the gains and losses.

4. Cline Company sells Hope's bonds costing $40,000 for $45,000, including $2,000 of accrued interest. In recording the sale, Cline books a $5,000 gain. Is this correct? Explain.

5. What is the cost of an investment in stock?

6. To acquire May Corporation stock, B. Mallon pays $60,000 in cash plus $1,500 broker's fees. What entry should be made for this investment, assuming the stock is readily marketable?

7. (a) When should a long-term investment in common stock be accounted for by the equity method? (b) When is revenue recognized under this method?

8. Marx Corporation uses the equity method to account for its ownership of 25% of the common stock of Welch Packing. During 2001 Welch reported a net income of $80,000 and declares and pays cash dividends of $10,000. What recognition should Marx Corporation give to these events?

9. What constitutes "significant influence" when an investor's financial interest is below the 50% level?

10. Distinguish between the cost and equity methods of accounting for investments in stocks.

11. What are consolidated financial statements?

12. What are the valuation guidelines for investments at a balance sheet date?

13. Kim Carley is the controller of Roarke, Inc. At December 31, the company's investments in trading securities cost $74,000 and have a fair value of $68,000. Indicate how Kim would report these data in the financial statements prepared on December 31.

14. Using the data in question 13, how would Kim report the data if the investment were long-term and the securities were classified as available-for-sale?

15. Colby Company's investments in available-for-sale securities at December 31 shows total cost of $192,000 and total fair value of $205,000. Prepare the adjusting entry.

16. Using the data in question 15, prepare the adjusting entry assuming the securities are classified as trading securities.

17. What is the proper statement presentation of the account Unrealized Loss—Equity?

18. What purposes are served by reporting Unrealized Gains (Losses)—Equity in the stockholders' equity section?

19. Kiley Wholesale Supply owns stock in Sharp Corporation, which it intends to hold indefinitely because of some negative tax consequences if sold. Should the investment in Sharp be classified as a temporary investment? Why?

*20. (a) What asset and stockholders' equity balances are eliminated in preparing a consolidated balance sheet for a parent and a wholly owned subsidiary? (b) Why are they eliminated?

*21. Weller Company pays $320,000 to purchase all the outstanding common stock of Wood Corporation. At the date of purchase the net assets of Wood have a book value of $290,000. Weller's management allocates $20,000 of the excess cost to undervalued land on the books of Wood. What should be done with the rest of the excess?

BRIEF EXERCISES

Journalize entries for debt investments.
(SO 2)

Journalize entries for stock investments.
(SO 3)

Record transactions under the equity method of accounting.
(SO 3)

Prepare adjusting entry using fair value.
(SO 5)

Indicate statement presentation using fair value.
(SO 5, 6)
Prepare adjusting entry using fair value.
(SO 5)
Indicate statement presentation using fair value.
(SO 5, 6)

Prepare investment section of balance sheet.
(SO 5, 6)

Prepare partial consolidated work sheet when cost equals book value.
(SO 7)

Prepare partial consolidated work sheet when cost exceeds book value.
(SO 7)

BE13–1 DeShields Corporation purchased debt investments for $41,500 on January 1, 2001. On July 1, 2001, DeShields received cash interest of $2,490. Journalize the purchase and the receipt of interest. Assume that no interest has been accrued.

BE13–2 On August 1, Lolich Company buys 1,000 shares of Stead common stock for $36,000 cash plus brokerage fees of $600. On December 1, the stock investments are sold for $38,000 in cash. Journalize the purchase and sale of the common stock.

BE13–3 Arkin Company owns 30% of Hines Company. For the current year Hines reports net income of $180,000 and declares and pays a $50,000 cash dividend. Record Arkin's equity in Hines's net income and the receipt of dividends from Hines.

BE13–4 Cost and fair value data for the trading securities of Mingo Company at December 31, 2001, are $64,000 and $59,000, respectively. Prepare the adjusting entry to record the securities at fair value.

BE13–5 For the data presented in BE13–4, show the financial statement presentation of the trading securities and related accounts.

BE13–6 Dexter Corporation holds available-for-sale stock securities costing $72,000 as a long-term investment. At December 31, 2001, the fair value of the securities is $68,000. Prepare the adjusting entry to record the securities at fair value.

BE13–7 For the data presented in BE13–6, show the financial statement presentation of the available-for-sale securities and related accounts. Assume the available-for-sale securities are noncurrent.

BE13–8 Thesh Corporation has the following long-term investments: common stock of Kubek Co. (10% ownership) held as available-for-sale securities, cost $108,000, fair value $110,000; common stock of Ely Inc. (30% ownership), cost $210,000, equity $250,000; and a bond sinking fund of $150,000. Prepare the investments section of the balance sheet.

*BE13–9 Provo Company acquires 100% of the common stock of Stanton Company for $180,000 cash. On the acquisition date, Stanton's ledger shows Common Stock $120,000 and Retained Earnings $60,000. Complete the work sheet for the following accounts: Provo—Investment in Stanton Common Stock, Stanton—Common Stock, and Stanton—Retained Earnings.

*BE13–10 Data for the Provo and Stanton companies are given in BE13–9. Instead of paying $180,000, assume that Provo pays $200,000 to acquire the 100% interest in Stanton Company. Complete the work sheet for the accounts identified in BE13–9 and for the excess of cost over book value.

EXERCISES

Journalize debt investment transactions and accrue interest.
(SO 2)

E13–1 Greer Corporation had the following transactions pertaining to debt investments:

Jan. 1   Purchased 90 10%, $1,000 Ford Co. bonds for $90,000 cash plus brokerage fees of $900. Interest is payable semiannually on July 1 and January 1.
July 1   Received semiannual interest on Ford Co. bonds.
July 1   Sold 30 Ford Co. bonds for $32,000 less $400 brokerage fees.

Instructions
(a) Journalize the transactions.
(b) Prepare the adjusting entry for the accrual of interest at December 31.

Journalize stock investment transactions.
(SO 3)

E13–2 Jacobs Company had the following transactions pertaining to stock investments:

Feb. 1   Purchased 800 shares of Aber common stock (2%) for $9,000 cash plus brokerage fees of $200.
July 1   Received cash dividends of $1 per share on Aber common stock.
Sept. 1   Sold 300 shares of Aber common stock for $4,000 less brokerage fees of $100.
Dec. 1   Received cash dividends of $1 per share on Aber common stock.

Instructions

   (a) Journalize the transactions.

   (b) Explain how dividend revenue and the gain (loss) on sale should be reported in the income statement.

E13–3 Crosby Inc. had the following transactions pertaining to investments in common stock:

Journalize transactions for investments in stocks.
(SO 3)

  Jan. 1 Purchased 1,000 shares of Hannah Corporation common stock (5%) for $70,000 cash plus $2,100 broker's commission.

  July 1 Received a cash dividend of $9 per share.

  Dec. 1 Sold 500 shares of Hannah Corporation common stock for $37,000 cash less $800 broker's commission.

  Dec. 31 Received a cash dividend of $9 per share.

Instructions

Journalize the transactions.

E13–4 On January 1 Howell Corporation purchased a 30% equity in Louise Corporation for $150,000. At December 31 Louise declared and paid a $60,000 cash dividend and reported net income of $200,000.

Journalize and post transactions and contrast cost and equity method results.
(SO 3)

Instructions

   (a) Journalize the transactions.

   (b) Determine the amount to be reported as an investment in Louise stock at December 31.

E13–5 Presented below are two independent situations:

Journalize entries under cost and equity methods.
(SO 3)

  1. Ritter Cosmetics acquired 10% of the 200,000 shares of common stock of Mai Fashion at a total cost of $13 per share on March 18, 2001. On June 30, Mai declared and paid a $75,000 dividend. On December 31, Mai reported net income of $122,000 for the year. At December 31, the market price of Mai Fashion was $15 per share. The stock is classified as available-for-sale.

  2. Somer, Inc., obtained significant influence over Ortiz Corporation by buying 40% of Ortiz's 30,000 outstanding shares of common stock at a total cost of $9 per share on January 1, 2001. On June 15, Ortiz declared and paid a cash dividend of $35,000. On December 31, Ortiz reported a net income of $80,000 for the year.

Instructions

Prepare all the necessary journal entries for 2001 for (a) Ritter Cosmetics and (b) Somer, Inc.

E13–6 At December 31, 2001, the trading securities for Yanik, Inc., are as follows:

Prepare adjusting entry to record fair value and indicate statement presentation.
(SO 5, 6)

Security	Cost	Fair Value
A	$17,500	$16,000
B	12,500	14,000
C	23,000	21,000
	$53,000	$51,000

Instructions

   (a) Prepare the adjusting entry at December 31, 2001, to report the securities at fair value.

   (b) Show the balance sheet and income statement presentation at December 31, 2001, after adjustment to fair value.

E13–7 Data for investments in stock classified as trading securities are presented in E13–6. Assume instead that the investments are classified as available-for-sale securities with the same cost and fair value data. The securities are considered to be a long-term investment.

Prepare adjusting entry to record fair value and indicate statement presentation.
(SO 5, 6)

Instructions

   (a) Prepare the adjusting entry at December 31, 2001, to report the securities at fair value.

   (b) Show the statement presentation at December 31, 2001, after adjustment to fair value.

   (c) ▓▓▶ M. Wise, a member of the board of directors, does not understand the reporting of the unrealized gains or losses. Write a letter to Mr. Wise explaining the reporting and the purposes that it serves.

Prepare adjusting entries for fair value and indicate statement presentation for two classes of securities.
(SO 5, 6)

E13–8 Quayle Company has the following data at December 31, 2001:

Securities	Cost	Fair Value
Trading	$120,000	$128,000
Available-for-sale	100,000	94,000

The available-for-sale securities are held as a long-term investment.

Instructions
(a) Prepare the adjusting entries to report each class of securities at fair value.
(b) Indicate the statement presentation of each class of securities and the related unrealized gain (loss) accounts.

Prepare consolidated work sheet when cost equals book value.
(SO 7, 8)

*E13–9 On January 1, 2001, Swiss Corporation acquires 100% of Arco Inc. for $200,000 in cash. The condensed balance sheets of the two corporations immediately following the acquisition are as follows:

	Swiss Corporation	Acro Inc.
Current assets	$ 60,000	$ 40,000
Investment in Arco Inc. common stock	200,000	
Plant and equipment (net)	300,000	210,000
	$560,000	$250,000
Current liabilities	$180,000	$ 50,000
Common stock	225,000	75,000
Retained earnings	155,000	125,000
	$560,000	$250,000

Instructions
Prepare a work sheet for a consolidated balance sheet.

Prepare consolidated work sheet when cost exceeds book value.
(SO 7, 8)

*E13–10 Data for the Swiss and Arco corporations are presented in E13–9. Assume that instead of paying $200,000 in cash for Arco Inc., Swiss Corporation pays $215,000 in cash. Thus, at the acquisition date, the assets of Swiss Corporation are: Current assets $45,000, Investment in Arco Inc. Common Stock $215,000, and Plant and Equipment (net) $300,000.

Instructions
Prepare a work sheet for a consolidated balance sheet.

PROBLEMS: SET A
....

Journalize debt investment transactions and show statement presentations.
(SO 2, 5, 6)

P13–1A Marvel Davis Farms, is a grower of hybrid seed corn for DeKalb Genetics Corporation. It has had two exceptionally good years and has elected to invest its excess funds in bonds. The following selected transactions relate to bonds acquired as an investment by Marvel Davis Farms, whose fiscal year ends on December 31:

2001

Jan. 1   Purchased at par $1,000,000 of Sycamore Corporation 10-year, 9% bonds dated January 1, 2001, directly from the issuing corporation.
July 1   Received the semiannual interest on the Sycamore bonds.
Dec. 31 Accrual of interest at year-end on the Sycamore bonds.

(Assume that all intervening transactions and adjustments have been properly recorded and the number of bonds owned has not changed from December 31, 2001, to December 31, 2003.)

2004

Jan. 1   Received the semiannual interest on the Sycamore bonds.
Jan. 1   Sold $500,000 Sycamore bonds at 114. The broker deducted $7,000 for commissions and fees on the sale.
July 1   Received the semiannual interest on the Sycamore bonds.
Dec. 31 Accrual of interest at year-end on the Sycamore bonds.

Instructions
(a) Journalize the listed transactions for the years 2001 and 2004.

(b) Assume that the fair value of the bonds at December 31, 2001, was $960,000. These bonds are classified as available-for-sale securities. Prepare the adjusting entry to record these bonds at fair value.

(c) Show the balance sheet presentation of the bonds and interest receivable at December 31, 2001, and indicate where any unrealized gain or loss is reported in the financial statements.

P13–2A   In January 2001, the management of Mann Company concludes that it has sufficient cash to purchase some temporary investments in debt and stock securities. During the year, the following transactions occurred:

Journalize investment transactions, prepare adjusting entry, and show statement presentation.
(SO 2, 3, 5, 6)

Feb. 1	Purchased 800 shares of SRI common stock for $32,000 plus brokerage fees of $800.
Mar. 1	Purchased 500 shares of FGH common stock for $15,000 plus brokerage fees of $300.
Apr. 1	Purchased 60 $1,000, 12% XYZ bonds for $60,000 plus $1,200 brokerage fees. Interest is payable semiannually on April 1 and October 1.
July 1	Received a cash dividend of $.60 per share on the SRI common stock.
Aug. 1	Sold 200 shares of SRI common stock at $42 per share less brokerage fees of $350.
Sept. 1	Received a $1 per share cash dividend on the FGH common stock.
Oct. 1	Received the semiannual interest on the XYZ bonds.
Oct. 1	Sold the XYZ bonds for $63,000 less $1,000 brokerage fees.

At December 31, the fair value of the SRI and FGH common stocks were $39 and $30 per share, respectively.

Instructions
(a) Journalize the transactions and post to the accounts Debt Investments and Stock Investments. (Use the T-account form.)
(b) Prepare the adjusting entry at December 31, 2001, to report the investments at fair value. All securities are considered to be trading securities.
(c) Show the balance sheet presentation of investment securities at December 31, 2001.
(d) Identify the income statement accounts and give the statement classification of each account.

P13–3A   On December 31, 2001, Kern Associates owned the following securities that are held as long-term investments:

Journalize transactions and adjusting entry for stock investments.
(SO 3, 5, 6)

Common Stock	Shares	Cost
A Co.	1,000	$50,000
B Co.	6,000	36,000
C Co.	1,200	24,000

On this date, the total fair value of the securities was equal to its cost. The securities are not held for influence or control over the investees. In 2002, the following transactions occurred:

July 1	Received $1 per share semiannual cash dividend on B Co. common stock.
Aug. 1	Received $.50 per share cash dividend on A Co. common stock.
Sept. 1	Sold 500 shares of B Co. common stock for cash at $7 per share less brokerage fees of $100.
Oct. 1	Sold 400 shares of A Co. common stock for cash at $56 per share less brokerage fees of $600.
Nov. 1	Received $1 per share cash dividend on C Co. common stock.
Dec. 15	Received $.50 per share cash dividend on A Co. common stock.
31	Received $1 per share semiannual cash dividend on B Co. common stock.

At December 31, the fair values per share of the common stocks were: A Co. $47, B Co. $6, and C Co. $19.

Instructions
(a) Journalize the 2002 transactions and post to the account Stock Investments. (Use the T-account form.)
(b) Prepare the adjusting entry at December 31, 2002, to show the securities at fair value. The stock should be classified as available-for-sale securities.
(c) Show the balance sheet presentation of the investments at December 31, 2002. At this date, Kern Associates has common stock $2,000,000 and retained earnings $1,200,000.

Prepare entries at cost and at equity and prepare memorandum.
(SO 3)

P13–4A   Jantz Concrete acquired 20% of the outstanding common stock of Hawes, Inc., on January 1, 2001, by paying $1,200,000 for 50,000 shares. Hawes declared and paid a $0.60 per share cash dividend on June 30 and again on December 31, 2001. Hawes reported net income of $800,000 for the year.

Instructions
(a) Prepare the journal entries for Jantz Concrete for 2001 assuming Jantz cannot exercise significant influence over Hawes. (Use the cost method.)
(b) Prepare the journal entries for Jantz Concrete for 2001, assuming Jantz can exercise significant influence over Hawes. (Use the equity method.)
(c) ▨▨▨▷ The board of directors of Jantz Concrete is confused about the differences between the cost and equity methods. Prepare a memorandum for the board that (1) explains each method and (2) shows, in tabular form, the account balances under each method at December 31, 2001.

Journalize stock investment transactions and show statement presentation.
(SO 3, 5, 6)

P13–5A   The following securities are in Sammy Sosa Company's portfolio of long-term available-for-sale securities at December 31, 2001:

	Cost
1,000 shares of McGwire Inc. common stock	$52,000
1,400 shares of B. Ruth Company common stock	84,000
800 shares of H. Aaron Inc. preferred stock	33,600

On December 31, 2001, the total cost of the portfolio equaled total fair value. Sosa had the following transactions related to the securities during 2002:

Jan. 20   Sold 1,000 shares of McGwire Inc. common stock at $56 per share less brokerage fees of $600.
     28   Purchased 400 shares of $70 par value common stock of M. Mantle Corporation at $78 per share, plus brokerage fees of $480.
     30   Received a cash dividend of $1.15 per share on B. Ruth Corp. common stock.
Feb. 8   Received cash dividends of $.40 per share on H. Aaron Inc. preferred stock.
     18   Sold all 800 shares of H. Aaron Inc. preferred stock at $30.00 per share less brokerage fees of $360.
July 30   Received a cash dividend of $1.00 per share on B. Ruth Company common stock.
Sept. 6   Purchased an additional 800 shares of $10 par value common stock of M. Mantle Corporation at $82 per share, plus brokerage fees of $800.
Dec. 1   Received a cash dividend of $1.50 per share on M. Mantle Corporation common stock.

At December 31, 2002, the fair values of the securities were:

B. Ruth Company common stock	$64 per share
M. Mantle Corporation common stock	$72 per share

Sosa Company uses separate account titles for each investment, such as "Investment in B. Ruth Company Common Stock."

Instructions
(a) Prepare journal entries to record the transactions.
(b) Post to the investment accounts. (Use T accounts.)
(c) Prepare the adjusting entry at December 31, 2002, to report the portfolio at fair value.
(d) Show the balance sheet presentation at December 31, 2002.

Prepare a balance sheet.
(SO 5, 6)

P13–6A   The following data are taken from the records of Claudia Jackson Corporation.

Accounts payable	$ 220,000
Accounts receivable	90,000
Accumulated depreciation—building	180,000
Accumulated depreciation—equipment	52,000
Allowance for doubtful accounts	6,000
Bonds payable (10%, due 2014)	400,000
Bond investments	360,000
Buildings	900,000
Cash	92,000
Common stock ($5 par value; 500,000 shares authorized, 300,000 shares issued)	1,500,000

Discount on bonds payable	$ 20,000
Dividends payable	50,000
Equipment	275,000
Goodwill	200,000
Income taxes payable	120,000
Investment in ComEd Inc, stock (30% ownership), at equity	240,000
Land	500,000
Temporary stock investment, at fair value	185,000
Merchandise inventory	170,000
Notes payable (due 2002)	70,000
Patents	50,000
Paid-in capital in excess of par value	200,000
Prepaid insurance	16,000
Retained earnings	300,000

Instructions
Prepare a balance sheet at December 31, 2001.

*P13–7A   Terry Duffy Corporation purchased all the outstanding common stock of Henning Plastics, Inc., on December 31, 2001. Just before the purchase, the condensed balance sheets of the two companies appeared as follows:

Prepare consolidated work sheet and balance sheet when cost exceeds book value.
(SO 7, 8)

	Terry Duffy Corporation	**Henning Plastics, Inc.**
Current assets	$1,480,000	$ 439,500
Plant and equipment (net)	2,100,000	672,000
	$3,580,000	$1,111,500
Current liabilities	$ 578,000	$ 92,500
Common stock	1,950,000	525,000
Retained earnings	1,052,000	494,000
	$3,580,000	$1,111,500

Duffy used current assets of $1,200,000 to acquire the stock of Henning Plastics. The excess of this purchase price over the book value of Henning Plastics' net assets is determined to be attributable $81,000 to Henning Plastics' plant and equipment and the remainder to goodwill.

Instructions
(a) Prepare the entry for Terry Duffy's acquisition of Henning Plastics, Inc., stock.
(b) Prepare a consolidated work sheet at December 31, 2001.
(c) Prepare a consolidated balance sheet at December 31, 2001.

PROBLEMS: SET B
....

P13–1B   Omega Carecenters Inc. provides financing and capital to the healthcare industry, with a particular focus on nursing homes for the elderly. The following selected transactions relate to bonds acquired as an investment by Omega, whose fiscal year ends on December 31:

Journalize debt investment transactions and show statement presentations.
(SO 2, 5, 6)

2001

Jan. 1 Purchased at par $5,000,000 of Friendship Nursing Centers, Inc., 10-year, 10% bonds dated January 1, 2001, directly from Friendship.
July 1 Received the semiannual interest on the Friendship bonds.
Dec. 31 Accrual of interest at year-end on the Friendship bonds.

(Assume that all intervening transactions and adjustments have been properly recorded and that the number of bonds owned has not changed from December 31, 2001, to December 31, 2003.)

2004

Jan. 1 Received the semiannual interest on the Friendship bonds.
Jan. 1 Sold $2,500,000 Friendship bonds at 106. The broker deducted $10,000 for commissions and fees on the sale.
July 1 Received the semiannual interest on the Friendship bonds.
Dec. 31 Accrual of interest at year-end on the Friendship bonds.

Instructions
(a) Journalize the listed transactions for the years 2001 and 2004.

(b) Assume that the fair value of the bonds at December 31, 2001, was $5,500,000. These bonds are classified as available-for-sale securities. Prepare the adjusting entry to record these bonds at fair value.

(c) Show the balance sheet presentation of the bonds and interest receivable at December 31, 2001, and indicate where any unrealized gain or loss is reported in the financial statements.

Journalize investment transactions, prepare adjusting entry, and show statement presentation.
(SO 2, 3, 5, 6)

P13–2B In January 2001, the management of Norris Company concludes that it has sufficient cash to purchase some temporary investments in debt and stock securities. During the year, the following transactions occurred:

Feb. 1   Purchased 600 shares of CBA common stock for $31,800 plus brokerage fees of $600.
Mar. 1   Purchased 800 shares of GHI common stock for $20,000 plus brokerage fees of $400.
Apr. 1   Purchased 50 $1,000, 12% UVW bonds for $50,000 plus $1,000 brokerage fees. Interest is payable semiannually on April 1 and October 1.
July 1   Received a cash dividend of $.60 per share on the CBA common stock.
Aug. 1   Sold 200 shares of CBA common stock at $58 per share less brokerage fees of $200.
Sept. 1   Received a $1 per share cash dividend on the GHI common stock.
Oct. 1   Received the semiannual interest on the UVW bonds.
Oct. 1   Sold the UVW bonds for $51,000 less $1,000 brokerage fees.

At December 31, 2001, the fair value of the CBA and GHI common stocks were $55 and $23 per share, respectively.

Instructions

(a) Journalize the transactions and post to the accounts Debt Investments and Stock Investments. (Use the T-account form.)

(b) Prepare the adjusting entry at December 31, 2001, to report the investments securities at fair value. All securities are considered to be trading securities.

(c) Show the balance sheet presentation of investment securities at December 31, 2001.

(d) Identify the income statement accounts and give the statement classification of each account.

Journalize transactions and adjusting entry for stock investments.
(SO 3, 5, 6)

P13–3B On December 31, 2001, Milner Associates owned the following securities that are held as a long-term investment. The securities are not held for influence or control of the investee.

Common Stock	Shares	Cost
X Co.	2,000	$90,000
Y Co.	5,000	45,000
Z Co.	1,500	30,000

On this date, the total fair value of the securities was equal to its cost. In 2002, the following transactions occurred:

July 1   Received $1 per share semiannual cash dividend on Y Co. common stock.
    8   Received 4,000 shares of X Co. common stock in a 3-for-1 stock split.
Aug. 1   Received $.50 per share cash dividend on X Co. common stock.
Sept. 1   Sold 700 shares of Y Co. common stock for cash at $8 per share less brokerage fees of $200.
Oct. 1   Sold 600 shares of X Co. common stock for cash at $17 per share less brokerage fees of $500.
Nov. 1   Received $1 per share cash dividend on Z Co. common stock.
Dec. 15   Received $.50 per share cash dividend on X Co. common stock.
    31   Received $1 per share semiannual cash dividend on Y Co. common stock.

At December 31, the fair values per share of the common stocks were: X Co. $16, Y Co. $8, and Z Co. $18.

Instructions

(a) Journalize the 2002 transactions and post to the account Stock Investments. (Use the T-account form.)

(b) Prepare the adjusting entry at December 31, 2002, to show the securities at fair value. The stock should be classified as available-for-sale securities.

(c) Show the balance sheet presentation of the investments at December 31, 2002. At this date, Milner Associates has common stock $1,500,000 and retained earnings $1,000,000.

P13–4B Nayler Services acquired 30% of the outstanding common stock of Quinn Company on January 1, 2001, by paying $800,000 for 40,000 shares. Quinn declared and paid a $0.40 per share cash dividends on March 15, June 15, September 15, and December 15, 2001. Quinn reported net income of $360,000 for the year.

Prepare entries under the cost and equity methods and tabulate differences.
(SO 3)

Instructions
(a) Prepare the journal entries for Nayler Services for 2001 assuming Nayler cannot exercise significant influence over Quinn. (Use the cost method.)
(b) Prepare the journal entries for Nayler Services for 2001, assuming Nayler can exercise significant influence over Quinn. (Use the equity method.)
(c) In tabular form, indicate the investment and income statement account balances at December 31, 2001, under each method of accounting.

P13–5B The following are in Hyatt Company's portfolio of long-term available-for-sale securities at December 31, 2001:

Journalize stock transactions and show statement presentation.
(SO 3, 5, 6)

	Cost
500 shares of Aglar Corporation common stock	$26,000
700 shares of BAL Corporation common stock	42,000
400 shares of Hicks Corporation preferred stock	16,800

On December 31, the total cost of the portfolio equaled total fair value. Hyatt had the following transactions related to the securities during 2002:

Jan. 7 Sold 500 shares of Aglar Corporation common stock at $56 per share less brokerage fees of $700.
Jan. 10 Purchased 200 shares, $70 par value common stock of Miley Corporation at $78 per share, plus brokerage fees of $240.
26 Received a cash dividend of $1.15 per share on BAL Corporation common stock.
Feb. 2 Received cash dividends of $.40 per share on Hicks Corporation preferred stock.
10 Sold all 400 shares of Hicks Corporation preferred stock at $30.00 per share less brokerage fees of $180.
July 1 Received a cash dividend of $1.00 per share on BAL Corporation common stock.
Sept. 1 Purchased an additional 400 shares of the $70 par value common stock of Miley Corporation at $82 per share, plus brokerage fees of $400.
Dec. 15 Received a cash dividend of $1.50 per share on Miley Corporation common stock.

At December 31, 2002, the fair values of the securities were:

BAL Corporation common stock	$64 per share
Miley Corporation common stock	$72 per share

Hyatt uses separate account titles for each investment, such as Investment in BAL Corporation Common Stock.

Instructions
(a) Prepare journal entries to record the transactions.
(b) Post to the investment accounts. (Use T accounts.)
(c) Prepare the adjusting entry at December 31, 2002, to report the portfolio at fair value.
(d) Show the balance sheet presentation at December 31, 2002.

P13–6B The following data are taken from the records of Jana Corporation.

Prepare a balance sheet.
(SO 5, 6)

Accounts payable	$ 270,000
Accounts receivable	140,000
Accumulated depreciation—building	180,000
Accumulated depreciation—equipment	52,000
Allowance for doubtful accounts	6,000
Bonds payable (10%, due 2012)	500,000
Bond investments	150,000
Buildings	950,000
Cash	92,000
Common stock ($10 par value; 500,000 shares authorized, 150,000 shares issued)	1,500,000
Dividends payable	80,000
Equipment	275,000

Goodwill	$200,000
Income taxes payable	120,000
Investment in Thebeau Inc. common stock (10% ownership), at cost	278,000
Investment in Comex Co. common stock (30% ownership), at equity	230,000
Land	500,000
Market adjustment—available-for-sale securities (Dr)	8,000
Merchandise inventory	170,000
Notes payable (due 2002)	70,000
Patents	50,000
Paid-in capital in excess of par value	200,000
Premium on bonds payable	40,000
Prepaid insurance	16,000
Retained earnings	213,000
Temporary stock investment, at fair value	180,000
Unrealized gain—available-for-sale securities	8,000

The investment in Thebeau Inc. common stock is considered to be a long-term available-for-sale security.

Instructions
Prepare a balance sheet at December 31, 2001.

Prepare consolidated work sheet and balance sheet when cost exceeds book value.
(SO 6, 7, 8)

*P13–7B   Naperville Company purchased all the outstanding common stock of Peoria Company on December 31, 2001. Just before the purchase, the condensed balance sheets of the two companies were as follows:

	Naperville Company	Peoria Company
Current assets	$1,476,000	$379,000
Plant and equipment (net)	1,882,000	353,000
	$3,358,000	$732,000
Current liabilities	$ 868,000	$ 92,000
Common stock	1,947,000	360,000
Retained earnings	543,000	280,000
	$3,358,000	$732,000

Naperville used current assets of $726,000 to acquire the stock of Peoria. The excess of this purchase price over the book value of Naperville's net assets is determined to be attributable $30,000 to Peoria's plant and equipment and the remainder to goodwill.

Instructions
(a) Prepare the entry for Naperville Company's acquisition of Peoria Company stock.
(b) Prepare a consolidated work sheet at December 31, 2001.
(c) Prepare a consolidated balance sheet at December 31, 2001.

BROADENING YOUR PERSPECTIVE

FINANCIAL REPORTING AND ANALYSIS

FINANCIAL REPORTING PROBLEM: Kellogg Company

BYP13–1   The 1998 Annual Report of Kellogg Company is presented in Appendix A.

Instructions
Answer the following questions:

(a) What information about investments is reported in the consolidated balance sheet?
(b) Based on the information in Note 1 accompanying the financial statements, what is the nature of Kellogg's short-term investments?
(c) How much was spent in acquisition of new businesses in 1998 compared with 1997 and 1996?

COMPARATIVE ANALYSIS PROBLEM: Kellogg Company vs. General Mills

BYP13-2 Kellogg's financial statements are presented in Appendix A; General Mills's financial statements are presented in Appendix B.

Instructions
(a) Based on the information contained in these financial statements, determine each of the following for each company:
   (1) Cash used in (by) investing (investment) activities during 1998 (from the Statement of Cash Flows).
   (2) Cash used for acquisitions and investments in businesses during 1998.
(b) Based on the information contained in the notes to the financial statements, explain the major acquisitions made by these two companies in the last three years.

RESEARCH ASSIGNMENT

BYP 13-3 The January 9, 1999, issue of *The Economist* includes an article entitled "How to Make Mergers Work."

Instructions
Read the article and answer the following questions:

(a) What percentage of mergers actually added value to the combined firm? Which investors tend to gain from the merger, and which tend to lose?
(b) The article suggests that mergers in the past tended to be undertaken to create diversified conglomerates, but that mergers of today tend to be defensive in nature. Give examples of motivations for defensive mergers and industries where they have taken place.
(c) What are some reasons why mergers often fail?
(d) What are some methods for increasing the likelihood of success?

INTERPRETING FINANCIAL STATEMENTS: Xerox Corporation

BYP13-4 Xerox Corporation has a 50% investment interest in a joint venture with the Japanese corporation Fuji, called Fuji Xerox. Xerox accounts for this investment using the equity method. The following additional information regarding this investment was taken from Xerox's 1995 annual report:

Investment in Fuji Xerox per balance sheet	$ 1,223
Xerox's equity in Fuji Xerox net income	88
Xerox total assets	25,969
Xerox total liabilities	21,328
Fuji Xerox total assets	6,603
Fuji Xerox total liabilities	4,153

Instructions
(a) What alternative approaches are available for accounting for long-term investments in stock? Discuss whether Xerox is correct in using the equity method to account for this investment.
(b) Under the equity method, how does Xerox reports its investment in Fuji Xerox? If Xerox owned a majority of Fuji Xerox, it then would have to consolidate Fuji Xerox instead of using the equity method. Discuss how this would change Xerox's financial statements. That is, in what way and by how much would assets and liabilities change?
(c) The use of 50% joint ventures is becoming a fairly common practice. Why might companies like Xerox prefer to participate in a joint venture rather than own a majority share?

REAL-WORLD FOCUS: SPS Technologies, Inc.

BYP13-5 **SPS Technologies, Inc.,** was formed in 1903 as Standard Pressed Steel. Today the company is engaged in the design, manufacture, and marketing of high-strength mechanical fasteners, superalloys, and magnetic materials for the aerospace, automotive, and off-highway equipment industries. The company owns plants in the United States, United Kingdom, Ireland, Australia, and Spain, and has minority interests in facilities in Brazil and India.

The following note to the financial statements appears in a recent SPS annual report:

SPS TECHNOLOGIES
Notes to the Financial Statements

Investments: The Company's investments in affiliates consist of a 16.75% interest in Precision Fasteners Ltd., Bombay, India; a 46.49% interest in Metalac S.A. Industria e Comercio, Sao Paulo, Brazil; a 51.0% interest in Pacific Products Limited, Guernsey, Channel Islands, United Kingdom; and a 51.0% interest in National-Arnold Magnetics Company, Adelanto, California, United States. In three consecutive years, dividends received from these companies were $42,000, $44,000, and $66,000.

Instructions
(a) Does the investment in these companies represent short- or long-term investments? Are these investments in stocks or in bonds of these companies?
(b) The ownership percentages in these companies vary. Based upon the information given, which accounting method would appear appropriate for each company? What other information would you like to know before deciding how to account for each investment?
(c) What is the most likely method used to account for dividends received from Precision Fasteners? From National-Arnolds Magnetics Company?

CRITICAL THINKING
GROUP DECISION CASE

BYP13–6 At the beginning of the question and answer portion of the annual stockholders' meeting of Powell Corporation, stockholder Cindy Olson asks, "Why did management sell the holdings in BMA Company at a loss when this company has been very profitable during the period its stock was held by Powell?"

Since president Tony Perez has just concluded his speech on the recent success and bright future of Powell, he is taken aback by this question and responds, "I remember we paid $1,100,000 for that stock some years ago, and I am sure we sold that stock at a much higher price. You must be mistaken."

Olson retorts, "Well, right here in footnote number 7 to the annual report it shows that 240,000 shares, a 25% interest in BMA, were sold on the last day of the year. Also, it states that BMA earned $550,000 this year and paid out $150,000 in cash dividends. Further, a summary statement indicates that in past years, while Powell held BMA stock, BMA earned $1,240,000 and paid out $440,000 in dividends. Finally, the income statement for this year shows a loss on the sale of BMA stock of $180,000. So, I doubt that I am mistaken."

Red-faced, president Perez turns to you.

Instructions
With the class divided into groups, answer the following:
(a) What dollar amount did Powell receive upon the sale of the BMA stock?
(b) Explain why both stockholder Olson and president Perez are correct.

COMMUNICATION ACTIVITY

BYP13–7 Ramariz Corporation has purchased two securities for its portfolio. The first is a stock investment in Thome Corporation, one of its suppliers. Ramariz purchased 10% of Thome with the intention of holding it for a number of years, but has no intention of purchasing more shares. The second investment was a purchase of debt securities. Ramariz purchased the debt securities because its analysts believe that changes in market interest rates will cause these securities to increase in value in a short period of time. Ramariz intends to sell the securities as soon as they have increased in value.

Instructions

Write a memo to Crus Carey, the chief financial officer, explaining how to account for each of these investments, and what the implications for reported income are from this accounting treatment.

ETHICS CASE

BYP13–8   Kimble Financial Services Company holds a large portfolio of debt and stock securities as an investment. The total fair value of the portfolio at December 31, 2001, is greater than total cost, with some securities having increased in value and others having decreased. Ann Osborn, the financial vice president, and Sue Ling, the controller, are in the process of classifying for the first time the securities in the portfolio.

Osborn suggests classifying the securities that have increased in value as trading securities in order to increase net income for the year. She also wants to classify the securities that have decreased in value as long-term available-for-sale securities so that the decreases in value will not affect 2001 net income.

Ling disagrees. She recommends classifying the securities that have decreased in value as trading securities and those that have increased in value as long-term available-for-sale securities. Ling argues that the company is having a good earnings year and that recognizing the losses now will help to smooth income for this year. Moreover, for future years, when the company may not be as profitable, the company will have built-in gains.

Instructions

(a) Will classifying the securities as Osborn and Ling suggest actually affect earnings as each says it will?

(b) Is there anything unethical in what Osborn and Ling propose? Who are the stakeholders affected by their proposals?

(c) Assume that Osborn and Ling properly classify the portfolio. Assume, at year-end, that Osborn proposes to sell the securities that will increase 2001 net income, and that Ling proposes to sell the securities that will decrease 2001 net income. Is this unethical?

SURFING THE NET

BPY13–9   Most publicly traded companies are analyzed by numerous analysts. These analysts often don't agree about a company's future prospects. In this exercise you will find analysts' ratings about companies and make comparisons over time and across companies in the same industry. You will also see to what extent the analysts experienced "earnings surprises." Earnings surprises can cause changes in stock prices.

Address: http://biz.yahoo.com/i (or go to www.wiley.com/college/weygandt)

Steps:

1. Choose a company.
2. Use the index to find the company's name.
3. Choose **Research**.

Instructions

Answer the following questions:

(a) How many brokers rated the company?

(b) What percentage rated it a strong buy?

(c) What was the average rating for the week?

(d) Did the average rating improve or decline relative to the prior week?

(e) How do the brokers rank this company among all the companies in its industry?

(f) What was the amount of the earnings surprise during the last quarter (that is, to what extent were analysts' expectations of earnings incorrect)?

(g) Are earnings expected to increase or decrease this quarter compared to last?

Answers to Self-Study Questions
1. a   2.   3. c   4. a   5. a   6. c   7. b   8. c   *9. d   *10. d   *11. d

Answer to Kellogg Review It Question 4, page 576
In Note 1, the following statement is made regarding the consolidation policy of Kellogg Company: "The consolidated financial statements include the accounts of Kellogg Company and its majority-owned subsidiaries. Intercompany balances and transactions are eliminated. Certain amounts in the prior year financial statements have been reclassified to conform to the current year presentation."

Remember to go back to the Navigator box on the chapter-opening page and check off your completed work.

Before studying this chapter, you should know or, if necessary, review:

a. The difference between the accrual basis and the cash basis of accounting. (Ch. 3, pp. 112–113)

b. The major items included in a corporation's classified balance sheet. (Ch. 4, p. 161)

c. The major items included in a corporation's multiple-step income statement. (Ch. 5, p. 207)

THE
NAVIGATOR

FEATURE STORY

"Cash Is Cash, and Everything Else Is Accounting"

For Gerald Biby, vice president and chief financial officer of Kilian Community College in Sioux Falls, South Dakota, the statement of cash flows was the difference between being able to refinance a mortgage and being turned down by six local banks. "We recently wanted to refinance a $125,000 mortgage on a piece of property that we own," he says. "It was the statement of cash flows that finally showed our lender that we had the cash flow to service the debt."

As he explains, the traditional financial statement for a not-for-profit, educational institution shows revenues and all expenditures, even the capital expenditures. According to this format, which the banks focused on initially, Kilian Community College was just breaking even. "In the business world, if we had spent $250,000 on a computer system, then we would have put that on a depreciation schedule. But in the non-profit arena, it's typical that the entire $250,000 is written off as an expense against the general fund." The statement of cash flows showed the bankers that one of the uses of funds was really the purchase of computer equipment that had several years of life.

The college's statement of cash flows has over 30 classifications including tuition, fees, bookstore revenues, and so on. The school has 250 students, charges $70 a credit hour (12 hours is a full-time schedule), and has five terms each year.

The bankers granted the refinancing when they saw that the college's sources of funds exceeded the loan repayments, including principal and interest, by a ratio of 3-to-1. Not only did the school get the loan, but it did so at a favorable rate. "We were able to cut the mortgage rate to prime plus 1% from prime plus 3%."

THE
NAVIGATOR

CHAPTER 14

THE STATEMENT OF CASH FLOWS

THE NAVIGATOR ✔

- Understand *Concepts for Review*
- Read *Feature Story*
- Scan *Study Objectives*
- Read *Preview*
- Read text and answer *Before You Go On*
  p. 615 ☐ p. 625 ☐ p. 638 ☐ p. 643 ☐
- Work *Demonstration Problem*
- Review *Summary of Study Objectives*
- Answer *Self-Study Questions*
- Complete assignments

STUDY OBJECTIVES

After studying this chapter, you should be able to:

1. *Indicate the primary purpose of the statement of cash flows.*
2. *Distinguish among operating, investing, and financing activities.*
3. *Prepare a statement of cash flows using the indirect method.*
4. *Prepare a statement of cash flows using the direct method.*
5. *Analyze the statement of cash flows.*

THE NAVIGATOR

*A*s the story about Kilian Community College indicates, the balance sheet, income statement, and retained earnings statement do not always show the whole picture of the financial condition of a company or institution. In fact, looking at the three traditional financial statements of some well-known companies, a thoughtful investor might have questions like the following: How did Eastman Kodak finance cash dividends of $649 million in a year in which it earned only $17 million? How could Delta Airlines purchase new planes costing $900 million in a year in which it reported a net loss of $86 million? How did the companies that were involved in the 7,000 mergers and acquisitions worth over $1 trillion in 1998 finance those business combinations? Answers to these and similar questions can be found in this chapter, which presents the **statement of cash flows**. The content and organization of this chapter are as follows:

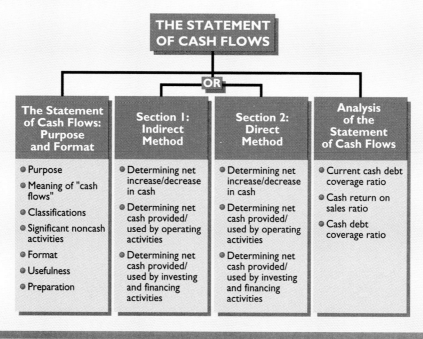

THE NAVIGATOR

THE STATEMENT OF CASH FLOWS: PURPOSE AND FORMAT

The three basic financial statements we've studied so far present only limited and fragmentary information about a company's cash flows (cash receipts and cash payments). For example, comparative balance sheets show the increase in property, plant, and equipment during the year, but they do not show how the additions were financed or paid for. The income statement shows net income, but it does not indicate the amount of cash generated by operating activities. Similarly, the retained earnings statement shows cash dividends declared but not the cash dividends paid during the year. None of these statements presents a detailed summary of the net change in cash as a result of operating, investing, and financing activities during the period.

Purpose of the Statement of Cash Flows

The primary purpose of the statement of cash flows is to provide information about the cash receipts and cash payments of an entity during a period. A secondary objective is to provide information about the operating, investing, and financing activities of the entity during the period.[1] The statement of cash flows reports the cash receipts, cash payments, and net change in cash resulting from the operating, investing, and financing activities of an enterprise during a period in a format that reconciles the beginning and ending cash balances.

Reporting the causes of changes in cash is considered useful because investors, creditors, and other interested parties want to know what is happening to a company's most liquid resource—its cash. As the Feature Story about Kilian Community College demonstrates, a statement of cash flows helps us understand what is happening. It provides answers to the following simple, but important, questions about the enterprise:

1. Where did the cash come from during the period?
2. What was the cash used for during the period?
3. What was the change in the cash balance during the period?

1
STUDY
OBJECTIVE
....
Indicate the primary purpose of the statement of cash flows.

Meaning of "Cash Flows"

The statement of cash flows is generally prepared using "**cash and cash equivalents**" as its basis. Cash equivalents are short-term, highly liquid investments that are both:

1. Readily convertible to known amounts of cash, and
2. So near their maturity that their market value is relatively insensitive to changes in interest rates.

Generally, only investments with original maturities of three months or less qualify under this definition. Examples of cash equivalents are Treasury bills, commercial paper (short-term corporate notes), and money market funds. All typically are purchased with cash that is in excess of immediate needs. Note that since cash and cash equivalents are viewed as the same, transfers between cash and cash equivalents are not treated as cash receipts and cash payments—i.e., they are not reported in the statement of cash flows. The term "cash" when used in this chapter includes cash and cash equivalents.

Classification of Cash Flows

The statement of cash flows classifies cash receipts and cash payments by operating, investing, and financing activities. Transactions and other events characteristic of each kind of activity are described in the list below and pictured in Illustration 14-1:

2
STUDY
OBJECTIVE
....
Distinguish among operating, investing, and financing activities.

1. Operating activities include the cash effects of transactions that create revenues and expenses and thus enter into the determination of net income.
2. Investing activities include (a) acquiring and disposing of investments and productive long-lived assets, and (b) lending money and collecting the loans.
3. Financing activities include (a) obtaining cash from issuing debt and repaying the amounts borrowed, and (b) obtaining cash from stockholders and providing them with a return on their investment.

---

[1]"Statement of Cash Flows," *Statement of Financial Accounting Standards No. 95* (Stamford, Conn.: FASB, 1987).

ILLUSTRATION 14-1

Business activities shown on the statement of cash flows

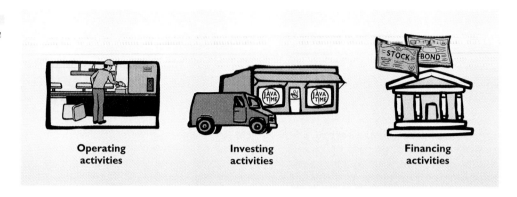

The category of operating activities is the most important because it shows the cash provided by company operations. This source of cash is generally considered to be the best measure of a company's ability to generate sufficient cash to continue as a going concern.

Illustration 14-2 lists typical cash receipts and cash payments within each of the three classifications. Study the list carefully. It will prove very useful in solving homework exercises and problems.

ILLUSTRATION 14-2

Typical receipts and payments classified by activity

Types of Cash Inflows and Outflows

Operating activities
Cash inflows:
From sale of goods or services.
From returns on loans (interest received) and on equity securities (dividends received).
Cash outflows:
To suppliers for inventory.
To employees for services.
To government for taxes.
To lenders for interest.
To others for expenses.

Investing activities
Cash inflows:
From sale of property, plant, and equipment.
From sale of debt or equity securities of other entities.
From collection of principal on loans to other entities.
Cash outflows:
To purchase property, plant, and equipment.
To purchase debt or equity securities of other entities.
To make loans to other entities.

Financing activities
Cash inflows:
From issuance of equity securities (company's own stock).
From issuance of debt (bonds and notes).
Cash outflows:
To stockholders as dividends.
To redeem long-term debt or reacquire capital stock.

HELPFUL HINT
Operating activities generally relate to changes in current assets and current liabilities. Investing activities generally relate to changes in noncurrent assets. Financing activities relate to changes in noncurrent liabilities and stockholders' equity accounts.

As you can see, some cash flows relating to investing or financing activities are classified as operating activities. For example, **receipts of investment revenue (interest and dividends) and payments of interest to lenders are classified as operating activities because these items are reported in the income statement.**

ACCOUNTING IN ACTION
Business Insight

Differences between net income and net cash provided by operating activities are illustrated by the following results from recent annual reports for the same fiscal year (all data are in millions of dollars):

Company	Net Income	Net Cash from Operations
Kmart Corporation	$ 296	$ 76
Wal-Mart Stores, Inc.	2,681	2,906
Gap Inc.	824	1,394
J.C. Penney Company, Inc.	1,057	738
Sears, Roebuck & Co.	1,454	1,930
The May Department Stores Company	782	999

Note the wide disparity among the companies that engaged in similar types of retail merchandising.

Note that, generally, (1) operating activities involve income determination (income statement) items, (2) investing activities involve cash flows resulting from changes in investments and long-term asset items, and (3) financing activities involve cash flows resulting from changes in long-term liability and stockholders' equity items.

Significant Noncash Activities

Not all of a company's significant activities involve cash. Examples of significant noncash activities are:

1. Issuance of common stock to purchase assets.
2. Conversion of bonds into common stock.
3. Issuance of debt to purchase assets.
4. Exchanges of plant assets.

Significant financing and investing activities that do not affect cash are not reported in the body of the statement of cash flows. However, these activities are reported in either a separate schedule at the bottom of the statement of cash flows or in a separate note or supplementary schedule to the financial statements.

The reporting of these activities in a separate note or supplementary schedule satisfies the **full disclosure principle** because it identifies significant noncash investing and financing activities of the enterprise. In solving homework assignments you should present significant noncash investing and financing activities in a separate schedule at the bottom of the statement of cash flows. (See lower section of Illustration 14-3, on page 612, for an example.)

HELPFUL HINT
Do not include noncash investing and financing activities in the body of the statement of cash flows. Report this information in a separate schedule at the bottom of the statement.

Format of the Statement of Cash Flows

The three activities discussed previously—operating, investing, and financing—plus the significant noncash investing and financing activities constitute the general format of the statement of cash flows. A widely used form of the statement of cash flows is shown in Illustration 14-3.

ILLUSTRATION 14-3

Format of statement of cash flows

COMPANY NAME Statement of Cash Flows Period Covered		
Cash flows from operating activities		
(List of individual items)	XX	
Net cash provided (used) by operating activities		XXX
Cash flows from investing activities		
(List of individual inflows and outflows)	XX	
Net cash provided (used) by investing activities		XXX
Cash flows from financing activities		
(List of individual inflows and outflows)	XX	
Net cash provided (used) by financing activities		XXX
Net increase (decrease) in cash		XXX
Cash at beginning of period		XXX
Cash at end of period		XXX
Noncash investing and financing activities		
(List of individual noncash transactions)		XXX

As illustrated, the cash flows from operating activities section always appears first, followed by the investing activities and the financing activities sections. Also, **the individual inflows and outflows from investing and financing activities are reported separately**. Thus, cash outflow for the purchase of property, plant, and equipment is reported separately from the cash inflow from the sale of property, plant, and equipment. Similarly, the cash inflow from the issuance of debt securities is reported separately from the cash outflow for the retirement of debt. If a company did not report the inflows and outflows separately, it would obscure the investing and financing activities of the enterprise and thus make it more difficult to assess future cash flows.

The reported operating, investing, and financing activities result in either net cash **provided or used** by each activity. The net cash provided or used by each activity is totaled to show the net increase (decrease) in cash for the period. The net increase (decrease) in cash for the period is then added to or subtracted from the beginning-of-the-period cash balance to obtain the end-of-the-period cash balance. Finally, any significant noncash investing and financing activities are reported in a separate schedule at the bottom of the statement.

Usefulness of the Statement of Cash Flows

The information in a statement of cash flows should help investors, creditors, and others assess various aspects of the firm's financial position:

1. **The entity's ability to generate future cash flows.** By examining relationships between such items as sales and net cash provided by operating activities, or cash provided by operations and increases or decreases in cash, investors and others can make predictions of the amounts, timing, and uncertainty of future cash flows better than from accrual basis data.

2. **The entity's ability to pay dividends and meet obligations.** Simply put, if a company does not have adequate cash, employees cannot be paid, debts settled, or dividends paid. Employees, creditors, stockholders, and customers should be particularly interested in this statement, because it alone shows the flows of cash in a business.

3. **The reasons for the difference between net income and net cash provided (used) by operating activities.** Net income is important, because it provides information on the success or failure of a business enterprise. However, some are critical of accrual basis net income because it requires many estimates; as a result, the reliability of the number is often challenged. Such is not the case with cash. Thus, many readers of the financial statements want to know the reasons for the difference between net income and net cash provided by operating activities. Then they can assess for themselves the reliability of the income number.

4. **The cash investing and financing transactions during the period.** By examining a company's investing activities and its financing transactions, a financial statement reader can better understand why assets and liabilities increased or decreased during the period. In summary, the information in the statement of cash flows is useful in answering the following questions:

> How did cash increase when there was a net loss for the period?
> How were the proceeds of the bond issue used?
> How was the expansion in the plant and equipment financed?
> Why were dividends not increased?
> How was the retirement of debt accomplished?
> How much money was borrowed during the year?
> Is cash flow greater or less than net income?

HELPFUL HINT

Income from operations and cash flow from operating activities are different. Income from operations is based on accrual accounting; cash flow from operating activities is prepared on a cash basis.

ACCOUNTING IN ACTION
Business Insight

Cash flow is also sometimes used to determine the price of a company. Page Net, a company in the telephone beeper business, had an initial public offering (IPO) in which $590 million of stock was sold. In December 1993 the stock had a market value of $1.5 billion. Yet Page Net reported losses in every quarter since it went public. However, its cash flow the year before the IPO was $39 million, $57 million in the IPO year, $75 million in 1992, and approximately $99 million in 1993. As one expert noted, "It is a classic example of a company valued by cash flow."

Preparing the Statement of Cash Flows

The statement of cash flows is prepared differently from the three other basic financial statements. First, it is not prepared from an adjusted trial balance. Because the statement requires detailed information concerning the changes in account balances that occurred between two periods of time, an adjusted trial balance will not provide the necessary data for the statement. Second, the statement of cash flows deals with cash receipts and payments. As a result, **the accrual concept is not used in the preparation of a statement of cash flows**.

The information to prepare this statement usually comes from three sources:

Comparative balance sheet. Information in this statement indicates the amount of the changes in assets, liabilities, and stockholders' equities from the beginning to the end of the period.

Current income statement. Information in this statement helps the reader determine the amount of cash provided by or used by operations during the period.

Additional information. Additional information includes transaction data that are needed to determine how cash was provided or used during the period.

ILLUSTRATION 14-4

Three major steps in preparing the statement of cash flows

Preparing the statement of cash flows from these data sources involves three major steps, explained in Illustration 14-4.

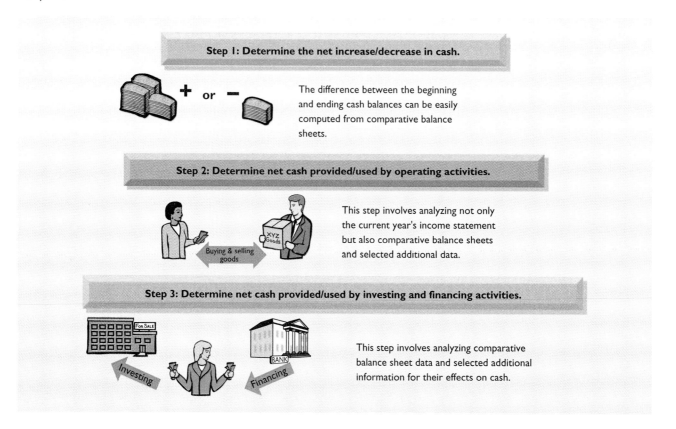

Step 1: Determine the net increase/decrease in cash.

The difference between the beginning and ending cash balances can be easily computed from comparative balance sheets.

Step 2: Determine net cash provided/used by operating activities.

Buying & selling goods

This step involves analyzing not only the current year's income statement but also comparative balance sheets and selected additional data.

Step 3: Determine net cash provided/used by investing and financing activities.

Investing   Financing

This step involves analyzing comparative balance sheet data and selected additional information for their effects on cash.

Indirect and Direct Methods

In order to perform step 2, the operating activities section of the statement of cash flows **must be converted from an accrual basis to a cash basis**. This conversion may be done by either of two methods: (1) the indirect method or (2) the direct method. **Both methods arrive at the same total amount** for "Net cash provided by operating activities," but they differ in disclosing the items that comprise the total amount.

The indirect method is used extensively in practice, as shown in the nearby chart.[2] Companies (98%) favor the indirect method for two reasons: (1) it is easier to prepare, and (2) it focuses on the differences between net income and net cash flow from operating activities.

Others, however, favor the direct method. The direct method shows operating cash receipts and payments. Thus, it is more consistent with the objective of a statement of cash flows. The FASB has expressed a preference for the direct method, but allows the use of either method. However, when the direct method is used, the net cash flow from operating activities as computed using the indirect method must also be reported in a separate schedule.

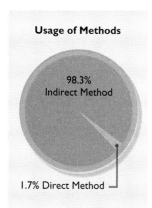

Usage of Methods

98.3%
Indirect Method

1.7% Direct Method

---

[2]*Accounting Trends and Techniques—1998* survey of 600 companies indicated that 590 use the indirect method and 10 use the direct method.

BEFORE YOU GO ON . . .

Review It

1. What is the primary purpose of a statement of cash flows?
2. What are the major classifications of cash flows on the statement of cash flows?
3. What are the three major steps in the preparation of a statement of cash flows?
4. Why is the statement of cash flows useful? What key information does it convey?

Do It

During its first week of existence, Plano Molding Company had the following transactions:

1. Issued 100,000 shares of $5 par value common stock for $800,000 cash.
2. Borrowed $200,000 from Sandwich State Bank, signing a 5-year note bearing 8% interest.
3. Purchased two semi-trailer trucks for $170,000 cash.
4. Paid employees $12,000 for salaries and wages.
5. Collected $20,000 cash for services rendered.

Classify by type of cash flow activity each of these transactions.

Reasoning: All cash flows are classified into three types of activities for purposes of reporting cash inflows and outflows: operating activities, investing activities, and financing activities. Operating activities include the cash effects of transactions that create revenues and expenses and thus enter into the determination of net income. Investing activities include (a) acquiring and disposing of investments and productive long-lived assets, and (b) lending money and collecting the loans. Financing activities include (a) obtaining cash from issuing debt and repaying the amounts borrowed, and (b) obtaining cash from stockholders and providing them with a return on their investment.

Solution:

1. Financing activity.   4. Operating activity.
2. Financing activity.   5. Operating activity.
3. Investing activity.

Related exercise material: BE14–3, BE14–5, E14–1, and E14–6.

INTERNATIONAL NOTE

International accounting requirements are quite similar in most respects with regard to the cash flow statement. Some interesting exceptions: In Japan, operating and investing activities are combined; in Australia, the direct method is mandatory; in Spain, the indirect method is mandatory. Also, in a number of European and Scandinavian countries a cash flow statement is not required at all, although in practice most publicly traded firms provide one.

On the following pages, in two separate sections, we describe the use of the two alternative methods of preparing the operating activities section of the statement of cash flows. Section 1 illustrates the indirect method, and Section 2 illustrates the direct method. These sections are independent of each other; *only one or the other* need be covered in order to understand and prepare the statement of cash flows. When you have finished the section assigned by your instructor, turn to the next topic, on page 640—"Analysis of the Statement of Cash Flows."

SECTION 1   STATEMENT OF CASH FLOWS— INDIRECT METHOD

To explain and illustrate the indirect method, we will use the transactions of the Computer Services Company for two years—2000 and 2001. Annual statements of cash flows will be prepared. Basic transactions will be used in the first year with additional transactions added in the second year.

3
STUDY
OBJECTIVE

Prepare a statement of cash flows using the direct method.

....
FIRST YEAR OF OPERATIONS—2000

Computer Services Company started on January 1, 2000, when it issued 50,000 shares of $1.00 par value common stock for $50,000 cash. The company rented its office space and furniture and performed consulting services throughout the first year. The comparative balance sheets at the beginning and end of 2000, showing increases or decreases, appear in Illustration 14-5.

ILLUSTRATION 14-5

Comparative balance sheet, 2000, with increases and decreases

COMPUTER SERVICES COMPANY
Comparative Balance Sheet

Assets	Dec. 31, 2000	Jan. 1, 2000	Change Increase/Decrease
Cash	$34,000	$ –0–	$34,000 Increase
Accounts receivable	30,000	–0–	30,000 Increase
Equipment	10,000	–0–	10,000 Increase
Total	$74,000	$ –0–	
Liabilities and Stockholders' Equity			
Accounts payable	$ 4,000	$ –0–	$ 4,000 Increase
Common stock	50,000	–0–	50,000 Increase
Retained earnings	20,000	–0–	20,000 Increase
Total	$74,000	$ –0–	

HELPFUL HINT
Note that although each of the balance sheet items of Computer Sevices increased, their individual effects are not the same. Some of these increases are cash inflows, and some are cash outflows.

The income statement and additional information for Computer Services Company are shown in Illustration 14-6.

ILLUSTRATION 14-6

Income statement and additional information, 2000

COMPUTER SERVICES COMPANY
Income Statement
For the Year Ended December 31, 2000

Revenues	$85,000
Operating expenses	40,000
Income before income taxes	45,000
Income tax expense	10,000
Net income	$35,000

Additional information:
(a) A dividend of $15,000 was declared and paid during the year.
(b) The equipment was purchased at the end of 2000. No depreciation was taken in 2000.

HELPFUL HINT
You may wish to insert the beginning and ending cash balances and the increase/decrease in cash necessitated by these balances immediately into the statement of cash flows. The net increase/decrease is the target amount. The net cash flows from the three classes of activities must equal the target amount.

Determining the Net Increase/Decrease in Cash (Step 1)

To prepare a statement of cash flows, the first step to **determine the net increase or decrease in cash**. This is a simple computation. For example, Computer Services Company had no cash on hand at the beginning of 2000, but had $34,000 on hand at the end of 2000. Thus, the change in cash for 2000 was an increase of $34,000.

Determining Net Cash Provided/Used by Operating Activities (Step 2)

To determine net cash provided by operating activities under the indirect method, **net income is adjusted for items that did not affect cash**. A useful starting point in determining net cash provided by operating activities is to understand **why** net income must be converted. Under generally accepted accounting principles, most companies use the accrual basis of accounting. As you have learned, this basis requires that revenue be recorded when earned and that expenses be recorded when incurred. Earned revenues may include credit sales that have not been collected in cash and expenses incurred that may not have been paid in cash. Thus, under the accrual basis of accounting, net income does not indicate the net cash provided by operating activities. Therefore, under the indirect method, net income must be adjusted to convert certain items to the cash basis.

The indirect method (or reconciliation method) starts with net income and converts it to net cash provided by operating activities. In other words, **the indirect method adjusts net income for items that affected reported net income but did not affect cash**, as shown in Illustration 14-7. That is, noncash charges in the income statement are added back to net income and noncash credits are deducted to compute net cash provided by operating activities. A useful starting point in identifying the adjustments to net income is the current asset and current liability accounts other than cash. Those accounts—receivables, payables, prepayments, and inventories—should be analyzed for their effects on cash.

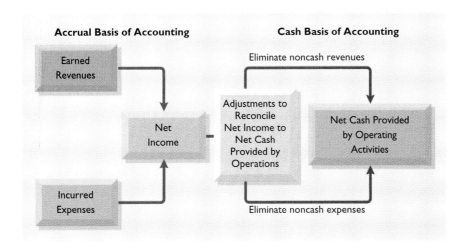

ILLUSTRATION 14-7

Net income versus net cash provided by operating activities

Increase in Accounts Receivable.   When accounts receivable increase during the year, revenues on an accrual basis are higher than revenues on a cash basis. In other words, operations of the period led to increased revenues, **but not all of these revenues resulted in an increase in cash**; some of the increase in revenues resulted in an increase in accounts receivable.

Illustration 14-8 shows that Computer Services Company had $85,000 in revenues, but it collected only $55,000 in cash. Therefore, to convert net income to net cash provided by operating activities, the increase of $30,000 in accounts receivable must be deducted from net income.

ILLUSTRATION 14-8

*Analysis of accounts
receivable*

Accounts Receivable

1/1/00	Balance	-0-	Receipts from customers	55,000
	Revenues	85,000		
12/31/00	Balance	30,000		

Increase in Accounts Payable.   In the first year, operating expenses incurred on account were credited to Accounts Payable. When accounts payable increase during the year, operating expenses on an accrual basis are higher than they are on a cash basis. For Computer Services, operating expenses reported in the income statement were $40,000. However, since Accounts Payable increased $4,000, only $36,000 ($40,000 − $4,000) of the expenses were paid in cash. To adjust net income to net cash provided by operating activities, the increase of $4,000 in accounts payable must be added to net income.

A T-account analysis also indicates that payments to creditors are less than operating expenses.

ILLUSTRATION 14-9

Analysis of accounts payable

Accounts Payable

Payments to creditors	36,000	1/1/00	Balances	-0-
			Operating expenses	40,000
		12/31/00	Balance	4,000

For Computer Services Company, the changes in accounts receivable and accounts payable were the only changes in current asset and current liability accounts. This means that any other revenues or expenses reported in the income statement were received or paid in cash. Thus, Computer Services' income tax expense of $10,000 was paid in cash, and no adjustment of net income is necessary.

The operating activities section of the statement of cash flows for Computer Services Company is shown in Illustration 14-10.

ILLUSTRATION 14-10

*Presentation of net cash
provided by operating
activities, 2000—indirect
method*

COMPUTER SERVICES COMPANY
Partial Statement of Cash Flows—Indirect Method
For the Year Ended December 31, 2000

Cash flows from operating activities		
Net income		$35,000
Adjustments to reconcile net income to net cash provided		
by operating activities:		
Increase in accounts receivable	$(30,000)	
Increase in accounts payable	4,000	(26,000)
Net cash provided by operating activities		**$ 9,000**

Determining Net Cash Provided/Used by Investing and Financing Activities (Step 3)

The third and final step in preparing the statement of cash flows begins with a study of the balance sheet to determine changes in noncurrent accounts. The changes in each noncurrent account are then analyzed using selected transaction data to determine the effect, if any, the changes had on cash.

In Computer Services Company, the three noncurrent accounts are Equipment, Common Stock, and Retained Earnings, and all three have increased during the year. What caused these increases? No transaction data are given for the increases in Equipment of $10,000 and Common Stock of $50,000. In solving your homework, you can conclude that **any unexplained differences in noncurrent accounts involve cash**. Thus, the increase in equipment is assumed to be a purchase of equipment for $10,000 cash. This purchase is reported as a cash outflow in the investing activities section. The increase in common stock is assumed to result from the issuance of common stock for $50,000 cash. It is reported as an inflow of cash in the financing activities section of the statement of cash flows.

The reasons for the net increase of $20,000 in the Retained Earnings account are determined by analysis. First, net income increased retained earnings by $35,000. Second, the additional information provided below the income statement in Illustration 14-6 indicates that a cash dividend of $15,000 was declared and paid. The $35,000 increase due to net income is reported in the operating activities section. The cash dividend paid is reported in the financing activities section.

This analysis can also be made directly from the Retained Earnings account in the ledger of Computer Services Company as shown in Illustration 14-11:

ILLUSTRATION 14-11

Analysis of retained earnings

Retained Earnings				
12/31/00　Cash dividend	15,000	1/1/00　Balance		–0–
		12/31/00　Net income		35,000
		12/31/00　Balance		20,000

The $20,000 increase in Retained Earnings in 2000 is a **net** change. When a net change in a noncurrent balance sheet account has occurred during the year, it generally is necessary to report the causes of the net change separately in the statement of cash flows.

Statement of Cash Flows—2000

Having completed the three steps above, we can prepare the statement of cash flows. The statement starts with the operating activities section, followed by the investing activities section, and then the financing activities section. The 2000 statement of cash flows for Computer Services is shown in Illustration 14-12.

Computer Services' statement of cash flows for 2000 shows that operating activities **provided** $9,000 cash; investing activities **used** $10,000 cash; and financing activities **provided** $35,000 cash. The increase in cash of $34,000 reported in the statement of cash flows agrees with the increase of $34,000 shown as the change in the cash account in the comparative balance sheet.

ILLUSTRATION 14-12

Statement of cash flows, 2000—indirect method

COMPUTER SERVICES COMPANY
Statement of Cash Flows—Indirect Method
For the Year Ended December 31, 2000

Cash flows from operating activities		
Net income		$35,000
Adjustments to reconcile net income to net cash provided by operating activities:		
Increase in accounts receivable	$(30,000)	
Increase in accounts payable	4,000	(26,000)
Net cash provided by operating activities		9,000
Cash flows from investing activities		
Purchase of equipment	(10,000)	
Net cash used by investing activities		(10,000)
Cash flows from financing activities		
Issuance of common stock	50,000	
Payment of cash dividends	(15,000)	
Net cash provided by financing activities		35,000
Net increase in cash		34,000
Cash at beginning of period		–0–
Cash at end of period		$34,000

....

SECOND YEAR OF OPERATIONS—2001

Presented in Illustrations 14-13 and 14-14 is information related to the second year of operations for Computer Services Company.

ILLUSTRATION 14-13

Comparative balance sheet, 2001, with increases and decreases

COMPUTER SERVICES COMPANY
Comparative Balance Sheet
December 31

Assets	2001	2000	Change Increase/Decrease
Cash	$ 56,000	$34,000	$ 22,000 Increase
Accounts receivable	20,000	30,000	10,000 Decrease
Prepaid expenses	4,000	–0–	4,000 Increase
Land	130,000	–0–	130,000 Increase
Building	160,000	–0–	160,000 Increase
Accumulated depreciation—building	(11,000)	–0–	11,000 Increase
Equipment	27,000	10,000	17,000 Increase
Accumulated depreciation—equipment	(3,000)	–0–	3,000 Increase
Total	$383,000	$74,000	
Liabilities and Stockholders' Equity			
Accounts payable	$ 59,000	$ 4,000	$ 55,000 Increase
Bonds payable	130,000	–0–	130,000 Increase
Common stock	50,000	50,000	–0–
Retained earnings	144,000	20,000	124,000 Increase
Total	$383,000	$74,000	

COMPUTER SERVICES COMPANY Income Statement For the Year Ended December 31, 2001		
Revenues		$507,000
Operating expenses (excluding depreciation)	$261,000	
Depreciation expense	15,000	
Loss on sale of equipment	3,000	279,000
Income from operations		228,000
Income tax expense		89,000
Net income		$139,000

Additional information:
(a) In 2001, the company declared and paid a $15,000 cash dividend.
(b) The company obtained land through the issuance of $130,000 of long-term bonds.
(c) A building costing $160,000 was purchased for cash; equipment costing $25,000 was also purchased for cash.
(d) During 2001, the company sold equipment with a book value of $7,000 (cost $8,000, less accumulated depreciation $1,000) for $4,000 cash.

ILLUSTRATION 14-14

Income statement and additional information, 2001

Determining the Net Increase/Decrease in Cash (Step 1)

To prepare a statement of cash flows from this information, the first step is to **determine the net increase or decrease in cash**. As indicated from the information presented, cash increased $22,000 ($56,000 − $34,000).

Determining Net Cash Provided/Used by Operating Activities (Step 2)

As in step 2 in 2000, net income on an accrual basis must be adjusted to arrive at net cash provided/used by operating activities. Explanations for the adjustments to net income for Computer Services in 2001 are as follows:

Decrease in Accounts Receivable. Accounts receivable decreases during the period because cash receipts are higher than revenues reported on an accrual basis. To adjust net income to net cash provided by operating activities, the decrease of $10,000 in accounts receivable must be added to net income.

Increase in Prepaid Expenses. Prepaid expenses increase during a period because cash paid for expenses is higher than expenses reported on an accrual basis. Cash payments have been made in the current period, but expenses (as charges to the income statement) have been deferred to future periods. To adjust net income to net cash provided by operating activities, the increase of $4,000 in prepaid expenses must be deducted from net income. An increase in prepaid expenses results in a decrease in cash during the period.

Increase in Accounts Payable. Like the increase in 2000, the 2001 increase of $55,000 in accounts payable must be added to net income to convert to net cash provided by operating activities.

Depreciation Expense. During 2001, Computer Services Company reported depreciation expense of $15,000. Of this amount, $11,000 related to the building and $4,000 to the equipment. These two amounts were determined by analyzing the accumulated depreciation accounts.

HELPFUL HINT
Decrease in accounts receivable indicates that cash collections were greater than sales. **Increase in accounts receivable** indicates that sales were greater than cash collections. **Increase in prepaid expenses** indicates that the amount paid for the prepayments exceeded the amount that was recorded as an expense. **Decrease in prepaid expenses** indicates that the amount recorded as an expense exceeded the amount of cash paid for the prepayments. **Increase in accounts payable** indicates that expenses incurred exceed the cash paid for expenses that period.

Increase in Accumulated Depreciation—Building. As shown in Illustration 14-13, accumulated depreciation increased $11,000. This change represents the depreciation expense on the building for the year. **Because depreciation expense is a noncash charge, it is added back to net income** in order to arrive at net cash provided by operating activities.

Increase in Accumulated Depreciation—Equipment. The increase in the Accumulated Depreciation—Equipment account was $3,000. This amount does not represent depreciation expense for the year because the additional information indicates that this account was decreased (debited $1,000) as a result of the sale of some equipment. Thus depreciation expense for 2001 was $4,000 ($3,000 + $1,000). This amount is added to net income to determine net cash provided by operating activities. The T-account below provides information about the changes that occurred in this account in 2001.

ILLUSTRATION 14-15

Analysis of accumulated depreciation—equipment

Accumulated Depreciation—Equipment

Accumulated depreciation on equipment sold	1,000	1/1/01	Balance	–0–
			Depreciation expense	**4,000**
		12/31/01	Balance	3,000

Depreciation expense on the building of $11,000 plus depreciation expense on the equipment of $4,000 equals the depreciation expense of $15,000 reported on the income statement.

Other charges to expense that do not require the use of cash, such as the amortization of intangible assets and depletion expense, are treated in the same manner as depreciation. Depreciation and similar noncash charges are frequently listed in the statement of cash flows as the first adjustments to net income.

Loss on Sale of Equipment. On the income statement, Computer Services Company reported a $3,000 loss on the sale of equipment (book value $7,000, less cash proceeds $4,000). The loss reduced net income but **did not reduce cash**. Thus the loss is **added to net income** in determining net cash provided by operating activities.[3]

As a result of the previous adjustments, net cash provided by operating activities is $218,000 as computed in Illustration 14-16.

Determining Net Cash Provided/Used by Investing and Financing Activities (Step 3)

After finding net cash provided by operating activities, the next step involves analyzing the remaining changes in balance sheet accounts to determine net cash provided (used) by investing and financing activities.

---

[3]If a gain on sale occurs, a different situation results. To allow a gain to flow through to net cash provided by operating activities would be double-counting the gain—once in net income and again in the investing activities section as part of the cash proceeds from sale. As a result, a gain is deducted from net income in reporting net cash provided by operating activities.

ILLUSTRATION 14-16

Presentation of net cash provided by operating activities, 2001—indirect method

COMPUTER SERVICES COMPANY
Partial Statement of Cash Flows—Indirect Method
For the Year Ended December 31, 2001

Cash flows from operating activities		
Net income		$139,000
Adjustments to reconcile net income to net cash provided by operating activities:		
Depreciation expense	$15,000	
Loss on sale of equipment	3,000	
Decrease in accounts receivable	10,000	
Increase in prepaid expenses	(4,000)	
Increase in accounts payable	55,000	79,000
Net cash provided by operating activities		$218,000

Increase in Land. As indicated from the change in the Land account, land of $130,000 was purchased through the issuance of long-term bonds. Although the issuance of bonds payable for land has no effect on cash, it is a significant non-cash investing and financing activity that merits disclosure. As indicated earlier, these activities are disclosed in a separate schedule at the bottom of the statement of cash flows.

Increase in Building. As indicated in the additional data, an office building was acquired using cash of $160,000. This transaction is a cash outflow reported in the investing section.

Increase in Equipment. The Equipment account increased $17,000. Based on the additional information, this was a net increase that resulted from two transactions: (1) a purchase of equipment of $25,000 and (2) the sale for $4,000 of equipment costing $8,000. These transactions are classified as investing activities, and each transaction should be reported separately. Thus the purchase of equipment should be reported as an outflow of cash for $25,000, and the sale should be reported as an inflow of cash for $4,000. The T-account below shows the reasons for the change in this account during the year.

ILLUSTRATION 14-17

Analysis of equipment

Equipment

1/1/01 Balance	10,000	Cost of equipment sold	8,000
Purchase of equipment	25,000		
12/31/01 Balance	27,000		

The following entry shows the details of the equipment sale transaction:

Cash	4,000	
Accumulated Depreciation	1,000	
Loss on Sale of Equipment	3,000	
Equipment		8,000

A	=	L	+	SE
+4,000				−3,000
+1,000				
−8,000				

Increase in Bonds Payable. The Bonds Payable account increased $130,000. As shown in the additional information, land was acquired from the issuance of these bonds. As indicated earlier, this noncash transaction is reported in a separate schedule at the bottom of the statement.

Increase in Retained Earnings. Retained earnings increased $124,000 during the year. This increase can be explained by two factors: (1) net income of $139,000 increased retained earnings, and (2) dividends of $15,000 decreased retained earnings. Net income is adjusted to net cash provided by operating activities in the operating activities section. Payment of the dividends is a **cash outflow that is reported as a financing activity**.

Statement of Cash Flows—2001

Combining the previous items, we obtain a statement of cash flows for 2001 for Computer Services Company as presented in Illustration 14-18.

COMPUTER SERVICES COMPANY
Statement of Cash Flows—Indirect Method
For the Year Ended December 31, 2001

Cash flows from operating activities		
Net income		$139,000
Adjustments to reconcile net income to net cash provided by operating activities:		
Depreciation expense	$ 15,000	
Loss on sale of equipment	3,000	
Decrease in accounts receivable	10,000	
Increase in prepaid expenses	(4,000)	
Increase in accounts payable	55,000	79,000
Net cash provided by operating activities		218,000
Cash flows from investing activities		
Purchase of building	(160,000)	
Purchase of equipment	(25,000)	
Sale of equipment	4,000	
Net cash used by investing activities		(181,000)
Cash flows from financing activities		
Payment of cash dividends	(15,000)	
Net cash used by financing activities		(15,000)
Net increase in cash		22,000
Cash at beginning of period		34,000
Cash at end of period		$ 56,000
Noncash investing and financing activities		
Issuance of bonds payable to purchase land		$130,000

Summary of Conversion to Net Cash Provided by Operating Activities—Indirect Method

As shown in the previous illustrations, the statement of cash flows prepared by the indirect method starts with net income and adds (or deducts) items not affecting cash to arrive at net cash provided by operating activities. The additions and deductions consist of (1) changes in specific current assets and current liabilities and (2) noncash charges reported in the income statement. A summary of the adjustments for current assets and current liabilities is provided in Illustration 14-19.

Current Assets and Current Liabilities	Adjustments to Convert Net Income to Net Cash Provided by Operating Activities	
	Add to Net Income	Deduct from Net Income
Accounts receivable	Decrease	Increase
Inventory	Decrease	Increase
Prepaid expenses	Decrease	Increase
Accounts payable	Increase	Decrease
Accrued expenses payable	Increase	Decrease

ILLUSTRATION 14-19

Adjustments for current assets and current liabilities

HELPFUL HINT
1. Increase in a current asset is deducted from net income.
2. Decrease in a current asset is added to net income.
3. Increase in a current liability is added to net income.
4. Decrease in a current liability is deducted from net income.

Adjustments for the noncash charges reported in the income statement are made as shown in Illustration 14-20.

Noncash Charges	Adjustments to Convert Net Income to Net Cash Provided by Operating Activities
Depreciation expense	Add
Patent amortization expense	Add
Depletion expense	Add
Loss on sale of asset	Add

ILLUSTRATION 14-20

Adjustments for noncash charges

BEFORE YOU GO ON ...

Review It

1. What is the format of the operating activities section of the statement of cash flows using the indirect method?
2. Where is depreciation expense shown on a statement of cash flows using the indirect method?
3. Where are significant noncash investing and financing activities shown in a statement of cash flows? Give some examples.
4. Which method of computing net cash provided by operating activities does Kellogg use? What single item provided the largest amount of cash inflow for Kellogg in 1998? The answers to these questions are provided on page 669.

Do It

Presented below is information related to Reynolds Company. Use it to prepare a statement of cash flows using the indirect method.

REYNOLDS COMPANY
Comparative Balance Sheet
December 31

Assets	2001	2000	Change Increase/Decrease
Cash	$ 54,000	$ 37,000	$ 17,000 Increase
Accounts receivable	68,000	26,000	42,000 Increase
Inventories	54,000	–0–	54,000 Increase
Prepaid expenses	4,000	6,000	2,000 Decrease
Land	45,000	70,000	25,000 Decrease
Buildings	200,000	200,000	–0–
Accumulated depreciation—buildings	(21,000)	(11,000)	10,000 Increase
Equipment	193,000	68,000	125,000 Increase
Accumulated depreciation—equipment	(28,000)	(10,000)	18,000 Increase
Totals	$569,000	$386,000	

Liabilities and Stockholders' Equity			
Accounts payable	$ 23,000	$ 40,000	$ 17,000 Decrease
Accrued expenses payable	10,000	–0–	10,000 Increase
Bonds payable	110,000	150,000	40,000 Decrease
Common stock ($1 par)	220,000	60,000	160,000 Increase
Retained earnings	206,000	136,000	70,000 Increase
Totals	$569,000	$386,000	

HELPFUL HINT
You may wish to insert the beginning and ending cash balances and the increase/decrease in cash necessitated by these balances immediately into the statement of cash flows. The net increase/decrease is the target amount. The net cash flows from the three classes of activities must equal the target amount.

REYNOLDS COMPANY
Income Statement
For the Year Ended December 31, 2001

Revenues		$890,000
Cost of goods sold	$465,000	
Operating expenses	221,000	
Interest expense	12,000	
Loss on sale of equipment	2,000	700,000
Income from operations		190,000
Income tax expense		65,000
Net income		$125,000

Additional information:
(a) Operating expenses include depreciation expense of $33,000 and charges from prepaid expenses of $2,000.
(b) Land was sold at its book value for cash.
(c) Cash dividends of $55,000 were declared and paid in 2001.
(d) Interest expense of $12,000 was paid in cash.
(e) Equipment with a cost of $166,000 was purchased for cash. Equipment with a cost of $41,000 and a book value of $36,000 was sold for $34,000 cash.
(f) Bonds of $10,000 were redeemed at their book value for cash; bonds of $30,000 were converted into common stock.
(g) Common stock ($1 par) of $130,000 was issued for cash.
(h) Accounts payable pertain to merchandise suppliers.

Reasoning: As you have learned, the balance sheet and the income statement are prepared from an adjusted trial balance of the general ledger. The statement of cash flows is prepared from an analysis of the content and changes in the balance sheet and the income statement.

Solution:

REYNOLDS COMPANY
Statement of Cash Flows—Indirect Method
For the Year Ended December 31, 2001

Cash flows from operating activities		
Net income		$125,000
Adjustments to reconcile net income to net cash provided		
by operating activities:		
Depreciation expense	$ 33,000	
Increase in accounts receivable	(42,000)	
Increase in inventories	(54,000)	
Decrease in prepaid expenses	2,000	
Decrease in accounts payable	(17,000)	
Increase in accrued expenses payable	10,000	
Loss on sale of equipment	2,000	(66,000)
Net cash provided by operating activities		59,000
Cash flows from investing activities		
Sale of land	25,000	
Sale of equipment	34,000	
Purchase of equipment	(166,000)	
Net cash used by investing activities		(107,000)
Cash flows from financing activities		
Redemption of bonds	(10,000)	
Sale of common stock	130,000	
Payment of dividends	(55,000)	
Net cash provided by financing activities		65,000
Net increase in cash		17,000
Cash at beginning of period		37,000
Cash at end of period		$ 54,000
Noncash investing and financing activities		
Conversion of bonds into common stock		$ 30,000

HELPFUL HINT
To prepare the statement of cash flows:
1. Determine the net increase/decrease in cash.
2. Determine net cash provided/used by operating activities.
3. Operating activities generally relate to changes in current assets and current liabilities.
4. Determine net cash provided/used by investing and financing activities.
5. Investing activities generally relate to changes in noncurrent assets.
6. Financing activities generally relate to changes in noncurrent liabilities and stockholders' equity accounts.

THE NAVIGATOR

Related exercise material: BE14–1, BE14–2, BE14–4, E14–2, E14–3, E14–4, and E14–5.

Note: This concludes Section 1 on preparation of the statement of cash flows using the indirect method. Unless your instructor assigns Section 2, you should turn to the concluding section of the chapter, "Analysis of the Statement of Cash Flows," on page 640.

SECTION 2   STATEMENT OF CASH FLOWS— DIRECT METHOD

To explain and illustrate the direct method, we will use the transactions of Juarez Company for two years, 2000 and 2001. Annual statements of cash flow will be prepared. Basic transactions will be used in the first year with additional transactions added in the second year.

4
STUDY
OBJECTIVE

Prepare a statement of cash flows using the direct method.

FIRST YEAR OF OPERATIONS—2000

Juarez Company began business on January 1, 2000, when it issued 300,000 shares of $1 par value common stock for $300,000 cash. The company rented office and sales space along with equipment. The comparative balance sheet at the beginning and end of 2000 and the changes in each account are shown in Illustration 14-21. The income statement and additional information for Juarez Company are shown in Illustration 14-22.

ILLUSTRATION 14-21

Comparative balance sheet, 2000, with increases and decreases

JUAREZ COMPANY
Comparative Balance Sheet

Assets	Dec. 31, 2000	Jan. 1, 2000	Change Increase/Decrease
Cash	$159,000	$ –0–	$159,000 Increase
Accounts receivable	15,000	–0–	15,000 Increase
Inventory	160,000	–0–	160,000 Increase
Prepaid expenses	8,000	–0–	8,000 Increase
Land	80,000	–0–	80,000 Increase
Total	$422,000	$ –0–	

Liabilities and Stockholders' Equity

	Dec. 31, 2000	Jan. 1, 2000	Change Increase/Decrease
Accounts payable	$ 60,000	$ –0–	$ 60,000 Increase
Accrued expenses payable	20,000	–0–	20,000 Increase
Common stock	300,000	–0–	300,000 Increase
Retained earnings	42,000	–0–	42,000 Increase
Total	$422,000	$ –0–	

ILLUSTRATION 14-22

Income statement and additional information, 2000

JUAREZ COMPANY
Income Statement
For the Year Ended December 31, 2000

Revenues	$780,000
Cost of goods sold	450,000
Gross profit	330,000
Operating expenses	170,000
Income before income taxes	160,000
Income tax expense	48,000
Net income	$112,000

Additional information:
(a) Dividends of $70,000 were declared and paid in cash.
(b) The accounts payable increase resulted from the purchase of merchandise.

The three steps cited on page 614 for preparing the statement of cash flows are used in the direct method.

Determining the Net Increase/Decrease in Cash (Step 1)
The comparative balance sheet for Juarez Company shows a zero cash balance at January 1, 2000, and a cash balance of $159,000 at December 31, 2000. Thus, the change in cash for 2000 was a net increase of $159,000.

Determining Net Cash Provided/Used by Operating Activities (Step 2)

Under the direct method, net cash provided by operating activities is computed by **adjusting each item in the income statement** from the accrual basis to the cash basis. To simplify and condense the operating activities section, **only major classes of operating cash receipts and cash payments are reported**. The difference between these major classes of cash receipts and cash payments is the net cash provided by operating activities as shown in Illustration 14-23.

ILLUSTRATION 14-23

Major classes of cash receipts and payments

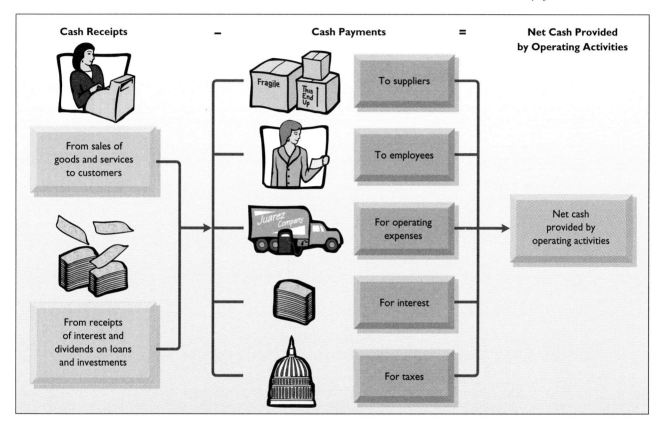

An efficient way to apply the direct method is to analyze the revenues and expenses reported in the income statement in the order in which they are listed. Cash receipts and cash payments related to these revenues and expenses are then determined. The direct method adjustments for Juarez Company in 2000 to determine net cash provided by operating activities are presented in the following sections.

Cash Receipts from Customers. The income statement for Juarez Company reported revenues from customers of $780,000. To determine cash receipts from customers, it is necessary to consider the change in accounts receivable during the year. When accounts receivable increase during the year, revenues on an accrual basis are higher than cash receipts from customers. In other words, operations led to increased revenues, but not all of these revenues resulted in cash receipts. To determine the amount of cash receipts, the increase in accounts receivable is deducted from sales revenues. Conversely, a decrease in accounts receivable is added to sales revenues, because cash receipts from customers then exceed sales revenues.

For Juarez Company, accounts receivable increased $15,000. Thus, cash receipts from customers were $765,000, computed as follows:

ILLUSTRATION 14-24

Computation of cash receipts from customers

Revenues from sales	$780,000
Deduct: Increase in accounts receivable	15,000
Cash receipts from customers	$765,000

Cash receipts from customers may also be determined from an analysis of the Accounts Receivable account as shown in Illustration 14-25.

ILLUSTRATION 14-25

Analysis of accounts receivable

Accounts Receivable

1/1/00 Balance	–0–	Receipts from customers	765,000
Revenues from sales	780,000		
12/31/00 Balance	15,000		

HELPFUL HINT
The T-account shows that revenue less increase in receivables equals cash receipts.

The relationships between cash receipts from customers, revenues from sales, and changes in accounts receivable are shown in Illustration 14-26.

ILLUSTRATION 14-26

Formula to compute cash receipts from customers— direct method

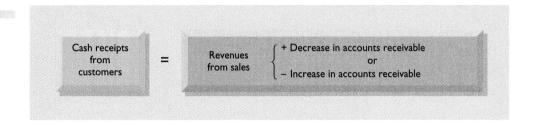

Cash Payments to Suppliers.   Juarez Company reported cost of goods sold on its income statement of $450,000. To determine cash payments to suppliers, it is first necessary to find purchases for the year. To find purchases, cost of goods sold is adjusted for the change in inventory. When inventory increases during the year, it means that purchases this year exceed cost of goods sold. As a result, the increase in inventory is added to cost of goods sold to arrive at purchases.

In 2000, Juarez Company's inventory increased $160,000. Purchases, therefore, are computed as follows:

ILLUSTRATION 14-27

Computation of purchases

Cost of goods sold	$450,000
Add: Increase in inventory	160,000
Purchases	$610,000

After purchases are computed, cash payments to suppliers are determined by adjusting purchases for the change in accounts payable. When accounts payable increase during the year, purchases on an accrual basis are higher than they are on a cash basis. As a result, an increase in accounts payable is deducted from purchases to arrive at cash payments to suppliers. Conversely, a decrease in accounts payable is added to purchases because cash payments to suppliers exceed purchases. Cash payments to suppliers were $550,000, computed as follows:

Purchases	$610,000
Deduct: Increase in accounts payable	60,000
Cash payments to suppliers	$550,000

ILLUSTRATION 14-28

Computation of cash payments to suppliers

Cash payments to suppliers may also be determined from an analysis of the Accounts Payable account as shown in Illustration 14-29.

Accounts Payable

Payments to suppliers	550,000	1/1/00 Balance	–0–
		Purchases	610,000
		12/31/00 Balance	60,000

ILLUSTRATION 14-29

Analysis of accounts payable

HELPFUL HINT
The T-account shows that purchases less increase in accounts payable equals payments to suppliers.

The relationship between cash payments to suppliers, cost of goods sold, changes in inventory, and changes in accounts payable is shown in the following formula:

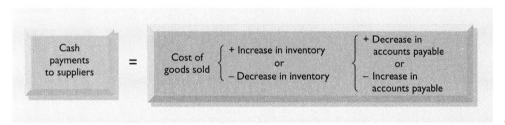

HELPFUL HINT
Decrease in accounts receivable indicates that cash collections were greater than sales. **Increase in accounts receivable** indicates that sales were greater than cash collections. **Increase in prepaid expenses** indicates that the amount paid for the prepayments exceeded the amount that was recorded as an expense. **Decrease in prepaid expenses** indicates that the amount recorded as an expense exceeded the amount of cash paid for the prepayments. **Increase in accounts payable** indicates that expenses incurred exceed the cash paid for expenses that period.

Cash Payments for Operating Expenses. Operating expenses of $170,000 were reported on Juarez's income statement. To determine the cash paid for operating expenses, this amount must be adjusted for any changes in prepaid expenses and accrued expenses payable. For example, when prepaid expenses increased $8,000 during the year, cash paid for operating expenses was $8,000 higher than operating expenses reported on the income statement. To convert operating expenses to cash payments for operating expenses, the increase of $8,000 must be added to operating expenses. Conversely, if prepaid expenses decrease during the year, the decrease must be deducted from operating expenses.

Operating expenses must also be adjusted for changes in accrued expenses payable. When accrued expenses payable increase during the year, operating expenses on an accrual basis are higher than they are in a cash basis. As a result, an increase in accrued expenses payable is deducted from operating expenses to arrive at cash payments for operating expenses. Conversely, a decrease in accrued expenses payable is added to operating expenses because cash payments exceed operating expenses.

Juarez Company's cash payments for operating expenses were $158,000, computed as follows:

Operating expenses	$170,000
Add: Increase in prepaid expenses	8,000
Deduct: Increase in accrued expenses payable	(20,000)
Cash payments for operating expenses	$158,000

ILLUSTRATION 14-31

Computation of cash payments for operating expenses

The relationships among cash payments for operating expenses, changes in prepaid expenses, and changes in accrued expenses payable are shown in the following formula.

ILLUSTRATION 14-32

Formula to compute cash payments for operating expenses—direct method

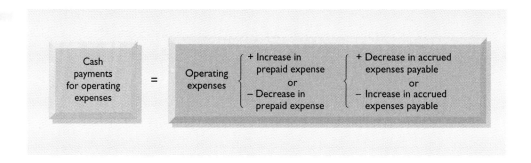

Cash Payments for Income Taxes.   The income statement for Juarez shows income tax expense of $48,000. This amount equals the cash paid because the comparative balance sheet indicated no income taxes payable at either the beginning or end of the year.

All of the revenues and expenses in the 2000 income statement have now been adjusted to a cash basis. The operating activities section of the statement of cash flows is as follows:

ILLUSTRATION 14-33

Operating activities section—direct method

JUAREZ COMPANY Partial Statement of Cash Flows—Direct Method For the Year Ended December 31, 2000		
Cash flows from operating activities		
Cash receipts from customers		$765,000
Cash payments:		
To suppliers	$550,000	
For operating expenses	158,000	
For income taxes	48,000	756,000
Net cash provided by operating activities		$ 9,000

Determining Net Cash Provided/Used by Investing and Financing Activities (Step 3)

Preparing the investing and financing activities sections of the statement of cash flows begins with a determination of the changes in noncurrent accounts reported in the comparative balance sheet. The change in each account is then analyzed using the additional information to determine the effect, if any, the change had on cash.

HELPFUL HINT

This is the same procedure used under the indirect method; the investing and financing activities are measured and reported the same under both methods.

Increase in Land.   No additional information is given for the increase in land. In such case, you should assume that the increase affected cash. You should also make the same assumption in solving homework problems when the cause of a change in a noncurrent account is not explained. The purchase of land is an investing activity. Thus, an outflow of cash of $80,000 for the purchase of land should be reported in the investing activities section.

Increase in Common Stock.   As indicated earlier, 300,000 shares of $1 par value stock were sold for $300,000 cash. The issuance of common stock is a financing activity. Thus, a cash inflow of $300,000 from the issuance of common stock is reported in the financing activities section.

Increase in Retained Earnings.   For the Retained Earnings account, the reasons for the net increase of $42,000 are determined by analysis. First, net income increased retained earnings by $112,000. Second, the additional information section indicates that a cash dividend of $70,000 was declared and paid. The adjustment of revenues and expenses to arrive at net cash provided by operations was done in step 2 above. The cash dividend paid is reported as an outflow of cash in the financing activities section.

This analysis can also be made directly from the Retained Earnings account in the ledger of Juarez Company as shown in Illustration 14-34.

HELPFUL HINT
It is the **payment** of dividends, not the declaration, that appears on the cash flow statement.

ILLUSTRATION 14-34

Analysis of retained earnings

Retained Earnings

12/31/00	Cash dividend	70,000	1/ 1/00 Balance	–0–	
			12/31/00 Net income	112,000	
			12/31/00 Balance	42,000	

The $42,000 increase in Retained Earnings in 2000 is a net change. When a net change in a noncurrent balance sheet account has occurred during the year, it generally is necessary to report the individual items that cause the net change.

Statement of Cash Flows—2000

The statement of cash flows can now be prepared. The operating activities section is reported first, followed by the investing and financing activities sections. The statement of cash flows for Juarez Company for 2000 is shown in Illustration 14-35.

ILLUSTRATION 14-35

Statement of cash flows, 2000—direct method

JUAREZ COMPANY Statement of Cash Flows—Direct Method For the Year Ended December 31, 2000		
Cash flows from operating activities		
Cash receipts from customers		$765,000
Cash payments:		
To suppliers	$550,000	
For operating expenses	158,000	
For income taxes	48,000	756,000
Net cash provided by operating activities		9,000
Cash flows from investing activities		
Purchase of land	(80,000)	
Net cash used by investing activities		(80,000)
Cash flows from financing activities		
Issuance of common stock	300,000	
Payment of cash dividend	(70,000)	
Net cash provided by financing activities		230,000
Net increase in cash		159,000
Cash at beginning of period		–0–
Cash at end of period		$159,000

HELPFUL HINT
Note that in the investing and financing activities sections, positive numbers indicate cash inflows (receipts) and negative numbers indicate cash outflows (payments).

The statement of cash flows shows that operating activities provided $9,000 of the net increase in cash of $159,000. Financing activities **provided** $230,000 of cash, and investing activities **used** $80,000 of cash. The net increase in cash for the year of $159,000 agrees with the increase in cash of $159,000 reported in the comparative balance sheet.

SECOND YEAR OF OPERATIONS — 2001

Illustrations 14-36 and 14-37 present the comparative balance sheet, the income statement, and additional information pertaining to the second year of operations for Juarez Company.

ILLUSTRATION 14-36

Comparative balance sheet, 2001, with increases and decreases

JUAREZ COMPANY
Comparative Balance Sheet
December 31

Assets	2001	2000	Change Increase/Decrease
Cash	$191,000	$159,000	$ 32,000 Increase
Accounts receivable	12,000	15,000	3,000 Decrease
Inventory	130,000	160,000	30,000 Decrease
Prepaid expenses	6,000	8,000	2,000 Decrease
Land	180,000	80,000	100,000 Increase
Equipment	160,000	–0–	160,000 Increase
Accumulated depreciation—equipment	(16,000)	–0–	16,000 Increase
Total	$663,000	$422,000	

Liabilities and Stockholders' Equity			
Accounts payable	$ 52,000	$ 60,000	$ 8,000 Decrease
Accrued expenses payable	15,000	20,000	5,000 Decrease
Income taxes payable	12,000	–0–	12,000 Increase
Bonds payable	90,000	–0–	90,000 Increase
Common stock	400,000	300,000	100,000 Increase
Retained earnings	94,000	42,000	52,000 Increase
Total	$663,000	$422,000	

ILLUSTRATION 14-37

Income statement and additional information, 2001

JUAREZ COMPANY
Income Statement
For the Year Ended December 31, 2001

Revenues		$975,000
Cost of goods sold	$660,000	
Operating expenses (excluding depreciation)	176,000	
Depreciation expense	18,000	
Loss on sale of equipment	1,000	855,000
Income before income taxes		120,000
Income tax expense		36,000
Net income		$ 84,000

Additional information:
(a) In 2001, the company declared and paid a $32,000 cash dividend.
(b) Bonds were issued at face value for $90,000 in cash.
(c) Equipment costing $180,000 was purchased for cash.
(d) Equipment costing $20,000 was sold for $17,000 cash when the book value of the equipment was $18,000.
(e) Common stock of $100,000 was issued to acquire land.

Determining the Net Increase/Decrease in Cash (Step 1)

The comparative balance sheet shows a beginning cash balance of $159,000 and an ending cash balance of $191,000. Thus, there was a net increase in cash in 2001 of $32,000.

Determining Net Cash Provided/Used by Operating Activities (Step 2)

Cash Receipts from Customers.   Revenues from sales were $975,000. Since accounts receivable decreased $3,000, cash receipts from customers were greater than sales revenues. Cash receipts from customers were $978,000, computed as follows:

Revenues from sales	$975,000
Add: Decrease in accounts receivable	3,000
Cash receipts from customers	$978,000

ILLUSTRATION 14-38

Computation of cash receipts from customers

Cash Payments to Suppliers.   The conversion of cost of goods sold to purchases and purchases to cash payments to suppliers is similar to the computations made in 2000. For 2001, purchases are computed using cost of goods sold of $660,000 from the income statement and the decrease in inventory of $30,000 from the comparative balance sheet. Purchases are then adjusted by the decrease in accounts payable of $8,000. Cash payments to suppliers were $638,000, computed as follows:

Cost of goods sold	$660,000
Deduct: Decrease in inventory	30,000
Purchases	630,000
Add: Decrease in accounts payable	8,000
Cash payments to suppliers	$638,000

ILLUSTRATION 14-39

Computation of cash payments to suppliers

Cash Payments for Operating Expenses.   Operating expenses (exclusive of depreciation expense) for 2001 were reported at $176,000. This amount is then adjusted for changes in prepaid expenses and accrued expenses payable to arrive at cash payments for operating expenses.

As indicated from the comparative balance sheet, prepaid expenses decreased $2,000 during the year. This means that $2,000 was allocated to operating expenses (thereby increasing operating expenses), but cash payments did not increase by that $2,000. To arrive at cash payments for operating expenses, the decrease in prepaid expenses is deducted from operating expenses.

Accrued operating expenses decreased $5,000 during the period. As a result, cash payments were higher by $5,000 than the amount reported for operating expenses. The decrease in accrued expenses payable is added to operating expenses. Cash payments for operating expenses were $179,000, computed as follows:

ILLUSTRATION 14-40

Computation of cash payments for operating expenses

Operating expenses, exclusive of depreciation	$176,000
Deduct: Decrease in prepaid expenses	(2,000)
Add: Decrease in accrued expenses payable	5,000
Cash payments for operating expenses	**$179,000**

Depreciation Expense and Loss on Sale of Equipment.   Operating expenses are shown exclusive of depreciation. Depreciation expense in 2001 was $18,000. Depreciation expense is not shown on a statement of cash flows because it is a noncash charge. If the amount for operating expenses includes depreciation expense, operating expenses must be reduced by the amount of depreciation to determine cash payments for operating expenses.

The loss on sale of equipment of $1,000 is also a noncash charge. The loss on sale of equipment reduces net income, but it does not reduce cash. Thus, the loss on sale of equipment is not reported on a statement of cash flows.

Other charges to expense that do not require the use of cash, such as the amortization of intangible assets and depletion expense, are treated in the same manner as depreciation.

Cash Payments for Income Taxes.   Income tax expense reported on the income statement was $36,000. Income taxes payable, however, increased $12,000 which means that $12,000 of the income taxes have not been paid. As a result, income taxes paid were less than income taxes reported on the income statement. Cash payments for income taxes were, therefore, $24,000 as shown below.

ILLUSTRATION 14-41

Computation of cash payments for income taxes

Income tax expense	$36,000
Deduct: Increase in income taxes payable	12,000
Cash payments for income taxes	**$24,000**

The relationships of cash payments for income taxes, income tax expense, and changes in income taxes payable are shown in the following formula:

ILLUSTRATION 14-42

Formula to compute cash payments for income taxes—direct method

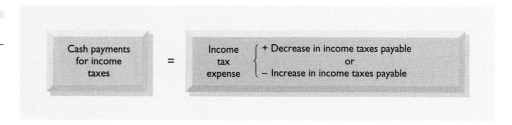

Determining Net Cash Provided/Used
by Investing and Financing Activities (Step 3)

Increase in Land.   Land increased $100,000. The additional information section indicates that common stock was issued to purchase the land. Although the issuance of common stock for land has no effect on cash, it is a **significant non-cash investing and financing transaction**. This transaction requires disclosure in a separate schedule at the bottom of the statement of cash flows.

Increase in Equipment.   The comparative balance sheet shows that equipment increased $160,000 in 2001. The additional information in Illustration 14-37 indicates that the increase resulted from two investing transactions: (1) equipment costing $180,000 was purchased for cash, and (2) equipment costing $20,000 was sold for $17,000 cash when its book value was $18,000. The relevant data for the statement of cash flows is the cash paid for the purchase and the cash proceeds from the sale. For Juarez Company, the investing activities section will show: Purchase of equipment $180,000, as an outflow of cash; and sale of equipment $17,000, as an inflow of cash. The two amounts **should not be netted** because one is an outflow of cash and the other is an inflow of cash; **both flows should be shown**.

The analysis of the changes in equipment should include the related Accumulated Depreciation account. These two accounts for Juarez Company are shown in Illustration 14-43.

Equipment

1/1/01	Balance	–0–	Cost of equipment sold	20,000
	Cash purchase	180,000		
12/31/01	Balance	160,000		

Accumulated Depreciation—Equipment

Sale of equipment	2,000	1/1/01	Balance	–0–
			Depreciation expense	18,000
		12/31/01	Balance	16,000

ILLUSTRATION 14-43

Analysis of equipment and related accumulated depreciation

Increase in Bonds Payable.   Bonds Payable increased $90,000. The additional information in Illustration 14-37 indicates that bonds with a face value of $90,000 were issued for $90,000 cash. The issuance of bonds is a financing activity. For Juarez Company, there is an inflow of cash of $90,000 from the issuance of bonds.

Increase in Common Stock.   The Common Stock account increased $100,000. As indicated from the additional information, land was acquired from the issuance of common stock. This transaction is a **significant noncash investing and financing transaction** that should be reported in a separate schedule at the bottom of the statement.

Increase in Retained Earnings.   The net increase in Retained Earnings of $52,000 resulted from net income of $84,000 and the declaration and payment of a cash dividend of $32,000. **Net income is not reported in the statement of cash flows**

under the direct method. Cash dividends paid of $32,000 are reported in the financing activities section as an outflow of cash.

Statement of Cash Flows—2001

The statement of cash flows for Juarez Company is shown in Illustration 14-44.

ILLUSTRATION 14-44

*Statement of cash flows,
2001—direct method*

JUAREZ COMPANY Statement of Cash Flows—Direct Method For the Year Ended December 31, 2001		
Cash flows from operating activities		
Cash receipts from customers		$978,000
Cash payments:		
To suppliers	$638,000	
For operating expenses	179,000	
For income taxes	24,000	841,000
Net cash provided by operating activities		137,000
Cash flows from investing activities		
Purchase of equipment	(180,000)	
Sale of equipment	17,000	
Net cash used by investing activities		(163,000)
Cash flows from financing activities		
Issuance of bonds payable	90,000	
Payment of cash dividends	(32,000)	
Net cash provided by financing activities		58,000
Net increase in cash		32,000
Cash at beginning of period		159,000
Cash at end of period		$191,000
Noncash investing and financing activities		
Issuance of common stock to purchase land		$100,000

BEFORE YOU GO ON ...

Review It

1. What is the format of the operating activities section of the statement of cash flows using the direct method?
2. Where is depreciation expense shown on a statement of cash flows using the direct method?
3. Where are significant noncash investing and financing activities shown on a statement of cash flows? Give some examples.

Do It

Presented below is information related to Reynolds Company. Use it to prepare a statement of cash flows using the direct method.

REYNOLDS COMPANY
Comparative Balance Sheet
December 31

Assets	2001	2000	Change Increase/Decrease
Cash	$ 54,000	$ 37,000	$ 17,000 Increase
Accounts receivable	68,000	26,000	42,000 Increase
Inventories	54,000	–0–	54,000 Increase
Prepaid expenses	4,000	6,000	2,000 Decrease
Land	45,000	70,000	25,000 Decrease
Buildings	200,000	200,000	–0–
Accumulated depreciation—buildings	(21,000)	(11,000)	10,000 Increase
Equipment	193,000	68,000	125,000 Increase
Accumulated depreciation—equipment	(28,000)	(10,000)	18,000 Increase
Totals	$569,000	$386,000	

Liabilities and Stockholders' Equity			
Accounts payable	$ 23,000	$ 40,000	$ 17,000 Decrease
Accrued expenses payable	10,000	–0–	10,000 Increase
Bonds payable	110,000	150,000	40,000 Decrease
Common stock ($1 par)	220,000	60,000	160,000 Increase
Retained earnings	206,000	136,000	70,000 Increase
Totals	$569,000	$386,000	

REYNOLDS COMPANY
Income Statement
For the Year Ended December 31, 2001

Revenues		$890,000
Cost of goods sold	$465,000	
Operating expenses	221,000	
Interest expense	12,000	
Loss on sale of equipment	2,000	700,000
Income from operations		190,000
Income tax expense		65,000
Net income		$125,000

Additional information:
(a) Operating expenses include depreciation expense of $33,000 and charges from prepaid expenses of $2,000.
(b) Land was sold at its book value for cash.
(c) Cash dividends of $55,000 were declared and paid in 2001.
(d) Interest expense of $12,000 was paid in cash.
(e) Equipment with a cost of $166,000 was purchased for cash. Equipment with a cost of $41,000 and a book value of $36,000 was sold for $34,000 cash.
(f) Bonds of $10,000 were redeemed at their book value for cash; bonds of $30,000 were converted into common stock.
(g) Common stock ($1 par) of $130,000 was issued for cash.
(h) Accounts payable pertain to merchandise suppliers.

Reasoning: The indirect and the direct methods differ primarily in their presentation of the cash flows from the operating activities. The direct method reports cash receipts less cash payments to arrive at net cash provided by operating activities.

Solution:

REYNOLDS COMPANY
Statement of Cash Flows—Direct Method
For the Year Ended December 31, 2001

Cash flows from operating activities		
Cash receipts from customers		$848,000[a]
Cash payments:		
To suppliers	$536,000[b]	
For operating expenses	176,000[c]	
For interest expense	12,000	
For income taxes	65,000	789,000
Net cash provided by operating activities		59,000
Cash flows from investing activities		
Sale of land	25,000	
Sale of equipment	34,000	
Purchase of equipment	(166,000)	
Net cash used by investing activities		(107,000)
Cash flows from financing activities		
Redemption of bonds	(10,000)	
Sale of common stock	130,000	
Payment of dividends	(55,000)	
Net cash provided by financing activities		65,000
Net increase in cash		17,000
Cash at beginning of period		37,000
Cash at end of period		$ 54,000
Noncash investing and financing activities		
Conversion of bonds into common stock		$ 30,000

Computations:

[a]$848,000 = $890,000 − $42,000
[b]$536,000 = $465,000 + $54,000 + $17,000
[c]$176,000 = $221,000 − $33,000 − $2,000 − $10,000

Technically, an additional schedule reconciling net income to net cash provided by operating activities should be presented as part of the statement of cash flows when using the direct method.

THE
NAVIGATOR

Related exercise material: BE14–6, BE14–7, BE14–8, E14–7, E14–8, E14–9, and E14–10.

Note: This concludes Section 2 on preparation of the statement of cash flows using the direct method. You should now turn to the next—and con-cluding—section of the chapter, "Analysis of the Statement of Cash Flows."

5
STUDY
OBJECTIVE

Analyze the statement of cash flows.

ANALYSIS OF THE STATEMENT OF CASH FLOWS

The statement of cash flows provides information about a company's financial health that is not evident from analysis of the balance sheet or the income statement. Bankers, creditors, and other users of the statement of cash flows are as concerned with cash flow from operations as they are with net income because they are interested in a company's ability to pay its bills. Does accrual account ing conceal cash flow problems? What can be learned about a company and its management from the statement of cash flows?

In the following discussion of cash flow analysis, we use financial informa- tion from the fiscal 1999 annual report of Gap Inc. (manufacturer and retailer of Gap, Banana Republic, and Old Navy brands). Gap Inc. reported the following relevant information:

Gap Inc.
Gap
Banana Republic
Old Navy

GAP INC.

($ in millions)	Fiscal 1999	Fiscal 1998
Current liabilities	$1,553	$ 992
Total liabilities	2,390	1,754
Net sales	9,054	6,508
Net cash provided by operating activities	1,394	845

ILLUSTRATION 14-45

Gap Inc. data used in cash flow analysis

As with the balance sheet and the income statement, ratio analysis of the statement of cash flows can evaluate Gap Inc.'s liquidity, profitability, and sol- vency. Three cash flow ratios that contribute to these evaluations are (a) the cur- rent cash debt coverage ratio, (b) the cash return on sales ratio, and (c) the cash debt coverage ratio. Each of these ratios uses net cash provided by operating ac- tivities as the numerator.

Current Cash Debt Coverage Ratio

A disadvantage of the current ratio is that it employs year-end balances of cur- rent asset and current liability accounts. These year-end balances may not be representative of what the company's current position was during most of the year. A ratio that partially corrects for this problem is the ratio of net cash pro- vided by operating activities to average current liabilities, referred to as the cur- rent cash debt coverage ratio. Because it uses net cash provided by operating activities during the period, rather than a balance at a point in time, it may pro- vide a better representation of **liquidity**. Using Gap Inc.'s financial data, the cur- rent cash debt coverage ratio is computed as follows:

HELPFUL HINT

Recall that the current ratio is current assets divided by current liabilities.

ILLUSTRATION 14-46

Current cash debt coverage ratio

This ratio indicates that for every dollar of debt due during the year, $1.10 of cash was generated from operations to pay that debt.

Cash Return on Sales Ratio

One measure of profitability using accrual accounting is the profit margin ratio. This ratio is defined as net income divided by net sales and measures net income generated by each dollar of sales. The cash-based ratio that is the counterpart of the profit margin ratio is the cash return on sales ratio (sometimes referred to as "cash flow margin"), computed by dividing net cash provided by operating activities by net sales. For Gap Inc., this ratio is computed as follows:

ILLUSTRATION 14-47

Cash return on sales ratio

Although differences are expected between cash and accrual accounting, significant differences should be investigated. When Gap Inc.'s cash flow margin—its cash return on sales—of 15.4% is compared with its profit margin of 9.1%, it appears that Gap Inc. is efficient at turning sales into cash—since its cash flow margin is nearly 70% greater than its profit margin (accrual basis).

Cash Debt Coverage Ratio

In Chapter 11 we introduced the debt to total assets ratio as one measure of long-term **solvency**. The cash basis measure of solvency is the cash debt coverage ratio—the ratio of net cash provided by operating activities to average total liabilities. This ratio demonstrates a company's ability to repay its liabilities from net cash provided by operating activities, without having to liquidate the assets employed in its operations. Gap Inc.'s cash debt coverage ratio is computed as follows:

ILLUSTRATION 14-48

Cash debt coverage ratio

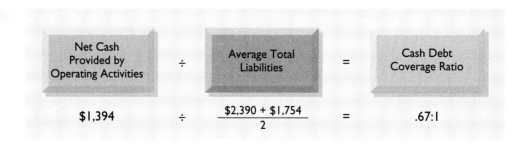

The three cash-based ratios illustrated above show that Gap Inc. is efficiently generating cash, and its cash flow coverage ratios are in line with or higher than industry averages. These ratios indicate that the company is liquid, profitable, and solvent.

BEFORE YOU GO ON . . .

Review It

1. Why might an analyst want to supplement accrual-based ratios with cash-based ratios?
2. What cash-basis ratios may be prepared to evaluate liquidity, profitability, and solvency?

A LOOK BACK AT OUR FEATURE STORY

Refer to the Feature Story of Gerald Biby's attempt to refinance Kilian Community College's mortgage, and answer the following questions:

1. How was the purchase of the $250,000 computer system presented on the "traditional educational institution financial statement" so that it negatively affected Biby's ability to refinance the mortgage?
2. How was the purchase of the $250,000 computer system presented on the statement of cash flows? How did the preparation of the statement of cash flows aid Biby in securing the refinancing of the mortgage?

Solution:

1. A traditional financial statement for a not-for-profit, educational institution reports receipts as revenues and all expenditures as expenses, even capital expenditures such as the $250,000 computer system. That is, the traditional financial statement reported the entire $250,000 as an expense in one year, making it look like the college was just breaking even.
2. When the computer purchase was classified as an investing activity, the statement of cash flows showed the bankers that one of the uses of funds was really the purchase of computer equipment that had several years of life. In addition, the bankers noted from the statement of cash flows "that the college's sources of funds exceeded the loan repayments, including principal and interest, by a ratio of 3-to-1."

THE
NAVIGATOR

DEMONSTRATION PROBLEM

The income statement for the year ended December 31, 2001, for John Kosinski Manufacturing Company contains the following condensed information:

JOHN KOSINSKI MANUFACTURING COMPANY
Income Statement

Revenues		$6,583,000
Operating expenses (excluding depreciation)	$4,920,000	
Depreciation expense	880,000	5,800,000
Income before income taxes		783,000
Income tax expense		353,000
Net income		$ 430,000

Included in operating expenses is a $24,000 loss resulting from the sale of machinery for $270,000 cash. Machinery was purchased at a cost of $750,000. The following balances are reported on Kosinski's comparative balance sheet at December 31:

JOHN KOSINSKI MANUFACTURING COMPANY
Balance Sheet (partial)

	2001	2000
Cash	$672,000	$130,000
Accounts receivable	775,000	610,000
Inventories	834,000	867,000
Accounts payable	521,000	501,000

Income tax expense of $353,000 represents the amount paid in 2001. Dividends declared and paid in 2001 totaled $200,000.

Instructions
(a) Prepare the statement of cash flows using the indirect method.

OR

(b) Prepare the statement of cash flows using the direct method.

This demonstration problem illustrates both the direct and indirect methods using the same basic data. Note the similarities and the differences between the two methods. Both methods report the same information in the investing and financing activities sections. The cash flow from operating activities section reports different information, but the amount—net cash provided by operating activities—is the same for both methods.

SOLUTION TO DEMONSTRATION PROBLEM

(a)
JOHN KOSINSKI MANUFACTURING COMPANY
Statement of Cash Flows—Indirect Method
For the Year Ended December 31, 2001

Cash flows from operating activities		
Net income		$ 430,000
Adjustments to reconcile net income to net cash provided by operating activities:		
Depreciation expense	$880,000	
Loss on sale of machinery	24,000	
Increase in accounts receivable	(165,000)	
Decrease in inventories	33,000	
Increase in accounts payable	20,000	792,000
Net cash provided by operating activities		1,222,000
Cash flows from investing activities		
Sale of machinery	270,000	
Purchase of machinery	(750,000)	
Net cash used by investing activities		(480,000)
Cash flows from financing activities		
Payment of cash dividends		(200,000)
Net increase in cash		542,000
Cash at beginning of period		130,000
Cash at end of period		$ 672,000

(b)
JOHN KOSINSKI MANUFACTURING COMPANY
Statement of Cash Flows—Direct Method
For the Year Ended December 31, 2001

Cash flows from operating activities		
Cash collections from customers		$6,418,000*
Cash payments:		
For operating expenses	$4,843,000**	
For income taxes	353,000	5,196,000
Net cash provided by operating activities		1,222,000
Cash flows from investing activities		
Sale of machinery	270,000	
Purchase of machinery	(750,000)	
Net cash used by investing activities		(480,000)
Cash flows from financing activities		
Payment of cash dividends		(200,000)
Net increase in cash		542,000
Cash at beginning of period		130,000
Cash at end of period		$ 672,000

Direct Method Computations:
* Computation of cash collections from customers:

Revenues per the income statement	$6,583,000
Less increase in accounts receivable	165,000
Cash collections from customers	$6,418,000

** Computation of cash payments for operating expenses:

Operating expenses per the income statement	$4,920,000
Deduct loss from sale of machinery	(24,000)
Deduct decrease in inventories	(33,000)
Deduct increase in accounts payable	(20,000)
Cash payments for operating expenses	$4,843,000

THE NAVIGATOR

SUMMARY OF STUDY OBJECTIVES

1. Indicate the primary purpose of the statement of cash flows. The primary purpose of the statement of cash flows is to provide information about the cash receipts and cash payments of an entity during a period. A secondary objective is to provide information about the operating, investing, and financing activities of the entity during the period.

2. Distinguish among operating, investing, and financing activities. Operating activities include the cash effects of transactions that enter into the determination of net income. Investing activities involve cash flows resulting from changes in investments and long-term asset items. Financing activities involve cash flows resulting from changes in long-term liability and stockholders' equity items.

3. Prepare a statement of cash flows using the indirect method. The preparation of a statement of cash flows involves three major steps: (1) determine the net increase or decrease in cash; (2) determine net cash provided (used) by operating activities; and (3) determine net cash flows provided (used) by investing and financing activities. Under the indirect method, accrual basis net income is adjusted to net cash provided by operating activities.

4. Prepare a statement of cash flows using the direct method. The preparation of the statement of cash flows involves three major steps: (1) determine the net increase or decrease in cash; (2) determine net cash provided (used) by operating activities; and (3) determine net cash flows provided (used) by investing and financing activities. The direct method reports cash receipts less cash payments to arrive at net cash provided by operating activities.

5. Analyze the statement of cash flows. Ratio analysis of the statement of cash flows can evaluate liquidity, profitability, and solvency by computing (a) the current cash debt coverage ratio, (b) the cash return on sales ratio, and (c) the cash debt coverage ratio.

THE NAVIGATOR

GLOSSARY
· ·

Cash debt coverage ratio A cash-basis measure of solvency, computed as net cash provided by operating activities divided by average total liabilities. (p. 642)

Cash return on sales ratio A cash-basis measure of profitability, computed as net cash provided by operating activities divided by net sales. Also called *cash flow margin.* (p. 642)

Current cash debt coverage ratio A cash-basis measure of liquidity, computed as net cash provided by operating activities divided by average current liabilities. (p. 641)

Direct method A method of determining the "net cash provided by operating activities" by adjusting each item in the income statement from the accrual basis to the cash basis. (p. 629)

Financing activities Cash flow activities that include (a) obtaining cash from issuing debt and repaying the amounts borrowed and (b) obtaining cash from stockholders and providing them with a return on their investment. (p. 609)

Indirect method A method of preparing a statement of cash flows in which net income is adjusted for items that did not affect cash, to determine net cash provided by operating activities. (p. 617)

Investing activities Cash flow activities that include (a) acquiring and disposing of investments and productive long-lived assets and (b) lending money and collecting on those loans. (p. 609)

Operating activities Cash flow activities that include the cash effects of transactions that create revenues and expenses and thus enter into the determination of net income. (p. 609)

Statement of cash flows A basic financial statement that provides information about the cash receipts and cash payments of an entity during a period, classified as operating, investing, and financing activities, in a format that reconciles the beginning and ending cash balances. (p. 609)

APPENDIX USING A WORK SHEET TO PREPARE THE STATEMENT OF CASH FLOWS— INDIRECT METHOD

6

STUDY

OBJECTIVE

Explain the guidelines and procedural steps in using a work sheet to prepare the statement of cash flows.

When numerous adjustments of net income are necessary, **a work sheet is often used to assemble and classify the data that will appear on the statement of cash flows.** The work sheet is merely a device that aids in the preparation of the statement; its use is optional. The skeleton format of the work sheet for preparation of the statement of cash flows is shown in Illustration 14A-1.

XYZ COMPANY
Work Sheet
Statement of Cash Flows
For the Year Ended . . .

Balance Sheet Accounts	End of Last Year Balances	Reconciling Items Debits	Reconciling Items Credits	End of Current Year Balances
Debit balance accounts	XX	XX	XX	XX
	XX	XX	XX	XX
Totals	XXX			XXX
Credit balance accounts	XX	XX	XX	XX
	XX	XX	XX	XX
Totals	XXX			XXX

Statement of Cash Flows Effects

Operating activities			
Net income		XX	
Adjustments to net income		XX	XX
Investing activities			
Receipts and payments		XX	XX
Financing activities			
Receipts and payments		XX	XX
Totals		XXX	XXX
Increase (decrease) in cash		(XX)	XX
Totals		XXX	XXX

ILLUSTRATION 14A-1

Format of work sheet

The following guidelines are important in using a work sheet:

1. In the balance sheet accounts section, **accounts with debit balances are listed separately from those with credit balances.** This means, for example, that Accumulated Depreciation is listed under credit balances and not as a contra account under debit balances. The beginning and ending balances of each account are entered in the appropriate columns. The transactions that caused the change in the account balance during the year are entered as reconciling items in the two middle columns. After all reconciling items have been entered, each line pertaining to a balance sheet account should "foot across." That is, the beginning balance plus or minus the reconciling item(s) must equal the ending balance. When this agreement exists for all balance sheet accounts, all changes in account balances have been reconciled.

2. The bottom portion of the work sheet consists of the operating, investing, and financing activities sections. Accordingly, it provides the information necessary to prepare the formal statement of cash flows. **Inflows of cash are entered as debits in the reconciling columns, and outflows of cash are entered as credits in the reconciling columns.** Thus, in this section, the sale of equipment for cash at book value is entered as a debit under investing activities. Similarly, the purchase of land for cash is entered as a credit under investing activities.

3. **The reconciling items shown in the work sheet are not entered in any journal or posted to any account.** They do not represent either adjustments or corrections of the balance sheet accounts. They are used only to facilitate the preparation of the statement of cash flows.

PREPARING THE WORK SHEET

As in the case of work sheets illustrated in earlier chapters, the preparation of a work sheet involves a series of prescribed steps. The steps in this case are:

1. Enter in the balance sheet accounts section the balance sheet accounts and their beginning and ending balances.

2. Enter in the reconciling columns of the work sheet the data that explain the changes in the balance sheet accounts other than cash and their effects on the statement of cash flows.

3. Enter on the cash line and at the bottom of the work sheet the increase or decrease in cash. This entry should enable the totals of the reconciling columns to be in agreement.

To illustrate the preparation of a work sheet, we will use the 2001 data for Computer Services Company. Your familiarity with these data should help you understand the use of a work sheet. For ease of reference, the comparative balance sheets, income statement, and selected data for 2001 are presented in Illustrations 14A-2 and 14A-3.

ILLUSTRATION 14A-2

Comparative balance sheet, 2001, with increases and decreases

COMPUTER SERVICES COMPANY Comparative Balance Sheet December 31			
Assets	2001	2000	Change Increase/Decrease
Cash	$ 56,000	$34,000	$ 22,000 Increase
Accounts receivable	20,000	30,000	10,000 Decrease
Prepaid expenses	4,000	–0–	4,000 Increase
Land	130,000	–0–	130,000 Increase
Building	160,000	–0–	160,000 Increase
Accumulated depreciation—building	(11,000)	–0–	11,000 Increase
Equipment	27,000	10,000	17,000 Increase
Accumulated depreciation—equipment	(3,000)	–0–	3,000 Increase
Totals	$383,000	$74,000	
Liabilities and Stockholders' Equity			
Accounts payable	$ 59,000	$ 4,000	55,000 Increase
Bonds payable	130,000	–0–	130,000 Increase
Common stock	50,000	50,000	–0–
Retained earnings	144,000	20,000	124,000 Increase
Totals	$383,000	$74,000	

COMPUTER SERVICES COMPANY		
Income Statement		
For the Year Ended December 31, 2001		
Revenues		$507,000
Operating expenses (excluding depreciation)	$261,000	
Depreciation expense	15,000	
Loss on sale of equipment	3,000	279,000
Income from operations		228,000
Income tax expense		89,000
Net income		$139,000

Additional information:
(a) In 2001, the company declared and paid a $15,000 cash dividend.
(b) The company obtained land through the issuance of $130,000 of long-term bonds.
(c) A building costing $160,000 was purchased for cash; equipment costing $25,000 was also purchased for cash.
(d) During 2001, the company sold equipment with a book value of $7,000 (cost $8,000, less accumulated depreciation $1,000) for $4,000 cash.

Determining the Reconciling Items

Several approaches may be used to determine the reconciling items. For example, the changes affecting net cash provided by operating activities could be completed first and then the effects of financing and investing transactions could be determined. Alternatively, the balance sheet accounts can be analyzed in the order in which they are listed on the work sheet. We will follow this latter approach for Computer Services, except for cash. As indicated above, **cash is handled last**.

Accounts Receivable.   The decrease of $10,000 in accounts receivable means that cash collections from revenues are higher than the revenues reported in the income statement. To convert net income to net cash provided by operating activities, the decrease of $10,000 is added to net income. The entry in the reconciling columns of the work sheet is:

(a)	Operating—Decrease in Accounts Receivable	10,000	
	Accounts Receivable		10,000

Prepaid Expenses.   An increase of $4,000 in prepaid expenses means that expenses deducted in determining net income are less than expenses that were paid in cash. Thus, the increase of $4,000 must be deducted from net income in determining net cash provided by operating activities. The work sheet entry is:

(b)	Prepaid Expenses	4,000	
	Operating—Increase in Prepaid Expenses		4,000

HELPFUL HINT

These amounts are asterisked in the work sheet to indicate that they result from a significant noncash transaction.

Land.   The increase in land of $130,000 resulted from a purchase through the issuance of long-term bonds. This transaction should be reported as a significant noncash investing and financing activity. The work sheet entry is:

(c)	Land	130,000	
	Bonds Payable		130,000

Building.   The cash purchase of a building for $160,000 is an investing activity cash outflow. The entry in the reconciling columns of the work sheet is:

| (d) | Building | 160,000 | |
| | Investing—Purchase of Building | | 160,000 |

Equipment. The increase in equipment of $17,000 resulted from a cash purchase of $25,000 and the sale of equipment costing $8,000. The book value of the equipment was $7,000, the cash proceeds were $4,000, and a loss of $3,000 was recorded. The work sheet entries are:

| (e) | Equipment | 25,000 | |
| | Investing—Purchase of Equipment | | 25,000 |

(f)	Investing—Sale of Equipment	4,000	
	Operating—Loss on Sale of Equipment	3,000	
	Accumulated Depreciation—Equipment	1,000	
	Equipment		8,000

Accounts Payable. The increase of $55,000 in accounts payable must be added to net income to obtain net cash provided by operating activities. The following work sheet entry is made:

| (g) | Operating—Increase in Accounts Payable | 55,000 | |
| | Accounts Payable | | 55,000 |

Bonds Payable. The increase of $130,000 in this account resulted from the issuance of bonds for land. This is a significant noncash investing and financing activity. Work sheet entry (c) above is the only entry necessary.

Accumulated Depreciation—Building, and Accumulated Depreciation—Equipment. The increases in these accounts of $11,000 and $4,000, respectively, resulted from depreciation expense. Depreciation expense is a **noncash charge that must be added to net income** in determining net cash provided by operating activities. The work sheet entries are:

| (h) | Operating—Depreciation Expense—Building | 11,000 | |
| | Accumulated Depreciation—Building | | 11,000 |

| (i) | Operating—Depreciation Expense—Equipment | 4,000 | |
| | Accumulated Depreciation—Equipment | | 4,000 |

Retained Earnings. The $124,000 increase in retained earnings resulted from net income of $139,000 and the declaration of a $15,000 cash dividend that was paid in 2001. Net income is included in net cash provided by operating activities, and the dividends are a financing activity cash outflow. The entries in the reconciling columns of the work sheet are:

| (j) | Operating—Net Income | 139,000 | |
| | Retained Earnings | | 139,000 |

| (k) | Retained Earnings | 15,000 | |
| | Financing—Payment of Dividends | | 15,000 |

Disposition of Change in Cash. The firm's cash increased $22,000 in 2001. The final entry on the work sheet, therefore, is:

| (l) | Cash | 22,000 | |
| | Increase in cash | | 22,000 |

As shown in the work sheet, the increase in cash is entered in the reconciling credit column as a balancing amount. This entry should complete the reconciliation of the changes in the balance sheet accounts. In addition, it should permit the totals of the reconciling columns to be in agreement. When all changes have been explained and the reconciling columns are in agreement, the reconciling columns are ruled to complete the work sheet. The completed work sheet for Computer Services Company is shown in Illustration 14A-4.

ILLUSTRATION 14A-4

*Completed work sheet—
indirect method*

COMPUTER SERVICES COMPANY
Work Sheet
Statement of Cash Flows
For the Year Ended December 31, 2001

Balance Sheet Accounts	Balance 12/31/00	Reconciling Items Debit	Reconciling Items Credit	Balance 12/31/01
Debits				
Cash	34,000	(l) 22,000		56,000
Accounts Receivable	30,000		(a) 10,000	20,000
Prepaid Expenses	–0–	(b) 4,000		4,000
Land	–0–	(c) 130,000*		130,000
Building	–0–	(d) 160,000		160,000
Equipment	10,000	(e) 25,000	(f) 8,000	27,000
Total	74,000			397,000
Credits				
Accounts Payable	4,000		(g) 55,000	59,000
Bonds Payable	–0–		(c) 130,000*	130,000
Accumulated Depreciation—Building	–0–		(h) 11,000	11,000
Accumulated Depreciation—Equipment	–0–	(f) 1,000	(i) 4,000	3,000
Common Stock	50,000			50,000
Retained Earnings	20,000	(k) 15,000	(j) 139,000	144,000
Total	74,000			397,000

Statement of Cash Flows Effects

Operating activities				
Net income		(j) 139,000		
Decrease in accounts receivable		(a) 10,000		
Increase in prepaid expenses			(b) 4,000	
Increase in accounts payable		(g) 55,000		
Depreciation expense—building		(h) 11,000		
Depreciation expense—equipment		(i) 4,000		
Loss on sale of equipment		(f) 3,000		
Investing activities				
Purchase of building			(d) 160,000	
Purchase of equipment			(e) 25,000	
Sale of equipment		(f) 4,000		
Financing activities				
Payment of dividends		_____	(k) 15,000	
Totals		583,000	561,000	
Increase in cash		_____	(l) 22,000	
Totals		583,000	583,000	

*Significant noncash investing and financing activity.

PREPARING THE STATEMENT

The statement of cash flows is prepared primarily from the data that appear in the work sheet under Statement of Cash Flows Effects. The reconciling columns should also be scanned for any asterisked items that designate significant non-cash activities. The formal statement was shown in Illustration 14-18.

SUMMARY OF STUDY OBJECTIVES

6. *Explain the guidelines and procedural steps in using a work sheet to prepare the statement of cash flows.* When there are numerous adjustments, a work sheet can be a helpful tool in preparing the statement of cash flows. Key guidelines for using a work sheet are: (1) list accounts with debit balances separately from those with credit balances; (2) in the reconciling columns in the bottom portion of the work sheet, show cash inflows as debits and cash outflows as credits; (3) do not enter reconciling items in any journal or account but use them only to help prepare the statement of cash flows.

The steps in preparing the work sheet are: (1) enter beginning and ending balances of balance sheet accounts; (2) enter debits and credits in reconciling columns; (3) enter the increase or decrease in cash in two places as a balancing amount.

*****Note:** All asterisked Questions, Exercises, and Problems relate to material in the appendix to the chapter.

SELF-STUDY QUESTIONS

Answers are at the end of the chapter.

(SO 1) 1. Which of the following is *incorrect* about the statement of cash flows?
    a. It is a fourth basic financial statement.
    b. It provides information about cash receipts and cash payments of an entity during a period.
    c. It reconciles the ending cash account balance to the balance per the bank statement.
    d. It provides information about the operating, investing, and financing activities of the business.

(SO 2) 2. The statement of cash flows classifies cash receipts and cash payments by the following activities:
    a. operating and nonoperating.
    b. investing, financing, and operating.
    c. financing, operating, and nonoperating.
    d. investing, financing, and nonoperating.

(SO 2) 3. An example of a cash flow from an operating activity is:
    a. payment of cash to lenders for interest.
    b. receipt of cash from the sale of capital stock.
    c. payment of cash dividends to the company's stockholders.
    d. none of the above.

(SO 2) 4. An example of a cash flow from an investing activity is:
    a. receipt of cash from the issuance of bonds payable.
    b. payment of cash to repurchase outstanding capital stock.
    c. receipt of cash from the sale of equipment.
    d. payment of cash to suppliers for inventory.

5. Cash dividends paid to stockholders are classified on (SO 2) the statement of cash flows as:
    a. operating activities.
    b. investing activities.
    c. a combination of the above.
    d. financing activities.

6. An example of a cash flow from a financing activity is: (SO 2)
    a. receipt of cash from sale of land.
    b. issuance of debt for cash.
    c. purchase of equipment for cash.
    d. none of the above.

7. Which of the following about the statement of cash (SO 2) flows is *incorrect?*
    a. The direct method may be used to report cash provided by operations.
    b. The statement shows the cash provided (used) for three categories of activity.
    c. The operating section is the last section of the statement.
    d. The indirect method may be used to report cash provided by operations.

Questions 8 and 9 apply only to the indirect method.

8. Net income is $132,000, accounts payable increased (SO 3) $10,000 during the year, inventory decreased $6,000 during the year, and accounts receivable increased $12,000 during the year. Under the indirect method, net cash provided by operations is:

a. $102,000.
b. $112,000.
c. $124,000.
d. $136,000.

(SO 3) 9. Noncash charges that are added back to net income in determining cash provided by operations under the indirect method do *not* include:
a. depreciation expense.
b. an increase in inventory.
c. amortization expense.
d. loss on sale of equipment.

Questions 10 and 11 apply only to the direct method.

(SO 4) 10. The beginning balance in accounts receivable is $44,000, and the ending balance is $42,000. Sales during the period are $129,000. Cash receipts from customers are:
a. $127,000.
b. $129,000.
c. $131,000.
d. $141,000.

11. Which of the following items is reported on a cash flow statement prepared by the direct method? (SO 4)
a. Loss on sale of building.
b. Increase in accounts receivable.
c. Depreciation expense.
d. Cash payments to suppliers.

12. The statement of cash flows should *not* be used to evaluate an entity's ability to: (SO 3)
a. earn net income.
b. generate future cash flows.
c. pay dividends.
d. meet obligations.

*13. In a work sheet for the statement of cash flows, a decrease in accounts receivable is entered in the reconciling columns as a credit to Accounts Receivable and a debit in the: (SO 5)
a. investing activities section.
b. operating activities section.
c. financing activities section.
d. none of the above.

THE NAVIGATOR

QUESTIONS

1. (a) What is the statement of cash flows? (b) Alice Weiseman maintains that the statement of cash flows is an optional financial statement. Do you agree? Explain.

2. What questions about cash are answered by the statement of cash flows?

3. What are "cash equivalents"? How do cash equivalents affect the statement of cash flows?

4. Distinguish among the three types of activities reported in the statement of cash flows.

5. What are the major sources (inflows) of cash in a statement of cash flows? What are the major uses (outflows) of cash?

6. Why is it important to disclose certain noncash transactions? How should they be disclosed?

7. Wilma Flintstone and Barny Rublestone were discussing the presentation format of the statement of cash flows of Stone Candy Co. At the bottom of Stone Candy's statement of cash flows was a separate section entitled "Noncash investing and financing activities." Give three examples of significant noncash transactions that would be reported in this section.

8. Why is it necessary to use comparative balance sheets, a current income statement, and certain transaction data in preparing a statement of cash flows?

9. Contrast the advantages and disadvantages of the direct and indirect methods. Are both methods acceptable? Which method is preferred by the FASB? Which method is more popular?

10. When the total cash inflows exceed the total cash outflows in the statement of cash flows, how and where is this excess identified?

11. Describe the indirect method for determining net cash provided by operating activities.

12. Why is it necessary to convert accrual based net income to cash basis income when preparing a statement of cash flows?

13. The president of Styx Company is puzzled. During the last year, the company experienced a net loss of $800,000, yet its cash increased $300,000 during the same period of time. Explain to the president how this situation could occur.

14. Identify five items that are adjustments to reconcile net income to net cash provided by operating activities under the indirect method.

15. Why and how is depreciation expense reported in a statement prepared using the indirect method?

16. Why is the statement of cash flows useful?

17. During 2001, James Brown Company converted $1,600,000 of its total $2,000,000 of bonds payable into common stock. Indicate how the transaction would be reported on a statement of cash flows, if at all.

18. Describe the direct method for determining net cash provided by operating activities.

19. Give the formulas under the direct method for computing (a) cash receipts from customers and (b) cash payments to suppliers.

20. Sharon Stone Inc. reported sales of $2 million for 2001. Accounts receivable decreased $100,000 and accounts payable increased $325,000. Compute cash receipts from customers, assuming that the receivable and payable transactions related to operations.

21. Why is depreciation expense not reported in the direct-method cash flow from operating activities section?

22. Give an example of one accrual-based ratio and one cash-based ratio to measure these characteristics of a company: (a) liquidity, (b) solvency, and (c) profitability.

*23. Why is it advantageous to use a work sheet when preparing a statement of cash flows? Is a work sheet required to prepare a statement of cash flows?

BRIEF EXERCISES

●●●

BE14–1 DiCaprio Co., reported net income of $2.5 million in 2001. Depreciation for the year was $280,000, accounts receivable decreased $350,000, and accounts payable decreased $310,000. Compute net cash provided by operating activities using the indirect approach.

Compute cash provided by operating activities—indirect method.
(SO 3)

BE14–2 The net income for Kate Winslet Co. for 2001 was $280,000. For 2001, depreciation on plant assets was $60,000, and the company incurred a loss on sale of plant assets of $10,000. Compute net cash provided by operating activities under the indirect method.

Compute cash provided by operating activities—indirect method.
(SO 3)

BE14–3 Each of the following items must be considered in preparing a statement of cash flows for Matt Damon Co. for the year ended December 31, 2001. For each item, state how it should be shown in the statement of cash flows for 2001.

Indicate statement presentation of selected transactions.
(SO 2)

(a) Issued bonds for $200,000 cash.
(b) Purchased equipment for $180,000 cash.
(c) Sold land costing $20,000 for $20,000 cash.
(d) Declared and paid a $50,000 cash dividend.

BE14–4 The comparative balance sheet for Amistad Company shows the following changes in noncash current asset accounts: accounts receivable decrease $95,000, prepaid expenses increase $12,000, and inventories increase $30,000. Compute net cash provided by operating activities using the indirect method assuming that net income is $220,000.

Compute net cash provided by operating activities using indirect method.
(SO 3)

BE14–5 Classify the following items as an operating, investing, or financing activity. Assume all items involve cash unless there is information to the contrary.

Classify items by activities.
(SO 2)

(a) Purchase of equipment.
(b) Sale of building.
(c) Redemption of bonds.
(d) Depreciation
(e) Payment of dividends.
(f) Issuance of capital stock

BE14–6 Julie Christie Co. has accounts receivable of $14,000 at Janury 1, 2001, and $24,000 at December 31, 2001. Sales revenues were $490,000 for the year 2001. What is the amount of cash receipts from customers in 2001?

Compute receipts from customers using direct method.
(SO 4)

BE14–7 Joe Pesci Company reported income taxes of $90,000 on its 2001 income statement and income taxes payable of $12,000 at December 31, 2000, and $9,000 at December 31, 2001. What amount of cash payments was made for income taxes during 2001?

Compute cash payments for income taxes using direct method.
(SO 4)

BE14–8 Titanic Company reports operating expenses of $100,000 excluding depreciation expense of $15,000 for 2001. During the year prepaid expenses decreased $6,600 and accrued expenses payable increased $4,400. Compute the cash payments for operating expenses in 2001.

Compute cash payments for operating expenses using direct method.
(SO 4)

BE14–9 The T-accounts for Equipment and the related Accumulated Depreciation for Kim Bassinger Company at the end of 2001 are as follows:

Determine cash received in sale of equipment.
(SO 3, 4)

Equipment				Accumulated Depreciation			
Beg. bal.	80,000	Disposals	22,000	Disposals	5,500	Beg. bal.	44,500
Acquisitions	41,600					Depr.	12,000
End. bal.	99,600					End. bal.	51,000

In addition, Kim Bassinger Company's income statement reported a loss on the sale of equipment of $6,900. What amount was reported on the statement of cash flows as "cash flow from sale of equipment"?

Identify financing activity transactions.
(SO 2)

BE14–10   The following T-account is a summary of the cash account of Robin Williams Company.

Cash (Summary Form)

Balance, 1/1/01	8,000		
Receipts from customers	364,000	Payments for goods	200,000
Dividends on stock investments	6,000	Payments for operating expenses	140,000
Proceeds from sale of equipment	36,000	Interest paid	10,000
Proceeds from issuance of bonds		Taxes paid	8,000
payable	100,000	Dividends paid	45,000
Balance, 12/31/01	111,000		

For Robin Williams Company what amount of net cash provided (used) by financing activities should be reported in the statement of cash flows?

Calculate cash-based ratios.
(SO 5)

BE14–11   Alice Weiseman Company reported cash from operations of $300,000, net sales $1,500,000, average current liabilities of $150,000 and average total liabilities of $225,000. Calculate these ratios:
(a) Current cash debt coverage ratio.
(b) Cash debt coverage ratio.
(c) Cash return on sales ratio.

Indicate entries in work sheet.
(SO 6)

***BE14–12**   Using the data in BE14–8, indicate how the changes in prepaid expenses and accrued expenses payable should be entered in the reconciling columns of a work sheet. Assume that beginning balances were: prepaid expenses, $18,600 and accrued expenses payable, $8,200.

EXERCISES
....

Classify transactions by type of activity.
(SO 2)

E14–1   Depeche Mode Corporation had the following transactions during 2001:
1. Issued $50,000 par value common stock for cash.
2. Collected $16,000 of accounts receivable.
3. Declared and paid a cash dividend of $25,000.
4. Sold a long-term investment with a cost of $15,000 for $15,000 cash.
5. Issued $200,000 par value common stock upon conversion of bonds having a face value of $200,000.
6. Paid $18,000 on accounts payable.
7. Purchased a machine for $30,000, giving a long-term note in exchange.

Instructions
Analyze the transactions above and indicate whether each transaction is reported as (a) operating activities, (b) investing activities, (c) financing activities, or (d) noncash investing and financing activities.

Prepare the operating activities section—indirect method.
(SO 3)

E14–2   Burt Reynolds Company reported net income of $195,000 for 2001. Reynolds also reported depreciation expense of $45,000, and a loss of $5,000 on the sale of equipment. The comparative balance sheet shows an increase in accounts receivable of $15,000 for the year, an $8,000 increase in accounts payable, and a decrease in prepaid expenses $4,000.

Instructions
Prepare the operating activities section of the statement of cash flows for 2001. Use the indirect method.

E14–3 The current sections of Greg Kinnear Co. balance sheets at December 31, 2000 and 2001, arc prcscntcd bclow.

Prepare the operating activities section—indirect method.
(SO 3)

GREG KINNEAR CO.
Balance Sheet (partial)
December 31

	2001	2000
Current assets		
Cash	$105,000	$ 99,000
Accounts receivable	110,000	89,000
Inventory	171,000	186,000
Prepaid expenses	27,000	32,000
Total current assets	$413,000	$406,000
Current liabilities		
Accrued expenses payable	$ 15,000	$ 5,000
Accounts payable	$ 85,000	$ 92,000
Total current liabilities	$100,000	$ 97,000

Kinnear's net income for 2001 was $153,000. Depreciation expense was $24,000.

Instructions

Prepare the net cash provided by operating activities section of Kinnear's statement of cash flows for the year ended December 31, 2001, using the indirect method.

E14–4 Presented below are three accounts that appear in the general ledger of Anthony Hopkins Co. during 2001:

Prepare a partial statement of cash flows—indirect method.
(SO 3)

Equipment

Date		Debit	Credit	Balance
Jan. 1	Balance			160,000
July 31	Purchase of equipment	70,000		230,000
Sept. 2	Cost of equipment constructed	53,000		283,000
Nov. 10	Cost of equipment sold		45,000	238,000

Accumulated Depreciation—Equipment

Date		Debit	Credit	Balance
Jan. 1	Balance			71,000
Nov. 10	Accumulated depreciation on equipment sold	30,000		41,000
Dec. 31	Depreciation for year		24,000	65,000

Retained Earnings

Date		Debit	Credit	Balance
Jan. 1	Balance			105,000
Aug. 23	Dividends (cash)	14,000		91,000
Dec. 31	Net income		67,000	158,000

Instructions

From the postings in the accounts above, indicate how the information is reported on a statement of cash flows by preparing a partial statement of cash flows using the indirect method. The loss on sale of equipment was $6,000.

E14–5 A comparative balance sheet for Rupert Everett Company is presented below.

Prepare a statement of cash flows—indirect method.
(SO 3, 5)

RUPERT EVERETT COMPANY
Balance Sheet
December 31

Assets	2001	2000
Cash	$ 63,000	$ 22,000
Accounts receivable	85,000	76,000
Inventories	180,000	189,000
Land	75,000	100,000
Equipment	260,000	200,000
Accumulated depreciation	(66,000)	(42,000)
Total	$597,000	$545,000

Liabilities and Stockholders' Equity	2001	2000
Accounts payable	$ 34,000	$ 47,000
Bonds payable	150,000	200,000
Common stock ($1 par)	214,000	164,000
Retained earnings	199,000	134,000
Total	$597,000	$545,000

Additional information:

1. Net income for 2001 was $105,000.
2. Cash dividends of $40,000 were declared and paid.
3. Bonds payable amounting to $50,000 were redeemed for cash $50,000.
4. Common stock was issued for $50,000 cash.
5. Depreciation expense was $24,000.
6. Sales for the year were $978,000.

Instructions
(a) Prepare a statement of cash flows for 2001 using the indirect method.
(b) Compute the following cash-basis ratios:
    (1) Current cash debt coverage ratio.
    (2) Cash return on sales ratio.
    (3) Cash debt coverage ratio.

Classify transactions by type of activity.
(SO 2)

E14–6 An analysis of comparative balance sheets, the current year's income statement, and the general ledger accounts of Kevin Spacey Corp. uncovered the following items. Assume all items involve cash unless there is information to the contrary.

(a) Issuance of capital stock.
(b) Amortization of patent.
(c) Issuance of bonds for land.
(d) Payment of interest on notes payable.
(e) Conversion of bonds into common stock.
(f) Sale of land at a loss.
(g) Receipt of dividends on investment in stock.
(h) Purchase of land.
(i) Payment of dividends.
(j) Sale of building at book value.
(k) Exchange of land for patent.
(l) Depreciation.
(m) Redemption of bonds.
(n) Receipt of interest on notes receivable.

Instructions
Indicate how the above items should be classified in the statement of cash flows using the following four major classifications: operating activity (indirect method), investing activity, financing activity, and significant noncash investing and financing activity.

Compute cash provided by operating activities—direct method.
(SO 4)

E14–7 Judi Dench Company has just completed its first year of operations on December 31, 2001. Its initial income statement showed that Judi Dench had revenues of $157,000 and operating expenses of $88,000. Accounts receivable and accounts payable at year-end were $42,000 and $33,000, respectively. Assume that accounts payable related to operating expenses. Ignore income taxes.

Instructions
Compute net cash provided by operating activities using the direct method.

E14–8 The income statement for Helen Hunt Company shows cost of goods sold $355,000 and operating expenses (exclusive of depreciation) $250,000. The comparative balance sheet for the year shows that inventory increased $6,000, prepaid expenses decreased $6,000, accounts payable (merchandise suppliers) decreased $8,000, and accrued expenses payable increased $8,000.

Compute cash payments— direct method.
(SO 4)

Instructions
Using the direct method, compute (a) cash payments to suppliers and (b) cash payments for operating expenses.

E14–9 The 2001 accounting records of Helena Bonham Co. reveal the following transactions and events.

Compute cash flow from operating activities—direct method.
(SO 2, 4)

Payment of interest	$ 6,000	Collection of accounts receivable	$180,000
Cash sales	48,000	Payment of salaries and wages	68,000
Receipt of dividend revenue	14,000	Depreciation expense	18,000
Payment of income taxes	15,000	Proceeds from sale of aircraft	812,000
Net income	38,000	Purchase of equipment for cash	22,000
Payment of accounts payable for		Loss on sale of aircraft	3,000
merchandise	90,000	Payment of dividends	14,000
Payment for land	74,000	Payment of operating expenses	20,000

Instructions
Prepare the cash flows from operating activities section using the direct method. (Not all of the above items will be used.)

E14–10 The following information is taken from the 2001 general ledger of Robert Duvall Company:

Calculate cash flows—direct method.
(SO 4)

Rent	Rent expense	$ 33,000
	Prepaid rent, January 1	5,900
	Prepaid rent, December	3,000
Salaries	Salaries expense	54,000
	Salaries payable, January 1	5,000
	Salaries payable, December 31	8,000
Sales	Revenue from sales	180,000
	Accounts receivable, January 1	12,000
	Accounts receivable, December 31	9,000

Instructions
In each of above cases, compute the amount that should be reported in the operating activities section of the statement of cash flows applying the direct method.

E14–11 Presented here is information for two companies in the same industry: Morgan Corporation and Cole Corporation.

Compare two companies by using cash-basis ratios.
(SO 5)

	Morgan Corporation	Cole Corporation
Cash provided by operations	$200,000	$200,000
Average current liabilities	50,000	100,000
Average total libilities	200,000	250,000
Net income	200,000	200,000
Sales	400,000	800,000

Instructions
Using the cash-basis ratios presented in this chapter, compare and discuss the (a) liquidity, (b) solvency, and (c) profitability of the two companies.

*E14–12 Information for Rupert Everett Company is presented in E14–5.

Prepare a work sheet.
(SO 6)

Instructions
Use the data in E14–5 to prepare a work sheet for a statement of cash flows for 2001. Enter the reconciling items directly on the work sheet, identifying the entries alphabetically.

PROBLEMS: SET A

· ·

Prepare the operating activities section—indirect method.
(SO 3)

P14–1A   The income statement of Emma Thompson Company is shown below:

EMMA THOMPSON COMPANY
Income Statement
For the Year Ended December 31, 2001

Sales		$7,100,000
Cost of goods sold		
Beginning inventory	$1,700,000	
Purchases	5,430,000	
Goods available for sale	7,130,000	
Ending inventory	1,920,000	
Cost of goods sold		5,210,000
Gross profit		1,890,000
Operating expenses		
Selling expenses	380,000	
Administrative expense	525,000	
Depreciation expense	75,000	
Amortization expense	30,000	1,010,000
Net income		$ 880,000

Additional information:

1. Accounts receivable increased $510,000 during the year.
2. Prepaid expenses increased $170,000 during the year.
3. Accounts payable to merchandise suppliers increased $50,000 during the year.
4. Accrued expenses payable decreased $180,000 during the year.

Instructions
Prepare the operating activities section of the statement of cash flows for the year ended December 31, 2001, for Emma Thompson Company using the indirect method.

Prepare the operating activities section—direct method.
(SO 4)

P14–2A   Data for the Emma Thompson Company are presented in P14–1A.

Instructions
Prepare the operating activities section of the statement of cash flows using the direct method.

Prepare the operating activities section—direct method.
(SO 4)

P14–3A.   Pierce Brosnan Company's income statement for the year ended December 31, 2001, contained the following condensed information:

Revenue from fees		$900,000
Operating expenses (excluding depreciation)	$624,000	
Depreciation expense	60,000	
Loss on sale of equipment	26,000	710,000
Income before income taxes		190,000
Income tax expense		40,000
Net income		$150,000

Brosnan's balance sheet contained the following comparative data at December 31:

	2001	2000
Accounts receivable	$47,000	$55,000
Accounts payable	41,000	33,000
Income taxes payable	4,000	9,000

(Accounts payable pertains to operating expenses.)

Instructions
Prepare the operating activities section of the statement of cash flows using the direct method.

Prepare the operating activities section—indirect method.
(SO 3)

P14–4A   Data for Pierce Brosnan Company are presented in P14–3A.

Instructions
Prepare the operating activities section of the statement of cash flows for Pierce Brosnan Company using the indirect method.

P14–5A   The financial statements of Joan E. Robinson Company appear below:

Prepare a statement of cash flows—indirect method and compute ratios.
(SO 3, 5)

JOAN E. ROBINSON COMPANY
Comparative Balance Sheet
December 31

Assets	2001	2000
Cash	$ 29,000	$ 13,000
Accounts receivable	28,000	14,000
Merchandise inventory	25,000	35,000
Property, plant, and equipment	60,000	78,000
Accumulated depreciation	(20,000)	(24,000)
Total	$122,000	$116,000

Liabilities and Stockholders' Equity		
Accounts payable	$ 29,000	$ 23,000
Income taxes payable	5,000	8,000
Bonds payable	27,000	33,000
Common stock	18,000	14,000
Retained earnings	43,000	38,000
Total	$122,000	$116,000

JOAN E. ROBINSON COMPANY
Income Statement
For the Year Ended December 31, 2001

Sales		$220,000
Cost of goods sold		180,000
Gross profit		40,000
Selling expenses	$14,000	
Administrative expenses	10,000	24,000
Income from operations		16,000
Interest expense		2,000
Income before income taxes		14,000
Income tax expense		4,000
Net income		$ 10,000

The following additional data were provided:

1. Dividends declared and paid were $5,000.
2. During the year equipment was sold for $8,500 cash. This equipment cost $18,000 originally and had a book value of $8,500 at the time of sale.
3. All depreciation expense is in the selling expense category.
4. All sales and purchases are on account.

Instructions
(a) Prepare a statement of cash flows using the indirect method.
(b) Compute the following cash-basis ratios:
   (1) Current cash debt coverage ratio.
   (2) Cash return on sales ratio.
   (3) Cash debt coverage ratio.

P14–6A   Data for the Joan E. Robinson Company are presented in P14–5A. Further analysis reveals the following:

1. Accounts payable pertain to merchandise suppliers.
2. All operating expenses except for depreciation were paid in cash.

Prepare a statement of cash flows—direct method and compute ratios.
(SO 4, 5)

Instructions

(a) Prepare a statement of cash flows for Joan E. Robinson Company using the direct method.

(b) Compute the following cash-basis ratios:
   (1) Current cash debt coverage ratio.
   (2) Cash return on sales ratio.
   (3) Cash debt coverage ratio.

Prepare a statement of cash flows—indirect method.
(SO 3)

P14–7A   The financial statements of Charlie Brown Company appear below:

CHARLIE BROWN COMPANY
Balance Sheet
December 31

Assets	2001	2000
Cash	$ 25,000	$ 11,000
Accounts receivable	22,000	33,000
Merchandise inventory	20,000	29,000
Prepaid expenses	15,000	13,000
Land	40,000	40,000
Property, plant, and equipment	210,000	225,000
Less: Accumulated depreciation	(55,000)	(67,500)
Total	$277,000	$283,500

Liabilities and Stockholders' Equity		
Accounts payable	$ 11,000	$ 18,500
Accrued expenses payable	9,500	7,500
Interest payable	1,000	1,500
Income taxes payable	3,000	2,000
Bonds payable	50,000	80,000
Common stock	125,000	105,000
Retained earnings	77,500	69,000
Total	$277,000	$283,500

CHARLIE BROWN COMPANY
Income Statement
For the Year Ended December 31, 2001

Revenues		
Sales	$600,000	
Gain on sale of plant assets	2,500	$602,500
Less: Expenses		
Cost of goods sold	$500,000	
Operating expenses (excluding depreciation)	60,000	
Depreciation expense	7,500	
Interest expense	5,000	
Income tax expense	9,000	581,500
Net income		$ 21,000

Additional information:

1. Plant assets were sold at a sales price of $37,500.
2. Additional equipment was purchased at a cost of $40,000.
3. Dividends of $12,500 were paid.
4. All sales and purchases were on account.
5. Bonds were redeemed at face value.
6. Additional shares of stock were issued for cash.

Instructions
Prepare a statement of cash flows for Charlie Brown Company for the year ended December 31, 2001, using the indirect method.

P14–8A Data for Charlie Brown Company is presented in P14–7A. Further analysis reveals the following:

Prepare a statement of cash flows—direct method.
(SO 4)

1. Accounts payable relates to merchandise creditors.
2. All operating expenses, except depreciation expense, were paid in cash.

Instructions
Prepare a statement of cash flows for Charlie Brown Company for the year ended December 31, 2001, using the direct method.

P14–9A Presented below is the comparative balance sheet for Karin Weigle Company as of December 31:

Prepare a statement of cash flows—indirect method and compute ratios.
(SO 3, 5)

KARIN WEIGLE COMPANY
Comparative Balance Sheet
December 31

Assets	2001	2000
Cash	$ 41,000	$ 45,000
Accounts receivable	47,500	52,000
Inventory	151,450	142,000
Prepaid expenses	16,780	21,000
Land	100,000	130,000
Equipment	228,000	155,000
Accumulated depreciation—equipment	(45,000)	(35,000)
Building	200,000	200,000
Accumulated depreciation—building	(60,000)	(40,000)
	$679,730	$670,000
Liabilities and Stockholders' Equity		
Accounts payable	$ 43,730	$ 40,000
Bonds payable	250,000	300,000
Common stock, $1 par	200,000	150,000
Retained earnings	186,000	180,000
	$679,730	$670,000

Additional information:

1. Operating expenses include depreciation expense of $42,000.
2. Land was sold for cash at book value.
3. Cash dividends of $32,000 were paid.
4. Net income for 2001 was $38,000.
5. Equipment was purchased for $95,000 cash. In addition, equipment costing $22,000 with a book value of $10,000 was sold for $8,100 cash.
6. Bonds were converted at face value by issuing 50,000 shares of $1 par value common stock.
7. Net sales for 2001 totaled $420,000.

Instructions
(a) Prepare a statement of cash flows for the year ended December 31, 2001, using the indirect method.
(b) Compute the following cash-basis ratios for 2001:
    (1) Current cash debt coverage ratio.
    (2) Cash return on sales ratio.
    (3) Cash debt coverage ratio.

*P14–10A Data for Charlie Brown Company are presented in P14–7A.

Prepare a work sheet.
(SO 6)

Instructions
Prepare a work sheet for a statement of cash flows for 2001. Enter the reconciling entries directly on the work sheet, identifying the entries alphabetically.

PROBLEMS: SET B

Prepare the operating activities section—indirect method.
(SO 3)

14–1B   The income statement of Oprah Winfrey Company is shown below:

OPRAH WINFREY COMPANY
Income Statement
For the Year Ended November 30, 2001

Sales		$6,900,000
Cost of goods sold		
Beginning inventory	$2,000,000	
Purchases	4,300,000	
Goods available for sale	6,300,000	
Ending inventory	1,600,000	
Cost of goods sold		4,700,000
Gross profit		2,200,000
Operating expenses		
Selling expenses	450,000	
Administrative expenses	700,000	1,150,000
Net income		$1,050,000

Additional information:

1. Accounts receivable decreased $290,000 during the year.
2. Prepaid expenses increased $150,000 during the year.
3. Accounts payable to suppliers of merchandise decreased $300,000 during the year.
4. Accrued expenses payable decreased $100,000 during the year.
5. Administrative expenses include depreciation expense of $90,000.

Instructions
Prepare the operating activities section of the statement of cash flows for the year ended November 30, 2001, for Oprah Winfrey Company using the indirect method.

Prepare the operating activities section—direct method.
(SO 4)

P14–2B   Data for the Oprah Winfrey Company are presented in P14–1B.

Instructions
Prepare the operating activities section of the statement of cash flows using the direct method.

Prepare the operating activities section—direct method.
(SO 4)

P14–3B   The income statement of Kanapilei International Co. for the year ended December 31, 2001, reported the following condensed information:

Revenue from fees	$470,000
Operating expenses	280,000
Income from operations	190,000
Income tax expense	47,000
Net income	$143,000

Kanapilei's balance sheet contained the following comparative data at December 31:

	2001	2000
Accounts receivable	$50,000	$40,000
Accounts payable	30,000	41,000
Income taxes payable	6,000	4,000

Kanapilei has no depreciable assets. (Accounts payable pertains to operating expenses.)

Instructions
Prepare the operating activities section of the statement of cash flows using the direct method.

P14–4B   Data for Kanapilei International Co. are presented in P14–3B.

Instructions

Prepare the operating activities section of the statement of cash flows using the indirect method.

Prepare the operating activities section—indirect method.
(SO 3)

P14–5B   The financial statements of Adam Sandler Company appear below:

Prepare a statement of cash flows—indirect method and compute ratios.
(SO 3, 5)

ADAM SANDLER COMPANY
Comparative Balance Sheet
December 31

Assets		2001		2000
Cash		$ 26,000		$ 13,000
Accounts receivable		18,000		14,000
Merchandise inventory		38,000		35,000
Property, plant, and equipment	$70,000		$78,000	
Less: Accumulated depreciation	(30,000)	40,000	(24,000)	54,000
Total		$122,000		$116,000

Liabilities and Stockholders' Equity			
Accounts payable		$ 29,000		$ 33,000
Income taxes payable		15,000		20,000
Bonds payable		20,000		10,000
Common stock		25,000		25,000
Retained earnings		33,000		28,000
Total		$122,000		$116,000

ADAM SANDLER COMPANY
Income Statement
For the Year Ended December 31, 2001

Sales		$240,000
Cost of goods sold		180,000
Gross profit		60,000
Selling expenses	$24,000	
Administrative expenses	10,000	34,000
Income from operations		26,000
Interest expense		2,000
Income before income taxes		24,000
Income tax expense		7,000
Net income		$ 17,000

The following additional data were provided:

1. Dividends of $12,000 were declared and paid.
2. During the year equipment was sold for $10,000 cash. This equipment cost $15,000 originally and had a book value of $10,000 at the time of sale.
3. All depreciation expense, $11,000, is in the selling expense category.
4. All sales and purchases are on account.
5. Additional equipment was purchased for $7,000 cash.

Instructions

(a) Prepare a statement of cash flows using the indirect method.
(b) Compute the following cash-basis ratios:
  (1) Current cash debt coverage ratio.
  (2) Cash return on sales ratio.
  (3) Cash debt coverage ratio.

Prepare a statement of cash flows—direct method and compute ratios.
(SO 4, 5)

P14–6B Data for the Adam Sandler Company are presented in P14–5B. Further analysis reveals the following:

1. Accounts payable pertains to merchandise creditors.
2. All operating expenses except for depreciation are paid in cash.

Instructions

(a) Prepare a statement of cash flows using the direct method.
(b) Compute the following cash-basis ratios:
   (1) Current cash debt coverage ratio.
   (2) Cash return on sales ratio.
   (3) Cash debt coverage ratio.

Prepare a statement of cash flows—indirect method.
(SO 3)

P14–7B Condensed financial data of Dan Aykroyd Company appear below:

DAN AYKROYD COMPANY
Comparative Balance Sheet
December 31

Assets	2001	2000
Cash	$ 96,700	$ 47,250
Accounts receivable	86,800	57,000
Inventories	121,900	102,650
Investments	84,500	87,000
Plant assets	250,000	205,000
Accumulated depreciation	(49,500)	(40,000)
	$590,400	$458,900

Liabilities and Stockholders' Equity	2001	2000
Accounts payable	$ 52,700	$ 48,280
Accrued expenses payable	12,100	18,830
Bonds payable	100,000	70,000
Common stock	250,000	200,000
Retained earnings	175,600	121,790
	$590,400	$458,900

DAN AYKROYD COMPANY
Income Statement Data
For the Year Ended December 31, 2001

Sales		$297,500
Gain on sale of plant assets		8,750
		306,250
Less:		
Cost of goods sold	$ 99,460	
Operating expenses (excluding depreciation expense)	14,670	
Depreciation expense	49,700	
Income taxes	7,270	
Interest expense	2,940	174,040
Net income		$132,210

Additional information:

1. New plant assets costing $92,000 were purchased for cash during the year.
2. Investments were sold at cost.
3. Plant assets costing $47,000 were sold for $15,550, resulting in a gain of $8,750.
4. A cash dividend of $78,400 was declared and paid during the year.

Instructions
Prepare a statement of cash flows using the indirect method.

P14–8B   Data for Dan Aykroyd Company are presented in P14–7B. Further analysis reveals that accounts payable pertains to merchandise creditors.

Instructions
Prepare a statement of cash flows for Dan Aykroyd Company using the direct method.

P14–9B   Presented below is the comparative balance sheet for Andy Garcia Company at December 31:

ANDY GARCIA COMPANY
Comparative Balance Sheet
December 31

Assets	2001	2000
Cash	$ 40,000	$ 57,000
Accounts receivable	77,000	64,000
Inventory	132,000	140,000
Prepaid expenses	12,140	16,540
Land	125,000	150,000
Equipment	200,000	175,000
Accumulated depreciation—equipment	(60,000)	(42,000)
Building	250,000	250,000
Accumulated depreciation—building	(75,000)	(50,000)
	$701,140	$760,540

Liabilities and Stockholders' Equity	2001	2000
Accounts payable	$ 33,000	$ 45,000
Bonds payable	235,000	265,000
Common stock, $1 par	280,000	250,000
Retained earnings	153,140	200,540
	$701,140	$760,540

Additional information:
1. Operating expenses include depreciation expense of $70,000 and charges from prepaid expenses of $4,400.
2. Land was sold for cash at cost.
3. Cash dividends of $74,290 were paid.
4. Net income for 2001 was $26,890.
5. Equipment was purchased for $65,000 cash. In addition, equipment costing $40,000 with a book value of $13,000 was sold for $14,000 cash.
6. Bonds were converted at face value by issuing 30,000 shares of $1 par value common stock.
7. Net sales in 2001 were $367,000.

Instructions
 (a) Prepare a statement of cash flows for 2001 using the indirect method.
 (b) Compute the following cash-basis ratios for 2001:
   (1) Current cash debt coverage ratio.
   (2) Cash return on sales ratio.
   (3) Cash debt coverage ratio.

*P14–10B   Data for Dan Aykroyd Company are presented in P14–7B.

Instructions
Prepare a work sheet for a statement of cash flows. Enter the reconciling items directly in the work sheet columns, identifying the debit and credit amounts alphabetically.

BROADENING YOUR PERSPECTIVE

FINANCIAL REPORTING AND ANALYSIS

FINANCIAL REPORTING PROBLEM: Kellogg Company

BYP14–1 Refer to the financial statements of Kellogg Company, presented in Appendix A and answer the following questions:

(a) What was the amount of net cash provided by operating activities for the year 1998? For the year 1997?
(b) What was the amount of increase or decrease in cash and cash equivalents for the year 1998? For the year 1997?
(c) Which method of computing net cash provided by operating activities does Kellogg use?
(d) From your analysis of the 1998 statement of cash flows, did the change in accounts receivable require or provide cash? Did the change in inventories require or provide cash? Did the change in accounts payable require or provide cash?
(e) What was the net outflow or inflow of cash from investing activities for 1998?
(f) What was the amount of interest paid in 1998? What was the amount of income taxes paid in 1998?

COMPARATIVE ANALYSIS PROBLEM: Kellogg Company vs. General Mills

BYP14–2 Kellogg's financial statements are presented in Appendix A; General Mills's financial statements are presented in Appendix B.

Instructions

(a) Based on the information contained in these financial statements, compute the following 1998 ratios for each company:
(1) Current cash debt coverage ratio
(2) Cash return on sales ratio
(3) Cash debt coverage ratio
(b) What conclusions concerning the management of cash can be drawn from these data?

RESEARCH ASSIGNMENT

BYP14–3 The March 21, 1997, issue of *The Wall Street Journal* contains an article by Greg Ip entitled "Cash Flow Rise Could Be Prop to Stock Prices."

Instructions
Read the article and answer the following questions:

(a) How is "free cash flow" defined in the article?
(b) What has been the recent trend in free cash flow relative to earnings in the 1990s?
(c) How are stock prices related to companies' cash flows?
(d) Are there any negatives related to large free cash flows?

INTERPRETING FINANCIAL STATEMENTS: Vermont Teddy Bear Co.

BYP14–4 Founded in the early 1980s, the Vermont Teddy Bear Co. designs and manufactures American-made teddy bears and markets them primarily as gifts called Bear-Grams or Teddy Bear-Grams. Bear-Grams are personalized teddy bears delivered directly to the recipient for special occasions such as birthdays and anniversaries. The Shelburne, Vermont, company's primary markets are New York, Boston, and Chicago. Sales have jumped dramatically in recent years, exceeding 50% increases in several consecutive years prior to 1994. Such dramatic growth has significant implications for cash flows. Provided on page 667 are the company's cash flow statements for 1993 and 1994.

Instructions

(a) Note that net income in 1994 was only $17,523 compared to 1993 income of $838,955, but cash flow from operations was $236,480 in 1994 and a negative $700,957 in 1993. Explain the causes of this apparent paradox.
(b) Evaluate Vermont Teddy Bear's liquidity, solvency, and profitability for 1994 using cash-basis ratios.

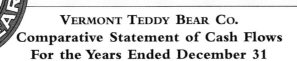

VERMONT TEDDY BEAR CO. Comparative Statement of Cash Flows For the Years Ended December 31		
	1994	**1993**
Cash flows from operating activities		
Net income	$17,523	$838,955
Adjustments to reconcile net income to net cash provided by operating activities		
Deferred income taxes	(69,524)	(146,590)
Depreciation and amortization	316,416	181,348
Changes in assets and liabilities		
Accounts receivable, trade	(38,267)	(25,947)
Inventories	(1,599,014)	(1,289,293)
Prepaid and other current assets	(444,794)	(113,205)
Deposit and other assets	(24,240)	(83,044)
Accounts payable	2,017,059	(284,567)
Accrued expenses	61,321	170,755
Accrued interest payable, debentures	—	(58,219)
Other	—	(8,960)
Income taxes payable	—	117,810
Net cash provided by (used for) operating activities	236,480	(700,957)
Net cash used for investing activities	(2,102,892)	(4,422,953)
Net cash (used for) provided by financing activities	(315,353)	9,685,435
Net change in cash and cash equivalents	$(2,181,765)	$4,561,525
Other information:		
	1994	**1993**
Current liabilities	$4,055,465	$1,995,600
Total liabilities	4,620,085	2,184,386
Net sales	20,560,566	17,025,856

REAL-WORLD FOCUS: Praxair Incorporated

BYP14–5 Praxair was founded in 1907 as Linde-Air Products Company and was a pioneer in separating oxygen from air. It was purchased and run as a division of Union Carbide. In 1992 Praxair became an independent public company. Today, the company is one of the top three largest suppliers of industrial gases worldwide. Praxair has operations in all regions of the world, with half of its sales occurring outside of the United States.

The management discussion on page 668 was included in a recent annual report.

Instructions
   (a) What method has Praxair changed from?
   (b) What will the newly prepared cash flow statement show that the former one did not?
   (c) Will the cash flows from investing and financing appear any differently under the new method of preparation than they did under the old method?

PRAXAIR INCORPORATED
Management Discussion and Analysis

Liquidity, Capital Resources and Other Financial Data: This year, Praxair changed its presentation of the Statement of Cash Flows to the direct method to report major classes of cash receipts and payments from operations. Praxair believes the direct method more clearly presents its operating cash flows. Prior years' cash flow information has been reclassified to conform to the current year presentation.

CRITICAL THINKING

GROUP DECISION CASE

BYP14-6　Greg Rhoda and Debra Sondgeroth are examining the following statement of cash flows for K.K. Bean Trading Company for the year ended January 31, 1999.

K.K. BEAN TRADING COMPANY
Statement of Cash Flows
For the Year Ended January 31, 1999

Sources of cash	
From sales of merchandise	$370,000
From sale of capital stock	420,000
From sale of investment (purchased below)	80,000
From depreciation	55,000
From issuance of note for truck	20,000
From interest on investments	6,000
Total sources of cash	951,000
Uses of cash	
For purchase of fixtures and equipment	340,000
For merchandise purchased for resale (all sold)	258,000
For operating expenses (including depreciation)	160,000
For purchase of investment	75,000
For purchase of truck by issuance of note	20,000
For purchase of treasury stock	10,000
For interest on note payable	3,000
Total uses of cash	866,000
Net increase in cash	$ 85,000

Greg claims that K.K. Bean's statement of cash flows is an excellent portrayal of a superb first year with cash increasing $85,000. Debra replies that it was not a superb first year—but rather, that the year was an operating failure, that the statement was incorrectly presented, and that $85,000 is not the actual increase in cash. The cash balance at the beginning of the year was $140,000.

Instructions
With the class divided into groups, answer the following:

(a) With whom do you agree, Greg or Debra? Explain your position.
(b) Using the data provided, prepare a statement of cash flows in proper form using the indirect method. The only noncash items in the income statement are depreciation and the gain from the sale of the investment.

COMMUNICATION ACTIVITY

BYP14-7　Arnold Byte, the owner-president of Computer Services Company, is unfamiliar with the statement of cash flows which you, as his accountant, prepared. He asks for further explanation.

Instructions
Write him a brief memo explaining the form and content of the statement of cash flows as shown in Illustration 14-18 on page 624.

ETHICS CASE

BYP14–8 Puebla Corporation is a medium-sized wholesaler of automotive parts. It has 10 stockholders, who have been paid a total of $1 million in cash dividends for 8 consecutive years. The policy of the Board of Directors requires that in order for this dividend to be declared, net cash provided by operating activities as reported in Puebla's current year's statement of cash flows must be in excess of $1 million. President and CEO Phil Monat's job is secure so long as he produces annual operating cash flows to support the usual dividend.

At the end of the current year, controller Rick Rodgers presents president Monat with some disappointing news—the net cash provided by operating activities is calculated by the indirect method to be only $970,000. The president says to Rick, "We must get that amount above $1 million. Isn't there some way to increase operating cash flow by another $30,000?" Rick answers, "These figures were prepared by my assistant. I'll go back to my office and see what I can do." The president replies, "I know you won't let me down, Rick."

Upon close scrutiny of the statement of cash flows, Rick concludes that he can get the operating cash flows above $1 million by reclassifying a $60,000, 2-year note payable listed in the financing activities section as "Proceeds from bank loan—$60,000." He will report the note instead as "Increase in payables—$60,000" and treat it as an adjustment of net income in the operating activities section. He returns to the president saying, "You can tell the Board to declare their usual dividend. Our net cash flow provided by operating activities is $1,030,000." "Good man, Rick! I knew I could count on you," exults the president.

Instructions
- (a) Who are the stakeholders in this situation?
- (b) Was there anything unethical about the president's actions? Was there anything unethical about the controller's actions?
- (c) Are the Board members or anyone else likely to discover the misclassification?

SURFING THE NET

BYP14–9 The Securities and Exchange Commission (SEC) is the primary regulatory agency of U.S. financial markets. Its job is to ensure that the markets remain fair for all investors. The following SEC site provides useful information for investors.

Address: http://www.sec.gov/consumer/weisktc.htm (or go to www.wiley.com/college/weygandt)

Steps:
1. Go to the site shown above.
2. Choose **Glossary**.

Instructions
Using the glossary, find the definition of:

- (a) ask.
- (b) margin account.
- (c) prospectus.
- (d) yield.

Answers to Self-Study Questions
1. c   2. b   3. a.   4. c   5. d   6. b   7. c   8. d.   9. b   10. c   11. d
12. a   *13. b

Answer to Kellogg Review It Question 4, p. 625
4. Kellogg uses the indirect method of computing net cash provided by operating activities. The largest single item of cash flow for Kellogg in 1998 is "Issuance of long-term debt, $600 million."

 Remember to go back to the Navigator box on the chapter-opening page and check off your completed work.

Before studying this chapter, you should know or, if necessary, review:

a. The contents and classification of a corporate balance sheet. (Ch. 4, pp. 157–161)

b. The contents and classification of a corporate income statement. (Ch. 5, pp. 206–209)

c. Who are the various users of financial statement information. (Ch. 1, pp. 3–5)

d. How to compute earnings per share (EPS). (Ch. 7, p. 300)

e. How the liquidity of a company is determined. (Ch. 4, p. 160)

THE NAVIGATOR

FEATURE STORY

Just Fooling Around?

The information superhighway added a new lane recently when two brothers, Tom and David Gardner, created an online investor service called the Motley Fool. The name comes from Shakespeare's *As You Like It*. The fool in Shakespeare's plays was the only one who could speak unpleasant truths to kings and queens without being killed. Tom and David view themselves as 20th-century "fools," revealing the

"truths" of Wall Street to the small investor, who they feel has been taken advantage of by Wall Street insiders. They provide a bulletin board service where America Online subscribers can exchange information and insights about companies that may be of interest to investors.

One company, Iomega, has captured the interest of Motley Fool subscribers more than all others. Iomega makes a new kind of computer disk drive called a Zip drive. In less than one year, Iomega's stock price soared by a multiple of 16; that is, a $1,000 investment was suddenly

worth $16,000! Many people suggest that this tremendous run-up in price (one of the highest increases experienced by any U.S. company during that period) was caused by the attention the stock received on the Motley Fool bulletin board. Supporters of the Motley Fool say that this is an example of how the Internet can be used by small investors to make the kind of returns that the "big guys" make. Participants share any information they can find about the company and its product: Are Zip drive users happy with the product? How quickly are Zip drives moving off store shelves? How full is the employee parking lot at Iomega on Sundays?

Critics, however, contend that the bulletin board is merely a high-tech rumor mill that has built a speculative house of cards. One potentially troubling aspect of the bulletin board is that participants on the board don't have to give their identities. Consequently, there is little to stop people from putting misinformation on the board to influence the price in the direction they desire.

As information services such as Motley Fool proliferate, gathering information will become easier, and evaluating it will become the harder task. THE NAVIGATOR

On the World Wide Web
http://www.fool.com
http://www.iomega.com

CHAPTER 15

FINANCIAL STATEMENT ANALYSIS

THE NAVIGATOR ✔

- Understand *Concepts for Review* ☐
- Read *Feature Story* ☐
- Scan *Study Objectives* ☐
- Read *Preview* ☐
- Read text and answer *Before You Go On*
  p. 679 ☐ p. 695 ☐ p. 701 ☐
- Work *Demonstration Problems* ☐
- Review *Summary of Study Objectives* ☐
- Answer *Self-Study Questions* ☐
- Complete assignments ☐

STUDY OBJECTIVES

After studying this chapter, you should be able to:

1. *Discuss the need for comparative analysis.*
2. *Identify the tools of financial statement analysis.*
3. *Explain and apply horizontal analysis.*
4. *Describe and apply vertical analysis.*
5. *Identify and compute ratios and describe their purpose and use in analyzing a firm's liquidity, profitability, and solvency.*
6. *Understand the concept of earning power and indicate how material items not typical of regular operations are presented.*
7. *Recognize the limitations of financial statement analysis.*

THE NAVIGATOR

*I*f you are thinking of purchasing Iomega Corporation stock, or the stock of any company, how can you determine the worth of the stock? How can you determine the company's financial soundness or its profitability? How does Iomega compare financially with other companies in the high-tech industry of computer disk-drive manufacturers? To answer these types of questions, it is helpful for you to understand how to analyze financial statement information.

Financial statement analysis, the topic of this chapter, enhances the usefulness of published financial statements in making decisions about a company. The content and organization of this chapter are shown below.

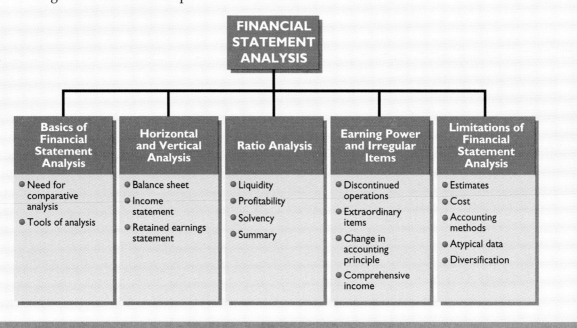

THE NAVIGATOR

BASICS OF FINANCIAL STATEMENT ANALYSIS

Analyzing financial statements involves evaluating three characteristics of a company: its liquidity, its profitability, and its solvency. For example, a **short-term creditor**, such as a bank, is primarily interested in the ability of the borrower to pay obligations when they come due. The liquidity of the borrower in such a case is extremely important in evaluating the safety of a loan. A **long-term creditor**, such as a bondholder, however, looks to indicators such as profitability and solvency that indicate the firm's ability to survive over a long period of time. Long-term creditors consider such measures as the amount of debt in the company's capital structure and the ability to meet interest payments. Similarly, **stockholders** are interested in the profitability and solvency of the enterprise when they assess the likelihood of dividends and the growth potential of the stock.

Need for Comparative Analysis

Every item reported in a financial statement has significance. For example, when Iomega Corporation reports cash of $108 million on its balance sheet, we know the company had that amount of cash on the balance sheet date. However, we do not know whether the amount represents an increase over prior years or whether the amount is adequate in relation to the company's need for cash. To obtain this information, it is necessary to compare the amount of cash with other financial statement data.

Comparisons can be made on a number of different bases—three are illustrated in this chapter:

1. **Intracompany basis.** This basis compares an item or financial relationship **within a company** in the current year with the same item or relationship in one or more prior years. For example, a comparison of Iomega's cash balance at the end of the current year with last year's balance will show the amount of the increase or decrease. Likewise, Iomega can compare the percentage of cash to current assets at the end of the current year with the percentage in one or more prior years. Intracompany comparisons are useful in detecting changes in financial relationships and significant trends.

2. **Industry averages.** This basis compares an item or financial relationship of a company with **industry averages** (or **norms**) published by financial ratings organizations such as Dun & Bradstreet, Moody's, and Standard & Poor's. For example, Iomega's net income can be compared with the average net income of all companies in the computer hard-drive and storage solutions industry. Comparisons with industry averages provide information as to a company's relative performance within the industry.

3. **Intercompany basis.** This basis compares an item or financial relationship of one company with the same item or relationship in **one or more competing companies**. The comparisons are made on the basis of the published financial statements of the individual companies. For example, Iomega's total sales for the year can be compared with the total sales of its major competitors such as IBM and Nomai. Intercompany comparisons are useful in determining a company's competitive position.

Tools of Financial Statement Analysis

Various tools are used to evaluate the significance of financial statement data. Three commonly used tools are these:

Horizontal analysis is a technique for evaluating a series of financial statement data over a period of time.

Vertical analysis is a technique for evaluating financial statement data that expresses each item in a financial statement in terms of a percent of a base amount.

Ratio analysis expresses the relationship among selected items of financial statement data.

Horizontal analysis is used primarily in intracompany comparisons. Two features in published financial statements facilitate this type of comparison: First, each of the basic financial statements is presented on a comparative basis for a minimum of two years. Second, a summary of selected financial data is presented for a series of 5 to 10 years or more. Vertical analysis is used in both intra- and intercompany comparisons. Ratio analysis is used in all three types of

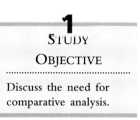

1
STUDY
OBJECTIVE

Discuss the need for comparative analysis.

Intracompany

2000 ↔ 2001

Industry averages

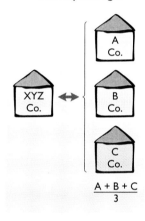

Intercompany

2
STUDY
OBJECTIVE

Identify the tools of financial statement analysis.

comparisons. In the following sections, we will explain and illustrate each of the three types of analysis.

HORIZONTAL ANALYSIS

3
STUDY
OBJECTIVE

Explain and apply
horizontal analysis.

Horizontal analysis, also called **trend analysis**, is a technique for evaluating a series of financial statement data over a period of time. Its purpose is to determine the increase or decrease that has taken place, expressed as either an amount or a percentage. For example, the recent net sales figures of Sears, Roebuck and Co. are as follows:

ILLUSTRATION 15-1

Sears, Roebuck's net sales

SEARS, ROEBUCK AND CO. Net Sales (in millions)				
1998	**1997**	**1996**	**1995**	**1994**
$41,322	$41,296	$38,064	$34,835	$33,110

If we assume that 1994 is the base year, we can measure all percentage increases or decreases from this base period amount as follows:

ILLUSTRATION 15-2

Formula for horizontal analysis of changes since base period

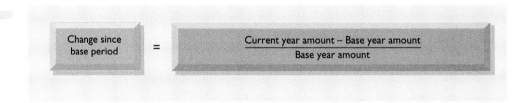

For example, we can determine that net sales for Sears, Roebuck increased approximately 5.2% [($34,835 − $33,110) ÷ $33,110] from 1994 to 1995. Similarly, we can determine that net sales increased over 24.8% [($41,322 − $33,110) ÷ $33,110] from 1994 to 1998.

Alternatively, we can express current year sales as a percentage of the base period by dividing the current year amount by the base year amount, as shown below:

ILLUSTRATION 15-3

Formula for horizontal analysis of current year in relation to base year

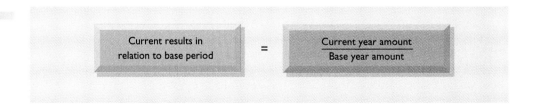

Illustration 15-4 presents this analysis for Sears for a 5-year period using 1994 as the base period.

SEARS, ROEBUCK AND CO.
Net Sales (in millions)
in relation to base period 1994

1998	1997	1996	1995	1994
$41,322	$41,296	$38,064	$34,835	$33,110
124.8%	124.7%	115%	105%	100%

ILLUSTRATION 15-4

Horizontal analysis of Sears, Roebuck's net sales in relation to base period

Balance Sheet

To further illustrate horizontal analysis, we will use the financial statements of Quality Department Store Inc., a downtown full-line department store in a southeastern city of 55,000 population. Its 2-year condensed balance sheets for 1998 and 1997 showing dollar and percentage changes are presented in Illustration 15-5.

QUALITY DEPARTMENT STORE INC.
Condensed Balance Sheet
December 31

	1998	1997	Increase or (Decrease) during 1998 Amount	Percent
Assets				
Current assets	$1,020,000	$ 945,000	$ 75,000	7.9%
Plant assets (net)	800,000	632,500	167,500	26.5%
Intangible assets	15,000	17,500	(2,500)	(14.3%)
Total assets	$1,835,000	$1,595,000	$240,000	15.0%
Liabilities				
Current liabilities	$ 344,500	$ 303,000	$ 41,500	13.7%
Long-term liabilities	487,500	497,000	(9,500)	(1.9%)
Total liabilities	832,000	800,000	32,000	4.0%
Stockholders' Equity				
Common stock, $1 par	275,400	270,000	5,400	2.0%
Retained earnings	727,600	525,000	202,600	38.6%
Total stockholders' equity	1,003,000	795,000	208,000	26.2%
Total liabilities and stockholders' equity	$1,835,000	$1,595,000	$240,000	15.0%

ILLUSTRATION 15-5

Horizontal analysis of a balance sheet

HELPFUL HINT It is difficult to comprehend the significance of a change when only the dollar amount of change is examined. When the change is expressed in percentage form, it is easier to grasp the true magnitude of the change.

The comparative balance sheet in Illustration 15-5 shows that a number of significant changes have occurred in Quality Department Store's financial structure from 1997 to 1998. In the asset section, plant assets (net) increased $167,500, or 26.5%. In the liabilities section, current liabilities increased $41,500, or 13.7%. In the stockholders' equity section, we find that retained earnings increased $202,600, or 38.6%. This suggests that the company expanded its asset base during 1998 and financed this expansion primarily by retaining income in the business rather than assuming additional long-term debt.

Income Statement

Presented in Illustration 15-6 is a 2-year comparative income statement of Quality Department Store Inc. for the years 1998 and 1997, in a condensed format.

ILLUSTRATION 15-6

Horizontal analysis of an income statement

	1998	1997	Amount	Percent
QUALITY DEPARTMENT STORE INC.				
Condensed Income Statement				
For the Years Ended December 31				
			Increase or (Decrease) during 1998	
Sales	$2,195,000	$1,960,000	$235,000	12.0%
Sales returns and allowances	98,000	123,000	(25,000)	(20.3%)
Net sales	2,097,000	1,837,000	260,000	14.2%
Cost of goods sold	1,281,000	1,140,000	141,000	12.4%
Gross profit	816,000	697,000	119,000	17.1%
Selling expenses	253,000	211,500	41,500	19.6%
Administrative expenses	104,000	108,500	(4,500)	(4.1%)
Total operating expenses	357,000	320,000	37,000	11.6%
Income from operations	459,000	377,000	82,000	21.8%
Other revenues and gains				
Interest and dividends	9,000	11,000	(2,000)	(18.2%)
Other expenses and losses				
Interest expense	36,000	40,500	(4,500)	(11.1%)
Income before income taxes	432,000	347,500	84,500	24.3%
Income tax expense	168,200	139,000	29,200	21.0%
Net income	$ 263,800	$ 208,500	$ 55,300	26.5%

HELPFUL HINT

Note that while the amount column is additive (the total is $55,300), the percentage column is not additive (26.5% is not the total). A separate percentage has been calculated for each item.

Horizontal analysis of the income statements shows the following changes:

1. Net sales increased $260,000, or 14.2% ($260,000 ÷ $1,837,000).
2. Cost of goods sold increased $141,000, or 12.4% ($141,000 ÷ $1,140,000).
3. Total operating expenses increased $37,000, or 11.6% ($37,000 ÷ $320,000).

Overall, gross profit and net income were up substantially. Gross profit, for example, increased 17.1% and net income increased 26.5%. It appears, therefore, that Quality's profit trend is favorable.

Retained Earnings Statement

Quality Department Store's comparative retained earnings statement for the years 1998 and 1997 is presented in Illustration 15-7. Analyzed horizontally, net income increased $55,300, or 26.5%, whereas dividends on the common stock increased only $1,200, or 2%. Ending retained earnings, as shown in the horizontal analysis of the balance sheet, increased 38.6%. As indicated earlier, Quality Department Store Inc. retained a significant portion of its net income to finance expenditures for additional plant facilities.

			Increase (or Decrease) during 1998	
QUALITY DEPARTMENT STORE INC.				
Retained Earnings Statement				
For the Years Ended December 31				
	1998	1997	Amount	Percent
Retained earnings, Jan. 1	$525,000	$376,500	$148,500	39.4%
Add: Net income	263,800	208,500	55,300	26.5%
	788,800	585,000	203,800	
Deduct: Dividends	61,200	60,000	1,200	2.0%
Retained earnings, Dec. 31	$727,600	$525,000	$202,600	38.6%

ILLUSTRATION 15-7
Horizontal analysis of a retained earnings statement

The measurement of changes from period to period in terms of percentages is relatively straightforward and is quite useful. However, complications can result in making the computations. For example, if an item has no value in a base year or preceding year and a value in the next year, no percentage change can be computed. Similarly, if a negative amount appears in the base or preceding period and a positive amount exists the following year, or vice versa, no percentage change can be computed.

VERTICAL ANALYSIS

Vertical analysis, sometimes referred to as **common size analysis**, is a technique for evaluating financial statement data that expresses each item within a financial statement in terms of a percent of a base amount. For example, on a balance sheet we might say that current assets are 22% of total assets (total assets being the base amount). Or on an income statement, we might say that selling expenses are 16% of net sales (net sales being the base amount).

4
STUDY
OBJECTIVE
....
Describe and apply vertical analysis.

Balance Sheet
Presented in Illustration 15-8 on page 678 is the comparative balance sheet of Quality Department Store Inc. for 1998 and 1997, analyzed vertically. The base for the asset items is **total assets**, and the base for the liability and stockholders' equity items is **total liabilities and stockholders' equity**.

In addition to showing the relative size of each category on the balance sheet, vertical analysis may show the **percentage change** in the individual asset, liability, and stockholders' equity items. In this case, even though current assets increased $75,000 from 1997 to 1998, they decreased from 59.2% to 55.6% of total assets. Plant assets (net) have increased from 39.7% to 43.6% of total assets, and retained earnings have increased from 32.9% to 39.7% of total liabilities and stockholders' equity. These results reinforce the earlier observations that Quality is choosing to finance its growth through retention of earnings rather than through the issuance of additional debt.

Income Statement
Vertical analysis of the comparative income statements of Quality, shown in Illustration 15-9 on page 678, reveals that cost of goods sold as a percentage of

ILLUSTRATION 15-8

Vertical analysis of a balance sheet

QUALITY DEPARTMENT STORE INC.
Condensed Balance Sheet
December 31

	1998		1997	
	Amount	Percent	Amount	Percent
Assets				
Current assets	$1,020,000	55.6%	$ 945,000	59.2%
Plant assets (net)	800,000	43.6%	632,500	39.7%
Intangible assets	15,000	.8%	17,500	1.1%
Total assets	$1,835,000	100.0%	$1,595,000	100.0%
Liabilities				
Current liabilities	$ 344,500	18.8%	$ 303,000	19.0%
Long-term liabilities	487,500	26.5%	497,000	31.2%
Total liabilities	832,000	45.3%	800,000	50.2%
Stockholders' Equity				
Common stock, $1 par	275,400	15.0%	270,000	16.9%
Retained earnings	727,600	39.7%	525,000	32.9%
Total stockholders' equity	1,003,000	54.7%	795,000	49.8%
Total liabilities and stockholders' equity	$1,835,000	100.0%	$1,595,000	100.0%

HELPFUL HINT

The formula for calculating these balance sheet percentages is:

$$\frac{\text{Each item on B/S}}{\text{Total assets}} = \%$$

net sales declined 1% (62.1% vs. 61.1%) and total operating expenses declined 0.4% (17.4% vs. 17.0%). As a result, it is not surprising to see net income as a percent of net sales increase from 11.4% to 12.6%. As indicated from the horizontal analysis, Quality appears to be a profitable enterprise that is becoming even more successful.

ILLUSTRATION 15-9

Vertical analysis of an income statement

QUALITY DEPARTMENT STORE INC.
Condensed Income Statement
For the Years Ended December 31

	1998		1997	
	Amount	Percent	Amount	Percent
Sales	$2,195,000	104.7%	$1,960,000	106.7%
Sales returns and allowances	98,000	4.7%	123,000	6.7%
Net sales	2,097,000	100.0%	1,837,000	100.0%
Cost of goods sold	1,281,000	61.1%	1,140,000	62.1%
Gross profit	816,000	38.9%	697,000	37.9%
Selling expenses	253,000	12.0%	211,500	11.5%
Administrative expenses	104,000	5.0%	108,500	5.9%
Total operating expenses	357,000	17.0%	320,000	17.4%
Income from operations	459,000	21.9%	377,000	20.5%
Other revenues and gains				
Interest and dividends	9,000	0.4%	11,000	0.6%
Other expenses and losses				
Interest expense	36,000	1.7%	40,500	2.2%
Income before income taxes	432,000	20.6%	347,500	18.9%
Income tax expense	168,200	8.0%	139,000	7.5%
Net income	$ 263,800	12.6%	$ 208,500	11.4%

HELPFUL HINT

The formula for calculating these income statement percentages is:

$$\frac{\text{Each item on I/S}}{\text{Net Sales}} = \%$$

An associated benefit of vertical analysis is that it enables you to compare companies of different sizes. For example, Quality's main competitor is a Sears store in a nearby town. Using vertical analysis, the condensed income statements of the small local retail enterprise, Quality Department Store Inc., can be more meaningfully compared with the 1998 income statement of the giant international retailer, Sears, Roebuck and Co., as shown in Illustration 15-10.

ILLUSTRATION 15-10

Intercompany income statement comparison

Condensed Income Statements
(in thousands)

	Quality Department Store Inc.		Sears, Roebuck and Co.	
	Dollars	**Percent**	**Dollars**	**Percent**
Net sales	$2,097	**100.0%**	$41,322,000	**100.0%**
Cost of goods sold	1,281	**61.1%**	27,257,000	**66.0%**
Gross profit	816	**38.9%**	14,065,000	**34.0%**
Selling and administrative expenses	357	**17.0%**	10,787,000	**26.1%**
Income from operations	459	**21.9%**	3,278,000	**7.9%**
Other expenses and revenues (including income taxes)	195	**9.3%**	2,230,000	**5.4%**
Net income	$ 264	**12.6%**	$ 1,048,000	**2.5%**

Although Sears' net sales are 19,704 times greater than the net sales of relatively tiny Quality Department Store, vertical analysis eliminates this difference in size. The percentages show that Quality's and Sears' gross profit rates were somewhat comparable at 38.9% and 34%, although the percentages related to income from operations were significantly different at 21.9% and 7.9%. This disparity can be attributed to Quality's selling and administrative expense percentage (17%) which is much lower than Sears' (26.1%). Although Sears earned net income nearly 3,970 times larger than Quality's, Sears' net income as a **percent of each sales dollar** (2.5%) is only 20% of Quality's (12.6%).

BEFORE YOU GO ON...

Review It

1. What are the different tools that might be used to compare financial information?
2. What is horizontal analysis?
3. What is vertical analysis?
4. Identify the specific sections in Kellogg's 1998 Annual Report where horizontal and vertical analysis of financial data is presented. The answer to this question is provided on page 731.

Do It

Summary financial information for Rosepatch Company is as follows:

	December 31, 2000	December 31, 1999
Current assets	$234,000	$180,000
Plant assets (net)	756,000	420,000
Total assets	$990,000	$600,000

Compute the amount and percentage changes in 2000 using horizontal analysis, assuming 1999 is the base year.

Reasoning: Since 1999 is the base year, the percentage change is found by dividing the amount of the increase by the 1999 amount.

Solution:

	Increase in 2000	
	Amount	**Percent**
Current assets	$ 54,000	30% [($234,000 − $180,000) ÷ $180,000]
Plant assets (net)	336,000	80% [($756,000 − $420,000) ÷ $420,000]
Total assets	$390,000	65% [($990,000 − $600,000) ÷ $600,000]

Related exercise material: BE15–1, BE15–3, BE15–4, BE15–6, E15–1, E15–3, and E15–4.

RATIO ANALYSIS

Ratio analysis expresses the relationship among selected items of financial statement data. A ratio expresses the mathematical relationship between one quantity and another. The relationship is expressed in terms of either a percentage, a rate, or a simple proportion. To illustrate, recently Nike, Inc., had current assets of $3,533 million and current liabilities of $1,703.8 million. The relationship is determined by dividing current assets by current liabilities. The alternative means of expression are:

Percentage: Current assets are 207% of current liabilities.
Rate: Current assets are 2.07 times greater than current liabilities.
Proportion: The relationship of current assets to liabilities is 2.07:1.

TECHNOLOGY IN ACTION

Many general ledger accounting programs include the generation of financial ratios as routine output. All the ratio computations presented in this chapter can be done with electronic spreadsheets as well. There are also many programs written specifically for financial statement analysis. These packages are written for both general purpose use and use in specific industries. For example, financial institutions routinely use over 60 ratios geared specifically to the banking industry.

For analysis of the primary financial statements, ratios can be classified as pictured in Illustration 15-11.

Ratios can provide clues to underlying conditions that may not be apparent from inspection of the individual components of a particular ratio. However, a single ratio by itself is not very meaningful. Accordingly, in the following discussion we will use:

1. **Intracompany comparisons** covering 2 years for the Quality Department Store.

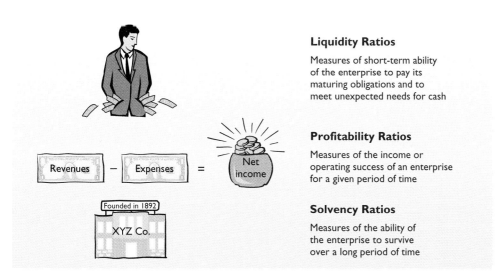

ILLUSTRATION 15-11

Financial ratio classifications

Liquidity Ratios

Measures of short-term ability of the enterprise to pay its maturing obligations and to meet unexpected needs for cash

Profitability Ratios

Measures of the income or operating success of an enterprise for a given period of time

Solvency Ratios

Measures of the ability of the enterprise to survive over a long period of time

2. **Industry average comparisons** based on Dun & Bradstreet's median ratios for department stores and Robert Morris Associates' median ratios for department stores.

3. **Intercompany comparisons** based on Sears, Roebuck and Co. as Quality Department Store's principal competitor.

Liquidity Ratios

Liquidity ratios measure the short-term ability of the enterprise to pay its maturing obligations and to meet unexpected needs for cash. Short-term creditors such as bankers and suppliers are particularly interested in assessing **liquidity.** The ratios that can be used to determine the enterprise's short-term debt-paying ability are the current ratio, the acid-test ratio, the current cash debt coverage ratio, receivables turnover, and inventory turnover.

1. Current Ratio

The current ratio is a widely used measure for evaluating a company's liquidity and short-term debt-paying ability. The ratio is computed by dividing current assets by current liabilities. It is sometimes referred to as the **working capital ratio** because **working capital** is the excess of current assets over current liabilities. The current ratio is a more dependable indicator of liquidity than working capital. Two companies with the same amount of working capital may have significantly different current ratios. The 1998 and 1997 current ratios for Quality Department Store and comparative data are shown in Illustration 15-12 on page 682.

What does the ratio actually mean? The 1998 ratio of 2.96:1 means that for every dollar of current liabilities, Quality has $2.96 of current assets. Quality's current ratio has decreased in the current year. However, compared to the industry average of 3.2:1, and Sears' 2.07:1 current ratio, Quality appears to be reasonably liquid.

The current ratio is only one measure of liquidity. It does not take into account the composition of the current assets. For example, a satisfactory current ratio does not disclose the fact that a portion of the current assets may be tied up in slow-moving inventory. A dollar of cash is more readily available to pay the bills than is a dollar of slow-moving inventory.

ILLUSTRATION 15-12

Current ratio

HELPFUL HINT

Can any corporation operate successfully without working capital? Yes, if it has very predictable cash flows and solid earnings. A surprising number of companies, including Whirlpool, American Standard, and Campbell's Soup, are pursuing this goal. The rationale: Less money tied up in working capital means more money to invest in the business.

$$\textbf{CURRENT RATIO} = \frac{\textbf{CURRENT ASSETS}}{\textbf{CURRENT LIABILITIES}}$$

Quality Department Store

1998	1997
$\dfrac{\$1,020,000}{\$344,500} = 2.96{:}1$	$\dfrac{\$945,000}{\$303,000} = 3.1{:}1$
Industry average 3.2:1	Sears, Roebuck and Co. 2.07:1

2. Acid-Test Ratio

ALTERNATIVE TERMINOLOGY

The acid-test ratio is also called the *quick ratio.*

The acid-test ratio is a measure of a company's immediate short-term liquidity, computed by dividing the sum of cash, temporary investments, and net receivables by current liabilities. Thus, it is an important complement to the current ratio. For example, assume that the current assets of Quality Department Store for 1998 and 1997 consist of the following items:

ILLUSTRATION 15-13

Current assets of Quality Department Store

QUALITY DEPARTMENT STORE INC.
Balance Sheet (partial)

	1998	1997
Current assets		
Cash	$ 100,000	$155,000
Temporary investments	20,000	70,000
Receivables (net)	230,000	180,000
Inventory	620,000	500,000
Prepaid expenses	50,000	40,000
Total current assets	$1,020,000	$945,000

ACCOUNTING IN ACTION
Business Insight

The apparent simplicity of the current ratio can have real-world limitations because an addition of equal amounts to both the numerator and the denominator causes the ratio to decrease. Assume, for example, that a company has $2,000,000 of current assets and $1,000,000 of current liabilities; its current ratio is 2:1. If it purchases $1,000,000 of inventory on account, it will have $3,000,000 of current assets and $2,000,000 of current liabilities; its current ratio will decrease to 1.5:1. If, instead, the company pays off $500,000 of its current liabilities, it will have $1,500,000 of current assets and $500,000 of current liabilities, and its current ratio will increase to 3:1. Thus, any trend analysis should be done with care, since the ratio is susceptible to quick changes and is easily influenced by management.

Cash, temporary investments, and receivables (net) are highly liquid compared to inventory and prepaid expenses. The inventory may not be readily saleable and the prepaid expenses may not be transferable to others. Thus, the acid-test ratio measures **immediate** liquidity. The 1998 and 1997 acid-test ratios for Quality Department Store and comparative data are as follows:

ILLUSTRATION 15-14

Acid-test ratio

$$\text{ACID-TEST RATIO} = \frac{\text{CASH + TEMPORARY INVESTMENTS + RECEIVABLES (NET)}}{\text{CURRENT LIABILITIES}}$$

Quality Department Store

1998	1997
$\dfrac{\$100{,}000 + \$20{,}000 + \$230{,}000}{\$344{,}500} = 1.0{:}1$	$\dfrac{\$155{,}000 + \$70{,}000 + \$180{,}000}{\$303{,}000} = 1.3{:}1$
Industry average 1.3:1	Sears, Roebuck and Co. 1.3:1

Is an acid-test ratio of 1.0:1 adequate? The ratio has declined in 1998. However, when compared with the industry median of 1.3:1 and Sears' of 1.3:1, Quality's acid-test ratio seems adequate.

3. Current Cash Debt Coverage Ratio

A disadvantage of the current and acid-test ratios is that they use year-end balances of current asset and current liability accounts. These year-end balances may not be representative of what the company's current position was during most of the year. A ratio that partially corrects for this problem is the ratio of net cash provided by operating activities to average current liabilities, referred to as the current cash debt coverage ratio. Because it uses net cash provided by operating activities rather than a balance at a point in time, it may provide a better representation of liquidity.

To illustrate the computation of this ratio, assume that Quality Department Store's statement of cash flows shows net cash flows provided by operating activities of $404,000 in 1998 and $340,000 in 1997 and that current liabilities at January 1, 1997, are $290,000. The current cash debt coverage ratio for Quality Department Store and comparative data are as follows:

ILLUSTRATION 15-15

Current cash debt coverage ratio

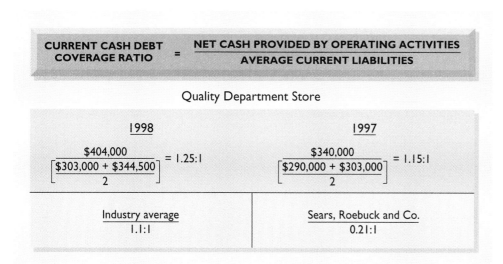

$$\text{CURRENT CASH DEBT COVERAGE RATIO} = \frac{\text{NET CASH PROVIDED BY OPERATING ACTIVITIES}}{\text{AVERAGE CURRENT LIABILITIES}}$$

Quality Department Store

1998	1997
$\dfrac{\$404{,}000}{\left[\dfrac{\$303{,}000 + \$344{,}500}{2}\right]} = 1.25{:}1$	$\dfrac{\$340{,}000}{\left[\dfrac{\$290{,}000 + \$303{,}000}{2}\right]} = 1.15{:}1$
Industry average 1.1:1	Sears, Roebuck and Co. 0.21:1

The ratio has increased in 1998. Is the coverage adequate? Probably so. Quality's operating cash flow coverage of average current liabilities is slightly greater than the industry average and considerably greater than Sears' coverage.

4. Receivables Turnover

Liquidity may be measured by how quickly certain assets can be converted to cash. How liquid, for example, are the receivables? The ratio used to assess the liquidity of the receivables is the receivables turnover ratio. This ratio measures the number of times, on average, receivables are collected during the period. The receivables turnover ratio is computed by dividing net credit sales (net sales less cash sales) by the average net receivables during the year. Unless seasonal factors are significant, average net receivables outstanding can be computed from the beginning and ending balance of the net receivables.[1]

Assuming that all sales are credit sales and the balance of accounts receivable (net) at the beginning of 1997 is $200,000, the receivables turnover ratio for Quality Department Store and comparative data are shown in Illustration 15-16. Quality's receivables turnover improved in 1998. The turnover of 10.2 times compares quite favorably with Sears' 2.18 times and the department store industry's average of 7.0 times.

ILLUSTRATION 15-16

Receivables turnover

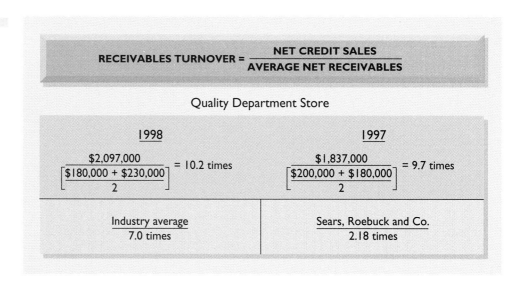

$$\text{RECEIVABLES TURNOVER} = \frac{\text{NET CREDIT SALES}}{\text{AVERAGE NET RECEIVABLES}}$$

Quality Department Store

1998	1997
$\dfrac{\$2,097,000}{\left[\dfrac{\$180,000 + \$230,000}{2}\right]} = 10.2$ times	$\dfrac{\$1,837,000}{\left[\dfrac{\$200,000 + \$180,000}{2}\right]} = 9.7$ times
Industry average 7.0 times	Sears, Roebuck and Co. 2.18 times

ACCOUNTING IN ACTION
Business Insight

In some cases, receivables turnover may be misleading. Some companies, especially large retail chains, encourage credit and revolving charge sales, and they slow collections in order to earn a healthy return on the outstanding receivables in the form of interest at rates of 18% to 22%. This may explain why Sears' turnover is only 2.18 times. In general, however, the faster the turnover, the greater the reliance that can be placed on the current and acid-test ratios for assessing liquidity.

---

[1]If seasonal factors are significant, the average receivables balance might be determined by using monthly amounts.

A popular variant of the receivables turnover ratio is to convert it into an **average collection period** in terms of days. This is done by dividing the receivables turnover ratio into 365 days. For example, the receivables turnover in 1998 of 10.2 times is divided into 365 days to obtain approximately 35.8 days. This means that the average collection period for receivables is 36 days, or approximately every 5 weeks. The average collection period is frequently used to assess the effectiveness of a company's credit and collection policies. The general rule is that the collection period should not greatly exceed the credit term period (i.e., the time allowed for payment).

5. Inventory Turnover

The inventory turnover ratio measures the number of times on average the inventory is sold during the period. Its purpose is to measure the liquidity of the inventory. The inventory turnover is computed by dividing cost of goods sold by the average inventory during the period. Unless seasonal factors are significant, average inventory can be computed from the beginning and ending inventory balances. Assuming that the inventory balance for Quality Department Store at the beginning of 1997 was $450,000, its inventory turnover and comparative data are as shown in Illustration 15-17. Quality's inventory turnover declined slightly in 1998. The turnover ratio of 2.3 times is relatively low compared with the industry average of 3.4 and Sears' 5.5. Generally, the faster the inventory turnover, the less cash that is tied up in inventory and the less the chance of inventory obsolescence.

ILLUSTRATION 15-17

Inventory turnover

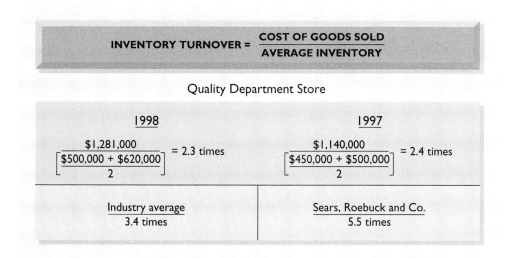

A variant of the inventory turnover ratio is the **average days to sell the inventory**. For example, the inventory turnover in 1998 of 2.3 times divided into 365 is approximately 159 days. An average selling time of 159 days is also relatively high compared with the industry average of 107 days (365 ÷ 3.4) and Sears' 66 days (365 ÷ 5.5).

Profitability Ratios

Profitability ratios measure the income or operating success of an enterprise for a given period of time. Income, or the lack of it, affects the company's ability to obtain debt and equity financing, the company's liquidity position, and the com-

ACCOUNTING IN ACTION
Business Insight

Inventory turnover ratios vary considerably among industries. For example, grocery store chains have a turnover of 10 times and an average selling period of 37 days. In contrast, jewelry stores have an average turnover of 1.3 times and an average selling period of 281 days. Within a company there may be significant differences in inventory turnover among different types of products. Thus, in a grocery store the turnover of perishable items such as produce, meats, and dairy products will be faster than the turnover of soaps and detergents.

pany's ability to grow. As a consequence, creditors and investors alike are interested in evaluating earning power (profitability). Profitability is frequently used as the ultimate test of management's operating effectiveness.

6. Profit Margin

The profit margin ratio is a measure of the percentage of each dollar of sales that results in net income. It is computed by dividing net income by net sales for the period. Quality Department Store's profit margin ratios and comparative data are shown in Illustration 15-18.

ALTERNATIVE TERMINOLOGY

The profit margin ratio is also called the *rate of return on sales.*

ILLUSTRATION 15-18

Profit margin ratio

$$\text{PROFIT MARGIN ON SALES} = \frac{\text{NET INCOME}}{\text{NET SALES}}$$

Quality Department Store

1998	1997
$\frac{\$263,800}{\$2,097,000} = 12.6\%$	$\frac{\$208,500}{\$1,837,000} = 11.4\%$
Industry average 3.6%	Sears, Roebuck and Co. 2.5%

Quality experienced an increase in its profit margin from 1997 to 1998. Its profit margin is unusually high in comparison with the industry average of 3.6% and Sears' 2.5%.

High-volume (high inventory turnover) enterprises such as grocery stores (Safeway or Kroger) and discount stores (Kmart or Wal-Mart) generally experience low profit margins, whereas low-volume enterprises such as jewelry stores (Tiffany & Co.) or airplane manufacturers (Boeing Aircraft) have high profit margins.

7. Cash Return on Sales Ratio

The profit margin ratio discussed above is an accrual-based ratio using net income as the numerator. The cash-basis counterpart to that ratio is the cash return on sales ratio which uses net cash provided by operating activities as the numerator and net sales as the denominator. The difference between these two ratios should be explainable as differences between accrual accounting and cash-basis accounting, i.e., differences in the timing of revenue and expense recognition. Using net cash provided by operating activities of $404,000 in 1998 and $340,000 in 1997, Quality Department Store's cash return on sales ratios are computed as follows:

ILLUSTRATION 15-19

Cash return on sales ratio

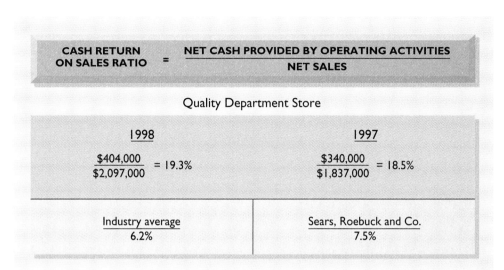

Quality's cash return on sales is considerably higher than its profit margin on sales. The difference of 6.7% (19.3% − 12.6%) in 1998 is due to excess noncash charges over noncash credits to the income statement. Quality appears to have a very healthy cash return on sales.

8. Asset Turnover

The asset turnover ratio measures how efficiently a company uses its assets to generate sales. It is determined by dividing net sales by average assets for the period. The resulting number shows the dollars of sales produced by each dollar invested in assets. Unless seasonal factors are significant, average total assets can be computed from the beginning and ending balance of total assets. Assuming that the total assets at the beginning of 1997 were $1,446,000, the 1998 and 1997 asset turnover ratios for Quality Department Store and comparative data are as follows:

ILLUSTRATION 15-20

Asset turnover

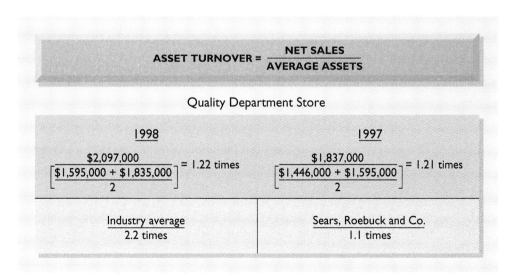

The asset turnover ratio shows that Quality generated sales of $1.22 in 1998 for each dollar it had invested in assets. The ratio changed little from 1997 to 1998. Quality's asset turnover ratio is below the industry average of 2.2 times and above Sears' ratio of 1.1 times.

Asset turnover ratios vary considerably among industries. For example, a large utility company like Consolidated Edison (New York) has a ratio of 0.49 times, the large grocery chain Kroger Stores has a ratio of 4.3 times, and the large sports shoe manufacturer and marketer Nike, Inc. has an asset turnover ratio of 1.78 times.

9. Return on Assets Ratio

An overall measure of profitability is the return on assets ratio. This ratio is computed by dividing net income by average assets. The 1998 and 1997 return on assets for Quality Department Store and comparative industry and Sears data are shown below.

ILLUSTRATION 15-21

Return on assets

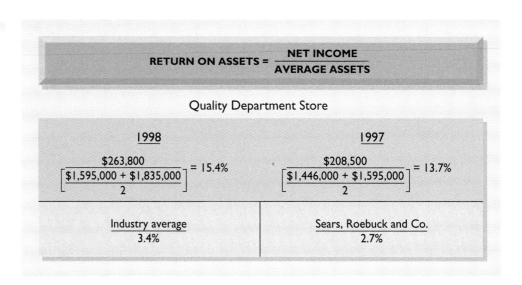

Quality's return on assets improved from 1997 to 1998. Its return of 15.4% is very high, compared with the department store industry average of 3.4% and Sears' 2.7%.

10. Return on Common Stockholders' Equity

Another widely used ratio that measures profitability from the common stockholder's viewpoint is return on common stockholders' equity. This ratio shows how many dollars of net income were earned for each dollar invested by the owners. It is computed by dividing net income by average common stockholders' equity. Assuming that common stockholders' equity at the beginning of 1997 was $667,000, the 1998 and 1997 ratios for Quality Department Store and comparative data are shown in Illustration 15-22.

Quality's rate of return on common stockholders' equity is unusually high at 29.3%, considering an industry average of 12.9% and a rate of 17.6% for Sears, Roebuck and Co.

When preferred stock is present, **preferred dividend** requirements are deducted from net income to compute income available to common stockholders.

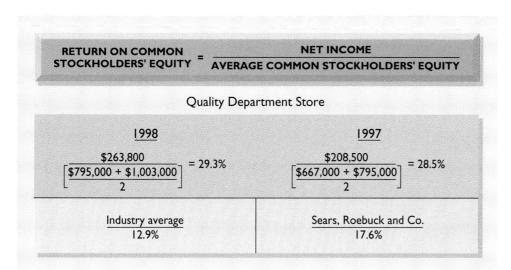

ILLUSTRATION 15-22

Return on common stockholders' equity

Similarly, the par value of preferred stock (or call price, if applicable) must be deducted from total stockholders' equity to arrive at the amount of common stock equity used in this ratio. The ratio then appears as follows:

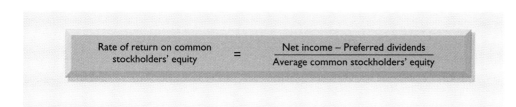

Note that Quality's rate of return on stockholders' equity (29.3%) is substantially higher than its rate of return on assets (15.38%). The reason is that Quality has made effective use of leverage or trading on the equity at a gain. Trading on the equity at a gain means that the company has borrowed money through the issuance of bonds or notes at a lower rate of interest than it is able to earn by using the borrowed money. Leverage is using money supplied by nonowners to increase the return to the owners. A comparison of the rate of return on total assets with the rate of interest paid for borrowed money indicates the profitability of trading on the equity. Quality Department Store earns more on its borrowed funds than it has to pay in the form of interest. Thus the return to stockholders exceeds the return on the assets, benefiting from the positive leveraging.

11. Earnings per Share (EPS)

Earnings per share of stock is a measure of the net income earned on each share of common stock. It is computed by dividing net income by the number of weighted average common shares outstanding during the year. Reducing net income earned to a per share basis provides a useful perspective for determining profitability. Assuming that there is no change in the number of outstanding shares during 1997 and that the 1998 increase occurred midyear, the net income per share for Quality Department Store for 1998 and 1997 is computed as shown in Illustration 15-24 on page 690.

Note that no industry or Sears data are presented. Such comparisons are not meaningful because of the wide variations in the number of shares of outstanding stock among companies. Quality's earnings per share increased 20 cents per share

ILLUSTRATION 15-24

Earnings per share

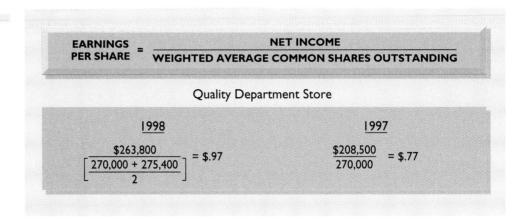

in 1998. This represents a 26% increase over the 1997 earnings per share of 77 cents.

When the term "net income per share" or "earnings per share" is used, it refers to the amount of net income applicable to each share of **common stock**. Therefore, in computing net income per share, if there are preferred dividends declared for the period, they must be deducted from net income to arrive at income available to the common stockholders.

12. Price-Earnings Ratio

The price-earnings ratio is an oft-quoted statistic that measures the ratio of the market price of each share of common stock to the earnings per share. The price-earnings (PE) ratio reflects investors' assessments of a company's future earnings. It is computed by dividing the market price per share of the stock by earnings per share. Assuming that the market price of Quality Department Store Inc. stock is $8 in 1997 and $12 in 1998, the price-earnings ratio is computed as follows:

ILLUSTRATION 15-25

Price-earnings ratio

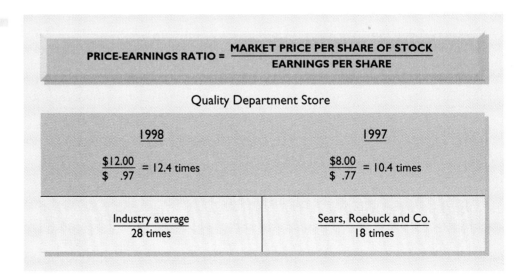

In 1998 each share of Quality's stock sold for 12.4 times the amount that was earned on each share. Quality's price-earnings ratio is significantly lower than the industry average of 28 times, and it is less than the ratio of 18 times for Sears. The average price-earnings ratio for the stocks that constitute the Dow-Jones industrial average on the New York Stock Exchange in June 1999 was an unusually high 25 times.

ACCOUNTING IN ACTION
Business Insight

For the stock of some companies, investors are willing to pay high multiples of per-share earnings because they feel the future growth in earnings will provide an adequate return on the investment. Examples of companies with high price-earnings ratios are America Online (110), Microsoft (60), Coca-Cola (50), and Gillette Co. (49). Examples of companies with low price-earnings ratios are Ford Motor (10), General Motors (9), and Northwest Airlines (7).

13. Payout Ratio

The payout ratio measures the percentage of earnings distributed in the form of cash dividends. It is computed by dividing cash dividends by net income. Companies that have high growth rates are characterized by low payout ratios because they reinvest most of their net income into the business. The 1998 and 1997 payout ratios for Quality Department Store are computed as follows:

ILLUSTRATION 15-26

Payout ratio

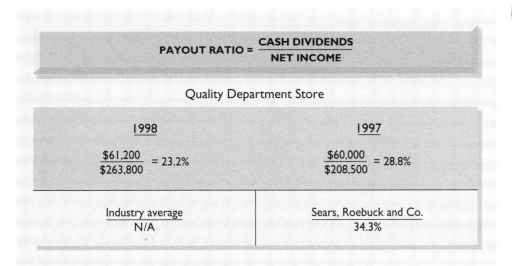

$$\text{PAYOUT RATIO} = \frac{\text{CASH DIVIDENDS}}{\text{NET INCOME}}$$

Quality Department Store

1998	1997
$\frac{\$61,200}{\$263,800} = 23.2\%$	$\frac{\$60,000}{\$208,500} = 28.8\%$
Industry average N/A	Sears, Roebuck and Co. 34.3%

Quality's payout ratio is lower than Sears' payout ratio of 34.3%. As indicated earlier, the company has apparently decided to fund its purchase of plant assets through retention of earnings.

ACCOUNTING IN ACTION
Business Insight

Many companies with stable earnings have high payout ratios. For example, Baltimore Gas and Electric has had an 84% payout ratio over the last 5 years, and Omega Healthcare's dividends exceeded net income over the same period. Conversely, companies that are expanding rapidly, such as Toys `R' Us, Microsoft, and Telecommunications Inc. (TCI) have never paid a cash dividend.

Solvency Ratios

Solvency ratios measure the ability of the enterprise to survive over a long period of time. Long-term creditors and stockholders are interested in a company's long-run solvency, particularly its ability to pay interest as it comes due and to repay the face value of the debt at maturity. Debt to total assets, times interest earned, and cash debt coverage are three ratios that provide information about debt-paying ability.

14. Debt to Total Assets Ratio

The debt to total assets ratio measures the percentage of the total assets provided by creditors (this ratio indicates the degree of leveraging). It is computed by dividing total debt (both current and long-term liabilities) by total assets. This ratio provides some indication of the company's ability to withstand losses without impairing the interests of creditors. The higher the percentage of debt to total assets, the greater the risk that the company may be unable to meet its maturing obligations. The 1998 and 1997 ratios for Quality Department Store and comparative data are as follows:

ILLUSTRATION 15-27

Debt to total assets

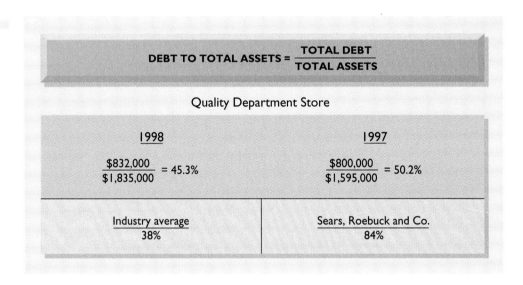

A ratio of 45.3% means that creditors have provided 45.3% of Quality Department Store's total assets. Quality's 45.3% is above the industry average of 38%, but it is considerably below the incredibly high 84% ratio of Sears. The lower the ratio, the more equity "buffer" there is available to the creditors if the company becomes insolvent. Thus, from the creditors' point of view, a low ratio of debt to total assets is usually desirable.

The adequacy of this ratio is often judged in the light of the company's earnings. Generally, companies with relatively stable earnings, such as public utilities, have higher debt to total assets ratios than cyclical companies with widely fluctuating earnings, such as many high-tech companies. (See the following *Accounting in Action* for examples of debt to total assets ratios for selected companies.)

ACCOUNTING IN ACTION
Business Insight

Examples of debt to total assets ratios for selected companies are:

	Total Debt to Total Assets as a Percent
Advanced Micro Devices	19%
Ford Motor Company	42%
Merck	9%
Caterpillar	37%
Bob Evans Farms	0%
Revlon	56%

Another means used in practice to measure this same leverage phenomenon is the debt to equity ratio. It shows the relative use of borrowed funds (total liabilities) as compared to resources invested by the owners. Because this ratio may be computed in several ways, care should be taken when making comparisons.

15. Times Interest Earned Ratio

The times interest earned ratio provides an indication of the company's ability to meet interest payments as they come due. It is computed by dividing income before interest expense and income taxes by interest expense. The 1998 and 1997 ratios for Quality Department Store and comparative data are shown in Illustration 15-28. Note that the times interest earned ratio uses income before income taxes and interest expense, because this amount represents the amount available to cover interest. For Quality Department Store the 1998 amount of $468,000 is computed by taking the income before income taxes of $432,000 and adding back the $36,000 of interest expense. The interest expense of Quality is well covered at 13 times relative to the industry average of 2.7 times and Sears' 2.27 times.

ALTERNATIVE TERMINOLOGY

The times interest earned ratio is also called the *interest coverage ratio.*

ILLUSTRATION 15-28

Times interest earned

$$\text{TIMES INTEREST EARNED} = \frac{\text{INCOME BEFORE INCOME TAXES AND INTEREST EXPENSE}}{\text{INTEREST EXPENSE}}$$

Quality Department Store

1998	1997
$\frac{\$468,000}{\$36,000} = 13$ times	$\frac{\$388,000}{\$40,500} = 9.6$ times

Industry average	Sears, Roebuck and Co.
2.7 times	2.27 times

16. Cash Debt Coverage Ratio

The ratio of net cash provided by operating activities to average total liabilities, referred to as the cash debt coverage ratio, is a cash-basis measure of **solvency**. This ratio demonstrates a company's ability to repay its liabilities from cash generated from operating activities, without having to liquidate the assets employed in its operations. Using Quality's net cash provided by operating activities of $404,000 in 1998 and $340,000 in 1997 and assuming total liabilities of $740,000 on January 1, 1997, the cash debt coverage ratios are computed as follows:

ILLUSTRATION 15-29

Cash debt coverage ratio

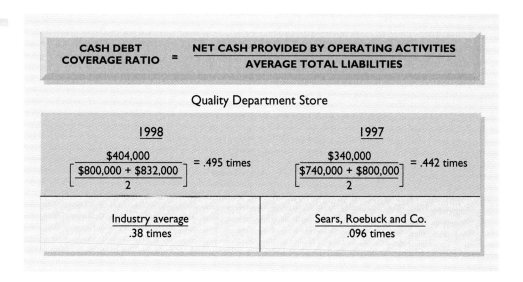

Based on net cash generated from operations in 1998, it would take Quality approximately 2 years to generate enough cash to pay off all its liabilities (assuming all of the net cash generated was used for that purpose only). Its ratio is also superior to that of the retail industry and Sears.

Summary of Ratios

ILLUSTRATION 15-30

Summary of liquidity, profitability, and solvency ratios

A summary of the ratios discussed in the chapter is presented in Illustration 15-30. The summary includes the formula and purpose or use of each ratio.

Ratio	Formula	Purpose or Use
Liquidity Ratios		
1. Current ratio	$\dfrac{\text{Current assets}}{\text{Current liabilities}}$	Measures short-term debt-paying ability.
2. Acid-test or quick ratio	$\dfrac{\text{Cash + temporary investments + receivables (net)}}{\text{Current liabilities}}$	Measures immediate short-term liquidity.
3. Current cash debt coverage ratio	$\dfrac{\text{Net cash provided by operating activities}}{\text{Average current liabilities}}$	Measures short-term debt-paying ability (cash basis).
4. Receivables turnover	$\dfrac{\text{Net credit sales}}{\text{Average net receivables}}$	Measures liquidity of receivables.
5. Inventory turnover	$\dfrac{\text{Cost of goods sold}}{\text{Average inventory}}$	Measures liquidity of inventory.

Illustration 15-30

Summary of liquidity, profitability, and solvency ratios (continued)

Ratio	Formula	Purpose or Use
Profitability Ratios		
6. Profit margin	$\dfrac{\text{Net income}}{\text{Net sales}}$	Measures net income generated by each dollar of sales.
7. Cash return on sales ratio	$\dfrac{\text{Net cash provided by operating activities}}{\text{Net sales}}$	Measures the net cash flow generated by each dollar of sales.
8. Asset turnover	$\dfrac{\text{Net sales}}{\text{Average assets}}$	Measures how efficiently assets are used to generate sales.
9. Return on assets	$\dfrac{\text{Net income}}{\text{Average assets}}$	Measures overall profitability of assets.
10. Return on common stockholders' equity	$\dfrac{\text{Net income}}{\text{Average common stockholders' equity}}$	Measures profitability of stockholders' investment.
11. Earnings per share	$\dfrac{\text{Net income}}{\text{Weighted average common shares outstanding}}$	Measures net income earned on each share of common stock.
12. Price-earnings ratio	$\dfrac{\text{Market price per share of stock}}{\text{Earnings per share}}$	Measures the ratio of the market price per share to earnings per share.
13. Payout ratio	$\dfrac{\text{Cash dividends}}{\text{Net income}}$	Measures percentage of earnings distributed in the form of cash dividends.
Solvency Ratios		
14. Debt to total assets	$\dfrac{\text{Total debt}}{\text{Total assets}}$	Measures the percentage of total assets provided by creditors.
15. Times interest earned	$\dfrac{\text{Income before income taxes and interest expense}}{\text{Interest expense}}$	Measures ability to meet interest payments as they come due.
16. Cash debt coverage ratio	$\dfrac{\text{Net cash provided by operating activities}}{\text{Average total liabilities}}$	Measures the long-term debt-paying ability (cash basis).

Before You Go On...

Review It

1. What are liquidity ratios? Explain the current ratio, acid-test ratio, current cash debt coverage ratio, receivables turnover ratio, and inventory turnover ratio.
2. What are profitability ratios? Explain the profit margin ratio, cash return on sales ratio, asset turnover ratio, return on assets ratio, return on common stockholders' equity ratio, earnings per share, price-earnings ratio, and payout ratio.
3. What are solvency ratios? Explain the debt to total assets ratio, times interest earned ratio, and cash debt coverage ratio.

Do It

Selected financial data for Drummond Company at December 31, 2001, are as follows: cash $60,000; receivables (net) $80,000; inventory $70,000; current liabilities $140,000. Compute the current and acid-test ratios.

Reasoning: The formula for the current ratio is: current assets ÷ current liabilities. The formula for the acid-test ratio is: cash + temporary investments + receivables (net) ÷ current liabilities.

Solution: The current ratio is 1.5:1 ($210,000 ÷ $140,000). The acid-test ratio is 1:1 ($140,000 ÷ $140,000).

*Related exercise material:*BE15–7, BE15–8, BE15–9, BE15–10, BE15–11, E15–5, E15–6, and E15–7.

THE NAVIGATOR

EARNING POWER AND IRREGULAR ITEMS

6

STUDY

OBJECTIVE

Understand the concept of earning power and indicate how material items not typical of regular operations are presented.

Users of financial statements are interested in the concept of "earning power." Earning power means the normal level of income to be obtained in the future. Earning power differs from actual net income by the amount of irregular revenues, expenses, gains, and losses. Users are interested in earning power because it helps them derive an estimate of future earnings without the "noise" of irregular items.

For users of financial statements to determine "earning power" or regular income, the irregular items are separately identified on the income statement. Three types of irregular items are reported:

1. Discontinued operations.
2. Extraordinary items.
3. Changes in accounting principle.

All these irregular items are reported net of income taxes. That is, the applicable income tax expense or tax savings is shown for income before income taxes and for each of the listed irregular items. The general concept is "let the tax follow income or loss."

Discontinued Operations

To downsize its operations, General Dynamics Corp. sold its missile business to Hughes Aircraft Co. for $450 million. In its income statement, General Dynamics was required to report the sale in a separate section entitled "discontinued operations."

Discontinued operations refers to the disposal of a **significant segment** of a business, such as the cessation of an entire activity or the elimination of a major class of customers. Thus, Kmart's decision to terminate its interest in four business activities including PACE Membership Warehouse, Inc., and PayLess Drug Stores Northwest, Inc., were reported as discontinued operations. On the other hand, the phasing out of a model such as the GM Chevette or part of a line of business is not considered to be a disposal of a segment.

When the disposal of a significant segment occurs, the income statement should report both income from continuing operations and income (or loss) from discontinued operations. **The income (loss) from discontinued operations con-**

sists of the income (loss) from operations and the gain (loss) on disposal of the segment. To illustrate, assume that Acro Energy Inc. has revenues of $2.5 million and expenses of $1.7 million from continuing operations in 2001. The company, therefore, has income before income taxes of $800,000. During 2001 the company discontinued and sold its unprofitable chemical division. The loss in 2001 from chemical operations (net of $60,000 taxes) was $140,000, and the loss on disposal of the chemical division (net of $30,000 taxes) was $70,000. Assuming a 30% tax rate on income before income taxes, the income statement presentation is shown below.

ILLUSTRATION 15-31

Statement presentation of discontinued operations

ACRO ENERGY INC. Income Statement (partial) For The Year Ended December 31, 2001		
Income before income taxes		$800,000
Income tax expense		240,000
Income from continuing operations		560,000
Discontinued operations		
Loss from operations of chemical division, net of $60,000 income tax savings	$140,000	
Loss from disposal of chemical division, net of $30,000 income tax savings	70,000	210,000
Net income		$350,000

HELPFUL HINT

Observe the dual disclosures: (1) the results of operations of the discontinued division must be eliminated from the results of continuing operations, and (2) the disposal of the operation.

Note that the caption "Income from continuing operations" is used and that a section "Discontinued operations" is added. **Within the new section, both the operating loss and the loss on disposal are reported net of applicable income taxes.** This presentation clearly indicates the separate effects of continuing operations and discontinued operations on net income.

Extraordinary Items

Extraordinary items are events and transactions that meet two conditions: they are (1) **unusual in nature** and (2) **infrequent in occurrence.** To be considered unusual, the item should be abnormal and be only incidentally related to the customary activities of the entity. To be regarded as infrequent, the event or transaction should not be reasonably expected to recur in the foreseeable future. Both criteria must be evaluated in terms of the environment in which the entity operates. Thus, Weyerhaeuser Co. reported the $36 million in damages to its timberland caused by the volcanic eruption of Mount St. Helens as an extraordinary item because the event was both unusual and infrequent. In contrast, Florida Citrus Company does not report frost damage to its citrus crop as an extraordinary item because frost damage is not viewed as infrequent. Illustration 15-32 on page 698 shows the appropriate classification of extraordinary and ordinary items.

Extraordinary items are reported net of taxes in a separate section of the income statement immediately below discontinued operations. To illustrate, assume that in 2001 a revolutionary foreign government expropriated property held as an investment by Acro Energy Inc. If the loss is $70,000, before applicable income taxes of $21,000, the income statement presentation will show a deduction of $49,000 as shown in Illustration 15-33 on page 698.

ILLUSTRATION 15-32

Examples of extraordinary and ordinary items

Extraordinary items	Ordinary items

Extraordinary items

1. Effects of major casualties (acts of God), if rare in the area.

2. Expropriation (takeover) of property by a foreign government.

3. Effects of a newly enacted law or regulation, such as a condemnation action.

Ordinary items

1. Effects of major casualties (acts of God), not uncommon in the area.

2. Write-down of inventories or write-off of receivables.

3. Losses attributable to labor strikes.

4. Gains or losses from sales of property, plant, or equipment.

ILLUSTRATION 15-33

Statement presentation of extraordinary items

HELPFUL HINT

Ordinary gains and losses are reported at pretax amounts in arriving at income before income taxes. For example, gains from sales of property, plant, and equipment are reported under other revenues and gains.

ACRO ENERGY INC.
Income Statement (partial)
For the Year Ended December 31, 2001

Income before income taxes		$800,000
Income tax expense		240,000
Income from continuing operations		560,000
Discontinued operations		
Loss from operations of chemical division, net of $60,000		
income tax savings	$140,000	
Loss from disposal of chemical division, net of $30,000		
income tax savings	70,000	210,000
Income before extraordinary item		350,000
Extraordinary item		
Expropriation of investment, net of $21,000 income tax		
savings		49,000
Net income		$301,000

As illustrated above, the caption "Income before extraordinary item" is added immediately before the section for the extraordinary item. This presentation clearly indicates the effect of the extraordinary item on net income. If there are no discontinued operations, the third line of the income statement in Illustration 15-33 would be labeled "Income before extraordinary item."

If a transaction or event meets one (but not both) of the criteria for an extraordinary item, it is reported under either "Other revenues and gains" or "Other expenses and losses" at its gross amount (not net of tax). This is true, for example, of gains (losses) resulting from the sale of property, plant, and equipment, as explained in Chapter 10.

Change in Accounting Principle

For ease of comparison, financial statements are expected to be prepared on a basis **consistent** with that used for the preceding period. That is, where a choice of accounting principles is available, the principle initially chosen should be consistently applied from period to period. A change in an accounting principle occurs when the principle used in the current year is different from the one used in the preceding year. A change is permitted, when (1) management can show that the new principle is preferable to the old principle, and (2) the effects of the change are clearly disclosed in the income statement. Examples of a change in accounting principle include a change in depreciation methods (e.g., declining-balance to straight-line) and a change in inventory costing methods (e.g., FIFO to average cost). The effect of a change in an accounting principle on net income may be significant.

When a change in an accounting principle has occurred,

1. The new principle should be used in reporting the results of operations of the current year.
2. The cumulative effect of the change on all prior year income statements should be disclosed net of applicable taxes in a special section immediately preceding net income.

To illustrate, we will assume that at the beginning of 2001, Acro Energy Inc. changes from the straight-line method of depreciation to the declining-balance method for equipment purchased on January 1, 1998. The cumulative effect on prior year income statements (statements for 1998–2000) is to increase depreciation expense and decrease income before income taxes by $24,000. Assuming a 30% tax rate, the net of tax effect of the change is $16,800 ($24,000 x 70%). The income statement presentation is shown in Illustration 15-34.

ILLUSTRATION 15-34

Statement presentation of cumulative effect of change in accounting principle

ACRO ENERGY INC. Income Statement (partial) For the Year Ended December 31, 2001		
Income before income taxes		$800,000
Income tax expense		240,000
Income from continuing operations		560,000
Discontinued operations		
Loss from operations of chemical division, net of $60,000 income tax savings	$140,000	
Loss from disposal of chemical division, net of $30,000 income tax savings	70,000	210,000
Income before extraordinary item and cumulative effect of change in accounting principle		350,000
Extraordinary item		
Expropriation of investment, net of $21,000 income tax savings		49,000
Cumulative effect of change in accounting principle		
Effect on prior years of change in depreciation method, **net of $7,200 income tax savings**		**16,800**
Net income		$284,200

HELPFUL HINT

Study this illustration carefully for sequencing, labeling, descriptions, and amounts.

ETHICS NOTE

Changes in accounting principles should result in financial statements that are more informative for statement users. They should not be used to artificially improve the reported performance and financial position of the corporation.

The income statement for Acro Energy will also show depreciation expense for the current year. The amount is based on the new depreciation method. In this case the caption "Income before extraordinary item and cumulative effect of change in accounting principle" is inserted immediately following the effects of discontinued operations. This presentation clearly indicates the cumulative effect of the change on prior years' income. If a company does not have either discontinued operations or extraordinary items, the label "Income before cumulative effect of change in accounting principle" is used in place of "Income from continuing operations." A complete income statement showing all material items not typical of regular operations is illustrated in the second demonstration problem (pp. 704–705).

ACCOUNTING IN ACTION
Business Insight

Sometimes a change in accounting principle is mandated by the Financial Accounting Standards Board. An example is the change in accounting for interperiod income taxes required by Statement of Financial Accounting Standards 109. Such changes can significantly affect net income. For example, in its income statement, Consolidated Natural Gas Company reported an increase to income of $17,422,000 under "Cumulative Effect of Accounting Change." An accompanying note explained that the increase in income resulted from a required "change" from the deferred method to an asset and liability approach for accounting for and reporting of income taxes."

Comprehensive Income

Most revenues, expenses, gains, and losses recognized during the period are included in income. However, over time, specific exceptions to this general practice have developed so that certain items now bypass income and are reported directly in stockholders' equity. For example, in Chapter 13 you learned that unrealized gains and losses on available-for-sale securities are not included in income, but rather are reported in the balance sheet as adjustments to stockholders' equity.

Why are these gains and losses on available-for-sale securities excluded from net income? Because disclosing them separately (1) reduces the volatility of net income due to fluctuations in fair value, yet (2) informs the financial statement user of the gain or loss that would be incurred if the securities were sold at fair value.

Many analysts have expressed concern that the number of items that bypass the income statement has increased significantly. They feel that this has reduced the usefulness of the income statement. To address this concern, the FASB now requires that, in addition to reporting net income, a company must also report comprehensive income. Comprehensive income includes all changes in stockholders' equity during a period except those resulting from investments by stockholders and distributions to stockholders. A number of alternative formats for reporting comprehensive income are allowed. These formats are discussed in advanced accounting courses.

7
STUDY OBJECTIVE

Recognize the limitations of financial statement analysis.

LIMITATIONS OF FINANCIAL STATEMENT ANALYSIS

Significant business decisions are frequently made using one or more of the three analytical tools illustrated in this chapter. However, you should be aware of some of the limitations of these tools and of the financial statements on which they are based.

Estimates

Financial statements contain numerous estimates. Estimates, for example, are used in determining the allowance for uncollectible receivables, periodic depreciation, the costs of warranties, and contingent losses. To the extent that these estimates are inaccurate, the financial ratios and percentages are inaccurate.

Cost

Traditional financial statements are based on cost and are not adjusted for price-level changes. Comparisons of unadjusted financial data from different periods may be rendered invalid by significant inflation or deflation. For example, a 5-year comparison of Sears' revenues might show a growth of 36%. But this growth trend would be misleading if the general price-level had increased significantly during the same 5-year period.

Alternative Accounting Methods

Variations among companies in the application of generally accepted accounting principles may hamper comparability. For example, one company may use the FIFO method of inventory costing, whereas another company in the same industry may use LIFO. If inventory is a significant asset to both companies, it is unlikely that their current ratios are comparable. For example, if General Motors Corporation had used FIFO instead of LIFO in valuing its inventories, its inventories would have been valued 26% higher, significantly affecting the current ratio (and other ratios as well). In addition to differences in inventory costing methods, differences also exist in reporting such items as depreciation, depletion, and amortization. Although these differences in accounting methods might be detectable from reading the notes to the financial statements, adjusting the financial data to compensate for the different methods is difficult, if not impossible in some cases.

INTERNATIONAL NOTE

In many industries competition is global: To evaluate a firm's standing, an investor or analyst must make comparisons to firms from other countries. However, given the many differences in accounting practices, these comparisons can be both difficult and misleading.

Atypical Data

Fiscal year-end data may not be typical of the financial condition during the year. Firms frequently establish a fiscal year-end that coincides with the low point in operating activity or in inventory levels. Therefore, certain account balances (cash, receivables, payables, and inventories) may not be representative of the balances in the accounts during the year.

ETHICS NOTE

When investigating diversified firms, investors are often most interested to learn about the results of particular divisions. Firms are required to disclose the results of distinct lines of business separately if they are a material part of operations. Unfortunately, some companies shift revenues and expenses across divisions to achieve desired results. This reduces the usefulness of this information for financial statement analysis.

Diversification of Firms

Diversification in American industry also limits the usefulness of financial analysis. Many firms today are so diversified that they cannot be classified by a single industry—they are true conglomerates. Others appear to be comparable but are not.

BEFORE YOU GO ON...

Review It

1. What is comprehensive income?
2. What are some limitations of financial statement analysis?
3. Give examples of alternative accounting methods that hamper comparability.
4. In what way does diversification limit the usefulness of financial statement analysis?

A LOOK BACK AT OUR FEATURE STORY

Refer to the Feature Story and answer the following questions:

1. How is the Motley Fool bulletin board like the fool in Shakespeare's plays?

2. What makes the Motley Fool bulletin board attractive to Internet subscribers?

3. What are the dangers of using the Motley Fool bulletin board for investment purposes?

Solution:

1. The fool in Shakespeare's play was the only one who could speak unpleasant truths to kings and queens without being killed. The creators of the Motley Fool bulletin board view themselves as twentieth-century "fools," revealing the "truths" of Wall Street to the small investor, who the Gardner brothers believe has been taken advantage of by Wall Street insiders. That is, both Shakespeare's fools and the Motley Fool are irreverent attacks on the establishment.

2. The Motley Fool provides a bulletin board service where America Online subscribers can exchange information and insights about companies of interest to investors and potential investors. The information sources are endless (grassroots, insiders, anyone), worldwide, and nearly costless.

3. Critics contend that the bulletin board is nothing more than a high-tech rumor mill that tends to build a speculative house of cards. Participants on the board don't have to give their identities. Consequently, there is little to stop people from putting misinformation on the board to influence stock prices in the direction they want. Much of the information is soft and stands in sharp contrast to the data and ratios provided by analysis of financial statements as illustrated in this chapter.

THE NAVIGATOR

DEMONSTRATION PROBLEM 1

The condensed financial statements of The Estée Lauder Companies, Inc., for the years ended June 30, 1998 and 1997 are presented below:

THE ESTÉE LAUDER COMPANIES, INC.
Balance Sheet
June 30

| | (in millions) | |
Assets	1998	1997
Current assets		
Cash and cash equivalents	$ 277.5	$ 255.6
Accounts receivable (net)	497.8	471.7
Inventories	513.2	440.6
Prepaid expenses and other current assets	166.1	143.2
Total current assets	1,454.6	1,311.1
Property, plant, and equipment (net)	335.8	265.0
Investments	27.7	25.9
Intangibles and other assets	694.7	271.1
Total assets	$2,512.8	$1,873.1
Liabilities and Stockholders' Equity		
Current liabilities	$ 837.4	$ 759.5
Long-term liabilities	619.0	565.9
Stockholders' equity—common	1,056.4	547.7
Total liabilities and stockholders' equity	$2,512.8	$1,873.1

THE ESTÉE LAUDER COMPANIES, INC. Income Statement For the Year Ended June 30		
	(in millions)	
	1998	1997
Revenues	$3,618.0	$3,381.6
Costs and expenses		
Cost of goods sold	819.5	765.1
Selling and administrative expenses	2,383.1	2,224.6
Interest expense and royalties	0	52.4
Total costs and expenses	3,202.6	3,042.1
Income before income taxes	415.4	339.5
Income tax expense	178.6	165.3
Net income	$ 236.8	$ 174.2

Instructions

Compute the following ratios for 1998 and 1997.

(a) Current ratio.

(b) Inventory turnover (Inventory 6/30/96, $452.8).

(c) Profit margin ratio.

(d) Return on assets (Assets 6/30/96, $1,779.4).

(e) Return on common stockholders' equity (Equity 6/30/96, $394.2).

(f) Debt to total assets.

(g) Times interest earned.

SOLUTION TO DEMONSTRATION PROBLEM 1

	1998	1997
(a) Current ratio:		
$1,454.6 ÷ $837.4 =	1.7:1	
$1,311.1 ÷ $759.5 =		1.7:1
(b) Inventory turnover:		
$819.5 ÷ [$513.2 + $440.6) ÷ 2] =	1.7 times	
$765.1 ÷ [($440.6 + $452.8) ÷ 2] =		1.7 times
(c) Profit margin:		
$236.8 ÷ $3,618.0 =	6.5%	
$174.2 ÷ $3,381.6 =		5.2%
(d) Return on assets:		
$236.8 ÷ [($2,512.8 + $1,873.1) ÷ 2] =	10.8%	
$174.2 ÷ [($1,873.1 + $1,779.4) ÷ 2] =		9.5%
(e) Return on common stockholders' equity:		
$236.8 ÷ [($1,056.4 + $547.7) ÷ 2] =	30%	
$174.2 ÷ [($547.7 + $394.2) ÷ 2] =		37%
(f) Debt to total assets:		
$1,456.4 ÷ $2,512.8 =	58%	
$1,325.4 ÷ $1,873.1 =		71%
(g) Times interest earned:		
No interest expense in 1998.		
($174.2 + $165.3 + $52.4) ÷ $52.4 =		7.5 times

PROBLEM-SOLVING STRATEGIES

1. Remember that the current ratio includes all current assets; acid-test ratio uses only cash, temporary investments, and net receivables.

2. Use average balances for turnover ratios like inventory, receivables, and assets.

3. Return on assets is greater or smaller than return on common stockholders' equity depending on cost of debt.

THE NAVIGATOR

DEMONSTRATION PROBLEM 2

The events and transactions of the Dever Corporation for the year ending December 31, 2001, resulted in the following data:

Cost of goods sold	$2,600,000
Net sales	4,400,000
Other expenses and losses	9,600
Other revenues and gains	5,600
Selling and administrative expenses	1,100,000
Income from operations of plastics division	70,000
Gain on sale of plastics division	500,000
Loss from tornado disaster (extraordinary loss)	600,000
Cumulative effect of changing from the straight-line depreciation to double-declining-balance (increase in depreciation expense)	300,000

Analysis reveals that:

1. All items are before the applicable income tax rate of 30%.
2. The plastics division was sold on July 1.
3. All operating data for the plastics division have been segregated.
4. There were 100,000 shares of common stock outstanding during the year.

Instructions
Prepare an income statement for the year, including the presentation of earnings per share data.

PROBLEM-SOLVING STRATEGIES

1. Remember that material items not typical of operations are reported in separate sections net of taxes.
2. Income taxes should be associated with the item that affects the taxes.
3. A corporation income statement will have income tax expense when there is income before income tax.
4. All data presented in determining income before income taxes are the same as for unincorporated companies.

SOLUTION TO DEMONSTRATION PROBLEM 2

Dever Corporation
Income Statement
For the Year Ended December 31, 2001

Net sales		$4,400,000
Cost of goods sold		2,600,000
Gross profit		1,800,000
Selling and administrative expenses		1,100,000
Income from operations		700,000
Other revenues and gains	$ 5,600	
Other expenses and losses	9,600	4,000
Income before income taxes		696,000
Income tax expense ($696,000 × 30%)		208,800
Income from continuing operations		487,200
Discontinued operations		
Income from operations of plastics division, net of		
$21,000 income taxes ($70,000 × 30%)	49,000	
Gain on sale of plastics division, net of $150,000		
income taxes ($500,000 × 30%)	350,000	399,000
Income before extraordinary item and cumulative effect of		
change in accounting principle		886,200
Extraordinary item		
Tornado loss, net of income tax savings $180,000		
($600,000 × 30%)		420,000
Cumulative effect of change in accounting principle		
Effect on prior years of change in depreciation method,		
net of $90,000 income tax savings ($300,000 × 30%)		210,000
Net income		$ 256,200

Earnings per share
  Income from continuing operations $4.87
  Gain from discontinued operations   3.99
  Income before extraordinary item and cumulative effect
    of change in accounting principle   8.86
  Extraordinary loss   (4.20)
  Cumulative effect of change in accounting principle   (2.10)
  Net income $2.56

Summary of Study Objectives

1. Discuss the need for comparative analysis. There are three bases of comparison: (1) Intracompany, which compares an item or financial relationship with other data within a company. (2) Industry, which compares company data with industry averages. (3) Intercompany, which compares an item or financial relationship of a company with data of one or more competing companies.

2. Identify the tools of financial statement analysis. Financial statements may be analyzed horizontally, vertically, and with ratios.

3. Explain and apply horizontal (trend) analysis. Horizontal analysis is a technique for evaluating a series of data over a period of time to determine the increase or decrease that has taken place, expressed as either an amount or a percentage.

4. Describe and apply vertical analysis. Vertical analysis is a technique that expresses each item within a financial statement in terms of a percentage of a relevant total or a base amount.

5. Identify and compute ratios and describe their purpose and use in analyzing a firm's liquidity, profitability, and solvency. The formula and purpose of each ratio is presented in Illustration 15-30.

6. Understand the concept of earning power and indicate how material items not typical of regular operations are presented. Earning power refers to a company's ability to sustain its profits from operations. Irregular items—discontinued operations, extraordinary items, and changes in accounting principles—are presented net of tax below income from continuing operations to highlight their unusual nature.

7. Recognize the limitations of financial statement analysis. The usefulness of analytical tools is limited by the use of estimates, the cost basis, the application of alternative accounting methods, atypical data at year-end, and the diversification of firms.

GLOSSARY

Acid-test ratio A measure of a company's immediate short-term liquidity, computed by dividing the sum of cash, temporary investments, and (net) receivables by current liabilities. (p. 682).

Asset turnover ratio A measure of how efficiently a company uses its assets to generate sales, computed by dividing net sales by average assets. (p. 687).

Cash debt coverage ratio A cash-basis measure of long-term debt-paying ability, computed as net cash provided by operating activities divided by average total liabilities. (p. 693).

Cash return on sales ratio A measure of the cash generated by each dollar of sales, computed as net cash provided by operating activities divided by net sales. (p. 686).

Change in accounting principle Use of an accounting principle in the current year different from the one used in the preceding year. (p. 699).

Comprehensive income Includes all changes in stockholders' equity during a period except those resulting from investments by stockholders and distributions to stockholders. (p. 700).

Current cash debt coverage ratio A cash-basis measure of short-term debt-paying ability, computed as net cash provided by operating activities divided by average current liabilities. (p. 683).

Current ratio A measure used to evaluate a company's liquidity and short-term debt-paying ability, computed by dividing current assets by current liabilities. (p. 681).

Debt to total assets ratio Measures the percentage of total assets provided by creditors, computed by dividing total debt by total assets. (p. 692).

Discontinued operations The disposal of a significant segment of a business. (p. 696).

Earnings per share The net income earned by each share of common stock, computed by dividing net income by the weighted average common shares outstanding. (p. 689).

Extraordinary items Events and transactions that meet two conditions: (1) unusual in nature, and (2) infrequent in occurrence. (p. 697).

Horizontal analysis A technique for evaluating a series of financial statement data over a period of time to determine the increase (decrease) that has taken place, expressed as either an amount or a percentage. (p. 674).

Inventory turnover ratio   A measure of the liquidity of inventory, computed by dividing cost of goods sold by average inventory. (p. 685).

Liquidity ratios   Measures of the short-term ability of the enterprise to pay its maturing obligations and to meet unexpected needs for cash. (p. 681).

Payout ratio   Measures the percentage of earnings distributed in the form of cash dividends, computed by dividing cash dividends by net income. (p. 691).

Price-earnings ratio   Measures the ratio of the market price of each share of common stock to the earnings per share, computed by dividing the market price of the stock by earnings per share. (p. 690).

Profitability ratios   Measures of the income or operating success of an enterprise for a given period of time. (p. 685).

Profit margin ratio   Measures the percentage of each dollar of sales that results in net income, computed by dividing net income by net sales. (p. 686).

Ratio   An expression of the mathematical relationship between one quantity and another. The relationship may be expressed either as a percentage, a rate, or a simple proportion. (p. 680).

Ratio analysis   A technique for evaluating financial statements that expresses the relationship among selected financial statement data. (p. 680).

Receivables turnover ratio   A measure of the liquidity of receivables, computed by dividing net credit sales by average net receivables. (p. 684).

Return on assets ratio   An overall measure of profitability, computed by dividing net income by average assets. (p. 688).

Return on common stockholders' equity   Measures the dollars of net income earned for each dollar invested by the owners, computed by dividing net income by average common stockholders' equity. (p. 688).

Solvency ratios   Measures of the ability of the enterprise to survive over a long period of time. (p. 692).

Times interest earned ratio   Measures a company's ability to meet interest payments as they come due, computed by dividing income before interest expense and income taxes by interest expense. (p. 693).

Trading on the equity (leverage)   Borrowing money at a lower rate of interest than can be earned by using the borrowed money. (p. 689).

Vertical analysis   A technique for evaluating financial statement data that expresses each item within a financial statement in terms of a percent of a base amount. (p. 677).

SELF-STUDY QUESTIONS

Answers are at the end of the chapter.

(SO 1) 1. Comparisons of data within a company are an example of the following comparative basis:
   a. Industry averages.
   b. Intracompany.
   c. Intercompany.
   d. Both (b) and (c).

(SO 2) 2. In horizontal analysis, each item is expressed as a percentage of the:
   a. net income amount.
   b. stockholders' equity amount.
   c. total assets amount.
   d. base year amount.

(SO 4) 3. In vertical analysis, the base amount for depreciation expense is generally:
   a. net sales.
   b. depreciation expense in a previous year.
   c. gross profit.
   d. fixed assets.

(SO 4) 4. The following schedule is a display of what type of analysis?

	Amount	Percent
Current assets	$200,000	25%
Property, plant, and equipment	600,000	75%
Total assets	$800,000	

   a. Horizontal analysis.
   b. Differential analysis.
   c. Vertical analysis.
   d. Ratio analysis.

(SO 3) 5. Oswego Corporation reported net sales of $300,000, $330,000, and $360,000 in the years 1998, 1999, and 2000, respectively. If 1998 is the base year, what is the trend percentage for 2000?
   a. 77%.
   b. 108%.
   c. 120%.
   d. 130%.

(SO 5) 6. Which of the following measures is an evaluation of a firm's ability to pay current liabilities?
   a. Acid-test ratio.
   b. Current ratio.
   c. Both (a) and (b).
   d. None of the above.

(SO 5) 7. A measure useful in evaluating the efficiency in managing inventories is:
   a. inventory turnover ratio.
   b. average days to sell inventory.
   c. Both (a) and (b).
   d. None of the above.

(SO 5) 8. Which of the following is *not* a liquidity ratio?
   a. Current ratio.
   b. Asset turnover.
   c. Inventory turnover.
   d. Receivables turnover.

(SO 5) 9. Plainfield Corporation reported net income $24,000, net sales $400,000, and average assets $600,000 for 2001. The 2001 profit margin was:
   a. 6%.
   b. 12%.
   c. 40%.
   d. 200%.

(SO 6) 10. In reporting discontinued operations, the income statement should show in a special section:
   a. gains and losses on the disposal of the discontinued segment.
   b. gains and losses from operations of the discontinued segment.
   c. Neither (a) nor (b).
   d. Both (a) and (b).

11. Sugar Grove Corporation has income before taxes of (SO 6) $400,000 and an extraordinary loss of $100,000. If the income tax rate is 25% on all items, the income statement should show income before extraordinary items and extraordinary items, respectively, of
   a. $325,000 and $100,000.
   b. $325,000 and $75,000.
   c. $300,000 and $100,000.
   d. $300,000 and $75,000.

12. Which of the following is generally *not* considered to be (SO 7) a limitation of financial analysis?
   a. Use of estimates.
   b. Use of ratio analysis.
   c. Use of cost.
   d. Use of alternative accounting methods.

THE
NAVIGATOR

QUESTIONS

1. (a) Tara Goff believes that the analysis of financial statements is directed at two characteristics of a company: liquidity and profitability. Is Tara correct? Explain.
   (b) Are short-term creditors, long-term creditors, and stockholders interested primarily in the same characteristics of a company? Explain.

2. (a) Distinguish among the following bases of comparison: (1) intracompany, (2) industry averages, and (3) intercompany.
   (b) Give the principal value of using each of the three bases of comparison.

3. Two popular methods of financial statement analysis are horizontal analysis and vertical analysis. Explain the difference between these two methods.

4. (a) If Roy Company had net income of $480,000 in 2000 and it experienced a 24.5% increase in net income for 2001, what is its net income for 2001?
   (b) If six cents of every dollar of Roy's revenue is net income in 2000, what is the dollar amount of 2000 revenue?

5. What is a ratio? What are the different ways of expressing the relationship of two amounts? What information does a ratio provide?

6. Name the major ratios useful in assessing (a) liquidity and (b) solvency.

7. Bob Thebeau is puzzled. His company had a profit margin of 10% in 2001. He feels that this is an indication that the company is doing well. Loren Foelske, his accountant, says that more information is needed to determine the firm's financial well-being. Who is correct? Why?

8. What do the following classes of ratios measure? (a) Liquidity ratios. (b) Profitability ratios. (c) Solvency ratios.

9. What is the difference between the current ratio and the acid-test ratio?

10. Payne Company, a retail store, has a receivables turnover ratio of 4.5 times. The industry average is 12.5 times. Does Payne have a collection problem with its receivables?

11. Which ratios should be used to help answer the following questions?
   (a) How efficient is a company in using its assets to produce sales?
   (b) How near to sale is the inventory on hand?
   (c) How many dollars of net income were earned for each dollar invested by the owners?
   (d) How able is a company to meet interest charges as they fall due?

12. The price-earnings ratio of General Motors (automobile builder) was 9, and the price-earnings ratio of Microsoft (computer software) was 49. Which company did the stock market favor? Explain.

13. What is the formula for computing the payout ratio? Would you expect this ratio to be high or low for a growth company?

14. Holding all other factors constant, indicate whether each of the following changes generally signals good or bad news about a company:
   (a) Increase in profit margin.
   (b) Decrease in inventory turnover.
   (c) Increase in the current ratio.
   (d) Decrease in earnings per share.
   (e) Increase in price-earnings ratio.
   (f) Increase in debt to total assets ratio.
   (g) Decrease in times interest earned.
   (h) Increase in book value per share.

15. The return on total assets for Matson Corporation is 7.6%. During the same year Matson's return on common stockholders' equity is 12.8%. What is the explanation for the difference in the two rates?

16. Which two ratios do you think should be of greatest interest to:
   (a) A pension fund considering the purchase of 20-year bonds?
   (b) A bank contemplating a short-term loan?
   (c) A common stockholder?

17. (a) What is meant by trading on the equity?
   (b) How would you determine the profitability of trading on the equity?

18. Kiser Inc. has net income of $210,000, weighted average shares of common stock outstanding of 50,000, and preferred dividends for the period of $40,000. What is Kiser's earnings per share of common stock? Jim Akins, the president of Kiser Inc., believes the computed EPS of the company is high. Comment.

19. Identify and briefly explain five limitations of financial analysis.

20. Explain how the choice of one of the following accounting methods over the other raises or lowers a company's net income during a period of continuing inflation:
    (a) Use of FIFO instead of LIFO for inventory costing.
    (b) Use of a 6-year life for machinery instead of a 9-year life.
    (c) Use of straight-line depreciation instead of accelerated declining-balance depreciation.

21. What three ratios are partially dependent on cash-basis data, that is, data from the statement of cash flows?

22. Explain "earning power." What relationship does this concept have to the treatment of irregular items on the income statement?

23. Indicate which of the following items would be reported as an extraordinary item on Fine & Fancy Food Corporation's income statement?
    (a) Loss from damages caused by a volcano eruption.
    (b) Loss from the sale of temporary investments.
    (c) Loss attributable to a labor strike.
    (d) Loss caused when the Food and Drug Administration prohibited the manufacture and sale of a product line.
    (e) Loss of inventory from flood damage because a warehouse is located on a flood plain that floods every five to ten years.
    (f) Loss on the write-down of outdated inventory.
    (g) Loss from a foreign government's expropriation of a production facility.
    (h) Loss from damage to a warehouse in southern California from a minor earthquake.

24. Iron Ingots Inc. reported 1999 earnings per share of $3.26 and had no extraordinary items. In 2000, earnings per share on income before extraordinary items was $2.99, and earnings per share on net income was $3.49. Do you consider this trend to be favorable? Why or why not?

25. Rodger Robotics Inc. has been in operation for three years. All of its manufacturing equipment, which has a useful life of 10 to 12 years, has been depreciated on a straight-line basis. During the 4th year, Rodger Robotics changes to an accelerated depreciation method for all of its equipment.
    (a) Will Rodger Robotics post a gain or a loss on this change?
    (b) How will this change be reported?

BRIEF EXERCISES*

....

Prepare horizontal analysis.
(SO 3)

BE15–1 Using the following data from the comparative balance sheet of Jackie Remmers Company, illustrate horizontal analysis:

	December 31, 2001	December 31, 2000
Accounts receivable	$ 500,000	$ 400,000
Inventory	$ 840,000	$ 600,000
Total assets	$3,220,000	$2,800,000

Prepare vertical analysis.
(SO 4)

BE15–2 Using the same data presented above in BE15–1 for Jackie Remmers Company, illustrate vertical analysis.

Calculate percentage of change.
(SO 3)

BE15–3 Net income was $500,000 in 1999, $400,000 in 2000, and $504,000 in 2001. What is the percentage of change from (1) 1999 to 2000 and (2) 2000 to 2001? Is the change an increase or a decrease?

Calculate net income.
(SO 3)

BE15–4 If Hal Adelman Company had net income of $662,500 in 2001 and it experienced a 25% increase in net income over 2000, what was its 2000 net income?

Calculate change in net income.
(SO 4)

BE15–5 Vertical analysis (common size) percentages for Domingo Company's sales, cost of goods sold, and expenses are shown below:

Vertical Analysis	2001	2000	1999
Sales	100.0	100.0	100.0
Cost of goods sold	59.5	61.4	64.5
Expenses	25.0	26.6	28.5

Did Domingo's net income as a percent of sales increase, decrease, or remain unchanged over the 3-year period presented above? Provide numerical support for your answer.

Calculate change in net income.
(SO 3)

BE15–6 Horizontal analysis (trend analysis) percentages for Foltz Company's sales, cost of goods sold, and expenses are shown on page 709:

―――――――――
*Follow the rounding procedures used in the chapter.

Horizontal Analysis	2001	2000	1999
Sales	96.2	106.8	100.0
Cost of goods sold	102.0	97.0	100.0
Expenses	110.6	95.4	100.0

Did Foltz's net income increase, decrease, or remain unchanged over the 3-year period presented above?

BE15–7 Selected condensed data taken from a recent balance sheet of Jensen Farms are as follows: *Calculate liquidity ratios.*
(SO 5)

JENSEN FARMS
Balance Sheet (partial)

Cash	$ 8,241,000
Marketable securities	1,947,000
Accounts receivable	12,545,000
Inventories	14,814,000
Other current assets	5,371,000
Total current assets	$42,918,000
Total current liabilities	$45,844,000

What are the (1) working capital, (2) current, and (3) acid-test ratios?

BE15–8 Hawkins Corporation has net income of $12 million and net revenue of $100 million in 2001. Its assets were $12 million at the beginning of the year and $18 million at the end of the year. What are (a) the Hawkins' asset turnover ratio and (b) profit margin ratio? (Round to two decimals.) *Calculate profitability ratios.*
(SO 5)

BE15–9 The following data are taken from the financial statements of Geitz Company: *Evaluate collection of accounts receivable.*
(SO 5)

	2001	2000
Accounts receivable (net), end of year	$ 560,000	$ 540,000
Net sales on account	4,400,000	3,100,000
Terms for all sales are 1/10, n/60.		

Compute for each year (1) the receivables turnover and (2) the average collection period. What conclusions about the management of accounts receivable can be drawn from these data? At the end of 1999, accounts receivable (net) was $490,000.

BE15–10 The following data were taken from the income statements of Lester Fredrick Company: *Evaluate management of inventory.*
(SO 5)

	2001	2000
Sales	$6,420,000	$6,240,000
Beginning inventory	980,000	860,000
Purchases	4,440,000	4,661,000
Ending inventory	1,020,000	980,000

Compute for each year (1) the inventory turnover ratio and (2) the average days to sell the inventory. What conclusions concerning the management of the inventory can be drawn from these data?

BE15–11 McCarty Company has stockholders' equity of $400,000 and net income of $60,000. It has a payout ratio of 20% and a rate of return on assets of 16%. How much did McCarty pay in cash dividends, and what were its average assets? *Calculate profitability ratios.*
(SO 5)

BE15–12 Selected data taken from the year 2000 financial statements of Shirley Denson Manufacturing Company are as follows: *Calculate cash-basis liquidity, profitability, and solvency ratios.*
(SO 5)

Net sales for 2000	$6,860,000
Current liabilities, January 1, 2000	180,000
Current liabilities, December 31, 2000	240,000
Net cash provided by operating activities	760,000
Total liabilities, January 1, 2000	1,500,000
Total liabilities, December 31, 2000	1,300,000

Compute the following ratios at December 31, 2000: (a) the current cash debt coverage ratio, (b) the cash return on sales ratio, and (c) the cash debt coverage ratio.

Prepare a discontinued
operations section of an
income statement.
(SO 6)

BE15–13   On June 30, Osborn Corporation discontinued its operations in Mexico. During the year, the operating loss was $400,000 before taxes. On September 1, Osborn disposed of the Mexico facility at a pretax loss of $150,000. The applicable tax rate is 30%. Show the discontinued operations section of Osborn's income statement.

Prepare a corrected income
statement with an
extraordinary item.
(SO 6)

BE15–14   An inexperienced accountant for John McKee Corporation showed the following in McKee's income statement: Income before income taxes, $300,000; Income tax expense, $72,000; Extraordinary loss from flood (before taxes), $60,000; and Net income, $168,000. The extraordinary loss and taxable income are both subject to a 30% tax rate. Prepare a corrected income statement beginning with "Income before income taxes."

Prepare change in accounting
principles section of an income
statement.
(SO 6)

BE15–15   On January 1, 2000, Ricky Inc. changed from the straight-line method of depreciation to the declining-balance method. The cumulative effect of the change was to increase prior years' depreciation by $40,000 and 2000 depreciation by $8,000. Show the change in accounting principle section of the 2000 income statement, assuming the tax rate is 30%.

EXERCISES*

Prepare horizontal analysis.
(SO 3)

E15–1   Financial information for Lister Inc. is presented below:

	December 31, 2001	December 31, 2000
Current assets	$125,000	$100,000
Plant assets (net)	400,000	330,000
Current liabilities	91,000	70,000
Long-term liabilities	144,000	95,000
Common stock, $1 par	155,000	115,000
Retained earnings	135,000	150,000

Instructions
Prepare a schedule showing a horizontal analysis for 2001 using 2000 as the base year.

Prepare vertical analysis.
(SO 4)

E15–2   Operating data for Khan Corporation are presented below:

	2001	2000
Sales	$800,000	$600,000
Cost of goods sold	464,000	378,000
Selling expenses	120,000	72,000
Administrative expenses	80,000	54,000
Income tax expense	38,400	25,200
Net income	97,600	70,800

Instructions
Prepare a schedule showing a vertical analysis for 2001 and 2000.

Prepare horizontal and vertical
analyses.
(SO 3, 4)

E15–3   The comparative balance sheets of Barkley Corporation are presented below:

BARKLEY CORPORATION
Comparative Balance Sheets
December 31

	2001	2000
Assets		
Current assets	$ 76,000	$ 80,000
Property, plant, & equipment (net)	99,000	90,000
Intangibles	25,000	40,000
Total assets	$200,000	$210,000
Liabilities & stockholders' equity		
Current liabilities	$ 45,800	$ 48,000
Long-term liabilities	138,000	150,000
Stockholders' equity	16,200	12,000
Total liabilities & stockholders' equity	$200,000	$210,000

*Follow the rounding procedures used in the chapter.

Instructions

(a) Prepare a horizontal analysis of the balance sheet data for Barkley Corporation using 2000 as a base. (Show the amount of increase or decrease as well.)

(b) Prepare a vertical analysis of the balance sheet data for Barkley Corporation in columnar form for 2001.

E15–4 The comparative income statements of LaGalle Corporation are shown below:

Prepare horizontal and vertical analyses. (SO 3, 4)

LAGALLE CORPORATION
Comparative Income Statements
For the Years Ended December 31

	2001	2000
Net sales	$550,000	$500,000
Cost of goods sold	440,000	420,000
Gross profit	110,000	80,000
Operating expenses	57,200	44,000
Net income	$ 52,800	$ 36,000

Instructions

(a) Prepare a horizontal analysis of the income statement data for LaGalle Corporation using 2000 as a base. (Show the amounts of increase or decrease.)

(b) Prepare a vertical analysis of the income statement data for LaGalle Corporation in columnar form for both years.

E15–5 Nordstrom, Inc., operates department stores in numerous states. Selected financial statement data in millions of dollars for a recent year are as follows:

Compute liquidity ratios and compare results. (SO 5)

NORDSTROM, INC.
Balance Sheet (partial)

	End-of-Year	Beginning-of-Year
Cash and cash equivalents	$ 33	$ 91
Receivables (net)	676	586
Merchandise inventory	628	586
Prepaid expenses	61	52
Total current assets	$1,398	$1,315
Total current liabilities	$690	$627

For the year, net sales were $3,894 and cost of goods sold was $2,600. Net cash provided by operating activities was $800.

Instructions

(a) Compute the five liquidity ratios at the end of the current year.

(b) Using the data in the chapter, compare Nordstrom's liquidity with (1) Sears, Roebuck and (2) the industry averages for department stores.

E15–6 Fargo Incorporated had the following transactions occur involving current assets and current liabilities during February 2001:

Perform current and acid-test ratio analysis. (SO 5)

Feb. 3 Accounts receivable of $15,000 are collected.
     7 Equipment is purchased for $25,000 cash.
    11 Paid $3,000 for a 3-year insurance policy.
    14 Accounts payable of $14,000 are paid.
    18 Cash dividends are declared, $6,000.

Additional information:

1. As of February 1, 2001, current assets were $120,000 and current liabilities were $50,000.
2. As of February 1, 2001, current assets included $15,000 of inventory and $5,000 of pre-paid expenses.

Instructions
(a) Compute the current ratio as of the beginning of the month and after each transaction.
(b) Compute the acid-test ratio as of the beginning of the month and after each transaction.

Compute selected ratios.
(SO 5)

E15–7   Georgette Company has the following comparative balance sheet data:

GEORGETTE COMPANY
Balance Sheet
December 31

	2001	2000
Cash	$ 20,000	$ 30,000
Receivables (net)	65,000	60,000
Inventories	60,000	50,000
Plant assets (net)	200,000	180,000
	$345,000	$320,000
Accounts payable	$ 50,000	$ 60,000
Mortgage payable (15%)	100,000	100,000
Common stock, $10 par	140,000	120,000
Retained earnings	55,000	40,000
	$345,000	$320,000

Additional information for 2001:

1. Net income was $25,000.
2. Sales on account were $420,000. Sales returns and allowances amounted to $20,000.
3. Cost of goods sold was $198,000.
4. Net cash provided by operating activities was $44,000.

Instructions
Compute the following ratios at December 31, 2001:

(a) Current.   (e) Cash return on sales.
(b) Acid-test.   (f) Cash debt coverage.
(c) Receivables turnover. (g) Current cash debt coverage.
(d) Inventory turnover.

Compute selected ratios.
(SO 5)

E15–8   Selected comparative statement data for Meng Products Company are presented below. All balance sheet data are as of December 31.

	2001	2000
Net sales	$800,000	$720,000
Cost of goods sold	480,000	40,000
Interest expense	7,000	5,000
Net income	64,000	42,000
Accounts receivable	120,000	100,000
Inventory	85,000	75,000
Total assets	600,000	500,000
Total common stockholders' equity	450,000	310,000

Instructions

Compute the following ratios for 2001:

(a) Profit margin.

(b) Asset turnover.

(c) Return on assets.

(d) Return on common stockholders' equity.

E15-9 The income statement for Cheryl Countryman, Inc., appears below.

Compute selected ratios.
(SO 5)

CHERYL COUNTRYMAN, INC.
Income Statement
For the Year Ended December 31, 2001

Sales	$400,000
Cost of goods sold	230,000
Gross profit	170,000
Expenses (including $20,000 interest and $24,000 income taxes)	100,000
Net income	$ 70,000

Additional information:

1. Common stock outstanding January 1 and December 31, 2001, was 35,000 shares.
2. The market price of Cheryl Countryman, Inc., stock was $15 in 2001.
3. Cash dividends of $21,000 were paid, $5,000 of which were to preferred stockholders.
4. Net cash provided by operating activities $98,000.

Instructions

Compute the following ratios for 2001:

(a) Earnings per share.   (d) Times interest earned.

(b) Price-earnings.   (e) Cash return on sales.

(c) Payout.

E15-10 Perez Corporation experienced a fire on December 31, 2001, in which its financial records were partially destroyed. It has been able to salvage some of the records and has ascertained the following balances:

Compute amounts from ratios.
(SO 5)

	December 31, 2001	December 31, 2000
Cash	$ 30,000	$ 10,000
Receivables (net)	72,500	126,000
Inventory	200,000	180,000
Accounts payable	50,000	90,000
Notes payable	30,000	60,000
Common stock, $100 par	400,000	400,000
Retained earnings	115,000	101,000

Additional information:

1. The inventory turnover is 3.8 times.
2. The return on common stockholders' equity is 22%. The company had no additional paid-in capital.
3. The receivables turnover is 8.4 times.
4. The return on assets is 20%.
5. Total assets at December 31, 2000, were $605,000.

Instructions

Compute the following for Perez Corporation:

   (a) Cost of goods sold for 2001.
   (b) Net sales for 2001.
   (c) Net income for 2001.
   (d) Total assets at December 31, 2001.

Prepare irregular items portion of an income statement.
(SO 6)

E15–11   The Davis Company has income from continuing operations $240,000 for the year ended December 31, 2001. It also has the following items (before considering income taxes): (1) an extraordinary fire loss of $60,000, (2) a gain of $40,000 from the discontinuance of a division, which includes a $110,000 gain from the operation of the division and a $70,000 loss on its disposal, and (3) a cumulative change in accounting principle that resulted in an increase in prior year's depreciation of $30,000. Assume all items are subject to income taxes at a 30% tax rate.

Instructions

Prepare Davis Company's income statement for 2001, beginning with "Income from continuing operations."

Evaluate the effects of unusual or irregular items.
(SO 5, 6, 7)

E15–12   *The Wall Street Journal* routinely publishes summaries of corporate quarterly and annual earnings reports in a feature called the "Earnings Digest." A typical "digest" report takes the following form:

ENERGY ENTERPRISES (A)

	Quarter ending July 31,	
	2000	**1999**
Revenues	$2,049,000,000	$1,754,000,000
Net income	97,000,000	(a) 68,750,000
E.P.S.:		
Net income	1.31	.93

	9 months ending July 31,	
	2000	**1999**
Revenues	$5,578,500,000	$5,065,300,000
Extraord. item	(b) 1,900,000	
Net income	102,700,000	(a) 33,250,000
E.P.S.:		
Net income	1.39	.45

(a) Includes a net charge of $26,000,000 from loss on the sale of electrical equipment
(b) Extraordinary gain on Middle East property expropriation

The letter in parentheses following the company name indicates the exchange on which Energy Enterprises' stock is traded—in this case, the American Stock Exchange.

Instructions

Answer the following questions:

   (a) How was the loss on the electrical equipment reported on the income statement? Was it reported in the third quarter of 1999? How can you tell?
   (b) Why did *The Wall Street Journal* list the extraordinary item separately?
   (c) What is the extraordinary item? Was it included in income for the third quarter? How can you tell?
   (d) Did Energy Enterprises have an operating loss in any quarter of 1999? Of 2000? How do you know?
   (e) Approximately how many shares of stock were outstanding in 2000? Did the number of outstanding shares change from July 31, 1999, to July 31, 2000?

(f) As an investor, what numbers do you think should be used to determine Energy Enterprises' profit margin percentage (return on sales)? Calculate the 9-month profit margin percentage for 1999 and 2000 that you consider most useful. Explain your decision.

PROBLEMS: SET A*

P15–1A Comparative statement data for Catchem Company and Eatum Company, two competitors, appear below. All balance sheet data are as of December 31, 2001, and December 31, 2000.

Prepare vertical analysis and comment on profitability.
(SO 4, 5)

	Catchem Company		Eatum Company	
	2001	**2000**	**2001**	**2000**
Net sales	$1,549,035		$339,038	
Cost of goods sold	1,080,490		238,006	
Operating expenses	302,275		79,000	
Interest expense	6,800		1,252	
Income tax expense	51,030		6,650	
Current assets	325,975	$312,410	83,336	$ 79,467
Plant assets (net)	521,310	500,000	139,728	125,812
Current liabilities	66,325	75,815	35,348	30,281
Long-term liabilities	108,500	90,000	29,620	25,000
Common stock, $10 par	500,000	500,000	120,000	120,000
Retained earnings	172,460	146,595	38,096	29,998

Instructions
(a) Prepare a vertical analysis of the 2001 income statement data for Catchem Company and Eatum Company in columnar form.
(b) ▦▦▦▧➤ Comment on the relative profitability of the companies by computing the return on assets and the return on common stockholders' equity ratios for both companies.

P15–2A The comparative statements of Dorothy Fleming Company are presented below:

Compute ratios from balance sheet and income statement.
(SO 5)

DOROTHY FLEMING COMPANY
Income Statement
For the Year Ended December 31

	2001	2000
Net sales	$1,818,500	$1,750,500
Cost of goods sold	1,005,500	996,000
Gross profit	813,000	754,500
Selling and administrative expense	506,000	479,000
Income from operations	307,000	275,500
Other expenses and losses		
Interest expense	18,000	19,000
Income before income taxes	289,000	256,500
Income tax expense	86,700	77,000
Net income	$ 202,300	$ 179,500

*Follow the rounding procedures used in the chapter.

DOROTHY FLEMING COMPANY
Balance Sheet
December 31

Assets	2001	2000
Current assets		
Cash	$ 60,100	$ 64,200
Marketable securities	54,000	50,000
Accounts receivable (net)	107,800	102,800
Inventory	123,000	115,500
Total current assets	344,900	332,500
Plant assets (net)	625,300	520,300
Total assets	$970,200	$852,800

Liabilities and Stockholders' Equity	2001	2000
Current liabilities		
Accounts payable	$150,000	$145,400
Income taxes payable	43,500	42,000
Total current liabilities	193,500	187,400
Bonds payable	210,000	200,000
Total liabilities	403,500	387,400
Stockholders' equity		
Common stock ($5 par)	280,000	300,000
Retained earnings	286,700	165,400
Total stockholders' equity	566,700	465,400
Total liabilities and stockholders' equity	$970,200	$852,800

On April 1, 2001, 4,000 common shares were repurchased and canceled. All sales were on account. Net cash provided by operating activities for 2001 was $280,000.

Instructions
Compute the following ratios for 2001:

(a) Earnings per share (compute weighted average).
(b) Return on common stockholders' equity.
(c) Return on assets.
(d) Current.
(e) Acid-test.
(f) Receivables turnover.
(g) Inventory turnover.

(h) Times interest earned.
(i) Asset turnover.
(j) Debt to total assets.
(k) Current cash debt coverage.
(l) Cash return on sales.
(m) Cash debt coverage.

Perform ratio analysis.
(SO 5)

P15–3A Condensed balance sheet and income statement data for Roland Carlson Corporation appear below:

ROLAND CARLSON CORPORATION
Balance Sheet
December 31

	2001	2000	1999
Cash	$ 25,000	$ 20,000	$ 18,000
Receivables (net)	50,000	45,000	48,000
Other current assets	90,000	85,000	64,000
Investments	75,000	70,000	45,000
Plant and equipment (net)	400,000	370,000	358,000
	$640,000	$590,000	$533,000
Current liabilities	$ 75,000	$ 80,000	$ 70,000
Long-term debt	80,000	85,000	50,000
Common stock, $10 par	340,000	300,000	300,000
Retained earnings	145,000	125,000	113,000
	$640,000	$590,000	$533,000

ROLAND CARLSON CORPORATION
Income Statement
For the Years Ended December 31

	2001	2000
Sales	$740,000	$700,000
Less: Sales returns and allowances	40,000	50,000
Net sales	700,000	650,000
Cost of goods sold	420,000	400,000
Gross profit	280,000	250,000
Operating expenses (including income taxes)	230,000	215,000
Net income	$ 50,000	$ 35,000

Additional information:

1. The market price of Carlson's common stock was $4.00, $5.00, and $7.95 for 1999, 2000, and 2001, respectively.
2. All dividends were paid in cash.
3. On July 1, 2001, 4,000 shares of common stock were issued.

Instructions
(a) Compute the following ratios for 2000 and 2001:
   (1) Profit margin.
   (2) Asset turnover.
   (3) Earnings per share (compute weighted average).
   (4) Price-earnings.
   (5) Payout.
   (6) Debt to total assets.
(b) ▭▭▭▭▷ Based on the ratios calculated, discuss briefly the improvement or lack thereof in financial position and operating results from 2000 to 2001 of Roland Carlson Corporation.

P15–4A Financial information for Callaway Company is presented below:

Compute ratios, commenting on overall liquidity and profitability.
(SO 5)

CALLAWAY COMPANY
Balance Sheet
December 31

Assets	2001	2000
Cash	$ 60,000	$ 55,000
Short-term investments	45,000	40,000
Receivables (net)	94,000	90,000
Inventories	130,000	125,000
Prepaid expenses	25,000	23,000
Land	140,000	140,000
Building and equipment (net)	190,000	175,000
	$684,000	$648,000

Liabilities and Stockholders' Equity	2001	2000
Notes payable	$100,000	$100,000
Accounts payable	45,000	42,000
Accrued liabilities	40,000	40,000
Bonds payable, due 2003	150,000	150,000
Common stock, $10 par	200,000	200,000
Retained earnings	149,000	116,000
	$684,000	$648,000

CALLAWAY COMPANY
Income Statement
For the Years Ended December 31

	2001	2000
Sales	$850,000	$790,000
Cost of goods sold	610,000	570,000
Gross profit	240,000	220,000
Operating expenses	194,000	180,000
Net income	$ 46,000	$ 40,000

Additional information:

1. Inventory at the beginning of 2000 was $115,000.
2. Receivables at the beginning of 2000 were $88,000.
3. Total assets at the beginning of 2000 were $630,000.
4. No common stock transactions occurred during 2000 or 2001.
5. All sales were on account.

Instructions
   (a) Indicate, by using ratios, the change in liquidity and profitability of Callaway Company from 2000 to 2001. (*Note*: Not all profitability ratios can be computed.)
   (b) Given below are three independent situations and a ratio that may be affected. For each situation, compute the affected ratio (1) as of December 31, 2001, and (2) as of December 31, 2002, after giving effect to the situation. Net income for 2002 was $45,000. Total assets on December 31, 2002, were $700,000.

Situation	Ratio
1. 18,000 shares of common stock were sold at par on July 1, 2002.	Return on common stockholders' equity
2. All of the notes payable were paid in 2002.	Debt to total assets
3. Market price of common stock was $9 and $12.80 on December 31, 2001, and 2002, respectively.	Price-earnings ratio

Compute selected ratios and compare liquidity, profitability, and solvency for two companies.
(SO 5)

P15–5A Selected financial data of two intense competitors in a recent year are presented below in millions of dollars.

	Kmart Corporation	Wal-Mart Stores, Inc.
Income Statement Data for Year		
Net sales	$34,025	$82,494
Cost of goods sold	25,992	65,586
Selling and administrative expenses	7,701	12,858
Interest expense	494	706
Other income (net)	572	918
Income taxes	114	1,581
Net income	$ 296	$ 2,681
Balance Sheet Data (End-of-Year)		
Current assets	$ 9,187	$15,338
Property, plant, and equipment (net)	7,842	17,481
Total assets	$17,029	$32,819
Current liabilities	$ 5,626	$ 9,973
Long-term debt	5,371	10,120
Total stockholders' equity	6,032	12,726
Total liabilities and stockholders' equity	$17,029	$32,819

	Kmart Corporation	Wal-Mart Stores, Inc.
Beginning-of-Year Balances		
Total assets	$17,504	$26,441
Total stockholders' equity	6,093	10,753
Other Data		
Average net receivables	$ 1,570	$ 695
Average inventory	7,317	12,539
Net cash provided by operating activities	351	3,106
Average current liablilities	5,720	10,110
Average total liablilities	11,230	20,160

Instructions

(a) For each company, compute the following ratios:

(1) Current.	(7) Return on common stockholders' equity.
(2) Receivables turnover.	(8) Debt to total assets.
(3) Inventory turnover.	(9) Times interest earned.
(4) Profit margin.	(10) Current cash debt coverage.
(5) Asset turnover.	(11) Cash return on sales.
(6) Return on assets.	(12) Cash debt coverage.

(b) Compare the liquidity, profitability, and solvency of the two companies.

P15–6A Presented below are the incomplete income statement and comparative balance sheet for Buena Vista Corporation:

Compute missing information given a set of ratios.
(SO 5)

BUENA VISTA CORPORATION
Income Statement
For the Year Ended December 31, 2001

Net sales	$?
Cost of goods sold	3,500,000
Gross profit	?
Operating expenses	?
Income from operations	700,000
Other expenses and losses	
Interest expense	?
Income before income taxes	?
Income tax expense	?
Net income	$ 310,000

BUENA VISTA CORPORATION
Balance Sheet
December 31, 2001

	2001	2000
Assets		
Current assets		
Cash	$ 275,000	$ 214,270
Accounts receivable	625,000	?
Inventory	540,000	?
Total current assets	1,440,000	?
Plant assets (net)	2,310,000	2,000,000
Total assets	$3,750,000	$?

	2001	2000
Liabilities and Stockholders' Equity		
Current liabilities	$ 480,000	$?
Long-term liabilities	1,570,000	?
Total liabilities	2,050,000	?
Common stock, $2 par	1,500,000	1,500,000
Retained earnings	200,000	215,000
Total stockholders' equity	1,700,000	1,715,000
Total liabilities and stockholders' equity	$3,750,000	$?

Additional information:

1. Times interest earned for 2001 is 7 times.
2. Net cash provided by operating activities for 2001 is $750,000.
3. Cash return on sales ratio for 2001 is 15%.
4. Inventory turnover ratio for 2001 was 5 times.
5. Asset turnover ratio for 2001 was 1.37 times.
6. Working capital for 2000 was $960,000.

Instructions

Compute the missing information given the information above. Show computations. (*Note:* Start with one ratio and derive as much information as possible from it before trying another ratio. List all missing amounts under the ratio used to find the information.)

Compute numerous ratios.
(SO 5)

P15–7A The comparative statements of Swanson Company are presented below:

SWANSON COMPANY
Income Statement
For Year Ended December 31

	2001	2000
Net sales (all on account)	$650,000	$520,000
Expenses		
Cost of goods sold	415,000	354,000
Selling and administrative	150,800	114,800
Interest expense	7,200	6,000
Income tax expense	18,000	14,000
Total expenses	591,000	488,800
Net income	$ 59,000	$ 31,200

SWANSON COMPANY
Balance Sheet
December 31

Assets	2001	2000
Current assets		
Cash	$ 41,000	$ 18,000
Marketable securities	18,000	15,000
Accounts receivable (net)	92,000	74,000
Inventory	84,000	70,000
Total current assets	235,000	177,000
Plant assets (net)	403,000	383,000
Total assets	$638,000	$560,000

Liabilities and Stockholders' Equity	2001	2000
Current liabilities		
Accounts payable	$112,000	$110,000
Income taxes payable	23,000	20,000
Total current liabilities	135,000	130,000
Long-term liabilities		
Bonds payable	130,000	80,000
Total liabilities	265,000	210,000
Stockholders' equity		
Common stock ($5 par)	150,000	150,000
Retained earnings	223,000	200,000
Total stockholders' equity	373,000	350,000
Total liabilities and stockholders' equity	$638,000	$560,000

Additional data:
The common stock recently sold at $19.50 per share.

Instructions

Compute the following ratios for 2001:

(a) Current.
(b) Acid-test.
(c) Receivables turnover.
(d) Inventory turnover.
(e) Profit margin.
(f) Asset turnover.
(g) Return on assets.
(h) Return on common stockholders' equity.
(i) Earnings per share (weighted average).
(j) Price-earnings.
(k) Payout.
(l) Debt to total assets.
(m) Times interest earned.

PROBLEMS: SET B*

P15–1B Comparative statement data for Brooke Company and Shields Company, two competitors, appear below. All balance sheet data are as of December 31, 2001, and December 31, 2000.

Prepare vertical analysis and comment on profitability.
(SO 4, 5)

	Brooke Company		Shields Company	
	2001	2000	2001	2000
Net sales	$250,000		$1,200,000	
Cost of goods sold	160,000		720,000	
Operating expenses	51,000		252,000	
Interest expense	3,000		10,000	
Income tax expense	11,000		65,000	
Current assets	130,000	$110,000	700,000	$650,000
Plant assets (net)	305,000	270,000	800,000	750,000
Current liabilities	60,000	52,000	250,000	275,000
Long-term liabilities	50,000	68,000	200,000	150,000
Common stock	260,000	210,000	750,000	700,000
Retained earnings	65,000	50,000	300,000	275,000

Instructions

(a) Prepare a vertical analysis of the 2001 income statement data for Brooke Company and Shields Company in columnar form.

(b) Comment on the relative profitability of the companies by computing the return on assets and the return on common stockholders' equity ratios for both companies.

*Follow the rounding procedures used in the chapter.

Compute ratios from balance sheet and income statement (SO 5)

P15–2D The comparative statements of the Demac Company are presented below:

DEMAC COMPANY
Income Statement
For the Year Ended December 31

	2001	2000
Net sales	$660,000	$624,000
Cost of goods sold	440,000	405,600
Gross profit	220,000	218,400
Selling and administrative expense	143,880	149,760
Income from operations	76,120	68,640
Other expenses and losses		
Interest expense	7,920	7,200
Income before income taxes	68,200	61,400
Income tax expense	25,300	24,000
Net income	$ 42,900	$ 37,440

DEMAC COMPANY
Balance Sheet
December 31

Assets	2001	2000
Current assets		
Cash	$ 23,100	$ 21,600
Marketable securities	34,800	33,000
Accounts receivable (net)	106,200	93,800
Inventory	72,400	64,000
Total current assets	236,500	212,400
Plant assets (net)	465,300	459,600
Total assets	$701,800	$672,000

Liabilities and Stockholders' Equity	2001	2000
Current liabilities		
Accounts payable	$134,200	$132,000
Income taxes payable	25,300	24,000
Total current liabilities	159,500	156,000
Bonds payable	132,000	120,000
Total liabilities	291,500	276,000
Stockholders' equity		
Common stock ($10 par)	140,000	150,000
Retained earnings	270,300	246,000
Total stockholders' equity	410,300	396,000
Total liabilities and stockholders' equity	$701,800	$672,000

On July 1, 2001, 1,000 common shares were repurchased and canceled. All sales were on account. Net cash provided by operating activities was $36,000.

Instructions
Compute the following ratios for 2001:

(a) Earnings per share (weighted average).
(b) Return on common stockholders' equity.
(c) Return on assets.
(d) Current.
(e) Acid-test.
(f) Receivables turnover.
(g) Inventory turnover.

(h) Times interest earned.
(i) Asset turnover.
(j) Debt to total assets.
(k) Current cash debt.
(l) Cash return on sales.
(m) Cash debt coverage.

P15–3B   Condensed balance sheet and income statement data for El Camino Corporation appear below:

Perform ratio analysis
(SO 5)

EL CAMINO CORPORATION
Balance Sheet
December 31

	2001	2000	1999
Cash	$ 40,000	$ 24,000	$ 20,000
Receivables (net)	70,000	45,000	48,000
Other current assets	80,000	75,000	62,000
Investments	90,000	70,000	50,000
Plant and equipment (net)	450,000	400,000	360,000
	$730,000	$614,000	$540,000
Current liabilities	$ 98,000	$ 75,000	$ 70,000
Long-term debt	97,000	75,000	65,000
Common stock, $10 par	400,000	340,000	300,000
Retained earnings	135,000	124,000	105,000
	$730,000	$614,000	$540,000

EL CAMINO CORPORATION
Income Statement
For the Years Ended December 31

	2001	2000
Sales	$700,000	$750,000
Less: Sales return and allowances	40,000	50,000
Net sales	660,000	700,000
Cost of goods sold	420,000	400,000
Gross profit	240,000	300,000
Operating expenses (including income taxes)	194,000	237,000
Net income	$ 46,000	$ 63,000

Additional information:

1. The market price of El Camino's common stock was $5.00, $4.50, and $2.30 for 1999,
   2000, and 2001, respectively.
2. All dividends were paid in cash.
3. On July 1, 2000, 4,000 shares of common stock were issued, and on July 1, 2001, 6,000
   shares were issued.

Instructions
  (a) Compute the following ratios for 2000 and 2001:
      (1) Profit margin.
      (2) Asset turnover.
      (3) Earnings per share (weighted average).
      (4) Price-earnings.
      (5) Payout.
      (6) Debt to total assets.
  (b) Based on the ratios calculated, discuss briefly the improvement or lack
      thereof in financial position and operating results from 2000 to 2001 of El Camino
      Corporation.

Compute ratios, commenting on overall liquidity and profitability.
(SO 5)

P15–4B   Financial information for Skywalker Company is presented below:

SKYWALKER COMPANY
Balance Sheet
December 31

Assets	2001	2000
Cash	$ 50,000	$ 42,000
Short-term investments	80,000	100,000
Receivables (net)	100,000	87,000
Inventories	440,000	400,000
Prepaid expenses	25,000	31,000
Land	75,000	75,000
Building and equipment (net)	570,000	500,000
	$1,340,000	$1,235,000

Liabilities and Stockholders' Equity	2001	2000
Notes payable	$ 125,000	$ 125,000
Accounts payable	160,000	140,000
Accrued liabilities	50,000	50,000
Bonds payable, due 2004	200,000	200,000
Common stock, $5 par	500,000	500,000
Retained earnings	305,000	220,000
	$1,340,000	$1,235,000

SKYWALKER COMPANY
Income Statement
For the Years Ended December 31

	2001	2000
Sales	$1,000,000	$ 940,000
Cost of goods sold	650,000	635,000
Gross profit	350,000	305,000
Operating expenses	235,000	215,000
Net income	$ 115,000	$ 90,000

Additional information:

1. Inventory at the beginning of 2000 was $350,000.
2. Receivables at the beginning of 2000 were $80,000.
3. Total assets at the beginning of 2000 were $1,175,000
4. No common stock transactions occurred during 2000 or 2001.
5. All sales were on account.

Instructions
   (a) Indicate, by using ratios, the change in liquidity and profitability of Skywalker Company from 2000 to 2001. (*Note:* Not all profitability ratios can be computed nor can cash basis ratios be computed.)
   (b) Given below are three independent situations and a ratio that may be affected. For each situation, compute the affected ratio (1) as of December 31, 2001, and (2) as of December 31, 2002, after giving effect to the situation. Net income for 2002 was $125,000. Total assets on December 31, 2002, were $1,500,000.

Situation	Ratio
(1) 65,000 shares of common stock were sold at par on July 1, 2002.	Return on common stockholders' equity
(2) All of the notes payable were paid in 2002.	Debt to total assets
(3) Market price of common stock on December 31, 2002, was $6.25. Market price on December 31, 2001 was $5.	Price-earnings ratio

P15–5B   Selected financial data of two intense competitors in a recent year are presented below in millions of dollars.

*Compute selected ratios and
compare liquidity, profitability,
and solvency for two
companies.*
(SO 5)

	Bethlehem Steel Corporation	Inland Steel Company
Income Statement Data for Year		
Net sales	$4,819	$4,497
Cost of goods sold	4,548	3,991
Selling and administrative expenses	137	265
Interest expense	46	72
Other income (net)	7	0
Income taxes	14	62
Net income	$ 81	$ 107
Balance Sheet Data (End-of-Year)		
Current assets	$1,569	$1,081
Property, plant, and equipment (net)	2,759	1,610
Other assets	1,454	662
Total assets	$5,782	$3,353
Current liabilities	$1,011	$ 565
Long-term debt	3,615	2,056
Total stockholders' equity	1,156	732
Total liabilities and stockholders' equity	$5,782	$3,353
Beginning-of-Year Balances		
Total assets	$5,877	$3,436
Total stockholders' equity	697	623
Other Data		
Average net receivables	$ 511	$ 515
Average inventory	868	403
Net cash provided by operating activities	90	160

Instructions
   (a) For each company, compute the following ratios:

(1) Current.	(7) Return on common stockholders' equity.
(2) Receivables turnover.	(8) Debt to total assets.
(3) Inventory turnover.	(9) Times interest earned.
(4) Profit margin.	(10) Current cash debt.
(5) Asset turnover.	(11) Cash return on sales.
(6) Return on assets.	(12) Cash debt coverage

   (b) Compare the liquidity, profitability, and solvency of the two companies.

Compute missing information given a set of ratios.
(SO 5)

P15–6B   Presented below are the incomplete income statement and comparative balance sheet for Mira Mesa Corporation:

MIRA MESA CORPORATION
Income Statement
For the Year Ended December 31, 2001

Net sales	$?
Cost of goods sold	4,200,000
Gross profit	?
Operating expenses	?
Income from operations	840,000
Other expenses and losses:	
Interest expense	?
Income before income taxes	?
Income tax expense	?
Net income	$ 372,000

MIRA MESA CORPORATION
Balance Sheet
December 31, 2001

Assets	2001	2000
Current assets		
Cash	$ 385,000	$ 299,978
Accounts receivable	?	665,000
Inventory	?	1,204,000
Total current assets	?	2,168,978
Plant assets (net)	3,234,000	2,800,000
Total assets	$?	$4,968,978
Liabilities and Stockholders' Equity		
Current liabilities	$?	$ 824,978
Long-term liabilities	?	1,743,000
Total liabilities	?	2,567,978
Common stock, $2 par	2,100,000	2,100,000
Retained earnings	280,000	301,000
Total stockholders' equity	2,380,000	2,401,000
Total liabilities and stockholders' equity	$?	$4,968,978

Additional information:
1. Times interest earned for 2001 is 8 times.
2. Net cash provided by operating activities for 2001 is $840,000.
3. Cash return on sales ratio for 2001 is 14%.
4. Inventory turnover ratio for 2001 was 4.2 times.
5. Asset turnover ratio for 2001 was 1.2 times.
6. Working capital for 2000 was $1,344,000.

Instructions
Compute the missing information given the information above. Show computations. (*Note:* Start with one ratio and derive as much information as possible from it before trying another ratio. List all missing amounts under the ratio used to find the information.)

BROADENING YOUR PERSPECTIVE

FINANCIAL REPORTING AND ANALYSIS
∙∙
FINANCIAL REPORTING PROBLEM: Kellogg Company

BYP15–1   Your parents are considering investing in Kellogg Company, Inc., common stock. They ask you, as an accounting expert, to make an analysis of the company for them. Fortunately, excerpts from a current annual report of Kellogg are presented in Appendix A of this textbook. Note that all amounts omit 000,000's (i.e., all dollar amounts are in millions).

Instructions
(Follow the approach in the chapter for rounding numbers.)

(a) Make a 5-year trend analysis, using 1994 as the base year, of (1) net sales and (2) operating profit. Comment on the significance of the trend results.

(b) Compute for 1998 and 1997 the (1) profit margin, (2) asset turnover, (3) return on assets, and (4) return on common stockholders' equity. How would you evaluate Kellogg's profitability? Total assets at December 31, 1996, were $5,050, and total stockholders' equity at December 31, 1996, was $1,282.4.

(c) Compute for 1998 and 1997 the (1) debt to total assets and (2) times interest earned ratio. How would you evaluate Kellogg's long-term solvency?

(d) What information outside the annual report may also be useful to your parents in making a decision about Kellogg Company?

COMPARATIVE ANALYSIS PROBLEM: Kellogg Company vs. General Mills

BYP15–2   Kellogg's financial statements are presented in Appendix A; General Mills's financial statements are presented in Appendix B.

Instructions
(a) Based on the information contained in these financial statements, determine each of the following for each company:
   1. The percentage increase (decrease) in (i) net sales and (ii) net income from 1997 to 1998.
   2. The percentage increase in (i) total assets and (ii) total stockholders' (shareholders') equity from 1997 to 1998.
   3. The earnings per share and price-earnings ratio for 1998. General Mills's common stock had a market price of $68.25 at the end of fiscal 1998.

(b) What conclusions concerning the two companies can be drawn from these data?

RESEARCH ASSIGNMENT

BYP15–3   The chapter stresses the importance of comparing an individual firm's financial ratios to industry norms. Robert Morris Associates (RMA), a national association of bank loan and credit officers, publishes industry-specific financial data in its *Annual Statement Studies.* This publication includes common-size financial statements and various ratios classified by four-digit SIC code. (*Note*: An alternative source is Dun & Bradstreet's *Industry Norms and Key Business Ratios.*)

   Obtain the 1997 edition of *Annual Statement Studies* (covering fiscal years ended 4/1/96 through 3/31/97) and the 1997 (or 1998) Annual Report of Wal-Mart Stores, Inc.

Instructions
(a) Prepare a 1997 common-size (vertical analysis) balance sheet and income statement for Wal-Mart.

(b) Calculate those 1997 ratios for Wal-Mart which are covered by RMA. (*Note:* The specific ratio definitions used by RMA are described in the beginning of the book. Use ending values for balance sheet items.)

(c) What is Wal-Mart's SIC code? Use your answers from parts (a) and (b) to compare Wal-Mart to the appropriate current industry data. How does Wal-Mart compare to its competitors? (*Note:* RMA sorts current-year data by firm assets and sales, while five years of historical data are presented on an aggregate basis.)

(d) How many sets of financial statements did RMA use in compiling the current industry data sorted by sales?

INTERPRETING FINANCIAL STATEMENTS:
Manitowoc Company and Caterpillar Corp.

BYP15–4 The Manitowoc Company and Caterpillar Corporation are both producers and sellers of large fixed assets. Caterpillar is substantially larger than Manitowoc. Financial information taken from each company's financial statements is provided below.

	Caterpillar (in millions)		Manitowoc (in thousands)	
Financial highlights	Current Year	Prior Year	Current Year	Prior Year
Cash and short-term investments	$ 638	$ 419	$ 16,635	$ 16,163
Accounts receivable	4,285	4,290	51,011	29,500
Inventory	1,921	1,835	52,928	36,793
Other current assets	803	865	14,571	14,082
Current assets	7,647	7,409	135,145	96,538
Total assets	16,830	16,250	324,915	159,465
Current liabilities	6,049	5,498	110,923	54,064
Total liabilities	13,442	13,339	243,254	84,408
Total stockholders' equity	3,388	2,911	81,661	75,057
Sales	15,451		313,149	
Cost of goods sold	12,000		237,679	
Interest expense	191		1,865	
Income tax expense	501		8,551	
Net income	1,136		14,569	
Cash provided from operations	2,190		16,367	

Instructions

(a) Calculate the following liquidity ratios and discuss the relative liquidity of the two companies:
   1. Current ratio.
   2. Quick or acid-test ratio.
   3. Current cash debt coverage.
   4. Accounts receivable turnover.
   5. Inventory turnover.

(b) Calculate the following profitability ratios and discuss the relative profitability of the two companies:
   1. Asset turnover.
   2. Profit margin on sales.
   3. Return on assets.
   4. Return on common equity.

(c) Calculate the following solvency ratios and discuss the relative solvency of the two companies:
   1. Debt to assets.
   2. Times interest earned.

REAL-WORLD FOCUS: Coca-Cola Company and PepsiCo, Inc.

BYP15–5 Coca-Cola Company and **PepsiCo, Inc.** provide refreshments to every corner of the world. Both believe that great potential still exists—to satisfy the thirst of the world's population. Selected data from the consolidated financial statements for Coca-Cola Company and for PepsiCo, Inc., are presented below. (All dollars are in millions.)

	Coca-Cola	PepsiCo
Total current assets (including cash, accounts receivable, and marketable securities totaling $3,056 and $3,539, respectively)	$ 5,205	$ 5,546
Total current liabilities	6,177	5,230
Net sales	16,172	30,421
Cost of goods sold	6,167	14,886
Net income	2,554	1,606
Average receivables for the year	1,384	2,229
Average inventories for the year	1,048	1,011
Average total assets	12,947	25,112
Average common stockholders' equity	4,910	7,085
Net cash provided by operating activities	3,115	3,742
Average current liabilities	6,763	5,250
Total assets	13,873	25,432
Total liabilities	8,638	18,119
Income before income taxes	3,728	2,432
Interest expense	199	682

Instructions

(a) Compute the following liquidity ratios for Coca-Cola and for PepsiCo.:
  (1) Current.
  (2) Acid-test.
  (3) Current cash debt coverage.
  (4) Receivables turnover.
  (5) Inventory turnover.
(b) Comment on the relative liquidity of the two competitors.
(c) Compute the following profitability ratios for the two companies:
  (1) Profit margin.
  (2) Cash return on sales.
  (3) Asset turnover.
  (4) Return on assets.
  (5) Return on common stockholders' equity.
(d) Comment on the relative profitability of the two competitors.

CRITICAL THINKING

GROUP DECISION CASE

BYP15–6 As the CPA for L. Gonzalez Manufacturing Inc., you have been requested to develop some key ratios from the comparative financial statements. This information is to be used to convince creditors that L. Gonzalez Manufacturing Inc. is solvent and to support the use of going-concern valuation procedures in the financial statements.

The data requested and the computations developed from the financial statements follow:

	2001	2000
Current ratio	3.1 times	2.1 times
Acid-test ratio	.8 times	1.4 times
Asset turnover	2.8 times	2.2 times
Sales to stockholders' equity	2.3 times	2.7 times
Net income	Up 32%	Down 8%
Earnings per share	$3.30	$2.50
Book value per share	Up 8%	Up 11%

Instructions
With the class divided into groups, answer the following:
   (a) L. Gonzalez Manufacturing Inc. asks you to prepare a list of brief comments stating how each of these items supports the solvency and going-concern potential of the business. The company wishes to use these comments to support its presentation of data to its creditors. You are to prepare the comments as requested, giving the implications and the limitations of each item separately, and then the collective inference that may be drawn from them about L. Gonzales's solvency and going-concern potential.
   (b) What warnings should you offer these creditors about the limitations of ratio analysis for the purpose stated here?

COMMUNICATION ACTIVITY

BYP15–7   Ken Powell is the Chief Executive Officer of Midwest Electronics. Powell is an expert engineer but a novice in accounting. Powell asks you, as an accounting major, to explain (1) the bases for comparison in analyzing Midwest's financial statements and (2) the limitations, if any, in financial statement analysis.

Instructions
Write a memo to Powell that explains the bases for comparison and the limitations of financial statement analysis.

ETHICS CASE

BYP15–8   Ron Staub, president of Staub Industries, wishes to issue a press release to bolster his company's image and maybe even its stock price, which has been gradually falling. As controller, you have been asked to provide a list of twenty financial ratios along with some other operating statistics relative to Staub Industries' first quarter financials and operations.

   Two days after you provide the ratios and data requested, you are asked by Manny Alomar, the public relations director of Staub, to prove the accuracy of the financial and operating data contained in the press release written by the president and edited by Manny. In the news release, the president highlights the sales increase of 25% over last year's first quarter and the positive change in the current ratio from 1.5:1 last year to 3:1 this year. He also emphasizes that production was up 50% over the prior year's first quarter. You note that the release contains only positive or improved ratios and none of the negative or deteriorated ratios. For instance, no mention is made that the debt to total assets ratio has increased from 35% to 55%, that inventories are up 89%, and that while the current ratio improved, the acid-test ratio fell from 1:1 to .5:1. Nor is there any mention that the reported profit for the quarter would have been a loss had not the estimated lives of Staub's plant and machinery been increased by 30%. Manny emphasized, "The Pres wants this release by early this afternoon."

Instructions
   (a) Who are the stakeholders in this situation?
   (b) Is there anything unethical in president Staub's actions?
   (c) Should you as controller remain silent? Does Manny have any responsibility?

SURFING THE NET

BYP15–9   The Management Discussion and Analysis (MD&A) section of an annual report addresses corporate performance for the year, and sometimes uses financial ratios to support its claims.

Addresses: http://www.ibm.com/financialguide
              http://www.ge.com/investor/finance.htm (or go to
              www.wiley.com/college/weygandt)

Steps:
   1. From IBM's Financial Guide, choose Guides Contents.
   2. Choose **Anatomy of an Annual Report.**

3. Follow instruction (a).
4. From General Electric's website, choose the most recent annual report, then choose financial section, and then choose management discussion.
5. Follow instructions (b)–(e).

Instructions

(a) Using IBM's Financial Guide, describe the contents of the "Management's Discussion."
(b) Compare current year earnings with the previous year's earnings.
(c) What were some of management's explanations for the change in net earnings?

Answers to Self-Study Questions
1. b   2. d   3. a   4. c   5. c   6. c   7. c   8. b   9. a   10. d   11. d
12. b

Answer to Kellogg Review It Question 4, p. 679

4. Kellogg presents horizontal analyses in its "Financial Highlights" section and its Management's Discussion and Analysis section. Horizontal and vertical analysis are used in schedules presented in the Management's Discussion and Analysis section.

 Remember to go back to the Navigator box on the chapter-opening page and check off your completed work.

APPENDIXES A-F

APPENDIX A

SPECIMEN FINANCIAL STATEMENTS:
Kellogg Company

THE ANNUAL REPORT

Once each year a corporation communicates to its stockholders and other interested parties by issuing a complete set of audited financial statements. The **annual report**, as this communication is called, summarizes the financial results of its operations for the year and its plans for the future. Many such annual reports have become attractive, multicolored, glossy public relations ad pieces containing pictures of corporate officers and directors as well as photos and descriptions of new products and new buildings. Yet the basic function of every annual report is to report **financial information**, almost all of which is a product of the corporation's accounting system.

The content and organization of corporate annual reports have become fairly standardized. Excluding the public relations part of the report (pictures and products), the following items are the traditional financial portions of the annual report:

Financial Highlights
Letter to the Stockholders
Auditor's Report
Management Discussion and Analysis
Financial Statements and Accompanying Notes
Five- or Ten-Year Summary

In this appendix we illustrate current financial reporting with a comprehensive set of corporate financial statements that are prepared in accordance with generally accepted accounting principles and audited by an international independent certified public accounting firm. We are grateful for permission to use the actual financial statements and other accompanying financial information from the annual report of a large, publicly held company, Kellogg Company.

FINANCIAL HIGHLIGHTS

The financial highlights section is usually presented inside the front cover or on the first two pages of the annual report. This section generally reports the total or per share amounts for five to ten financial items for the current year and one or more previous years. Financial items from the income statement and the balance sheet that typically are presented are sales, income from continuing operations, net income, net income per share, dividends per common share, and the amount of capital expenditures. The financial highlights section from Kellogg's Annual Report is shown below:

Financial Highlights

(millions, except per share data)	1998	Change	1997	Change	1996	Change
Net sales	$6,762.1	-1%	$6,830.1	+2%	$6,676.6	-5%
Operating profit, excluding non-recurring charges (a)	965.6	-19%	1,193.2	+9%	1,095.0	-13%
Earnings, excluding non-recurring charges and other unusual items (a) and before cumulative effect of accounting change (b)	548.9	-22%	704.5	+8%	651.1	-14%
Earnings per share (basic and diluted), excluding non-recurring charges and other unusual items (a) and before cumulative effect of accounting change (b) (c)	1.35	-21%	1.70	+11%	1.53	-12%
Operating profit	895.1	-11%	1,009.1	+5%	958.9	+14%
Net earnings	502.6	-8%	546.0	+3%	531.0	+8%
Net earnings per share (basic and diluted) (c)	1.23	-7%	1.32	+6%	1.25	+12%
Net cash provided by operating activities	719.7	-18%	879.8	+24%	711.5	-32%
Capital expenditures	373.9	+20%	312.4	+2%	307.3	-3%
Average shares outstanding (c)	407.8		414.1		424.9	
Dividends per share (c)	$ .92	+6%	$ .87	+7%	$ .81	+8%
Year-end stock price (c)	$ 34⅛	-31%	$ 49⅝	+51%	$ 32¹³⁄₁₆	-15%

(a) Refer to Management's Discussion and Analysis and Notes 3 and 4 within Notes to Consolidated Financial Statements for further explanation of non-recurring charges and other unusual items for years 1996-1998.

(b) Refer to Management's Discussion and Analysis and Note 1 within Notes to Consolidated Financial Statements for further explanation of cumulative effect of accounting change in 1997.

(c) Restated for two-for-one stock split effective August 22, 1997.

As shown above, Kellogg chose also to present the percent change from last year to the current year for each of the reported items.

TO OUR SHAREOWNERS

*We are fully committed
to return to both top-line
and bottom-line growth.*

Carlos M. Gutierrez   Arnold G. Langbo

Growth

While we look to the future with great optimism at Kellogg Company, our performance in 1998 was disappointing, particularly following a year of growth in 1997.

Our level of cereal marketing investment early in 1998 was not sufficient in the face of extremely competitive market conditions. This situation hurt our volume performance for much of the year and, combined with other issues in markets around the world, led to a decline in both sales and earnings. Nonetheless, we continue to have the utmost confidence in the future of our grain-based businesses, and we are fully committed to return to both top-line and bottom-line growth.

Our Strategy for Growth

Although our 1998 business results were below our performance expectations, it was a year in which we put in place key elements of a stronger foundation for future growth. This included investments in new product development and a complete overhaul of our corporate headquarters and North American organizational structure.

Also in 1998, we adopted this five-point strategy for growth in 1999 and beyond:

Leading the food industry in innovation. Kellogg Company is rolling out a broader grain-based product portfolio, including great-tasting new cereals,

innovative convenience foods, and new grain-based products outside our traditional lines. We also are adding to the nutritional value delivered by our products, including reformulations that we believe will help many long-established *Kellogg's*® cereal brands return to growth. This report further describes some of our most important innovation initiatives.

Investing in our largest cereal markets. During 1999, we will invest in growth in our seven largest cereal markets: the United States, the United Kingdom, Mexico, Canada, Australia, Germany, and France. In addition to major product improvement programs, we are

INVESTING IN OUR LARGEST CEREAL MARKETS

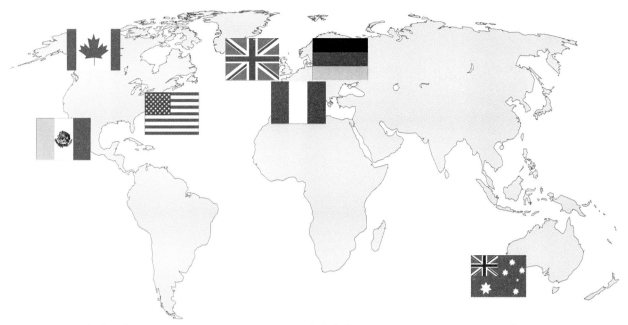

A high strategic priority for 1999 is promoting growth
in Kellogg Company's seven largest cereal markets:

1. ▦ *the United States,* 2. ✖ *the United Kingdom,* 3. ▦ *Mexico,*

4. ▦ *Canada,* 5. ▦ *Australia,* 6. ▬ *Germany, and* 7. ▮ *France.*

significantly increasing our overall marketing investment in these markets, which comprise nearly 70 percent of our business.

Accelerating the global growth of our convenience foods business. Around the world, consumption of food "on-the-go" continues to increase dramatically. We believe we are uniquely positioned to capitalize on this trend with products such as *Nutri-Grain*® bars, *Rice Krispies Treats*™ squares, and *Pop-Tarts*® toaster pastries. We are focusing both on expanded geographic distribution and new distribution channels, particularly single-serve channels.

Continuing to reduce costs. From ongoing cost-reduction programs, we anticipate more than $50 million in incremental savings in 1999. These savings need to be viewed as a requirement to remaining competitive. They will enable us to deliver still greater value to consumers and help fund business growth in 1999 and beyond.

Creating a more focused and accountable organization. Our objective is to develop a talented, diverse global workforce with every person focused on the largest, most important activities.

Dividend and Stock News

We are pleased to report that the Kellogg Company dividend rose in 1998 for the 42nd consecutive year, with an increase of 5 cents per share to $.92. We also continued our program of purchasing Kellogg shares, with 1998 purchases totaling $239.7 million.

Appointments and Recognition

We offer sincere thanks and best wishes to Russell G. Mawby, who retired from the Kellogg Company Board of Directors in April 1998 after 24 years of distinguished service, and to Donald H. Rumsfeld, who will retire from the Board in April 1999 after 14 years of distinguished service. We have benefited greatly from the wise counsel provided by Russ and Don during their long periods of service on the Board.

In April 1998, Dorothy A. Johnson, president and chief executive officer of the Council of Michigan Foundations, was elected to the Board.

William A. Camstra, vice chairman of Kellogg Company, retired during 1998 after 42 years of dedicated service to the Company around the world. Charles E. French, vice president, retired after 32 years of dedicated service in the United States and the United Kingdom. Also during 1998, John L. Forbis joined the Company as vice president – global convenience foods innovation.

CONVENIENCE FOODS SALES
(As a percentage of total sales)

Kellogg Company's global convenience foods sales, now $1.5 billion a year, are continuing to increase as a percentage of our total sales.

In January 1999, Jacobus Groot joined Kellogg as executive vice president and president – Kellogg Asia-Pacific. In February 1999, John D. Cook joined as executive vice president and president – Kellogg North America. We are excited about the energy and insight these two executives bring to our Company.

In addition, 1999 is an important year in top-leadership transition. In January 1999, Carlos M. Gutierrez, president and chief operating officer of Kellogg Company, was elected to the Board of Directors. Mr. Gutierrez will become chief executive officer of the Company at the Annual Meeting of Shareowners on April 23, 1999. I will continue as chairman of the board until the Annual Meeting scheduled for April 28, 2000.

We appreciate sincerely the resolve of Kellogg people amid difficulty and significant changes in 1998. We are most fortunate to have such a dedicated team that remains deeply committed to delivering superior growth and value to you, our shareowners.

Arnold G. Langbo
Chairman of the Board
Chief Executive Officer

Carlos M. Gutierrez
President
Chief Operating Officer

AUDITOR'S REPORT

All publicly held corporations, as well as many other enterprises and organizations (both profit and not-for-profit, large and small) engage the services of independent certified public accountants for the purpose of obtaining an objective, expert report on their financial statements. Based on a comprehensive examination of the company's accounting system and records, and of the financial statements, the outside CPA issues the auditor's report.

The standard auditor's report consists of three pieces of information, expressed in separate sentences or paragraphs: (1) a responsibilities statement, (2) a scope statement, and (3) the opinion. In the **responsibilities statement**, the auditor identifies who and what was audited and indicates the responsibilities of management and the auditor relative to the financial statements. In the **scope statement**, the auditor states that the audit was conducted in accordance with generally accepted auditing standards and discusses the nature and limitations of the audit. In the **opinion statement**, (which is first in Kellogg's auditor's report), the auditor expresses an informed opinion as to (1) the fairness of the financial statements and (2) their conformity with generally accepted accounting principles. The **Report of PricewaterhouseCoopers Independent Auditors** appearing in Kellogg's Annual Report is shown below:

Report of Independent Accountants

PricewaterhouseCoopers LLP

To the Shareholders and Board of Directors of Kellogg Company

In our opinion, the accompanying consolidated balance sheet and the related consolidated statements of earnings, of shareholders' equity and of cash flows present fairly, in all material respects, the financial position of Kellogg Company and its subsidiaries at December 31, 1998 and 1997, and the results of their operations and their cash flows for each of the three years in the period ended December 31, 1998, in conformity with generally accepted accounting principles. These financial statements are the responsibility of the Company's management; our responsibility is to express an opinion on these financial statements based on our audits. We conducted our audits of these statements in accordance with generally accepted auditing standards which require that we plan and perform the audit to obtain reasonable assurance about whether the financial statements

are free of material misstatement. An audit includes examining, on a test basis, evidence supporting the amounts and disclosures in the financial statements, assessing the accounting principles used and significant estimates made by management, and evaluating the overall financial statement presentation. We believe that our audits provide a reasonable basis for the opinion expressed above.

As discussed in Note 1 to the financial statements, the Company changed its method of accounting for business process reengineering costs effective October 1, 1997.

PricewaterhouseCoopers LLP

January 29, 1999

The auditor's report above contains an additional paragraph wherein PricewaterhouseCoopers reports that Kellogg changed its method of accounting for business process reengineering costs as discussed in notes to the financial statements.

The auditor's report issued on Kellogg's financial statements is **unqualified** or "clean"; that is, it contains no qualifications or exceptions. In other words, the auditor conformed completely with generally accepted auditing standards in performing the audit, and the financial statements conformed in all material respects with generally accepted accounting principles.

When the financial statements do not conform with generally accepted accounting principles, the auditor must issue a **qualified** opinion and describe the exception. If the lack of conformity with GAAP is sufficiently material, the auditor is compelled to issue an **adverse** or negative opinion. An adverse opinion means that the financial statements do not present fairly the company's financial condition and/or the results of the company's operations at the dates and for the periods reported.

In circumstances where the auditor is unable to perform all the auditing procedures necessary to reach a conclusion as to the fairness of the financial statements, a **disclaimer** must be issued. In these rare instances, the auditor must report the reason for failure to reach a conclusion on the fairness of the financial statements.

Companies strive to obtain an unqualified auditor's report. Hence, only infrequently are you likely to encounter anything other than this type of opinion on the financial statements.

MANAGEMENT DISCUSSION AND ANALYSIS

The management discussion and analysis (MD&A) section covers three financial aspects of a company: its results of operations, its ability to pay near-term obligations, and its ability to fund operations and expansion. Management must highlight favorable or unfavorable trends and identify significant events and uncertainties that affect these three factors. This discussion obviously involves a number of subjective estimates and opinions. The MD&A section of Kelloggs' annual report is presented on the following pages.

Management's Discussion and Analysis

Kellogg Company and Subsidiaries

Results of operations

Overview

Kellogg Company manufactures and markets ready-to-eat cereal and other grain-based convenience food products, including toaster pastries, frozen waffles, cereal bars, and bagels, throughout the world. Principal markets for these products include the United States and Great Britain. Operations are managed via four major geographic areas — North America, Europe, Asia-Pacific, and Latin America — which are the basis of the Company's reportable operating segment information. The Company leads the global ready-to-eat cereal category with an estimated 38% annualized share of worldwide volume. Additionally, the Company is the North American market leader in the toaster pastry, cereal/granola bar, frozen waffle, and pre-packaged bagel categories.

During 1998, the Company realized declines in earnings per share both with and without unusual items (discussed below). The Company experienced significant competitive pressure combined with category softness in its major ready-to-eat cereal markets, to which it responded by accelerating investment in long-term growth strategies, including product development, technology, and efficiency initiatives.

For the full year of 1998, Kellogg Company reported net earnings and earnings per share of $502.6 million and $1.23, respectively, compared to 1997 net earnings of $546.0 million and net earnings per share of $1.32. Net earnings and earnings per share for 1996 were $531.0 million and $1.25, respectively. (All per share amounts reflect the 2-for-1 stock split effective August 22, 1997. All earnings per share presented represent both basic and diluted earnings per share.)

During the current and prior years, the Company reported non-recurring charges and other unusual items that have been excluded from all applicable amounts presented below for purposes of comparison between years. Additionally, results for 1997 are presented before the cumulative effect of a change in the method of accounting for business process reengineering costs. Refer to the separate section below on non-recurring charges and other unusual items for further information.

1998 compared to 1997

Excluding non-recurring charges and other unusual items, the Company reported 1998 earnings per share of $1.35, a 21% decrease from the prior-year result of $1.70. The year-to-year decrease in earnings per share of $.35 resulted from $.33 of business decline, $.01 of unfavorable tax rate movements, and $.03 of unfavorable foreign currency movements, partially offset by a $.02 benefit from share repurchase. The business decline was principally attributable to cereal category softness and competitive pressures in North America and Europe, and continued global investments in brand-building marketing activities and streamlining initiatives. Foreign currency movements had a minimal net impact in Europe and negatively impacted earnings by 2% on a consolidated basis due to currency devaluation in Latin America and Asia-Pacific.

The Company realized the following volume results during 1998:

	Change
North America	-4.3%
Europe	-1.2%
Asia-Pacific	+6.9%
Latin America	+16.2%
Global total	-1.3%

	Change
Global cereal	-2.0%
Global convenience foods	+1.1%
Global total	-1.3%

Within North America and Europe, volume declines were principally due to softness in the ready-to-eat cereal business. Asia-Pacific experienced record volume due to a combination of cereal growth and new convenience food product introductions. Latin America continued to post double-digit increases in both ready-to-eat cereal and convenience foods, with record volume results throughout 1998.

The global convenience foods volume increase was driven by double-digit growth in the Company's international markets offset by softness within North America, primarily due to declines in the Lender's Bagels business

On an annualized basis, regional volume market share of the ready-to-eat cereal category was approximately 33% in North America, 43% in Europe, 43% in Asia-Pacific, and 61% in Latin America.

Consolidated net sales decreased 1% for 1998. Adjusted for unfavorable foreign currency translation, sales were even with the prior year, with the unfavorable impact of volume declines offset by favorable pricing and product mix movements. On an operating segment basis, net sales versus the prior year were:

	North America	Europe	Asia-Pacific	Latin America	Consolidated
Business	-1%	—	+7%	+16%	—
Foreign currency impact	-1%	—	-15%	-4%	-1%
Total change	**-2%**	**—**	**-8%**	**+12%**	**-1%**

Margin performance for 1998 and 1997 was:

	1998	1997	Change
Gross margin	+51.5%	+52.1%	-.6%
SGA%(a)	-37.2%	-34.6%	-2.6%
Operating margin	+14.3%	+17.5%	-3.2%

(a) Selling, general and administration expense as a percentage of net sales.

The gross margin decline was due to a combination of the fixed cost absorption impact of lower volumes combined with incremental costs related to launching new products in Europe and North America. The increase in SGA% reflects increased global research and development costs to support our ongoing innovation strategy combined with significant marketing investment and increased spending on streamlining initiatives.

Operating profit (loss) on an operating segment basis was:

(millions)	North America	Europe	Asia-Pacific	Latin America	Corporate and other	Consolidated
1998 operating profit (loss) as reported	$790.8	$208.1	$44.9	$107.2	($255.9)	$ 895.1
Non-recurring charges	40.8	3.3	3.4	—	23.0	70.5
1998 operating profit (loss) excluding non-recurring charges	**$831.6**	**$211.4**	**$48.3**	**$107.2**	**($232.9)**	**$965.6**
1997 operating profit (loss) as reported	$847.0	$189.9	$22.5	$111.6	($161.9)	$1,009.1
Non-recurring charges	37.8	115.9	28.6	.2	1.6	184.1
1997 operating profit (loss) excluding non-recurring charges	**$884.8**	**$305.8**	**$51.1**	**$111.8**	**($160.3)**	**$1,193.2**
% change – 1998 vs. 1997 excluding non-recurring charges						
Business	-6%	-31%	+11%	-1%	-45%	-18%
Foreign currency impact	—	—	-16%	-3%	—	-1%
Total change	**-6%**	**-31%**	**-5%**	**-4%**	**-45%**	**-19%**

Gross interest expense, prior to amounts capitalized, increased 8% versus the prior year to $127.3 million. The higher interest expense resulted from overall increased debt levels, partially offset by a lower effective interest rate.

Excluding the impact of non-recurring charges and other unusual items, the effective income tax rate was 35.7%, an increase of .4 percentage points versus the prior-year rate. The higher effective tax rate is primarily due to lower earnings and country mix. For both 1998 and 1997, the effective tax rate benefited from statutory rate reductions in the United Kingdom, as well as favorable adjustments in other jurisdictions. The effective income tax rate based on reported earnings (before cumulative effect of accounting change) was 35.8% in 1998 and 37.6% in 1997.

1997 compared to 1996
Excluding non-recurring charges and other unusual items, the Company reported 1997 earnings per share of $1.70, an 11% increase over the prior-year results of $1.53. The year-over-year increase in earnings per share of $.17 resulted from $.12 of business growth, $.03 of common stock repurchases, and $.04 of favorable tax rate movements, partially offset by $.02 of unfavorable foreign currency movements. The business growth was principally attributable to cereal volume growth in North America and Latin America, continued double-digit growth in convenience foods volume, and reductions in manufacturing and marketing costs. Foreign currency movements negatively impacted earnings 1% on a consolidated basis. The negative impact of the Lender's Bagels business, acquired in December 1996, was approximately $.05.

The Company achieved the following volume growth during 1997:

	Change
North America	+16.1%
Europe	+2.6%
Asia-Pacific	+1.5%
Latin America	+16.3%
Global total(a)	+11.3%

	Change
Global cereal	+3.4%
Global convenience foods(b)	+47.2%
Global total	+11.3%

(a) Excluding Lender's, acquired in December 1996, global volume growth was 5.0%.
(b) Excluding Lender's, global convenience foods growth was 12.5%.

Within North America, the Company recovered cereal volume declines of the prior year, and slightly exceeded 1995 results. Growth in Europe was partially offset by a decline in the United Kingdom, while Asia-Pacific was slowed by softness in Australia. Latin America achieved record annual volume results.

Consolidated net sales increased 2% for 1997. The favorable impact of strong volumes was partially offset by unfavorable pricing and product mix movements, and a negative foreign currency impact of 2%. Excluding the Lender's business, consolidated net sales were even with the prior year. On an operating segment basis, net sales versus the prior year were:

	North America	Europe	Asia-Pacific	Latin America	Consolidated
Business	+4%	+2%	+2%	+13%	+4%
Foreign currency impact	—	-5%	-7%	-1%	-2%
Total change	**+4%**	**-3%**	**-5%**	**+12%**	**+2%**

Margin performance for 1997 and 1996 was:

	1997	1996	Change
Gross margin	+52.1%	+53.2%	-1.1%
SGA%(a)	-34.6%	-36.8%	+2.2%
Operating margin	+17.5%	+16.4%	+1.1%

(a) Selling, general and administrative expense as a percentage of net sales.

Gross margin performance for 1997 benefited from volume increases and year-over-year operational cost savings. However, these favorable factors were outweighed by the negative impact of prior-year pricing actions. The reduction in SGA% primarily reflects reduced promotional spending in North America.

Operating profit (loss) on an operating segment basis was:

(millions)	North America	Europe	Asia-Pacific	Latin America	Corporate and other	Consolidated
1997 operating profit (loss) excluding non-recurring charges	**$884.8**	**$305.8**	**$51.1**	**$111.8**	**($160.3)**	**$1,193.2**
1996 operating profit (loss) as reported	$751.2	$249.8	$31.2	$ 93.5	($166.8)	$958.9
Non-recurring charges	11.1	55.3	30.1	.7	38.9	136.1
1996 operating profit (loss) excluding non-recurring charges	**$762.3**	**$305.1**	**$61.3**	**$94.2**	**($127.9)**	**$1,095.0**
% change – 1997 vs. 1996 excluding non-recurring charges						
Business	+16%	+4%	-9%	+20%	-25%	+11%
Foreign currency impact	—	-4%	-8%	-1%	—	-2%
Total change	**+16%**	**—**	**-17%**	**+19%**	**-25%**	**+9%**

Gross interest expense, prior to amounts capitalized, increased 70% versus the prior year to $117.9 million. The higher interest expense resulted from increased debt levels to fund the Lender's Bagels business acquisition and the Company's common stock repurchase program.

Excluding the impact of non-recurring charges and other unusual items, the effective income tax rate was 35.3%, 1.5 percentage points lower than the prior-year rate. The lower effective tax rate is primarily due to enactment of a 2% statutory rate reduction in the United Kingdom, effective April 1, 1997, as well as favorable adjustments in other jurisdictions. The effective income tax rate based on reported earnings (before cumulative effect of accounting change) was 37.6% in 1997 and 38.2% in 1996. For both 1997 and 1996, the higher reported rate (as compared to the rate excluding the impact of unusual items) primarily relates to certain non-recurring charges for which no tax benefit was provided, based on management's assessment of the likelihood of recovering such benefit in future years.

Other expense for 1996 included a charge of $35.0 million for a contribution to the Kellogg's Corporate Citizenship Fund, a private trust established for charitable donations.

Liquidity and capital resources

The Company's financial condition remained strong throughout 1998. A strong cash flow, combined with a program of issuing commercial paper and maintaining worldwide credit facilities, provides adequate liquidity to meet the Company's operational needs. In August 1998, Moody's lowered its rating on the Company's senior unsecured notes from Aa1 to Aa2 reflecting the Company's increased use of cash for investments in marketing, product development, and other initiatives in the highly competitive markets around the world. Management believes that this change will have an insignificant impact on future borrowing costs. The rating agency confirmed the Company's Prime-1 commercial paper rating.

Net cash provided by operating activities was $719.7 million during 1998, compared to $879.8 million in 1997, with the decrease due principally to lower earnings and unfavorable working capital movements. The ratio of current assets to current liabilities was .9 at December 31, 1998 and 1997.

Net cash used in investing activities was $398.0 million, compared to $329.3 million in 1997. The increase was primarily due to property additions, which increased from $312.4 million in 1997 to $373.9 million for 1998.

Net cash used in financing activities was $358.3 million, primarily related to common stock repurchases of $239.7 million and dividend payments of $375.3 million, partially offset by a net increase in total debt of $241.5 million. The Company's total 1998 per share dividend payment was $.92, a 5.7% increase over the prior-year payment of $.87.

On August 1, 1997, the Company's Board of Directors approved a 2-for-1 stock split to shareholders of record at the close of business August 8, 1997, effective August 22, 1997, and also authorized retirement of 105.3 million common shares (pre-split) held in treasury. All per share and shares outstanding data have been restated retroactively to reflect the stock split.

Under existing plans authorized by the Company's Board of Directors, management spent $239.7 million during 1998 to repurchase 6.3 million shares of the Company's common stock at an average price of $38 per share. The open repurchase authorization, which has been extended through December 31, 1999, was $149.4 million at year-end 1998.

Notes payable primarily consist of commercial paper borrowings in the United States and borrowings under a $200 million revolving credit agreement in Europe with several international banks initiated during December 1998. At December 31, 1998, outstanding borrowings under the revolving credit agreement were $148.5 million with an effective interest rate of 5.5%. U.S. borrowings at December 31, 1998, were $423.3 million with an effective interest rate of 5.2%. Associated with the U.S. borrowings, during September 1997, the Company purchased a $225 million notional, four-year fixed interest rate cap. Under the terms of the cap, if the Federal Reserve AA composite rate on 30-day commercial paper increases to 6.33%, the Company will pay this fixed rate on $225 million of its commercial paper borrowings. If the rate increases to 7.68% or above, the cap will expire. As of year-end 1998, the rate was 4.90%.

In October 1998, the Company issued $200 million of seven-year 4.875% fixed rate U.S. Dollar Notes. Management used the proceeds from this issuance to replace maturing long-term debt. Management entered into a series of interest rate hedges throughout 1998 to effectively fix the interest rate prior to issuance. The effect of the hedges, when combined with original issue discounts, resulted in an overall effective rate for this debt of 6.07%.

To reduce short-term borrowings, on February 4, 1998, the Company issued $400 million of three-year 5.75% fixed rate U.S. Dollar Notes. Accordingly, an equivalent amount of commercial paper borrowings was classified as long-term debt in the December 31, 1997, balance sheet. These Notes were issued under an existing "shelf registration" with the Securities and Exchange Commission, and provide an option to holders to extend the obligation for an additional four years at a predetermined interest rate of 5.63% plus the Company's then-current credit spread. As a result of this option, the effective interest rate on the three-year Notes is 5.23%. Concurrent with this issuance, the Company entered into a $400 million notional, three-year fixed-to-floating interest rate swap, indexed to the Federal Reserve AA composite rate on 30-day commercial paper.

On January 29, 1997, the Company issued $500 million of seven-year 6.625% fixed rate Euro Dollar Notes. This debt was issued primarily to fund the purchase of the Lender's Bagels business, acquired in December 1996. In conjunction with this issuance, the Company settled $500 million notional amount of interest rate forward swap agreements, which effectively fixed the interest rate on the debt at 6.354%. Associated with this debt, during September 1997, the Company entered into a $225 million notional, 4½-year fixed-to-floating interest rate swap, indexed to the three-month London Interbank Offered Rate (LIBOR). Under the terms of this swap, if three-month LIBOR decreases to 4.71% or below, the swap will expire. At year-end 1998, three-month LIBOR was 5.07%.

To replace other long-term debt maturing during 1997, the Company issued $500 million of four-year 6.125% Euro Dollar Notes on August 5, 1997. In conjunction with this issuance, the Company settled $400 million notional amount of interest rate forward swap agreements that effectively fixed the interest rate on the debt at 6.4%. Associated with this debt, during September 1997, the Company entered into a $200 million notional, four-year fixed-to-floating interest rate swap, indexed to three-month LIBOR.

The ratio of total debt to market capitalization at December 31, 1998, was 16%, up from 10% at December 31, 1997, due to a combination of a lower stock price and higher debt levels in 1998.

Non-recurring charges and other unusual items

From 1995 to the present, management has commenced major productivity and operational streamlining initiatives in an effort to optimize the Company's cost structure. The incremental costs of these programs have been reported throughout 1995-1998 as non-recurring charges.

In addition to the non-recurring charges reported for streamlining initiatives, the Company incurred charges for other unusual items. Furthermore, net earnings for 1997 included a cumulative effect of accounting change related to business process reengineering costs. In summary, the following charges were excluded from reported results for purposes of comparison within the "Results of operations" section above:

Non-recurring charges & other unusual items

Impact on (millions, except per share data)	Operating profit	Earnings before income taxes & cumulative effect of accounting change	Net earnings	Net earnings per share
1998:				
Streamlining initiatives	**$70.5**	**$70.5**	**$46.3**	**$.12**
1997:				
Streamlining initiatives	$161.1	$161.1		
Impairment losses	23.0	23.0		
Total non-recurring charges	**$184.1**	**$184.1**	**$140.5**	**$.34**
Cumulative effect of accounting change	—	—	**$ 18.0**	**$.04**
1996:				
Streamlining initiatives	$121.1	$121.1		
Litigation provision	15.0	15.0		
Private trust contribution(a)	—	35.0		
Total	**$136.1**	**$171.1**	**$120.1**	**$.28**

(a) Recorded in other income (expense), net.

The 1998 streamlining charges relate primarily to an overhead activity analysis that resulted in the elimination of approximately 550 employees and 240 contractors from the Company's headquarters and North American operations through a combination of involuntary early retirement and severance programs. The charges consist mainly of employee retirement and separation benefits, outplacement services, associated consulting and other related costs. This initiative is expected to result in annual pre-tax savings of $105 million, beginning in 1999. Cash outlays for the 1998 charges during 1998 were $8 million, with the remainder to be spent during 1999. Total cash outlays during 1998 for all streamlining initiatives were approximately $47 million. Refer to Note 3 within Notes to Consolidated Financial Statements for further information.

All streamlining programs commenced since 1995, including the aforementioned 1998 initiatives, are expected to result in the elimination of approximately 3,500 employee positions by the end of 1999, with approximately 95% of this reduction already achieved. These programs are expected to deliver average annual pre-tax savings in excess of $300 million by the year 2000, with approximately $250 million of that amount to be realized in 1999. These savings are not necessarily indicative of current and future incremental earnings due to management's commitment to invest in competitive business strategies, new markets, and growth opportunities.

In addition to the non-recurring charges reported during 1997 and 1996 for streamlining initiatives, the Company incurred charges for the following unusual items:

- During 1997, the Company included in non-recurring charges $23.0 million of asset impairment losses which resulted from an evaluation of the Company's ability to recover components of its investments in the emerging markets of Asia-Pacific.

- During 1996, the Company included in non-recurring charges a provision of $15.0 million for the potential settlement of certain litigation.

- During 1996, the Company included in other expense a charge of $35.0 million for a contribution to the Kellogg's Corporate Citizenship Fund, which is expected to satisfy the charitable-giving plans of this private trust through the year 2000.

The Company's streamlining initiatives will continue throughout 1999. The aforementioned overhead activity analysis will be extended to Europe and Latin America during the first half of 1999. Management believes these initiatives will result in the elimination of several hundred employee positions, requiring separation benefit costs to be incurred. Since the number of employees affected, their job functions, and their locations have not yet been identified, the costs that may result are not yet known. The combination of this Europe and Latin America overhead activity analysis and other ongoing cost-reduction programs is expected to result in more than $50 million in incremental savings in 1999.

The foregoing discussion of streamlining initiatives contains forward-looking statements regarding headcount reductions, cash requirements, and realizable savings. Actual amounts may vary depending on the final determination of important factors, such as identification of specific employees to be separated from pre-determined pools, actual amounts of asset removal and relocation costs, dates of asset disposal and costs to maintain assets up to the date of disposal, proceeds from asset disposals, final negotiation of third party contract buy-outs, and other items.

New accounting pronouncements

In March 1998, the Accounting Standards Executive Committee of the American Institute of Certified Public Accountants (AcSEC) issued Statement of Position (SOP) 98-1 "Accounting for the Costs of Computer Software Developed or Obtained for Internal Use." SOP 98-1 provides guidance on the classification of software project costs between expense and capital. During April 1998, AcSEC also issued SOP 98-5 "Reporting on Costs of Start-up Activities." SOP 98-5 prescribes that the costs of opening a new facility, commencing business in a new market, or similar start-up activities must be expensed as incurred. Both of these pronouncements are effective for fiscal years beginning after December 15, 1998. SOP 98-1 is to be applied on a prospective basis to costs incurred on or after the date of adoption. The initial application of SOP 98-5 is to be reported as a cumulative effect of a change in accounting principle, if material. Management intends to adopt SOP 98-1 and SOP 98-5 effective January 1, 1999, and does not expect the impact of adoption to have a significant impact on the Company's financial results.

In June 1998, the Financial Accounting Standards Board (FASB) issued Statement of Financial Accounting Standards (SFAS) #133 "Accounting for Derivative Instruments and Hedging Activities." This Statement establishes accounting and reporting standards for derivative instruments, requiring recognition of the fair value of all derivatives as assets or liabilities on the balance sheet. SFAS #133 is effective for fiscal years beginning after June 15, 1999. Management intends to adopt the provisions of SFAS #133 effective January 1, 2000, and does not expect the impact of adoption to have a significant impact on the Company's financial results.

On November 20, 1997, the Emerging Issues Task Force (EITF) of the FASB reached a consensus in EITF Issue 97-13 that the costs of business process reengineering activities are to be expensed as incurred. This consensus also applies to business process reengineering activities that are part of an information technology project. Beginning in 1996, the Company has undertaken an Enterprise Business Applications (EBA) initiative that combines design and installation of business processes and software packages to achieve global best practices. Under the EBA initiative, the Company had capitalized certain external costs associated with business process reengineering activities as part of the software asset. EITF Issue 97-13 prescribes that previously capitalized business process reengineering costs should be expensed and reported as a cumulative effect of a change in accounting principle. Accordingly, for the fourth quarter of 1997, the Company reported a charge of $18.0 million (net of tax benefit of $7.7 million) or $.04 per share for write-off of business process reengineering costs. Such costs were expensed as incurred during 1998 and the fourth quarter of 1997 and were insignificant.

Year 2000

The Company established a global program in 1997 to address the millennium date change issue (the inability of certain computer software, hardware, and other equipment with embedded computer chips to properly process two-digit year-date codes after 1999). The program is structured to address all date-related risks to the Company's business in four major categories: information technology systems, embedded technology systems, suppliers, and customers.

In the information technology and embedded systems categories, the inventories and detailed assessments are complete, remediation is 70% complete, and testing is 50% complete. Remediation and testing are on schedule with planned completion by June 30, 1999, for business critical and important systems.

The Company is spending approximately $70 million during 1998 and 1999 to become Year 2000 compliant. This amount includes the costs of activities described above, as well as costs to replace non-compliant systems for which replacement was accelerated to meet Year 2000 requirements. On a global basis, spending through December 31, 1998, is consistent with the overall percentage of program completion of approximately 70%. These amounts do not include the effect of other planned system initiatives that will contribute to the Year 2000 compliance effort. Management believes that to the extent these other planned system initiatives impact the Year 2000 project, they will be completed as scheduled by mid-1999.

The Company is continuing a contingency planning process started in 1998 designed to mitigate business risks due to unexpected date-related issues within any of the Year 2000 program categories across all key business units worldwide. The testing results for information technology and embedded systems are being coupled with risk assessments of the Company's suppliers, customers, and other internal initiatives, and incorporated into this contingency planning process. These plans are expected to be defined in each of the Company's four operating segments of North America, Europe, Asia-Pacific, and Latin America by April of 1999, for execution in preparation for the millennium transition.

While management believes that the estimated cost of becoming Year 2000 compliant is not significant to the Company's financial results, failure to complete all the work in a timely manner could result in material financial risk. While management expects all planned work to be completed, there can be no guarantee that all systems will be in compliance by the Year 2000, that the systems of other companies and government agencies on which the Company relies will be converted in a timely manner, or that contingency planning will be able to fully address all potential interruptions. Therefore, date-related issues could cause delays in the Company's ability to produce or ship its products, process transactions, or otherwise conduct business in any of its markets.

Euro conversion

On January 1, 1999, eleven European countries (Germany, France, Spain, Italy, Ireland, Portugal, Finland, Luxembourg, Belgium, Austria, and the Netherlands) implemented a single currency zone, the Economic and Monetary Union (EMU). The new currency, the Euro, has become the official currency of the participating countries. Those countries financial markets and banking systems are quoting financial and treasury data in Euros from January 1, 1999.

The Euro will exist alongside the old national currencies during a transition period from January 1, 1999, to January 1, 2002. During this period, entities within participating countries must complete changes which enable them to transact in the Euro. National currencies will be withdrawn no later than July 1, 2002. This transition to the Euro currency will involve changing budgetary, accounting, pricing, costing, and fiscal systems in companies and public administrations, as well as the simultaneous handling of parallel currencies and conversion of legacy data. During the first quarter of 1999, the Euro currency has demonstrated stability. However, this early stability needs to be observed over a longer period before conclusions can be drawn on the currency's long-term viability.

In early 1998, management formed a task force to monitor EMU developments, evaluate the impact of the Euro conversion on the Company's operations, and develop and execute action plans, as necessary. The task force has completed a full EMU impact assessment identifying company-wide, cross-functional effects of the Euro. Required business strategy, system, and process changes within the Company's European region are underway with certain markets already Euro compliant. Many of these changes will be made in conjunction with other significant technology initiatives currently under way, and will be completed in accordance with the Company's timetable for transacting with its suppliers and customers in the Euro. Results of task force assessments indicate that most suppliers and customers desire to initiate Euro transactions during 2000 and 2001.

Management expects to complete financial, operational, and manufacturing system conversions during 2001. Although Management currently believes the Company will be able to accommodate any required changes in its operations, there can be no assurance that the Company, its customers, suppliers, financial service providers, or government agencies will meet all of the Euro currency requirements on a timely basis. Such failure to complete the necessary work could result in material financial risk.

1999 outlook

Management is not aware of any adverse trends that would materially affect the Company's strong financial position. Should suitable investment opportunities or working capital needs arise that would require additional financing, management believes that the Company's strong credit rating, balance sheet, and earnings history provide a base for obtaining additional financial resources at competitive rates and terms. Based on the expectation of cereal volume growth, and strong results from product innovation and the continued global roll-out of convenience foods, management believes the Company is well-positioned to deliver sales and earnings growth for the full year 1999. The Company will continue to identify and pursue streamlining and productivity initiatives to optimize its cost structure.

The Company is currently reviewing strategies related to the Lender's Bagels business, given its performance since acquisition. The Company has evaluated the recoverability of Lender's long-lived assets as of December 31, 1998, and although this evaluation has not resulted in the recognition of an impairment loss, management expects to update its assessment during 1999.

Additional expectations for 1999 include a gross profit margin of 51-52%, an SGA% of 36-37%, an effective income tax rate of 36-37%, and capital spending of approximately $270 million.

The foregoing projections concerning impact of future borrowing costs, accounting changes, volume growth, profitability, capital spending, and common stock repurchase activity are forward-looking statements that involve risks and uncertainties. Actual results may differ materially due to the impact of competitive conditions, marketing spending and/or incremental pricing actions on actual volumes and product mix; the levels of spending on system initiatives, properties, business opportunities, continued streamlining initiatives, and other general and administrative costs; raw material price and labor cost fluctuations; foreign currency exchange rate fluctuations; changes in statutory tax law; interest rates available on short-term financing; the impact of stock market conditions on common stock repurchase activity; and other items.

FINANCIAL STATEMENTS AND ACCOMPANYING NOTES

The standard set of financial statements consists of: (1) a comparative income statement (statement of earnings) for 3 years, (2) a comparative balance sheet for 2 years, (3) a comparative statement of cash flows for 3 years, (4) a statement of retained earnings (or stockholders' equity) for 3 years, and (5) a set of accompanying notes that are considered an integral part of the financial statements. The auditor's report, unless stated otherwise, covers the financial statements and the accompanying notes. The financial statements and accompanying notes plus some supplementary data for Kellogg Company appear on the following pages.

Kellogg Company and Subsidiaries

Consolidated Statement of Earnings

Year ended December 31,

(millions, except per share data)	1998	1997	1996
Net sales	**$6,762.1**	$6,830.1	$6,676.6
Cost of goods sold	**3,282.6**	3,270.1	3,122.9
Selling and administrative expense	**2,513.9**	2,366.8	2,458.7
Non-recurring charges	**70.5**	184.1	136.1
Operating profit	**895.1**	1,009.1	958.9
Interest expense	**119.5**	108.3	65.6
Other income (expense), net	**6.9**	3.7	(33.4)
Earnings before income taxes and cumulative effect of accounting change	**782.5**	904.5	859.9
Income taxes	**279.9**	340.5	328.9
Earnings before cumulative effect of accounting change	**502.6**	564.0	531.0
Cumulative effect of accounting change (net of tax)	**—**	(18.0)	—
Net earnings	**$ 502.6**	$ 546.0	$ 531.0
Per share amounts (basic and diluted):			
Earnings before cumulative effect of accounting change	**$ 1.23**	$ 1.36	$ 1.25
Cumulative effect of accounting change	**—**	(.04)	—
Net earnings per share	**$ 1.23**	$ 1.32	$ 1.25

Refer to Notes to Consolidated Financial Statements.

Kellogg Company and Subsidiaries

Consolidated Statement of Shareholders' Equity

(millions)	Common stock shares	Common stock amount	Capital in excess of par value	Retained earnings	Treasury stock shares	Treasury stock amount	Accumulated other comprehensive income	Total shareholders' equity	Total comprehensive income
Balance, January 1, 1996	311.1	$ 77.8	$ 105.2	$ 3,963.0	94.4	($2,361.2)	($ 193.9)	$ 1,590.9	
Common stock repurchases					7.4	(535.7)		(535.7)	
Net earnings				531.0				531.0	$ 531.0
Dividends				(343.7)				(343.7)	
Other comprehensive income							27.6	27.6	27.6
Stock options exercised and other	.4	.1	18.7		.1	(6.5)		12.3	
Balance, December 31, 1996	**311.5**	**77.9**	**123.9**	**4,150.3**	**101.9**	**(2,903.4)**	**(166.3)**	**1,282.4**	**$558.6**
Common stock repurchases (pre-split)					3.9	(290.9)		(290.9)	
Stock options exercised and other (pre-split)	.6	.1	31.9		—	(3.9)		28.1	
Retirement of treasury stock	(105.3)	(26.3)	(55.8)	(3,095.8)	(105.3)	3,177.9		—	
Two-for-one stock split	206.8	51.7	(51.7)		.5	—		—	
Common stock repurchases (post-split)					3.1	(135.1)		(135.1)	
Net earnings				546.0				546.0	$ 546.0
Dividends				(360.1)				(360.1)	
Other comprehensive income							(115.6)	(115.6)	(115.6)
Stock options exercised and other (post-split)	1.2	.3	44.3		—	(1.9)		42.7	
Balance, December 31, 1997	**414.8**	**103.7**	**92.6**	**1,240.4**	**4.1**	**(157.3)**	**(281.9)**	**997.5**	**$430.4**
Common stock repurchases					6.3	(239.7)		(239.7)	
Net earnings				502.6				502.6	$ 502.6
Dividends				(375.3)				(375.3)	
Other comprehensive income							(10.5)	(10.5)	(10.5)
Stock options exercised and other	.5	.1	12.4		(.1)	2.7		15.2	
Balance, December 31, 1998	**415.3**	**$103.8**	**$105.0**	**$1,367.7**	**10.3**	**($ 394.3)**	**($292.4)**	**$ 889.8**	**$492.1**

Refer to Notes to Consolidated Financial Statements.

Kellogg Company and Subsidiaries

Consolidated Balance Sheet

At December 31,

(millions, except share data)	1998	1997
Current assets		
Cash and cash equivalents	$ 136.4	$ 173.2
Accounts receivable, less allowances of $12.9 and $7.5	693.0	587.5
Inventories	451.4	434.3
Other current assets	215.7	272.7
Total current assets	1,496.5	1,467.7
Property, net	2,888.8	2,773.3
Other assets	666.2	636.6
Total assets	$5,051.5	$4,877.6
Current liabilities		
Current maturities of long-term debt	$ 1.1	$ 211.2
Notes payable	620.4	368.6
Accounts payable	386.9	328.0
Other current liabilities	710.1	749.5
Total current liabilities	1,718.5	1,657.3
Long-term debt	1,614.5	1,415.4
Other liabilities	828.7	807.4
Shareholders' equity		
Common stock, $.25 par value, 500,000,000 shares authorized Issued: 415,343,626 shares in 1998 and 414,823,142 in 1997	103.8	103.7
Capital in excess of par value	105.0	92.6
Retained earnings	1,367.7	1,240.4
Treasury stock, at cost: 10,346,524 shares in 1998 and 4,143,124 shares in 1997	(394.3)	(157.3)
Accumulated other comprehensive income	(292.4)	(281.9)
Total shareholders' equity	889.8	997.5
Total liabilities and shareholders' equity	$5,051.5	$4,877.6

Refer to Notes to Consolidated Financial Statements.

Kellogg Company and Subsidiaries

Consolidated Statement of Cash Flows

Year ended December 31,

(millions)	1998	1997	1996
Operating activities			
Net earnings	$ 502.6	$ 546.0	$ 531.0
Items in net earnings not requiring (providing) cash:			
Depreciation and amortization	278.1	287.3	251.5
Deferred income taxes	46.2	38.5	58.0
Non-recurring charges, net of cash paid	62.2	133.8	90.6
Other	21.7	9.5	14.5
Pension and other postretirement benefit contributions	(88.8)	(114.5)	(156.8)
Changes in operating assets and liabilities	(102.3)	(20.8)	(77.3)
Net cash provided by operating activities	719.7	879.8	711.5
Investing activities			
Additions to properties	(373.9)	(312.4)	(307.3)
Acquisitions of businesses	(27.8)	(25.4)	(505.2)
Property disposals	6.8	5.9	11.6
Other	(3.1)	2.6	14.1
Net cash used in investing activities	(398.0)	(329.3)	(786.8)
Financing activities			
Net issuances (reductions) of notes payable, with maturities less than or equal to 90 days	(152.9)	(374.7)	906.6
Issuances of notes payable, with maturities greater than 90 days	5.5	4.8	137.0
Reductions of notes payable, with maturities greater than 90 days	(.8)	(14.1)	(79.0)
Issuances of long-term debt	600.0	1,000.0	—
Reductions of long-term debt	(210.3)	(507.9)	(3.4)
Net issuances of common stock	15.2	70.7	12.2
Common stock repurchases	(239.7)	(426.0)	(535.7)
Cash dividends	(375.3)	(360.1)	(343.7)
Net cash provided by (used in) financing activities	(358.3)	(607.3)	94.0
Effect of exchange rate changes on cash	(.2)	(13.8)	3.2
Increase (decrease) in cash and cash equivalents	(36.8)	(70.6)	21.9
Cash and cash equivalents at beginning of year	173.2	243.8	221.9
Cash and cash equivalents at end of year	$ 136.4	$ 173.2	$ 243.8

Refer to Notes to Consolidated Financial Statements.

Notes to Consolidated Financial Statements
Kellogg Company and Subsidiaries

Note 1 Accounting policies

Consolidation
The consolidated financial statements include the accounts of Kellogg Company and its majority-owned subsidiaries. Intercompany balances and transactions are eliminated.

Certain amounts in the prior year financial statements have been reclassified to conform to the current year presentation.

Cash and cash equivalents
Highly liquid temporary investments with original maturities of less than three months are considered to be cash equivalents. The carrying amount approximates fair value.

Inventories
Inventories are valued at the lower of cost (principally average) or market.

Property
Fixed assets are recorded at cost and depreciated over estimated useful lives using straight-line methods for financial reporting and accelerated methods for tax reporting. Cost includes an amount of interest associated with significant capital projects.

Goodwill and other intangible assets
Intangible assets are amortized principally on a straight-line basis over the estimated periods benefited, generally 40 years for goodwill and periods ranging from 5 to 40 years for other intangible assets. The realizability of goodwill and other intangibles is evaluated periodically when events or circumstances indicate a possible inability to recover the carrying amount. Evaluation is based on various analyses, including cash flow and profitability projections.

Advertising
The costs of advertising are generally expensed as incurred.

Recently adopted pronouncements
In 1998, the Company adopted several statements issued by the Financial Accounting Standards Board (FASB). In June 1997, the FASB issued Statement of Financial Accounting Standards (SFAS) #130 "Reporting Comprehensive Income," which requires companies to disclose all items recognized under accounting standards as components of comprehensive income. In June 1997, the FASB issued SFAS #131 "Disclosures about Segments of an Enterprise and Related Information," which requires certain information to be reported about operating segments consistent with management's internal view of the Company. In February 1998, the FASB issued SFAS #132 "Employers' Disclosures about Pensions and Other Postretirement Benefits," which revises and standardizes disclosures for pension and other postretirement benefit plans.

On November 20, 1997, the Emerging Issues Task Force (EITF) of the FASB reached a consensus in EITF Issue 97-13 that the costs of business process reengineering activities are to be expensed as incurred. This consensus also applies to business process reengineering activities that are part of an information technology project. Beginning in 1996, the Company has undertaken an Enterprise Business Applications (EBA) initiative that combines design and installation of business processes and software packages to achieve global best practices. Under the EBA initiative, the Company had capitalized certain external costs associated with business process reengineering activities as part of the software asset. EITF Issue 97-13 prescribes that previously capitalized business process reengineering costs should be expensed and reported as a cumulative effect of a change in accounting principle. Accordingly, for the fourth quarter of 1997, the Company reported a charge of $18.0 million (net of tax benefit of $7.7 million) or $.04 per share for write-off of business process reengineering costs. Such costs were expensed as incurred during 1998 and the fourth quarter of 1997 and were insignificant.

Recently issued pronouncements
In March 1998, the Accounting Standards Executive Committee of the American Institute of Certified Public Accountants (AcSEC) issued Statement of Position (SOP) 98-1 "Accounting for the Costs of Computer Software Developed or Obtained for Internal Use." SOP 98-1 provides guidance on the classification of software project costs between expense and capital. During April 1998, AcSEC also issued SOP 98-5 "Reporting on Costs of Start-up Activities." SOP 98-5 prescribes that the costs of opening a new facility, commencing business in a new market, or similar start-up activities must be expensed as incurred. Both of these pronouncements are effective for fiscal years beginning after December 15, 1998. SOP 98-1 is to be applied on a prospective basis to costs incurred on or after the date of adoption. The initial application of SOP 98-5 is to be reported as a cumulative effect of a change in accounting principle, if material. Management intends to adopt SOP 98-1 and SOP 98-5 effective January 1, 1999.

In June 1998, the FASB issued SFAS #133 "Accounting for Derivative Instruments and Hedging Activities." This Statement establishes accounting and reporting standards for derivative instruments, requiring recognition of the fair value of all derivatives as assets or liabilities on the balance sheet. SFAS #133 is effective for fiscal years beginning after June 15, 1999. Management intends to adopt the provisions of SFAS #133 effective January 1, 2000.

The impact of adoption of these pronouncements on the Company's financial results is not expected to be significant.

Common stock split
On August 1, 1997, the Company's Board of Directors approved a 2-for-1 stock split to shareholders of record at the close of business August 8, 1997, effective August 22, 1997, and also authorized retirement of 105.3 million common shares (pre-split) held in treasury. All per share and shares outstanding data in the Consolidated Statement of Earnings and Notes to Consolidated Financial Statements have been retroactively restated to reflect the stock split.

Stock compensation
The Company follows Accounting Principles Board Opinion (APB) #25, "Accounting for Stock Issued to Employees," in accounting for its employee stock options and other stock-based compensation. Under APB #25, because the exercise price of the Company's employee stock options equals the market price of the underlying stock on the date of the grant, no compensation expense is recognized. As permitted, the Company has elected to adopt the disclosure provisions only of SFAS #123, "Accounting for Stock-Based Compensation". (Refer to Note 7 for further information.)

Net earnings per share
Basic net earnings per share is determined by dividing net earnings by the weighted average number of common shares outstanding during the period. Weighted average shares outstanding, in millions, were 407.8, 414.1, and 424.9 for 1998, 1997, and 1996, respectively. Diluted net earnings per share is similarly determined except that the denominator is increased to include the number of additional common shares that would have been outstanding if all dilutive potential common shares had been issued. Dilutive potential common shares are principally comprised of employee stock options issued by the Company and had an insignificant impact on the computation of diluted net earnings per share during the periods presented. Weighted average shares outstanding, in millions, for purposes of computing diluted net earnings per share were 408.6, 415.2, and 426.4 for 1998, 1997, and 1996, respectively.

Comprehensive income
Comprehensive income includes all changes in equity during a period except those resulting from investments by or distributions to shareholders. For the Company, comprehensive income for all periods presented consists solely of net earnings and foreign currency translation adjustments pursuant to SFAS #52, "Foreign Currency Translation," as follows:

(millions)	1998	1997	1996
Net earnings	$502.6	$546.0	$531.0
Other comprehensive income (loss):			
Foreign currency translation adjustments	(11.1)	(112.1)	26.6
Related tax effect	.6	(3.5)	1.0
	(10.5)	(115.6)	27.6
Total comprehensive income	$492.1	$430.4	$558.6

Use of estimates

The preparation of financial statements in conformity with generally accepted accounting principles requires management to make estimates and assumptions that affect the reported amounts of assets and liabilities and disclosure of contingent assets and liabilities at the date of the financial statements and the reported amounts of revenues and expenses during the reporting period. Actual results could differ from those estimates.

Note 2 Acquisition

On December 16, 1996, the Company purchased certain assets and liabilities of the Lender's Bagels business from Kraft Foods, Inc. for $466 million in cash, including related acquisition costs. The acquisition was accounted for as a purchase. The results of Lender's operations from the date of the acquisition to December 31, 1996, were not significant. The acquisition was initially financed through commercial paper borrowings that were replaced with long-term debt in January 1997. Intangible assets included in the allocation of purchase price consisted of goodwill and trademarks of $329 million and non-compete covenants of $20 million. The goodwill and trademarks are being amortized over 40 years and the non-compete covenants are being amortized over 5 years.

The unaudited pro forma combined historical results, as if the Lender's Bagels business had been acquired at the beginning of fiscal 1996, are estimated to be net sales of $6.87 billion, net earnings of $524.3 million, and net earnings per share of $1.23. The pro forma results are not necessarily indicative of what actually would have occurred if the acquisition had been completed as of the beginning of the fiscal period presented, nor are they necessarily indicative of future consolidated results.

Note 3 Non-recurring charges

Operating profit for 1998 includes non-recurring charges of $70.5 million ($46.3 million after tax or $.12 per share) for streamlining initiatives.

Operating profit for 1997 includes non-recurring charges of $184.1 million ($140.5 million after tax or $.34 per share), comprised of $161.1 million for streamlining initiatives and $23.0 million for asset impairment losses.

Operating profit for 1996 includes non-recurring charges of $136.1 million ($97.8 million after tax or $.23 per share), comprised of $121.1 million for streamlining initiatives and $15.0 million for potential settlement of certain litigation.

Streamlining initiatives

From 1995 to the present, management has commenced major productivity and operational streamlining initiatives in an effort to optimize the Company's cost structure. The incremental costs of these programs have been reported throughout 1995-1998 as non-recurring charges.

The 1998 streamlining charges relate primarily to an overhead activity analysis that resulted in the elimination of approximately 550 employees and 240 contractors from the Company's headquarters and North American operations through a combination of involuntary early retirement and severance programs. The charges consist mainly of employee retirement and separation benefits, outplacement services, associated consulting and other related costs. Cash outlays for the 1998 charges during 1998 were $8 million, with the remainder to be spent during 1999. Total cash outlays during 1998 for all streamlining initiatives were approximately $47 million.

The 1997 charges for streamlining initiatives relate principally to management's plan to optimize the Company's pan-European operations, as well as ongoing productivity programs in the United States and Australia. A major component of the pan-European initiatives was the late-1997 closing of plants and separation of employees in Riga, Latvia; Svendborg, Denmark; and Verola, Italy. Approximately 50% of the total 1997 streamlining charges consist of manufacturing asset write-downs, with the balance comprised of current and anticipated cash outlays for employee separation benefits, equipment removal, production redeployment, associated management consulting, and similar costs. Total cash outlays during 1997 for streamlining initiatives were approximately $85 million.

The 1996 charges for streamlining initiatives result from management's actions to consolidate and reorganize operations in the United States, Europe, and other international locations. Cash outlays for streamlining initiatives were approximately $120 million in 1996. All streamlining programs commenced since 1995, including

the aforementioned 1998 initiatives, are expected to result in the elimination of approximately 3,500 employee positions by the end of 1999, with approximately 95% of this reduction already achieved.

The components of the streamlining charges, as well as reserve balances remaining at December 31, 1998, 1997, and 1996, were:

(millions)	Employee retirement & severance benefits (a)	Asset write-offs	Asset removal	Other costs	Total
Remaining reserve at December 31, 1995	$57.5	$ —	$36.5	$ —	$ 94.0
1996 streamlining charges (b)	31.4	37.5	13.5	38.7	121.1
Amounts utilized during 1996	(65.0)	(37.5)	(19.6)	(38.7)	(160.8)
Remaining reserve at December 31, 1996	23.9	—	30.4	—	54.3
1997 streamlining charges	22.4	78.1	19.3	41.3	161.1
Amounts utilized during 1997	(22.7)	(78.1)	(21.4)	(41.3)	(163.5)
Remaining reserve at December 31, 1997	23.6	—	28.3	—	51.9
1998 streamlining charges	59.8	5.5	3.0	2.2	70.5
Amounts utilized during 1998	(43.8)	(5.5)	(19.4)	(2.2)	(70.9)
Remaining reserve at December 31, 1998	$39.6	$ —	$11.9	$ —	$ 51.5

(a) Includes approximately $5 and $18 of pension and postretirement health care curtailment losses and special termination benefits recognized in 1996 and 1998, respectively. (Refer to Notes 8 and 9.)

(b) Includes $23 of reversals of prior-year reserves due to lower than expected employee severance payments and asset removal costs, and other favorable factors.

Other

In addition to the non-recurring charges reported for streamlining initiatives, the Company incurred charges for the following unusual items:

- During 1997, asset impairment losses of $23.0 million, which resulted from evaluation of the Company's ability to recover components of its investments in the emerging markets of Asia-Pacific.

- During 1996, a provision of $15.0 million for the potential settlement of certain litigation.

1999 events

The Company's streamlining initiatives will continue throughout 1999. The aforementioned overhead activity analysis will be extended to Europe and Latin America during the first half of 1999. Management believes these initiatives will result in the elimination of several hundred employee positions, requiring separation benefit costs to be incurred. Since the number of employees affected, their job functions, and their locations have not yet been identified, the costs that may result are not yet known.

Note 4 Other income and expense

Other income and expense includes non-operating items such as interest income, foreign exchange gains and losses, and charitable donations.

Other expense for 1996 includes a charge of $35.0 million ($22.3 million after tax or $.05 per share) for a contribution to the Kellogg's Corporate Citizenship Fund private trust established for charitable donations. This contribution is expected to satisfy the charitable-giving plans of this trust through the year 2000.

Note 5 Leases

Operating leases are generally for equipment and warehouse space. Rent expense on all operating leases was $36.5 million in 1998, $38.6 million in 1997, and $37 million in 1996. At December 31, 1998, future minimum annual rental commitments under non-cancelable operating leases totaled $62 million consisting of (in millions) 1999-$16; 2000-$12; 2001-$9; 2002-$8; 2003-$6; 2004 and beyond-$11.

Note 6 Debt

Notes payable consist of commercial paper borrowings in the United States at the highest credit rating available, borrowings against a revolving credit agreement in Europe and, to a lesser extent, bank loans of foreign subsidiaries at competitive market rates. U.S. borrowings at December 31, 1998, were $423.3 million with an effective interest rate of 5.2%. U.S. borrowings at December 31, 1997 (including $400 million classified in long-term debt, as discussed in (d) below), were $744.2 million with an effective interest rate of 5.7%. Associated with these borrowings, during September 1997, the Company purchased a $225 million notional, four-year fixed interest rate cap. Under the terms of the cap, if the Federal Reserve AA composite rate on 30-day commercial paper increases to 6.33%, the Company will pay this fixed rate on $225 million of its commercial paper borrowings. If the rate increases to 7.68% or above, the cap will expire. As of year-end 1998, the rate was 4.90%.

In December 1998, the Company entered into a $200 million, three-year revolving credit agreement with several international banks. At December 31, 1998, outstanding borrowings under this agreement were $148.5 million with an effective interest rate of 5.5%. Additionally, the Company has entered into financing arrangements which provide for the sale of future foreign currency revenues. As of December 31, 1998, the Company had committed to borrowings during 1999 in the cumulative principle amount of approximately $280 million. No borrowings were outstanding under these arrangements at December 31, 1998 or 1997. At December 31, 1998, the Company had $715.9 million of total short-term lines of credit, of which $543.6 million were unused and available for borrowing on an unsecured basis.

Long-term debt at year-end consisted of:

(millions)	1998	1997
(a) Seven-Year Notes due 2005	$ 200.0	$ —
(b) Seven-Year Notes due 2004	500.0	500.0
(c) Four-Year Notes due 2001	500.0	500.0
(d) Three-Year Notes due 2001	400.0	—
(e) Five-Year Notes due 1998	—	200.0
(d) Commercial paper	—	400.0
Other	15.6	26.6
	1,615.6	1,626.6
Less current maturities	(1.1)	(211.2)
Balance, December 31	$1,614.5	$1,415.4

(a) In October 1998, the Company issued $200 of seven-year 4.875% fixed rate U.S. Dollar Notes to replace maturing long-term debt. The Company entered into a series of interest rate hedges throughout 1998 to effectively fix the interest rate prior to issuance. The effect of the hedges, when combined with original issue discounts, resulted in an effective interest rate on this debt of 6.07%.

(b) In January 1997, the Company issued $500 of seven-year 6.625% fixed rate Euro Dollar Notes. In conjunction with this issuance, the Company settled $500 notional amount of interest rate forward swap agreements, which effectively fixed the interest rate on the debt at 6.354%. Associated with this debt, during September 1997, the Company entered into a $225 notional, 4½-year fixed-to-floating interest rate swap, indexed to the three-month London Interbank Offered Rate (LIBOR). Under the terms of this swap, if three-month LIBOR decreases to 4.71% or below, the swap will expire. At year-end 1998, three-month LIBOR was 5.07%.

(c) In August 1997, the Company issued $500 of four-year 6.125% Euro Dollar Notes. In conjunction with this issuance, the Company settled $400 notional amount of interest rate forward swap agreements which effectively fixed the interest rate on the debt at 6.4%. Associated with this debt, during September 1997, the Company entered into a $200 notional, four-year fixed-to-floating interest rate swap, indexed to three-month LIBOR.

(d) At December 31, 1997, $400 of the Company's commercial paper was classified as long-term, based on the Company's intent and ability to refinance as evidenced by an issuance of $400 of three-year 5.75% fixed rate U.S. Dollar Notes on February 4, 1998. These Notes were issued under an existing "shelf registration" with the Securities and Exchange Commission, and provide an option to holders to extend the obligation for an additional four years at a predetermined interest rate of 5.63% plus the Company's then-current credit spread. As a result of this option, the effective interest rate on the three-year Notes is 5.23%. Concurrent with this issuance, the Company entered into a $400 notional, three-year fixed-to-floating interest rate swap, indexed to the Federal Reserve AA Composite Rate on 30-day commercial paper.

(e) In October 1993, the Company issued $200 of five-year 6.25% Euro Canadian Dollar Notes which were swapped into 4.629% fixed rate U.S. Dollar obligations for the duration of the five-year term.

Scheduled principal repayments on long-term debt are (in millions): 1999-$1; 2000-$6; 2001-$900; 2002-$5; 2003-$2; 2004 and beyond-$702.

Interest paid was (in millions): 1998-$113; 1997-$85; 1996-$67. Interest expense capitalized as part of the construction cost of fixed assets was (in millions): 1998-$7.8; 1997-$9.6; 1996-$3.8.

Note 7 Stock options

The Key Employee Long-Term Incentive Plan provides for benefits to be awarded to executive-level employees in the form of stock options, performance shares, performance units, incentive stock options, restricted stock grants, and other stock-based awards. Options granted under this plan generally vest over two years and, prior to September 1997, vested at the date of grant. The Bonus Replacement Stock Option Plan allows certain key executives to receive stock options that generally vest immediately in lieu of part or all of their respective bonus. Options granted under this plan are issued from the Key Employee Long-Term Incentive Plan. The Kellogg Employee Stock Ownership Plan is designed to offer stock and other incentive awards based on Company performance to employees who are not eligible to participate in the Key Employee Long-Term Incentive Plan. Options awarded under the Kellogg Employee Stock Ownership Plan are subject to graded vesting over a five-year period. Under these plans (the "stock option plans"), options are granted with exercise prices equal to the fair market value of the Company's common stock at the time of grant, exercisable for a 10-year period following the date of grant, subject to vesting rules.

The Key Employee Long-Term Incentive Plan contains an accelerated ownership feature ("AOF"). An AOF option is granted when Company stock is surrendered to pay the exercise price of a stock option. The holder of the option is granted an AOF option for the number of shares surrendered. For all AOF options, the original expiration date is not changed but the options vest immediately.

As permitted by SFAS #123 "Accounting for Stock-Based Compensation," the Company has elected to account for the stock option plans under APB #25 "Accounting for Stock Issued to Employees." Accordingly, no compensation cost has been recognized for these plans.

For purposes of pro forma disclosures, the estimated fair value of the options is amortized to expense over the options' vesting period. Had compensation cost for the stock option plans been determined based on the fair value at the grant date consistent with SFAS #123, the Company's net earnings and earnings per share are estimated as follows:

(millions, except per share data)	1998	1997	1996
Net earnings			
As reported	$502.6	$546.0	$531.0
Pro forma	$484.4	$520.8	$514.1
Net earnings per share (basic and diluted)			
As reported	$1.23	$1.32	$1.25
Pro forma	$1.19	$1.26	$1.21

The fair value of each option grant was estimated at the date of grant using the Black-Scholes option pricing model with the following weighted average assumptions:

	1998	1997	1996
Risk-free interest rate	5.56%	6.31%	6.16%
Dividend yield	2.00%	1.97%	2.30%
Volatility	21.28%	19.83%	19.16%
Average expected term (years)	3.47	3.52	3.34
Fair value of options granted	$8.45	$7.48	$6.32

Under the Key Employee Long-Term Incentive Plan, options for 9.8 million and 13.2 million shares were available for grant at December 31, 1998 and 1997, respectively. Under the Kellogg Employee Stock Ownership Plan, options for 6.0 million and 6.9 million shares were available for grant at December 31, 1998 and 1997, respectively. Transactions under these plans were:

(millions, except per share data)	1990	1997	1006
Under option, January 1	12.4	11.2	8.4
Granted	6.8	6.0	5.2
Exercised	(1.7)	(4.5)	(2.1)
Cancelled	(1.1)	(.3)	(.3)
Under option, December 31	16.4	12.4	11.2
Exercisable, December 31	8.7	8.1	7.6
Shares available, December 31, for options that may be granted	15.8	20.1	23.8
	Average prices per share		
Under option, January 1	$35	$33	$30
Granted	43	36	38
Exercised	34	33	30
Cancelled	33	34	30
Under option, December 31	$38	$35	$33
Exercisable, December 31	$36	$36	$35

Employee stock options outstanding and exercisable under these plans as of December 31, 1998, were:

(millions, except per share data)	Outstanding			Exercisable	
Range of exercise prices	Number of Options	Weighted average exercise price	Weighted average remaining contractual life (yrs.)	Number of Options	Weighted average exercise price
$15 – 34	5.1	$31	5.0	3.5	$30
35 – 39	3.9	38	4.9	2.6	38
40 – 44	6.6	44	1.8	1.8	43
45 – 50	.8	48	5.7	.8	48
	16.4			8.7	

Note 8 Pension benefits

The Company has a number of U.S. and foreign pension plans to provide retirement benefits for its employees. Benefits for salaried employees are generally based on salary and years of service, while union employee benefits are generally a negotiated amount for each year of service. Plan funding strategies are influenced by tax regulations. Plan assets consist primarily of equity securities with smaller holdings of bonds, real estate, and other investments. Investment in Company common stock represented 2.4% and 4.2% of consolidated plan assets at December 31, 1998 and 1997, respectively.

The components of pension expense were:

(millions)	1998	1997	1996
Service cost	$ 41.3	$ 29.9	$27.6
Interest cost	81.3	79.6	72.8
Expected return on plan assets	(113.9)	(104.7)	(95.0)
Amortization of unrecognized transition obligation	.7	(.3)	(.5)
Amortization of unrecognized prior service cost	7.5	7.9	7.2
Recognized losses	10.0	4.7	5.2
Curtailment loss and special termination benefits	17.4	—	4.0
Pension expense – Company plans	44.3	17.1	21.3
Pension expense – multiemployer plans	1.2	1.9	2.0
Total pension expense	$ 45.5	$ 19.0	$23.3

The worldwide weighted average actuarial assumptions were:

	1998	1997	1996
Discount rate	6.7%	7.6%	7.9%
Long-term rate of compensation increase	4.9%	4.9%	5.2%
Long-term rate of return on plan assets	10.5%	10.5%	10.5%

The aggregate change in projected benefit obligation, change in plan assets, and funded status were:

(millions)	1998	1997
Change in projected benefit obligation		
Projected benefit obligation at beginning of year	$1,133.4	$1,036.3
Service cost	41.3	29.9
Interest cost	81.3	79.6
Plan participants' contributions	1.4	—
Amendments	9.6	1.3
Actuarial loss	133.6	41.1
Benefits paid	(70.5)	(62.7)
Other	1.1	7.9
Projected benefit obligation at end of year	$1,331.2	$1,133.4
Change in plan assets		
Fair value of plan assets at beginning of year	$1,209.0	$1,048.7
Actual return on plan assets	132.6	210.4
Employer contribution	54.7	38.8
Plan participants' contributions	1.4	—
Benefits paid	(70.5)	(62.7)
Other	(8.9)	(26.2)
Fair value of plan assets at end of year	$1,318.3	$1,209.0
Funded status	($ 12.9)	$ 75.6
Unrecognized net loss	111.5	7.4
Unrecognized transition amount	4.2	4.4
Unrecognized prior service cost	36.2	47.2
Prepaid pension	$ 139.0	$ 134.6
Amounts recognized in the statement of financial position consist of		
Prepaid benefit cost	$ 213.6	$ 185.4
Accrued benefit liability	(88.4)	(61.5)
Intangible asset	13.8	10.7
Net amount recognized	$ 139.0	$ 134.6

The projected benefit obligation, accumulated benefit obligation, and fair value of plan assets for pension plans with accumulated benefit obligations in excess of plan assets were, in millions, $104.6, $84.5, and $8.3, respectively, as of December 31, 1998, and $87.1, $69.1, and $15.4, respectively, as of December 31, 1997.

All gains and losses, other than curtailment losses and special termination benefits, are recognized over the average remaining service period of active plan participants. Curtailment losses and special termination benefits recognized in 1998 and 1996 relate to operational workforce reduction initiatives undertaken during these years and are recorded as a component of non-recurring charges. (Refer to Note 3 for further information.)

Certain of the Company's subsidiaries sponsor 401(k) or similar savings plans for active employees. Expense related to these plans was (in millions): 1998-$16; 1997-$16; 1996-$17.

Note 9 Nonpension postretirement benefits

Certain of the Company's North American subsidiaries provide health care and other benefits to substantially all retired employees, their covered dependents, and beneficiaries. Generally, employees are eligible for these benefits when one of the following service/age requirements is met: 30 years and any age; 20 years and age 55; 5 years and age 62. Plan assets consist primarily of equity securities with smaller holdings of bonds.

Components of postretirement benefit expense were:

(millions)	1998	1997	1996
Service cost	$ 9.1	$ 9.6	$11.2
Interest cost	36.8	37.2	40.2
Expected return on plan assets	(15.0)	(13.3)	—
Amortization of unrecognized prior service cost	(.5)	(.5)	.3
Recognized gains	(5.3)	(6.3)	—
Curtailment loss and special termination benefits	1.0	—	1.0
Postretirement benefit expense	$26.1	$26.7	$52.7

The worldwide weighted average actuarial assumptions were:

	1998	1997	1996
Discount rate	7.0%	7.25%	7.75%
Long-term rate of return on plan assets	10.5%	10.5%	n/a

The aggregate change in accumulated postretirement benefit obligation, change in plan assets, and funded status were:

(millions)	1998	1997
Change in accumulated benefit obligation		
Accumulated benefit obligation at beginning of year	$523.3	$494.1
Service cost	9.1	9.6
Interest cost	36.8	37.2
Actuarial loss	7.6	11.9
Amendments	2.2	—
Benefits paid	(29.5)	(29.0)
Other	(.7)	(.5)
Accumulated benefit obligation at end of year	$548.8	$523.3
Change in plan assets		
Fair value of plan assets at beginning of year	$150.7	$ 81.0
Actual return on plan assets	22.1	23.0
Employer contribution	34.1	75.7
Benefits paid	(29.5)	(29.0)
Fair value of plan assets at end of year	$177.4	$150.7
Funded status	($371.4)	($372.6)
Unrecognized net gain	(80.9)	(86.5)
Unrecognized prior service cost	(6.2)	(8.1)
Accrued postretirement benefit cost	($458.5)	($467.2)
Amounts recognized in the statement of financial position consist of		
Accrued benefit liability	($458.5)	($467.2)

The assumed health care cost trend rate was 7.0% for 1998, decreasing gradually to 4.2% by the year 2003 and remaining at that level thereafter. These trend rates reflect the Company's prior experience and management's expectation that future rates will decline. A one percentage point change in assumed health care cost trend rates would have the following effects:

(millions)	One percentage point increase	One percentage point decrease
Effect on total of service and interest cost components	$6.5	($4.2)
Effect on postretirement benefit obligation	$65.4	($54.5)

All gains and losses, other than curtailment losses and special termination benefits, are recognized over the average remaining service period of active plan participants. Curtailment losses and special termination benefits recognized in 1998 and 1996 relate to operational workforce reduction initiatives undertaken during these years and are recorded as a component of non-recurring charges. (Refer to Note 3 for further information.) Since December 1996, the Company has contributed to a voluntary employee benefit association (VEBA) trust for funding of its nonpension postretirement benefit obligations.

Note 10 Income taxes

Earnings before income taxes and cumulative effect of accounting change, and the provision for U.S. federal, state, and foreign taxes on these earnings, were:

(millions)	1998	1997	1996
Earnings before income taxes and cumulative effect of accounting change			
United States	$564.0	$576.4	$516.7
Foreign	218.5	328.1	343.2
	$782.5	$904.5	$859.9
Income taxes			
Currently payable			
Federal	$128.7	$129.4	$130.6
State	17.8	29.6	21.9
Foreign	87.2	143.0	118.4
	233.7	302.0	270.9
Deferred			
Federal	30.6	50.2	45.7
State	1.7	4.0	11.4
Foreign	13.9	(15.7)	.9
	46.2	38.5	58.0
Total income taxes	$279.9	$340.5	$328.9

The difference between the U.S. federal statutory tax rate and the Company's effective rate was:

	1998	1997	1996
U.S. statutory rate	35.0%	35.0%	35.0%
Foreign rates varying from 35%	(2.0)	(1.6)	.7
State income taxes, net of federal benefit	2.4	2.4	2.5
Net change in valuation allowances	2.9	1.6	(.1)
Statutory rate changes, deferred tax impact	(.3)	(.5)	—
Other	(2.2)	.7	.1
Effective income tax rate	35.8%	37.6%	38.2%

The 1998 and 1997 increases in valuation allowances on deferred tax assets and corresponding impacts on the effective income tax rate, as presented above, primarily result from management's assessment of the Company's ability to utilize certain operating loss and tax credit carryforwards. Total tax benefits of carryforwards at year-end 1998 and 1997 were $55.1 million and $30.4 million, respectively, and principally expire after five years.

The deferred tax assets and liabilities included in the balance sheet at year-end were:

(millions)	Deferred tax assets 1998	1997	Deferred tax liabilities 1998	1997
Current:				
Promotion and advertising	$ 26.0	$ 65.0	$ 9.9	$ 10.5
Wages and payroll taxes	27.3	13.8	—	—
Health and postretirement benefits	18.1	15.7	3.8	2.4
State taxes	5.7	8.1	—	—
Operating loss and credit carryforwards	1.5	2.1	—	—
Other	27.9	24.2	15.4	12.3
	106.5	128.9	29.1	25.2
Less valuation allowance	(1.5)	(4.1)	—	—
	105.0	124.8	29.1	25.2
Noncurrent:				
Depreciation and asset disposals	15.7	18.8	347.4	326.0
Health and postretirement benefits	164.3	163.5	58.8	56.2
Capitalized interest	—	—	28.3	28.8
State taxes	—	—	1.9	2.6
Operating loss and credit carryforwards	53.6	28.3	—	—
Other	36.4	26.6	9.9	5.8
	270.0	237.2	446.3	419.4
Less valuation allowance	(67.1)	(41.8)	—	—
	202.9	195.4	446.3	419.4
Total deferred taxes	$307.9	$320.2	$475.4	$444.6

At December 31, 1998, foreign subsidiary earnings of $1.2 billion were considered permanently invested in those businesses. Accordingly, U.S. income taxes have not been provided on these earnings. Foreign withholding taxes of approximately $75 million would be payable upon remittance of these earnings. Subject to certain limitations, the withholding taxes would then be available for use as credits against the U.S. tax liability.

Cash paid for income taxes was (in millions): 1998-$211; 1997-$332; 1996-$281.

Note 11 Financial instruments and credit risk concentration

The fair values of the Company's financial instruments are based on carrying value in the case of short-term items, quoted market prices for derivatives and investments, and, in the case of long-term debt, incremental borrowing rates currently available on loans with similar terms and maturities. The carrying amounts of the Company's cash, cash equivalents, receivables, notes payable, and long-term debt approximate fair value.

The Company is exposed to certain market risks which exist as a part of its ongoing business operations and uses derivative financial and commodity instruments, where appropriate, to manage these risks. In general, instruments used as hedges must be effective at reducing the risk associated with the exposure being hedged and must be designated as a hedge at the inception of the contract. Deferred gains or losses related to any instrument 1) designated but ineffective as a hedge of existing assets, liabilities, or firm commitments, or 2) designated as a hedge of an anticipated transaction which is no longer likely to occur, are recognized immediately in the statement of earnings.

For all derivative financial and commodity instruments held by the Company, changes in fair values of these instruments and the resultant impact on the Company's cash flows and/or earnings would generally be offset by changes in value of underlying exposures. The impact on the Company's results and financial position of holding derivative financial and commodity instruments was insignificant during the periods presented.

Foreign exchange risk
The Company is exposed to fluctuations in foreign currency cash flows primarily related to third party purchases, intercompany product shipments, and intercompany loans. The Company is also exposed to fluctuations in the value of foreign currency investments in subsidiaries and cash flows related to repatriation of these investments. Additionally, the Company is exposed to volatility in the translation of foreign currency earnings to U.S. Dollars.

The Company assesses foreign currency risk based on transactional cash flows and enters into forward contracts and other commitments to sell foreign currency revenues, all of generally less than twelve months duration, to reduce fluctuations in net long or short currency positions. Foreign currency contracts are marked-to-market with net amounts due to or from counterparties recorded in accounts receivable or payable. For contracts hedging firm commitments, mark-to-market gains and losses are deferred and recognized as adjustments to the basis of the transaction. For contracts hedging subsidiary investments, mark-to-market gains and losses are recorded in the accumulated other comprehensive income component of shareholders' equity. For all other contracts, mark-to-market gains and losses are recognized currently in other income or expense. Commitments to sell future foreign currency revenues are accounted for as contingent borrowings.

The notional amounts of open forward contracts were $22.2 million and $143.2 million at December 31, 1998 and 1997, respectively. No borrowings were outstanding under commitments to sell foreign currency revenues at December 31, 1998 or 1997. Refer to Supplemental Financial Information on pages 33 and 34 for further information regarding these contracts.

Interest rate risk
The Company is exposed to interest rate volatility with regard to future issuances of fixed rate debt and existing issuances of variable rate debt. The Company uses interest rate caps, and currency and interest rate swaps, including forward swaps, to reduce interest rate volatility and funding costs associated with certain debt issues, and to achieve a desired proportion of variable versus fixed rate debt, based on current and projected market conditions.

Interest rate forward swaps are marked-to-market with net amounts due to or from counterparties recorded in interest receivable or payable. Mark-to-market gains and losses are deferred and recognized over the life of the debt issue as a component of interest expense. For other caps and swaps entered into concurrently with the debt issue, the interest or currency differential to be paid or received on the instrument is recognized in the statement of earnings as incurred, as a component of interest expense. If a position were to be terminated prior to maturity, the gain or loss realized upon termination would be deferred and amortized to interest expense over the remaining term of the underlying debt issue or would be recognized immediately if the underlying debt issue was settled prior to maturity.

The notional amounts of currency and interest rate swaps were $1.05 billion and $875.0 million at December 31, 1998 and 1997, respectively. Refer to Note 6 and Supplemental Financial Information on pages 33 and 34 for further information regarding these swaps.

Price risk
The Company is exposed to price fluctuations primarily as a result of anticipated purchases of raw and packaging materials. The Company uses the combination of long cash positions with vendors, and exchange-traded futures and option contracts to reduce price fluctuations in a desired percentage of forecasted purchases over a duration of generally less than one year. Commodity contracts are marked-to-market with net amounts due to or from brokers recorded in accounts receivable or payable. Mark-to-market gains and losses are deferred and recognized as adjustments to the basis of the underlying material purchase.

Credit risk concentration
The Company is exposed to credit loss in the event of nonperformance by counterparties on derivative financial and commodity contracts. This credit loss is limited to the cost of replacing these contracts at current market rates. Management believes that the probability of such loss is remote.

Financial instruments which potentially subject the Company to concentrations of credit risk are primarily cash, cash equivalents, and accounts receivable. The Company places its investments in highly rated financial institutions and investment grade short-term debt instruments, and limits the amount of credit exposure to any one entity. Concentrations of credit risk with respect to accounts receivable are limited due to the large number of customers, generally short payment terms, and their dispersion across geographic areas.

Note 12 Quarterly financial data (unaudited)

(millions, except per share data)	Net sales 1998	Net sales 1997	Gross profit 1998	Gross profit 1997
First	$1,642.9	$1,688.9	$ 861.1	$ 860.9
Second	1,713.5	1,719.7	893.9	908.9
Third	1,805.8	1,803.8	936.9	944.4
Fourth	1,599.9	1,617.7	787.6	845.8
	$6,762.1	$6,830.1	$3,479.5	$3,560.0

	Earnings before cumulative effect of accounting change (a) 1998	1997	Earnings per share before cumulative effect of accounting change (a)(b) 1998	1997
First	$170.7	$160.6	$.42	$.38
Second	143.2	163.6	.35	.39
Third	141.9	207.2	.35	.50
Fourth	46.8	32.6	.11	.08
	$502.6	$564.0		

	Net earnings (a) 1998	1997	Earnings per share (a)(b) 1998	1997
First	$170.7	$160.6	$.42	$.38
Second	143.2	163.6	.35	.39
Third	141.9	207.2	.35	.50
Fourth	46.8	14.6	.11	.04
	$502.6	$546.0		

(a) The quarterly results of 1998 and 1997 include the following non-recurring charges and cumulative effect of accounting change. (Refer to Notes 1 and 3 for further information.)

	Net earnings 1998	1997	Earnings per share 1998	1997
Non-recurring charges:				
Second	$ —	($8.0)	$ —	($.02)
Third	—	(6.6)	—	(.02)
Fourth	(46.3)	(125.9)	(.12)	(.31)
Earnings before cumulative effect of accounting change	(46.3)	(140.5)		
Cumulative effect of accounting change – Fourth	—	(18.0)	—	(.04)
Net earnings	($46.3)	($158.5)		

(b) Earnings per share presented represent both basic and diluted earnings per share.

The principal market for trading Kellogg shares is the New York Stock Exchange (NYSE). The shares are also traded on the Boston, Chicago, Cincinnati, Pacific, and Philadelphia Stock Exchanges. At year-end 1998, the closing price (on the NYSE) was $34 1/8 and there were 24,634 shareholders of record.

Dividends paid and the quarterly price ranges on the NYSE during the last two years were:

1998 – Quarter	Dividend	Stock Price High	Low
Fourth	$.235	$37.63	$32.19
Third	.235	39.19	29.56
Second	.225	43.50	37.69
First	.225	49.69	41.81
	$.920		
1997 – Quarter			
Fourth	$.225	$50.38	$40.00
Third	.225	50.38	42.00
Second	.210	43.44	32.00
First	.210	36.38	32.06
	$.870		

Note 13 Operating segments

The Company manufactures and markets ready-to-eat cereal and other grain-based convenience food products, including toaster pastries, frozen waffles, cereal bars, and bagels, throughout the world. Principal markets for these products include the United States and Great Britain. Operations are managed via four major geographic areas – North America, Europe, Asia-Pacific, and Latin America – which are the basis of the Company's reportable operating segment information disclosed below. The measurement of operating segment results is generally consistent with the presentation of the Consolidated Statement of Earnings and Balance Sheet. Intercompany transactions between reportable operating segments were insignificant in all periods presented.

(millions)	1998	1997	1996
Net sales			
North America	$4,175.9	$4,260.8	$4,086.3
Europe	1,698.5	1,702.0	1,749.6
Asia-Pacific	377.0	411.9	433.2
Latin America	510.7	455.4	407.5
Consolidated	$6,762.1	$6,830.1	$6,676.6
Operating profit excluding non-recurring charges			
North America	$ 831.6	$ 884.8	$ 762.3
Europe	211.4	305.8	305.1
Asia-Pacific	48.3	51.1	61.3
Latin America	107.2	111.8	94.2
Corporate and other	(232.9)	(160.3)	(127.9)
Consolidated (a)	$ 965.6	$1,193.2	$1,095.0
Depreciation and amortization			
North America	$ 152.1	$ 153.7	$ 135.1
Europe	54.6	59.6	59.9
Asia-Pacific	21.3	21.9	20.7
Latin America	14.2	12.5	10.2
Corporate and other	35.9	39.6	25.6
Consolidated	$ 278.1	$ 287.3	$ 251.5
Total assets			
North America	$2,430.8	$2,519.2	$2,574.0
Europe	1,336.0	1,154.5	1,254.1
Asia-Pacific	328.4	309.5	449.2
Latin America	380.9	361.4	285.6
Corporate and other	1,516.7	1,405.1	1,316.5
Elimination entries	(941.3)	(872.1)	(829.4)
Consolidated	$5,051.5	$4,877.6	$5,050.0
Additions to long-lived assets			
North America	$ 82.5	$ 166.5	$ 544.6
Europe	169.1	60.7	71.9
Asia-Pacific	40.3	24.3	34.7
Latin America	41.7	43.3	17.7
Corporate and other	98.5	94.9	138.3
Consolidated	$ 432.1	$ 389.7	$ 807.2

(a) Reconciliation to operating profit as reported:

	1998	1997	1996
Operating profit excluding non-recurring charges	$965.6	$1,193.2	$1,095.0
Non-recurring charges	(70.5)	(184.1)	(136.1)
Operating profit as reported	$895.1	$1,009.1	$ 958.9

Supplemental geographic information is provided below for revenues from external customers and long-lived assets:

(millions)	1998	1997	1996
Net sales			
United States	**$3,858.0**	$3,922.2	$3,733.7
Great Britain	**743.6**	719.0	673.8
Other foreign countries	**2,160.5**	2,188.9	2,269.1
Consolidated	**$6,762.1**	$6,830.1	$6,676.6
Long-lived assets			
United States	**$1,644.2**	$1,707.1	$1,720.0
Great Britain	**553.0**	452.4	463.2
Other foreign countries	**1,330.3**	1,225.2	1,304.3
Consolidated	**$3,527.5**	$3,384.7	$3,487.5

Supplemental product information is provided below for revenues from external customers:

(millions)	1998	1997	1996
Ready-to-eat cereal net sales	**$5,265.4**	$5,435.8	$5,543.8
Convenience foods net sales	**1,496.7**	1,394.3	1,132.8
Consolidated	**$6,762.1**	$6,830.1	$6,676.6

Note 14 Supplemental financial statement data

(millions)			
Consolidated Statement of Earnings	**1998**	1997	1996
Research and development expense	**$121.9**	$106.1	$84.3
Advertising expense	**$695.3**	$780.4	$778.9

Consolidated Statement of Cash Flows	**1998**	1997	1996
Accounts receivable	**($102.6)**	$ 5.1	$10.9
Inventories	**(15.0)**	(8.1)	(35.4)
Other current assets	**33.2**	(11.0)	(0.5)
Accounts payable	**58.9**	(8.7)	(41.0)
Other current liabilities	**(76.8)**	1.9	(11.3)
Changes in operating assets and liabilities	**($102.3)**	($20.8)	($77.3)

Consolidated Balance Sheet	**1998**	1997
Raw materials and supplies	**$ 133.3**	$ 135.0
Finished goods and materials in process	**318.1**	299.3
Inventories	**$ 451.4**	$ 434.3
Deferred income taxes	**$ 89.9**	$ 113.4
Prepaid advertising and promotion	**69.9**	95.2
Other	**55.9**	64.1
Other current assets	**$ 215.7**	$ 272.7
Land	**$ 49.3**	$ 49.0
Buildings	**1,247.9**	1,213.8
Machinery and equipment	**3,608.2**	3,434.7
Construction in progress	**341.4**	283.1
Accumulated depreciation	**(2,358.0)**	(2,207.3)
Property, net	**$2,888.8**	$2,773.3
Goodwill	**$ 185.5**	$ 194.3
Other intangibles	**194.0**	191.2
Other	**286.7**	251.1
Other assets	**$ 666.2**	$ 636.6
Accrued income taxes	**$ 69.4**	$ 30.5
Accrued salaries and wages	**100.7**	99.7
Accrued advertising and promotion	**243.4**	308.8
Other	**296.6**	310.5
Other current liabilities	**$ 710.1**	$ 749.5
Nonpension postretirement benefits	**$ 435.2**	$ 444.1
Deferred income taxes	**259.2**	237.7
Other	**134.3**	125.6
Other liabilities	**$ 828.7**	$ 807.4

Supplemental Financial Information (unaudited)

Quantitative & qualitative disclosures related to market-risk-sensitive instruments

The Company is exposed to certain market risks which exist as a part of its ongoing business operations and uses derivative financial and commodity instruments, where appropriate, to manage these risks. The Company, as a matter of policy, does not engage in trading or speculative transactions. Refer to Note 11 within Notes to Consolidated Financial Statements for further information on accounting policies related to derivative financial and commodity instruments.

Foreign exchange risk

The Company is exposed to fluctuations in foreign currency cash flows related to third party purchases, intercompany product shipments, and intercompany loans. The Company is also exposed to fluctuations in the value of foreign currency investments in subsidiaries and cash flows related to repatriation of these investments. Additionally, the Company is exposed to volatility in the translation of foreign currency earnings to U.S. Dollars. Primary exposures include the U.S. Dollar versus the British Pound, member currencies of the European Monetary Union, Australian Dollar, Canadian Dollar, and Mexican Peso, and in the case of inter-subsidiary transactions, the British Pound versus other European currencies. The Company assesses foreign currency risk based on transactional cash flows and enters into forward contracts and other commitments to sell foreign currency revenues, all of generally less than twelve months duration, to reduce fluctuations in net long or short currency positions. No borrowings were outstanding under commitments to sell foreign currency revenues at December 31, 1998 or 1997. As of December 31, 1998, the Company had committed to borrowings during 1999 in the cumulative principle amount of approximately $280 million.

The tables below summarize forward contracts held at year-end 1998 and 1997. All contracts are valued in U.S. Dollars using year-end exchange rates, are hedges of anticipated transactions (unless indicated otherwise), and mature within one year.

Contracts to sell foreign currency

Currency sold	Currency received	Notional value (millions)		Exchange rate (fc/1US$)		Fair value (millions)	
		1998	1997	**1998**	1997	**1998**	1997
Belgian Franc	British Pound	**$ 1.9**	$ 11.7	**35.11**	35.19	**$ —**	$.5
Swiss Franc	German Deutschmark	**.3**	3.9	**2.08**	1.46	**—**	—
French Franc	German Deutschmark	**—**	4.3	**—**	6.08	**—**	—
French Franc	Danish Kroner	**—**	.6	**—**	6.06	**—**	—
Danish Kroner	British Pound	**3.2**	5.4	**6.60**	6.67	**(.1)**	.1
Belgian Franc	French Franc	**—**	1.0	**—**	36.87	**—**	—
French Franc	British Pound	**6.9**	48.0	**5.69**	5.70	**(.1)**	2.3
Irish Punt	British Pound	**3.4**	27.4	**.68**	.66	**—**	1.7
Spanish Peseta	British Pound	**—**	1.3	**—**	134.72	**—**	.2
Swedish Kroner	Danish Kroner	**1.6**	16.0	**7.41**	7.89	**.1**	.1
Venezuelan Bolivar	U.S. Dollar	**2.1**	—	**726.67**	—	**(.6)**	—
Total		**$19.4**	$119.6			**($.7)**	$4.9

Contracts to purchase foreign currency

Currency purchased	Currency exchanged	Notional value (millions)		Exchange rate (fc/1US$)		Fair value (millions)	
		1998	1997	**1998**	1997	**1998**	1997
Swiss Franc (a)	British Pound	**$ —**	$ 4.7	**—**	1.42	**$ —**	($.1)
German Deutschmark (a)	British Pound	**—**	.3	**—**	1.72	**—**	—
German Deutschmark	British Pound	**2.8**	18.6	**1.69**	1.71	**—**	(.8)
Total		**$ 2.8**	$23.6			**$ —**	($.9)

(a) Designated as hedge of firm commitment.

Interest rate risk

The Company is exposed to interest rate volatility with regard to future issuances of fixed rate debt and existing issuances of variable rate debt. Primary exposures include movements in U.S. Treasury rates, London Interbank Offered rates (LIBOR), and commercial paper rates. The Company uses interest rate caps, and currency and interest rate swaps, including forward swaps, to reduce interest rate volatility and funding costs associated with certain debt issues, and to achieve a desired proportion of variable versus fixed rate debt, based on current and projected market conditions.

The tables below provide information on the Company's significant debt issues and related hedging instruments at year-end 1998 and 1997. For foreign currency-denominated debt, the information is presented in U.S. Dollar equivalents. Variable interest rates are based on effective rates or implied forward rates as of year-end 1998. Refer to Note 6 within the Notes to Consolidated Financial Statements for further information.

Significant debt issues

Debt characteristics	Principal by year of maturity (millions)				12/31/98 Fair value (millions)	12/31/97 Fair value (millions)
	1999	2001	2004	2005		
Euro Dollar		$500.0			$505.8	$502.6
fixed rate		6.125%				
effective rate (a)		6.400%				
U.S. Dollar		$400.0			$435.9	$ —
fixed rate		5.75%				
effective rate (b)		5.23%				
Euro Dollar			$500.0		$510.2	$515.3
fixed rate			6.625%			
effective rate (a)			6.354%			
U.S. Dollar				$200.0	$198.4	$ —
fixed rate				4.875%		
effective rate (a)				6.070%		
U.S. commercial paper	$423.3				$423.3	$ —
weighted avg. variable	5.2%					
Multi-currency revolving credit facility	$148.5				$148.5	$ —
effective rate	5.5%					
Other debt issues maturing in 1998:						
Euro Canadian Dollar					$ —	$186.6
U.S. commercial paper (c)					$ —	$744.2

(a) Effective fixed interest rate paid, as a result of settlement of forward interest rate swap at date of debt issuance.

(b) Effective fixed interest rate paid, as a result of extendable feature. Refer to Note 6 within Notes to Consolidated Financial Statements for further information.

(c) $400 million of commercial paper classified in long-term debt as of year-end 1997. Refer to Note 6 within Notes to Consolidated Financial Statements for further information.

Interest & currency swaps & caps

Instrument characteristics		Year of maturity (millions)		12/31/98 Fair value (millions)	12/31/97 Fair value (millions)
		2001	2002		
Interest rate swap – pay variable/receive fixed – hedge of existing debt issue	Notional amt.	$200.0		$5.6	$ 1.3
	Pay	5.22%			
	Receive	6.40%			
Interest rate swap – pay variable/receive fixed – hedge of existing debt issue (a)	Notional amt.		$225.0	$1.1	$ 1.2
	Pay		4.86%		
	Receive		6.354%		
Interest rate swap – pay variable/receive fixed – hedge of existing debt issue	Notional amt.	$400.0		$5.2	$ —
	Pay	4.49%			
	Receive	5.23%			
Interest rate cap – pay fixed if 30-day C.P. rate rises to strike rate – hedge of U.S. commercial paper (b)	Notional amt.	$225.0		($.2)	($ .4)
	Strike	6.33%			
	Reference	4.90%			
Other swaps settling in 1998				$ —	($10.9)

(a) Under the terms of this swap, if three-month LIBOR falls to 4.71% or below, the swap will expire. At year-end 1998, three-month LIBOR was 5.07%.

(b) Under the terms of this cap, if the Federal Reserve AA composite rate on 30-day commercial paper increases to 7.68% or above, the cap will expire. At year-end 1998 the rate was 4.90%.

Price risk

The Company is exposed to price fluctuations primarily as a result of anticipated purchases of raw and packaging materials. Primary exposures include corn, wheat, soybean oil, and sugar. The Company uses the combination of long cash positions with vendors, and exchange-traded futures and option contracts to reduce price fluctuations in a desired percentage of forecasted purchases over a duration of generally less than one year. The fair values of commodity contracts held at year-end 1998 and 1997 were insignificant, and potential near-term changes in commodity prices are not expected to have a significant impact on the Company's future earnings or cash flows.

For all derivative financial instruments presented in the tables above, changes in fair values of these instruments and the resultant impact on the Company's cash flows and/or earnings would generally be offset by changes in values of underlying transactions and positions. Therefore, it should be noted that the exclusion of certain of the underlying exposures from the tables above may be a limitation in assessing the net market risk of the Company.

FIVE- OR TEN-YEAR SUMMARY

Usually presented in close proximity to the audited financial statements is a 5- or 10-year summary of selected financial data. From such a summary, one can determine trends and growth patterns over a fairly long period of time. Kellogg

Selected Financial Data

(millions, except per share data and number of employees)

	Net sales	% Growth	(a) Operating profit	% Growth	(a)(b) Earnings before accounting change	% Growth	Averag share outstandir
10-year 0 compound growth rate	5%		1%		—		
1998	**$6,762.1**	**(1)%**	**$ 895.1**	**(11)%**	**$ 502.6**	**(11)%**	**407.**
1997	6,830.1	2	1,009.1	5	564.0	6	414.
1996	6,676.6	(5)	958.9	14	531.0	8	424.
1995	7,003.7	7	837.5	(28)	490.3	(30)	438.
1994	6,562.0	4	1,162.6	16	705.4	4	448.
1993	6,295.4	2	1,004.6	(5)	680.7	—	463.
1992	6,190.6	7	1,062.8	3	682.8	13	477.
1991	5,786.6	12	1,027.9	16	606.0	21	482.
1990	5,181.4	11	886.0	21	502.8	19	483.
1989	4,651.7	7	732.5	(8)	422.1	(12)	488.
1988	4,348.8	15	794.1	15	480.4	21	492.

	Total assets	Return on average assets	Shareholders' equity	Return on average equity	Property, net	Capital expenditures	Depreci and amor
1998	**$5,051.5**	**10%**	**$ 889.8**	**53%**	**$2,888.8**	**$373.9**	**$278.**
1997	4,877.6	11	997.5	49	2,773.3	312.4	287
1996	5,050.0	11	1,282.4	37	2,932.9	307.3	251
1995	4,414.6	11	1,590.9	29	2,784.8	315.7	258
1994	4,467.3	16	1,807.5	40	2,892.8	354.3	256
1993	4,237.1	16	1,713.4	37	2,768.4	449.7	265
1992	4,015.0	11	1,945.2	21	2,662.7	473.6	231
1991	3,925.8	16	2,159.8	30	2,646.5	333.5	222
1990	3,749.4	14	1,901.8	28	2,595.4	320.5	200
1989	3,390.4	14	1,634.4	30	2,406.3	508.7	167
1988	3,297.9	16	1,483.2	36	2,131.9	538.1	139

presents selected financial data that includes operating data, financial position data, and selected statistics and ratios.

| Per Common Share Data (c) | | | | | | |
(a)(b) Earnings before accounting change	Cash dividends	(d) Price/ earnings ratio	Stock price range	Net cash provided by operating activities	Net cash provided by/ (used in) financing activities	Common stock repurchases
2%	9%					
$1.23	$.92	28	$30-50	$ 719.7	($358.3)	$239.7
1.36	.87	36	32-50	879.8	(607.3)	426.0
1.25	.81	26	31-40	711.5	94.0	535.7
1.12	.75	34	26-40	1,041.0	(759.2)	374.7
1.57	.70	18	24-30	966.8	(559.5)	327.3
1.47	.66	19	23-34	800.2	(464.2)	548.1
1.43	.60	23	27-37	741.9	(422.6)	224.1
1.26	.54	26	17-33	934.4	(537.7)	83.6
1.04	.48	18	14-19	819.2	(490.9)	86.9
.87	.43	20	14-20	533.5	(143.2)	78.6
.98	.38	16	12-17	492.3	52.1	33.6

Long-term debt	(e) Debt to market capitalization	Pretax interest coverage (times)	Current ratio	Advertising expense	R&D expense	Number of employees
$1,614.5	16%	7	.9	$695.3	$121.9	14,498
1,415.4	10	9	.9	780.4	106.1	14,339
726.7	14	13	.7	778.9	84.3	14,511
717.8	5	12	1.1	891.5	72.2	14,487
719.2	8	23	1.2*	856.9	71.7	15,657
521.6	7	27	1.0	772.4	59.2	16,151
314.9	3	33	1.2	782.3	56.7	16,551
15.2	3	17	.9	708.3	34.7	17,017
295.6	7	10	.9	648.5	38.3	17,239
371.4	10	10	.9	611.4	42.9	17,268
272.1	9	14	.9	560.9	42.0	17,461

SPECIMEN FINANCIAL STATEMENTS:
General Mills, Inc.

Continuing Operations

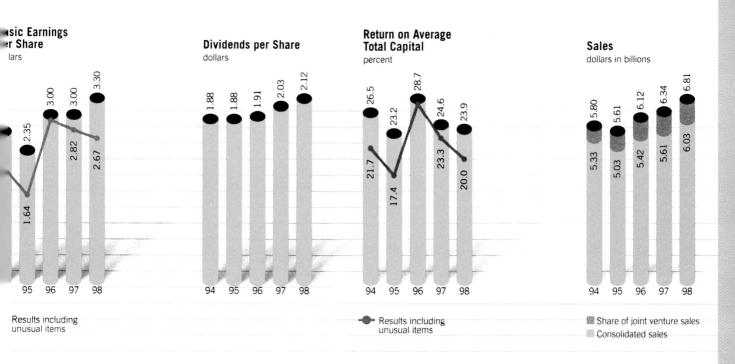

Basic Earnings per Share
dollars

2.35 3.00 3.00 3.30
1.64 2.82 2.67

95 96 97 98

Results including
unusual items

Dividends per Share
dollars

1.88 1.88 1.91 2.03 2.12

94 95 96 97 98

Return on Average Total Capital
percent

26.5 23.2 28.7 24.6 23.9
21.7 17.4 23.3 20.0

94 95 96 97 98

Results including
unusual items

Sales
dollars in billions

5.80 5.61 6.12 6.34 6.81
5.33 5.03 5.42 5.61 6.03

94 95 96 97 98

Share of joint venture sales
Consolidated sales

FINANCIAL HIGHLIGHTS

General Mills, Inc.

In Millions, Except per Share Data

Fiscal Year Ended	May 31, 1998	May 25, 1997	Change
Sales	$6,033.0	$5,609.3	8%
Net Earnings:			
Before unusual items	522.0	474.6	10
As reported	421.8	445.4	(5)
Earnings per Share:			
Basic, before unusual items	3.30	3.00	10
Diluted, before unusual items	3.22	2.94	10
Basic, as reported	2.67	2.82	(5)
Diluted, as reported	2.60	2.76	(6)
Average Common Shares Outstanding for Earnings per Share:			
Basic	158.1	158.2	–
Diluted	162.3	161.6	–
Dividends per Share	$ 2.12	$ 2.03	4
Common Shares Repurchased	7.5	6.2	21
Cash Flow from Operations	$ 775.3	$ 594.1	31
Fixed Charge Coverage (Times), Before Unusual Items	6.8X	6.9X	(.1)pt.
Cash Flow to Debt	34.6%	36.1%	(1.5)pts.

Fiscal 1998 includes 53 weeks; fiscal 1997 includes 52 weeks.

CONSOLIDATED STATEMENTS OF EARNINGS

General Mills, Inc.

In Millions, Except per Share Data, Fiscal Year Ended	May 31, 1998	May 25, 1997	May 26, 1996
Sales	$6,033.0	$5,609.3	$5,416.0
Costs and Expenses:			
Cost of sales	2,389.3	2,328.4	2,241.0
Selling, general and administrative	2,498.6	2,239.2	2,128.3
Depreciation and amortization	194.9	182.8	186.7
Interest, net	117.2	100.5	101.4
Unusual items	166.4	48.4	–
Total Costs and Expenses	5,366.4	4,899.3	4,657.4
Earnings before Taxes and Earnings (Losses) from Joint Ventures	666.6	710.0	758.6
Income Taxes	241.9	258.3	279.4
Earnings (Losses) from Joint Ventures	(2.9)	(6.3)	(2.8)
Net Earnings	$ 421.8	$ 445.4	$ 476.4
Earnings per Share	$ 2.67	$ 2.82	$ 3.00
Average Number of Common Shares	158.1	158.2	158.9
Earnings per Share – Assuming Dilution	$ 2.60	$ 2.76	$ 2.94
Average Number of Common Shares – Assuming Dilution	162.3	161.6	162.0

See accompanying notes to consolidated financial statements.

CONSOLIDATED STATEMENTS OF CASH FLOWS   General Mills, Inc.

In Millions, Fiscal Year Ended	May 31, 1998	May 25, 1997	May 26, 1996
Cash Flows – Operating Activities:			
Net earnings	$ 421.8	$ 445.4	$ 476.4
Adjustments to reconcile net earnings to cash flow:			
Depreciation and amortization	194.9	182.8	186.7
Deferred income taxes	(29.3)	20.9	42.4
Change in current assets and liabilities, net of effects			
from business acquired	54.5	(86.4)	(25.9)
Unusual items	166.4	48.4	–
Other, net	(33.0)	(17.0)	(3.2)
Cash provided by continuing operations	775.3	594.1	676.4
Cash used by discontinued operations	(5.8)	(6.8)	(16.6)
Net Cash Provided by Operating Activities	769.5	587.3	659.8
Cash Flows – Investment Activities:			
Purchases of land, buildings and equipment	(183.6)	(162.5)	(128.8)
Investments in businesses, intangibles and affiliates,			
net of investment returns and dividends	(9.5)	(42.0)	(40.0)
Purchases of marketable securities	(10.6)	(8.0)	(21.6)
Proceeds from sale of marketable securities	40.3	47.7	22.5
Proceeds from disposal of land, buildings and equipment	2.1	2.6	6.2
Proceeds from disposition of businesses	–	6.5	–
Other, net	(42.0)	(29.9)	(11.3)
Net Cash Used by Investment Activities	(203.3)	(185.6)	(173.0)
Cash Flows – Financing Activities:			
Change in notes payable	63.9	312.7	(42.4)
Issuance of long-term debt	286.6	76.2	42.3
Payment of long-term debt	(151.6)	(167.0)	(164.7)
Common stock issued	92.5	60.5	38.0
Purchases of common stock for treasury	(524.9)	(361.8)	(35.6)
Dividends paid	(336.3)	(320.7)	(303.6)
Other, net	(2.8)	(9.4)	(13.2)
Net Cash Used by Financing Activities	(572.6)	(409.5)	(479.2)
Increase (Decrease) in Cash and Cash Equivalents	(6.4)	(7.8)	7.6
Cash and Cash Equivalents – Beginning of Year	12.8	20.6	13.0
Cash and Cash Equivalents – End of Year	$ 6.4	$ 12.8	$ 20.6
Cash Flow from Changes in Current Assets and Liabilities:			
Receivables	$ 23.7	$ (80.0)	$ (59.5)
Inventories	(26.4)	45.0	(23.7)
Prepaid expenses and other current assets	1.6	2.5	(6.3)
Accounts payable	4.0	(27.8)	93.2
Other current liabilities	51.6	(26.1)	(29.6)
Change in Current Assets and Liabilities	$ 54.5	$ (86.4)	$ (25.9)

See accompanying notes to consolidated financial statements.

General Mills, Inc.

CONSOLIDATED BALANCE SHEETS

In Millions	May 31, 1998	May 25, 1997
Assets		
Current Assets:		
Cash and cash equivalents	$ 6.4	$ 12.8
Receivables, less allowance for doubtful accounts of $4.2 in 1998 and $4.1 in 1997	395.1	419.1
Inventories	389.7	364.4
Prepaid expenses and other current assets	107.2	107.3
Deferred income taxes	136.9	107.7
Total Current Assets	1,035.3	1,011.3
Land, Buildings and Equipment at cost, net	1,186.3	1,279.4
Other Assets	1,639.8	1,611.7
Total Assets	**$3,861.4**	**$3,902.4**
Liabilities and Equity		
Current Liabilities:		
Accounts payable	$ 593.1	$ 599.7
Current portion of long-term debt	153.2	139.0
Notes payable	264.1	204.3
Accrued taxes	148.5	97.0
Accrued payroll	129.7	129.4
Other current liabilities	155.1	123.1
Total Current Liabilities	1,443.7	1,292.5
Long-term Debt	1,640.4	1,530.4
Deferred Income Taxes	284.8	272.1
Deferred Income Taxes – Tax Leases	129.1	143.7
Other Liabilities	173.2	169.1
Total Liabilities	3,671.2	3,407.8
Stockholders' Equity:		
Cumulative preference stock, none issued	–	–
Common stock, 204.2 shares issued	619.6	578.0
Retained earnings	1,622.8	1,535.4
Less common stock in treasury, at cost, shares of 49.4 in 1998 and 44.3 in 1997	(1,935.7)	(1,501.9)
Unearned compensation and other	(48.1)	(58.0)
Cumulative foreign currency adjustment	(68.4)	(58.9)
Total Stockholders' Equity	190.2	494.6
Total Liabilities and Equity	**$3,861.4**	**$3,902.4**

See accompanying notes to consolidated financial statements.

In Millions, Except per Share Data	$.10 Par Value Common Stock (One Billion Shares Authorized) Issued Shares	Amount	Treasury Shares	Amount	Retained Earnings	Unearned Compensation and Other	Cumulative Foreign Currency Adjustment	Total
Balance at May 28, 1995	204.2	$379.5	(46.3)	$(1,372.1)	$1,233.3	$(57.9)	$(41.8)	$ 141.0
Net earnings					476.4			476.4
Cash dividends declared ($1.91 per share), net of income taxes of $2.5					(301.1)			(301.1)
Stock option, profit sharing and ESOP plans	–	4.6	1.7	40.3				44.9
Shares purchased on open market			(.6)	(35.6)				(35.6)
Put option premium/settlements, net	–	.2						.2
Unearned compensation related to restricted stock awards						(6.5)		(6.5)
Earned compensation and other						7.1		7.1
Change in unrealized gain, net of income taxes of $2.0, on available-for-sale securities						(3.1)		(3.1)
Minimum pension liability adjustment						(.8)		(.8)
Translation adjustments, net of income tax benefit of $.2							(14.8)	(14.8)
Balance at May 26, 1996	204.2	384.3	(45.2)	(1,367.4)	1,408.6	(61.2)	(56.6)	307.7
Net earnings					445.4			445.4
Cash dividends declared ($2.03 per share), net of income taxes of $2.1					(318.6)			(318.6)
Shares issued in acquisition	–	181.4	5.4	173.0				354.4
Stock option, profit sharing and ESOP plans	–	9.3	1.7	57.4				66.7
Shares purchased via puts, or on open market			(6.2)	(368.0)				(368.0)
Put and call option premium/settlements, net	–	3.0	–	3.1				6.1
Unearned compensation related to restricted stock awards						(7.9)		(7.9)
Earned compensation and other						13.1		13.1
Change in unrealized gain, net of income taxes of $.1, on available-for-sale securities						(.1)		(.1)
Minimum pension liability adjustment						(1.9)		(1.9)
Amount removed on disposition of foreign operation							6.1	6.1
Translation adjustments							(8.4)	(8.4)
Balance at May 25, 1997	204.2	578.0	(44.3)	(1,501.9)	1,535.4	(58.0)	(58.9)	494.6
Net earnings					421.8			421.8
Cash dividends declared ($2.12 per share), net of income taxes of $1.9					(334.4)			(334.4)
Stock option, profit sharing and ESOP plans	–	29.3	2.4	83.9				113.2
Shares purchased via puts, or on open market			(7.5)	(518.7)				(518.7)
Put and call option premium/settlements, net	–	12.3	–	1.0				13.3
Unearned compensation related to restricted stock awards						(7.3)		(7.3)
Earned compensation and other						11.9		11.9
Change in unrealized gain, net of income taxes of $5.2, on available-for-sale securities						8.2		8.2
Minimum pension liability adjustment						(2.9)		(2.9)
Translation adjustments							(9.5)	(9.5)
Balance at May 31, 1998	204.2	$619.6	(49.4)	$(1,935.7)	$1,622.8	$(48.1)	$(68.4)	$ 190.2

See accompanying notes to consolidated financial statements.

Appendix C

TIME VALUE OF MONEY

STUDY OBJECTIVES

After studying this appendix, you should be able to:

1. Distinguish between simple and compound interest.
2. Solve for future value of a single amount.
3. Solve for future value of an annuity.
4. Identify the variables fundamental to solving present value problems.
5. Solve for present value of a single amount.
6. Solve for present value of an annuity.
7. Compute the present value of notes and bonds.

Would you rather receive $1,000 today or a year from now? You should prefer to receive $1,000 today because you can invest the $1,000 and earn interest on it. As a result, you will have more than $1,000 a year from now. What this example illustrates is the concept of the **time value of money**. Everyone prefers to receive money today rather than in the future because of the interest factor.

NATURE OF INTEREST

Interest is payment for the use of another person's money. It is the difference between the amount borrowed or invested (called the principal) and the amount repaid or collected. The amount of interest to be paid or collected is usually stated as a rate over a specific period of time. The rate of interest is generally stated as an annual rate.

The amount of interest involved in any financing transaction is based on three elements:

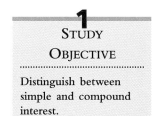

**STUDY
OBJECTIVE**

Distinguish between simple and compound interest.

1. **Principal (p)**: The original amount borrowed or invested.
2. **Interest Rate (i)**: An annual percentage of the principal.
3. **Time (n)**: The number of years that the principal is borrowed or invested.

Simple Interest

Simple interest is computed on the principal amount only. It is the return on the principal for one period. Simple interest is usually expressed as:

ILLUSTRATION C-1

Interest computation

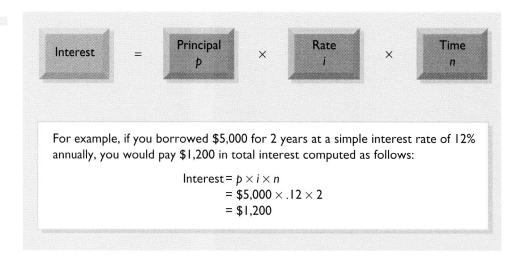

For example, if you borrowed $5,000 for 2 years at a simple interest rate of 12% annually, you would pay $1,200 in total interest computed as follows:

$$\text{Interest} = p \times i \times n$$
$$= \$5,000 \times .12 \times 2$$
$$= \$1,200$$

Compound Interest

Compound interest is computed on principal **and** on any interest earned that has not been paid or withdrawn. It is the return on (or growth of) the principal for two or more time periods. Compounding computes interest not only on the principal but also on the interest earned to date on that principal, assuming the interest is left on deposit.

To illustrate the difference between simple and compound interest, assume that you deposit $1,000 in Bank One, where it will earn simple interest of 9% per year, and you deposit another $1,000 in CityCorp, where it will earn compound interest of 9% per year compounded annually. Also assume that in both cases you will not withdraw any interest until 3 years from the date of deposit. The computation of interest to be received and the accumulated year-end balances are indicated in Illustration C-2.

ILLUSTRATION C-2

Simple vs. compound interest

Bank One				CityCorp.		
Simple Interest Calculation	Simple Interest	Accumulated Year-end Balance		Compound Interest Calculation	Compound Interest	Accumulated Year-end Balance
Year 1 $1,000.00 × 9%	$ 90.00	$1,090.00		Year 1 $1,000.00 × 9%	$ 90.00	$1,090.00
Year 2 $1,000.00 × 9%	90.00	$1,180.00		Year 2 $1,090.00 × 9%	98.10	$1,188.10
Year 3 $1,000.00 × 9%	90.00	$1,270.00		Year 3 $1,188.10 × 9%	106.93	$1,295.03
	$ 270.00		$25.03 Difference		$ 295.03	

Note in the illustration above that simple interest uses the initial principal of $1,000 to compute the interest in all 3 years. Compound interest uses the accumulated balance (principal plus interest to date) at each year-end to compute interest in the succeeding year—which explains why your compound interest account is larger.

Obviously, if you had a choice between investing your money at simple interest or at compound interest, you would choose compound interest, all other things—especially risk—being equal. In the example, compounding provides $25.03 of additional interest income. For practical purposes compounding assumes that unpaid interest earned becomes a part of the principal, and the accumulated balance at the end of each year becomes the new principal on which interest is earned during the next year.

As can be seen in Illustration C-2, you should invest your money at City-Corp which compounds interest annually. Compound interest is used in most business situations. Simple interest is generally applicable only to short-term situations of one year or less.

SECTION 1   FUTURE VALUE CONCEPTS

FUTURE VALUE OF A SINGLE AMOUNT

The future value of a single amount is the value at a future date of a given amount invested assuming compound interest. For example, in Illustration C-2, $1,295.03 is the future value of the $1,000 at the end of 3 years. The $1,295.03 could be determined more easily by using the following formula:

$$FV = p \times (1 + i)^n$$

2
STUDY
OBJECTIVE
....
Solve for future value of a single amount.

where:

FV = future value of a single amount
p = principal (or present value)
i = interest rate for one period
n = number of periods

The $1,295.03 is computed as follows:

$$FV = p \times (1 + i)^n$$
$$= \$1{,}000 \times (1 + i)^3$$
$$= \$1{,}000 \times 1.29503$$
$$= \$1{,}295.03$$

ILLUSTRATION C-3

Time diagram

The 1.29503 is computed by multiplying ($1.09 \times 1.09 \times 1.09$). The amounts in this example can be depicted in the following time diagram:

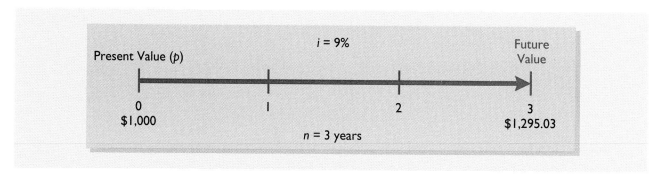

Another method that may be used to compute the future value of a single amount involves the use of a compound interest table. This table shows the future value of 1 for n periods. Such a table is shown below.

TABLE 1
FUTURE VALUE OF 1

(n) Periods	4%	5%	6%	8%	9%	10%	11%	12%	15%
1	1.04000	1.05000	1.06000	1.08000	1.09000	1.10000	1.11000	1.12000	1.15000
2	1.08160	1.10250	1.12360	1.16640	1.18810	1.21000	1.23210	1.25440	1.32250
3	1.12486	1.15763	1.19102	1.25971	1.29503	1.33100	1.36763	1.40493	1.52088
4	1.16986	1.21551	1.26248	1.36049	1.41158	1.46410	1.51807	1.57352	1.74901
5	1.21665	1.27628	1.33823	1.46933	1.53862	1.61051	1.68506	1.76234	2.01136
6	1.26532	1.34010	1.41852	1.58687	1.67710	1.77156	1.87041	1.97382	2.31306
7	1.31593	1.40710	1.50363	1.71382	1.82804	1.94872	2.07616	2.21068	2.66002
8	1.36857	1.47746	1.59385	1.85093	1.99256	2.14359	2.30454	2.47596	3.05902
9	1.42331	1.55133	1.68948	1.99900	2.17189	2.35795	2.55803	2.77308	3.51788
10	1.48024	1.62889	1.79085	2.15892	2.36736	2.59374	2.83942	3.10585	4.04556
11	1.53945	1.71034	1.89830	2.33164	2.58043	2.85312	3.15176	3.47855	4.65239
12	1.60103	1.79586	2.01220	2.51817	2.81267	3.13843	3.49845	3.89598	5.35025
13	1.66507	1.88565	2.13293	2.71962	3.06581	3.45227	3.88328	4.36349	6.15279
14	1.73168	1.97993	2.26090	2.93719	3.34173	3.79750	4.31044	4.88711	7.07571
15	1.80094	2.07893	2.39656	3.17217	3.64248	4.17725	4.78459	5.47357	8.13706
16	1.87298	2.18287	2.54035	3.42594	3.97031	4.59497	5.31089	6.13039	9.35762
17	1.94790	2.29202	2.69277	3.70002	4.32763	5.05447	5.89509	6.86604	10.76126
18	2.02582	2.40662	2.85434	3.99602	4.71712	5.55992	6.54355	7.68997	12.37545
19	2.10685	2.52695	3.02560	4.31570	5.14166	6.11591	7.26334	8.61276	14.23177
20	2.19112	2.65330	3.20714	4.66096	5.60441	6.72750	8.06231	9.64629	16.36654

In Table 1, n is the number of compounding periods, the percentages are the periodic interest rates, and the 5-digit decimal numbers in the respective columns are the future value of 1 factors. In using Table 1, the principal amount is multiplied by the future value factor for the specified number of periods and interest rate. For example, the future value factor for 2 periods at 9% is 1.18810. Multiplying this factor by $1,000 equals $1,188.10, which is the accumulated balance at the end of year 2 in the CityCorp example in Illustration C-2. The $1,295.03 accumulated balance at the end of the third year can be calculated from Table 1 by multiplying the future value factor for 3 periods (1.29503) by the $1,000.

The following demonstration problem illustrates how to use Table 1.

ILLUSTRATION C-4

Demonstration Problem—
Using Table 1 for FV of 1

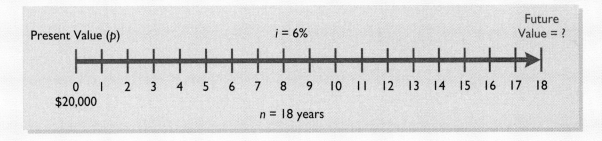

John and Mary Rich invested $20,000 in a savings account paying 6% interest at the time their son, Mike, was born. The money is to be used by Mike for his college education. On his 18th birthday, Mike withdraws the money from his savings account. How much did Mike withdraw from his account?

Present Value (p) $i = 6\%$ Future Value = ?

0 1 2 3 4 5 6 7 8 9 10 11 12 13 14 15 16 17 18
$20,000

$n = 18$ years

Answer: The future value factor from Table 1 is 2.85434 (18 periods at 6%). The future value of $20,000 earning 6% per year for 18 years is **$57,086.80** ($20,000 × 2.85434).

FUTURE VALUE OF AN ANNUITY

The preceding discussion involved the accumulation of only a single principal sum. Individuals and businesses frequently encounter situations in which a series of equal dollar amounts are to be paid or received periodically, such as loans or lease (rental) contracts. Such payments or receipts of equal dollar amounts are referred to as annuities. The future value of an annuity is the sum of all the payments (receipts) plus the accumulated compound interest on them. In computing the future value of an annuity, it is necessary to know the (1) interest rate, (2) the number of compounding periods, and (3) the amount of the periodic payments or receipts.

To illustrate the computation of the future value of an annuity, assume that you invest $2,000 at the end of each year for 3 years at 5% interest compounded annually. This situation is depicted in the following time diagram:

3
STUDY

OBJECTIVE

Solve for future value
of an annuity.

ILLUSTRATION C-5

Time diagram for a 3-year annuity

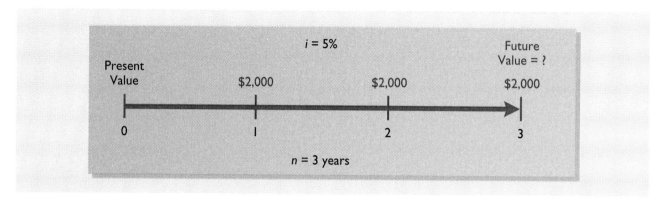

As can be seen from the preceding diagram, the $2,000 invested at the end of year 1 will earn interest for 2 years (years 2 and 3) and the $2,000 invested at the end of year 2 will earn interest for 1 year (year 3). However, the last $2,000 investment (made at the end of year 3) will not earn any interest. The future value of these periodic payments could be computed using the future value factors from Table 1 as shown below:

ILLUSTRATION C-6

Future value of periodic payment computation

Year Invested	Amount Invested	×	Future Value of 1 Factor at 5%	=	Future Value
1	$2,000	×	1.10250		$2,205
2	$2,000	×	1.05000		2,100
3	$2,000	×	1.00000		2,000
			3.15250		$6,305

The first $2,000 investment is multiplied by the future value factor for 2 periods (1.1025) because 2 years' interest will accumulate on it (in years 2 and 3). The second $2,000 investment will earn only 1 year's interest (in year 3) and therefore is multiplied by the future value factor for 1 year (1.0500). The final $2,000 investment is made at the end of the third year and will not earn any interest. Consequently, the future value of the last $2,000 invested is only $2,000 since it does not accumulate any interest.

This method of calculation is required when the periodic payments or receipts are not equal in each period. However, when the periodic payments (receipts) are the same in each period, the future value can be computed by using a future value of an annuity of 1 table. Such a table is shown on the next page.

Table 2 shows the future value of 1 to be received periodically for a given number of periods. From Table 2 it can be seen that the future value of an annuity of 1 factor for 3 periods at 5% is 3.15250. The future value factor is the total of the three individual future value factors as shown in Illustration C-6. Multiplying this amount by the annual investment of $2,000 produces a future value of $6,305.

The demonstration problem on the next page illustrates how to use Table 2.

TABLE 2
FUTURE VALUE OF AN ANNUITY OF 1

(n) Periods	4%	5%	6%	8%	9%	10%	11%	12%	15%
1	1.00000	1.00000	1.00000	1.00000	1.00000	1.00000	1.00000	1.00000	1.00000
2	2.04000	2.05000	2.06000	2.08000	2.09000	2.10000	2.11000	2.12000	2.15000
3	3.12160	3.15250	3.18360	3.24640	3.27810	3.31000	3.34210	3.37440	3.47250
4	4.24646	4.31013	4.37462	4.50611	4.57313	4.64100	4.70973	4.77933	4.99338
5	5.41632	5.52563	5.63709	5.86660	5.98471	6.10510	6.22780	6.35285	6.74238
6	6.63298	6.80191	6.97532	7.33592	7.52334	7.71561	7.91286	8.11519	8.75374
7	7.89829	8.14201	8.39384	8.92280	9.20044	9.48717	9.78327	10.08901	11.06680
8	9.21423	9.54911	9.89747	10.63663	11.02847	11.43589	11.85943	12.29969	13.72682
9	10.58280	11.02656	11.49132	12.48756	13.02104	13.57948	14.16397	14.77566	16.78584
10	12.00611	12.57789	13.18079	14.48656	15.19293	15.93743	16.72201	17.54874	20.30372
11	13.48635	14.20679	14.97164	16.64549	17.56029	18.53117	19.56143	20.65458	24.34928
12	15.02581	15.91713	16.86994	18.97713	20.14072	21.38428	22.71319	24.13313	29.00167
13	16.62684	17.71298	18.88214	21.49530	22.95339	24.52271	26.21164	28.02911	34.35192
14	18.29191	19.59863	21.01507	24.21492	26.01919	27.97498	30.09492	32.39260	40.50471
15	20.02359	21.57856	23.27597	27.15211	29.36092	31.77248	34.40536	37.27972	47.58041
16	21.82453	23.65749	25.67253	30.32428	33.00340	35.94973	39.18995	42.75328	55.71747
17	23.69751	25.84037	28.21288	33.75023	36.97351	40.54470	44.50084	48.88367	65.07509
18	25.64541	28.13238	30.90565	37.45024	41.30134	45.59917	50.39593	55.74972	75.83636
19	27.67123	30.53900	33.75999	41.44626	46.01846	51.15909	56.93949	63.43968	88.21181
20	29.77808	33.06595	36.78559	45.76196	51.16012	57.27500	64.20283	72.05244	102.44358

ILLUSTRATION C-7

Demonstration Problem—Using Table 2 for FV of an annuity of 1

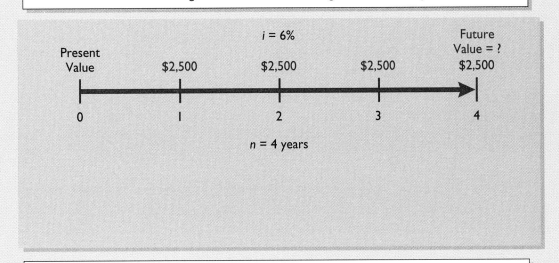

John and Char Lewis' daughter, Debra, has just started high school. They decide to start a college fund for her and will invest $2,500 in a savings account at the end of each year she is in high school (4 payments total). The account will earn 6% interest compounded annually. How much will be in the college fund at the time Debra graduates from high school?

Answer: The future value factor from Table 2 is 4.37462 (4 periods at 6%). The future value of $2,500 invested each year for 4 years at 6% interest is **$10,936.55** ($2,500 × 4.37462).

SECTION 2 PRESENT VALUE CONCEPTS

PRESENT VALUE VARIABLES

4
STUDY
OBJECTIVE

Identify the variables fundamental to solving present value problems.

The present value, like the future value, is based on three variables: (1) the dollar amount to be received (future amount), (2) the length of time until the amount is received (number of periods), and (3) the interest rate (the discount rate). The process of determining the present value is referred to as discounting the future amount.

In this textbook, present value computations are used in measuring several items. For example, in Chapter 11, to determine the market price of a bond, the present value of the principal and interest payments is computed. In addition, the determination of the amount to be reported for notes payable and lease liability (Appendix F) involves present value computations.

PRESENT VALUE OF A SINGLE AMOUNT

5
STUDY
OBJECTIVE

Solve for present value of a single amount.

To illustrate present value concepts, assume that you are willing to invest a sum of money that will yield $1,000 at the end of one year. In other words, what amount would you need to invest today to have $1,000 one year from now? If you want a 10% rate of return, the investment or present value is $909.09 ($1,000 ÷ 1.10). The computation of this amount is shown in Illustration C-8.

ILLUSTRATION C-8

Present value computation— $1,000 discounted at 10% for 1 year

$$\text{Present Value} = \text{Future Value} \div (1 + i)^n$$
$$\text{PV} = \text{FV} \div (1 + 10\%)^1$$
$$\text{PV} = \$1,000 \div 1.10$$
$$\text{PV} = \$909.09$$

The future amount ($1,000), the discount rate (10%), and the number of periods (1) are known. The variables in this situation can be depicted in the following time diagram:

ILLUSTRATION C-9

Finding present value if discounted for 1 period

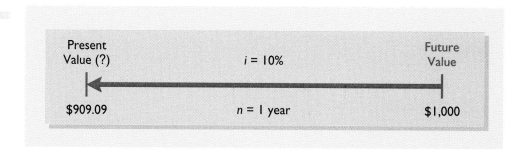

If the single amount of $1,000 is to be received **in 2 years** and discounted at 10% [PV = $1,000 ÷ (1 + 10%)²], its present value is $826.45 [($1,000 ÷ 1.10) ÷ 1.10], depicted as follows:

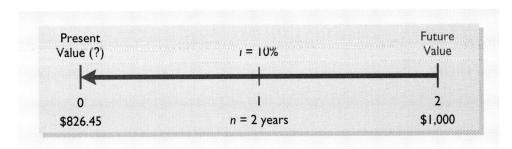

ILLUSTRATION C-10

Finding present value if discounted for 2 periods

The present value of 1 may also be determined through tables that show the present value of 1 for *n* periods. In Table 3, *n* is the number of discounting periods involved. The percentages are the periodic interest rates or discount rates, and the 5-digit decimal numbers in the respective columns are the present value of 1 factors.

TABLE 3
PRESENT VALUE OF 1

(*n*) Periods	4%	5%	6%	8%	9%	10%	11%	12%	15%
1	.96154	.95238	.94340	.92593	.91743	.90909	.90090	.89286	.86957
2	.92456	.90703	.89000	.85734	.84168	.82645	.81162	.79719	.75614
3	.88900	.86384	.83962	.79383	.77218	.75132	.73119	.71178	.65752
4	.85480	.82270	.79209	.73503	.70843	.68301	.65873	.63552	.57175
5	.82193	.78533	.74726	.68058	.64993	.62092	.59345	.56743	.49718
6	.79031	.74622	.70496	.63017	.59627	.56447	.53464	.50663	.43233
7	.75992	.71068	.66506	.58349	.54703	.51316	.48166	.45235	.37594
8	.73069	.67684	.62741	.54027	.50187	.46651	.43393	.40388	.32690
9	.70259	.64461	.59190	.50025	.46043	.42410	.39092	.36061	.28426
10	.67556	.61391	.55839	.46319	.42241	.38554	.35218	.32197	.24719
11	.64958	.58468	.52679	.42888	.38753	.35049	.31728	.28747	.21494
12	.62460	.55684	.49697	.39711	.35554	.31863	.28584	.25668	.18691
13	.60057	.53032	.46884	.36770	.32618	.28966	.25751	.22917	.16253
14	.57748	.50507	.44230	.34046	.29925	.26333	.23199	.20462	.14133
15	.55526	.48102	.41727	.31524	.27454	.23939	.20900	.18270	.12289
16	.53391	.45811	.39365	.29189	.25187	.21763	.18829	.16312	.10687
17	.51337	.43630	.37136	.27027	.23107	.19785	.16963	.14564	.09293
18	.49363	.41552	.35034	.25025	.21199	.17986	.15282	.13004	.08081
19	.47464	.39573	.33051	.23171	.19449	.16351	.13768	.11611	.07027
20	.45639	.37689	.31180	.21455	.17843	.14864	.12403	.10367	.06110

When Table 3 is used, the future value is multiplied by the present value factor specified at the intersection of the number of periods and the discount rate. For example, the present value factor for 1 period at a discount rate of 10% is .90909, which equals the $909.09 ($1,000 x .90909) computed in Illustration C-8. For 2 periods at a discount rate of 10%, the present value factor is .82645, which equals the $826.45 ($1,000 x .82645) computed previously.

Note that a higher discount rate produces a smaller present value. For example, using a 15% discount rate, the present value of $1,000 due one year from now is $869.57 versus $909.09 at 10%. It should also be recognized that the farther removed from the present the future value is, the smaller the present value.

For example, using the same discount rate of 10%, the present value of $1,000 due in **5 years** is $620.92 versus $1,000 due in **1 year** is $909.09.

The following two demonstration problems (Illustrations C-11, C-12) illustrate how to use Table 3.

ILLUSTRATION C-11

*Demonstration Problem—
Using Table 3 for PV of 1*

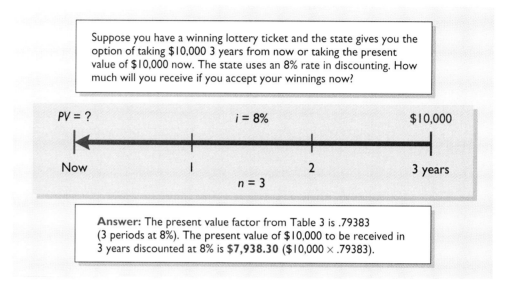

Suppose you have a winning lottery ticket and the state gives you the option of taking $10,000 3 years from now or taking the present value of $10,000 now. The state uses an 8% rate in discounting. How much will you receive if you accept your winnings now?

PV = ?   i = 8% $10,000

Now   1   2   3 years

n = 3

Answer: The present value factor from Table 3 is .79383 (3 periods at 8%). The present value of $10,000 to be received in 3 years discounted at 8% is **$7,938.30** ($10,000 × .79383).

ILLUSTRATION C-12

*Demonstration Problem—
Using Table 3 for PV of 1*

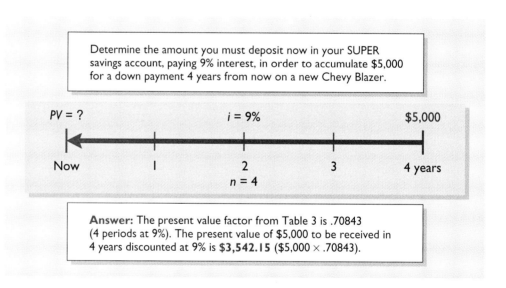

Determine the amount you must deposit now in your SUPER savings account, paying 9% interest, in order to accumulate $5,000 for a down payment 4 years from now on a new Chevy Blazer.

PV = ?   i = 9% $5,000

Now   1   2   3   4 years

n = 4

Answer: The present value factor from Table 3 is .70843 (4 periods at 9%). The present value of $5,000 to be received in 4 years discounted at 9% is **$3,542.15** ($5,000 × .70843).

PRESENT VALUE OF AN ANNUITY

**6
STUDY
OBJECTIVE**

Solve for present value of an annuity.

The preceding discussion involved the discounting of only a single future amount. Businesses and individuals frequently engage in transactions in which a series of equal dollar amounts are to be received or paid periodically. Examples of a series of periodic receipts or payments are loan agreements, installment sales, mortgage notes, lease (rental) contracts, and pension obligations. These series of periodic receipts or payments are called **annuities**. In computing the present value of an annuity, it is necessary to know the (1) discount rate, (2) the number of discount periods, and (3) the amount of the periodic receipts or payments. To illustrate the computation of the present value of an annuity, assume that you will receive $1,000 cash annually for 3 years at a time when the discount rate is 10%. This situation is depicted in the following time diagram:

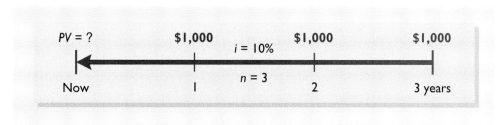

ILLUSTRATION C-13

Time diagram for a 3-year annuity

The present value in this situation may be computed as follows:

ILLUSTRATION C-14

Present value of a series of future amounts computation

Future Amount	×	Present Value of 1 Factor at 10%	=	Present Value
$1,000 (1 year away)		.90909		$ 909.09
1,000 (2 years away)		.82645		826.45
1,000 (3 years away)		.75132		751.32
		2.48686		$2,486.86

This method of calculation is required when the periodic cash flows are not uniform in each period. However, when the future receipts are the same in each period, there are two other ways to compute present value. First, the annual cash flow can be multiplied by the sum of the three present value factors. In the previous example, $1,000 x 2.48686 equals $2,486.86. Second, annuity tables may be used. As illustrated in Table 4 below, these tables show the present value of 1 to be received periodically for a given number of periods.

TABLE 4
PRESENT VALUE OF AN ANNUITY OF 1

(n) Periods	4%	5%	6%	8%	9%	10%	11%	12%	15%
1	.96154	.95238	.94340	.92593	.91743	.90909	.90090	.89286	.86957
2	1.88609	1.85941	1.83339	1.78326	1.75911	1.73554	1.73552	1.69005	1.62571
3	2.77509	2.72325	2.67301	2.57710	2.53130	2.48685	2.44371	2.40183	2.28323
4	3.62990	3.54595	3.46511	3.31213	3.23972	3.16986	3.10245	3.03735	2.85498
5	4.45182	4.32948	4.21236	3.99271	3.88965	3.79079	3.69590	3.60478	3.35216
6	5.24214	5.07569	4.91732	4.62288	4.48592	4.35526	4.23054	4.11141	3.78448
7	6.00205	5.78637	5.58238	5.20637	5.03295	4.86842	4.71220	4.56376	4.16042
8	6.73274	6.46321	6.20979	5.74664	5.53482	5.33493	5.14612	4.96764	4.48732
9	7.43533	7.10782	6.80169	6.24689	5.99525	5.75902	5.53705	5.32825	4.77158
10	8.11090	7.72173	7.36009	6.71008	6.41766	6.14457	5.88923	5.65022	5.01877
11	8.76048	8.30641	7.88687	7.13896	6.80519	6.49506	6.20652	5.93770	5.23371
12	9.38507	8.86325	8.38384	7.53608	7.16073	6.81369	6.49236	6.19437	5.42062
13	9.98565	9.39357	8.85268	7.90378	7.48690	7.10336	6.74987	6.42355	5.58315
14	10.56312	9.89864	9.29498	8.24424	7.78615	7.36669	6.98187	6.62817	5.72448
15	11.11839	10.37966	9.71225	8.55948	8.06069	7.60608	7.19087	6.81086	5.84737
16	11.65230	10.83777	10.10590	8.85137	8.31256	7.82371	7.37916	6.97399	5.95424
17	12.16567	11.27407	10.47726	9.12164	8.54363	8.02155	7.54879	7.11963	6.04716
18	12.65930	11.68959	10.82760	9.37189	8.75563	8.20141	7.70162	7.24967	6.12797
19	13.13394	12.08532	11.15812	9.60360	8.95012	8.36492	7.83929	7.36578	6.19823
20	13.59033	12.46221	11.46992	9.81815	9.12855	8.51356	7.96333	7.46944	6.25933

From Table 4 it can be seen that the present value factor of an annuity of 1 for three periods at 10% is 2.48685.[1] This present value factor is the total of the three individual present value factors as shown in Illustration C-14. Applying this amount to the annual cash flow of $1,000 produces a present value of $2,486.85.

The following demonstration problem (Illustration C-15) illustrates how to use Table 4.

ILLUSTRATION C-15

Demonstration Problem—Using Table 4 for PV of an annuity of 1

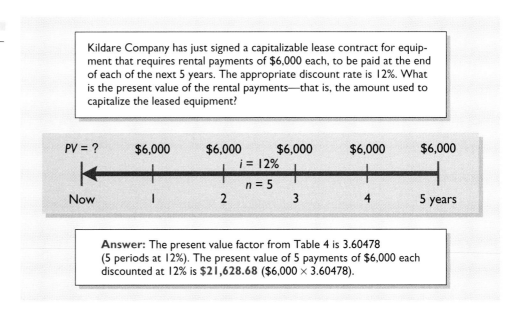

Kildare Company has just signed a capitalizable lease contract for equipment that requires rental payments of $6,000 each, to be paid at the end of each of the next 5 years. The appropriate discount rate is 12%. What is the present value of the rental payments—that is, the amount used to capitalize the leased equipment?

PV = ? $6,000 $6,000 $6,000 $6,000 $6,000

i = 12%
n = 5

Now   1   2   3   4   5 years

Answer: The present value factor from Table 4 is 3.60478 (5 periods at 12%). The present value of 5 payments of $6,000 each discounted at 12% is **$21,628.68** ($6,000 × 3.60478).

TIME PERIODS AND DISCOUNTING

In the preceding calculations, the discounting has been done on an annual basis using an annual interest rate. Discounting may also be done over shorter periods of time such as monthly, quarterly, or semiannually. When the time frame is less than one year, it is necessary to convert the annual interest rate to the applicable time frame. Assume, for example, that the investor in Illustration C-14 received $500 **semiannually** for 3 years instead of $1,000 annually. In this case, the number of periods becomes 6 (3 × 2), the discount rate is 5% (10% ÷ 2), the present value factor from Table 4 is 5.07569, and the present value of the future cash flows is $2,537.85 (5.07569 × $500). This amount is slightly higher than the $2,486.86 computed in Illustration C-14 because interest is computed twice during the same year; therefore interest is earned on the first half year's interest.

COMPUTING THE PRESENT VALUE OF A LONG-TERM NOTE OR BOND

7

STUDY OBJECTIVE

Compute the present value of notes and bonds.

The present value (or market price) of a long-term note or bond is a function of three variables: (1) the payment amounts, (2) the length of time until the amounts are paid, and (3) the discount rate. Our illustration uses a 5-year bond issue.

---

[1]The difference of .00001 between 2.48686 and 2.48685 is due to rounding.

The first variable (dollars to be paid) is made up of two elements: (1) a series of interest payments (an annuity) and (2) the principal amount (a single sum). To compute the present value of the bond, both the interest payments and the principal amount must be discounted—two different computations. The time diagrams for a bond due in 5 years are shown in Illustration C-16.

ILLUSTRATION C-16

Present value of a bond time diagram

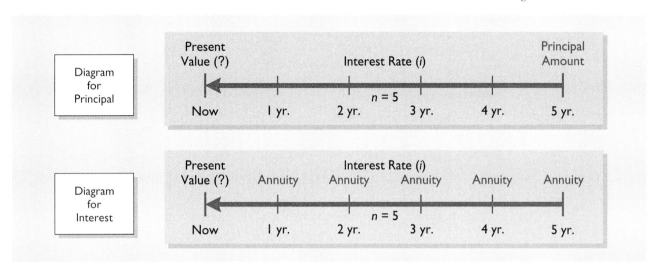

When the investor's discount rate is equal to the bond's contractual interest rate, the present value of the bonds will equal the face value of the bonds. To illustrate, assume a bond issue of 10%, 5-year bonds with a face value of $100,000 with interest payable **semiannually** on January 1 and July 1. If the discount rate is the same as the contractual rate, the bonds will sell at face value. In this case, the investor will receive (1) $100,000 at maturity and (2) a series of ten $5,000 interest payments [($100,000 × 10%) ÷ 2] over the term of the bonds. The length of time is expressed in terms of interest periods, in this case, 10, and the discount rate per interest period, 5%. The following time diagram (Illustration C-17) depicts the variables involved in this discounting situation:

ILLUSTRATION C-17

Time diagram for present value of a 10%, 5-year bond paying interest semiannually

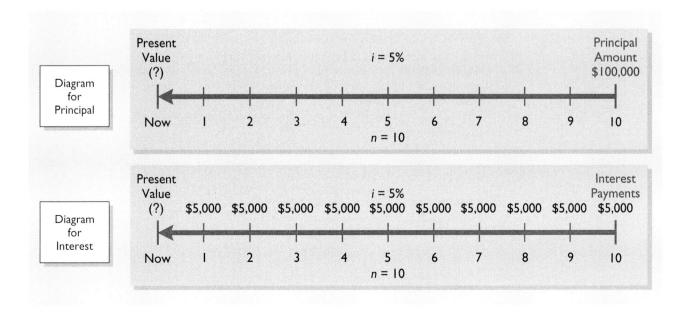

The computation of the present value of these bonds is shown below.

10% Contractual Rate—10% Discount Rate

Present value of principal to be received at maturity	
$100,000 × PV of 1 due in 10 periods at 5%	
$100,000 × .61391 (Table 3)	$ 61,391
Present value of interest to be received periodically	
over the term of the bonds	
$5,000 × PV of 1 due periodically for 10 periods at 5%	
$5,000 × 7.72173 (Table 4)	38,609*
Present value of bonds	**$100,000**

*(Rounded).

Now assume that the investor's required rate of return is 12%, not 10%. The future amounts are again $100,000 and $5,000, respectively, but now a discount rate of 6% (12% ÷ 2) must be used. The present value of the bonds is $92,639, as computed below:

10% Contractual Rate—12% Discount Rate

Present value of principal to be received at maturity	
$100,000 × .55839 (Table 3)	$55,839
Present value of interest to be received periodically	
over the term of the bonds	
$5,000 × 7.36009 (Table 4)	36,800
Present value of bonds	**$92,639**

Conversely, if the discount rate is 8% and the contractual rate is 10%, the present value of the bonds is $108,111, computed as follows:

10% Contractual Rate—8% Discount Rate

Present value of principal to be received at maturity	
$100,000 × .67556 (Table 3)	$ 67,556
Present value of interest to be received periodically	
over the term of the bonds	
$5,000 × 8.11090 (Table 4)	40,555
Present value of bonds	**$108,111**

TECHNOLOGY IN ACTION

As discussed in this appendix, the selling price of the bonds can be determined via present value formulas. Many computer spreadsheets and computer programs can perform the discounting functions given the basic information of the situation.

The above discussion relied on present value tables in solving present value problems. Hand-held calculators may also be used to compute present values without the use of these tables. Some calculators, especially the "business" or "MBA"-type calculators, have present value (PV) functions that allow you to calculate present values by merely inputting the proper amount, discount rate, periods, and pressing the PV key.

SUMMARY OF STUDY OBJECTIVES

1. *Distinguish between simple and compound interest.* Simple interest is computed on the principal only, whereas compound interest is computed on the principal and any interest earned that has not been withdrawn.

2. *Solve for future value of a single amount.* First, prepare a time diagram of the problem. Identify the principal amount, the number of compounding periods, and the interest rate. Using the future value of 1 table, multiply the principal amount by the future value factor specified at the intersection of the number of periods and the interest rate.

3. *Solve for future value of an annuity.* Prepare a time diagram of the problem. Identify the amount of the periodic payments, the number of compounding periods, and the interest rate. Using the future value of an annuity of 1 table, multiply the amount of the payments by the future value factor specified at the intersection of the number of periods and interest rate.

4. *Identify the variables fundamental to solving present value problems.* The following three variables are fundamental to solving present value problems: (1) the future amount, (2) the number of periods, and (3) the interest rate (the discount rate).

5. *Solve for present value of a single amount.* Prepare a time diagram of the problem. Identify the future amount, the number of discounting periods, and the discount (interest) rate. Using the present value of a single amount table, multiply the future amount by the present value factor specified at the intersection of the number of periods and the discount rate.

6. *Solve for present value of an annuity.* Prepare a time diagram of the problem. Identify the future amounts (annuities), the number of discounting periods, and the discount (interest) rate. Using the present value of an annuity of 1 table, multiply the amount of the annuity by the present value factor specified at the intersection of the number of periods and the interest rate.

7. *Compute the present value of notes and bonds.* Determine the present value of the principal amount: Multiply the principal amount (a single future amount) by the present value factor (from the present value of 1 table) intersecting at the number of periods (number of interest payments) and the discount rate. Determine the present value of the series of interest payments: Multiply the amount of the interest payment by the present value factor (from the present value of an annuity of 1 table) intersecting at the number of periods (number of interest payments) and the discount rate. Add the present value of the principal amount to the present value of the interest payments to arrive at the present value of the note or bond.

GLOSSARY

Annuity   A series of equal dollar amounts to be paid or received periodically. (p. C5).

Compound interest   The interest computed on the principal and any interest earned that has not been paid or received. (p. C2).

Discounting the future amount(s)   The process of determining present value. (p. C8).

Future value of a single amount   The value at a future date of a given amount invested assuming compound interest. (p. C3).

Future value of an annuity   The sum of all the payments or receipts plus the accumulated compound interest on them. (p. C5).

Interest   Payment for the use of another's money. (p. C2).

Present value   The value now of a given amount to be invested or received in the future assuming compound interest. (p. C8).

Present value of an annuity   A series of future receipts or payments discounted to their value now assuming compound interest. (p. C10).

Principal   The amount borrowed or invested. (p. C2).

Simple interest   The interest computed on the principal only. (p. C2).

BRIEF EXERCISES (Use Tables to Solve Exercises)

....

Compute the future value of a single amount.

BEC–1 Luke Skywalker invested $5,000 at 6% annual interest, and left the money invested without withdrawing any of the interest for 10 years. At the end of the 10 years, Luke withdrew the accumulated amount of money. (a) What amount did Luke withdraw assuming the investment earns simple interest? (b) What amount did Luke withdraw assuming the investment earns interest compounded annually?

Use future value tables.

BEC–2 For each of the following cases, indicate (a) to what interest rate columns and (b) to what number of periods you would refer in looking up the future value factor.

(a) In Table 1 (future value of 1)

	Annual Rate	Number of Years Invested	Compounded
(1)	6%	5	Annually
(2)	5%	3	Semiannually

(b) In Table 2 (future value of an annuity of 1):

	Annual Rate	Number of Years Invested	Compounded
(1)	5%	10	Annually
(2)	4%	6	Semiannually

Compute the future value of a single amount.

BEC–3 Galaxy Company signed a lease for an office building for a period of 10 years. Under the lease agreement, a security deposit of $10,000 is made. The deposit will be returned at the expiration of the lease with interest compounded at 5% per year. What amount will Galaxy receive at the time the lease expires?

Compute the future value of an annuity.

BEC–4 Darth Company issued $1,000,000, 10-year bonds and agreed to make annual sinking fund deposits of $80,000. The deposits are made at the end of each year into an account paying 5% interest. What amount will be in the sinking fund at the end of 10 years?

Compute the future value of a single amount and of an annuity.

BEC–5 Dawna and Marc Tucci invested $5,000 in a savings account paying 6% annual interest when their son, Tanner, was born. They also deposited $1,000 on each of his birthdays until he was 18 (including his 18th birthday). How much will be in the savings account on his 18th birthday (after the last deposit)?

Compute the future value of a single amount.

BEC–6 Ron Watson borrowed $20,000 on July 1, 2000. This amount plus accrued interest at 6% compounded annually is to be repaid on July 1, 2005. How much will Ron have to repay on July 1, 2005?

Use present-value tables.

BEC–7 For each of the following cases, indicate (a) to what interest rate columns and (b) to what number of periods you would refer in looking up the discount rate.

(a) In Table 3 (present value of 1):

	Annual Rate	Number of Years Involved	Discounts Per Year
(1)	12%	6	Annually
(2)	10%	15	Annually
(3)	8%	8	Semiannually

(b) In Table 4 (present value of an annuity of 1):

	Annual Rate	Number of Years Involved	Number of Payments Involved	Frequency of Payments
(1)	12%	20	20	Annually
(2)	10%	5	5	Annually
(3)	8%	4	8	Semiannually

Determine present values.

BEC–8 (a) What is the present value of $10,000 due 8 periods from now, discounted at 8%? (b) What is the present value of $10,000 to be received at the end of 6 periods, discounted at 9%?

BEC-9 Heather & Mark Company is considering an investment which will return a lump sum of $500,000 five years from now. What amount should Heather & Mark Company pay for this investment to earn a 15% return?

Compute the present value of a single amount investment.

BEC-10 Piazza Company earns 11% on an investment that will return $875,000 eight years from now. What is the amount Piazza should invest now to earn this rate of return?

Compute the present value of a single amount investment.

BEC-11 Remmers Company is considering investing in an annuity contract that will return $20,000 annually at the end of each year for 15 years. What amount should Remmer Company pay for this investment if it earns a 6% return?

Compute the present value of an annuity investment.

BEC-12 Zarita Enterprises earns 11% on an investment that pays back $110,000 at the end of each of the next four years. What is the amount Zarita Enterprises invested to earn the 11% rate of return?

Compute the present value of an annuity investment.

BEC-13 Hernandez Railroad Co. is about to issue $100,000 of 10-year bonds paying a 12% interest rate, with interest payable semiannually. The discount rate for such securities is 10%. How much can Hernandez expect to receive for the sale of these bonds?

Compute the present value of bonds.

BEC-14 Assume the same information as BEC–13 except that the discount rate was 12% instead of 10%. In this case, how much can Hernandez expect to receive from the sale of these bonds?

Compute the present value of bonds.

BEC-15 Caledonian Taco Company receives a $50,000, 6-year note bearing interest of 11% (paid annually) from a customer at a time when the discount rate is 12%. What is the present value of the note received by Caledonian?

Compute the present value of a note.

BEC-16 Rodriguez Enterprises issued 10%, 8-year, $2,000,000 par value bonds that pay interest semiannually on October 1 and April 1. The bonds are dated April 1, 2000, and are issued on that date. The discount rate of interest for such bonds on April 1, 2000, is 12%. What cash proceeds did Rodriguez receive from issuance of the bonds?

Compute the present value of bonds.

BEC-17 Barney Googal owns a garage and is contemplating purchasing a tire retreading machine for $16,280. After estimating costs and revenues, Barney projects a net cash flow from the retreading machine of $2,790 annually for 8 years. Barney hopes to earn a return of 11 percent on such investments. What is the present value of the retreading operation? Should Barney Googal purchase the retreading machine?

Compute the present value of a machine for purposes of making a purchase decision.

BEC-18 Hung-Chao Yu Company issues a 10%, 6-year mortgage note on January 1, 2000, to obtain financing for new equipment. Land is used as collateral for the note. The terms provide for semiannual installment payments of $112,825. What were the cash proceeds received from the issuance of the note?

Compute the present value of a note.

BEC-19 Denise Ramos Company is considering purchasing equipment. The equipment will produce the following cash flows: Year 1, $30,000; Year 2, $40,000; Year 3, $50,000. Ramos requires a minimum rate of return of 15%. What is the maximum price Ramos should pay for this equipment?

Compute the maximum price to pay for a machine.

BEC-20 If Caroline Remmers invests $1,827 now, she will receive $10,000 at the end of 15 years. What annual rate of interest will Caroline earn on her investment? (*Hint:* Use Table 3.)

Compute the interest rate on a single amount.

BEC-21 Maloney Cork has been offered the opportunity of investing $24,719 now. The investment will earn 15% per year and will at the end of that time return Maloney $100,000. How many years must Maloney wait to receive $100,000? (*Hint:* Use Table 3.)

Compute the number of periods of a single amount.

BEC-22 Annie Dublin purchased an investment for $11,469.92. From this investment, she will receive $1,000 annually for the next 20 years starting one year from now. What rate of interest will Annie's investment be earning for her? (*Hint:* Use Table 4.)

Compute the interest rate on an annuity.

BEC-23 Andy Sanchez invests $8,851.37 now for a series of $1,000 annual returns beginning one year from now. Andy will earn a return of 8% on the initial investment. How many annual payments of $1,000 will Andy receive? (*Hint:* Use Table 4.)

Compute the number of periods of an annuity.

APPENDIX D

PAYROLL ACCOUNTING

STUDY OBJECTIVES

After studying this appendix, you should be able to:

1. *Discuss the objectives of internal control for payroll.*
2. *Compute and record the payroll for a pay period.*
3. *Describe and record employer payroll taxes.*

Payroll and related fringe benefits often constitute a substantial percentage of current liabilities. In addition, employee compensation is often the most significant expense that a company incurs. For example, General Motors recently reported total employees of 516,000 and labor costs of $31.3 billion. Add to labor costs such fringe benefits as health insurance, life insurance, disability insurance, pensions, and so on, and you can see why proper accounting and control of payroll are so important.

It should be emphasized that payroll accounting involves more than paying employees' wages. Companies are required by law to maintain payroll records for each employee, file and pay payroll taxes, and comply with numerous state and federal tax laws applicable to employee compensation. Accounting for payroll has become much more complex as a result of these regulations.

PAYROLL DEFINED

The term "payroll" pertains to all salaries and wages paid to employees. Managerial, administrative, and sales personnel are generally paid salaries, which are often expressed in terms of a specified amount per month or per year. For example, the faculty and administrative personnel at your college or university are paid salaries. In contrast, store clerks, factory employees, and manual laborers are normally paid wages, which are based on a rate per hour, or on a piece-work basis (such as per unit of product). Frequently, the terms "salaries" and "wages" are used in interchangeably.

The term "payroll" does not extend to payments made for personal service by professionals such as certified public accountants, attorneys, and architects. Such professionals are independent contractors, and payments to them are called **fees**, rather than salaries and wages. This distinction is important because government regulations relating to the payment and reporting of payroll taxes apply only to employees.

IMPORTANCE OF INTERNAL CONTROL TO PAYROLL

1
STUDY
OBJECTIVE

Discuss the objectives of internal control for payroll.

Internal control was introduced in Chapter 8. As applied to payrolls, the objectives of internal control are (1) to safeguard company assets against unauthorized payments of payrolls and (2) to assure the accuracy and reliability of the accounting records pertaining to payrolls.

Unfortunately, irregularities often result if internal control is lax. Overstating hours, using unauthorized pay rates, adding fictitious employees to the payroll, continuing terminated employees on the payroll, and distributing duplicate payroll checks are all methods of stealing from a company. Moreover, inaccurate records will result in incorrect paychecks, financial statements, and payroll tax returns.

Payroll activities involve four functions: hiring employees, timekeeping, preparing the payroll, and paying the payroll. For an internal control system to work effectively, these four functions should be assigned to different departments or individuals. To illustrate these functions in more detail, we will examine the case of Academy Company and one of its employees, Michael Jordan.

TECHNOLOGY IN ACTION

A Senate hearing revealed that the U.S. Army spent $8 million on unauthorized pay, including payments to deserters and "ghost" soldiers. The underlying cause was a computer system so lax that it was possible to create new pay records and destroy old ones without leaving an audit trail.

Hiring Employees

Posting job openings, screening and interviewing applicants, and hiring employees are responsibilities of the personnel department. From a control standpoint, the personnel department provides significant documentation and authorization. When an employee is hired, the personnel department prepares an authorization form like the one used by Academy Company for Michael Jordan shown in Illustration D-1.

Hiring Employees

Personnel department documents and authorizes employment.

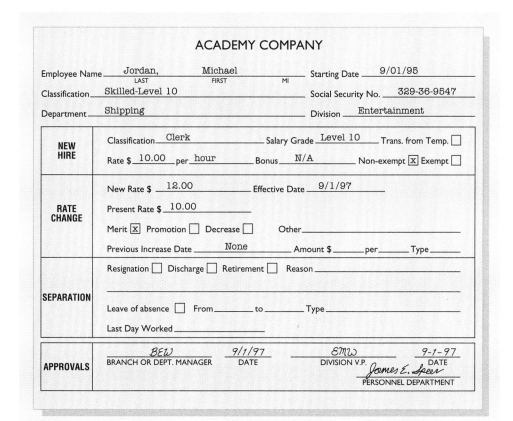

ILLUSTRATION D-1

Personnel authorization form

The authorization form is sent to the payroll department, where it is used to place the new employee on the payroll. A chief concern of the personnel department is ensuring the accuracy of this form. The reason is quite simple: one of the most common types of payroll frauds is adding fictitious employees to the payroll.

The personnel department is also responsible for authorizing (1) changes in pay rates during employment and (2) terminations of employment. In each instance, the authorization should be in writing, and a copy of the change in status should be sent to the payroll department. Note in Illustration D-1 that Jordan received a pay increase of $2 per hour.

Timekeeping

Supervisors monitor hours worked through time cards and time reports.

Timekeeping

Another area in which internal control is important is timekeeping. Hourly employees are usually required to record time worked by "punching" a time clock. The time of arrival and departure are automatically recorded by the employee when he or she inserts a time card into the clock. The time card for Michael Jordan is shown in Illustration D-2.

				PAY PERIOD ENDING

No. 17 — 1/14/99

NAME Michael Jordan

EXTRA TIME		REGULAR TIME	
	1st Day A.M. IN		8:58
	NOON OUT		12:00
	NOON IN		1:00
	P.M. OUT		5:01
	2nd Day A.M. IN		9:00
	NOON OUT		11:59
	NOON IN		12:59
	P.M. OUT		5:00
	3rd Day A.M. IN		8:59
	NOON OUT		12:01
	NOON IN		1:01
	P.M. OUT		5:00
5:00	4th Day A.M. IN		9:00
9:00	NOON OUT		12:00
	NOON IN		1:00
	P.M. OUT		5:00
	5th Day A.M. IN		8:57
	NOON OUT		11:58
	NOON IN		1:00
	P.M. OUT		5:01
	6th Day A.M. IN		8:00
	NOON OUT		1:00
	NOON IN		
	P.M. OUT		
	7th Day A.M. IN		
	NOON OUT		
	NOON IN		
	P.M. OUT		
TOTAL 4	TOTAL		40

THIS SIDE OUT

ILLUSTRATION D-2

Time card

In large companies, time clock procedures are often monitored by a supervisor or security guard to make sure an employee punches only one card. At the end of the pay period, the employee's supervisor is required to approve the hours shown by signing the time card. When overtime hours are involved, approval by a supervisor is usually mandatory to guard against unauthorized overtime. The approved time card is then sent to the payroll department. For salaried employees, a manually prepared weekly or monthly time record kept by a supervisor may be used to record time worked.

Preparing the Payroll

Two (or more) employees verify payroll amounts; supervisor approves.

Preparing the Payroll

The payroll is prepared in the payroll department on the basis of two sources of input: (1) personnel department authorizations and (2) approved time cards. Because of the numerous calculations involved in determining gross wages and payroll deductions, it is customary for a second payroll department employee, working independently, to verify all amounts, and a payroll department supervisor then approves the payroll. The payroll department is also responsible for preparing (but not signing) payroll checks, maintaining payroll records, and preparing payroll tax returns.

Paying the Payroll

The payroll is paid by the treasurer's department. **Payment by check minimizes the risk of loss from theft, and the endorsed check provides proof of payment.** For good internal control, payroll checks should be prenumbered, and all checks should be accounted for. All checks must be signed by the treasurer (or a designated agent), and their distribution to employees should be controlled by the treasurer's department. Checks may be distributed by the treasurer or paymaster.

If the payroll is paid in currency, it is customary to have a second person count the cash in each pay envelope and for the paymaster to obtain a signed receipt from the employee upon payment. Thus, if alleged discrepancies arise, adequate safeguards have been established to protect each party involved.

Paying the Payroll

Treasurer signs and distributes checks.

DETERMINING THE PAYROLL

Determining the payroll involves computing (1) gross earnings, (2) payroll deductions, and (3) net pay.

Gross Earnings

Gross earnings are the total compensation earned by an employee. There are three major types of gross earnings: wages, salaries, and bonuses.

Total **wages** for an employee are determined by multiplying the hours worked by the hourly rate of pay. In addition to the hourly pay rate, most companies are required by law to pay hourly workers a minimum of one and one-half times the regular hourly rate for overtime work in excess of 8 hours per day or 40 hours per week. For example, companies involved in interstate commerce are required by the Federal Fair Labor Standards Act to pay one and one-half times the regular wage rate. In addition, many employees pay overtime rates for work done at night, on weekends, and on holidays. The computation of Michael Jordan's gross earnings (total wages) for the 44 hours shown on his time card for the weekly pay period ending January 14 is as follows:

2
STUDY
OBJECTIVE

Compute and record the payroll for a pay period.

Type of Pay	Hours	×	Rate	=	Gross Earnings
Regular	40	×	$12.00	=	$480.00
Overtime	4	×	18.00	=	72.00
Total wages					$552.00

ILLUSTRATION D-3

Computation of total wages

This computation assumes that Jordan receives one and one-half times his regular hourly rate ($12.00 × 1.5) for his overtime hours. Union contracts often require that overtime rates be as much as twice the regular rates.

The **salary** for an employee is generally based on a monthly or yearly rate rather than on an hourly basis. These rates are then applied ratably to the payroll periods used by the company. Most executive and administrative positions are salaried. The Federal Fair Labor Standards Act does not require overtime pay for such positions.

Many companies have bonus agreements for management personnel and other employees. For example, a recent survey indicated that over 94% of the largest manufacturing companies in the United States provide annual bonuses to their key executives. Bonus arrangements may be based on such factors as in-

ETHICS NOTE

Bonuses often reward outstanding individual performance; however, a successful corporation also needs considerable teamwork. A challenge is to motivate individuals while preventing an unethical team member from taking another's idea for his or her own advantage.

creased sales or net income. Bonuses may be paid in cash and/or by granting executives and employees the opportunity to acquire shares of stock in the company at favorable prices (called stock option plans). Bonuses have become very lucrative, as companies attempt to retain the services of key executives—so lucrative, in fact, that they have come under intense public scrutiny.

ACCOUNTING IN ACTION
Business Insight

In a recent year Amoco Corporation employees received shares of the company's stock equal to 3.5% of their salaries as a result of the company's strong total return to shareholders in the previous year. Amoco's performance plan awards shares to employees when the return to shareholders meets or exceeds the average of seven major oil companies. Amoco's return of 18.8% was the second highest of the group of competitors.

Payroll Deductions

As anyone who has received a paycheck knows, gross earning are usually very different from the amount actually received. The difference is attributable to payroll deductions. Payroll deductions do not result in payroll tax expense to the employer. The employer serves only as a collection agency, and it subsequently transfers the deductions to the government and designated recipients. Payroll deductions may be mandatory or voluntary. The former are required by law and consist of FICA taxes and income taxes. The latter are at the option of the employee. Illustration D-4 summarizes the types of payroll deductions.

ILLUSTRATION D-4

Payroll deductions

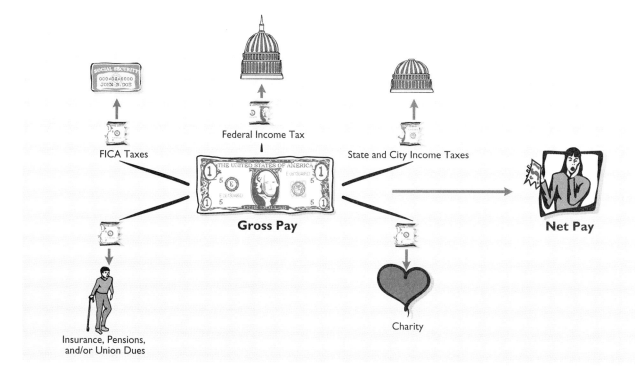

FICA Taxes

In 1937 Congress enacted the Federal Insurance Contribution Act (FICA). FICA taxes **are designed to provide workers with supplemental retirement, employment disability, and medical benefits.** In 1965, benefits were expanded to include Medicare for individuals over 65 years of age. The benefits are financed by a tax levied on employees' earnings. FICA taxes are commonly referred to as **Social Security taxes**.

The tax rate and the tax base for FICA taxes are set by Congress, and they are changed intermittently. When FICA taxes were first imposed, the rate was 1% on the first $3,000 of gross earnings, or a maximum of $30 per year. The rate and base have changed dramatically since that time! In 1998, that rate was 7.65% (6.2% Social Security and 1.45% Medicare) on the first $68,400 of gross earnings for each employee, or a maximum of $5,232.60.[1] For purpose of illustration in this chapter, we will assume a rate of 8% on the first $65,000 of gross earnings, or a maximum of $5,200. Using the 8% rate, the FICA withholding for Jordan for the weekly pay period ending January 14 is $44.16 ($552 × 8%).

Income Taxes

Under the United States pay-as-you-go system of federal income taxes, employers are required to withhold income taxes from employees each pay period. The amount to be withheld is determined by three variables: (1) the employee's gross earnings; (2) the number of allowances claimed by the employee for herself or himself, his or her spouse, and other dependents; and (3) the length of the pay period. **To indicate to the Internal Revenue Service the number of allowances claimed, the employee must complete an** Employee's Withholding Allowance Certificate (Form W-4). As shown in Illustration D-5, Michael Jordan claims two allowances on his W-4.

Form **W-4**	**Employee's Withholding Allowance Certificate**	OMB No. 1545-0010

Department of the Treasury
Internal Revenue Service
► For Privacy Act and Paperwork Reduction Act Notice, see page 2.

19**98**

1 Type or print your first name and middle initial — Michael
Last name — Jordan
2 Your social security number — 329-36-9547

Home address (number and street or rural route)
2345 Mifflin Ave.

3 ☐ Single ☒ Married ☐ Married, but withhold at higher Single rate.
Note: *If married, but legally separated, or spouse is a nonresident alien, check the Single box.*

City or town, State, and ZIP code
Hampton, MI 48292

4 If your last name differs from that on your social security card, check here and call 1-800-772-1213 for a new card . . . . . ► ☐

5 Total number of allowances you are claiming (from line H above or from the worksheet on page 2 if they apply) . . . 5 2
6 Additional amount, if any, you want withheld from each paycheck . . . . 6 $
7 I claim exemption from withholding for 1998, and I certify that I meet BOTH of the following conditions for exemption:
• Last year I had a right to a refund of ALL Federal income tax withheld because I had NO tax liability AND
• This year I expect a refund of ALL Federal income tax withheld because I expect to have NO tax liability.
If you meet both conditions, enter "Exempt" here . . . . ► 7

Under penalties of perjury, I certify that I am entitled to the number of withholding allowances claimed on this certificate or entitled to claim exempt status.

Employee's signature ► *Michael Jordan*
Date ► September 1, 19 99

8 Employer's name and address (Employer: Complete 8 and 10 only if sending to the IRS)
9 Office code (optional)
10 Employer identification number

Cat. No. 102200

Withholding tables furnished by the Internal Revenue Service indicate the amount of income tax to be withheld from gross wages based on the number of allowances claimed. Separate tables are provided for weekly, biweekly, semi-monthly, and monthly pay periods. The portion of the withholding tax table for Michael Jordan (assuming he earns $552 per week) is shown in Illustration D-6. As indicated in the table, for a weekly salary of $552 with two allowances, the income tax to be withheld is $49.

---

[1]The Medicare provision also includes a tax of 1.45% on gross earnings in excess of $68,400. In the interest of simplification, our end-of-chapter assignment material ignores this 1.45% charge. We assume zero withholdings on gross earnings above $65,000.

MARRIED Persons — **WEEKLY** Payroll Period
(For Wages Paid in 1998)

If the wages are –		And the number of withholding allowances claimed is –										
At least	But less than	0	1	2	3	4	5	6	7	8	9	10
		The amount of income tax to be withheld is –										
490	500	56	48	40	32	24	17	9	1	0	0	0
500	510	57	49	42	34	26	18	10	3	0	0	0
510	520	59	51	43	35	27	20	12	4	0	0	0
520	530	60	52	45	37	29	21	13	6	0	0	0
530	540	62	54	46	38	30	23	15	7	0	0	0
540	550	63	55	48	40	32	24	16	9	1	0	0
550	560	65	57	49	41	33	26	18	10	2	0	0
560	570	66	58	51	43	35	27	19	12	4	0	0
570	580	68	60	52	44	36	29	21	13	5	0	0
580	590	69	61	54	46	38	30	22	15	7	0	0
590	600	71	63	55	47	39	32	24	16	8	1	0
600	610	72	64	57	49	41	33	25	18	10	2	0
610	620	74	66	58	50	42	35	27	19	11	4	0
620	630	75	67	60	52	44	36	28	21	13	5	0
630	640	77	69	61	53	45	38	30	22	14	7	0
640	650	78	70	63	55	47	39	31	24	16	8	0
650	660	80	72	64	56	48	41	33	25	17	10	2
660	670	81	73	66	58	50	42	34	27	19	11	3
670	680	83	75	67	59	51	44	36	28	20	13	5
680	690	84	76	69	61	53	45	37	30	22	14	6

Most states and some cities also require employers to withhold income taxes from the earnings of employees. As a general rule, the amounts to be withheld are determined by applying a percentage specified in the state revenue code to the amount withheld for the federal income tax or to the employee's earnings. For the sake of simplicity, we have assumed that Jordan's wages are subject to state income taxes of 2%, or $11.04 (2% × $552).

There is no limit on the amount of gross earnings subject to income tax withholdings. In fact, the higher the earnings, the higher the amount of taxes withheld.

Other Deductions

Employees may voluntarily authorize withholdings for charitable, retirement, and other purposes. All voluntary deductions from gross earnings should be authorized in writing by the employee. The authorization(s) may be made individually or as part of a group plan. Deductions for charitable organizations, such as the United Way, or for financial arrangements, such as U.S. savings bonds and repayment of loans from company credit unions, are made individually. In contrast, deductions for union dues, health and life insurance, and pension plans are often made on a group basis. For purpose of illustration, we will assume that Jordan has voluntary deductions of $10 for the United Way and $5 for union dues.

ALTERNATIVE TERMINOLOGY

Net pay is also called *take-home pay.*

Net Pay

Net pay is determined by subtracting payroll deductions from gross earnings. For Michael Jordan, net pay for the pay period is $432.80, computed as follows:

Gross earnings		$552.00
Payroll deductions:		
FICA taxes	$44.16	
Federal income taxes	49.00	
State income taxes	11.04	
United Way	10.00	
Union dues	5.00	119.20
Net pay		**$432.80**

Assuming that Michael Jordan's wages for each week during the year are $552, total wages for the year are $28,704 (52 × $552). Thus, all of Jordan's wages are subject to FICA tax during the year. However, if an employee's wages are $1,350 per week, or $70,200 for the year, only the first $65,000 is subject to FICA taxes. In such case, the maximum FICA withholdings would be $5,200 ($65,000 × 8%).

RECORDING THE PAYROLL

Recording the payroll involves maintaining payroll department records, recognizing payroll expenses and liabilities, and recording payment of the payroll.

Maintaining Payroll Department Records

To comply with state and federal laws, an employer must keep a cumulative record of each employee's gross earnings, deductions, and net pay during the year. The record that provides this information and other essential data is the employee earnings record. Michael Jordan's employee earnings record is shown in Illustration D-8.

ACADEMY COMPANY
Employee Earnings Record
For the Year 1999

Name	Michael Jordan	Address	2345 Mifflin Ave.
Social Security Number	329-36-9547		Hampton, Michigan 48292
Date of Birth	December 24, 1962	Telephone	555-238-9051
Date Employed	September 1, 1995	Date Employment Ended	
Sex	Male	Exemptions	2
Single _____	Married X		

1999 Period Ending	Total Hours	Gross Earnings				Deductions						Payment	
		Regular	Overtime	Total	Cumulative	FICA	Fed. Inc. Tax	State Inc. Tax	United Way	Union Dues	Total	Net Amount	Check No.
1/7	42	480.00	36.00	516.00	516.00	41.28	43.00	10.32	10.00	5.00	109.60	406.40	974
1/14	44	480.00	72.00	552.00	1,068.00	44.16	49.00	11.04	10.00	5.00	119.20	432.80	1028
1/21	43	480.00	54.00	534.00	1,602.00	42.72	46.00	10.68	10.00	5.00	114.40	419.60	1077
1/28	42	480.00	36.00	516.00	2,118.00	41.28	43.00	10.32	10.00	5.00	109.60	406.40	1133
Jan. Total		1,920.00	198.00	2,118.00		169.44	181.00	42.36	40.00	20.00	452.80	1,665.20	

A separate earnings record is kept for each employee, and it is updated after each pay period. The cumulative payroll data on the earnings record are used by the employer in (1) determining when an employee has earned the maximum earnings subject to FICA taxes, (2) filing state and federal payroll tax returns (as explained later in the appendix), and (3) providing each employee with a statement of gross earnings and tax withholdings for the year, as shown in Illustration D-12 on page D15.

In addition to employee earnings records, many companies find it useful to prepare a payroll register to accumulate the gross earnings, deductions, and net pay by employee for each pay period. It provides the documentation for preparing a paycheck for each employee. The payroll register is presented in Illustration D-9, with the data for Michael Jordan shown in the wages section. In this example, Academy Company's total payroll is $17,210, as shown in the gross pay column.

Note that this record is a listing of each employee's payroll data for the pay period. In some companies, a payroll register is a journal or book of original entry, and postings are made directly to ledger accounts from the register. In other companies, the payroll register is a memorandum record that provides the data for a general journal entry and subsequent posting to the ledger accounts. In the Academy Company situation, the latter procedure is followed.

ILLUSTRATION D-9

Payroll register

ACADEMY COMPANY
Payroll Register
For the Week Ending January 14, 1999

Employee	Total Hours	Regular	Over-time	Gross	FICA	Federal Income Tax	State Income Tax	United Way	Union Dues	Total	Net pay	Check No.	Office Salaries Expense	Wages Expense
Office Salaries														
Arnold, Patricia	40	580.00		580.00	46.40	61.00	11.60	15.00		134.00	446.00	998	580.00	
Canton, Matthew	40	590.00		590.00	47.20	63.00	11.80	20.00		142.00	448.00	999	590.00	
Mueller, William	40	530.00		530.00	42.40	54.00	10.60	11.00		118.00	412.00	1000	530.00	
Subtotal		5,200.00		5,200.00	416.00	1,090.00	104.00	120.00		1,730.00	3,470.00		5,200.00	
Wages														
Bennett, Robin	42	480.00	36.00	516.00	41.28	43.00	10.32	18.00	5.00	117.60	398.40	1025		516.00
Jordan, Michael	44	480.00	72.00	552.00	44.16	49.00	11.04	10.00	5.00	119.20	432.80	1028		552.00
Milroy, Lee	43	480.00	54.00	534.00	42.72	46.00	10.68	10.00	5.00	114.40	419.60	1029		534.00
Subtotal		11,000.00	1,010.00	12,010.00	960.80	2,400.00	240.20	301.50	115.00	4,017.50	7,992.50			12,010.00
Total		16,200.00	1,010.00	17,210.00	1,376.80	3,490.00	344.20	421.50	115.00	5,747.50	11,462.50		5,200.00	12,010.00

Column groupings: Earnings (Total Hours, Regular, Over-time, Gross); Deductions (FICA, Federal Income Tax, State Income Tax, United Way, Union Dues, Total); Paid (Net pay, Check No.); Accounts Debited (Office Salaries Expense, Wages Expense)

Recognizing Payroll Expenses and Liabilities

From the payroll register in Illustration D-9, a journal entry is made to record the payroll. For the week ending January 14 the entry is:

Jan. 14	Office Salaries Expense		5,200.00	
	Wages Expense		12,010.00	
	FICA Taxes Payable			1,376.80
	Federal Income Taxes Payable			3,490.00
	State Income Taxes Payable			344.20
	United Way Payable			421.50
	Union Dues Payable			115.00
	Salaries and Wages Payable			11,462.50
	(To record payroll for the week ending January 14)			

```
A  =    L     +     SE
   + 1,376.80  −  5,200.00
   + 3,490.00  − 12,010.00
   +   344.20
   +   421.50
   +   115.00
   +11,462.50
```

Specific liability accounts are credited for the mandatory and voluntary deductions made during the pay period. In the example, debits to Office Salaries and Wages Expense are used for gross earnings because office workers are on a salary and other employees are paid on an hourly rate. In other cases, there may be additional debits such as Store Salaries and Sales Salaries. The amount credited to Salaries and Wages Payable is the sum of the individual checks the employees will receive.

Recording Payment of the Payroll

Payment by check is made either from the employer's regular bank account or a payroll bank account. Each check is usually accompanied by a detachable statement of earnings document that shows the employee's gross earnings, payroll deductions, and net pay. The Academy Company uses its regular bank account for payroll checks. The check and statement of earnings for Michael Jordan are shown in Illustration D-10.

AC	ACADEMY COMPANY 19 Center St. Hampton, MI 48291			No. 1028	

January 14, 1999 62—1113/610

Pay to the order of Michael Jordan $ 432.80

Four Hundred Thirty-two and 80/100 ———————— Dollars

City Bank & Trust
P.O. Box 3000
Hampton, MI 48291

For Payroll

Randall E. Barnes

00324477⑆ 7660

- - - - - - - - - - - - - - DETACH AND RETAIN THIS PORTION FOR YOUR RECORDS - - - - - - - - - - - - - -

NAME				SOC. SEC. NO.	EMPL. NUMBER	NO. EXEMP	PAY PERIOD ENDING
Michael Jordan				329-36-9547		2	1/14/99

REG. HRS.	O.T. HRS.	OTH. HRS. (1)	OTH. HRS. (2)	REG. EARNINGS	O.T. EARNINGS	OTH. EARNINGS (1)	OTH. EARNINGS (2)	GROSS
40	4			480.00	72.00			$552.00

FED. W/H TAX	FICA	STATE TAX	LOCAL TAX	OTHER DEDUCTIONS				NET PAY
49.00	44.16	11.04		(1) 10.00	(2) 5.00	(3)	(4)	432.80

YEAR TO DATE								
FED. W/H TAX	FICA	STATE TAX	LOCAL TAX	OTHER DEDUCTIONS				NET PAY
92.00	85.44	21.36		(1) 20.00	(2) 10.00	(3)	(4)	$839.20

HELPFUL HINT
Do any of the income tax liabilities result in payroll tax expense for the employer? Answer: No, the employer is acting only as a collection agency for the government.

Following payment of the payroll, the check numbers are entered in the payroll register. The entry to record payment of the payroll for Academy Company is as follows:

Jan. 14	Salaries and Wages Payable	11,462.50	
	Cash		11,462.50
	(To record payment of payroll)		

A	=	L	+	SE
−11,462.50		−11,462.50		

When currency is used in payment, one check is prepared for the net pay. The check is then cashed, and the coins and currency are inserted in individual pay envelopes for disbursement to individual employees.

TECHNOLOGY IN ACTION

In addition to supplying the entry to record the payroll, the output for a computerized payroll system would include (1) payroll checks, (2) a payroll check register sorted by check and department, and (3) updated employee earnings records which become the source for monthly, quarterly, and annual reporting of wages to taxing agencies.

BEFORE YOU GO ON ...

Review it

1. Identify two internal control procedures that are applicable to each payroll function.
2. What are the primary sources of gross earnings?
3. What payroll deductions are (a) mandatory and (b) voluntary?
4. What account titles are used in recording a payroll, assuming only mandatory payroll deductions are involved?

Do It

Your cousin Stan is establishing a house-cleaning business and will have a number of employees working for him. From his prior work experience, he is aware that documentation procedures are an important part of internal control. However, he is confused about the difference between an employee earnings record and a payroll register. He asks you to explain the principal differences, because he wants to be sure that he sets up the proper payroll procedures.

Reasoning: You may need to review the material on payroll department records and study Illustrations D-8 and D-9 in order to identify and explain the differences for Stan.

Solution: An employee earnings record is kept for *each* employee. It shows gross earnings, payroll deductions, and net pay for each pay period. It provides cumulative payroll data for that employee. In contrast, a payroll register is a listing of *all* employees' gross earnings, payroll deductions, and net pay for each pay period. It is the documentation for preparing paychecks and for recording the payroll. Of course, Stan will need to keep both documents.

Related exercise material: BED–1, BED–3, and ED–3.

EMPLOYER PAYROLL TAXES

3
STUDY
OBJECTIVE

Describe and record employer payroll taxes.

Payroll tax expense for businesses results from three taxes **levied on employers** by governmental agencies. These taxes are: FICA, federal unemployment tax, and state unemployment tax. Each of these taxes plus such items as paid vacations and pensions are collectively referred to as "fringe benefits." As indicated earlier, the cost of fringe benefits in many companies is substantial.

FICA Taxes

We have seen that each employee must pay FICA taxes. The employer must match each employee's FICA contribution. The matching contribution results in **payroll tax expense** to the employer. The employer's tax is subject to the same rate and maximum earnings applicable to the employee. The account, FICA Taxes Payable, is used for both the employee's and the employer's FICA contributions. For the January 14 payroll, Academy Company's FICA tax is $1,376.80 ($17,210.00 × 8%).

Federal Unemployment Taxes

The Federal Unemployment Tax Act (FUTA) is another feature of the federal Social Security program. Federal unemployment taxes provide benefits for a limited period of time to employees who lose their jobs through no fault of their own. Under provisions of the Act, the employer is required to pay a tax of 6.2% on the first $7,000 of gross wages paid to each employee during a calendar year. The law, however, allows the employer a maximum credit of 5.4% on the federal rate for contributions to state unemployment taxes. Because of this provision, state unemployment tax laws generally provide for a 5.4% rate, and the effective federal unemployment tax rate becomes 0.8% (6.2% − 5.4%). This tax is borne **entirely by the employer**; there is no deduction or withholding from employees. The account Federal Unemployment Taxes Payable is used to recognize this liability. The federal unemployment tax for Academy Company for the January 14 payroll is $137.68 ($17,210.00 × 0.8%).

State Unemployment Taxes

All states have unemployment compensation programs under state unemployment tax acts (SUTA). Like federal unemployment taxes, state unemployment taxes provide benefits to employees who lose their jobs. These taxes are levied on employers.[2] The basic rate is usually 5.4% on the first $7,000 of wages paid to an employee during the year. The basic rate is adjusted according to the employer's experience rating: Companies with a history of unstable employment may pay more than the basic rate. Companies with a history of stable employment may pay less than 5.4%. Regardless of the rate paid, the credit on the federal unemployment tax is still 5.4%. The account State Unemployment Taxes Payable is used for this liability. The state unemployment tax for Academy Company for the January 14 payroll is $929.34 ($17,210.00 × 5.4%). Illustration D-11 summarizes the types of employer payroll taxes.

HELPFUL HINT
FICA taxes are paid both by the employer and employee. Federal unemployment taxes and (in most states) the state unemployment taxes are borne entirely by the employer.

ILLUSTRATION D-11

Employer payroll taxes

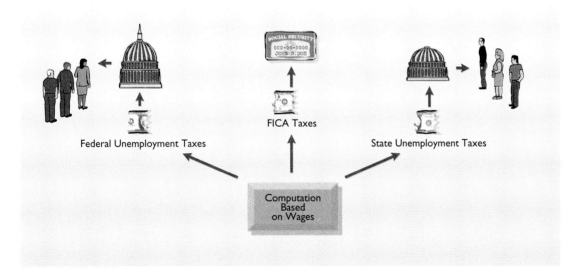

Recording Employer Payroll Taxes

Employer payroll taxes are usually recorded at the same time the payroll is journalized. The entire amount of gross pay ($17,210.00) shown in the payroll register in Illustration D-9 is subject to each of the three taxes mentioned above. Ac-

---

[2]In a few states, the employee is also required to make a contribution. In this textbook, including the homework, we will assume that the tax is only on the employer.

cordingly, the entry to record the payroll tax expense associated with the January 14 payroll is:

A	=	L	+	SE
		+1,376.80		−2,443.82
		+ 137.68		
		+ 929.34		

Jan. 14	Payroll Tax Expense	2,443.82	
	FICA Taxes Payable		1,376.80
	Federal Unemployment Taxes Payable		137.68
	State Unemployment Taxes Payable		929.34
	(To record employer's payroll taxes on January 14 payroll)		

Separate liability accounts are used instead of a single credit to Payroll Taxes Payable, because these liabilities are payable to different taxing authorities at different dates. The liability accounts are classified as current liabilities since they will be paid within the next year. Payroll Tax Expense is classified on the income statement as an operating expense.

FILING AND REMITTING PAYROLL TAXES

Preparation of payroll tax returns is the responsibility of the payroll department; payment of the taxes is made by the treasurer's department. Much of the information for the returns is obtained from employee earnings records.

For purposes of reporting and remitting, FICA taxes and federal income taxes withheld are combined. **The taxes must be reported quarterly**, no later than one month following the close of each quarter. The remitting requirements depend on the amount of taxes withheld and the length of the pay period. Remittances are made through deposits in either a Federal Reserve Bank or an authorized commercial bank.

ACCOUNTING IN ACTION
Business Insight

The owner of a newly restored Victorian hotel, nestled in a small Massachusetts town, skipped payment of withholding taxes for three quarters because of cash flow problems. Before long, he received a call from the IRS. After months of haggling, the hotel owner was told that unless he paid the $70,000 owed, the IRS would be forced to liquidate the hotel, the land, and dozens of antiques in the inn, which had taken him and his wife years to acquire.

As this story indicates, cash-hungry small businesses are often tempted to skip or delay paying withholding taxes. Increasingly, federal and state agencies are cracking down on such cheaters. Penalties for lateness or nonpayment can be devastating: Fines are levied at the rate of 5% of taxes owed for *each month* a payroll tax isn't filed. And in cases where nothing is paid, penalties of 100% can be applied, with interest added, to the unpaid balance. Under the 100% penalty, the government can padlock the doors, seize assets, and hold the officers or certain other employees personally responsible for the penalties.

What happened to the Massachusetts hotel owner? He's now working on a repayment plan, rather than lose his years of hard work.

Federal unemployment taxes are generally filed and remitted **annually** on or before January 31 of the subsequent year. Earlier payments are required, however, when the tax exceeds a specified amount. State unemployment taxes usually must be filed and paid by the **end of the month following each quarter**. When payroll taxes are paid, payroll liability accounts are debited and cash is credited.

The employer is also required to provide each employee with a Wage and Tax Statement (Form W-2) by January 31 following the end of a calendar year. This statement shows gross earnings, FICA taxes withheld, and income taxes withheld for the year. The required W-2 form for Michael Jordan, using assumed annual data, is shown in Illustration D-12.

ILLUSTRATION D-12

W-2 form

The employer must send a copy of each employee's Wage and Tax Statement to the Social Security Administration. This agency subsequently furnishes the Internal Revenue Service with the income data required.

BEFORE YOU GO ON ...

Review It

1. What payroll taxes are levied on employers?
2. What accounts are involved in accruing employer payroll taxes?

Do It

In January, the payroll supervisor determines that gross earnings in Halo Company are $70,000. All earnings are subject to 8% FICA taxes, 5.4% state unemployment taxes, and 0.8% federal unemployment taxes. You are asked to record the employer's payroll taxes.

Reasoning: In recording the taxes, you should remember that (1) the total expense can be debited to one account and (2) separate accounts are required for each of the three liabilities.

Solution: The entry to record the employer's payroll taxes is:

Payroll Tax Expense	9,940	
FICA Taxes Payable ($70,000 × 8%)		5,600
Federal Unemployment Taxes Payable ($70,000 × 0.8%)		560
State Unemployment Taxes Payable ($70,000 × 5.4%)		3,780
(To record employer's payroll taxes on January payroll)		

Related exercise material: BED–2, BED–3, BED–4, ED–1, ED–2, ED–3, ED–4, and ED–5.

DEMONSTRATION PROBLEM

Indiana Jones Company had the following payroll transactions:

Feb. 28   The payroll for the month consists of Sales Salaries $32,000 and Office Salaries $18,000. All wages are subject to 8% FICA taxes. A total of $8,900 federal income taxes are withheld. The salaries are paid on March 1.

28   Employer payroll taxes include 8% FICA taxes, a 5.4% state unemployment tax, and a .8% federal unemployment tax.

Instructions
(a) Journalize the February payroll transaction.
(b) Journalize the payroll adjusting entry at February 28.

SOLUTION TO DEMONSTRATION PROBLEM

(a) Feb. 28	Sales Salaries Expense		32,000	
	Office Salaries Expense		18,000	
	FICA Taxes Payable (8% × $50,000)			4,000
	Federal Income Taxes Payable			8,900
	Salaries Payable			37,100
	(To record February salaries)			
(b) Feb. 28	Payroll Tax Expense		7,100	
	FICA Taxes Payable			4,000
	Federal Unemployment Taxes Payable			400
	(.8% × $50,000)			
	State Unemployment Taxes Payable			2,700
	(5.4% × $50,000)			
	(To record employer's payroll taxes on February payroll)			

SUMMARY OF STUDY OBJECTIVES

1. Discuss the objectives of internal control for payroll. The objectives of internal control for payroll are (1) to safeguard company assets against unauthorized payments of payrolls, and (2) to assure the accuracy and reliability of the accounting records pertaining to payrolls.

2. Compute and record the payroll for a pay period. The computation of the payroll involves gross earnings, payroll deductions, and net pay. In recording the payroll, salaries (or wages) expense is debited for gross earnings, individual tax and other liability accounts are credited for payroll de-

ductions, and salaries (wages) payable is credited for net pay. When the payroll is paid, Salaries and Wages Payable is debited, and Cash is credited.

3. Describe and record employer payroll taxes. Employer payroll taxes consist of FICA, federal unemployment taxes, and state unemployment taxes. The taxes are usually accrued at the time the payroll is recorded by debiting Payroll Tax Expense and crediting separate liability accounts for each type of tax.

GLOSSARY

Bonus Compensation to management personnel and other employees, based on factors such as increased sales or the amount of net income. (p. D5)

Employee earnings record A cumulative record of each employee's gross earnings, deductions, and net pay during the year. (p. D9)

Employee's Withholding Allowance Certificate (Form W-4) An Internal Revenue Service form on which the employee indicates the number of allowances claimed for withholding federal income taxes. (p. D7)

Federal unemployment taxes Taxes imposed on the employer that provide benefits for a limited time period to employees who lose their jobs through no fault of their own. (p. D13)

FICA taxes Taxes designed to provide workers with supplemental retirement, employment disability, and medical benefits. (p. D6)

Gross earnings Total compensation earned by an employee. (p. D5)

Net pay Gross earnings less payroll deductions. (p. D8)

Payroll deductions   Deductions from gross earnings to determine the amount of a paycheck. (p. D6)

Payroll register   A payroll record that accumulates the gross earnings, deductions, and net pay by employee for each pay period. (p. D10)

Salaries   Specified amount per month or per year paid to executive and administrative personnel. (p. D2)

Statement of earnings   A document attached to a paycheck that indicates the employee's gross earnings, payroll deductions, and net pay. (p. D11)

State unemployment taxes   Taxes imposed on the employer that provide benefits to employees who lose their jobs. (p. D13)

Wage and Tax Statement (Form W-2)   A form showing gross earnings, FICA taxes withheld, and income taxes withheld which is prepared annually by an employer for each employee. (p. D15)

Wages   Amounts paid to employees based on a rate per hour or on a piece-work basis. (p. D2)

SELF-STUDY QUESTIONS

Answers are at the end of the appendix.

(SO 1) 1. The department that should pay the payroll is the:
   a. timekeeping department.
   b. personnel department.
   c. treasurer's department.
   d. payroll department

(SO 2) 2. Tyler Remmers earns $14 per hour for a 40-hour week and $21 per hour for any overtime work. If Tyler works 44 hours in a week, gross earnings are:

   a. $560.
   b. $616.
   c. $644.
   d. $666.

3. Employer payroll taxes do *not* include: (SO 3)
   a. federal unemployment taxes.
   b. state unemployment taxes.
   c. FICA taxes.
   d. federal income taxes.

QUESTIONS

1. You are a newly hired accountant with Schindlebeck Company. On your first day, the controller asks you to identify the main internal control objectives related to payroll accounting. How would you respond?

2. What are the four functions associated with payroll activities?

3. What is the difference between gross pay and net pay? Which amount should a company record as wages or salaries expense?

4. Which payroll tax is levied on both employers and employees?

5. Are the federal and state income taxes withheld from employee paychecks a payroll tax expense for the employer? Explain your answer.

6. What do the following acronyms stand for: FICA, FUTA, and SUTA?

7. What information is shown on a W-4 statement? A W-2 statement?

8. Distinguish between the two types of payroll deductions and give examples of each.

9. What are the primary uses of the employees earnings record?

10. (a) Identify the three types of employer payroll taxes. (b) How are tax liability accounts and payroll tax expense classified in the financial statements?

BRIEF EXERCISES

BED–1   Anakin Company has the following payroll procedures: *Identify payroll functions.*
                                                                        (SO 1)

   1. Supervisor approves overtime work.
   2. The personnel department prepares hiring authorization forms for new hires.
   3. A second payroll department employee verifies payroll calculations.
   4. The treasurer's department pays employees.

Identify the payroll function to which each procedure pertains.

BED–2   Maggie Sharrer's regular hourly wage rate is $14, and she receives an hourly rate   *Compute gross earnings and*
of $21 for work in excess of 40 hours. During a January pay period, Maggie works 43 hours.   *net pay.*
Maggie's federal income tax withholding is $70, and she has no voluntary deductions. FICA   *(SO 2)*
taxes are 8% on the first $60,000 of gross earnings. Compute Maggie Sharrer's gross earnings
and net pay for the pay period.

BED–3 Data for Maggie Sharrer are presented in BED–2. Prepare the journal entries to record (a) Maggie's pay for the period and (b) the payment of Maggie's wages. Use January 15 for the end of the pay period and the payment date.

BED–4 In January, gross earnings in the Dan Nagel Company totaled $50,000. All earnings are subject to 8% FICA taxes, 5.4% state unemployment taxes, and 0.8% federal unemployment taxes. Prepare the entry to record January payroll tax expense.

EXERCISES

ED–1 Rose Reed's regular hourly wage rate is $15.00, and she receives a wage of $1\frac{1}{2}$ times the regular hourly rate for work in excess of 40 hours. During a March weekly pay period Rose worked 42 hours. Her gross earnings prior to the current week were $7,000. Rose is married and claims three withholding allowances. Her only voluntary deduction is for group hospitalization insurance at $10.00 per week.

Instructions
  (a) Compute the following amounts for Rose's wages for the current week.
      1. Gross earnings.
      2. FICA taxes. (Assume 8% rate on maximum of $60,000.)
      3. Federal income taxes withheld. (Use wage-bracket table in text, p. D8.)
      4. State income taxes withheld. (Assume 2.0% rate.)
      5. Net pay.
  (b) Record Rose's pay, assuming she is an office computer operator.

ED–2 Employee earnings records for Kokomo Company reveal the following gross earnings for four employees through the pay period of December 15.

R. Sunberg	$58,500	D. Myers	$59,200
C. Carlsen	$59,700	P. Otto	$60,000

For the pay period ending December 31, each employee's gross earnings is $1,000. The FICA tax rate is 8% on gross earnings up to $60,000.

Instructions
Compute the FICA withholdings that should be made for each employee for the December 31 pay period. (Show computations.)

ED–3 Ahmad Company has the following data for the weekly payroll ending January 31.

	Hours						Hourly	Federal Income Tax	Health
Employee	M	T	W	T	F	S	Rate	Withholding	Insurance
A. Hope	8	8	9	8	10	0	$10	$34	$10
B. Innes	8	8	8	8	8	2	12	37	15
C. Stone	9	10	8	8	9	0	12	58	15

Employees are paid $1\frac{1}{2}$ times the regular hourly rate for all hours worked in excess of 40 hours per week. FICA taxes are 8% on the first $60,000 of gross earnings. Ahmad Company is subject to 5.4% state unemployment taxes and 0.8% federal unemployment taxes on the first $7,000 of gross earnings.

Instructions
  (a) Prepare the payroll register for the weekly payroll.
  (b) Prepare the journal entry to record the payroll and Ahmad's payroll tax expense.

ED–4 Selected data from a February payroll register for Tia Yue Company are presented below with some amounts intentionally omitted.

Gross earnings:

Regular	$8,900	State income taxes	$ (3)
Overtime	(1)	Union dues	100
Total	(2)	Total deductions	(4)
Deductions:		Net pay	7,310
FICA taxes	$ 760	Accounts debited:	
Federal income taxes	1,140	Warehouse wages	(5)
		Store wages	$4,000

FICA taxes are 8% and state income taxes are 2% of gross earnings.

Instructions
(a) Fill in the missing amounts.
(b) Journalize the February payroll and the payment of the payroll.

ED–5 According to a payroll register summary of Modesco Company, the amount of employee's gross pay in December was $700,000, of which $60,000 was not subject to FICA tax and $680,000 was not subject to state and federal unemployment taxes.

Determine employer's payroll taxes and record payroll tax expense.
(SO 3)

Instructions
(a) Determine the employer's payroll tax expense for the month, using the following rates: FICA, 8%; state unemployment, 5.4%; federal unemployment, 0.8%.
(b) Prepare the journal entry to record December payroll tax expense.

PROBLEMS: SET A

PD–1A The payroll procedures used by three different companies are described below:

Identify internal control weaknesses and make recommendations for improvement.
(SO 1)

1. In Lindy Company each employee is required to mark the hours worked on a clock card. At the end of each pay period, the employee must have this clock card approved by the department manager. The approved card is then given to the payroll department by the employee. Subsequently, the treasurer's department pays the employee by check.
2. In Selina Company clock cards and time clocks are used. At the end of each pay period, the department manager initials the cards, indicates the rates of pay, and sends them to payroll. A payroll register is prepared from the cards by the payroll department. Cash equal to the total net pay in each department is given to the department manager, who pays the employees in cash.
3. In Winker Company employees are required to record hours worked on clock cards by "punching" a time clock. At the end of each pay period, the clock cards are collected by the department manager. The manager prepares a payroll register in duplicate and forwards the original to payroll. In payroll, the summaries are checked for mathematical accuracy, and a payroll supervisor pays each employee by check.

Instructions
(a) ▰▰▰▱▶ Indicate the weakness(es) in internal control in each company.
(b) ▰▰▰▱▶ For each weakness, describe the control procedure(s) that will provide effective internal control. Use the following format for your answer:

(a) Weaknesses	(b) Recommended Procedures

PD–2A Banner Drug Store has four employees who are paid on an hourly basis plus time-and-one-half for all hours worked in excess of 40 a week. Payroll data for the week ended February 15, 2000, are presented below:

Prepare payroll register and payroll entries.
(SO 2, 3)

Employees	Hours Worked	Hourly Rate	Federal Income Tax Withholdings	United Way
B. Creek	39	$13.00	$?	$–0–
C. Crowley	42	12.00	?	5.00
E. Irvine	44	13.00	56	7.50
G. Klamath	46	12.00	33	5.00

Creek and Crowley are married. They claim 2 and 4 withholding allowances, respectively. The following tax rates are applicable: FICA 8%, state income taxes 3%, state unemployment taxes 5.4%, and federal unemployment 0.8%. The first three employees are sales clerks (store wages expense), and the other employee performs administrative duties (office wages expense).

Instructions

(a) Prepare a payroll register for the weekly payroll. (Use the wage-bracket withholding table in the text for federal income tax withholdings.)

(b) Journalize the payroll on February 15, 2000, and the accrual of employer payroll taxes.

(c) Journalize the payment of the payroll on February 16, 2000.

(d) Journalize the deposit in a Federal Reserve Bank on February 28, 2000, of the FICA and federal income taxes payable to the government.

Journalize payroll transactions and adjusting entries.
(SO 2, 3)

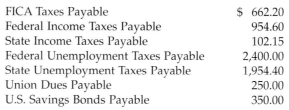

PD–3A   The following payroll liability accounts are included in the ledger of Carlos Costa Company on January 1, 2000:

FICA Taxes Payable	$ 662.20
Federal Income Taxes Payable	954.60
State Income Taxes Payable	102.15
Federal Unemployment Taxes Payable	2,400.00
State Unemployment Taxes Payable	1,954.40
Union Dues Payable	250.00
U.S. Savings Bonds Payable	350.00

In January, the following transactions occurred:

Jan. 10   Sent check for $250.00 to union treasurer for union dues.
    12   Deposited check for $1,616.80 in Federal Reserve Bank for FICA taxes and federal income taxes withheld.
    15   Purchased U.S. Savings Bonds for employees by writing check for $350.00.
    17   Paid state income taxes withheld from employees.
    20   Paid federal and state unemployment taxes.
    31   Completed monthly payroll register, which shows office salaries $14,600, store wages $27,400, FICA taxes withheld $3,360, federal income taxes payable $1,654, state income taxes payable $360, union dues payable $400, United Way contributions payable $1,688, and net pay $34,538.
    31   Prepared payroll checks for the net pay and distributed checks to employees.

At January 31, the company also makes the following accruals pertaining to employee compensation: FICA taxes (8%), state unemployment taxes (5.4%), and federal unemployment taxes (0.8%).

Instructions

(a) Journalize the January transactions.

(b) Journalize the adjustments pertaining to employee compensation at January 31.

Prepare entries for payroll and payroll taxes, and prepare W-2 data.
(SO 2, 3)

PD–4A   For the year ended December 31, 2000, Valley Electric Company reports the following summary payroll data:

Gross earnings:	
Administrative salaries	$180,000
Electricians' wages	370,000
Total	$550,000
Deductions:	
FICA taxes	$ 38,000
Federal income taxes withheld	168,000
State income taxes withheld (2.6%)	14,300
United Way contributions payable	27,500
Hospital insurance premiums	17,200
Total	$265,000

Valley Electric's payroll taxes are: FICA 8%, state unemployment 2.5% (due to a stable employment record), and 0.8% federal unemployment. Gross earnings subject to (1) FICA taxes total $475,000, and (2) unemployment taxes total $400,000.

Instructions
(a) Prepare a summary journal entry at December 31 for the full year's payroll.
(b) Journalize the adjusting entry at December 31 to record the employer's payroll taxes.
(c) The W-2 Wage and Tax Statement requires the following dollar data:

Wages, Tips, Other Compensation	Federal Income Tax Withheld	State Income Tax Withheld	FICA Wages	FICA Tax Withheld

Complete the required data for the following employees:

Employee	Gross Earnings	Federal Income Tax Withheld
A. Osa	$60,000	$27,500
B. Bama	26,000	10,200

PROBLEMS: SET B

PD–1B Selected payroll procedures of Chen Wee Company are described below:

1. Department managers interview applicants and on the basis of the interview either hire or reject the applicants. When an applicant is hired, the applicant fills out a W-4 form (Employer's Withholding Exemption Certificate). One copy of the form is sent to the personnel department and one copy is sent to the payroll department as notice that the individual has been hired. On the copy of the W-4 sent to payroll, the managers manually indicate the hourly pay rate for the new hire.
2. The payroll checks are manually signed by the chief accountant and given to the department managers for distribution to employees in their department. The managers are responsible for seeing that any absent employees receive their checks.
3. There are two clerks in the payroll department. The payroll is divided alphabetically with one clerk having employees A to L and the other employees M to Z. Each clerk computes the gross earnings, deductions, and net pay for employees in the section and posts the data to the employer earning records.

Identify internal control weaknesses and make recommendations for improvement. (SO 1)

Instructions
(a) ▦⟹ Indicate the weaknesses in internal control.
(b) ▦⟹ For each weakness, describe the control procedures that will provide effective internal control. Use the following format for your answer:

(a) Weaknesses   **(b) Recommended Procedures**

PD–2B Sure-Value Hardware has four employees who are paid on an hourly basis plus time-and-one-half for all hours worked in excess of 40 a week. Payroll data for the week ended March 15, 2000, are presented below:

Prepare payroll register and payroll entries. (SO 2, 3)

Employee	Hours Worked	Hourly Rate	Federal Income Tax Withholdings	United Way
A. Pima	40	$13.00	$?	$5.00
C. Zuni	42	13.00	?	5.00
E. Hopi	44	13.00	42	8.00
G. Mohav	46	13.00	48	5.00

Pima and Zuni are married. They claim 0 and 4 withholding allowances, respectively. The following tax rates are applicable: FICA 8%, state income taxes 3%, state unemployment taxes 5.4%, and federal unemployment 0.8%. The first three employees are sales clerks (store wages expense), and the other employee performs administrative duties (office wages expense).

Instructions
(a) Prepare a payroll register for the weekly payroll. (Use the wage-bracket withholding table in the text for federal income tax withholdings.)
(b) Journalize the payroll on March 15, 2000, and the accrual of employer payroll taxes.
(c) Journalize the payment of the payroll on March 16, 2000.
(d) Journalize the deposit in a Federal Reserve Bank on March 31, 2000, of the FICA and federal income taxes payable to the government.

Journalize payroll transactions and adjusting entries.
(SO 2, 3)

PD–3B The following payroll liability accounts are included in the ledger of Amora Company on January 1, 2000:

FICA Taxes Payable	$ 760.00
Federal Income Taxes Payable	954.60
State Income Taxes Payable	108.95
Federal Unemployment Taxes Payable	288.95
State Unemployment Taxes Payable	1,954.40
Union Dues Payable	870.00
U.S. Savings Bonds Payable	360.00

In January, the following transactions occurred:

Jan. 10 Sent check for $870.00 to union treasurer for union dues.
    12 Deposited check for $1,714.60 in Federal Reserve Bank for FICA taxes and federal income taxes withheld.
    15 Purchased U.S. Savings Bonds for employees by writing check for $360.00.
    17 Paid state income taxes withheld from employees.
    20 Paid federal and state unemployment taxes.
    31 Completed monthly payroll register, which shows office salaries $14,600, store wages $28,400, FICA taxes withheld $3,440, federal income taxes payable $1,684, state income taxes payable $360, union dues payable $400, United Way contributions payable $1,888, and net pay $35,228.
    31 Prepared payroll checks for the net pay and distributed checks to employees.

At January 31, the company also makes the following accrued adjustments pertaining to employee compensation: FICA taxes (8%), federal unemployment taxes (0.8%), and state unemployment taxes (5.4%).

Instructions
    (a) Journalize the January transactions.
    (b) Journalize the adjustments pertaining to employee compensation at January 31.

Prepare entries for payroll and payroll taxes and prepare W-2 data.
(SO 2, 3)

PD–4B For the year ended December 31, 2000, Wynn Electrical Repair Company reports the following summary payroll data:

Gross earnings:	
Administrative salaries	$180,000
Electricians' wages	470,000
Total	$650,000
Deductions:	
FICA taxes	$ 48,000
Federal income taxes withheld	188,000
State income taxes withheld (2.6%)	16,900
United Way contributions payable	32,500
Hospital insurance premiums	20,300
Total	$305,700

Wynn Company's payroll taxes are: FICA 8%, state unemployment 2.5% (due to a stable employment record), and 0.8% federal unemployment. Gross earnings subject to (1) FICA taxes total $600,000, and (2) unemployment taxes total $450,000.

Instructions
    (a) Prepare a summary journal entry at December 31 for the full year's payroll.
    (b) Journalize the adjusting entry at December 31 to record the employer's payroll taxes.
    (c) The W-2 Wage and Tax Statement requires the following dollar data:

Wages, Tips, Other Compensation	Federal Income Tax Withheld	State Income Tax Withheld	FICA Wages	FICA Tax Withheld

Complete the required data for the following employees:

Employee	Gross Earnings	Federal Income Tax Withheld
A. Ute	$62,000	$28,500
B. Yuma	28,000	10,800

BROADENING YOUR PERSPECTIVE

CRITICAL THINKING
. . . .
GROUP DECISION CASE

BYPD–1 Sauk Processing Company provides word-processing services for clients and students in a university community. The work for clients is fairly steady throughout the year, but the work for students peaks significantly in December and May as a result of term papers research project reports, and dissertations.

Two years ago, the company attempted to meet the peak demand by hiring part-time help. However, this led to numerous errors and considerable customer dissatisfaction. A year ago, the company hired four experienced employees on a permanent basis instead of using part-time help. This proved to be much better in terms of productivity and customer satisfaction. However, it has caused an increase in annual payroll costs and a significant decline in annual net income.

Recently, Tammy Berg, a sales representative of Harrington Services Inc., has made a proposal to the company. Under the plan, Harrington Services will provide up to four experienced workers at a daily rate of $105 per person for an 8-hour workday. Harrington workers are not available on an hourly basis. Sauk Processing would have to pay only the daily rate for the workers used.

The owner of Sauk Processing, Martha Bell, asks you, as the company's accountant, to prepare a report on the expenses that are pertinent to the decision. If the Harrington plan is adopted, Martha will terminate the employment of two permanent employees who are each earning an average annual salary of $30,000. The remaining permanent employees each earn an annual income of $30,000. Sauk Processing pays 8% FICA taxes, 0.8% federal unemployment taxes, and 5.4% state unemployment taxes. The unemployment taxes apply to only the first $7,000 of gross earnings. In addition, Sauk Processing pays $40 per month for each employee for medical and dental insurance.

Martha indicates that if the Harrington Services plan is accepted, her needs for workers will be as follows:

Months	Number	Working Days per Month
January–March	2	20
April–May	3	25
June–October	2	18
November–December	3	23

Instructions
With the class divided into groups, answer the following:

(a) Prepare a report showing the comparative payroll expense of continuing to employ permanent workers compared to adopting the Harrington Services Inc. plan.
(b) What other factors should Martha consider before finalizing her decision?

COMMUNICATION ACTIVITY

BYPD–2 Tim Harp, president of the Low Cloud Company, has recently hired a number of additional employees. He recognizes that additional payroll taxes will be due as a result of this hiring, and that the company will serve as the collection agent for other taxes.

Instructions
In a memorandum to Tim Harp, explain each of the taxes, and identify the taxes that result in payroll tax expense to the employer.

ETHICS CASE

BYPD–3 Harry Smith owns and manages Harry's Restaurant, a 24-hour restaurant near the city's medical complex. Harry employs nine full-time employees and sixteen part-time employees. He pays all of the full-time employees by check, the amounts of which are determined by Harry's public accountant, Pam Web. Harry pays all of his part-time employees in currency that he computes and withdraws directly from his cash register. Pam has repeatedly urged Harry to pay all employees by check. But as Harry has told his competitor and friend, Steve Hill, who owns the Greasy Diner, "First of all, my part-time employees prefer the currency over a check, and secondly I don't withhold or pay any taxes or workmen's compensation insurance on those wages because they go totally unrecorded and unnoticed."

Instructions
- (a) Who are the stakeholders in this situation?
- (b) What are the legal and ethical considerations regarding Harry's handling of his payroll?
- (c) Pam Web is aware of Harry's payment of the part-time payroll in currency. What are her ethical responsibilities in this case?
- (d) What internal control principle is violated in this payroll process?

SURFING THE NET

BYPD–4   The Internal Revenue Service provides considerable information over the Internet. The following demonstrates how useful one of its sites is in answering payroll tax questions faced by employers.

Address: http://www.irs.ustreas.gov/prod/forms_pubs/index.html

Steps
1. Go to the site shown above.
2. Choose **Publications Online**.
3. Choose **circular E, Employer's Tax Guide**.

Instructions
Answer each of the following questions:
- (a) How does the government define "employees"?
- (b) What are the special rules for Social Security and Medicare regarding children who are employed by their parents?
- (c) How can an employee obtain a Social Security card if he or she doesn't have one?
- (d) Must employees report tips received from customers to their employer? If so, what is the process?
- (e) Where should the employer deposit Social Security taxes withheld or contributed?

Answers to Self-Study Questions
1. c   2. c   3. d

APPENDIX E

SUBSIDIARY LEDGERS AND SPECIAL JOURNALS

STUDY OBJECTIVES

After studying this appendix, you should be able to:

1. *Describe the nature and purpose of a subsidiary ledger.*
2. *Explain how special journals are used in journalizing.*
3. *Indicate how a columnar journal is posted.*

SECTION 1 EXPANDING THE LEDGER— SUBSIDIARY LEDGERS

NATURE AND PURPOSE OF SUBSIDIARY LEDGERS

1

STUDY

OBJECTIVE

Describe the nature and purpose of a subsidiary ledger.

Imagine a business that has several thousand charge (credit) customers and shows the transactions with these customers in only one account—Accounts Receivable—in the general ledger. It would be virtually impossible to determine the balance owed by an individual customer at any specific time. Similarly, the amount payable to one creditor would be difficult to locate quickly from a single Accounts Payable account in the general ledger.

To provide such information, companies use subsidiary ledgers to keep track of individual balances. A subsidiary ledger is a group of accounts with a common characteristic (for example, all customer accounts—that is, accounts receivable). The subsidiary ledger frees the general ledger from the details of individual balances. A subsidiary ledger is an addition to, and an expansion of, the general ledger.

Two common subsidiary ledgers are:

1. The accounts receivable (or customers') ledger which accumulates transaction data with individual customers.
2. The accounts payable (or creditors') ledger which maintains transaction data with individual creditors.

In each of these subsidiary ledgers, individual accounts are usually arranged in alphabetical order.

The detailed data shown in a subsidiary ledger are summarized in a general ledger account. The accounts for the two ledgers above are Accounts Receivable and Accounts Payable, respectively. The general ledger account that summarizes subsidiary ledger data is called a control account. **Each general ledger control account balance must equal the composite balance of the individual accounts in the related subsidiary ledger at the end of an accounting period.** An overview of the relationship of subsidiary ledgers to the general ledger is shown in Illustration E-1, with the general ledger control accounts and subsidiary ledger accounts in green color.

ILLUSTRATION E-1

Relationship of general ledgers and subsidiary accounts

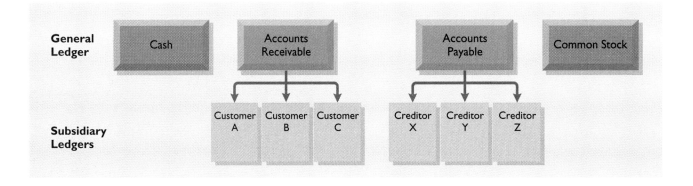

Note that cash and common stock in this illustration are not control accounts.

ILLUSTRATION OF SUBSIDIARY LEDGERS

An example of a control account and subsidiary ledger for Larson Enterprises is provided in Illustration E-2. The explanation column in these accounts is not shown in this and subsequent illustrations due to space considerations.

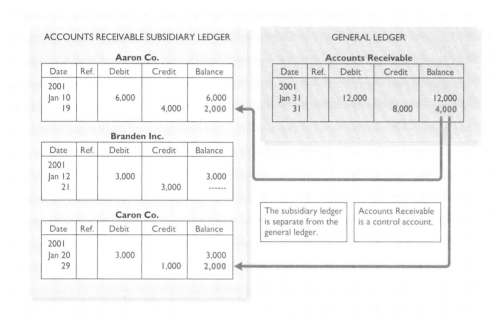

The example is based on the following transactions:

Credit Sales				Collections on Account		
Jan. 10	Aaron Co.	$ 6,000		Jan. 19	Aaron Co.	$ 4,000
12	Branden Inc.	3,000		21	Branden Inc.	3,000
20	Caron Co.	3,000		29	Caron Co.	1,000
		$12,000				$ 8,000

The total debits and credits in Accounts Receivable in the general ledger are reconcilable to the detailed debits and credits in the subsidiary accounts. In addition, the balance of $4,000 in the accounts receivable control account agrees with the total of the balances in the individual accounts (Aaron Co. $2,000 + Branden Inc. $0 + Caron Co. $2,000) in the subsidiary ledger.

As shown, postings are made monthly to the control accounts in the general ledger so that monthly financial statements may be prepared. Postings to the individual accounts in the subsidiary ledger are made daily. The rationale for posting daily is to ensure that current account information can be used as a basis for monitoring credit limits, billing customers, and answering inquiries from customers about their account balances.

ADVANTAGES OF SUBSIDIARY LEDGERS

The advantages of using subsidiary ledgers are that they:

1. **Show transactions affecting one customer or one creditor in a single account**, thus providing necessary up-to-date information on specific account balances.
2. **Free the general ledger of excessive details.** As a result, a trial balance of the general ledger does not contain vast numbers of individual account balances.
3. **Help locate errors in individual accounts** by reducing the number of accounts combined in one ledger and by using control accounts.
4. **Make possible a division of labor** in posting by having one employee post to the general ledger and someone else post to the subsidiary ledgers.

TECHNOLOGY IN ACTION

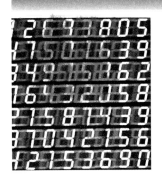

Rather than relying on customer or creditor names in a subsidiary ledger, a computer system expands the account number of the control account in a pre-specified manner. For example, if accounts receivable was numbered 10010, the first account in the accounts receivable subsidiary ledger might be numbered 10010-0001. Most systems allow inquiries about specific accounts in the subsidiary ledger (by account number) or about the control account. With the latter, the system would automatically total all the subsidiary accounts whenever an inquiry to the control account was made.

BEFORE YOU GO ON . . .

Review It

1. What is a subsidiary ledger, and what purpose does it serve?

Do It

Presented below is information related to Sims Company for its first month of operations. Identify the balances that appear in the accounts payable subsidiary ledger and the Accounts Payable balance that appears in the general ledger at the end of January.

Credit Purchases			Cash Paid		
Jan 5	Devon Co.	$11,000	Jan 9	Devon Co.	$7,000
Jan 11	Shelby Co.	7,000	Jan 14	Shelby Co.	2,000
Jan 22	Taylor Co.	14,000	Jan 27	Taylor Co.	9,000

Reasoning: Note that only one account appears in the general ledger, but the detail related to this account is shown in the subsidiary ledger.

Solution: Subsidiary ledger balances: Devon Co. $4,000 ($11,000 − $7,000); Shelby Co. $5,000 ($7,000 − $2,000); Taylor Co. $5,000 ($14,000 − $9,000). General ledger Accounts Payable balance $14,000 ($32,000 − $18,000).

Related exercise material: BEE–1, BEE–2, EE–1, EE–2, and EE–3.

SECTION 2   EXPANDING THE JOURNAL— SPECIAL JOURNALS

So far you have learned to journalize transactions in a two-column general journal and post these entries individually to the general ledger. This procedure is satisfactory in only the very smallest companies. To expedite journalizing and posting transactions, most companies use special journals **in addition to the general journal**.

NATURE AND PURPOSE OF SPECIAL JOURNALS

A special journal is used to record similar types of transactions, such as all sales of merchandise on account, or all cash receipts. The types of special journals used depend largely on the types of transactions that occur frequently in a business enterprise. Most merchandising enterprises use the journals shown in Illustration E-4 to record transactions daily:

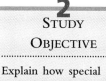

2
STUDY
OBJECTIVE

Explain how special journals are used in journalizing.

ILLUSTRATION E-4

Use of special journals and the general journal

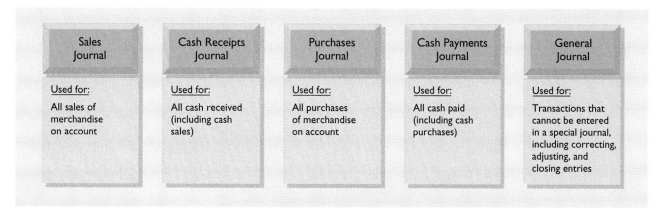

Sales Journal	Cash Receipts Journal	Purchases Journal	Cash Payments Journal	General Journal
Used for:	Used for:	Used for:	Used for:	Used for:
All sales of merchandise on account	All cash received (including cash sales)	All purchases of merchandise on account	All cash paid (including cash purchases)	Transactions that cannot be entered in a special journal, including correcting, adjusting, and closing entries

If a transaction cannot be recorded in a special journal, it is recorded in the general journal. For example, if you had special journals only for the four types of transactions listed above, purchase returns and allowances or sales returns and allowances would be recorded in the general journal. Similarly, **correcting, adjusting, and closing entries are recorded in the general journal**. Other types of special journals may be used in some situations. For example, when purchase returns and allowances or sales returns and allowances are frequent, special journals may be used to record these transactions.

Special journals **permit greater division of labor** because several individuals can record entries in different journals at the same time. For example, one employee may be responsible for journalizing all cash receipts, and another for journalizing credit sales. In addition, the use of special journals **reduces the time necessary to complete the posting process**. When special journals are used, monthly postings to some accounts may be substituted for daily postings, as will be illustrated later in the appendix.

HELPFUL HINT
In what journal would you record: (1) the cash purchase of merchandise inventory? (2) the purchase of inventory on credit? (3) a cash sale? Answers: (1) Cash payments journal; (2) purchases journal; (3) cash receipts journal.

SALES JOURNAL

The sales journal is used to record sales of merchandise on account. Cash sales of merchandise are entered in the cash receipts journal. Credit sales of assets other than merchandise are entered in the general journal.

Journalizing Credit Sales

Karns Wholesale Supply uses a **perpetual inventory** system. Under a perpetual inventory system, each entry in the sales journal results in one entry **at selling price**—a debit to Accounts Receivable (a control account) and a credit of equal amount to Sales—and another entry **at cost**—a debit to Cost of Goods Sold and a credit of equal amount to Merchandise Inventory (a control account). A sales journal with two amount columns can accommodate a sales transaction recognizing both selling price and cost using only one line. Assuming that Karns Wholesale Supply has the following credit sales transactions (per sales invoices 101–107), its two-column sales journal is shown in Illustration E-5.

HELPFUL HINT

Postings are also made daily to individual ledger accounts in the inventory subsidiary ledger to maintain a perpetual inventory.

ILLUSTRATION E-5

Journalizing the sales journal—perpetual inventory system

KARNS WHOLESALE SUPPLY
Sales Journal   **S1**

Date	Account Debited	Invoice No.	Ref.	Accts. Receivable Dr. Sales Cr.	Cost of Goods Sold Dr. Merchandise Inventory Cr.
2001					
May 3	Abbot Sisters	101		10,600	6,360
7	Babon Co.	102		11,350	7,370
14	Carson Bros.	103		7,800	5,070
19	Deli Co.	104		9,300	6,510
21	Abbot Sisters	105		15,400	10,780
24	Deli Co.	106		21,210	15,900
27	Babson Co.	107		14,570	10,200
				90,230	62,190

The reference (Ref.) column is not used in journalizing. It is used in posting the sales journal, as explained in the next section. Also, note that, unlike the general journal, an explanation is not required for each entry in a special journal. Finally, note that each invoice is prenumbered to ensure that all invoices are journalized.

Posting the Sales Journal

Postings from the sales journal are made **daily to the individual accounts receivable** in the subsidiary ledger and **monthly to the general ledger**, as shown in Illustration E-6.

A check mark (√) is inserted in the reference posting column to indicate that the daily posting to the customer's account has been made. A check mark (√) is used in this illustration because the subsidiary ledger accounts are not numbered. At the end of the month, the column totals of the sales journal are posted to the general ledger—as a debit of $90,230 to Accounts Receivable (account No. 4), a credit of $90,230 to Sales (account No. 60), a debit of $62,190 to Cost of Goods Sold (account No. 75), and a credit of $62,190 to Merchandise Inventory (account No. 6). The insertion of the respective account numbers below the column total indicates that the postings have been made. In both the general ledger and subsidiary ledger accounts, the reference **S1** indicates that the posting came from page 1 of the sales journal.

HELPFUL HINT

Additional columns may be provided in the sales journal, i.e., sales by department or by product line. Some companies add a separate column for sales taxes payable.

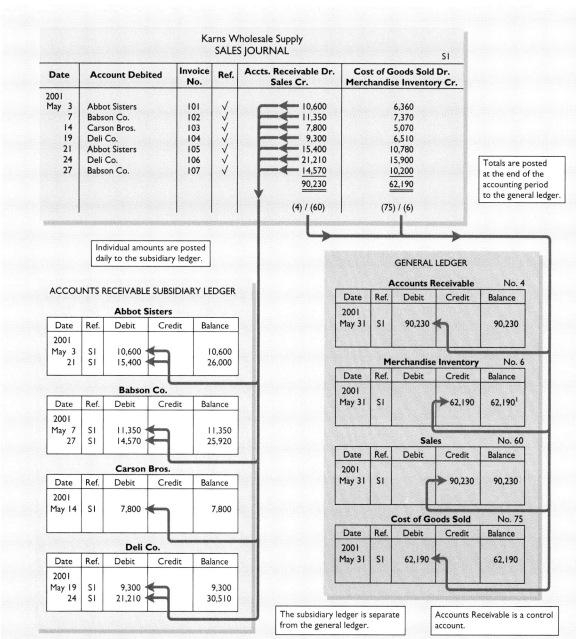

[1]The normal balance for Merchandise Inventory is a debit. But, because of the sequence in which we have posted the special journals, with the sales journals first, the credits to Merchandise Inventory are posted before the debits. This posting sequence explains the credit balance, in Merchandise Inventory, which exists only until the other journals are posted.

Proving the Ledgers

To prove the ledgers it is necessary to determine that (1) the total of the general ledger debit balances equals the total of the general ledger credit balances and (2) the sum of the subsidiary ledger balances equals the balance in the control accounts. The proof of the postings from the sales journal to the general ledger and the accounts receivable subsidiary ledger is shown in Illustration E-7 (on page E8).

ILLUSTRATION E-7

Proving the equality of the postings from the sales journal.

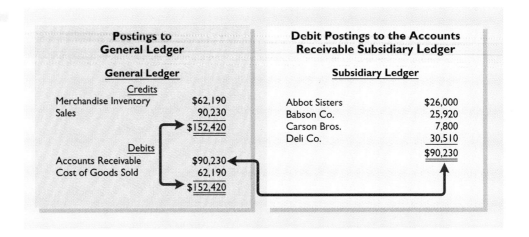

Advantages of the Sales Journal

The use of a special journal to record sales on account has a number of advantages. First, the one-line entry for each sales transaction **saves time**, because it is not necessary to write out the four account titles for each transaction. Second, only totals, rather than individual entries, are posted to the general ledger, thus **saving posting time and reducing the possibilities of errors in posting**. Finally, **a division of labor results**, because one individual can take responsibility for the sales journal.

HELPFUL HINT

Question: Do you see any other advantages of a sales journal? Answer: The prenumbering of sales invoices helps to ensure that all sales are recorded and that no sale is recorded more than once.

CASH RECEIPTS JOURNAL

All receipts of cash are recorded in the cash receipts journal. The most common types of cash receipts are cash sales of merchandise and collections of accounts receivable. Many other possibilities exist, however, such as receipt of money from bank loans and cash proceeds from disposals of equipment, buildings, or land. A one- or two-column cash receipts journal is not sufficient to accommodate all possible cash receipt transactions. Therefore, a multiple-column cash receipts journal is used.

Generally, a cash receipts journal includes debit columns for cash and sales discounts and credit columns for accounts receivable, sales, and "other" accounts. The other accounts category is used when the cash receipt does not involve a cash sale or a collection of accounts receivable. Under a perpetual inventory system, each sales entry is accompanied by another entry that debits Cost of Goods Sold and credits Merchandise Inventory for the cost of the merchandise sold. This entry may be recorded separately. A six-column cash receipts journal that accommodates both entries is shown in Illustration E-8. When a special journal has more than one account column it is referred to as a columnar journal.

Additional credit columns may be used if they significantly reduce postings to a specific account. For example, the cash receipts of a loan company, such as Household International, include thousands of collections from customers. These collections are credited to Loans Receivable and Interest Revenue. A significant saving in posting would result from using separate credit columns for Loans Receivable and Interest Revenue, rather than using the other accounts credit column for these amounts. In contrast, a retailer that has only one interest collection a month would not find it useful to have a separate column for interest revenue.

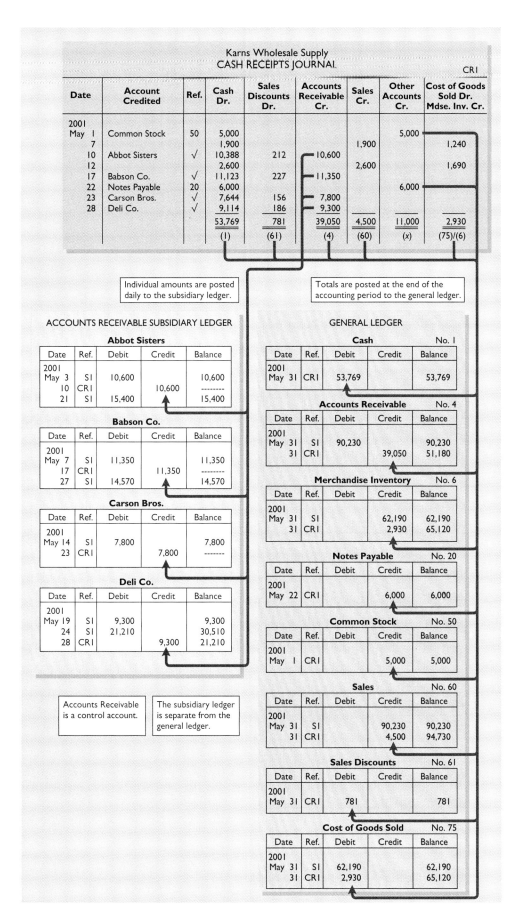

Journalizing Cash Receipts Transactions

To illustrate the journalizing of cash receipts transactions, we will continue with the transactions of Karns Wholesale Supply during the month of May. Collections from customers relate to the entries recorded in the sales journal in Illustration E-5. The entries in the cash receipts journal are based on the following cash receipts transactions:

May 1 Stockholders invest $5,000 in the business.

      7 Cash sales of merchandise total $1,900 (cost, $1,240).

    10 A check for $10,388 is received from Abbot Sisters in payment of invoice No. 101 for $10,600 less a 2% discount.

    12 Cash sales of merchandise total $2,600 (cost, $1,690).

    17 A check for $11,123 is received from Babson Co. in payment of invoice No. 102 for $11,350 less a 2% discount.

    22 Cash is received by signing a note for $6,000.

    23 A check for $7,644 is received from Carson Bros. in full for invoice No. 103 for $7,800 less a 2% discount.

    28 A check for $9,114 is received from Deli Co. in full for invoice No. 104 for $9,300 less a 2% discount.

Further information about the columns in the cash receipts journal (see Illustration E-8) is as follows:

Debit Columns:

1. **Cash.** The amount of cash actually received in each transaction is entered in this column; the column total indicates the total cash receipts for the month.
2. **Sales Discounts.** The Sales Discounts column is included so that it is not necessary to enter sales discount items in the general journal. As a result, the collection of an account receivable within the discount period is expressed on one line in the appropriate columns of the cash receipts journal.

Credit Columns:

3. **Accounts Receivable.** The Accounts Receivable column is used to record cash collections on account. The amount entered in this column is the amount to be credited to the individual customer's account.
4. **Sales.** The Sales column records all cash sales of merchandise. Cash sales of plant assets, for example, are not reported in this column.
5. **Other Accounts.** The Other Accounts column, often referred to as the **sundry accounts column**, is used whenever the credit is other than to Accounts Receivable or Sales. For example, in the first entry, $5,000 is entered as a credit to Common Stock.

Debit and Credit Column:

6. **Cost of Goods Sold and Merchandise Inventory.** This column records debits to Cost of Goods sold and credits to Merchandise Inventory.

In a columnar journal, as in a single-column journal, generally only one line is needed per entry. There must be equal debit and credit amounts for each line. When the collection from Abbot Sisters on May 10 is journalized, for example, three amounts are indicated. Note also that the Account Credited column is used to identify both general ledger and subsidiary ledger account titles. The former is illustrated in the May 1 entry for stockholders' investment; the latter is illustrated in the May 10 entry for the collection in full from Abbot Sisters.

When the journalizing of a columnar journal has been completed, the amount columns are totaled, and the totals are balanced to prove the equality of debits and credits. The proof of the equality of Karns's cash receipts journal is as follows:

HELPFUL HINT

When is an account title entered in the "Account Credited" column of the cash receipts journal? Answer: A *subsidiary ledger* title is entered there whenever the entry involves a collection of accounts receivable. A *general ledger* account title is entered there whenever the entry involves an account that is not the subject of a special column (and an amount must be entered in the "Other Accounts" column). No account title is entered there if neither of the foregoing applies.

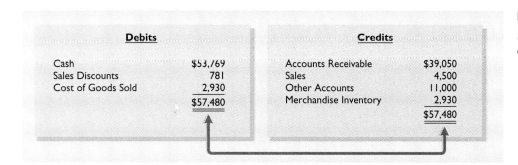

ILLUSTRATION E-9

Proving the equality of the cash receipts journal.

Totaling the columns of a journal and proving the equality of the totals is called **footing** and **cross-footing** a journal.

Posting the Cash Receipts Journal

Posting a columnar journal involves the following procedures.

3

STUDY

OBJECTIVE

Indicate how a columnar journal is posted.

1. All column totals except the total for the Other Accounts column are posted **once at the end of the month** to the account title or titles specified in the column heading, such as Cash or Accounts Receivable. Account numbers are entered below the column totals to show that they have been posted.
2. The total of the Other Accounts column is not posted. Instead, the **individual amounts comprising the total are posted separately** to the general ledger accounts specified in the Accounts Credited column. See, for example, the credit posting to Common Stock. The symbol (X) is inserted below the total to this column to indicate that the amount has not been posted.
3. The individual amounts in a column, posted in total to a control account (Accounts Receivable, in this case), are posted **daily to the subsidiary ledger** account specified in the Account Credited column. See, for example, the credit posting of $10,600 to Abbot Sisters.

Therefore, cash is posted to account No. 1, accounts receivable to account No. 4, merchandise inventory to account No. 6, sales to account No. 60, sales discounts to account No. 61, and cost of goods sold to account No. 75. The symbol **CR** is used in the ledgers to identify postings from the cash receipts journal.

Proving the Ledgers

After the posting of the cash receipts journal is completed, it is necessary to prove the ledgers. As shown in Illustration E-10, the general ledger totals are in agreement and the sum of the subsidiary ledger balances equals the control account balance.

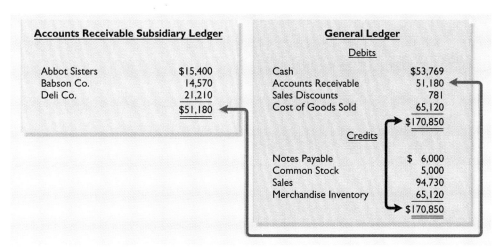

ILLUSTRATION E-10

Proving the ledgers after posting the sales and the cash receipts journals

PURCHASES JOURNAL

HELPFUL HINT

A single-column purchases journal needs only to be footed to prove the equality of debits and credits.

All purchases of merchandise on account are recorded in the purchases journal. Each entry in this journal results in a debit to Merchandise Inventory and a credit to Accounts Payable. When a one-column purchases journal is used, other types of purchases on account and cash purchases cannot be journalized in it. For example, credit purchases of equipment or supplies must be recorded in the general journal, and all cash purchases are entered in the cash payments journal. As illustrated later, where credit purchases for items other than merchandise are numerous, the purchases journal is often expanded to a multi-column format. The single-column purchases journal for Karns Wholesale Supply is shown in Illustration E-11.

ILLUSTRATION E-11

Journalizing and posting the purchases journal

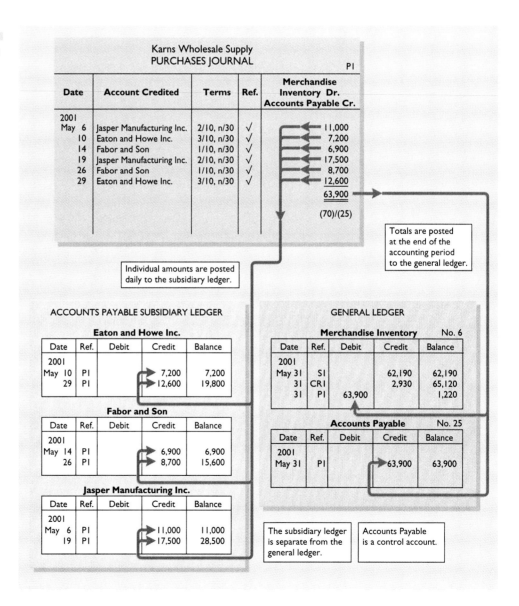

Journalizing Credit Purchases of Merchandise

Entries in the purchases journal are made from purchase invoices. The journalizing procedure is similar to the procedures for a single-column sales journal. In contrast to the sales journal, the purchases journal may not have an invoice number column, because invoices received from different suppliers will not be in numerical sequence. To assure that all purchase invoices are recorded, however, some companies consecutively number each invoice upon receipt and then provide for an internal document number column in the purchases journal.

The entries for Karns Wholesale Supply are based on the following assumed purchases on credit transactions.

Date	Supplier	Amount	Date	Supplier	Amount
5/6	Jasper Manufacturing Inc.	$11,000	5/19	Jasper Manufacturing Inc.	$17,500
5/10	Eaton and Howe, Inc.	7,200	5/26	Fabor and Son	8,700
5/14	Fabor and Son	6,900	5/29	Eaton and Howe, Inc.	12,600

ILLUSTRATION E-12

Credit purchases transactions

Posting the Purchases Journal

The procedures for posting the purchases journal are similar to those for the sales journal. In this case, postings are made **daily** to the **accounts payable ledger** and **monthly** to Merchandise Inventory and Accounts Payable in the general ledger. In both ledgers, P1 is used in the reference column to show that the postings are from page 1 of the purchases journal.

Proof of the equality of the postings from the purchases journal to both ledgers in this example is shown by the following tabulation:

HELPFUL HINT
Postings to subsidiary ledger accounts are done daily because it is often necessary to know a current balance for the subsidiary accounts.

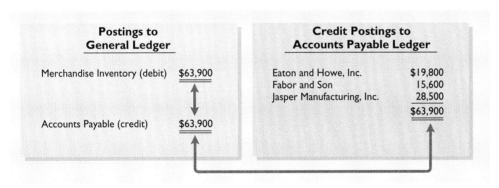

ILLUSTRATION E-13

Proving the equality of the purchases journal

Expanding the Purchases Journal

Some companies expand the purchases journal to include all types of purchases on account. Instead of one column for merchandise inventory and accounts payable, a multiple-column format is used. The multiple-column format usually includes a credit column for accounts payable and debit columns for purchases of merchandise, purchases of office supplies, purchases of store supplies, and other accounts. Illustration E-14 is an example of a multiple-column purchases journal for Hanover Co. The posting procedures are similar to those used for posting the cash receipts journal illustrated earlier.

HELPFUL HINT
A multiple-column purchases journal must be footed and cross-footed to prove the equality of debits and credits.

ILLUSTRATION E-14

Columnar purchases journal

HANOVER CO.
Purchases Journal   P1

Date	Account Credited	Ref.	Accounts Payable Cr.	Merchandise Inventory Dr.	Office Supplies Dr.	Store Supplies Dr.	Other Accounts Dr. Account	Ref.	Amount
2001									
June 1	Signe Audio	√	2,000		2,000				
3	Wright Co.	√	1,500	1,500					
5	Orange Tree Co.	√	2,600				Equipment	18	2,600
30	Sue's Business Forms	√	800			800			
			56,600	43,000	7,500	1,200			4,900

CASH PAYMENTS JOURNAL

ALTERNATIVE TERMINOLOGY
The cash payments journal is sometimes called the *cash disbursements journal*.

All disbursements of cash are entered in a cash payments journal. Entries in this journal are made from prenumbered checks. Because cash payments may be made for a variety of purposes, the cash payments journal has multiple columns. A four-column journal is shown in Illustration E-15.

Journalizing Cash Payments Transactions

The procedures for journalizing transactions in this journal are similar to those described earlier for journalizing transactions in the cash receipts journal. For example, each transaction is entered on one line, and for each line there must be equal debit and credit amounts. The entries in the cash payments journal shown in Illustration E-15 are based on the following transactions for Karns Wholesale Supply:

May 1   Check No. 101 for $1,200 issued for the annual premium on a fire insurance policy.
       3   Check No. 102 for $100 issued in payment of freight when terms were FOB shipping point.
       8   Check No. 103 for $4,400 issued for the purchase of merchandise.
       10   Check No. 104 for $10,780 sent to Jasper Manufacturing Inc. in payment of May 6 invoice for $11,000 less a 2% discount.
       19   Check No. 105 for $6,984 mailed to Eaton and Howe, Inc. in payment of May 10 invoice for $7,200 less a 3% discount.
       23   Check No. 106 for $6,831 sent to Fabor and Son in payment of May 14 invoice for $6,900 less 1% discount.
       28   Check No. 107 for $17,150 sent to Jasper Manufacturing Inc. in payment of May 19 invoice for $17,500 less a 2% discount.
       30   Check No. 108 for $500 issued to stockholders as a cash dividend.

Note that whenever an amount is entered in the Other Accounts column, a specific general ledger account must be identified in the Accounts Debited column. The entries for check Nos. 101, 102, and 103 illustrate this situation. Similarly, a subsidiary account must be identified in the Account Debited column whenever an amount is entered in the Accounts Payable column, as, for example, the entry for check No. 104.

When the journalizing of the cash payments journal has been completed, the amount columns are totaled. The totals are then balanced to prove the equality of debits and credits.

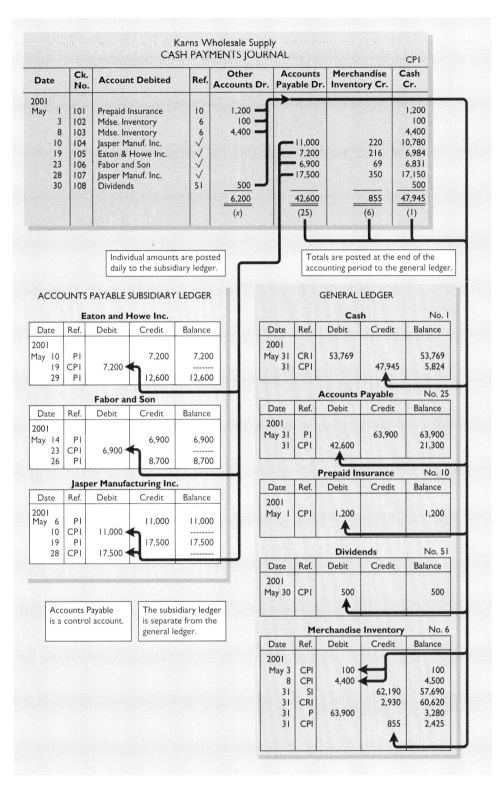

Posting the Cash Payments Journal

The procedures for posting the cash payments journal are similar to those for posting the cash receipts journal. Specifically, the amounts recorded in the Accounts Payable column are posted individually to the subsidiary ledger and in total to the control account. Merchandise Inventory and Cash are posted only in

HELPFUL HINT
If a company has a subsidiary ledger for merchandise inventory, amounts in the merchandise inventory column would be posted daily.

total at the end of the month. When a transaction is recorded in the Other Accounts column, it is posted individually to the appropriate account(s) affected. No totals are posted for this column.

The posting of the cash payments journal is shown in Illustration E-15. Note that the symbol **CP** is used as the posting reference for this journal. After postings from the journals are completed, the equality of the debit and credit balances in the general ledger should be determined. In addition, the control account balances should agree with the subsidiary ledger total balance. The agreement of these balances is shown in Illustration E-16.

ILLUSTRATION E-16

Proving the ledgers after postings from the sales, cash receipts, purchases, and cash payments journals

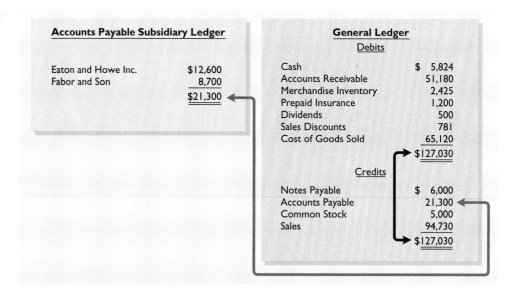

EFFECTS OF SPECIAL JOURNALS ON GENERAL JOURNAL

Special journals for sales, purchases, and cash substantially reduce the number of entries that are made in the general journal. **Only transactions that cannot be entered in a special journal are recorded in the general journal.** For example, the general journal may be used to record such transactions as granting of credit to a customer for a sales return or allowance, granting of credit from a supplier for purchases returned, acceptance of a note receivable from a customer, and purchase of equipment by issuing a note payable. In addition, correcting, adjusting, and closing entries are made in the general journal.

The general journal has columns for date, account titles and explanation, reference, and debit and credit amounts. When control and subsidiary accounts are not involved, the procedures for journalizing and posting of transactions are identical with those described in earlier chapters. However, when control and subsidiary accounts are involved, two modifications of earlier procedures are required:

1. In **journalizing**, both the control and the subsidiary accounts must be identified.

2. In **posting**, there must be a **dual posting**: once to the control account and once to the subsidiary account.

To illustrate, assume that on May 31, Karns Wholesale Supply returns $500 of merchandise for credit to Fabor and Son because of an error in filling its May 26 order. The entry in the general journal and the posting of the entry are shown in Illustration E-17. Note that if cash is received instead of credit granted on this return, then the transaction is recorded in the cash receipts journal.

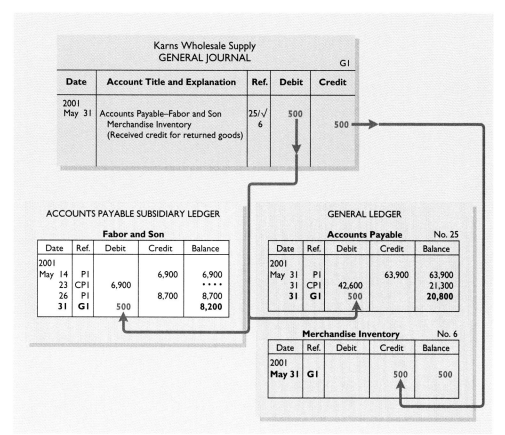

Observe in the journal that two accounts are indicated for the debit and two postings are indicated in the reference column. One amount is posted to the control account and the other to the creditor's account in the subsidiary ledger.

BEFORE YOU GO ON ...

Review It

1. What types of special journals are usually used to record transactions? Why are special journals used?
2. Explain how transactions recorded in the sales journal and the cash receipts journal are posted.
3. Indicate the types of transactions that are recorded in the general journal when special journals are used.

Do It

The Vilas Company has the following selected transactions: (1) purchase of equipment for cash, (2) cash sales, (3) sales returns and allowances, (4) payment of cash dividends, and (5) sales of merchandise on account. Identify the journals in which each transaction should be entered.

Reasoning: It is necessary to know the content of each special journal and the effect of special journals on the general journal. For example, the sales journal contains only sales on account, and the cash payments journal is used for all cash payments.

Solution: (1)Purchase of equipment for cash—cash payments journal. (2) Cash sale—cash receipts journal. (3) Sales return and allowance—general journal. (4) Payment of cash dividends—cash payments journal. (5) Sale of merchandise on account—sales journal.

Related exercise material: BEE–4, BEE–5, BEE–6, BEE–7, EE–1, EE–2, EE–3, EE–4, EE–5, EE–6, EE–7, and EE–8.

DEMONSTRATION PROBLEM

Celine Dion Company uses a six-column cash receipts journal with columns for Cash (Dr.), Sales Discounts (Dr.), Accounts Receivable (Cr.), Sales (Cr.), Other Accounts (Cr.), Cost of Goods Sold (Dr.), and Merchandise Inventory (Cr.). Cash receipts transactions for the month of July 2001 are as follows:

PROBLEM-SOLVING STRATEGIES

1. All cash receipts are recorded in the cash receipts journal.
2. The "account credited" indicates items posted individually to the subsidiary ledger or general ledger.
3. Cash sales are recorded in the cash receipts journal—not in the sales journal.
4. The total debits must equal the total credits.

July 3 Cash sales total $5,800 (cost, $3,480).
      5 A check for $6,370 is received from the Jeltz Company in payment of invoice dated June 26 for $6,500 terms 2/10, n/30.
      9 An additional investment of $5,000 in cash is made in the business by stockholders.
     10 Cash sales total $12,519 (cost, $7,511).
     12 A check for $7,275 is received from R. Eliot & Co. in payment of a $7,500 invoice dated July 3, terms 3/10, n/30.
     15 A customer advance of $700 cash is received for future sales.
     20 Cash sales total $15,472 (cost, $9,283).
     22 A check for $5,880 is received from Beck Company in payment of $6,000 invoice dated July 13, terms 2/10, n/30.
     29 Cash sales total $17,660 (cost $10,596).
     31 Cash of $200 is received on interest earned for July.

Instructions
(a) Journalize the transactions in the cash receipts journal.
(b) Contrast the posting of the Accounts Receivable and Other Accounts columns.

SOLUTION TO DEMONSTRATION PROBLEM

(a)

CELINE DION COMPANY
Cash Receipts Journal   **CR1**

Date	Account Credited	Ref.	Cash Dr.	Sales Discounts Dr.	Accounts Receivable Cr.	Sales Cr.	Other Accounts Cr.	Cost of Goods Sold Dr. Mdse. Inv. Cr.
2001								
7/3			5,800			5,800		3,480
5	Jelt Company		6,370	130	6,500			
9	Common Stock		5,000				5,000	
10			12,519			12,519		7,511
12	R. Eliot & Co.		7,275	225	7,500			
15	Unearned Revenues		700				700	
20			15,472			15,472		9,283
22	Beck Company		5,880	120	6,000			
29			17,660			17,660		10,596
31	Interest Revenue		200				200	
			76,876	475	20,000	51,451	5,900	30,870

(b) The Accounts Receivable column is posted as a credit to Accounts Receivable. The individual amounts are credited to the customers' accounts identified in the Account Credited column, which are maintained in the accounts receivable subsidiary ledger.

The amounts in the Other Accounts Column are only posted individually. They are credited to the account titles identified in the Account Credited column.

SUMMARY OF STUDY OBJECTIVES

1. Describe the nature and purpose of a subsidiary ledger. A subsidiary ledger is a group of accounts with a common characteristic. It facilitates the recording process by freeing the general ledger from details of individual balances.

2. Explain how special journals are used in journalizing. A special journal is used to group similar types of transactions. In a special journal, generally only one line is used to record a complete transaction.

3. Indicate how a columnar journal is posted. In posting a columnar journal:

(a) all column total except for the Other Accounts column are posted once at the end of the month to the account title specified in the column heading.

(b) the total of the Other Accounts column is not posted. Instead, the individual amounts comprising the total are posted separately to the general ledger accounts specified in the Accounts column.

(c) the individual amounts in a column posted in total to a control account are posted daily to the subsidiary ledger accounts specified in the Accounts column.

GLOSSARY

Accounts payable (creditors') ledger A subsidiary ledger that contains accounts with individual creditors. (p. E2).

Accounts receivable (customers') ledger A subsidiary ledger that contains individual customer accounts. (p. E2).

Cash payments (disbursements) journal A special journal used to record all cash paid. (p. E14).

Cash receipts journal A special journal used to record all cash received. (p. E8).

Columnar journal A special journal with more than one column. (p. E8).

Control account An account in the general ledger that controls a subsidiary ledger. (p. E2).

Purchases journal A special journal used to record all purchases of merchandise on account. (p. E12).

Sales journal A special journal used to record all sales of merchandise on account. (p. E6).

Special journal A journal that is used to record similar types of transactions such as all credit sales. (p. E5).

Subsidiary ledger A group of accounts with a common characteristic. (p. E2).

SELF-STUDY QUESTIONS

Answers are at the end of the appendix.

(SO 1) 1. Which of the following is *incorrect* concerning subsidiary ledgers?
   a. The purchases ledger is a common subsidiary ledger for creditor accounts.
   b. The accounts receivable ledger is a subsidiary ledger.
   c. A subsidiary ledger is a group of accounts with a common characteristic.
   d. An advantage of the subsidiary ledger is that it permits a division of labor in posting.

(SO 2) 2. A sales journal will be used for:

	Credit Sales	Cash Sales	Sales Discounts
a.	no	yes	yes
b.	yes	no	yes
c.	yes	no	no
d.	yes	yes	no

3. Which of the following statements is correct?   (SO 3)
   a. The sales discount column is included in the cash receipts journal.
   b. The purchases journal records all purchases of merchandise whether for cash or on account.
   c. The cash receipts journal records sales on account.
   d. Merchandise returned by the buyer is recorded by the seller in the purchases journal.

4. Which of the following is *incorrect* concerning the posting of the cash receipts journal?   (SO 3)
   a. The total of the Other Accounts column is not posted.
   b. All column totals except the total for the Other Accounts column are posted once at the end of the month to the account title specified in the column heading.
   c. The total of all columns is posted daily to the accounts specified in the column heading.

d. The individual amounts in a column posted in total to a control account are posted daily to the subsidiary ledger account specified in the Accounts Credited column.

(SO 3) 5. Postings from the purchases journal to the subsidiary ledger are generally made:
   a. yearly.
   b. monthly.
   c. weekly.
   d. daily.

6. Which statement is *incorrect* regarding the general jour- (SO 2) nal?
   a. Only transactions that cannot be entered in a special journal are recorded in the general journal.
   b. Dual postings are always required in the general journal.
   c. The general journal may be used to record acceptance of a note receivable for an accounts receivable.
   d. Correcting, adjusting, and closing entries are made in the general journal.

QUESTIONS

1. What are the advantages of using subsidiary ledgers?

2. (a) When are postings normally made to (1) the subsidiary accounts and (2) the general ledger control accounts? (b) Describe the relationship between a control account and a subsidiary ledger.

3. Identify and explain the four specific journals discussed in the chapter. List an advantage of using each of these journals rather than using only a general journal.

4. A. Mega Company uses special journals. A sale made on account to K. Hansen for $435 was recorded in a single-column sales journal. A few days later, Hansen returns $70 worth of merchandise for credit. Where should A. Mega Company record the sales return? Why?

5. A $400 purchase of merchandise on account from Julia Company was properly recorded in the purchases journal. When posted, however, the amount recorded in the subsidiary ledger was $40. How might this error be discovered?

6. Why would special journals used in different business not be identical in format? Can you think of a business that would maintain a cash receipts journal but not include a column for accounts receivable?

7. The cash and the accounts receivable columns in the cash receipts journal were mistakenly overadded by $4,000 at the end of the month. (a) Will the customers' ledger agree with the Accounts Receivable control account? (b) Assuming no other errors, will the trial balance totals be equal?

8. One column total of a special journal is posted at month end to only two general ledger accounts. One of these two accounts is Accounts Receivable. What is the name of this special journal? What is the other general ledger account to which the month-end total is posted?

9. In what journal would the following transactions be recorded? (Assume that a single-column sales journal and a single-column purchases journal are used.)
   (a) Recording of depreciation expense for the year.
   (b) Gave credit to a customer for merchandise purchased on credit and returned.
   (c) Sales of merchandise for cash.
   (d) Sales of merchandise on account.
   (e) Collection of cash on account from a customer.
   (f) Purchase of office supplies on account.

10. In what journal would the following transactions be recorded? (Assume that a single-column sales journal and a single-column purchases journal are used.)
    (a) Cash received from signing a note payable.
    (b) Investment of cash by a stockholder of the company.
    (c) Closing of the expense accounts at the end of the year.
    (d) Purchase of merchandise on account.
    (e) Received credit for merchandise purchased and returned to supplier.
    (f) Payment of cash on account due a supplier.

11. What transactions might be included in a multiple-column purchases journal that would not be included in a single-column purchases journal?

12. Give an example of a transaction in the general journal that causes an entry to be posted twice (i.e., to two accounts), one in the general ledger, the other in the subsidiary ledger. Does this affect the debit/credit equality of the general ledger?

13. Give some examples of appropriate general journal transactions for an organization using special journals.

BRIEF EXERCISES

Identify subsidiary ledger balances.
(SO 1)

BEE–1   Presented below is information related to Bradley Company for its first month of operations. Identify the balances that appear in the accounts receivable subsidiary ledger and the accounts receivable balance that appears in the general ledger at the end of January.

Credit Sales			Cash Collections		
Jan. 7	Avon Co.	$9,000	Jan. 17	Avon Co.	$7,000
15	Barto Inc.	6,000	24	Barto Inc.	5,000
23	Cecil Co.	9,000	29	Cecil Co.	9,000

BEE–2 Identify in what ledger (general or subsidiary) the following accounts are shown.

1. Rent Expense
2. Accounts Receivable—Olivia
3. Notes Payable
4. Accounts Payable—Kerns

Identify subsidiary ledger accounts.
(SO 1)

BEE–3 Identify the journal in which each of the following transactions is recorded.

1. Cash sales
2. Payment of cash dividends
3. Cash purchase of land
4. Credit sales
5. Purchase of merchandise on account
6. Receipt of cash for services performed

Identify special journals.
(SO 2)

BEE–4 Indicate whether each of the following debits and credits is included in the Cash Receipts journal. (Use "Yes" or "No" to answer this question.)

1. Debit to Sales
2. Credit to Purchase Discounts
3. Credit to Accounts Receivable
4. Debit to Accounts Payable

Identify entries to cash receipts journal.
(SO 2)

BEE–5 Sterling Computer Components Inc. uses a columnar Cash Receipts journal. Indicate which column(s) is/are posted only in total, only daily, or both in total and daily.

1. Accounts Receivable
2. Sales Discounts
3. Cash
4. Other Accounts

Indicate postings to cash receipts journal.
(SO 3)

BEE–6 Cohen Co. uses special journals and a general journal. Identify the journal in which each of the following transactions is recorded.

1. Purchased equipment on account.
2. Purchased merchandise on account.
3. Paid utility expense in cash.
4. Sold merchandise on account.

Identify transactions for special journals.
(SO 2)

BEE–7 Identify the special journal(s) in which the following column headings appear.

1. Sales Discounts Dr.
2. Accounts Receivable Cr.
3. Cash Dr.
4. Purchase Discount Cr.
5. Purchase Dr.
6. Sales Cr.

Identify transactions for special journals.
(SO 2)

EXERCISES

EE–1 Valdes Company uses both special journals and a general journal. On June 30, after all monthly postings had been completed, the Accounts Receivable controlling account in the general ledger had a debit balance of $350,000 and the Accounts Payable controlling account had a credit balance of $87,000.

The July transactions recorded in the special journals are summarized below. No entries affecting accounts receivable and accounts payable were recorded in the general journal for July.

Determine control account balances and explain posting of special journals.
(SO 1, 2)

Sales journal	Total sales, $161,400
Purchases journal	Total purchases, $54,360
Cash receipts journal	Accounts receivable column total, $135,000
Cash payments journal	Accounts payable column total, $47,500

Instructions
(a) What is the balance of the Accounts Receivable control account after the monthly postings on July 31?
(b) What is the balance of the Accounts Payable control account after the monthly postings on July 31?
(c) To what account(s) is the column total of $161,400 in the sales journal posted?
(d) To what account(s) is the accounts receivable column total of $135,000 in the cash receipts journal posted?

EE–2 Presented below is the subsidiary accounts receivable account of Rico Perez.

Explain postings to subsidiary ledger.
(SO 1)

Date	Ref.	Debit	Credit	Balance
2001				
Sept. 2	S31	61,000		61,000
9	G4		12,000	49,000
27	CR8		49,000	—

Instructions
➡ Write a memo that explains each transaction.

EE–3   On September 1 the balance of the Accounts Receivable controlling account in the general ledger of Cremer Company was $10,960. The customers' subsidiary ledger contained account balances as follows: Alou, $1,440; Farr, $2,640; Keaton, $2,060; Skiles, $4,820. At the end of September the various journals contained the following information:

> **Sales journal**: Sales to Skiles, $800; to Alou, $1,350; to George, $1,030; to Keaton, $1,100.
>
> **Cash receipts journal**: Cash received from Keaton, $1,310; from Skiles, $2,300; from George, $410; from Farr, $1,800; from Alou, $1,240.
>
> **General journal**: An allowance is granted to Skiles, $220.

Instructions

(a) Set up control and subsidiary accounts and enter the beginning balances. Do not construct the journals.

(b) Post the various journals. Post the items as individual items or as totals, whichever would be the appropriate procedure. (No sales discounts given.)

(c) Prepare a list of customers and prove the agreement of the controlling account with the subsidiary ledger at September 30, 2001.

EE–4   Harris Company uses special journals and a general journal. The transactions presented below occurred during September 2001. (Harris uses a perpetual inventory system.)

Sept. 2 Sold merchandise on account to F. Vina, invoice no. 101, $500, terms n/30. The cost of the merchandise sold was $300.

  10 Purchased merchandise on account from F. Kotsch $600, terms 2/10, n/30.

  12 Purchased office equipment on account from J. Wells, $6,500.

  21 Sold merchandise on account to J. Rich, invoice no. 102 for $800, terms 2/10, n/30. The cost of the merchandise sold was $480.

  25 Purchased merchandise on account from M. Watt $900, terms n/30.

  27 Sold merchandise to R. Cowan for $700 cash. The cost of the merchandise sold was $420.

Instructions

(a) Draw a sales journal (see Illustration E-6) and a single-column purchase journal (see Illustration E-11). (Use page 1 for each journal.)

(b) Record the transaction(s) for September that should be journalized in the sales journal and the purchases journal.

EE–5   Briggs Co. uses special journals and a general journal. The transactions presented below occurred during May 2001. (Briggs uses a perpetual inventory system.)

May 1 J. Briggs invested $62,000 cash in the business in exchange for shares of common stock.

  2 Sold merchandise to L. Bean for $6,000 cash. The cost of the merchandise sold was $4,200.

  3 Purchased merchandise for $9,000 from R. L. Sanchez using check no. 101.

  14 Paid salary to F. Sparks $700 by issuing check no. 102.

  16 Sold merchandise on account to B. Ready for $900, terms n/30. The cost of the merchandise sold was $630.

  22 A check of $9,000 is received from M. Lane in full for invoice 101; no discount given.

Instructions

(a) Draw a multiple-column cash receipts journal (see Illustration E-8) and a multiple-column cash payments journal (see Illustration E-15). (Use page 1 for each journal.)

(b) Record the transaction(s) for May that should be journalized in the cash receipts journal and cash payments journal.

EE–6   Abbott Company uses the columnar cash journals illustrated in the textbook. In April, the following selected cash transactions occurred. (Abbott uses a perpetual inventory system.)

1. Made a refund to a customer for the return of damaged goods.
2. Received collection from customer within the 3% discount period.
3. Purchased merchandise for cash.
4. Paid a creditor within the 3% discount period.
5. Received collection from customer after the 3% discount period had expired.
6. Paid freight on merchandise purchased.
7. Paid cash for office equipment.

8. Received cash refund from supplier for merchandise returned.
9. Withdrew cash for personal use of owner.
10. Made cash sales.

Instructions

Indicate (a) the journal, and (b) the columns in the journal that should be used in recording each transaction.

EE–7 Warner Company uses a perpetual inventory system and has the following selected transactions during March:

Journalize transactions in general journal and post.
(SO 1, 2)

Mar. 2 Purchased equipment costing $5,000 from Pena Company on account.
5 Received credit memorandum for $300 from Simon Company for merchandise damaged in shipment to Warner.
7 Issued a credit memorandum for $400 to Farr Company for merchandise the customer returned. The returned merchandise had a cost of $260.

Warner Company uses a one-column purchases journal, a sales journal, the columnar cash journals used in the text, and a general journal.

Instructions

(a) Journalize the transactions in the general journal.
(b) ▭▭▭➤ In a brief memo to the president of Warner Company, explain the postings to the control and subsidiary accounts.

EE–8 Below are some typical transactions incurred by Littlejohn Company.

Indicate journalizing in special journals.
(SO 2)

1. Payment of creditors on account.
2. Return on merchandise sold for credit.
3. Collection on account from customers.
4. Sold land for cash.
5. Sales of merchandise on account.
6. Sale of merchandise for cash.
7. Received credit for merchandise purchased on credit.
8. Sales discount taken on goods sold.
9. Payment of employee wages.
10. Paid a dividend to stockholders.
11. Depreciation on building.
12. Purchase of office supplies for cash.
13. Purchase of merchandise on account.

Instructions

For each transaction, indicate whether it would normally be recorded in a cash receipts journal, cash payments journal, sales journal, single-column purchases journal, or general journal.

EE–9 The general ledger of the Torres Company contained the following Accounts Payable control account (in T-account form). Also shown is the related subsidiary ledger.

Explain posting to control account and subsidiary ledger.
(SO 1, 3)

GENERAL LEDGER

Accounts Payable

Feb. 15	General Journal	1,400	Feb. 1	Balance	26,025
28	?	?	5	General Journal	265
			11	General Journal	550
			28	Purchases	13,700
			Feb. 28	Balance	9,640

ACCOUNTS PAYABLE LEDGER

Sealy			Wolcott		
	Feb. 28 Bal. 4,600			Feb. 28 Bal. ?	

Gates	
	Feb. 28 Bal. 2,000

Instructions

(a) Indicate the missing posting reference and amount in the control account and the missing ending balance in the subsidiary ledger.
(b) Indicate the amounts in the control account that were dual-posted (i.e., posted to the control account and the subsidiary accounts).

Prepare purchases and general journals.
(SO 1, 2)

EE–10   Selected accounts from the ledgers of Moyer Company at July 31 are shown below. (Moyer uses a perpetual inventory system.)

GENERAL LEDGER

Store Equipment   No. 153

Date	Explanation	Ref.	Debit	Credit	Balance
July 1		G1	3,600		3,600

Merchandise Inventory   No. 120

Date	Explanation	Ref.	Debit	Credit	Balance
July 15		G1	400		400
18		G1		100	300
25		G1		200	100
31		P1	8,400		8,500

Accounts Payable   No. 201

Date	Explanation	Ref.	Debit	Credit	Balance
July 1		G1		3,600	3,600
15		G1		400	4,000
18		G1	100		3,900
25		G1	200		3,700
31		P1		8,400	12,100

ACCOUNTS PAYABLE LEDGER

Alcott Equipment Co.

Date	Explanation	Ref.	Debit	Credit	Balance
July 1		G1		3,600	3,600

Delco Co.

Date	Explanation	Ref.	Debit	Credit	Balance
July 14		P1		1,100	1,100
25		G1	200		900

Bradley Co.

Date	Explanation	Ref.	Debit	Credit	Balance
July 3		P1		2,000	2,000
20		P1		700	2,700

Erick Co.

Date	Explanation	Ref.	Debit	Credit	Balance
July 12		P1		500	500
21		P1		600	1,100

Costo Materials

Date	Explanation	Ref.	Debit	Credit	Balance
July 17		P1		1,400	1,400
18		G1	100		1,300
29		P1		2,100	3,400

Gaetti Transit

Date	Explanation	Ref.	Debit	Credit	Balance
July 15		G1		400	400

Instructions
From the data prepare:

(a) the single-column purchases journal for July.
(b) the general journal entries for July.

Determine correct posting amount to control account.
(SO 3)

EE–11   Yan Products uses both special journals and a general journal. Yan also posts customers' accounts in the accounts receivable subsidiary ledger. The postings for the most recent month are included in the subsidiary T accounts below.

Edmonds

Bal.	340	250
	180	

Roemer

Bal.	150	150
	290	

Schulz

Bal.	–0–	145
	145	

Park

Bal.	120	120
	190	
	170	

Instructions
Determine the correct amount of the end-of-month posting from the sales journal to the Accounts Receivable controlling account.

PROBLEMS

PE-1 Koslo Company's chart of accounts includes the following selected accounts:

*Journalize transactions in cash
receipts journal and post to
control account and subsidiary
ledger.*
(SO 1, 2, 3)

101 Cash	401 Sales
112 Accounts Receivable	414 Sales Discounts
120 Merchandise Inventory	505 Cost of Goods Sold
311 Common Stock	

On June 1 the accounts receivable ledger of the Koslo Company showed the following balances: Bell & Son, $2,500; Ellis Co., $1,900; Grant Bros., $1,600; and Meija Co., $1,000. The June transactions involving the receipt of cash were as follows:

June 1 T. Koslo invested additional cash for common stock, $9,000.
     3 Received check in full from Meija Co. less 2% cash discount.
     6 Received check in full from Ellis Co. less 2% cash discount.
     7 Made cash sales of merchandise totaling $6,135. The cost of the merchandise sold was $4,090.
     9 Received check in full from Bell & Son less 2% cash discount.
    11 Received cash refund from a supplier for damaged merchandise, $200.
    15 Made cash sales of merchandise totaling $5,250. The cost of the merchandise sold was $3,500.
    20 Received check in full from Gant Bros., $1,600.

Instructions (Assume the use of a perpetual inventory system.)
(a) Journalize the transactions above in a six-column cash receipts journal with columns for Cash Dr.; Sales Discounts Dr.; Accounts Receivable Cr.; Sales Cr.; Other Accounts Cr.; and Cost of Goods Sold Dr./Merchandise Inventory Cr. Foot and crossfoot the journal.
(b) Insert the beginning balances in the Accounts Receivable control and subsidiary accounts and post the June transactions to these accounts.
(c) Prove the agreement of the control account and subsidiary account balances.

PE-2 Cline Company's chart of accounts includes the following selected accounts:

*Journalize transactions in cash
payments journal and post to
the general and subsidiary
ledgers.*
(SO 1, 2, 3)

101 Cash	157 Equipment
120 Merchandise Inventory	201 Accounts Payable
130 Prepaid Insurance	322 Dividends

On November 1 the accounts payable ledger of the Cline Company showed the following balances: S. Haley & Co., $3,750; C. King, $2,350; W. Ortega, $1,000; and Welch Bros., $1,900. The November transactions involving the payment of cash were as follows:

Nov. 1 Purchased merchandise, check no. 11, $900.
     3 Purchased store equipment, check no. 12, $1,650.
     5 Paid Welch Bros. balance due of $1,900, less 1% discount, check no. 13, $1,881.
    11 Purchased merchandise, check no. 14, $2,000.
    15 Paid W. Ortega balance due of $1,000, less 3% discount, check no. 15, $970.
    16 A dividend is paid in the amount of $500, check no. 16.
    19 Paid C. King in full for invoice no. 1245, $1,300 less 2% discount, check no. 17, $1,274.
    25 Paid premium due on one year insurance policy, check no. 18, $3,000.
    30 Paid S. Haley & Co. in full for invoice no. 832, $2,250, check no. 19.

Instructions (Assume the use of a perpetual inventory system.)
(a) Journalize the transactions above in a four-column cash payments journal with columns for Other Accounts Dr.; Accounts Payable Dr.; Merchandise Inventory Cr.; and Cash Cr. Foot and crossfoot the journal.
(b) Insert the beginning balances in the Accounts Payable control and subsidiary accounts and post the November transactions to these accounts.
(c) Prove the agreement of the control account and the subsidiary account balances.

PE-3 The chart of accounts of Pagnozzi Company includes the following selected accounts:

*Journalize transactions in
multicolumn purchases
journal and post to the general
and subsidiary ledgers.*
(SO 1, 2, 3)

112 Accounts Receivable	401 Sales
120 Merchandise Inventory	412 Sales Returns and Allowances
126 Supplies	505 Cost of Goods Sold
157 Equipment	610 Advertising Expense
201 Accounts Payable	

In May the following selected transactions were completed. All purchases and sales were on account except as indicated. The cost of all merchandise sold was 70% of the sales price.

May 2 Purchased merchandise from Vena Company, $9,000.
      3 Received freight bill from Abel Freight on Vena purchase, $400.
      5 Sales were made to Potts Company, $1,600; Hogan Bros., $2,700; and Nance Company, $1,500.
      8 Purchased merchandise from Gore Company, $8,000 and Deleon Company, $8,700.
     10 Received credit on merchandise returned to Deleon Company, $500.
     15 Purchased supplies from Eaton Supply, $900.
     16 Purchased merchandise from Vena Company, $4,500; and Gore Company, $6,000.
     17 Returned supplies to Eaton Supply, receiving credit, $100. (*Hint:* Credit Supplies.)
     18 Received freight bills on May 16 purchases from Abel Freight, $500.
     20 Returned merchandise to Vena Company receiving credit, $300.
     23 Made sales to Hogan Bros., $2,400; and Nance Company, $2,200.
     25 Received bill for advertising from Beck Advertising, $900.
     26 Granted allowance to Nance Company for merchandise damaged in shipment, $200.
     28 Purchased equipment from Eaton Supply, $250.

Instructions (Assume the use of a perpetual inventory system.)
(a) Journalize the transactions above in a purchases journal, a sales journal, and a general journal. The purchases journal should have the following column headings: Date, Accounts Credited (Debited), Ref., Other Accounts Dr., Merchandise Inventory Dr., and Accounts Payable Cr.
(b) Post to both the general and subsidiary ledger accounts. (Assume that all accounts have zero beginning balances.)
(c) Prove the agreement of the control and subsidiary accounts.

Journalize transactions in special journals.
(SO 1, 2, 3)

PE–4 Selected accounts from the chart of accounts of Santos Company are shown below. (Santos uses a perpetual inventory system.)

101 Cash	201 Accounts Payable
112 Accounts Receivable	401 Sales
120 Merchandise Inventory	414 Sales Discounts
126 Supplies	505 Cost of Goods Sold
140 Land	610 Advertising Expense
145 Buildings	

The cost of all merchandise sold was 60% of the sales price. During October, Santos Company completed the following transactions:

Oct. 2 Purchased merchandise on account from Ming Company, $17,500.
      4 Sold merchandise on account to Pinka Co., $8,000. Invoice no. 204; terms 2/10, n/30.
      5 Purchased supplies for cash, $80.
      7 Made cash sales for the week totaling $9,160.
      9 Paid in full the amount owed the Ming Company less a 2% discount.
     10 Purchased merchandise on account from Quayle Corp., $4,200.
     12 Received payment from Pinka Co. for invoice no. 204.
     13 Issued a debit memorandum to Quayle Corp. and returned $250 worth of damaged goods.
     14 Made cash sales for the week totaling $8,180.
     16 Sold a parcel of land for $27,000 cash, the land's book value.
     17 Sold merchandise on account to C. Baden & Co., $5,350, invoice no. 205, terms 2/10, n/30.
     18 Purchased merchandise for cash, $2,125.
     21 Made cash sales for the week totaling $8,465.
     23 Paid in full the amount owed the Quayle Corp. for the goods kept (no discount).
     25 Purchased supplies on account from Flott Co., $260.
     25 Sold merchandise on account to Gregg Corp., $5,220, invoice no. 206, terms 2/10, n/30.
     25 Received payment from C. Baden & Co. for invoice no. 205.

26 Purchased for cash a small parcel of land and a building on the land to use as a storage facility. The total cost of $35,000 was allocated $21,000 to the land and $14,000 to the building.

27 Purchased merchandise on account from Singer Co., $8,500.

28 Made cash sales for the week totaling $8,540.

30 Purchased merchandise on account from Ming Company, $14,000.

30 Paid advertising bill for the month from the Gazette, $400.

30 Sold merchandise on account to C. Baden & Co., $4,600, invoice no. 207; terms 2/10, n/30.

Santos Company uses the following journals:

1. Sales journal.
2. Single-column purchases journal.
3. Cash receipts journal with columns for Cash Dr.; Sales Discounts Dr.; Accounts Receivable Cr.; Sales Cr.; Other Accounts Cr.; and Cost of Goods Sold Dr./Merchandise Inventory Cr.
4. Cash payments journal with columns for Other Accounts Dr.; Accounts Payable Dr.; Merchandise Inventory, Cr.; and Cash Cr.
5. General journal.

Instructions

Using the selected accounts provided:

(a) Record, in the appropriate journals, the October transactions.

(b) Foot and crossfoot all special journals.

(c) Show how postings would be made by placing ledger account numbers and check marks as needed in the journals. (Actual posting to ledger accounts is not required.)

Journalize in purchase and cash payments journals, post, prepare a trial balance, prove control to subsidiary, prepare adjusting entries, and prepare an adjusted trial balance.
(SO 1, 2, 3)

PE–5 Presented below are the sales and cash receipts journals for Tino Co. for its first month of operation. (Tino Co. uses a perpetual inventory system.)

SALES JOURNAL   S1

Date	Account Debited	Ref.	Accounts Receivable Dr. Sales Cr.	Cost of Goods Sold Dr. Merchandise Inventory Cr.
Feb. 3	D. Alco		5,000	3,300
9	P. Barber		6,500	4,290
12	D. Casey		8,000	5,280
26	K. Dennis		6,000	3,960
			25,500	16,830

CASH RECEIPTS JOURNAL   CR1

Date	Account Credited	Ref.	Cash Dr.	Sales Discounts Dr.	Accounts Receivable Cr.	Sales Cr.	Other Accounts Cr.	Cost of Goods Sold Dr. Merchandise Inventory Cr.
Feb. 1	Common Stock		30,000				30,000	
2			6,500			6,500		4,290
13	D. Alco		4,950	50	5,000			
18	Merchandise Inventory		150				150	
26	P. Barber		6,500		6,500			
			48,100	50	11,500	6,500	30,150	4,290

In addition, the following transactions have not been journalized for February 2001.

Feb. 2 Purchased merchandise on account from J. Carsen for $3,000, terms 1/10, n/30.

7 Purchased merchandise on account from K. Cooper for $30,000, terms 1/10, n/30.

9 Paid cash of $1,000 for purchase of supplies.

12 Paid $2,970 to J. Carsen in payment for $3,000 invoice, less 1% discount.

15 Purchased equipment for $8,000 cash.

16 Purchased merchandise on account from M. Kim, $2,400, terms 2/10, n/30.

17 Paid $29,700 to K. Cooper in payment of $30,000 invoice, less 1% discount.

20   Paid a cash dividend of $1,100.
21   Purchased merchandise on account from G. Azar for $6,500, terms 1/10, n/30.
28   Paid $2,400 to M. Kim in payment of $2,400 invoice.

Instructions

(a) Open the following accounts in the general ledger.

101 Cash
112 Accounts Receivable
120 Merchandise Inventory
126 Supplies
157 Equipment
158 Accumulated Depreciation—Equipment
201 Accounts Payable

311 Common Stock
332 Dividends
401 Sales
414 Sales Discounts
505 Cost of Goods Sold
631 Supplies Expense
711 Depreciation Expense

(b) Journalize the transactions that have not been journalized in a one-column purchases journal, and journalize the cash payments journal (see Illustration E-15).
(c) Post to the accounts receivable and accounts payable subsidiary ledgers. Follow the sequence of transactions as shown in the problem.
(d) Post the individual entries and totals to the general ledger.
(e) Prepare a trial balance at February 28, 2001.
(f) Determine that the subsidiary ledgers agree with the control accounts in the general ledger.
(g) The following adjustments at the end of February are necessary.
1. A count of supplies indicates that $300 is still on hand.
2. Depreciation on equipment for February is $200.
Prepare the adjusting entries and then post the adjusting entries to the general ledger.
(h) Prepare an adjusted trial balance.

BROADENING YOUR PERSPECTIVE

FINANCIAL REPORTING AND ANALYSIS

FINANCIAL REPORTING PROBLEM—A MINI PRACTICE SET

BYPE–1 (The working papers that accompany this textbook are needed in order to work this mini practice set. This practice set uses a **periodic inventory system**; therefore it should be assigned after coverage of Chapter 6.)

Hunt Co. uses both an accounts receivable and an accounts payable subsidiary ledger. Balances related to both the general ledger and the subsidiary ledger for Hunt are indicated in the working papers. Presented below are a series of transactions for Hunt Co. for the month of January. Credit sales terms are 2/10, n/30.

Jan. 3   Sell merchandise on credit to B. Sargent $3,100, invoice No. 510, and to J. Eaton $1,800, invoice No. 511.
5   Purchase merchandise from S. Walden $3,000 and D. Landell $2,200, terms n/30.
7   Receive checks from S. Lowell $4,000 and B. Jaggar $2,000 after discount period has lapsed.
8   Pay freight on merchandise purchased $180.
9   Send checks to S. Lee for $9,000 less 2% cash discount and D. Nordin for $11,000 less 1% cash discount.
9   Issue credit memo for $300 to J. Eaton for merchandise returned.
10   Summary daily cash sales total $15,500.
11   Sell merchandise on credit to R. Dansig $1,300, invoice No. 512, and to S. Lowell $900, invoice No. 513.
12   Pay rent of $1,000 for January.
13   Receive payment in full from B. Sargent and J. Eaton less cash discounts.
15   Paid cash dividends of $800.

15 Post all entries to the subsidiary ledgers.
16 Purchase merchandise from D. Nordin $15,000, terms 1/10, n/30; S. Lee $14,200, terms 2/10, n/30; and S. Walden $1,500, terms n/30.
17 Pay $400 cash for office supplies.
18 Return $200 of merchandise to S. Lee and receive credit.
20 Summary daily cash sales total $17,500.
21 Issue $15,000 note to R. Mannon in payment of balance due.
21 Receive payment in full from S. Lowell less cash discount.
22 Sell merchandise on credit to B. Sargent $1,700, invoice No. 514 and to R. Dansig $800, invoice No. 515.
22 Post all entries to the subsidiary ledger.
23 Send checks to D. Nordin and S. Lee in full payment less cash discounts.
25 Sell merchandise on credit to B. Jaggar $3,500, invoice No. 516 and to J. Eaton $6,100, invoice No. 517.
27 Purchase merchandise from D. Nordin $14,500, terms 1/10, n/30; D. Landell $1,200, terms n/30; and S. Walden $2,800, terms n/30.
27 Post all entries to the subsidiary ledger.
28 Pay $200 cash for office supplies.
31 Summary daily cash sales total $21,300.
31 Pay sales salaries $4,300 and office salaries $2,600.

Instructions
(a) Record the January transactions in a single-column sales journal, a single-column purchases journal, a cash receipts journal as shown in Illustration E-8, a cash payments journal as shown in Illustration E-15, and a two-column general journal.
(b) Post the journals to the general ledger.
(c) Prepare a trial balance at January 31, 2001, in the trial balance columns of the work sheet. Complete the work sheet using the following additional information. (A periodic inventory system is assumed.)
   (1) Office supplies at January 31 total $500.
   (2) Insurance coverage expires on October 31, 2001.
   (3) Annual depreciation on the equipment is $1,500.
   (4) Interest of $60 has accrued on the note payable.
   (5) Merchandise inventory at January 31 is $16,000.
(d) Prepare a multiple-step income statement and a retained earnings statement for January and a classified balance sheet at the end of January.
(e) Prepare and post adjusting and closing entries.
(f) Prepare a post-closing trial balance and determine whether the subsidiary ledgers agree with the controlling accounts in the general ledger.

REAL-WORLD FOCUS: Alco Standard Corporation

BYPE–2 Alco Standard Corporation's operations are divided into two business groups: Alco Office Products and Unisource. Alco Office Products sells, leases, and rents various electronic office machines; Unisource markets and distributes papers primarily for office use. The company owns or leases facilities in 49 states and 9 foreign countries.
   The president of Alco wrote the following in his letter in a recent annual report:

ALCO STANDARD CORPORATION
President's Letter to Stockholders

The creation of Unisource allows us to pursue strategies that are practical only on a unified basis. Our efforts to upgrade information technology, for example, will now be directed to building a common system throughout North America. This unified approach will give us online electronic link suppliers, cutting order entry costs and improving inventory management. As a result, we will be able to improve service to customers with more timely and more accurate order fulfillment, faster inquiry response and enhanced technical support.

Instructions

(a) When a company computerizes customer order entry, what equivalent special journal type must be programmed into such an electronic system?

(b) When a company computerizes inventory management (which involves more timely ordering of new merchandise), what special journal type must be programmed into such an electronic system?

CRITICAL THINKING

GROUP DECISION CASE

BYPE–3 Davis & Ruiz is a wholesaler of small appliances and parts. Davis & Ruiz is operated by two owners, Phil Davis and Tony Ruiz. In addition, the company has one employee, a repair specialist, who is on a fixed salary. Revenues are earned through the sale of appliances to retailers (approximately 75% of total revenues), appliance parts to do-it-yourselfers (10%), and the repair of appliances brought to the store (15%). Appliance sales are made on both a credit and cash basis. Customers are billed on prenumbered sales invoices. Credit terms are always net/30 days. All parts sales and repair work are cash only.

Merchandise is purchased on account from the manufacturers of both the appliances and the parts. Practically all suppliers offer cash discounts for prompt payments, and it is company policy to take all discounts. Most cash payments are made by check. Checks are most frequently issued to suppliers, to trucking companies for freight on merchandise purchases, and to newspapers, radio, and TV stations for advertising. All advertising bills are paid as received. The company pays dividends to its stockholders monthly. The salaried repairman is paid twice monthly.

Davis & Ruiz currently has a manual accounting system. However, the business is growing and some consideration is being given to an electronic accounting system.

Instructions
With the class divided into groups, answer the following:

(a) Identify the special journals that Davis & Ruiz should have in its manual system. List the column headings appropriate for each of the special journals.

(b) What control and subsidiary accounts should be included in Davis & Ruiz's manual system? Why?

(c) Identify for Phil and Tony the key points they should consider in deciding whether to install an electronic system.

COMMUNICATION ACTIVITY

BYPE–4 Sue Marsh, a classmate, has a part-time bookkeeping job. She is concerned about the inefficiencies in journalizing and posting transactions. Raul Hindi is the owner of the company where Sue works. In response to numerous complaints from Sue and others, Raul hired two additional bookkeepers a month ago. However, the inefficiencies have continued at an even higher rate. The accounting information system for the company has only a general journal and a general ledger. Raul refuses to install an electronic accounting system.

Instructions
Now that Sue is an expert in manual accounting information systems, she decides to send a letter to Raul Hindi explaining (1) why the additional personnel did not help and (2) what changes should be made to improve the efficiency of the accounting department. Write the letter that you think Sue should send.

ETHICS CASE

BYPE–5 Tyler Products Company operates three divisions, each with its own manufacturing plant and marketing/sales force. The corporate headquarters and central accounting office are in Tyler and the plants are in Freeport, Rockport, and Bayport, all within 50 miles of Tyler. Corporate management treats each division as an independent profit center and encourages competition among them. They each have similar but different product lines. As a competitive incentive, bonuses are awarded each year to the employees of the fastest growing and most profitable division.

Don Henke is the manager of Tyler's centralized computer accounting operation that keyboards the sales transactions and maintains the accounts receivable for all three divisions. Don came up in the accounting ranks from the Bayport division where his wife, several relatives, and many friends still work.

As sales documents are keyboarded into the computer, the originating division is identified by code. Most sales documents (95%) are coded, but some (5%) are not coded or are coded incorrectly. As the manager, Don has instructed the keyboard operators to assign the Bayport code to all uncoded and incorrectly coded sales documents. This is done he says, "in order to expedite processing and to keep the computer files current since they are updated daily." All receivables and cash collections for all three divisions are handled by Tyler as one subsidiary accounts receivable ledger.

Instructions
  (a) Who are the stakeholders in this situation?
  (b) What are the ethical issues in this case?
  (c) How might the system be improved to prevent this situation?

SURFING THE NET

BYPE–6 Great Plains Dynamics is one of the leading accounting software packages. Information related to this package is found at its web site.

Address: http://www.gps.com/dynamics (or go to www.wiley.com/college/weygandt)

Steps:
  1. Go to the site shown above.
  2. Choose **Product Details** then choose **General Ledger**. Perform instruction (a) below.
  3. Choose **Product Details** then choose **Payables Management**. Perform instruction (b) below.
  4. Choose **Product Details** then choose **Receivables Management**. Perform instruction (c) below.

Instructions
  (a) What are three key features of the general ledger module highlighted by the company?
  (b) What are three key features of the payables management module highlighted by the company?
  (c) What are three key features of the receivables management module highlighted by the company?

Answers to Self-Study Questions.
1. a   2. c   3. a   4. c   5. d   6. b

OTHER SIGNIFICANT LIABILITIES

STUDY OBJECTIVES

After studying this appendix, you should be able to:

1. *Describe the accounting and disclosure requirements for contingent liabilities.*
2. *Contrast the accounting for operating and capital leases.*
3. *Identify additional liabilities for fringe benefits associated with employee compensation.*

In addition to the current and long-term liabilities discussed in Chapter 11, several more types of liabilities may exist that could have a significant impact on a company's financial position and future cash flows. These other significant liabilities have been classified in this appendix as (a) contingent liabilities, (b) lease liabilities, and (c) additional liabilities for employee fringe benefits (paid absences and postretirement benefits).

CONTINGENT LIABILITIES

1

STUDY

OBJECTIVE

Describe the accounting and disclosure requirements for contingent liabilities.

With notes payable, interest payable, accounts payable, and sales taxes payable, we know that an obligation exists to make payment. But suppose that your company is currently involved in a dispute with the Internal Revenue Service (IRS) over the amount of its income tax liability. Do you have to report the disputed amount on the balance sheet as a liability? Or suppose your company is the defendant in a lawsuit in which an adverse decision might result in bankruptcy. How should this major contingency be reported? The answers to these questions are difficult, because these liabilities are dependent—contingent—upon some future event. In other words, a contingent liability is a potential liability that may become an actual liability in the future.

How, then, should contingent liabilities be reported? Guidelines have been adopted that are helpful in resolving these problems. The guidelines require that:

HELPFUL HINT

Another example of a contingency is toxic waste cleanup costs. Some expect that insurance will cover these costs, but insurance companies are arguing that general liability policies were never meant to cover this type of situation.

1. If the contingency is **probable**—if it is likely to occur—**and** the amount can be **reasonably estimated**, the liability should be recorded in the accounts.
2. If the contingency is only **reasonably possible**—if it could happen—then it need be disclosed only in the notes accompanying the financial statements.
3. If the contingency is **remote**—if it is unlikely to occur—it need not be recorded or disclosed.

ACCOUNTING IN ACTION
Business Insight

Contingent liabilities abound in the real world. Consider the following: Manville Corp. filed bankruptcy when it was hit by billions of dollars in asbestos product liability claims. Companies having multiple toxic waste sites are faced with cleanup costs that average $10 to $30 million and can reach as high as $500 million depending on the type of waste. For life and health insurance companies and their stockholders, the cost of AIDS is like an iceberg—everybody wonders how big it really is and what damage it might do in the future; according to the U.S. Centers for Disease Control treatment costs could be $8 billion to $16 billion. And frequent-flyer programs are so popular that airlines at one time owed participants more than 3 million round-trip domestic tickets. That's enough to fly at least 5.4 billion miles—free for the passengers but at what future cost to the airlines?

Recording a Contingent Liability

INTERNATIONAL NOTE

International accounting standards basically use criteria similar to those in the U.S. in determining how to account for contingencies.

Product warranties are a good example of a contingent liability that should be recorded in the accounts. Warranty contracts result in future costs that may be incurred in replacing defective units or repairing malfunctioning units without charge to the customer for a specified period after the product is sold. Generally, a manufacturer, such as Black & Decker, knows that some warranty costs will be incurred. Moreover, on the basis of prior experience with the product (or similar products), the company usually can make a reasonable estimate of the anticipated cost of servicing (honoring) the contract.

The accounting for warranty costs is based on the matching principle. To comply with this principle, **the estimated cost of honoring product warranty contracts should be recognized as an expense in the period in which the sale occurs**. To illustrate, assume that in 2000 Denson Manufacturing Company sells 10,000 washers and dryers at an average price of $600 each. The selling price includes a one-year warranty on parts. It is expected that 500 units (5%) will be defective and that warranty repair costs will average $80 per unit. In the year of sale, warrant contracts are honored on 300 units at a total cost of $24,000.

At December 31, it is necessary to accrue the estimated warranty costs on the 2000 sales. The computation is as follows:

Number of units sold	10,000
Estimated rate of defective units	× 5%
Total estimated defective units	500
Average warranty repair cost	× $80
Estimated product warranty liability	$40,000

ILLUSTRATION F-1

Computation of estimated product warranty liability

The adjusting entry, therefore, is:

Dec. 31	Warranty Expense	40,000	
	Estimated Warranty Liability		40,000
	(To accrue estimated warranty costs)		

A = L + SE
   +40,000 −40,000

The entry to record repair costs incurred in 2000 to honor warranty contracts on 2000 sales is shown in summary form below:

Jan. 1– Dec. 31	Estimated Warranty Liability	24,000	
	Repair Parts		24,000
	(To record honoring of 300 warranty contracts on 2000 sales)		

A = L + SE
−24,000 −24,000

Warranty expense of $40,000 is reported under selling expenses in the income statement, and estimated warranty liability of $16,000 ($40,000 − $24,000) is classified as a current liability on the balance sheet.

In the following year, all expenses incurred in honoring warranty contracts on 2000 sales should be debited to Estimated Warranty Liability. To illustrate, assume that 20 defective units are replaced in January 2001, at an average cost of $80 in parts and labor. The summary entry for the month of January is:

Jan. 31	Estimated Warranty Liability	1,600	
	Repair Parts		1,600
	(To record honoring of 20 warranty contracts on 2000 sales)		

A = L + SE
−1,600 −1,600

Disclosure of Contingent Liabilities

When it is probable that a contingent liability will be incurred but the amount cannot be reasonably estimated, or when the contingent liability is only reasonably possible, only disclosure of the contingency is required. Examples of contingencies that may require disclosure are pending or threatened lawsuits and assessment of additional income taxes pending an IRS audit of the tax return.

The disclosure should identify the nature of the item, and if known, the amount of the contingency and the expected outcome of the future event. Disclosure is usually accomplished through a note to the financial statements, as illustrated by the following:

ILLUSTRATION F-2

Disclosure of contingent liability

USAIR
Notes to the Financial Statements

Legal Proceedings

The Company and various subsidiaries have been named as defendants in various suits and proceedings which involve, among other things, environmental concerns about noise and air pollution and employment matters. These suits and proceedings are in various stages of litigation, and the status of the law with respect to several of the issues involved is unsettled. For these reasons the outcome of these suits and proceedings is difficult to predict. In the Company's opinion, however, the disposition of these matters is not likely to have a material adverse effect on its financial condition.

LEASE LIABILITIES

2

STUDY OBJECTIVE

Contrast the accounting for operating and capital leases.

A lease is a contractual arrangement between the lessor (owner of the property) and a lessee (renter of the property) that grants the right to use specific property for a period of time in return for cash payments. Leasing is a big business. For example, an estimated $125 billion of capital equipment was leased in a recent year. This represents approximately one-third of equipment financed that year. The two most common types of leases are operating leases and capital leases.

ACCOUNTING IN ACTION
Business Insight

As an excellent example of the magnitude of leasing, leased planes account for nearly 40% of the U.S. fleet of commercial airlines. The reasons for leasing include favorable tax treatment, increased flexibility, and low airline income. As passenger volume is expected to double in the next 20 years, some industry analysts estimate that approximately $400 billion in airplanes will be needed, and it is anticipated that much of the financing will be done through leasing. Leasing is particularly attractive to lessors because airplanes have relatively long lives, a ready secondhand market, and a significant resale value. Or take the commercial truck fleet—over one-third of heavy-duty trucks are presently leased.

Operating Leases

The renting of an apartment and the rental of a car at an airport are examples of operating leases. **In an operating lease the intent is temporary use of the property by the lessee with continued ownership of the property by the lessor.** The lease (or rental) payments are recorded as an expense by the lessee and as revenue by the lessor. For example, assuming that a sales representative for Western Inc. leases a car from Hertz Car Rental at the Los Angeles airport and that Hertz charges a total of $275, the entry by the lessee, Western Inc., is:

A	=	L	+	SE
−275				−275

Car Rental Expense	275	
Cash		275
(To record payment of lease rental charge)		

In addition, the lessee may incur other costs during the lease period. For example, in the case above, the lessee may be required to pay for gas and oil. These costs are also reported as an expense.

Capital Leases

In most lease contracts, a periodic payment is made by the lessee and is recorded as rent expense in the income statement. However, in some cases, the lease contract transfers substantially all the benefits and risks of ownership to the lessee, so that the lease is in effect a purchase of the property. This type of lease is called a capital lease because the present value of the cash payments for the lease are capitalized and recorded as an asset. Illustration F-3 indicates the major difference between an operating and a capital lease.

ILLUSTRATION F-3

Types of leases

The lessee must record the lease **as an asset**—that is, as a capital lease—if any **one** of the following conditions exists:

1. **The lease transfers ownership of the property to the lessee.** *Rationale*: If during the lease term, the lessee receives ownership of the asset, the leased asset should be reported as an asset on the lessee's books.
2. **The lease contains a bargain purchase option.** *Rationale*: If during the term of the lease, the lessee can purchase the asset at a price substantially below its fair market value, the lessee will obviously exercise this option. Thus, the lease should be reported as a leased asset on the lessee's books.
3. **The lease term is equal to 75% or more of the economic life of the leased property.** *Rationale*: If the lease term is for much of the asset's useful life, the asset should be recorded by the lessee.
4. **The present value of the lease payments equals or exceeds 90% of the fair market value of the leased property.** *Rationale*: If the present value of the lease payments is equal to or almost equal to the fair market value of the asset, the lessee has essentially purchased the asset. As a result, the leased asset should be recorded on the books of the lessee.

To illustrate, assume that Gonzalez Company decides to lease new equipment. The lease period is 4 years; the economic life of the leased equipment is

HELPFUL HINT

What are the effects on the lessee's balance sheet if a lease meets the criteria to be classified as a capital lease but is incorrectly accounted for as an operating lease? Assets and liabilities are understated.

A	=	L	+	SE
+190,000		+190,000		

HELPFUL HINT

Off-balance sheet financing is a major reporting problem. Some other off-balance sheet items are guarantees, pensions, and long-term commitments.

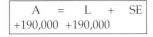

3

STUDY

OBJECTIVE

Identify additional liabilities for fringe benefits associated with employee compensation.

estimated to be 5 years. The present value of the lease payments is $190,000 which is equal to the fair market value of the equipment. There is no transfer of ownership during the lease term nor is there any bargain purchase option.

In this example, Gonzalez has essentially purchased the equipment. Conditions 3 and 4 have been met: First, the lease term is 75% or more of the economic life of the asset, and second, the present value of cash payments is equal to the equipment's fair market value. The entry to record the transaction is as follows:

Leased Asset—Equipment	190,000	
Lease Liability		190,000
(To record leased asset and lease liability)		

The leased asset is reported on the balance sheet under plant assets. The lease liability is reported as a liability on the balance sheet. **The portion of the lease liability expected to be paid in the next year is reported as a current liability. The remainder is classified as a long-term liability.**

Most lessees do not like to report leases on their balance sheets. The reason is that the lease liability increases the company's total liabilities. This, in turn, may make it more difficult for the company to obtain needed funds from lenders. As a result, companies attempt to keep leased assets and lease liabilities off the balance sheet by not meeting any one of the four conditions mentioned above. This procedure of keeping liabilities off the balance sheet is often referred to as **off-balance sheet financing**.

··

ADDITIONAL LIABILITIES FOR EMPLOYEE FRINGE BENEFITS

In addition to the three payroll tax fringe benefits, employers incur other substantial fringe benefit costs. Two of the most important are paid absences and postretirement benefits.

Paid Absences

Employees often have rights to receive compensation for future absences when certain conditions of employment are met. The compensation may pertain to paid vacations, sick pay benefits, and paid holidays. When the payment of such compensation is **probable** and the amount can be **reasonably estimated**, a liability should be accrued for paid future absences. When the amount cannot be reasonably estimated, the potential liability should be disclosed. Ordinarily, vacation pay is the only paid absence that is accrued; the other types of paid absences are only disclosed.[1]

To illustrate, assume that Academy Company employees are entitled to one day's vacation for each month worked. If thirty employees earn an average of $110 per day in a given month, the accrual for vacation benefits in one month is $3,300. The liability is recognized at the end of the month by the following adjusting entry:

A	=	L	+	SE
		+3,300		−3,300

Jan. 31	Vacation Benefits Expense	3,300	
	Vacation Benefits Payable		3,300
	(To accrue vacation benefits expense)		

---

[1]The typical U.S. company provides an average of 12 days of paid vacations for its employees, at an average cost of 5% of gross earnings.

This accrual is required by the matching principle. Vacation Benefits Expense is reported as an operating expense in the income statement, and Vacation Benefits Payable is reported as a current liability in the balance sheet. When vacation benefits are paid, Vacation Benefits Payable is debited and Cash is credited. For example if the above benefits for ten employees are paid in July, the entry is:

July 31	Vacation Benefits Payable	1,100	
	Cash		1,100
	(To record payment of vacation benefits)		

A	=	L	+	SE
−1,100		−1,100		

The magnitude of unused paid absences has gained employers' attention. Consider the case of an assistant superintendent of schools who worked for around 20 years and rarely took a vacation or sick day. A month or so before she retired, the school district discovered that she was due nearly $30,000 in accrued benefits. Yet the liability was never accrued.

Postretirement Benefits

Postretirement benefits consist of benefits provided by employers to retired employees for (1) health care and life insurance and (2) pensions. For many years the accounting for postretirement benefits was on a cash basis. However, both types of postretirement benefits are now accounted for on the accrual basis.

Postretirement Health Care and Life Insurance Benefits

Providing medical and related health care benefits for retirees—at one time an inexpensive and highly effective way of generating employee goodwill—has turned into one of corporate America's most worrisome financial problems. Runaway medical costs, early retirement, and increased longevity are sending the liability for retiree health plans through the roof.

Many companies began offering retiree health care coverage in the form of Medicare supplements in the 1960s. Almost all plans operated on a pay-as-you-go basis—the companies simply paid the bills as they came in, rather than setting aside funds to meet the cost of future benefits. These plans were accounted for on the cash basis rather than the accrual basis. However, the FASB concluded that shareholders and creditors should know the amount of the employer's obligations. As a result, employers must now use the **accrual basis** in accounting for postretirement health care and life insurance benefits.

HELPFUL HINT
These costs should be expensed during the working years of the employee because the company benefits during this period.

HELPFUL HINT
Recognizing the impact of retiree health costs on net income, companies are increasingly changing their health plans to shift costs and reduce benefits.

ACCOUNTING IN ACTION
Business Insight

The battle over fringe benefits is increasing in intensity as benefits outpace wages and salaries. Growing faster than pay, benefits equaled 38% of wages and salaries in a recent year. While vacations and other forms of paid leave still take the biggest bite of the benefits pie, medical costs are the fastest-growing item.

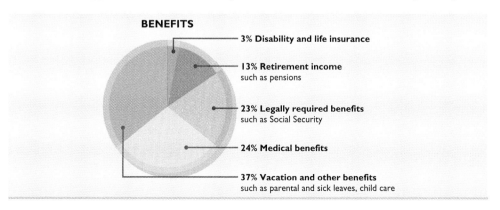

BENEFITS

- 3% Disability and life insurance
- 13% Retirement income such as pensions
- 23% Legally required benefits such as Social Security
- 24% Medical benefits
- 37% Vacation and other benefits such as parental and sick leaves, child care

Pension Plans

A pension plan is an agreement whereby an employer provides benefits (payments) to employees after they retire. Over 50 million workers currently participate in pension plans in the United States. The need for proper administration of and good accounting for pension plans becomes apparent when one appreciates the size of existing pension funds. Most pension plans are subject to the provisions of ERISA (Employee Retirement Income Security Act), a law enacted to curb abuses in the administration and funding of such plans.

Three parties are generally involved in a pension plan. The **employer** (company) sponsors the pension plan. The **plan administrator** receives the contributions from the employer, invests the pension assets, and makes the benefit payments to the **pension recipients** (retired employees). Illustration F-4 shows the three distinct parties involved in a pension plan and indicates the flow of cash among them.

ILLUSTRATION F-4

Parties in a pension plan

An employer-financed pension is part of the employee's compensation. The provisions of ERISA establish the minimum contribution that a company must make each year toward employee pensions. The company records the pension costs as an expense while the employees are working because that is when the company receives benefits from the employees' services. Generally the pension expense is reported as an operating expense in the company's income statement. Frequently, the amount contributed by the company to the pension plan is different from the amount of the pension expense. A **liability** is recognized when the pension expense to date is **more than** the company's contributions to date; an **asset** is recognized when the pension expense to date is **less than** the company's contributions to date.

The two most common types of pension arrangements for providing benefits to employees after they retire are defined contribution plans and defined benefit plans.

Defined Contribution Plan

In a defined contribution plan, the employer's contribution to the plan is defined by the terms of the plan. That is, the employer agrees to contribute a certain sum each period based on a formula.

The accounting for a defined contribution plan is straightforward: The employer simply makes a contribution each year based on the formula established in the plan. As a result, the employer's obligation is easily determined. It follows that **the amount of the contribution required each period is reported as pension expense. A liability is reported by the employer only if the contribution has not been made in full.**

To illustrate, assume that Alba Office Interiors Corp. has a defined contribution plan in which it contributes $200,000 each year to the pension fund for its employees. The entry to record this transaction is:

Pension Expense	200,000		
Cash		200,000	
(To record pension expense and contribution to pension fund)			

A	=	L	+	SE
−200,000				−200,000

To the extent that Alba did not contribute the $200,000 defined contribution, a liability would be recorded. Pension payments to retired employees are made from the pension fund by the plan administrator.

Defined Benefit Plan

In a defined benefit plan, the benefits that the employee will receive at the time of retirement are defined by the terms of the plan. Benefits are typically calculated using a formula that considers an employee's compensation level when he or she nears retirement and the employee's years of service. Because the benefits in this plan are defined in terms of uncertain future variables, an appropriate funding pattern is established to assure that enough funds are available at retirement to meet the benefits promised. This funding level depends on a number of factors such as employee turnover, length of service, mortality, compensation levels, and investment earnings. **The proper accounting for these plans is complex and is considered in more advanced accounting courses.**

Postretirement Benefits as Long-term Liabilities

While part of the liability associated with (1) postretirement health care and life insurance benefits and (2) pension plans is generally a current liability, the greater portion of these liabilities extends many years into the future. Therefore, many companies are required to report significant amounts as long-term liabilities for postretirement benefits.

BEFORE YOU GO ON ...

Review It

1. What is a contingent liability?
2. How are contingent liabilities reported in financial statements.
3. What accounts are involved in accruing and paying vacation benefits?
4. What basis should be used in accounting for postretirement benefits?

SUMMARY OF STUDY OBJECTIVES

1. Describe the accounting and disclosure requirements for contingent liabilities. If it is probable that the contingency will happen (if it is likely to occur) and the amount is reasonably estimable, the liability should be recorded in the accounts. However, if it is only reasonably possible (it could occur), then it need be disclosed only in the notes to the financial statements. If the possibility that the contingency will happen is remote (unlikely to occur), it need not be recorded or disclosed.

2. Contrast the accounting for operating and capital leases. For an operating lease, lease (or rental) payments are recorded as an expense by the lessee (renter). For a capital lease, the lessee records the asset and related obligation at the present value of the future lease payments.

3. Identify additional liabilities for fringe benefits associated with employee compensation. Additional liabilities for fringe benefits associated with wages are paid absences (paid vacations, sick pay benefits, and paid holidays), postretirement health care and life insurance, and pensions. The two most common types of pension arrangements are a defined contribution plan and a defined benefit plan.

GLOSSARY

Capital lease A contractual arrangement that transfers substantially all the benefits and risks of ownership to the lessee so that the lease is in effect a purchase of the property. (p. F5).

Contingent liability A potential liability that may become an actual liability in the future. (p. F2).

Defined benefit plan A pension plan in which the benefits that the employee will receive at retirement are defined by the terms of the plan. (p. F9).

Defined contribution plan A pension plan in which the employer's contribution to the plan is defined by the terms of the plan. (p. F8).

Operating lease A contractual arrangement giving the lessee temporary use of the property with continued ownership of the property by the lessor. (p. F4).

Pension plan An agreement whereby an employer provides benefits to employees after they retire. (p. F8).

Postretirement benefits Payments by employers to retired employees for health care, life insurance, and pensions. (p. F7).

SELF-STUDY QUESTIONS

Answers are at the end of the appendix.

(SO 1) 1. A contingency should be recorded in the accounts when:
a. It is probable the contingency will happen but the amount cannot be reasonably estimated.
b. It is reasonably possible the contingency will happen and the amount can be reasonably estimated.
c. It is reasonably possible the contingency will happen but the amount cannot be reasonably estimated.
d. It is probable the contingency will happen and the amount can be reasonably estimated.

(SO 1) 2. At December 31, Hanes Company prepares an adjusting entry for a product warranty contract. Which of the following accounts are included in the entry?
a. Warranty Expense.
b. Estimated Warranty Liability.
c. Repair Parts/Wages Payable.
d. Both (a) and (b).

(SO 2) 3. Lease A does not contain a bargain purchase option, but the lease term is equal to 90 percent of the estimated economic life of the leased property. Lease B does not transfer ownership of the property to the lessee by the end of the lease term, but the lease term is equal to 75 percent of the estimated economic life of the lease property. How should the lessee classify these leases?

	Lease A	Lease B
a.	Operating lease	Capital lease
b.	Operating lease	Operating lease
c.	Capital lease	Capital lease
d.	Capital lease	Operating lease

4. Which of the following is *not* an additional fringe benefit? (SO 3)
a. Salaries.
b. Paid absences.
c. Paid vacations.
d. Postretirement pensions.

QUESTIONS

1. What is a contingent liability? Give an example of a contingent liability that is usually recorded in the accounts.

2. Under what circumstances is a contingent liability disclosed only in the notes to the financial statements? Under what circumstances is a contingent liability not recorded in the accounts nor disclosed in the notes to the financial statements?

3. (a) What is a lease agreement? (b) What are the two most common types of leases? (c) Distinguish between the two types of leases.

4. Mitchell Company rents a warehouse on a month-to-month basis for the storage of its excess inventory. The company periodically must rent space when its production greatly exceeds actual sales. What is the nature of this type of lease agreement, and what accounting treatment should be accorded it?

5. Rodriguez Company entered into an agreement to lease 12 computers from Rochester Electronics Inc. The present value of the lease payments is $186,300. Assuming that this is a capital lease, what entry would Rodriguez Company make on the date of the lease agreement?

6. Identify three additional types of fringe benefits associated with employees' compensation.

7. Often during job interviews, the candidate asks the potential employer about the firm's paid absences policy. What are paid absences? How are they accounted for?

8. What are the two types of postretirement benefits? During what years does the FASB advocate expensing the employer's costs of these postretirement benefits?

9. What basis of accounting for the employer's cost of postretirement health care and life insurance benefits has been used by most companies and what basis does

the FASB advocate in the future? Explain the basic difference between these methods in recognizing postretirement benefit costs.

10. Identify the three parties in a pension plan. What role does each party have in the plan?

11. Tom Broka and Bryant Gumbs are reviewing pension plans. They ask your help in distinguishing between a defined contribution plan and a defined benefit plan. Explain the principal differences to Tom and Bryant.

BRIEF EXERCISES

• •

BEF–1 On December 1, Filgas Company introduces a new product that includes a 1-year warranty on parts. In December 1,000 units are sold. Management believes that 3% of the units will be defective and that the average warranty costs will be $60 per unit. Prepare the adjusting entry at December 31 to accrue the estimated warranty cost.

Prepare adjusting entry for warranty costs.
(SO 1)

BEF–2 Prepare the journal entries that the lessee should make to record the following transactions:

1. The lessee makes a lease payment of $100,000 to the lessor in an operating lease transaction.
2. Goldberg Company leases a new building from Brace Construction, Inc. The present value of the lease payments is $600,000. The lease qualifies as a capital lease.

Contrast accounting for operating and capital lease.
(SO 2)

BEF–3 In the Reid Company, employees are entitled to 1 day's vacation for each month worked. In January, 50 employees worked the full month. Record the vacation pay liability for January assuming the average daily pay for each employee is $100.

Record estimated vacation benefits.
(SO 3)

EXERCISES

• •

EF–1 Red Cliff Company sells automatic can openers under a 75-day warranty for defective merchandise. Based on past experience, Red Cliff Company estimates that 3% of the units sold will become defective during the warranty period. Management estimates that the average cost of replacing or repairing a defective unit is $10. The units sold and units defective that occurred during the last 2 months of 2001 are as follows:

Record estimated liability and expense for warranties.
(SO 1)

Month	Units Sold	Units Defective Prior to December 31
November	30,000	600
December	32,000	400

Instructions
(a) Determine the estimated warranty liability at December 31 for the units sold in November and December.
(b) Prepare the journal entries to record the estimated liability for warranties and the costs (assume actual costs of $10,000) incurred in honoring 1,000 warranty claims.
(c) Give the entry to record the honoring of 350 warranty contracts in January at an average cost of $10.

EF–2 Murphy Company has the following liability accounts after posting adjusting entries: Accounts Payable $62,000, Unearned Ticket Revenue $24,000, Estimated Warranty Liability $18,000, Interest Payable $12,000, Mortgage Payable $120,000, Notes Payable $80,000, and Sales Taxes Payable $12,000.

Prepare the current liability section of the balance sheet.
(SO 1)

Instructions
(a) Prepare the current liability section of the balance sheet, assuming $30,000 of the mortgage is payable next year.
(b) Comment on Murphy Company's liquidity, assuming total current assets are $300,000.

EF–3 Presented below are two independent situations.

Journal entries for operating lease and capital lease.
(SO 2)

1. Plante Car Rental leased a car to Rockefeller Company for 1 year. Terms of the operating lease agreement call for monthly payments of $600.
2. On January 1, 2001, Wizard Inc. entered into an agreement to lease 20 computers from Kilgust Electronics. The terms of the lease agreement require three annual rental pay-

ments of $120,00 (including 10% interest) beginning December 31, 2001. The present value of the three rental payments is $298,422. Wizard considers this a capital lease.

Instructions

(a) Prepare the appropriate journal entry to be made by Rockefeller Company for the first lease payment.
(b) Prepare the journal entry to record the lease agreement on the books of Wizard Inc. on January 1, 2001.

Prepare adjusting entries for fringe benefits.
(SO 3)

EF–4 Mercer Company has two fringe benefit plans for its employees:

1. It grants employees 2 days' vacation for each month worked. Ten employees worked the entire month of March at an average daily wage of $100 per employee.
2. It has a defined contribution pension plan in which the company contributes 10% of gross earnings. Gross earnings in March were $35,000. The payment to the pension fund has not been made.

Instructions
Prepare the adjusting entries at March 31.

PROBLEMS: SET A

Prepare current liability entries, adjusting entries, and current liability section.
(SO 1)

PF–1A On January 1, 2001, the ledger of Carroll Company contains the following liability accounts.

Accounts Payable	$42,500
Sales Taxes Payable	5,600
Unearned Service Revenue	15,000

During January the following selected transactions occurred:

Jan. 1 Borrowed $15,000 in cash from Midland Bank on a 4-month, 12%, $15,000 note.
     5 Sold merchandise for cash totaling $7,800 which includes 4% sales taxes.
    12 Provided services for customers who had made advance payments of $8,000. (Credit Service Revenue.)
    14 Paid state treasurer's department for sales taxes collected in December 2000 ($5,600).
    20 Sold 500 units of a new product on credit at $52 per unit, plus 4% sales tax. This new product is subject to a 1-year warranty.
    25 Sold merchandise for cash totaling $11,440, which includes 4% sales taxes.

Instructions

(a) Journalize the January transactions.
(b) Journalize the adjusting entries at January 31 for (1) the outstanding notes payable, and (2) estimated warranty liability, assuming that the estimated rate of defective units is 10% and the average warranty repair cost is $41.60.
(c) Prepare the current liability section of the balance sheet at January 31, 2001.

Analyze three different lease situations and prepare journal entries.
(SO 2)

PF–2A Presented below are three different lease transactions in which Casper Enterprises engaged in 2001. Assume that all lease transactions start on January 1, 2001. In no case does Casper receive title to the properties leased during or at the end of the lease term.

	Lessor		
	Lornegren Associates	**Potter Co.**	**Haskell Inc.**
Type of property	Bulldozer	Truck	Furniture
Bargain purchase option	None	None	None
Lease term	4 years	6 years	3 years
Estimated economic life	8 years	7 years	5 years
Yearly rental	$13,000	$ 6,000	$ 5,000
Fair market value of leased asset	$80,000	$29,000	$27,500
Present value of the lease rental payments	$48,000	$27,000	$12,000

Instructions
(a) Identify the leases above as operating or capital leases. Explain.
(b) How should the lease transaction for Potter Co. be recorded on January 1, 2001?
(c) How should the lease transactions for Haskell Inc. be recorded in 2001?

PROBLEMS: SET B

PF-1B   On January 1, 2001, the ledger of Midler Company contains the following liability accounts:

Accounts Payable	$52,000
Sales Taxes Payable	7,500
Unearned Service Revenue	16,000

Prepare current liability entries, adjusting entries, and current liability section.
(SO 1)

During January the following selected transactions occurred:

Jan. 5   Sold merchandise for cash totaling $16,632, which includes 8% sales taxes.
   12   Provided services for customers who had made advance payments of $9,000. (Credit Service Revenue.)
   14   Paid state revenue department for sales taxes collected in December 2000 ($7,500).
   20   Sold 500 units of a new product on credit at $50 per unit, plus 8% sales tax. This new product is subject to a 1-year warranty.
   21   Borrowed $18,000 from Midland Bank on a 3-month, 12%, $18,000 note.
   25   Sold merchandise for cash totaling $11,340, which includes 8% sales taxes.

Instructions
(a) Journalize the January transactions.
(b) Journalize the adjusting entries at January 31 for (1) the outstanding notes payable, and (2) estimated warranty liability, assuming that the estimated rate of defective units is 10% and the average warranty repair cost is $40. (*Hint:* Use one-half of a month for the City Bank note and one-third of a month for the Midland Bank note.)
(c) Prepare the current liability section of the balance sheet at January 31, 2001.

PF-2B   Presented below are three different lease transactions that occurred for Brett Inc. in 2001. Assume that all lease contracts start on January 1, 2001. In no case does Brett receive title to the properties leased during or at the end of the lease term.

Analyze three different lease situations and prepare journal entries.
(SO 2)

	Lessor		
	Hung Delivery	**Williams Co.**	**Cecil Auto**
Type of property	Computer	Delivery equipment	Automobile
Yearly rental	$ 8,000	$ 4,000	$ 3,700
Lease term	6 years	4 years	2 years
Estimated economic life	7 years	7 years	5 years
Fair market value of lease asset	$44,000	$19,000	$11,000
Present value of the lease rental payments	$43,000	$13,000	$ 6,400
Bargain purchase option	None	None	None

Instructions
(a) Which of the leases above are operating leases and which are capital leases? Explain.
(b) How should the lease transaction for Williams Co. be recorded in 2001?
(c) How should the lease transaction for Hung Delivery be recorded on January 1, 2001?

BROADENING YOUR PERSPECTIVE

FINANCIAL REPORTING AND ANALYSIS
••

FINANCIAL REPORTING PROBLEMS
Kellogg Company

BYPF–1   Refer to the financial statements of Kellogg and the Notes to Consolidated Financial Statements in Appendix A to answer the following questions about contingent liabilities, lease liabilities, and pension costs.

(a) Where does Kellogg report its contingent liabilities?

(b) What is management's opinion as to the ultimate effect of the "various claims and legal proceedings" pending against the company?

(c) Where did Kellogg report the details of its lease obligations? What amount of rent expense from operating leases did Kellogg incur in 1998? What was Kellogg's total future minimum annual rental commitment under noncancelable operating leases at December 31, 1998?

(d) What type of employee pension plan does Kellogg have?

(e) What is the amount of postretirement benefit expense (other than pensions) for 1998?

CF Industries, Inc.

BYPF–2   Presented below is the lease portion of the notes to the financial statements of CF Industries, Inc.

CF INDUSTRIES, INC.
Notes to the Financial Statements

Leases   The present value of future minimum capital lease payments and the future minimum lease payments under noncancelable operating leases at December 31, 2000, are:

	Capital Lease Payments	Operating Lease Payments
2001	$ 7,733	$3,067
2002	6,791	2,052
2003	6,730	1,056
2004	6,788	918
2005	6,785	86
Thereafter	13,441	6
Future minimum lease payments	48,268	$7,185
Less: Equivalent interest	11,391	
Present value	36,877	
Less: Current portion	5,570	
	$31,307	

Rent expense for operating leases was $7.0 million for the year ended December 31, 2000, $5.3 million for 1999, and $5.6 million for 1998.

Instructions
What type of leases does CF Industries, Inc. use? What is the amount of the current portion of the lease obligation?

CRITICAL THINKING

. . . .

GROUP DECISION CASE

BYPF–3 Presented below is the condensed balance sheet for Express, Inc. as of December 31, 2001:

EXPRESS, INC.
Balance Sheet
December 31, 2001

Current assets	$ 800,000	Current liabilities	$1,200,000
Plant assets	1,600,000	Long-term liabilities	700,000
		Common stock	400,000
		Retained earnings	100,000
Total	$2,400,000	Total	$2,400,000

Express has decided that it needs to purchase a new crane for its operations. The new crane costs $900,000 and has a useful life of 15 years. However, Express' bank has refused to provide any help in financing the purchase of the new equipment, even though Express is willing to pay an above-market interest rate for the financing.

The chief financial officer for Express, Lisa Colder, has discussed with the manufacturer of the crane the possibility of a lease agreement. After some negotiation, the manufacturer of the equipment agrees to lease the crane to Express under the following terms: length of the lease, 7 years; payments, $100,000 per year. The present value of the lease payments is $548,732.

The board of directors at Express is delighted with this new lease. They reason they have the use of the crane for the next seven years. In addition, Lisa Colder notes that this type of financing is a good deal because it will keep debt off the balance sheet.

Instructions

With the class divided into groups, answer the following:

(a) Why do you think the bank decided not to lend money to Express, Inc.?
(b) How should this lease transaction be reported in the financial statements?
(c) What did Lisa Colder mean when she said "leasing will keep debt off the balance sheet"?

Answers to Self-Study Questions
1. d   2. d   3. c   4. a

PHOTO CREDITS

Chapter 1
Opener: John Kelly/Tony Stone Images/New York, Inc. Page 5: Garry Hunter, Tony Stone Images/New York, Inc. Page 6: Ivan Chermayeff/Nonstock, Inc. Page 7: Ann Sates/SABA. Page 11: Laurence Dutton/Tony Stone Images/New York, Inc. Page 22: Will Crocker/The Image Bank.

Chapter 2
Opener: Courtesy Foster's Restaurants. Reproduced with permission. Page 47: Wes Thompson/The Stock Market. Page 50: AP/Wide World Photos. Page 56: Diana Walker/Gamma Liaison. Page 58: Stephen Marks/The Image Bank. Page 59: Arthur Meyerson/The Image Bank. Page 68: Frank Wing/Sock, Boston/PNI.

Chapter 3
Opener: John Martin/The Stock Market. Page 94: AP/Wide World Photos. Page 98: Neil Rabinowitz/Corbis-Bettmann. Page 107: Ralph Mercer/Tony Stone Images/New York, Inc.

Chapter 4
Opener: Bartee/Stock Imagery. Page 142: © 99 Lotus Development Corporation. Used with permission of Lotus Development Corporation. Lotus and 1-2-3 are registered trademarks of Lotus Development Corporation. Page 148: John Chiasson/Gamma Liaison. Page 156: Kunio Owaki/The Stock Market. Page 158 (top): Courtesy United Airlines. Page 158 (bottom): Leland Bobbe/Tony Stone Images/New York, Inc. Page 159 (top): John Fiordalisi/SUPERSTOCK. Page 159 (bottom): Zigy Kaluzny/Tony Stone Images/New York, Inc. Page 160 (top): Courtesy United Airlines. Page 160 (bottom): Courtesy Consolidated Freightways. Page 161: Michel Tcherevkoff/The Image Bank. Page 167: Lonnie Duka/Tony Stone Images/New York, Inc. Page 182: Courtesy Case Corporation.

Chapter 5
Opener: Ed Honowitz/Tony Stone Images/New York, Inc. Page 191: Alex Bartel/FPG International. Page 194: G. Covian/The Image Bank. Page 197: David Young Wolff/Tony Stone Images/New York, Inc. Page 198: T. Cordoza/Gamma Liaison. Page 204: Murray Alcosser/The Image Bank. Page 208: © Gamma Liaison. Page 225: Courtesy McDonnell Douglas.

Chapter 6
Opener: Courtesy Mountain Equipment Co-op. Page 234: Charles Schmidt/Stock Imagery. Page 235: Stewart Cohen/Tony Images/New York, Inc. Page 250: James Schnepf/Gamma Liaison. Page 251: Bob Krist/Tony Stone Images/New York, Inc. Page 252: Arnulf Husmo/Tony Stone Images/New York, Inc. Page 280: Courtesy General Motors Corporation.

Chapter 7
Opener: Ron Chappel/FPG International/PNI. Page 287: Donald Struthers/Tony Stone Images/New York, Inc. Page 289: Ken Wilde/The Image Bank. Page 293: Leif Skoogfors/Corbis-Bettmann. Page 294: Andy Zito/The Image Bank. Page 303: Steve Forney/SUPERSTOCK. Page 305: Olney Vasan/Tony Stone Images/New York, Inc.

Chapter 8
Opener: Rosanne Olson/Tony Stone Images/New York, Inc. Page 333 (top): Mike Blank/Tony Stone Images/New York, Inc. Page 333 (bottom): Robert Slack/International Stock Photo. Page 336: Michael Murphy/The Image Bank. Page 341: M.J. Cardenas/The Image Bank. Page 346: David Leach/Tony Stone Images/New York, Inc. Page 347: Jon Riley/Tony Stone Images/New York, Inc. Page 348 (top): Petrified Collection/The Image Bank. Page 348 (bottom): Comstock, Inc. Page 352: Courtesy Eastman Kodak Company. Page 369 (top): Courtesy Microsoft. Page 369 (bottom): Courtesy Oracle Corporation.

Chapter 9
Opener: Peter Poulides/Tony Stone Images/New York, Inc. Page 376: Jay Belmore/The Image Bank. Page 378: Jed & Kaoru Share/Tony Stone Images/New York, Inc. Page 380: Zefa/Stock Imagery. Page 383: Brian Smale Photography. Page 388: John Lund/Tony Stone Images/New York, Inc. Page 390: Laurence Dutton/Tony Stone Images/New York, Inc. Page 406: Courtesy Sears, Roebuck and Co.

Chapter 10
Opener: Bob Krist/Tony Stone Images/New York, Inc. Page 422: Bill Losh/FPG International. Page 430: N. Cotton/International Stock Photo. Page 433: Evan Kafka/Gamma Liaison. Page 434: Tristan Paviot/Tony Stone Images/New York, Inc. Page 456: Courtesy Clark Equipment Company.

Chapter 11
Opener: Scott Barrow Scott Barrow Photography. Page 464: Laurence Dutton/Tony Stone Images/New York, Inc. Page 472: AP/Wide World Photos. Page 483: Historical Picture Archive/Corbis-Bettmann. Page 494: Ken Whitmore/Tony Stone Images/New York, Inc. Page 508: Courtesy Apache Corporation.

Chapter 12
Opener: Mike Powell/Tony Stone Images/New York, Inc. Page 515: AP/Wide World Photos. Page 516: Courtesy Delaware State Travel Service. Page 517: Paul Van Riel/Black Star. Page 520: Jon Riley/Tony Stone Images/New York, Inc. Page 530: Will Crocker/The Image Bank. Page 531: Sandra Baker/Tony Stone Images/New York, Inc. Page 537: John Labbe/The Image Bank. Page 539 (top): Courtesy Lockheed Martin. Page 539 (bottom): Ken Whitmore/Tony Stone Images/New York, Inc. Page 543: Courtesy Knight-Ridder, Inc.

Chapter 13
Opener: © Photofest. Page 587: Ralph Mercer/Tony Stone Images/New York, Inc. Page 589: John Van Hasselt/Sygma. Page 602: Courtesy SPS Technologies.

Chapter 14
Opener: John Lund/Tony Stone Images/New York, Inc. Page 611: Jonathan Elderfield/Gamma Liaison. Page 613: Janis Christie/PhotoDisc. Page 641: © William Waldron. Page 667: Courtesy The Vermont Teddy Bear Company. Page 668: Courtesy Praxair, Inc.

Chapter 15
Opener: Photo by Jeanne Strongin. Permission from The Motley Fool, Inc. Page 680: D. Sarraute/The Image Bank. Page 682: Lightscapes/The Stock Market. Page 684: Christopher Morris/Black Star. Page 686: Phil Banko/Tony Stone Images/New York, Inc. Page 691 (top): Ray Massey/Tony Stone Images/New York, Inc. Page 691 (bottom): Steve Cole/PhotoDisc. Page 693: Andy Whale/Tony Stone Images/New York, Inc. Page 700: Mitchell Funk/The Image Bank. Page 702: Jan Cobb/The Image Bank

Appendix D
Page D3: Steve Bronstein/The Image Bank. Page D6: Adam Woolfitt/Woodfin Camp & Associates. Page D12: © 1994 Turner & Devries/The Image Bank. Page D14: Randy O'Rourke/The Stock Market.

Appendix E
Page E4: Earl Glass/Stock, Boston/PNI.

Appendix F
Page F2: Peter Gridley/FPG International. Page F4 (top): © The Image Bank. Page F4 (bottom): Mitchell Funk/The Image Bank.

INDEX

COMPANY INDEX

Ace Hardware, 260
A.D. Makepeace, 537
Advanced Micro Devices, 693
Airbus, 454
Air Transportation Holding Company Inc., 41–42
A.L. Laboratories, 226
Alcatel-Alsthom, 291
Alco Standard Corporation, E29
Alternative Distributor Corp., 369
Aluminum Company of America (Alcoa), 555
American Air Lines, 101
American Brands, Inc., 575
American Cancer Society, 512
American Exploration Company, 457
American Express Company, 382, 383–385, 484
American Petrofina, 429
American Standard, 682
American Telephone and Telegraph (AT&T), 303, 334, 464, 575
American Water Works Company, 412
America Online (AOL), 284, 306, 691
AMICO Co., 234
Amoco Corporation, D6
AOL, see America Online
Apache Corporation, 507–508
Apple Computer, Inc., 279, 512
Archer Daniels Midland Co., 8
Art World Industries, Inc., 406
Atlantic, 566
Atlas Distributing Inc., 250
AT&T, see American Telephone and Telegraph
Automated Security Holdings, 86

Balitmore Gas and Electric, 691
Barrister Information Systems Corp., 563
Beatrice Foods, 575
Berkshire Hathaway, 537
Bethlehem Corporation, 183
Bethlehem Steel Corporation, 725
Black and Decker Manufacturing Company, 248
Bob Evans Farms, Inc., 86, 693
Boeing Company, 225, 454, 531
Boise Cascade Corporation, 420
Book-of-the-Month Club, 566
Boston Beer Company, 185
Bristol-Myers Squibb Co., 248, 303
Brunswick Corporation, 159
Burlington Northern Santa Fe Corporation, 412–413
Buy.com, 186, 209–210

Callahan Mining, 429
Callaway Golf, 549
Cambridge Biotech Corp., 90, 113
Campbell Soup Company, 248, 305, 419, 525, 579, 682
Case Corporation, 182
Caterpillar Inc., 471, 513, 693, 728
CF Industries Inc., F14

Checkmate Electronic Inc., 347
Chemical Bank, 348, 388
Chicago Heights Steel Co., 250
Chrysler, 54
Citibank, 348, 388
Citicorp, 11, 155
Clark Equipment Company, 455–456
Club Med, 434
The Coca-Cola Company, 305, 525, 589, 691, 728–729
Commonwealth Edison, 530
Compaq Computer, 12
Consolidated Freightways, Inc., 160
Consolidated Natural Gas Company, 700
Coopers and Lybrand, 204
Copperweld, 429
Crane Company, 529

Daimler Benz, 54
Daimler-Chrysler Corporation, 482
Dayton-Hudson, 197
Dell Computer Corporation, 161
Del Monte Corporation, 248
Delta Airlines, Inc., 22, 93, 101, 158–159, 412–413, 425, 608
Digital Equipment Corporation, 577
Diners Club, 382
Disney, 305
Dow Jones & Company, Inc., 40
Dunkin' Donuts, Inc., 22, 93

Eastman Kodak Company, 185, 352, 433, 549, 578, 608
E.I. duPont de Nemours, 305, 429, 529
Electrolux Company, 266
The Estée Lauder Companies, 702–703
E-Trade, 186
Exxon, 11, 288, 334, 344

Federal Express, 235
Florafax International Inc., 198
Florida Citrus Company, 697
FMCC (Ford Motor Credit Corp.), 382
Ford Foundation, 29, 512
Ford Motor Company, 58, 185, 305, 382, 521, 531, 691, 693
Ford Motor Credit Corp. (FMCC), 382
Forster's Restaurants, 44
Frito Lay, 307

Gap Inc., 611, 641–642
GE Capital Services (GECS), 382
General Dynamics Corp., 696
General Electric, 294, 305, 382, 513
General Mills, Inc., 12, 22, 419, B1–B5
General Motors Acceptance Corp. (GMAC), 382
General Motors Corporation, 11, 233, 280, 382, 412–413, 424, 434, 484, 512, 516, 521, 529, 691, D2
Gillette Co., 691
Gingiss Formal West, 422

GMAC (General Motors Acceptance Corp.), 382
Goodyear Tire & Rubber Company, 59
Greyhound Corporation, 9
Gulf Oil, 517

Harold's Club, 293
HBO (Home Box Office) Corporation, 566
Henredon Furniture, 383
Hershey Corporations, 579
Home Box Office (HBO) Corporation, 566, 575
The Home Depot, 538
Hughes Aircraft Co., 696

IBM, see International Business Machines
Imax, 433
Imperial Oil, 429
Inland Steel Company, 725
Intel, 208
International Business Machines (IBM), 334, 424, 434, 473, 513, 518, 521
Internet Direct, 284
Iomega, 670
Irkutsk Energo, 5

J.C. Penney Company, Inc., 232, 288, 338, 347, 375–376, 611
Johnson & Johnson, 303, 455

Kellogg Company, xxxiv, 3, 8, 11, 25, 85, 93, 98, 254–255, 282, 391–392, 405, 436, 437, 468–469, 485, 509, 512, 520, 547, 563, 565, A2-A29
Kentucky Fried Chicken, 432
Kmart Corporation, 22, 93, 188, 191, 260, 303, 338, 344, 506–507, 611, 696, 718–719
Kolff Medical, 519–520
Krogers, 248, 303

Laser Recording Systems, Inc., 134–135
Lincoln Village Properties, Inc, 41
Linde-Air Products Company
Little, Brown & Co., 566
Long Island Lighting Company, 530

Manitowoc, 728
Manville Corp., F2
Marriott Corporation, 419
Martin Lockheed Corporation, 539
MasterCard, 382, 383, 384
McDonald's Corporation, 98, 412, 432, 444, 445, 484, 512, 525
McDonnell Douglas, 225, 454
MCI Communications, 303
McKesson HBOC, 90, 113
McKessonHMOC, 188
MEC, see Mountain Equipment Co-op
Mechanics Bank, 537
Media Vision Technology, Inc., 90, 113
Merck Co., Inc., 303, 455, 693
Microsoft, Inc., 368–369, 691
Minnesota Mining and Manufacturing Company (3M), 397, 432
Mobil, 429

Montgomery Ward, 288
Moody's Investment Service, 509
Motley Fool, 670
Motorola, Inc., 182, 215, 248, 498
Mountain Equipment Co-op (MEC), 230, 256
Mug and Musket, 44, 70

National Cash Register Co., 333
Neiman-Marcus, 347
Netscape, 538
Nike, Inc., 98, 279–280, 314, 510, 512, 531, 536, 544, 680
North American Van Lines, 521
Northern Illinois Gas Company, 412
Northwest Airlines, 691

Office Depot, 188
O'Hare International Airport, 416
Omega Healthcare, 691
Oracle, 368–369
Owens-Illinois, 436–437

PACE Membership Warehouse, Inc., 696
Page Net, 613
Paramount Communications Inc., 515
PayLess Drug Stores Northwest, Inc., 696
Penguin USA, 90, 113
PepsiCo, Inc., 307, 521, 728–729
Peugeot Company, 266
Pharmacy Fund, 372, 392
PharMor, 204
Phillip Morris, 294, 305, 325
Pier 1 Imports, 347
Polaroid, 432, 433
Pratt & Lambert, 539
Praxair Incorporated, 667–668
Procter & Gamble, 98, 521

Quaker Oats Company, 250
Quality Department Store Inc., 675–694

Red Cross, 29
Reebok International, Ltd., 279–280, 305, 510
Reprise, 566
Republic Carloading, 156
Revlon, 693
Rhino, 566
Rite Aid, 368
RJR Nabisco, 294, 305, 325
RMA (Robert Morris Associates), 727
Robert Half International, 7
Robert Morris Associates (RMA), 727

Safeway, 188, 303
Salvation Army, 512
Seagram, 569
Sears, Roebuck and Company, 8, 11, 98, 191, 194, 288, 305, 338, 375, 376, 378, 382, 383, 406, 412, 538, 549, 611, 674, 679, 681–694
Sears Roebuck Acceptance Corp. (SRAC), 382
Smith's Food and Drug Centers, Inc., 134
Softbank, 186
Somonauk Fashions, 407
Sprint, 303

SPS Technologies, Inc., 601–602
SRAC (Sears Roebuck Acceptance Corp.), 382
SRC Corporation, 138, 162
Standard Oil Company, 420, 434
Standard Pressed Steel, 601
Stephanie's Gourmet Coffee and More, 329, 331–334, 353–354
Sumitomo Corporation, 333

Telecommunications Inc. (TCI), 691
Texaco Oil Company, 396, 429
Texas Instruments, 507
The May Department Stores Company, 611
3M, *see* Minnesota Mining and Manufacturing Company
Time Inc., 515
Time-Life Books, 566
Time Warner Corporation, 566, 568, 569, 573, 575
Toys'R'Us, 188, 691
Trans World Airlines Inc. (TWA), 472
Turner Broadcasting, 566, 569, 573, 575
TWA (Trans World Airlines Inc.), 472
Twentieth Century Fox, 93

UAL, *see* United Airlines, Inc.
Union Carbide, 251, 667
United Airlines, Inc. (UAL), 101, 158–160, 467
United Stationers, 188

United Way, 29
USAir, 482, F4
USX Corp., 482, 516

Vermont Teddy Bear Co., 666–667
VISA, 382, 383, 384
Volvo Company, 266

Walgreen Drug Co., 188, 248, 529
Wal-Mart Stores, Inc., 56, 148, 188, 191, 232, 260, 303, 344, 611, 718–719, 727
The Walt Disney Company, 538, 575
Walt Disney Productions, 22, 93
Warner Bros., 566
Warner Communications, 515
Wells Fargo Bank, 330
Wendy's International, 248, 434
Weyerhaeuser Company, 324–325, 697
Whirlpool, 682
Willamette Industries, Inc., 417
Woolworth Corporation, 347
W.R. Grace and Company, 11

Xerox Corporation, 601

Yahoo!, 186
Yale Express, 156
Yorkville Company, 578

SUBJECT INDEX

Accelerated-depreciation methods, 421
Accounts, 46–47
  contra revenue, 199
  nominal, 146–147
  permanent, 146–147, 149
  real, 146–147
  temporary, 146–147, 149
Accounts payable, 12
Accounts payable ledger, E2
Accounts receivable, 374–385
  definition of, 374
  disposing of, 382–385
  recognizing, 375–376
  uncollectible, 376–382
  valuing, 376–382
Accounts receivable ledger, E2
Accounts receivables turnover ratio, 391
Account form (of balance sheet), 161
Accounting:
  assumptions of, 10–11, 290–291
  bookkeeping vs., 6
  and careers, 6–7
  constraints in, 290, 295–297
  ethics in, 8–9
  history of, 5–6
  not-for-profit, 29–30
  principles of, 290–295
    cost principle, 294–295
    full disclosure principle, 294
    matching principle, 292–293
    revenue recognition principle, 292
  private, 29
  as process, 2–3
  as profession, 29–30
  public, 29
  standards for, 9–10, 305–306
Accounting cycle, 151, 154–156
Accounting information, 3–5
  comparability/consistency of, 288–289
  external users of, 4–5
  internal users of, 4
  relevance of, 288
  reliability of, 288
Accounting information systems, 29
Accounting year, 22
Accruals, adjusting entries for, 103–106
  expenses, accrued, 104–106
  revenues, accrued, 103–104
Accrual basis of accounting, 112
Accrued expenses, 104–106
  interest, 104–105
  salaries, 105–106
Accrued revenues, 103–104
Acid-test ratio, 682–683
Additions and improvements, 424
Adjusted trial balance, 110–112, 201
Adjusting entries, 95–109
  for accruals, 103–106
    expenses, accrued, 104–106
    revenues, accrued, 103–104
  alternative, 115–119
  illustrations of, 108–109

  for merchandising operations, 204
  preparation of, from work sheet, 146
  for prepayments, 96–101
    expenses, prepaid, 97–101
    revenues, unearned, 101
  types of, 95–96, 108
Administrative expenses, 208
Advertising, 6–7
Advertising supplies, 97–98
Aggregate data, 3
Aging schedule, 380
Allowances:
  purchase, 192, 237
  sales, 197–198, 238
Allowance method, 377–381
  bases used for, 379–381
    receivables, percentage of, 380–381
    sales, percentage of, 380
  estimated collectibles, recording of,
      377–378
  recovery of uncollectible amount, 379
  write-off of uncollectible amount,
      recording of, 378
Alternative adjusting entries, 115–119
Amortization:
  of bond discount, 477, 491–493
  of bond premium, 479–480, 493–494
  effective-interest, 490–494
  of intangible assets, 432–433
Analysis, 3, 672–696
  comparative, 673
  of current liabilities, 467–469
  horizontal, 674–677
    of balance sheet, 675
    of income statement, 676
    of retained earnings statement, 676–677
  of inventory, 254–255
  limitations of, 700–701
  of long-term liabilities, 485–486
  of plant assets, 437–438
  ratio, see Ratios
  of receivables, 391–392
  of shareholders' equity, 532–533
  of statement of cash flows, 640–643
    cash debt coverage ratio, 642
    cash return on sales ratio, 642
    current cash debt coverage ratio, 641
  transaction, 16–21, 59
  vertical, 677–680
    of balance sheet, 677
    of income statement, 677–679
Annual report, A2–A29
  auditor's report in, A8–A9
  definition of, A2
  financial highlights section of, A3
  five- or ten-year summary in, A28–A29
  management discussion and analysis
      section of, A9–A15
  notes to consolidated financial statements
      in, A19–A27
  standard set of financial statements in,
      A15–A18, B1–B5

Annuities:
 future value of, C5–C7
 present value of, C10–C12
Articles of incorporation, 516
Assets:
 in basic accounting equation, 12
 current, 157–158
 and debit/credit balance, 48
 definition of, 12
 intangible, *see* Intangible assets
 plant, *see* Plant assets
 total, 13
 wasting, 429
Asset turnover ratio, 437–438, 687–688
Assumed cost flow methods, 244–248,
     262–265
 average cost method, 247–248
 consistent use of, 250
 effects of, on financial statements,
     248–250
  balance sheet, 249–250
  income statement, 248–249
 First-in, First-out (FIFO), 245–246
 Last-in, First-out (LIFO), 246–247
 tax effects of, 250
Assumptions, accounting, 10–11, 290–291
Auditing, 29
Auditor's report, A8–A9
Authorized stock, 519
Available-for-sale securities, 578–579
Average age, 437
Average collection period, 391–392, 685
Average cost method, 247–248, 263
Average life, 437

Bad debt expense, 376
Balance sheet, 22–24. *See also* Classified
     balance sheet
 consolidated, 585–589
  content of, 588–589
  work sheets for, 587–588
 and cost flow method, 249–250
 horizontal analysis of, 675
 inventory errors on, 253, 254
 inventory on, 232
 presentation of investments on, 579–582
 vertical analysis of, 677
 on work sheet, 202–203
Bankers, 7
Banking, 344–352
 check writing, 345–346
 deposits, 344–345
 reconciliations, 347–352
 statements, bank, 346–347
Bank service charges, 347, 351
Basic accounting equation, 12–14, 51
Basis of accounting, 112–113
Batching, 69
Bearer (coupon) bonds, 471
Bonds, 469–483
 advantages/disadvantages of, 470
 bearer, 471
 callable, 471
 convertible, 471
 converting, into common stock, 482–483
 definition of, 469

 discount on, 475–478, 491–493
 as investment, 570–571
 issuance of, 471–472
  at discount, 476–478
  at face value, 474–475
  between interest dates, 480–481
  at premium, 478–480
 market value of, 473–474
 premium on, 475, 478–480, 493–494
 redemption of
  at maturity, 482
  before maturity, 482
 registered, 471
 retirement of, 481–483
 secured, 471
 serial, 471
 term, 471
 trading of, 473
 types of, 471
 unsecured, 471
Bond certificates, 472
Bond indenture, 471
Bonding (of employees), 335
Bonuses, D5–D6
Book (carrying) value, 476, 482
Book error, 351
Bookkeeping, accounting vs., 6
Book value, 426–427
Book value method, 483
Book value per share, 547–549
 definition of, 547–548
 market value vs., 549
Brokers, 7
Budgeting, 29
Buildings, 414, 622, 623, 648–649
Business documents, 52, 196
Business transactions, 15–16
By-laws, corporate, 516

Calendar year, 93
Callable bonds, 471
Capital, paid-in, 13
Capital leases, F5–F6
Capital stock, 542
Capital surplus, 543
Careers, and accounting, 6–7
Carrying (book) value, 476, 482
Carrying value method, 483
Cash:
 as current asset, 157
 reporting, 352–353
Cash basis of accounting, 112–113
Cash control(s), 336–352
 and banking, 344–352
  check writing, 345–346
  deposits, 344–345
  reconciliations, 347–352
  statements, bank, 346–347
 with disbursements, 340–343
  EFT system, 341
  petty cash fund, 341–343
  voucher system, 340–341
 with receipts, 337–340
  mail receipts, 339–340
  over-the-counter receipts, 338–339
Cash debt coverage ratio, 642, 693–694

Cash dividends, 531–534
Cash equivalents, 352, 609
Cash flow statement, *see* Statement of cash flows
Cash (net) receivable value, 376
Cash payments journal, E14–E16
Cash receipts journal, E8–E11
Cash register, electronic, 70
Cash register tapes, 196, 338
Cash return on sales ratio, 642, 686–687
Cash sales, 198
Certified public accountants (CPAs), 29
Change in accounting principle, 699–700
"Channel stuffing," 198
Charter, corporate, 516
Chart of accounts, 58–59
Checks, writing, 345–346
Check register, 341
Classified balance sheet, 157–161
    account form of, 161
    current assets on, 157–158
    current liabilities on, 159–160
    illustration of, 161
    intangible assets on, 159
    long-term investments on, 158
    long-term liabilities on, 160
    property, plant, and equipment on, 158–159
    report form of, 161
    stockholders' equity on, 160–161
Closing entries, 147–153
    illustration of, 148–149
    for merchandising operations, 204
    post-closing trial balance, 150–153
    posting of, 149–150
    preparation of, 147–148
Closing the books, 146–153
Collection agents, 464
Collusion, 335–336
Common stock, 517, 522–525
    converting bonds into, 482–483
    and debit/credit balance, 49
    definition of, 49
Communicating (as accounting activity), 3
Comparability of accounting information, 288–289
Compensating balances, 353
Compound entry, 54–55
Compound interest, C2–C3
Comprehensive income, 700
Computer fraud, 336
Computerized accounting information systems, 68–70, 167
Computers, 6
Conservatism, 251, 296, 297
Consigned goods, 235
Consistency of accounting information, 288–289
Consolidated financial statements, 585–589
    balance sheet, 585–589
        content of, 588–589
        work sheets for, 587–588
    income statement, 589
    notes to, A19–A27
Constraints, 290, 295–297
Construction costs, 414

Consulting, management, 29
Contingent liabilities, F2–F4
Continuous life (of corporation), 514
Contra revenue accounts, 199
Controller, 514
Controlling interest, 574
Convertible bonds, 471
Copyrights, 433–434
Corporation(s), 11, 512–517. *See also* Stock(s)
    advantages/disadvantages of, 516
    characteristics of, 513–515
    classification of, 512–513
    continuous life of, 514
    Delaware, 516–517
    formation of, 516–517
    investment by, 568–569
    as legal entity, 512, 513
    management of, 514–515
    nonprofit, 512
    privately held, 513
    publicly held, 512–513
Correcting entries, 154–156
Cost(s):
    depreciable, 418
    expired vs. unexpired, 293
    organization, 517
    research and development, 435–436
Cost accounting, 29
Cost flow assumptions, *see* Assumed cost flow methods
Costing, inventory, 242–251
    assumed cost flow methods, 244–248
    consistent use of, 250, 251
    financial statement effects of, 248–250
    physical flow costing, 243–244
Cost of goods available for sale, 240
Cost of goods on hand, 240
Cost of goods purchased, 239–240
Cost of goods sold, 188, 190, 238–241
Cost principle, 9, 294–295, 524, 570
Coupon (bearer) bonds, 471
CPAs (certified public accountants), 29
Credit(s):
    definition of, 47
    equality of debits and, 48
Credit balance, 47
Credit card sales, 383–385
Crediting, 47
Credit memorandum, 197, 347
Creditors, 13
Creditors' ledger, E2
Credit sales, 198, E6
Credit terms, 193
Cumulative dividend, 529–530
Current assets, 157–158
Current cash debt coverage ratio, 641, 683–684
Current liabilities, 159–160, 462–469
    analysis of, 467–469
    definition of, 462
    long-term debt, current maturities of, 467
    notes payable, 463–464
    payroll taxes payable, 465–466
    presentation of, 467, 468
    sales taxes payable, 464
    unearned revenues, 466–467

wages and salaries payable, 465
Current ratio, 301–302, 468–469, 681–682
Current replacement cost, 251–252
Customers, as users of accounting
    information, 4–5
Customers' ledger, E2
Cycle(s):
    accounting, 151, 154–156
    operating, 157, 189–190

Data, 3. *See also* Accounting information
Debit(s):
    definition of, 47
    equality of credits and, 48
Debit balance, 47
Debiting, 47
Debit memorandum, 192, 347
Debts, 12, 160
Debt investments, 570–571
Debt to total assets ratio, 304, 485, 692–693
Declaration date, 532
Declining-balance depreciation method,
    420–421
Deductions, payroll, D6–D8
Defined benefit plans, F9
Defined contribution plans, F8–F9
Delaware corporations, 516–517
Depletion, 430–431
Deposits, bank, 344–345
Depreciation, 415–423
    adjusting entries for, 99–100
    computational factors in, 416–417
    and income taxes, 423
    methods for, 418–422
        declining-balance method, 420–421
        double-declining-balance method, 421
        straight-line depreciation, 418–419
        units-of-activity method, 419–420
    as prepaid expense, 99–101
    and revision of periodic depreciation, 423
    in statement of cash flows, 621–622
    statement presentation of, 100–101
Direct write-off method, 382
Disbursements, cash, 340–343
    EFT system, 341
    petty cash fund, 341–343
    voucher system, 340–341
Discontinued operations, 696–697
Discount(s):
    on bonds, 475–478, 491–493
    purchase, 193–195, 237–238
    sales, 198–199, 238
Discounting, 473, C12
Discount period, 193
Dishonored notes, 389–390
Dividend(s), 13–14, 529–536
    in arrears, 529–530
    cash, 531–534
    cumulative, 529–530
    and debit/credit balance, 49–50
    definition of, 49
    preferred, 544, 688–689
    recording, 573
    stock, 534–536
Documentation procedures, 332–333

Documents, business, 52, 196
Dollar signs, use of, 68
Double-declining-balance depreciation
    method, 421
Double-entry system, 48
Duties, segregation of, 332

Earning power, 696
Earnings per share (EPS), 300, 689–690
Economic entity assumption, 10–11, 291
Economic planners, 5
Effective-interest method, 491
Effective-interest rate, 491
EFT (electronic funds transfer), 341
Electronic cash register, 70
Electronic controls, 333
Electronic data processing, 68–70
Electronic funds transfer (EFT), 341
Electronic home banking, 346
Employees:
    bonding of, 335
    fringe benefits for, F6–F9
        paid absences, F6–F7
        postretirement benefits, F7–F9
    hiring, D3
EPS, *see* Earnings per share
Equipment, 414–415, 622, 623, 637, 649
Equity, stockholders', 12, 13
Error(s):
    book, 351
    inventory, 252–254
        balance sheet effects, 253, 254
        income statement effects, 253, 254
    locating, from trial balance, 67–68
    processing, 69
"ESP method," 148
Ethics, 8–9, 11, 612
Excel, 142
Exchange (of plant assets), 426–428
Exclusive right, 159
Expense(s), 13, 208
    accrued, 104–106
    and debit/credit balance, 50
    operating, 188–189, 200, 242
    prepaid, 97–101, 115–117
Expense recognition, 292–293
Expired costs, 293
External transactions, 15
External users of accounting information,
    4–5
Extraordinary items, 697–699

Face value, 388
Factors, 383
Fair market value, 426–427
FASB, *see* Financial Accounting Standards
    Board
FBI, *see* Federal Bureau of Investigation
Federal Bureau of Investigation (FBI), 7, 30
Federal Insurance Contribution Act (FICA),
    D6–D7
Federal Trade Commission, 4
Federal Unemployment Tax Act (FUTA),
    D13
Federal unemployment taxes, D13
Feedback value, 288

FICA, *see* Federal Insurance Contribution Act
FICA taxes, D6–D7, D12
FIFO, *see* First in, First out
Finance, 7
Financial Accounting Standards Board (FASB), 9, 286–287
Financial highlights, A3
Financial reporting:
　database concept of, 294
　objectives of, 287–288
Financial statements, 3, 22–27
　adjusted trial balance for preparation of, 111–112
　and adjusting entries, 95
　analysis of, *see* Analysis
　consolidated, 574–575, 585–589
　　balance sheet, 585–589
　　　content of, 588–589
　　　work sheets for, 587–588
　　income statement, 589
　　notes to, A19–A27
　elements of, 289–290
　for merchandising operations, 203
　presentation of, 298–300
　　classified balance sheet, 298–299
　　classified income statement, 299–300
　　and international business, 304–306
　standard set of, A15–A18, B1–B5
　work sheets for preparation of, *see* Work sheet(s)
Finished goods, 233
First-in, First-out (FIFO), 245–246, 248–251, 262–263
Fiscal year, 93
Fixed assets, *see* Plant assets
FOB destination, 195, 234, 235
FOB shipping point, 195, 234, 235
"For Deposit Only," 339
Foreign Corrupt Practices Act of 1977, 331
Form W-2, D15
Form W-4, D7
Franchises, 434–435
Free on board (FOB), 195
Freight costs, 195, 237
Freight-in, 237
Full-cost approach, 429
Full disclosure principle, 294, 611
FUTA (Federal Unemployment Tax Act), D13
Future value, C3–C7
　of annuity, C5–C7
　of single amount, C3–C5

GAAP, *see* Generally accepted accounting principles
Gardner, David, 670
Gardner, Tom, 670
General accounting, 29
General Accounting Office, 30
General journal, 53
　adjusting entries in, 108
　effect of special journals on, E16–E18
General ledger, 55, 109
Generally accepted accounting principles (GAAP), 9–10, 112, 286
General managers, 6

Going concern assumption, 291
Goods in transit, 234–235
Goodwill, 435
Government regulation (of corporations), 515
Gross earnings, D5–D6
Gross profit, 188, 199–200
Gross profit method, 259–260
Guidelines, operating, 290

Health benefits, postretirement, F7
Historical cost principle, *see* Cost principle
History of accounting, 5–6
Honored notes, 389
Horizontal analysis, 674–677
　of balance sheet, 675
　of income statement, 676
　of retained earnings statement, 676–677
Human element, 335–336

IASC (International Accounting Standards Committee), 306
Identifying (as accounting activity), 2
Imprest system, 341
Improvements, land, 414
Income:
　comprehensive, 700
　net, 13–14, 199–200
Income statement, 22–24
　classified, 299–300
　consolidated, 589
　and cost flow method, 248–249
　horizontal analysis of, 676
　inventory on, 232, 241–242, 253, 254
　for merchandising operations, 206–209
　　multi-step income statement, 206–208
　　single-step income statement, 208–209
　for retailers/wholesalers, 200
　vertical analysis of, 677–679
　on work sheet, 201–202
Income Summary, 147
Income taxes, 299–300, D7–D8
　cash payments for, 632, 636
　and depreciation, 423
Independent internal verification, 334–335
Industrial age, 5–6
Information, accounting, *see* Accounting information
Information age, 6
Insurance, 98–99
Intangible assets, 159, 432–435
　amortization of, 432–433
　copyrights, 433–434
　franchises/licenses, 434–435
　goodwill, 435
　patents, 433
　trademarks/trade names, 434
　useful life of, 432
Interest, C2–C3
　accrued, 104–105
　annual rate of, 387–388
　compound, C2–C3
　on notes receivable, 387–388
　simple, C2
Internal auditing, 29

Internal auditors, 334
Internal control, 330–336. *See also* Cash
    control(s)
    documentation procedures for, 332–333
    and establishment of responsibility,
        331–332
    goals of, 330–331
    and independent internal verification,
        334–335
    limitations of, 335–336
    and payroll, D2–D5
    physical/mechanical/electronic controls,
        333, 334
    and segregation of duties, 332
Internal Revenue Service, 4, 30
Internal transactions, 15
Internal users of accounting information, 4
International accounting:
    cash flow statement, 615
    corporations, designations for, 517
    financial statement presentation,
        304–306
International Accounting Standards
    Committee (IASC), 306
Interpretation, 3
Inventory(-ies), 232–257
    on balance sheet, 232
    classification of, 233
    errors in, 252–254
        balance sheet effects, 253, 254
        income statement effects, 253, 254
    estimation of, 259–261
        gross profit method, 259–260
        retail inventory method, 260–261
    on income statement, 232
    LCM valuation of, 251–252
    merchandise, 190, 233
    ownership of, 234–235
    periodic inventory system, *see* Periodic
        inventory system
    perpetual inventory system, 190,
        235–236, 262–265, E6
    physical, 233–234
    statement presentation/analysis of,
        254–255
Inventory summary sheets, 234
Inventory turnover ratio, 685
Investment(s), 568–584
    balance sheet presentation of, 579–582
    and categories of securities, 577–579
    by corporations, 568–569
    debt, 570–571
    long-term, 158, 580
    presentation of realized/unrealized
        gain/loss on, 580–581
    stock, 572–576
        with holdings between 20% and 50%,
            573–574
        with holdings of less than 20%,
            572–573
        with holdings of more than 50%,
            574–575
    temporary, 579–580
    valuation of, 577
Invoices, 191, 192, 196

Irregular items, 696–700

Journal, 53–55, 58
Journalizing, 53–55, 147
Just-in-time inventory management systems,
    191

Labor unions, 5
Land, 623, 632, 636–637, 648
    cost of, 413–414
    improvements to, 414
    value of, 416
Last-in, First-out (LIFO), 246–251, 263
LCM, *see* Lower of cost or market
Lease liabilities, F4–F6
    capital leases, F5–F6
    operating leases, F4–F5
Ledger, 55–58, 58
Leonardo da Vinci, 5
Liability(-ies):
    in basic accounting equation, 12–13
    contingent, F2–F4
    current, *see* Current liabilities
    and debit/credit balance, 48
    definition of, 12
    for employee fringe benefits, F6–F9
        paid absences, F6–F7
        postretirement benefits, F7–F9
    lease, F4–F6
    limited, 11, 513
    long-term, *see* Long-term liabilities
Licenses, 434–435
Life insurance benefits, postretirement, F7
LIFO, *see* Last-in, First-out
Limited liability, 11, 513
Liquidity ratios, 301–302, 681–685
    acid-test ratio, 682–683
    current cash debt coverage ratio, 683–684
    current ratio, 681–682
    inventory turnover ratio, 685
    receivables turnover ratio, 684–685
Long-term debt, current maturities of, 467
Long-term investments, 158, 580
Long-term liabilities, 160. *See also* Bonds
    analysis of, 485–486
    definition of, 469
    notes payable, 484–485
    postretirement benefits as, F9
    presentation of, 485
Long-term notes/bonds, present value of,
    C12–C15
LOTUS 1–2–3, 142
Lower of cost or market (LCM), 251–252

MACRS (Modified Accelerated Cost
    Recovery System), 423
Mail receipts, 339–340
Maker (of check), 345
Management consulting, 29
Management discussion and analysis
    (MD&A), A9–A15
Managerial accounting, 29
Manual accounting systems, 68–69
Manufacturing enterprises, inventory in, 233
Marketable securities, 157

Marketing specialists, 6
Market value, 9
   book value per share vs., 549
   of stock, 520
Matching principle, 94, 292–293
Materiality, 295–297
MD&A, *see* Management discussion and analysis
Mechanical controls, 333
Merchandise inventory, 191, 233
Merchandising operations, 188–211. *See also* Inventory(-ies)
   accounting cycle for, 188
   adjusting entries for, 204
   closing entries for, 204
   cost of goods sold in, 188
   gross profit in, 188, 199–200
   income statements for, 200, 206–209
      multi-step income statement, 206–208
      single-step income statement, 208–209
   inventory system for, 190
   measurement of net income in, 199–200
   operating cycles in, 189–190
   operating expenses in, 188–189, 200
   post-closing trial balance for, 205
   preparing financial statements for, 203
   recording purchases in, 191–196
      alternative accounting for, 195–196
      cash purchases, 191
      credit purchases, 191
      discounts, 193–195
      freight costs, 195
      returns and allowances, 191–193
   recording sales in, 196–199
      discounts, 198–199
      returns and allowances, 197–198
      statement presentation, 199
   work sheets for, 201–203
Merchandising profit, 200
Modified Accelerated Cost Recovery System (MACRS), 423
Monetary unit assumptions, 10, 291
Mortgages, 484
Mortgage notes payable, 484
Moving average method, 263–264
Multi-step income statement, 206–208

NAFTA (North American Free Trade Agreement), 9
Natural resources, 429–431
   acquisition cost, 429–430
   analysis of, 437–438
   definition of, 429
   depletion of, 430–431
   statement presentation of, 436–437
Net (cash) receivable value, 376
Net income, 13–14, 199–200
Net pay, D8–D9
Net sales, 199
Neutrality of accounting information, 288
Nominal accounts, 146–147
Noncash activities, 611
Nonoperating activities, operating vs., 207–208
Nonprofit corporations, 512

No-par value stock, 521, 523
North American Free Trade Agreement (NAFTA), 9
Notes payable, 12–13, 463–464, 484–485
Notes receivable, 385–390
   computing interest on, 387–388
   definition of, 374
   dishonor of, 389–390
   disposing of, 388–390
   honor of, 389
   maturity date for, 386–387
   recognizing, 388
   sale of, 390
   valuing, 388
Notes to consolidated financial statements, A19–A27
Not-for-profit accounting, 29–30
NSF, 347, 351

Obligations, 12
Office supplies, 97
Operating activities, nonoperating vs., 207–208
Operating cycles, 157, 189–190
Operating expenses, 188–189, 200, 208, 242
Operating guidelines, 290
Operating leases, F4–F5
Organization costs, 517
Over-the-counter receipts, 338–339
Owners' equity, *see* Stockholders' equity
Ownership:
   of corporation, 513, 517–519
   of goods, 234–235

Pacioli, Luca, 5
Paid absences, F6–F7
Paid-in capital, 13
Paper profit, 249
Parent company, 574
Partnerships, 11
Par value stock, 521
Patents, 433
Patterson, John, 333
Payee (of check), 345
Payment date (dividends), 532–533
Payout ratio, 691
Payroll, D2–D16
   computation of, D5–D9
      deductions, D6–D8
      gross earnings, D5–D6
      net pay, D8–D9
   definition of, D2
   and hiring, D3
   and internal control, D2–D5
   paying, D5
   preparation of, D4
   recording of, D9–D12
      expenses/liabilities, D10–D11
      payment, D11
      requirements, D9–D10
   and timekeeping, D4
Payroll taxes, 465–466
   filing/remitting, D14–D15
   types of, D11–D14
Pension plans, F8

PE ratio, *see* Price-earnings ratio
Periodic inventory system, 190, 236–251
    costing methods in, 242–251
        assumed cost flow method, 244–248
        consistent use of, 250, 251
        financial statement effects of, 248–250
        physical flow costing, 243–244
    cost of goods sold in, 238–241
    income statement presentation in,
        241–242
    recording transactions in, 236–241
        purchases, 237–238
        sales, 238
Periodicity assumption, 93
Permanent accounts, 146–147, 149
Perpetual inventory system, 190, 235–236,
    262–265, E6
Petty cash fund, 341–343
Phantom profit, 249
Physical controls, 333
Physical flow costing, 243–244
Physical inventory, taking, 233–234
Plant assets, 412–429
    analysis of, 437–438
    depreciation of, 415–423
        computational factors, 416–417
        and income taxes, 423
        methods for, 418–422
        and revision of periodic depreciation, 423
    determining cost of, 413–415
        buildings, 414
        equipment, 414–415
        land, 413–414
        land improvements, 414
    disposal of, 424–428
        exchange, 426–428
        retirement, 424–425
        sale, 425–426
    statement presentation of, 436–437
    useful life of, 417, 423–424
Post-closing trial balance, 150–153, 205
Posting, 57–58, 147, 149–150
Postretirement benefits, F7–F9
Predictive value, 288
Preferred dividends, 544, 688–689
Preferred stock, 528–530
Premiums, bonds, 475, 478–480, 493–494
Prepaid expenses, 97–101
    alternative treatment of, 115–117
    as current asset, 158
    depreciation, 99–101
    insurance, 98–99
    supplies, 97–98
Prepayments, adjusting entries for,
    96–101
    expenses, prepaid, 97–101
    revenues, unearned, 101
Present value, 473, C8–C15
    of annuity, C10–C12
    and discounting, C12
    of long-term note/bond, C12–C15
    of single amount, C8–C10
President (of corporation), 514
Price-earnings (PE) ratio, 690–691
Principles, accounting, 290–295
    cost principle, 294–295

full disclosure principle, 294
matching principle, 292–293
revenue recognition principle, 292
Prior period adjustments, 539–540
Private accounting, 29
Privately held corporations, 513
Profit:
    gross, 188, 199–200
    merchandising, 200
    paper, 249
Profitability ratios, 302–304, 685–691
    asset turnover ratio, 687–688
    cash return on sales ratio, 686–687
    earnings per share, 689–690
    payout ratio, 691
    price-earnings ratio, 690–691
    profit margin ratio, 686
    return on assets ratio, 688
    return on common stockholders' equity,
        688–689
Profit margin ratio, 302–303, 686
Property, plant, and equipment, 158–159
Proprietorships, 11
Public accounting, 29
Publicly held corporations, 512–513
Purchases:
    in merchandising operations, 191–196
        alternative accounting, 195–196
        cash purchases, 191
        credit purchases, 191
        discounts, 193–195
        freight costs, 195
        returns and allowances, 191–193
    in periodic inventory systems, 237–238
        discounts, purchase, 237–238
        freight costs, 237
        returns and allowances, 237
Purchases journal, E12–E14
Purchase allowances, 192
Purchase returns, 192, 237

Ratios, 680–696
    liquidity, 301–302, 681–685
        acid-test ratio, 682–683
        current cash debt coverage ratio,
            683–684
        current ratio, 681–682
        inventory turnover ratio, 685
        receivables turnover ratio, 684–685
    profitability, 302–304, 685–691
        asset turnover ratio, 687–688
        cash return on sales ratio, 686–687
        earnings per share, 689–690
        payout ratio, 691
        price-earnings ratio, 690–691
        profit margin ratio, 686
        return on assets ratio, 688
        return on common stockholders' equity,
            688–689
    solvency, 692–694
        cash debt coverage ratio, 693–694
        debt to total assets ratio, 692–693
        times interest earned ratio, 693
Ratio analysis, 680
Raw materials, 233
Real accounts, 146–147

Real estate, 7
Real-time processing systems, 69
Reasonable assurance, 335
Receipts, cash, 337–340
    mail receipts, 339–340
    over-the-counter receipts, 338–339
Receivables. *See also* Accounts receivable;
        Notes receivable
    analysis of, 391–392
    as current asset, 157–158
    definition of, 374
    presentation of, 391
    types of, 374–375
Receivables turnover ratio, 684–685
Reconciliation, 347–352
    entries from, 351–352
    illustration of, 350
    procedure for, 348–350
Record date (dividends), 532
Recording process, 2, 46, 52–66
    chart of accounts, 58–59
    illustration of, 59–66
    journalizing, 53–55
    posting, 57–58
    steps in, 52–53
Registered bonds, 471
Regulation (of corporations), 515
Regulatory agencies, 4
Relevance of accounting information, 288
Reliability of accounting information, 288
Reports:
    accounting, 3
    generating, with computerized vs. manual
        systems, 69
Report form (of balance sheet), 161
Reporting:
    cash, 352–353
    financial, 287–288, 294
Research and development costs, 435–436
Responsibility, establishment of, 331–332
Restrictive endorsements, 339
Retailers, 188
Retail inventory method, 260–261
Retained earnings, 13, 538–541
    and debit/credit balance, 49
    definition of, 49, 538
    and dividends, 531
    prior period adjustments to, 538–539
    restrictions on, 538
    statement of, 540–541
Retained earnings statement, 22–24,
        676–677
Retirement:
    of bonds, 481–483
    of plant assets, 424–425
Returns and allowances:
    purchase, 191–193, 237
    sales, 197–198, 238
Return on assets, 303, 688
Return on common stockholders' equity,
        303–304, 543–544, 688–689
Revenues, 13, 208
    accrued, 103–104
    and debit/credit balance, 50
    unearned, 101, 115, 117–118
Revenue expenditures, 424

Revenue recognition principle, 93–94, 292
Reversing entries, 154, 165–167

Salary(-ies), 105–106, D5
Sale(s):
    of bonds, 570–571
    cash, 198
    credit, 198, E6
    credit card, 383–385
    in merchandising operations, 196–199
        discounts, 198–199
        returns and allowances, 197–198
        statement presentation, 199
    net, 199
    of notes receivable, 390
    in periodic inventory systems, 238
    of plant assets, 425–426
    of receivables, 383
    statement presentation of, 199
    of stock, 573
    of treasury stock, 527–528
Sales allowances, 197–198
Sales and real estate taxes payable, 13
Sales basis, 292
Sales discounts, 198–199, 238
Sales invoice, 196
Sales journal, E6–E8
    advantages of, E8
    posting, E6–E7
Sales returns, 197
Sales taxes payable, 464
Salvage value, 417
SEC, *see* Securities and Exchange
        Commission
Secured bonds, 471
Securities:
    available-for-sale, 578–579
    trading, 577–578
Securities and Exchange Commission (SEC),
        4, 9, 30
Segregation of duties, 332
Selling expenses, 208
Serial bonds, 471
Shareholders' equity, *see* Stockholders'
        equity
Shipping costs, 195
Shoplifting, 197
Signature cards, 344
Simple entry, 54
Simple interest, C2
Single-step income statement, 208–209
Social Security taxes, D6–D7
Solvency, 304
Solvency ratios, 692–694
    cash debt coverage ratio, 693–694
    debt to total assets ratio, 692–693
    times interest earned ratio, 693
Special journals, E5–E18
    cash payments journal, E14–E16
    cash receipts journal, E8–E11
    definition of, E5
    effects of, on general journal, E16–E18
    purchases journal, E12–E14
    sales journal, E6–E8
Splits, stock, 536–538
Standards, accounting, 9–10, 305–306

Stated value, 521
Statements:
    bank, 346–347
    financial, *see* Financial statements
Statement of cash flows, 22–25, 608–645
    analysis of, 640–643
        cash debt coverage ratio, 642
        cash return on sales ratio, 642
        current cash debt coverage ratio, 641
    direct method, 614, 627–640
        first year of operations, 628–634
        indirect method vs., 614
        second year of operations, 634–640
    format of, 611–612
    indirect method, 614–627
        direct method vs., 614
        first year of operations, 616–620
        second year of operations, 620–627
        work sheets, 646–651
    preparation of, 613–614
    purpose of, 609
    scope of, 609–611
    usefulness of, 612–613
    work sheet for preparation of, 646–651
State unemployment taxes, D13
Stock(s), 517–538
    authorized, 519
    capital, 542
    certificates of, 517–518
    common, *see* Common stock
    dividends on, *see* Dividend(s)
    as investment, 572–576
        with holdings between 20% and 50%,
            573–574
        with holdings of less than 20%,
            572–573
        with holdings of more than 50%,
            574–575
    issuance of, 519–520
    market value of, 520
    no-par value, 521, 523
    par value, 521
    preferred, 528–530
    splits, 536–538
    treasury, 525–528
        disposal of, 527–528
        purchase of, 525–527
Stock certificates, 517–518
Stock dividends, 534–536
Stockholders' equity, 12, 13, 51, 160–161, 517
    analysis of, 543–544
    presentation of, 541–542
    statement of, 547
    subdivisions of, 49–50
Straight-line amortization, 477
Straight-line depreciation, 418–419
Subsidiary ledgers, E2–E4
    advantages of using, E4
    definition of, E2
    illustration of, E3
    purpose of, E2
Successful efforts approach, 429
Supplies, 97–98

T accounts, 46–47
Tax accounting, 29

Taxation:
    as area of public accounting, 29
    and assumed cost flow methods, 250
    of corporations, 515–516
    income taxes, 299–300, 423, 632, 636,
        D7–D8
    payroll taxes, 465–466
        filing/remitting, D14–D15
        types of, D11–D14
Taxing authorities, 4
Temporary accounts, 146–147, 149
Temporary investments, 579–580
Term bonds, 471
Three-column form of account, 56–57
Timekeeping, D4
Timeliness of accounting information, 288
Time periods, accounting, 93
Time period assumption, 291
Times interest earned ratio, 485, 693
Time value of money, 473, C1–C15
    future value, C3–C7
        of annuity, C5–C7
        of single amount, C3–C5
    and nature of interest, C1–C2
    present value, C8–C15
        of annuity, C10–C12
        and discounting, C12
        of long-term note/bond, C12–C15
        of single amount, C8–C10
Timing issues, 92–94
Total assets, 13
Trademarks, 434
Trade names, 434
Trading, bond, 473
Trading securities, 577–578
Transactions, 15–16
    external, 15
    internal, 15
Transaction analysis, 16–21, 59
Transit, goods in, 234–235
Treasury stock, 525–528
    disposal of, 527–528
    purchase of, 525–527
Trial balance, 66–68
    adjusted, 110–112, 201
    example of, 67
    limitations of, 67–68
    post-closing, 150–153
    purpose of, 66–67
    on work sheet, 141, 201
Trustees, 471

Uncollectible accounts receivable, 376–382
Unearned revenues, 101, 115, 117–118,
    466–467
Unemployment taxes, D13
Unexpired costs, 293
U.S. Department of Commerce, 232
Units-of-activity depreciation method,
    419–420
Unsecured bonds, 471
Useful life, 417, 423–424

Valuation:
    of accounts receivable, 376–382

of investments, 577
LCM, 251–252
of notes receivable, 388
Value, market, 9
Verifiability of accounting information, 288
Vertical analysis, 677–680
of balance sheet, 677
of income statement, 677–679
Voucher register, 341
Voucher system, 340–341

Wages, D5
Wages payable, 13, 465
Walton, Sam, 56, 148
Wasting assets, 429
Wear and tear, 416
Weighted average unit cost, 247–248

Wholesalers, 188
Working capital, 302, 468, 681
Work in process, 233
Work sheet(s), 140–146
adjusting entries prepared from, 146
basic form of, 140, 141
for consolidated balance sheet, 587–588
decision to use, 140
definition of, 140
financial statements prepared from, 143, 145
for merchandising operations, 201–203
statement of cash flows prepared from, 646–651
steps in preparation of, 141–144

Year, fiscal/calendar, 22, 93